DATE DUE		

THEME AND FORM

THEME AND FORM

An Introduction to Literature

Fourth Edition

MONROE C. BEARDSLEY
Temple University

ROBERT W. DANIEL
Kenyon College

GLENN LEGGETT
Grinnell College

"I always have two things in my head—
I always have a theme and the form,"
said W.H. Auden. "The form looks for the theme,
theme looks for the form,
and when they come together you're able to write."

Prentice-Hall, Inc., *Englewood Cliffs, New Jersey*

Library of Congress Cataloging in Publication Data

BEARDSLEY, MONROE C.   ed.
    Theme and form.

    Includes indexes.
    1. Literature—Collections.   I. Daniel, Robert
Woodham, 1915–   joint ed. II. Leggett, Glenn H.,
1918–   joint ed. III. Title.
PN6014.B39 1975   808.8   74–30026
ISBN   0-13-912972-3

PRENTICE-HALL ENGLISH LITERATURE SERIES
Maynard Mack, editor

10 9 8 7 6 5 4 3 2 1

Prentice-Hall International, Inc., *London*
Prentice-Hall of Australia, Pty. Ltd., *Sydney*
Prentice-Hall of Canada, Ltd., *Toronto*
Prentice-Hall of India Private Limited, *New Delhi*
Prentice-Hall of Japan, Inc., *Tokyo*

ACKNOWLEDGMENTS

Peter Abrahams, "Tell Freedom." Reprinted by permission of John Farquharson Ltd.

James Agee, "Knoxville: Summer 1915," from *A Death in the Family* by James Agee, copyright © 1957 by James Agee Trust. First published in *The Partisan Review*. Reprinted by permission of the publisher, Grosset & Dunlap, Inc.

W. H. Auden, "Musée des Beaux Arts." Copyright 1940 and renewed 1968 by W. H. Auden. Reprinted from *Collected Shorter Poems 1927–1957*, by W. H. Auden, by permission of Random House, Inc. and Faber and Faber Ltd.

W. H. Auden, "September 1, 1939," copyright 1940 and renewed 1968 by W. H. Auden. Reprinted from *The Collected Poetry of W. H. Auden* by permission of Random House, Inc. Also by permission of Faber and Faber Ltd., from *Collected Shorter Poems 1930–44.*

James Baldwin, "Sonny's Blues," reprinted from *Going to Meet the Man* by James Baldwin. Copyright © 1948, 1950, 1957, 1958, 1960, 1965 by James Baldwin and used by permission of the publisher, The Dial Press, Inc. and Robert Lantz–Candida Donadio Literary Agency, Inc.

Donald Barthelme, "At the End of the Mechanical Age," reprinted by permission of International Famous Agency and Donald Barthelme. Copyright © 1973 by The Atlantic Monthly Company, Boston, Mass.

Charles Baudelaire, "The Albatross," reprinted by permission of the translator, Richard Wilbur.

Charles Baudelaire, "The Seven Old Men," from *The Flowers of Evil* translated by F. P. Sturm from *Baudelaire, His Prose and Poetry* edited by T. R. Smith. © 1919 by Boni & Liveright, Inc.; © 1925 by The Modern Library, Inc. Reprinted by permission of Random House, Inc.

Stephen Vincent Benét, "The Blood of the Martyrs," from *The Selected Works of Stephen Vincent Benét* (Holt, Rinehart and Winston, Inc.), copyright 1936, 1937 by Stephen Vincent Benét. Reprinted by permission of Brandt & Brandt.

Henry Beston, "The Headlong Wave," from *The Outermost House* by Henry Beston. Copyright 1928, 1949, © 1956 by Henry Beston. Reprinted by permission of Holt, Rinehart and Winston, Inc.

Georges Blond, "An Odyssey of Birds," reprinted by permission of Macmillan Publishing Co., Inc. from *The Great Migrations* by Georges Blond. © Macmillan Publishing Co., Inc., 1956.

Laura Bohannon, "Shakespeare in the Bush," from *Conformity and Conflict: Readings in Cultural Anthropology*, eds. James P. Spradley and David W. McCurdy (Boston: Little Brown and Company, 1971). Copyright Laura Bohannon. Reprinted with permission.

Roy Bongartz, "Twelve Chases on West Ninety-Ninth Street." Copyright © 1965 by Roy Bongartz. Reprinted by permission of the publisher, Houghton Mifflin Company.

Bertolt Brecht, "Life of Galileo." Copyright © 1972 by Stefan S. Brecht. Reprinted from *Collected Plays*, Vol. 5, by Bertolt Brecht, edited by Ralph Manheim and John Willett, by permission of Pantheon Books, a Division of Random House, Inc. Original work entitled "Leben des Galileo." Copyright 1940 by Arvic Englind Teaterforlag AB, renewed June 1967 by Stefan S. Brecht. © 1955 by Suhrkamp Verlag, Frankfurt am Main. Reprinted by permission of Methuen & Co. publisher.

Gwendolyn Brooks, "The Ballad of Rudolph Reed" and "The Chicago Defender Sends a Man to Little Rock," from *The World of Gwendolyn Brooks.* Copyright © 1960 by Gwendolyn Brooks Blakely.

Albert Camus, "The Guest," © copyright 1957, 1958, by Alfred A. Knopf, Inc. Reprinted from *Exile and the Kingdom* by Albert Camus and translated by Justin O'Brien, by permission of the publisher and Hamish Hamilton Ltd., London.

Robert Cantwell, "Believing in Bluegrass." Reprinted with permission of the author. Copyright © 1972 by The Atlantic Monthly Company, Boston, Mass.

Guy Wetmore Carryl, "The Sycophantic Fox and the Gullible Raven," from *Fables for the Frivolous* by Guy Wetmore Carryl. Published by Harper & Bros., 1898.

Rachel Carson, "Nature Fights Back," from *Silent Spring* by Rachel Carson. Copyright © 1962 by Rachel L. Carson. Reprinted by permission of the publisher, Houghton Mifflin Company and Marie Rodell.

Anton Chekhov, "A Day in the Country," reprinted with permission of Macmillan Publishing Co., Inc., the Estate of Constance Garnett and Chatto & Windus Ltd. from *The Cook's Wedding and Other Stories* by Anton Chekhov. Translated from the Russian by Constance Garnett. Copyright 1922 by Macmillan Publishing Co., Inc., renewed 1950 by David Garnett.

Anton Chekhov, "A Trifling Occurrence," from *The Short Stories of Anton Chekhov*, edited by Robert N. Linscott. Copyright 1932 and renewed 1960 by The Modern Library, Inc. Reprinted by permission of Random House, Inc.

Arthur C. Clarke, "If I Forget Thee, O Earth," from *Across the Sea of Stars* by Arthur C. Clarke. Copyright 1951 by Columbia Publications, Inc. Reprinted by permission of the author and his agents, Scott Meredith Literary Agency, Inc., and David Higham Associates, Ltd.

John Collier, "The Chaser." Copyright 1940 by John Collier. Reprinted by permission of The Harold Matson Company, Inc.

Joseph Conrad, "The Secret Sharer," from *'Twixt Land and Sea* by Joseph Conrad. Reprinted by permission of J. M. Dent & Sons Ltd. and the Trustees of the Joseph Conrad Estate.

Stephen Crane, "An Episode of War," from *Stephen Crane: An Omnibus*, edited by Robert Wooster Stallman. Published by Alfred A. Knopf, Inc.

E. E. Cummings, "Pity this Busy Monster." Copyright 1944 by E. E. Cummings; copyright 1972 by Nancy Andrews. Reprinted from *Complete Poems 1913–1962* by E. E. Cummings by permission of Harcourt Brace Jovanovich, Inc. and MacGibbon Kee.

C. Day-Lewis, "When Nature Plays," from *Selected Poems* by C. Day-Lewis. Copyright 1929 by C. Day-Lewis. Reprinted by permission of Harper & Row, Publishers, Inc., and the Harold Matson Company, Inc.

Emily Dickinson, "Because I Could Not Stop for Death," from *Poems by Emily Dickinson*, ed. Martha Dickinson Bianchi. Published by Little, Brown and Company.

Emily Dickinson, "Going to Him," from *The Complete Poems of Emily Dickinson.* Published by Little, Brown and Company.

Emily Dickinson, "A Narrow Fellow in the Grass," from *Poems by Emily Dickinson*, ed. Martha Dickinson Bianchi. Published by Little, Brown and Company.

T. S. Eliot, "The Hollow Men," from *Collected Poems 1909–1962* by T. S. Eliot. Copyright 1936 by Harcourt Brace Jovanovich, Inc.; copyright © 1963, 1964 by T. S. Eliot. Reprinted by permission of Harcourt Brace Jovanovich, Inc. and Faber and Faber Ltd.

T. S. Eliot, "The Love Song of J. Alfred Prufrock," from *Collected Poems 1909–1962* by T. S. Eliot. Copyright 1936 by Harcourt Brace Jovanovich, Inc.; copyright © 1963, 1964 by T. S. Eliot. Reprinted by permission of Harcourt Brace Jovanovich, Inc., and Faber and Faber Ltd.

T. S. Eliot, "Preludes," from *Collected Poems 1909–1962* by T. S. Eliot; copyright 1936 by Harcourt Brace Jovanovich, Inc.; copyright © 1963, 1964 by T. S. Eliot. Reprinted by permission of the publisher and Faber and Faber Ltd.

William Faulkner, "A Rose for Emily." Copyright 1930 and renewed 1958 by William Faulkner. Reprinted from *Collected Stories of William Faulkner* by permission of Random House, Inc., and Curtis Brown Ltd.

William Faulkner, "Spotted Horses." Copyright 1931 and renewed 1959 by William Faulkner. Reprinted by permission of Random House, Inc., and Curtis Brown Ltd. An expanded version of this story appears in *The Hamlet* by William Faulkner.

E. M. Forster, "Troublesome Molluscs," from *Abinger Harvest*, copyright 1936, 1964 by E. M. Forster. Reprinted by permission of Harcourt Brace Jovanovich, Inc. and Edward Arnold (Publishers) Ltd.

Robert Frost, "Birches," "Out, Out—," and "Desert Places" from *The Poetry of Robert Frost* edited by Edward Connery Lathem. Copyright 1916, © 1969 by Holt, Rinehart and Winston, Inc. Copyright 1936, 1944 by Robert Frost. Copyright © 1964 by Lesley Frost Ballantine. Reprinted by permission of Holt, Rinehart and Winston, Inc.

Robert Frost, "Desert Places," from *The Poetry of Robert Frost*, edited by Edward Connery Lathem. Copyright 1916, © 1969 by Holt, Rinehart and Winston, Inc. Copyright 1936, 1944 by Robert Frost. Copyright © 1964 by Lesley Frost Ballantine. Reprinted by permission of Holt, Rinehart and Winston, Inc. and Laurence Pollinger Ltd.

John Kenneth Galbraith, "Economics and Art," from *The Liberal Hour* by John Kenneth Galbraith, pp. 44–62. Reprinted by permission of Houghton Mifflin Company.

Harry Golden, "Marriages Were Made in Heaven," from *Only in America* by Harry Golden. Copyright © 1958 by Harry Golden, with permission of Thomas Y. Crowell Company, Inc., publisher.

Robert Graves, "The Persian Version," from *Collected Poems 1955* by Robert Graves (Garden City, N.Y.: Doubleday & Company, Inc.). Reprinted by permission of Collins Knowlton-Wing, Inc. Copyright © 1955 by Robert Graves.

Alex Haley, "My Furthest Back Person—the African." Copyright 1972 by Alex Haley. Reprinted by permission of Paul R. Reynolds, Inc., 599 Fifth Ave., New York, N.Y., 10017.

Thomas Hardy, "Channel Firing." Reprinted with permission of Macmillan Publishing Co., Inc. and of the Estate, Macmillan & Co., Ltd., London and The Macmillan Company of Canada Limited from *Collected Poems* by Thomas Hardy. Copyright 1925 by Macmillan Publishing Co., Inc.

Thomas Hardy, "Nature's Questioning," reprinted with permission of Macmillan Publishing Co., Inc. and of the Estate, Macmillan & Co., Ltd., London, and the Macmillan Company of Canada Limited, from *Collected Poems* by Thomas Hardy. Copyright 1925 by Macmillan Publishing Co., Inc.

Ernest Hemingway, "The Undefeated," from *Men Without Women* by Ernest Hemingway. Copyright 1927 by Charles Scribner's Sons, 1955 by Ernest Hemingway. Reprinted by permission of Charles Scribner's Sons.

James Herndon, "The Price of Amphibians," copyright © 1971 by James Herndon. Reprinted by permission of Simon and Schuster.

Gerard Manley Hopkins, "God's Grandeur," "Spring," "The Windhover," from *The Poems of Gerard Manley Hopkins* by Gerard Manley Hopkins, published by Oxford University Press.

Gerard Manley Hopkins, "Spring and Fall to a Young Child," from *The Poems of Gerard Manley Hopkins* published by Oxford University Press.

A. E. Housman, "Be Still, My Soul," "On Wenlock Edge," "Terence, This is Stupid Stuff," and "To an Athlete Dying Young," from "A Shropshire Lad," Authorized Edition, from *Collected Poems of A. E. Housman*. Copyright 1939, 1940, © 1965 by Holt, Rinehart and Winston, Inc. Copyright © 1967, 1968 by Robert E. Symons. By permission of the Society of Authors as the literary representative of the Trustees of the estate of the late A. E. Housman and Jonathan Cape Ltd., London, and Holt, Rinehart and Winston, Inc., New York.

A. E. Housman, "My Dreams are of a Field Afar," from *The Collected Poems of A. E. Housman*. Copyright 1936 by Barclays Bank Ltd. Copyright © 1964 by Robert E. Symons. By permission of the Society of Authors as the literary representative of the Trustees of the estate of the late A. E. Housman, and Jonathan Cape Ltd., London, and Holt, Rinehart and Winston, Inc., New York.

Helen Hudson, "After Cortes," from *Stories for the Sixties*, Richard Yates, editor. Copyright © 1963, Helen Hudson. By permission of Bantom Books, Inc.

Glyn Hughes, "No Superficial Change." Reprinted by permission of the author.

Thomas Henry Huxley, "The Faith of a Scientist," from *Life and Letters of Thomas Henry Huxley* by Leonard Huxley. Originally published in 1903 by Appleton-Century-Crofts, Inc.

Shirley Jackson, "Pillar of Salt," reprinted with permission of Farrar,

Strauss & Giroux, Inc. and Brandt & Brandt from *The Lottery* by Shirley Jackson. Copyright 1948, 1949 by Shirley Jackson.

William James, "Footnote on Science," from *Principles of Psychology* by William James. Published by Holt, Rinehart and Winston, Inc., 1890.

Josephine Johnson, "December," from *The Inland Island* by Josephine Johnson. Copyright © 1969 by Josephine W. Johnson. Reprinted by permission of Simon & Schuster, Inc.

James Joyce, "Araby," from *Dubliners* by James Joyce. Originally published by B. W. Huebsch, Inc. in 1916. All rights reserved. Reprinted by permission of The Viking Press, Inc.

Franz Kafka, "A Hunger–Artist," trans. Marion Nielsen. From *Rocky Mountain Review*, 1946. Reprinted by permission of Marion Nielsen.

X. J. Kennedy, "Nude Descending a Staircase," copyright © 1960 by X. J. Kennedy from the book *Nude Descending a Staircase* by X. J. Kennedy. Reprinted by permission of Doubleday & Company, Inc.

Galway Kinnell, "The Correspondence School Instructor Says Goodbye to his Poetry Students." © 1967 by Galway Kinnell. Reprinted by permission of the publisher, Houghton Mifflin Company.

L. C. Knights, "In Search of Fundamental Values," from *The Critical Moment* by L. C. Knights. Published in the *Times Literary Supplement*. Reprinted by permission of Times Newspapers Limited, London.

Victor Kolpacoff, "The Room," from *The Prisoners of Quai Dong* by Victor Kolpacoff. Copyright © 1967 by Victor Kolpacoff. Reprinted by arrangement with The New American Library, Inc., New York, New York.

R. D. Laing, "The Schizophrenic Experience" from *The Politics of Experience* (Penguin Books Ltd., 1967) Chapter 5: "The Schizophrenic Experience." Copyright © 1967 by R. D. Laing. Reprinted by permission of Penguin Books, Ltd.

Philip Larkin, "Church Going," from *The Less Deceived*, reprinted by permission of The Marvell Press, England.

Philip Larkin, "I Remember, I Remember," from *The Less Deceived*. Reprinted by permission of The Marvell Press, England.

D. H. Lawrence, "The Blind Man," from *The Complete Short Stories of D. H. Lawrence*, Vol. II, copyright 1922 by Thomas B. Seltzer, Inc., copyright renewed 1950 by Frieda Lawrence. Reprinted by permission of The Viking Press, Inc., Laurence Pollinger Ltd and the Estate of the late Mrs. Frieda Lawrence.

Doris Lessing, "The Woman," reprinted from *The Habit of Loving* by Doris Lessing. Copyright © 1957 by Doris Lessing. Reprinted with permission of the publishers, Thomas Y. Crowell Co., Inc., and John Cushman Associates, Inc.

Denise Levertov, "February Evening in New York," from *With Eyes at the Back of Our Heads*. Copyright © 1958 by Denise Levertov Goodman. Reprinted by permission of The New Directions Publishing Corporation.

Denise Levertov, "Merritt Parkway," from *The Jacob's Ladder*. Copyright © 1958 by Denise Levertov Goodman. Reprinted by permission of The New Directions Publishing Corporation and Laurence Pollinger Ltd.

Walter Lippmann, "The Indispensable Opposition." Copyright © 1939, renewed 1967 by The Atlantic Monthly Company, Boston, Mass. Reprinted by permission of the author.

Robert Lowell, "Central Park." Reprinted by permission of Farrar, Straus & Giroux, Inc., from *Near the Ocean* by Robert Lowell. Copyright © 1965 by Robert Lowell.

Robert Lowell, "Christmas Eve Under Hooker's Statue," from *Lord Weary's Castle*, copyright 1946 by Robert Lowell. Reprinted by permission of Harcourt Brace Jovanovich, Inc.

Robert Lowell, "For the Union Dead," reprinted with permission of Farrar, Straus & Giroux, Inc. from *For the Union Dead* by Robert Lowell. Copyright © 1960 by Robert Lowell.

Archibald MacLeish, "The End of the World," from *The Collected Poems of Archibald MacLeish*, reprinted by permission of the publisher, Houghton Mifflin Company.

Louis MacNeice, "Leaving Barra," from *The Collected Poems of Louis MacNeice*, edited by E. R. Dodds. Copyright © 1966 by The Estate of Louis MacNeice. Reprinted by permission of Oxford University Press, Inc., and Faber and Faber Limited.

Terrence McNally, "Botticelli," reprinted by permission of William Morris Agency, Inc. Copyright © 1968 by Terrence McNally. Caution: Professionals and amateurs are hereby warned that "Boticelli," being fully protected under the copyright laws of the United States of America, The British Commonwealth, including the Dominion of Canada, and all other countries of the copyright union, The Berne Convention, The Pan-American Copyright Convention and the Universal Copyright Convention, is subject to license and royalty. All rights including, but not limited to, reproduction in whole or in part by a process or method, professional use, amateur use, film, recitation, lecturing, public reading, recording, taping, radio & television broadcasting, and the rights of translation into foreign languages, are strictly reserved. Particular emphasis is laid on the matter of readings, permission for which must be obtained in writing from the author's representative.

Stanley Milgram and Paul Hollander, "The Murder They Heard." Originally appeared in *The Nation*, June 15, 1964. Reprinted by permission of *The Nation*.

Yukio Mishima, "Three Million Yen," translated by Edward G. Seidensticker from *Death in Midsummer and Other Stories*. Copyright © 1966 by New Directions Publishing Corporation. Reprinted by permission of New Directions Publishing Corporation.

Marianne Moore, "Poetry," reprinted with permission of Macmillan Publishing Co., Inc., from *Collected Poems* by Marianne Moore. Copyright 1935 by Marianne Moore, renewed 1963 by Marianne Moore and T. S. Eliot.

Ogden Nash, "Song to Be Sung by the Father of Infant Female Children," from *Verses from 1929 on* by Ogden Nash. Copyright 1933 by Ogden Nash. Reprinted by permission of Little, Brown and Company and J. M. Dent & Sons Ltd.

Flannery O'Connor, "Greenleaf." Reprinted with permission of Farrar, Straus & Giroux, Inc., from *Everything that Rises Must Converge* by Flannery O'Connor, copyright © 1956, 1965 by the Estate of Mary Flannery O'Connor.

Liam O'Flaherty, "The Old Woman," from *The Stories of Liam O'Flaherty* by Liam O'Flaherty. Copyright 1956 by The Devin-Adair Company, Old Greenwich, Conn., reprinted by permission.

José Ortega y Gasset, "Landscape with a Deer in the Background," reprinted by permission of The World Publishing Company and Laurence Pollinger Ltd., from *On Love* by José Ortega y Gasset, translated by Toby Talbot. Copyright © 1957 by The World Publishing Company.

Wilfred Owen, "Dulce et Decorum Est," from *Collected Poems*. Copyright Chatto & Windus Ltd. 1946, © 1963. Reprinted by permission of the New Directions Publishing Corporation and the Executors of the Estate of Harold Owen and Chatto & Windus Ltd.

Plato, "The Death of Socrates," from *The Dialogues of Plato*, translated by Benjamin Jowett, 4th ed., 1953. Reprinted by permission of The Clarendon Press, Oxford.

Katherine Anne Porter, "The Grave," from *The Leaning Tower and Other Stories*, copyright 1944, 1972 by Katherine Anne Porter. Reprinted by permission of Harcourt Brace Jovanovich, Inc.

Theodore R. Poston, "Rat Joiner Routs the Klan," from *Modern Black Stories* by Theodore R. Poston (Woodbury, N.Y.: Barron's Educational Series, Inc., 1971). Reprinted by permission of the Estate of Theodore R. Poston.

John Crowe Ransom, "Dead Boy," copyright 1927 by Alfred A. Knopf, Inc. and renewed 1955 by John Crowe Ransom. Reprinted from *Selected Poems*, Third Edition, Revised and Enlarged by John Crowe Ransom, by permission of the publisher and Laurence Pollinger Ltd.

Adrienne Rich, "A Marriage in the 'Sixties," reprinted from *Snapshots of a Daughter-in-Law, Poems, 1954–1962* by Adrienne Rich, by permission of W. W. Norton & Co., Inc. Copyright © 1956, 1957, 1958, 1959, 1960, 1961, 1962, 1963, 1967 by Adrienne Rich Conrad.

Adrienne Rich, "A Marriage in the 'Sixties," reprinted from *Snapshots Daughter-in-Law, Poems, 1954–1962* by Adrienne Rich. By permission of W. W. Norton & Company, Inc. Copyright © 1956, 1957, 1958, 1959, 1960, 1961, 1962, 1963, 1967 by Adrienne Rich Conrad.

Edwin Arlington Robinson, "The Mill." Reprinted with permission of the Macmillan Publishing Co., Inc., from *Collected Poems* by Edwin Arlington Robinson. Copyright 1920 by Edwin Arlington Robinson, renewed 1948 by Ruth Nivison.

Edwin Arlington Robinson, "Mr. Flood's Party," reprinted with permission of Macmillan Publishing Co., Inc., from *Collected Poems* by Edwin Arlington Robinson. Copyright 1921 by Edwin Arlington Robinson, renewed 1949 by Ruth Nivison.

Theodore Roethke, "The Abyss," copyright © 1963 by Beatrice Roethke, Administratrix of the Estate of Theodore Roethke, from the book *The Collected Poems of Theodore Roethke*. Reprinted by permission of Doubleday & Company, Inc.

Theodore Roethke, "Elegy for Jane," copyright 1950 by Theodore Roethke from the book *The Collected Poems of Theodore Roethke*. Reprinted by permission of Doubleday & Company, Inc.

Theodore Roethke, "My Papa's Waltz," copyright 1942 by Hearst Magazines, Inc., and "Frau Bauman, Frau Schmidt, and Frau Schwartze," copyright 1952 by Theodore Roethke from the book *Collected Poems of Theodore Roethke*. Reprinted by permission of Doubleday & Company, Inc.

Philip Roth, "The Conversion of the Jews," from *Goodbye Columbus*. Copyright © 1959 by Philip Roth. Reprinted by permission of the publisher, Houghton Mifflin Company.

Berton Roueché, "S. Miami," from *A Man Named Hoffman* by Berton Roueché. Copyright © 1958, 1960, 1961, 1963, 1964, 1965, by Berton Roueché. Reprinted by permission of Little, Brown and Company and Harold Ober, Associates, Inc.

Franklin Russell, "A Madness of Nature," *New American Review*, No. 2, (1968). Reprinted by permission of John Cushman Associates, Inc. Copyright © 1968 by Franklin Russell.

Bernard Shaw, "Duse and Bernhardt," from *The Saturday Review*, 1895. Reprinted by permission of The Shaw Estate and The Society of Authors.

Louis Simpson, "John the Baptist," (copyright 1951 by Louis Simpson) is reprinted with the permission of Charles Scribner's Sons from Good News of Death and Other Poems by Louis Simpson, *Poets of Today, II*.

Louis Simpson, "The Man Who Married Magdalene," (copyright 1951 by Louis Simpson) is reprinted with permission of Charles Scribner's Sons from *Good News of Death and Other Poems* by Louis Simpson, *Poets of Today II*.

Isaac Bashevis Singer, "I Place My Reliance on No Man," reprinted by permission of Farrar Straus & Giroux, Inc., from *Short Friday and Other Stories* by Isaac Bashevis Singer, copyright © 1961, 1962, 1963, 1964 by Isaac Bashevis Singer. Also with permission of Laurence Pollinger Ltd.

Sophocles, "Oedipus the King," translated by Dudley Fitts and Robert Fitzgerald, copyright 1949 by Harcourt Brace Jovanovich, Inc., and reprinted with their permission. Caution: All rights, including professional, amateur, motion picture, recitation, lecturing, public reading, radio broadcasting, and television are strictly reserved. Inquiries on all rights should be addressed to Harcourt Brace Jovanovich, Inc., 757 Third Avenue, New York, N.Y., 10017.

Wallace Stevens, "Sunday Morning." Copyright 1923 and renewed 1951 by Wallace Stevens. Reprinted from *The Collected Poems of Wallace Stevens* by permission of Alfred A. Knopf, Inc.

Andre M. Tao-Kim-Hai, "Orientals are Stoic." Reprinted by permission; © 1957 The New Yorker Magazine, Inc.

Dylan Thomas, "Fern Hill," from *The Poems of Dylan Thomas*. Copyright 1946 by New Directions Publishing Corporation. Reprinted by permission of New Directions Publishing Corporation and J. M. Dent & Sons Ltd. and the Trustees for the Copyrights of the late Dylan Thomas.

James Thurber, "The Figgerin' of Aunt Wilma." Copyright © 1953 by James Thurber. From *Thurber Country*, published by Simon and Schuster. Originally printed in the New Yorker. Also from *Vintage Thurber* by James Thurber, copyright © 1963 Hamish Hamilton, London.

James Thurber, "The Secret Life of Walter Mitty." Copyright © 1942 by James Thurber; copyright © 1970 by Helen Thurber. From *My World—And Welcome to It*, published by Harcourt Brace Jovanovich. Originally printed in *The New Yorker*. Also from *Vintage Thurber* by James Thurber, copyright © 1963 by Hamish Hamilton, London.

John Updike, "The Persistence of Desire," copyright © 1959 by John Updike. Reprinted from *Pigeon Feathers and Other Stories* by John Updike, by permission of Alfred A. Knopf, Inc. Originally appeared in *The New Yorker*.

Robert Penn Warren, "Blackberry Winter," from *The Circus in the Attic and Other Stories*, copyright 1947 by Robert Penn Warren. Reprinted by permission of Harcourt Brace Jovanovich, Inc.

Eudora Welty, "Why I Live at the P.O." Copyright 1941, 1969 by Eudora Welty. Reprinted from her volume, *A Curtain of Green and Other Stories* by permission of Harcourt Brace Jovanovich, Inc.

E. B. White, "Walden: June 1939," from *One Man's Meat* by E. B. White. Copyright 1939 by E. B. White. Reprinted by permission of Harper & Row, Publishers, Inc.

Richard Wilbur, "June Light," from *The Beautiful Changes and Other Poems*, copyright 1947 by Richard Wilbur. Reprinted by permission of Harcourt Brace Jovanovich, Inc.

William Carlos Williams, "Asphodel, That Greeny Flower: Coda," from *Pictures from Brueghel and Other Poems* by William Carlos Williams. Copyright 1954 by William Carlos Williams. Reprinted by permission of New Directions Publishing Corporation.

William Carlos Williams, "Tract," from *Collected Earlier Poems* by William Carlos Williams. Copyright 1938 by New Directions Publishing Corporation. Reprinted by permission of New Directions Publishing Corporation.

William Butler Yeats, "An Irish Airman Foresees his Death," from *The Collected Poems of William Butler Yeats*. Reprinted by permission of M. B. Yeats, Miss Anne Yeats, the Macmillan Co. of Canada, and Macmillan Publishing Co., Inc. Copyright 1919 by Macmillan Publishing Co., Inc., renewed 1947 by Bertha Georgia Yeats.

William Butler Yeats, "Sailing to Byzantium," from *The Collected Poems of William Butler Yeats*. Reprinted by permission of M. B. Yeats, Miss Anne Yeats, the Macmillan Co. of Canada and Macmillan Publishing Co., Inc. Copyright 1928 by Macmillan Publishing Co., Inc., renewed 1956 by Bertha Georgia Yeats.

William Butler Yeats, "The Second Coming," from *The Collected Poems of William Butler Yeats*. Reprinted by permission of M. B. Yeats, Miss Anne Yeats, the Macmillan Co. of Canada, and Macmillan Publishing Co., Inc. Copyright 1924 by Macmillan Publishing Co., Inc., renewed 1952 by Bertha Georgia Yeats.

CONTENTS

Chapter 2   MAN AND WOMAN   47

Chapter 3   THE WORLD AROUND US   85

Chapter 4   THE CITY   132

Chapter 5   INDIVIDUAL AND SOCIETY   169

Chapter 6   COMMUNITY AND CONFLICT   232

Chapter 7 PEACE AND WAR   290

Chapter 8 ARTS AND THE MAN   331

Chapter 11   AT THE END OF LIFE   565

Chapter 12   ACHIEVEMENT AND REALIZATION   591

ANALYTIC CONTENTS

POETRY

Ballads and Narratives

DRAMA

PREFACE

When a book goes through several editions, each considerably revised, it may occur to some sardonic readers to wonder whether those responsible for it are ever going to get it right. But fortunately the editors of a literary anthology are not in the position of aiming at, and constantly missing, a target of frozen perfection. New combinations of works suggest themselves and new candidates beg to be included—one of the literature teacher's greatest satisfactions, after all, being to discover fresh examples to offer his students. And the editors, being human, change their interpretations and judgments as their experience of literature broadens and their study deepens.

This fourth edition of *Theme and Form,* like its predecessors, includes discursive writing, prose fiction, poetry, and drama. In our revision we have again introduced new subject areas, while consolidating the earlier ones to preserve the size of the volume. Roughly a third of the selections appear in *Theme and Form* for the first time, and most of these are the work of currently active writers. The old favorites should take on additional meaning from association with their new companions.

The introductory essay, "The Study of Literature," and the concluding exemplary analyses of an essay, a short story, a play, and a lyric poem have undergone various degrees of rewriting. With minor changes we have retained the Index of Critical Terms, which clarifies the terms that are most useful in literary discussion. As before, we offer the reader editorial assistance in coping with difficulties—unusual foreign words, puzzling allusions, and the like—that lie beyond the scope of his desk dictionary.

As "The Study of Literature" explains, the title *Theme and Form* links two fundamental aspects of literature. Both of these aspects, we believe, must be kept in view while studying any literary work, since they are intimately connected and derive their artistic value from their connection. One who enjoys literature at any level of artistry is implicitly acknowledging that literary works deal with the stuff of human experience and carry themes that resound and reverberate through all human life. But as one comes to enjoy more complex and therefore more rewarding works, one also comes to recognize that it is the way these experiences and themes are shaped that transforms the elementary matter of literature into art. It might be said that it is form that extracts thematic meaning from experience, and it is the theme that breathes life into form. By arranging our selections under broad thematic headings, we invite the teacher and the student to intensify their awareness of the human import of literature; by providing an alternate table of contents classifying the selections by genre, and by including examples of various types, structures, and styles, we also call attention to the formal aspects of literature.

Again we thank the many friends and colleagues who have given us help, both solicited and unsolicited, especially the teachers who have shared with us their valued reflections on their classroom experience with earlier editions. We also thank Ms. June Siegel for her helpful comments on our proposal for this edition. We acknowledge our continuing indebtedness to Professor Maynard Mack of Yale University, our series editor, and our new obligations to Mss. Marilyn Brauer and Sandra Messik of Prentice-Hall, Inc.

M. C. B. / R. W. D. / G. L.

THE STUDY
OF LITERATURE

A college student who opens this book may feel a little offended by its subtitle. The offer to introduce him to literature is perhaps a generous one, but does it not imply that he and literature have never met before? And surely if that were true, he would never have arrived in college.

Certainly the student comes to this book having already had many experiences of literature. These will have been of two distinct sorts: he has studied literature and he has enjoyed it. Occasionally, we hope, he has both studied and enjoyed it. . . . On the simplest level of enjoyment, all of us have laughed at jokes and watched stories unfold on the television screen. This is fun—but it is also a special kind of fun, the kind that comes from responding to a work, in however elementary a way, as literature. We have to grasp the point of the joke; we have to feel the suspense of the television story. These are specifically literary pleasures, but they are not the only, or the greatest, pleasures of literature. Many of us recall novels that we read long ago—and especially some of the characters in them—more vividly than we recall last month's television episode. To some books we return again and again because of the profound impression they made on us. Here also is the enjoyment of literature, more intense and lasting because deeper and more complex.

The other sort of experience, the study of literature, is familiar through years of schooling. We have been presented with certain acknowledged masterpieces or outstanding literary works—novels by Hardy and George Eliot, plays by Shakespeare, poems by Tennyson and Browning—and asked to analyze and explain them. This approach is detached and intellectual rather than immediate and emotional; instead of letting the work sweep us along, we examine its workings—its plot, its imagery, its rhyme-scheme.

Study and enjoyment, of course, do not necessarily go together. Some works we can enjoy though we have never closely examined them; how absurd it would be to anatomize a joke whose point is perfectly clear! Some works we study hard without managing to enjoy them at all—and no doubt certain pedantic ways of studying literature even interfere with enjoyment. Many students, indeed, come to college with a deep sense of conflict between the two approaches: they enjoy some works without understanding, they analyze others without enjoyment. And yet these two approaches are closely connected and should work co-operatively. Comparatively simple and easy works, whose pleasures lie on the surface, are fruits that are easily gathered. But there are others that cannot be enjoyed without concentration, thought, and skill. If their fruits are harder to reach, they reward the effort to grasp them, as those who have enjoyed them testify. Hence the study of literature: its purpose is to make understandable the subtler, less obvious aspects on which the pleasure of reading a literary work depends.

THE LITERARY WORKS

When we survey the writings that we have enjoyed reading for their own sakes—apart from any information they gave us, of the kind an encyclopedia article or almanac gives—we are struck by their great variety. There are works of prose fiction, ranging from jokes and short stories in the magazines of mass circulation to elaborate novels that follow a family through several generations; poems, including everything from nursery rhymes and light verse to the great epic poems, ancient and modern; drama, either read in the library or seen on stage or screen; and finally the essay, which also exists in numerous forms. All these works may be comprised under the general heading of "literature," though, as we shall see later, there are important differences among them.

But when we begin the study of literature, we must focus on the elements shared by all these various works—and especially the elements that make them literature, that distinguish them from other writings that are not literature, such as street-signs, advertisements, and chemistry textbooks. What, we must ask, are the essential features of a literary work?

A work of literature is, at the very least, a series of sentences, spoken or written. And the essence of a sentence is that in it someone is talking about something. It will help us to get our bearings if we begin with this basic distinction: in every work there is an implicit SPEAKER, and there is always a SITUATION about which he is speaking.[1] Consider, for example, the well-known anonymous poem that begins:

Frankie and Johnny were lovers.
O Lawdy how they did love!
They swore to be true to each other,
As true as the stars above.
He was her man, but he done her wrong.

The situation, baldly summarized, is a love affair that comes to grief because one of the parties is unfaithful and the other jealous. The speaker tells the story with some sympathy for both lovers, and with wonder at the unusual intensity of their relationship; he also makes it clear that he blames Johnny for what happens. And the reader is invited to share these feelings. The speaker and the situation together, and in relation to each other, make up the substance of the work: the speaker confronts certain violent events, and the poem embodies his response to what he observes and reports.

The Situation

The situation in a literary work may be anything that can be contemplated or thought about: a single object such as a wooded hill, as in A. E. Housman's "On Wenlock Edge,"[2] or a complex series of events, as in Shakespeare's *Othello*. Although the title may single out some salient or notable feature of the situation, as the title of "The Secret Life of Walter Mitty" tells us, in summary fashion, what the story is about, the situation consists of everything that happens or that appears in the work. It is thus unique to that work.

Yet when we compare two works with respect to their situations, we may find that they have a good deal in common: they are both about a love affair or about the same battle. In this case we may say that they are the same, or similar, in SUBJECT. A subject is not a particular situation, but a kind of situation. The situation in "Frankie and Johnny" includes such characters as the bartender and Nellie Bly; *Othello* includes not only Desdemona and Iago but all the lesser characters. Yet the subject, sexual jealousy leading to murder, is common to both works. It is the kind of situation, together with the genre, that may determine the way we classify a literary work. We say it is a love poem or a story of jealousy; in short, a literary work whose principal subject is love or jealousy. Or it is a war play, an elegy, a sports story.

The people referred to in a literary work need not, of course, ever have existed; the events reported need not have occurred. The death of Socrates was a historical event; the death of Peyton Farquhar in "An Occurrence at Owl Creek Bridge" is fictitious. It makes no difference, as far as the work itself is concerned. For the situation of the work is not something outside of it, something that the author read about or experienced. It is just what is presented in the work itself.

The situation in a work of literature is always a human situation of some kind. Even if the characters in a story are animals, like Snoopy in the *Peanuts* cartoon or the Houyhnhnms in *Gulliver's Travels*, or visitors from another planet, they speak English if the author's language is English, and act in ways that involve reflections or distortions or exaggerations of human motives. When they act or speak or suffer, they do so in a human way. Every literary work has the same subject: namely, human life.

One of the dimensions of the work is the scope of its situation: the range of human ex-

[1] See Index of Critical Terms, page 696, for further explanations of words in small capitals.

[2] All examples except a few very familiar ones will be found in this book.

perience it encompasses. The scope may be gauged in any of several ways: by the variety of character, incident, emotion that the work presents or implies; by the extent of time and space it covers; by the subtlety and depth of its penetration into the details of a single episode.

The Speaker

Every literary work implies, more or less distinctly, a speaker, who is the apparent or ostensible utterer of the words: in a lyric poem, the "I" of the poem; in a novel or short story, the narrator; in a drama, a kind of invisible impresario, the presumed selector and arranger of the scenes. Any understandable sentence or series of sentences comes to us as though written or spoken by a human being, and tells us, if we listen carefully, something about the sort of human being who might have uttered it.

The most obvious sort of example, of course, is dialect or regional slang like the expressions in the story "Blackberry Winter" that mark the narrator as one brought up in the rural South. More importantly, the speaker may reveal his personality by what he says, or does not say. He may take part in the action, reporting it in the first person, as happens in "The Secret Sharer" and "Araby." Or, without being actually involved, he may write about the events in such a way as to imply some relationship to them; perhaps he lives in the same village and has heard the story, as in "The Girl in Arles" and "A Rose for Emily."

Although it is often convenient to refer to the speaker of a literary work by the name of the author, this practice may be misleading. The speaker is not to be confused with the actual author, however similar they may be in character or point of view. Sometimes speaker and author are indeed very similar: no doubt William James really believed what he put into his essay "The Moral Equivalent of War," and Theodore Roethke may actually have felt about his student the way the speaker in "Elegy for Jane" does. But the speaker in "Why I Live at the P.O." bears little resemblance to Eudora Welty, and Browning's bishop is not Browning. A literary work is a performance of a particular kind; the author is playing a role, like an actor on the stage, and we are to keep our eyes, not on the actor, but on the part he is playing. All we can know about Eudora Welty's postmistress or the teacher in Roethke's poem is what the work itself reveals.

Just as a work has an implicit speaker, so it may have an implicit AUDITOR, who is also part of the work, though only hinted at. Browning's bishop, ordering his tomb at Saint Praxed's, ostensibly speaks to his illegitimate sons, whom he calls "nephews." Not many works have so specific an audience, but it is often illuminating to think of this aspect: after reading "Sonny's Blues," for example, to ask ourselves whom we imagine the narrator to be addressing.

Attitude

Another important dimension of a literary work involves the relationship between its speaker and the situation. A significant characteristic of literature is that the speaker does more than merely report or notify, announce or catalog. He shows—sometimes specifically and strongly, sometimes by suggestion—his ATTITUDE toward the events and persons he tells about.

Used in this way, the word "attitude" has a wide meaning, and especially it encompasses both emotional and intellectual relationships: that is, the speaker's *feelings* about the situation and his *beliefs* about it. These are so bound together that only conscious analysis can distinguish them, yet often they must be distinguished if they are to be seen clearly. An attitude that is reasonably well articulated becomes an appraisal of the situation: it consists of a moral condemnation or an acceptance of what is happening, or it suggests that actions are to be judged by certain definite standards. "He was her man, but he done her wrong" is a clear-cut example. In other works we may find an appraisal, not so explicitly stated, but even more clearly and powerfully present: the amused tolerance of the narrator in "The Figgerin' of Aunt Wilma," the ecstatic response of the speaker in "The Windhover." Not every work makes a moral judgment, of course, but every work deals with human acts and choices, and the speaker never wholly conceals the way in which these move and affect him.

The speaker's feelings are largely embodied in what is called the TONE of the literary work. When we say that a remark is bitter, envious, carefree, angry, hurt, or joyous, we are describing its tone. The speaker, to be sure, may simply tell us how he feels; in "The Faith of a Scientist" Thomas Henry Huxley expresses his attitude explicitly. On the other hand, feelings may only be suggested, as Plato's admiration of Socrates is revealed in the tone of his dialogues. The tone of "Spotted Horses" is evidently quite different from the tone of "A Rose for Emily," though the two stories have the same author. Tone is basically a function of STYLE and is to be understood by analyzing the stylistic components through which one tone differs from another. We shall come to style shortly.

Theme and Thesis

Besides considering a speaker's feelings, the affective elements in his attitude, we may examine its cognitive or intellectual element— which is to ask: What does he *believe* about the situation?

The two questions that are involved here must be distinguished. When in ordinary life we encounter an object or situation having some striking characteristic—a familiar house sadly in need of paint and repairs, a married couple quarreling bitterly—we may be reminded of one of the recurring aspects of human experience: the prevalence of change and decay, the blindness of human beings to what is in the hearts of others. Similarly, the speaker in a literary work may emphasize and focus attention upon something in the situation that makes us think, as he is supposedly thinking, of an abstract concept. The concrete images of the poem, the significant object on the stage, the climactic events of the story thus become symbolic, the bearers of broader meanings. These meanings are known as the THEMES of the work.

When someone mentions the name of a novel we have not read, we often ask, "What is it about?" Two different sorts of answer may be given. One of them we have already examined: we can say what the situation is, what is happening, what characters appear, and so on. The situation is the CONCRETE SUBJECT. But we may also answer by naming the general concepts or themes in the novel: it is about the riskiness of love, the mutability of things, the emptiness of pride or honor. The themes are the ABSTRACT SUBJECTS of the novel. After reading a difficult and complex work, we may have to pause and reflect before we are sure what the themes, or at least what the dominant themes, of that work may be. That is part of understanding it. There are many subtle themes implicit in the story "A Hunger-Artist" that do not emerge readily from it, yet when they are grasped they add enormously to its interest.

The speaker may, however, not merely convey a theme; he may advance a proposition.

"Young Goodman Brown," for example, is not merely about evil; it suggests that dwelling upon the evil in man, as the Puritans did, may itself be corrupting. This is the THESIS—or one of the theses—of the story. When we speak of the religious or philosophical content of a literary work, its social or ideological message, we mean its thesis. Almost any essay, of course, advances a thesis—often a number of them— but a poem that states no opinions explicitly may nevertheless convey them implicitly, as Auden's "September 1, 1939" suggests a critical view of recent history. A thesis, then, is a proposition—true or false, acceptable or unacceptable—that can be abstracted from a work and considered separately: although the proposition may appear crude and bare when stripped of the refinements it possesses in its literary context. Yet the coherence of a set of theses running connectedly through a large work may be one of its most important aspects; the system of beliefs may contribute to the unity of the work and enhance its depth and complexity. Here is another important dimension of the work: the largeness of its themes and theses; its penetration, its profundity, its capacity to explain and give significance to a wide range of human experience. Not all literary works have theses; some only consider their subjects without commenting on them, at least very definitely. But all works have themes, and it is always profitable to identify these and consider how they are related, and how broad and deep they are.

FORM IN LITERATURE

Even the simplest literary work is made up of parts: of paragraphs or stanzas, of scenes or episodes. And its situation is made up of elements: few or many characters, who may change much or little as they are involved in incidents that are violent or calm, long or short, funny or sad—characters who project aims and hopes, who succeed or fail. The FORM of the work is just the ways in which all these parts and elements are connected with one another. When we say that the sestet of a sonnet is an answer to a question or doubt raised in the octave, or that a play contains two distinct plots that parallel or contrast with each other, we are talking about form.

Much of the study of literature consists in the study of form, and that is understandable when we consider the two essential roles that form plays in our enjoyment of literature. First, much of the enjoyment is precisely enjoyment of form. Some people, to be sure, are so fond of horses that they read anything about horses and presumably enjoy it; and doubtless this enjoyment is an enjoyment of subject, rather than form. But usually we enjoy a story because it builds up suspense toward an exciting climax, or because the plot works out neatly to a conclusion that seems somehow right and inevitable, or because of other such factors. On these occasions, it is the form of the work that we are responding to. The form, moreover, plays a basic psychological role: it permits us, for instance, to respond without fear even to a fearful subject—and hence to enjoy our response.

This second point requires explanation. When we read a literary work, we are human beings reading about human beings; we follow the work with interest because something is happening, is developing. The moving force in that development is conflict, either between persons or within one person's mind; it is conflict, often painful and severe conflict, that generates powerful emotions and drives people to actions. Some of these actions are bloody and evil, and we in turn, in reading about them, are deeply moved—to pity, to indignation, to fear or sadness. If the work is to engage us in this way, evoking a strong emotional response, we must feel a deeply sympathetic kind of identification with the characters, both heroes and villains. But in so doing we are playing a dangerous game: if in real life we encountered betrayals of love, or lynchings, or murders, we should be struck by terror or despair. The work must therefore preserve in us, as readers, some detachment or distance from what is happening, despite our emotional state; and all the varieties and resources of form are marshaled by the literary artist for just this purpose—to keep the emotions under control, to help us master and thus enjoy them, instead of succumbing to them. That is how our imaginative apprehension of Frankie's feelings about Johnny's unfaithfulness takes on a very different, and far more valuable, quality than our experience of reading, as we may do every day in the newspaper, that some man or woman has been shot by a lover for running around with somebody else.

Kinds of Structure

The parts of a literary work may themselves consist of parts, and those parts may in turn be analyzed. So we may speak of the dominant or subordinate parts of the work: the major sections or the smaller sequences that make them up. Since the form of the work is the whole set of relationships among its parts, form may be considered at two levels. The distinction is not sharp, but it is very useful. The relationships among the dominant parts constitute the STRUCTURE of the work; the relationships among the smaller parts constitute its TEXTURE.

Oedipus the King, for example, consists of a series of scenes, in each of which a new fact is revealed to Oedipus. Part of its structure, then, is the sequence of changes in his knowledge, and of stages of increasing intensity in the pervasive sense of impending doom. Shirley Jackson's "Pillar of Salt" is built upon a simple reversal: the narrator's original attitude is turned upside down. These are examples of structure. They play a crucial role in making the works interesting and satisfying to read, and they do so in part by making them unified.

To ask about the structure of a literary work is to ask what its main binding principles are: what makes it hang together, connects its beginning with its end, and defines for it a shape that the reader's mind can grasp. It might be possible to divide and subdivide the varieties of literary structure in an elaborate way; for our purposes it will be sufficient to define three main categories.

(1) PLOT STRUCTURE. A plot, defined succinctly, is a sequence of events in which a person forms a purpose and tries to realize it against obstacles. These elements seem to be essential. The activity that consists of a man's walking down the street is not a plot, even if he has a purpose in mind; but if something happens to hinder his efforts to reach his goal, then we have a plot, albeit a simple one. A plot may of course be complicated enormously by being extended through many incidents and combined with other plots, and other, related purposes may supersede the original one.

A literary work may or may not have a plot; but if it has, that plot will have a more or less definite structure, and that structure will play a crucial part in determining how coherent and complete the work is. It is in the nature of a plot as we have defined it to have a beginning, a middle, and an end. The beginning is the point at which the purpose is formed, or at which we first discern the purpose. The first sentence may tell us that a tall, well-dressed man turned the corner into Market Street; a little later we may become aware that he is going to meet a man he has determined to kill. The emergence of obstacles to his purpose makes up the middle of the story: the appearance of the police or the victim's reluctance to be killed. The end is the resolution of the conflict, the ultimate success or failure of the initial purpose; the murder occurs, or the would-be murderer is effectually frustrated.

Within this broad pattern, a great variety of plot structures can be found, depending on the number and interconnections of the purposes, the characters, the obstacles, and so forth. Our sense of the coherence of the work will depend on such matters as the invention of adequate motivation for the characters, the extent to which the events grow inevitably out of developing situations, the plausibility of the characters and their actions. Our sense of the completeness and self-sufficiency of the work will depend on such effects as our impression that the beginning is really a beginning, with nothing left unexplained that we feel needs to be explained, and the decisiveness and finality of the consummation—the completeness of our feeling that the story has been wholly written.

(2) LOGICAL STRUCTURE. Statements put together in the same discourse must have some coherent relationship. A literary work that is not a narrative and therefore has no plot will have to be held together in another fashion —as by having some form of logical structure.

Logical structure is more apparent in literary works—verse as well as prose essays—that are essentially arguments. Such a work contains not only a thesis or group of theses but also a set of reasons that support the conclusions. If the reasons are truly reasons, they must have some logical connection with the conclusions they are supposed to support. The argument, in short, will be inductive or deductive; it may be an argument from analogy or a syllogistic argument, or it may have some other logical form.

Even if the work is not an argument but a description of something, it will have some logical structure. It may be based, for example, on a system of classification, by which different aspects of the object are discussed in sequence; it may proceed from a consideration of parts to a consideration of the whole, from description to evaluation, from cause to effect—or vice versa. It may consist only of true statements beginning with "George Washington" or "He," yet these may be said to be logically parallel

since they refer to the same person—though if that is the only principle of organization, and the statements jumble together otherwise unrelated facts about George Washington, the work will not, of course, be very unified.

(3) KINETIC (RHETORICAL) STRUCTURE. A third kind of structure is less easy to recognize than the first two, and less easy to describe. It depends partly upon them, though it may exist even in a lyric poem which has neither plot nor, in the strict sense, a logical structure. Milton's sonnet "On His Blindness," for instance, begins with the speaker's brooding over his misfortune; it ends with a realization that reconciles him to it. If we trace the pattern of emotional intensity, we find that the speaker's feeling rises to a height of despair through the first seven lines; at that point a new and opposite feeling emerges, and by the last line the despair has been overcome. We are here describing the movement of the poem, the pattern of its emotional development; and this pattern is its kinetic or rhetorical structure.

A plot moves, too, of course—and indeed the most fundamental part of our response to it is our attention to the fortunes of its characters: What are they up to? Will their purposes be achieved? So there are crises and CLIMAXES as the plot develops—moments of high tension, turning points in the action with periods of comparative quiet between; there are changes of pace and changes in the scope and size of the action.

Texture and Style

Turning from the structure of literature to its TEXTURE is like turning from a small-scale road map of the Eastern United States to a large-scale map of New York City. An important fact about literary works, as we have seen, is that they deal with persons and their actions; it is also an important fact that they are written in words. To study the language of a work, the details of its workmanship, is to study its texture.

Since a word is a sound with meaning, it presents two aspects for consideration. Especially when we study poetry do we realize the extent to which the power that words may have over us depends upon their sound, their qualities of smoothness and harshness, their metrical patterns, their rhymes and alliterations. At present, however, we are concerned with the other aspects of words, their meanings, and the ways in which these can mesh with each other to produce some of the most characteristic qualities of literature. We are concerned, not with the sound-texture, but with the meaning-texture.

When we speak of the STYLE of a literary work, or of a writer, we mean certain recurrent features of the texture. The style of a writer includes his preference for a certain diction (colloquial expressions, for example, or words of Latin origin) and his preference for certain constructions (compound-complex sentences, parallel clauses, parenthetical expressions). And it includes the devices he employs to obtain what we shall call, in the most general sense, MULTIPLE MEANING: that is, suggestions of meaning in addition to the expressed, literal meaning. There are a great many such devices, including IRONY, SIMILE, and ALLUSION, but the general principle can be illustrated by an example of the most complex sort, METAPHOR. T. S. Eliot's poem "The Hollow Men" begins,

> We are the hollow men
> We are the stuffed men. . . .

The important fact about a metaphorical expression is that it presents, on its primary level of meaning, a manifest impossibility. Perhaps a man may be imagined as hollowed out, or as stuffed like an owl or a moose. But obviously it is impossible for a living, speaking man, like the speaker in the poem, to be literally hollow or stuffed. It is even more obvious that he could not be both hollow and stuffed at the same time. So when we try to take such a remark seriously, as the grave tone of the poem seems to demand, we find ourselves driven to explore a secondary level of potential meaning, the metaphorical senses of "hollow" and "stuffed." We think of the connotations of these words, of the spiritual emptiness, the moral deadness, the creative incapacity that the words mean when applied to human beings. A hollow tree is simply what it is; a hollow man is rich in implied significance.

When, in this way, we understand the metaphor, we are reading the lines in their full sense. Words put together in novel metaphorical combinations generate new meanings that have never existed before. An effective metaphor is not simply a decoration or a play on words; there is no substitute for it. It contributes a complex of meanings to the work, helping the work to become an example of meaning condensed and compacted beyond the ability

of ordinary, literal language. In a similar way, other rhetorical devices and figures of speech enrich discourse by multiplying its capacity to mean.

THE MODES OF LITERATURE

One literary work, as we have seen, may differ from another in any of several ways: in the sort of situation it involves, in the speaker's relation to the situation, in its structure or texture, in its theme or thesis. Even if we consider only the possible varieties of form—and of course we cannot foresee what forms future writers may invent—there are many theoretical combinations. But certain of these have proved more fruitful aesthetically than others, and hence more durable. We shall refer to them as MODES of literature; they are also called "genres." Literature exists in four chief modes.

Since all four modes are represented in this book, we must briefly describe them,[3] showing how they are distinguished from one another and what their significant characteristics are.

Poetry

The mode of literature called POETRY is notoriously hard to define, yet the following statements would probably meet with general acceptance: (1) such works as "On His Blindness" and "The Hollow Men" are poems, though the form of the first is regular and that of the second is irregular; (2) the mode of literature made up of works like these is distinct from other modes; (3) "On His Blindness" is written in VERSE, "The Hollow Men" in free verse—but it is not the verse that makes them poetry. Let us first examine the distinctions contained in the third statement.

To say that a work is written in verse—regular, not free—implies that it is metered. Not everyone agrees about the nature of METER in English verse, but it is widely believed to depend upon the fact that the syllables of English words are, as dictionaries tell us, either stressed or unstressed. When the stressed syllables of a discourse occur regularly enough to be felt as a pattern, the result is meter. (Characteristically, the pattern is reinforced by division of the sentences into lines having an equal number of syl-

---

[3] For a more extensive discussion of each one, see pages 670–95.

lables.) Accenting the first line of "On His Blindness,"

/		/		/		/		/	
When	I	con·sid·er	how	my	light	is	spent,
1	2	3	4	5	6	7	8	9	10

we see that only the even-numbered syllables are stressed. Moreover, each of the other lines has ten syllables; and though the pattern of stresses is not precisely maintained throughout —it is very freely handled in line 10, "Either man's work or his own gifts. Who best"—it is everywhere approximated.

Verse, then, is metrical discourse; it emphasizes the sounds of words to a greater extent than is normal in ordinary language. (It may also contain rhyme, as "On His Blindness" does, but it need not.) FREE VERSE is a term devised to label what is near the borderline: although "free" of the regular recurrence of stressed syllables and of syllabic equality from line to line, it nevertheless exhibits some form of unusual rhythmic organization. Its phrases may be printed on separate lines, emphasizing the groups of sounds that compose its sentences. It may rely heavily on repetition: except for one word, the second line of "The Hollow Men" is identical with the first.

Poetry is verse, regular or free, but not all verse is poetry. The following would be generally considered to be one and not the other:

> Simple Simon met a pieman
>   Going to the Fair.
> Said Simple Simon to the pieman,
>   "Let me taste your ware."

Although some readers might differ, this stanza appears to be something less than poetry, or at any rate something different from it. It is metrical fiction, but it lacks two qualities that together are essential for poetry.

The sentences in "Simple Simon" are plain and clear, but convey little beyond the surface. The ballad "Frankie and Johnny," on the other hand, which is also a straightforward report of a series of incidents, contains a good deal of implied meaning as well. Even in its first stanza we encounter a simile, "As true as the stars above"; a pungent colloquialism with considerable secondary meaning ("He was her man"); and a sudden, dramatic shift (". . . but he done her wrong") that foreshadows the development of the theme. Verse tends to be poetry when it is characterized by figurative language,

by irony, by an emergent theme that its imagery conveys. If complication and enrichment of the language of "Simple Simon" could turn Simon into a symbol of the Common Man faced with the stern economic doctrine of *caveat emptor,* the verses would acquire an additional level of meaning, and come nearer to being a poem.

Along with complexity of meaning, poetry exhibits a second characteristic: namely, feeling. The speaker in "Simple Simon" merely states; in the first stanza, at least, he does not seem to care about what he is telling. The speaker in "Frankie and Johnny," by contrast, cannot suppress his emotion; it comes out in the exclamation "O Lawdy" and in the bitter tone of the refrain. One reason there is no feeling in "Simple Simon," of course, is that it lacks conflict; the first stanza promises no important purpose, no obstacles. But the moment we learn that Frankie and Johnny are caught in an intense, possessive love, we realize that the situation has risks and can lead to trouble. The speaker is concerned, and so may the reader be.

A poem, then, is a discourse having these characteristics: it is verse, it involves feeling, and its language tends to be rich in figures of speech and other devices that produce complexity of meaning. In this book, nevertheless, *poem* and *poetry* are used as descriptive rather than evaluative terms. Those who dislike the works of Edgar A. Guest sometimes say that they are not poetry, but merely verse. Here they would be called bad poems.

Prose Fiction

Prose FICTION, including short stories and novels, may be distinguished from the other modes of literature by four criteria. The first two are simple and plain. A prose fiction is a narrative; it contains a plot. And it is written in prose, or nonmetrical language.

In the third place, it is fiction. Unlike the historian and the journalist, the writer of fiction lets us know, by various devices, that he is telling a made-up story; the events he relates could have happened, but actually never did. Perhaps woven into the story are historical persons and actual happenings—even friends or enemies of the writer, in disguise. But they have become part of the tale; the writer makes no claim of literal truth; he says, "Let me tell you a story."

A fourth important feature of prose fiction is that it implies a spatial and temporal PERSPECTIVE upon the events described. Fiction is characteristically told in the past tense, as of events gone by; it is make-believe history. This perspective, looking back as though on the past, is established by the descriptive passages, within which the dramatic scenes—dialogue and detailed descriptions of action—are embedded. When we read these dramatic passages, the scene unrolls as though happening now, before our eyes, but we are not permitted to forget for long that the events are supposed to have occurred some time before they are reported. Verbs in the past tense—"He said," "She said"—characterize even the scenes of dialogue and action narrated in detail.

The narrator's spatial point of view is the vantage-point from which he surveys what is going on. The substance of fiction is, broadly speaking, a CONFLICT—sometimes an overt conflict between two people, as in "Greenleaf," sometimes an inner, psychological one, as in "Three Million Yen," sometimes a confrontation of life's inexorable forces of time and change, as in "Blackberry Winter." The conflict always takes place against a particular background, or SETTING, which helps to define its terms, to sharpen its point. Setting includes the physical scene, the climate and weather, and the objects or properties (in the theatrical sense): the Greenleafs' bull, the "three-million-yen" cracker, the drowned cow. The narrator himself has, at all times, a distinct position from which he observes the conflict in its setting: he may speak as though inside one of the characters, seeing the others from the outside only ("After Cortes"), or switch from one to another ("The Blind Man"), or remain purely objective, outside them all ("The Undefeated").

The Drama

Drama in its primary sense is something that takes place on a stage or screen. That is the drama as produced. In a second, derived sense, the drama is the script, what the dramatist writes and the producer starts with in casting the parts, designing the scenes, rehearsing the actors. The script is the drama as literature. It is, of course, in the second sense that the plays included in this book are drama.

Since plays, like prose fiction, are narratives, what has been said about conflict and setting applies as well to the drama. The difference lies in what may be called degree of immediacy. When a prose fiction is dramatized the purely narrative passages disappear, except for brief indications of actions that the dialogue does

not imply. Descriptive passages are reduced to indications of the setting and a few of the characters' movements. Dialogue is accompanied by little more than the names of the speakers. Some plays, such as those of Bernard Shaw's, exist in special reading versions, which describe what is presented on stage by costume, scene, and action; others, such as *Oedipus*, leave almost everything except their dialogue to the reader's imagination. But in either case, to read a play is to experience not a series of events already concluded—the experience of a story—but an action happening now, before our eyes. The tense of drama is the present, or the future becoming the present.

In a drama the speaker withdraws to the wings, but he does not disappear entirely. We see the evidence of his controlling hand in the way the scenes are selected and developed, in what he chooses to reveal to us; and we may discern something of his thought in the implied theses of the play.

The Essay

The term ESSAY covers a large body of writings, ranging in length from a few paragraphs to a book and embracing some religious meditations ("A Discourse of Bells"), some scientific writings (Berton Roueché's "S. Miami"), and some history ("My Furthest Back Person—the African").

What distinguishes the essay from the other three modes of literature is its essential claim to truth. Unlike poetry, fiction, and drama, it does not pretend. Even when it is rather playful, like "Shakespeare in the Bush," it sets forth a basically serious thesis, which it invites the reader to accept. This is quite evident in the REFLECTIVE ESSAY ("In Search of Fundamental Values"), which is an argument: it states its thesis and defends it by reasons. But it is also true of the other main variety, the NARRATIVE ESSAY ("The Price of Amphibians"), which narrates a plot as a work of fiction does, but asserts that the events really happened or that the situation actually exists and draws, implicitly if not explicitly, a general conclusion.

A harder problem is to distinguish the literary essay from other works that purport to convey truth—from history and science that are not literature, from newspaper stories and advertisements. No very sharp line can be drawn here, and a few of the selections in this book may be considered borderline cases. Yet regarding them as literary essays can be defended on three grounds. First, their tone is to some extent personal: a speaker is present, and we are aware of him as a human being, with human feelings and convictions, as we are not when we read a carefully depersonalized scientific report. If there is some feeling, some human warmth, in a work, then it is more than a scientific document—though it may be that, too—and can be responded to as literature. Second, these are literary essays in that they have style, in the broad sense; they exhibit some subtlety in their awareness of meanings and distinctions, and some complexity in their development of secondary meanings through figures of speech and other devices. Third, these works have, to a greater extent than nonliterary essays, articulated and satisfactory form—especially kinetic form, a sense of movement and climax, a placing of points so that they are cumulative in their effect, a contrasting of points that produces irony and surprise.

Any work, whether a scientific paper, a piece of historical scholarship, or a newspaper item, that shows some of these qualities can lay claim to being a literary work—though, of course, not necessarily a great one.

THE AIMS AND METHODS OF LITERARY STUDY

Works of literature, like all other things, can be the objects of systematic, disinterested study. Like the chemist or the anthropologist, the literary critic or scholar is moved by the simple but absorbing desire to know and to understand. To him, the distinctions we have been making are part of a large scheme of concepts and categories that he uses in probing the nature of literature and its varieties.

To the rest of us, however, literature is worth studying because it is worth reading. From this point of view literary study is a process of preparing oneself for a fruitful encounter with literary works. It is a training of the intellect and the feelings so that they become capable of possessing what literary works have to offer in and through an adequate experience of them.

The Values of Literature

A simple source of satisfaction, such as a chocolate ice-cream cone, has but one dimension of value: it can be enjoyed in just one way. Literary works, even the simplest of them, are comparatively complex; they may have various values, of diverse sorts. In order to know what one can expect to obtain from the study of literature, and to decide how this study ought to be conducted, we must understand what the main values of literature are and how they are related. We may represent these values by three concentric circles.

The central and distinctive value of literature —in the innermost circle—is its AESTHETIC value. When we speak of "a good poem," "a first-rate novel," "an excellent play," we refer to this kind of value, for we have in mind the special kind of goodness that a poem, a novel, or a play can have as a work of literature. This kind of value, which depends primarily on the structure and texture of the work and consists in its capacity to provide the qualified reader with an experience that is unified, complex, and intense, is therefore inherently satisfying.

The aesthetic value of literature is, of course, a value shared with the other arts, for a musical composition or a painting can also yield the sort of experience that we think of as "an experience." But the wide resources of literature —of story and description, of emotional appeal and logical argument, of word-sound and multiple meaning—enable it to range over the whole of human thought, action, and feeling. Hence the experiences that it creates may be more complicated and profound than those of the other arts. There is evidence, moreover, that literature reaches us on unconscious levels, where it touches repressed impulses, helping us to face them indirectly and thereby to satisfy them without loss of control. If this is so, it partly accounts for both the conscious delight of reading and the less obvious liberating, inspiriting, and harmonizing effect that readers of literature experience.

We move outward to the second circle of our diagram when we consider the relationship of the literary work to the real world, through the implications of its themes and theses. Far more than the arts of vision and hearing, literature bears on the whole life of the human being: it says something, it makes a comment on the world and especially the human world—or, at the very least, it exemplifies an attitude, a point of view, toward the world. In this way it can give us insights into ourselves and our lives, helping us to understand ourselves and others. This kind of value, which depends mainly on the substance of the work, is its value as knowledge, its *cognitive* value.

It is not that stories and poems are capable of proving psychological generalizations in the way a psychologist does; they are not substitutes for science. But they often propose ideas about human nature and, explicitly or implicitly, invite the reader to try them out in his own experience. Literature enlarges our acquaintance with human beings—with possible if not actual ones—and sharpens our perceptions of human motives and feelings. Consider four examples. The subtle ingredients of jealousy and the various forms it takes are revealed in "Frankie and Johnny," "A Rose for Emily," "The Blind Man," and *Othello*. These works may not teach us about jealousy directly, but by stimulating and refining our awareness they may enormously enhance our ability to win knowledge and understanding from our own experience. By confronting us with poignant examples of moral choice, and exploring their implications, literary works can increase our moral sensitivity and deepen our ethical insight. (See, for instance, such stories as "The Guest" and "The Blood of the Martyrs.") One reason some literary works are called great—better than merely good—is that they deal with profound and universal human problems in a way which brings the reader understanding.

The outermost circle of our diagram comprises those more peripheral values of literature that arise from its capacity for inspiring us to change ourselves or the world around us. Such a work possesses *social* values, including moral, political, and religious ones; and these depend on its substance and form combined. A literary work need not be a call to action in order to be good or great; and of course if it is only a call to action, without being good or great, it is mere propaganda or advertising. But a novel that is good simply as a novel may also, in times of social crisis or social need, serve other ends as well: it may arouse the reader's indignation against some flagrant injustice to which he has been blind or indifferent; it may awaken him to a new religious awareness that changes the direction of his life and his work. Many evils in the world—brutality, slavery, economic exploitations—have been pointed out in literary works, and the emotions thus aroused have hastened amelioration of those evils. This is evident with writings that, primarily aimed at social action, became literature, as it were, despite themselves: Rachel Carson's "Nature Fights Back." But social values inhere equally in some famous novels and plays. Even some of the short stories in this book may arouse readers against the conditions they describe; consider, for instance, "A Trifling Occurrence," "If I Forget Thee, O Earth," and "Rat Joiner Routs the Klan."

The Thematic Method

There are various methods of studying literature, or avenues by which it may be fruitfully approached. The historical approach considers literary works in chronological sequence, from *The Iliad* to *Catch-22* and beyond. It stresses the influence of one writer on another and the development of modes and sub-modes. The social-psychological approach relates literary works to the milieus in which they were written, exploring the biography of the writer and the political and social conditions under which he wrote, in an effort to explain how the work came to be what it is.

Both of these methods are difficult and unenlightening unless the reader has already approached literature, and given it considerable attention, in a third way. This is the formal approach, which groups works according to their modes (short stories, lyric poems, and so on) and studies each mode separately, with respect to its principles of design and techniques of construction. This kind of study is surely indispensable for the other two, but, like them, it offers difficulties at the start. If forms are considered apart from the subjects they shape and the themes they embody and define, the reasons for studying them will be far from clear, and the works may come to seem abstract and lifeless. That is why this book proposes and recommends a fourth method of study.

The fundamental tool of the student of literature is comparison. It is comparison that enables him to understand a work of literature, both its form and its subject. The special and significant aspects of a work show up more plainly when it is compared with others. The more ways in which two works are similar, the more their differences emerge and become clear. At some stage in the study of a work it must be compared with others having similar formal features: a lyric with a lyric, a short story with a short story. But at an early stage of fairly serious and intensive literary study, we look for comparisons that will bring us most quickly to a comprehensive grasp of all the important aspects of the work. And what first strikes us about a story or poem, as a kind of solid center—and what is most likely to make one work remind us of another—is its central situation and the themes that radiate from it: its concern with growing out of childhood, or falling in love, or becoming aware of artistic beauty. This consideration has led to the organization adopted for this book.

The works making up each chapter—essays, stories, poems, and in some chapters a play—are grouped together because they have similar subjects and share a cluster of related themes that grow out of these. Thus, one chapter is concerned with persons in love, another with the relationship of the individual to his society, another with experience of the arts. We suggest that the works in each chapter be read and discussed together. A careful consideration of the similarities and differences in their treatment of the subject and their development of the themes will lead to discussion of the significant aspects of structure and texture that give form to the situation, and precision and vitality to the themes. The discussion of literary form can, if desired, be made the occasion for excursions into the history of literary modes, as well as the relation between literature and social conditions. This way of gaining access to literature may be called the *thematic method*.

Comparison of two short stories with similar themes, such as "After Cortes" and "I Place My Reliance on No Man," illuminates the differences in the way each theme is worked out; and some truths about the nature of the short story and its range also emerge. When an essay, a short story, and a poem with similar themes are compared ("The Murder They Heard," "Pillar of Salt," and "Preludes," for instance), certain essential differences between these modes become clear. Reading a few essays that deal abstractly with a topic such as the nature of science also leads to a better grasp of the

themes and theses that are implicit in related stories and poems.

We have not tried to force literary works into arbitrarily defined categories; the situations that unify each chapter are those with which literature has always been greatly concerned. Even less do we advocate a limited view of each work. If *Oedipus the King* is placed in the chapter on "Achievement and Realization," it is because that seems to us one fruitful way of considering some of its most important aspects. But it can fruitfully be compared to works in other chapters, too. Nor do we insist that the contents be read in a particular order, though the modes are kept distinct within each chapter. The simplest and easiest essays are put first. The order of chapters is equally discretionary. In general, the themes become more complex and the writings more profound as the book moves on; the plays occur in the natural order of study, from the most accessible to the least.

For students and instructors who prefer to study these works in some other order—to bring out themes or formal patterns that we have not emphasized—we have provided an alternate table of contents in which the modes are grouped and subdivided. Indeed, we urge the reader to experiment with various combinations, looking for illuminating comparisons that have not occurred to the editors. But whatever order he follows, it is our hope that he will finish his study of this book with a strong sense of the unity of literature—the fundamental worth that underlies all its differences. We believe he will take away with him a better understanding of both the older and acknowledged masterpieces and the new, contemporary works that are here. And we hope that through the wide variety of literary enjoyments that these selections afford, he will be helped to count the values of literature among his permanent possessions.

THEME AND FORM

Chapter 1

EARLY YEARS

A serious literary work is one in which the thoughtful reader can discern a general significance: whatever specific situations and happenings it may be about, its ultimate subject is the human condition itself—the natural, social, and cosmic situation within which human beings act and suffer. It conveys something of the wonder, the humor, the irony, the peril, or the challenge of our common predicament. More often than not, these universal meanings are not stated, but suggested; yet they are there to be grasped, and must be grasped if the work is to be fully realized.

One of the most pervasive characteristics of human experience is change: contingent change, such as may be brought about by accident, by a determined will, by natural forces impinging on our lives; or necessary change, such as we see in the natural rhythms and processes of birth, growth, maturity, decline, and death. Many writers, trying in their middle years to understand the shape of their own lives and to discover what they have learned from that about the life of mankind in general, turn to memories of their youth for experiences that can illuminate the persistent questions and can become the material of literature.

Early experiences, through their sharpness of outline and directness of feeling, can often with little shaping be made into literature; but always they are transformed in some degree: rearranged, concentrated, combined, their qualities heightened by literary art. "The Figgerin' of Aunt Wilma" and "The Price of Amphibians" appear to be reports of actual events; yet when we study the details of their structure and texture, we see how they are made larger than life, more interesting than life, by selection and emphasis, by focus on significant features, by control of style. And an essay like "Knoxville: Summer 1915," or a poem like "There Was a Boy" or "Birches," clearly as it draws upon personal experience, makes of the original experience something far more meaningful than it could have been originally.

The selections in this chapter deal with a number of aspects of the life of those who are learning to find their way about in the strange and sometimes terrifying world of adults: youthful zest and search for identity in "Knoxville: Summer 1915" and "Fern Hill"; the experience of the first betrayal by adults, in "A Trifling Occurrence"; inarticulate vain longing, in "Araby"; ways of being protectively loved, in "Blackberry Winter" and "My Papa's Waltz"; and the endless struggle of the child to fit somehow into the scheme of things laid out by grown-ups, in "The Price of Amphibians."

James Thurber

THE FIGGERIN' OF AUNT WILMA

When I was a boy, John Hance's grocery stood on the south side of Town Street, just east of Fourth, in the Central Market region of Columbus, Ohio. It was an old store even then, forty-five years ago, and its wide oak floor boards had been worn pleasantly smooth by the shoe soles of three generations of customers. The place smelled of coffee, peppermint, vinegar, and spices. Just inside the door on the left, a counter with a rounded glass front held all the old-fashioned penny candies—gumdrops, licorice whips, horehound, and the rest—some of them a little pale with age. On the rear wall, between a barrel of dill pickles and a keg of salt mackerel in brine, there was an iron coffee grinder, whose handle I was sometimes allowed to turn.

Once, Mr. Hance gave me a stick of Yucatan gum, an astonishing act of generosity, since he had a sharp sense of the value of a penny. Thrift was John Hance's religion. His store was run on a strictly cash basis. He shared the cost of his telephone with the Hays Carriage Shop, next door. The instrument was set in a movable wooden cubicle that could be whirled through an opening in the west wall of the store. When I was ten, I used to hang around the grocery on Saturday afternoons, waiting for the telephone to disappear into the wall. Then I would wait for it to swing back again. It was a kind of magic, and I was disappointed to learn of its mundane purpose—the saving of a few dollars a month.

Mr. Hance was nearly seventy, a short man with white hair and a white mustache and the most alert eyes that I can remember, except perhaps Aunt Wilma Hudson's. Aunt Wilma lived on South Sixth Street and always shopped at Mr. Hance's store.

Mr. Hance's eyes were blue and capable of a keen concentration that could make you squirm. Aunt Wilma had black agate eyes that moved restlessly and scrutinized everybody with bright suspicion. In church, her glance would dart around the congregation seeking out irreverent men and women whose expressions showed that they were occupied with worldly concerns, or even carnal thoughts, in the holy place. If she lighted on a culprit, her heavy, dark brows would lower, and her mouth would tighten in righteous disapproval. Aunt Wilma was as honest as the day is long and as easily confused, when it came to what she called figgerin', as the night is dark. Her clashes with Mr. Hance had become a family legend. He was a swift and competent calculator, and nearly fifty years of constant practice had enabled him to add up a column of figures almost at a glance. He set down his columns swiftly on an empty paper sack with a stubby black pencil. Aunt Wilma, on the other hand, was slow and painstaking when it came to figgerin'. She would go over and over a column of numbers, her glasses far down on her nose, her lips moving soundlessly. To her, rapid calculation, like all the other reckless and impulsive habits of men, was tainted with a kind of godlessness. Mr. Hance always sighed when he looked up and saw her coming into his store. He knew that she could lift a simple dollar transaction into a dim and mystic realm of confusion all her own.

I was fortunate enough to be present one day in 1905 when Mr. Hance's calculating and Aunt Wilma's figgerin' came together in memorable single combat. She had wheedled me into carrying her market basket, on the ground that it was going to be too heavy for her to manage. Her two grandsons, boys around my own age, had skipped out when I came to call at their house, and Aunt Wilma promptly seized on me. A young'un, as she called everybody under seventeen, was not worth his salt if he couldn't help a body about the house. I had shopped with her before, under duress, and I knew her accustomed and invariable route on Saturday mornings, when Fourth Street, from Main to State, was lined with the stands of truck gardeners. Prices were incredibly low in those days, but Aunt Wilma questioned the cost, the quality, and the measure of everything. By the time she had finished her long and tedious purchases of fresh produce from the country, and we had turned east into Town Street and headed for Mr. Hance's store, the weight of the market basket was beginning to pain my arm. "Come along, child, come along," Aunt Wilma snapped, her eyes shining with the look of the Middle Western housewife engaged in hard but virtuous battle with the wicked forces of the merchandising world.

I saw Mr. Hance make a small involuntary gesture with his right hand as he spied Aunt Wilma coming through the door. He had just finished with a customer, and since his assistant was busy, he knew he was in for it. It took a good half hour for Aunt Wilma to complete her shopping for groceries, but at length everything wanted was stacked on the counter in sacks and cans and boxes. Mr. Hance set deftly to work with his paper sack and pencil, jotting down the price of each article as he fitted it into the basket. Aunt Wilma watched his expert movements closely, like a hostile baseball fan waiting for an error in the infield. She regarded adroitness in a man as "slick" rather than skillful.

Aunt Wilma's purchases amounted to ninety-eight cents. After writing down this sum, Mr. Hance, knowing my aunt, whisked the paper bag around on the counter so that she could examine his addition. It took her some time, bending over and peering through her glasses, to arrive at a faintly reluctant corroboration of his figgerin'. Even when she was satisfied that all was in order, she had another go at the column of numbers, her lips moving silently as she added them up for the third time. Mr. Hance waited patiently, the flat of his hands on the counter. He seemed to be fascinated by the movement of her lips. "Well, I guess it's all right," said Aunt Wilma, at last, "but everything *is* so dear." What she had bought for less than a dollar made the market basket bulge. Aunt Wilma took her purse out of her bag and drew out a dollar bill slowly and handed it over, as if it were a hundred dollars she would never see again.

Mr. Hance deftly pushed the proper keys of the cash register, and the red hand on the indicator pointed to $.98. He studied the cash drawer, which had shot out at him. "Well, well," he said, and then, "Hmm. Looks like I haven't got any pennies." He turned back to Aunt Wilma. "Have you got three cents, Mrs. Hudson?" he asked.

That started it.

Aunt Wilma gave him a quick look of distrust. Her Sunday suspicion gleamed in her eyes. *"You* owe *me two* cents," she said sharply.

"I know that, Mrs. Hudson," he sighed, "but I'm out of pennies. Now, if you'll give me three cents, I'll give you a nickel."

Aunt Wilma stared at him cautiously.

"It's all right if you give him three cents and he gives you a nickel," I said.

"Hush up," said Aunt Wilma. "I'm figgerin'." She figgered for several moments, her mouth working again.

Mr. Hance slipped a nickel out of the drawer and placed it on the counter. "There is your nickel," he said firmly. "Now you just have to give me three cents."

Aunt Wilma pecked about in her purse and located three pennies, which she brought out carefully, one at a time. She laid them on the counter beside the nickel, and Mr. Hance reached for them. Aunt Wilma was too quick for him. She covered the eight cents with a lean hand. "Wait, now!" she said, and she took her hand away slowly. She frowned over the four coins as if they were a difficult hand in bridge whist. She ran her lower lip against her upper teeth.

"Maybe if I give you a dime," she said, "and take the eight cents. . . . It is *two* cents you're short, ain't it?"

Mr. Hance began to show signs of agitation. One or two amused customers were now taking in the scene out of the corners of their eyes. "No, no," said Mr. Hance. "That way, you would be making me a present of seven cents!" This was too much for Aunt Wilma. She couldn't understand the new and preposterous sum of seven cents that had suddenly leaped at her from nowhere. The notion that she was about to do herself out of some money staggered her, and her eyes glazed for a moment like a groggy prizefighter's. Neither Mr. Hance nor I said anything, out of fear of deepening the tangle. She made an uncertain move of her right hand and I had the wild thought that she was going to give Mr. Hance one of the pennies and scoop up the seven cents, but she didn't. She fell into a silent clinch with the situation and then her eyes cleared. "Why, of *course*!" she cried brightly. "I don't know what got into me! You take the eight cents and give me a dime. Then I'll have the two cents that's coming to me." One of the customers laughed, and Aunt Wilma cut him down with a swift glare. The diversion gave me time to figure out that whereas Mr. Hance had been about to gain seven cents, he was now going to lose a nickel. "That way, *I* would be making *you* a present of *five* cents, Mrs. Hudson," he said stiffly. They stood motionless for several seconds, each trying to stare the other down.

"Now, here," said Mr. Hance, turning and taking her dollar out of the still open cash drawer. He laid it beside the nickel and the pennies. "Now, here," he said again. "You gave me a dollar three, but you don't owe me a dollar three—you owe me five cents less than that. Here is the five cents." He snatched it up and handed it to her. She held the nickel between thumb and forefinger, and her eyes gleamed briefly, as if she at last comprehended the peculiar

deal, but the gleam faded. Suddenly she handed him his nickel and picked up her dollar and her three cents. She put the pennies back in her purse. "I've rung up the ninety-eight cents, Mrs. Hudson," said Mr. Hance quickly. "I must put the dollar back in the till." He turned and pointed at the $.98 on the indicator. "I tell you what. If you'll give me the dollar, I'll give you the nickel and we'll call it square." She obviously didn't want to take the nickel or give up the dollar, but she did, finally. I was astounded at first, for here was the penny-careful Mr. Hance knocking three cents off a bill, but then I realized he was afraid of losing the dollar and was willing to settle for the lesser of two evils.

"Well," said Aunt Wilma irritably, "I'm sure I don't know what you're trying to do."

I was a timid boy, but I had to plunge into the snarl, if only on behalf of the family honor. "Gee, Aunt Wilma," I told her, "if you keep the nickel, he's giving you everything for ninety-five cents."

Mr. Hance scowled hard at me. He was afraid I was going to get him in deeper than he already was. "It's all right, son," he said. "It's all right." He put the dollar in the till and shoved the drawer shut with a decisive bang, but I wasn't going to give up.

"Gee whiz, Aunt Wilma," I complained, "you still owe him three cents. Don't you see that?"

She gave me the pitying glance of a superior and tired intelligence. "I never owed him three cents in my life," she said tartly. "He owes me two cents. You stay out of things you don't understand."

"It's all right," said Mr. Hance again, in a weary voice. He was sure that if she scrabbled in her purse again for the three pennies, she would want her dollar back, and they would be right where they had started. I gave my aunt a look of disenchantment.

"Now, wait!" she cried suddenly. "Maybe I have the exact change! I don't know what's got into me. I didn't think of that! I think I have the right change after all." She put back on the counter the nickel she had been clutching in her left hand, and then she began to peck at the coins in her purse and, after a good minute, arranged two quarters, four dimes, Mr. Hance's nickel, and three pennies on the counter. "There," she said, her eyes flashing triumph. "Now you give me my dollar back."

Mr. Hance sighed deeply, rang out the cash drawer by pushing "No Sale," and handed her the dollar. Then he hastily scraped up the change, deposited each coin in its proper place in the till, and slammed the drawer shut again. I was only ten, and mathematics was not my best study, but it wasn't hard to figure that Mr. Hance, who in the previous arrangement had been out three cents, was now out five cents. "Good day, Mrs. Hudson," he said grimly. He felt my sympathetic eyes on him, and we exchanged a brief, knowing masculine glance of private understanding.

"Good day, Mr. Hance," said Aunt Wilma, and her tone was as grim as the grocer's.

I took the basket from the counter, and Mr. Hance sighed again, this time with relief. "Goodbye, goodbye," he said with false heartiness, glad to see us on our way. I felt I should slip him the parsley, or whatever sack in the basket had cost a nickel.

"Come on, child," said Aunt Wilma. "It's dreadfully late. I declare it's taken hours to shop today." She muttered plaintively all the way out of the store.

I noticed as I closed the door behind us that Mr. Hance was waiting on a man customer. The man was laughing. Mr. Hance frowned and shrugged.

As we walked east on Town Street, Aunt Wilma let herself go. "I never heard of such a thing in all the born days of my life," she said. "I don't know where John Hance got his schooling, if he got any. The very idea— a grown man like that getting so mixed up. Why, I could have spent the whole day in that store and he'd never of figgered it out. Let him keep the two cents, then. It was worth it to get out of that store."

"*What* two cents, Aunt Wilma?" I almost squealed.

"Why, the two cents he still owes me!" she said. "I don't know what they teach you young'uns nowadays. Of course he owes me two cents. It come to ninety-eight cents and I give him a dollar. He owed me two cents in the beginning and he still owes me two cents. Your Uncle Herbert will explain it to you. Any man in the world could figger it out except John Hance."

I walked on beside her in silence, thinking of Uncle Herbert, a balding, choleric man of high impatience and quick temper.

"Now, you let *me* explain it to your Uncle Herbert, child," she said. "I declare you were as mixed up as John Hance was. If I'd of listened to you and given him the three cents, like you said, I'd never of got my dollar back. He'd owe me five cents instead of two. Why, it's as plain as day."

I thought I had the solution for her now, and I leaped at it. "That's right, Aunt Wilma," I almost yelled. "He owed you a nickel and he gave you the nickel."

Aunt Wilma stabbed me with her indignation. "I gave *him* the nickel," she said. "I put it on the counter right there under your very eyes, and you saw him scoop it up."

I shifted the market basket to my left arm. "I know, Aunt Wilma," I said, "but it was *his* nickel all the time."

She snorted. "Well, he's got his precious nickel, ain't he?" she demanded. I shifted the basket again. I thought I detected a faint trace of uneasiness in her tone. She fell silent and quickened her cadence, and it was hard for me to keep up with her. As we turned south into Sixth Street, I glanced up and saw that she was frowning and that her lips were moving again. She was rehearsing the story of the strange transaction for Uncle Herbert. I began to whistle. "Hush up, child," she said. "I'm figgerin'."

Uncle Herbert was sitting in the living room, eating an apple. I could tell from his expression that he was in one of his rare amiable moods. Aunt Wilma grabbed the basket away from me. "Now, you let me explain it to your uncle," she said. "You wait till I get back." She sailed out of the room on her way to the kitchen.

A little breathlessly, I told Uncle Herbert the saga of Aunt Wilma's complicated financial quandary. He was chuckling when she came back into the room.

Uncle Herbert's amusement nettled her. "The boy got it wrong," she said accusingly. "He didn't tell it right. He was ever' bit as mixed up as John Hance." Uncle Herbert's chuckle increased to full and open laughter. Aunt Wilma glared at him until he subsided. "Now, Herbert, you listen to me," she began, but he cut in on her.

"If Hance ever gives you that two cents he owes you, Wilma," he said, "I tell you what you have to do to square accounts. Someday you're going to have to give him a dime for three cents." He began to laugh again.

Aunt Wilma Hudson stared at each of us in turn, with a look of fine, cold scorn, and then she raised both her hands and let them fall helplessly. "I declare," she said, "I don't know how the world gets along with the men runnin' it."

James Herndon

THE PRICE OF AMPHIBIANS

An expression only has meaning within the stream of life.

—Wittgenstein[1]

This chapter is about the fact that it is so, that an expression only has meaning

[1] Ludwig Wittgenstein (1889–1951), Austrian philosopher, whose *Philosophical Investigations* (1953) is largely concerned with problems about meaning and language.

within the stream of life. It is also about the logical notion that in order, roughly, to know what something is (within the stream of life) you ought to be able to know what would be the case if it were not.

Alienation is such an expression. Within that particular tributary which is a school, it has the meaning that an individual gives up his Self (denying what he knows to be so in favor of what the school says is so) in order to achieve success and avoid failure. Of course, success and failure are expressions too and only have meaning within the stream in question, but by the time anyone remembers that, he is usually forty and reduced to writing about it.

For my students, and for myself, this alienation from ourselves means in practice that they (we) do or don't do things as a matter of reaction—as if we came in to school each day as so many blanks, having wiped ourselves clean of desire between breakfast and getting off the bus or out of our car. We turn ourselves off as I turn off the car radio just when the front wheels hit the curb at the teachers' parking lot. Once officially in the school we dispose of our cans of Coke and our smokes and await the presentation of our daily (streams of) lives by the school, and it is to that presentation that we respond. Re-act. We don't act first ourselves, and let the school respond (while we watch it), for the reason that we are alienated (as presupposed) and because we are sane.

What would we be like (what would be the case) if we were not? Not alienated. From ourSelves.

In September of 1967 I looked through the cumulative folders of the kids we were going to have at Rabbit Mountain for the coming year, that is to say, the next Monday. I read what I already knew—the first grader with testable high IQ, the remarked bright student, leader, reads-at-third-grade-level, headed for the big time; and the fourth grader with low-average capability,

IQ 89, lazy kid, must-be-pushed-to-achieve, reads-at-second-grade-level, discipline-problem, parents cooperative. The first grader and the fourth grader are the same kid.

I was not prepared for the phrase *identifies with amphibians*. The rest of the remarks on this kid's folder were indefinite. It was as if the folder was composed entirely of question marks. *Lazy, bright, success, leader, follower, reading level, achievement, cooperation* apparently didn't come into it, so the teachers wrote what amounted to nothing. Only the one teacher, having written out (I imagined) some thirty such folders before, bored and maddened by the effort, had torn this one remark out of the systematic abstraction of the school's nature. It was as if, in the middle of the seventh grade social studies book about the amount of flax cultivated by Palestinian Arabs in their refugee camps, I could come across a page from *The Golden Bough*[2] or an engraving of a priapus.[3]

Monday mornings on the first day of school all kids come in and sit down to await announcement by the teacher of their daily lives in that class, that period. It is surprising how beautiful they are, even as blanks —or as they wait, filling in the blanks with future re-actions as you talk—and all the teachers every first day are full of enthusiasm and even hope, as if they finally had gotten a Good Class and now, they seem to say, Watch me teach! Richard didn't come in and sit down and await anything. He came in the door and straight up to me, smiling and holding an eight-inch brown-backed yellow-bellied water dog out to me in his right hand, saying Did you ever see a water dog before?

A water dog is a kind of newt or salamander common to all warm-water California coastal streams. I used to catch them all the

time. Its skin is sandpapery. Perhaps it gets its name from the fact that its visage seems not to be reptilian but gives an odd impression of warm-bloodedness—you get the notion, if you hold a water dog, that it likes you. If you go underwater in streams like the Navarro you'll see them in deep holes, legs outspread, sinking slowly towards the bottom from which, when they reach it, they will push off and swim upwards; orange-bellied, towards the surface. They are amphibians.

Richard was a medium-sized twelve-year-old boy with a pleasant face, a wide smile, a blue jacket zipped up all the way. After showing me the water dog and telling me where he got it, he went back to the cabinets and began looking around for something to put the water dog in. While I called the roll and mispronounced names he found one of the aquariums and ran some water in it and put the water dog in it and while I talked about the school and its formalities he went outside and came back in with some rocks and some dirt for the aquarium and then he watched the water dog swim and crawl around. He took it out a couple of times and held it, but he didn't do any landscaping on the dirt and rocks because he knew the water dog didn't give a damn about that, and he didn't give a damn about that. He didn't make any noise and didn't disturb anyone, but all of us felt how utterly wrong his entire behavior was, since I was there in front of the class talking and they were sitting down pretending to listen and he was wandering around inside and outside with dirt and rocks and fooling with the water dog and all of us wanted to do it too and so we knew it was wrong. He didn't seem to be listening to what I was saying but when I got to the part where I explained that if you were absent you had to bring a note the next day, or if you were leaving school to go to the dentist or something you had to bring a note and give it to the health office, Richard raised his hand. What about, he asked, if you were going to your

2 By Sir James Frazer (1854–1941); anthropological work containing much information about the sexual practices of primitive peoples.
3 Statue of the Greek god symbolizing male sexuality.

psychiatrist? Well. That told us all we wanted to know. The water dog, roaming around, that dirt, wandering in and out, not sitting down—things all the kids would be doing or wanting to do all the time, but which no one would do on the first day. We were dealing with a nut. That made it easy to understand.

I've always wondered what made Richard ask that. He never again referred to any psychiatrist or to therapy or anything of the sort. Perhaps he really wanted to know if the procedure was the same. I don't know.

For the first weeks of that year, Richard got along very badly. Everything he did seemed to be odd and not with it—everything he did got to be the focus of everyone's resentment and terror in the first few weeks of What To Do? In a very direct way he was ruining me as the teacher, or in the way I was trying to work with the kids as their teacher. That is, the kids attacked him precisely where I couldn't stand it, as if they (the other kids and Richard) had conspired to involve my personal terrors from the start. The kids attacked the water dog, they attacked Richard, and they revenged themselves on the thin black blind worm-salamanders which he brought into the aquarium, divebombing them with rocks, putting them on the heater, throwing them against the wall.

They attacked things he made. We had a big box of wood scraps from the shop and of beautiful odds and ends from a picture-framing shop and everyone was gluing them together with white glue and making constructions. But whereas everyone else made abstract architectural monuments (having already been to school art classes where any image of the real had been forbidden for some years) Richard preferred to make little toy trains and streetcars and tracks for them and then he played with them. He didn't play with them for long, though, for the kids smashed them almost as quickly as he made them, threw them, stomped them, broke them, laughing and with anger.

Richard reacted to these acts with squeals of rage, with tears, with demands to me. He made placards from construction paper on which he wrote appeals to public opinion and to authority in the form of the vice-principal:

Some kids in the eighth grade, like [followed by a list of names] are wrecking trains made by Richard S. All people in the school must get together and beat them up so they can never do it again.

To the V.P.! Cruelty to animals is against nature. These kids are killing salamanders by heat and by bombing with rocks. They are [list of names]. Call them into the office and suspend them for ten days.

He taped these placards up on the walls of the room, he put them up in the halls outside, he hung them in the office, he even took them into the V.P.'s office and put them on his desk. The placards drove the other kids wild. They couldn't stand to see their names up there in public association with cruel acts, and they were really afraid that the V.P. *would* call them in, *would* suspend them, *would* call their mothers (it was the beginning, I can see now, of Richard's magical power) and so they tore the placards down, they threatened Richard, they hit him, killed the water dog, approached me with demands.

In the middle of all that. Richard displayed another eccentricity which provided excuse for revenge—namely, he had a great love for a kind of small-time obscenity. It mainly revolved around the word *dick*. (He never said any of the other common kid swear words; he said fucking, but never fuck, and he only used it to mean actual intercourse, never as just another vulgarity.)

So anyway, my memory has an image of Richard in an ebullient mood, having forgotten for the moment about cruelty, going around to kids talking about their dicks, and inevitably being persuaded by boys to go up to the girls and say something dirty. What Richard usually said was *Take out your dick!* The girls, the very same girls who were saying all the words Richard didn't say all the time and writing Fuck and Fuck you and Let's fuck in lipstick on the walls of the girls' bathroom, reacted with indignation and slapped Richard and made demands of me. When I foolishly told them to forget it, they counterattacked by going to see the V.P. and telling him (with what mixture of sexuality and prudishness can be imagined) about Richard told them to take out their dicks, and so he called in Richard and talked to him warily about dicks and girls and forbade Richard to say dick . . . and of course this counterattack enabled him to totally ignore Richard's own public complaints about kids who tortured amphibians to death and broke things you made, for somehow that didn't count alongside some nut or freak kid who told girls to take out their dicks! That was something you could get involved with! That you could take seriously! But dead salamanders, well . . .

(See man, this is what an American public school *is.* Let's cut out talking that shit about curriculum and learning about flax and all. The above is a School. Get it through your heads.)

All of this put me in the middle. I had to get mad at the kids who bombed the salamanders. I had to get mad at the kids who broke Richard's stuff. I had to discuss the phony outrage about dicks. I had to hear from the V.P. about should Richard be in EH classes. The worst thing was that my anger was real. I felt capable of killing a kid who stood there laughing while a moist salamander fried on the heater. I did hate the chickenshit girls. And I also began to hate Richard for his utter childishness, his ignorance of what the other kids were up to, his failure to respond as a twelve-year-old ought, his total remoteness from group custom and behavior. For, instead of staying neutral (which was my plan) while the kids sweated out the crucial problem of Who Are We In This Room and What Shall We Do, I was being forced into the position of forbidding stuff all the time, of threatening, of being angry, or moralizing. It didn't matter, somehow, that it was real—that is I really did think the killing and breaking was wrong. It didn't matter that I really thought everyone should be able to tolerate Richard. And it especially didn't matter that what I was really furious about was true—that they were attacking Richard as a substitute, as an excuse for not attacking those things which were at the root of their anxiety and frenzy, but which involved some risk in attacking, namely their parents and teachers and their lives at school eight hours a day.

So it was really quite nutty. On the one hand, I kept wishing Richard would start building abstract junk, call people assholes when he thought I wasn't listening (or deny it if I heard it), pitch pennies against the wall, smoke in the bathroom, break other kids' stuff or throw chalk, torture the water dog, make hip teen-age sexual innuendo to the girls, complain about mean teachers and grades and that he wasn't learning anything, and speak sagely of marijuana, using the words *pot* and *lid* a lot . . . in fact, become just like the other kids. Then I could *work with him, straighten him out,* get him to face his *real situation*—in short, do what I was ready to do, what the class was for, what I figured to do with the group. What was that? Why, merely to force them, through my existence in the room as *person* rather than giver of daily streams of life against which to react, rather than as successful or unsuccessful entertainer, to decide the course of their own lives.

On the other hand, that goddamn Richard was already at the point I hoped the other kids would reach. He already knew what he wanted to do, every moment of the day, he was prepared to do it, and could do it, did do it, liked to do it, it harmed no one, it wasn't isolated from his total life (he continued at school the things he did at home), he used the school's resources (science books, films, maps, geographics, aquarium, dirt and rocks)—he knew what he wanted, learned from it, required no instruction, shared his knowledge and experience, asked advice . . . he was there! It was great! It was also intolerable, because he was nuts. No one planned to put up with a nut who was also content. He wasn't alienated. No one could stand it. He was fair game.

Then changes began to happen. Richard made some of them. He stopped building trains and stuff. He didn't bring any more salamanders or water dogs. He began to concentrate on drawing cartoons and drawing maps. He made the cartoons on ordinary school paper, and the maps on huge pieces of butcher paper which he got from the office. They had a weird kind of association. The maps covered eight-foot-long pieces of paper with streets, freeways, alleys, telephone poles, street signs, street lights, bridges, underpasses, streetcar lines, depots, bus stations, bus stops, train stations and airports. The main characters in the cartoons were automobiles—generally old, famous makes like Duesenberg and Rolls ("Hey, Duse," a Rolls would ask, "What happened to you?")—and talking fireplugs and talking telephone poles and talking buildings, plus an occasional human who was usually identified as one of the members of the class or as myself and who had a bit part. Events in the classroom always played a role—someone who had attacked Richard found himself being run over by a Duesenberg somewhere in the cartoon, for instance, and when a lot of kids began to play chess later on, talking chesspieces began to enter into the action.

In itself, this changed nothing. The car-

toons and maps only emphasized what everyone knew—that Richard was a nut and a babyish nut to boot. He kept wanting to show them to everyone and everyone kept being disgusted and upset. His writing, for one thing, was quite illegible; it was too large, too crowded, didn't go in a straight line. (The school nurse, confronted with some of it, wanted to talk about brain damage.) He writes like a baby! everyone wanted to say. That didn't matter to Richard, since he wanted to read it out loud to everyone anyway. (Looked at from this standpoint, it was rather literate, involved somewhat sophisticated puns and was at least as interesting as the average comic book.)

The change had more to do with Tizzo and Junior and Karl, who were the Big Three of the class, and who had a certain identity in the school as a Big Three. It's odd how these combinations occur among kids. The three were in no way alike and there seemed no objective reason for either their association or their identification as a unit. Perhaps it was a question of superlatives. Tizzo, for instance, was the toughest kid in school, with the possible exception of one other boy. (All year long kids tried to instigate a fight between the two, but it never happened.) Karl was the hippest kid in school, in the superficial sense of hipness which prevails among twelve- and thirteen-years-olds. He had the longest hair, knew all the music, associated with musicians (but did not play) and was one of the few kids (at that time) who actually smoked, rather than just talked about, grass. Junior could only be called the charming-est, or perhaps the carefree-est. He was beautiful, for one thing—dark curly hair, an open, friendly face, smiling, unworried, not angry, expressive of some term like happy-go-lucky.

In their relations to the school, they were equally diverse. Tizzo was a kid from an earlier age and another place. He didn't criticize the existence of the school, didn't question the rightness of its principles, didn't object to his place in it, which was to get (as he saw it) average grades (not too many D's and F's) and stay out of trouble. His trouble was his great anger at injustices within the system, as they affected him. He took it for granted that teachers were mean (else how would they control guys like him?) but there were limits. If a teacher didn't let him out of class every day to go to the bathroom (and have a smoke) that was reasonable; if the teacher never let him out, or gave him moral lectures when he asked, that was unreasonable. If he didn't try in a class and got an F or a D, that was O.K. If he *tried* (at least sometimes) and still got an F or D, that was unreasonable. When it was unreasonable, he got angry, slammed books. cursed the teacher, hit other kids, and got in trouble.

Karl was a critic. His aim was to get out of school as soon as possible. He wasn't concerned about degrees of things. He resented being made to go to class and was uninterested in whether the teacher was good or bad, nice or mean. His goal was the Continuation School, where his older brother had gone and where all the hip kids went (according to Karl), where they let you smoke in class, and where you could learn what's happening. He constantly criticized the structure of the school and the curriculum. His grounds for discontent were that it was useless and irrelevant. His philosophy was direct and simple, and also typical; he did nothing to hurt anyone else, therefore he should be allowed to do as he pleased. It was his business; he had nothing to learn from anyone.

Tizzo and Karl, however, both attended regularly, Tizzo in order to keep out of trouble and stick to his Roman sense of order, and Karl because only at school could you get a sizable audience for existential criticism of it. Junior, by contrast, came when he felt like it, almost always late, sometimes not at all. My image of Junior is of him coming in the room at eleven and saying that he thought he'd drop by for lunch. When he dropped in, he was immediately the center of attention. What did you do all morning? everyone would ask. Well, Junior hadn't done anything. I just watched Captain Kangaroo, he'd say smiling, and then I went back to sleep and got up and ate some stuff and got dressed and thought I'd come on over here for lunch. Hey, Mr. Herndon, he'd say, can I go out to the bathroom? And then Junior and five or six other lucky kids would go over to the bathroom and smoke and talk until lunchtime. I always felt good when Junior wandered in, and so I knew the kids felt it also. It was good to have him around (that's all you can say), you missed him when he wasn't there, and that was his superlative quality.

I want to remark here about fathers or upon the absence of them. Unlike black inner-city ghetto pore deprived (choose your term) schools, most kids officially had fathers in our district, but in fact fathers were rarely mentioned. Kids talked about mothers. It was mothers they tried to satisfy, mothers who got mad if you got in trouble, mothers who came (with few exceptions) to the school, mothers who wanted you to get good grades and go to college, mothers who wrote you fake excuses (like Junior) or who you didn't want to feel ashamed of you (like Karl). I think I can tell a kid who has a real relationship with his father within a week of having him in class, it is that unusual. The point, for the present story, is that Tizzo was such a kid. He had an Italian father. His father was (according to Tizzo) rough and tough and would beat the hell out of him if he got in trouble. He wanted to avoid it. His father thought he ought to go to school, be clean and neat, get there on time, not smart off to the teachers, and not flunk. Period. Tizzo had a lot of tales about how strong his father was, even though he was smaller than Tizzo, who was at thirteen already a man physically, being about five feet ten and weighing perhaps a hundred and seventy. He also had a lot of tales about working with his father, going around with his father, fixing up the house with his father—in short, of manly relations with his father. In fact, he was learning how to be a father himself. He knew what his father did at work, what he did at home, what he thought, and how to please him. His concern was uncritical. His father was right, his demands not impossible; he Tizzo was imperfect and couldn't always control his temper and when he couldn't, deserved to be punished, deserved his father's anger, deserved to have to stay home instead of spending the day fishing for striped bass off the beaches of San Francisco. He didn't like the punishments, he thought the school could let up on him a bit and didn't have to be quite so tight, and he hoped continually for a break, a little luck in getting through, but he didn't criticize its general right to exist.

So the Three approached me one day. All of a sudden they were concerned about Richard. All these other little punks keep picking on him, they told me, and they had decided to do something about it. Richard has a right to exist even if he is nuts. He isn't hurting anyone else, said Karl, and so he has a right to do his thing. And everyone picks on him just because they are chickenshit, said Junior. They pick on him because he can't take up for himself, and because Richard is so nutty that the vice-principal won't do anything to them when they bug Richard, because he thinks it's all Richard's fault because he is so crazy and tells the girls to take out their dicks. Tizzo said, They do it because they can get away with it!

So their analysis was that all kids would torment anyone and anything if they could get away with it. The only reason kids would act decently toward other creatures was if they were afraid of punishment for acting otherwise. That was what their lives, in and

out of school, had taught them. They didn't treat Tizzo badly, because they were afraid he'd beat the shit out of them. They didn't treat Karl badly, because he'd put them down for being wimps and had the reputation to make it stick. They didn't treat Junior badly, because then he wouldn't smile at them and ask them to come along to the bathroom. Richard, having no saving graces of that kind, and having no protection from adults because he was nuts, had to take it.

Tizzo et al planned to turn things around. They proposed to supply the punishment to any kids who *bothered* Richard. Well, I said O.K. Why shouldn't I? It was a step in another, if not the right, direction. It also meant that Tizzo and Karl, who had been (to be honest) among Richard's chief persecutors, wouldn't be doing it any more, and that would be a break for Richard.

It became, immediately, an instrument of terror. All the kids became fair game themselves; they were in the same relationship to Tizzo and Karl and Junior as Richard had been to them. As soon as they had conferred with me, the Three foraged out firing on kids. They belted them for what they'd done a week ago to Richard, for what they'd told the V.P. a couple of days ago, for what they were planning on doing to Richard tomorrow. The three were full of anger. They hit half the kids and threatened the rest. If kids who were physically (if not morally) tougher than Karl or Junior protested, they were confronted with Tizzo. Girls, who were not to be hit according to Tizzo, were made to sit down in desks and not move. (If they moved, they were hit anyway. It was their own fault; they were told to stay put.)

We spent perhaps a week under the Terror, a week of outcry and protest and attempted discussion. Why was I allowing goon squad rule?

Why are you tormenting Richard?

How come Tizzo et al, who had been tormenting Richard, were all of a sudden allowed to hit kids for tormenting Richard?

How come you are all tormenting Richard?

How come we have to have some nutty kid in our room?

How come you bomb water dogs?

How come Richard get to tell us to take out our dicks?

How come you want to write Let's fuck! on the bathroom walls?

How come Richard has to make all that nutty stuff?

How come you care what he does?

How come Tizzo and Karl and Junior, who are part of us, i.e., our leaders to whom we look up, turn against us when all we are doing is exercising our normal white sane American middle-class, or almost middle-class, prerogative of tormenting anyone and anything that isn't clearly us and tormenting it *without any fear of retribution*? What other good reason could there be for remaining this normal white, etc., with all its load of fear, guilt and alienation, than daily assurance of this reward? Why, considering our own agreement that everything we want to do—everything from writing Fuck you to talking to each other in class—is wrong and deserves punishment, ought some kid to be doing whatever he wants and think it is O.K.?

After about a week, the Terror began to peter out. Junior, having come to school regularly and early in order to keep Ordnung,[4] began to arrive at noon. Tizzo and Karl found their interest beginning to flag. Perhaps they had only wanted to re-establish their Big Threeness in concrete terms; having done so, they didn't figure to keep up this eternal slugging. They weren't cruel, only angry. Still, it worked, in a way. Prevented by the goon squad from pinning the sins of the world on Richard, the class began to look elsewhere for something to do.

4 Order. The German word suggests the repression that the "Terror" has imposed.

In the meantime, Richard, left relatively alone, had not been idle. He began to exploit his three major aptitudes—natural history, maps and magic. Indeed, he began to gain grudging admirers. He scoured the library and came up with fantastic photos of snakes devouring other beasts, or magnified tarantulas' jaws, or piranhas, cobras, moccasins and other death-dealing reptiles. No one could resist them. Since Richard was the only kid willing, at that time, to do the work necessary to produce this fascinating material, everyone had to gather around him in order to look, everyone had to hear his stock of snake lore and no one could just snatch the book and run and look at it by himself because of the Terror.

It was the same with his maps. He had begun to make huge maps on fifteen-foot lengths of butcher paper. To his great pleasure and astonishment he discovered that the school could afford butcher paper, as much as you wanted, in whatever lengths you wanted, as often as you wanted. Life was good. He spread the paper out on our long table, the ends drooping over, and covered it with freeways, overpasses, bridges, streets, alleys, stop signs, turnoffs, thoroughfares, bus stops, streetcar tracks, depots, and the rest. Up until this time, we had all figured it was fantasy; our judgment was variously that it was interesting or nutty or disgusting but, either way, predicated on the fact of fantasy. When it was discovered that it was not fantasy, it was like revelation. How that happened I'm not sure, but, in any case, I recall kids coming up to me and saying that goddamn Richard says his maps are real and what did I think of that? So for a while we all stood around interrogating Richard about maps. Sometimes he was eager to answer—to trace the beginnings of a freeway in South San Francisco and show where it went, where bus connections could be made, where turnoffs to Tierra Firma could be expected—but at other times he displayed irritation, an irritation directed at dilettantes who were (1) not serious and (2) *bothering* him by getting in the way of his work. Still, he was convincing. If a kid asked, Rich (all of a sudden it was Rich, not Richard-you-nut), how would you get from here to Haight-Ashbury (mentioning one of the few places in the city that all the kids had heard of), what bus would you take? then Richard would stop working and get serious and answer the question in detail; what jitney to take, where to get off, what number bus to get on then, what street to transfer at, where to get off and then walk two blocks north . . . or kids who had once lived in San Francisco would say, Look, Rich, I used to live at such and such a street, number so and so, tell me what bus goes by there and where it came from and where it goes. Richard would think a bit and then say, Well, it would be Muni bus Number 48 (or whatever) coming from . . . and then go ahead and trace the entire route of the bus, street by street, finally allowing the bus to go right past the kid's former house on its journey into the mysteries of the city.

Then Richard's maps, having the decisive quality of the real, began to attract co-workers. It turned out that Richard was not against having houses drawn in on streets, or Doggie Diners or movie theaters. So that one morning I was treated to the sight of a bunch of kids sitting by the table over Richard's map, eagerly drawing in Marin's Travel Agency, Holt's Conservatory, Kohl's Burlesque (20—girls—20), Grand's Nursery (Exotic Plants), Stroud's Orpheum and Foundation, Spino's Health Farm, Perry's Gym, and so on. Other kids rushed me with demands for pencils, pens, marking pens and crayons and I got in a little sarcasm about *students* being *prepared* for work but in the end, not being prepared with any such items myself, had to send to the office for them. For I too had plans for Richard's map, and spent some time later elbow to elbow with kids (Move over! I can't move over, I'm drawing right here! Well I got to

have room to draw! Well, I have to have room too!) drawing in Herndon's French Restaurant, a medieval affair with towers and moat and an immense menu featuring Sole Marguery with Petits Pois, which (I admit) was much admired.

Thus did Richard triumph momentarily over us all, a triumph in which we were happy to acquiesce. Richard's (now our) map was completed in perhaps a week and was hung up on the wall and admired, not only by us but by counselors and administrators and art consultants and visiting firemen from San Fransisco State. It had a Fillmore district with soul food and dance halls and it had a Chinatown with opium dens and curio shops and it had museums and movies and Aquatic Park with bongo drummers and naked-lady sunbathers and it had a Haight-Ashbury with poster shops and drug emporiums and it had suburbs with shopping centers and houses with the kids' names on them and police stations and a gigantic Juvenile Hall with guard towers and machine guns and a big sign out front which said Junior's Juvi.

All in all it was pleasant to come in and watch fifteen or so kids sitting along the table opposite space on the map, drawing and coloring and looking at one another's stuff. Naturally we had incidents. There were bad guys who wanted to write Fuck on the map, and there were objections to the tyranny and unfairness of Richard, who, acting as Planning Board, allotted drawing space according to some design in his mind not readily apparent to the rest of us. There was also some outcry about Richard's naming of the streets (a job he allowed no one else to do) wherein inevitably some kids had major freeways named after them (Tizzo Memorial Parkway) and others were only allotted minor streets or even alleys. Still, the map was finished, with an awful decrepit falling-down tenement named after the vice-principal, located on a tiny alley of the same name which was carefully decorated with garbage cans, old whiskey bottles and refuse. Two days later Tizzo got mad at Richard because of the Memorial Parkway. Some brave kid had pointed out to him that *Memorial* meant that he, Tizzo, was dead. What the hell, Rich, I thought I was your friend, said Tizzo. Sure, Tizzo, said Richard, you are. But that map's in the future! It's all in the future.

I doubt that Tizzo was satisfied by that answer, but all he could do about it was to remember some kid who had written a passing Fuck on the end of the Parkway and threaten him a bit.

Richard was probably the only kid who was not completely satisfied by the map. I could see he liked the attention and un-accustomed feeling of working with other kids on a project of his invention. At the same time, he made it clear that they *bothered* him. He had to keep watch over them so that they didn't encroach on space he had allotted for something else. He had to argue with them about details. He had to take them into account, and that was a *bother*. More important, I think, he had to compromise his idea of reality—the map was now clearly a fantasy, could only be a fantasy, at best something of the future. It *might* come true; that was as close to the real as Richard could make it.

I said magic. Free of persecution and momentarily full of power as Director of Map Activities, Richard indulged himself. Kids began to rush me with complaints in a new key. Tell that fucking Rich to stop turning me into a frog! Richard said I was turned into a fart! He said I am immobile!

It's true, ain't it? I remembered to answer slyly. It's true, you *are* a frog, a fart, you can't move! No it ain't, they said, of course it isn't. What are you worried about then? I would say. But they *were* worried. Richard had them in the old grip of the Logos,[5] and they genuinely didn't want him to do it.

5 The Word, thought of as an independent power.

The ritual was simple, Richard would come up to kids, walking on his toes and grinning with secret delight as usual, and ask them Say Om. (Or Say X or antidis-establishmentarianism or Shazam.) The kids couldn't ever resist and so they'd say it. Then Richard would say, You are now a frog, or Now you don't exist. Then the kids would disprove it (they hoped) by running hollering to me. They were prevented from solving it more simply by the memory of the Terror.

I enjoyed this action quite a bit, but in the end I could see everyone was really quite bugged and I began to tell Richard to lay off. I expected it to be difficult. All of a sudden we were some nomadic tribe caught between Attila-the-Big-Three and Richard-the-shaman. We alienated folk were in danger. I called Richard over and began to explain why he had to stop turning everyone into frogs. But Richard just said, innocently and quite reasonably, After all, Mr. Herndon, it's only a joke!

It was as if that remark, turning us almost against our will away from our urge towards supernatural explanations of all our difficulties, loaning us sanity and the real, just as mothers soothe their children at bed-time by telling them that TV program, that Monster, Vampire, The Glob, Murderer, they aren't real, they are just stories, they are made up, just pretend . . . the kids still have nightmares, of course, since nightmares can't be done away with by applications of reason like wet compresses, but they can be recognized and talked about as nightmares, given a name apart from breakfast or play or sunshine . . . as if that remark turned us off of Richard, diffused our focus on him, and let us back into our own lives in the classroom. Most likely, of course, it wasn't that at all, there was no actual moment of turning away but only some gradual release, unclear as to its moments, from our obsession. But memory wants to pinpoint its feeling of history, so as to make art. (The Muses are the daughters of Memory.) We began to go our own ways, ways which only occasionally touched Richard's or his ours. Kids occasionally did some drawing on Richard's maps. I occasionally stapled his cartoons up on the board alongside other stuff. Richard occasionally gave informal lectures on the habits of amphibians. When a group of kids developed a flourishing business making ceramic chesspieces he joined them, but not as a co-businessman. He made his own clay chesspieces alongside them, using the same clay at the same time, but that was all. His knights looked like sea horses, his pawns like tiny fireplugs.

The year went on. Richard wasn't the only kid in the class. Maps were not the only projects. Salamander torturing wasn't the only barbarism. Richard's mother came to see us a couple of times. She reminded us all of Richard; she gave the impression of being too placid, perhaps a bit vague, not worried enough. Naturally we had to see her in contrast to the mothers we usually saw who were mad for success, were outraged or wept, wanted to settle and fix everything in their kids' lives in half-hour conferences on their way to afternoon league play at the bowling alley. She mainly hoped that he would make some friends. She was happy with our program without knowing or caring to know much about it since Richard told her the school didn't bother him. I got a few calls from Richard's therapist, who wanted to know how he was getting along. It became clear that the therapist saw Rich as a pretty hopeless case, i.e., that he was never going to be a "normal" kid, that the best that could be hoped for with all the therapy in the world was that he could keep out of an institution and perhaps hold some kind of job like the ones social workers invent for severely retarded adults. Later in the year I worked up courage enough (and believed it enough) to tell the therapist about Richard's real ability and, more important to him (for

Richard's intelligence didn't seem to him to be the issue so much as what he could *do* with it), about his actual acquired knowledge of the real world in concrete terms of geography and science. I told him I thought that if Richard could get through the age of being a kid and a teen-ager without being physically or spiritually murdered, that he might emerge (to a startled society composed of the therapist and ex-classmates and aging teachers) as a perfectly reasonable thirty-year-old citizen, albeit a bit eccentric like many another citizen, working at some fairly unusual job, one which very few other people could do. The therapist seemed to like the idea and in fact we both got a little excited about it then and there. He seemed to have visions of museums and classifying salamanders. I thought about the post office, where I used to work, and the difficulty of memorizing mail-routing schemes, the contests in the coffee rooms among supervisors and old hands about where certain streets were, what they used to be called, what routes served them, and so on, and I conjured up Richard, the Grey Eminence of the P.O. in a dusty back office drawing charts and schemes, settling disputes and reading the archives. In fact, when I thought of the future of America in terms of science-fiction (the predictions of which I always believe), I rather thought that Richard was one of the few kids in the class who had any real chance of having a job, of having work to do that a machine couldn't do and wouldn't be doing. Richard and Junior, by the way, whose uncle was a bail-bondsman.

P.S. Because the rest I write about Richard appears here like a postscript. Of course it ain't a postscript to Richard, or to Tizzo or to Richard's dad, or in fact at all to anyone, really. Readers ought to beware of the trouble with books. Still later in the year Richard's mother came to see us again, and she was quite upset for the first time. Richard's dad was upset, that was the thing.

There was this report which Richard was supposed to write for his music class (a kind of music appreciation which all kids in the seventh grade take at our school, twelve weeks) and which he was in fact writing. Well, I'd seen him writing it in class and heard about it from him. Naturally he was writing about all sorts of old instruments and drawing pictures of talking Sackbuts and Serpents and Viols d'Amore and coming up to me with his sly and expectant grin and wanting to know if I knew what this and that was? But he was also writing it at home, and one evening his father took a look at Richard's report and apparently it was just the last straw for the father—there it was all scribbly and you couldn't read lots of it and there were maps and streets interspersed with accounts of Theobald Boehm inventing the flute—so the father got really angry and decided to show Richard how reports ought to be written and they sat down and talked about headings and footnotes and theses and paragraphs and documentation and clarity and so when that was all done and Richard indicated yes he understood what the issue was, the father told Richard to get going and rewrite that report and he did. I felt the father understood about Richard's real ability and intelligence and knowledge and curiosity and couldn't stand it, as we all can't, that Richard wouldn't put this all to use in normal bright-kid fashion, earning normal bright-kid success and evaluation. Along with that, I could imagine the father hoping Richard would get busy and play a little ball, get in a little normal trouble for smoking in the bathroom or cutting class.

So Richard did, but in the end wasn't able to hold to it and finally produced his big music report, name up in the right-hand corner and a title and skip a space and start in with a paragraph about sackbuts and a drawing centered nicely on the page and some more writing and then *Misericordia!* sprawled across the page, as Richard's mind

made some irresistible connections in Xanadu, marched a procession of talking fireplugs, of cartoon frames enclosing Duesenbergs lecturing a crowd of applauding sea horses or chesspieces about musical instruments—Oh man, give a thought to fathers at this moment!

What is a teacher's part in this whole thing? It is only to pay attention and give protection. The rest I was able to leave to Tizzo. Tizzo maintained his relationship to Richard; he insisted on remaining Richard's friend. He kept an eye out for him, instructed him on what to do or what not to do, and he played with him. They played a game in the room where Richard was a bad ill-tempered car, speeding and going through red lights and being a road hog, and Tizzo was a police car and afterwards a judge who sentenced Richard-the-car to jail and locked him up in the closet. Then he would extract promises from the bad car about being good and reforming and let him out, at which the bad car would immediately start speeding around the room and have to get arrested all over again. Richard thought he'd like to play this game every day, but Tizzo saw that was no good. He restricted Richard to one day a week, usually Friday, and only one period. Often other kids would get into the game too. Although most kids complained about Richard's childishness all week long, many of them in fact found such childishness very attractive. Since Tizzo was doing it, they could often permit themselves to play.

Tizzo, who had a father, was practicing up to be a father. He had a good use for Richard. Richard had a good use for Tizzo too, since he was learning to be a kid. Unlike the therapist and myself and Richard's own father, Tizzo didn't want Richard to turn into some other person, but only to accept the human condition. I can still hear him telling Richard forthrightly that he wasn't really a car (I know it, Tizzo, Richard would say, it's only a game) and that he could only pretend to be a car on Fridays. *That's the only day you can be a car!* Or, *Rich, I thought you were going to stop telling people to take out their dicks!* Oh, yeah, Richard would say, *I was, but I forgot. Bullshit, Rich, you didn't forget*, Tizzo would say, *you just wanted to and went ahead and did it.* Sometimes Tizzo would try to explain to Richard why it was that he could call people assholes and it would be O.K., and once in a while he'd try to get Richard to call someone an asshole, just to try it out and see if he got any satisfaction out of it, but Richard didn't want to call anyone an asshole, couldn't see any reason for it, and couldn't understand what Tizzo was getting at. In the end, all Tizzo was trying to get Richard to see was that human beings had to accept the idea of being *bothered* once in a while—that was what it was about. That if you accepted that, then you also could revolt against being bothered *all* the time, and that was as free as you could be.

Occasionally Richard would get mad at the tyranny of Tizzo and produce a placard:

Some person in the eighth grade who thinks he is tough is trying to be Julius Caesar and tell other people what to do. The whole eighth grade should get together and make him stop doing this.

Then Tizzo would get mad and say he didn't care what Richard did and if the vice-principal got him it was just tough shit and Richard would indulge himself and be a car on Monday or Tuesday. Then suddenly it would be over and I could tell when it was. The bell would ring and it would be time for Tizzo to go to Reading, which he was mad at because Eileen wouldn't let him go to the bathroom—the bell would ring and Tizzo would just stand there in the room and I'd say Get going, Tizzo, and he'd say Sorry, Mr. Herndon, I can't go to Reading, Rich just turned me into a frog! And whenever that happened,

Tizzo and Richard and I and many another kid standing around would laugh like hell and I would bang Tizzo on the back as he went out and he would hit me in the ribs and Richard would skip out grinning with his arms raised up like a cheering section and we would all recognize for an instant the foolishness and absurdity of our way through the world and feel the impact of the great, occasional and accidental joy which would be our only reward along those paths.

Anton Chekhov

A TRIFLING OCCURRENCE

Nikolay Ilyich Bieliayev, a Petersburg landlord, very fond of the racecourse, a well fed, pink young man of about thirty-two, once called towards evening on Madame Irnin—Olga Ivanovna—with whom he had a *liaison*, or, to use his own phrase, spun out a long and tedious romance. And indeed the first pages of his romance, pages of interest and inspiration, had been read long ago; now they dragged on and on, and presented neither novelty nor interest.

Finding that Olga Ivanovna was not at home, my hero lay down a moment on the drawing-room sofa and began to wait.

"Good evening, Nikolay Ilyich," [6] he suddenly heard a child's voice say. "Mother will be in in a moment. She's gone to the dressmaker's with Sonya."

In the same drawing-room on the sofa lay Olga Ivanovna's son, Aliosha, a boy about eight years old, well built, well looked after, dressed up like a picture in a velvet jacket and long black stockings. He lay on a satin pillow, and apparently imitating an acrobat whom he had lately seen in the circus, lift-

[6] In Russia it is respectfully formal to address a person by his first two names.

ing up first one leg, then the other. When his elegant legs began to be tired, he moved his hands, or he jumped up impetuously and then went on all fours, trying to stand with his legs in the air. All this he did with a most serious face, breathing heavily, as if he himself found no happiness in God's gift of such a restless body.

"Ah, how do you do, my friend?" said Bieliayev. "Is it you? I didn't notice you. Is your mother well?"

At the moment Aliosha had just taken hold of the toe of his left foot in his right hand and got into a most awkward pose. He turned head over heels, jumped up, and glanced from under the big, fluffy lamp-shade at Bieliayev.

"How can I put it?" he said, shrugging his shoulders. "As a matter of plain fact Mother is never well. You see she's a woman, and women, Nikolay Ilych, have always some pain or another."

For something to do, Bieliayev began to examine Aliosha's face. All the time he had been acquainted with Olga Ivanova he had never once turned his attention to the boy and had completely ignored his existence. A boy is stuck in front of your eyes, but what is he doing here, what is his role?— you don't want to give a single thought to the question.

In the evening dusk Aliosha's face with a pale forehead and steady black eyes unexpectedly reminded Bieliayev of Olga Ivanovna as she was in the first pages of the romance. He had the desire to be affectionate to the boy.

"Come here, whipper-snapper," he said. "Come and let me have a good look at you, quite close."

The boy jumped off the sofa and ran to Bieliayev.

"Well?" Nikolay Ilyich began, putting his hand on the thin shoulders. "And how are things with you?"

"How shall I put it? . . . They used to be much better before."

"How?"

"Quite simple. Before, Sonya and I only had to do music and reading, and now we're given French verses to learn. You've had your hair cut lately?"

"Yes, just lately."

"That's why I noticed it. Your beard's shorter. May I touch it . . . Doesn't it hurt?"

"No, not a bit."

"Why is it that it hurts if you pull one hair and when you pull a whole lot, it doesn't hurt a bit? Ah, ah! You know it's a pity you don't have side-whiskers. You should shave here, and at the sides . . . and leave the hair just here."

The boy pressed close to Bieliayev and began to play with his watch-chain.

"When I go to the gymnasium,"[7] he said, "Mother is going to buy me a watch. I'll ask her to buy me a chain just like this. What a fine locket! Father has one just the same, but yours has stripes, here, and his has got letters . . . Inside it's Mother's picture. Father has another chain now, not in links, but like a ribbon . . ."

"How do you know? Do you see your father?"

"I? Mm . . . no . . . I . . ."

Aliosha blushed and in the violent confusion of being detected in a lie began to scratch the locket busily with his finger-nail. Bieliayev looked steadily at his face and asked:

"Do you see your father?"

"No . . . No!"

"But, be honest—on your honor. By your face I can see you're not telling me the truth. If you made a slip of the tongue by mistake, what's the use of shuffling? Tell me, do you see him? As one friend to another."

Aliosha mused.

"And you won't tell Mother?" he asked.

"What next."

"On your word of honor."

7 Secondary school.

"My word of honor."

"Swear an oath."

"What a nuisance you are! What do you take me for?"

Aliosha looked round, made big eyes and began to whisper.

"Only for God's sake don't tell Mother! Never tell it to anyone at all, because it's a secret. God forbid that Mother should ever get to know; then I and Sonya and Pelagueya will pay for it. . . . Listen. Sonya and I meet Father every Tuesday and Friday. When Pelagueya takes us for a walk before dinner, we go into Apfel's sweet-shop and Father's waiting for us. He always sits in a separate room, you know, where there's a splendid marble table and an ash-tray shaped like a goose without a back . . ."

"And what do you do there?"

"Nothing!—First, we welcome one another, then we sit down at a little table and Father begins to treat us to coffee and cakes. You know, Sonya eats meat-pies, and I can't bear pies with meat in them! I like them made of cabbage and eggs. We eat so much that afterwards at dinner we try to eat as much as we possibly can so that Mother shan't notice."

"What do you talk about there?"

"To Father? About anything. He kisses us and cuddles us, tells us all kinds of funny stories. You know, he says that he will take us to live with him when we are grown up. Sonya doesn't want to go, but I say 'Yes.' Of course, it'll be lonely without Mother; but I'll write letters to her. How funny: we could go to her for our holidays then— couldn't we? Besides, Father says that he'll buy me a horse. He's a splendid man. I can't understand why Mother doesn't invite him to live with her or why she says we mustn't meet him. He loves Mother very much indeed. He's always asking us how she is and what she's doing. When she was ill, he took hold of his head like this . . . and ran, ran, all the time. He is always telling us to obey and respect her. Tell me, is it true that we're unlucky?"

"H'm . . . how?"

"Father says so. He says: 'You are unlucky children.' It's quite strange to listen to him. He says: 'You are unhappy, I'm unhappy, and Mother's unhappy.' He says: 'Pray to God for yourselves and for her.' "

Aliosha's eyes rested upon the stuffed bird and he mused.

"Exactly . . ." snorted Bieliayev. "This is what you do. You arrange conferences in sweet-shops. And your mother doesn't know?"

"No—no . . . How could she know? Pelagueya won't tell for anything. The day before yesterday Father stood us pears. Sweet, like jam. I had two."

"H'm . . . well, now . . . tell me, doesn't your father speak about me?"

"About you? How shall I put it?"

Aliosha gave a searching glance to Bieliayev's face and shrugged his shoulders.

"He doesn't say anything in particular."

"What does he say, for instance?"

"You won't be offended?"

"What next? Why, does he abuse me?"

"He doesn't abuse you, but you know . . . he is cross with you. He says that it's through you that Mother's unhappy and that you . . . ruined Mother. But he is so queer! I explain to him that you are good and never shout at Mother, but he only shakes his head."

"Does he say those very words: that I ruined her?"

"Yes. Don't be offended, Nikolay Ilyich!"

Bieliayev got up, stood still a moment, and then began to walk about the drawing-room.

"This is strange, and . . . funny," he murmured, shrugging his shoulders and smiling ironically. "He is to blame all round, and now *I've* ruined her, eh? What an innocent lamb! Did he say those very words to you: that I ruined your mother?"

"Yes, but . . . you said that you wouldn't get offended."

"I'm not offended, and . . . and it's none of your business! No, it . . . it's quite funny, though. I fell into the trap, yet I'm to be blamed as well."

The bell rang. The boy dashed from his place and ran out. In a minute a lady entered the room with a little girl. It was Olga Ivanovna, Aliosha's mother. After her, hopping, humming noisily, and waving his hands, followed Aliosha.

"Of course, who is there to accuse except me?" he murmured, sniffing. "He's right, he's the injured husband."

"What's the matter?" asked Olga Ivanovna.

"What's the matter! Listen to the kind of sermon your dear husband preaches. It appears I'm a scoundrel and a murderer, I've ruined you and the children. All of you are unhappy, and only I am awfully happy! Awfully, awfully happy!"

"I don't understand, Nikolay! What is it?"

"Just listen to this young gentleman," Bieliayev said, pointing to Aliosha.

Aliosha blushed, then became pale suddenly, and his whole face was twisted in fright.

"Nikolay Ilyich," he whispered loudly. "Shh!"

"Ask him, if you please," went on Bieliayev. "That stupid fool Pelagueya of yours takes them to sweet-shops and arranges meetings with their dear father there. But that's not the point. The point is that the dear father is a martyr, and I'm a murderer, I'm a scoundrel, who broke the lives of both of you. . . ."

"Nikolay Ilyich!" moaned Aliosha. "You gave your word of honor!"

"Ah, let me alone!" Bieliayev waved his hand. "This is something more important than any words of honor. The hypocrisy revolts me, the lie!"

"I don't understand," muttered Olga Ivanovna, and tears began to glimmer in her eyes. "Tell me, Liolka,"—she turned to her son, "Do you see your father?"

Aliosha did not hear and looked with horror at Bieliayev.

"It's impossible," said the mother. "I'll go and ask Pelagueya."

Olga Ivanovna went out.

"But, but you gave me your word of honor," Aliosha said, trembling all over.

Bieliayev waved his hand at him and went on walking up and down. He was absorbed in his insult, and now, as before, he did not notice the presence of the boy. He, a big serious man, had nothing to do with boys. And Aliosha sat down in a corner and in terror told Sonya how he had been deceived. He trembled, stammered, wept. This was the first time in his life that he had been set, roughly, face to face with a lie. He had never known before that in this world, besides sweet pears and cakes and expensive watches, there exist many things which have no name in children's language.

James Agee

KNOXVILLE: SUMMER 1915

We are talking now of summer evenings in Knoxville, Tennessee in the time that I lived there so successfully disguised to myself as a child. It was a little bit mixed sort of block, fairly solidly lower middle class, with one or two juts apiece on either side of that. The houses corresponded: middle-sized gracefully fretted wood houses built in the late nineties and early nineteen hundreds, with small front and side and more spacious back yards, and trees in the yards, and porches. These were softwooded trees,

poplars, tulip trees, cottonwoods. There
were fences around one or two of the houses,
but mainly the yards ran into each other
with only now and then a low hedge that
wasn't doing very well. There were few good
friends among the grown people, and they
were not poor enough for the other sort of
intimate acquaintance, but everyone nodded and spoke, and even might talk short-
times, trivially, and at the two extremes of
the general or the particular, and ordinarily
next-door neighbors talked quite a bit when
they happened to run into each other, and
never paid calls. The men were mostly
small businessmen, one or two very modestly
executives, one or two worked with their
hands, most of them clerical, and most of
them between thirty and forty-five.

But it is of these evenings, I speak.

Supper was at six and was over by half
past. There was still daylight, shining softly
and with a tarnish, like the lining of a shell;
and the carbon lamps lifted at the corners
were on in the light, and the locusts were
started, and the fire flies were out, and a
few frogs were flopping in the dewy grass,
by the time the fathers and the children
came out. The children ran out first hell
bent and yelling those names by which they
were known; then the fathers sank out leisurely in crossed suspenders, their collars
removed and their necks looking tall and
shy. The mothers stayed back in the kitchen
washing and drying, putting things away, re-
crossing their traceless footsteps like the lifetime journeys of bees, measuring out the
dry cocoa for breakfast. When they came out
they had taken off their aprons and their
skirts were dampened and they sat in
rockers on their porches quietly.

It is not of the games children played in
the evening that I want to speak now, it is
of a contemporaneous atmosphere that has
little to do with them: that of the fathers
of families, each in his space of lawn, his
shirt fish-like pale in the unnatural light and
his face nearly anonymous, hosing their

lawns. The hoses were attached at spigots
that stood out of the brick foundations of
the houses. The nozzles were variously set
but usually so there was a long sweet stream
of spray, the nozzle wet in the hand, the
water trickling the right forearm and the
peeled-back cuff, and the water whishing
out a long loose and low-curved cone, and
so gentle a sound. First an insane noise of
violence in the nozzle, then the still irregular sound of adjustment, then the
smoothing into steadiness and a pitch as accurately tuned to the size and style of stream
as any violin. So many qualities of sound
out of one hose: so many choral differences
out of those several hoses that were in earshot. Out of any one hose, the almost dead
silence of the release, and the short still arch
of the separate big drops, silent as a held
breath, and the only noise the flattering
noise on leaves and the slapped grass at the
fall of each big drop. That, and the intense
hiss with the intense stream; that, and that
same intensity not growing less but growing
more quiet and delicate with the turn of the
nozzle, up to that extreme tender whisper
when the water was just a wide bell of film.
Chiefly, though, the hoses were set much
alike, in a compromise between distance and
tenderness of spray (and quite surely a sense
of art behind this compromise, and a quiet
deep joy, too real to recognize itself), and
the sounds therefore were pitched much
alike; pointed by the snorting start of a new
hose; decorated by some man playful with
the nozzle; left empty, like God by the
sparrow's fall, when any single one of them
desists: and all, though near alike, of various
pitch; and in this unison. These sweet pale
streamings in the light lift out their pallors
and their voices all together, mothers hushing their children, the hushing unnaturally
prolonged, the men gentle and silent and
each snail-like withdrawn into the quietude
of what he singly is doing, the urination of
huge children stood loosely military against
an invisible wall, and gentle happy and

peaceful, tasting the mean goodness of their living like the last of their suppers in their mouths; while the locusts carry on this noise of hoses on their much higher and sharper key. The noise of the locust is dry, and it seems not to be rasped or vibrated but urged from him as if through a small orifice by breath that can never give out. Also there is never one locust but an illusion of at least a thousand. The noise of each locust is pitched in some classic locust range out of which none of them varies more than two full tones: and yet you seem to hear each locust discrete from all the rest, and there is a long, slow, pulse in their noise, like the scarcely defined arch of a long and high set bridge. They are all around in every tree, so that the noise seems to come from no-where and everywhere at once, from the whole shell heaven, shivering in your flesh and teasing your eardrums, the boldest of all the sounds of night. And yet it is habitual to summer nights, and is of the great order of noises, like the noises of the sea and of the blood of her precocious grand-child, which you realize you are hearing only when you catch yourself listening. Meantime from low in the dark, just out-side the swaying horizons of the hoses, con-veying always grass in the damp of dew and its strong green-black smear of smell, the regular yet spaced noises of the crickets, each a sweet cold silver noise three-noted, like the slipping each time of three matched links of a small chain.

But the men by now, one by one, have silenced their hoses and drained and coiled them. Now only two, and now only one, is left, and you see only ghostlike shirt with the sleeve garters, and sober mystery of his mild face like the lifted face of large cattle enquiring of your presence in a pitchdark pool of meadow; and now he too is gone; and it has become that time of evening when people sit on their porches, rocking gently and talking gently and watching the street and the standing up into their sphere of possession of the trees, of birds, hung havens, hangars. People go by; things go by. A horse, drawing a buggy, breaking his hollow iron music on the asphalt; a loud auto; a quiet auto; people in pairs, not in a hurry, scuffling, switching their weight of aestival body, talking casually, the taste hovering over them of vanilla, strawberry, pasteboard and starched milk, the image upon them of lovers and horsemen, squared with clowns in hueless amber. A street car raising its iron moan; stopping, belling and starting; stertorous; rousing and raising again its iron increasing moan and swim-ming its gold windows and straw seats on past and past and past, the bleak spark crackling and cursing above it like a small malignant spirit set to dog its tracks; the iron whine rises on rising speed; still risen, faints; halts; the faint stinging bell; rises again, still fainter; fainting, lifting, lifts, faints forgone: forgotten. Now is the night one blue dew.

Now is the night one blue dew, my father has drained, he has coiled the hose.

Low on the length of lawns, a frailing of fire who breathes.

Content, silver, like peeps of light, each cricket makes his comment over and over in the drowned grass.

A cold toad thumpily flounders.

Within the edges of damp shadows of side yards are hovering children nearly sick with joy of fear, who watch the unguarding of a telephone pole.

Around white carbon corner lamps bugs of all sizes are lifted elliptic, solar systems. Big hardshells bruise themselves, assailant: he is fallen on his back, legs squiggling.

Parents on porches: rock and rock: From damp strings morning glories: hang their ancient faces.

The dry and exalted noise of the locusts from all the air at once enchants my eardrums.

On the rough wet grass of the back yard my father and mother have spread quilts. We all lie there, my mother, my father, my uncle, my aunt, and I too am lying there. First we were sitting up, then one of us lay down, and then we all lay down, on our stomachs, or on our sides, or on our backs, and they have kept on talking. They are not talking much, and the talk is quiet, of nothing in particular, of nothing at all in particular, of nothing at all. The stars are wide and alive, they seem each like a smile of great sweetness, and they seem very near. All my people are larger bodies than mine, quiet, with voices gentle and meaningless like the voices of sleeping birds. One is an artist, he is living at home. One is a musician, she is living at home. One is my mother who is good to me. One is my father who is good to me. By some chance, here they are, all on this earth; and who shall ever tell the sorrow of being on this earth, lying, on quilts, on the grass, in a summer evening, among the sounds of the night. May God bless my people, my uncle, my aunt, my mother, my good father, oh, remember them kindly in their time of trouble; and in the hour of their taking away.

After a little I am taken in and put to bed. Sleep, soft smiling, draws me unto her: and those receive me, who quietly treat me, as one familiar and well beloved in that home: but will not, oh, will not, not now, not ever; but will not ever tell me who I am.

James Joyce

ARABY

North Richmond Street, being blind, was a quiet street except at the hour when the Christian Brothers' School set the boys free. An uninhabited house of two stories stood at the blind end, detached from its neigh-bors in a square ground. The other houses of the street, conscious of decent lives within them, gazed at one another with brown imperturbable faces.

The former tenant of our house, a priest, had died in the back drawing room. Air, musty from having been long enclosed, hung in all the rooms, and the waste room behind the kitchen was littered with old useless papers. Among these I found a few paper-covered books, the pages of which were curled and damp: *The Abbot*, by Walter Scott, *The Devout Communicant*, and *The Memoirs of Vidocq*. I liked the last best because its leaves were yellow. The wild garden behind the house contained a central apple tree and a few straggling bushes, under one of which I found the late tenant's rusty bicycle pump. He had been a very charitable priest; in his will he had left all his money to institutions and the furniture of his house to his sister.

When the short days of winter came, dusk fell before we had well eaten our dinners. When we met in the street the houses had grown somber. The space of sky above us was the color of ever-changing violet, and towards it the lamps of the street lifted their feeble lanterns. The cold air stung us and we played till our bodies glowed. Our shouts echoed in the silent street. The career of our play brought us through the dark muddy lanes behind the houses where we ran the gantlet of the rough tribes from the cottages, to the back doors of the dark dripping gardens where odors arose from the ashpits, to the dark odorous stables where a coachman smoothed and combed the horse or shook music from the buckled harness. When we returned to the street, light from the kitchen windows had filled the areas. If my uncle was seen turning the corner we hid in the shadow until we had seen him safely housed. Or if Mangan's sister came out on the doorstep to call her brother in to his tea we watched her from our shadow peer up and down the street.

We waited to see whether she would remain or go in and, if she remained, we left our shadow and walked up to Mangan's steps resignedly. She was waiting for us, her figure defined by the light from the half-opened door. Her brother always teased her before he obeyed, and I stood by the railings looking at her. Her dress swung as she moved her body, and the soft rope of her hair tossed from side to side.

Every morning I lay on the floor in the front parlor watching her door. The blind was pulled down to within an inch of the sash so that I could not be seen. When she came out on the doorstep my heart leaped. I ran to the hall, seized my books, and followed her. I kept her brown figure always in my eye and, when we came near the point at which our ways diverged, I quickened my pace and passed her. This happened morning after morning. I had never spoken to her, except for a few casual words, and yet her name was like a summons to all my foolish blood.

Her image accompanied me even in places the most hostile to romance. On Saturday evenings when my aunt went marketing I had to go to carry some of the parcels. We walked through the flaring streets, jostled by drunken men and bargaining women, amid the curses of laborers, the shrill litanies of shop boys who stood on guard by the barrels of pigs' cheeks, the nasal chanting of street singers, who sang a *come-all-you* about O'Donovan Rossa, or a ballad about the troubles in our native land. These noises converged in a single sensation of life for me: I imagined that I bore my chalice safely through a throng of foes. Her name sprang to my lips at moments in strange prayers and praises which I myself did not understand. My eyes were often full of tears (I could not tell why), and at times a flood from my heart seemed to pour itself out into my bosom. I thought little of the future. I did not know whether I would ever speak to her or not or, if I spoke to her, how I could tell her of my confused adoration. But my body was like a harp and her words and gestures were like fingers running upon the wires.

One evening I went into the back drawing room in which the priest had died. It was a dark, rainy evening and there was no sound in the house. Through one of the broken panes I heard the rain impinge upon the earth, the fine incessant needles of water playing in the sodden beds. Some distant lamp or lighted window gleamed below me. I was thankful that I could see so little. All my senses seemed to desire to veil themselves and, feeling that I was about to slip from them, I pressed the palms of my hands together until they trembled, murmuring: *"O love! O love!"* many times.

At last she spoke to me. When she addressed the first words to me I was so confused that I did not know what to answer. She asked me was I going to *Araby*. I forget whether I answered yes or no. It would be a splendid bazaar, she said; she would love to go.

"And why can't you?" I asked.

While she spoke she turned a silver bracelet round and round her wrist. She could not go, she said, because there would be a retreat that week in her convent. Her brother and two other boys were fighting for their caps and I was alone at the railings. She held one of the spikes, bowing her head towards me. The light from the lamp opposite our door caught the white curve of her neck, lit up her hair that rested there and, falling, lit up the hand upon the railing. It fell over one side of her dress and caught the white border of a petticoat, just visible as she stood at ease.

"It's well for you," she said.

"If I go," I said, "I will bring you something."

What innumerable follies laid waste my waking and sleeping thoughts after that evening! I wished to annihilate the tedious intervening days. I chafed against the work of school. At night in my bedroom and by day in the classroom her image came between me and the page I strove to read. The syllables of the word *Araby* were called to me through the silence in which my soul luxuriated and cast an Eastern enchantment over me. I asked for leave to go to the bazaar on Saturday night. My aunt was surprised and hoped it was not some Freemason affair. I answered few questions in class. I watched my master's face pass from amiability to sternness; he hoped I was not beginning to idle. I could not call my wandering thoughts together. I had hardly any patience with the serious work of life which, now that it stood between me and my desire, seemed to me child's play, ugly monotonous child's play.

On Saturday morning I reminded my uncle that I wished to go to the bazaar in the evening. He was fussing at the hall stand, looking for the hat brush, and answered me curtly:

"Yes, boy, I know."

As he was in the hall I could not get into the front parlor and lie at the window. I left the house in bad humor and walked slowly toward the school. The air was pitilessly raw and already my heart misgave me.

When I came home to dinner my uncle had not yet been home. Still it was early. I sat staring at the clock for some time and, when its ticking began to irritate me, I left the room. I mounted the staircase and gained the upper part of the house. The high cold empty gloomy rooms liberated me and I went from room to room singing. From the front window I saw my companions playing below in the street. Their cries reached me weakened and indistinct and, leaning my forehead against the cool glass, I looked over at the dark house where she lived. I may have stood there for an hour, seeing nothing but the brown-clad figure cast by my imagination, touched discreetly by the lamplight at the curved neck, at the hand upon the railings, and at the border below the dress.

When I came downstairs again I found Mrs. Mercer sitting at the fire. She was an old garrulous woman, a pawnbroker's widow, who collected used stamps for some pious purpose. I had to endure the gossip of the tea table. The meal was prolonged beyond an hour and still my uncle did not come. Mrs. Mercer stood up to go: she was sorry she couldn't wait any longer, but it was after eight o'clock and she did not like to be out late, as the night air was bad for her. When she had gone I began to walk up and down the room, clenching my fists. My aunt said:

"I'm afraid you may put off your bazaar for this night of Our Lord."

At nine o'clock I heard my uncle's latchkey in the hall door. I heard him talking to himself and heard the hall stand rocking when it had received the weight of his overcoat. I could interpret these signs. When he was midway through his dinner I asked him to give me the money to go to the bazaar. He had forgotten.

"The people are in bed and after their first sleep now," he said.

I did not smile. My aunt said to him energetically:

"Can't you give him the money and let him go? You've kept him late enough as it is."

My uncle said he was very sorry he had forgotten. He said he believed in the old saying: "All work and no play makes Jack a dull boy." He asked me where I was going and, when I had told him a second time, he asked me did I know *The Arab's Farewell to His Steed*. When I left the kitchen he was about to recite the opening lines of the piece to my aunt.

I held a florin tightly in my hand as I strode down Buckingham Street towards the station. The sight of the streets thronged with buyers and glaring with gas recalled to me the purpose of my journey. I took my seat in a third-class carriage of a deserted train. After an intolerable delay the train moved out of the station slowly. It crept onward among ruinous houses and over the twinkling river. At Westland Row Station a crowd of people pressed to the carriage doors; but the porters moved them back, saying that it was a special train for the bazaar. I remained alone in the bare carriage. In a few minutes the train drew up beside an improvised wooden platform. I passed out on to the road and saw by the lighted dial of a clock that it was ten minutes to ten. In front of me was a large building which displayed the magical name.

I could not find any sixpenny entrance and, fearing that the bazaar would be closed, I passed in quickly through a turnstile, handing a shilling to a weary-looking man. I found myself in a big hall girdled at half its height by a gallery. Nearly all the stalls were closed and the greater part of the hall was in darkness. I recognized a silence like that which pervades a church after a service. I walked into the center of the bazaar timidly. A few people were gathered about the stalls which were still open. Before a curtain, over which the words *Café Chantant* were written in colored lamps, two men were counting money on a salver. I listened to the fall of the coins.

Remembering with difficulty why I had come I went over to one of the stalls and examined porcelain vases and flowered tea sets. At the door of the stall a young lady was talking and laughing with two young gentlemen. I remarked their English accents and listened vaguely to their conversation.

"O, I never said such a thing!"

"O, but you did!"

"O, but I didn't!"

"Didn't she say that?"

"Yes. I heard her."

"O, there's a . . . fib!"

Observing me, the young lady came over and asked me did I wish to buy anything. The tone of her voice was not encouraging; she seemed to have spoken to me out of a sense of duty. I looked humbly at the great jars that stood like eastern guards at either side of the dark entrance to the stall and murmured:

"No, thank you."

The young lady changed the position of one of the vases and went back to the two young men. They began to talk of the same subject. Once or twice the young lady glanced at me over her shoulder.

I lingered before her stall, though I knew my stay was useless, to make my interest in her wares seem the more real. Then I turned away slowly and walked down the middle of the bazaar. I allowed the two pennies to fall against the sixpence in my pocket. I heard a voice call from one end of the gallery that the light was out. The upper part of the hall was now completely dark.

Gazing up into the darkness I saw myself as a creature driven and derided by vanity; and my eyes burned with anguish and anger.

Robert Penn Warren

BLACKBERRY WINTER

It was getting into June and past eight o'clock in the morning, but there was a fire —even if it wasn't a big fire, just a fire of chunks—on the hearth of the big stone fireplace in the living room. I was standing on the hearth, almost into the chimney, hunched over the fire, working my bare toes slowly on the warm stone. I relished the heat which made the skin of my bare legs warp and creep and tingle, even as I called to my mother, who was somewhere back in the dining room or kitchen, and said: "But it's June, I don't have to put them on!"

"You put them on if you are going out," she called.

I tried to assess the degree of authority and conviction in the tone, but at that distance it was hard to decide. I tried to analyze the tone, and then I thought what a fool I had been to start out the back door and let her see that I was barefoot. If I had gone out the front door or the side door she would never have known, not till dinner time anyway, and by then the day would have been half gone and I would have been all over the farm to see what the storm had done and down to the creek to see the flood. But it had never crossed my mind that they would try to stop you from going barefoot in June, no matter if there had been a gully-washer and a cold spell.

Nobody had ever tried to stop me in June as long as I could remember, and when you are nine years old, what you remember seems forever; for you remember everything and everything is important and stands big and full and fills up Time and is so solid that you can walk around and around it like a tree and look at it. You are aware that time passes, that there is a movement in time, but that is not what Time is. Time is not a movement, a flowing, a wind then, but is, rather, a kind of climate in which things are, and when a thing happens it begins to live and keeps on living and stands solid in Time like the tree that you can walk around. And if there is a movement, the movement is not Time itself, any more than a breeze is climate, and all the breeze does is to shake a little the leaves on the tree which is alive and solid. When you are nine, you know that there are things that you don't know, but you know that when you know something you know it. You know how a thing has been and you know that you can go barefoot in June. You do not understand that voice from back in the kitchen which says that you cannot go barefoot outdoors and run to see what has happened and rub your feet over the wet shivery grass and make the perfect mark of your foot in the smooth, creamy, red mud and

then muse upon it as though you had suddenly come upon that single mark on the glistening auroral beach of the world. You have never seen a beach, but you have read the book and how the footprint was there.

The voice had said what it had said, and I looked savagely at the black stockings and the strong, scuffed brown shoes which I had brought from my closet as far as the hearth rug. I called once more, "But it's June," and waited.

"It's June," the voice replied from far away, "but it's blackberry winter."

I had lifted my head to reply to that, to make one more test of what was in that tone, when I happened to see the man.

The fireplace in the living room was at the end; for the stone chimney was built, as in so many of the farmhouses in Tennessee, at the end of a gable, and there was a window on each side of the chimney. Out of the window on the north side of the fireplace I could see the man. When I saw the man I did not call out what I had intended, but, engrossed by the strangeness of the sight, watched him, still far off, come along the path by the edge of the woods.

What was strange was that there should be a man there at all. That path went along the yard fence, between the fence and the woods which came right down to the yard, and then on back past the chicken runs and on by the woods until it was lost to sight where the woods bulged out and cut off the back field. There the path disappeared into the woods. It led on back, I knew, through the woods and to the swamp, skirted the swamp where the big trees gave way to sycamores and water oaks and willows and tangled cane, and then led on to the river. Nobody ever went back there except people who wanted to gig frogs in the swamp or to fish in the river or to hunt in the woods, and those people, if they didn't have a standing permission from my father, always stopped to ask permission to cross the farm. But the man whom I now saw wasn't, I could tell even at that distance, a sportsman. And what would a sportsman have been doing down there after a storm? Besides, he was coming from the river, and nobody had gone down there that morning. I knew that for a fact, because if anybody had passed, certainly if a stranger had passed, the dogs would have made a racket and would have been out on him. But this man was coming up from the river and had come up through the woods. I suddenly had a vision of him moving up the grassy path in the woods, in the green twilight under the big trees, not making any sound on the path, while now and then, like drops off the eaves, a big drop of water would fall from a leaf or bough and strike a stiff oak leaf lower down with a small, hollow sound like a drop of water hitting tin. That sound, in the silence of the woods, would be very significant.

When you are a boy and stand in the stillness of woods, which can be so still that your heart almost stops beating and makes you want to stand there in the green twilight until you feel your very feet sinking into and clutching the earth like roots and your body breathing slow through its pores like the leaves—when you stand there and wait for the next drop to drop with its small, flat sound to a lower leaf, that sound seems to measure out something, to put an end to something, to begin something, and you cannot wait for it to happen and are afraid it will not happen, and then when it has happened, you are waiting again, almost afraid.

But the man whom I saw coming through the woods in my mind's eye did not pause and wait, growing into the ground and breathing with the enormous, soundless breathing of the leaves. Instead, I saw him moving in the green twilight inside my head as he was moving at that very moment along the path by the edge of the woods, coming toward the house. He was moving steadily, but not fast, with his shoulders hunched a little and his head thrust forward, like a man who has come a long way and has a long way to go. I shut my eyes for a couple of seconds, thinking that when I opened them he would not be there at all. There was no place for him to have come from, and there was no reason for him to come where he was coming, toward our house. But I opened my eyes, and there he was, and he was coming steadily along the side of the woods. He was not yet even with the back chicken yard.

"Mama," I called.

"You put them on," the voice said.

"There's a man coming," I called, "out-back."

She did not reply to that, and I guessed that she had gone to the kitchen window to look. She would be looking at the man and wondering who he was and what he wanted, the way you always do in the country, and if I went back there now she would not notice right off whether or not I was barefoot. So I went back to the kitchen.

She was standing by the window. "I don't recognize him," she said, not looking around at me.

"Where could he be coming from?" I asked.

"I don't know," she said.

"What would he be doing down at the river? At night? In the storm?"

She studied the figure out the window, then said, "Oh, I reckon maybe he cut across from the Dunbar place."

That was, I realized, a perfectly rational explanation. He had not been down at the river in the storm, at night. He had come over this morning. You could cut across from the Dunbar place if you didn't mind breaking through a lot of elder and sassafras and blackberry bushes which had about taken over the old cross path, which nobody ever used any more. That satisfied me for a moment, but only for a moment. "Mama," I asked, "what would he be doing over at the Dunbar place last night?"

Then she looked at me, and I knew I had

made a mistake, for she was looking at my bare feet. "You haven't got your shoes on," she said.

But I was saved by the dogs. That instant there was a bark which I recognized as Sam, the collie, and then a heavier, churning kind of bark which was Bully, and I saw a streak of white as Bully tore round the corner of the back porch and headed out for the man. Bully was a big, bone-white bull dog, the kind of dog that they used to call a farm bull dog but that you don't see any more, heavy chested and heavy headed, but with pretty long legs. He could take a fence as light as a hound. He had just cleared the white paling fence toward the woods when my mother ran out to the back porch and began calling, "Here you Bully! Here you!"

Bully stopped in the path, waiting for the man, but he gave a few more of those deep, gargling, savage barks that reminded you of something down a stone-lined well. The red clay mud, I saw, was splashed up over his white chest and looked exciting, like blood.

The man, however, had not stopped walking even when Bully took the fence and started at him. He had kept right on coming. All he had done was to switch a little paper parcel which he carried from the right hand to the left, and then reach into his pants pocket to get something. Then I saw the glitter and knew that he had a knife in his hand, probably the kind of mean knife just made for devilment and nothing else, with a blade as long as the blade of a frog-sticker, which will snap out ready when you press a button in the handle. That knife must have had a button in the handle, or else how could he have had the blade out glittering so quick and with just one hand?

Pulling his knife against the dogs was a funny thing to do, for Bully was a big, powerful brute and fast, and Sam was all right. If those dogs had meant business, they might have knocked him down and ripped him before he got a stroke in. He ought to have picked up a heavy stick, something to take a swipe at them with and something which they could see and respect when they came at him. But he apparently did not know much about dogs. He just held the knife blade close against the right leg, low down, and kept on moving down the path.

Then my mother had called, and Bully had stopped. So the man let the blade of the knife snap back into the handle, and dropped it into his pocket, and kept on coming. Many women would have been afraid with the strange man who they knew had that knife in his pocket. That is, if they were alone in the house with nobody but a nine-year-old boy. And my mother was alone, for my father had gone off, and Dellie, the cook, was down at her cabin because she wasn't feeling well. But my mother wasn't afraid. She wasn't a big woman, but she was clear and brisk about everything she did and looked everybody and everything right in the eye from her own blue eyes in her tanned face. She had been the first woman in the country to ride a horse astride (that was back when she was a girl and long before I was born), and I have seen her snatch up a pump gun and go out and knock a chicken hawk out of the air like a busted skeet when he came over her chicken yard. She was a steady and self-reliant woman, and when I think of her now after all the years she has been dead, I think of her brown hands, not big, but somewhat square for a woman's hands, with square-cut nails. They looked, as a matter of fact, more like a young boy's hands than a grown woman's. But back then it never crossed my mind that she would ever be dead.

She stood on the back porch and watched the man enter the back gate, where the dogs (Bully had leaped back into the yard) were dancing and muttering and giving sidelong glances back to my mother to see if she meant what she had said. The man walked right by the dogs, almost brushing them, and didn't pay them any attention. I could see now that he wore old khaki pants, and a dark wool coat with stripes in it, and a gray felt hat. He had on a gray shirt with blue stripes in it, and no tie. But I could see a tie, blue and reddish, sticking in his side coat-pocket. Everything was wrong about what he wore. He ought to have been wearing blue jeans or overalls, and a straw hat or an old black felt hat, and the coat, granting that he might have been wearing a wool coat and not a jumper, ought not to have had those stripes. Those clothes, despite the fact that they were old enough and dirty enough for any tramp, didn't belong there in our back yard, coming down the path, in Middle Tennessee, miles away from any big town, and even a mile off the pike.

When he got almost to the steps, without having said anything, my mother, very matter-of-factly, said, "Good morning."

"Good morning," he said, and stopped and looked her over. He did not take off his hat, and under the brim you could see the perfectly unmemorable face, which wasn't old and wasn't young, or thick or thin. It was grayish and covered with about three days of stubble. The eyes were a kind of nondescript, muddy hazel, or something like that, rather bloodshot. His teeth, when he opened his mouth, showed yellow and uneven. A couple of them had been knocked out. You knew that they had been knocked out, because there was a scar, not very old, there on the lower lip just beneath the gap.

"Are you hunting work?" my mother asked him.

"Yes," he said—not "yes, mam"—and still did not take off his hat.

"I don't know about my husband, for he isn't here," she said, and didn't mind a bit telling the tramp, or whoever he was, with the mean knife in his pocket, that no man was around, "but I can give you a few things to do. The storm has drowned a lot of my chicks. Three coops of them. You can

gather them up and bury them. Bury them deep so the dogs won't get at them. In the woods. And fix the coops the wind blew over. And down yonder beyond that pen by the edge of the woods are some drowned poults. They got out and I couldn't get them in. Even after it started to rain hard. Poults haven't got any sense."

"What are them things—poults?" he demanded, and spat on the brick walk. He rubbed his foot over the spot, and I saw that he wore a black, pointed-toe low shoe, all cracked and broken. It was a crazy kind of shoe to be wearing in the country.

"Oh, they're young turkeys," my mother was saying. "And they haven't got any sense. I oughtn't to try to raise them around here with so many chickens, anyway. They don't thrive near chickens, even in separate pens. And I won't give up my chickens." Then she stopped herself and resumed briskly on the note of business. "When you finish that, you can fix my flower beds. A lot of trash and mud and gravel has washed down. Maybe you can save some of my flowers if you are careful."

"Flowers," the man said, in a low, impersonal voice which seemed to have a wealth of meaning, but a meaning which I could not fathom. As I think back on it, it probably was not pure contempt. Rather, it was a kind of impersonal and distant marveling that he should be on the verge of grubbing in a flower bed. He said the word, and then looked off across the yard.

"Yes, flowers," my mother replied with some asperity, as though she would have nothing said or implied against flowers. "And they were very fine this year." Then she stopped and looked at the man. "Are you hungry?" she demanded.

"Yeah," he said.

"I'll fix you something," she said, "before you get started." She turned to me. "Show him where he can wash up," she commanded, and went into the house.

I took the man to the end of the porch

where a pump was and where a couple of wash pans sat on a low shelf for people to use before they went into the house. I stood there while he laid down his little parcel wrapped in newspaper and took off his hat and looked around for a nail to hang it on. He poured the water and plunged his hands into it. They were big hands, and strong looking, but they did not have the creases and the earth-color of the hands of men who work outdoors. But they were dirty, with black dirt ground into the skin and under the nails. After he had washed his hands, he poured another basin of water and washed his face. He dried his face, and with the towel still dangling in his grasp, stepped over to the mirror on the house wall. He rubbed one hand over the stubble on his face. Then he carefully inspected his face, turning first one side and then the other, and stepped back and settled his striped coat down on his shoulders. He had the movements of a man who has just dressed up to go to church or a party—the way he settled his coat and smoothed it and scanned himself in the mirror.

Then he caught my glance on him. He glared at me for an instant out of the bloodshot eyes, then demanded in a low, harsh voice, "What you looking at?"

"Nothing," I managed to say, and stepped back a step from him.

He flung the towel down, crumpled, on the shelf, and went toward the kitchen door and entered without knocking.

My mother said something to him which I could not catch. I started to go in again, then thought about my bare feet, and decided to go back of the chicken yard, where the man would have to come to pick up the dead chicks. I hung around behind the chicken house until he came out.

He moved across the chicken yard with a fastidious, not quite finicking motion, looking down at the curdled mud flecked with bits of chicken-droppings. The mud curled up over the soles of his black shoes. I stood

back from him some six feet and watched him pick up the first of the drowned chicks. He held it up by one foot and inspected it.

There is nothing deader looking than a drowned chick. The feet curl in that feeble, empty way which back when I was a boy, even if I was a country boy who did not mind hog-killing or frog-gigging, made me feel hollow in the stomach. Instead of looking plump and fluffy, the body is stringy and limp with the fluff plastered to it, and the neck is long and loose like a little string of rag. And the eyes have that bluish membrane over them which makes you think of a very old man who is sick about to die.

The man stood there and inspected the chick. Then he looked all around as though he didn't know what to do with it.

"There's a great big old basket in the shed," I said, and pointed to the shed attached to the chicken house.

He inspected me as though he had just discovered my presence, and moved toward the shed.

"There's a spade there, too," I added.

He got the basket and began to pick up the other chicks, picking each one up slowly by a foot and then flinging it into the basket with a nasty, snapping motion. Now and then he would look at me out of the bloodshot eyes. Every time he seemed on the verge of saying something, but he did not. Perhaps he was building up to say something to me, but I did not wait that long. His way of looking at me made me so uncomfortable that I left the chicken yard.

Besides, I had just remembered that the creek was in flood, over the bridge, and that people were down there watching it. So I cut across the farm toward the creek. When I got to the big tobacco field I saw that it had not suffered much. The land lay right and not many tobacco plants had washed out of the ground. But I knew that a lot of tobacco round the country had been washed right out. My father had said so at breakfast.

My father was down at the bridge. When I came out of the gap in the osage hedge into the road, I saw him sitting on his mare over the heads of the other men who were standing around, admiring the flood. The creek was big here, even in low water; for only a couple of miles away it ran into the river, and when a real flood came, the red water got over the pike where it dipped down to the bridge, which was an iron bridge, and high over the floor and even the side railings of the bridge. Only the upper iron work would show, with the water boiling and frothing red and white around it. That creek rose so fast and so heavy because a few miles back it came down out of the hills, where the gorges filled up with water in no time when a rain came. The creek ran in a deep bed with limestone bluffs along both sides until it got within three quarters of a mile of the bridge, and when it came out from between those bluffs in flood it was boiling and hissing and steaming like water from a fire hose.

Whenever there was a flood, people from half the county would come down to see the sight. After a gully-washer there would not be any work to do anyway. If it didn't ruin your crop, you couldn't plow and you felt like taking a holiday to celebrate. If it did ruin your crop, there wasn't anything to do except to try to take your mind off the mortgage, if you were rich enough to have a mortgage, and if you couldn't afford a mortgage you needed something to take your mind off how hungry you would be by Christmas. So people would come down to the bridge and look at the flood. It made something different from the run of days.

There would not be much talking after the first few minutes of trying to guess how high the water was this time. The men and kids just stood around, or sat their horses or mules, as the case might be, or stood up in the wagon beds. They looked at the strangeness of the flood for an hour or two, and then somebody would say that he had better

be getting on home to dinner and would start walking down the gray, puddled limestone pike, or would touch heel to his mount and start off. Everybody always knew what it would be like when he got down to the bridge, but people always came. It was like church or a funeral. They always came, that is, if it was summer and the flood unexpected. Nobody ever came down in winter to see high water.

When I came out of the gap in the bodock hedge, I saw the crowd, perhaps fifteen or twenty men and a lot of kids, and saw my father sitting his mare, Nellie Gray. He was a tall, limber man and carried himself well. I was always proud to see him sit a horse, he was so quiet and straight, and when I stepped through the gap of the hedge that morning, the first thing that happened was, I remember, the warm feeling I always had when I saw him up on a horse, just sitting. I did not go toward him, but skirted the crowd on the far side, to get a look at the creek. For one thing, I was not sure what he would say about the fact that I was barefoot. But the first thing I knew, I heard his voice calling, "Seth!"

I went toward him, moving apologetically past the men, who bent their large, red or thin, sallow faces above me. I knew some of the men, and knew their names, but because those I knew were there in a crowd, mixed with the strange faces, they seemed foreign to me, and not friendly. I did not look up at my father until I was almost within touching distance of his heel. Then I looked up and tried to read his face, to see if he was angry about my being barefoot. Before I could decide anything from that impassive, high-boned face, he had leaned over and reached a hand to me. "Grab on," he commanded.

I grabbed on and gave a little jump, and he said, "Up-see-daisy!" and whisked me, light as a feather, up to the pommel of his McClellan saddle.

"You can see better up here," he said,

slid back on the cantle a little to make me more comfortable, and then, looking over my head at the swollen, tumbling water, seemed to forget all about me. But his right hand was laid on my side, just above my thigh, to steady me.

I was sitting there as quiet as I could, feeling the faint stir of my father's chest against my shoulders as it rose and fell with his breath, when I saw the cow. At first, looking up the creek, I thought it was just another big piece of driftwood steaming down the creek in the ruck of water, but all at once a pretty good-size boy who had climbed part way up a telephone pole by the pike so that he could see better yelled out, "Golly-damn, look at that-air cow!"

Everybody looked. It was a cow all right, but it might just as well have been driftwood; for it was dead as a chunk, rolling and rolling down the creek, appearing and disappearing, feet up or head up, it didn't matter which.

The cow started up the talk again. Somebody wondered whether it would hit one of the clear places under the top girder of the bridge and get through or whether it would get tangled in the drift and trash that had piled against the upright girders and braces. Somebody remembered how about ten years before so much driftwood had piled up on the bridge that it was knocked off its foundations. Then the cow hit. It hit the edge of the drift against one of the girders, and hung there. For a few seconds it seemed as though it might tear loose, but then we saw it was really caught. It bobbed and heaved on its side there in a slow, grinding, uneasy fashion. It had a yoke around its neck, the kind made out of a forked limb to keep a jumper behind fence.

"She shore jumped one fence," one of the men said.

And another: "Well, she done jumped her last one, fer a fack."

Then they began to wonder about whose cow it might be. They decided it must be-

long to Milt Alley. They said that he had a cow that was a jumper, and kept her in a fenced-in piece of ground up the creek. I had never seen Milt Alley, but I knew who he was. He was a squatter and lived up the hills a way, on a shirt-tail patch of set-on-edge land, in a cabin. He was pore white trash. He had lots of children. I had seen the children at school, when they came. They were thin-faced, with straight, sticky-looking, dough-colored hair, and they smelled something like old sour buttermilk, not because they drank so much buttermilk but because that is the sort of smell which children out of those cabins tend to have. The big Alley boy drew dirty pictures and showed them to the little boys at school.

That was Milt Alley's cow. It looked like the kind of cow he would have, a scrawny, old, sway-backed cow, with a yoke around her neck. I wondered if Milt Alley had another cow.

"Poppa," I said, "do you think Milt Alley has got another cow?"

"You say 'Mr. Alley,' " my father said quietly.

"Do you think he has?"

"No telling," my father said.

Then a big gangly boy, about fifteen, who was sitting on a scraggly little old mule with a piece of croker sack thrown across the saw-tooth spine, and who had been staring at the cow, suddenly said to nobody in particular, "Reckin anybody ever et drownt cow?"

He was the kind of boy who might just as well as not have been the son of Milt Alley, with his faded and patched overalls ragged at the bottom of the pants and the mud-stiff brogans hanging off his skinny, bare ankles at the level of the mule's belly. He had said what he did, and then looked embarrassed and sullen when all the eyes swung at him. He hadn't meant to say it, I am pretty sure now. He would have been too proud to say it, just as Milt Alley would have been too proud. He had just been thinking out loud, and the words had dropped out.

There was an old man standing there on the pike, an old man with a white beard. "Son," he said to the embarrassed and sullen boy on the mule, "you live long enough and you'll find a man will eat anything when the time comes."

"Time gonna come fer some folks this year," another man said.

"Son," the old man said, "in my time I et things a man don't like to think on. I was a sojer and I rode with Gin'l Forrest, and them things we et when the time come. I tell you. I et meat what got up and run when you taken out yore knife to cut a slice to put on the fire. You had to knock it down with a carbeen butt, it was so active. That-air meat would jump like a bullfrog, it was so full of skippers."

But nobody was listening to the old man. The boy on the mule turned his sullen sharp face from him, dug a heel into the side of the mule and went off up the pike with a motion which made you think that any second you would hear mule bones clashing inside that lank and scrofulous hide.

"Cy Dundee's boy," a man said, and nodded toward the figure going up the pike on the mule.

"Reckin Cy Dundee's young-uns seen times they'd settle fer drownt cow," another man said.

The old man with the beard peered at them both from his weak, slow eyes, first at one and then at the other. "Live long enough," he said, "and a man will settle fer what he kin git."

Then there was silence again, with the people looking at the red, foam-flecked water.

My father lifted the bridle rein in his left hand, and the mare turned and walked around the group and up the pike. We rode on up to our big gate, where my father dismounted to open it and let me myself ride Nellie Gray through. When he got to the lane that led off from the drive about two

hundred yards from our house, my father said, "Grab on." I grabbed on, and he let me down to the ground. "I'm going to ride down and look at my corn," he said. "You go on." He took the lane, and I stood there on the drive and watched him ride off. He was wearing cowhide boots and an old hunting coat, and I thought that that made him look very military, like a picture. That and the way he rode.

I did not go to the house. Instead, I went by the vegetable garden and crossed behind the stables, and headed down for Dellie's cabin. I wanted to go down and play with Jebb, who was Dellie's little boy about two years older than I was. Besides, I was cold. I shivered as I walked, and I had gooseflesh. The mud which crawled up between my toes with every step I took was like ice. Dellie would have a fire, but she wouldn't make me put on shoes and stockings.

Dellie's cabin was of logs, with one side, because it was on a slope, set on limestone chunks, with a little porch attached to it, and had a little whitewashed fence around it and a gate with plow-points on a wire to clink when somebody came in, and had two big white oaks in the yard and some flowers and a nice privy in the back with some honeysuckle growing over it. Dellie and Old Jebb, who was Jebb's father and who lived with Dellie and had lived with her for twenty-five years even if they never had got married, were careful to keep everything nice around their cabin. They had the name all over the community for being clean and clever Negroes. Dellie and Jebb were what they used to call "whitefolks' niggers." There was a big difference between their cabin and the other two cabins farther down where the other tenants lived. My father kept the other cabins weatherproof, but he couldn't undertake to go down and pick up after the litter they strewed. They didn't take the trouble to have a vegetable patch like Dellie and Jebb or to make preserves from wild plum, and jelly from crab apple the way Dellie did. They were shiftless, and my father was always threatening to get shed of them. But he never did. When they finally left, they just up and left on their own, for no reason, to go and be shiftless somewhere else. Then some more came. But meanwhile they lived down there, Matt Rawson and his family, and Sid Turner and his, and I played with their children all over the farm when they weren't working. But when I wasn't around they were mean sometimes to Little Jebb. That was because the other tenants down there were jealous of Dellie and Jebb.

I was so cold that I ran the last fifty yards to Dellie's gate. As soon as I had entered the yard, I saw that the storm had been hard on Dellie's flowers. The yard was, as I have said, on a slight slope, and the water running across had gutted the flower beds and washed out all the good black woods-earth which Dellie had brought in. What little grass there was in the yard was plastered sparsely down on the ground, the way the drainage water had left it. It reminded me of the way the fluff was plastered down on the skin of the drowned chicks that the strange man had been picking up, up in my mother's chicken yard.

I took a few steps up the path to the cabin, and then I saw that the drainage water had washed a lot of trash and filth out from under Dellie's house. Up toward the porch, the ground was not clean any more. Old pieces of rag, two or three rusted cans, pieces of rotten rope, some hunks of old dog dung, broken glass, old paper, and all sorts of things like that had washed out from under Dellie's house to foul her clean yard. It looked just as bad as the yards of the other cabins, or worse. It was worse, as a matter of fact, because it was a surprise. I had never thought of all that filth being under Dellie's house. It was not anything against Dellie that the stuff had been under the cabin. Trash will get under any house. But I did not think of that when I saw the

foulness which had washed out on the ground which Dellie sometimes used to sweep with a twig broom to make nice and clean.

I picked my way past the filth, being careful not to get my bare feet on it, and mounted to Dellie's door. When I knocked, I heard her voice telling me to come in.

It was dark inside the cabin, after the daylight, but I could make out Dellie piled up in bed under a quilt, and Little Jebb crouched by the hearth, where a low fire simmered. "Howdy," I said to Dellie, "how you feeling?"

Her big eyes, the whites surprising and glaring in the black face, fixed on me as I stood there, but she did not reply. It did not look like Dellie, or act like Dellie, who would grumble and bustle around our kitchen, talking to herself, scolding me or Little Jebb, clanking pans, making all sorts of unnecessary noises and mutterings like an old-fashioned black steam thrasher engine when it has got up an extra head of steam and keeps popping the governor and rumbling and shaking on its wheels. But now Dellie just lay up there on the bed, under the patch-work quilt, and turned the black face, which I scarcely recognized, and the glaring white eyes to me.

"How you feeling?" I repeated.

"I'se sick," the voice said croakingly out of the strange black face which was not attached to Dellie's big, squat body, but stuck out from under a pile of tangled bedclothes. Then the voice added: "Mighty sick."

"I'm sorry, I managed to say."

The eyes remained fixed on me for a moment, then they left me and the head rolled back on the pillow. "Sorry," the voice said, in a flat way which wasn't question or statement of anything. It was just the empty word put into the air with no meaning or expression, to float off like a feather or a puff of smoke, while the big eyes, with the whites like the peeled white of hard-boiled eggs, stared at the ceiling.

"Dellie," I said after a minute, "there's a tramp up at the house. He's got a knife."

She was not listening. She closed her eyes.

I tiptoed over to the hearth where Jebb was and crouched beside him. We began to talk in low voices. I was asking him to get out his train and play train. Old Jebb had put spool wheels on three cigar boxes and put wire links between the boxes to make a train for Jebb. The box that was the locomotive had the top closed and a length of broom stick for a smoke stack. Jebb didn't want to get the train out, but I told him I would go home if he didn't. So he got out the train, and the colored rocks, and fossils of crinoid stems, and other junk he used for the load, and we began to push it around, talking the way we thought trainmen talked, making a chuck-chucking sound under the breath for the noise of the locomotive and now and then uttering low, cautious toots for the whistle. We got so interested in playing train that the toots got louder. Then, before he thought, Jebb gave a good, loud *toot-toot*, blowing for a crossing.

"Come here," the voice said from the bed.

Jebb got up slow from his hands and knees, giving me a sudden, naked, inimical look.

"Come here!" the voice said.

Jebb went to the bed. Dellie propped herself weakly up on one arm, muttering, "Come closer."

Jebb stood closer.

"Last thing I do, I'm gonna do it," Dellie said. "Done tole you to be quiet."

Then she slapped him. It was an awful slap, more awful for the kind of weakness which it came from and brought to focus. I had seen her slap Jebb before, but the slapping had always been the kind of easy slap you would expect from a good-natured, grumbling Negro woman like Dellie. But this was different. It was awful. It was so awful that Jebb didn't make a sound. The tears just popped out and ran down his face, and his breath came sharp, like gasps.

Dellie fell back. "Cain't even be sick," she said to the ceiling. "Git sick and they won't even let you lay. They tromp all over you. Cain't even be sick." Then she closed her eyes.

I went out of the room. I almost ran getting to the door, and I did run across the porch and down the steps and across the yard, not caring whether or not I stepped on the filth which had washed out from under the cabin. I ran almost all the way home. Then I thought about my mother catching me with the bare feet. So I went down to the stables.

I heard a noise in the crib, and opened the door. There was Big Jebb, sitting on an old nail keg, shelling corn into a bushel basket. I went in, pulling the door shut behind me, and crouched on the floor near him. I crouched there for a couple of minutes before either of us spoke, and watched him shelling the corn.

He had very big hands, knotted and grayish at the joints, with calloused palms which seemed to be streaked with rust with the rust coming up between the fingers to show from the back. His hands were so strong and tough that he could take a big ear of corn and rip the grains right off the cob with the palm of his hand, all in one motion, like a machine. "Work long as me," he would say, "and the good Lawd'll give you a hand lak cass-ion won't nuthin' hurt." And his hands did look like cast iron, old cast iron streaked with rust.

He was an old man, up in his seventies, thirty years or more older than Dellie, but he was strong as a bull. He was a squat sort of man, heavy in the shoulders, with remarkably long arms, the kind of build they say the river natives have on the Congo from paddling so much in their boats. He had a round bullet-head, set on powerful shoulders. His skin was very black, and the thin hair on his head was now grizzled like tufts of old cotton batting. He had small eyes and a flat nose, not big, and the kindest and wisest old face in the world, the blunt, sad, wise face of an old animal peering tolerantly out on the goings-on of the merely human creatures before him. He was a good man, and I loved him next to my mother and father. I crouched there on the floor of the crib and watched him shell corn with the rusty cast-iron hands, while he looked down at me out of the little eyes set in the blunt face.

"Dellie says she's mighty sick," I said.

"Yeah," he said.

"What's she sick from?"

"Woman-mizry," he said.

"What's woman-mizry?"

"Hit comes on 'em," he said. "Hit just comes on 'em when the time comes."

"What is it?"

"Hit is the change," he said. "Hit is the change of life and time."

"What changes?"

"You too young to know."

"Tell me."

"Time come and you find out everything."

I knew that there was no use in asking him any more. When I asked him things and he said that, I always knew that he would not tell me. So I continued to crouch there and watch him. Now that I had sat there a little while, I was cold again.

"What you shiver fer?" he asked me.

"I'm cold. I'm cold because it's blackberry winter," I said.

"Maybe 'tis and maybe 'tain't," he said.

"My mother says it is."

"Ain't sayen Miss Sallie doan know and ain't sayen she do. But folks doan know everthing."

"Why isn't it blackberry winter?"

"Too late fer blackberry winter. Blackberries done bloomed."

"She said it was."

"Blackberry winter just a leetle cold spell. Hit come and then hit go away, and hit is growed summer of a sudden lak a gunshot. Ain't no tellen hit will go way this time."

"It's June," I said.

"June," he replied with great contempt. "That what folks say. What June mean? Maybe hit is come cold to stay."

"Why?"

" 'Cause this-here old yearth is tahrd. Hit is tahrd and ain't gonna perduce. Lawd let hit come rain one time forty days and forty nights, 'cause He was tahrd of sinful folks. Maybe this-here old yearth say to the Lawd, Lawd, I done plum tahrd, Lawd, lemme rest. And Lawd say, Yearth, you done your best, you give 'em cawn and you give 'em taters, and all they think on is they gut, and, Yearth, you kin take a rest."

"What will happen?"

"Folks will eat up everthing. The yearth won't perduce no more. Folks cut down all the trees and burn 'em 'cause they cold, and the yearth won't grow no more. I been tellen 'em. I been tellen folks. Sayen, maybe this year, hit is the time. But they doan listen to me, how the yearth is tahrd. Maybe this year they find out."

"Will everything die?"

"Everthing and everbody, hit will be so."

"This year?"

"Ain't no tellen. Maybe this year."

"My mother said it is blackberry winter," I said confidently, and got up.

"Aint sayen nuthin' agin Miss Sallie," he said.

I went to the door of the crib. I was really cold now. Running, I had got up a sweat and now I was worse.

I hung on the door, looking at Jebb, who was shelling corn again.

"There's a tramp came to the house," I said. I had almost forgotten the tramp.

"Yeah."

"He came by the back way. What was he doing down there in the storm?"

"They comes and they goes," he said, "and ain't no tellen."

"He had a mean knife."

"The good ones and the bad ones, they

comes and they goes. Storm or sun, light or dark. They is folks and they comes and they goes lak folks."

I hung on the door, shivering.

He studied me a moment, then said, "You git on to the house. You ketch yore death. Then what yore mammy say?"

I hesitated.

"You git," he said.

When I came to the back yard, I saw that my father was standing by the back porch and the tramp was walking toward him. They began talking before I reached them, but I got there just as my father was saying, "I'm sorry, but I haven't got any work. I got all the hands on the place I need now. I won't need any extra until wheat thrashing."

The stranger made no reply, just looked at my father.

My father took out his leather coin purse, and got out a half-dollar. He held it toward the man. "This is for half a day," he said.

The man looked at the coin, and then at my father, making no motion to take the money. But that was the right amount. A dollar a day was what you paid them back in 1910. And the man hadn't even worked half a day.

Then the man reached out and took the coin. He dropped it into the right side pocket of his coat. Then he said, very slowly and without feeling: "I didn't want to work on your ——— farm."

He used the word which they would have frailed me to death for using.

I looked at my father's face and it was streaked white under the sunburn. Then he said, "Get off this place. Get off this place or I won't be responsible."

The man dropped his right hand into his pants pocket. It was the pocket where he kept the knife. I was just about to yell to my father about the knife when the hand came back out with nothing in it. The man gave a kind of twisted grin, showing where

the teeth had been knocked out above the new scar. I thought that instant how maybe he had tried before to pull a knife on somebody else and had got his teeth knocked out.

So now he just gave that twisted, sickish grin out of the unmemorable grayish face, and then spat on the brick path. The blob landed just about six inches from the toe of my father's right boot. My father looked down at it, and so did I. I thought that if the glob had hit my father's boot something would have happened. I looked down and saw the bright glob, and on one side of it my father's strong cowhide boots, with the brass eyelets and the leather thongs, heavy boots splashed with good red mud and set solid on the bricks, and on the other side the pointed-toe, broken, black shoes, on which the mud looked so sad and out of place. Then I saw one of the black shoes move a little, just a twitch first, then a real step backward.

The man moved in a quarter circle to the end of the porch, with my father's steady gaze upon him all the while. At the end of the porch, the man reached up to the shelf where the wash pans were to get his little newspaper-wrapped parcel. Then he disappeared around the corner of the house and my father mounted the porch and went into the kitchen without a word.

I followed around the house to see what the man would do. I wasn't afraid of him now, no matter if he did have the knife. When I got around in front, I saw him going out the yard gate and starting up the drive toward the pike. So I ran to catch up with him. He was sixty yards or so up the drive before I caught up.

I did not walk right up even with him at first, but trailed him, the way a kid will, about seven or eight feet behind, now and then running two or three steps in order to hold my place against his longer stride. When I first came up behind him, he turned to give me a look, just a meaningless look, and then fixed his eyes up the drive and kept on walking.

When we had got around the bend in the drive which cut the house from sight, and were going along by the edge of the woods, I decided to come up even with him. I ran a few steps, and was by his side, or almost, but some feet off to the right. I walked along in this position for a while, and he never noticed me. I walked along until we got within sight of the big gate that let on the pike.

Then I said: "Where did you come from?"

He looked at me then with a look which seemed almost surprised that I was there. Then he said, "It ain't none of your business."

We went on another fifty feet.

Then I said, "Where are you going?"

He stopped, studied me dispassionately for a moment, then suddenly took a step toward me and leaned his face down at me. The lips jerked back, but not in any grin, to show where the teeth were knocked out and to make the scar on the lower lip come white with the tension.

He said: "Stop following me. You don't stop following me and I cut yore throat, you little son-of-a-bitch."

Then he went on to the gate, and up the pike.

That was thirty-five years ago. Since that time my father and mother have died. I was still a boy, but a big boy, when my father got cut on the blade of a mowing machine and died of lockjaw. My mother sold the place and went to town to live with her sister. But she never took hold after my father's death, and she died within three years, right in middle life. My aunt always said, "Sallie just died of a broken heart, she was so devoted." Dellie is dead, too, but she died, I heard, quite a long time after we sold the farm.

As for Little Jebb, he grew up to be a mean and ficey Negro. He killed another Negro in a fight and got sent to the penitentiary, where he is yet, the last I heard tell. He probably grew up to be mean and ficey from just being picked on so much by the children of the other tenants, who were jealous of Jebb and Dellie for being thrifty and clever and being white-folks' niggers.

Old Jebb lived forever. I saw him ten years ago and he was about a hundred then, and not looking much different. He was living in town then, on relief—that was back in the Depression—when I went to see him. He said to me: "Too strong to die. When I was a young feller just comen on and seen how things wuz, I prayed the Lawd. I said, Oh, Lawd, gimme strength and meke me strong fer to do and to in-dure. The Lawd hearkened to my prayer. He give me strength. I was in-duren proud fer being strong and me much man. The Lawd give me my prayer and my strength. But now He done gone off and fergot me and left me alone with my strength. A man doan know what to pray fer, and him mortal."

Jebb is probably living yet, as far as I know.

That is what has happened since the morning when the tramp leaned his face down at me and showed his teeth and said: "Stop following me. You don't stop following me and I cut yore throat, you little son-of-a-bitch." That was what he said, for me not to follow him. But I did follow him, all the years.

Ogden Nash

SONG TO BE SUNG BY THE FATHER OF INFANT FEMALE CHILDREN

My heart leaps up when I behold
A rainbow in the sky;
Contrariwise, my blood runs cold
When little boys go by.

For little boys as little boys,
No special hate I carry,
But now and then they grow to men,
And when they do, they marry.
No matter how they tarry.
Eventually they marry. 10
And, swine among the pearls,
They marry little girls.

Oh, somewhere, somewhere, an infant plays
With parents who feed and clothe him.
Their lips are sticky with pride and praise,
But I have begun to loathe him.
Yes, I loathe with a loathing shameless
This child who to me is nameless.
This bachelor child in his carriage
Gives never a thought to marriage, 20
But a person can hardly say knife
Before he will hunt him a wife.

I never see an infant (male),
A-sleeping in the sun,
Without I turn a trifle pale
And think, is he the one?
Oh, first he'll want to crop his curls,
And then he'll want a pony,
And then he'll think of pretty girls
And holy matrimony. 30
He'll put away his pony,
And sigh for matrimony.
A cat without a mouse
Is he without a spouse.

Oh, somewhere he bubbles, bubbles of milk,
And quietly sucks his thumbs;
His cheeks are roses painted on silk,
And his teeth are tucked in his gums.
But alas, the teeth will begin to grow,
And the bubbles will cease to bubble; 40
Given a score of years or so,
The roses will turn to stubble.
He'll sell a bond, or he'll write a book,
And his eyes will get that acquisitive look,
And raging and ravenous for the kill,
He'll boldly ask for the hand of Jill.
This infant whose middle

Is diapered still
Will want to marry
My daughter Jill. 50
Oh sweet be his slumber and moist his middle!
My dreams, I fear, are infanticiddle.
A fig for embryo Lohengrins!
I'll open all of his safety pins,
I'll pepper his powder and salt his bottle,
And give him readings from Aristotle,
Sand for his spinach I'll gladly bring,
And tabasco sauce for his teething ring,
And an elegant, elegant alligator
To play with in his perambulator. 60
Then perhaps he'll struggle through fire and
        water
To marry somebody *else's* daughter!

Henry Vaughan

THE RETREAT

Happy those early days, when I
Shined in my angel-infancy!
Before I understood this place
Appointed for my second race,
Or taught my soul to fancy aught
But a white, celestial thought;
When yet I had not walked above
A mile or two from my first love,
And looking back—at that short space—
Could see a glimpse of his bright face; 10
When on some gilded cloud or flower
My gazing soul would dwell an hour,
And in those weaker glories spy
Some shadows of eternity;
Before I taught my tongue to wound
My conscience with a sinful sound,
Or had the black art to dispense
A several sin to every sense,
But felt through all this fleshly dress
Bright shoots of everlastingness. 20

19 *fleshly dress:* body.

O, how I long to travel back,
And tread again that ancient track!
That I might once more reach that plain
Where first I left my glorious train;
From whence the enlightened spirit sees
That shady city of palm trees.
But ah! my soul with too much stay
Is drunk, and staggers in the way!
Some men a forward motion love,
But I by backward steps would move;   30
And when this dust falls to the urn,
In that state I came, return.

This boy was taken from his mates, and died
In childhood, ere he was full twelve years old.
Pre-eminent in beauty is the vale
Where he was born and bred: the churchyard
    hangs
Upon a slope above the village-school;   30
And through that churchyard when my way has
    led
On summer evenings, I believe that there
A long half-hour together I have stood
Mute—looking at the grave in which he lies!

William Wordsworth

THERE WAS A BOY

There was a Boy; ye know him well, ye cliffs
And islands of Winander!—many a time,
At evening, when the earliest stars began
To move along the edges of the hills,
Rising or setting, would he stand alone,
Beneath the trees, or by the glimmering lake;
And there, with fingers interwoven, both hands
Pressed closely palm to palm and to his mouth
Uplifted, he, as through an instrument,
Blew mimic hootings to the silent owls,   10
That they might answer him.—And they would
    shout
Across the watery vale, and shout again,
Responsive to his call,—with quivering peals,
And long halloos, and screams, and echoes loud
Redoubled and redoubled; concourse wild
Of jocund din! And, when there came a pause
Of silence such as baffled his best skill:
Then sometimes, in that silence, while he hung
Listening, a gentle shock of mild surprise
Has carried far into his heart the voice   20
Of mountain-torrents; or the visible scene
Would enter unawares into his mind
With all its solemn imagery, its rocks,
Its woods, and that uncertain heaven received
Into the bosom of the steady lake.

Robert Frost

BIRCHES

When I see birches bend to left and right
Across the lines of straighter darker trees,
I like to think some boy's been swinging them.
But swinging doesn't bend them down to stay
As ice storms do. Often you must have seen them
Loaded with ice a sunny winter morning
After a rain. They click upon themselves
As the breeze rises, and turn many-colored
As the stir cracks and crazes their enamel.
Soon the sun's warmth makes them shed crystal
    shells   10
Shattering and avalanching on the snowcrust—
Such heaps of broken glass to sweep away
You'd think the inner dome of heaven had
    fallen.
They are dragged to the withered bracken by the
    load,
And they seem not to break; though once they
    are bowed
So low for long, they never right themselves:
You may see their trunks arching in the woods
Years afterwards, trailing their leaves on the
    ground
Like girls on hands and knees that throw their
    hair

Before them over their heads to dry in the
    sun. 20
But I was going to say when Truth broke in
With all her matter of fact about the ice-storm,
I should prefer to have some boy bend them
As he went out and in to fetch the cows—
Some boy too far from town to learn baseball,
Whose only play was what he found himself,
Summer or winter, and could play alone.
One by one he subdued his father's trees
By riding them down over and over again
Until he took the stiffness out of them, 30
And not one but hung limp, not one was left
For him to conquer. He learned all there was
To learn about not launching out too soon
And so not carrying the tree away
Clear to the ground. He always kept his poise
To the top branches, climbing carefully
With the same pains you use to fill a cup
Up to the brim, and even above the brim.
Then he flung outward, feet first, with a
    swish
Kicking his way down through the air to the 40
    ground.
So was I once myself a swinger of birches.
And so I dream of going back to be.
It's when I'm weary of considerations,
And life is too much like a pathless wood
Where your face burns and tickles with the
    cobwebs
Broken across it, and one eye is weeping
From a twig's having lashed across it open,
I'd like to get away from earth a while
And then come back to it and begin over.
May no fate wilfully misunderstand me 50
And half grant what I wish and snatch me away
Not to return. Earth's the right place for love:
I don't know where it's likely to go better.
I'd like to go by climbing a birch tree,
And climb black branches up a snow-white
    trunk
Toward heaven, till the tree could bear no
    more,
But dipped its top and set me down again.
That would be good both going and coming
    back.
One could do worse than be a swinger of
    birches.

Robert Frost

"OUT, OUT—"

The buzz saw snarled and rattled in the yard
And made dust and dropped stove-lengths of
    wood,
Sweet-scented stuff when the breeze drew across
    it.
And from there those that lifted eyes could count
Five mountain ranges one behind the other
Under the sunset far into Vermont.
And the saw snarled and rattled, snarled and
    rattled,
As it ran light, or had to bear a load.
And nothing happened: day was all but done.
Call it a day, I wish they might have said 10
To please the boy by giving him the half hour
That a boy counts so much when saved from
    work.
His sister stood beside them in her apron
To tell them "Supper." At the word, the saw,
As if to prove saws knew what supper meant,
Leaped out at the boy's hand, or seemed to
    leap—
He must have given the hand. However it was,
Neither refused the meeting. But the hand!
The boy's first outcry was a rueful laugh,
As he swung toward them holding up the
    hand, 20
Half in appeal, but half as if to keep
The life from spilling. Then the boy saw all—
Since he was old enough to know, big boy
Doing a man's work, though a child at heart—
He saw all spoiled. "Don't let him cut my hand
    off—
The doctor, when he comes. Don't let him, sister!"
So. But the hand was gone already.
The doctor put him in the dark of ether.
He lay and puffed his lips out with his breath.
And then—the watcher at his pulse took
    fright. 30
No one believed. They listened at his heart.
Little—less—nothing!—and that ended it.
No more to build on there. And they, since they
Were not the one dead, turned to their affairs.

"OUT, OUT—": See *Macbeth* V, v.

Dylan Thomas

FERN HILL

Now as I was young and easy under the apple boughs
About the lilting house and happy as the grass was green,
    The night above the dingle starry,
Time let me hail and climb
      Golden in the heydays of his eyes,
And honored among wagons I was prince of the apple towns
And once below a time I lordly had the trees and leaves
        Trail with daisies and barley
    Down the rivers of the windfall light.

And as I was green and carefree, famous among the barns 10
About the happy yard and singing as the farm was home,
    In the sun that is young once only,
      Time let me play and be
    Golden in the mercy of his means,
And green and golden I was huntsman and herdsman, the calves
Sang to my horn, the foxes on the hills barked clear and cold,
      And the sabbath rang slowly
    In the pebbles of the holy streams.

All the sun long it was running, it was lovely, the hay-
Fields high as the house, the tunes from the chimneys, it was air 20
    And playing, lovely and watery
      And fire green as grass.
    And nightly under the simple stars
As I rode to sleep the owls were bearing the farm away,
All the moon long I heard, blessed among stables, the nightjars
    Flying with the ricks, and the horses
      Flashing into the dark.

And then to awake, and the farm, like a wanderer white
With the dew, come back, and cock on his shoulder: it was all
    Shining, it was Adam and maiden, 30
      The sky gathered again
    And the sun grew round that very day.
So it must have been after the birth of the simple light
In the first, spinning place, spellbound horses walking warm
    Out of the whinnying green stable
      On to the fields of praise.

And honored among foxes and pheasants by the gay house
Under the new-made clouds and happy as the heart was long,
     In the sun born over and over,
          I ran my heedless ways,
     My wishes raced through the house-high hay
And nothing I cared, at my sky-blue trades, that time allows
In all his tuneful turning so few and such morning songs
     Before the children green and golden
          Follow him out of grace.

40

Nothing I cared, in the lamb-white days, that time would take me
.Up to the swallow-thronged loft by the shadow of my hand,
     In the moon that is always rising,
          Nor that riding to sleep
     I should hear him fly with the high fields
And wake to the farm forever fled from the childless land.
Oh as I was young and easy in the mercy of his means,
     Time held me green and dying
          Though I sang in my chains like the sea.

50

Theodore Roethke

MY PAPA'S WALTZ

The whiskey on your breath
Could make a small boy dizzy;
But I hung on like death:
Such waltzing was not easy.

We romped until the pans
Slid from the kitchen shelf;
My mother's countenance
Could not unfrown itself.

The hand that held my wrist
Was battered on one knuckle;
At every step you missed
My right ear scraped a buckle.

10

You beat time on my head
With a palm caked hard by dirt,
Then waltzed me off to bed
Still clinging to your shirt.

Theodore Roethke

FRAU BAUMAN,
FRAU SCHMIDT,
AND FRAU SCHWARTZE

Gone the three ancient ladies
Who creaked on the greenhouse ladders,
Reaching up white strings
To wind, to wind
The sweet-pea tendrils, the smilax,

Nasturtiums, the climbing
Roses, to straighten
Carnations, red
Chrysanthemums; the stiff
Stems, jointed like corn,   10
They tied and tucked, —
These nurses of nobody else.
Quicker than birds, they dipped
Up and sifted the dirt;
They sprinkled and shook;
They stood astride pipes,
Their skirts billowing out wide into tents,
Their hands twinkling with wet;
Like witches they flew along rows
Keeping creation at ease;   20
With a tendril for needle
They sewed up the air with a stem;
They teased out the seed that the cold kept
   asleep. —

All the coils, loops, and whorls.
They trellised the sun; they plotted for more
   than themselves.

I remember how they picked me up, a spindly
   kid,
Pinching and poking my thin ribs
Till I lay in their laps, laughing,
Weak as a whiffet,
Now, when I'm alone and cold in my bed,   30
They still hover over me,
These ancient leathery crones,
With their bandannas stiffened with sweat,
And their thorn-bitten wrists,
And their snuff-laden breath blowing lightly over
   me in my first sleep.

29 *Whiffet:* insignificant dog or person.

Chapter 2

MAN
AND
WOMAN

The common names of emotions (*love, fear, hate*) are general labels for phenomena of unlimited variety. The precise quality of an emotion depends on the person, the object, and the circumstances: to hate ruthless politicians feels different from hating to pretend you like your least favorite cousin. General terms have their uses, certainly, but it is one of the functions of literature to lead us back to the individual, concrete feelings that underlie the abstractions. We understand, not love in general, but Romeo's love for Juliet or Desdemona's love for Othello. The concept of love, of course, can encompass many dimensions, as well as species, of attraction or devotion: love of God, of mankind, of country. Here we take it in a more restricted, though by no means narrow, sense in which it designates a relationship between one human being and another, and more specifically between a man and a woman. Love in this context may still be many things: an unselfish desire to serve, a common-sense give-and-take arrangement, a narcissistic projection of the self, a clutching dependence, an unconscious wish to dominate.

Probably no two literary works present identical conceptions of love. Bacon's prudential observations on marriage versus the single life and Byron's cynical comments about the alleged amorousness of womankind are attempts to find dependable generalizations about the relationship between the sexes. Ortega y Gasset is as cynical, in his own way, as Byron, but at the expense of men. "Marriages Were Made in Heaven" and "A Marriage in the 'Sixties" share a compassionate realism, yet they are worlds apart in their assumptions about what is to be expected in marriage.

In spite of all these differences, a single theme dominates the treatment of love in literature: the relationship between love and time. In many of Shakespeare's sonnets, in "To His Coy Mistress," in the ambiguous flashbacks of "The Woman," in the powerful fixations depicted in "The Persistence of Desire," and suggested ominously in "The Chaser," one or another facet of this eternal tension is marked out for contemplation and reflection. We see the fickleness of a lover's constancy; the integrity of love or its illusoriness; love's triumph over time or its succumbing to the corruption, betrayal, or deadening that the passage of time may bring about.

Of all human relationships, those involving sex and love have exercised the most compelling fascination for writers, from Homer's time to our own. No subject is more constantly and continuously celebrated in stories that are printed, filmed, or videotaped. These love stories, which human beings have always wanted to hear and will no doubt always want to hear again and again and again, differ enormously in quality: some are among the greatest literature, some the purest trash. But here is one of the values to be found in this chapter: by comparing the following works with one another, and with the love stories encountered elsewhere, the reader may come to see more clearly, to enjoy more fully, the subtlety, intensity, and formal beauty from which works of literary artistry derive their lasting interest.

John Collier

THE CHASER

Alan Austen, as nervous as a kitten, went up certain dark and creaky stairs in the neighborhood of Pell Street, and peered about for a long time on the dim landing before he found the name he wanted written obscurely on one of the doors.

He pushed open this door, as he had been told to do, and found himself in a tiny room, which contained no furniture but a plain kitchen table, a rocking-chair, and an ordinary chair. On one of the dirty buff-colored walls were a couple of shelves, containing in all perhaps a dozen bottles and jars.

An old man sat in the rocking-chair, reading a newspaper. Alan, without a word, handed him the card he had been given. "Sit down, Mr. Austen," said the old man very politely. "I am glad to make your acquaintance."

"Is it true," asked Alan, "that you have a certain mixture that has—er—quite extraordinary effects?"

"My dear sir," replied the old man, "my stock in trade is not very large—I don't deal in laxatives and teething mixtures—but such as it is, it is varied. I think nothing I

sell has effects which could be precisely described as ordinary."

"Well, the fact is—" began Alan.

"Here, for example," interrupted the old man, reaching for a bottle from the shelf. "Here is a liquid as colorless as water, almost tasteless, quite imperceptible in coffee, milk, wine, or any other beverage. It is also quite imperceptible to any known method of autopsy."

"Do you mean it is a poison?" cried Alan, very much horrified.

"Call it a glove-cleaner if you like," said the old man indifferently. "Maybe it will clean gloves. I have never tried. One might call it a life-cleaner. Lives need cleaning sometimes."

"I want nothing of that sort," said Alan.

"Probably it is just as well," said the old man. "Do you know the price of this? For one teaspoonful, which is sufficient, I ask five thousand dollars. Never less. Not a penny less."

"I hope all your mixtures are not so expensive," said Alan apprehensively.

"Oh dear, no," said the old man. "It would be no good charging that sort of price for a love potion, for example. Young people who need a love potion very seldom have five thousand dollars. Otherwise they would not need a love potion."

"I am glad to hear that," said Alan.

"I look at it like this," said the old man. "Please a customer with one article, and he will come back when he needs another. Even if it *is* more costly. He will save up for it, if necessary."

"So," said Alan, "you really do sell love potions?"

"If I did not sell love potions," said the old man, reaching for another bottle, "I should not have mentioned the other matter to you. It is only when one is in a position to oblige that one can afford to be so confidential."

"And these potions," said Alan. "They are not just—just—er——"

"Oh, no," said the old man. "Their effects

are permanent, and extend far beyond casual impulse. But they include it. Bountifully, insistently. Everlastingly."

"Dear me!" said Alan, attempting a look of scientific detachment. "How very interesting!"

"But consider the spiritual side," said the old man.

"I do, indeed," said Alan.

"For indifference," said the old man, "they substitute devotion. For scorn, adoration. Give one tiny measure of this to the young lady—its flavor is imperceptible in orange juice, soup, or cocktails—and however gay and giddy she is, she will change altogether. She will want nothing but solitude, and you."

"I can hardly believe it," said Alan. "She is so fond of parties."

"She will not like them any more," said the old man. "She will be afraid of the pretty girls you may meet."

"She will actually be jealous?" cried Alan in a rapture. "Of me?"

"Yes, she will want to be everything to you."

"She is, already. Only she doesn't care about it."

"She will, when she has taken this. She will care intensely. You will be her sole interest in life."

"Wonderful!" cried Alan.

"She will want to know all you do," said the old man. "All that has happened to you during the day. Every word of it. She will want to know what you are thinking about, why you smile suddenly, why you are looking sad."

"That is love!" cried Alan.

"Yes," said the old man. "How carefully she will look after you! She will never allow you to be tired, to sit in a draught, to neglect your food. If you are an hour late, she will be terrified. She will think you are killed, or that some siren has caught you."

"I can hardly imagine Diana like that!" cried Alan, overwhelmed with joy.

"You will not have to use your imagina-

tion," said the old man. "And, by the way, since there are always sirens, if by any chance you *should*, later on, slip a little, you need not worry. She will forgive you, in the end. She will be terribly hurt, of course, but she will forgive you—in the end."

"That will not happen," said Alan fervently.

"Of course not," said the old man. "But, if it did, you need not worry. She would never divorce you. Oh no! And, of course, she herself will never give you the least, the very least, grounds for—uneasiness."

"And how much," said Alan, "is this wonderful mixture?"

"It is not as dear," said the old man, "as the glove-cleaner, or life-cleaner, as I sometimes call it. No. That is five thousand dollars, never a penny less. One has to be older than you are, to indulge in that sort of thing. One has to save up for it."

"But the love potion?" said Alan.

"Oh, that," said the old man, opening the drawer in the kitchen table, and taking out a tiny, rather dirty-looking phial. "That is just a dollar."

"I can't tell you how grateful I am," said Alan, watching him fill it.

"I like to oblige," said the old man. "Then customers come back, later in life, when they are rather better off, and want more expensive things. Here you are. You will find it very effective."

"Thank you again," said Alan. "Goodbye."

"*Au revoir,*" said the old man.

Sir Francis Bacon

OF MARRIAGE AND SINGLE LIFE

He that hath wife and children hath given hostages to fortune; for they are impediments to great enterprises, either of virtue or mischief. Certainly the best works, and of greatest merit for the public, have proceeded from the unmarried or childless men, which both in affection and means have married and endowed the public. Yet it were great reason that those that have children should have greatest care of future times, unto which they know they must transmit their dearest pledges.

Some there are who, though they lead a single life, yet their thoughts do end with themselves, and account future times impertinences. Nay, there are some other that account wife and children but as bills of charges. Nay more, there are some foolish rich covetous men that take a pride in having no children, because they may be thought so much the richer. For perhaps they have heard some talk, "Such a one is a great rich man," and another except to it, "Yes, but he hath a great charge of children"; as if it were an abatement to his riches. But the most ordinary cause of a single life is liberty, especially in certain self-pleasing and humorous[1] minds, which are so sensible of every restraint, as they will go near to think their girdles and garters to be bonds and shackles.

Unmarried men are best friends, best masters, best servants, but not always best subjects, for they are light to run away, and almost all fugitives are of that condition. A single life doth well with churchmen, for charity will hardly water the ground where it must first fill a pool. It is indifferent for judges and magistrates, for if they be facile and corrupt, you shall have a servant five times worse than a wife. For soldiers, I find the generals commonly in their hortatives put men in mind of their wives and children; and I think the despising of marriage amongst the Turks maketh the vulgar soldier more base. Certainly wife and children are a kind of discipline of humanity; and single men, though they be many times more charitable, because their means are less exhaust, yet, on the other side, they are more cruel and hard-hearted (good to make

severe inquisitors), because their tenderness is not so oft called upon. Grave natures, led by custom and therefore constant, are commonly loving husbands, as was said of Ulysses, *Vetulam suam praetulit immortalitati*.[2]

Chaste women are often proud and froward, as presuming upon the merit of their chastity. It is one of the best bonds, both of chastity and obedience, in the wife if she think her husband wise, which she will never do if she find him jealous. Wives are young men's mistresses, companions for middle age, and old men's nurses, so as a man may have a quarrel[3] to marry when he will. But yet he[4] was reputed one of the wise men that made answer to the question when a man should marry. "A young man not yet, an elder man not at all."

It is often seen that bad husbands have very good wives; whether it be that it raiseth the price of their husbands' kindness when it comes, or that the wives take a pride in their patience. But this never fails, if the bad busbands were of their own choosing, against their friends'[5] consent; for then they will be sure to make good their own folly.

Harry Golden

MARRIAGES WERE MADE IN HEAVEN

The shadkhan was an important member of the first-generation society which I knew as a boy.

The "outside" people whom the young immigrant met immediately after settling

---

[1] Eccentric, self-willed.

[2] He preferred his aged wife to immortality— Plutarch, *Gryllus* I. Odysseus refused the nymph Calypso's offer to make him immortal if he would remain with her (*Odyssey* v. 209ff.).

[3] Reason, pretext.

[4] Diogenes Laertius tells the story about Thales of Miletus, 640?–546 B.C.

[5] Parents', relatives'.

himself with his relatives were first, the fellow who sold him a gold watch and chain "so you'll become a real American," and then the Tammany Hall worker who advised him about night study classes "so you can become a citizen and vote"; and, finally, the shadkhan—the marriage broker.

Usually the shadkhan entered into the preliminary negotiations with the parents of the boy and girl, and in cases of a "single" boy, an orphan, or whose parents were still in Europe, the shadkhan dealt with an aunt or other relatives. After these initial discussions the parents of the girl told her of the negotiations and a formal meeting was arranged. The immediate reaction of the girl was based on an old East Side shadkhan joke: At the age of eighteen she asks, "What does he look like?" At the age of twenty-five, she asks, "What does he do for a living?" And at the age of thirty, she asks, "Where is he?"

The shadkhan's biggest headache was the amateur competition. Everybody was a part-time shadkhan. The average housewife, with a million things to do for a family of a half-dozen children, always had a few irons in the fire with at least one shidduch (match) on tap for a niece, a nephew, or even a boarder.

But the professionals, too, started out on a part-time basis. This was not a business which offered an immediate return. The remuneration was based on a small fee in the early days of the negotiations, followed by a percentage of the dowry involved, payable on the evening of the wedding. The shadkhan could not depend upon this profession for a livelihood. Often it was a rabbi or a cantor who embarked on this career as a side line, as well as for its purely religious value: a mitzvah (a good deed added to the final reckoning). A part-time shadkhan I knew on my block operated a small cleaning-and-dyeing establishment. Eventually, his many successful matches gave him a good reputation and he branched out as a full-time shadkhan.

Eventually the shadkhan adopted certain symbols of his office: namely, a beard, a derby hat, and an umbrella. No one ever saw a shadkhan without an umbrella.

The umbrella was of tremendous importance to the immigrant people of the East Side. Folks bought an umbrella even before they bought a pair of eyeglasses, for the umbrella was the symbol of urban middle-class life.

The shadkhan had no sense of humor at all. In the milieu which practiced humor on a grand scale this fellow never cracked a smile. There were many jokes about the shadkhan and he was determined to do nothing that would add to the hilarity. "This is no laughing matter." No matter how two people are brought together, they will have the usual stormy courtship: quarrels, breaking off the engagement, making up, saying "good-bye forever," etc.

The great anxiety in a Jewish household was concerned with marrying off the daughter, and the anxiety increased a hundredfold for each additional daughter. And they had to be married off in proper sequence according to their age, the eldest first, and so on. The greatest fear of the family was that the eldest would be "left"—spinsterhood. The idea that a younger sister's marrying out of turn was bad luck for the older girl was based on fact rather than superstition. The word got around that the younger sister could no longer wait; this meant the family had abandoned hope for the older girl; therefore, there must be something wrong with her.

The whole operation required great tact. The first meeting of the couple was usually a Friday evening Sabbath dinner at the girl's home. Often the shadkhan came along, casual-like, just an old friend of the family bringing along a young stranger to a Sabbath meal. No one gave the slightest indication of what it was all about.

The younger children of school age were urged and bribed to be on their good behavior. But now for the problem. The younger sister who was PRETTY. The young man could very well come to see the older sister but fall in love with the younger one. The mother used tact. She began planning this the previous Wednesday; "Rachel, this Friday night go to spend the evening with your friend Naomi. I'll tell her mother when I see her in the market tomorrow." The younger sister had raised all kinds of hell for this very privilege many times, but now she is hesitant; she wants to know *why*. She knows why, of course, but before she is through, her mother will have to spell it out to her, every detail. The younger sister goes off to "hide" from her sister's fellow and she is very happy about the whole thing. She is very happy about it because she's a woman who has been told she is pretty.

At the inception of the shadkhan's activities, the mother went into the details of her daughter's qualifications. She can cook, sew, take care of children, and play the piano.

There were other virtues. "Mein Sarah is alle drei" (My Sarah is all three). This meant that the girl had completed a course in business school and was now—"ah stenographerinn, ah bookkeeperinn, und a typewriterka." These Yiddish words need no translation. It was a big thing on the East Side for the girls to become "all three," and it makes me feel a little sad when I think of the drive behind it; the saving, the scrimping, the intensity, and the anxiety. Of course, when a mother extolled her daughter with all these qualifications, it meant one thing; that the girl was not what you would call pretty. But the shadkhan listened politely—all the time waiting for takhlis, a wonderful word which means "goal," "purpose," "essence"—the dowry.

The dowry (nadan) was not a "gift." These are two separate words in Hebrew. Neither should this nadan, in cash or real estate, be confused with the centuries-old custom in Eastern lands of the purchase price in money or goods for a wife. The nadan may or may not have been brought into

Europe by the Jews, but it has long been part of the culture of the West. In fact, the nadan was a mark of *status*; and a girl in France, Ireland, Spain, and Italy would tease her friends if her parents had a larger dowry set aside for her. Often the dowry was part of the marriage contract, even when the bridegroom had not requested or expected it, or if he had independent means of his own. The situation added another English word to the Yiddish language. The word was "millionaire," and was used indiscriminately for any boy or man who made more than sixty dollars a week. "My Yetta is marrying a regular millionaire," said the mother to all her friends and neighbors. The use of this word became so widespread that it was modified eventually to "Jewish millionaire," which meant anyone worth $2,500 and up.

Basically the dowry was for the son-in-law so that he could continue to read or study the *Torah*—the Law—as free from financial care as possible. With the expansion of the commercial world, however, the purpose was extended to help the son-in-law get a start in some business. There is many a vast business enterprise in our country today which was started with a bride's dowry.

Since the negotiations involved many people—the two principals, the four parents, a few aunts, and the shadkhan—there were many areas of misunderstanding, perhaps even a bit of chicanery once in a while. A middle-aged widower calls on a widow. During the six or seven weeks of the courtship he has been her guest at the Friday evening Sabbath supper. On each of these Friday evenings, the widower sees the widow's little boy, a cute, curly-haired, eight-year-old child, and the widower grows very fond of the boy. Now could he suddenly break the spell of a pleasant evening and, out of a clear sky, ask, "Do you happen to have other children?" What kind of a stupid question is that? They are married and the day following, the widow's married sister brings over the other children, three little girls, probably. The widow smiles and says to her new husband: "Can you imagine such a thing, every Friday the three girls yell and holler that they want to visit their aunt, so what could I do?" The new-husband-widower listens to this tale as he watches the charming little boy joined by his three little sisters. If the guy has imagination and a sense of humor, he goes along and makes the best of it like a gentleman. But if he's a grubbe yung (ignoramus), he'll sue.

The philanthropists had set up a Jewish court on the East Side, still doing great work, which has saved the State of New York millions of dollars in court costs over a half century.

A groom may have misunderstood the terms of the dowry. The bride's parents may have promised to pay it in installments; the groom may have expected it all in one sum. There were all sorts of problems before the court. I examined the minutes of one such case tried in 1921. The wedding guests were all assembled and the bride looked lovely. The rabbi was there and so were the musicians and the caterers, but no groom. Finally a message came from the groom. It was addressed to the bride's father and later was read into the court records: "You'll not see me there tonight, you faker. You promised a dowry of two thousand dollars cash and I haven't received it." The poor man was staggered and had to make an embarrassing excuse to his two hundred guests. The proprietor of the hall demanded payment for his outlay for one hundred couples. The jeweler was there. He had sold the ring to the bridegroom on credit. He immediately changed his status from guest to jeweler and wanted to know where he stood in the matter. During the hearing before the Jewish court, the bride's father testified that he had never promised a dowry of two thousand dollars. "My daughter," he said, "is known as the belle of Washington Heights, and the bridgegroom is a window cleaner. Is it rea-

sonable that I, the father of the belle of Washington Heights, would offer a window cleaner a dowry of two thousand dollars? For two thousand dollars I could get a doctor, a lawyer, or a whatnot." The bride's father was suing the family of the groom for one thousand dollars' damages for the wedding arrangements. The court tried a reconciliation between the two young people and when that failed, it decided against the bride's father, stating that "dowry was ordained by rabbis, and each man *must* give part of his property to his marriageable daughter." The court also ordered the bride to return the ring to the jeweler, because the man was an innocent bystander. The court further publicly reprimanded the shadkhan as incompetent.

Most of the litigation before that court today involves business disputes or domestic relations complaints by litigants who want a quick decision or who cannot afford the legal expenses to see their matter through the State courts. There are not many dowry arguments today. The kids born in America have acquired great resourcefulness. They eased themselves into the American milieu with dances, proms, parties, socials, clubs, introductions, blind dates; and they bring home their own fellows.

José Ortega y Gasset

LANDSCAPE WITH A DEER IN THE BACKGROUND

Around 1793 there were many men in Europe; but of all, the consummate man was probably Captain Nelson.[6] And what of Napoleon? you may ask. Napoleon, rather than a man, was a superman or demigod.

6 Horatio Nelson, 1758–1805. He was made a rear admiral in 1797 and a viscount in 1801.

For the very reason that Nelson was so exclusively and enormously a man, he seems to have been many other things. A man who is a "measure of all things" is a crossroads of the Universe, and the starting point for roads leading everywhere. By extending his features, in one sense or another, one can achieve splendid and extraordinary images. Human fantasy is a dense atmosphere in which the phenomenon of the *fata morgana*[7] is always produced. Thus, for the neoclassic provincial, abundant in that period, who read the gazettes, Nelson was an Atlantic genius imposing order upon the seas. Seen in this way, from a distance, Nelson was Neptune. The provincial man read the gazette sitting before a fireplace upon which stood a bronze clock; the dial of the clock was encased in the round hollow of a metal wave, upon which a floating naked god, with a trident in his hand, was reclining. It was Nelson. But, seen from close up, he was something else. He was many other things: a small man with a hard expression, as tough as the shell of a mollusk, and with the smoldering spirit of an English Triton. He was a being who does not need poetry to live, but detests it and shakes it off like dust from the road by day or the whirring mosquitoes by night. (After living the best moments of his life in Naples—moments of amorous fire upon the already desert-like stretch of maturity—all that occurs to him to say about Italy is that it is an intolerable country of violinists, poets, and scoundrels.) His seafaring life is composed of violent gusts of wind which pass over him and each time take something away: first one limb, then another. Away with his arm! Away with his eye! And the curious thing is that each one of these amputations and losses emphasizes more strongly how much of one piece this man was. His courage became concentrated in the remaining limbs.

Before conquering Bonaparte's fleet in Abukir, he draws into the Bay of Naples one day with his big-bellied frigates. He goes to the English embassy, where he is received by the ambassador, Sir William Hamilton.

Humanity is a vast, expansive concept: Admiral Nelson and Ambassador Hamilton can be placed at its opposite extremes, and one does not hinder the other.

We would like to have known this gentleman, to have been one of his friends, and to have had a talk with him. For Hamilton was a man of the world, a great collector and a great skeptic. The skeptic is the man with the fullest, richest, and most complete life. Some foolish idea leads us to suppose that the skeptic does not believe in anything. Quite the contrary! The skeptic differs from the dogmatic in that the latter believes in only one thing and the former in many, in almost everything. And this multitude of beliefs, acting as mutual restraints, make the mind flexible and prolific. Hamilton was one of the first to collect "classical" objects, and it is he who began the excavations of Pompeii. His unequaled collection is now, I believe, in the British Museum.

Nelson is introduced to the ambassador's wife, and for the first time the Triton feels gnawed at by an indefinable power. Here we have the fable in motion, a fundamental fable which all writers and philosophers have striven to avoid; I, too, of course. The fable is this: Nelson and Hamilton, the two most opposite male types that can be imagined, have fallen in love with the same Lady Hamilton. Naturally all the other intermediary types have also succumbed to her magic.

The fable is complete if we answer this question: Who is Lady Hamilton?

Lady Hamilton is that lady with the white plume, now galloping past us upon a bay steed. She is the intimate, over-intimate friend of the Neapolitan Queen María Carolina, the sister of Marie Antoinette, who has produced eighteen children and still has

---

[7] Sea mirage.

enough reserved vigor for her attachment to this Englishwoman. Emma Hamilton is the most beautiful lady in the United Kingdom, an "official beauty," whom people point out to each other from afar as if she were a national monument. She sings with a pleasing voice and at parties she assumes "poses." With a few shawls and dressed in the Greek manner, she poses as Clytemnestra or Cassandra. She wrinkles her brow tragically or makes her divine face appear melancholy, reflecting light slant-wise from her eyes, as do the figures of Guido Reni. Her triumph is enormous: these "poses" are spoken about all over Europe. Let it not be forgotten: we are about to enter the age of Romanticism. The heart is going to the head. Emotion is accepted as a sort of alcohol; it is a new inebriating taste, and people are now, more than anything else, seeking inebriation. The woman is about to serve as a subject or pretext for the exaltation of the sentiments. The tenor of the epoch is proclaimed in its vocabulary: at every moment you hear "divine," "sublime," "ecstatic," "fatal." Tears and pearls are the fashion.

All this, when seen from afar, is appealing and attractive. The theater merges with life, and life puffs up and swells like a sail in the wind blowing from off-stage. I do not know; but I think that this theatricality of life—which explains the romantic success of the "poses" executed by Emma Hamilton—is more admirable than the opposite principle, in force one hundred years later, when the theater is preoccupied with imitating life.

Now this Emma, the friend of the Queen, the Ambassador's wife, and Lady Hamilton, who was she before? She was the mistress of Hamilton's nephew, Grenville,[8] who passed her on to his uncle. He had met her at the home of a healer who, by means of electric shocks, restored vitality to decrepit men. Standing before the healing sofa on

which the patient received the shocks, this marvelous girl, who had been humbly raised and born of a cook, posed as "Hygeia," or "Health." Now she is the wife of the Ambassador of England. It is not easy to rise from the depths to the heights.

"Beauty is not enough," the reader will say, "to explain such a glorious ascent. This woman must have had a great talent."

For me this is the decisive point of the fable, the one we all usually avoid. The plain truth is that Lady Hamilton had neither talent nor even a fine upbringing and scarcely any taste or good judgment. She is the perfect feather-brain. Living for her is putting on and taking off dresses, coming and going from one party to another party. Spending money. Never standing still. Dances, little gestures, inviting and being invited. She is the eternal worldly woman who, in one form or another, we have all known and with whom almost all of us have fallen in love at some time. That is why I say that the fable is fundamental, and not a mere anecdote.

The reader, faced with this, turns around and says: "She must have been an extraordinary beauty." Yes, so it seems; but this does not explain, either, why men like Nelson and Hamilton fell in love with her so completely. Extraordinary beauty acts as an obstacle to men of fine sensibilities feeling attracted by a woman. The excessive perfection of a face encourages us to objectify its possessor and to keep at a distance from her in order to admire her as an aesthetic object. The only ones who fall in love with "official beauties" are fools and drugstore clerks. They are public monuments, curiosities which one views momentarily and from a distance. In their presence one feels like a tourist and not a lover.

It is advisable, then, for us not to evade the question by way of the avenue of beauty. If she had not possessed some degree of beauty, these two very different heroes—Nelson and Hamilton—would not have

---

[8] Actually Charles Greville, younger son of the Earl of Warwick.

loved Emma; but what really attracted them was something else. I hope that the reader resists the plebeian and commonplace temptation to suppose that love in men of this rank springs from sexual appetite. But then we run into an enigma. . . .

Lady Hamilton, agile, sprightly, with an animated little head full of devious means, appears in the background of the landscape like a deer. This is the landscape which hangs in almost all the houses in England. Lady Hamilton does not have much more sense than a deer. Why do two men like Nelson and Hamilton fall in love with her?

The probable solution to the enigma is quite serious, and I do not know if I dare to promise it for the next number.

OLMEDO'S SOLUTION

I have met Olmedo. Who is Olmedo? To my taste, an admirable man. He is intelligent, yet he is not an intellectual. I do not know if others have had the same experience; but from what I have seen of life I have the disturbing conviction that, at least in our time, there are no intelligent men other than intellectuals. And since the majority of intellectuals are not intelligent either, it turns out that intelligence is an exceedingly rare event on this planet. This conviction, the pronouncement of which will probably, and justly so, irritate the reader, is also extremely painful and upsetting for the one who holds it. This is true for many reasons, but especially because, taking it as a point of departure, it becomes enormously probable that one's own self is not at all intelligent and, consequently, that all of one's ideas are false (including this one which judges intelligence to be a rare occurrence). But it is unavoidable. No one can jump outside of his shadow nor have convictions other than those he has. All that one can ask is that each one sing his song with fidelity. And my present song could bear the same title as Massillon's famous ser-

mon, *sur le petit nombre des élus.*[9] Nothing has instilled more melancholy in me than the discovery that the number of intelligent men is extremely small.

I am not seeking genius in the next man. By intelligence I mean only that the mind react to happenings with a certain sharpness and precision, that the radish not be perpetually seized by its leaves, that the gray not be confused with brown and, above all, that objects in front of one be seen with a little exactness and accuracy, without supplanting sight by mechanically repeated words. But, ordinarily, one has the impression of living amid somnambulists who advance through life buried in a hermetic sleep from which it is impossible to stir them in order to make them aware of their surroundings. Probably, humanity has almost always lived in this somnambulistic state in which ideas are not a wide-awake, conscious reaction to things, but a blind, automatic habit, drawn from a repertory of formulae which the atmosphere infuses into the individual.

It is undeniable that a large part of science and literature has also been produced in a somnambulistic trance; that is to say, by creatures who are not at all intelligent. Science, particularly in our day, at once specialized and systematized, permits the utilization of the fool, so that we constantly see undistinguished people performing admirable work. Science and literature, as such, do not imply perspicacity; but, undoubtedly, their cultivation is a stimulant which favors the awakening of the mind and preserves it in that luminous state of alertness which constitutes intelligence. The difference between the intelligent man and the fool is, after all, that the former lives on guard against his own foolishness, recognizes it as soon as it appears, and strives to elim-

9 "On the Small Number of the Elect"—those destined for Heaven. Jean Baptiste Massillon (1663–1742) was a French bishop.

inate it, whereas the fool enchantedly surrenders to his foolishness without reservations.

Due to the fact of a constant stimulus, there is a greater probability that an intellectual will be intelligent; but I consider it a grave misfortune if, in any period or nation, intelligence remains, practically speaking, reduced to the limits of the intellectual. Intelligence asserts itself above all not in art, nor in science, but in intuition of life. The intellectual, however, barely lives; he is usually a man with poverty of intuition; his acts in the world are few and he has very little knowledge of women, business, pleasure, and passion. He leads an abstract existence, and can rarely throw a morsel of authentic live meat to the sharp-pointed teeth of his intellect.

The intellectual's intelligence is of very little use to us: it almost always acts upon unreal subjects, matters of his own profession. It is, therefore, a delight for me to meet Olmedo, to see him arrive smiling, preceded by the double-edged foil of his glance—a penetrating and almost cynical glance, which seems to lift the skirts of everything to see what it is like underneath. Olmedo is a banker and a man of the great world. When he passes rapidly through my squalid intellectual existence, he seems to me to be a glittering meteorite arriving laden with golden sidereal dust. Wherever he comes from, I know that he is always coming from the universe, and that during his journey he has caught a side glance of what was happening in Venus and has given Neptune a pat on the backside. Olmedo knows a great deal about books; he knows as much as the intellectual; but he knows it, not as an intellectual, but as a man of the world. He has never permitted the axis of his being to remain fixed and thereby limited to any profession, but he lets it wander in the drift of his uni-personal destiny. In other periods—for example, in the eighteenth century—there must have been many men like this: noblemen, financiers, property-holders, magistrates, who were, nevertheless, intelligent and who took pleasure in distilling clear, individual ideas out of their vital experiences. (The present situation in Europe—its incapacity to resolve gracefully the problems before it—can only be explained if one supposes that today men of this class are lacking. Thus as there are periods, *verbi gratia* [for instance], the end of Roman history, in which bravery becomes so rare that finally no one is brave other than military men, so there are other periods in which intelligence becomes restricted to intellectuals and hence a profession.)

A great deal is said about Olmedo in a yet unpublished (perhaps never to be published) history in which certain aspects of present-day life in Madrid are described with disturbing accuracy.

"I just saw your article on Lady Hamilton," Olmedo said to me. "You did very well to stress the essential paradigm in the situation; but now, out with the solution to the problem!"

"The fact is, my friend Olmedo, that I don't have the solution."

"Are you saying this seriously?"

"Completely seriously!"

"Then you are the bourgeois gentleman of psychology."

"Why?"

"Because you resolve problems without knowing it."

"How's that?"

"In stating the problem you actually give the solution. After all, it almost always happens that way. Our enigmas and questions are usually disguised answers with the false curlicues of question marks. That is what is happening now. Nelson and Hamilton, two men of opposite but first-class temperaments, fall in love with a woman who, by her graceful charm and her lack of sense, turns out to be more or less a deer. Here is the problem, you say."

"In fact. . . ."

"However, I do not see any problem here; rather, a fact as clear and perfect as a mathematical equation. You are the one who adds the problem because you approach so clear a fact with a preconceived idea, which is this: worthwhile men do not fall in love with deer."

"It seems natural that a man with a complex, disciplined mind could not feel attracted by a flighty, fickleminded creature who is, as one of Baroja's characters says, 'without substance'!"

"Yes, yes; it seems natural; but what is natural is not what appears so to us, but what appears so to Nature, who is much more natural than all our mental symmetries and has much more sense. After all, what reason is there for an intelligent man to fall in love with an intelligent woman? If one is trying to establish a business, a political party, or a scientific school, it is understandable that a clear mind will try to link itself to other clear minds; but the need for love—even leaving aside its sexual dimension—has nothing to do with these things; it is precisely the opposite of all rational preoccupations. Far from being an enigma, the situation you present is the key to amorous experience. Men fall in love with deer, with what there is of the deer in a woman. I would not say this in front of the ladies, because they would feign great anger, although deep down nothing could flatter them more."

"Then, for you, a woman's talent, her capacity for sacrifice, her nobility, are unimportant qualities . . . ?"

"No, no; they are very important, they are wonderful, most admirable—we look for them and exalt them in the mother, the wife, the sister, the daughter. When it's a question, however, strictly speaking, of falling in love, one falls in love with the hidden deer which lies in a woman."

"What the deuce are you saying?"

"The more of a man one is, the more is he filled to the brim with rationality. Everything he does and achieves he does and achieves for a reason, especially for a practical reason. A woman's love, that divine surrender of her ultra-inner being which the impassioned woman makes, is perhaps the only thing which is not achieved by reasoning. The core of the feminine mind, no matter how intelligent the woman may be, is occupied by an irrational power. If the male is the rational being, the female is the irrational being. And that is the supreme delight which we find in her! The animal is also irrational, but it is not a person; it is incapable of self-awareness and of responding to us, of being aware of us. There is no room for relating or being intimate with it. The woman offers the man the magic opportunity of relating with another being *without reasoning*, of influencing, dominating, surrendering to another, without any reason entering into it. Believe me: if birds had the minimum personality necessary for being able to respond to us, we would all fall in love with birds and not with women. And, vice versa, if the normal male does not fall in love with another male, it is because he sees that the other man's mind is made up completely of rationality, logic, mathematics, poetry, business, and economy. What, from a masculine point of view, we call absurd and a woman's whim is precisely what attracts us. The world is admirably made by an excellent supervisor, and all of its parts are assembled and adjusted like a charm!"

"You are stupefying, Olmedo, my friend!"

"The idea, then, that the worthwhile man has to fall in love with a worthwhile woman, in the rational sense, is pure geometry. The intelligent man feels a slight revulsion for the very talented woman, unless her over-rationality is compensated for by over-irrationality. The over-rational in a woman smacks of masculinity and, rather than love, he feels friendship and admiration for her. It is just as false to assume that the eminent man attracts the 'very clever' woman as it is to embrace the other idea that women propagate without involvement and, therefore, above all, seek beauty in a man. The ugly, but intelligent, man knows very well that, finally, he must cure women of the boredom contracted in their love affairs with handsome men. One after another, he sees them forced to rebound, infinitely fed up with their sally through the landscape of masculine beauty."

"Olmedo, my friend, if you were a writer and wrote all this that you're telling me, they'd hang you from a lamppost. . . ."

"That is why I don't write. Why write? It is impossible to instil in others what is obvious to oneself. It is very rare for someone to attempt sympathetically to understand us exactly. But, after all, what I am saying was already said in substance many years ago, by our friend *Fede*. [Olmedo calls Friedrich Nietzsche *Fede*.] Where he enumerates the characteristic traits of the superior man, whom he calls the 'distinguished man,' we find this:

Complacency is in women as in beings of a lesser, perhaps, but finer and lighter species. What a delight to encounter creatures who have their heads always filled with dancing and whims and clothes! They are the charm of all overtense and serious masculine souls, whose life is filled with enormous responsibilities."

Alphonse Daudet

THE GIRL IN ARLES

The road leading down from my mill to the village passes near a farmhouse at the other end of a big courtyard planted with hackberry trees. It is a typical Provençal farmer's house, with its red tiles, great brown irregular front, and, at the very top, the weathervane, the pulley for hoisting the hay, and some brown tufts of hay sticking out of the loft.

Why had this house arrested my attention? Why did its shut gate make my heart ache? Though I could not have explained why, the place gave me a chill. It was too quiet. . . .When you passed by, the dogs did not bark and the guinea-fowl ran away without a sound. On the inside not a word was spoken. No sound at all, not even the tinkle of a mule's bell. Had there not been white curtains at the windows and smoke rising above the roof, you would have thought the place deserted.

Yesterday, just at noon, I was returning from the village, and to get out of the sunlight I walked beside the wall of the farm in the shade of the hackberry trees. On the road in front of the house some farm hands were silently finishing the loading of a haywagon. The gate had been left open. I glanced in as I passed and saw, at the other end of the courtyard, with his elbows on a big stone table and his head in his hands, a tall, white-haired old man, wearing a vest that was too short and a pair of tattered breeches. I stopped. One of the men said to me in a low voice, "Shh. It's the master. He's been that way ever since his son's tragedy."

At this moment a woman and a little boy, dressed in black and carrying huge gilt prayerbooks, passed by us and went into the farmhouse.

". . . the mistress and the younger son coming home from mass," the man added. "They go every day, ever since the boy killed himself. Oh, sir, what an affliction! The father is still wearing his funeral clothes; we can't get him to take them off. . . . Get up, horse!"

The wagon began to move away. Wishing to hear more, I asked the driver if I might get up beside him, and there, atop the load of hay, I learned the whole heart-breaking story. . . .

His name was Jan. He was a fine peasant lad, twenty years old, discreet as a girl, steady and of an open countenance. As he was very good-looking, women would stare at him; but he had no thought for any of them but one—a little girl in Arles, dressed always in velvet and lace, whom he had once met in the stadium there. At first nobody at the farm approved of this love affair. The girl was considered a flirt, and her family were not country people. But Jan wanted his Arlésienne, no matter what. He would say, "I'll die if they don't let me have her."

They had to give in. It was decided that the wedding should take place after the harvest.

One Sunday evening, in the courtyard of the farmhouse, the family were finishing dinner. It was almost a wedding feast. Jan's fiancée was not present but they had drunk her health many times. . . . A man came to the gate and in a shaky voice asked to speak to Master Estève, to him only. Estève got up and went out to the road.

"Master," said the man, "you are about to marry your boy to a deceiver, who for two years has been my mistress. I will prove what I say: here are her letters! . . . Her parents know all about it and had promised her to me; but since your son has been courting her, neither they nor that fine girl want any more of me. . . . It would seem to me, though, that after that she couldn't be anyone else's wife."

"Very well," said Master Estève after looking at the letters. "Come in and drink a glass of muscatel."

The man answered: "No, thanks! I am too unhappy to drink." And he went away.

The father came back in, his face expressionless, and resumed his place at the table. The feast ended cheerfully.

That evening Master Estève and his son went out together into the fields. They stayed out a long while; when they came back, the mother was waiting up for them.

"Wife," said the farmer, taking her son to her, "give him a kiss. He is unhappy. . . ."

Jan spoke no more of the girl in Arles. He still loved her, however, all the more that he had been made to see her in someone else's arms. Only he was too proud to say anything; that is what killed him, poor fellow. Sometimes he would spend whole days alone in a corner, without moving. Other days he would rush out into the fields and by himself do the work of ten laborers. When evening came, he would set out toward Arles and walk straight ahead till he saw the slender spires of the town rising in the sunset. Then he would come back. He never went any farther.

Seeing him like this, always sad and lonely, the people at the farm did not know what to do. They were afraid something frightful would happen. At the table one day his mother, looking at him with her eyes full of tears, said to him:

"All right. Listen, Jan, if you want her in spite of everything, we'll let you have her. . . ."

His father, red-faced with shame, lowered his head. Jan made a gesture that meant "No," and went out.

From that day on he changed his manner, pretending to be gay all the time, so as to reassure his parents. Once more he was to be seen at dances, in the tavern, and at the fair. On election day at Fonvieille, he was the one who led the dancing of the *farandole*.

His father said, "He is cured." His mother, though, was still worried, and kept an eye on her child more carefully than ever. Jan slept with his younger brother, very near the silkworm nursery; the poor old woman made a bed for herself near their room—she said that the silkworms might need her during the night.

The feast of Eloi, patron saint of farmers, came around. There was a great celebration at the farm: *château neuf* for everybody, and the mulled wine flowed like water. Fireworks of all sorts, the hackberry trees full of colored lanterns . . . hurrah for Saint Eloi! They almost farandoled themselves to death. The young brother burned a hole in his new blouse. Even Jan seemed to be happy; he tried to make his mother dance, and the poor woman cried for joy.

At midnight everybody went to bed. They needed sleep. Jan did not go to sleep, though. His brother said afterwards that he sobbed all night. Oh, he had it bad, let me tell you.

At dawn the next day his mother heard someone running across his room. She seemed to have a presentiment: "Jan, is that you?"

Jan did not reply, he was already on the ladder.

Instantly his mother got out of bed: "Jan, where are you going?"

He climbed up to the hayloft, she climbing after him.

"Son, in the name of heaven!"

He shut the door and bolted it.

"Jan, my little Jan, answer me. What are you going to do?"

She groped for the latch with her old, shaking hands. . . . A window opening, the thud of a body on the flagstones of the courtyard, and that was all.

The poor fellow had said to himself, "I love her too much; I am going away. . . ." Ah, wretched souls that we are! It is a pretty hard thing that contempt cannot extinguish love.

That morning the village people were asking each other who could be screaming that way, down at the Estève farm.

In front of the stone table in the courtyard, covered with dew and blood, the mother, quite naked, was wailing with her dead child in her arms.

Doris Lessing

THE WOMAN

Two elderly gentlemen emerged on to the hotel terrace at the same moment. They stopped, and checked movements which suggested they wished to retreat. Their first involuntary glances had been startled, even troubled. Now they allowed their eyes to exchange a long formal glare of hate, before turning deliberately away from each other.

They surveyed the terrace. A problem! Only one of the tables still remained in sunlight. They stiffly marched towards it, pulled out chairs, seated themselves. At once they opened newspapers and lifted them up like screens.

A pretty waitress came sauntering across to take the orders. The two newspapers remained stationary. Around the edge of one Herr Scholtz ordered warmed wine; from the shelter of the other Captain Forster from England demanded tea—with milk.

When she returned with these fluids, neatly disposed on similar metal trays, both walls of print slightly lowered themselves. Captain Forster, with an aggressive flicker of uneasy blue eyes towards his opponent, suggested that it was a fine evening. Herr Scholtz remarked with warm freemasonry that it was a shame such a pretty girl should not be free to enjoy herself on such an evening. Herr Scholtz appeared to consider that he had triumphed, for his look towards the Englishman was boastful. To both remarks, however, Rosa responded with an amiable but equally perfunctory smile. She strolled away to the balustrade where she leaned indolently, her back to them.

Stirring sugar into tea, sipping wine, was difficult with those stiff papers in the way. First Herr Scholtz, then the Captain, folded his and placed it on the table. Avoiding each other's eyes, they looked away towards the mountains, which however were partly blocked by Rosa.

She wore a white blouse, low on the shoulders; a black skirt, with a tiny white apron; smart red shoes. It was at her shoulders that the gentlemen gazed. They coughed, tapped on the table with their fingers, narrowed their eyes in sentimental appreciation at the mountains, looked at Rosa again. From time to time their eyes almost met but quickly slid away. Since they could not fight, civilization demanded they should speak. Yes, conversation appeared imminent.

A week earlier they had arrived on the same morning, and were given rooms at either end of a long corridor. The season was nearly over, the hotel half empty. Rosa therefore had plenty of time to devote to Herr Scholtz, who demanded it: he wanted bigger towels, different pillows, a glass of water. But soon the bell pealed from the other side of the corridor, and she excused herself and hastened over to Captain Forster, who was also dissatisfied with the existing arrangements for his comfort. Before she had finished with him, Herr Scholtz' bell rang again. Between the two of them Rosa was kept busy until the midday meal, and not once did she suggest by her manner that she had any other desire in this world than to readjust Captain Forster's reading light or bring Herr Scholtz cigarettes and newspapers.

That afternoon Captain Forster happened to open his door, and found he had a clear view into the room opposite, where Rosa stood at the window smiling in what seemed to him charming surrender at Herr Scholtz, who was reaching out a hand towards her elbow. The hand dropped, Herr Scholtz scowled, walked across, indignantly closed his door as if it were the Captain's fault it had been left open. . . . Almost at once the Captain's painful jealousy was eased, for Rosa emerged from that door smiling with perfect indifference, and wished him good day.

That night, very late, quick footsteps sounded on the floor of the corridor, the two doors gently opened at the same moment, and Rosa, midway between them, smiled placidly at first Herr Scholtz, then the Captain, who gave each other contemptuous looks after she had passed. They both slammed their doors.

Next day Herr Scholtz asked her if she would care to come with him up the funicular on her afternoon off, but unfortunately she was engaged. The day after Captain Forster made the same suggestion.

Finally, there was a repetition of that earlier incident. Rosa was passing along the corridor late at night on her way to her own bed, when those two doors cautiously opened and the two urgent faces appeared. This time she stopped, smiled politely, wished them a very good night. Then she yawned. It was a slight gesture, but perfectly timed. Both gentlemen solaced themselves with the thought that it must have been earned by his rival; for Herr Scholtz considered the Captain ridiculously gauche, while the Captain thought Herr Scholtz' attitude towards Rosa disgustingly self-assured and complacent. They were therefore able to retire to their beds with philosophy.

Since then Herr Scholtz had been observed in conversation with a well-preserved widow of fifty who unfortunately was obliged to retire to her own room every evening at nine o'clock for reasons of health and was therefore unable to go dancing with him, as he longed to do. Captain Forster took his tea every afternoon in a café where there was a charming waitress who might have been Rosa's sister.

The two gentlemen looked through each other in the dining-room, and crossed over the street if one saw the other approaching. There was a look about them which suggested that they might be thinking Switzerland—at any rate so late in the season—was not all that it had been.

Gallant, however, they both continued to be; and might continually be observed observing the social scene of flirtations and failures and successes with the calm authority of those well-qualified by long familiarity with it to assess and make judgments. Men of weight, they were; men of substance; men who expected deference.

And yet . . . here they were seated on opposite sides of that table in the last sunlight, the mountains rising about them all mottled white and brown and green with melting spring, the warm sun folding delicious but uncertain arms around them— and surely they were entitled to feel aggrieved? Captain Forster, a lean, tall, military man, carefully suntanned, spruced, brushed—was handsome still, no doubt of it. And Herr Scholtz, large, rotund, genial, with infinite resources of experience, was certainly worth more than the tea-time confidences of a widow of fifty?

Unjust to be sixty on such a spring evening; particularly hard with Rosa not ten paces away, shrugging her shoulders in a low embroidered blouse.

And almost as if she were taking a pleasure in the cruelty, she suddenly stopped humming, and leaned forward over the balustrade. With what animation did she wave and call down the street, while a very handsome young man below waved and called back. Rosa watched him stride away, and then she sighed and turned, smiling dreamily.

There sat Herr Scholtz and Captain Forster gazing at her with hungry resentful appreciation.

Rosa narrowed her blue eyes with anger, and her mouth went thin and cold, in disastrous contrast with her tenderness of a moment before. She shot bitter looks from one gentleman to the other, and then she yawned again. This time it was a large, contemptuous prolonged yawn, and she tapped the back of her hand against her mouth for emphasis, and let out her breath in a long descending note which however was cut off short as if to say that she really had no time to waste even on this small demonstration. She then swung past them in a crackle of starched print, her heels tapping. She went inside.

The terrace was empty. Gay painted tables, striped chairs, flowery sun-umbrellas —all were in cold shadow, save for the small corner where the gentlemen sat. At the same moment, from the same impulse, they rose and pushed the table forward into the last well of golden sunlight. And now they looked at each other straight and frankly laughed.

"Will you have a drink?" enquired Herr Scholtz in English, and his jolly smile was tightened by a consciously regretful stoicism. After a moment's uncertainty, during which Captain Forster appeared to be thinking that the stoicism was too early an admission of defeat, he said, "Yes, yes. Thanks, I will."

Herr Scholtz raised his voice sharply, and Rosa appeared from indoors, ready to be partly defensive. But now Herr Scholtz was no longer a suppliant. Master to servant, a man who habitually employed labor, he ordered wine without looking at her once. And Captain Forster was the picture of a silky gentleman.

When she reappeared with the wine they were so deep in good fellowship they might have been saying aloud how foolish it was to allow the sound companionship of men to be spoiled, even for a week, on account of the silly charm of women. They were roaring with laughter at some joke. Or rather, Herr Scholtz was roaring, a good stomach laugh from depths of lusty enjoyment. Captain Forster's laugh was slightly nervous, emitted from the back of his throat, and suggested that Herr Scholtz' warm Bavarian geniality was all very well, but that there were always reservations in any relationship.

It soon transpired that during the war— the First War, be it understood—they had been enemies on the same sector of the front at the same time. Herr Scholtz had been wounded in his arm. He bared it now, holding it forward under the Captain's nose to show the long white scar. Who knew but that it was the Captain who had dealt that blow—indirectly, of course—thirty-five years before? Nor was this all. During the Second War Captain Forster had very nearly been sent to North Africa, where he would certainly have had the pleasure of fighting Herr, then Oberst-leutnant [Lieutenant Colonel], Scholtz. As it happened, the fortunes of war had sent him to India instead. While these happy coincidences were being established, it was with the greatest amity on both sides, and if the Captain's laugh tended to follow Herr Scholtz' just a moment late, it could easily be accounted for by those unavoidable differences of temperament. Before half an hour was out, Rosa was despatched for a second flask of the deep crimson wine.

When she returned with it, she placed the glasses so, the flasks so, and was about to turn away when she glanced at the Captain and was arrested. The look on his face certainly invited comment. Herr Scholtz was just remarking, with that familiar smiling geniality, how much he regretted that the "accidents of history"—a phrase which caused the Captain's face very slightly to tighten—had made it necessary for them to be enemies in the past. In the future, he hoped, they would fight side by side, comrades in arms against the only possible foe for either. . . . But now Herr Scholtz stopped, glanced swiftly at the Captain, and after the briefest possible pause, and without a change of tone, went on to say that as for himself he was a man of peace, a man of creation: he caused innumerable tubes of toothpaste to reach the bathrooms of his country, and he demanded nothing more of life than to be allowed to continue to do so. Besides, had he not dropped his war-title, the Oberst-leutnant, in proof of his fundamentally civilian character?

Here, as Rosa still remained before them, contemplating them with a look which can only be described as ambiguous, Herr Scholtz blandly enquired what she wanted. But Rosa wanted nothing. Having enquired if that was all she could do for the gentlemen, she passed to the end of the terrace and leant there, looking down into the street where the handsome young man might pass.

Now there was a pause. The eyes of both men were drawn painfully towards her. As painful was the effort to withdraw them. Then, as if reminded that any personal differences were far more dangerous than the national ones, they plunged determinedly into gallant reminiscences. How pleasant, said that hearty masculine laughter—how pleasant to sit here in snug happy little Switzerland, comfortable in easy friendship, and after such fighting, such obviously meaningless hostilities! Citizens of the world they were, no less, human beings enjoying civilized friendship on equal terms. And each time Herr Scholtz or the Captain succumbed to that fatal attraction and glanced towards the end of the terrace, he as quickly withdrew his eyes and as it were set his teeth to offer another gauge of friendship across the table.

But fate did not intend this harmony to continue.

Cruelly, the knife was turned again. The young man appeared at the bottom of the street, and waved smiling towards Rosa. Rosa leaned forward, arms on the balustrade, the picture of bashful coquetry, rocking one heel up and down behind her, and shaking her hair forward to conceal the frankness of her response.

There she stood, even after he had gone, humming lightly to herself, looking after him. The crisp white napkin over her arm shone in the sunlight, her bright white apron shone, her mass of rough fair curls glowed. She stood there in the last sunlight, and looked away into her own thoughts, and softly sang as if she were quite alone.

Certainly she had completely forgotten the existence of Herr Scholtz and Captain Forster.

The Captain and the ex-Oberst-leutnant

had apparently come to the end of their shareable memories. One cleared his throat; the other, Herr Scholtz, tapped his signet ring irritatingly on the table.

The Captain shivered. "It's getting cold," he said, for now they were in the blue evening shadow. He made a movement, as if ready to rise.

"Yes," said Herr Scholtz. But he did not move. For a while he tapped his ring on the table, and the Captain set his teeth against the noise. Herr Scholtz was smiling. It was a smile which announced a new trend in the drama. Obviously. And obviously the Captain disapproved of it in advance. A blatant fellow, he was thinking, altogether too noisy and vulgar. He glanced impatiently towards the inside room, which would be warm and quiet.

Herr Scholtz remarked: "I always enjoy coming to this place. I always come here."

"Indeed?" asked the Captain, taking his cue in spite of himself. He wondered why Herr Scholtz was suddenly speaking German. Herr Scholtz spoke an excellent English, learned while he was interned in England during the latter part of the Second World War. Captain Forster had already complimented him on it. His German was not nearly so fluent, no.

But Herr Scholtz, for reasons of his own, was speaking his own language, and rather too loudly, one might have thought. Captain Forster looked at him, wondering, and was attentive.

"It is particularly pleasant for me to come to this resort," remarked Herr Scholtz in that loud voice, as if to an inner listener who was rather deaf, "because of the happy memories I have of it."

"Really?" enquired Captain Forster, listening with nervous attention. Herr Scholtz, however, was speaking very slowly, as if out of consideration for him.

"Yes," said Herr Scholtz, "of course during the war it was out of bounds for both of us, but now. . . ."

The Captain suddenly interrupted: "Ac-tually I'm very fond of it myself. I come here every year it is possible."

Herr Scholtz inclined his head, admitting that Captain Forster's equal right to it was incontestable, and continued: "I associate with it the most charming of my memories —perhaps you would care to. . . ."

"But certainly," agreed Captain Forster hastily. He glanced involuntarily towards Rosa—Herr Scholtz was speaking with his eyes on Rosa's back. Rosa was no longer humming. Captain Forster took in the situation and immediaely colored. He glanced protestingly towards Herr Scholtz. But it was too late.

"I was eighteen," said Herr Scholtz very loudly. "Eighteen." He paused, and for a moment it was possible to resurrect, in the light of his rueful reminiscent smile, the delightful, ingenuous bouncing youth he had certainly been at eighteen. "My parents allowed me, for the first time, to go alone for a holiday. It was against my mother's wishes, but my father on the other hand. . . ."

Here Captain Forster necessarily smiled, in acknowledgement of that international phenomenon, the sweet jealousy of mothers.

"And here I was, for a ten days' holiday, all by myself—imagine it!"

Captain Forster obligingly imagined it, but almost at once interrupted: "Odd, but I had the same experience. Only I was twenty-five."

Herr Scholtz exclaimed: "Twenty-five!" He cut himself short, covered his surprise, and shrugged as if to say: Well, one must make allowances. He at once continued to Rosa's listening back. "I was in this very hotel. Winter. A winter holiday. There was a woman. . . ." He paused, smiling, "How can I describe her?"

But the Captain, it seemed, was not pre-pared to assist. He was frowning uncom-fortably towards Rosa. His expression said quite clearly: "Really, *must* you?"

Herr Scholtz appeared not to notice it. "I was even in those days not backward—you understand?" The Captain made a movement of his shoulders which suggested that to be forward at eighteen was not a matter for congratulation, whereas at twenty-five. . . .

"She was beautiful, beautiful," continued Herr Scholtz with enthusiasm. "And she was obviously rich, a woman of the world, and her clothes. . . ."

"Quite," said the Captain.

"She was alone. She told me she was here for her health. Her husband unfortunately could not get away, for reasons of business. And I too was alone."

"Quite," said the Captain.

"Even at that age I was not too surprised at the turn of events. A woman of thirty . . . a husband so much older than herself . . . and she was beautiful . . . and intelligent. . . . Ah, but she was magnificent!" He almost shouted this, and drained his glass reminiscently towards Rosa's back. "Ah . . ." he breathed gustily. "And now I must tell you. All that was good enough, but now there is even better. Listen. A week passed. And what a week! I loved her as I never loved anyone. . . ."

"Quite," said the Captain fidgeting.

But Herr Scholtz swept on. "And then one morning I wake, and I am alone." Herr Scholtz shrugged and groaned.

The Captain observed that Herr Scholtz was being carried away by the spirit of his own enjoyment. This tale was by now only half for the benefit of Rosa. That rich dramatic groan—Herr Scholtz might as well be in the theatre, thought the Captain uncomfortably.

"But there was a letter, and when I read it. . . ."

"A letter?" interrupted the Captain suddenly.

"Yes, a letter. She thanked me so that the tears came into my eyes. I wept."

One could have sworn that the sentimental German eyes swam with tears, and Captain Forster looked away. With eyes averted he asked nervously: "What was in the letter?"

"She said how she hated her husband. She had married him against her will—to please her parents. In those days, this thing happened. And she had sworn a vow to herself never to have his child. But she wanted a child. . . ."

"*What?*" exclaimed the Captain. He was leaning forward over the table now, intent on every syllable.

This emotion seemed unwelcome to Herr Scholtz, who said blandly: "Yes, that was how it was. That was my good fortune, my friend."

"*When* was that?" enquired the Captain hungrily.

"I beg your pardon?"

"When was it? What year?"

"What year? Does it matter? She told me she had arranged this little holiday on grounds of her bad health, so that she might come by herself to find the man she wanted as the father of her child. She had chosen me. I was her choice. And now she thanked me and was returning to her husband." Herr Scholtz stopped in triumph, and looked at Rosa. Rosa did not move. She could not possibly have failed to hear every word. Then he looked at the Captain. But the Captain's face was scarlet, and very agitated.

"What was her name?" barked the Captain.

"Her name?" Herr Scholtz paused. "Well, she would clearly have used a false name?" he enquired. As the Captain did not respond, he said firmly: "That is surely obvious, my friend. And I did not know her address." Herr Scholtz took a slow sip of his wine, then another. He regarded the Captain for a moment thoughtfully, as if wondering whether he could be trusted to behave according to the rules, and then continued: "I ran to the hotel manager—no, there was no information. The lady had left unexpectedly, early that morning. No address. I was frantic. You can imagine. I wanted to rush after her, find her, kill her husband, marry her!" Herr Scholtz laughed in amused, regretful indulgence at the follies of youth.

"You *must* remember the year," urged the Captain.

"But my friend . . ." began Herr Scholtz after a pause, very annoyed. "What can it matter, after all?"

Captain Forster glanced stiffly at Rosa, and spoke in English, "As it happened, the same thing happened to me."

"Here?" enquired Herr Scholtz politely.

"Here."

"In this valley?"

"In this hotel."

"Well," shrugged Herr Scholtz, raising his voice even more, "Well women—women you know. At eighteen of course—and perhaps even at twenty-five—" Here he nodded indulgently towards his opponent—"Even at twenty-five perhaps one takes such things as miracles that happen only to oneself. But at our age. . . ?"

He paused, as if hoping against hope that the Captain might recover his composure.

But the Captain was speechless.

"I tell you, my friend," continued Herr Scholtz, good-humoredly relishing the tale, "I tell you I was crazy, I thought I would go mad, I wanted to shoot myself, I rushed around the streets of every city I happened to be in, looking into every face, I looked at photographs in the papers, actresses, society women, I used to follow a woman I had glimpsed in the street thinking that perhaps this was she at last. But no," said Herr Scholtz dramatically, bringing down his hand on the table, so that his ring clicked again, "No, never, never was I successful!"

"What did she look like?" asked the Captain agitatedly in English, his anxious eyes searching the by now very irritated eyes of Herr Scholtz.

Herr Scholtz moved his chair back slightly, looked towards Rosa, and said loudly in German: "Well, she was beautiful, as I have told you." He paused, for thought. "And she was an aristocrat."

"Yes, yes," said the Captain impatiently.

"She was tall, very slim, with a beautiful body—beautiful! She had that black hair, you know, black, black! And black eyes, and beautiful teeth." He added loudly and spitefully towards Rosa: "She was not the country bumpkin type, not at all. One has some taste."

With extreme discomfort did the Captain glance towards the plump village Rosa. He said, pointedly using English even at this late stage: "Mine was fair. Tall and fair. A lovely girl. Lovely!" he insisted with a glare. "Might have been an English girl."

"Which was entirely to her credit," suggested Herr Scholtz, with a smile.

"That was in 1913," said the Captain insistently, and then: "You say she had *black* hair?"

"Certainly, black hair. On that occasion —but that was not the last time it happened to me." He laughed. "I had three children by my wife, a fine woman—she is now dead, unfortunately." Again, there was no doubt tears filled his eyes. At the sight, the Captain's indignation soared. But Herr Scholtz had recovered and was speaking: "But I ask myself, how many children in addition to the three? Sometimes I look at a young man in the streets who has a certain resemblance, and I ask myself: Perhaps he is my son? Yes, yes, my friend, this is a question that every man must ask himself, sometimes, is it not?" He put back his head and laughed wholeheartedly, though with an undertone of rich regret.

The Captain did not speak for a moment. Then he said in English: "It's all very well, but it did happen to me, it *did*." He sounded like a defiant schoolboy, and Herr Scholtz shrugged.

"It happened to me, here. In this hotel."

Herr Scholtz controlled his irritation, glanced at Rosa, and for the first time since the beginning of this regrettable incident, he lowered his voice to a reasonable tone and spoke English. "Well," he said, in frank irony, smiling gently, with a quiet shrug, "Well, and perhaps if we are honest we must say that this is a thing that has happened to every man? Or rather, if it did not exist, it was necessary to invent it?"

And now—said his look towards the Captain, and now, for heaven's sake!—for the sake of decency, masculine solidarity, for the sake of our dignity in the eyes of that girl over there, who has so wounded us both —pull yourself together, my friend, and consider what you are saying!

But the Captain was oblivious in memories. "No," he insisted. "No. Speak for yourself. It *did* happen. Here." He paused, and then brought out, with difficulty: "I never married."

Herr Scholtz shrugged, at last, and was silent. Then he called out, "Fräulein, Fräulein—may I pay?" It was time to put an end to it.

Rosa did not immediately turn herself around. She patted her hair at the back. She straightened her apron. She took her napkin from one forearm and arranged it prettily on the other. Then she turned and came smiling towards them. It could at once be seen that she intended her smile to be noticed.

"You wish to pay?" she asked Herr Scholtz. She spoke calmly and deliberately in English, and the Captain started, and looked extremely uncomfortable. But Herr Scholtz immediately adjusted himself and said in English: "Yes, I am paying."

She took the note he held out, and counted out the change from the small satchel under her apron. Having laid the last necessary coin on the table, she stood squarely in front of them, smiling down equally at both, her hands folded in front of her. At last, when they had had the full benefit of her amused maternal smile, she suggested in English: "Perhaps the lady changed the color of her hair to suit what you both like best?" Then she laughed. She put back her head and laughed a full, wholehearted laugh.

Herr Scholtz, accepting the defeat with equanimity, smiled a rueful, appreciative smile.

The Captain sat stiffly in his chair, regarding them both with hot hostility, clinging tight to his own, authentic memories.

But Rosa laughed at him, until with a final swish of her dress she clicked past them both, and away off the terrace.

John Updike

THE PERSISTENCE OF DESIRE

Pennypacker's office still smelled of linoleum, a clean, sad scent that seemed to lift from the checkerboard floor in squares of alternating intensity; this pattern had given Clyde as a boy a funny nervous feeling of intersection, and now he stood crisscrossed by a double sense of himself, his present identity extending down from Massachusetts to meet his disconsolate youth in Pennsylvania, projected upward from a distance of years. The enlarged, tinted photograph of a lake in the Canadian wilderness still covered one whole wall, and the walnut-stained chairs and benches continued their vague impersonation of the Shaker manner. The one new thing, set squarely on an orange end table, was a compact black clock constructed like a speedometer; it showed in Arabic numerals the present minute—1:28 —and coiled invisibly in its works the two infinities of past and future. Clyde was early; the waiting room was empty. He sat down on a chair opposite the clock. Already it was 1:29, and while he watched, the digits slipped again: another drop into the brimming void. He glanced around for the comfort of a clock with a face and gracious, gradual hands. A stopped grandfather matched the other imitation antiques. He opened a magazine and immediately read, "Science reveals that the cells of the normal human body are replaced *in toto* every seven years."

The top half of a Dutch door at the other

end of the room opened, and, framed in the square, Pennypacker's secretary turned the bright disc of her face toward him. "Mr. Behn?" she asked in a chiming voice. "Dr. Pennypacker will be back from lunch in a minute." She vanished backward into the maze of little rooms where Pennypacker, an eye, ear, nose, and throat man, had arranged his fabulous equipment. Through the bay window Clyde could see traffic, gayer in color than he remembered, hustle down Grand Avenue. On the sidewalk, haltered girls identical in all but name with girls he had known strolled past in twos and threes. Small town perennials, they moved rather mournfully under their burdens of bloom. In the opposite direction packs of the opposite sex carried baseball mitts.

Clyde became so lonely watching his old street that when, with a sucking exclamation, the door from the vestibule opened, he looked up gratefully, certain that the person, this being his home town, would be a friend. When he saw who it was, though every cell in his body had been replaced since he had last seen her, his hands jerked in his lap and blood bounded against his skin.

"Clyde Behn," she pronounced, with a matronly and patronizing yet frightened finality, as if he were a child and these words the moral of a story.

"Janet." He awkwardly rose from his chair and crouched, not so much in courtesy as to relieve the pressure on his heart.

"Whatever brings you back to these parts?" She was taking the pose that she was just anyone who once knew him.

He slumped back. "I'm always coming back. It's just you've never been here."

"Well, I've"—she seated herself on an orange bench and crossed her plump legs cockily—"been in Germany with my husband."

"He was in the Air Force."

"Yes." It startled her a little that he knew.

"And he's out now?" Clyde had never met him, but having now seen Janet again, he felt he knew him well—a slight, literal fellow, to judge from the shallowness of the marks he had left on her. He would wear eyebrow-style glasses, be a griper, have some not quite negotiable talent, like playing the clarinet or drawing political cartoons, and now be starting up a drab avenue of business. Selling insurance, most likely. Poor Janet, Clyde felt; except for the interval of himself—his splendid, perishable self—she would never see the light. Yet she had retained her beautiful calm, a sleepless tranquility marked by that pretty little blue puffiness below the eyes. And either she had grown slimmer or he had grown more tolerant of fat. Her thick ankles and the general *obstinacy* of her flesh used to goad him into being cruel.

"Yes." Her voice indicated that she had withdrawn; perhaps some ugliness of their last parting had recurred to her.

"I was 4-F." He was ashamed of this, and his confessing it, though she seemed unaware of the change, turned their talk inward. "A peacetime slacker," he went on, "what could be more ignoble?"

She was quiet a while, then asked, "How many children do you have?"

"Two. Age three and one. A girl and a boy; very symmetrical. Do you"—he blushed lightly, and brushed at his forehead to hide it—"have any?"

"No, we thought it wouldn't be fair, until we were more fixed."

Now the quiet moment was his to hold; she had matched him failing for failing. She recrossed her legs, and in a quaint strained way smiled.

"I'm trying to remember," he admitted, "the last time we saw each other. I can't remember how we broke up."

"I can't either," she said. "It happened so often."

Clyde wondered if with that sarcasm she intended to fetch his eyes to the brink of tears of grief. Probably not; premeditation had never been much of a weapon for her, though she had tried to learn it from him.

He moved across the linoleum to sit on the bench beside her. "I can't tell you," he said, "how much, of all the people in this town, you were the one I wanted to see." It was foolish, but he had prepared it to say, in case he ever saw her again.

"Why?" This was more like her: blunt, puckerlipped curiosity. He had forgotten it.

"Well, hell. Any number of reasons. I wanted to say something."

"What?"

·"Well, that if I hurt you, it was stupidity, because I was young. I've often wondered since if I did, because it seems now that you were the only person outside my family who ever, actually, *liked* me."

"Did I?"

"If you think by doing nothing but asking monosyllabic questions you're making an effect, you're wrong."

She averted her face, leaving, in a sense, only her body—the pale, columnar breadth of arm, the freckled crescent of shoulder muscle under the cotton strap of her summer dress—with him. "You're the one who's making effects." It was such a wan, senseless thing to say to defend herself; Clyde, virtually paralyzed by so heavy an injection of love, touched her arm icily.

With a quickness that suggested she had foreseen this, she got up and went to the table by the bay window, where rows of overlapping magazines were laid. She bowed her head to their titles, the nape of her neck in shadow beneath a half-collapsed bun. She had always had trouble keeping her hair pinned.

Clyde was blushing intensely. "Is your husband working around here?"

"He's looking for work." That she kept her back turned while saying this gave him hope.

"Mr. Behn?" The petite secretary-nurse, switching like a pendulum, led him back through the sanctums and motioned for him to sit in a high hinged chair padded with black leather. Pennypacker's equipment had always made him nervous; tons of it were marshalled through the rooms. A complex tree of tubes and lenses leaned over his left shoulder, and by his right elbow a porcelain basin was cupped expectantly. An eye chart crisply stated gibberish. In time Pennypacker himself appeared: a tall, stooped man with mottled cheekbones and an air of suppressed anger.

"Now what's the trouble, Clyde?"

"It's nothing; I mean it's very little," Clyde began, laughing inappropriately. During his adolescence he had developed a joking familiarity with his dentist and his regular doctor, but he had never become intimate with Pennypacker, who remained, what he had seemed at first, an aloof administrator of expensive humiliations. In the third grade he had made Clyde wear glasses. Later, he annually cleaned, with a shrill push of hot water, wax from Clyde's ears, and once had thrust two copper straws up Clyde's nostrils in a futile attempt to purge his sinuses. Clyde always felt unworthy of Pennypacker, felt himself a dirty conduit balking the smooth onward flow of the doctor's reputation and apparatus. He blushed to mention his latest trivial stoppage. "It's just that for over two months I've had this eyelid that twitters and it makes it difficult to think."

Pennypacker drew little circles with a pencil-sized flashlight in front of Clyde's right eye.

"It's the left lid," Clyde said, without daring to turn his head. "I went to a doctor up where I live, and he said it was like a rattle in the fender and there was nothing to do. He said it would go away, but it didn't and didn't, so I had my mother make an appointment for when I came down here to visit."

Pennypacker moved to the left eye and drew even closer. The distance between the doctor's eyes and the corners of his mouth was very long; the emotional impression of his face close up was like that of those first photographs taken from rockets, in which the earth's curvature was made apparent. "How do you like being in your home territory?" Pennypacker asked.

"Fine."

"Seem a little strange to you?"

The question itself seemed strange. "A little."

"Mm. That's interesting."

"About the eye, there were two things I thought. One was, I got some glasses made in Massachusetts by a man nobody else ever went to, and I thought his prescription might be faulty. His equipment seemed so ancient and kind of full of cobwebs; like a Dürer print." He never could decide how cultured Pennypacker was; the Canadian lake argued against it, but he was county-famous in his trade, in a county where doctors were as high as the intellectual scale went.

The flashlight, a tepid sun girdled by a grid of optical circles behind which Pennypacker's face loomed dim and colorless, came right to the skin of Clyde's eye, and the vague face lurched forward angrily, and Clyde, blind in a world of light, feared that Pennypacker was inspecting the floor of his soul. Paralyzed by panic, he breathed, "The other was that something might be in it. At night it feels as if there's a tiny speck deep in under the lid."

Pennypacker reared back and insolently raked the light back and forth across Clyde's face. "How long have you had this flaky stuff on your lids?"

The insult startled Clyde. "Is there any?"

"How long have you had it?"

"Some mornings I notice little grains like salt that I thought were what I used to call sleepy-dust—"

"This isn't sleepy-dust," the doctor said. He repeated, "This isn't sleepy-dust." Clyde started to smile at what he took to be kidding of his childish vocabulary, but Pennypacker cut him short with "Cases of this can lead to loss of the eyelashes."

"Really?" Clyde was vain of his lashes, which in his boyhood had been exceptionally long, giving his face the alert and tender look of a girl's. "Do you think it's the reason for the tic?" He imagined his face with the lids bald and the lashes lying scattered on his cheeks like insect legs. "What can I do?"

"Are you using your eyes a great deal?"

"Some. No more than I ever did."

Pennypacker's hands, blue after Clyde's dazzlement, lifted an intense brown bottle from a drawer. "It may be bacteria, it may be allergy; when you leave I'll give you something that should knock it out either way. Do you follow me? Now, Clyde"—his voice became murmurous and consolatory as he placed a cupped hand, rigid as an electrode, on the top of Clyde's head—"I'm going to put some drops in your eyes so we can check the prescription of the glasses you bought in Massachusetts."

Clyde didn't remember that the drops stung so; he gasped outright and wept while Pennypacker held the lids apart with his fingers and worked them gently open and shut, as if he were playing with snapdragons. Pennypacker set preposterously small, circular dark brown glasses on Clyde's face and in exchange took away the stylish horn-rims Clyde had kept in his pocket. It was Pennypacker's method to fill his little rooms with waiting patients and wander from one to another like a dungeon-keeper.

Clyde heard, far off, the secretary's voice tinkle, and, amplified by the hollow hall, Pennypacker's rumble in welcome and Janet's respond. The one word "headaches," petulantly emphasized, stood up in her answer. Then a door was shut. Silence.

Clyde admired how matter-of-fact she had sounded. He had always admired this competence in her, her authority in the world peripheral to the world of love in which she was so servile. He remembered how she could outface waitresses and how she would bluff her mother when this vicious woman unexpectedly entered the screened porch where they were supposed to be playing cribbage. Potted elephant plants sat in the corners of the porch like faithful dwarfs; robins had built a nest in the lilac outside, inches from the screen. It had been taken as an omen, a blessing, when one evening their being on the glider no longer distressed the birds.

Unlike, say, the effects of Novocain, the dilation of pupils is impalpable. The wallpaper he saw through the open door seemed as distinct as ever. He held his fingernails close to his nose and was unable to distinguish the cuticles. He touched the sides of his nose, where tears had left trails. He looked at his fingers again, and they seemed fuzzier. He couldn't see his fingerprint whorls. The threads of his shirt had melted into an elusive liquid surface.

A door opened and closed, and another patient was ushered into a consulting room and imprisoned by Pennypacker. Janet's footsteps had not mingled with the others. Without ever quite sacrificing his reputation for good behavior, Clyde in high school had become fairly bold in heckling teachers he considered stupid or unjust. He got out of his chair, looked down the hall to where a white splinter of secretary showed, and quickly walked past a closed door to one ajar. His blood told him, This one.

Janet was sitting in a chair as upright as the one he had left, a two-pronged comb in her mouth, her back arched and her arms up, bundling her hair. As he slipped around the door, she plucked the comb from between her teeth and laughed at him. He saw in a little rimless mirror cocked above her head his own head, grimacing with stealth and grotesquely costumed in glasses like two chocolate coins, and appreciated her laughter, though it didn't fit with what he had prepared to say. He said it anyway: "Janet, are you happy?"

She rose with a practical face and walked past him and clicked the door shut. As she stood facing it, listening for a reaction from outside, he gathered her hair in his hand and lifted it from the nape of her neck, which he had expected to find in shadow but which was instead, to his distended eyes, bright as a candle. He clumsily put his lips to it.

"Don't you love your wife?" she asked.

"Incredibly much," he murmured into the neck-down.

She moved off, leaving him leaning awkwardly, and in front of the mirror smoothed her hair away from her ears. She sat down again, crossing her wrists in her lap.

"I just got told my eyelashes are going to fall out," Clyde said.

"Your pretty lashes," she said somberly.

"Why do you hate me?"

"Shh. I don't hate you now."

"But you did once."

"No, I did *not* once. Clyde, what *is* this bother? What are you after?"

"Son of a bitch, so I'm a bother. I knew it. You've just forgotten, all the time I've been remembering; you're so *damn* dense. I come in here a bundle of pain to tell you I'm sorry and I want you to be happy, and all I get is the back of your neck." Affected by what had happened to his eyes, his tongue had loosened, pouring out impressions; with culminating incoherence he dropped to his knees beside her chair, wondering if the thump would bring Pennypacker. "I must see you again," he blurted.

"Shh."

"I come back here and the only person who was ever pleasant to me I discover I maltreated so much she hates me."

"Clyde," she said, "you didn't maltreat me. You were a good boy to me."

Straightening up on his knees, he fumbled his fingers around the hem of the neck of her dress and pulled it out and looked down into the blurred cavity between her breasts. He had a remembrance of her freckles going down from her shoulders into her bathing suit. His glasses hit her cheek.

She stabbed the back of his hand with the points of her comb and he got to his feet, rearing high into a new, less sorrowful atmosphere. "When?" he asked, short of breath.

"No," she said.

"What's your married name?"

"Clyde, I thought you were successful. I thought you had beautiful children. Aren't you happy?"

"I am, I am; but"—the rest was so purely inspired its utterance only grazed his lips— "happiness isn't everything."

Footsteps ticked down the hall, toward their door, past it. Fear emptied his chest, yet with an excellent imitation of his old high-school flippancy he blew her a kiss, waited, opened the door, and whirled through it. His hand had left the knob when the secretary, emerging from the room where he should have been, confronted him in the linoleum-smelling hall. "Where could I get a drink of water?" he asked plaintively, assuming the hunch and whine of a blind beggar. In truth, he had, without knowing it, become thirsty.

"Once a year I pass through your territory," Pennypacker intoned as he slipped a growing weight of lenses into the tin frame on Clyde's nose. He had returned to Clyde more relaxed and chatty, now that all his little rooms were full. Clyde had tried to figure out from the pattern of noise if Janet had been dismissed. He believed she had. The thought made his eyelid throb. He didn't even know her married name. "Down the Turnpike," Pennypacker droned on, while his face flickered in and out of focus, "up the New Jersey Pike, over the George Washington Bridge, up the Merritt, then up Route 7 all the way to Lake Champlain. To hunt the big bass. There's an experience for you."

"I notice you have a new clock in your waiting room."

"That's a Christmas present from the Alton Optical Company. Can you read that line?"

"H, L, F, Y, T, something that's either an S or an E—"

"K," Pennypacker said without looking. The poor devil, he had all those letters memorized, all that gibberish—abruptly, Clyde wanted to love him. The oculist altered one lens. "Is it better this way? . . . Or this way?"

At the end of the examination, Pennypacker said, "Though the man's equipment was dusty, he gave you a good prescription. In your right eye the axis of astigmatism has rotated several degrees, which is corrected in the lenses. If you have been experiencing a sense of strain, part of the reason, Clyde, is that these heavy frames are slipping down on your nose and giving you a prismatic effect. For a firm fit you should have metal frames, with adjustable nose pads."

"They leave such ugly dents on the sides of your nose."

"You should have them. Your bridge, you see"—he tapped his own—"is recessed. It takes a regular face to support unarticulated frames. Do you wear your glasses all the time?"

"For the movies and reading. When I got them in the third grade you told me that was all I needed them for."

"You should wear them all the time."

"Really? Even just for walking around?"

"All the time, yes. You have middle-aged eyes."

Pennypacker gave him a little plastic squeeze bottle of drops. "That is for the fungus on your lids."

"Fungus? There's a brutal thought. Well, will it cure the tic?"

Pennypacker impatiently snapped, "The tic is caused by muscular fatigue."

Thus Clyde was dismissed into a tainted

world where things evaded his focus. He went down the hall in his sunglasses and was told by the secretary that he would receive a bill. The waiting room was full now, mostly with downcast old men and myopic children gnawing at their mothers. From out of this crowd a ripe young woman arose and came against his chest, and Clyde, included in the intimacy of the aroma her hair and skin gave off, felt weak and broad and grand, like a declining rose. Janet tucked a folded note into the pocket of his shirt and said conversationally, "He's waiting outside in the car."

The neutral, ominous "he" opened wide a conspiracy Clyde instantly entered. He stayed behind a minute, to give her time to get away. Ringed by the judging eyes of the young and old, he felt like an actor snug behind the blinding protection of the footlights; he squinted prolongedly at the speedometer-clock, which, like a letter delivered on the stage, in fact was blank. Then, smiling ironically toward both sides, he left the waiting room, coming into Pennypacker's entrance hall, a cubicle equipped with a stucco umbrella stand and a red rubber mat saying, in letters so large he could read them, WALK IN.

He had not expected to be unable to read her note. He held it at arm's length and slowly brought it toward his face, wiggling it in the light from outdoors. Though he did this several times, it didn't yield even the simplest word. Just wet blue specks. Under the specks, however, in their intensity and disposition, he believed he could make out the handwriting—slanted, open, unoriginal—familiar to him from other notes received long ago. This glimpse, through the skin of the paper, of her plain self quickened and sweetened his desire more than touching her had. He tucked the note back into his shirt pocket and its stiffness there made a shield for his heart. In this armor he stepped into the familiar street. The maples, macadam, shadows, houses, cement, were to his violated eyes as brilliant as a

scene remembered; he became a child again in this town, where life was a distant adventure, a rumor, an always imminent joy.

William Shakespeare

WHEN IN DISGRACE

When, in disgrace with fortune and men's eyes,
I all alone beweep my outcast state
And trouble deaf heaven with my bootless cries
And look upon myself and curse my fate,
Wishing me like to one more rich in hope,
Featured like him, like him with friends
    possessed,
Desiring this man's art and that man's scope,
With what I most enjoy contented least;
Yet in these thoughts myself almost despising,
Haply I think on thee, and then my state,   10
Like to the lark at break of day arising
From sullen earth, sings hymns at heaven's gate;
  For thy sweet love remembered such wealth
    brings
  That then I scorn to change my state with
    kings.

William Shakespeare

THAT TIME OF YEAR

That time of year thou may'st in me behold
When yellow leaves, or none, or few, do hang
Upon those boughs which shake against the cold,
Bare ruined choirs, where late the sweet birds
    sang.
In me thou seest the twilight of such day
As after sunset fadeth in the west,
Which by and by black night doth take away,
Death's second self, that seals up all in rest.
In me thou seest the glowing of such fire,
That on the ashes of his youth doth lie   10
As the death-bed whereon it must expire,

Consumed with that which it was nourished by.
   This thou perceiv'st, which makes thy love
      more strong
   To love that well which thou must leave ere
      long.

12 *Consumed, etc.:* The ashes stifle the flame that
their wood had fed.   14 *leave:* give up.

William Shakespeare

LET ME NOT TO THE MARRIAGE

Let me not to the marriage of true minds
Admit impediments. Love is not love
Which alters when it alteration finds,
Or bends with the remover to remove:
Oh no! it is an ever-fixed mark,
That looks on tempests and is never shaken;
It is the star to every wandering bark,
Whose worth's unknown, although his height be
   taken.
Love's not time's fool, though rosy lips and
   cheeks
Within his bending sickle's compass come;   10
Love alters not with his brief hours and weeks,
But bears it out even to the edge of doom.
   If this be error and upon me proved,
   I never writ, nor no man ever loved.

4 *bends, etc.:* changes when the beloved changes.
5 *mark:* the North Star, for instance. 8 *worth:* as-
trological influence.

William Shakespeare

THE EXPENSE OF SPIRIT

The expense of spirit in a waste of shame
Is lust in action; and till action, lust
Is perjured, murderous, bloody, full of blame,
Savage, extreme, rude, cruel, not to trust;

1 *expense:* consumption. 2 *till:* even before.
4 *trust:* be trusted.

Enjoyed no sooner but despisèd straight;
Past reason hunted; and no sooner had,
Past reason hated, as a swallowed bait
On purpose laid to make the taker mad:
Mad in pursuit, and in possession so;
Had, having, and in quest to have, extreme;   10
A bliss in proof—and proved, a very woe;
Before, a joy proposed, behind, a dream.
   All this the world well knows; yet none knows
      well
   To shun the heaven that leads men to this
      hell.

11 *proof:* practice.   12 *proposed:* imagined.

John Donne

A VALEDICTION FORBIDDING MOURNING

As virtuous men pass mildly away
   And whisper to their souls to go,
Whilst some of their sad friends do say,
   "The breath goes now," and some say, "No":

So let us melt and make no noise,
   No tear-floods nor sigh-tempests move;
'Twere profanation of our joys
   To tell the laity our love.

Moving of th' earth brings harms and fears;
   Men reckon what it did and meant;   10
But trepidation of the spheres,
   Though greater far, is innocent.

Dull sublunary lovers' love
   (Whose soul is sense) cannot admit
Absence, because it doth remove
   Those things which elemented it.

11 *spheres:* the invisible crystal spheres that were
believed to surround the earth. 14 *sense:* physical
contact. 16 *elemented:* composed.

But we by a love so much refined
  That ourselves know not what it is,
Inter-assurèd of the mind,
  Care less, eyes, lips, and hands to miss.   20

Our two souls therefore, which are one,
  Though I must go, endure not yet
A breach, but an expansion,
  Like gold to airy thinness beat.

If they be two, they are two so
  As stiff twin compasses are two;
Thy soul, the fixed foot, makes no show
  To move, but doth, if th' other do.

And though it in the center sit,
  Yet when the other far doth roam,   30
It leans and hearkens after it
  And grows erect as that comes home.

Such wilt thou be to me, who must
  Like th' other foot, obliquely run;
Thy firmness make my circle just
  And makes me end where I begun.

26 *twin compasses:* the feet of a drawing compass.

John Donne

THE ECSTASY

Where, like a pillow on a bed,
  A pregnant bank swelled up to rest
The violet's reclining head,
  Sat we two, one another's best.
Our hands were firmly cemented
  With a fast balm which thence did spring;
Our eye-beams twisted and did thread
  Our eyes upon one double string.
So to intergraft our hands, as yet
  Was all the means to make us one;   10
And pictures in our eyes to get
  Was all our propagation.
As, 'twixt two equal armies, fate
  Suspends uncertain victory,

Our souls, which, to advance their state,
  Were gone out, hung 'twixt her and me.
And whilst our souls negotiate there,
  We like sepulchral statues lay;
All day, the same our postures were,
  And we said nothing, all the day.   20
If any, so by love refined
  That he soul's language understood,
And by good love were grown all mind,
  Within convenient distance stood,
He, though he knew not which soul spake,
  Because both meant, both spake, the same,
Might thence a new concoction take,
  And part far purer than he came.
"This ecstasy doth unperplex,"
  We said, "and tell us what we love;   30
We see by this it was not sex;
  We see, we saw not what did move;
But as all several souls contain
  Mixture of things, they know not what,
Love these mixed souls doth mix again
  And makes both one, each this and that."
A single violet transplant,
  The strength, the color, and the size,
All which before was poor and scant,
  Redoubles still and multiplies.   40
When love with one another so
  Interinanimates two souls,
That abler soul, which thence doth flow,
  Defects of loneliness controls.
We then, who are this new soul, know
  Of what we are composed and made,
For the atomies of which we grow
  Are souls, whom no change can invade.
But O alas! so long, so far,
  Our bodies why do we forbear?   50
They are ours, though they are not we; we are
  The intelligences, they the spheres.
We owe them thanks, because they thus
  Did us, to us, at first convey,
Yielded their forces, sense, to us,
  Nor are dross to us, but allay.
On man heaven's influence works not so,
  But that it first imprints the air;

17 *negotiate:* communed. 27 *concoction:* maturing treatment. 32 *we saw, etc.:* i.e., that we did not understand what made us fall in love. 52 *intelligences:* the angels that govern the heavenly bodies. 56 *allay:* alloy.

For soul into the soul may flow,
   Though it to body first repair.   60
As our blood labors to beget
   Spirits, as like souls as it can,
Because such fingers need to knit
   That subtle knot which makes us man,
So must pure lovers' souls descend
   To affections and to faculties
Which sense may reach and apprehend;
   Else a great prince in prison lies.
To our bodies turn we then, that so
   Weak men on love revealed may look;   70
Love's mysteries in souls do grow,
   But yet the body is his book.
And if some lover, such as we,
   Have heard this dialogue of one,
Let him still mark us; he shall see
   Small change when we're to bodies gone.

57 *not so, etc.*: i.e., not until it has been transmitted through air—as astrology taught; so our souls work through bodily contact.

Robert Herrick

UPON JULIA'S CLOTHES

Whenas in silks my Julia goes,
Then, then, methinks, how sweetly flows
That liquefaction of her clothes.

Next, when I cast mine eyes and see
That brave vibration each way free,
O how that glittering taketh me!

Robert Herrick

DELIGHT IN DISORDER

A sweet disorder in the dress
Kindles in clothes a wantonness:
A lawn about the shoulders thrown
Into a fine distractiön,

2 *wantonness*: enticing freedom. 3 *lawn*: thin scarf. 4 *distraction*: disarray.

An erring lace which here and there
Enthralls the crimson stomacher,
A cuff neglectful and thereby
Ribbands to flow confusedly,
A winning wave (deserving note)
In the tempestuous petticoat,   10
A careless shoestring in whose tie
I see a wild civility,
Do more bewitch me than when art
Is too precise in every part.

Edmund Waller

GO, LOVELY ROSE

   Go, lovely rose,
Tell her that wastes her time and me
   That now she knows,
When I resemble her to thee,
   How sweet and fair she seems to be.

   Tell her that's young
And shuns to have her graces spied
   That hadst thou sprung
In deserts, where no men abide,
   Thou must have uncommended died.   10

   Small is the worth
Of beauty from the light retired;
   Bid her come forth,
Suffer herself to be desired,
   And not blush so to be admired.

   Then die, that she
The common fate of all things rare
   May read in thee;
How small a part of time they share,
   That are so wondrous sweet and fair.   20

4 *resemble*: liken, compare.

Andrew Marvell

TO HIS COY MISTRESS

Had we but world enough, and time,
This coyness, Lady, were no crime.
We would sit down and think which way
To walk and pass our long love's day.
Thou by the Indian Ganges' side
Shouldst rubies find; I by the tide
Of Humber would complain. I would
Love you ten years before the Flood,
And you should, if you please, refuse
Till the conversion of the Jews.   10
My vegetable love should grow
Vaster than empires and more slow;
A hundred years should go to praise
Thine eyes and on thy forehead gaze,
Two hundred to adore each breast,
But thirty thousand to the rest;
An age at least to every part,
And the last age should show your heart.
For, Lady, you deserve this state,
Nor would I love at lower rate.   20

   But at my back I always hear
Time's wingèd chariot hurrying near;
And yonder all before us lie
Deserts of vast eternity.
Thy beauty shall no more be found,
Nor, in thy marble vault, shall sound
My echoing song; then worms shall try
That long-preserved virginity,
And your quaint honor turn to dust,
And into ashes all my lust: 30
The grave's a fine and private place,
But none, I think, do there embrace.

   Now therefore, while the youthful hue
Sits on thy skin like morning dew,
And while thy willing soul transpires
At every pore with instant fires,

MISTRESS: sweetheart, not paramour. 11 *vege-table:* plantlike, inhuman. 19 *state:* honor. 20 *rate:* cost.

Now let us sport us while we may,
And now, like amorous birds of prey,
Rather at once our time devour
Than languish in his slow-chapped power.   40
Let us roll all our strength and all
Our sweetness up into one ball
And tear our pleasures with rough strife
Thorough the iron gates of life;
Thus, though we cannot make our sun
Stand still, yet we will make him run.

   36 *instant:* eager. 40 *slow-chapped:* slow-jawed, slowly devouring. 44 *Thorough:* through. 46 *Stand:* as Jehovah did at Gibeon (*Joshua* x, 12) and as Zeus did to prolong his night with Amphitryon's wife, Alcmene.

George Gordon, Lord Byron

WOMEN IN LOVE

I

Hail, Muse! *et cetera.*—We left Juan sleeping,
   Pillowed upon a fair and happy breast,
And watched by eyes that never yet knew
      weeping,
   And loved by a young heart, too deeply blest
To feel the poison through her spirit creeping,
   Or know who rested there, a foe to rest,
Had soiled the current of her sinless years
And turned her pure heart's purest blood to
      tears!

II

Oh, Love! what is it in this world of ours
   Which makes it fatal to be loved? Ah,
      why   10
With cypress branches hast thou wreathed thy
      bowers,

WOMEN IN LOVE: *Don Juan* III, I-XXV.
   1 *Hail, Muse:* a burlesque of the classic beginning, in which the poet begs the aid of the goddess Calliope. 2 *breast:* that of Haidée, daughter of a Greek pirate; the story is resumed in St. XII. 6 *who:* that he who.

And made thy best interpreter a sigh?
As those who dote on odors pluck the flowers
   And place them on their breast—but place to
     die—
Thus the frail beings we would fondly cherish
Are laid within our bosoms but to perish.

III

In her first passion woman loves her lover;
   In all others all she loves is love,
Which grows a habit she can ne'er get over,
   And fits her loosely—like an easy glove,   20
As you may find whene'er you like to prove her:
   One man alone at first her heart can move;
She then prefers him in the plural number,
Not finding that the additions much encumber.

IV

I know not if the fault be men's or theirs;
   But one thing's pretty sure; a woman planted
(Unless at once she plunge for life in prayers)
   After a decent time must be gallanted;
Although, no doubt, her first of love affairs
   Is that to which her heart is wholly
     granted;   30
Yet there are some, they say, who have had *none*,
But those who have ne'er end with only *one*.

V

'Tis melancholy, and a fearful sign
   Of human frailty, folly, also crime,
That love and marriage rarely can combine,
   Although they both are born in the same clime;
Marriage from love, like vinegar from wine—
   A sad, sour, sober beverage—by time
Is sharpened from its high celestial flavor
Down to a very homely household savor.   40

VI

There's something of antipathy, as 't were,
   Between their present and their future state;
A kind of flattery that's hardly fair
   Is used until the truth arrives too late—

26 *planted:* abandoned by her lover.

Yet what can people do, except despair?
   The same things change their names at such a
     rate;
For instance—passion in a lover's glorious,
But in a husband is pronounced uxorious.

VII

Men grow ashamed of being so very fond;
   They sometimes also get a little tired   50
(But that, of course, is rare) and then despond:
   The same things cannot always be admired,
Yet 'tis "so nominated in the bond"
   That both are tied till one shall have expired.
Sad thought! to lose the spouse that was
     adorning
Our days, and put one's servants into mourning.

VIII

There's doubtless something in domestic doings
   Which forms, in fact, true love's antithesis;
Romances paint at full length people's wooings
   But only give a bust of marriages,   60
For no one cares for matrimonial cooings;
   There's nothing wrong in a connubial kiss:
Think you, if Laura had been Petrarch's wife,
He would have written sonnets all his life?

IX

All tragedies are finished by a death,
   All comedies are ended by a marriage;
The future states of both are left to faith,
   For authors fear description might disparage
The worlds to come of both, or fall beneath,
   And then both worlds would punish their
     miscarriage;   70
So leaving each their priest and prayer-book
     ready,
They say no more of Death or of the Lady.

X

The only two that in my recollection
   Have sung of heaven and hell, or marriage, are

53 *nominated, etc.:* specified in the contract (*The Merchant of Venice* IV, 1).   63 *Laura:* idealized lady to whom Petrarch addressed his sonnets.

Dante and Milton, and of both the affection
 Was hapless in their nuptials, for some bar
Of fault or temper ruined the connection
 (Such things, in fact, it don't ask much to mar),
But Dante's Beatrice and Milton's Eve
Were not drawn from their spouses, you
   conceive.   80

XI

Some persons say that Dante meant theology
 By Beatrice, and not a mistress—I,
Although my opinion may require apology,
 Deem this a commentator's fantasy,
Unless indeed it was from his own knowledge he
 Decided thus, and showed good reason why;
I think that Dante's more abstruse ecstatics
Meant to personify the mathematics.

XII

Haidée and Juan were not married, but
 The fault was theirs, not mine; it is not
  fair,   90
Chaste reader, then, in any way to put
 The blame on me, unless you wish they were;
Then if you'd have them wedded, please to shut
 The book which treats of this erroneous pair
Before the consequences grow too awful;
'Tis dangerous to read of loves unlawful.

XIII

Yet they were happy—happy in the illicit
 Indulgence of their innocent desires;
But more imprudent grown with every visit,
 Haidée forgot the island was her sire's; 100
When we have what we like, 'tis hard to miss it,
 At least in the beginning, ere one tires;
Thus she came often, not a moment losing,
Whilst her piratical papa was cruising.

76 *hapless:* Dante's marriage to Gemma Donati is
not known to have been unhappy—though Milton's first marriage. to Mary Powell was.

XIV

Let not his mode of raising cash seem strange,
 Although he fleeced the flags of every nation,
For into a prime minister but change
 His title, and 'tis nothing but taxation;
But he, more modest, took an humbler range
 Of life, and in an honester vocation 110
Pursued o'er the high seas his watery journey,
And merely practised as a sea-attorney.

XV

The good old gentleman had been detained
 By winds and waves, and some important
  captures;
And, in the hope of more, at sea remained,
 Although a squall or two had damped his
  raptures,
By swamping one of the prizes; he had chained
 His prisoners, dividing them like chapters
In numbered lots; they all had cuffs and collars
And averaged each from ten to a hundred
  dollars.   120

XVI

Some he disposed of off Cape Matapan,
 Among his friends the Mainots; some he sold
To his Tunis correspondents, save one man
 Tossed overboard unsaleable (being old);
The rest—save here and there some richer one,
 Reserved for future ransom—in the hold
Were linked alike, as for the common people he
Had a large order from the Dey of Tripoli.

XVII

The merchandise was served in the same way,
 Pieced out for different marts in the
  Levant;   130
Except some certain portions of the prey,
 Light classic articles of female want,
French stuffs, lace, tweezers, toothpicks,
  teapot, tray,
 Guitars and castanets from Alicant,
All which selected from the spoil he gathers,
Robbed for his daughter by the best of fathers.

XVIII

A monkey, a Dutch mastiff, a mackaw,
  Two parrots, with a Persian cat and kittens,
He chose from several animals he saw—
  A terrier, too, which once had been a
    Briton's,   140
Who dying on the coast of Ithaca,
  The peasants gave the poor dumb thing a
    pittance;
These to secure in this strong blowing weather,
He caged in one huge hamper altogether.

XIX

Then having settled his marine affairs,
  Despatching single cruisers here and there,
His vessel having need of some repairs,
  He shaped his course to where his daughter
    fair
Continued still her hospitable cares;
  But that part of the coast being shoal and
    bare,   150
And rough with reefs which ran out many a
    mile,
His port lay on the other side o' the isle.

XX

And there he went ashore without delay,
  Having no custom-house nor quarantine
To ask him awkward questions on the way
  About the time and place where he had been:
He left his ship to be hove down next day,
  With orders to the people to careen;
So that all hands were busy beyond measure
In getting out goods, ballast, guns, and
    treasure.   160

XXI

Arriving at the summit of a hill
  Which overlooked the white walls of his home,
He stopped.—What singular emotions fill
  Their bosoms who have been induced to roam!
With fluttering doubts if all be well or ill—
  With love for many, and with fears for some;
All feelings which o'erleap the years long lost
And bring our hearts back to their starting-post.

XXII

The approach of home to husbands and to sires,
  After long travelling by land or water,   170
Most naturally some small doubt inspires—
  A female family's a serious matter
(None trusts the sex more, or so much admires—
  But they hate flattery, so I never flatter) ;
Wives in their husbands' absences grow subtler,
And daughters sometimes run off with the butler.

XXIII

An honest gentleman at his return
  May not have the good fortune of Ulysses;
Not all lone matrons for their husbands mourn
  Or show the same dislike to suitors'
    kisses;   180
The odds are that he finds a handsome urn
  To his memory—and two or three young
    misses
Born to some friend, who holds his wife and
    riches—
And that *his* Argus—bites him by the breeches.

XXIV

If single, probably his plighted fair
  Has in his absence wedded some rich miser;
But all the better, for the happy pair
  May quarrel, and the lady growing wiser,
He may resume his amatory care
  As cavalier servente, or despise her;   190
And that his sorrow may not be a dumb one,
Write odes on the Inconstancy of Woman.

XXV

And oh! ye gentlemen who have already
  Some chaste *liaison* of the kind—I mean
An honest friendship with a married lady—
  The only thing of this sort ever seen

178 *Ulysses:* who, after twenty years' absence,
found his wife, Penelope, faithful to him despite her
suitors' importunities; and who was welcomed by
his aged hound, Argus. 190 *cavalier servente:* lover.

To last—of all connections the most steady,
  And the true Hymen (the first's but a
    screen)—
Yet for all that keep not too long away;
I've known the absent wronged four times a
  day.   200

Emily Dickinson

GOING TO HIM

Going to him—happy letter!
Tell him,
Tell him the page I didn't write.
Tell him I only said the syntax
And left the verb and the pronoun out.

Tell him just how the fingers hurried,
Then how they waded slow, slow;
And then you wished you had eyes in your page
So you could see what moved them so.

Tell him it wasn't a practiced writer—   10
You guessed from the way the sentence
    toiled.
You could hear the bodice tug behind you
As if it held but the might of a child.
You almost pitied it, you it worked so.
Tell him—no, you may quibble there,
For it would split his heart to know it,
And then you and I were silenter.

Tell him night finished before we finished,
And the old clock kept neighing "Day!"
And you got sleepy and begged to be
    ended.   20
What could hinder it, so to say?
Tell him just how she sealed you, cautious.
But if he ask where you are hid
Until tomorrow, happy letter,
Gesture coquette, and shake your head.

George Meredith

MARK WHERE THE PRESSING WIND

Mark where the pressing wind shoots javelin-like
Its skeleton shadow on the broad-backed wave!
Here is a fitting spot to dig Love's grave,
Here where the ponderous breakers plunge and
    strike
And dart their hissing tongues high up the sand:
In hearing of the ocean and in sight
Of those ribbed wind-streaks running into white.
If I the death of Love had deeply planned,
I never could have made it half so sure
As by the unblest kisses which upbraid   10
The full-waked sense; or failing that, degrade!
'Tis morning: but no morning can restore
What we have forfeited. I see no sin:
The wrong is mixed. In tragic life, God wot,
No villain need be! Passions spin the plot:
We are betrayed by what is false within.

Louis MacNeice

LEAVING BARRA

The dazzle on the sea, my darling,
Leads from the western channel
A carpet of brilliance taking
My leave for ever of the island.

I never shall visit that island
Again with its easy tempo—
The seal sunbathing, the circuit
Of gulls on the wing for garbage.

I go to a different garbage
And scuffle for scraps of notice,   10
Pretend to ignore the stigma
That stains my life and my leisure.

BARRA: island northwest of Scotland, in the outer
Hebrides.

For fretful even in leisure
I fidget for different values,
Restless as a gull and haunted
By a hankering after Atlantis.

I do not know that Atlantis
Unseen and uncomprehended,
Dimly divined but keenly
Felt with a phantom hunger.   20

If only I could crush the hunger
If only I could lay the phantom
Then I should no doubt be happy
Like a fool or a dog or a buddha.

O the self-abnegation of Buddha
The belief that is disbelieving
The denial of chiaroscuro
Not giving a damn for existence!

But I would cherish existence
Loving the beast and the bubble   30
Loving the rain and the rainbow,
Considering philosophy alien.

For all the religions are alien
That allege that life is a fiction,
And when we agree in denial
The cock crows in the morning.

If only I could wake in the morning
And find I had learned the solution,
Wake with the knack of knowledge
Who as yet have only an inkling.   40

Though some facts foster the inkling—
The beauty of the moon and music,
The routine courage of the worker,
The gay endurance of women.

And you who to me among women
Stand for so much that I wish for,
I thank you, my dear, for the example
Of living like a fugue and moving.

36 *crows*: cf. Peter's denial, *Gospel of St. Matthew*
XXVI, 74.

For few are able to keep moving,
They drag and flag in the traffic;   50
While you are alive beyond question
Like the dazzle on the sea, my darling.

Richard Wilbur

JUNE LIGHT

Your voice, with clear location of June days,
Called me—outside the window. You were there,
Light yet composed, as in the just soft stare
Of uncontested summer all things raise
Plainly their seeming into seamless air.

Then your love looked as simple and entire
As that picked pear you tossed me, and your face
As legible as pearskin's fleck and trace,
Which promise always wine, by mottled fire
More fatal fleshed than ever human grace.   10

And your gift—Oh when I saw it fall
Into my hands, through all that naïve light,
It seemed as blessed with truth and new delight
As must have been the first great gift of all.

Louis Simpson

THE MAN WHO MARRIED MAGDALENE

The man who married Magdalene
Had not forgiven her.
God might pardon every sin . . .
Love is no pardoner.

Her hands were hollow, pale and blue,
Her mouth like watered wine.
He watched to see if she were true
And waited for a sign.

It was old harlotry, he guessed,
That drained her strength away,   10
So gladly for the dark she dressed,
So sadly for the day.

Their quarrels made her dull and weak
And soon a man might fit
A penny in the hollow cheek
And never notice it.

At last, as they exhausted slept,
Death granted the divorce,
And nakedly the woman leapt
Upon that narrow horse.   20

But when he woke and woke alone
He wept and would deny
The loose behavior of the bone
And the immodest thigh.

Adrienne Rich

A MARRIAGE IN THE 'SIXTIES

As solid-seeming as antiquity,
you frown above
the *New York Sunday Times*
where Castro, like a walk-on out of *Carmen,*
mutters into a bearded henchman's ear.

They say the second's getting shorter—
I knew it in my bones—
and pieces of the universe are missing.
I feel the gears of this late afternoon
slip, cog by cog, even as I read.   10
"I'm old," we both complain,
half-laughing, oftener now.

Time serves you well. That face—
part Roman emperor, part Raimu—
nothing this side of Absence can undo.
Bliss, revulsion, your rare angers can
only carry through what's well begun.

When
I read your letters long ago
In that half-defunct   20
hotel in Magdalen Street
every word primed my nerves.
A geographical misery
composed of oceans, fogbound planes
and misdelivered cablegrams
lay round me, a Nova Zembla
only your live breath could unfreeze.
Today we stalk
in the raging desert of our thought
whose single drop of mercy is   30
each knows the other there.
Two strangers, thrust for life upon a rock,
may have at last the perfect hour of talk
that language aches for; still—
two minds, two messages.

Your brows knit into flourishes. Some piece
of mere time has you tangled there.
Some mote of history has flown into your eye.
Will nothing ever be the same,
even our quarrels take a different key,   40
our dreams exhume new metaphors?
The world breathes underneath our bed.
Don't look. We're at each other's mercy too.

Dear fellow-particle, electric dust
I'm blown with—ancestor
to what euphoric cluster—
see how particularity dissolves
in all that hints of chaos. Let one finger
hover toward you from There
and see this furious grain   50
suspend its dance to hang
beside you like your twin.

Chapter 3

THE WORLD AROUND US

Nature, in one of its several tangled but powerful senses, is everything that is not mankind or made by mankind. Of course, in another sense, human beings have a nature, too—that which is fixed in us or inseparable from our being and ways. Humanity's attitude toward its natural setting has always been ambivalent, as the selections in this chapter show well: fear and love mixed in different proportions, trust and mistrust, a determination to dominate and a deep sense of dependence. "Nature never did betray the heart that loved her," says one of Wordsworth's poems; but one of Tennyson's poems speaks of "Nature red in tooth and claw." Contrast the deep love of nature expressed in Keats's "To Autumn" and Blake's "To Spring" with the awe in "The Headlong Wave" and the fear in Emily Dickinson's "A narrow Fellow in the Grass."

We regard nature, inevitably, in many different ways and from many points of view, as our interests and our circumstances influence us. Perhaps the four most basic points of view are these: aesthetic (we perceive and enjoy the beauty or sublimity of nature), ethical (we take nature as a lesson or model for ideals of human conduct), cognitive (we want to understand its workings and marvel at the intricate complexity of its inner laws), and technological (we try to master nature and bend its resources and its powers to our own purposes). With the cognitive point of view this chapter has little to do, for that view gives rise to the scientific enterprise, which is to be the subject of Chapter 9. But each of the others is clearly exhibited in the selections that follow.

The beauty of nature is appreciated in most of the selections in this chapter—no less in "A Day in the Country," in which the characters feel so much at home in, and a part of, the world around them, than in the sonnets by Hopkins, in which nature is perceived as the visible image of divinity. For Thoreau and E. B. White, the Walden woods are cherished for their potential influence on human beings, and a similar attitude is present in "The Garden" and "Ode to Evening"; but in "December," the order of nature gives rise to painful reflections on man's inhumanity to man; and "A Madness of Nature," for all its sense of the grandeur of natural processes, warns us that nature's ways are not to be taken as a model for human society. What our technological exploitation has done to nature—or a small part of this enormous story—is brought out in "Nature Fights Back," and underlined in the implicit warning of "If I Forget Thee, O Earth."

Henry David Thoreau

SOLITUDE

This is a delicious evening, when the whole body is one sense, and imbibes delight through every pore. I go and come with a strange liberty in Nature, a part of herself. As I walk along the stony shore of the pond in my shirt sleeves, though it is cool as well as cloudy and windy, and I see nothing special to attract me, all the elements are unusually congenial to me. The bull frogs trump to usher in the night, and the note of the whippoorwill is borne on the rippling wind from over the water. Sympathy with the fluttering alder and poplar leaves almost takes away my breath; yet, like the lake, my serenity is rippled but not ruffled. These small waves raised by the evening wind are as remote from storm as the smooth reflecting surface. Though it is now dark, the wind still blows and roars in the wood, the waves still dash, and some creatures lull the rest with their notes. The repose is never complete. The wildest animals do not repose, but seek their prey now; the fox, and skunk, and rabbit, now roam the fields and woods without fear. They are Nature's watchmen,—links which connect the days of animated life.

When I return to my house I find that visitors have been there and left their cards, either a bunch of flowers, or a wreath of evergreen, or a name in pencil on a yellow walnut leaf or a chip. They who come rarely to the woods take some little piece of the forest into their hands to play with by the way, which they leave, either intentionally or accidentally. One has peeled a willow wand, woven it into a ring, and dropped it on my table. I could always tell if visitors had called in my absence, either by the bended twigs or grass, or the print of their shoes, and generally of what sex or age or

quality they were by some slight trace left, as a flower dropped, or a bunch of grass plucked and thrown away, even as far off as the railroad, half a mile distant, or by the lingering odor of a cigar or pipe. Nay, I was frequently notified of the passage of a traveller along the highway sixty rods off by the scent of his pipe.

There is commonly sufficient space about us. Our horizon is never quite at our elbows. The thick wood is not just at our door, nor the pond, but somewhat is always clearing, familiar and worn by us, appropriated and fenced in some way, and reclaimed from Nature. For what reason have I this vast range and circuit, some square miles of unfrequented forest, for my privacy, abandoned to me by men? My nearest neighbor is a mile distant, and no home is visible from any place but the hill-tops within half a mile of my own. I have my horizon bounded by woods all to myself; a distant view of the railroad where it touches the pond on the one hand, and of the fence which skirts the woodland road on the other. But for the most part it is as solitary where I live as on the prairies. It is as much Asia or Africa as New England. I have, as it were, my own sun and moon and stars, and a little world all to myself. At night there was never a traveller passed my house, or knocked at my door, more than if I were the first or last man; unless it were in the spring, when at long intervals some came from the village to fish for pouts,—they plainly fished much more in the Walden Pond of their own natures, and baited their hooks with darkness,—but they soon retreated, usually with light baskets, and left "the world to darkness and to me," [1] and the black kernel of the night was never profaned by any human neighborhood. I believe that men are generally still a little afraid of the dark, though the witches are

[1] Thomas Gray, "Elegy Written in a Country Churchyard," 1. 4.

all hung, and Christianity and candles have been introduced.

Yet I experienced sometimes that the most sweet and tender, the most innocent and encouraging society may be found in any natural object, even for the poor misanthrope and most melancholy man. There can be no very black melancholy to him who lives in the midst of Nature and has his senses still. There was never yet such a storm but it was Æolian[2] music to a healthy and innocent ear. Nothing can rightly compel a simple and brave man to a vulgar sadness. While I enjoy the friendship of the seasons I trust that nothing can make life a burden to me. The gentle rain which waters my beans and keeps me in the house to-day is not drear and melancholy, but good for me too. Though it prevents my hoeing them, it is of far more worth than my hoeing. If it should continue so long as to cause the seeds to rot in the ground and destroy the potatoes in the low lands, it would still be good for the grass on the uplands, and, being good for the grass, it would be good for me. Sometimes, when I compare myself with other men, it seems as if I were more favored by the gods than they, beyond any deserts that I am conscious of; as if I had a warrant and surety at their hands which my fellows have not, and were especially guided and guarded. I do not flatter myself, but if it be possible they flatter me. I have never felt lonesome, or in the least oppressed by a sense of solitude, but once, and that was a few weeks after I came to the woods, when, for an hour, I doubted if the near neighborhood of man was not essential to a serene and healthy life. To be alone was something unpleasant. But I was at the same time conscious of a slight insanity in my mood, and seemed to foresee my recovery. In the midst of a gentle rain while these thoughts prevailed, I was suddenly sensible of such sweet and beneficent society in Nature, in the very

pattering of the drops, and in every sound and sight around my house, an infinite and unaccountable friendliness all at once like an atmosphere sustaining me, as made the fancied advantages of human neighborhood insignificant, and I have never thought of them since. Every little pine needle expanded and swelled with sympathy and befriended me. I was so distinctly made aware of the presence of something kindred to me, even in scenes which we are accustomed to call wild and dreary, and also that the nearest of blood to me and humanest was not a person nor a villager, that I thought no place could ever be strange to me again.—

"Mourning untimely consumes the sad;
    Few are their days in the land of the living,
    Beautiful daughter of Toscar." [3]

Some of my pleasantest hours were during the long rain storms in the spring or fall, which confined me to the house for the afternoon as well as the forenoon, soothed by their ceaseless roar and pelting; when an early twilight ushered in a long evening in which many thoughts had time to take root and unfold themselves. In those driving north-east rains which tried the village houses so, when the maids stood ready with mop and pail in front entries to keep the deluge out, I sat behind my door in my little house, which was all entry, and thoroughly enjoyed its protection. In one heavy thunder shower the lightning struck a large pitch-pine across the pond, making a very conspicuous and perfectly regular spiral groove from top to bottom, an inch or more deep, and four or five inches wide, as you would groove a walking-stick. I passed it again the other day, and was struck with awe on looking up and beholding that mark, now more distinct than ever, where a terrific and re-

2 Aeolus is the Greek god of the winds.

3 Quoted from a modernized version of the works of Ossian, a legendary Gaelic poet of the third century.

sistless bolt came down out of the harmless sky eight years ago. Men frequently say to me, "I should think you would feel lonesome down there, and want to be nearer to folks, rainy and snowy days and nights especially." I am tempted to reply to such, —This whole earth which we inhabit is but a point in space. How far apart, think you, dwell the two most distant inhabitants of yonder star, the breadth of whose disk cannot be appreciated by our instruments? Why should I feel lonely? is not our planet in the Milky Way? This which you put seems to me not to be the most important question. What sort of space is that which separates a man from his fellows and makes him solitary? I have found that no exertion of the legs can bring two minds much nearer to one another. What do we want most to dwell near to? Not to many men surely, the depot, the post-office, the bar-room, the meeting-house, the school-house, the grocery, Beacon Hill,[4] or the Five Points,[5] where men most congregate, but to the perennial source of our life, whence in all our experience we have found that to issue, as the willow stands near the water and sends out its roots in that direction. This will vary with different natures, but this is the place where a wise man will dig his cellar. . . . I one evening overtook one of my townsmen, who has accumulated what is called "a handsome property,"—though I never got a *fair* view of it,—on the Walden road, driving a pair of cattle to market, who inquired of me how I could bring my mind to give up so many of the comforts of life. I answered that I was very sure I liked it passably well; I was not joking. And so I went home to my bed, and left him to pick his way through the darkness and the mud to Brighton,[6]—or Bright-town,[7]—which place he would reach some time in the morning.

4 Fashionable residential district of Boston.
5 Section of New York notorious for vice.
6 Suburb of Boston.
7 "Bright" was a pet name for an ox.

Any prospect of awakening or coming to life to a dead man makes indifferent all times and places. The place where that may occur is always the same, and indescribably pleasant to all our senses. For the most part we allow only outlying and transient circumstances to make our occasions. They are, in fact, the cause of our distraction. Nearest to all things is that power which fashions their being. *Next* to us the grandest laws are continually being executed. *Next* to us is not the workman whom we have hired, with whom we love so well to talk, but the workman whose work we are.

"How vast and profound is the influence of the subtle powers of Heaven and of Earth!

"We seek to perceive them, and we do not see them; we seek to hear them, and we do not hear them; identified with the substance of things, they cannot be separated from them.

"They cause that in all the universe men purify and sanctify their hearts, and clothe themselves in their holiday garments to offer sacrifices and oblations to their ancestors. It is an ocean of subtle intelligences. They are everywhere, above us, on our left, on our right; they environ us on all sides." [8]

We are the subjects of an experiment which is not a little interesting to me. Can we not do without the society of our gossips a little while under these circumstances,— have our own thoughts to cheer us? Confucius says truly, "Virtue does not remain as an abandoned orphan; it must of necessity have neighbors." [9]

With thinking we may be beside ourselves in a sane sense. By a conscious effort of the mind we can stand aloof from actions and their consequences; and all things, good and bad, go by us like a torrent. We are not wholly involved in Nature. I may be either the driftwood in the stream, or Indra[10] in

8 Confucius, *The Doctrine of the Mean*, XVI, 1–3.
9 Confucius, *Analects*, IV, xxv.
10 Hindu god of the air.

the sky looking down on it. I *may* be affected by a theatrical exhibition; on the other hand, I *may not* be affected by an actual event which appears to concern me much more. I only know myself as a human entity; the scene, so to speak, of thoughts and affections; and am sensible of a certain doubleness by which I can stand as remote from myself as from another. However intense my experience, I am conscious of the presence and criticism of a part of me, which, as it were, is not a part of me, but spectator, sharing no experience, but taking note of it; and that is no more I than it is you. When the play, it may be the tragedy, of life is over, the spectator goes his way. It was a kind of fiction, a world of the imagination only, so far as he was concerned. This doubleness may easily make us poor neighbors and friends sometimes.

I find it wholesome to be alone the greater part of the time. To be in company, even with the best, is soon wearisome and dissipating. I love to be alone. I never found the companion that was so companionable as solitude. We are for the most part more lonely when we go abroad among men than when we stay in our chambers. A man thinking or working is always alone, let him be where he will. Solitude is not measured by the miles of space that intervene between a man and his fellows. The really diligent student in one of the crowded hives of Cambridge College[11] is as solitary as a dervish in the desert. The farmer can work alone in the field or the woods all day, hoeing or chopping, and not feel lonesome, because he is employed; but when he comes home at night he cannot sit down in a room alone, at the mercy of his thoughts, but must be where he can "see the folks," and recreate, and as he thinks remunerate himself for his day's solitude; and hence he wonders how the student can sit alone in the house all night and most of the day without ennui

11 Harvard University.

and "the blues"; but he does not realize that the student, though in the house, is still at work in *his* field, and chopping in *his* woods, as the farmer in his, and in turn seeks the same recreation and society that the latter does, though it may be a more condensed form of it.

Society is commonly too cheap. We meet at very short intervals, not having had time to acquire any new value for each other. We meet at meals three times a day, and give each other a new taste of that old musty cheese that we are. We have had to agree on a certain set of rules, called etiquette and politeness, to make this frequent meeting tolerable, and that we need not come to open war. We meet at the post-office, and at the sociable, and about the fireside every night; we live thick and are in each other's way, and stumble over one another, and I think that we thus lose some respect for one another. Certainly less frequency would suffice for all important and hearty communications. Consider the girls in a factory,—never alone, hardly in their dreams. It would be better if there were but one inhabitant to a square mile, as where I live. The value of a man is not in his skin, that we should touch him.

I have heard of a man lost in the woods and dying of famine and exhaustion at the foot of a tree, whose loneliness was relieved by the grotesque visions with which, owing to bodily weakness, his diseased imagination surrounded him, and which he believed to be real. So also, owing to bodily and mental health and strength, we may be continually cheered by a like but more normal and natural society, and come to know that we are never alone.

I have a great deal of company in my house; especially in the morning, when nobody calls. Let me suggest a few comparisons, that some one may convey an idea of my situation. I am no more lonely than the loon in the pond that laughs so loud, or than Walden Pond itself. What company has that lonely lake, I pray? And yet it has not the blue devils,[12] but the blue angels in it, in the azure tint of its waters. The sun is alone, except in thick weather, when there sometimes appear to be two, but one is a mock sun. God is alone,—but the devil, he is far from being alone; he sees a great deal of company; he is legion. I am no more lonely than a single mullein or dandelion in a pasture, or a bean leaf, or sorrel, or a horse-fly, or a humble-bee. I am no more lonely than the Mill Brook, or a weathercock, or the north star, or the south wind, or an April shower, or a January thaw, or the first spider in a new house.

I have occasional visits in the long winter evenings, when the snow falls fast and the wind howls in the wood, from an old settler[13] and original proprietor, who is reported to have dug Walden Pond, and stoned it, and fringed it with pine woods; who tells me stories of old time and of new eternity; and between us we manage to pass a cheerful evening with social mirth and pleasant views of things, even without apples or cider,—a most wise and humorous friend, whom I love much, who keeps himself more secret than ever did Goffe or Whalley;[14] and though he is thought to be dead, none can show where he is buried. An elderly dame,[15] too, dwells in my neighborhood, invisible to most persons, in whose odorous herb garden I love to stroll sometimes, gathering simples and listening to her fables; for she has a genius of unequalled fertility, and her memory runs back farther than mythology, and she can tell me the original of every fable, and on what fact every one is founded, for the incidents occurred when she was young. A ruddy and lusty old dame, who delights in all weathers and seasons, and is likely to outlive all her children yet.

The indescribable innocence and beneficence of Nature,—of sun and wind and rain, of summer and winter,—such health, such cheer, they afford forever! and such sympathy have they ever with our race, that all Nature would be affected, and the sun's brightness fade, and the winds would sigh humanely, and the clouds rain tears, and the woods shed their leaves and put on mourning in midsummer, if any man should ever for a just cause grieve. Shall I not have intelligence with the earth? Am I not partly leaves and vegetable mould myself?

What is the pill which will keep us well, serene, contented? Not my or thy great-grandfather's, but our great-grandmother Nature's universal, vegetable, botanic medicines, by which she has kept herself young always, outlived so many old Parrs[16] in her day, and fed her health with their decaying fatness. For my panacea, instead of one of those quack vials[17] of a mixture dipped from Acheron[18] and the Dead Sea, which come out of those long shallow black-schooner looking wagons which we sometimes see made to carry bottles, let me have a draught of undiluted morning air. Morning air! If men will not drink of this at the fountain-head of the day, why, then, we must even bottle up some and sell it in the shops, for the benefit of those who have lost their subscription ticket to morning time in this world. But remember, it will not keep quite till noon-day even in the coolest cellar, but drive out the stoples long ere that and fol-

12 "The blues," as in the earlier paragraph.

13 Apparently the Creator—but according to Walter Harding, whose notes have here been freely borrowed, the Greek Pan, god of the woods. ("The great god Pan is dead"—Plutarch.)

14 William Goffe and Edward Whalley, two judges who signed the death warrant of Charles I, fled to New England after the Restoration of Charles II (1660) and hid in various parts of Massachusetts and Connecticut.

15 Cf. "our great-grandmother" in the last paragraph.

16 Thomas Parr, supposedly born in 1483, died in 1635.

17 Patent medicines.

18 River bordering Hades.

low westward the steps of Aurora. I am no worshipper of Hygeia,[19] who was the daughter of that old herb-doctor Æsculapius,[20] and who is represented on monuments holding a serpent in one hand, and in the other a cup out of which the serpent sometimes drinks; but rather of Hebe, cupbearer to Jupiter, who was the daughter of Juno and wild lettuce,[21] and who had the power of restoring gods and men to the vigor of youth. She was probably the only thoroughly sound-conditioned, healthy, and robust young lady that ever walked the globe, and wherever she came it was spring.

E. B. White

WALDEN: JUNE 1939

Miss Nims take a letter to Henry David Thoreau. Dear Henry: I thought of you the other afternoon as I was approaching Concord doing fifty on Route 62. That is a high speed at which to hold a philosopher in one's mind, but in this century we are a nimble bunch.

On one of the lawns in the outskirts of the village a woman was cutting the grass with a motorized lawn mower. What made me think of you was that the machine had rather got away from her, although she was game enough, and in the brief glimpse I had of the scene it appeared to me that the lawn was mowing the lady. She kept a tight grip on the handles, which throbbed violently with every explosion of the one-cylinder motor, and as she sheered around bushes and lurched along at a reluctant trot behind her impetuous servant, she looked like a puppy who had grabbed something that was too much for him. Concord hasn't changed much, Henry; the farm implements and the animals still have the upper hand.

I may as well admit that I was journeying to Concord with the deliberate intention of visiting your woods; for although I have never knelt at the grave of a philosopher nor placed wreaths on moldy poets, and have often gone a mile out of my way to avoid some place of historical interest, I have always wanted to see Walden Pond. The account which you left of your sojourn there is, you will be amused to learn, a document of increasing pertinence; each year it seems to gain a little headway, as the world loses ground. We may all be transcendental yet, whether we like it or not. As our common complexities increase, any tale of individual simplicity (and yours is the best written and the cockiest) acquires a new fascination; as our goods accumulate, but not our well-being, your report of an existence without material adornment takes on a certain awkward credibility.

My purpose in going to Walden Pond, like yours, was not to live cheaply or to live dearly there, but to transact some private business with the fewest obstacles. Approaching Concord, doing forty, doing forty-five, doing fifty, the steering wheel held snug in my palms, the highway held grimly in my vision, the crown of the road now serving me (on the right-hand curves), now defeating me (on the left-hand curves), I began to rouse myself from the stupefaction which a day's motor journey induces. It was a delicious evening, Henry, when the whole body is one sense, and imbibes delight through every pore, if I may coin a phrase.[22] Fields were richly brown where the harrow, drawn by the stripped Ford, had lately sunk its teeth; pastures were green; and overhead

[19] Greek goddess of health—but Thoreau means medicines.

[20] Physician in Homer's *Iliad*.

[21] Juno supposedly conceived Hebe after eating lettuce.

[22] Actually White is quoting the first sentence of "Solitude," the fifth chapter of *Walden*. The essay is full of such sly allusions to Thoreau's work.

the sky had that same everlasting great look which you will find on Page 144 of the Oxford pocket edition. I could feel the road entering me, through tire, wheel, spring, and cushion; shall I not have intelligence with earth too? Am I not partly leaves and vegetable mold myself?—a man of infinite horsepower, yet partly leaves.

Stay with me on 62 and it will take you into Concord. As I say, it was a delicious evening. The snake had come forth to die in a bloody S on the highway, the wheel upon its head, its bowels flat now and exposed. The turtle had come up too to cross the road and die in the attempt, its hard shell smashed under the rubber blow, its intestinal yearning (for the other side of the road) forever squashed. There was a sign by the wayside which announced that the road had a "cotton surface." You wouldn't know what that is, but neither, for that matter, did I. There is a cryptic ingredient in many of our modern improvements—we are awed and pleased without knowing quite what we are enjoying. It is something to be traveling on a road with a cotton surface.

The civilization round Concord today is an odd distillation of city, village, farm, and manor. The houses, yards, fields look not quite suburban, not quite rural. Under the bronze beech and the blue spruce of the departed baron grazes the milch goat of the heirs. Under the porte-cochère stands the reconditioned station wagon; under the grape arbor sit the puppies for sale. But why do men degenerate ever? What makes families run out?)

It was June and everywhere June was publishing her immemorial stanza; in the lilacs, in the syringa, in the freshly edged paths and the sweetness of moist beloved gardens, and the little wire wickets that preserve the tulips' front. Farmers were already moving the fruits of their toil into their yards, arranging the rhubarb, the asparagus, the strictly fresh eggs on the painted stands under the little shed roofs with the patent shingles. And though it was almost a hundred years since you had taken your ax and started cutting out your home on Walden Pond, I was interested to observe that the philosophical spirit was still alive in Massachusetts: in the center of a vacant lot some boys were assembling the framework of a rude shelter, their whole mind and skill concentrated in the rather inauspicious helter-skeleton of studs and rafters. They too were escaping from town, to live naturally, in a rich blend of savagery and philosophy.

That evening, after supper at the inn, I strolled out into the twilight to dream my shapeless transcendental dreams and see that the car was locked up for the night (first open the right front door, then reach over, straining, and pull up the handles of the left rear and the left front till you hear the click, then the handle of the right rear, then shut the right front but open it again, remembering that the key is still in the ignition switch, remove the key, shut the right front again with a bang, push the tiny keyhole cover to one side, insert key, turn, and withdraw). It is what we all do, Henry. It is called locking the car. It is said to confuse thieves and keep them from making off with the laprobe. Four doors to lock behind one robe. The driver himself never uses a laprobe, the free movement of his legs being vital to the operation of the vehicle; so that when he locks the car it is a pure and unselfish act. I have in my life gained very little essential heat from laprobes, yet I have ever been at pains to lock them up.

The evening was full of sounds, some of which would have stirred your memory. The robins still love the elms of New England villages at sundown. There is enough of the thrush in them to make song inevitable at the end of day, and enough of the tramp to make them hang round the dwellings of men. A robin, like many another American, dearly loves a white house with green blinds. Concord is still full of them.

Your fellow-townsmen were stirring abroad—not many afoot, most of them in their cars; and the sound which they made in Concord at evening was a rustling and a whispering. The sound lacks steadfastness and is wholly unlike that of a train. A train, as you know who lived so near the Fitchburg line, whistles once or twice sadly and is gone, trailing a memory in smoke, soothing to ear and mind. Automobiles, skirting a village green, are like flies that have gained the inner ear—they buzz, cease, pause, start, shift, stop, halt, brake, and the whole effect is a nervous polytone curiously disturbing.

As I wandered along, the toc toc of ping-pong balls drifted from an attic window. In front of the Reuben Brown house a Buick was drawn up. At the wheel, motionless, his hat upon his head, a man sat, listening to Amos and Andy on the radio (it is a drama of many scenes and without an end). The deep voice of Andrew Brown, emerging from the car, although it originated more than two hundred miles away, was unstrained by distance. When you used to sit on the shore of your pond on Sunday morning, listening to the church bells of Acton and Concord, you were aware of the excellent filter of the intervening atmosphere. Science has attended to that, and sound now maintains its intensity without regard for distance. Properly sponsored, it goes on forever.

A fire engine, out for a trial spin, roared past Emerson's house, hot with readiness for public duty. Over the barn roofs the martins dipped and chittered. A swarthy daughter of an asparagus grower, in culottes, shirt, and bandanna, pedalled past on her bicycle. It was indeed a delicious evening, and I returned to the inn (I believe it was your house once) to rock with the old ladies on the concrete veranda.

Next morning early I started afoot for Walden, out Main Street and down Thoreau, past the depot and the Minuteman Chevrolet Company. The morning was fresh, and in a bean field along the way I flushed an agriculturalist, quietly studying his beans. Thoreau Street soon joined Number 126, an artery of the State. We number our highways nowadays, our speed being so great we can remember little of their quality or character and are lucky to remember their number. (Men have an indistinct notion that if they keep up this activity long enough all will at length ride somewhere, in next to no time.) Your pond is on 126.

I knew I must be nearing your woodland retreat when the Golden Pheasant lunchroom came into view—Sealtest ice cream, toasted sandwiches, hot frankfurters, waffles, tonics, and lunches. Were I the proprietor, I should add rice, Indian meal, and molasses —just for old time's sake. The Pheasant. incidentally, is for sale: a chance for some nature lover who wishes to set himself up beside a pond in the Concord atmosphere and live deliberately, fronting only the essential facts of life on Number 126. Beyond the Pheasant was a place called Walden Breezes, an oasis whose porch pillars were made of old green shutters sawed into lengths. On the porch was a distorting mirror, to give the traveler a comical image of himself, who had miraculously learned to gaze in an ordinary glass without smiling. Behind the Breezes, in a sun-parched clearing, dwelt your philosophical descendants in their trailers, each trailer the size of your hut, but all grouped together for the sake of congeniality. Trailer people leave the city, as you did, to discover solitude and in any weather, at any hour of the day or night, to improve the nick of time; but they soon collect in villages and get bogged deeper in the mud than ever. The camp behind Walden Breezes was just rousing itself to the morning. The ground was packed hard under the heel, and the sun came through the clearing to bake the soil and enlarge the wry smell of cramped housekeeping. Cushman's bakery truck had stopped to deliver an early basket of rolls. A camp dog, seeing me in the road, barked petulantly. A man emerged from one of the trailers and set forth with a bucket to draw water from some forest tap.

Leaving the highway I turned off into the woods toward the pond, which was apparent through the foliage. The floor of the forest was strewn with dried old oak leaves and *Transcripts*.[23] From beneath the flattened popcorn wrapper (*granum explosum*) peeped the frail violet. I followed a footpath and descended to the water's edge. The pond lay clear and blue in the morning light, as you have seen it so many times. In the shallows a man's waterlogged shirt undulated gently. A few flies came out to greet me and convoy me to your cove, past the No Bathing signs on which the fellows and the girls had scrawled their names. I felt strangely excited suddenly to be snooping around your premises, tiptoeing along watchfully, as though not to tread by mistake upon the intervening century. Before I got to the cove I heard something which seemed to me quite wonderful: I heard your frog, a full, clear *troonk*, guiding me, still hoarse and solemn, bridging the years as the robins had bridged them in the sweetness of the village evening. But he soon quit, and I came on a couple of young boys throwing stones at him.

Your front yard is marked by a bronze tablet set in a stone. Four small granite posts, a few feet away, show where the house was. On top of the tablet was a pair of faded blue bathing trunks with a white stripe. Back of it is a pile of stones, a sort of cairn, left by your visitors as a tribute I suppose. It is a rather ugly little heap of stones, Henry. In fact the hillside itself seems faded, browbeaten; a few tall skinny pines bare of lower limbs, a smattering of young maples in suitable green, some birches and oaks, and a number of trees felled by the last big wind. It was from the bole of one of these fallen pines, torn up by

the roots, that I extracted the stone which I added to the cairn—a sentimental act in which I was interrupted by a small terrier from a nearby picnic group, who confronted me and wanted to know about the stone.

I sat down for a while on one of the posts of your house to listen to the bluebottles and the dragonflies. The invaded glade sprawled shabby and mean at my feet, but the flies were tuned to the old vibration. There were the remains of a fire in your ruins, but I doubt that it was yours; also two beer bottles trodden into the soil and become part of earth. A young oak had taken root in your house, and two or three ferns, unrolling like the ticklers at a banquet. The only other furnishings were a DuBarry pattern sheet, a page torn from a picture magazine, and some crusts in wax paper.

Before I quit I walked clear round the pond and found the place where you used to sit on the northeast side to get the sun in the fall, and the beach where you got sand for scrubbing your floor. On the eastern side of the pond, where the highway borders it, the State has built dressing rooms for swimmers, a float with diving towers, drinking fountains of porcelain, and rowboats for hire. The pond is in fact a State Preserve, and carries a twenty-dollar fine for picking wild flowers, a decree signed in all solemnity by your fellow citizens Walter C. Wardwell, Erson B. Barlow, and Nathaniel I. Bowditch. There was a smell of creosote where they had been building a wide wooden stairway to the road and the parking area. Swimmers and boaters were arriving; bodies plunged vigorously into the water and emerged wet and beautiful in the bright air. As I left, a boatload of town boys were splashing about in mid-pond, kidding and fooling, the young fellows singing at the tops of their lungs in a wild chorus:

Amer-ica, Amer-ica, God shed his grace on thee,
And crown thy good with brotherhood
From sea to shi-ning sea!

---

[23] I.e., copies of a Boston newspaper.

I walked back to town along the railroad, following your custom. The rails were expanding noisily in the hot sun, and on the slope of the roadbed the wild grape and the blackberry sent up their creepers to the track.

The expense of my brief sojourn in Concord was:

Canvas shoes $1.95
Baseball bat...... .25
Left-handed
   fielder's glove .. 1.25 } gifts to take back to a boy
Hotel and meals .. 4.24
_____
In all $7.70

As you see, this amount was almost what you spent for food for eight months. I cannot defend the shoes or the expenditure for shelter and food: they reveal a meanness and grossness in my nature which you would find contemptible. The baseball equipment, however, is the kind of impediment with which you were never on even terms. You must remember that the house where you practiced the sort of economy which I respect was haunted only by mice and squirrels. You never had to cope with a shortstop.

Henry Beston

THE HEADLONG WAVE

I

This morning I am going to try my hand at something that I do not recall ever having encountered either in a periodical or in a book, namely, a chapter on the ways, the forms, and the sounds of ocean near a beach. Friends are forever asking me about the surf on the great beach[24] and if I am not some-

24 The author's house, which he called The Fo'castle, stood on the outer shore of Cape Cod, Massachusetts, near the village of Eastham.

times troubled or haunted by its sound. To this I reply that I have grown unconscious of the roar, and though it sounds all day long in my waking ears, and all night long in my sleeping ones, my ears seldom send on the long tumult to the mind. I hear the roar the instant I wake in the morning and return to consciousness, I listen to it a while consciously, and then accept and forget it; I hear it during the day only when I stop again to listen, or when some change in the nature of the sound breaks through my acceptance of it to my curiosity.

They say here that great waves reach this coast in threes. Three great waves, then an indeterminate run of lesser rhythms, then three great waves again. On Celtic coasts it is the seventh wave that is seen coming like a king out of the grey, cold sea. The Cape tradition, however, is no half-real, half-mystical fancy, but the truth itself. Great waves do indeed approach this beach by threes. Again and again have I watched three giants roll in one after the other out of the Atlantic, cross the outer bar, break, form again, and follow each other into fulfilment and destruction on this solitary beach. Coast-guard crews are all well aware of this triple rhythm and take advantage of the lull that follows the last wave to launch their boats.

It is true that there are single giants as well. I have been roused by them in the night. Waked by their tremendous and unexpected crash, I have sometimes heard the last of the heavy overspill, sometimes only the loud, withdrawing roar. After the roar came a briefest pause, and after the pause the return of ocean to the night's long cadences. Such solitary titans, flinging their green tons down upon a quiet world, shake beach and dune. Late one September night, as I sat reading, the very father of all waves must have flung himself down before the house, for the quiet of the night was suddenly overturned by a gigantic, tumbling crash and an earthquake rumbling; the beach trembled beneath the avalanche, the dune shook, and my house so shook in its dune that the flame of a lamp quivered and pictures jarred on the wall.

The three great elemental sounds in nature are the sound of rain, the sound of wind in a primeval wood, and the sound of outer ocean on a beach. I have heard them all, and of the three elemental voices, that of ocean is the most awesome, beautiful, and varied. For it is a mistake to talk of the monotone of ocean or of the monotonous nature of its sound. The sea has many voices. Listen to the surf, really lend it your ears, and you will hear in it a world of sounds: hollow booming and heavy roarings, great watery tumblings and tramplings, long hissing seethes, sharp, rifle-shot reports, splashes, whispers, the grinding undertone of stones, and sometimes vocal sounds that might be the half-heard talk of people in the sea. And not only is the great sound varied in the manner of its making, it is also constantly changing its tempo, its pitch, its accent, and its rhythm, being now loud and thundering, now almost placid, now furious, now grave and solemn-slow, now a simple measure, now a rhythm monstrous with a sense of purpose and elemental will.

Every mood of the wind, every change in the day's weather, every phase of the tide— all these have subtle sea musics all their own. Surf of the ebb, for instance, is one music, surf of the flood another, the change in the two musics being most clearly marked during the first hour of a rising tide. With the renewal of the tidal energy, the sound of the surf grows louder, the fury of battle returns to it as it turns again on the land, and beat and sound change with the renewal of the war.

Sound of surf in these autumnal dunes— the continuousness of it, sound of endless charging, endless incoming and gathering, endless fulfilment and dissolution, endless fecundity, and endless death. I have been trying to study out the mechanics of that mighty resonance. The dominant note is the great spilling crash made by each arriving wave. It may be hollow and booming, it may be heavy and churning, it may be a tumbling roar. The second fundamental sound is the wild seething cataract roar of the wave's dissolution and the rush of its foaming waters up the beach—this second sound *diminuendo*. The third fundamental sound is the endless dissolving hiss of the inmost slides of foam. The first two sounds reach the ear as a unisonance—the booming impact of the tons of water and the wild roar of the up-rush blending—and this mingled sound dissolves into the foam-bubble hissing of the third. Above the tumult, like birds, fly wisps of watery noise, splashes and counter splashes, whispers, seethings, slaps, and chucklings. An overtone sound of other breakers, mingled with a general rumbling, fills earth and sea and air.

Here do I pause to warn my reader that although I have recounted the history of a breaker—an ideal breaker—the surf process must be understood as mingled and continuous, waves hurrying after waves, interrupting waves, washing back on waves, overwhelming waves. Moreover, I have described the sound of a high surf in fair weather. A storm surf is mechanically the same thing, but it *grinds*, and this same long, sepulchral grinding—sound of utter terror to all mariners—is a development of the second fundamental sound; it is the cry of the breaker water roaring its way ashore and dragging at the sand. A strange underbody of sound when heard through the high, wild screaming of a gale.

Breaking waves that have to run up a steep tilt of the beach are often followed by a dragging, grinding sound—the note of the baffled water running downhill again to the sea. It is loudest when the tide is low and breakers are rolling beach stones up and down a slope of the lower beach.

I am, perhaps, most conscious of the sound of surf just after I have gone to bed. Even here I read myself to drowsiness, and, reading, I hear the cadenced trampling roar filling all the dark. So close is the Fo'castle to the ocean's edge that the rhythm of sound I hear oftenest in fair weather is not so much a general tumult as an endless arrival, overspill, and dissolution of separate great seas. Through the dark, mathematic square of the screened half window, I listen to the rushes and the bursts, the tramplings, and the long, intermingled thunderings, never wearying of the sonorous and universal sound.

Away from the beach, the various sounds of the surf melt into one great thundering symphonic roar. Autumnal nights in Eastham village are full of this ocean sound. The "summer people" have gone, the village rests and prepares for winter, lamps shine from kitchen windows, and from across the moors, the great levels of the marsh, and the bulwark of the dunes resounds the long wintry roaring of the sea. Listen to it a while, and it will seem but one remote and formidable sound; listen still longer and you will discern in it a symphony of breaker thunderings, an endless, distant, elemental cannonade. There is beauty in it, and ancient terror. I heard it last as I walked through the village on a starry October night; there was no wind, the leafless trees were still, all the village was abed, and the whole sombre world was awesome with the sound.

II

The seas are the heart's blood of the earth. Plucked up and kneaded by the sun and the moon; the tides are systole and diastole of earth's veins.

The rhythm of waves beats in the sea like a pulse in living flesh. It is pure force, forever embodying itself in a succession of watery shapes which vanish on its passing.

I stand on my dune top watching a great wave coursing in from sea, and know that I am watching an illusion, that the distant water has not left its place in ocean to advance upon me, but only a force shaped in water, a bodiless pulse beat, a vibration.

Consider the marvel of what we see. Somewhere in ocean, perhaps a thousand miles and more from this beach, the pulse beat of earth liberates a vibration, an ocean wave. Is the original force circular, I wonder? and do ocean waves ring out from the creative beat as they do on a quiet surface broken by a stone? Are there, perhaps, ocean circles so great and so intricate that they are unperceived? Once created, the wave or the arc of a wave begins its journey through the sea. Countless vibrations precede it, countless vibrations follow after. It approaches the continent, swings into the coast line, courses ashore, breaks, dissolves, is gone. The innermost waters it last inhabited flow back in marbly foam to become a body to another beat, and to be again flung down. So it goes night and day, and will go till the secret heart of earth strikes out its last slow beat and the last wave dissolves upon the last forsaken shore.

As I stand on my dune top, however, I do not think of the illusion and the beat of earth, for I watch the waves with my outer rather than my inner eye. After all, the illusion is set off by an extraordinary, an almost miraculous thing—the embodiment of the wave beat in an almost constant shape. We see a wave a quarter of a mile off, then a few hundred yards nearer in, then just offshore; we seem to have been watching the same travelling mass of water—there has been no appreciable change in mass or in shape—yet all the while the original beat has taken on a flowing series of liquid bodies, bodies so alike, so much the same, that our eye will individualize them and follow them in—the third wave, we say, or the second wave behind the great wave. How strange it is that this beat of earth, this mysterious undulation of the seas, moving through and among the other forces stirring the waters close off the continent, should thus keep its constancy of form and mass, and how odd a blend of illusion and reality it all is! On the whole, the outer eye has the best of it.

Blowing all day long, a northwest wind yesterday swept the sky clear of every tatter and wisp of cloud. Clear it still is, though the wind has shifted to the east. The sky this afternoon is a harmony of universal blue, bordered with a surf rim of snowiest blue white. Far out at sea, in the northeast and near the horizon, is a pool of the loveliest blue I have ever seen here—a light blue, a petal blue, blue of the emperor's gown in a Chinese fairy tale. If you would see waves at their best, come on such a day, when the ocean reflects a lovely sky, and the wind is light and onshore; plan to arrive in the afternoon so that you will have the sun facing the breakers. Come early, for the glints on the waves are most beautiful and interesting when the light is oblique and high. And come with a rising tide.

The surf is high, and on the far side of it, a wave greater than its fellows is shouldering out of the blue, glinting immensity of sea.

Friends tell me that there are certain tropic beaches where waves miles long break all at once in one cannonading crash: a little of this, I imagine, would be magnificent; a constancy of it, unbearable. The surf here is broken; it approaches the beach in long intercurrent parallels, some a few hundred feet long, some an eighth of a mile long, some, and the longest, attaining the quarter-mile length and perhaps just over. Thus, at all times and instants of the day, along the five miles of beach visible from the Fo'castle deck, waves are to be seen breaking, coursing in to break, seething up and sliding back.

But to return to the blue wave rolling in out of the blue spaciousness of sea. On the other side of the world, just opposite the Cape, lies the ancient Spanish province of Galicia, and the town of Pontevedra and St. James Compostella, renowned of pilgrims. (When I was there they offered me a silver cockle shell, but I would have none of it, and got myself a sea shell from some Galician fisherfolk.) Somewhere between this Spanish land and Cape Cod the pulse of earth has engendered this wave and sent it coursing westward through the seas. Far off the coast, the spray of its passing has, perhaps, risen on the windward bow of some rusty freighter and fallen in rainbow drops upon her plates; the great liners have felt it course beneath their keels.

A continent rises in the west, and the pulse beat approaches this bulwark of Cape Cod. Two thirds of a mile out, the wave is still a sea vibration, a billow. Slice it across, and its outline will be that of a slightly flattened semicircle; the pulse is shaped in a long, advancing mound. I watch it approach the beach. Closer and closer in, it is rising with the rise of the beach and the shoaling of the water; closer still, it is changing from a mound to a pyramid, a pyramid which swiftly distorts, the seaward side lengthening, the landward side incurving—the wave is now a breaker. Along the ridge of blue forms a rippling crest of clear, bright water; a little spray flies off. Under the racing foam churned up by the dissolution of other breakers the beach now catches at the last shape of sea inhabited by the pulse—the wave is *tripped* by the shoaling sand—the giant stumbles, crashes, and is pushed over and ahead by the sloping line of force behind. The fall of a breaker is never the work of gravity alone.

It is the last line of the wave that has captured the decorative imagination of the world—the long seaward slope, the curling crest, the incurved volute ahead.

Toppling over and hurled ahead, the wave crashes, its mass of glinting blue falling down in a confusion of seething, splendid white, the tumbling water rebounding from the sand to a height almost always a little above that of the original crest. Out of the wild, crumbling confusion born of the dissolution of the force and the last great shape, foamy fountains spurt, and ringlets of spray. The mass of water, still all furiously a-churn and seething white, now rushes for the rim of the beach as it might for an inconceivable cataract. Within thirty-five feet the water shoals from two feet to dry land. The edge of the rush thins, and the last impulse disappears in inch-deep slides of foam which reflect the sky in one last moment of energy and beauty and then vanish all at once into the sands.

Another thundering, and the water that has escaped and withdrawn is gathered up and swept forward again by another breaking wave. Night and day, age after age, so works the sea, with infinite variation obeying an unalterable rhythm moving through an intricacy of chance and law.

I can watch a fine surf for hours, taking pleasure in all its wild plays and variations. I like to stand on my beach, watching a long wave start breaking in many places, and see the curling water run north and south from the several beginnings, and collide in furious white pyramids built of the opposing energies. Splendid fountains often delight the eye. A towering and deep-bellied wave, toppling, encloses in its volute a quantity of air, and a few seconds after the spill this prisoned and compressed vapor bursts up through the boiling rush in feathery, foamy jets and geyser plumes. I have seen fountains here, on a September day, twenty and twenty-five and even thirty feet high. Sometimes a curious thing happens. Instead of escaping vertically, the rolled-up air escapes horizontally, and the breaker suddenly blows, as from a dragon's mouth, a great lateral puff of steamy spray. On sunny days, the toppling crest is often mirrored in the glassy volute as the wave is breaking. One lovely autumn afternoon, I saw a beautiful white gull sailing along the volute of a breaker accompanied by his reflection in the wave.

I add one curious effect of the wind. When the wind is directly offshore or well offshore, the waves approach fighting it; when the wind is offshore but so little off that its angle with the coast line is oblique —say an angle never greater than twenty-two degrees and never less than about twelve— the waves that approach the coast do not give battle, but run in with their long axis parallel to the wind. Sitting in the Fo'castle, I can often tell the exact quarter of an offshore wind simply by looking at this oblique alignment of the waves.

The long miles of beach are never more beautiful that when waves are rolling in fighting a strong breeze. Then do the breakers actually seem to charge the coast. As they approach, the wind meets them in a shock of war, the chargers rear but go on, and the wind blows back their manes. North and south, I watch them coursing in, the manes of white, sun-brilliant spray streaming behind them for thirty and even forty feet. Sea horses do men call such waves on every coast of the world. If you would see them at their best, come to this beach on a bright October day when a northwest wind is billowing off to sea across the moors.

III

I will close my chapter with a few paragraphs about heavy surf.

It is best to be seen, I think, when the wind is not too high. A gale blows up a surf, but it also flattens out the incoming rollers, making monstrous, foamy travelling mounds of them much like those visible from a ship at sea. Not until the wind has dropped do the breakers gather form. The finest surf I have ever seen here—it was a northern recoil of the great Florida hurricane—broke on three pleasant and almost windless autumn days. The storm itself had passed us, but our seas had been stirred to their deeps. Returning to the Cape at night from a trip to town, I heard the roar of the ocean in

Orleans, and on arriving at Nauset, found the beach flooded to the dunes, and covered with a churn of surf and moonlight. Dragging a heavy suitcase and clad in my go-to-town clothes, I had an evil time getting to the Fo'castle over the dune tops and along the flooded marsh.

Many forces mingle in the surf of a storm —the great earth rhythm of the waves, the violence of wind, the struggle of water to obey its own elemental law. Out of the storm at sea come the giants and, being giants, trip far out, spilling first on the outer bar. Shoreward then they rush, breaking all the way. Touching the beach, they tumble in a roar lost in a general noise of storm. Trampled by the wind and everlastingly moved and lifted up and flung down by the incoming seas, the water offshore becomes a furious glassiness of marbly foam; wild, rushing sheets of seethe fifty feet wide border it; the water streams with sand.

Under all this move furious tidal currents, the longshore undertow of outer Cape Cod. Shore currents here move in a southerly direction; old wreckage and driftwood is forever being carried down here from the north. Coast guard friends often look at a box or stick I have retrieved, and say, "Saw that two weeks ago up by the light."

After an easterly, I find things on the beach which have been blown from the Gulf of Maine—young, uprooted spruce trees, lobster buoys from Matinicus, and, after one storm, a great strewing of empty sea-urchin shells. Another easterly washed up a strewing of curious wooden pebbles shaped by the sea out of the ancient submerged forests which lie just off the present coast. They were brown-black, shaped like beach stones, and as smooth as such stones.

The last creature I found in the surf was a huge horseshoe crab, the only one I have ever chanced to find on the outside. Poor *Limulus polyphemus!* The surf having turned him upside down, he had as usual doubled up, and the surf had then filled

with sand the angle of his doubling. When I discovered him, he was being bullied by a foam slide, and altogether in a desperate way. So I picked him up, rinsed the sand out of his waving gills, held him up all dripping by the tail, and flung him as far as I could to seaward of the breakers. A tiny splash, and I had seen the last of him, a moment more, and the surf had filled the hollow in which he had lain.

Autumnal easterlies and November tides having scoured from the beach its summer deeps of sand, the high seasonal tides now run clear across to the very foot of the dunes. Under this daily overflow of cold, the last of the tide-rim hoppers and foragers vanish from the beach. An icy wind blusters; I hear a dry tinkle of sand against my western wall; December nears, and winter closes in upon the coast.

Rachel Carson

NATURE FIGHTS BACK

To have risked so much in our efforts to mold nature to our satisfaction and yet to have failed in achieving our goal would indeed be the final irony. Yet this, it seems, is our situation. The truth, seldom mentioned but there for anyone to see, is that nature is not so easily molded and that the insects are finding ways to circumvent our chemical attacks on them.

"The insect world is nature's most astonishing phenomenon," said the Dutch biologist C. J. Briejèr. "Nothing is impossible to it; the most improbable things commonly occur there. One who penetrates deeply into its mysteries is continually breathless with wonder. He knows that anything can happen, and that the completely impossible often does."

The "impossible" is now happening on

two broad fronts. By a process of genetic selection, the insects are developing strains
resistant to chemicals. . . . But the broader
problem, which we shall look at now, is that
our chemical attack is weakening the defenses inherent in the environment itself,
defenses designed to keep the various species
in check. Each time we breach these defenses
a horde of insects pours through.

From all over the world come reports that
make it clear we are in a serious predicament. At the end of a decade or more of intensive chemical control, entomologists were
finding that problems they had considered
solved a few years earlier had returned to
plague them. And new problems had arisen
as insects once present only in insignificant
numbers had increased to the status of serious pests. By their very nature chemical
controls are self-defeating, for they have
been devised and applied without taking
into account the complex biological systems
against which they have been blindly
hurled. The chemicals may have been pre-
tested against a few individual species, but
not against living communities.

In some quarters nowadays it is fashionable to dismiss the balance of nature as a
state of affairs that prevailed in an earlier,
simpler world—a state that has now been so
thoroughly upset that we might as well forget it. Some find this a convenient assumption, but as a chart for a course of action it is
highly dangerous. The balance of nature is
not the same today as in Pleistocene times,
but it is still there: a complex, precise, and
highly integrated system of relationships between living things which cannot safely be
ignored any more than the law of gravity can
be defied with impunity by a man perched
on the edge of a cliff. The balance of nature
is not a *status quo;* it is fluid, ever shifting,
in a constant state of adjustment. Man, too, is
part of this balance. Sometimes the balance
is in his favor; sometimes—and all too often
through his own activities—it is shifted to
his disadvantage.

Two critically important facts have been
overlooked in designing the modern insect-
control programs. The first is that the really
effective control of insects is that applied by
nature, not by man. Populations are kept in
check by something the ecologists call the resistance of the environment, and this has
been so since the first life was created. The
amount of food available, conditions of
weather and climate, the presence of com-
peting or predatory species, all are critically
important. "The greatest single factor in preventing insects from overwhelming the rest
of the world is the internecine warfare which
they carry out among themselves," said the
entomologist Robert Metcalf. Yet most of
the chemicals now used kill all insects, our
friends and enemies alike.

The second neglected fact is the truly explosive power of a species to reproduce once
the resistance of the environment has been
weakened. The fecundity of many forms of
life is almost beyond our power to imagine,
though now and then we have suggestive
glimpses. I remember from student days the
miracle that could be wrought in a jar containing a simple mixture of hay and water
merely by adding to it a few drops of material from a mature culture of protozoa. Within a few days the jar would contain a whole
galaxy of whirling, darting life—uncount-
able trillions of the slipper animalcule,
Paramecium, each small as a dust grain,
all multiplying without restraint in their
temporary Eden of favorable temperatures,
abundant food, absence of enemies. Or I
think of shore rocks white with barnacles as
far as the eye can see, or of the spectacle of
passing through an immense school of jelly-
fish, mile after mile, with seemingly no end
to the pulsing, ghostly forms scarcely more
substantial than the water itself.

We see the miracle of nature's control at
work when the cod move through winter
seas to their spawning grounds, where each
female deposits several millions of eggs. The
sea does not become a solid mass of cod as it

would surely do if all the progeny of all the cod were to survive. The checks that exist in nature are such that out of the millions of young produced by each pair only enough, on the average, survive to adulthood to replace the parent fish.

Biologists used to entertain themselves by speculating as to what would happen if, through some unthinkable catastrophe, the natural restraints were thrown off and all the progeny of a single individual survived. Thus Thomas Huxley a century ago calculated that a single female aphis (which has the curious power of reproducing without mating) could produce progeny in a single year's time whose total weight would equal that of the inhabitants of the Chinese empire of his day.

Fortunately for us such an extreme situation is only theoretical, but the dire results of upsetting nature's own arrangements are well known to students of animal populations. The stockman's zeal for eliminating the coyote has resulted in plagues of field mice, which the coyote formerly controlled. The oft-repeated story of the Kaibab deer in Arizona is another case in point. At one time the deer population was in equilibrium with its environment. A number of predators—wolves, pumas, and coyotes—prevented the deer from outrunning their food supply. Then a campaign was begun to "conserve" the deer by killing off their enemies. Once the predators were gone, the deer increased prodigiously and soon there was not enough food for them. The browse line on the trees went higher and higher as they sought food, and in time many more deer were dying of starvation than had formerly been killed by predators. The whole environment, moreover, was damaged by their desperate efforts to find food.

The predatory insects of field and forests play the same role as the wolves and coyotes of the Kaibab. Kill them off and the population of the prey insect surges upward.

No one knows how many species of insects inhabit the earth because so many are yet to be identified. But more than 700,000 have already been described. This means that in terms of the number of species, 70 to 80 per cent of the earth's creatures are insects. The vast majority of these insects are held in check by natural forces, without any intervention by man. If this were not so, it is doubtful that any conceivable volume of chemicals—or any other methods—could possibly keep down their populations.

The trouble is that we are seldom aware of the protection afforded by natural enemies until it fails. Most of us walk unseeing through the world, unaware alike of its beauties, its wonders, and the strange and sometimes terrible intensity of the lives that are being lived about us. So it is that the activities of the insect predators and parasites are known to few. Perhaps we may have noticed an oddly shaped insect of ferocious mien on a bush in the garden and been dimly aware that the praying mantis lives at the expense of other insects. But we see with understanding eye only if we have walked in the garden at night and here and there with a flashlight have glimpsed the mantis stealthily creeping upon her prey. Then we sense something of the drama of the hunter and the hunted. Then we begin to feel something of that relentlessly pressing force by which nature controls her own.

The predators—insects that kill and consume other insects—are of many kinds. Some are quick and with the speed of swallows snatch their prey from the air. Others plod methodically along a stem, plucking off and devouring sedentary insects like the aphids. The yellowjackets capture soft-bodied insects and feed the juices to their young. Muddauber wasps build columned nests of mud under the eaves of houses and stock them with insects on which their young will feed. The horseguard wasp hovers above herds of grazing cattle, destroying the blood-sucking flies that torment them. The loudly buzzing syrphid fly, often mistaken for a bee, lays its eggs on leaves of aphis-infested plants; the hatching larvae then consume immense numbers of aphids. Ladybugs or lady beetles are among the most effective destroyers of aphids, scale insects, and other plant-eating insects. Literally hundreds of aphids are consumed by a single ladybug to stoke the little fires of energy which she requires to produce even a single batch of eggs.

Even more extraordinary in their habits are the parasitic insects. These do not kill their hosts outright. Instead, by a variety of adaptations they utilize their victims for the nurture of their own young. They may deposit their eggs within the larvae or eggs of their prey, so that their own developing young may find food by consuming the host. Some attach their eggs to a caterpillar by means of a sticky solution; on hatching, the larval parasite bores through the skin of the host. Others, led by an instinct that simulates foresight, merely lay their eggs on a leaf so that a browsing caterpillar will eat them inadvertently.

Everywhere, in field and hedgerow and garden and forest, the insect predators and parasites are at work. Here, above a pond, the dragonflies dart and the sun strikes fire from their wings. So their ancestors sped through swamps where huge reptiles lived. Now, as in those ancient times, the sharp-eyed dragonflies capture mosquitoes in the air, scooping them in with basket-shaped legs. In the waters below, their young, the dragonfly nymphs, or naiads, prey on the aquatic stages of mosquitoes and other insects.

Or there, almost invisible against a leaf, is the lacewing, with green gauze wings and golden eyes, shy and secretive, descendant of an ancient race that lived in Permian times. The adult lacewing feeds mostly on plant nectars and the honeydew of aphids, and in time she lays her eggs, each on the end of a long stalk which she fastens to a leaf. From these emerge her children—strange, bristled larvae called aphis lions, which live by preying on aphids, scales, or mites, which they capture and suck dry of fluid. Each may consume several hundred aphids before the ceaseless turning of the cycle of its life brings the time when it will spin a white silken cocoon in which to pass the pupal stage.

And there are many wasps, and flies as well, whose very existence depends on the destruction of the eggs or larvae of other insects through parasitism. Some of the egg parasites are exceedingly minute wasps, yet by their numbers and their great activity they hold down the abundance of many crop-destroying species.

All these small creatures are working—working in sun and rain, during the hours of darkness, even when winter's grip has damped down the fires of life to mere embers. Then this vital force is merely smoldering, awaiting the time to flare again into activity when spring awakens the insect world. Meanwhile, under the white blanket of snow, below the frost-hardened soil, in crevices in the bark of trees, and in sheltered caves, the parasites and the predators have found ways to tide themselves over the season of cold.

The eggs of the mantis are secure in little cases of thin parchment attached to the branch of a shrub by the mother who lived her life span with the summer that is gone.

The female *Polistes* wasp, taking shelter in a forgotten corner of some attic, carries in her body the fertilized eggs, the heritage on which the whole future of her colony depends. She, the lone survivor, will start a small paper nest in the spring, lay a few eggs in its cells, and carefully rear a small force of workers. With their help she will then enlarge the nest and develop the colony. Then the workers, foraging ceaselessly through the hot days of summer, will destroy countless caterpillars.

Thus, through the circumstances of their lives, and the nature of our own wants, all these have been our allies in keeping the balance of nature tilted in our favor. Yet we have turned our artillery against our friends. The terrible danger is that we have grossly underestimated their value in keeping at bay a dark tide of enemies that, without their help, can overrun us.

The prospect of a general and permanent lowering of environmental resistance becomes grimly and increasingly real with each passing year as the number, variety, and destructiveness of insecticides grows. With the passage of time we may expect progressively more serious outbreaks of insects, both disease-carrying and crop-destroying species, in excess of anything we have ever known.

"Yes, but isn't this all theoretical?" you may ask. "Surely it won't really happen—not in my lifetime, anyway."

But it is happening, here and now. Scientific journals had already recorded some fifty species involved in violent dislocations of nature's balance by 1958. More examples are being found every year. A recent review of the subject contained references to 215 papers reporting or discussing unfavorable upsets in the balance of insect populations caused by pesticides.

Sometimes the result of chemical spraying has been a tremendous upsurge of the very insect the spraying was intended to control, as when blackflies in Ontario became seventeen times more abundant after spraying than they had been before. Or when in England an enormous outbreak of the cabbage aphid—an outbreak that had no parallel on record—followed spraying with one of the organic phosphorus chemicals.

At other times spraying, while reasonably effective against the target insect, has let loose a whole Pandora's box of destructive pests that had never previously been abundant enough to cause trouble. The spider mite, for example, has become practically a worldwide pest as DDT and other insecticides have killed off its enemies. The spider mite is not an insect. It is a barely visible eight-legged creature belonging to the group that includes spiders, scorpions, and ticks. It has mouth parts adapted for piercing and sucking, and a prodigious appetite for the chlorophyll that makes the world green. It inserts these minute and stiletto-sharp mouth parts into the outer cells of leaves and evergreen needles and extracts the chlorophyll. A mild infestation gives trees and shrubbery a mottled or salt-and-pepper appearance; with a heavy mite population, foliage turns yellow and falls.

This is what happened in some of the western national forests a few years ago, when in 1956 the United States Forest Service sprayed some 885,000 acres of forested lands with DDT. The intention was to control the spruce budworm, but the following summer it was discovered that a problem worse than the budworm damage had been created. In surveying the forests from the air, vast blighted areas could be seen where the magnificent Douglas firs were turning brown and dropping their needles. In the Helena National Forest and on the western slopes of the Big Belt Mountains, then in other areas of Montana and down into Idaho the forests looked as though they had been scorched. It was evident that this summer of 1957 had brought the most extensive and spectacular infestation of spider mites in history. Almost all of the sprayed area was affected. Nowhere else was the damage evident. Searching for precedents, the foresters could remember other scourges of spider mites, though less dramatic than this one. There had been similar trouble along the Madison River in Yellowstone Park in 1929, in Colorado twenty years later, and then in New Mexico in 1956. *Each of these outbreaks had followed forest spraying with insecticides.* (The 1929 spraying, occurring before the DDT era, employed lead arsenate.)

Why does the spider mite appear to thrive on insecticides? Besides the obvious fact that it is relatively insensitive to them, there seem to be two other reasons. In nature it is kept in check by various predators such as ladybugs, a gall midge, predaceous mites, and several pirate bugs, all of them extremely sensitive to insecticides. The third reason has to do with population pressure within the spider mite colonies. An undisturbed colony of mites is a densely settled community, huddled under a protective concealment from its enemies. When sprayed, the colonies disperse as the mites, irritated though not killed by the chemicals, scatter out in search of places where they will not be disturbed. In so doing they find a far greater abundance of space and food than was available in the former colonies. Their enemies are now dead, so there is no need for the mites to spend their energy in secreting protective webbing. Instead, they pour all their energies into producing more mites. It is not uncommon for the egg production to be increased threefold—all through the beneficent effect of insecticides.

In the Shenandoah Valley of Virginia, a famous apple-growing region, hordes of a small insect called the red-banded leaf roller arose to plague the growers as soon as DDT began to replace arsenate of lead. Its depredations had never before been important; soon its toll rose to 50 per cent of the crop and it achieved the status of the most destructive pest of apples, not only in this region but throughout much of the East and Midwest, as the use of DDT increased.

The situation abounds in ironies. In the apple orchards of Nova Scotia in the late 1940's the worst infestations of the codling moth (cause of "wormy apples") were in the orchards regularly sprayed. In unsprayed orchards the moths were not abundant enough to cause real trouble.

Diligence in spraying had a similarly unsatisfactory reward in the eastern Sudan, where cotton growers had a bitter experience with DDT. Some 60,000 acres of cotton were being grown under irrigation in the Gash Delta. Early trials of DDT having

given apparently good results, spraying was intensified. It was then that trouble began. One of the most destructive enemies of cotton is the bollworm. But the more cotton was sprayed, the more bollworms appeared. The unsprayed cotton suffered less damage to fruits and later to mature bolls than the sprayed, and in twice-sprayed fields the yield of seed cotton dropped significantly. Although some of the leaf-feeding insects were eliminated, any benefit that might thus have been gained was more than offset by bollworm damage. In the end the growers were faced with the unpleasant truth that their cotton yield would have been greater had they saved themselves the trouble and expense of spraying.

In the Belgian Congo and Uganda the results of heavy applications of DDT against an insect pest of the coffee bush were almost "catastrophic." The pest itself was found to be almost completely unaffected by the DDT, while its predator was extremely sensitive.

In America, farmers have repeatedly traded one insect enemy for a worse one as spraying upsets the population dynamics of the insect world. Two of the mass-spraying programs recently carried out have had precisely this effect. One was the fire ant eradication program in the South; the other was the spraying for the Japanese beetle in the Midwest.

When a wholesale application of heptachlor was made to the farmlands in Louisiana in 1957, the result was the unleashing of one of the worst enemies of the sugarcane crop—the sugarcane borer. Soon after the heptachlor treatment, damage by borers increased sharply. The chemical aimed at the fire ant had killed off the enemies of the borer. The crop was so severely damaged that farmers sought to bring suit against the state for negligence in not warning them that this might happen.

The same bitter lesson was learned by Illinois farmers. After the devastating bath of dieldrin recently administered to the farmlands in eastern Illinois for the control of the Japanese beetle, farmers discovered that corn borers had increased enormously in the treated area. In fact, corn grown in fields within this area contained almost twice as many of the destructive larvae of this insect as did the corn grown outside. The farmers may not yet be aware of the biological basis of what has happened, but they need no scientists to tell them they have made a poor bargain. In trying to get rid of one insect, they have brought on a scourge of a much more destructive one. According to Department of Agriculture estimates, total damage by the Japanese beetle in the United States adds up to about 10 million dollars a year, while damage by the corn borer runs to about 85 million.

It is worth noting that natural forces had been heavily relied on for control of the corn borer. Within two years after this insect was accidentally introduced from Europe in 1917, the United States Government had mounted one of its most intensive programs for locating and importing parasites of an insect pest. Since that time twenty-four species of parasites of the corn borer have been brought in from Europe and the Orient at considerable expense. Of these, five are recognized as being of distinct value in control. Needless to say, the results of all this work are now jeopardized as the enemies of the corn borer are killed off by the sprays.

If this seems absurd, consider the situation in the citrus groves of California, where the world's most famous and successful experiment in biological control was carried out in the 1880's. In 1872 a scale insect that feeds on the sap of citrus trees appeared in California and within the next fifteen years developed into a pest so destructive that the fruit crop in many orchards was a complete loss. The young citrus industry was threatened with destruction. Many farmers gave up and pulled out their trees. Then a parasite of the scale insect was imported from Australia, a small lady beetle called the vedalia. Within only two years after the first shipment of the beetles, the scale was under complete control throughout the citrus-growing sections of California. From that time on one could search for days among the orange groves without finding a single scale insect.

Then in the 1940's the citrus growers began to experiment with glamorous new chemicals against other insects. With the advent of DDT and the even more toxic chemicals to follow, the populations of the vedalia in many sections of California were wiped out. Its importation had cost the government a mere $5,000. Its activities had saved the fruit growers several millions of dollars a year, but in a moment of heedlessness the benefit was canceled out. Infestations of the scale insect quickly reappeared and damage exceeded anything that had been seen for fifty years.

"This possibly marked the end of an era," said Dr. Paul DeBach of the Citrus Experiment Station in Riverside. Now control of the scale has become enormously complicated. The vedalia can be maintained only by repeated releases and by the most careful attention to spray schedules, to minimize their contact with insecticides. And regardless of what the citrus growers do, they are more or less at the mercy of the owners of adjacent acreages, for severe damage has been done by insecticidal drift.

All these examples concern insects that attack agricultural crops. What of those that carry disease? There have already been warnings. On Nissan Island in the South Pacific, for example, spraying had been carried on intensively during the Second World War, but was stopped when hostilities came to an end. Soon swarms of malaria-carrying mosquitos reinvaded the island. All of its predators had been killed off and there had not been time for new populations to become established. The way was therefore clear for a tremendous population explosion. Marshall Laird, who has described this incident, compares chemical control to a treadmill; once we have set foot on it we are unable to stop for fear of the consequences.

In some parts of the world disease can be linked with spraying in quite a different way. For some reason, snail-like mollusks seem to be almost immune to the effects of insecticides. This has been observed many times. In the general holocaust that followed the spraying of salt marshes in eastern Florida, aquatic snails alone survived. The scene as described was a macabre picture—something that might have been created by a surrealist brush. The snails moved among the bodies of the dead fishes and the moribund crabs, devouring the victims of the death rain of poison.

But why is this important? It is important because many aquatic snails serve as hosts of dangerous parasitic worms that spend part of their life cycle in a mollusk, part in a human being. Examples are the blood flukes, or schistosoma, that cause serious disease in man when they enter the body by way of drinking water or through the skin when people are bathing in infested waters. The flukes are released into the water by the host snails. Such diseases are especially prevalent in parts of Asia and Africa. Where they occur, insect-control measures that favor a vast increase of snails are likely to be followed by grave consequences.

And of course man is not alone in being subject to snail-borne disease. Liver disease in cattle, sheep, goats, deer, elk, rabbits, and various other warm-blooded animals may be caused by liver flukes that spend parts of their life cycles in fresh-water snails. Livers infested with these worms are unfit for use as human food and are routinely condemned. Such rejections cost American cattlemen about three and one-half million dollars annually. Anything that acts to increase the number of snails can obviously make this problem an even more serious one.

Over the past decade these problems have cast long shadows, but we have been slow to recognize them. Most of those best fitted to develop natural controls and assist in putting them into effect have been too busy laboring in the more exciting vineyards of chemical control. It was reported in 1960 that only two per cent of all the economic entomologists in the country were then working in the field of biological controls. A substantial number of the remaining ninety-eight per cent were engaged in research on chemical insecticides.

Why should this be? The major chemical companies are pouring money into the universities to support research on insecticides. This creates attractive fellowships for graduate students and attractive staff positions. Biological-control studies, on the other hand, are never so endowed—for the simple reason that they do not promise anyone the fortunes that are to be made in the chemical industry. These are left to state and federal agencies, where the salaries paid are far less.

This situation also explains the otherwise mystifying fact that certain outstanding entomologists are among the leading advocates of chemical control. Inquiry into the background of some of these men reveals that their entire research program is supported by the chemical industry. Their professional prestige, sometimes their very jobs depend on the perpetuation of chemical methods. Can we then expect them to bite the hand that literally feeds them? But knowing their bias, how much credence can we give to their protests that insecticides are harmless?

Amid the general acclaim for chemicals as the principal method of insect control, minority reports have occasionally been filed by those few entomologists who have not lost sight of the fact that they are neither chemists nor engineers, but biologists.

F. H. Jacob in England has declared that "the activities of many so-called economic entomologists would make it appear that they operate in the belief that salvation lies at the end of a spray nozzle . . . that when they have created problems of resurgence or resistance or mammalian toxicity, the chemist will be ready with another pill. That view is not held here . . . Ultimately only the biologist will provide the answers to the basic problems of pest control."

"Economic entomologists must realize," wrote A. D. Pickett of Nova Scotia, "that they are dealing with living things . . . their work must be more than simply insecticide testing or a quest for highly destructive chemicals." Dr. Pickett himself was a pioneer in the field of working out sane methods of insect control that take full advantage of the predatory and parasitic species. The method which he and his associates evolved is today a shining model but one too little emulated. Only in the integrated control programs developed by some California entomologists do we find anything comparable in this country.

Dr. Pickett began his work some thirty-five years ago in the apple orchards of the Annapolis Valley in Nova Scotia, once one of the most concentrated fruit-growing areas in Canada. At that time it was believed that insecticides—then inorganic chemicals—would solve the problems of insect control, that the only task was to induce fruit growers to follow the recommended methods. But the rosy picture failed to materialize. Somehow the insects persisted. New chemicals were added, better spraying equipment was devised, and the zeal for spraying increased, but the insect problem did not get any better. Then DDT promised to "obliterate the nightmare" of codling moth outbreaks. What actually resulted from its use was an unprecedented scourge of mites. "We move from crisis to crisis,

merely trading one problem for another," said Dr. Pickett.

At this point, however, Dr. Pickett and his associates struck out on a new road instead of going along with other entomologists who continued to pursue the will-o'-the-wisp of the ever more toxic chemical. Recognizing that they had a strong ally in nature, they devised a program that makes maximum use of natural controls and minimum use of insecticides. Whenever insecticides are applied, only minimum dosages are used— barely enough to control the pest without avoidable harm to beneficial species. Proper timing also enters in. Thus, if nicotine sulphate is applied before rather than after the apple blossoms turn pink one of the important predators is spared, probably because it is still in the egg stage.

Dr. Pickett uses special care to select chemicals that will do as little harm as possible to insect parasites and predators. "When we reach the point of using DDT, parathion, chlordane, and other new insecticides as routine control measures in the same way as we have used the inorganic chemicals in the past, entomologists interested in biological control may as well throw in the sponge," he says. Instead of these highly toxic, broad-spectrum insecticides, he places chief reliance on ryania (derived from ground stems of a tropical plant), nicotine sulphate, and lead arsenate. In certain situations very weak concentrations of DDT or malathion are used (one or two ounces per hundred gallons—in contrast to the usual one or two pounds per hundred gallons). Although these two are the least toxic of the modern insecticides, Dr. Pickett hopes by further research to replace them with safer and more selective materials.

How well has this program worked? Nova Scotia orchardists who are following Dr. Pickett's modified spray program are producing as high a proportion of first-grade fruit as are those who are using intensive chemical applications. They are also getting as good production. They are getting these results, moreover, at a substantially lower cost. The outlay for insecticides in Nova Scotia apple orchards is only from ten to twenty per cent of the amount spent in most other apple-growing areas.

More important than even these excellent results is the fact that the modified program worked out by these Nova Scotian entomologists is not doing violence to nature's balance. It is well on the way to realizing the philosophy stated by the Canadian entomologist G. C. Ullyett a decade ago: "We must change our philosophy, abandon our attitude of human superiority, and admit that in many cases in natural environments we find ways and means of limiting populations of organisms in a more economical way than we can do it ourselves."

Franklin Russell

A MADNESS OF NATURE

Beyond the northern beach, a gray swell rolls in from Greenland and runs softly along the shore. The horizon is lost in a world of gray, and gulls glide, spectral in the livid air. Watching, I am enveloped in the sullen waiting time and feel the silence, drawn out long and thin. I wait for the sea to reveal a part of itself.

A capelin is perhaps the best-hunted creature on earth. It is not more than five inches long, about the size of a young herring, and undistinguished in appearance, except that when it is freshly caught, it is the color of mercury. As the capelin dies, its silvery scales tarnish and the glitter goes out like a light, ending a small allegory about nature, a spectacle of victims, victors, and an imperative of existence. Its death illuminates a dark process of biology in which there are shadows of other, more complex lives.

The capelin are born to be eaten. They transform oceanic plankton into flesh which is then hunted greedily by almost every sea creature that swims or flies. Their only protection is fecundity. One capelin survives to adulthood from every ten thousand eggs laid, and yet a single school may stir square miles of sea.

In mid-June, the capelin gather offshore. They can be seen everywhere and at all times in history, symbols of summer and fertility, of Providence and danger. I see them along the shores of Greenland, Iceland, Norway, and near Spitsbergen. I follow them across the northern coast of Russia. Chill air, gray seas, the northern silence are the capelin's world in Alaska, in the Aleutians, around Hudson Bay, and along the northeastern shores of North America. But the capelin of the Newfoundland coast are the most visible. Here, they spawn on the beaches rather than in deep water offshore, and I have come to see their rush for eternity.

They gather a thousand feet offshore, coalescing into groups of a hundred thousand to break the water's surface with bright chuckling sounds. They gather, and grow. Soon they are in the millions, with other millions swimming up from the offshore deeps. They gather, now in the billions, so densely packed together in places that the sea shimmers silver for miles and flows, serpentine, with the swelling body of a single, composite creature.

The fish do, in fact, possess a common sense of purpose. Nothing can redirect their imperative to breed. I once swam among them and saw them parting reluctantly ahead of me, felt their bodies flicking against my hands. Looking back, I saw them closing in, filling up the space created by my passage. The passive fish tolerated me, in their anticipation of what they were about to do.

At this time of the year they are so engrossed that they barely react when a host of creatures advances to kill them. Beneath and beyond them, codfish pour up out of the deep. They overtake the capelin, eat them, plunge their sleek, dark bodies recklessly into shallow water. Some have swum so rapidly from such depths that their swim bladders are distended by the sudden drop in water pressure. The cod are gigantic by comparison with the capelin. Many weigh one hundred pounds or more, and will not be sated until they have eaten scores of capelin each. The water writhes with movement and foam where cod, headlong in pursuit, drive themselves clear out of the sea and fall back with staccato slaps.

The attack of the codfish is a brutal opening to a ritual, and a contradiction in their character. Normally, they are sedentary feeders on the sea floor. Now, however, they are possessed. Their jaws rip and tear; the water darkens with capelin blood: the shredded pieces of flesh hang suspended or rise to the surface.

Now a group of seabirds, the parrotlike puffins, clumsy in flight, turn over the capelin, their grotesque, axlike beaks probing from side to side as they watch the upper layers of the massacre. They are joined by new formations of birds until several thousand puffins are circling. They are silent, and there is no way of knowing how they were summoned from their nesting burrows on an island that is out of sight. They glide down to the water—stub-winged cargo planes—land awkwardly, taxi with fluttering wings and stamping paddle feet, then dive.

At the same time, the sea view moves with new invasions of seabirds. Each bird pumps forward with an urgency that suggests it has received the same stimulus as the cod. The gulls that breed on cliffs along a southern bay come first, gracefully light of wing, with raucous voice as they cry out their anticipation. Beneath them, flying flat, direct, silent, come murres, black-bodied, short-tailed, close relatives of the puffins. The murres

land and dive without ceremony. Well offshore, as though waiting confirmation of the feast, shearwaters from Tristan da Cunha turn long, pointed wings across the troughs of waves and cackle like poultry.

The birds converge, and lose their identity in the mass thickening on the water. Small gulls—the kittiwakes, delicate in flight—screech and drop and rise and screech and drop like snowflakes on the sea. They fall among even smaller birds, lighter than they, which dangle their feet and hover at the water's surface, almost walking on water as they seek tiny pieces of shredded flesh. These are the ocean-flying petrels, the Mother Carey's chickens of mariners' legends, which rarely come within sight of land. All order is lost in the shrieking tumult of the hundreds of thousands of birds.

Underwater, the hunters meet among their prey. The puffins and murres dive below the capelin and attack, driving for the surface. The cod attack at mid-depth. The gulls smother the surface and press the capelin back among the submarine hunters. The murres and puffins fly underwater, their beating wings turning them rapidly back and forth. They meet the cod, flail wings in desperate haste, are caught, crushed, and swallowed. Now seabirds as well as capelin become the hunted. Puffin and murre tangle wings. Silver walls of capelin flicker, part, re-form. Some seabirds surface abruptly, broken wings dangling. Others, with a leg or legs torn off, fly frantically, crash, skitter in shock across the water.

I see the capelin hunters spread across the sea, but also remember them in time. Each year the hunters are different because many of them depend on a fortuitous meeting with their prey. A group of small whales collides with the capelin, and in a flurry of movement they eat several tons of them. Salmon throw themselves among the capelin with the same abandon as the codfish, and in the melee become easy victims for a score of seals that kill dozens of them, then turn to the capelin and gorge themselves nearly stuporous. They rise, well beyond the tumult of the seabirds, their black heads jutting like rocks from the swell, to lie with distended bellies and doze away their feast. Capelin boil up around them for a moment but now the animals ignore them.

The capelin are hosts in a ceremony so ancient that a multitude of species have adapted to seeking a separate share of the host's bounty. The riotous collision of cod, seal, whale, and seabird obscures the smaller guests at the feast. Near the shore wait small brown fish—the cunner—one of the most voracious species. Soon they will be fighting among themselves for pieces of flesh as the capelin begin their run for the beach, or when the survivors of the spawning reel back into deep water, with the dead and dying falling to the bottom. If the water is calm and the sun bright, the cunner can be seen in two fathoms, ripping capelin corpses to pieces and scattering translucent scales like silver leaves in a wind of the sea.

Closer inshore, at the wave line, the flounder wait. They know the capelin are coming and their role is also predetermined. They cruise rapidly under the purling water in uncharacteristic excitement. They are not interested in capelin flesh. They want capelin eggs, and they will gorge as soon as spawning starts.

Now, the most voracious of all the hunters appear. Fishing vessels come up over the horizon. They brought the Portuguese of the fifteenth century, who anchored offshore, dropped their boats, and rowed ashore to take the capelin with handnets, on beaches never before walked by white men. They brought Spaniards and Dutchmen, Englishmen and Irish, from the sixteenth to the twentieth centuries. Americans, Nova Scotians, Gloucestermen, schoonermen, bankermen, longliner captains have participated in the ritual. All of them knew that fresh capelin is the finest

bait when it is skillfully used, and can attract a fortune in codfish flesh, hooked on the submarine banks to the south.

But presently, these hunters are Newfoundlanders. They bring their schooners flying inshore like great brown-and-white birds, a hundred, two hundred, three hundred sail. They heel through the screaming seabirds, luff, anchor, and drop their dories with the same precision of movement of the other figures in the ritual. In an hour, three thousand men are at work from the boats. They work as the codfish work, with a frenzy that knots forearms and sends nets spilling over the sterns to encircle the capelin. They lift a thousand tons of capelin out of the sea, yet they do not measurably diminish the number of fish.

Meanwhile, landbound hunters wait for the fish to come within range of their lead-weighted handnets. Women, children, and old people crowd the beach with the able-bodied men. The old people have ancestral memories of capelin bounty. In the seventeenth and eighteenth centuries, when food was often short, only the big capelin harvest stood between them and starvation during the winter.

Many of the shore people are farmers who use the capelin for fertilizers as well as for food. Capelin corpses, spread to rot over thin northern soils, draw obedient crops of potatoes and cabbages out of the ground, and these, mixed with salted capelin flesh, become winter meals.

The children, who remember dried capelin as their candy, share the excitement of waiting. They chase one another up and down the beach and play with their own nets and fishing rods. Some are already asleep because they awoke before dawn to rouse the village, as they do every capelin morning, with the cry: "They've a-come, they've a-come!"

At the top of the beach, old women lie asleep or sit watching the seabirds squabbling and the dorymen rowing. They are

Aunt Sadie and Little Nell and Bessie Blue and Mother Taunton, old ladies from several centuries. They know the capelin can save children in hard winters when the inshore cod fishery fails. They get up at two o'clock in the morning when the capelin are running, to walk miles to the nearest capelin beach. They net a barrel of fish, then roll the barrel, which weighs perhaps a hundred pounds, back home. They have finished spreading the fish on their gardens, or salting them, before the first of their grandchildren awakes.

They have clear memories of catching capelin in winter, when the sea freezes close inshore and the tide cracks the ice in places. Then millions of capelin, resting out the winter, rise in the cracks. An old woman with a good net can take tons of passive fish out of the water for as long as her strength lasts and for as far as her net reaches.

A cry rises from the beach: "Here they come!"

The ritual must be played out, according to habit. The dorymen and the seabirds, the rampaging cod and cunner cannot touch or turn the purpose of the capelin. At a moment, its genesis unknown, they start for the shore. From the top of some nearby cliffs I watch and marvel at the precision of their behavior. The capelin cease to be a great, formless mass offshore. They split into groups that the Newfoundlanders call *wads* —rippling gray lines, five to fifty feet wide— and run for the shore like advancing infantry lines. One by one, they peel away from their surviving comrades and advance, thirty to forty wads at a time.

Each wad has its discipline. The fish prepare to mate. Each male capelin seeks a female, darting from one fish to another. When he finds one, he presses against her side. Another male, perhaps two males, press against her other side. The males urge the female on toward the beach. Some are struck down by diving seabirds but others take their places. Cod dash among them and

smash their sexual formations; they re-form immediately. Cunner rise and rip at them; flounder dart beneath them toward the beach.

The first wad runs into beach wavelets, and a hundred nets hit the water together; a silver avalanche of fish spills out on the beach. In each breaking wavelet the capelin maintain their formations, two or three males pressed tightly against their female until they are all flung up on the beach. There, to the whispering sound of tiny fins and tails vibrating, the female convulsively digs into the sand, which is still moving in the wake of the retreating wave. As she goes down, she extrudes up to fifty thousand eggs, and the males expel their milt.

The children shout; their bare feet fly over the spawning fish; the nets soar; sea boots grind down; the fish spill out; gulls run in the shallows under the children's feet; the flounder gorge. A codfish, two feet long, leaps out of the shallows and hits the beach. An old man scoops it up. The wads keep coming. The air is filled with birds. The dorymen shout and laugh.

The flood of eggs becomes visible. The sand glistens, then is greasy with eggs. They pile in driftlines that writhe back and forth in each wave. The female capelin wriggle into masses of eggs. The shallows are permeated with eggs. The capelin breathe eggs. Their mouths fill with eggs. Their stomachs are choked with eggs. The wads keep pouring onwards, feeding the disaster on the beach.

Down come the boots and the nets, and the capelin die, mouths open and oozing eggs. The spawning is a fiasco. The tide has turned. Instead of spawning on the shore with the assurance of rising water behind them, each wad strikes ashore in retreating water. Millions are stranded but the wads keep coming.

In the background, diminished by the quantity of fish, other players gasp and pant at their nets. Barrels stack high on the beach. Horses whinny, driven hard up the bank at the back of the beach. Carts laden with barrels weave away. Carts bringing empty barrels bounce and roar down. The wads are still coming. Men use shovels to lift dead and dying fish from driftlines that are now two and three feet high. The easterly wind is freshening. The wavelets become waves. The capelin are flung up on the beach without a chance to spawn. They bounce and twist and the water flees beneath them.

It is twilight, then dark; torches now spot the beach, the offshore dories, and the schooners. The waves grow solidly and pile the capelin higher. The men shovel the heaps into pyramids, then reluctantly leave the beach. Heavy rain blots out beach and sea.

I remain to watch the blow piling up the sea. At the lowest point of the tide, it is driving waves high up on the beach, roiling the sand, digging up the partially buried eggs, and carrying them out to sea. By dawn most of the eggs are gone. The capelin have disappeared. The seabirds, the schooners, the cod, flounder, cunner, seals, whales have gone. Nothing remains except the marks of human feet, the cart tracks on the high part of the beach, the odd pyramid of dead fish. The feast is done.

The empty arena of the beach suggests a riddle. If the capelin were so perfectly adapted to spawn on a rising tide, to master the task of burying eggs in running sand between waves, to *know* when the tide was rising, why did they continue spawning after the tide turned? Was that, by the ancient rules of the ritual, intentional? If it was, then it indicated a lethal error of adaptation that did not jibe with the great numbers of capelin.

I wonder, then, if the weak died and the strong survived, but dismiss the notion after recalling the indiscriminate nature of all capelin deaths. There was no Darwinian selection for death of the stupid or the inexperienced. Men slaughtered billions, this year and last year and for three hundred years before, but the capelin never felt this pinpricking on their colossal corporate bodies. Their spawning was a disaster for reasons well beyond the influence of men.

A nineteenth-century observer, after seeing a capelin-spawning, recorded his amazement at "the astonishing *prosperity* of these creatures, cast so wilfully away. . . ." It was in the end, and indeed throughout the entire ritual, the sheer numbers of capelin that scored the memory. The *prosperity* of the capelin preceded the disaster but then, it seemed, created it. Prosperity was not beneficial or an assurance of survival. The meaning of the ritual was slowly growing into sense. Prosperity unhinges the capelin. Prosperity, abundance, success, drive them on. They become transformed and throw themselves forward blindly. . . .

I turn from the beach, warm and secure, and take a blind step forward.

Josephine Johnson

DECEMBER

Hoarfrost is silver all over the trees, twigs, and grass. Silver-violet shadows. Silver-blue hills. A great woodpecker comes, the pileated giant. Flattens his body against the bark. He is the blackest thing in the woods. He has a flaming crest and a probing bill. But he is timid, he hugs the bark to him. I can see the black quilting of his feathers. Then suddenly he lifts his wings. The whiteness is startling. He takes flight like a great ship in sail. Magnificent!

On a tree, bright bitter green with moss and pale-green scabs of lichen from head to foot, a squirrel is cleaning himself in the sunlight. He turns his back. His arched tail is hinged in two parts. One part is round, a big furry circle, and concentric furry circles within, white, grey and brown, and in the center the tail's tip hangs down like another tail, white, brown and grey. He is scratching and biting, thriftily eating his fleas.

The margin of the hill is a moving and flickering line of birds, strung out restlessly through the frosty leaves. Juncos, sparrows, chickadees, wrens and titmice and woodpeckers. The leaves jump up and down from prying and flickering bills. The goldfinches are around, in winter feathers of such marvelous subtlety that the shades of brown and yellow and green flow in and out under the black and orange wing bars.

High up in the sun, a starling is singing. Singing? Holding forth, putting out sounds. His throat vibrates. His peacock colors of purple and green ripple. He has a frosting of flecks over the royal black, and his eyes are mean and stupid.

A dove is on the ground. In this winter light it is very brown. Snow is frozen on its long, thin tail. The dove ruffles the brown feathers of its back, opens them like a pine cone. It walks slowly on its raspberry feet. A delicate white rim circles its eyes. Pink patches are on its cheeks. When other birds fly over it, the dove flinches. I think it is wounded. It pecks the grain and then slowly walks away. It settles in the leaves at the edge of the wood, and faces the cold, early sun. Slowly the dove's head sinks in its feathers. They expand around it like the petals of a great brown rose. Only one eye, white-rimmed, anxious, is still visible. After awhile the dove is gone.

I look for bluebirds. Might they not seem auspicious omens in this hour? An auspice is a bird seer. One who tells omens from the flight or feeding of birds. An omen usually favorable, or predicting good. (Is it not the function of such omens to fill with happy thoughts that time between the prophecy and the disaster?)

In finding the meaning of auspicious, I got hung up on *hate*, and from thence to *hathi*, meaning elephant, and *hathi, grey*, a color which is yellowish green, and *hat homage*, a Quaker phrase, and *Hathor*, a cowheaded goddess of love, mirth, and social joy. I like the simple definition of hater: One who hates.

Slipped out quietly to avoid the cat, Pussywillow. Walked quietly past the glazed pond with its frozen plume forms in the ice. Walked over the December dandelion. A large gold one. A defiant cold gold object in the cold green grass. Saw the goldfinches, now brown, in the bleached cattail sedges— very sedgy, very beat-up, beaten down. Approached the cottage, and there on the window ledge sat Pussywillow, an enormous silver-grey dandelion with cold green eyes. She had been surveying my arrival from the time I left the house. I, visible as I peered about to avoid her, visible as I walked softly on the gravel not to arouse her, visible as I crept by the willows of the pond.

From thence she followed—or preceded —me. A great mass of all this puffy silver fur—before—behind. Peering down holes, leaping over leaves, knowing what was there invisible, who had come, who had hidden, in what mood the wild thing that had walked before us. Telling me nothing.

Some honeysuckle was still rose and green and saddle-brown. Had bright black berries of surprising size and softness. Big clusters of unwinking eyes. The masses of honeysuckle vines that mat out and are moving down the once-pasture from the fence line do not have berries. They are a great bushy crawling thing without eyes. The goldenrod is being pushed downhill.

The cedars grow all through the goldenrod, whose galls are woody, polished knobs. I searched each cedar for a little owl, Saw-whet or screech. The cedars have increased in numbers, come in every size now, the new growth is a delicate blue-green, almost a smoke put out by the prickly flame. The old nest of the cardinals that housed the cowbird orphan was tipped over to one side. No owls. Came back through honeysuckle strongholds that hold up the pasture from below. When the vine tides meet we will have a Sargasso Sea of vines. (Will the center vines live forever, as the seaweed lives in the heart of the Sargasso Sea? Or will they embrace and strangle each other, as the higher forms of life find it best to do?)

The coralberry bush is leafless now, a delicate scaffolding of red berries. Odd that the birds don't seem to want them yet. The fallen walnuts look like iron or blackened copper. Soot-black. As black as any vegetable thing can be before it hardens into coal.

I found my screech owl in an evergreen near the house. Was led to it by a cloud of jays and chickadees, screeching and probing. There he sat, brown-and-white feathers flattened against the trunk, his ear tufts thinned high to make him as small as possible. His eyes half shut. The chickadees stitched in and out the needles, very close. The jays shouted. He did not move, and at last they went away and left him with his delicate ears ringing.

December, the white boles of sycamores. The blue-and-white sky. The white-and-blue frost. The early snow, more a frost than a snow. A rime of silver. The sky is blue, the land seems shrunken since the leaves have fallen. My blood is still thin. Water is frozen. The creek still runs, will always run from its great sewer source.

Two years ago I started the path through the walnut grove with a corn knife. That path was made in an agony of spirit, a coming to terms with the concept of oneself as murderer. The stark taking to heart of this knowledge, as one would take a wild animal with poisonous teeth or fangs, and holding it there, this knowledge that as long as you pay the bills for this war, you are a part of it and whatever it results in. You cannot say (as we would say of Hiroshima),

I did not know. *I know*. You know. It is known.

What, then, is the result of this embrace? Knowledge and knower become one. In the ensuing darkness that follows this question, dim forms move about. There is comfort in the vast company in which we find ourselves. We are all murderers here. You, I, my neighbor, and all the law's trustees. An unwilling, restless throng. But a warm throng. We are all engaged in keeping warm, keeping the lights low, keeping the soul's terminal sickness a secret.

Who is outside this huddle? The hope of the world is outside. The sons who will not go to war. The young who throw themselves in front of the war machine. The men and women who do not pay war taxes. They are outside the warm huddle and some are inside the walls of prisons. But they are free. They are the only free people in this nation.

On this planet Pain, the season of Christmas is upon us. The men of the communications media are gathering on the parapets with paper bags full of sugar water and mother's molasses. Their pens and voices are beginning to choke up as they see "time-honored traditions" being trotted out, wiped off, set up.

Orphan children are given a buying spree for Christ's birthday. The children leave the buses, their little faces radiant and eager. They are greeted by the genial owners of the store with fistfuls of five-dollar bills. Each child, the commentator tells us, may buy whatever he wishes. Some children can't decide. "But here's a little fellow who knows just what he wants. . . ." The voice is filled with patronizing, fatherly indulgence, and the camera focuses on a small child of eight, his innocent round face smiling, his arms filled by a toy machine gun as large as he is.

The manger scene is being set up in the park. I think it is a fine idea to recall this certain child on his natal day. Of all who come to stroll, or stand and stare at this plastic replica of God's son, some will be weighted down by monstrous ironies they feel, but cannot understand or really bear. To find this child, we are told, and to wipe out his dangerous power to come, Herod ordered the slaughter of young children throughout his kingdom. The child was not found, and he lived. Today the slaughter goes on in this child's name.

We think of children in this Christmas season. There should be services in all the churches for the children. For the children blinded and homeless in Vietnam, for the children robbed of childhood and turned into thieves and prostitutes, orphaned and mutilated. For the children who have been burned to death. There should be services in the churches for the children of the poor here at home, who have been robbed of their education, robbed of their heritage, to pay for this vast, mindless sinning. Childhood and manhood wiped out by war.

We think of the thousands of young men dead in the war as of this hour. The young men wounded, burned, blinded, paralyzed in the strange perversion of this child's teaching.

The Pentagon is the greatest power on earth today. We cannot absorb the Pentagon into an image. We cannot fit it anywhere in the natural world, relate it, compare it. There it sits, a terrible mass of concrete, on our minds, on our hearts, squat on top of our lives. Its power penetrates into every single life. It is in the very air we breathe. The water we drink. Because of its insatiable demands we are drained and we are polluted.

Nothing in the world is like this concrete monster. It is not a mountain. It is not a storm, it is not a hurricane, a pack of wolves, a flood. It is like the great god Moloch into which the children were thrown as sacrifice. It is the greatest unnatural disaster of the world.

We can call it a cancer in the body of the world — this five-sided concrete sore, full of neatly dressed and tidy human beings, who work to spread its malignant cells throughout the life of the world. Who work to substitute death for life. And make no mistake about this. No matter what is said is happening, this is what is happening — death instead of life. Death of the heart, death of the mind, and death of the body. We cannot even probe the final mystery of the cancer cell in the human flesh because of this great Thing's demand.

I set out to circle and crisscross the land in this last month of the year. Visit the three great stones. The oak. The mink crossing. Find the hornet's nest again. The quiet valley. Cross the ruined creek, the pure creek. Climb the snail hill, the north pasture, come home through the walnut grove and the woodchuck's small ravine.

That barren stretch of land, where the hornet's nest was found, I like the least of all the acres. This piece of land is strange. A graveyard of the woods. Here is where, if ever, the murdered traveler will be found. On this desolate dying patch of witch-rent.

There are thorns here, great clusters, grey and brittle, bouquets of swords. The underbrush is made of high weeds and raspberry hoops. Fallen trees and fallen limbs of trees litter the hill. Young trees are bent over by old trees, and all are diseased, covered with an unpleasant moss. A moss not truly green, but a whitishness. There is a purplish film over the one pine tree in all that mess of broken limbs. The Virginia creeper strangles the living and the dead. Its hairy roots spray out, dig in the bark. Some plants bleach to white, some blacken in death. This is a fit place for a rape, a murder, or the culmination of despair. Do the old trees come here to die? Why is this piece of land so cursed?

I could not find the hornet's nest. Each tangle of dead vines and branches; rotting logs and decaying snakeroot, looked alike.

And then suddenly it was there, right in front of me. But an awful change had come over it. The great nest, like grey whipped cream, smooth whorls of paper cleverly designed, was torn and shredded. A dreadful pagoda, a thatched thing hung there, with its whole bottom torn away, exposing the open cells. Shreds and clumps of torn grey paper were scattered in the weeds. Was it birds? Squirrels? The branch it hung by was too delicate to hold anything heavier. Birds, I would say. Hanging on it and shredding away to eat the delicious white things within.

Everything seemed gnawed in these woods, rotten wood pulp exposed. Dead leaves of beeches rattling. Paths of hunters following the flat land above. Some harmony of hate here. I shall not come back unless I am still searching for some elusive darkness, some concentration of that vague enveloping misery which is my mortal cloak (shirt, skirt, socks, shoes, sweater and cap). Not even to watch this strange ecology develop. Here the witches come to die. Or to gather thorns for their winter weddings. They love it here. It has that fungoid nourishment they need. But not in the summer, it is dry and dusty.

Once over the ridge, a change begins. A profound change. Is it shadows in summer, or the way the water runs? The trees stop dying in confusion. They lie down and rest silently. The pure creek runs with rain. The moss is greener than Ireland. The rocks are green and clean. Great oaks are here. Whole and healthy. The shedding and scaling that went on before, like a tide of disease and dandruff, is all gone. The very fallen leaves are different.

It is a ravine, and very quiet except for the sound of the water. No birds. No chipmunks. Nothing moves but the water; nothing speaks but the water. It is clean water. The leaves are wet and deep and soft underfoot. That great tree leaning from one side of the creek to the other is a mossy bridge, thick green moss from root to crown where it was rimmed with snow last January. Bright green moss covers the roots of the bitter-nut tree that hold the bank both north and south and plunge straight down like thick legs of elephants into the small stream. Spectacular and almost grotesque, the velvet green of these roots. They are so powerful they disturb and satisfy. A rock holds a fossil shell, blue and silver, delicately veined.

I sit and rearrange the days, the words, the acts of all last week. Placing things as they should have been. Saying the things I should have said. Undoing that which should not ever have been done. But it's no good. It is only pain.

It is better to push on down the stream course with the banks dripping with sword ferns. This is winter. This is December. And here are all those green ferns in the warm grey sunlight! And tree trunks sprouting a fox fire of orange fungus, fat fleshy knobs like ears of corn.

The dead thicket of wild plum is green with lichen. Moss is bright green over all the stones. Michaelmas winter. Weather warm enough for the slime mold to be on the move. Humping and inching its film along the floor of the woods, flowing over and under the bark of fallen trees. Grey-violet shadows move along the ridge. Large unsubstantial clouds dissolve into a spring-blue sky, the sun moves downward to the grey grass, where the ground is littered with the big pocky balls of mock orange. Lavish in size, smelling faintly of bitter fruit. A yellow-green that shines like the sun. Nothing eats them that I know of, and they lie there all exposed and tempting. A wild mock. The trunks of osage oranges are always twisted, the bark shredded; they are bent and tortured as though they fought from the hour of seed. They are very tough.

The doves are flocking. Easily frightened, ripping in and out of the fir trees as one passes. wheeling and tearing the air with their wild wings. Pinheads.

Now, tired from walking, befuddled by something that seems to come from the leaves — an emanation — eyes hurting, I hunt a tree, a spot to lean against and sit down. Approach the rose-crystal granite rock cautiously. Observe its wet shining loveliness, keep my eyes on the log where the great blacksnake lives. A few steps forward and there is Old Scratch himself — long, moist, and coiled, savoring the warmth of this late spring, this intermittent sunlight. What an event! He does not move. I pass and sit on the ground against the tree.

Two old reptiles, we doze in silence. Nothing moves. Nothing calls.

The sunlight falls like a gold sweater on the shoulders. It dries the chilly mud. It is reflected in the bright pin eyes of the chickadee. It is a free and mindless benediction over the winter world. The dry pods of vines move with a small music in the breeze, not a wintry rattle.

What interval is this? What curious hollow that is happiness? The heart is a warm and humming hollow. I live. I am. This is not holy, this is not heaven. This is the ancient pagan hollow of the hand that holds the sun.

After a while I get up and go through the warm brown spongy twilight. The creek is a rushing of tan clay. Old Scratch still lies there coiled. What will he do if he cools to torpor before he knows it and cannot make it back to his hole on time? In the west, a curious tower of clouds rises like a smoke signal, a brassy gold. And behind it, the blue sky opens before the night comes down.

Once in the year there comes *the snow*.

There are all manner of snows, both cruel and kind. There is the snow that falls like needles and drifts in hard ridges on the dead cornfields, is bitterly cold, coming down from the northwest and driving into the earth like knives. And there is the snow that people think of as *snow*, that actually comes very seldom, but is the symbol of all snows, the childhood miracle that remains forever an image larger than all the dreary, bitter or halfhearted snows that come before and after.

The snow falls slowly in soft, descending clusters like fairy snowballs. It falls slowly, almost thoughtfully, and far apart. So slow, so far apart that children can stand and choose which cluster they want to catch on their tongues. The snow clings where it falls, lovingly and coldly to the barren twigs, pure as wool blankets over the dead grass. The wild-raspberry wires become tunnels of silver whiteness, the browning pine trees become white trees, and the grapevines are a still, white fountain of flowers.

Everything is still, so unbelievably still. We brush away snow from sheltered spots and spread out crumbs, and the chickadees, whose seedy voices are muffled in the snow, come, and the redbirds and winter wrens and quail. The thistles become flowers. The wild carrot blooms again.

The snow falls to the proper depth, to the exact moment when all ugliness is covered, to the weight that the twig and branch can bear and be beautiful without breaking. It knows precisely when to stop, when the moment of absolute perfection has been attained, and there it stops.

All night the snow remains motionless, unless a twig is shaken by an owl or a weasel. It hardens a little with a light, pure crust, to bear the weight of the wild things walking in the night, and to preserve itself for the daylight.

The morning comes slowly through the arches of whiteness in the woods, and comes more silently. It begins with a grey whiteness, and the sun is late. The ground is stitched with tiny tracks that end suddenly in round, damp holes, or stop and vanish as a small thing flew upward. The oval tracks of rabbits wander purposefully along the raspberry thickets, and the sycamore balls have little caps of fur.

It is best in this white greyness before the sun has come through the ascending clouds. The brooding, silent, closed-in world of snow and whiteness, motionless except for the birds, the grey juncos and the wrens, a timeless moment like an enormous pearl, a moment of stillness before the sun, and the thousand-diamond glitter and the rain-bowed sound of light.

Even children, whose first thought is to tramp it with their big galoshes and scrape it into balls, stand for a moment in awe at their windows, on their porches, and drink in the miracle that is to become forever *snow* for the rest of their lives. The snow that is almost too beautiful to be borne.

In the year's end, without faith, without expecting an answer, we find ourselves crying, "Almighty and most merciful God, Maker of heaven and earth — Maker of this beautiful and awesome world, stop this terrible and disgusting march of Thy people to destruction. Stop the killing!"

And God answers, "Mighty and unmerciful man, stop your own killing."

Which leaves us here in this white cold winter, in this orderly world of nature with its fine and intricate chains of life which man has broken, screwed up, and is preparing to strangle himself with, to find an answer. An imperfect answer.

We are dying of preconceptions, outworn rules, decaying flags, venomous religions, and sentimentalities. We need a new world. We've wrenched up all the old roots. The old men have no roots. They don't know it. They just go on talking and flailing away and falling down on the young with their tons of dead weight and their power. For the power is still there, in their life-in-death. But the roots are dead, and the land is poisoned for miles around them.

How can I hold such bitterness in this white snow on this lovely darkened land? Because there is nothing in all of nature that can compare to this enormous dying of the nation's soul.

In the last day of the old year a snow came down, a thin, grey snow. Very cold. In the late afternoon, this falling snow came down straight as rain. Fell straight like white rain down one's collar to the shuddering spine. Down on the crumbling cottage. Down on the dog tracks, down on the thistle leaves and over the wild green mint. It fell down like a blank white curtain, a final curtain over the last day of the year. Rung down, blotted out. And the coldness of night poured in from the dark ravines. It went down to zero in the night. And the new year began with awesome clarity.

Anton Chekhov

A DAY IN THE COUNTRY

Between eight and nine o'clock in the morning.

A dark leaden-colored mass is creeping over the sky towards the sun. Red zigzags of lightning gleam here and there across it. There is a sound of far-away rumbling. A warm wind frolics over the grass, bends the trees, and stirs up the dust. In a minute there will be a spurt of May rain and a real storm will begin.

Fyokla, a little beggar-girl of six, is running through the village, looking for Terenty the cobbler. The white-haired, barefoot child is pale. Her eyes are wide-open, her lips are trembling.

"Uncle, where is Terenty?" she asks everyone she meets. No one answers. They are all preoccupied with the approaching storm and take refuge in their huts. At last she meets Silanty Silitch, the sacristan. Terenty's bosom friend. He is coming along, staggering from the wind.

"Uncle, where is Terenty?"

"At the kitchen-gardens," answers Silanty.

The beggar-girl runs behind the huts to the kitchen-gardens and there finds Terenty; the tall old man with a thin, pock-marked face, very long legs, and bare feet, dressed in a woman's tattered jacket, is standing near the vegetable plots, looking with drowsy, drunken eyes at the dark storm cloud. On his long crane-like legs he sways in the wind like a starling-cote.

"Uncle Terenty!" the white-headed beggar-girl addresses him. "Uncle, darling!"

Terenty bends down to Fyokla, and his grim, drunken face is overspread with a smile, such as comes into people's faces when they look at something little, foolish, and absurd, but warmly loved.

"Ah! servant of God, Fyokla," he says, lisping tenderly, "where have you come from?"

"Uncle Terenty," says Fyokla, with a sob, tugging at the lapel of the cobbler's coat. "Brother Danilka has had an accident! Come along!"

"What sort of accident? Ough, what thunder! Holy, holy, holy. . . . What sort of accident?"

"In the count's copse Danilka stuck his hand into a hole in a tree, and he can't get it out. Come along, uncle, do be kind and pull his hand out!"

"How was it he put his hand in? What for?"

"He wanted to get a cuckoo's egg out of the hole for me."

"The day has hardly begun and already you are in trouble. . . ." Terenty shook his head and spat deliberately. "Well, what am I to do with you now? I must come . . . I must, may the wolf gobble you up, you naughty children! Come, little orphan!"

Terenty comes out of the kitchen-garden and, lifting high his long legs, begins striding down the village street. He walks quickly without stopping or looking from side to side, as though he were shoved from behind or afraid of pursuit. Fyokla can hardly keep up with him.

They come out of the village and turn along the dusty road towards the count's copse that lies dark blue in the distance. It is about a mile and a half away. The clouds have by now covered the sun, and soon afterwards there is not a speck of blue left in the sky. It grows dark.

"Holy, holy, holy . . ." whispers Fyokla, hurrying after Terenty. The first rain-drops, big and heavy, lie, dark dots on the dusty road. A big drop falls on Fyokla's cheek and glides like a tear down her chin.

"The rain has begun," mutters the cobbler, kicking up the dust with his bare, bony feet. "That's fine, Fyokla, old girl. The grass and the trees are fed by the rain, as we are by bread. And as for the thunder, don't you be frightened, little orphan. Why should it kill a little thing like you?"

As soon as the rain begins, the wind drops. The only sound is the patter of rain dropping like fine shot on the young rye and the parched road.

"We shall get soaked, Fyokla," mutters Terenty. "There won't be a dry spot left on us. . . . Ho-ho, my girl! It's run down my neck! But don't be frightened, silly. . . . The grass will be dry again, the earth will be dry again, and we shall be dry again. There is the same sun for us all."

A flash of lightning, some fourteen feet long, gleams above their heads. There is a loud peal of thunder, and it seems to Fyokla that something big, heavy, and round is rolling over the sky and tearing it open, exactly over her head.

"Holy, holy, holy . . ." says Terenty, crossing himself. "Don't be afraid, little orphan! It is not from spite that it thunders."

Terenty's and Fyokla's feet are covered with lumps of heavy, wet clay. It is slippery and difficult to walk, but Terenty strides on more and more rapidly. The weak little beggar-girl is breathless and ready to drop.

But at last they go into the count's copse. The washed trees, stirred by a gust of wind, drop a perfect waterfall upon them. Terenty stumbles over stumps and begins to slacken his pace.

"Whereabouts is Danilka?" he asks. "Lead me to him."

Fyokla leads him into a thicket, and, after going a quarter of a mile, points to Danilka. Her brother, a little fellow of eight, with hair as red as ochre and a pale sickly face, stands leaning against a tree, and, with his head on one side, looking sideways at the sky. In one hand he holds his shabby old cap, the other is hidden in an old lime tree. The boy is gazing at the stormy sky, and apparently not thinking of his trouble. Hearing footsteps and seeing the cobbler he gives a sickly smile and says:

"A terrible lot of thunder, Terenty. . . . I've never heard so much thunder in all my life."

"And where is your hand?"

"In the hole. . . . Pull it out, please, Terenty!"

The wood had broken at the edge of the hole and jammed Danilka's hand: he could push it farther in, but could not pull it out. Terenty snaps off the broken piece, and the boy's hand, red and crushed, is released.

"It's terrible how it's thundering," the boy says again, rubbing his hand. "What makes it thunder, Terenty?"

"One cloud runs against the other," answers the cobbler. The party come out of the copse, and walk along the edge of it towards the darkened road. The thunder gradually abates, and its rumbling is heard far away beyond the village.

"The ducks flew by here the other day, Terenty," says Danilka, still rubbing his hand. "They must be nesting in the Gniliya Zaimishtcha marshes. . . . Fyokla, would you like me to show you a nightingale's nest?"

"Don't touch it, you might disturb them,"

says Terenty, wringing the water out of his cap. "The nightingale is a singing-bird, without sin. He has had a voice given him in his throat, to praise God and gladden the heart of man. It's a sin to disturb him."

"What about the sparrow?"

"The sparrow doesn't matter, he's a bad, spiteful bird. He is like a pickpocket in his ways. He doesn't like man to be happy. When Christ was crucified it was the sparrow brought nails to the Jews, and called 'alive! alive!' "

A bright patch of blue appears in the sky.

"Look!" says Terenty. "An ant-heap burst open by the rain! They've been flooded, the rogues!"

They bent over the ant-heap. The downpour has damaged it; the insects are scurrying to and fro in the mud, agitated, and busily trying to carry away their drowned companions.

"You needn't be in such a taking, you won't die of it!" says Terenty, grinning. "As soon as the sun warms you, you'll come to your senses again. . . . It's a lesson to you, you stupids. You won't settle on low ground another time."

They go on.

"And here are some bees," cries Danilka, pointing to the branch of a young oak tree.

The drenched and chilled bees are huddled together on the branch. There are so many of them that neither bark nor leaf can be seen. Many of them are settled on one another.

"That's a swarm of bees," Terenty informs them. "They were flying looking for a home, and when the rain came down upon them they settled. If a swarm is flying, you need only sprinkle water on them to make them settle. Now if, say, you wanted to take the swarm, you would bend the branch with them into a sack and shake it. and they all fall in."

Little Fyokla suddenly frowns and rubs her neck vigorously. Her brother looks at her neck, and sees a big swelling on it.

"Hey-hey!" laughs the cobbler. "Do you know where you got that from, Fyokla, old girl? There are Spanish flies on some tree in the wood. The rain has trickled off them, and a drop has fallen on your neck—that's what has made the swelling."

The sun appears from behind the clouds and floods the wood, the fields, and the three friends with its warm light. The dark menacing cloud has gone far away and taken the storm with it. The air is warm and fragrant. There is a scent of bird-cherry, meadowsweet, and lilies-of-the-valley.

"That herb is given when your nose bleeds," says Terenty, pointing to a woolly-looking flower. "It does good."

They hear a whistle and a rumble, but not such a rumble as the storm-clouds carried away. A freight train races by before the eyes of Terenty, Danilka, and Fyokla. The engine, panting and puffing out black smoke, drags more than twenty cars after it. Its power is tremendous. The children are interested to know how an engine, not alive and without the help of horses, can move and drag such weights, and Terenty undertakes to explain it to them:

"It's all the steam's doing, children. . . . The steam does the work. . . . You see, it shoves under that thing near the wheels, and it . . . you see . . . it works. . . ."

They cross the railway line, and, going down from the embankment, walk towards the river. They walk not with any object, but just at random, and talk all the way. . . . Danilka asks questions, Terenty answers them. . . .

Terenty answers all his questions, and there is no secret in Nature which baffles him. He knows everything. Thus, for example, he knows the names of all the wild flowers, animals, and stones. He knows what herbs cure diseases, he has no difficulty in telling the age of a horse or a cow. Looking at the sunset, at the moon, or the birds, he can tell what sort of weather it will be next day. And indeed, it is not only Terenty who is so wise. Silanty Silitch, the innkeeper,

the market-gardener, the shepherd, and all the villagers, generally speaking, know as much as he does. These people have learned not from books, but in the fields, in the wood, on the river bank. Their teachers have been the birds themselves, when they sang to them, the sun when it left a glow of crimson behind it at setting, the very trees, and wild herbs.

Danilka looks at Terenty and greedily drinks in every word. In spring, before one is weary of the warmth and the monotonous green of the fields, when everything is fresh and full of fragrance, who would not want to hear about the golden may-beetles, about the cranes, about the gurgling streams, and the corn mounting into ear?

The two of them, the cobbler and the orphan, walk about the fields, talk unceasingly, and are not weary. They could wander about the world endlessly. They walk, and in their talk of the beauty of the earth do not notice the frail little beggar-girl tripping after them. She is breathless and moves with a lagging step. There are tears in her eyes; she would be glad to stop these inexhaustible wanderers, but to whom and where can she go? She has no home or people of her own; whether she likes it or not, she must walk and listen to their talk.

Towards midday, all three sit down on the river bank. Danilka takes out of his bag a piece of bread, soaked and reduced to a mash, and they begin to eat. Terenty says a prayer when he has eaten the bread, then stretches himself on the sandy bank and falls asleep. While he is asleep, the boy gazes at the water, pondering. He has many different things to think of. He has just seen the storm, the bees, the ants, the train. Now, before his eyes, fishes are whisking about. Some are two inches long and more, others are no bigger than one's nail, A viper, with its head held high, is swimming from one bank to the other.

Only towards the evening our wanderers return to the village. The children go for the night to a deserted barn, where the corn of the commune used to be kept, while Terenty, leaving them, goes to the tavern. The children lie huddled together on the straw, dozing.

The boy does not sleep. He gazes into the darkness, and it seems to him that he is seeing all that he has seen in the day: the storm-clouds, the bright sunshine, the birds, the fish, lanky Terenty. The number of his impressions, together with exhaustion and hunger, are too much for him; he is as hot as though he were on fire, and tosses from side to side. He longs to tell someone all that is haunting him now in the darkness and agitating his soul, but there is no one to tell. Fyokla is too little and could not understand.

"I'll tell Terenty tomorrow," thinks the boy.

The children fall asleep thinking of the homeless cobbler, and, in the night, Terenty comes to them, makes the sign of the cross over them, and puts bread under their heads. And no one sees his love. It is seen only by the moon which floats in the sky and peeps caressingly through the holes in the wall of the deserted barn.

Arthur C. Clarke

IF I FORGET THEE, O EARTH[25]

When Marvin was ten years old, his father took him through the long, echoing corridors that led up through Administration and Power, until at last they came to the uppermost levels of all and were among the swiftly growing vegetation of the Farmlands. Marvin liked it here: it was fun watching the great, slender plants creeping with almost visible eagerness toward the

[25] For the title, compare *Psalms* CXXXVII, 5.

sunlight as it filtered down through the plastic domes to meet them. The smell of life was everywhere, awakening inexpressible longings in his heart: no longer was he breathing the dry, cool air of the residential levels, purged of all smells but the faint tang of ozone. He wished he could stay here for a little while, but Father would not let him. They went onward until they had reached the entrance to the Observatory. which he had never visited: but they did not stop, and Marvin knew with a sense of rising excitement that there could be only one goal left. For the first time in his life, he was going Outside.

There were a dozen of the surface vehicles, with their wide balloon tires and pressurized cabins, in the great servicing chamber. His father must have been expected, for they were led at once to the little scout car waiting by the huge circular door of the airlock. Tense with expectancy, Marvin settled himself down in the cramped cabin while his father started the motor and checked the controls. The inner door of the lock slid open and then closed behind them: he heard the roar of the great air pumps fade slowly away as the pressure dropped to zero. Then the "Vacuum" sign flashed on, the outer door parted, and before Marvin lay the land which he had never yet entered.

He had seen it in photographs, of course: he had watched it imaged on television screens a hundred times. But now it was lying all around him, burning beneath the fierce sun that crawled so slowly across the jet-black sky. He stared into the west, away from the blinding splendor of the sun—and there were the stars, as he had been told but had never quite believed. He gazed at them for a long time, marveling that anything could be so bright and yet so tiny. They were intense unscintillating points, and suddenly he remembered a rhyme he had once read in one of his father's books:

Twinkle, twinkle, little star,
How I wonder what you are.

Well, *he* knew what the stars were. Whoever asked that question must have been very stupid. And what did they mean by "twinkle"? You could see at a glance that all the stars shone with the same steady, unwavering light. He abandoned the puzzle and turned his attention to the landscape around him.

They were racing across a level plain at almost a hundred miles an hour, the great balloon tires sending up little spurts of dust behind them. There was no sign of the Colony: in the few minutes while he had been gazing at the stars, its domes and radio towers had fallen below the horizon. Yet there were other indications of man's presence, for about a mile ahead Marvin could see the curiously shaped structures clustering round the head of a mine. Now and then a puff of vapor would emerge from a squat smokestack and would instantly disperse.

They were past the mine in a moment: Father was driving with a reckless and exhilarating skill as if—it was a strange thought to come into a child's mind—he were trying to escape from something. In a few minutes they had reached the edge of the plateau on which the Colony had been built. The ground fell sharply away beneath them in a dizzying slope whose lower stretches were lost in shadow. Ahead, as far as the eye could reach, was a jumbled wasteland of craters, mountain ranges, and ravines. The crests of the mountains, catching the low sun, burned like islands of fire in a sea of darkness: and above them the stars still shone as steadfastly as ever.

There could be no way forward—yet there was. Marvin clenched his fists as the car edged over the slope and started the long descent. Then he saw the barely visible track leading down the mountainside, and relaxed a little. Other men, it seemed, had gone this way before.

Night fell with a shocking abruptness as they crossed the shadow line and the sun dropped below the crest of the plateau. The twin searchlights sprang into life, casting blue-white bands on the rocks ahead, so that there was scarcely need to check their speed. For hours they drove through valleys and past the foot of mountains whose peaks seemed to comb the stars, and sometimes they emerged for a moment into the sunlight as they climbed over higher ground.

And now on the right was a wrinkled, dusty plain, and on the left, its ramparts and terraces rising mile after mile into the sky, was a wall of mountains that marched into the distance until its peaks sank from sight below the rim of the world. There was no sign that men had ever explored this land, but once they passed the skeleton of a crashed rocket, and beside it a stone cairn surmounted by a metal cross.

It seemed to Marvin that the mountains stretched on forever: but at last, many hours later, the range ended in a towering, precipitous headland that rose steeply from a cluster of little hills. They drove down into a shallow valley that curved in a great arc toward the far side of the mountains: and as they did so, Marvin slowly realized that something very strange was happening in the land ahead.

The sun was now low behind the hills on the right; the valley before them should be in total darkness. Yet it was awash with a cold white radiance that came spilling over the crags beneath which they were driving. Then, suddenly, they were out in the open plain, and the source of the light lay before them in all its glory.

It was very quiet in the little cabin now that the motors had stopped. The only sound was the faint whisper of the oxygen feed and an occasional metallic crepitation as the outer walls of the vehicle radiated away their heat. For no warmth at all came from the great silver crescent that floated low above the far horizon and flooded all this land with pearly light. It was so brilliant that minutes passed before Marvin could accept its challenge and look steadfastly into its glare, but at last he could discern the outlines of continents, the hazy border of the atmosphere, and the white islands of cloud. And even at this distance, he could see the glitter of sunlight on the polar ice.

It was beautiful, and it called to his heart across the abyss of space. There in that shining crescent were all the wonders that he had never known—the hues of sunset skies, the moaning of the sea on pebbled shores, the patter of falling rain, the unhurried benison of snow. These and a thousand others should have been his rightful heritage, but he knew them only from the books and ancient records, and the thought filled him with the anguish of exile.

Why could they not return? It seemed so peaceful beneath those lines of marching cloud. Then Marvin, his eyes no longer blinded by the glare, saw that the portion of the disk that should have been in darkness was gleaming faintly with an evil phosphorescence: and he remembered. He was looking upon the funeral pyre of a world—upon the radioactive aftermath of Armageddon. Across a quarter of a million miles of space, the glow of dying atoms was still visible, a perennial reminder of the ruinous past. It would be centuries yet before that deadly glow died from the rocks and life could return again to fill that silent, empty world.

And now Father began to speak, telling Marvin the story which until this moment had meant no more to him than the fairy tales he had once been told. There were many things he could not understand: it was impossible for him to picture the glowing, multi-colored pattern of life on the planet he had never seen. Nor could he comprehend the forces that had destroyed it in the end, leaving the Colony, preserved by its isolation, as the sole survivor. Yet he could share the agony of those final days, when the Colony had learned at last that never again would the supply ships come flaming down through the stars with gifts from home. One by one the radio stations had ceased to call: on the shadowed globe the lights of the cities had dimmed and died, and they were alone at last, as no men had ever been alone before, carrying in their hands the future of the race.

Then had followed the years of despair, and the long-drawn battle for survival in this fierce and hostile world. That battle had been won, though barely: this little oasis of life was safe against the worst that Nature could do. But unless there was a goal, a future toward which it could work, the Colony would lose the will to live, and neither machines nor skill nor science could save it then.

So, at last, Marvin understood the purpose of this pilgrimage. He would never walk beside the rivers of that lost and legendary world, or listen to the thunder raging above its softly rounded hills. Yet one day—how far ahead?—his children's children would return to claim their heritage. The winds and the rains would scour the poisons from the burning lands and carry them to the sea, and in the depths of the sea they would waste their venom until they could harm no living things. Then the great ships that were still waiting here on the silent, dusty plains could lift once more into space, along the road that led to home.

That was the dream: and one day, Marvin knew with a sudden flash of insight, he would pass it on to his own son, here at this same spot with the mountains behind him and the silver light from the sky streaming into his face.

He did not look back as they began the homeward journey. He could not bear to see the cold glory of the crescent Earth fade from the rocks around him, as he went to rejoin his people in their long exile.

Andrew Marvell

THE GARDEN

How vainly men themselves amaze
To win the palm, the oak, or bays;
And their incessant labors see
Crowned from some single herb, or tree,
Whose short and narrow-vergèd shade
Does prudently their toils upbraid;
While all flowers and all trees do close
To weave the garlands of repose!

Fair Quiet, have I found thee here,
And Innocence, thy sister dear?   10
Mistaken long, I sought you then
In busy companies of men.
Your sacred plants, if here below,
Only among the plants will grow;
Society is all but rude
To this delicious solitude.

No white nor red was ever seen
So amorous as this lovely green.
Fond lovers, cruel as their flame,
Cut in these trees their mistress' name: 20
Little, alas! they know or heed
How far these beauties hers exceed!
Fair trees! wheres'e'er your barks I wound
No name shall but your own be found.

When we have run our passion's heat,
Love hither makes his best retreat.
The gods, that mortal beauty chase,
Still in a tree did end their race;
Apollo hunted Daphne so,
Only that she might laurel grow;   30
And Pan did after Syrinx speed,
Not as a nymph, but for a reed.

What wondrous life is this I lead!
Ripe apples drop about my head;

The luscious clusters of the vine
Upon my mouth do crush their wine;
The nectarine and curious peach
Into my hands themselves do reach;
Stumbling on melons, as I pass,
Insnared with flowers, I fall on grass.   40

Meanwhile the mind, from pleasure less,
Withdraws into its happiness;
The mind, that ocean where each kind
Does straight its own resemblance find;
Yet it creates, transcending these,
Far other worlds, and other seas,
Annihilating all that's made
To a green thought in a green shade.

Here at the fountain's sliding foot,
Or at some fruit tree's mossy root,   50
Casting the body's vest aside,
My soul into the boughs does glide:
There, like a bird, it sits and sings,
Then whets and combs its silver wings,
And, till prepared for longer flight,
Waves in its plumes the various light.

Such was that happy garden state,
While man there walked without a mate.
After a place so pure and sweet,
What other help could yet be meet?   60
But 'twas beyond a mortal's share
To wander solitary there:
Two paradises 'twere in one
To live in paradise alone.

How well the skillful gardener drew,
Of flowers and herbs, this dial new!
Where, from above, the milder sun
Does through a fragrant zodiac run,
And, as it works, the industrious bee
Computes its time as well as we.   70
How could such sweet and wholesome hours
Be reckoned but with herbs and flowers?

---

1 *amaze:* perplex, confuse. 2 *palm . . . bays:* i.e.,
fame. 16 *To:* compared with. 17 *white . . . red:*
i.e., of a female face. 29,31 *Daphne, Syrinx:* nymphs
thus transformed to save them from the advances
of Apollo and Pan.

37 *curious:* delicate, exquisite. 41 *less:* inferior.
43 *kind:* land species, each of which was thought to
have its counterpart in the sea. 51 *vest:* costume.
54 *whets:* smooths with its beak. 58 *man:* Adam.
66 *dial:* flowerbed shaped like a sundial.

William Collins

ODE TO EVENING

If aught of oaten stop, or pastoral song,
May hope, chaste Eve, to soothe thy modest ear,
　Like thy own solemn springs,
　Thy springs, and dying gales,
O nymph reserved, while now the bright-haired
　　sun
Sits in yon western tent, whose cloudy skirts,
　With brede ethereal wove,
　O'erhang his wavy bed:
Now air is hushed, save where the weak-eyed bat
With short shrill shrieks flits by on leathern
　　wing,　　　　　　　　　　　　　　　　10
　Or where the beetle winds
　His small but sullen horn,
As oft he rises midst the twilight path,
Against the pilgrim born in heedless hum:
　Now teach me, maid composed,
　To breathe some softened strain,
Whose numbers, stealing through thy darkening
　　vale,
May not unseemly with its stillness suit,
　As, musing slow, I hail
　Thy genial loved return!　　　　　　　　20
For when thy folding star arising shows
His paly circlet, at his warning lamp
　The fragrant Hours, and elves
　Who slept in flowers the day,
And many a nymph who wreathes her brows
　　with sedge,
And sheds the freshening dew, and, lovelier still,
　The pensive Pleasures sweet
　Prepare thy shadowy car.
Then lead, calm votaress, where some sheety lake
Cheers the lone heath, or some time-hallowed
　　pile,　　　　　　　　　　　　　　　　30

1 *aught of oaten stop:* any music from a shepherd's straw flute. 7 *brede:* garland. 21 *folding star:* Venus, whose appearance shows that the sheep must be led to their folds. 29 *votaress:* nun; *sheety:* smooth. 30 *pile:* ruined castle.

Or upland fallows gray
Reflect its last cool gleam.
But when chill blustering winds, or driving rain,
Forbid my willing feet, be mine the hut,
　That from the mountain's side
　Views wilds, and swelling floods,
And hamlets brown, and dim-discovered spires,
And hears their simple bell, and marks o'er all
　Thy dewy fingers draw
　The gradual dusky veil.　　　　　　　　40
While Spring shall pour his showers, as oft he
　　wont,
And bathe thy breathing tresses, meekest Eve;
　While Summer loves to sport
Beneath thy lingering light;
While sallow Autumn fills thy lap with leaves;
Or Winter, yelling through the troublous air,
　Affrights thy shrinking train
　And rudely rends thy robes;
So long, sure-found beneath the sylvan shed,
Shall Fancy, Friendship, Science, rose-lipped
　　Health,　　　　　　　　　　　　　　　50
　Thy gentlest influence own
　And hymn thy favorite name!

34 *Forbid:* deter me from my desired walk.　41 *as oft he wont:* as is often his custom.　49 *shed:* roof made by tree limbs. 50 *Science:* learning, study. 52 *favorite:* preferred (to all other times of day).

William Blake

TO SPRING

O thou with dewy locks, who lookest down
Through the clear windows of the morning, turn
Thine angel eyes upon our western isle,
Which in full choir hails thy approach, O
　　Spring!

The hills tell each other, and the listening
Valleys hear; all our longing eyes are turned
Up to thy bright pavilions: issue forth,
And let thy holy feet visit our clime.

Come o'er the eastern hills, and let our winds
Kiss thy perfumèd garments;! let us taste   10
Thy morn and evening breath; scatter thy pearls
Upon our love-sick land that mourns for thee.

O deck her forth with thy fair fingers; pour
Thy soft kisses on her bosom; and put
Thy golden crown upon her languished head,
Whose modest tresses were bound up for thee.

William Blake

NIGHT

The sun descending in the west,
The evening star does shine;
The birds are silent in their nest,
And I must seek for mine.
The moon, like a flower,
In heaven's high bower,
With silent delight
Sits and smiles on the night.

Farewell, green fields and happy groves,
Where flocks have took delight.   10
Where lambs have nibbled, silent moves
The feet of angels bright;
Unseen they pour blessing,
And joy without ceasing,
On each bud and blossom,
And each sleeping bosom.

They look in every thoughtless nest,
Where birds are covered warm;
They visit caves of every beast,
To keep them all from harm.   20
If they see any weeping
That should have been sleeping,
They pour sleep on their head,
And sit down by their bed.

When wolves and tigers howl for prey,
They pitying stand and weep;
Seeking to drive their thirst away,

And keep them from the sheep.
But if they rush dreadful,
The angels, most heedful,   30
Receive each mild spirit,
New worlds to inherit.

And there the lion's ruddy eyes
Shall flow with tears of gold,
And pitying the tender cries,
And walking round the fold,
Saying: "Wrath, by His meekness,
And, by His health, sickness
Is driven away
From our immortal day.   40

"And now beside thee, bleating lamb,
I can lie down and sleep;
Or think on Him who bore thy name,
Graze after thee and weep.
For, washed in life's river,
My bright mane for ever
Shall shine like the gold
As I guard o'er the fold."

William Wordsworth

LINES WRITTEN IN
EARLY SPRING

I heard a thousand blended notes,
While in a grove I sat reclined,
In that sweet mood when pleasant thoughts
Bring sad thoughts to the mind.

To her fair works did Nature link
The human soul that through me ran;
And much it grieved my heart to think
What man has made of man.

Through primrose tufts, in that green bower,
The periwinkle trailed its wreaths;   10
And 'tis my faith that every flower
Enjoys the air it breathes.

The birds around me hopped and played,
Their thoughts I cannot measure—
But the least motion which they made,
It seemed a thrill of pleasure.

The budding twigs spread out their fan,
To catch the breezy air;
And I must think, do all I can,
That there was pleasure there.   20

If this belief from heaven be sent,
If such be Nature's holy plan,
Have I not reason to lament
What man has made of man?

John Keats

TO AUTUMN

Season of mists and mellow fruitfulness,
  Close bosom-friend of the maturing sun;
Conspiring with him how to load and bless
    With fruit the vines that round the thatch-
      eaves run;
To bend with apples the mossed cottage-trees,
    And fill all fruit with ripeness to the core;
      To swell the gourd, and plump the hazel
        shells
    With a sweet kernel; to set budding more,
And still more, later flowers for the bees,
Until they think warm days will never cease,   10
      For Summer has o'er-brimmed their clammy
        cells.

Who hath not seen thee oft amid thy store?
  Sometimes whoever seeks abroad may find
Thee sitting careless on a granary floor,
  Thy hair soft-lifted by the winnowing wind;
Or on a half-reaped furrow sound asleep,
  Drowsed with the fume of poppies, while thy
    hook

12 *Thee*: Autumn, personified as a woman or a
goddess.

Spares the next swath and all its twinèd
  flowers;
And sometimes like a gleaner thou dost keep
  Steady thy laden head across a brook;   20
  Or by a cider-press, with patient look,
    Thou watchest the last oozings, hours by
      hours.

Where are the songs of Spring? Ay, where are
  they?
  Think not of them, thou hast thy music too,—
While barrèd clouds bloom the soft-dying day,
  And touch the stubble-plains with rosy hue;
Then in a wailful choir, the small gnats mourn
  Among the river sallows, borne aloft
    Or sinking as the light wind lives or dies;
And full-grown lambs loud bleat from hilly
  bourn;   30
  Hedge-crickets sing; and now with treble soft
  The redbreast whistles from a garden-croft,
    And gathering swallows twitter in the skies.

Emily Dickinson

A NARROW FELLOW
IN THE GRASS

A narrow fellow in the grass
Occasionally rides;
You may have met him—did you not?
His notice sudden is.

The grass divides as with a comb,
A spotted shaft is seen;
And then it closes at your feet
And opens further on.

He likes a boggy acre,
A floor too cool for corn.   10
Yet when a child, and barefoot,
I more than once, at morn,

Have passed, I thought, a whip-lash
Unbraiding in the sun—

When, stooping to secure it,
It wrinkled, and was gone.

Several of nature's people
I know, and they know me;
I feel for them a transport
Of cordiality;   20

But never met this fellow,
Attended or alone,
Without a tighter breathing,
And zero at the bone.

Gerard Manley Hopkins

GOD'S GRANDEUR

The world is charged with the grandeur of God.
   It will flame out, like shining from shook foil,
   It gathers to a greatness, like the ooze of oil
Crushed. Why do men then now not reck his
      rod?
Generations have trod, have trod, have trod;
   And all is seared with trade; bleared, smeared
      with toil;
   And wears man's smudge and shares man's
      smell: the soil
Is bare now, nor can foot feel, being shod.

And for all this, nature is never spent;
   There lives the dearest freshness deep down
      things;   10
And though the last lights off the black west
      went
   Oh, morning, at the brown brink eastward,
      springs—
Because the Holy Ghost over the bent
   World broods with warm breast and with ah!
      bright wings.

Gerard Manley Hopkins

SPRING

Nothing is so beautiful as spring—
   When weeds, in wheels, shoot long and lovely
      and lush;
   Thrush's eggs look little low heavens, and
      thrush
Through the echoing timber does so rinse and
      wring
The ear, it strikes like lightning to hear him
      sing;
   The glassy peartree leaves and blooms, they
      brush
   The descending blue; that blue is all in a rush
With richness; the racing lambs too have fair
      their fling.

What is all this juice and all this joy?
   A strain of the earth's sweet being in the
      beginning   10
In Eden garden.—Have, get, before it cloy,
   Before it cloud, Christ, lord, and sour with
      sinning,
Innocent mind and Mayday in girl and boy,
   Most, O maid's child, thy choice and worthy
      the winning.

Gerard Manley Hopkins

THE WINDHOVER

To Christ Our Lord

I caught this morning morning's minion, king-
    dom of daylight's dauphin, dapple-dawn-drawn Falcon, in his riding
    Of the rolling level underneath him steady air, and striding
High there, how he rung upon the rein of a wimpling wing
In his ecstasy! then off, off forth on swing,
    As a skate's heel sweeps smooth on a bow-bend: the hurl and gliding
    Rebuffed the big wind. My heart in hiding
Stirred for a bird—the achieve of, the mastery of the thing!

Brute beauty and valor and act, oh, air, pride, plume, here
    Buckle! AND the fire that breaks from thee then, a billion   10
Times told lovelier, more dangerous, O my chevalier!

    No wonder of it: shéer plód makes plough down sillion
Shine, and blue-bleak embers, ah my dear,
    Fall, gall themselves, and gash gold-vermilion.

C. Day-Lewis

WHEN NATURE PLAYS

  When nature plays hedge-schoolmaster,
Shakes out the gaudy map of summer
And shows me charabanc, rose, barley-ear
And every bright-winged hummer,

He only would require of me
To be the sponge of natural laws
And learn no more of that cosmography
Than passes through the pores.

Why must I then unleash my brain
To sweat after some revelation   10
Behind the rose, heedless if truth maintain
On the rose-bloom her station?

When bullying April bruised mine eyes
With sleet-bound appetites and crude
Experiments of green, I still was wise
And kissed the blossoming rod.

Now summer brings what April took,
Riding with fanfares from the south,
And I should be no Solomon to look
My Sheba in the mouth.   20

Charabancs shout along the lane
And summer gales bay in the wood
No less superbly because I can't explain
What I have understood.

Let logic analyze the hive,
Wisdom's content to have the honey:
So I'll go bite the crust of things and thrive
While hedgerows still are sunny.

Chapter 4

THE CITY

The number of people, and the percentage of people, who live in cities is constantly increasing; the cityscape becomes the inevitable environment for more and more of us. People's feelings about their urban environment are as deep and varied as their feelings about the natural world; and the literary expression of these feelings has called forth a variety of symbols. To middle-class city dwellers—so "The Murder They Heard" tells us—the street symbolizes vulgarity and danger. For the young couple in "Three Million Yen," the popular cracker and the amusement area embody a measure of their hope and their horizon of possibility. In "Twelve Chases on West Ninety-Ninth Street," the pace and personal interaction of city life is humorously epitomized as a series of chases. To Jonathan Swift, the rainwater coursing through the gutters climaxes the impressions of London with which "A City Shower" presents us.

Admirers of the city acclaim its wealth of opportunity, its richness of choice, its stimuli to creativity, its freedom from small-town and suburban interferences. Critics of the city cite its dirt, decay, danger, confusion, ugliness, and indifference to human needs. Some admirers and detractors have been poets, usually mixing ironically implicit criticism with praise and acknowledg-

ment of virtues with an attack on faults—as we see in Blake's "London," Wordsworth's "Composed upon Westminster Bridge," and other, contemporary, poems in this chapter. A similar ambivalence turns up in other works: Milgram and Hollander, for instance, call city life "harsh," but they find cities not lacking in human relationships—it is just that such relationships are organized on different principles from those found in small towns. And the protagonist of "Pillar of Salt," though the city ultimately overwhelms her, was initially magnetized by its "speed, luxury, and gaiety."

The works in this chapter, then, may be compared with those in "The World Around Us," for both chapters center on questions of the relationships of human beings to their physical environments. Both show us ways in which lives are shaped by their settings. But since the city is the man-made environment, it raises its own questions for the writer's literary appropriation and for the reader's reflection. What is a city, essentially? What features of city life are most distinctive and characteristic? In what specific ways can it be a sustainer of life on a truly human plane, and in what other ways does it threaten to destroy those values and qualities that make life worth living? Works of literature, though they cannot provide conclusive answers to such questions, can bring them home to us by offering dramatic presentations of issues as they have appeared to many writers of varying sensibilities.

Stanley Milgram and Paul Hollander

THE MURDER THEY HEARD

Catherine Genovese, coming home from a night job in the early hours of an April morning, was stabbed repeatedly and over an extended period of time. Thirty-eight residents of a respectable New York City neighborhood admit to having witnessed at least a part of the attack but not one of them went to her aid or even so much as called the police until after she was dead.

We are all certain that we would have done better. Our indignation toward the residents of Kew Gardens swells to a sense of outrage. The crime, or more precisely, the lack of civic response to it, was so vile that Senator Russell of Georgia read *The New York Times* account of it into the *Congressional Record*. The fact that it *was* Senator Russell is an indication of the complex social reactions touched off by this neighborhood tragedy.

It is noteworthy, first, that anger is directed, not toward the crime, nor the criminal, but toward those who failed to halt the criminal's actions. It is a curious shift, reminiscent of recent trends in moralizing about the Nazi era. Writers once focused on the sins of the Nazis; it is now more fashionable to discuss the complicity of their victims. The event is significant, also, for the way it is being exploited. Senator Russell is but one case in point. In his home state, several brutal murders of Negroes have taken place before large crowds of unprotesting white onlookers, but the Senator has never felt called upon to insert reports of

these brutalities into the *Record*. The crime against Miss Genovese no longer exists in and of itself. It is rapidly being assimilated to the uses and ideologies of the day.

For example, the Kew Gardens incident has become the occasion for a general attack on the city. It is portrayed as callous, cruel, indifferent to the needs of the people, and wholly inferior to the small town in the quality of its personal relationships. The abrasiveness of urban life cannot be argued; it is not true, however, that personal relationships are necessarily inferior in the city. They are merely organized on a different principle. Urban friendships and associations are not primarily formed on the basis of physical proximity. A person with numerous close friends in different parts of the city may not know the occupant of an adjacent apartment. Some hold this to be an advantage of the city: men and women can conduct lives unmonitored by the constant scrutiny of neighbors. This does not mean that a city dweller has fewer friends than does a villager, or knows fewer persons who will come to his aid; however, it does mean that his allies are not constantly at hand. Miss Genovese required immediate aid from those physically present; her predicament was desperate and not typical of the occasions when we look for the support of friends. There is no evidence that the city had deprived Miss Genovese of human associations, but the friends who might have rushed to her side were miles from the scene of her tragedy.

A truly extraordinary aspect of the case is the general readiness to forget the man who committed a very foul crime. This is typical of social reactions in present-day America. It begins to seem that everyone, having absorbed a smattering of sociology, looks at once beyond the concrete case in an eager quest for high-sounding generalizations that imply an enlightened social vista. What gets lost in many of these discussions—and what needs at least a partial restoration—is the notion that people may occasionally be responsible for what they do, even if their acts are criminal. In our righteous denunciation of the thirty-eight witnesses we should not forget that they did not commit the murder; they merely failed to prevent it. It is no more than clear thinking to bear in mind the moral difference.

A related and equally confusing error is to infer ethical values from the actual behavior of people in concrete situations. For example, in the case of Miss Genovese we must ask: Did the witnesses remain passive because they thought it was the right thing to do, or did they refrain from action *despite* what they thought or felt they should do? We cannot take it for granted that people always do what they consider right. It would be more fruitful to inquire why, in general and in this particular case, there is so marked a discrepancy between values and behavior. What makes people choose a course of action that probably shames them in retrospect? How do they become reduced to resignation, acquiescence and helplessness?

Those who vilify the residents of Kew Gardens measure them against the standard of their own ability to formulate high-minded moral prescriptions. But that is hardly a fair standard. It is entirely likely that many of the witnesses, at the level of stated opinion, feel quite as strongly as any of us about the moral requirement of aiding a helpless victim. They too, in general terms, know what *ought* to be done, and can state their values when the occasion arises. This has little, if anything, to do with actual behavior under the press of circumstances.

Furthermore, we must distinguish between the facts of the murder as finally known and reported in the press and the events of the evening as they were experienced by the Kew Gardens residents. We can now say that if the police had been called after the first attack, the woman's life might have been saved, and we tend to judge the inaction of the Kew Gardens residents in the light of this lost possibility. That is natural, perhaps, but it is unrealistic. If those men and women had had as clear a grasp of the situation as we have now, the chances are that many of them would have acted to save Miss Genovese's life. What they had, instead, were fragments of an ambiguous, confusing and doubtless frightening episode —one, moreover, that seemed totally incongruous in a respectable neighborhood. The very lack of correspondence between the violence of the crime and the character of the neighborhood must have created a sense of unreality which inhibited rational action. A lesser crime, one more in character with the locale—say, after-hours rowdiness from a group of college students—might have led more readily to a call for the police.

The incongruity, the sheer improbability of the event predisposed many to reject the most extreme interpretation: that a young woman was in fact being murdered outside the window. How much more probable, not to say more consoling, was the interpretation that a drunken party was sounding off, that two lovers were quarreling, or that youths were playing a nasty prank. Bruno Bettelheim, in *The Informed Heart*,[1] describes how resistant many German Jews were to the signs around them of impending disaster. Given any possibility for fitting events into an acceptable order of things, men are quick to seize it. It takes courage to perceive clearly and without distortion. We cannot justly condemn all the Kew Gardens residents in the light of a horrible outcome which only the most perspicacious could have foreseen.

Why didn't the group of onlookers band together, run out into the street, and subdue the assailant? Aside from the fact that such organization takes time, and that the on-

[1] A study (1960) of the individual vs. the state, based on the author's experiences in the concentration camps of Buchenwald and Dachau.

lookers were not in communication (who in such a community knows his neighbor's phone number?), there is another factor that would render such action almost impossible. Despite our current fears about the contagion of violence in the mass media, the fact remains that the middle-class person is totally unequipped to deal with its actual occurrence. More especially, he is unable to use personal violence, either singly or collectively, even when it is required for productive and socially valued ends.

More generally, modern societies are so organized as to discourage even the most beneficial, spontaneous group action. This applies with particular sharpness to the law-abiding, respectable segments of the population—such as the people of Kew Gardens—who have most thoroughly accepted the admonition: "do not take the law into your own hands." In a highly specialized society such people take it for granted that certain functions and activities—from garbage collection to fire protection, from meat certification to the control of criminals—are taken care of by specially trained people. The puzzle in the case under consideration is the reluctance to supply to the police even the barest information which it was essential they have if they were to fulfill their acknowledged functions.

Many facts of the case have not been made public, such as the quality of the relationship between Miss Genovese and the community, the extent to which she was recognized that night, and the number of persons who knew her. It is known that her cries for help were not directed to a specific person: they were general. But only individuals can act, and as the cries were not specifically directed, no particular person felt a special responsibility. The crime and the failure of community response seem absurd to us. At the time, it may well have seemed equally absurd to the Kew Gardens residents that not one of the neighbors would have called the police. A collective paralysis may have developed from the belief of each of the witnesses that someone else must surely have taken that obvious step.

If we ask why they did not call the police, we should also ask what were the alternatives. To be sure, phoning from within an apartment was the most prudent course of action, one involving the minimum of both physical inconvenience and personal involvement with a violent criminal. And yet, one has to assume that in the minds of many there lurked the alternative of going down to the street and defending the helpless woman. This, indeed, might have been felt as the ideal response. By comparison, a mere phone call from the safety of home may have seemed a cowardly compromise with what should be done. As often happens, the ideal solution was difficult, probably dangerous; but, as also happens, the practical, safe alternative may have seemed distasteful in the light of the ideal. Awareness of an ideal response often paralyzes a move toward the less than ideal alternative. Rather than accept the belittling second-best, the person so beset prefers to blot out the whole issue. Therefore, he pretends that there is nothing to get upset about. Probably it was only a drunken brawl.

The symbolic significance of "the street" for the middle-class mentality may have some relevance to the case. Although it cannot explain in full the failure to grab the telephone and call the police, it may account in part for the inertia and indifference. For the middle-class resident of a big city the street and what happens on the street are often symbolic of all that is vulgar and perilous in life. The street is the antithesis of privacy, security, and the support one derives from contemplating and living amidst prized personal possessions. The street represents the world of pushing and shoving crowds, potentially hostile strangers, sweat, dust, and noise. Those who spend much time on the street have nothing better to do and nowhere better to go: the poor,

the foot-loose, the drifters, juvenile delinquents. Therefore, the middle-class person
seeks almost automatically to disengage himself from the life of the street; he is on it
only from necessity, rarely for pleasure. Such
considerations help explain the genesis of
attitudes that prevented the witnesses from
making the crucial phone call. The tragic
drama was taking place on the street, hence
hardly relevant to their lives; in fact, in
some ways radically opposed to their outlook and concerns.

In an effort to make the strongest possible
case against the Kew Gardens citizens, the
press has ignored actual dangers of involvement, even at the level of calling the police.
They have treated the "fears" of the residents as foolish rationalizations, utterly
without basis. In doing so they have con-
veniently forgotten instances in which involvement did not turn out well for the hero.
One spectacular case in the early fifties,
amply publicized by the press, concerned the
misfortune of Arnold Schuster. While riding
in the subway this young Brooklyn man
spotted Willie Sutton, an escaped criminal.
He reported this information to the police,
and it led to Sutton's arrest. Schuster was
proclaimed a hero, but before a month was
up Schuster was dead—murdered in reprisal
for his part in Sutton's recapture. Schuster
had done nothing more than phone the
police.

The fact is that there *are* risks even in
minimal forms of involvement, and it is dishonest to ignore them. One becomes involved with the police, with the general
agents of publicity that swarm to such
events, and possibly with the criminal. If
the criminal is not caught immediately,
there is the chance that he will learn who
called the police (which apartment did they
enter first, whose pictures are in the papers,
etc.) and may fear that the caller can identify him. The caller, then, is of special concern to the criminal. If a trial is held, the
person who telephoned is likely to be a

witness. Even if he is jailed, the criminal
may have underworld friends who will act
to avenge him. One is a responsible citizen
and a worthy human being, not because of
the absence of risk but because one acts in
the face of it.

In seeking explanations for their inaction,
we have not intended to defend, certainly
not to excuse, Kew Gardens' passive witnesses. We have sought, rather, to put ourselves in their place, to try to understand
their response. The causes we have suggested
are in no way sufficient reason for inaction.
Perhaps we should have started with a more
fundamental question: Why should anyone
have gone to the aid of the victim? Why
should anyone have taken the trouble to call
the police? The answer must be that it is
a matter of common decency to help those
who are in distress. It is a humane and compassionate requirement in the relations between people. Yet how generally is it
observed? In New York City it is not at all
unusual to see a man, sick with alcohol,
lying in a doorway; he does not command
the least attention or interest from those
who pass by. The trouble here, as in Kew
Gardens, is that the individual does not perceive that his interests are identified with
others or with the community at large. And
is such a perception possible? What evidence
is there in the American community that
collective interests have priority over personal advantage?

There are, of course, practical limitations
to the Samaritan impulse in a major city. If
a citizen attended to every needy person, if
he were sensitive to and acted on every
altruistic impulse that was evoked in the
city, he could scarcely keep his own affairs
in order. A calculated and strategic indifference is an unavoidable part of life in our
cities, and it must be faced without sentimentality or rage. At most, each of us can
resolve to extend the range of his responsibilities in some perceptible degree, to rise
a little more adequately to moral obliga-

tions. City life is harsh; still, we owe it to ourselves and our fellows to resolve that it be no more harsh than is inevitable.

Shirley Jackson

PILLAR OF SALT

For some reason a tune was running through her head when she and her husband got on the train in New Hampshire for their trip to New York; they had not been to New York for nearly a year, but the tune was from further back than that. It was from the days when she was fifteen or sixteen, and had never seen New York except in movies, when the city was made up, to her, of penthouses filled with Noel Coward people; when the height and speed and luxury and gaiety that made up a city like New York were confused inextricably with the dullness of being fifteen, and beauty unreachable and far in the movies.

"What *is* that tune?" she said to her husband, and hummed it. "It's from some old movie, I think."

"I know it," he said, and hummed it himself. "Can't remember the words."

He sat back comfortably. He had hung up their coats, put the suitcases on the rack, and had taken his magazine out. "I'll think of it sooner or later," he said.

She looked out the window first, tasting it almost secretly, savoring the extreme pleasure of being on a moving train with nothing to do for six hours but read and nap and go into the dining-car, going farther and farther every minute from the children, from the kitchen floor, with even the hills being incredibly left behind, changing into fields and trees too far away from home to be daily. "I love trains," she said, and her

PILLAR OF SALT: *Genesis* XIX: 26.

husband nodded sympathetically into his magazine.

Two weeks ahead, two unbelievable weeks, with all arrangements made, no further planning to do, except perhaps what theaters or what restaurants. A friend with an apartment went on a convenient vacation, there was enough money in the bank to make a trip to New York compatible with new snow suits for the children; there was the smoothness of unopposed arrangements, once the initial obstacles had been overcome, as though when they had really made up their minds, nothing dared stop them. The baby's sore throat cleared up. The plumber came, finished his work in two days, and left. The dresses had been altered in time; the hardware store could be left safely, once they had found the excuse of looking over new city products. New York had not burned down, had not been quarantined, their friend had gone away according to schedule, and Brad had the keys to the apartment in his pocket. Everyone knew where to reach everyone else; there was a list of plays not to miss and a list of items to look out for in the stores—diapers, dress materials, fancy canned goods, tarnish-proof silverware boxes, And, finally, the train was there, performing its function, pacing through the afternoon, carrying them legally and with determination to New York.

Margaret looked curiously at her husband, inactive in the middle of the afternoon on a train, at the other fortunate people traveling, at the sunny country outside, looked again to make sure, and then opened her book. The tune was still in her head, she hummed it and heard her husband take it up softly as he turned a page in his magazine.

In the dining-car she ate roast beef, as she would have done in a restaurant at home, reluctant to change over too quickly to the new, tantalizing food of a vacation. She had ice cream for dessert but became uneasy over her coffee because they were due in

New York in an hour and she still had to put on her coat and hat, relishing every gesture, and Brad must take the suitcases down and put away the magazines. They stood at the end of the car for the interminable underground run, picking up their suitcases and putting them down again, moving restlessly inch by inch.

The station was a momentary shelter, moving visitors gradually into a world of people and sound and light to prepare them for the blasting reality of the street outside. She saw it for a minute from the sidewalk before she was in a taxi moving into the middle of it, and then they were bewilderingly caught and carried on uptown and whirled out on to another sidewalk and Brad paid the taxi driver and put his head back to look up at the apartment house. "This is it, all right," he said, as though he had doubted the driver's ability to find a number so simply given. Upstairs in the elevator, and the key fit the door. They had never seen their friend's apartment before, but it was reasonably familiar—a friend moving from New Hampshire to New York carries private pictures of a home not erasable in a few years, and the apartment had enough of home in it to settle Brad immediately in the right chair and comfort her with instinctive trust of the linen and blankets.

"This is home for two weeks," Brad said, and stretched. After the first few minutes they both went to the windows automatically; New York was below, as arranged, and the houses across the street were apartment houses filled with unknown people.

"It's wonderful," she said. There were cars down there, and people, and the noise was there. "I'm so happy," she said, and kissed her husband.

They went sight-seeing the first day; they had breakfast in an Automat and went to the top of the Empire State Building. "Got it all fixed up now," Brad said, at the top. "Wonder just where that plane hit."

They tried to peer down on all four sides, but were embarrassed about asking. "After all," she said reasonably, giggling in a corner, "if something of mine got broken I wouldn't want people poking around asking to see the pieces."

"If you owned the Empire State Building you wouldn't care," Brad said.

They traveled only in taxis the first few days, and one taxi had a door held on with a piece of string; they pointed to it and laughed silently at each other, and on about the third day, the taxi they were riding in got a flat tire on Broadway and they had to get out and find another.

"We've only got eleven days left," she said one day, and then, seemingly minutes later, "we've already been here six days."

They had got in touch with the friends they had expected to get in touch with, they were going to a Long Island summer home for a week end. "It looks pretty dreadful right now," their hostess said cheerfully over the phone, "and we're leaving in a week ourselves, but I'd never *forgive* you if you didn't see it *once* while you were here." The weather had been fair but cool, with a definite autumn awareness, and the clothes in the store windows were dark and already hinting at furs and velvets. She wore her coat every day, and suits most of the time. The light dresses she had brought were hanging in the closet in the apartment, and she was thinking now of getting a sweater in one of the big stores, something impractical for New Hampshire, but probably good for Long Island.

"I have to do some shopping, at least one day," she said to Brad, and he groaned.

"Don't ask me to carry packages," he said.

"You aren't up to a good day's shopping," she told him, "not after all this walking around you've been doing. Why don't you go to a movie or something?"

"I want to do some shopping myself," he said mysteriously. Perhaps he was talking about her Christmas present; she had thought vaguely of getting such things done in New York; the children would be pleased with novelties from the city, toys not seen in their home stores. At any rate she said, "You'll probably be able to get to your wholesalers at last."

They were on their way to visit another friend, who had found a place to live by a miracle and warned them consequently not to quarrel with the appearance of the building, or the stairs, or the neighborhood. All three were bad, and the stairs were three flights, narrow and dark, but there was a place to live at the top. Their friend had not been in New York long, but he lived by himself in two rooms, and had easily caught the mania for slim tables and low bookcases which made his rooms look too large for the furniture in some places, too cramped and uncomfortable in others.

"What a lovely place," she said when she came in, and then was sorry when her host said, "Some day this damn situation will let up and I'll be able to settle down in a really decent place."

There were other people there; they sat and talked companionably about the same subjects then current in New Hampshire, but they drank more than they would have at home and it left them strangely unaffected; their voices were louder and their words more extravagant; their gestures, on the other hand, were smaller, and they moved a finger where in New Hampshire they would have waved an arm. Margaret said frequently, "We're just staying here for a couple of weeks, on a vacation," and she said, "It's wonderful, so *exciting*," and she said, "We were *terribly* lucky; this friend went out of town just at the right. . . ."

Finally the room was very full and noisy, and she went into a corner near a window to catch her breath. The window had been opened and shut all evening, depending on whether the person standing next to it had both hands free; and now it was shut, with the clear sky outside. Someone came and stood next to her, and she said, "Listen to the noise outside. It's as bad as it is inside."

He said, "In a neighborhood like this someone's always getting killed."

She frowned. "It sounds different than before. I mean, there's a different sound to it."

"Alcoholics," he said. "Drunks in the streets. Fighting going on across the way." He wandered away, carrying his drink.

She opened the window and leaned out, and there were people hanging out of the windows across the way shouting and people standing in the street looking up and shouting, and from across the way she heard clearly, "Lady, lady." They must mean me, she thought, they're all looking this way. She leaned out farther and the voices shouted incoherently but somehow making an audible whole, "Lady, your house is on fire, lady, lady."

She closed the window firmly and turned around to the other people in the room, raising her voice a little. "Listen," she said, "they're saying the house is on fire." She was desperately afraid of their laughing at her, of looking like a fool while Brad across the room looked at her blushing. She said again, "The *house* is on *fire*," and added, "They say," for fear of sounding too vehement. The people nearest to her turned and someone said, "She says the house is on fire."

She wanted to get to Brad and couldn't see him; her host was not in sight either, and the people all around were strangers. They don't listen to me, she thought, I might as well not be here, and she went to the outside door and opened it. There was no smoke, no flame, but she was telling herself, I might as well not be here, so she abandoned Brad in panic and ran without her hat and coat down the stairs, carrying a glass in one hand and a package of matches in the other. The stairs were insanely long, but they were clear and safe, and she opened the street door and ran out. A man caught her arm and said, "Everyone out of the house?" and she said, "No, Brad's still there." The fire engines swept around the corner, with people leaning out of the windows watching them, and the man holding her arm said, "It's down here," and left her. The fire was two houses away; they could see flames behind the top windows, and smoke against the night sky, but in ten minutes it was finished and the fire engines pulled away with an air of martyrdom for hauling out all their equipment to put out a ten-minute fire.

She went back upstairs slowly and with embarrassment, and found Brad and took him home.

"I was so frightened," she said to him when they were safely in bed, "I lost my head completely."

"You should have tried to find someone," he said.

"They wouldn't listen," she insisted. "I kept telling them and they wouldn't listen and then I thought I must have been mistaken. I had some idea of going down to see what was going on."

"Lucky it was no worse," Brad said sleepily.

"I felt trapped," she said. "High up in that old building with a fire; it's like a nightmare. And in a strange city."

"Well, it's all over now," Brad said.

The same faint feeling of insecurity tagged her the next day; she went shopping alone and Brad went off to see hardware, after all. She got on a bus to go downtown and the bus was too full to move when it came time for her to get out. Wedged standing in the aisle she said, "Out, please," and, "Excuse me," and by the time she was loose and near the door the bus had started again and she got off a stop beyond. "No one *listens* to me," she said to herself. "Maybe it's because I'm too polite." In the stores the prices were all too high and the sweaters looked disarmingly like New Hampshire ones. The toys for the children filled her with dismay; they were so obviously for New York children: hideous little parodies of adult life, cash registers, tiny pushcarts with imitation fruit, telephones that really worked (as if there weren't enough phones in New York that really worked), miniature milk bottles in a carrying case. "We get our milk from cows," Margaret told the salesgirl.

"My children wouldn't know what these were." She was exaggerating, and felt guilty for a minute, but no one was around to catch her.

She had a picture of small children in the city dressed like their parents, following along with a miniature mechanical civilization, toy cash registers in larger and larger sizes that eased them into the real thing, millions of clattering jerking small imitations that prepared them nicely for taking over the large useless toys their parents lived by. She bought a pair of skis for her son, which she knew would be inadequate for the New Hampshire snow, and a wagon for her daughter inferior to the one Brad could make at home in an hour. Ignoring the toy mailboxes, the small phonographs with special small records, the kiddie cosmetics, she left the store and started home.

She was frankly afraid by now to take a bus; she stood on the corner and waited for a taxi. Glancing down at her feet, she saw a dime on the sidewalk and tried to pick it up, but there were too many people for her to bend down, and she was afraid to shove to make room for fear of being stared at. She put her foot on the dime and then saw a quarter near it, and a nickel. Someone dropped a pocketbook, she thought, and put her other foot on the quarter, stepping quickly to make it look natural; then she saw another dime and another nickel, and a third dime in the gutter. People were passing her, back and forth, all the time, rushing, pushing against her, not looking at her, and she was afraid to get down and start gathering up the money. Other people saw it and went past, and she realized that no one was going to pick it up. They were all embarrassed, or in too much of a hurry, or too crowded. A taxi stopped to let someone off, and she hailed it. She lifted her feet off the dime and the quarter, and left them there when she got into the taxi. This taxi went slowly and bumped as it went; she had begun to notice that the gradual decay was not peculiar to the taxis. The buses were cracking open in unimportant seams, the leather seats broken and stained. The buildings were going, too—in one of the nicest stores there had been a great gaping hole in the tiled foyer, and you walked around it. Corners of the buildings seemed to be crumbling away into fine dust that drifted downward, the granite was eroding unnoticed. Every window she saw on her way uptown seemed to be broken; perhaps every street corner was peppered with small change. The people were moving faster than ever before; a girl in a red hat appeared at the upper side of the taxi window and was gone beyond the lower side before you could see the hat; store windows were so terribly bright because you only caught them for a fraction of a second. The people seemed hurled on in a frantic action that made every hour forty-five minutes long, every day nine hours, every year fourteen days. Food was so elusively fast, eaten in such a hurry, that you were always hungry, always speeding to a new meal with new people. Everything was imperceptibly quicker every minute. She stepped into the taxi on one side and stepped out the other side at her home; she pressed the fifth-floor button on the elevator and was coming down again, bathed and dressed and ready for dinner with Brad. They went out for dinner and were coming in again, hungry and hurrying to bed in order to get to breakfast with lunch beyond. They had been in New York nine days; tomorrow was Saturday and they were going to Long Island, coming home Sunday, and then Wednesday they were going home, really home. By the time she had thought of it they were on the train to Long Island; the train was broken, the seats torn and the floor dirty; one of the doors wouldn't open and the windows wouldn't shut. Passing through the outskirts of the city, she thought, It's as though everything were traveling so fast that the solid stuff couldn't stand it and were going to pieces under the strain, cornices blowing off and windows caving in. She knew she was afraid to say it truly, afraid to face the knowledge that it was a voluntary neck-breaking speed, a deliberate whirling faster and faster to end in destruction.

On Long Island, their hostess led them into a new piece of New York, a house filled with New York furniture as though on rubber bands, pulled this far, stretched taut, and ready to snap back to the city, to an apartment, as soon as the door was opened and the lease, fully paid, had expired. "We've had this place every year for simply ages," their hostess said. "Otherwise we couldn't have gotten it *possibly* this year."

"It's an awfully nice place," Brad said. "I'm surprised you don't live here all year round."

"Got to get back to the city *some* time," their hostess said, and laughed.

"Not much like New Hampshire," Brad said. He was beginning to be a little homesick, Margaret thought; he wants to yell, just once. Since the fire scare she was apprehensive about large groups of people gathering together; when friends began to drop in after dinner she waited for a while, telling herself they were on the ground floor, she could run right outside, all the windows were open; then she excused herself and went to bed. When Brad came to bed much later she woke up and he said irritably, "We've been playing anagrams. Such crazy people." She said sleepily, "Did you win?" and fell asleep before he told her.

The next morning she and Brad went for a walk while their host and hostess read the Sunday papers. "If you turn to the right outside the door," their hostess said encouragingly, "and walk about three blocks down, you'll come to our beach."

"What do they want with our beach?" their host said. "It's too damn cold to do anything down there."

"They can look at the *water*," their hostess said.

They walked down to the beach; at this time of year it was bare and windswept, yet still nodding hideously under traces of its

summer plumage, as though it thought itself
warmly inviting. There were occupied
houses on the way there, for instance, and
a lonely lunchstand was open, bravely advertising hot dogs and root beer. The man in
the lunchstand watched them go by, his face
cold and unsympathetic. They walked far
past him, out of sight of houses, on to a
stretch of grey pebbled sand that lay between the grey water on one side and the
grey pebbled sand dunes on the other.

"Imagine going swimming here," she said
with a shiver. The beach pleased her; it was
oddly familiar and reassuring and at the
same time that she realized this, the little
tune came back to her, bringing a double
recollection. The beach was the one where
she had lived in imagination, writing for
herself dreary love-broken stories where the
heroine walked beside the wild waves; the
little tune was the symbol of the golden
world she escaped into to avoid the everyday
dreariness that drove her into writing
depressing stories about the beach. She
laughed out loud and Brad said, "What on
earth's so funny about this Godforsaken
landscape?"

"I was just thinking how far away from
the city it seems," she said falsely.

The sky and the water and the sand were
grey enough to make it feel like late afternoon instead of midmorning; she was tired
and wanted to go back, but Brad said suddenly, "Look at that," and she turned and
saw a girl running down over the dunes,
carrying her hat, and her hair flying behind
her.

"Only way to get warm on a day like
this," Brad remarked, but Margaret said,
"She looks frightened."

The girl saw them and came toward them,
slowing down as she approached them. She
was eager to reach them but when she came
within speaking distance the familiar embarrassment, the not wanting to look like a
fool, made her hesitate and look from one to
the other of them uncomfortably.

"Do you know where I can find a policeman?" she asked finally.

Brad looked up and down the bare rocky
beach and said solemnly, "There don't seem
to be any around. Is there something we can
do?"

"I don't think so," the girl said. "I really
need a policeman."

They go to the police for everything, Margaret thought, these people, these New York
people, it's as though they had selected a
section of the population to act as problem-
solvers, and so no matter what they want
they look for a policeman.

"Be glad to help you if we can," Brad
said.

The girl hesitated again. "Well, if you
must know," she said crossly, "there's a leg
up there."

They waited politely for the girl to explain, but she only said, "Come *on*, then,"
and waved to them to follow her. She led
them over the dunes to a spot near a small
inlet, where the dunes gave way abruptly to
an intruding head of water. A leg was lying
on the sand near the water, and the girl
gestured at it and said, "There," as though it
were her own property and they had insisted
on having a share.

They walked over to it and Brad bent
down gingerly. "It's a leg all right," he said.
It looked like part of a wax dummy, a death-
white wax leg neatly cut off at top-thigh
and again just above the ankle, bent comfortably at the knee and resting on the sand.
"It's real," Brad said, his voice slightly different. "You're right about that policeman."

They walked together to the lunchstand
and the man listened unenthusiastically
while Brad called the police. When the police came they all walked out again to where
the leg was lying and Brad gave the police
their names and addresses, and then said,
"Is it all right to go home?"

"What the hell you want to hang around
for?" the policeman inquired with heavy
humor. "You waiting for the rest of him?"

They went back to their host and hostess, talking about the leg, and their host apologized, as though he had been guilty of a breach of taste in allowing his guests to come on a human leg; their hostess said with interest, "There was an arm washed up in Bensonhurst, I've been reading about it."

"One of these killings," the host said.

Upstairs Margaret said abruptly, "I suppose it starts to happen first in the suburbs," and when Brad said, "What starts to happen?" she said hysterically, "People starting to come apart."

In order to reassure their host and hostess about their minding the leg, they stayed until the last afternoon train to New York. Back in their apartment again it seemed to Margaret that the marble in the house lobby had begun to age a little; even in two days there were new perceptible cracks. The elevator seemed a little rusty, and there was a fine film of dust over everything in the apartment. They went to bed feeling uncomfortable, and the next morning Margaret said immediately, "I'm going to stay in today."

"You're not upset about yesterday, are you?"

"Not a bit," Margaret said. "I just want to stay in and rest."

After some discussion Brad decided to go off again by himself; he still had people it was important to see and places he must go in the few days they had left. After breakfast in the Automat Margaret came back alone to the apartment, carrying the mystery story she had bought on the way. She hung up her coat and hat and sat down by the window with the noise and the people far below, looking out at the sky where it was grey beyond the houses across the street.

I'm not going to worry about it, she said to herself, no sense thinking all the time about things like that, spoil your vacation and Brad's too. No sense worrying, people get ideas like that and then worry about them.

The nasty little tune was running through her head again, with its burden of suavity and expensive perfume. The houses across the street were silent and perhaps unoccupied at this time of day; she let her eyes move with the rhythm of the tune, from window to window along one floor. By gliding quickly across two windows, she could make one line of the tune fit one floor of windows, and then a quick breath and a drop down to the next floor; it had the same number of windows and the tune had the same number of beats, and then the next floor and the next. She stopped suddenly when it seemed to her that the windowsill she had just passed had soundlessly crumpled and fallen into fine sand; when she looked back it was there as before but then it seemed to be the windowsill above and to the right, and finally a corner of the roof.

No sense worrying, she told herself, forcing her eyes down to the street, stop thinking about things all the time. Looking down at the street for long made her dizzy and she stood up and went into the small bedroom of the apartment. She had made the bed before going out to breakfast, like any good housewife, but now she deliberately took it apart, stripping the blankets and sheets off one by one, and then she made it again, taking a long time over the corners and smoothing out every wrinkle. "That's done," she said when she was through, and went back to the window. When she looked across the street the tune started again, window to window, sills dissolving and falling downward. She leaned forward and looked down at her own window, something she had never thought of before, down to the sill. It was partly eaten away; when she touched the stone a few crumbs rolled off and fell.

It was eleven o'clock; Brad was looking at blowtorches by now and would not be back before one, if even then. She thought of writing a letter home, but the impulse left her before she found paper and pen. Then it occurred to her that she might take a nap, a thing she had never done in the morning in her life, and she went in and lay down on the bed. Lying down, she felt the building shaking.

No sense worrying, she told herself again, as though it were a charm against witches, and got up and found her coat and hat and put them on. I'll just get some cigarettes and some letter paper, she thought, just run down to the corner. Panic caught her going down in the elevator; it went too fast, and when she stepped out in the lobby it was only the people standing around who kept her from running. As it was, she went quickly out of the building and into the street. For a minute she hesitated, wanting to go back. The cars were going past so rapidly, the people hurrying as always, but the panic of the elevator drove her on finally. She went to the corner and, following the people flying along ahead, ran out into the street, to hear a horn almost overhead and a shout from behind her, and the noise of brakes. She ran blindly on and reached the other side where she stopped and looked around. The truck was going on its appointed way around the corner, the people going past on either side of her, parting to go around her where she stood.

No one even noticed me, she thought with reassurance, everyone who saw me has gone by long ago. She went into the drugstore ahead of her and asked the man for cigarettes; the apartment now seemed safer to her than the street—she could walk up the stairs. Coming out of the store and walking to the corner, she kept as close to the buildings as possible, refusing to give way to the rightful traffic coming out of the doorways. On the corner she looked carefully at the light; it was green, but it looked as though it were going to change. Always safer to wait, she thought, don't want to walk into another truck.

People pushed past her and some were caught in the middle of the street when the light changed. One woman, more cowardly than the rest, turned and ran back to the curb, but the others stood in the middle of the street, leaning forward and then backward according to the traffic moving past them on both sides. One got to the farther curb in a brief break in the line of cars, the others were a fraction of a second too late and waited. Then the light changed again and as the cars slowed down Margaret put a foot on the street to go, but a taxi swinging wildly around her corner frightened her back and she stood on the curb again. By the time the taxi had gone the light was due to change again and she thought, I can wait once more, no sense getting caught out in the middle. A man beside her tapped his foot impatiently for the light to change back; two girls came past her and walked out in the street a few steps to wait, moving back a little when cars came too close, talking busily all the time. I ought to stay right with them, Margaret thought, but then they moved back against her and the light changed and the man next to her charged into the street and the two girls in front waited a minute and then moved slowly on, still talking, and Margaret started to follow and then decided to wait. A crowd of people formed around her suddenly; they had come off a bus and were crossing here, and she had a sudden feeling of being jammed in the center and forced out into the street when all of them moved as one with the light changing, and she elbowed her way desperately out of the crowd and went off to lean against a building and wait. It seemed to her that people passing were beginning to look at her. What do they think of me, she wondered, and stood up straight as though she were waiting for someone. She looked at her watch and frowned, and then thought, What a fool I must look like, no one here ever saw me before, they all go by too fast. She went back to the curb again but the green light was just changing to red and she thought, I'll go back to the drugstore and have a Coke, no sense going back to that apartment.

The man looked at her unsurprised in the drugstore and she sat and ordered a Coke but suddenly as she was drinking it the panic caught her again and she thought of the people who had been with her when she first started to cross the street, blocks away by now, having tried and made perhaps a dozen lights while she had hesitated at the first; people by now a mile or so downtown, because they had been going steadily while she had been trying to gather her courage. She paid the man quickly, restrained an impulse to say that there was nothing wrong with the Coke, she just had to get back, that was all, and she hurried down to the corner again.

The minute the light changes, she told herself firmly; there's no sense. The light changed before she was ready and in the minute before she collected herself traffic turning the corner overwhelmed her and she shrank back against the curb. She looked longingly at the cigar store on the opposite corner, with her apartment house beyond; she wondered, How do people ever manage to get there, and knew that by wondering, by admitting a doubt, she was lost. The light changed and she looked at it with hatred, a dumb thing, turning back and forth, back and forth, with no purpose and no meaning. Looking to either side of her slyly, to see if anyone were watching, she stepped quietly backward, one step, two, until she was well away from the curb. Back in the drugstore again she waited for some sign of recognition from the clerk and saw none; he regarded her with the same apathy as he had the first time. He gestured without interest at the telephone; he doesn't care, she thought, it doesn't matter to him who I call.

She had no time to feel like a fool, because they answered the phone immediately and agreeably and found him right away. When he answered the phone, his voice sounding surprised and matter-of-fact, she could only say miserably, "I'm in the drugstore on the corner. Come and get me."

"What's the matter?" He was not anxious to come.

"Please come and get me," she said into the black mouthpiece that might or might not tell him, "please come and get me, Brad. *Please*."

Yukio Mishima

THREE MILLION YEN

"We're to meet her at nine?" asked Kenzō.

"At nine, she said, in the toy department on the ground floor," replied Kiyoko. "But it's too noisy to talk there, and I told her about the coffee shop on the third floor instead."

"That was a good idea."

The young husband and wife looked up at the neon pagoda atop the New World Building, which they were approaching from the rear.

It was a cloudy, muggy night, of a sort common in the early-summer rainy season. Neon lights painted the low sky in rich colors. The delicate pagoda, flashing on and off in the softer of neon tones, was very beautiful indeed. It was particularly beautiful when, after all the flashing neon tubes had gone out together, they suddenly flashed on again, so soon that the after-image had scarcely disappeared. To be seen from all over Asakusa, the pagoda had replaced Gourd Pond, now filled in, as the main landmark of the Asakusa night.

To Kenzō and Kiyoko the pagoda seemed to encompass in all its purity some grand, inaccessible dream of life. Leaning against the rail of the parking lot, they looked absently up at it for a time.

Kenzō was in an undershirt, cheap trousers, and wooden clogs. His skin was fair but the lines of the shoulders and chest were powerful, and bushes of black hair showed between the mounds of muscle at the armpits. Kiyoko, in a sleeveless dress, always had her own armpits carefully shaved. Kenzō was very fussy. Because they hurt when the hair began to grow again, she had become almost obsessive about keeping them shaved, and there was a faint flush on the white skin.

She had a round little face, the pretty features as though woven of cloth. It reminded one of some earnest, unsmiling little animal. It was a face which a person trusted immediately, but not one on which to read thoughts. On her arm she had a large pink plastic handbag and Kenzō's pale blue sports shirt. Kenzō liked to be empty-handed.

From her modest coiffure and make-up one sensed the frugality of their life. Her eyes were clear and had no time for other men.

They crossed the dark road in front of the parking lot and went into the New World. The big market on the ground floor was filled with myriad-colored mountains of splendid, gleaming, cheap wares, and salesgirls peeped from crevices in the mountains. Cool fluorescent lighting poured over the scene. Behind a grove of antimony models of the Tokyo Tower was a row of mirrors painted with Tokyo scenes, and in them, as the two passed, were rippling, waving images of the mountain of ties and summer shirts opposite.

"I couldn't stand living in a place with so many mirrors," said Kiyoko. "I'd be embarrassed."

"Nothing to be embarrassed about." Though his manner was gruff, Kenzō was not one to ignore what his wife said, and his answers were generally perceptive. The two had come to the toy department.

"She knows how you love the toy depart-

ment. That's why she said to meet her here,"

Kenzō laughed. He was fond of the trains and automobiles and space missiles, and he always embarrassed Kiyoko, getting an explanation for each one and trying each one out, but never buying. She took his arm and steered him some distance from the counter.

"It's easy to see that you want a boy. Look at the toys you pick."

"I don't care whether it's a boy or a girl. I just wish it would come soon."

"Another two years, that's all."

"Everything according to plan."

They had divided the savings account they were so assiduously building up into several parts, labeled Plan X and Plan Y and Plan Z and the like. Children must come strictly according to plan. However much they might want a child now, it would have to wait until sufficient money for Plan X had accumulated. Seeing the inadvisability, for numerous reasons, of installment buying, they waited until the money for Plan A or Plan B or Plan C had accumulated, and then paid cash for an electric washing machine or refrigerator or a television set. Plan A and Plan B had already been carried out . Plan D required little money, but, since it had as its object a low-priority clothes cupboard, it was always being pushed back. Neither of them was much interested in clothes. What they had they could hang in the closet, and all they really needed was enough to keep them warm in the winter.

They were very cautious when making a large purchase. They collected catalogues and looked at various possibilities and asked the advice of people who had already made the purchase, and, when the time for buying finally came, went off to a wholesaler in Okachimachi.

A child was still more serious. First there had to be a secure livelihood and enough money, more than enough money, to see that the child had surroundings of which a parent need not be ashamed, if not, perhaps,

enough to see it all the wáy to adulthood.
Kenzō had already made thorough inquiries
with friends who had children, and knew
what expenditures for powdered milk could
be considered reasonable.

With their own plans so nicely formed,
the two had nothing but contempt for the
thoughtless, floundering ways of the poor.
Children were to be produced according to
plan in surroundings ideal for rearing them,
and the best days were waiting after a child
had arrived. Yet they were sensible enough
not to pursue their dreams too far. They
kept their eyes on the light immediately before them.

There was nothing that enraged Kenzō
more than the view of the young that life in
contemporary Japan was without hope. He
was not a person given to deep thinking, but
he had an almost religious faith that if a
man respected nature and was obedient to
it, and if he but made an effort for himself,
the way would somehow open. The first
thing was reverence for nature, founded on
connubial affection. The greatest antidote
for despair was the faith of a man and
woman in each other.

Fortunately, he was in love with Kiyoko.
To face the future hopefully, therefore, he
had only to follow the conditions laid down
by nature. Now and then some other woman
made a motion in his direction, but he
sensed something unnatural in pleasure for
the sake of pleasure. It was better to listen to
Kiyoko complaining about the dreadful
price these days of vegetables and fish.

The two had made a round of the market
and were back at the toy department.

Kenzō's eyes were riveted to the toy before him, a station for flying saucers. On the
sheet-metal base the complicated mechanism
was painted as if viewed through a window,
and a revolving light flashed on and off inside the control tower. The flying saucer, of
deep-blue plastic, worked on the old principle of the flying top. The station was

apparently suspended in space, for the background of the metal base was covered with
stars and clouds, among the former the
familiar rings of Saturn.

The bright stars of the summer night were
splendid. The painted metal surface was indescribably cool, and it was as if all the discomfort of the muggy night would go if a
person but gave himself up to that sky.

Before Kiyoko could stop him, Kenzō had
resolutely snapped a spring at one corner of
the station.

The saucer went spinning toward the
ceiling.

The salesgirl reached out and gave a little
cry.

The saucer described a gentle arc toward
the pastry counter across the aisle and
settled square on the million-yen crackers.

"We're in!" Kenzō ran over to it.

"What do you mean, we're in?" Embarrassed, Kiyoko turned quickly away from
the salesgirl and started after him.

"Look. Look where it landed. This means
good luck. Not a doubt about it."

The oblong crackers were in the shape of
decidedly large banknotes, and the baked-in
design, again like a banknote, carried the
words "One Million Yen." On the printed
label of the cellophane wrapper, the figure
of a bald shopkeeper took the place of
Prince Shōtoku, who decorates most banknotes. There were three large crackers in
each package.

Over the objections of Kiyoko, who
thought fifty yen for three crackers ridiculous, Kenzō bought a package to make
doubly sure of the good luck. He immediately broke the wrapping, gave a cracker to
Kiyoko, and took one himself. The third
went into her handbag.

As his strong teeth bit into the cracker, a
sweet, slightly bitter taste flowed into his
mouth. Kiyoko took a little mouse-like bite
from her own cracker, almost too large for
her grasp.

Kenzō brought the flying saucer back to the toy counter. The salesgirl, out of sorts, looked away as she reached to take it.

Kiyoko had high, arched breasts, and, though she was small, her figure was good. When she walked with Kenzō she seemed to be hiding in his shadow. At street crossings he would take her arm firmly, look to the right and the left, and help her across, pleased at the feel of the rich flesh.

Kenzō liked the pliant strength in a woman who, although she could perfectly well do things for herself, always deferred to her husband. Kiyoko had never read a newspaper, but she had an astonishingly accurate knowledge of her surroundings. When she took a comb in her hand or turned over the leaf of a calendar or folded a summer kimono, it was not as if she were engaged in housework, but rather as if, fresh and alert, she were keeping company with the "things" known as comb and calendar and kimono. She soaked in her world of things as she might soak in a bath.

"There's an indoor amusement park on the fourth floor. We can kill time there," said Kenzō. Kiyoko followed silently into a waiting elevator, but when they reached the fourth floor she tugged at his belt.

"It's a waste of money. Everything seems so cheap, but it's all arranged so that you spend more money than you intend to."

"That's no way to talk. This is our good night, and if you tell yourself it's like a first-run movie it doesn't seem so expensive."

"What's the sense in a first-run movie? If you wait a little while you can see it for half as much."

Her earnestness was most engaging. A brown smudge from the cracker clung to her puckered lips.

"Wipe your mouth," said Kenzō. "You're making a mess of yourself."

Kiyoko looked into a mirror on a near-by pillar and removed the smear with the nail of her little finger. She still had two thirds of a cracker in her hand.

They were at the entrance to "Twenty Thousand Leagues Under the Sea." Jagged rocks reached to the ceiling, and the porthole of a submarine on the sea floor served as the ticket window: forty yen for adults, twenty yen for children.

"But forty yen is too high," said Kiyoko, turning away from the mirror. "You aren't any less hungry after you look at all those cardboard fish, and for forty yen you can get a hundred grams of the best kind of real fish."

"Yesterday they wanted forty for a cut of black snapper. Oh, well. When you're chewing on a million yen you don't talk like a beggar."

The brief debate finished, Kenzō bought the tickets.

"You've let that cracker go to your head."

"But it isn't bad at all. Just right when you're hungry."

"You just ate."

At a landing like a railway platform five or six little boxcars, each large enough for two people, stood at intervals along a track. Three or four other couples were waiting, but the two climbed unabashedly into a car. It was in fact a little tight for two, and Kenzō had to put his arm around his wife's shoulders.

The operator was whistling somewhat disdainfully. Kenzō's powerful arm, on which the sweat had dried, was solid against Kiyoko's naked shoulders and back. Naked skin clung to naked skin like the layers of some intricately folded insect's wing. The car began to shake.

"I'm afraid," said Kiyoko, with the expression of one not in the least afraid.

The cars, each some distance from the rest, plunged into a dark tunnel of rock. Immediately inside there was a sharp curve, and the reverberations were deafening.

A huge shark with shining green scales passed, almost brushing their heads, and Kiyoko ducked away. As she clung to her young husband he gave her a kiss. After the shark had passed, the car ground around a curve in pitch darkness again, but his lips landed unerringly on hers, little fish speared in the dark. The little fish jumped and were still.

The darkness made Kiyoko strangely shy. Only the violent shaking and grinding sustained her. As she slipped deep into the tunnel, her husband's arms around her, she felt naked and flushed crimson. The darkness, dense and impenetrable, had a strength that seemed to render clothes useless. She thought of a dark shed she had secretly played in as a child.

Like a flower springing from the darkness, a red beam of light flashed at them, and Kiyoko cried out once more. It was the wide, gaping mouth of a big angler fish on the ocean floor. Around it, coral fought with the poisonous dark green of seaweed.

Kenzō put his cheek to his wife's—she was still clinging to him—and with the fingers of the arm around her shoulders played with her hair. Compared to the motion of the car the motion of the fingers was slow and deliberate. She knew that he was enjoying the show and enjoying her fright at it as well.

"Will it be over soon? I'm afraid." But her voice was drowned out in the roar.

Once again they were in darkness. Though frightened, Kiyoko had her store of courage. Kenzō's arms were around her, and there was no fright and no shame she could not bear. Because hope had never left them, the state of happiness was for the two of them just such a state of tension.

A big, muddy octopus appeared before them. Once again Kiyoko cried out. Kenzō promptly kissed the nape of her neck. The great tentacles of the octopus filled the cave, and a fierce lightning darted from its eyes.

At the next curve a drowned corpse was standing disconsolately in a seaweed forest.

Finally the light at the far end began to show, the car slowed down, and they were liberated from the unpleasant noise. At the

bright platform the uniformed attendant waited to catch the forward handle of the car.

"Is that all?" asked Kenzō.

The man said that it was.

Arching her back, Kiyoko climbed to the platform and whispered in Kenzō's ear: "It makes you feel like a fool, paying forty yen for that."

At the door they compared their crackers. Kiyoko had two thirds left, and Kenzō more than half.

"Just as big as when we came in," said Kenzō. "It was so full of thrills that we didn't have time to eat."

"If you think about it that way, it doesn't seem so bad after all."

Kenzō's eyes were already on the gaudy sign by another door. Electric decorations danced around the word "Magicland," and green and red lights flashed on and off in the startled eyes of a cluster of dwarfs, their domino costumes shining in gold and silver dust. A bit shy about suggesting immediately that they go in, Kenzō leaned against the wall and munched away at his cracker.

"Remember how we crossed the parking lot? The light brought out our shadows on the ground, maybe two feet apart, and a funny idea came to me. I thought to myself how it would be if a little boy's shadow bobbed up and we took it by the hand. And just then a shadow really did break away from ours and come between them."

"No!"

"Then I looked around, and it was someone behind us. A couple of drivers were playing catch, and one of them had dropped the ball and run after it."

"One of these days we really will be out walking, three of us."

"And we'll bring it here." Kenzō motioned toward the sign. "And so we ought to go in and have a look at it first."

Kiyoko said nothing this time as he started for the ticket window.

Possibly because it was a bad time of the

day, Magicland was not popular. On both sides of the path as they entered there were flashing banks of artificial flowers. A music box was playing.

"When we build our house this is the way we'll have the path."

"But it's in very bad taste," objected Kiyoko.

How would it feel to go into a house of your own? A building fund had not yet appeared in the plans of the two, but in due course it would. Things they scarcely dreamed of would one day appear in the most natural way imaginable. Usually so prudent, they let their dreams run on this evening, perhaps, as Kiyoko said, because the million-yen crackers had gone to their heads.

Great artificial butterflies were taking honey from the artificial flowers. Some were as big as brief cases, and there were yellow and black spots on their translucent red wings. Tiny bulbs flashed on and off in their protuberant eyes. In the light from below, a soft aura as of sunset in a mist bathed the plastic flowers and grasses. It may have been dust rising from the floor.

The first room they came to, following the arrow, was the leaning room. The floor and all the furnishings leaned so that when one entered upright there was a grating, discordant note to the room.

"Not the sort of house I'd want to live in," said Kenzō, bracing himself against a table on which there were yellow wooden tulips. The words were like a command. He was not himself aware of it, but his decisiveness was that of the privileged one whose hope and well-being refuse to admit outsiders. It was not strange that in the hope there was a scorn for the hopes of others and that no one was allowed to lay a finger on the well-being.

Braced against the leaning table, the determined figure in the undershirt made Kiyoko smile. It was a very domestic scene. Kenzō was like an outraged young man who,

having built an extra room on his Sunday holidays, had made a mistake somewhere and ended up with the windows and floors all askew .

"You *could* live in a place like this, though," said Kiyoko. Spreading her arms like a mechanical doll, she leaned forward as the room leaned, and her face approached Kenzō's broad left shoulder at the same angle as the wooden tulips.

His brow wrinkled in a serious young frown, Kenzō smiled. He kissed the cheek that leaned toward him and bit roughly into his million-yen cracker.

By the time they had emerged from the wobbly staircases, the shaking passageways, the log bridges from the railings of which monster heads protruded, and numerous other curious places as well, the heat was too much for them. Kenzō finished his own cracker, took what was left of his wife's between his teeth, and set out in search of a cool evening breeze. Beyond a row of rocking horses a door led out to a balcony.

"What time is it?" asked Kiyoko.

"A quarter to nine. Let's go out and cool off till nine."

"I'm thirsty. The cracker was so dry." She fanned at her perspiring white throat with Kenzō's sports shirt.

"In a minute you can have something to drink."

The night breeze was cool on the wide balcony. Kenzō yawned a wide yawn and leaned against the railing beside his wife. Bare young arms caressed the black railing, wet with the night dew.

"It's much cooler than when we came in."

"Don't be silly," said Kenzō. "It's just higher."

Far below, the black machines of the outdoor amusement park seemed to slumber. The bare seats of the merry-go-round, slightly inclined, were exposed to the dew. Between the iron bars of the aerial observation car, suspended chairs swayed gently in the breeze.

The liveliness of the restaurant to the left was in complete contrast. They had a bird's-eye view into all the corners of the wide expanse inside its walls. Everything was there to look at, as if on a stage: the roofs of the separate cottages, the passages joining them, the ponds and brooks in the garden, the stone lanterns, the interiors of the Japanese rooms, some with serving maids whose kimono sleeves were held up by red cords, others with dancing geisha. The strings of lanterns at the eaves were beautiful, and their white lettering was beautiful too.

The wind carried away the noises of the place, and there was something almost mystically beautiful about it, congealed in delicate detail there at the bottom of the murky summer night.

"I'll bet it's expensive," Kiyoko was once more at her favorite romantic topic.

"Naturally. Only a fool would go there."

"I'll bet they say that cucumbers are a great delicacy, and they charge some fantastic price. How much?"

"Two hundred, maybe." Kenzō took his sports shirt and started to put it on.

Buttoning it for him, Kiyoko continued: "They must think their customers are fools. Why, that's ten times what cucumbers are worth. You can get three of the very best for twenty yen."

"Oh? They're getting cheap."

"The price started going down a week or so ago."

It was five to nine. They went out to look for a stairway to the coffee shop on the third floor. Two of the crackers had disappeared. The other was too large for Kiyoko's very large handbag, and protruded from the unfastened clasp.

The old lady, an impatient person, had arrived early and was waiting. The seats from which the loud jazz orchestra could best be seen were all taken, but there were vacant places where the bandstand was out of sight, beside the potted palm probably rented from some gardener. Sitting alone in a summer kimono, the old lady seemed wholly out of place.

She was a small woman not far past middle age, and she had the clean, well-tended face of the plebeian lowlands. She spoke briskly with many delicate gestures. She was proud of the fact that she got along so nicely with young people.

"You'll be treating me, of course, so I ordered something expensive while I was waiting." Even as she spoke the tall glass arrived, pieces of fruit atop a parfait.

"Now that was generous of you. All we needed was soda water."

Her outstretched little finger taut, the old lady plunged in with her spoon and skillfully brought out the cream beneath. Meanwhile she was talking along at her usual brisk pace.

"It's nice that this place is so noisy and no one can hear us. Tonight we go to Nakano —I think I mentioned it over the phone. An ordinary private house and—can you imagine it?—the customers are housewives having a class reunion. There's not much that the rich ladies don't know about these days. And I imagine they walk around pretending the idea never entered their heads. Anyway, I told them about you, and they said they had to have you and no one else. They don't want someone who's all beaten up by the years, you know. And I must say that I can't blame them. So I asked a good stiff price and she said it was low and if they were pleased they'd give you a good tip. They haven't any idea what the market rate is, of course. But I want you to do your best, now. I'm sure I don't need to tell you, but if they're pleased we'll get all sorts of rich customers. There aren't many that go as well together as you two do, of course, and I'm not worried, but don't do anything to make me ashamed of you. Well, anyhow, the woman of the house is the wife of some important person or other, and she'll be waiting for us at the coffee shop in front of Nakano station. You know what will happen next. She'll send the taxi through all sorts of back alleys to get us mixed up. I don't imagine she'll blindfold us, but she'll pull us through the back door so we don't have a chance to read the sign on the gate. I won't like it any better than you will, but she has herself to consider, after all. Don't let it bother you. Me? Oh, I'll be doing the usual thing, keeping watch in the hall. I can bluff my way through, I don't care who comes in. Well, maybe we ought to get started. And let me say it again, I want a good performance from you."

It was late in the night, and Kiyoko and Kenzō had left the old lady and were back in Asakusa. They were even more exhausted than usual. Kenzō's wooden clogs dragged along the street. The billboards in the park were a poisonous black under the cloudy sky.

Simultaneously, they looked up at the New World. The neon pagoda was dark.

"What a rotten bunch. I don't think I've ever seen such a rotten, stuck-up bunch," said Kenzō.

Her eyes on the ground, Kiyoko did not answer.

"Well? Did you ever see a worse bunch of affected old women?"

"No. But what can you do? The pay was good."

"Playing around with money they pry from their husbands. Don't get to be that way when you have money."

"Silly." Kiyoko's smiling face was sharply white in the darkness.

"A really nasty bunch." Kenzō spat in a strong white arc. "How much?"

"This." Kiyoko reached artlessly into her handbag and pulled out some bills.

"Five thousand? We've never made that much before. And the old woman took three thousand. Damn! I'd like to tear it up, that's what I'd like to do. That would really feel good."

Kiyoko took the money back in some consternation. Her finger touched the last of the million-yen crackers.

"Tear this up in its place," she said softly.

Kenzō took the cracker, wadded the cellophane wrapper, and threw it to the ground. It crackled sharply on the silent, deserted street. Too large for one hand, he took the cracker in both hands and tried to break it. It was damp and soggy, and the sweet surface stuck to his hands. The more it bent the more it resisted. He was in the end unable to break it.

Roy Bongartz

TWELVE CHASES ON WEST NINETY-NINTH STREET

Everybody is running in New York; "the pace is fast," they say. What they are doing is chasing one another. Every one of them is either after somebody or running away from somebody. Once in a while, one of them manages, with careful timing, to do both at the same time. But on the upper West Side, between Broadway and Riverside Drive, the timing is only fair. On the 300 block of West Ninety-ninth Street, the residents chase each other up and down the steep hill that rises from the Drive to West End Avenue, and then, between chases, they rest, and sit on the front stoops or lean out of their windows and passively absorb the chaotic racket and motion of dogs, children, cats, fire engines, police cars, garbage trucks, moving vans, blocked and klaxoning cars, and rusty-wheeled grocery carts. Beat-up two-toned cars with North Carolina plates and cracked safety glass in the side windows park in broken brown-bottle glass. Everything is cracked, knocked in, busted on West Ninety-ninth. Two buildings on opposite sides of the street in the middle of the block are Negro rooming houses, one high-class and one low-class. The other buildings on the block exclude Negroes but are open to examples of all the other groups that exist.

When the people there chase, they usually pick out someone of their own type to go after; it is a rare sight to see a white chasing a Negro, or a Negro chasing a white. Even the children scattered about in front of the buildings ordinarily chase within their own groups. In one way, these barriers were attacked when a Negro named Ray fell twelve feet from a porch railing into a concrete-floored cellarway and broke his neck.

Ray lives in the low-class rooming house, where a torn, flapping canvas marquee proclaims its name—the Ritz. Across the street, the high-class rooming house, unnamed, displays only a neat red-lettered sign—"NO LOITERING IN THIS DOORWAY." The sign is obeyed, and altogether that building sustains a higher tone of amenities. Screams and violent threats are unusual, and among all the residents there is clear evidence of good taste in bathrobes and other night-dress, as everyone on the block can see when a fire breaks out in the basement or in one of the rooms and firemen rout the inhabitants out into the night. (Within one year, five fires broke out in one rooming house. In the whole of the 300 block, there were over two dozen.) The nightdress and other comparisons can be made among the residents even though direct, inter-building, man-to-man relationships are, as has been noted, rare.

There is no way to examine all of these people at a given moment so as to come up with a truthful and complete account of what is going on here. All that can be done is to take a sample of, say, three of these people: a wide-brim-hatted man in his late forties named Benny, who runs an inefficient parking lot; a very thin young woman named Flo, with good-looking dark eyes; and a young cop who actually lives in the Bronx but has made himself at home in the neighborhood. Broken-necked Ray does not figure in the sample, but he is in this scene nevertheless; all those people on the block, forever riding up and down in the elevators or wandering up to Broadway twenty times a day for small, obscure purposes—all those people are in it. The trouble, of course, is that nobody stays put in this slice-of-life 300 block; people are forever leaking out at each end of it (and sometimes, as with the local juvenile delinquents, they cut out of the scene laterally, via the rooftops). Never mind. We have, all lined up, Benny, Flo, and the cop. These three sample people, taken as chasers and also as chased, can work into an arithmetical maximum of twelve relationships, twelve chases.

What is the thin-limbed young woman Flo doing on West Ninety-ninth Street this Saturday evening, arguing with Benny out in front of his apartment building? She doesn't even live on this street; she lives on Amsterdam Avenue. (Nothing is perfect; of the three sample 300-block people, two of them live elsewhere. It's nowhere *near* perfect.) Flo is a waitress in the Crosstown Bar, on West Ninety-sixth Street, another world.

"Come on up," Benny says. "Come on, Flo. I thought you wanted to come up."

Flo looks out to the cars streaming along the Henry Hudson Parkway but doesn't focus her eyes on them. She's thinking. She says, "Don't rush me. You're always in a hurry."

"Already I know you over a year and I'm in a hurry?"

"Yes, you're in a hurry."

There they go, they're chasing now. Flo is going up the hill toward Broadway. She heads for the Cake Masters bakery to pick up a loaf of seeded rye with which eventually to carry out a secret plan to end Chase No. 1 by making sandwiches up in Benny's so-called studio apartment (where the stove is on top of the refrigerator). As she goes into the bakery, she sweeps a glance over the throng of beanbag women customers, all under five feet tall, scarves over their hair, jumping up and down waving exploding coins in their fists, and she hears a strong, oily-voiced baritone singing out from somewhere in a ululating vibrato. Flo takes a pink ticket from the Takacheck machine just inside the door and glances at her number—44. She compares this with the changing number in the frame behind the counter —3. Flo, although of a stolid, unimaginative nature, has nevertheless absorbed from the circuslike variety in the city around her a certain resiliency when she finds herself in untoward situations so that at first she hardly remarks the presence of a singer in the Cake Masters. This is a long-faced, rheumy-eyed singer with thatchy brown hair and bony red wrists and unstable lips, a gawky, sentimental bakery singer, with good strong lungs. "My Yiddishe Momme" and "When Irish Eyes Are Smiling" he sings while Flo waits for her number to come up. When it does, she whispers to the baker, "Why is he singing?" The baker replies loudly, embarrassing Flo, "He wants to sing, let him sing, why shouldn't he sing?" He gazes in amused speculation into Flo's handsome dark eyes. "Let him *sing*, he wants to sing." All the jolting little women are asking each other the same question, "Why is he singing?" Flo thinks, If he is singing, he must want money. She whispers to the baker, "But does he want money?" The baker smiles at her and says, "Give him money, you got too much. He's singing. He asks nothing." Flo at this point begins to suspect a kind of existence beyond her own, but then she leaves the bakery with the rye bread, and the process is interrupted. Flo, almost unchanged, now returns to the 300 block, late for the chase with Benny.

Chase No. 1 continues. Benny is again chasing Flo up that 300-block hill, Flo running awkwardly on spike heels, jerkily twisting her elbows as she goes. Her lips are tight as she flounces past the open doorway of the Ritz, where the lounging Negroes eye her implacably. As she clicks past, she shoots a sharp look at them, a chastising what-are-*you*-looking-at look, but they don't mind the look; they have seen Flo before and they have seen her look before, too. At the Cake Masters, we discovered Flo to be of a square state of mind, yet ready to consider giving a bakery singer a tip for singing she did not enjoy (though she would remember it). Here she is now giving Benny a hard time, giving the Negroes a cold eye, flouncing up the hill like a girl of no substance, like some floppy suburban teenager. She gives Benny a hard time but she doesn't turn him off altogether, as one ought to expect. Flo, who insists on a bakery singer giving an account of himself, insists on logic and rightness. When one considers Benny's overripe gambit to Flo six months ago (a blizzardy evening, and Benny emboldened by a rare access of ambition: "Say, young lady, how about taking in a show after you get off work, and before that maybe some Chinese food at the Gung Ho?"), it is clear that Flo should have frozen him solid. But that is not what Flo did; she accepted him, conditionally, accepted a little of him. She goes on up past the areaway of an apartment house and stops. Benny runs up to her, and Chase No. 1 ends, statistically, at least. Flo is going to come to his apartment. Benny opens his hands outward in a gesture of hopeless generosity—anything-you-say-is-O.K.-by-me. Now Flo wonders why she ever set foot in this 300 block. Benny is too old and his nose is too big and he talks too loud. But she had nothing better to do.

"Come on up for a little while," Benny persists.

Flo realizes that going with Benny means nothing to her one way or the other. She is altogether uninvolved with him. "No," she says, her lips forming the word completely by chance; it could just as easily have been "yes" or "green." This refusal is so unemotional that Benny receives it unquestioningly. He turns and heads for home.

Chase No. 2 takes up as Flo uncertainly retraces her steps and follows Benny down the hill. They go Indian file, loping along. Just before the Ritz entrance, Flo hears a groan, and stops. She looks around. The Negroes on the steps of the Ritz are watching her. Benny, sensing he is no longer being chased, turns around. All the figurants turn to stone momentarily until the next groan releases them. High above them, his elbows leaning on a blue-and-white striped pillow on the window ledge, a sallow-cheeked old man, immutable Cro-Magnon street watcher, gazes down, drawing no conclusions, one sight worth another—fat woman with shopping cart, nimble-footed television-set repossessors, jingling Good Humor man, busted Negro. Flo looks in every direction, trying to trace that groan, and notices this old man in his window, unblinkingly eying her, a gargoyle cemented to his window ledge. There is another groan. Flo peers down into a cellarway between the sidewalk and the wall of the Ritz. A man is lying down there.

She runs down the narrow stairs to him, and Benny runs up and peers over the railing at her, then looks up at the porch railing from which the man has fallen. Flo kneels beside the fallen Negro. "Where are you hurt?" she demands. The Negro mumbles. "Are you all right?" she demands more loudly.

"Of course he isn't all right," Benny interrupts. "He fell from way up here. We better call a cop."

Flo tugs at the Negro's arm. The Negro lies in sooty wetness. "Gimme a drink," he says. Flo clicks up the stairs and runs in her rag-doll run to the Ritz Negroes and commands in her thin voice, "Get some blankets, there's a man hurt down here!" Heads appear in Ritz windows, lounging Negroes stir, faces press against windows of parked cars; the gargoyle turns his head away from his late-afternoon-sun watching. Negroes clatter into the cellarway to help their fallen comrade, now moaning and cursing, as busy thin-legged Flo and useless wide-brimmed Benny run off (No. 3) to find a cop.

Flo runs blindly down West End Avenue, Benny protesting that they should go on over to Broadway. He will protest all his life; he has created a protesting existence for himself with this dark-haired, sharp-chinned girl—Benny the follower, the whiner, the pleader, would-be seducer of a Ninety-sixth Street waitress, operator of lousy parking lot. He cannot even catch a cop to save a busted Negro that his girl found, Benny himself never having noticed a single fallen human being in all his humdrum life. ("But if somebody would just let me know what I'm supposed to do," Benny is always complaining, and shrugging, his hands outstretched in that gesture of facile generosity.) Then he puts his hand in the side pocket of his checked jacket, where he can feel the silky, grainy texture of some crumpled dollar bills. He thinks, Maybe I will give this money to the Negro. But Benny won't actually give the money, because later he will decide the city will take care of the Negro.

Flo finds the cop, who follows her back to the Ritz and descends to kneel, in his turn, beside the fallen Negro. "How do you feel, buddy?" says the cop.

The Negro pronounces barely audible curses, velvet-caressing curses, in a sad, rambling, uninterested voice, as if someone else were doing his cursing for him and was falling asleep at the task. "Sons of bitches," he murmurs, "gimme a drink ma wine, man." He passes out, then passes in again.

The cop tests the articulation of the man's arms and legs. "How does that feel, buddy?" No answer.

Above, Benny and Flo and many Negro neighbors peer down, the Negroes according a preferred vantage point to Benny and Flo because of their central role in the diversion. Benny stands back, suddenly impatient of this intrusion into his plans by fallen Negro and cop-chasing, which anyway is done with. The victim is being attended by a city official. Good, thinks Benny, grasping Flo's arm, but even after a year she still acts as if he were a stranger molesting her. Has he not taken this girl to the Gung Ho, to movies at the Midtown, to Pizza Burger Pete's? Yet a little favor, a little friendliness like coming up to his place for a drink and sandwiches, becomes impossible. Benny now imagines the soft light of dusk in his room becoming dimmer; the two of them hear pigeons cooing, and the clapping of car tires over manhole covers, and the hum of weekend motorists on the Henry Hudson Parkway. But the cop shouts up at Flo, "Call an ambulance!"

Benny sees it is his and Flo's duty to call the ambulance, because they had called the cop in the first place. So now the cop is bringing them *his* troubles, chasing (No. 4) *them* with orders and demands. It is *their* fallen Negro now. But that's not true, Benny thinks protestingly. Still, nobody in the crowd offers to take the job from them, and Flo has already gone into the Ritz to telephone. Benny follows, as he follows all his life, to no purpose. Imperious Flo calls the ambulance: "Come right away! Man hurt, West-Ninety-ninth" Negro residents crowd the doorway and the stairs and stare at Flo, who returns to the railing above the cellarway; the people make room for her. There is enough residue of respect for Benny, as Flo's associate, to warrant him a place at the railing as well. The ambulance arrives; two wiry Puerto Rican interns jump out, clatter out a stretcher, and exchange bursts of Spanish. They, too, test his bones and joints. Ray curses them in his phenomenally soft voice. The interns grab his shoulders and lift him up; Ray screams in a

cruel, hopeless spasm, and they edge him onto their stretcher. Flo pulls away from the cellarway, and a Negro next to her says, "Thanks a lot for helping." She says, "I just hope those guys don't kill him." She goes off toward Broadway without looking back, and a few minutes later Benny follows.

The Negroes watch Benny depart as if he were the mayor of West Ninety-ninth Street —the mayor of West Ninety-ninth Street who has lost his girl. He sees the cop about to get into a police cruiser at the top of the hill. Benny chases (No. 5) him to ask where Flo might have gone—if she has gone to the police station to make a report, or something. Benny gets no information here, and goes on up to the end of the 300 block before the cop yells after him and chases (No. 6) him calling, "Hey, wait a minute." He wants to know the exact time the victim was found in the cellarway. But even this small usefulness Benny cannot produce. His watch is not working—not wound, probably, or just clogged. The cop lets him go. Benny gazes along the street hoping for the sight of a black skirt, thin legs. If it hadn't been for the cop, I should have caught her, he thinks. Still, the cop *had* come to him for information—important information. He glows a bit. He crosses West End Avenue and goes down to Albert's Liquor Store, source of Ray-toppling Gallo. Benny tells the proprietor of having found the busted Negro—"Probably saved his life," he boasts. A general conversation ensues on the subject of hard falls. Benny is looking for the girl, but he buys a bottle of J. W Dant anyway.

Flo returns to the 300 block, where the Negroes welcome her "Let the lady pass," they cry. After a round-the-world trip along escaping-from-Benny West End Avenue up to 100th Street, and then down unknown who-are-those-people-in-the-window-watching 300 block of 100th Street, she comes with relief into the safe, known world, past the firemen's memorial, to Ninety-ninth Street.

She knows she has found a home away from home in this place where the ambulance she had summoned has only just rolled away with damaged Negro aboard, Ray enthroned inside with Puerto Rican attendant cooling him with a palm fan, Ray waving a hand to all faithful subjects outside, and these Negroes, having been blessed by Ray, and by his rescue mollified, now retreat into their welcome-to-the-North furnished cages in the Ritz. Flo looks up at the façade of the Ritz, the bottles of beer, cartons of orange juice, cans of evaporated milk littering the sills. It's not good enough, she thinks, mumbles aloud; she isn't precisely sure what that means. The rooming house is included, and so is Benny, and Ray falling down drunk into the cellarway is in it, too. Somebody is responsible, she thinks; the nearest representative of organizing forces is that cop. So she chases (No. 7) off after him. She wants to make a general complaint.

Up the hill she goes. "Where's that cop?" she asks her new Negro neighbors. "Where's the cop?" the Negroes repeat to one another. A tall Negro girl in a thin red flower-printed dress, with a gold cap over one front tooth, and auburn-dyed hair, and high Indian cheekbones, grins at Flo and says, "What do you want that cop for, honey? Can we help you some way?" But Flo clicks up the street alone. She finds the cop leaning on the police car door. "That ambulance took an hour to arrive," she complains.

The cop says, "Lady, anybody in this whole city calls in with even a stomach ache, anything, we got to rush to him, and you can figure it takes a lot of ambulances, a city this size, and this being Saturday, and a hot Saturday, with people out in the parks and in the streets. We get a lot of calls, and there's just so many ambulances to go around. That boy there, he'll be all right."

"What is your name?" Flo demands, these being the only words she can think of by

way of explaining that she really wants to saddle him with the responsibility of having made none of it good enough; the dirty hot street not good enough, the hot-roast-beef and steam-table-pastrami waitress job not good enough, soggy-brained Ray fallen in that cellarway not good enough, and Benny —my God, Benny, he's not good enough, either—but that isn't the cop's fault, none of it is the cop's fault, leave him alone, the poor guy; this won't be his only case today. "Never mind," she tells him, and goes off toward Broadway.

The cop says something to his colleagues in the police car and then follows (No. 8) Flo across West End Avenue. She passes a group of Haitians, shadowy French phrases echoing up and down the 200 block. The cop catches up. "If you want my name, I'll give it to you," he tells her challengingly. "Never mind," says Flo. "I didn't mean to bother you again."

Benny returns to the 300 block with his bottle of bourbon and stops to talk with a Ritz resident, a tall, gangling Negro with a beret, Charlie Chan mustache, and thick-lensed horn-rimmed glasses, who says, "Ray he fell right off this railing like a sack of meal and nobody heard him till you came along, he could have died down there you hadn't heard him call out and then go on down there to see what it was." Benny modestly shakes his head; he doesn't know what to say, and he wonders why Flo has run out on him like this. Why could he never get the girl to come home with him? Why? Nothing worked out. He returns to the chase.

The cop is leaning on the door of the synagogue at the corner of West End Avenue; he raises an indolent finger at Benny, "Who is that girl friend of yours?"

"Ah," Benny replies, pained, the memory of her too much for him to communicate in a word. He wants to put out his two hands there in front of him like *that* and force her to appear—right there where he can take hold of her. Women always have somewhere else to go, Benny thinks.

"She wanted to take down my name," the cop says aggressively.

"So what do you want me to do about it?" says Benny.

"Well, what does she want with my name? She going to report me?" asks the cop.

"I don't know what she's going to do. Me, I'm the last person in the world you should ask what she's going to do. You want to talk to her again? I'll tell you something, *I'd* like to talk to her."

"Let's find her," the cop suggests. They go off together, looking for her, an unspoken threat eating into the cop's silver-badge mind, his chief receiving an unfounded report of neglect of duty or of cruelty to fallen Negro, as if *he* had pushed the Negro into the cellarway. The cop and Benny (the lover) go after (No. 9) Flo and find her in a drugstore on Broadway having a Coke.

"I won't report you for it," she tells the cop, having decided that the cop is slightly responsible for nothing being good enough; he deserves a little needling. (And here is Benny again, she thinks.)

"For *what?*" says the cop. "What won't you report me for?"

Flo won't tell him what it is. She won't tell the cop what he wants to know, nor will she go up to Benny's place for the drinks and sandwiches. It is too late to do that, though she has nothing else to do. Her plans lead through a white blank into tomorrow's table-waiting at the Crosstown Bar, unless, by good fortune, another fallen citizen should be lying in her path for her to retrieve. "I don't want to know your name," she tells the cop, absolving him and then sending both him and Benny away as if she owns the drugstore. The cop goes out, ready for a quiet stand in front of the cigar store half a block down Broadway, where life is both more colorful and more peaceful than on the cross streets.

Benny goes out with him. They get only to the corner before Flo chases (No. 10) after them. "What hospital did that hurt man go to?" she asks the cop.

"Roosevelt Hospital," he replies.

Benny says, "What, you still worried about that fellow? He'll get the best care in the world, best care in the world. Right, Officer?"

The cop says, "Do me a favor, the next time you hear something like that, somebody groaning, take my advice, just keep on walking, save yourself a lot of trouble."

"But he would have died," Flo protests.

"They never die," the cop says. "You can't kill them as easy as that."

He goes off and leaves outraged Flo in the incapable hands of Benny, who is wondering how he is going to make off with her, how to make the most of her anger. "Come on up to my place and cool off a little," he suggests. Flo is indecisive. A chink appears in her armor. Patience, thinks Benny. But I'll put my foot in it again, thinks Benny, remembering the time he had brought her some carnations while she was at work and she had stared at them as if she had never seen a flower before in her life, saying, "I don't like carnations!" Another time, during a walk in Riverside Park, he had grasped her hand in what was supposed to be an affectionate gesture, but he had done it too abruptly, it had been too grabby there in the dusk of the park, and she had simply been scared, briefly but sharply. All he had ever succeeded in doing was to wait until she finished work so as to take her to a movie. Now he has two cases of beer in his kitchen, and this bottle of bourbon. He is all ready for her. They walk together down West Ninety-ninth, past the two Chinese laundries, Benny keeping his mouth shut for fear of ruining everything. She's not the only broad in this town, he tries to convince himself. Springily he walks along, clapping his perforated brown-and-white shoes down on the concrete. Anyway, he thinks, he is *with* Flo. She isn't looking at him, doesn't adjust her pace to his—he can sense that, he is not insensitive to such tips of bad news. "Bought some *bourbon*," he says tantalizingly, pulling the neck of the bottle from his coat pocket so that she may see it. "Good for you," she says. There is no use in his kidding himself, he thinks; she is lost to him. What has happened, he wonders. She was on her way up to his place, then a man falls into a cellarway, and now she might as well be on another planet. Suddenly Flo is talking to him: "I'll have a drink with you; let's go to a bar somewhere." Benny understands nothing at all. They turn back, he takes her arm, and they go to a bar at 100th Street and Broadway to have Manhattans. Before they finish their first round, Benny orders another. Flo sighs a why-did-I-start-*this* sigh. Later, outside, Benny tries to pull her along with him; she resists, becomes angry, and then Benny becomes ugly and drags her a little way down Broadway. "Waste of *time!*" he shouts at her. Flo jerks away and runs down the street, past the cop, who calls out, "Where's the fire?" She stops, points accusingly, and she and the cop, in unrehearsed concert, move toward oncoming, lumbering Benny, on his way into another of his inconsequential disasters. Benny turns away from them, from secure and civilized Broadway, and runs (No. 11) down West Ninety-ninth Street, heading for home.

On the 300 block the old-man gargoyle leans on his pillowed elbows and gazes, with the stone lions in the cornices, blankly down to the warm asphalt of the darkened street. Empty garbage cans, one inside another like Dixie cups, are piled up before each building; a broken lamppost leans stupidly at the end of the street, and abruptly, with all the others on the street, it lights up. Benny walks along disgruntled, wondering what to do with his bourbon and his cold beer. Only three residents of the Ritz on the stoop now. One is the whiskered, bereted one, who looks up and says formally, "Evening."

Benny pulls himself out of his vindictive

trance, stops, and says, "Any word about our friend?"

"Busted his neck," says the bereted one. "What they said there at the hospital. We called. He ought to be all right, though."

"That's pretty rough," says Benny. "Well, I hope he—he comes out of it, comes through it all right."

"We hope so, too."

"Well, good night," Benny says uneasily. The three residents all reply, "Good night." Benny goes on down the hill.

When he gets to his building, he looks back to the Ritz marquee flapping in the warm wind, then gazes out at the red neon Spry sign on the Jersey shore. Then, as if chasing were the easiest thing in the world, he thinks his way back up (No. 12) to Broadway, where Flo, like a wise guy, has called the cop on him—*him*, Benny, who is greeted good evening by all the people on the street. And she already *agreed* to come up here, he says to himself once more. What did that busted Negro have to do with them? But now he knows how to handle her; he sees himself, as in a dream, striding right up to Flo and that cop and he hands the cop a five-dollar bill. Thank you, Copper, he says. You've done your duty, Copper. Then Benny takes the girl's arm, and the two of them stroll along the street, everybody saying hello, and then they go up to his place and open up that bottle of bourbon.

Jonathan Swift

A CITY SHOWER

Careful observers may foretell the hour
By sure prognostics when to dread a shower.
While rain depends, the pensive cat gives o'er
Her frolics and pursues her tail no more.
Returning home at night, you'll find the sink

5 *sink:* gutter or sewer.

Strike your offended sense with double stink.
If you be wise, then go not far to dine:
You'll spend in coach-hire more than save in
    wine.
A coming shower your shooting corns presage,
Old aches throb, your hollow tooth will
    rage.   10
Sauntering in coffee-house is Dulman seen;
He damns the climate and complains of spleen.

Meanwhile the south, rising with dappled wings,
A sable cloud athwart the welkin flings,
That swilled more liquor than it could contain
And like a drunkard gives it up again.
Brisk Susan whips her linen from the rope,
While the first drizzling shower is born aslope;
Such is that sprinkling which some careless
    quean
Flirts on you from her mop, but not so
    clean.   20
You fly, invoke the gods, then, turning, stop
To rail; she, singing, still whirls on her mop.
Not yet the dust had shunned th'unequal strife,
But, aided by the wind, fought still for life;
And, wafted with its foe by violent gust,
'Twas doubtful which was rain and which was
    dust.
Ah, where must needy poet seek for aid
When dust and rain at once his coat invade;
His only coat, where dust confused with rain
Roughen the nap and leave a mingled
    stain.   30
Now in contiguous drops the flood comes down,
Threatening with deluge this devoted town.
To shops in crowds the dagged females fly,
Pretend to cheapen goods, but nothing buy.
The Templar spruce, while every spout's
    a-broach,
Stays till 'tis fair, yet seems to call a coach.
The tucked-up seamstress walks with hasty
    strides
While streams run down her oiled umbrella's
    sides.

Here various kinds by various fortunes led
Commence acquaintance underneath a
    shed.   40
Triumphant Tories and desponding Whigs
Forget their feuds and join to save their wigs.
Boxed in a chair, the beau impatient sits
While spouts run clattering o'er the roof by fits.
And ever and anon with frightful din
The leather sounds; he trembles from within.
So when Troy chair-men bore the wooden steed,
Pregnant with Greeks, impatient to be freed
(Those bully Greeks, who, as the moderns do,
Instead of paying chair-men run them
    through),   50
Laocoön struck the outside with his spear
And each imprisoned hero quaked for fear.

Now from all parts the swelling kennels flow
And bear their trophies with them as they go:
Filth of all hues and odors seem to tell
What street they sailed from by their sight and
    smell.
They, as each torrent drives, with rapid force
From Smithfield or St. Pulchre's shape their
    course
And in huge confluence join at Snow Hill
    Ridge,
Fall from the conduit prone to Holborn
    Bridge.   60
Sweepings from butchers' stalls, dung, guts, and
    blood,
Drowned puppies, stinking sprats, all drenched
    in mud,
Dead cats and turnip-tops come tumbling down
    the flood.

39 *kinds:* classes of people. 41 *Tories:* "A City Shower" was published in 1710, soon after the Tories had taken over the government from the Whigs. 43 *chair:* sedan chair, a covered chair carried on poles. 44 *spouts:* downpours of rain. 53 *kennels:* gutters. 58 *Smithfield:* London's market district. *St. Pulchre's:* the Church of St. Sepulchre.

10 *aches:* pronounced "aitches." 12 *spleen:* melancholy. 32 *devoted:* doomed (to be drenched). 33 *dagged:* sprinkled. 35 *Templar:* lawyer.

Jonathan Swift

MORNING

Now hardly here and there a hackney coach
Appearing showed the ruddy morn's approach.
Now Betty from her master's bed had flown
And softly stole to discompose her own.
The slipshod 'prentice from his master's door
Had pared the dirt and sprinkled round the
    floor.
Now Moll had whirled her mop with dexterous
    airs,
Prepared to scrub the entry and the stairs.
The youth with broomy stumps began to trace
The kennel-edge, where wheels had worn the
    place.   10
The small-coal man was heard with cadence
    deep,
Till drowned in shriller notes of chimney sweep.
Duns at his lordship's gate began to meet,
And brickdust Moll had screamed through half
    the street.
The turnkey now his flock returning sees,
Duly let out a-nights to steal for fees;
The watchful bailiffs take their silent stands,
And schoolboys lag with satchels in their hands.

    3 *Betty:* a housemaid. 10 *kennel-edge:* rim of
the gutter. 14 *brickdust Moll:* hawker of brickdust,
used for scouring doorsills and the like. 16 *fees:*
i.e., payments of the turnkey for better food and
other luxuries. 17 *bailiffs:* sheriff's officers, here
probably preparing to serve processes.

William Blake

LONDON

I wander through each chartered street,
Near where the chartered Thames does flow,
And mark in every face I meet
Marks of weakness, marks of woe.

    1 *Chartered:* leased, monopolized.

In every cry of every man,
In every infant's cry of fear,
In every voice, in every ban,
The mind-forged manacles I hear:

How the chimney-sweeper's cry
Every blackening church appalls,   10
And the hapless soldier's sigh
Runs in blood down palace walls.

But most, through midnight streets I hear
How the youthful harlot's curse
Blasts the new-born infant's tear,
And blights with plagues the marriage hearse.

William Wordsworth

COMPOSED UPON
WESTMINSTER BRIDGE

SEPTEMBER 3, 1802

Earth has not anything to show more fair:
Dull would he be of soul who could pass by
A sight so touching in its majesty:
This City now doth, like a garment, wear
The beauty of the morning; silent, bare,
Ships, towers, domes, theatres, and temples lie
Open unto the fields and to the sky;
All bright and glittering in the smokeless air.
Never did sun more beautifully steep
In his first splendor, valley, rock, or hill;   10
Ne'er saw I, never felt, a calm so deep!
The river glideth at his own sweet will:
Dear God! the very houses seem asleep;
And all that mighty heart is lying still!

    WESTMINSTER BRIDGE: over the Thames River, con-
necting west-central London with the district of
Lambeth.

Charles Baudelaire

THE SEVEN OLD MEN

O swarming city, city full of dreams,
Where in full day the spectre walks and speaks;
Mighty colossus, in your narrow veins
My story flows as flows the rising sap.

One morn, disputing with my tired soul,
And like a hero stiffening all my nerves,
I trod a suburb shaken by the jar
Of rolling wheels, where the fog magnified
The houses either side of that sad street,
So they seemed like two wharves the ebbing
    flood   10
Leaves desolate by the river-side. A mist,
Unclean and yellow, inundated space—
A scene that would have pleased an actor's soul.

Then suddenly an aged man, whose rags
Were yellow as the rainy sky, whose looks
Should have brought alms in floods upon his
    head,
Without the misery gleaming in his eye,
Appeared before me; and his pupils seemed
To have been washed with gall; the bitter frost
Sharpened his glance; and from his chin a
    beard   20
Sword-stiff and ragged, Judas-like stuck forth.
He was not bent but broken: his backbone
Made a so true right angle with his legs,
That, as he walked, the tapping stick which gave
The finish to the picture, made him seem
Like some infirm and stumbling quadruped
Or a three-legged Jew. Through snow and mud
He walked with troubled and uncertain gait,
As though his sabots trod upon the dead,
Indifferent and hostile to the world.   30

His double followed him: tatters and stick
And back and eye and beard, all were the same;
Out of the same Hell, indistinguishable,
These centenarian twins, these spectres odd,
Trod the same pace toward some end
    unknown.

To what fell complot was I then exposed?
Humiliated by what evil chance?
For as the minutes one by one went by
Seven times I saw this sinister old man
Repeat his image there before my eyes!   40

Let him who smiles at my inquietude,
Who never trembled at a fear like mine,
Know that in their decrepitude's despite
These seven old hideous monsters had the mien
Of immortal beings.

Then, I thought, must I,
Undying, contemplate the awful eighth;
Inexorable, fatal, and ironic double;
Disgusting phœnix, father of himself
And his own son? In terror then I turned   50
My back upon the infernal band, and fled
To my own place, and closed my door;
    distraught
And like a drunkard who sees all things double,
With feverish troubled spirit, chilly and sick,
Wounded by mystery and absurdity!

In vain my reason tried to cross the bar,
The whirling storm but drove her back again;
And my soul tossed, and tossed, an outworn
    wreck,
Mastless, upon a monstrous, shoreless sea.

THE SEVEN OLD MEN: Translated by F. P. Sturm.
  48 *phoenix:* fabled Egyptian bird that consumes
itself by fire every five hundred years and is then
resurrected. Baudelaire accordingly considers the
phoenix its own father and own son.

T. S. Eliot

PRELUDES

I

The winter evening settles down
With smell of steaks in passageways.
Six o'clock.
The burnt-out ends of smoky days.
And now a gusty shower wraps
The grimy scraps

Of withered leaves about your feet
And newspapers from vacant lots;
The showers beat
On broken blinds and chimney-pots,   10
And at the corner of the street
A lonely cab-horse steams and stamps.
And then the lighting of the lamps.

II

The morning comes to consciousness
Of faint stale smells of beer
From the sawdust-trampled street
With all its muddy feet that press
To early coffee-stands.
With the other masquerades
That time resumes,   20
One thinks of all the hands
That are raising dingy shades
In a thousand furnished rooms.

III

You tossed a blanket from the bed,
You lay upon your back, and waited;
You dozed, and watched the night revealing
The thousand sordid images
Of which your soul was constituted;
They flickered against the ceiling.
And when all the world came back   30
And the light crept up between the shutters
And you heard the sparrows in the gutters,
You had such a vision of the street
As the street hardly understands;
Sitting along the bed's edge, where
You curled the papers from your hair,
Or clasped the yellow soles of feet
In the palms of both soiled hands.

IV

His soul stretched tight across the skies
That fade behind a city block,   40
Or trampled by insistent feet
At four and five and six o'clock;
And short square fingers stuffing pipes,

And evening newspapers, and eyes
Assured of certain certainties,
The conscience of a blackened street
Impatient to assume the world.

I am moved by fancies that are curled
Around these images, and cling:
The notion of some infinitely gentle   50
Infinitely suffering thing.

Wipe your hand across your mouth, and
      laugh;
The worlds revolve like ancient women
Gathering fuel in vacant lots.

Robert Lowell

FOR THE UNION DEAD

"RELINQUUNT OMNIA SERVARE
REM PUBLICAM."

The old South Boston Aquarium stands
in a Sahara of snow now. Its broken windows
      are boarded.
The bronze weathervane cod has lost half its
      scales.
The airy tanks are dry.

Once my nose crawled like a snail on the glass:
my hand tingled
to burst the bubbles
drifting from the noses of the cowed,
      compliant fish.

My hand draws back. I often sigh still
for the dark downward and vegetating
      kingdom   10
of the fish and reptile. One morning last March,
I pressed against the new barbed and galvanized

RELINQUUNT, etc.: "They leave everything to preserve the nation." Slightly altered from the motto on
the Shaw memorial.

fence of the Boston Common. Behind their cage,
yellow dinosaur steamshovels were grunting
as they cropped up tons of mush and grass
to gouge their underworld garage.

Parking spaces luxuriate like civic
sandpiles in the heart of Boston.
A girdle of orange, Puritan-pumpkin colored
   girders
braces the tingling Statehouse,   20

shaking over the excavations, as it faces Colonel
   Shaw
and his bell-cheeked Negro infantry
on St. Gaudens' shaking Civil War relief,
propped by a plank splint against the garage's
   earthquake.

Two months after marching through Boston,
half the regiment was dead;
at the dedication,
William James could almost hear the bronze
   Negroes breathe.

Their monument sticks like a fishbone
in the city's throat.   30
Its Colonel is as lean
as a compass-needle.

He has an angry wrenlike vigilance,
a greyhound's gentle tautness;
he seems to wince at pleasure,
and suffocate for privacy.

13 *Common:* Park in downtown Boston overlooked
by the Statehouse (capitol building). At one entrance
stands a bas-relief commemorating Col. Robert G.
Shaw and his troops; he was killed 18 July 1863
while leading an assault on Battery Wagner, near
Charleston, S.C. 23 *St. Gaudens':* The bas-relief is
the work of Augustus St. Gaudens (1848–1907). 28
William James: James (1842–1910) was the speaker
when the bas-relief was dedicated in 1897. Entitled
"Robert Gould Shaw," his address is printed in his
Memories and Studies, 1911.

He is out of bounds now. He rejoices in man's
   lovely,
peculiar power to choose life and die—
when he leads his black soldiers to death,
he cannot bend his back.   40

On a thousand small town New England greens,
the old white churches hold their air
of sparse, sincere rebellion; frayed flags
quilt the graveyards of the Grand Army of the
   Republic.

The stone statues of the abstract Union soldier
grow slimmer and younger each year—
wasp-waisted, they doze over muskets
and muse through their sideburns . . .

Shaw's father wanted no monument
except the ditch,   50
where his son's body was thrown
and lost with his "niggers."

The ditch is nearer.
There are no statues for the last war here;
on Boylston Street, a commercial photograph
shows Hiroshima boiling

over a Mosler Safe, the "Rock of Ages"
that survived the blast. Space is nearer.
When I crouch to my television set,
the drained faces of Negro school-children
   rise like balloons.   60

Colonel Shaw
is riding on his bubble,
he waits
for the blessèd break.

The Aquarium is gone. Everywhere,
giant finned cars nose forward like fish;
a savage servility
slides by on grease.

60 *school-children:* The poem was written at the
time of the disorders caused by the integration of
previously white schools.

Robert Lowell

CENTRAL PARK

Scaling small rocks, exhaling smog,
gasping at game-scents like a dog,
now light as pollen, now as white
and winded as a grounded kite—
I watched the lovers occupy
every inch of earth and sky:
one figure of geometry,
multiplied to infinity
straps down, and sunning openly . . .
each precious, public, pubic tangle   10
an equilateral triangle,
lost in the park, half covered by
the shade of some low stone or tree.
The stain of fear and poverty
spread through each trapped anatomy,
and darkened every mote of dust.
All wished to leave this drying crust,
borne on the delicate wings of lust
like bees, and cast their fertile drop
into the overwhelming cup.   20
Drugged and humbled by the smell
of zoo-straw mixed with animal,
the lion prowled his slummy cell,
serving his life-term in jail—
glaring, grinding, on his heel,
with tingling step and testicle . . .

Behind a dripping rock, I found
a one-day kitten on the ground—
deprived, weak, ignorant and blind,
squeaking, tubular, left behind—   30
dying with its deserter's rich
Welfare lying out of reach:
milk cartons, kidney heaped to spoil,
two plates sheathed with silver foil.
Shadows had stained the afternoon;
high in an elm, a snagged balloon
wooed the attraction of the moon.

Scurrying from the mouth of night,
a single, fluttery, paper kite
grazed Cleopatra's Needle, and sailed   40
where the light of the sun had failed.
Then night, the night—the jungle hour,
the rich in his slit-windowed tower . . .
Old Pharaohs starving in your foxholes,
with painted banquets on the walls,
fists knotted in your captives' hair,
tyrants with little food to spare—
all your embalming left you mortal,
glazed, black, and hideously eternal,
all your plunder and gold leaf   50
only served to draw the thief . . .

We beg delinquents for our life.
Behind each bush, perhaps a knife;
each landscaped crag, each flowering shrub,
hides a policeman with a club.

Philip Larkin

I REMEMBER, I REMEMBER

Coming up England by a different line
For once, early in the cold new year,
We stopped, and watching men with
        number-plates
Sprint down the platform to familiar gates,
"Why, Coventry!" I exclaimed. "I was born
        here."

I leant far out, and squinnied for a sign
That this was still the town that had been
        "mine"
So long, but found I wasn't even clear
Which side was which. From where those cycle-
        crates
Were standing, had we annually
        departed   10

22 *zoo-straw:* The Park has a zoo in its southeast
corner. 40 *Needle:* Egyptian obelisk in the Park.

I REMEMBER, I REMEMBER: ironic allusion to the
poem of the same name by Charles Lamb.

For all those family hols? . . . A whistle went:
Things moved. I sat back, staring at my boots.
"Was that," my friend smiled, "where you have
    your roots?"
No, only where my childhood was unspent,
I wanted to retort, just where I started:

By now I've got the whole place clearly charted.
Our garden, first: where I did not invent
Blinding theologies of flowers and fruits,
And wasn't spoken to by an old hat.
And here we have that splendid family   20

I never ran to when I got depressed,
The boys all biceps and the girls all chest,
Their comic Ford, their farm where I could be
"Really myself." I'll show you, come to that,
The bracken where I never trembling sat,

Determined to go through with it; where she
Lay back, and "all became a burning mist."
And, in those offices, my doggerel
Was not set up in blunt ten-point, nor read
By a distinguished cousin of the mayor,   30

Who didn't call and tell my father *There
Before us, had we the gift to see ahead*—
"You look as if you wished the place in Hell,"
My friend said, "judging from your face." "Oh
    well,
I suppose it's not the place's fault," I said.

"Nothing, like something, happens anywhere."

    11 *hols:* holidays.

Denise Levertov

MERRITT PARKWAY

      As if it were
forever that they move, that we
      keep moving—

MERRITT PARKWAY: Expressway in Connecticut, between New York and New Haven.

Under a wan sky where
as the lights went on a star
     pierced the haze & now
follows steadily
        a constant
above our six lanes
the dreamlike continuum . . .   10

And the people—ourselves!
   the humans from inside the
   cars, apparent
only at gasoline stops
        unsure,
   eyeing each other

      drink coffee hastily at the
     slot machines & hurry
back to the cars
   vanish   20
   into them forever, to
   keep moving—

Houses now & then beyond the
sealed road, and trees/trees, bushes
passing by, passing
     the cars that
      keep moving ahead of
     us, past us, pressing behind us
        and
     over left, those that come   30
     toward us shining too brightly
moving relentlessly

   in six lanes, gliding
north & south, speeding with
a slurred sound—

Denise Levertov

FEBRUARY EVENING IN NEW YORK

As the stores close, a winter light
  opens air to iris blue,
  glint of frost through the smoke,
  grains of mica, salt of the sidewalk.
As the buildings close, released autonomous
  feet pattern the streets
  in hurry and stroll; balloon heads
  drift and dive above them the bodies
  aren't really there.

As the lights brighten, as the sky darkens,   10
  a woman with crooked heels says to another
    woman
  while they step along at a fair pace,
  "You know, I'm telling you, what I love best
  is life. I love life! Even if I ever get
  to be old and wheezy—or limp! You know?
  Limping along?—I'd still . . ." Out of hearing.
To the multiple disordered tones
  of gears changing, a dance
  to the compass points, out, four-way river.
  Prospect of sky   20
  wedged into avenues, left at the ends of
    streets,
  west sky, east sky: more life tonight! A range
  of open time at winter's outskirts.

Glyn Hughes

NO SUPERFICIAL CHANGE

The town's soot-eaten platitudes
collapse, as "SCIENCE AND ART"
and stone, Greek generalities
are bulldozed; I awake each day
to a new space flowing with dust.

Tough letters dissolve to a bruise
of fume and dust, making way
for a racetrack of one-way streets
and the new frontier
of bungalows gripping the moor.   10

Even Wesley, "brand plucked from the burning"
that scorched the West Riding, whose mind
was architect of Satanic Mills,
has lost his gross stone box
that glowered from the hill.

11 *brand:* burning stick. Cf. Amos ɪᴠ, 11 and Zechariah ɪɪɪ, 2. John Wesley: (1703–1791), founder of Methodism, so regarded himself in part because, at the age of six, he narrowly escaped death in a fire at his father's rectory. 12 *West Riding:* district in Yorkshire, England. 13 *Satanic Mills:* William Blake. "And Did Those Feet in Ancient Times," 8.

Barnacled with iron, stone mottoes and nudes,
like old liners a few mills stay
anchored in sludge;
their chimneys still pump
black blood from snapped arteries.   20

How irrepressibly the weeds
bloom on waste whilst the town
is metamorphosed through the sixties!
Only those clinical planners
and the Salvationists think: what next?

The kids don't care. From the change
they bounce like hard peas on a drum:
immigrant, part-immigrant, they queue for rubberfaced
monsters at the scrat-and-laugh
cinemas soon to become   30

warehouses and amusement centers.
"Las Vegas of The North"
the vicar called it;
but the great milltown
is demoralized by petty industries.

Those who bled it left
the workers, who vote Conservative:
like Isaac Bell, who tends his shop from his bed
under the new College Block
and the glass Insurance Office.   40

With nervous carp's lips and pale skin blotched like a damp
front room awaiting demolition
he grips his stick that opens the door:
they say his donkey just got used
to living without eating, when it died.

It's a cold plunge from the South:
there's a view
of a reservoir, like a knife in a disemboweled
gray fowl; there are monotonies
of day-long sooty twilights;   50

and the great stone letters that spelled
the comfort of Culture
lie on the closed street,
fallen from lofts of factories where
pikes were sharpened after Peterloo.

29 *scrat:* scratch. The movie-houses had fleas and mainly showed comedies.   55
Peterloo: nickname (after "Waterloo") of a massacre in St. Peter's Fields, near
Manchester, in 1819, of citizens assembled to protest repressive policies of the
British government.

Chapter 5

INDIVIDUAL AND SOCIETY

Among the most memorable characters in literature are those who fulfill their destinies in the midst of uncomprehending or hostile social environments—the dissenter, the rebel, the loner, the saint, the hero, the villain. The dramatic conflict in such works is generated by tensions, not so much between two or more individuals as between an individual and social groups. And what gives depth and significance to the conflict is that the individual is not simply good or bad, but interacts in complex ways with others of his group, and embodies in his rebelliousness hints of some general truth about individuality. He may be a comic misfit ("Why I Live at the P.O."), one who feels an impulse to resist the pressures to conformity ("The Conversion of the Jews"), or an evil exploiter of others ("Spotted Horses"). In other works—"The Secret Life of Walter Mitty," "A Rose for Emily," "The Love Song of J. Alfred Prufrock"—the conflict takes other forms, and the responsibilities may be very mixed and ambiguous.

In a struggle of this sort, the parties are never evenly matched. Society is the immovable body, existing before the individual comes into it and after he is gone; a body whose enveloping power he must resist to forge his own identity yet which is an essential support for his growth. The individual may embody the integrity, initiative, and revolutionary ardor that represent irresistible, and indispensable, forces of change and progress. In the paradoxes of this human situation writers have found limitless varieties of material. In between the individual's total defeat and his total victory countless other outcomes are possible. The rebel may be overwhelmed, or flee, or fall into madness, or change decisively the society's character and development: compare, for instance, Plato's account of Socrates, "A Rose for Emily," "Dover Beach," "Richard Cory," and "The Mill."

When the conflict between individual and society embodies explicit general principles and standards, it becomes political, ethical, religious. It takes on a universal relevance to human life. At the same time the work also becomes more difficult to understand; it requires reflective thought to be fully appreciated. In the collision between Socrates and his ancient Greek contemporaries, in the symbolic plight of the Hunger-Artist, in the problems about the rights and duties of dissent discussed by Walter Lippmann, the issues are reducible to divergent philosophies and ways of life.

169

Plato

THE DEATH OF SOCRATES

I

[*Part of Socrates' speech to the Athenian court, before which he was brought in 399* B.C. *on the charge of impiety and corrupting the youth of Athens by his teaching.*]

How you, O Athenians, have been affected by my accusers, I cannot tell; but I know that they almost made me forget who I was —so persuasively did they speak; and yet they have hardly uttered a word of truth. But of the many falsehoods told by them, there was one which quite amazed me: I mean when they said that you should be upon your guard and not allow yourselves to be deceived by the force of my eloquence. To say this, when they were certain to be detected as soon as I opened my lips and proved myself to be anything but a great speaker did indeed appear to me most shameless—unless by the force of eloquence they mean the force of truth; for if such is their meaning, I admit that I am eloquent. But in how different a way from theirs! Well, as I was saying, they have scarcely spoken the truth at all; but from me you shall hear the whole truth: not, however, delivered after their manner in a set oration duly ornamented with words and phrases. No, by heaven! but I shall use the words and arguments which occur to me at the moment; for I am confident in the justice of my cause: at my time of life I ought not to be appearing before you, O men of Athens, in the character of a juvenile orator—let no one expect it of me. And I must beg of you to grant me a favor: If I defend myself in my accustomed manner and you hear me using the words which I have been in the habit of using in the agora,

at the tables of the money-changers, or anywhere else, I would ask you not to be surprised, and not to interrupt me on this account. For I am more than seventy years of age, and appearing now for the first time in a court of law, I am quite a stranger to the language of the place; and therefore I would have you regard me as if I were really a stranger, whom you would excuse if he spoke in his native tongue, and after the fashion of his country. Am I making an unfair request of you? Never mind the manner, which may or may not be good; but think only of the truth of my words, and give heed to that: let the speaker speak truly and the judge decide justly.

I will begin at the beginning, and ask what is the accusation which has given rise to the slander of me, and in fact has encouraged Meletus to prefer this charge against me. Well, what do the slanderers say? They shall be my prosecutors, and I will sum up their words in an affidavit: "Socrates is an evildoer, and a curious person, who searches into things under the earth and in heaven, and he makes the worse appear the better cause; and he teaches the aforesaid doctrines to others." Such is the nature of the accusation: it is just what you have yourselves seen in the comedy of Aristophanes,[1] who has introduced a man whom he calls Socrates, going about and saying that he walks in air, and talking a deal of nonsense concerning matters of which I do not pretend to know either much or little—not that I mean to speak disparagingly of anyone who is a student of natural philosophy. I should be very sorry if Meletus could bring so grave a charge against me. But the simple truth is, O Athenians, that I have nothing to do with physical speculations. Very many of those here present are witnesses to the truth of this, and to them I appeal. Speak then, you who have heard me,

[1] *The Clouds* (423 B.C.), in which Aristophanes makes fun of Socrates.

and tell your neighbors whether any of you have ever known me hold forth in few words or in many upon such matters. . . . You hear their answer. And from what they say of this part of the charge you will be able to judge of the truth of the rest.

As little foundation is there for the report that I am a teacher, and take money; this accusation has no more truth in it than the other. Although, if a man were really able to instruct mankind, to receive money for giving instruction would, in my opinion, be an honor to him. There is Gorgias of Leontium, and Prodicus of Ceos, and Hippias of Elis, who go the round of the cities, and are able to persuade the young men to leave their own citizens by whom they might be taught for nothing, and come to them whom they not only pay, but are thankful if they may be allowed to pay them. There is at this time a Parian[2] philosopher residing in Athens, of whom I have heard; and I came to hear of him in this way: I came across a man who has spent a world of money on the Sophists, Callias, the son of Hipponicus, and knowing that he had sons, I asked him: "Callias," I said, "if your two sons were foals or calves, there would be no difficulty in finding some one to put over them; we should hire a trainer of horses, or a farmer, probably, who would improve and perfect them in their own proper virtue and excellence; but as they are human beings, whom are you thinking of placing over them? Is there anyone who understands human and political virtue? You must have thought about the matter, for you have sons; is there anyone?" "There is," he said. "Who is he?" said I, "and of what country? and what does he charge?" "Evenus the Parian," he replied; "he is the man, and his charge is five minae." Happy is Evenus, I said to myself, if he really has this wisdom, and teaches at such a moderate charge. Had

I the same, I should have been very proud and conceited; but the truth is that I have no knowledge of the kind.

I dare say, Athenians, that someone among you will reply, "Yes, Socrates, but what is the origin of these accusations which are brought against you; there must have been something strange which you have been doing? All these rumors and this talk about you would never have arisen if you had been like other men: tell us, then, what is the cause of them, for we should be sorry to judge hastily of you." Now, I regard this as a fair challenge, and I will endeavor to explain to you the reason why I am called wise and have such an evil fame. Please to attend then. And although some of you may think that I am joking, I declare that I will tell you the entire truth. Men of Athens, this reputation of mine has come of a certain sort of wisdom which I possess. If you ask me what kind of wisdom, I reply, wisdom such as may perhaps be attained by man, for to that extent I am inclined to believe that I am wise; whereas the persons of whom I was speaking have a superhuman wisdom, which I may fail to describe because I have it not myself; and he who says that I have, speaks falsely and is taking away my character. And here, O men of Athens, I must beg you not to interrupt me, even if I seem to say something extravagant. For the word which I will speak is not mine. I will refer you to a witness who is worthy of credit; that witness shall be the god of Delphi—he will tell you about my wisdom, if I have any, and of what sort it is. You must have known Chaerephon; he was early a friend of mine, and also a friend of yours, for he shared in the recent exile of the people,[3] and returned with you. Well, Chaerephon, as you know, was very im-

---

[2] From Paros, one of the Cyclades islands, southeast of Athens.

[3] In 404 B.C. Athens fell under the rule of thirty oligarchs, and the leading democrats were forced into exile. A year later the democracy was re-established.

petuous in all his doings, and he went to Delphi and boldly asked the oracle to tell him whether—as I was saying, I must beg you not to interrupt—he asked the oracle to tell him whether anyone was wiser than I was, and the Pythian prophetess answered that there was no man wiser. Chaerephon is dead himself; but his brother, who is in court, will confirm the truth of what I am saying.

Why do I mention this? Because I am going to explain to you why I have such an evil name. When I heard the answer, I said to myself, What can the god mean? and what is the interpretation of his riddle? For I know that I have no wisdom, small or great. What then can he mean when he says that I am the wisest of men? And yet he is a god, and cannot lie; that would be against his nature. After long consideration, I thought of a method of trying the question. I reflected that if I could only find a man wiser than myself, then I might go to the god with a refutation in my hand. I should say to him, "Here is a man who is wiser than I am; but you said that I was the wisest." Accordingly I went to one who had the reputation of wisdom, and observed him—his name I need not mention; he was a politician whom I selected for examination—and the result was as follows: When I began to talk with him, I could not help thinking that he was not really wise, although he was thought wise by many, and still wiser by himself; and thereupon I tried to explain to him that he thought himself wise, but was not really wise; and the consequence was that he hated me, and his enmity was shared by several who were present and heard me. So I left him, saying to myself, as I went away: Well, although I do not suppose that either of us knows anything really beautiful and good, I am better off than he is, for he knows nothing, and thinks that he knows; I neither know nor think that I know. In this latter particular, then, I seem to have slightly the advantage of him.

Then I went to another who had still higher pretensions to wisdom, and my conclusion was exactly the same. Whereupon I made another enemy of him, and of many others besides him.

Then I went to one man after another, being not unconscious of the enmity which I provoked, and I lamented and feared this: but necessity was laid upon me—the word of God, I thought, ought to be considered first. And I said to myself, Go I must to all who appear to know, and find out the meaning of the oracle. And I swear to you, Athenians, by the dog[4] I swear!—for I must tell you the truth—the result of my mission was just this: I found that the men most in repute were all but the most foolish; and that others less esteemed were really wiser and better. I will tell you the tale of my wanderings and of the Herculean labors, as I may call them, which I endured only to find at last the oracle irrefutable. After the politicians, I went to the poets; tragic, dithyrambic, and all sorts. And there, I said to myself, you will be instantly detected; now you will find out that you are more ignorant than they are. Accordingly I took them some of the most elaborate passages in their own writings and asked what was the meaning of them—thinking that they would teach me something. Will you believe me? I am almost ashamed to confess the truth, but I must say that there is hardly a person present who would not have talked better about their poetry than they did themselves. Then I knew that not by wisdom do poets write poetry, but by a sort of genius and inspiration; they are like diviners or soothsayers who also say many fine things, but do not understand the meaning of them. The poets appeared to me to be much in the same case; and I further observed that upon the strength of their poetry they believed themselves to be the wisest of men in other things in which they were not wise.

---

4 An oath that avoids profanity.

So I departed, conceiving myself to be superior to them for the same reason that I was superior to the politicians.

At last I went to the artisans. I was conscious that I knew nothing at all, as I may say, and I was sure that they knew many fine things; and here I was not mistaken, for they did know many things of which I was ignorant, and in this they certainly were wiser than I was. But I observed that even the good artisans fell into the same error as the poets: because they were good workmen they thought that they also knew all sorts of high matters, and this defect in them overshadowed their wisdom; and therefore I asked myself on behalf of the oracle, whether I would like to be as I was, neither having their knowledge nor their ignorance, or like them in both; and I made answers to myself and to the oracle that I was better off as I was.

This inquisition has led to my having many enemies of the worst and most dangerous kind, and has given occasion also to many calumnies. And I am called wise, for my hearers always imagine that I myself possess the wisdom which I find wanting in others: but the truth is, O men of Athens, that God only is wise; and by his answer he intends to show that the wisdom of men is worth little or nothing; he is not speaking of Socrates, he is only using my name by way of illustration, as if he said, "He, O men, is the wisest. who, like Socrates, knows that his wisdom is in truth worth nothing." And so I go about the world obedient to the god, and search and make enquiry into the wisdom of anyone, whether citizen or stranger, who appears to be wise; and if he is not wise, then in vindication of the oracle I show him that he is not wise; and my occupation quite absorbs me, and I have no time to give either to any public matter of interest or to any concern of my own, but I am in utter poverty by reason of my devotion to the god.

Someone will say: "And are you not ashamed, Socrates, of a course of life which is likely to bring you to an untimely end?" To him I may fairly answer: "There you are mistaken: a man who is good for anything ought not to calculate the chances of living or dying; he ought only to consider whether in doing anything he is doing right or wrong—acting the part of a good man or of a bad. Whereas, upon your view, the heroes who fell at Troy were not good for much, and the son of Thetis [Achilles] above all, who altogether despised danger in comparison with disgrace; and when he was so eager to slay Hector, his goddess mother said to him that if he avenged his companion Patroclus and slew Hector, he would die himself—'Fate,' she said, in these or the like words, 'waits for you next after Hector'; he, receiving this warning, utterly despised danger and death, and instead of fearing them, feared rather to live in dishonor, and not to avenge his friend. 'Let me die forthwith,' he replies, 'and be avenged of my enemy, rather than abide here by the beaked ships, a laughing-stock and a burden of the earth.' Had Achilles any thought of death and danger? For wherever a man's place is, whether the place which he has chosen or that in which he has been placed by a commander, there he ought to remain in the hour of danger; he should not think of death or of anything but of disgrace." And this, O men of Athens, is a true saying.

Strange, indeed, would be my conduct, O men of Athens, if I, who, when I was ordered by the generals whom you chose to command me at Potidaea and Amphipolis and Delium,[5] remained where they placed me, like any other man, facing death—if now, when, as I conceive and imagine, God orders me to fulfill the philosopher's mission of searching into myself and other men, I were to desert my post through fear of death, or any other fear; that would indeed

5 Sites of engagements early in the Peloponnesian War, 431–404 B.C.

be strange and I might justly be arraigned in court for denying the existence of the gods, if I disobeyed the oracle because I was afraid of death, fancying that I was wise when I was not wise. For the fear of death is indeed the pretence of wisdom and not real wisdom, being a pretence of knowing the unknown; and no one knows whether death, which men in their fear apprehend to be the greatest evil, may not be the greatest good. Is not this ignorance of a disgraceful sort, the ignorance which is the conceit that a man knows what he does not know? And in this respect only I believe myself to differ from men in general, and may perhaps claim to be wiser than they are: that whereas I know but little of the world below, I do not suppose that I know; but I do know that injustice and disobedience to a better, whether God or man, is evil and dishonorable, and I will never fear or avoid a possible good rather than a certain evil. And therefore if you let me go now and are not convinced by Anytus, who said that since I had been prosecuted I must be put to death (or if not that I ought never to have been prosecuted at all); and that if I escape now, your sons will all be utterly ruined by listening to my words—if you say to me, Socrates, this time we will not mind Anytus, and you shall be let off, but upon one condition, that you are not to enquire and speculate in this way any more, and that if you are caught doing so again you shall die; if this was the condition on which you let me go, I should reply: "Men of Athens, I honor and love you; but I shall obey God rather than you, and while I have life and strength I shall never cease from the practice and teaching of philosophy, exhorting anyone whom I meet and saying to him after my manner: 'You, my friend, a citizen of the great and mighty and wise city of Athens, are you not ashamed of heaping up the greatest amount of money and honor and reputation, and caring so little about wisdom and truth and the greatest improve-

ment of the soul, which you never regard or heed at all?'" And if the person with whom I am arguing says: 'Yes, but I do care'; then I do not leave him or let him go at once; but I proceed to interrogate and examine and cross-examine him, and if I think that he has no virtue in him, but only says that he has, I reproach him with undervaluing the greater and overvaluing the less. And I shall repeat the same words to everyone whom I meet, young and old, citizen and alien, but especially to the citizens, inasmuch as they are my brethren. For know that this is the command of God; and I believe that no greater good has ever happened in the State than my service to the god. For I do nothing but go about persuading you all, old and young alike, not to take thought for your persons or your properties, but first and chiefly to care about the greatest improvement of the soul. I tell you that virtue is not given by money, but that from virtue comes money and every other good of man, public as well as private. This is my teaching, and if this is the doctrine which corrupts the youth, I am a mischievous person. But if anyone says that this is not my teaching, he is speaking an untruth. Wherefore, O men of Athens, I say to you, do as Anytus bids or not as Anytus bids, and either acquit me or not; but whichever you do, understand that I shall never alter my ways, not even if I have to die many times.

II

[*The trial of Socrates concluded with the death penalty. The account of his final hours is given by one of his young friends, Phaedo, to another, Echecrates.*]

When he had done speaking, Crito said: "And have you any commands for us, Socrates—anything to say about your children, or any other matter in which we can serve you?"

"Nothing particular, Crito," he replied; "only, as I have always told you, take care of yourselves; that is a service which you may be ever rendering to me and mine and to all of us, whether you promise to do so or not. But if you have no thought for yourselves and care not to walk according to the rule which I have prescribed for you, not now for the first time, however much you may profess or promise at the moment, it will be of no avail."

"We will do our best," said Crito. "And in what way shall we bury you?"

"In any way that you like; but you must get hold of me, and take care that I do not run away from you." Then he turned to us and added with a smile: "I cannot make Crito believe that I am the same Socrates who has been talking and conducting the argument; he fancies that I am the other Socrates whom he will soon see, a dead body—and he asks, 'How shall he bury me?' And though I have spoken many words in the endeavor to show that when I have drunk the poison I shall leave you and go to the joys of the blessed—these words of mine, with which I was comforting you and myself, have had, as I perceive, no effect upon Crito. And therefore I want you to be surety for me to him now, as at the trial he was surety to the judges for me: but let the promise be of another sort; for he was surety for me to the judges that I would remain, and you must be my surety to him that I shall not remain, but go away and depart; and then he will suffer less at my death and not be grieved when he sees my body being burned or buried. I would not have him sorrow at my hard lot or say at the burial, Thus we lay out Socrates, or, Thus we follow him to the grave or bury him: for false words are not only evil in themselves, but they inflict the soul with evil. Be of good cheer then, my dear Crito, and say that you are burying my body only, and do with that whatever is usual, and what you think best."

When he had spoken these words, he arose and went into a chamber to bathe; Crito followed him and told us to wait. So we remained behind, talking and thinking of the subject of discourse and also of the greatness of our sorrow; he was like a father of whom we were being bereaved, and we were about to pass the rest of our lives as orphans. When he had taken the bath his children were brought to him (he had two young sons and an elder one); and the women of his family also came, and he talked to them and gave them a few directions in the presence of Crito; then he dismissed them and returned to us.

Now the hour of sunset was near, for a good deal of time had passed while he was within. When he came out, he sat down with us again after his bath, but not much was said. Soon the jailer, who was the servant of the Eleven,[6] entered and stood by him, saying: "To you, Socrates, whom I know to be the noblest and gentlest and best of all who ever came to this place, I will not impute the angry feeling of other men, who rage and swear at me, when, in obedience to the authorities, I bid them drink the poison—indeed, I am sure that you will not be angry with me; for others, as you are aware, and not I, are to blame. And so fare you well, and try to bear lightly what must needs be—you know my errand." Then bursting into tears he turned away and went out.

Socrates looked at him and said: "I return your good wishes, and will do as you bid." Then turning to us, he said, "How charming the man is: since I have been in prison he has always been coming to see me, and at times he would talk to me, and was as good to me as could be, and now see how generously he sorrows on my account. We must do as he says, Crito; and therefore let the cup be brought, if the poison is prepared: if not, let the attendant prepare some."

"Yet," said Crito, "the sun is still upon

---

6 The administrative government of Athens.

the hilltops, and I know that many a one has taken the draught late, and after the announcement has been made to him, he has eaten and drunk, and enjoyed the society of his beloved: do not hurry—there is time enough."

Socrates said: "Yes, Crito, and they of whom you speak are right in so acting, for they think that they will be gainers by the delay; but I am right in not following their example, for I do not think that I should gain anything by drinking the poison a little later; I should only be ridiculous in my own eyes for sparing and saving a life which is already forfeit. Please then to do as I say, and not to refuse me."

Crito made a sign to the servant, who was standing by; and he went out, and having been absent for some time, returned with the jailer carrying the cup of poison. Socrates said: "You, my good friend, who are experienced in these matters, shall give me directions how I am to proceed." The man answered: "You have only to walk about until your legs are heavy, and then to lie down, and the poison will act." At the same time he handed the cup to Socrates, who in the easiest and gentlest manner, without the least fear or change of color or feature, looking at the man with all his eyes, Echecrates, as his manner was, took the cup and said: "What do you say about making a libation out of this cup to any god? May I, or not?" The man answered: "We only prepare, Socrates, just so much as we deem enough." "I understand," he said; "but I may and must ask the gods to prosper my journey from this to the other world—even so—and so be it according to my prayer." Then raising the cup to his lips, quite readily and cheerfully he drank off the poison. And hitherto most of us had been able to control our sorrow; but now when we saw him drinking, and saw too that he had finished the draught, we could no longer forbear, and in spite of myself my own tears were flowing fast; so that I cov-

ered my face and wept, not for him, but at the thought of my own calamity in having to part from such a friend. Nor was I the first; for Crito, when he found himself unable to restrain his tears, had got up, and I followed; and at that moment Apollodorus, who had been weeping all the time, broke out in a loud and passionate cry which made cowards of us all. Socrates alone retained his calmness: "What is this strange outcry?" he said. "I sent away the women mainly in order that they might not misbehave in this way, for I have been told that a man should die in peace. Be quiet then, and have patience." When we heard his words we were ashamed, and refrained our tears; and he walked about until, as he said, his legs began to fail, and then he lay on his back, according to directions, and the man who gave him the poison now and then looked at his feet and legs; and after a while he pressed his foot hard, and asked him if he could feel; and he said, "No"; and then his leg, and so upwards and upwards, and showed us that he was cold and stiff. And he felt them himself, and said: "When the poison reaches the heart, that will be the end." He was beginning to grow cold about the groin, when he uncovered his face, for he had covered himself up, and said—they were his last words—he said: "Crito, I owe a cock to Asclepius;[7] will you remember to pay the debt?" "The debt shall be paid," said Crito; "is there anything else?" There was no answer to this question; but in a minute or two a movement was heard, and the attendants uncovered him; his eyes were set, and Crito closed his eyes and mouth.

Such was the end, Echecrates, of our friend; concerning whom I may truly say, that of all men of his time whom I have known, he was the wisest and justest and best.

[7] It was the custom on recovering from an illness to make an offering to the god of health. Socrates perhaps means that death is curing him of the illness of life.

Walter Lippmann

THE INDISPENSABLE OPPOSITION

I

Were they pressed hard enough, most men would probably confess that political freedom—that is to say, the right to speak freely and to act in opposition—is a noble ideal rather that a practical necessity. As the case for freedom is generally put today, the argument lends itself to this feeling. It is made to appear that, whereas each man claims his freedom as a matter of right, the freedom he accords to other men is a matter of toleration. Thus, the defense of freedom of opinion tends to rest not on its substantial, beneficial, and indispensable consequences, but on a somewhat eccentric, a rather vaguely benevolent, attachment to an abstraction.

It is all very well to say with Voltaire, "I wholly disapprove of what you say, but will defend to the death your right to say it," but as a matter of fact most men will not defend to the death the rights of other men: if they disapprove sufficiently what other men say, they will somehow suppress those men if they can.

So, if this is the best that can be said for liberty of opinion, that a man must tolerate his opponents because everyone has a "right" to say what he pleases, then we shall find that liberty of opinion is a luxury, safe only in pleasant times when men can be tolerant because they are not deeply and vitally concerned.

Yet actually, as a matter of historic fact, there is a much stronger foundation for the great constitutional right of freedom of speech, and as a matter of practical human experience there is a much more compelling reason for cultivating the habits of free men. We take, it seems to me, a naïvely self-righteous view when we argue as if the right of our opponents to speak were something that we protect because we are magnanimous, noble, and unselfish. The compelling reason why, if liberty of opinion did not exist, we should have to invent it, why it will eventually have to be restored in all civilized countries where it is now suppressed, is that we must protect the right of our opponents to speak because we must hear what they have to say.

We miss the whole point when we imagine that we tolerate the freedom of our political opponents as we tolerate a howling baby next door, as we put up with the blasts from our neighbor's radio because we are too peaceable to heave a brick through the window. If this were all there is to freedom of opinion, that we are too good-natured or too timid to do anything about our opponents and our critics except to let them talk, it would be difficult to say whether we are tolerant because we are magnanimous or because we are lazy, because we have strong principles or because we lack serious convictions, whether we have the hospitality of an inquiring mind or the indifference of an empty mind. And so, if we truly wish to understand why freedom is necessary in a civilized society, we must begin by realizing that, because freedom of discussion improves our own opinions, the liberties of other men are our own vital necessity.

We are much closer to the essence of the matter, not when we quote Voltaire, but when we go to the doctor and pay him to ask us the most embarrassing questions and to prescribe the most disagreeable diet. When we pay the doctor to exercise complete freedom of speech about the cause and cure of our stomachache, we do not look upon ourselves as tolerant and magnanimous, and worthy to be admired by ourselves. We have enough common sense to know that if we threaten to put the doctor in jail because we do not like the diagnosis and the prescription it will be unpleasant for the doctor, to be sure, but equally unpleasant for our own stomachache. That is why even the most ferocious dictator would rather be treated by a doctor who was free to think and speak the truth than by his own Minister of Propaganda. For there is a point, the point at which things really matter, where the freedom of others is no longer a question of their right but of our own need.

The point at which we recognize this need is much higher in some men than in others. The totalitarian rulers think they do not need the freedom of an opposition: they exile, imprison, or shoot their opponents. We have concluded on the basis of practical experience, which goes back to Magna Carta and beyond, that we need the opposition. We pay the opposition salaries out of the public treasury.

In so far as the usual apology for freedom of speech ignores this experience, it becomes abstract and eccentric rather than concrete and human. The emphasis is generally put on the right to speak, as if all that mattered were that the doctor should be free to go out into the park and explain to the vacant air why I have a stomachache. Surely that is a miserable caricature of the great civic right which men have bled and died for. What really matters is that the doctor should tell *me* what ails me, that I should listen to him; that if I do not like what he says I should be free to call in another doctor; and that then the first doctor should have to listen to the second doctor; and that out of all the speaking and listening, the give-and-take of opinions, the truth should be arrived at.

This is the creative principle of freedom of speech, not that it is a system for the tolerating of error, but that it is a system for finding the truth. It may not produce the truth, or the whole truth all the time, or often, or in some cases ever. But if the truth can be found, there is no other system which

will normally and habitually find so much truth. Until we have thoroughly understood this principle, we shall not know why we must value our liberty, or how we can protect and develop it.

II

Let us apply this principle to the system of public speech in a totalitarian state. We may, without any serious falsification, picture a condition of affairs in which the mass of the people are being addressed through one broadcasting system by one man and his chosen subordinates. The orators speak. The audience listens but cannot and dare not speak back. It is a system of one-way communication; the opinions of the rulers are broadcast outwardly to the mass of the people. But nothing comes back to the rulers from the people except the cheers; nothing returns in the way of knowledge of forgotten facts, hidden feelings, neglected truths, and practical suggestions.

But even a dictator cannot govern by his own one-way inspiration alone. In practice, therefore, the totalitarian rulers get back the reports of the secret police and of their party henchmen down among the crowd. If these reports are competent, the rulers may manage to remain in touch with the public sentiment. Yet that is not enough to know what the audience feels. The rulers have also to make great decisions that have enormous consequences, and here their system provides virtually no help from the give-and-take of opinion in the nation. So they must either rely on their own intuition, which cannot be permanently and continually inspired, or, if they are intelligent despots, encourage their trusted advisers and their technicians to speak and debate freely in their presence.

On the walls of the houses of Italian peasants one may see inscribed in large letters the legend, "Mussolini is always right." But if that legend is taken seriously by Italian ambassadors, by the Italian General Staff, and by the Ministry of Finance, then all one can say is heaven help Mussolini, heaven help Italy, and the new Emperor of Ethiopia.

For at some point, even in a totalitarian state, it is indispensable that there should exist the freedom of opinion which causes opposing opinions to be debated. As time goes on, that is less and less easy under a despotism; critical discussion disappears as the internal opposition is liquidated in favor of men who think and feel alike. That is why the early successes of despots, of Napoleon I and of Napoleon III, have usually been followed by an irreparable mistake. For in listening only to his yes men —the others being in exile or in concentration camps, or terrified—the despot shuts himself off from the truth that no man can dispense with.

We know all this well enough when we contemplate the dictatorships. But when we try to picture our own system, by way of contrast, what picture do we have in our minds? It is, is it not, that anyone may stand up on his own soapbox and say anything he pleases, like the individuals in Kipling's poem[8] who sit each in his separate star and draw the Thing as they see it for the God of Things as they are. Kipling, perhaps, could do this, since he was a poet. But the ordinary mortal isolated on his separate star will have an hallucination, and a citizenry declaiming from separate soapboxes will poison the air with hot and nonsensical confusion.

If the democratic alternative to the totalitarian one-way broadcasts is a row of separate soapboxes, then I submit that the alternative is unworkable, is unreasonable, and is humanly unattractive. It is above all a false alternative. It is not true that liberty has developed among civilized men when anyone is free to set up a soapbox, is free to

8 "When Earth's Last Picture Is Painted," 1892.

hire a hall where he may expound his opinions to those who are willing to listen. On the contrary, freedom of speech is established to achieve its essential purpose only when different opinions are expounded in the same hall to the same audience.

For, while the right to talk may be the beginning of freedom, the necessity of listening is what makes the right important. Even in Russia and Germany a man may still stand in an open field and speak his mind. What matters is not the utterance of opinions. What matters is the confrontation of opinions in debate. No man can care profoundly that every fool should say what he likes. Nothing has been accomplished if the wisest man proclaims his wisdom in the middle of the Sahara Desert. This is the shadow. We have the substance of liberty when the fool is compelled to listen to the wise man and learn; when the wise man is compelled to take account of the fool, and to instruct him; when the wise man can increase his wisdom by hearing the judgment of his peers.

That is why civilized men must cherish liberty—as a means of promoting the discovery of truth. So we must not fix our whole attention on the right of anyone to hire his own hall, to rent his own broadcasting station, to distribute his own pamphlets. These rights are incidental; and though they must be preserved, they can be preserved only by regarding them as incidental, as auxiliary to the substance of liberty that must be cherished and cultivated.

Freedom of speech is best conceived, therefore, by having in mind the picture of a place like the American Congress, an assembly where opposing views are represented, where ideas are not merely uttered but debated, or the British Parliament, where men who are free to speak are also compelled to answer. We may picture the true condition of freedom as existing in a place like a court of law, where witnesses testify and are cross-examined, where the lawyer argues against the opposing lawyer before the same judge and in the presence of one jury. We may picture freedom as existing in a forum where the speaker must respond to questions; in a gathering of scientists where the data, the hypothesis, and the conclusion are submitted to men competent to judge them; in a reputable newspaper which not only will publish the opinions of those who disagree but will reëxamine its own opinion in the light of what they say.

Thus the essence of freedom of opinion is not in mere toleration as such, but in the debate which toleration provides: it is not in the venting of opinion, but in the confrontation of opinion. That this is the practical substance can readily be understood when we remember how differently we feel and act about the censorship and regulation of opinion purveyed by different media of communication. We find then that, in so far as the medium makes difficult the confrontation of opinion in debate, we are driven towards censorship and regulation.

There is, for example, the whispering campaign, the circulation of anonymous rumors by men who cannot be compelled to prove what they say. They put the utmost strain on our tolerance, and there are few who do not rejoice when the anonymous slanderer is caught, exposed, and punished. At a higher level there is the moving picture, a most powerful medium for conveying ideas, but a medium which does not permit debate. A moving picture cannot be answered effectively by another moving picture; in all free countries there is some censorship of the movies, and there would be more if the producers did not recognize their limitations by avoiding political controversy. There is then the radio. Here debate is difficult: it is not easy to make sure that the speaker is being answered in the presence of the same audience. Inevitably, there is some regulation of the radio.

When we reach the newspaper press, the opportunity for debate is so considerable that discontent cannot grow to the point where under normal conditions there is any disposition to regulate the press. But when newspapers abuse their power by injuring people who have no means of replying, a disposition to regulate the press appears. When we arrive at Congress we find that, because the membership of the House is so large, full debate is impracticable. So there are restrictive rules. On the other hand, in the Senate, where the conditions of full debate exist, there is almost absolute freedom of speech.

This shows us that the preservation and development of freedom of opinion are not only a matter of adhering to abstract legal rights, but also, and very urgently, a matter of organizing and arranging sufficient debate. Once we have a firm hold on the central principle, there are many practical conclusions to be drawn. We then realize that the defense of freedom of opinion consists primarily in perfecting the opportunity for an adequate give-and-take of opinion; it consists also in regulating the freedom of those revolutionists who cannot or will not permit or maintain debate when it does not suit their purposes.

We must insist that free oratory is only the beginning of free speech; it is not the end, but a means to an end. The end is to find the truth. The practical justification of civil liberty is not that self-expression is one of the rights of man. It is that the examination of opinion is one of the necessities of man. For experience tells us that it is only when freedom of opinion becomes the compulsion to debate that the seed which our fathers planted has produced its fruit. When that is understood, freedom will be cherished not because it is a vent for our opinions but because it is the surest method of correcting them.

The unexamined life, said Socrates, is unfit to be lived by man. This is the virtue of liberty, and the ground on which we may best justify our belief in it, that it tolerates error in order to serve the truth. When men are brought face to face with their opponents, forced to listen and learn and mend their ideas, they cease to be children and savages and begin to live like civilized men. Then only is freedom a reality, when men may voice their opinions because they must examine their opinions.

III

The only reason for dwelling on all this is that if we are to preserve democracy we must understand its principles. And the principle which distinguishes it from all other forms of government is that in a democracy the opposition not only is tolerated as constitutional but must be maintained because it is in fact indispensable.

The democratic system cannot be operated without effective opposition. For, in making the great experiment of governing people by consent rather than by coercion, it is not sufficient that the party in power should have a majority. It is just as necessary that the party in power should never outrage the minority. That means that it must listen to the minority and be moved by the criticisms of the minority. That means that its measures must take account of the minority's objections, and that in administering measures it must remember that the minority may become the majority.

The opposition is indispensable. A good statesman, like any other sensible human being, always learns more from his opponents than from his fervent supporters. For his supporters will push him to disaster unless his opponents show him where the dangers are. So if he is wise he will often pray to be delivered from his friends, because they will ruin him. But, though it hurts, he ought also to pray never to be left without opponents; for they keep him on the path of reason and good sense.

The national unity of a free people depends upon a sufficiently even balance of political power to make it impracticable for the administration to be arbitrary and for the opposition to be revolutionary and irreconcilable. Where that balance no longer exists, democracy perishes. For unless all the citizens of a state are forced by circumstances to compromise, unless they feel that they can affect policy but that no one can wholly dominate it, unless by habit and necessity they have to give and take, freedom cannot be maintained.

Franz Kafka

A HUNGER-ARTIST

In recent decades there has been a distinct falling-off in the interest shown in hunger-artists. Whereas in earlier times one could stage such exhibitions at one's own expense and be quite sure of success, today such a thing is utterly impossible. Those were other times. In those days the entire city occupied itself with the hunger-artist; the interest in him grew from fast day to fast day; everyone wanted to see the hunger-artist at least once a day, and in the latter stages there were regular subscribers who sat before the small, latticed cage for days on end. Performances were given at night too, in order to heighten the effect by torchlight. On sunny days the cage was carried out into the open, and on these occasions it was especially the children to whom the hunger-artist was exhibited. But whereas for the adults he was often no more than a source of amusement, of which they partook only because it was the stylish thing to do, the children would gaze upon him open-mouthed, holding one another by the hand for safety's sake, as he sat there on his straw, scorning even so much as a chair, deathly pale, dressed in black tights, his ribs protruding powerfully, sometimes nodding politely and answering questions with a forced smile, even thrusting his arm through the bars to let them feel his emaciation, then lapsing once more into complete self-absorption and paying attention to no one, ignoring even the striking of the clock which was the cage's sole decoration, looking straight before him with eyes almost closed, and sipping occasionally from a tiny glass of water to wet his lips.

Besides the spectators who merely came and went, there were also regular guards chosen by the public—usually butchers, for some remarkable reason, and always by threes—to whom was assigned the task of watching the hunger-artist day and night, lest he might succeed after all in surreptitiously partaking of nourishment. But that was no more than a formality, introduced to satisfy the masses, because the initiated were well aware that the hunger-artist would never under any circumstances, not even under compulsion, partake of any nourishment during the period of fasting. His honor as an artist forbade such a thing. Of course not every guard could comprehend this. Sometimes there were groups of watchers who were very lax in their guard duty, who would purposely sit down together in a distant corner and absorb themselves in a game of cards with the obvious intention of allowing the hunger-artist a little refreshment which they seemed to believe he could produce from some secret supply. To the hunger-artist nothing was more painful than such guards; they filled him with unspeakable sadness; they made fasting terribly difficult for him. Sometimes he would overcome his weakness and sing during such a watch as this, sing as long as his strength held out, just to show the people how unjust were their suspicions. But it availed him little; in such cases they would simply marvel at the cleverness which enabled him to eat even while singing. Much more to his liking were the guards who sat down close to the cage, and not satisfied with the gloomy illumination of the hall, turned upon him

the pocket torches with which they had been provided by the impresario. The bright light bothered him not at all. Sleep was impossible in any case, and he could always drowse a little, under any illumination and at any hour, even when the hall was noisy and overcrowded. He was only too willing to pass the night with such watchers entirely without sleep; he would put himself out to joke with them, to tell them tales of his wanderings or on the other hand to listen to their stories: anything to stay awake, to be able to show them again and again that he had nothing edible in his cage and that he was fasting as none of them could possibly do. But his happiest moment was when morning came and a sumptuous breakfast was brought to them at his expense, and he saw them fall upon it with the appetite of healthy men who had spent a tiresome night in wakeful watching. To be sure there were people who pretended to see in this breakfast an unseemly attempt to influence the guards, but that was going too far, and when they were asked whether they would be willing to take upon themselves the task of watching through the night for the sake of the thing itself and without the breakfast, they made a wry face, though they continued to harbor their suspicions just the same.

After all, this was simply one of the suspicions unavoidably connected with fasting. Obviously no one was in a position to spend every day and night as a watchman at the side of the hunger-artist, and no one could be sure from his own observation that the fasting was really uninterrupted and complete; only the hunger-artist himself could know that, and so only he who was the faster could be at the same time a completely satisfied spectator of his fasting. And yet for another reason he never was satisfied. Perhaps it wasn't fasting at all which made him so emaciated that some people to their great regret had to stay away because they couldn't bear the sight of him; perhaps his emaciation came solely from his dissatisfaction with himself. For the fact was that only he and no one else, not even the initiated, knew how easy a thing it was to fast. It was the easiest thing in the world. He didn't keep it a secret either, but no one would believe him. At best people said he was modest, but usually he was accused of being a publicity hound or even an out-and-out fraud for whom fasting was easy because he knew how to make it easy, and who had the cheek on top of that practically to admit as much. All this he was forced to accept; he had become accustomed to it in the course of years; but inside him was the constant gnawing of dissatisfaction.

And yet never, never once at the end of any hunger period—this all were forced to admit—had he left his cage willingly. The impresario had set forty days as the maximum period for fasting; beyond that he would never let the fasting go, not even in the great world centers—and for a very good reason. Experience had shown that for about forty days, through the use of gradually intensified publicity, the interest of a city could be brought to an ever higher pitch, but that at the end of that time public enthusiasm began to wane and a marked decrease in patronage became apparent. There were of course minor differences in this respect from city to city and country to country, but the rule was that forty days was the maximum time. And so on the fortieth day the door of the flower-bedecked cage was opened, an enthusiastic audience filled the amphitheater, a military band played, two doctors entered the cage to carry out the necessary measurements on the body of the hunger-artist, the results were announced to the hall through a megaphone, and finally there came two young ladies, happy in the knowledge that they and no one else had been chosen for the task, whose duty it was to lead the hunger-artist from his cage and down a few steps, at the bottom of which stood a tiny table set with a carefully chosen invalid's repast. And at this moment the

hunger-artist invariably rebelled. He was willing enough to place his bony arms into the helping hands which the young ladies extended as they bent over him, but he didn't want to stand up. Why stop just now, at the end of forty days? He could have borne it much longer, immeasurably longer; why stop just now, at the point when his fasting was at its best—no, not even yet at its best? Why did they want to rob him of the honor of fasting on, of becoming not only the greatest hunger-artist of all time, which he probably was already, but of surpassing himself beyond measure? For he sensed that there was no limit to his capacity for fasting. Why did this throng, which pretended to marvel so at his feat, have so little patience with him? If he could bear to go on fasting, why could they not bear with him? Besides, he was weary, his seat in the straw was comfortable, and now they wanted him to rouse himself, stand up, and go to the meal, the very thought of which induced in him a nausea which he was barely able to suppress out of respect for the women. And he looked into the eyes of the women, who appeared so friendly but were in reality so cruel, and wearily shook the head which was so much too heavy for the fragile neck. But now there happened the thing which always happened at this point. The impresario would come, and silently—for the music rendered speech impossible—he would raise his arms over the hunger-artist as if inviting heaven to look down upon its work here upon the straw, this pitiful martyr—and martyr the hunger-artist was, to be sure, though in an entirely different sense. Then he would grasp the hunger-artist about his frail waist, trying as he did to make it obvious by his exaggerated caution with what a fragile object he was dealing, and, after surreptitiously shaking him a little and causing his legs to wobble and his body to sway uncontrollably, would turn him over to the ladies, who had meanwhile turned as pale as death. Now the hunger-artist offered no further resistance. His head lay on his chest, as if it had rolled there and somehow inexplicably stuck fast; his torso was cavernous; his legs, impelled by the urge to self-preservation, were pressed tightly together at the knees, and yet his feet scraped the earth as if it were not real, as if they were seeking the real one. And the entire weight of his body, light though it was, rested upon one of the ladies, who, breathless and looking about imploringly for help (she had not pictured this post of honor thus) first tried to avoid contact with the hunger-artist by stretching her neck as far as possible, and then—since this availed her nothing and her more fortunate companion did nothing to help her, but simply contented herself with carrying the hand of the hunger-artist, a mere bundle of bones, in her own trembling hand—she broke into tears to the accompaniment of delighted laughter from the audience, and had to be relieved at her post by an attendant who had long been held in readiness. Then came the meal, a little of which the impresario managed to force down the half-unconscious hunger-artist, the while he chattered amiably to divert attention from his condition; then a toast was spoken to the public, which the impresario pretended had been whispered to him by the hunger-artist; the orchestra provided a mighty climax with a flourish of trumpets; the crowd broke up, and no one had the right to be dissatisfied with what he had seen, no one but the hunger-artist, always only he.

And so it went on for many years, with only brief intervals of recuperation. He lived in apparent glory, honored by the world, but for the most part filled with a gloomy melancholy which was deepened by the fact that no one understood it. And indeed what comfort could one offer him? What else could he wish for? And when sometimes a good-natured person appeared who felt sorry for him and tried to explain to him that his sadness was caused by the lack of food, it was quite likely—especially if the fasting period was far advanced—that the hunger-artist would answer by flying into a rage and terrifying all those around him by shaking the bars of his cage like a wild animal. But for such outbreaks the impresario had a method of punishment which he was very fond of employing. He would apologize to the assembled public on behalf of the hunger-artist and admit that his conduct could be pardoned only by understanding the irritability caused by fasting, an irritability which would be less easy to understand in a well-fed person; then he would lead logically to the hunger-artist's claim—also to be explained by his overwrought state—that he could fast much longer, and would praise the lofty endeavor, worthy determination, and great self-denial which were evidenced by this claim. But then he would attempt to refute this claim simply by passing around photographs— which at the same time were offered for sale —in which one could see the hunger-artist on the fortieth day of fasting, lying in bed and so weak that he was on the point of expiring. This perversion of the truth, so well known to the hunger-artist and yet so unnerving when applied, was more than he could bear. That which was the effect of the premature ending of the fasting was here being set forth as its cause! Against this lack of understanding, this universal lack of understanding, it was impossible to fight. Each time, he would stand at the bars and listen eagerly to what the impresario was saying, but always when the photographs were brought forth he would relax his hold on the bars and sink back onto the straw, and once more the reassured public could come near and view him undisturbed.

When the witnesses of such scenes thought back on them a few years later, they found it hard to understand themselves. For meanwhile the aforementioned transformation had taken place. Perhaps there were deep-lying reasons for it; but who was interested in seeking them out? At any rate, the pampered hunger-artist one day found himself abandoned by the pleasure-seeking multitude, which preferred to flock to other spectacles. Once again the impresario raced through half of Europe with him to see whether the old interest would not here and there manifest itself. But in vain; as if by some secret agreement a genuine dislike for fasting exhibitions had everywhere developed. In reality of course it couldn't have come as suddenly as all that, and now one tardily remembered certain warning signs which at the time, in the intoxication of success, had not been sufficiently heeded or sufficiently combatted—but it was too late now to do anything about it. To be sure it was certain that one day the time for fasting would come again, but for the living that was no comfort. What was the hunger-artist to do now? He whom thousands had acclaimed couldn't put himself on display in the exhibition booths at small annual fairs, and as for going into some other profession he was not only too old but above all too fanatically devoted to fasting. And so he dismissed the impresario, the companion of a brilliant career, and hired himself out to a great circus. In order to spare his feelings, he did not even examine the terms of his contract.

A great circus with its huge throng of contrasting yet complementary men and animals and its masses of equipment can always find a place for another attraction, even a hunger-artist—that is, if his claims are modest enough. But in this case it was not only the hunger-artist who was engaged, but also his old and well-known name itself. Indeed it wasn't even possible to say, in view of the peculiar nature of this art which showed no flagging with increasing age, that a superannuated artist no longer at the height of his powers had taken refuge in a quiet position with a circus. On the contrary: the hunger-artist gave assurance that he could fast as well as he ever could—a thoroughly credible claim—indeed, he even maintained that, if allowed to go his own way (a privilege immediately granted to him), he would only now for the first time set the world in justifiable astonishment, a claim which, in view of the temper of the times, forgotten by the hunger-artist in his zeal, evoked no more than a smile from those who were in the know.

Actually, however, even the hunger-artist did not lose sight of the true state of affairs, and he was not at all surprised when he saw that his cage was stationed not in the middle of the circus as a feature attraction but out in the vicinity of the menagerie, a place which in its own way certainly was accessible enough. Large, gaily colored signs surrounded the cage and proclaimed what was to be seen there. During the intermissions in the performances, when the crowds thronged to see the animals fed, it was almost unavoidable that they should pass by the hunger-artist and pause there for a little. Perhaps they would have stayed there longer had it not been for the fact that the people who were pushing impatiently from the rear in the narrow alley-way, not understanding the reason for the delay on the way to the eagerly awaited stalls, made a longer and more leisurely view impossible. This explained too why the hunger-artist, though longing impatiently for these visits, which he naturally saw as his reason for existence, couldn't help feeling at the same time a certain apprehension. At first he could scarcely wait for the intermissions; he would note the approach of the throng with charmed anticipation; but only too soon he became convinced of the fact that again and again, without exception, they were on their way to the animals, and his experience in this matter overcame even the most stubborn, almost conscious self-deception. And this view of the throng from a distance continued to be the most agreeable one. For once they had reached his cage, he was immediately submerged in a sea of shouting, cursing people who formed ever-changing groups, one made up of those who wanted to view him at their leisure—not because they had any understanding for him, but simply impelled by a whim or out of sheer willfulness (and these soon became for the hunger-artist the more unpleasant)—and the other consisting of those who were bent on getting immediately to the stalls. Once the great crowd had passed by, there would come the stragglers, and these, of course, for whom there was no obstacle to stopping had they only felt the desire, strode by with hurried steps in order not to be late at the stalls. And it was no more than a fortunate but infrequent stroke of luck when the father of a family would come by with his children, point to the hunger-artist, and explain in detail what it was all about; and he would tell about earlier times when he had been present at similar but incomparably finer exhibitions. But naturally the children, on account of inadequate preparation in the schools and in life, always remained without any understanding. What did fasting mean to them? And yet in the sparkling of their penetrating eyes they gave a hint of new and more merciful days to come. Perhaps, the hunger-artist would say to himself on such occasions, everything would be better if his station were not quite so close to the animals. It made the choice too easy for the people, to say nothing of the fact that the evil odors from the stalls, the restlessness of the animals at night, the sight of pieces of raw meat for the beasts of prey being carried by, and the screams of the animals at feeding time offended him and kept him in a constant state of depression. But he didn't venture to complain to the management; after all, he owed to the animals the fact that he had so many visitors, among whom there might be now and then one destined for him. And who knew to what spot they might banish him if he reminded them of his existence and of the fact that, when seen

aright, he served only as a hindrance on the way to the animals?

A minor hindrance, to be sure, and one that was constantly growing smaller. People came to take for granted the novelty of having anyone demand attention for a hunger-artist in modern times, and this taking-for-granted spelled his doom. Let him fast with all the skill of which he was capable—and he did—but nothing could save him now, people simply passed him by. Just try to explain the art of fasting to someone! He who has no feeling for it simply cannot comprehend it. The beautiful signs grew dirty and illegible; they were torn down, and it occurred to no one to replace them. The little board showing the number of days of fasting achieved, which at first had been conscientiously changed, had remained the same for weeks on end, for the attendants had grown weary even of this little task. And so the hunger-artist fasted on without hindrance, as he had once dreamed of doing, and was able to do it without difficulty, just as he had once predicted, but no one counted the days; no one, not even the hunger-artist himself, knew how great his achievement actually was, and his heart grew heavy. And if on occasion some idler stopped, ridiculed the old numbers on the board, and spoke of fraud, it was the most stupid lie which indifference and inborn malice could possibly invent, because it was not the hunger-artist who was cheating; he was doing his duty honorably, but the world was cheating him of his reward.

And yet more days passed, but that too had its end. Once one of the managers happened to notice the cage, and he asked the attendants why such a good serviceable cage with its putrid straw should be left standing unused. No one could say, until one of them, with the help of the numbered board, remembered the hunger-artist. The straw was probed with poles, and inside they found the hunger-artist. "You're still fasting?" asked the manager. "When in heaven's name will you be done?" "Forgive me, all of you," whispered the hunger-artist. "Certainly," said the manager, and he pointed to his head with his finger to indicate the hunger-artist's condition to the attendants, "we forgive you." "I always wanted you to admire my fasting," said the hunger-artist. "And we do admire it," replied the manager obligingly. "But you shouldn't admire it," said the hunger-artist. "Well, then, we don't admire it," said the manager, "but why shouldn't we admire it?" "Because I have to fast, I can't help myself," said the hunger-artist. "Just listen to that," said the manager; "and why can't you help yourself?" "Because," said the hunger-artist, and he lifted his dainty head a little, and, thrusting his lips forward as if for a kiss, spoke directly into the manager's ear so that no word would be lost, "because I could find no food to my liking. If I had found it, believe me, I should have caused no stir; I should have eaten my fill just as you do, and all others." Those were his last words, but in his glazed eyes there remained the firm, though no longer proud, conviction that he was still fasting.

"Well, now clean things up!" said the manager, and they buried the hunger-artist together with the straw. And into the cage they put a young panther. It was perceptibly refreshing even to the dullest temperament to see this wild animal hurl itself about in this cage which so long had been desolate. He lacked for nothing. Without any delay, the keepers brought him just the kind of food he craved. And he appeared not even to miss his freedom. This noble body, healthy to the point of bursting, seemed in fact to carry its own freedom around with it (a freedom which appeared to reside somewhere in the region of its teeth); and its joy in living issued forth from its throat with such fierceness that it wasn't easy for those who watched it to stand firm. But they overcame their hesitation, crowded about the cage, and just couldn't tear themselves away.

William Faulkner

A ROSE FOR EMILY

I

When Miss Emily Grierson died, our whole town went to her funeral: the men through a sort of respectful affection for a fallen monument, the women mostly out of curiosity to see the inside of her house, which no one save an old manservant—a combined gardener and cook—had seen in at least ten years.

It was a big, squarish frame house that had once been white, decorated with cupolas and spires and scrolled balconies in the heavily lightsome style of the Seventies, set on what had once been our most select street. But garages and cotton gins had encroached and obliterated even the august names of that neighborhood; only Miss Emily's house was left, lifting its stubborn and coquettish decay above the cotton wagons and the gasoline pumps—an eyesore among eyesores. And now Miss Emily had gone to join the representatives of those august names where they lay in the cedar-bemused cemetery among the ranked and anonymous graves of Union and Confederate soldiers who fell at the battle of Jefferson.

Alive, Miss Emily had been a tradition, a duty, and a care; a sort of hereditary obligation upon the town, dating from that day in 1894 when Colonel Sartoris, the mayor—he who fathered the edict that no Negro woman should appear on the streets without an apron—remitted her taxes, the dispensation dating from the death of her father on into perpetuity. Not that Miss Emily would have accepted charity. Colonel Sartoris invented an involved tale to the effect that Miss Emily's father had loaned money to the town, which the town, as a matter of business, preferred this way of repaying. Only a man of Colonel Sartoris' generation and thought could have invented it, and only a woman could have believed it.

When the next generation, with its more modern ideas, became mayors and aldermen, this arrangement created some little dissatisfaction. On the first of the year they mailed her a tax notice. February came, and there was no reply. They wrote her a formal letter, asking her to call at the sheriff's office at her convenience. A week later the mayor wrote her himself, offering to call or to send his car for her, and received in reply a note on paper of an archaic shape, in a thin, flowing calligraphy in faded ink, to the effect that she no longer went out at all. The tax notice was also enclosed, without comment.

They called a special meeting of the Board of Aldermen. A deputation waited upon her, knocked at the door through which no visitor had passed since she ceased giving china-painting lessons eight or ten years earlier. They were admitted by the old Negro into a dim hall from which a stairway mounted into still more shadow. It smelled of dust and disuse—a close, dank smell. The Negro led them into the parlor. It was furnished in heavy, leather-covered furniture. When the Negro opened the blinds of one window, they could see that the leather was cracked; and when they sat down, a faint dust rose sluggishly about their thighs, spinning with slow motes in the single sunray. On a tarnished gilt easel before the fireplace stood a crayon portrait of Miss Emily's father.

They rose when she entered—a small, fat woman in black, with a thin gold chain descending to her waist and vanishing into her belt, leaning on an ebony cane with a tarnished gold head. Her skeleton was small and spare; perhaps that was why what would have been merely plumpness in another was obesity in her. She looked bloated, like a body long submerged in motionless water, and of that pallid hue. Her eyes, lost in the fatty ridges of her face, looked like two small pieces of coal pressed into a lump of dough as they moved from one face to another while the visitors stated their errand.

She did not ask them to sit. She just stood in the door and listened quietly until the spokesman came to a stumbling halt. Then they could hear the invisible watch ticking at the end of the gold chain.

Her voice was dry and cold. "I have no taxes in Jefferson. Colonel Sartoris explained it to me. Perhaps one of you can gain access to the city records and satisfy yourselves."

"But we have. We are the city authorities, Miss Emily. Didn't you get a notice from the sheriff, signed by him?"

"I received a paper, yes," Miss Emily said. "Perhaps he considers himself the sheriff. . . . I have no taxes in Jefferson."

"But there is nothing on the books to show that, you see. We must go by the—"

"See Colonel Sartoris. I have no taxes in Jefferson."

"But, Miss Emily—"

"See Colonel Sartoris." (Colonel Sartoris had been dead almost ten years.) "I have no taxes in Jefferson. Tobe!" The Negro appeared. "Show these gentlemen out."

II

So she vanquished them, horse and foot, just as she had vanquished their fathers thirty years before about the smell. That was two years after her father's death and a short time after her sweetheart—the one we believed would marry her—had deserted her. After her father's death she went out very little; after her sweetheart went away, people hardly saw her at all. A few of the ladies had the temerity to call, but were not received, and the only sign of life about the place was the Negro man—a young man then—going in and out with a market basket.

"Just as if a man—any man—could keep a kitchen properly," the ladies said; so they were not surprised when the smell developed. It was another link between the gross, teeming world and the high and mighty Griersons.

A neighbor, a woman, complained to the mayor, Judge Stevens, eighty years old.

"But what will you have me do about it, madam?" he said.

"Why, send her word to stop it," the woman said. "Isn't there a law?"

"I'm sure that won't be necessary," Judge Stevens said. "It's probably just a snake or a rat that nigger of hers killed in the yard. I'll speak to him about it."

The next day he received two more complaints, one from a man who came in diffident deprecation. "We really must do something about it, Judge. I'd be the last one in the world to bother Miss Emily, but we've got to do something." That night the Board of Aldermen met—three graybeards and one younger man, a member of the rising generation.

"It's simple enough," he said. "Send her word to have her place cleaned up. Give her a certain time to do it in, and if she don't. . . ."

"Dammit, sir," Judge Stevens said, "will you accuse a lady to her face of smelling bad?"

So the next night, after midnight, four men crossed Miss Emily's lawn and slunk about the house like burglars, sniffing along the base of the brickwork and at the cellar openings while one of them performed a regular sowing motion with his hand out of a sack slung from his shoulder. They broke open the cellar door and sprinkled lime there, and in all the outbuildings. As they recrossed the lawn, a window that had been dark was lighted and Miss Emily sat in it, the light behind her, and her upright torso motionless as that of an idol. They crept quietly across the lawn and into the shadow of the locusts that lined the street. After a week or two the smell went away.

That was when people had begun to feel really sorry for her. People in our town, remembering how Old Lady Wyatt, her great-aunt, had gone completely crazy at last, believed that the Griersons held themselves a little too high for what they really were. None of the young men were quite good enough for Miss Emily and such. We had long thought of them as a tableau: Miss Emily a slender figure in white in the background, her father a spraddled silhouette in the foreground, his back to her and clutching a horsewhip, the two of them framed by the back-flung front door. So when she got to be thirty and was still single, we were not pleased exactly, but vindicated; even with insanity in the family she wouldn't have turned down all of her chances if they had really materialized.

When her father died, it got about that the house was all that was left to her; and in a way, people were glad. At last they could pity Miss Emily. Being left alone, and a pauper, she had become humanized. Now she too would know the old thrill and the old despair of a penny more or less.

The day after his death all the ladies prepared to call at the house and offer condolence and aid, as is our custom. Miss Emily met them at the door, dressed as usual and with no trace of grief on her face. She told them that her father was not dead. She did that for three days, with the ministers calling on her, and the doctors, trying to persuade her to let them dispose of the body. Just as they were about to resort to law and force, she broke down, and they buried her father quickly.

We did not say she was crazy then. We believed she had to do that. We remembered all the young men her father had driven away, and we knew that with nothing left, she would have to cling to that which had robbed her, as people will.

III

She was sick for a long time. When we saw her again, her hair was cut short, making her look like a girl, with a vague resemblance to those angels in colored church windows—sort of tragic and serene.

The town had just let the contracts for paving the sidewalks, and in the summer after her father's death they began the work. The construction company came with niggers and mules and machinery, and a foreman named Homer Barron, a Yankee—a big, dark, ready man, with a big voice and eyes lighter than his face. The little boys would follow in groups to hear him cuss the niggers, and the niggers singing in time to the rise and fall of picks. Pretty soon he knew everybody in town. Whenever you heard a lot of laughing anywhere about the square, Homer Barron would be in the center of the group. Presently we began to see him and Miss Emily on Sunday afternoons driving in the yellow-wheeled buggy and the matched team of bays from the livery stable.

At first we were glad that Miss Emily would have an interest, because the ladies all said, "Of course a Grierson would not think seriously of a Northerner, a day laborer." But there were still others, older people, who said that even grief could not cause a real lady to forget *noblesse oblige*—without calling it *noblesse oblige*. They just said, "Poor Emily. Her kinsfolk should come to her." She had some kin in Alabama; but years ago her father had fallen out with them over the estate of Old Lady Wyatt, the crazy woman, and there was no communication between the two families. They

had not even been represented at the funeral.

And as soon as the old people said, "Poor Emily," the whispering began. "Do you suppose it's really so?" they said to one another. "Of course it is. What else could. . . ." This behind their hands; rustling of craned silk and satin behind jalousies closed upon the sun of Sunday afternoon as the thin, swift clop-clop-clop of the matched team passed: "Poor Emily."

She carried her head high enough—even when we believed that she was fallen. It was as if she demanded more than ever the recognition of her dignity as the last Grierson; as if it had wanted that touch of earthiness to reaffirm her imperviousness. Like when she bought the rat poison, the arsenic. That was over a year after they had begun to say "Poor Emily," and while the two female cousins were visiting her.

"I want some poison," she said to the druggist. She was over thirty then, still a slight woman, though thinner than usual, with cold, haughty black eyes in a face the flesh of which was strained across the temples and about the eye-sockets as you imagine a lighthouse-keeper's face ought to look. "I want some poison," she said.

"Yes, Miss Emily. What kind? For rats and such? I'd recom—"

"I want the best you have. I don't care what kind."

The druggist named several. "They'll kill anything up to an elephant. But what you want is—"

"Arsenic," Miss Emily said. "Is that a good one?"

"Is . . . arsenic? Yes, ma'am. But what you want—"

"I want arsenic."

The druggist looked down at her. She looked back at him, erect, her face like a strained flag. "Why, of course," the druggist said. "If that's what you want. But the law requires you to tell what you are going to use it for."

Miss Emily just stared at him, her head tilted back in order to look him eye for eye, until he looked away and went and got the arsenic and wrapped it up. The Negro delivery boy brought her the package; the druggist didn't come back. When she opened the package at home there was written on the box, under the skull and bones: "For rats."

IV

So the next day we all said, "She will kill herself"; and we said it would be the best thing. When she had first begun to be seen with Homer Barron, we had said, "She will marry him." Then we said, "She will persuade him yet," because Homer himself had remarked—he liked men, and it was known that he drank with the younger men in the Elks' Club—that he was not a marrying man. Later we said "Poor Emily" behind the jalousies as they passed on Sunday afternoon in the glittering buggy, Miss Emily with her head high and Homer Barron with his hat cocked and a cigar in his teeth, reins and whip in a yellow glove.

Then some of the ladies began to say that it was a disgrace to the town and a bad example to the young people. The men did not want to interfere, but at last the ladies forced the Baptist minister—Miss Emily's people were Episcopal—to call upon her. He would never divulge what happened during that interview, but he refused to go back again. The next Sunday they again drove about the streets, and the following day the minister's wife wrote to Miss Emily's relations in Alabama.

So she had blood-kin under her roof again and we sat back to watch developments. At first nothing happened. Then we were sure that they were to be married. We learned that Miss Emily had been to the jeweler's and ordered a man's toilet set in silver, with the letters H. B. on each piece. Two days later we learned that she had bought a complete outfit of men's clothing, including a nightshirt, and we said, "They are married." We were really glad. We were glad because the two female cousins were even more Grierson than Miss Emily had ever been.

So we were not surprised when Homer Barron—the streets had been finished some time since—was gone. We were a little disappointed that there was not a public blowing-off, but we believed that he had gone on to prepare for Miss Emily's coming, or to give her a chance to get rid of the cousins. (By that time it was a cabal, and we were all Miss Emily's allies to help circumvent the cousins.) Sure enough, after another week they departed. And, as we had expected all along, within three days Homer Barron was back in town. A neighbor saw the Negro man admit him at the kitchen door at dusk one evening.

And that was the last we saw of Homer Barron. And of Miss Emily for some time. The Negro man went in and out with the market basket, but the front door remained closed. Now and then we would see her at a window for a moment, as the men did that night when they sprinkled the lime, but for almost six months she did not appear on the streets. Then we knew that this was to be expected too; as if that quality of her father which had thwarted her woman's life so many times had been too virulent and too furious to die.

When we next saw Miss Emily, she had grown fat and her hair was turning gray. During the next few years it grew grayer and grayer until it attained an even pepper-and-salt iron-gray, when it ceased turning. Up to the day of her death at seventy-four it was still that vigorous iron-gray, like the hair of an active man.

From that time on her front door remained closed, save for a period of six or seven years, when she was about forty, during which she gave lessons in china-painting. She fitted up a studio in one of the downstairs rooms, where the daughters and granddaughters of Colonel Sartoris' contemporaries were sent to her with the same regularity and in the same spirit that they were sent to church on Sundays with a twenty-five-cent piece for the collection plate. Meanwhile her taxes had been remitted.

Then the newer generation became the backbone and the spirit of the town, and the painting pupils grew up and fell away and did not send their children to her with boxes of color and tedious brushes and pictures cut from the ladies' magazines. The front door closed upon the last one and remained closed for good. When the town got free postal delivery, Miss Emily alone refused to let them fasten metal numbers above her door and attach a mailbox to it. She would not listen to them.

Daily, monthly, yearly we watched the Negro grow grayer and more stooped, going in and out with the market basket. Each December we sent her a tax notice, which would be returned by the post office a week later, unclaimed. Now and then we would see her in one of the downstairs windows—she had evidently shut up the top floor of the house—like the carven torso of an idol in a niche, looking or not looking at us, we could never tell which. Thus she passed from generation to generation—dear, inescapable, impervious, tranquil, and perverse.

And so she died. Fell ill in the house filled with dust and shadows, with only a doddering Negro man to wait on her. We did not even know she was sick; we had long since given up trying to get any information from the Negro. He talked to no one, probably not even to her, for his voice had grown harsh and rusty, as if from disuse.

She died in one of the downstairs rooms, in a heavy walnut bed with a curtain, her gray head propped on a pillow yellow and moldy with age and lack of sunlight.

V

The Negro met the first of the ladies at the front door and let them in, with their hushed, sibilant voices and their quick, curious glances, and then he disappeared. He walked right through the house and out the back and was not seen again.

The two female cousins came at once. They held the funeral on the second day, with the town coming to look at Miss Emily beneath a mass of bought flowers, with the crayon face of her father musing profoundly above the bier and the ladies sibilant and macabre; and the very old men—some in their brushed Confederate uniforms—on the porch and the lawn, talking of Miss Emily as if she had been a contemporary of theirs, believing that they had danced with her and courted her perhaps, confusing time with its mathematical progression, as the old do, to whom all the past is not a diminishing road but, instead, a huge meadow which no winter ever quite touches, divided from them now by the narrow bottle-neck of the most recent decade of years.

Already we knew that there was one room in that region above the stairs which no one had seen in forty years, and which would have to be forced. They waited until Miss Emily was decently in the ground before they opened it.

The violence of breaking down the door seemed to fill this room with pervading dust. A thin, acrid pall as of the tomb seemed to lie everywhere upon this room decked and furnished as for a bridal: upon the valence curtains of faded rose color, upon the rose-shaded lights, upon the dressing table, upon the delicate array of crystal and the man's toilet things backed with tarnished silver, silver so tarnished that the monogram was obscured. Among them lay a collar and tie, as if they had just been removed, which, lifted, left upon the surface a pale crescent in the dust. Upon a chair hung the suit, carefully folded; beneath it the two mute shoes and the discarded socks.

The man himself lay in the bed.

For a long while we just stood there, looking down at the profound and fleshless grin. The body had apparently once lain in the attitude of an embrace, and now the long sleep that outlasts love, that conquers even the grimace of love, had cuckolded him. What was left of him, rotted beneath what was left of the nightshirt, had become inextricable from the bed in which he lay; and upon him and upon the pillow beside him lay that even coating of the patient and biding dust.

Then we noticed that in the second pillow was the indentation of a head. One of us lifted something from it and leaning forward, that faint and invisible dust dry and acrid in the nostrils, we saw a long strand of iron-gray hair.

William Faulkner

SPOTTED HORSES

Yes sir. Flem Snopes has filled that whole country full of spotted horses. You can hear folks running them all day and all night, whooping and hollering, and the horses running back and forth across them little wooden bridges ever now and then kind of like thunder. Here I was this morning pretty near half way to town, with the team ambling along and me setting in the buckboard about half asleep, when all of a sudden something came swurging up outen the bushes and jumped the road clean, without touching hoof to it. It flew right over my team big as a billboard and flying through the air like a hawk. It taken me thirty minutes to stop my team and untangle the harness and the buckboard and hitch them up again.

That Flem Snopes. I be dog if he ain't a case, now. One morning about ten years ago the boys was just getting settled down on Varner's porch for a little talk and tobacco, when here come Flem out from behind the counter, with his coat off and his hair all parted, like he might have been clerking for Varner for ten years already. Folks all knowed him; it was a big family of them about five miles down the bottom. That year, at least. Share-cropping. They never stayed on any place over a year. Then they would move on to another place, with the chap or maybe the twins of that year's litter. It was a regular nest of them. But Flem. The rest of them stayed tenant farmers, moving ever year, but here come Flem one day, walking out from behind Jody Varner's counter like he owned it. And he wasn't there but a year or two before folks knowed that if him and Jody was both still in that store in ten years more it would be Jody clerking for Flem Snopes. Why, that fellow could make a nickel where it wasn't but four cents to begin with. He skun me in two trades myself, and the fellow that can do that, I just hope he'll get rich before I do; that's all.

All right. So here Flem was, clerking at Varner's, making a nickel here and there and not telling nobody about it. No, sir. Folks never knowed when Flem got the better of somebody lessen the fellow he beat told it. He'd just set there in the store-chair, chewing his tobacco and keeping his own business to hisself, until about a week later we'd find out it was somebody else's business he was keeping to hisself—provided the fellow he trimmed was mad enough to tell it. That's Flem.

We give him ten years to own ever thing Jody Varner had. But he never waited no ten years. I reckon you-all know that gal of Uncle Billy Varner's, the youngest, Eula.

Jody's sister. Ever Sunday ever yellow-wheeled buggy and curried riding horse in that country would be hitched to Bill Varner's fence, and the young bucks setting on the porch, swarming around Eula like bees around a honey pot. One of these here kind of big, soft-looking gals that could giggle richer than plowed new-ground. Wouldn't none of them leave before the others, and so they would set there on the porch until time to go home, with some of them with nine and ten miles to ride and then get up tomorrow and go back to the field. So they would all leave together and they would ride in a clump down to the creek ford and hitch them curried horses and yellow-wheeled buggies and get out and fight one another. Then they would get in the buggies again and go on home.

Well, one day about a year ago, one of them yellow-wheeled buggies and one of them curried saddle-horses quit this country. We heard they was heading for Texas. The next day Uncle Billy and Eula and Flem come into town in Uncle Bill's surrey, and when they come back, Flem and Eula was married. And on the next day we heard that two more of them yellow-wheeled buggies had left the country. They mought have gone to Texas, too. It's a big place.

Anyway, about a month after the wedding, Flem and Eula went to Texas, too. They was gone pretty near a year. Then one day last month, Eula come back, with a baby. We figgered up, and we decided that it was as well-growed a three-months-old baby as we ever see. It can already pull up on a chair. I reckon Texas makes big men quick, being a big place. Anyway, if it keeps on like it started, it'll be chewing tobacco and voting time it's eight years old.

And so last Friday here come Flem himself. He was on a wagon with another fellow. The other fellow had one of these two-gallon hats and a ivory-handled pistol and a box of gingersnaps sticking out of his hind pocket, and tied to the tail-gate of the wagon was about two dozen of them Texas ponies, hitched to one another with barbed wire. They was colored like parrots and they was quiet as doves, and ere a one of them would kill you quick as a rattlesnake. Nere a one of them had two eyes the same color, and nere a one of them had ever see a bridle, I reckon; and when that Texas man got down offen the wagon and walked up to them to show how gentle they was, one of them cut his vest clean offen him, same as with a razor.

Flem had done already disappeared; he had went on to see his wife, I reckon, and to see if that ere baby had done gone on to the field to help Uncle Billy plow, maybe. It was the Texas man that taken the horses on to Mrs. Littlejohn's lot. He had a little trouble at first, when they come to the gate, because they hadn't never see a fence before, and when he finally got them in and taken a pair of wire cutters and unhitched them and got them into the barn and poured some shell corn into the trough, they durn nigh tore down the barn. I reckon they thought that shell corn was bugs, maybe. So he left them in the lot and he announced that the auction would begin at sunup tomorrow.

That night we was setting on Mrs. Littlejohn's porch. You-all mind the moon was nigh full that night, and we could watch them spotted varmints swirling along the fence and back and forth across the lot same as minnows in a pond. And then now and then they would all kind of huddle up against the barn and rest themselves by biting and kicking one another. We would hear a squeal, and then a set of hoofs would go Bam! against the barn, like a pistol. It sounded just like a fellow with a pistol, in a nest of cattymounts, taking his time.

II

It wasn't ere a man knowed yet if Flem owned them things or not. They just knowed one thing: that they wasn't never goin to know for sho if Flem did or not, or if maybe he didn't just get on that wagon at the edge of town, for the ride or not. Even Eck Snopes didn't know, Flem's own cousin. But wasn't nobody surprised at that. We knowed that Flem would skin Eck quick as he would ere a one of us.

They was there by sunup next morning, some of them come twelve and sixteen miles, with seed-money tied up in tobacco sacks in their overalls, standing along the fence, when the Texas man come out of Mrs. Littlejohn's after breakfast and clumb onto the gate post with that ere white pistol butt sticking outen his hind pocket. He taken a new box of gingersnaps outen his pocket and bit the end offen it like a cigar and spit out the paper, and said the auction was open. And still they was coming up in wagons and a horse- and mule-back and hitching the teams across the road and coming to the fence. Flem wasn't nowhere in sight.

But he couldn't get them started. He begun to work on Eck, because Eck holp him last night to get them into the barn and feed them that shell corn. Eck got out just in time. He come outen that barn like a chip on the crest of a busted dam of water, and clumb into the wagon just in time.

He was working on Eck when Henry Armstid come up in his wagon. Eck was saying he was skeered to bid on one of them, because he might get it, and the Texas man says, "Them ponies? Them little horses?" He clumb down offen the gate post and went toward the horses. They broke and run, and him following them, kind of chirping to them, with his hand out like he was fixing to catch a fly, until he got three or four of them cornered. Then he jumped into them, and then we couldn't see nothing for a while because of the dust. It was a big cloud of it, and them blare-eyed, spotted things swoaring outen it twenty foot to a jump, in forty directions without counting up. Then the

dust settled and there they was, that Texas man and the horse. He had its head twisted clean around like a owl's head. Its legs was braced and it was trembling like a new bride and groaning like a sawmill, and him holding its head wrung clean around on its neck so it was snuffing sky. "Look it over," he says, with his heels dug too and that white pistol sticking outen his pocket and his neck swole up like a spreading adder's until you could just tell what he was saying, cussing the horse and talking to us all at once: "Look him over, the fiddle-headed son of fourteen fathers. Try him, buy him; you will get the best—" Then it was all dust again, and we couldn't see nothing but spotted hide and mane, and that ere Texas man's boot-heels like a couple of walnuts on two strings, and after a while that two-gallon hat come sailing out like a fat old hen crossing a fence.

When the dust settled again, he was just getting outen the far fence corner, brushing himself off. He come and got his hat and brushed it off and come and clumb onto the gate post again. He was breathing hard. The hammer-head horse was still running round and round the lot like a merry-go-round at a fair. That was when Henry Armstid come shoving up to the gate in them patched over-alls and one of them dangle-armed shirts of hisn. Hadn't nobody noticed him until then. We was all watching the Texas man and the horses. Even Mrs. Littlejohn; she had done come out and built a fire under the wash-pot in her back yard, and she would stand at the fence a while and then go back into the house and come out again with a arm full of wash and stand at the fence again. Well, here come Henry shoving up, and then we see Mrs. Armstid right behind him, in that ere faded wrapper and sunbonnet and them tennis shoes. "Git on back to that wagon," Henry says.

"Henry," she says.

"Here, boys," the Texas man says, "make room for missus to get up and see. Come on

Henry," he says, "here's your chance to buy that saddle-horse missus has been wanting. What about ten dollars, Henry?"

"Henry," Mrs. Armstid says. She put her hand on Henry's arm. Henry knocked her hand down.

"Git on back to that wagon, like I told you," he says.

Mrs. Armstid never moved. She stood behind Henry, with her hands rolled into her dress, not looking at nothing. "He hain't no more despair than to buy one of them things," she says. "And us not five dollars ahead of the pore house, he hain't no more despair." It was the truth, too. They ain't never made more than a bare living offen that place of theirs, and them with four chaps and the very clothes they wears she earns by weaving by the firelight at night while Henry's asleep.

"Shut your mouth and git on back to that wagon," Henry says. "Do you want I taken a wagon stake to you here in the big road?"

Well, that Texas man taken one look at her. Then he begun on Eck again, like Henry wasn't even there. But Eck was skeered. "I can git me a snapping turtle or a water moccasin for nothing. I ain't going to buy none."

So the Texas man said he would give Eck a horse. "To start the auction, and because you help me last night. If you'll start the bidding on the next horse," he says, "I'll give you that fiddle-head horse."

I wish you could have seen them, standing there with their seed-money in their pockets, watching that Texas man give Eck Snopes a live horse, all fixed to call him a fool if he taken it or not. Finally Eck says he'll take it. "Only I just starts the bidding," he says. "I don't have to buy the next one lessen I ain't overtopped." The Texas man said all right, and Eck bid a dollar on the next one, with Henry Armstid standing there with his mouth already open, watching Eck and the

Texas man like a mad-dog or something. "A dollar," Eck says.

The Texas man looked at Eck. His mouth was already open too, like he had started to say something and what he was going to say had up and died on him. "A dollar? You mean, *one* dollar, Eck?"

"Durn it," Eck says, "two dollars, then."

Well, sir, I wish you could a seen that Texas man. He taken out that gingersnap box and held it up and looked into it, careful, like it might have been a diamond ring in it, or a spider. Then he throwed it away and wiped his face with a bandanna. "Well," he says. "Well. Two dollars. Two dollars. Is your pulse all right, Eck?" he says. "Do you have ager-sweats at night, maybe?" he says. "Well," he says, "I got to take it. But are you boys going to stand there and see Eck get two horses at a dollar a head?"

That done it. I be dog if he wasn't nigh as smart as Flem Snopes. He hadn't no more than got the words outen his mouth before here was Henry Armstid, waving his hand. "Three dollars," Henry says. Mrs. Armstid tried to hold him again. He knocked her hand off, shoving up to the gate post.

"Mister," Mrs. Armstid says, "we got chaps in the house and not corn to feed the stock. We got five dollars I earned my chaps a-weaving after dark, and him snoring in the bed. And he hain't no more despair."

"Henry bid three dollars," the Texas man says. "Raise him a dollar, Eck, and the horse is yours."

"Henry," Mrs. Armstid says.

"Raise him, Eck," the Texas man says.

"Four dollars," Eck says.

"Five dollars," Henry says, shaking his fist. He shoved up right under the gate post. Mrs. Armstid was looking at the Texas man too.

"Mister," she says, "if you take that five dollars I earned my chaps a-weaving for one of them things, it'll be a curse onto you and yourn during all the time of man."

But it wasn't no stopping Henry. He had shoved up, waving his fist at the Texas man. He opened it; the money was in nickels and quarters, and one dollar bill that looked like a cow's cud. "Five dollars," he says. "And the man that raises it'll have to beat my head off, or I'll beat hisn."

"All right," the Texas man says. "Five dollars is bid. But don't you shake your hand at me."

III

It taken till nigh sundown before the last one was sold. He got them hotted up once and the bidding got up to seven dollars and a quarter, but most of them went around three or four dollars, him setting on the gate post and picking the horses out one at a time by mouth-word, and Mrs. Littlejohn pumping up and down at the tub and stopping and coming to the fence for a while and going back to the tub again. She had done got done too, and the wash was hung on the line in the back yard, and we could smell supper cooking. Finally they was all sold; he swapped the last two and the wagon for a buckboard.

We was all kind of tired, but Henry Armstid looked more like a mad-dog than ever. When he bought, Mrs. Armstid had went back to the wagon, setting in it behind them two rabbit-sized, bone-pore mules, and the wagon itself looking like it would fall all to pieces soon as the mules moved. Henry hadn't even waited to pull it outen the road; it was still in the middle of the road and her setting in it, not looking at nothing, ever since this morning.

Henry was right up against the gate. He went up to the Texas man. "I bought a horse and I paid cash," Henry says. "And yet you expect me to stand around here until they are all sold before I can get my horse. I'm going to take my horse outen that lot."

The Texas man looked at Henry. He talked like he might have been asking for a cup of coffee at the table. "Take your horse," he says.

Then Henry quit looking at the Texas man. He began to swallow, holding onto the gate. "Ain't you going to help me?" he says.

"It ain't my horse," the Texas man says.

Henry never looked at the Texas man again, he never looked at nobody. "Who'll help me catch my horse?" he says. Never nobody said nothing. "Bring the plowline," Henry says. Mrs. Armstid got outen the wagon and brought the plowline. The Texas man got down offen the post. The woman made to pass him, carrying the rope.

"Don't you go in there, missus," the Texas man says.

Henry opened the gate. He didn't look back. "Come on here," he says.

"Don't you go in there, missus," the Texas man says.

Mrs. Armstid wasn't looking at nobody, neither, with her hands across her middle, holding the rope. "I reckon I better," she says. Her and Henry went into the lot. The horses broke and run. Henry and Mrs. Armstid followed.

"Get him into the corner," Henry says. They got Henry's horse cornered finally, and Henry taken the rope, but Mrs. Armstid let the horse get out. They hemmed it up again, but Mrs. Armstid let it get out again, and Henry turned and hit her with the rope. "Why didn't you head him back?" Henry says. He hit her again. "Why didn't you?" It was about that time I looked around and see Flem Snopes standing there.

It was the Texas man that done something. He moved fast for a big man. He caught the rope before Henry could hit the third time, and Henry whirled and made like he would jump at the Texas man. But he never jumped. The Texas man went and taken Henry's arm and led him outen the lot. Mrs. Armstid come behind them and the Texas man taken some money outen his pocket and he give it into Mrs. Armstid's hand. "Get him into the wagon and take him on home," the Texas man says, like he might have been telling them he enjoyed his supper.

Then here come Flem. "What's that for, Buck?" Flem says.

"Thinks he bought one of them ponies," the Texas man says. "Get him on away, missus."

But Henry wouldn't go. "Give him back that money," he says. "I bought that horse and I aim to have him if I have to shoot him."

And there was Flem, standing there with his hands in his pockets, chewing like he had just happened to be passing.

"You take your money and I take my horse," Henry says. "Give it back to him," he says to Mrs. Armstid.

"You don't own no horse of mine," the Texas man says. "Get him on home, missus."

Then Henry seen Flem. "You got something to do with these horses," he says. "I bought one. Here's the money for it." He taken the bill outen Mrs. Armstid's hand. He offered it to Flem. "I bought one. Ask him. Here. Here's the money," he says, giving the bill to Flem.

When Flem taken the money, the Texas man dropped the rope he had snatched outen Henry's hand. He had done sent Eck Snopes's boy up to the store for another box of gingersnaps, and he taken the box outen his pocket and looked into it. It was empty and he dropped it on the ground. "Mr. Snopes will have your money for you to-morrow," he says to Mrs. Armstid. "You can get it from him tomorrow. He don't own no horse. You get him into the wagon and get him on home." Mrs. Armstid went back to the wagon and got in. "Where's that ere

buckboard I bought?" the Texas man says. It was after sundown then. And then Mrs. Littlejohn come out on the porch and rung the supper bell.

IV

I come on in and et supper. Mrs. Littlejohn would bring in a pan of bread or something, then she would go out to the porch a minute and come back and tell us. The Texas man had hitched his team to the buckboard he had swapped them last two horses for, and him and Flem had gone, and then she told that the rest of them that never had ropes had went back to the store with I. O. Snopes to get some ropes, and wasn't nobody at the gate but Henry Armstid, and Mrs. Armstid setting in the wagon in the road, and Eck Snopes and that boy of hisn. "I don't care how many of them fool men gets killed by them things," Mrs. Littlejohn says, "but I ain't going to let Eck Snopes take that boy into that lot again." So she went down to the gate, but she come back without the boy or Eck neither.

"It ain't no need to worry about that boy," I says. "He's charmed." He was right behind Eck last night when Eck went to help feed them. The whole drove of them jumped clean over that boy's head and never touched him. It was Eck that touched him. Eck snatched him into the wagon and taken a rope and frailed the tar outen him.

So I had done et and went to my room and was undressing, long as I had a long trip to make next day; I was trying to sell a machine to Mrs. Bundren up past Whiteleaf; when Henry Armstid opened up that gate and went in by hisself. They couldn't make him wait for the balance of them to get back with their ropes. Eck Snopes said he tried to make Henry wait, but Henry wouldn't do it. Eck said Henry walked right up to them and that when they broke, they run clean over Henry like a haymow breaking down. Eck said he snatched that boy of hisn out of the way just in time and that them things went through that gate like a creek flood and into the wagons and teams hitched side the road, busting wagon tongues and snapping harness like it was fishing-line, with Mrs. Armstid still setting in their wagon in the middle of it like something carved outen wood. Then they scattered, wild horses and tame mules with pieces of harness and single trees dangling offen them, both ways up and down the road.

"There goes ourn, paw!" Eck said his boy said. "There it goes, into Mrs. Littlejohn's house." Eck says it run right up the steps and into the house like a boarder late for supper. I reckon so. Anyway, I was in my room, in my underclothes, with one sock on and one sock in my hand, leaning out the window when the commotion busted out, when I heard something run into the melodeon in the hall; it sounded like a railroad engine. Then the door to my room come sailing in like when you throw a tin bucket top into the wind and I looked over my shoulder and see something that looked like a fourteen-foot pinwheel a-blaring its eyes at me. It had to blare them fast, because I was already done jumped out the window.

I reckon it was anxious, too. I reckon it hadn't never seen barbed wire or shell corn before, but I know it hadn't never seen underclothes before, or maybe it was a sewing-machine agent it hadn't never seen. Anyway, it whirled and turned to run back up the hall and outen the house, when it met Eck Snopes and that boy just coming in, carrying a rope. It swirled again and run down the hall and out the back door just in time to meet Mrs. Littlejohn. She had just gathered up the clothes she had washed, and she was coming onto the back porch with a armful of washing in one hand and a scrubbing-board in the other, when the horse skidded up to her, trying to stop and swirl again. It never taken Mrs. Littlejohn no time a-tall.

"Git outen here, you son," she says. She hit it across the face with the scrubbing-board; that ere scrubbing-board split as neat as ere a axe could have done it, and when the horse swirled to run back up the hall, she hit it again with what was left of the scrubbing-board, not on the head this time. "And stay out," she says.

Eck and that boy was halfway down the hall by this time. I reckon that horse looked like a pinwheel to Eck too. "Git to hell outen here, Ad!" Eck says. Only there wasn't time. Eck dropped flat on his face, but the boy never moved. The boy was about a yard tall maybe, in overalls just like Eck's; that horse swoared over his head without touching a hair. I saw that, because I was just coming back up the front steps, still carrying that ere sock and still in my underclothes, when the horse come onto the porch again. It taken one look at me and swirled again and run to the end of the porch and jumped the banisters and the lot fence like a hen-hawk and lit in the lot running and went out the gate again and jumped eight or ten upside-down wagons and went on down the road. It was a full moon then. Mrs. Armstid was still setting in the wagon like she had done been carved outen wood and left there and forgot.

That horse. It ain't never missed a lick. It was going about forty miles a hour when it come to the bridge over the creek. It would have had a clear road, but it so happened that Vernon Tull was already using the bridge when it got there. He was coming back from town; he hadn't heard about the auction; him and his wife and three daughters and Mrs. Tull's aunt, all setting in chairs in the wagon bed, and all asleep, including the mules. They waked up when the horse hit the bridge one time, but Tull said the first he knew was when the mules tried to turn the wagon around in the middle of the bridge and he seen that spotted varmint run right twixt the mules and run up the wagon tongue like a squirrel. He said he just had time to hit it across the face with his whip-stock, because about that time the mules turned the wagon around on that ere one-way bridge and that horse clumb across onto the bridge again and went on, with Vernon standing up in the wagon and kicking at it.

Tull said the mules turned in the harness and clumb back into the wagon too, with Tull trying to beat them out again, with the reins wrapped around his wrist. After that he says all he seen was overturned chairs and womenfolks' legs and white drawers shining in the moonlight, and his mules and that spotted horse going up the road like a ghost.

The mules jerked Tull outen the wagon and drug him a spell on the bridge before the reins broke. They thought at first that he was dead, and while they was kneeling around him, picking the bridge splinters outen him, here come Eck and that boy, still carrying the rope. They was running and breathing a little hard. "Where'd he go?" Eck said.

V

I went back and got my pants and shirt and shoes on just in time to go and help get Henry Armstid outen the trash in the lot. I be dog if he didn't look like he was dead, with his head hanging back and his teeth showing in the moonlight, and a little rim of white under his eyelids. We could still hear them horses, here and there; hadn't none of them got more than four-five miles away yet, not knowing the country, I reckon. So we could hear them and folks yelling now and then: "Whooey. Head him!"

We toted Henry into Mrs. Littlejohn's. She was in the hall; she hadn't put down the armful of clothes. She taken one look at us, and she laid down the busted scrubbing-board and taken up the lamp and opened a empty door. "Bring him in here," she says.

We toted him in and laid him on the bed. Mrs. Littlejohn set the lamp on the dresser,

still carrying the clothes. "I'll declare, you men," she says. Our shadows was way up the wall, tip toeing too; we could hear ourselves breathing. "Better get his wife," Mrs. Littlejohn says. She went out, carrying the clothes.

"I reckon we had," Quick says. "Go get her, somebody."

"Whyn't you go?" Winterbottom says.

"Let Ernest git her," Durley says. "He lives neighbors with them."

Ernest went to fetch her. I be dog if Henry didn't look like he was dead. Mrs. Littlejohn come back, with a kettle and some towels. She went to work on Henry, and then Mrs. Armstid and Ernest come in. Mrs. Armstid come to the foot of the bed and stood there, with her hands rolled into her apron, watching what Mrs. Littlejohn was doing, I reckon.

"You men get outen the way," Mrs. Littlejohn says. "Git outside," she says. "See if you can't find something else to play with that will kill some more of you."

"Is he dead?" Winterbottom says.

"It ain't your fault if he ain't," Mrs. Littlejohn says. "Go tell Will Varner to come up here. I reckon a man ain't so different from a mule, come long come short. Except maybe a mule's got more sense."

We went to get Uncle Billy. It was a full moon. We could hear them, now and then, four miles away: "Whooey. Head him." The country was full of them, one on ever wooden bridge in the land, running across it like thunder: "Whooey. There he goes. Head him."

We hadn't got far before Henry begun to scream. I reckon Mrs. Littlejohn's water had brung him to; anyway, he wasn't dead. We went on to Uncle Billy's. The house was dark. We called to him, and after a while the window opened and Uncle Billy put his head out, peart as a peckerwood, listening. "Are they still trying to catch them durn rabbits?" he says.

He come down, with his britches on over his night-shirt and his suspenders dangling, carrying his horse-doctoring grip. "Yes, sir," he says, cocking his head like a woodpecker; "they're still a-trying."

We could hear Henry before we reached Mrs. Littlejohn's. He was going Ah-Ah-Ah. We stopped in the yard. Uncle Billy went on in. We could hear Henry. We stood in the yard, hearing them on the bridges, this-a-way and that: "Whooey. Whooey."

"Eck Snopes ought to caught hisn," Ernest says.

"Looks like he ought," Winterbottom said.

Henry was going Ah-Ah-Ah steady in the house; then he begun to scream. "Uncle Billy's started," Quick says. We looked into the hall. We could see the light where the door was. Then Mrs. Littlejohn come out.

"Will needs some help," she says. "You, Ernest. You'll do." Ernest went into the house.

"Hear them?" Quick said. "That one was on Four Mile bridge." We could hear them; it sounded like thunder a long way off; it didn't last long:

"Whooey."

We could hear Henry: "Ah-Ah-Ah-Ah-Ah."

"They are both started now," Winterbottom says. "Ernest too."

That was early in the night. Which was a good thing, because it taken a long night for folks to chase them things right and for Henry to lay there and holler, being as Uncle Billy never had none of this here chloryfoam to set Henry's leg with. So it was considerate in Flem to get them started early. And what do you reckon Flem's comment was?

That's right. Nothing. Because he wasn't there. Hadn't nobody see him since that Texas man left.

VI

That was Saturday night. I reckon Mrs. Armstid got home about daylight, to see

about the chaps. I don't know where they thought her and Henry was. But lucky the oldest one was a gal, about twelve, big enough to take care of the little ones. Which she did for the next two days. Mrs. Armstid would nurse Henry all night and work in the kitchen for hern and Henry's keep, and in the afternoon she would drive home (it was about four miles) to see to the chaps. She would cook up a pot of victuals and leave it on the stove, and the gal would bar the house and keep the little ones quiet. I would hear Mrs. Littlejohn and Mrs. Armstid talking in the kitchen. "How are the chaps making out?" Mrs. Littlejohn says.

"All right," Mrs. Armstid says.

"Don't they git skeered at night?" Mrs. Littlejohn says.

"Ina May bars the door when I leave," Mrs. Armstid says. "She's got the axe in bed with her. I reckon she can make out."

I reckon they did. And I reckon Mrs. Armstid was waiting for Flem to come back to town; hadn't nobody seen him until this morning; to get her money the Texas man said Flem was keeping for her. Sho. I reckon she was.

Anyway, I heard Mrs. Armstid and Mrs. Littlejohn talking in the kitchen this morning while I was eating breakfast. Mrs. Littlejohn had just told Mrs. Armstid that Flem was in town. "You can ask him for that five dollars," Mrs. Littlejohn says.

"You reckon he'll give it to me?" Mrs. Armstid says.

Mrs. Littlejohn was washing dishes, washing them like a man, like they was made out of iron. "No," she says. "But asking him won't do no hurt. It might shame him. I don't reckon it will, but it might."

"If he wouldn't give it back, it ain't no use to ask," Mrs. Armstid says.

"Suit yourself," Mrs. Littlejohn says. "It's your money."

I could hear the dishes.

"Do you reckon he might give it back to me?" Mrs. Armstid says. "That Texas man said he would. He said I could get it from Mr. Snopes later."

"Then go and ask him for it," Mrs. Littlejohn says.

I could hear the dishes.

"He won't give it back to me," Mrs. Armstid says.

"All right," Mrs. Littlejohn says. "Don't ask him for it, then."

I could hear the dishes; Mrs. Armstid was helping. "You don't reckon he would, do you?" she says. Mrs. Littlejohn never said nothing. It sounded like she was throwing the dishes at one another. "Maybe I better go and talk to Henry about it," Mrs. Armstid says.

"I would," Mrs. Littlejohn says. I be dog if it didn't sound like she had two plates in her hands, beating them together. "Then Henry can buy another five-dollar horse with it. Maybe he'll buy one next time that will out and out kill him. If I thought that, I'd give you back the money, myself."

"I reckon I better talk to him first," Mrs. Armstid said. Then it sounded like Mrs. Littlejohn taken up all the dishes and throwed them at the cook-stove, and I come away.

That was this morning. I had been up to Bundren's and back, and I thought that things would have kind of settled down. So after breakfast, I went up to the store. And there was Flem, setting in the store chair and whittling, like he might not have ever moved since he come to clerk for Jody Varner. I. O. was leaning in the door, in his shirt sleeves and with his hair parted too, same as Flem was before he turned the clerking job over to I. O. It's a funny thing about them Snopes: they all looks alike, yet there ain't ere a two of them that claims brothers. They're always just cousins, like Flem and Eck and Flem and I. O. Eck was there too, squatting against the wall, him and that boy, eating cheese and crackers outen a sack; they told me that Eck hadn't been home a-tall. And that Lon Quick hadn't got back to town, even. He followed his horse clean

down to Samson's Bridge, with a wagon and a camp outfit. Eck finally caught one of hisn. It run into a blind lane at Freeman's and Eck and the boy taken and tied their rope across the end of the lane, about three foot high. The horse come to the end of the lane and whirled and run back without ever stopping. Eck says it never seen the rope a-tall. He says it looked just like one of these here Christmas pinwheels. "Didn't it try to run again?" I says.

"No," Eck says, eating a bite of cheese offen his knife blade. "Just kicked some."

"Kicked some?" I says.

"It broke its neck," Eck says.

Well, they was squatting there, about six of them, talking, talking, talking at Flem; never nobody knowed yet if Flem had ere a interest in them horses or not. So finally I come right out and asked him. "Flem's done skun all of us so much," I says, "that we're proud of him. Come on, Flem," I says, "how much did you and that Texas man make offen them horses? You can tell us. Ain't nobody here but Eck that bought one of them; the others ain't got back to town yet, and Eck's your own cousin; he'll be proud to hear, too. How much did you-all make?"

They was all whittling, not looking at Flem, making like they was studying. But you could a heard a pin drop. And I. O. He had been rubbing his back up and down on the door, but he stopped now, watching Flem like a pointing dog. Flem finished cutting the sliver offen his stick. He spit across the porch, into the road. "Twarn't none of my horses," he said.

I. O. cackled, like a hen, slapping his legs with both hands. "You boys might just as well quit trying to get ahead of Flem," he said.

Well, about that time I see Mrs. Armstid come outen Mrs. Littlejohn's gate, coming up the road. I never said nothing. I says, "Well, if a man can't take care of himself in a trade, he can't blame the man that trims him."

Flem never said nothing, trimming at the

stick. He hadn't seen Mrs. Armstid. "Yes, sir," I says. "A fellow like Henry Armstid ain't got nobody but hisself to blame."

"Course he ain't," I. O. says. He ain't seen her, either. "Henry Armstid's a born fool. Always is been. If Flem hadn't a got his money, somebody else would."

We looked at Flem. He never moved. Mrs. Armstid come on up the road.

"That's right," I says. "But come to think of it, Henry never bought no horse." We looked at Flem; you could a heard a match drop. "That Texas man told her to get that five dollars back from Flem next day. I reckon Flem's done already taken that money to Mrs. Littlejohn's and give it to Mrs. Armstid."

We watched Flem. I. O. quit rubbing his back against the door again. After a while Flem raised his head and spit across the porch, into the dust. I. O. cackled, just like a hen. "Ain't he a beating fellow, now?" I. O. says.

Mrs. Armstid was getting closer, so I kept on talking, watching to see if Flem would look up and see her. But he never looked up. I went on talking about Tull, about how he was going to sue Flem, and Flem setting there, whittling his stick, not saying nothing else after he said they wasn't none of his horses.

Then I. O. happened to look around. He seen Mrs. Armstid. "Psssst!" he says. Flem looked up. "Here she comes!" I. O. says. "Go out the back. I'll tell her you done went in to town today."

But Flem never moved. He just set there, whittling, and we watched Mrs. Armstid come up onto the porch, in that ere faded sunbonnet and wrapper and them tennis shoes that make a kind of hissing noise on the porch. She come onto the porch and stopped, her hands rolled into her dress in front, not looking at nothing.

"He said Saturday," she says, "that he wouldn't sell Henry no horse. He said I could get the money from you."

Flem looked up. The knife never stopped.

It went on trimming off a sliver same as if he was watching it. "He taken that money off with him when he left," Flem says.

Mrs. Armstid never looked at nothing. We never looked at her, neither, except that boy of Eck's. He had a half-et cracker in his hand, watching her, chewing.

"He said Henry hadn't bought no horse," Mrs. Armstid says. "He said for me to get the money from you today."

"I reckon he forgot about it," Flem said. "He taken that money off with him Saturday." He whittled again. I. O. kept on rubbing his back, slow. He licked his lips. After a while the woman looked up the road, where it went on up the hill, toward the graveyard. She looked up that way for a while, with that boy of Eck's watching her and I. O. rubbing his back slow against the door. Then she turned back toward the steps.

"I reckon it's time to get dinner started," she says.

"How's Henry this morning, Mrs. Armstid?" Winterbottom says.

She looked at Winterbottom; she almost stopped. "He's resting, I thank you kindly," she says.

Flem got up, outen the chair, putting his knife away. He spit across the porch. "Wait a minute, Mrs. Armstid," he says. She stopped again. She didn't look at him. Flem went on into the store, with I. O. done quit rubbing his back now, with his head craned after Flem, and Mrs. Armstid standing there with her hands rolled into her dress, not looking at nothing. A wagon come up the road and passed; it was Freeman, on the way to town. Then Flem come out again, with I. O. still watching him. Flem had one of these little striped sacks of Jody Varner's candy; I bet he still owes Jody that nickel, too. He put the sack into Mrs. Armstid's hand, like he would have put it into a hollow stump. He spit again across the porch. "A little sweetening for the chaps," he says.

"You're right kind," Mrs. Armstid says.

She held the sack of candy in her hand, not looking at nothing. Eck's boy was watching the sack, the half-et cracker in his hand; he wasn't chewing now. He watched Mrs. Armstid roll the sack into her apron. "I reckon I better get on back and help with dinner," she says. She turned and went back across the porch. Flem set down in the chair again and opened his knife. He spit across the porch again, past Mrs. Armstid where she hadn't went down the steps yet. Then she went on, in that ere sunbonnet and wrapper all the same color, back down the road toward Mrs. Littlejohn's. You couldn't see her dress move, like a natural woman walking. She looked like a old snag still standing up and moving along on a high water. We watched her turn in at Mrs. Littlejohn's and go outen sight. Flem was whittling. I. O. begun to rub his back on the door. Then he begun to cackle, just like a durn hen.

"You boys might just as well quit trying," I. O. says. "You can't git ahead of Flem. You can't touch him. Ain't he a sight, now?"

I be dog if he ain't. If I had brung a herd of wild cattymounts into town and sold them to my neighbors and kinfolks, they would have lynched me. Yes, sir.

Eudora Welty

WHY I LIVE AT THE P.O.

I was getting along fine with Mama, Papa-Daddy, and Uncle Rondo until my sister Stella-Rondo just separated from her husband and came back home again. Mr. Whitaker! Of course I went with Mr. Whitaker first, when he first appeared here in China Grove, taking "Pose-Yourself" photos, and Stella-Rondo broke us up. Told him I was one sided. Bigger on one side than the other, which is a deliberate, calculated false-

hood: I'm the same. Stella-Rondo is exactly twelve months to the day younger that I am and for that reason she's spoiled.

She'd always had anything in the world she wanted and then she'd throw it away. Papa-Daddy gave her this gorgeous Add-a-Pearl necklace when she was eight years old and she threw it away playing baseball when she was nine, with only two pearls.

So as soon as she got married and moved away from home the first thing she did was separate! From Mr. Whitaker! This photographer with the pop-eyes she said she trusted. Came home from one of those towns up in Illinois and to our complete surprise brought this child of two.

Mama said she like to made her drop dead for a second. "Here you had this marvelous blonde child and never so much as wrote your mother a word about it," says Mama. "I'm thoroughly ashamed of you." But of course she wasn't.

Stella-Rondo just calmly takes off this *hat*, I wish you could see it. She says, "Why, Mama, Shirley-T.'s adopted, I can prove it."

"How?" says Mama, but all I says was, "H'm!" There I was over the hot stove, trying to stretch two chickens over five people and a completely unexpected child into the bargain, without one moment's notice.

"What do you mean—'H'm'?" says Stella-Rondo, and Mama says, "I heard that, Sister."

I said that oh, I didn't mean a thing, only that whoever Shirley-T. was, she was the spit-image of Papa-Daddy if he'd cut off his beard, which of course he'd never do in the world. Papa-Daddy's Mama's papa and sulks.

Stella-Rondo got furious! She said, "Sister, I don't need to tell you you got a lot of nerve and always did have and I'll thank you to make no future reference to my adopted child whatsoever."

"Very well," I said. "Very well, very well. Of course I noticed at once she looks like Mr. Whitaker's side too. That frown. She looks like a cross between Mr. Whitaker and Papa-Daddy."

"Well, all I can say is she isn't."

"She looks exactly like Shirley Temple to me," says Mama, but Shirley-T. just ran away from her.

So the first thing Stella-Rondo did at the table was turn Papa-Daddy against me.

"Papa-Daddy," she says. He was trying to cut up his meat. "Papa-Daddy!" I was taken completely by surprise. Papa-Daddy is about a million years old and's got this long-long beard. "Papa-Daddy. Sister says she fails to understand why you don't cut off your beard."

So Papa-Daddy l-a-y-s down his knife and fork! He's real rich. Mama says he is, he says he isn't. So he says, "Have I heard correctly? You don't understand why I don't cut off my beard?"

"Why," I says, "Papa-Daddy, of course I understand, I did not say any such a thing, the idea!"

He says, "Hussy!"

I says, "Papa-Daddy, you know I wouldn't any more want you to cut off your beard than the man in the moon. It was the farthest thing from my mind! Stella-Rondo sat there and made that up while she was eating breast of chicken."

But he says, "So the postmistress fails to understand why I don't cut off my beard. Which job I got you through my influence with the government. 'Bird's nest'—is that what you call it?"

Not that it isn't the next-to-smallest P.O. in the entire state of Mississippi.

I says, "Oh, Papa-Daddy," I says, "I didn't say any such of a thing, I never dreamed it was a bird's nest, I have always been grateful though this is the next-to-smallest P.O. in the state of Mississippi, and I do not enjoy being referred to as a hussy by my own grandfather."

But Stella-Rondo says, "Yes, you did say it too. Anybody in the world could of heard you, that had ears."

"Stop right there," says Mama, looking at *me*.

So I pulled my napkin straight back through the napkin ring and left the table.

As soon as I was out of the room Mama says, "Call her back, or she'll starve to death," but Papa-Daddy says, "This is the beard I started growing on the Coast when I was fifteen years old." He would of gone on till nightfall if Shirley-T. hadn't lost the Milky Way she ate in Cairo.

So Papa-Daddy says, "I am going out and lie in the hammock, and you can all sit here and remember my words: I'll never cut off my beard as long as I live, even one inch, and I don't appreciate it in you at all." Passed right by me in the hall and went straight out and got in the hammock.

It would be a holiday. It wasn't five minutes before Uncle Rondo suddenly appeared in the hall in one of Stella-Rondo's flesh-colored kimonos, all cut on the bias, like something Mr. Whitaker probably thought was gorgeous.

"Uncle Rondo!" I says. "I didn't know who that was! Where are you going?"

"Sister," he says, "get out of my way, I'm poisoned."

"If you're poisoned stay away from Papa-Daddy," I says. "Keep out of the hammock. Papa-Daddy will certainly beat you on the head if you come within forty miles of him. He thinks I deliberately said he ought to cut off his beard after he got me the P.O., and I've told him and told him and told him, and he acts like he just don't hear me. Papa-Daddy must of gone stone deaf."

"He picked a fine day to do it then," says Uncle Rondo, and before you could say "Jack Robinson" flew out in the yard.

What he'd really done, he'd drunk another bottle of that prescription. He does it every single Fourth of July as sure as shooting, and it's horribly expensive. Then he falls over in the hammock and snores. So he insisted on zig-zagging right on out to the hammock, looking like a half-wit.

Papa-Daddy woke up with this horrible yell and right there without moving an inch he tried to turn Uncle Rondo against me. I heard every word he said. Oh, he told Uncle Rondo I didn't learn to read till I was eight years old and he didn't see how in the world I ever got the mail put up at the P.O., much less read it all, and he said if Uncle Rondo could only fathom the lengths he had gone to to get me that job! And he said on the other hand he thought Stella-Rondo had a brilliant mind and deserved credit for getting out of town. All the time he was just lying there swinging as pretty as you please and looping out his beard, and poor Uncle Rondo was *pleading* with him to slow down the hammock, it was making him as dizzy as a witch to watch it. But that's what Papa-Daddy likes about a hammock. So Uncle Rondo was too dizzy to get turned against me for the time being. He's Mama's only brother and is a good case of a one-track mind. Ask anybody. A certified pharmacist.

Just then I heard Stella-Rondo raising the upstairs window. While she was married she got this peculiar idea that it's cooler with the windows shut and locked. So she has to raise the window before she can make a soul hear her outdoors.

So she raises the window and says, *"Oh!"* You would have thought she was mortally wounded.

Uncle Rondo and Papa-Daddy didn't even look up, but kept right on with what they were doing. I had to laugh.

I flew up the stairs and threw the door open! I says, "What in the wide world's the matter, Stella-Rondo? You mortally wounded?"

"No," she says, "I am not mortally wounded but I wish you would do me the favor of looking out that window there and telling me what you see."

So I shade my eyes and look out the window.

"I see the front yard," I says.

"Don't you see any human beings?" she says.

"I see Uncle Rondo trying to run Papa-Daddy out of the hammock," I says. "Nothing more. Naturally, it's so suffocating-hot in the house, with all the windows shut and locked, everybody who cares to stay in their right mind will have to go out and get in the hammock before the Fourth of July is over."

"Don't you notice anything different about Uncle Rondo?" asks Stella-Rondo.

"Why, no, except he's got on some terrible-looking flesh-colored contraption I wouldn't be found dead in, is all I can see," I says.

"Never mind, you won't be found dead in it, because it happens to be part of my trousseau, and Mr. Whitaker took several dozen photographs of me in it," says Stella-Rondo. "What on earth could Uncle Rondo *mean* by wearing part of my trousseau out in the broad open daylight without saying so much as 'Kiss my foot,' *knowing* I only got home this morning after my separation and hung my negligee up on the bathroom door, just as nervous as I could be?"

"I'm sure I don't know, and what do you expect me to do about it?" I says. "Jump out the window?"

"No, I expect nothing of the kind. I simply declare that Uncle Rondo looks like a fool in it, that's all," she says. "It makes me sick to my stomach."

"Well, he looks as good as he can," I says. "As good as anybody in reason could." I stood up for Uncle Rondo, please remember. And I said to Stella-Rondo, "I think I would do well not to criticize so freely if I were you and came home with a two-year-old child I had never said a word about, and no explanation whatever about my separation."

"I asked you the instant I entered this house not to refer one more time to my adopted child, and you gave me your word of honor you would not," was all Stella-Rondo would say, and started pulling out every one of her eyebrows with some cheap Kress tweezers.

So I merely slammed the door behind me and went down and made some green-tomato pickle. Somebody had to do it. Of course Mama had turned both the niggers loose; she always said no earthly power could hold one anyway on the Fourth of July, so she wouldn't even try. It turned out that Jaypan fell in the lake and came within a very narrow limit of drowning.

So Mama trots in. Lifts up the lid and says, "H'm! Not very good for your Uncle Rondo in his precarious condition, I must say. Or poor little adopted Shirley-T. Shame on you!"

That made me tired. I says, "Well, Stella-Rondo had better thank her lucky stars it was her instead of me came trotting in with that very peculiar-looking child. Now if it had been me that trotted in from Illinois and brought a peculiar-looking child of two, I shudder to think of the reception I'd of got, much less controlled the diet of an entire family."

"But you must remember, Sister, that you were never married to Mr. Whitaker in the first place and didn't go up to Illinois to live," says Mama, shaking a spoon in my face. "If you had I would of been just as overjoyed to see you and your little adopted girl as I was to see Stella-Rondo, when you wound up with your separation and came on back home."

"You would not," I says.

"Don't contradict me, I would," says Mama.

But I said she couldn't convince me though she talked till she was blue in the face. Then I said, "Besides, you know as well as I do that that child is not adopted."

"She most certainly is adopted," says Mama, stiff as a poker.

I says, "Why, Mama, Stella-Rondo had

her just as sure as anything in this world, and just too stuck up to admit it."

"Why, Sister," said Mama. "Here I thought we were going to have a pleasant Fourth of July, and you start right out not believing a word your own baby sister tells you!"

"Just like Cousin Annie Flo. Went to her grave denying the facts of life," I remind Mama.

"I told you if you ever mentioned Annie Flo's name I'd slap your face," says Mama, and slaps my face.

"All right, you wait and see," I says.

"I," says Mama, "*I* prefer to take my children's word for anything when it's humanly possible." You ought to see Mama, she weighs two hundred pounds and has real tiny feet.

Just then something perfectly horrible occurred to me.

"Mama," I says, "can that child talk?" I simply had to whisper! "Mama, I wonder if that child can be—you know—in any way? Do you realize," I says, "that she hasn't spoken one single solitary word to a human being up to this minute? This is the way she looks," I says, and I looked like this.

Well, Mama and I just stood there and stared at each other. It was horrible!

"I remember well that Joe Whitaker frequently drank like a fish," says Mama. "I believed to my soul he drank *chemicals*." And without another word she marches to the foot of the stairs and calls Stella-Rondo.

"Stella-Rondo? O-o-o-o-o! Stella-Rondo!"

"What?" says Stella-Rondo from upstairs. Not even the grace to get up off the bed.

"Can that child of yours talk?" asks Mama.

Stella-Rondo says, "Can she what?"

"Talk! Talk!" says Mama. "Burdyburdy-burdyburdy!"

So Stella-Rondo yells back, "Who says she can't talk?"

"Sister says so," says Mama.

"You didn't have to tell me, I know whose word of honor don't mean a thing in this house," says Stella-Rondo.

And in a minute the loudest Yankee voice I ever heard in my life yells out, "OE-m Pop-OE the Sailor-r-r-r Ma-a-an!" and then somebody jumps up and down in the upstairs hall. In another second the house would of fallen down.

"Not only talks, she can tap-dance!" calls Stella-Rondo. "Which is more than some people I won't name can do."

"Why, the little precious darling thing!" Mama says, so surprised. "Just as smart as she can be!" Starts talking baby talk right there. Then she turns on me. "Sister, you ought to be thoroughly ashamed! Run upstairs this instant and apologize to Stella-Rondo and Shirley-T."

"Apologize for what?" I says. "I merely wondered if the child was normal, that's all. Now that she's proved she is, why, I have nothing further to say."

But Mama just turned on her heel and flew out, furious. She ran right upstairs and hugged the baby. She believed it was adopted. Stella-Rondo hadn't done a thing but turn her against me from upstairs while I stood there helpless over the hot stove. So that made Mama, Papa-Daddy, and the baby all on Stella-Rondo's side.

Next, Uncle Rondo.

I must say that Uncle Rondo has been marvelous to me at various times in the past and I was completely unprepared to be made to jump out of my skin, the way it turned out. Once Stella-Rondo did something perfectly horrible to him—broke a chain letter from Flanders Field—and he took the radio back he had given her and gave it to me. Stella-Rondo was furious! For six months we all had to call her Stella instead of Stella-Rondo, or she wouldn't answer. I always thought Uncle Rondo had all the brains of the entire family. Another time he sent me to Mammoth Cave, with all expenses paid.

But this would be the day he was drinking that prescription, the Fourth of July.

So at supper Stella-Rondo speaks up and says she thinks Uncle Rondo ought to try to eat a little something. So finally Uncle Rondo said he would try a little cold biscuits and ketchup, but that was all. So *she* brought it to him.

"Do you think it wise to disport with ketchup in Stella-Rondo's flesh-colored kimono?" I says. Trying to be considerate! If Stella-Rondo couldn't watch out for her trousseau, somebody had to.

"Any objections?" asks Uncle Rondo, just about to pour out all the ketchup.

"Don't mind what she says, Uncle Rondo," says Stella-Rondo. "Sister has been devoting this solid afternoon to sneering out my bedroom window at the way you look."

"What's that?" says Uncle Rondo. Uncle Rondo has got the most terrible temper in the world. Anything is liable to make him tear the house down if it comes at the wrong time.

So Stella-Rondo says, "Sister says, 'Uncle Rondo certainly does look like a fool in that pink kimono!'"

Do you remember who it was really said that?

Uncle Rondo spills out all the ketchup and jumps out of his chair and tears off the kimono and throws it down on the dirty floor and puts his foot on it. It had to be sent all the way to Jackson to the cleaners and repleated.

"So that's your opinion of your Uncle Rondo, is it?" he says. "I look like a fool, do I? Well, that's the last straw. A whole day in this house with nothing to do, and then to hear you come out with a remark like that behind my back!"

"I didn't say any such of a thing, Uncle Rondo," I says, "and I'm not saying who did, either. Why, I think you look all right. Just try to take care of yourself and not talk and eat at the same time," I says. "I think you better go lie down."

"Lie down my foot!" says Uncle Rondo. I ought to of known by that he was fixing to do something perfectly horrible.

So he didn't do anything that night in the precarious state he was in—just played casino with Mama and Stella-Rondo and Shirley-T. and gave Shirley-T. a nickel with a head on both sides. It tickled her nearly to death, and she called him "Papa." But at 6:30 A.M. the next morning, he threw a whole five-cent package of some unsold one-inch firecrackers from the store as hard as he could into my bedroom and they every one went off. Not one bad one in the string. Anybody else, there'd be one that wouldn't go off.

Well, I'm just terribly susceptible to noise of any kind, the doctor has always told me I was the most sensitive person he had ever seen in his whole life, and I was simply prostrated. I couldn't eat! People tell me they heard it as far as the cemetery, and old Aunt Jep Patterson, that had been holding her own so good, thought it was Judgment Day and she was going to meet her whole family. It's usually so quiet here.

And I'll tell you it didn't take me any longer than a minute to make up my mind what to do. There I was with the whole entire house on Stella-Rondo's side and turned against me. If I have anything at all I have pride.

So I just decided I'd go straight down to the P.O. There's plenty of room there in the back, I says to myself.

Well! I made no bones about letting the family catch on to what I was up to. I didn't try to conceal it.

The first thing they knew, I marched in where they were all playing Old Maid and pulled the electric oscillating fan out by the plug, and everything got real hot. Next I snatched the pillow I'd done the needle-point on right off the davenport from behind Papa-Daddy. He went "Ugh!" I beat Stella-Rondo up the stairs and finally found my charm bracelet in her bureau drawer under a picture of Nelson Eddy.

"So that's the way the land lies," says Uncle Rondo. There he was, piecing on the ham. "Well, Sister, I'll be glad to donate my army cot if you got any place to set it up, providing you'll leave right this minute and let me get some peace." Uncle Rondo was in France.

"Thank you kindly for the cot and 'peace' is hardly the word I would select if I had to resort to firecrackers at 6:30 A.M. in a young girl's bedroom," I says back to him. "And as to where I intend to go, you seem to forget my position as postmistress of China Grove, Mississippi," I says. "I've always got the P.O."

Well, that made them all sit up and take notice.

I went out front and started digging up some four-o'clocks to plant around the P.O.

"Ah-ah-ah!" says Mama, raising the window. "Those happen to be my four-o'clocks. Everything planted in that star is mine. I've never known you to make anything grow in your life."

"Very well," I says. "But I take the fern. Even you, Mama, can't stand there and deny that I'm the one watered that fern. And I happen to know where I can send in a box top and get a packet of one thousand mixed seeds, no two the same kind, free."

"Oh, where?" Mama wants to know.

But I says, "Too late. You 'tend to your house and I'll 'tend to mine. You hear things like that all the time if you know how to listen to the radio. Perfectly marvelous offers. Get anything you want free."

So I hope to tell you I marched in and got that radio, and they could of all bit a nail in two, especially Stella-Rondo, that it used to belong to, and she well knew she couldn't get it back, I'd sue for it like a shot. And I very politely took the sewing-machine motor I helped pay the most on to give Mama for Christmas back in 1929, and a good big calendar, with the first-aid remedies on it. The thermometer and the Hawaiian ukulele certainly were rightfully mine, and I stood on the stepladder and got all my watermelon-rind preserves and every fruit and vegetable I'd put up, every jar. Then I began to pull the tacks out of the bluebird wall vases on the archway to the dining room.

"Who told you you could have those, Miss Priss?" says Mama, fanning as hard as she could.

"I bought 'em and I'll keep track of 'em," I says. "I'll tack 'em up one on each side the post-office window, and you can see 'em when you come to ask me for your mail, if you're so dead to see 'em."

"Not I! I'll never darken the door to that post office again if I live to be a hundred," Mama says. "Ungrateful child! After all the money we spent on you at the Normal."

"Me either," says Stella-Rondo. "You can just let my mail lie there and *rot*, for all I care. I'll never come and relieve you of a single solitary piece."

"I should worry," I says. "And who you think's going to sit down and write you all those big fat letters and postcards, by the way? Mr. Whitaker? Just because he was the only man ever dropped down in China Grove and you got him—unfairly—is he going to sit down and write you a lengthy correspondence after you come home giving no rhyme nor reason whatsoever for your separation and no explanation for the presence of that child? I may not have your brilliant mind, but I fail to see it."

So Mama says, "Sister, I've told you a thousand times that Stella-Rondo simply got homesick, and this child is far too big to be

hers," and she says, "Now, why don't you all just sit down and play casino?"

Then Shirley-T. sticks out her tongue at me in this perfectly horrible way. She has no more manners than the man in the moon. I told her she was going to cross her eyes like that some day and they'd stick.

"It's too late to stop me now," I says. "You should have tried that yesterday. I'm going to the P.O. and the only way you can possibly see me is to visit me there."

So Papa-Daddy says, "You'll never catch me setting foot in that post office, even if I should take a notion into my head to write a letter some place." He says, "I won't have you reachin' out of that little old window with a pair of shears and cuttin' off any beard of mine. I'm too smart for you!"

"We all are," says Stella-Rondo.

But I said, "If you're so smart, where's Mr. Whitaker?"

So then Uncle Rondo says, "I'll thank you from now on to stop reading all the orders I get on postcards and telling everybody in China Grove what you think is the matter with them," but I says, "I draw my own conclusions and will continue in the future to draw them." I says, "If people want to write their inmost secrets on penny postcards, there's nothing in the wide world you can do about it, Uncle Rondo."

"And if you think we'll ever *write* another postcard, you're sadly mistaken," says Mama.

"Cutting off your nose to spite your face then," I says. "But if you're all determined to have no more to do with the U.S. mail, think of this: What will Stella-Rondo do now, if she wants to tell Mr. Whitaker to come after her?"

"Wah!" says Stella-Rondo. I knew she'd cry. She had a conniption fit right there in the kitchen.

"It will be interesting to see how long she holds out," I says. "And now—I am leaving."

"Good-by," says Uncle Rondo.

"Oh, I declare," says Mama, "to think that a family of mine should quarrel on the Fourth of July, or the day after, over Stella-Rondo leaving old Mr. Whitaker and having the sweetest little adopted child! It looks like we'd all be glad!"

"Wah!" says Stella-Rondo, and has a fresh conniption fit.

"*He* left *her*—you mark my words," I says. "That's Mr. Whitaker. I know Mr. Whitaker. After all, I knew him first. I said from the beginning he'd up and leave her. I foretold every single thing that's happened."

"Where did he go?" asks Mama.

"Probably to the North Pole, if he knows what's good for him," I says.

But Stella-Rondo just bawled and wouldn't say another word. She flew to her room and slammed the door.

"Now look what you've gone and done, Sister," says Mama. "You go apologize."

"I haven't got time, I'm leaving," I says.

"Well, what are you waiting around for?" asks Uncle Rondo.

So I just picked up the kitchen clock and marched off, without saying "Kiss my foot" or anything, and never did tell Stella-Rondo good-by.

There was a nigger girl going along on a little wagon right in front.

"Nigger girl," I says, "come help me haul these things down the hill, I'm going to live in the post office."

Took her nine trips in her express wagon. Uncle Rondo came out on the porch and threw her a nickel.

And that's the last I've laid eyes on any of my family or my family laid eyes on me for five solid days and nights. Stella-Rondo may be telling the most horrible tales in the world about Mr. Whitaker, but I haven't heard them. As I tell everybody, I draw my own conclusions.

But oh, I like it here. It's ideal, as I've been saying. You see, I've got everything cater-cornered, the way I like it. Hear the radio? All the war news. Radio, sewing machine, book ends, ironing board and that great big piano lamp—peace, that's what I like. Butter-bean vines planted all along the front where the strings are.

Of course, there's not much mail. My family are naturally the main people in China Grove, and if they prefer to vanish from the face of the earth, for all the mail they get or the mail they write, why, I'm not going to open my mouth. Some of the folks here in town are taking up for me and some turned against me. I know which is which. There are always people who will quit buying stamps just to get on the right side of Papa-Daddy.

But here I am, and here I'll stay. I want the world to know I'm happy.

And if Stella-Rondo should come to me this minute, on bended knees, and *attempt* to explain the incidents of her life with Mr. Whitaker, I'd simply put my fingers in both my ears and refuse to listen.

Philip Roth

THE CONVERSION OF THE JEWS

"You're a real one for opening your mouth in the first place," Itzie said. "What do you open your mouth all the time for?"

"I didn't bring it up, Itz, I didn't," Ozzie said.

"What do you care about Jesus Christ for anyway?"

"I didn't bring up Jesus Christ. He did. I

THE CONVERSION OF THE JEWS. The story whimsically contradicts line 10 of Andrew Marvell's "To His Coy Mistress."

didn't even know what he was talking about. Jesus is historical, he kept saying. Jesus is historical." Ozzie mimicked the monumental voice of Rabbi Binder.

"Jesus was a person that lived like you and me," Ozzie continued. "That's what Binder said—"

"Yeah? . . . So what! What do I give two cents whether he lived or not. And what do you gotta open your mouth!" Itzie Lieberman favored closed-mouthedness, especially when it came to Ozzie Freedman's questions. Mrs. Freedman had to see Rabbi Binder twice before about Ozzie's questions and this Wednesday at four-thirty would be the third time. Itzie preferred to keep *his* mother in the kitchen; he settled for behind-the-back subtleties such as gestures, faces, snarls and other less delicate barnyard noises.

"He was a real person, Jesus, but he wasn't like God, and we don't believe he is God." Slowly, Ozzie was explaining Rabbi Binder's position to Itzie, who had been absent from Hebrew School the previous afternoon.

"The Catholics," Itzie said helpfully, "they believe in Jesus Christ, that he's God." Itzie Lieberman used "the Catholics" in its broadest sense—to include the Protestants.

Ozzie received Itzie's remark with a tiny head bob, as though it were a footnote, and went on. "His mother was Mary, and his father probably was Joseph," Ozzie said. "But the New Testament says his real father was God."

"His *real* father?"

"Yeah," Ozzie said, "that's the big thing, his father's supposed to be God."

"Bull."

"That's what Rabbi Binder says, that it's impossible—"

"Sure it's impossible. That stuff's all bull. To have a baby you gotta get laid," Itzie theologized. "Mary hadda get laid."

"That's what Binder says: 'The only way a woman can have a baby is to have intercourse with a man.' "

"He said *that*, Ozz?" For a moment it appeared that Itzie had put the theological question aside. "He said that, intercourse?" A little curled smile shaped itself in the lower half of Itzie's face like a pink mustache. "What you guys do, Ozz, you laugh or something?"

"I raised my hand."

"Yeah? Whatja say?"

"That's when I asked the question."

Itzie's face lit up. "Whatja ask about—intercourse?"

"No, I asked the question about God, how if He could create the heaven and earth in six days, and make all the animals and the fish and the light in six days—the light especially, that's what always gets me, that He could make the light. Making fish and animals, that's pretty good—"

"That's damn good." Itzie's appreciation was honest but unimaginative: it was as though God had just pitched a one-hitter.

"But making light . . . I mean when you think about it, it's really something," Ozzie said. "Anyway, I asked Binder if He could make all that in six days, and He could *pick* the six days he wanted right out of nowhere, why couldn't He let a woman have a baby without having intercourse."

"You said intercourse, Ozz, to Binder?"

"Yeah."

"Right in class?"

"Yeah."

Itzie smacked the side of his head.

"I mean, no kidding around," Ozzie said, "that'd really be nothing. After all that other stuff, that'd practically be nothing."

Itzie considered a moment. "What'd Binder say?"

"He started all over again explaining how Jesus was historical and how he lived like you and me but he wasn't God. So I said I under*stood* that. What I wanted to know was different."

What Ozzie wanted to know was always different. The first time he had wanted to know how Rabbi Binder could call the Jews

"The Chosen People" if the Declaration of Independence claimed all men to be created equal. Rabbi Binder tried to distinguish for him between political equality and spiritual legitimacy, but what Ozzie wanted to know, he insisted vehemently, was different. That was the first time his mother had to come.

Then there was the plane crash. Fifty-eight people had been killed in a plane crash at La Guardia. In studying a casualty list in the newspaper his mother had discovered among the list of those dead eight Jewish names (his grandmother had nine but she counted Miller as a Jewish name); because of the eight she said the plane crash was "a tragedy." During free-discussion time on Wednesday Ozzie had brought to Rabbi Binder's attention this matter of "some of his relations" always picking out the Jewish names. Rabbi Binder had begun to explain cultural unity and some other things when Ozzie stood up at his seat and said that what he wanted to know was different. Rabbi Binder insisted that he sit down and it was then that Ozzie shouted that he wished all fifty-eight were Jews. That was the second time his mother came.

"And he kept explaining about Jesus being historical, and so I kept asking him. No kidding, Itz, he was trying to make me look stupid."

"So what he finally do?"

"Finally he starts screaming that I was deliberately simple-minded and a wise guy, and that my mother had to come, and this was the last time. And that I'd never get bar-mitzvahed[9] if he could help it. Then, Itz, then he starts talking in that voice like a statue, real slow and deep, and he says that I better think over what I said about the Lord. He told me to go to his office and think it over." Ozzie leaned his body towards

[9] Bar mitzvah is the Jewish ceremony through which thirteen-year-old boys are declared responsible adult.

Itzie. "Itz, I thought it over for a solid hour, and now I'm convinced God could do it."

Ozzie had planned to confess his latest transgression to his mother as soon as she came home from work. But it was a Friday night in November and already dark, and when Mrs. Freedman came through the door she tossed off her coat, kissed Ozzie quickly on the face, and went to the kitchen table to light the three yellow candles, two for the Sabbath and one for Ozzie's father.

When his mother lit the candles she would move her two arms slowly towards her, dragging them through the air, as though persuading people whose minds were half made up. And her eyes would get glassy with tears. Even when his father was alive Ozzie remembered that her eyes had gotten glassy, so it didn't have anything to do with his dying. It had something to do with lighting the candles.

As she touched the flaming match to the unlit wick of a Sabbath candle, the phone rang, and Ozzie, standing only a foot from it, plucked it off the receiver and held it muffled to his chest. When his mother lit candles Ozzie felt there should be no noise; even breathing, if you could manage it, should be softened. Ozzie pressed the phone to his breast and watched his mother dragging whatever she was dragging, and he felt his own eyes get glassy. His mother was a round, tired, gray-haired penguin of a woman whose gray skin had begun to feel the tug of gravity and the weight of her own history. Even when she was dressed up she didn't look like a chosen person. But when she lit candles she looked like something better; like a woman who knew momentarily that God could do anything.

After a few mysterious minutes she was finished. Ozzie hung up the phone and walked to the kitchen table where she was beginning to lay the two places for the four-course Sabbath meal. He told her that she would have to see Rabbi Binder next

Wednesday at four-thirty, and then he told her why. For the first time in their life together she hit Ozzie across the face with her hand.

All through the chopped liver and chicken soup part of the dinner Ozzie cried; he didn't have any appetite for the rest.

On Wednesday, in the largest of the three basement classrooms of the synagogue, Rabbi Marvin Binder, a tall, handsome, broad-shouldered man of thirty with thick strong-fibered black hair, removed his watch from his pocket and saw that it was four o'clock. At the rear of the room Yakov Blotnik, the seventy-one-year-old custodian, slowly polished the large window, mumbling to himself, unaware that it was four o'clock or six o'clock, Monday or Wednesday. To most of the students Yakov Blotnik's mumbling, along with his brown curly beard, scythe nose, and two heel-trailing black cats, made of him an object of wonder, a foreigner, a relic, towards whom they were alternatively fearful and disrespectful. To Ozzie the mumbling had always seemed a monotonous, curious prayer; what made it curious was that old Blotnik had been mumbling so steadily for so many years, Ozzie suspected he had memorized the prayers and forgotten all about God.

"It is now free-discussion time," Rabbi Binder said. "Feel free to talk about any Jewish matter at all—religion, family, politics, sports—"

There was silence. It was a gusty, clouded November afternoon and it did not seem as though there ever was or could be a thing called baseball. So nobody this week said a word about that hero from the past, Hank Greenberg—which limited free discussion considerably.

And the soul-battering Ozzie Freedman had just received from Rabbi Binder had imposed its limitation. When it was Ozzie's turn to read aloud from the Hebrew book the rabbi had asked him petulantly why he didn't read more rapidly. He was showing no progress. Ozzie said he could read faster but that if he did he was sure not to understand what he was reading. Nevertheless, at the rabbi's repeated suggestion Ozzie tried, and showed a great talent, but in the midst of a long passage he stopped short and said he didn't understand a word he was reading, and started in again at a drag-footed pace. Then came the soul-battering.

Consequently when free-discussion time rolled around none of the students felt too free. The rabbi's invitation was answered only by the mumbling of feeble old Blotnik.

"Isn't there anything at all you would like to discuss?" Rabbi Binder asked again, looking at his watch. "No questions or comments?"

There was a small grumble from the third row. The rabbi requested that Ozzie rise and give the rest of the class the advantage of his thought.

Ozzie rose. "I forget it now," he said, and sat down in his place.

Rabbi Binder advanced a seat towards Ozzie and poised himself on the edge of the desk. It was Itzie's desk and the rabbi's frame only a dagger's-length away from his face snapped him to sitting attention.

"Stand up again, Oscar," Rabbi Binder said calmly, "and try to assemble your thoughts."

Ozzie stood up. All his classmates turned in their seats and watched as he gave an unconvincing scratch to his forehead.

"I can't assemble any," he announced, and plunked himself down.

"Stand up!" Rabbi Binder advanced from Itzie's desk to the one directly in front of Ozzie; when the rabbinical back was turned Itzie gave it five-fingers off the tip of his nose, causing a small titter in the room. Rabbi Binder was too absorbed in squelching Ozzie's nonsense once and for all to bother with titters. "Stand up, Oscar. What's your question about?"

Ozzie pulled a word out of the air. It was the handiest word. "Religion."

"Oh, now you remember?"

"Yes."

"What is it?"

Trapped, Ozzie blurted the first thing that came to him. "Why can't He make anything He wants to make!"

As Rabbi Binder prepared an answer, a final answer, Itzie, ten feet behind him, raised one finger on his left hand, gestured it meaningfully towards the rabbi's back, and brought the house down.

Binder twisted quickly to see what had happened and in the midst of the commotion Ozzie shouted into the rabbi's back what he couldn't have shouted to his face. It was a loud, toneless sound that had the timbre of something stored inside for about six days.

"You don't know! You don't know anything about God!"

The rabbi spun back towards Ozzie. "What?"

"You don't know—you don't—"

"Apologize, Oscar, apologize!" It was a threat.

"You don't—"

Rabbi Binder's hand flicked out at Ozzie's cheek. Perhaps it had only been meant to clamp the boy's mouth shut, but Ozzie ducked and the palm caught him squarely on the nose.

The blood came in a short, red spurt on to Ozzie's shirt front.

The next moment was all confusion. Ozzie screamed, "You bastard, you bastard!" and broke for the classroom door. Rabbi Binder lurched a step backwards, as though his own blood had started flowing violently in the opposite direction, then gave a clumsy lurch forward and bolted out the door after Ozzie. The class followed after the rabbi's huge blue-suited back, and before old Blotnik could turn from his window, the room was empty and everyone was headed full speed up the three flights leading to the roof.

If one should compare the light of day to the life of man: sunrise to birth; sunset—the dropping down over the edge—to death; then as Ozzie Freedman wiggled through the trapdoor of the synagogue roof, his feet kicking backwards bronco-style at Rabbi Binder's outstretched arms—at that moment the day was fifty years old. As a rule, fifty or fifty-five reflects accurately the age of late afternoons in November, for it is in that month, during those hours, that one's awareness of light seems no longer a matter of seeing, but of hearing: light begins clicking away. In fact, as Ozzie locked shut the trapdoor in the rabbi's face, the sharp click of the bolt into the lock might momentarily have been mistaken for the sound of the heavier gray that had just throbbed through the sky.

With all his weight Ozzie kneeled on the locked door; any instant he was certain that Rabbi Binder's shoulder would fling it open, splintering the wood into shrapnel and catapulting his body into the sky. But the door did not move and below him he heard only the rumble of feet, first loud then dim, like thunder rolling away.

A question shot through his brain. "Can this be *me*?" For a thirteen-year-old who had just labeled his religious leader a bastard, twice, it was not an improper question. Louder and louder the question came to him—"Is it me? Is it me?"—until he discovered himself no longer kneeling, but racing crazily towards the edge of the roof, his eyes crying, his throat screaming, and his arms flying everywhichway as though not his own.

"Is it me? Is it me Me ME ME ME! It has to be me—but is it!"

It is the question a thief must ask himself the night he jimmies open his first window, and it is said to be the question with which bridegrooms quiz themselves before the altar.

In the few wild seconds it took Ozzie's body to propel him to the edge of the roof, his self-examination began to grow fuzzy. Gazing down at the street, he became confused as to the problem beneath the question: was it, is-it-me-who-called-Binder-a-bastard? or, is-it-me-prancing-around-on-the-roof? However, the scene below settled all, for there is an instant in any action when whether it is you or somebody else is academic. The thief crams the money in his pockets and scoots out the window. The bridegroom signs the hotel register for two. And the boy on the roof finds a streetful of people gaping at him, necks stretched backwards, faces up, as though he were the ceiling of the Hayden Planetarium. Suddenly you know it's you.

"Oscar! Oscar Freedman!" A voice rose from the center of the crowd, a voice that, could it have been seen, would have looked like the writing on scroll. "Oscar Freedman, get down from there. Immediately!" Rabbi Binder was pointing one arm stiffly up at him; and at the end of that arm, one finger aimed menacingly. It was the attitude of a dictator, but one—the eyes confessed all—whose personal valet had spit neatly in his face.

Ozzie didn't answer. Only for a blink's length did he look towards Rabbi Binder. Instead his eyes began to fit together the world beneath him, to sort out people from places, friends from enemies, participants from spectators. In little jagged starlike clusters his friends stood around Rabbi Binder, who was still pointing. The topmost point on a star compounded not of angels but of five adolescent boys was Itzie. What a world it was, with those stars below, Rabbi Binder below . . . Ozzie, who a moment earlier hadn't been able to control his own body, started to feel the meaning of the word control: he felt Peace and he felt Power.

"Oscar Freedman, I'll give you three to come down."

Few dictators give their subjects three to do anything; but, as always, Rabbi Binder only looked dictatorial.

"Are you ready, Oscar?"

Ozzie nodded his head yes, although he had no intention in the world—the lower one of the celestial one he'd just entered—of coming down even if Rabbi Binder should give him a million.

"All right then," said Rabbi Binder. He ran a hand through his black Samson hair as though it were the gesture prescribed for uttering the first digit. Then, with his other hand cutting a circle out of the small piece of sky around him, he spoke. "One!"

There was no thunder. On the contrary, at that moment, as though "one" was the cue for which he had been waiting, the world's least thunderous person appeared on the synagogue steps. He did not so much come out the synagogue door as lean out, onto the darkening air. He clutched at the doorknob with one hand and looked up at the roof.

"Oy!"

Yakov Blotnik's old mind hobbled slowly, as if on crutches, and though he couldn't decide precisely what the boy was doing on the roof, he knew it wasn't good—that is, it wasn't-good-for-the-Jews. For Yakov Blotnik life had fractionated itself simply: things were either good-for-the-Jews or no-good-for-the-Jews.

He smacked his free hand to his in-sucked cheek, gently. "Oy, Gut!" And then quickly as he was able, he jacked down his head and surveyed the street. There was Rabbi Binder (like a man at an auction with only three dollars in his pocket, he had just delivered a shaky "Two!"); there were the students, and that was all. So far it-wasn't-so-bad-for-the-

Jews. But the boy had to come down immediately, before anybody saw. The problem: how to get the boy off the roof?

Anybody who has ever had a cat on the roof knows how to get him down. You call the fire department. Or first you call the operator and you ask her for the fire department. And the next thing there is great jamming of brakes and clanging of bells and shouting of instructions. And then the cat is off the roof. You do the same thing to get a boy off the roof.

That is, you do the same thing if you are Yakov Blotnik and you once had a cat on the roof.

When the engines, all four of them, arrived, Rabbi Binder had four times given Ozzie the count of three. The big hook-and-ladder swung around the corner and one of the firemen leaped from it, plunging head-long towards the yellow fire hydrant in front of the synagogue. With a huge wrench he began to unscrew the top nozzle. Rabbi Binder raced over to him and pulled at his shoulder.

"There's no fire . . ."

The fireman mumbled back over his shoulder and, heatedly, continued working at the nozzle.

"But there's no fire, there's no fire . . ." Binder shouted. When the fireman mumbled again, the rabbi grasped his face with both his hands and pointed it up at the roof.

To Ozzie it looked as though Rabbi Binder was trying to tug the fireman's head out of his body, like a cork from a bottle. He had to giggle at the picture they made: it was a family portrait—rabbi in black skull-cap, fireman in red fire hat, and the little yellow hydrant squatting beside like a kid brother, bareheaded. From the edge of the roof Ozzie waved at the portrait, a one-handed, flapping, mocking wave; in doing it his right foot slipped from under him. Rabbi Binder covered his eyes with his hands.

Firemen work fast. Before Ozzie had even regained his balance, a big, round, yellowed net was being held on the synagogue lawn. The firemen who held it looked up at Ozzie with stern, feelingless faces.

One of the firemen turned his head towards Rabbi Binder. "What, is the kid nuts or something?"

Rabbi Binder unpeeled his hands from his eyes, slowly, painfully, as if they were tape. Then he checked: nothing on the sidewalk, no dents in the net.

"Is he gonna jump, or what?" the fireman shouted.

In a voice not at all like a statue, Rabbi Binder finally answered. "Yes, Yes, I think so . . . He's been threatening to . . ."

Threatening to? Why, the reason he was on the roof, Ozzie remembered, was to get away; he hadn't even thought about jumping. He had just run to get away, and the truth was that he hadn't really headed for the roof as much as he'd been chased there.

"What's his name, the kid?"

"Freedman," Rabbi Binder answered. "Oscar Freedman."

The fireman looked up at Ozzie. "What is it with you, Oscar? You gonna jump, or what?"

Ozzie did not answer. Frankly, the question had just arisen.

"Look, Oscar, if you're gonna jump, jump—and if you're not gonna jump, don't jump. But don't waste our time, willya?"

Ozzie looked at the fireman and then at Rabbi Binder. He wanted to see Rabbi Binder cover his eyes one more time.

"I'm going to jump."

And then he scampered around the edge of the roof to the corner, where there was no net below, and he flapped his arms at his sides, swishing the air and smacking his palms to his trousers on the downbeat. He began screaming like some kind of engine, "Wheeeee . . . wheeeeee," and leaning way out over the edge with the upper half of his body. The firemen whipped around to cover the ground with the net. Rabbi Binder mumbled a few words to Somebody and covered his eyes. Everything happened quickly, jerkily, as in a silent movie. The crowd, which had arrived with the fire engines, gave out a long, Fourth-of-July fire-works oooh-aahhh. In the excitement no one had paid the crowd much heed, except, of course, Yakov Blotnik, who swung from the doorknob counting heads. "Fier und tsvansik . . . finf und tsvantsik . . . Oy, Gut!" [10] It wasn't like this with the cat.

Rabbi Binder peeked through his fingers, checked the sidewalk and net. Empty. But there was Ozzie racing to the other corner. The firemen raced with him but were un-able to keep up. Whenever Ozzie wanted to he might jump and splatter himself upon the sidewalk, and by the time the firemen scooted to the spot all they could do with their net would be to cover the mess.

"Wheeeee . . . wheeeee . . ."

"Hey, Oscar," the winded fireman yelled, "What the hell is this, a game or something?"

"Wheeeee . . . wheeeee . . ."

"Hey, Oscar—"

But he was off now to the other corner, flapping his wings fiercely. Rabbi Binder couldn't take it any longer—the fire engines from nowhere, the screaming suicidal boy, the net. He fell to his knees, exhausted, and with his hands curled together in front of his chest like a little dome, he pleaded, "Oscar, stop it, Oscar. Don't jump, Oscar. Please come down . . . Please don't jump."

And further back in the crowd a single voice, a single young voice, shouted a lone word to the boy on the roof.

"Jump!"

It was Itzie. Ozzie momentarily stopped flapping.

"Go ahead, Ozz—jump!" Itzie broke off his point of the star and courageously, with the inspiration not of a wise-guy but of a disciple, stood alone. "Jump, Ozz, jump!"

Still on his knees, his hands still curled,

10 "Twenty-four . . . twenty-five . . . Oh, good!"

Rabbi Binder twisted his body back. He looked at Itzie, then, agonizingly, back to Ozzie.

"OSCAR, DON'T JUMP! PLEASE, DON'T JUMP . . . please please . . ."

"Jump!" This time it wasn't Itzie but another point of the star. By the time Mrs. Freedman arrived to keep her four-thirty appointment with Rabbi Binder, the whole little upside down heaven was shouting and pleading for Ozzie to jump, and Rabbi Binder no longer was pleading with him not to jump, but was crying into the dome of his hands.

Understandably Mrs. Freedman couldn't figure out what her son was doing on the roof. So she asked.

"Ozzie, my Ozzie, what are you doing? My Ozzie, what is it?"

Ozzie stopped wheeeeeing and slowed his arms down to a cruising flap, the kind birds use in soft winds, but he did not answer. He stood against the low, clouded, darkening sky—light clicked down swiftly now, as on a small gear—flapping softly and gazing down at the small bundle of a woman who was his mother.

"What are you doing, Ozzie?" She turned towards the kneeling Rabbi Binder and rushed so close that only a paper-thickness of dusk lay between her stomach and his shoulders.

"What is my baby doing?"

Rabbi Binder gaped up at her but he too was mute. All that moved was the dome of his hands; it shook back and forth like a weak pulse.

"Rabbi, get him down! He'll kill himself. Get him down, my only baby . . ."

"I can't," Rabbi Binder said, "I can't . . ." and he turned his handsome head towards the crowd of boys behind him. "It's them. Listen to them."

And for the first time Mrs. Freedman saw the crowd of boys, and she heard what they were yelling.

"He's doing it for them. He won't listen to me. It's them." Rabbi Binder spoke like one in a trance.

"For them?"

"Yes."

"Why for them?"

"They want him to . . ."

Mrs. Freedman raised her two arms upward as though she were conducting the sky. "For them he's doing it!" And then in a gesture older than pyramids, older than prophets and floods, her arms came slapping down to her sides. "A martyr I have. Look!" She tilted her head to the roof. Ozzie was still flapping softly. "My martyr."

"Oscar, come down, *please*," Rabbi Binder groaned.

In a startlingly even voice Mrs. Freedman called to the boy on the roof. "Ozzie, come down, Ozzie. Don't be a martyr, my baby."

As though it were a litany, Rabbi Binder repeated her words. "Don't be a martyr, my baby. Don't be a martyr."

"Gawhead, Ozz—*be* a Martin!" It was Itzie. "Be a Martin, be a Martin," and all the voices joined in singing for Martindom, whatever *it* was. "Be a Martin, be a Martin . . ."

Somehow when you're on a roof the darker it gets the less you can hear. All Ozzie knew was that two groups wanted two new things: his friends were spirited and musical about what they wanted; his mother and the rabbi were even-toned, chanting, about what they didn't want. The rabbi's voice was without tears now and so was his mother's.

The big net stared up at Ozzie like a sightless eye. The big, clouded sky pushed down. From beneath it looked like a gray corrugated board. Suddenly, looking up into that unsympathetic sky, Ozzie realized all the strangeness of what these people, his friends, were asking: they wanted him to jump, to kill himself; they were singing about it now —it made them that happy. And there was

an even greater strangeness: Rabbi Binder was on his knees, trembling. If there was a question to be asked now it was not "Is it me?" but rather "Is it us? . . . Is it us?"

Being on the roof, it turned out, was a serious thing. If he jumped would the singing become dancing? Would it? What would jumping stop? Yearningly, Ozzie wished he could rip open the sky, plunge his hands through, and pull out the sun; and on the sun, like a coin, would be stamped JUMP or DON'T JUMP.

Ozzie's knees rocked and sagged a little under him as though they were setting him for a dive. His arms tightened, stiffened, froze, from shoulders to fingernails. He felt as if each part of his body were going to vote as to whether he should kill himself or not— and each part as though it were independent of *him*.

The light took an unexpected click down and the new darkness, like a gag, hushed the friends singing for this and the mother and rabbi chanting for that.

Ozzie stopped counting votes, and in a curiously high voice, like one who wasn't prepared for speech, he spoke.

"Mamma?"

"Yes, Oscar."

"Mamma, get down on your knees, like Rabbi Binder."

"Oscar—"

"Get down on your knees," he said, "or I'll jump."

Ozzie heard a whimper, then a quick rustling, and when he looked down where his mother had stood he saw the top of a head and beneath that a circle of dress. She was kneeling beside Rabbi Binder.

He spoke again. "Everybody kneel." There was the sound of everybody kneeling.

Ozzie looked around. With one hand he pointed towards the synagogue entrance. "Make *him* kneel."

There was a noise, not of kneeling, but of body-and-cloth stretching. Ozzie could hear Rabbi Binder saying in a gruff whisper,

". . . or he'll *kill* himself," and when next he looked there was Yakov Blotnik off the door-knob and for the first time in his life upon his knees in the Gentile posture of prayer.

As for the firemen—it is not as difficult as one might imagine to hold a net taut while you are kneeling.

Ozzie looked around again; and then he called to Rabbi Binder.

"Rabbi?"

"Yes, Oscar."

"Rabbi Binder, do you believe in God?"

"Yes."

"Do you believe God can do Anything?" Ozzie leaned his head out into the darkness. "Anything?"

"Oscar, I think—"

"Tell me you believe God can do Anything."

There was a second's hesitation. Then: "God can do Anything."

"Tell me you believe God can make a child without intercourse."

"He can."

"Tell me!"

"God," Rabbi Binder admitted, "can make a child without intercourse."

"Mamma, you tell me."

"God can make a child without intercourse," his mother said.

"Make *him* tell me." There was no doubt who *him* was.

In a few moments Ozzie heard an old comical voice say something to the increasing darkness about God.

Next, Ozzie made everybody say it. And then he made them all say they believed in Jesus Christ—first one at a time, then all together.

When the catechizing was through it was the beginning of evening. From the street it sounded as if the boy on the roof might have sighed.

"Ozzie?" A woman's voice dared to speak. "You'll come down now?"

There was no answer, but the woman waited, and when a voice finally did speak it was thin and crying, and exhausted as that of an old man who had just finished pulling the bells.

"Mamma, don't you see—you shouldn't hit me. He shouldn't hit me. You shouldn't hit me about God, Mamma. You should never hit anybody about God—"

"Ozzie, please come down now."

"Promise me, promise me you'll never hit anybody about God."

He had asked only his mother, but for some reason everyone kneeling in the street promised he would never hit anybody about God.

Once again there was silence.

"I can come down now, Mamma," the boy on the roof finally said. He turned his head both ways as though checking the traffic lights. "Now I can come down . . ."

And he did, right into the center of the yellow net that glowed in the evening's edge like an overgrown halo.

Oliver Goldsmith

EPITAPH FOR EDMUND BURKE

Here lies our good Edmund, whose genius was
    such,
We scarcely can praise it or blame it too much;
Who, born for the universe, narrowed his mind
And to party gave up what was meant for
    mankind.
Though fraught with all learning, yet straining
    his throat
To persuade Tommy Townshend to lend him a
    vote;
Who, too deep for his hearers, still went on
    refining

6 *Townshend:* Thomas Townshend (1733–1800) later Lord Sydney, a Whig Member of Parliament.

And thought of convincing while they thought
    of dining;
Though equal to all things, for all things unfit,
Too nice for a statesman, too proud for a
    wit;   10
For a patriot too cool; for a drudge, disobedient,
And too fond of the right to pursue the
    expedient.
In short, 'twas his fate, unemployed or in place,
    sir,
To eat mutton cold and cut blocks with a razor.

10 *nice:* scrupulous. 13 *unemployed:* out of office.

Robert Burns

HOLY WILLIE'S PRAYER

O Thou, wha in the heavens dost dwell,
Wha, as it pleases best thysel',
Sends ane to heaven and ten to hell,
    A' for thy glory,
And no for ony guid or ill
    They've done afore thee!

I bless and praise thy matchless might,
Whan thousands thou hast left in night,
That I am here afore thy sight,
    For gifts an' grace   10
A burnin' an' a shinin' light,
    To a' this place.

What was I, or my generation,
That I should get sic exaltation?
I, wha deserve most just damnation
    For broken laws
Sax thousand years 'fore my creation,
    Thro' Adam's cause.

1 *wha:* who. 2 *as it pleases:* Calvinists believed that God arbitrarily divides mankind into two groups, the Elect and the Damned. 3. *ane:* one. 4 *A':* all. 5 *guid:* good. 13 *generation:* birth. 14 *sic:* such. 17 *Sax:* six. The events in *Genesis* I–III supposedly began in 4004 B.C.

When frae my mither's womb I fell,
Thou might hae plungèd me in hell,   20
To gnash my gums, to weep and wail,
    In burnin' lakes,
Where damnèd devils roar and yell,
    Chained to their stakes;

Yet I am here a chosen sample,
To show thy grace is great and ample:
I'm here a pillar in thy temple,
    Strong as a rock,
A guide, a buckler, an example
    To a' thy flock.   30

O Lord, thou kens what zeal I bear,
When drinkers drink, and swearers swear,
And singin' there and dancin' here,
    Wi' great an' sma':
For I am keepit by thy fear
    Free frae them a'.

But yet, O Lord! confess I must
At times I'm fashed wi' fleshly lust;
An' sometimes too, in warldly trust,
    Vile self gets in;   40
But thou remembers we are dust,
    Defiled wi' sin.

O Lord! yestreen, thou kens, wi' Meg—
Thy pardon I sincerely beg;
O! may 't ne'er be a livin' plague
    To my dishonor,
An' I'll ne'er lift a lawless leg
    Again upon her.

Besides, I farther maun avow,
Wi' Leezie's lass, three times, I trow—   50
But Lord, that Friday I was fou
    When I cam near her;
Or else, Thou kens, Thy servant true
    Wad never steer her.

Maybe Thou lets this fleshly thorn
Buffet Thy servant e'en and morn,

19 *frae:* from 20 *hae:* have. 31 *kens:* knowest. 34 *sma':* small. 43 *yestreen:* last night. 49 *maun:* must. 51 *fou:* full (of drink). 54 *steer:* molest.

Lest he owre proud and high should turn
    That he's sae gifted:
If sae, Thy han' maun e'en be borne,
    Until Thou lift it.   60

Lord, bless Thy chosen in this place,
For here Thou has a chosen race:
But God confound their stubborn face
    An' blast their name
Wha bring Thy elders to disgrace
    An' public shame.

Lord, mind Gaw'n Hamilton's deserts;
He drinks, an' swears, an' plays at cartes,
Yet has sae mony takin arts,
    Wi' great and sma',   70
Frae God's ain priest the people's hearts
    He steals awa.

An' when we chastened him therefor,
Thou kens how he bred sic a splore
An' set the warld in a roar
    O' laughin' at us;—
Curse Thou his basket and his store,
    Kail an' potatoes.

Lord, hear my earnest cry and pray'r
Against that Presbyt'ry o' Ayr;   80
Thy strong right hand, Lord, make it bare
    Upo' their heads;
Lord, visit them, an' dinna spare
    For their misdeeds.

O Lord my God, that glib-tongued Aiken—
My very heart and soul are quakin'
To think how we stood sweatin', shakin',
    An' pissed wi' dread,
While he, wi' hingin' lips and snakin',
    Held up his head.   90

57 *owre:* excessively. 58 *gifted:* see lines 9–12.
67 *Gaw'n:* Gavin Hamilton (1753–1805) was a
friend of Burns; *deserts:* pronounced "desarts." 69
mony takin arts: many attractive wiles. 71 *ain:*
own. 74 *splore:* commotion. 80 *Presbyt'ry:* i.e.,
the one which tried Hamilton for immorality. 83
dinna: do not. 85 *Aiken:* Hamilton's lawyer. 89
hingin: hanging; *snakin':* sneering.

Lord, in the day of vengeance try him;
Lord, visit him wha did employ him,
And pass not in thy mercy by them,
    Nor hear their pray'r:
But, for thy people's sake, destroy them,
    And dinna spare.

But, Lord, remember me and mine
Wi' mercies temp'ral and divine,
That I for gear and grace may shine
    Excelled by nane,   100
And a' the glory shall be thine;
    Amen, Amen!

99 *for gear:* on account of property. 100 *nane:*
none.

Percy Bysshe Shelley

ODE TO THE WEST WIND

I

O wild west wind, thou breath of autumn's being,
Thou from whose unseen presence the leaves
    dead
Are driven like ghosts from an enchanter fleeing,

Yellow, and black, and pale, and hectic red,
Pestilence-stricken multitudes: O thou,
Who chariotest to their dark wintry bed

The wingèd seeds, where they lie cold and low,
Each like a corpse within its grave, until
Thine azure sister of the spring shall blow

Her clarion o'er the dreaming earth, and
    fill   10
(Driving sweet buds like flocks to feed in air)
With living hues and odors plain and hill:

Wild spirit, which art moving
    everywhere;
Destroyer and preserver, hear, oh hear!

II

Thou on whose stream mid the steep sky's
    commotion
Loose clouds like earth's decaying leaves are shed,
Shook from the tangled boughs of heaven and
    ocean,

Angels of rain and lightning, there are spread
On the blue surface of thine aëry surge,
Like the bright hair uplifted from the head   20

Of some fierce maenad, even from the dim verge
Of the horizon to the zenith's height,
The locks of the approaching storm. Thou dirge

Of the dying year, to which this closing night
Will be the dome of a vast sepulchre,
Vaulted with all thy congregated might

Of vapors, from whose solid atmosphere
Black rain, and fire, and hail will burst: oh, hear!

III

Thou who didst waken from his summer dreams
The blue Mediterranean, where he lay,   30
Lulled by the coil of his crystàlline streams,

Beside a pumice isle in Baiae's bay,
And saw in sleep old palaces and towers
Quivering within the wave's intenser day,

All overgrown with azure moss and flowers
So sweet, the sense faints picturing them! Thou
For whose path the Atlantic 's level powers

Cleave themselves into chasms, while far below
The sea-blooms and the oozy woods, which wear
The sapless foliage of the ocean, know   40

Thy voice and suddenly grow gray with fear,
And tremble and despoil themselves: oh, hear!

    32 *Baiae:* ancient name of Baia, a town near
Naples.

IV

If I were a dead leaf thou mightest bear;
If I were a swift cloud to fly with thee,
A wave to pant beneath thy power and share

The impulse of thy strength, only less free
Than thou, O uncontrollable! If even
I were as in my boyhood and could be

The comrade of thy wanderings over heaven,
As then, when to outstrip thy skiey speed   50
Scarce seemed a vision, I would ne'er have striven

As thus with thee in prayer in my sore need.
Oh, lift me as a wave, a leaf, a cloud!
I fall upon the thorns of life! I bleed!

A heavy weight of hours has chained and bowed
One too like thee: tameless, and swift, and proud.

V

Make me thy lyre, even as the forest is.
What if my leaves are falling like its own!
The tumult of thy mighty harmonies

Will take from both a deep, autumnal tone,   60
Sweet though in sadness. Be thou, spirit fierce,
My spirit! Be thou me, impetuous one!

Drive my dead thoughts over the universe
Like withered leaves to quicken a new birth!
And by the incantation of this verse

Scatter, as from an unextinguished hearth
Ashes and sparks, my words among mankind!
Be through my lips to unawakened earth

The trumpet of a prophecy! O wind,
If winter comes, can spring be far behind?   70

    55 *weight of hours:* the passage of time, cares
brought by maturity.

Matthew Arnold

DOVER BEACH

The sea is calm tonight.
The tide is full, the moon lies fair
Upon the straits; on the French coast the light
Gleams and is gone; the cliffs of England stand,
Glimmering and vast, out in the tranquil bay.
Come to the window, sweet is the night-air!
Only, from the long line of spray
Where the sea meets the moon-blanched land,
Listen! you hear the grating roar
Of pebbles which the waves draw back, and
    fling,   10
At their return, up the high strand,
Begin, and cease, and then again begin,
With tremulous cadence slow, and bring
The eternal note of sadness in.

Sophocles long ago
Heard it on the Ægean, and it brought
Into his mind the turbid ebb and flow
Of human misery; we
Find also in the sound a thought,
Hearing it by this distant northern sea.   20

The Sea of Faith
Was once, too, at the full, and round earth's
    shore
Lay like the folds of a bright girdle furled.
But now I only hear
Its melancholy, long, withdrawing roar,
Retreating, to the breath
Of the night-wind, down the vast edges drear
And naked shingles of the world.

Ah, love, let us be true
To one another! for the world, which seems   30
To lie before us like a land of dreams,
So various, so beautiful, so new,
Hath really neither joy, nor love, nor light,

18 *misery:* supposedly a reference to Ode II of
Antigone, by Sophocles. 21 *Faith:* religious belief.

Nor certitude, nor peace, nor help for pain;
And we are here as on a darkling plain
Swept with confused alarms of struggle and
    flight,
Where ignorant armies clash by night.

Edwin Arlington Robinson

RICHARD CORY

Whenever Richard Cory went down town,
    We people on the pavement looked at him:
He was a gentleman from sole to crown,
    Clean-favored, and imperially slim.

And he was always quietly arrayed,
    And he was always human when he talked;
But still he fluttered pulses when he said,
    "Good morning," and he glittered when he
        walked.

And he was rich—yes, richer than a king,
    And admirably schooled in every grace: 10
In fine, we thought that he was everything
    To make us wish that we were in his place.

So on we worked, and waited for the light,
    And went without the meat, and cursed the
        bread;
And Richard Cory, one calm summer night,
    Went home and put a bullet through his head.

Edwin Arlington Robinson

THE MILL

The miller's wife had waited long:
    The tea was cold, the fire was dead,
And there might yet be nothing wrong
    In how he went and what he said:
"There are no millers any more,"

Was all that she had heard him say;
And he had lingered at the door
   So long that it seemed yesterday.

Sick with a fear that had no form
   She knew that she was there at last;   10
And in the mill there was a warm
   And mealy fragrance of the past.
What else there was would only seem
   To say again what he had meant;
And what was hanging from a beam
   Would not have heeded where she went.

And if she thought it followed her,
   She may have reasoned in the dark
That one way of the few there were
   Would hide her and would leave no
      mark: 20
Black water, smooth above the weir
   Like starry velvet in the night,
Though ruffled once, would soon appear
   The same as ever to the sight.

A. E. Housman

BE STILL, MY SOUL

Be still, my soul, be still; the arms you bear are
      brittle,
   Earth and high heaven are fixt of old and
      founded strong.
Think rather—call to thought, if now you grieve
      a little,
   The days when we had rest, O soul, for they
      were long.

Men loved unkindness then, but lightless in the
      quarry
   I slept and saw not; tears fell down, I did not
      mourn;
Sweat ran and blood sprang out and I was never
      sorry:
   Then it was well with me, in days ere I was
      born.

Now, and I muse for why and never find the
      reason,
   I pace the earth, and drink the air, and feel
      the sun.   10
Be still, be still, my soul; it is but for a season:
   Let us endure an hour and see injustice done.

Ay, look: high heaven and earth ail from the
      prime foundation;
   All thoughts to rive the heart are here, and all
      are vain:
Horror and scorn and hate and fear and
      indignation—
   Oh why did I awake? when shall I sleep again?

T. S. Eliot

THE LOVE SONG OF
J. ALFRED PRUFROCK

S'io credesse che mia risposta fosse
A persona che mai tornasse al mondo,
Questa fiamma staria senza piu scosse.
Ma perciocche giammai di questo fondo
Non torno vivo alcun, s'i' odo il vero,
Senza tema d'infamia ti rispondo.

[If I thought I were answering someone who would
ever return to the upper world, this flame would
shake no more; but since no one ever did return
alive from this pit, if what I hear be true, I answer
you without fear of infamy.

Dante, *Inferno* XXVII, 61–6]

Let us go then, you and I,
When the evening is spread out against the sky
Like a patient etherized upon a table;
Let us go, through certain half-deserted streets,
The muttering retreats
Of restless nights in one-night cheap hotels
And sawdust restaurants with oyster-shells:
Streets that follow like a tedious argument
Of insidious intent
To lead you to an overwhelming question . . .   10
Oh, do not ask, "What is it?"
Let us go and make our visit.

In the room the women come and go
Talking of Michelangelo.

The yellow fog that rubs its back upon the windowpanes,
The yellow smoke that rubs its muzzle on the windowpanes
Licked its tongue into the corners of the evening,
Lingered upon the pools that stand in drains,
Let fall upon its back the soot that falls from chimneys,

Epigraph: The answer Dante receives when he asks Count Guido da Monte-
feltro, who is guilty of having broken an oath, why he is condemned to the
Inferno. *This flame:* my tongue. The implication is that Prufrock's love will
never be declared.

Slipped by the terrace, made a sudden leap,   20
And seeing that it was a soft October night,
Curled once about the house, and fell asleep.

And indeed there will be time
For the yellow smoke that slides along the street,
Rubbing its back upon the windowpanes;
There will be time, there will be time
To prepare a face to meet the faces that you meet;

There will be time to murder and create,
And time for all the works and days of hands   30
That lift and drop a question on your plate
Time for you and time for me,
And time yet for a hundred indecisions,
And for a hundred visions and revisions,
Before the taking of a toast and tea.

In the room the women come and go
Talking of Michelangelo.

And indeed there will be time
To wonder, "Do I dare?" and, "Do I dare?"
Time to turn back and descend the stair,
With a bald spot in the middle of my hair—   40
(They will say: "How his hair is growing thin!")
My morning coat, my collar mounting firmly to the chin,
My necktie rich and modest, but asserted by a simple pin—
(They will say: "But how his arms and legs are thin!")
Do I dare
Disturb the universe?
In a minute there is time
For decisions and revisions which a minute will reverse.

For I have known them all already, known them all:—
Have known the evenings, mornings, afternoons,   50
I have measured out my life with coffee spoons;
I know the voices dying with a dying fall
Beneath the music from a farther room.
    So how should I presume?

And I have known the eyes already, known them all—
The eyes that fix you in a formulated phrase,
And when I am formulated, sprawling on a pin,
When I am pinned and wriggling on the wall,
Then how should I begin

To spit out all the butt-ends of my days and ways?   60
   And how should I presume?

And I have known the arms already, known them all—
Arms that are braceleted and white and bare
(But in the lamplight, downed with light brown hair!)

Is it perfume from a dress
That makes me so digress?
Arms that lie along a table, or wrap about a shawl.
   And should I then presume?
   And how should I begin?

      .   .   .   .   .

Shall I say, I have gone at dusk through narrow streets   70
And watched the smoke that rises from the pipes
Of lonely men in shirt-sleeves, leaning out of windows? . . .

I should have been a pair of ragged claws
Scuttling across the floors of silent seas.

      .   .   .   .   .

And the afternoon, the evening, sleeps so peacefully!
Smoothed by long fingers,
Asleep . . . tired . . . or it malingers,
Stretched on the floor, here beside you and me.
Should I, after tea and cakes and ices,
Have the strength to force the moment to its crisis?   80
But though I have wept and fasted, wept and prayed,
Though I have seen my head (grown slightly bald) brought in upon a platter,
I am no prophet—and here's no great matter;
I have seen the moment of my greatness flicker,
And I have seen the eternal Footman hold my coat, and snicker,
And in short, I was afraid.

And would it have been worth it, after all,
After the cups, the marmalade, the tea,
Among the porcelain, among some talk of you and me,
Would it have been worth while,   90
To have bitten off the matter with a smile,
To have squeezed the universe into a ball
To roll it toward some overwhelming question,

   82 *head:* like that of John the Baptist: *Gospel of St. Matthew* xiv, 11.

To say: "I am Lazarus, come from the dead,
Come back to tell you all, I shall tell you all"—
If one, settling a pillow by her head,
    Should say: "That is not what I meant at all,
    That is not it, at all."

And would it have been worth it, after all,
Would it have been worth while,   100
After the sunsets and the dooryards and the sprinkled streets,
After the novels, after the teacups, after the skirts that trail along the floor—
And this, and so much more?—
It is impossible to say just what I mean!
But as if a magic lantern threw the nerves in patterns on a screen:
Would it have been worth while
If one, settling a pillow or throwing off a shawl,
And turning toward the window, should say:
    "That is not it, at all,
    That is not what I meant, at all."   110

.   .   .   .   .

No! I am not Prince Hamlet, nor was meant to be;
Am an attendant lord, one that will do
To swell a progress, start a scene or two,
Advise the prince; no doubt, an easy tool,
Deferential, glad to be of use,
Politic, cautious, and meticulous;
Full of high sentence, but a bit obtuse;
At times, indeed, almost ridiculous—
Almost, at times, the Fool.

                                                                                    120

I grow old . . . I grow old . . .
I shall wear the bottoms of my trousers rolled.

Shall I part my hair behind? Do I dare to eat a peach?
I shall wear white flannel trousers, and walk upon the beach.
I have heard the mermaids singing, each to each.

I do not think that they will sing to me.

I have seen them riding seaward on the waves
Combing the white hair of the waves blown back
When the wind blows the water white and black.

   117 *full of high sentence:* sententious like Polonius in *Hamlet* I. III.

We have lingered in the chambers of the sea
By sea-girls wreathed with seaweed red and brown   130
Till human voices wake us, and we drown.

Louis Simpson

JOHN THE BAPTIST

The Prophet, scourged by his own hand,
        progressed
Through wilderness inhabited by brutes
Whose hollow voices would not let him rest,
Feeding on honeycombs and cactus roots.

The leopard frolicked in her leafy marking;
A multitude of undetermined shapes
Walked parallel. He fled the wild dog's barking,
The buzzard's black umbrella and collapse.

And as he fled from white Jerusalem
"Make straight the crooked way!" would loudly
        cry,   10
And fled from people and discovered them
As shadows at the corner of the eye.

Against the gaudy red edge of the world
There came a caravan. The camels kneeled
Under the drivers' blows; the fires curled
And to and fro the white-robed Arabs wheeled.

Their melody the rocks replied again.
In veils and silver serpents at the fire
The women sinuated; the tall men
Danced arm in arm, apart from their
        desire.   20

A Negro, shaking like an epilept,
Beat with his bleeding knuckles on a gourd,
Two naked dancers in the circle leapt
Swinging a supple child across a sword.

Then, at a long-drawn bray from throats of
        bronze

1 *Prophet:* see *Gospel of St. Matthew* III, 1.

A Roman legion rapidly debouched.
The drums, the piercing flutes, were stopped at
        once,
The dancers in a sullen silence crouched.

They carried on the column of their necks
The stone dome of the sky, their naked
        knees   30
Rolled out an iron street. Triumphant specks!
Their echoes had increased the silences.

A fearful discipline of little swords
And buckled mouths . . . The shields had shifted
        place
With the quick ruffle of an angry bird,
A slant of lances like one man's grimace.

They ruled the living and revered the dead . . .
These were the last reflectors of the sun
And carried him in purple and in red,
Their praying shadows rampant at the
        throne.   40

The Prophet for his supper parched the locust
And of her little burden robbed the bee,
And laid his hairy cloak beneath a cactus
On the bright margin of eternity.

And all his dreams were of a marshy pool
Where the old Vices run with backward glance:
Ingratitude, and Gluttony an owl
With human face, pot-bellied Ignorance.

An idiot with slack jaw and soiled rump
Was led upon a leash by sister crones—   50
Blind eye, flat dug, and amputated stump.
And there were mountain nymphs as smooth as
        stones

That kneel for centuries beside the waters
Under the leaves in the Italian wind,
Vases of clear song, the swan-necked daughters
Turned by divinity without a mind.

A centaur plashed in dappled dignity
Balancing a statue on his withers.
The forest flocked with gay stupidity,
The hoofs of goats and fluttering of feathers.   60

There, double-rooted, dark and ominous
The Tree of Knowledge screamed her triple text.
A pigmy, with a quiver of long arrows,
A monkey's head, both male and female sexed,

Fled from the shadow of pursuing Wisdom,
From the stained spear and the destroying shape,
And all the gods were guttural or dumb
To see Man separated from the Ape.

But was this Wisdom, with a woman's face?
She was not Wisdom, for she followed
    dancing.   70
Her mouth was smiling, an unholy grace

Flashed from her hands and from her eyes fell
    glancing.

And lightly lightly went the dancer's foot,
And as she danced she dazzled through a veil,
And softly played an Arab flute,
And on his throne a king sat stricken pale.

The Prophet woke. The stars were large with
    rain,
The moon upon a cloud lay soft and bright,
The pagan fires smouldered on the plain,
The tiger swung his lantern through the
    night.   80

And to the valley's winding ways he ran
Crying "Prepare the straight path for the Lord!"
And came to shallow Jordan, where began
The matter of the platter and the sword.

84 *matter:* see ibid., xiv, 10.

Chapter 6

COMMUNITY AND CONFLICT

Though mankind is not the only social species—we share this property with bees and timber wolves—the need to belong to a group, and the capacity to relate to others on various levels within a group are greatest in human beings among the creatures of the earth. When a group takes on enterprises of its own, larger than an individual can conduct, it becomes an *institution* in which the individual plays a role, or roles, which can help to differentiate him from others and increase his individuality. When a group is bound together by basic common values and interests and a sense of mutual belonging, it is a *community*. And genuine community seems to be an important element in the most satisfying human life.

But the formation of groups is often exclusive as well as inclusive: the "we" set off against the "they," the ins against the outs. The values that bind the members of one group are felt as contrasted to alien and opposed values of other groups. Clashes of personal aims and needs take on intensified acuteness when the persons think of themselves as representing, or embodying, a common cause. A single person may be torn by divided group loyalties, conflicts of duty or of duty to the group with strong inclinations to escape or transcend its limited concerns. In the perennial love-story

plot from *Romeo and Juliet* to its contemporary version, *West Side Story*, the hero or heroine (Juliet, a member of the Capulet family; Maria, the Puerto Rican) comes to a tragic end because of a love forbidden by group rivalry.

Some of the works in this chapter portray various sorts of group conflict: racial, as in "Tell Freedom" and "Rat Joiner Routs the Klan"; religious, as in Milton's "On the Late Massacre in Piedmont"; national, as in "The Guest." Other works present the subtler but often equally strong barriers set up by difference of family, economic status, social class (as in "Greenleaf").

One of the great rewards of literature is that it can help us to reach across those man-made walls that divide culture from culture, or class from class (as the children are able to do briefly in "Tell Freedom"), and to mitigate that emotional blindness which consists of our inability to sympathize with the feelings and aspirations of others who have different life-goals and life-styles. Literature is a remedy for that hardness of heart that shuts us in and keeps us apart. We can understand and sympathize a little, perhaps, with both sides in "Greenleaf," while at the same time understanding how their conflict is inevitable. We gain insight into the colonialist and those he rules (as in

"The Guest"); the white supremacist and his victim (as in "The Chicago *Defender* Sends a Man to Little Rock"). We become aware of the extent to which our own thinking is dominated by such stereotypes as those which are gently mocked, and pointedly rejected, in "Orientals are Stoic." And we may wonder whether human nature is, in some fundamental way, everywhere the same—the idea that is questioned, and yet ironically affirmed, in "Shakespeare in the Bush."

Laura Bohannon

SHAKESPEARE IN THE BUSH

Just before I left Oxford for the Tiv in West Africa,[1] conversation turned to the season at Stratford. "You Americans," said a friend, "often have difficulty with Shakespeare. He was, after all, a very English poet, and one can easily misinterpret the universal by misunderstanding the particular."

I protested that human nature is pretty much the same the whole world over; at least the general plot and motivation of the greater tragedies would always be clear—everywhere—although some details of custom might have to be explained and difficulties of translation might produce other slight changes. To end an argument we could not conclude, my friend gave me a copy of *Hamlet* to study in the African bush: it would, he hoped, lift my mind above its primitive surroundings, and possibly I might, by prolonged meditation, achieve the grace of correct interpretation.

It was my second field trip to that African tribe, and I thought myself ready to live in one of its remote sections—an area difficult

[1] I.e., northern Nigeria.

to cross even on foot. I eventually settled on the hillock of a very knowledgeable old man, the head of a homestead of some hundred and forty people, all of whom were either his close relatives or their wives and children. Like the other elders of the vicinity, the old man spent most of his time performing ceremonies seldom seen these days in the most accessible parts of the tribe. I was delighted. Soon there would be three months of enforced isolation and leisure, between the harvest that takes place just before the rising of the swamps and the clearing of new farms when the water goes down. Then, I thought, they would have even more time to perform ceremonies and explain them to me.

I was quite mistaken. Most of the ceremonies demanded the presence of elders from several homesteads. As the swamps rose, the old men found it too difficult to walk from one homestead to the next, and the ceremonies gradually ceased. As the swamps rose even higher, all activities but one came to an end. The women brewed beer from maize and millet. Men, women, and children sat on their hillocks and drank it.

People began to drink at dawn. By midmorning the whole homestead was singing, dancing, and drumming. When it rained, people had to sit inside their huts: there they drank and sang or they drank and told stories. In any case, by noon or before, I either had to join the party or retire to my own hut and my books. "One does not discuss serious matters when there is beer. Come, drink with us." Since I lacked their capacity for the thick native beer, I spent more and more time with *Hamlet*. Before the end of the second month, grace descended on me. I was quite sure that *Hamlet* had only one possible interpretation, and that one universally obvious.

Early every morning, in the hope of having some serious talk before the beer party. I used to call on the old man at his reception hut—a circle of posts supporting a thatched roof above a low mud wall to keep out wind and rain. One day I crawled through the low doorway and found most of the men of the homestead sitting huddled in their ragged cloths on stools, low plank beds, and reclining chairs, warming themselves against the chill of the rain around a smoky fire. In the center were three pots of beer. The party had started.

The old man greeted me cordially. "Sit down and drink." I accepted a large calabash full of beer, poured some into a small drinking gourd, and tossed it down. Then I poured some more into the same gourd for the man second in seniority to my host before I handed my calabash over to a young man for further distribution. Important people shouldn't ladle beer themselves.

"It is better like this," the old man said, looking at me approvingly and plucking at the thatch that had caught in my hair. "You should sit and drink with us more often. Your servants tell me that when you are not with us, you sit inside your hut looking at a paper."

The old man was acquainted with four kinds of "papers": tax receipts, bride price receipts, court free receipts, and letters. The messenger who brought him letters from the chief used them mainly as a badge of office, for he always knew what was in them and told the old man. Personal letters for the few who had relatives in the government or mission stations were kept until someone went to a large market where there was a letter writer and reader. Since my arrival, letters were brought to me to be read. A few men also brought me bride price receipts, privately, with requests to change the figures to a higher sum. I found moral arguments were of no avail, since in-laws are fair game, and the technical hazards of forgery difficult to explain to an illiterate people. I did not wish them to think me silly enough to look at any such papers for days on end, and I hastily explained that my "paper" was one of the "things of long ago" of my country.

"Ah," said the old man. "Tell us."

I protested that I was not a storyteller. Storytelling is a skilled art among them; their standards are high, and the audiences critical—and vocal in their criticism. I protested in vain. This morning they wanted to hear a story while they drank. They threatened to tell me no more stories until I told them one of mine. Finally, the old man promised that no one would criticize my style "for we know you are struggling with our language." "But," put in one of the elders, "you must explain what we do not understand, as we do when we tell you our stories." Realizing that here was my chance to prove *Hamlet* universally intelligible, I agreed.

The old man handed me some more beer to help me on with my storytelling. Men filled their long wooden pipes and knocked coals from the fire to place in the pipe bowls; then, puffing contentedly, they sat back to listen. I began in the proper style, "Not yesterday, not yesterday, but long ago, a thing occurred. One night three men were keeping watch outside the homestead of the great chief, when suddenly they saw the former chief approach them."

"Why was he no longer their chief?"

"He was dead," I explained. "That is why they were troubled and afraid when they saw him."

"Impossible," began one of the elders, handing his pipe on to his neighbor, who interrupted, "Of course it wasn't the dead chief. It was an omen sent by a witch. Go on."

Slightly shaken, I continued. "One of these three was a man who knew things"— the closest translation for scholar, but unfortunately it also meant witch. The second elder looked triumphantly at the first. "So he spoke to the dead chief saying, 'Tell us what we must do so you may rest in your grave,' but the dead chief did not answer. He vanished, and they could see him no more. Then the man who knew things—his name was Horatio—said this event was the affair of the dead chief's son, Hamlet."

There was a general shaking of heads round the circle. "Had the dead chief no living brothers? Or was this son the chief?"

"No," I replied. "That is, he had one living brother who became the chief when the elder brother died."

The old men muttered: such omens were matters for chiefs and elders, not for youngsters; no good could come of going behind a chief's back; clearly Horatio was not a man who knew things.

"Yes, he was," I insisted, shooing a chicken away from my beer. "In our country the son is next to the father. The dead chief's younger brother had become the great chief. He had also married his elder brother's widow only about a month after the funeral."

"He did well," the old man beamed and announced to the others, "I told you that if we knew more about Europeans, we would find they really were very like us. In our country also," he added to me, "the younger brother marries the elder brother's widow and becomes the father of his children. Now, if your uncle, who married your widowed mother, is your father's full brother, then he will be a real father to you. Did Hamlet's father and uncle have one mother?"

His question barely penetrated my mind; I was too upset and thrown too far off balance by having one of the most important elements of *Hamlet* knocked straight out of the picture. Rather uncertainly I said that I thought they had the same mother, but I wasn't sure—the story didn't say. The old man told me severely that these genealogical details made all the difference and that when I got home I must ask the elders about it. He shouted out the door to one of his younger wives to bring his goatskin bag.

Determined to save what I could of the

mother motif, I took a deep breath and began again. "The son Hamlet was very sad because his mother had married again so quickly. There was no need for her to do so, and it is our custom for a widow not to go to her next husband until she has mourned for two years."

"Two years is too long," objected the wife, who had appeared with the old man's battered goatskin bag. "Who will hoe your farms for you while you have no husband?"

"Hamlet," I retorted without thinking, "was old enough to hoe his mother's farms himself. There was no need for her to remarry." No one looked convinced. I gave up. "His mother and the great chief told Hamlet not to be sad, for the great chief himself would be a father to Hamlet. Furthermore, Hamlet would be the next chief: therefore he must stay to learn the things of a chief. Hamlet agreed to remain, and all the rest went off to drink beer."

While I paused, perplexed at how to render Hamlet's disgusted soliloquy to an audience convinced that Claudius and Gertrude had behaved in the best possible manner, one of the younger men asked me who had married the other wives of the dead chief.

"He had no other wives," I told him.

"But a chief must have many wives! How else can he brew beer and prepare food for all his guests?"

I said firmly that in our country even chiefs had only one wife, that they had servants to do their work, and that they paid them from tax money.

It was better, they returned, for a chief to have many wives and sons who would help him hoe his farms and feed his people; then everyone loved the chief who gave much and took nothing—taxes were a bad thing.

I agreed with the last comment, but for the rest fell back on their favorite way of fobbing off my questions: "That is the way it is done, so that is how we do it."

I decided to skip the soliloquy. Even if

Claudius was here thought quite right to marry his brother's widow, there remained the poison motif, and I knew they would disapprove of fratricide. More hopefully I resumed, "That night Hamlet kept watch with the three who had seen his dead father. The dead chief again appeared, and although the others were afraid, Hamlet followed his dead father off to one side. When they were alone, Hamlet's dead father spoke."

"Omens can't talk!" The old man was emphatic.

"Hamlet's dead father wasn't an omen. Seeing him might have been an omen, but he was not." My audience looked as confused as I sounded. "It *was* Hamlet's dead father. It was a thing we call a 'ghost'." I had to use the English word, for unlike many of the neighboring tribes, these people didn't believe in the survival after death of any individuating part of the personality.

"What is a 'ghost?' An omen?"

"No, a 'ghost' is someone who is dead but who walks around and can talk, and people can hear him and see him but not touch him."

They objected. "One can touch zombis."

"No, no! It was not a dead body the witches had animated to sacrifice and eat. No one else made Hamlet's dead father walk. He did it himself."

"Dead men can't walk," protested my audience as one man.

I was quite willing to compromise. "A 'ghost' is the dead man's shadow."

But again they objected. "Dead men cast no shadows."

"They do in my country," I snapped.

The old man quelled the babble of disbelief that arose immediately and told me with that insincere, but courteous, agreement one extends to the fancies of the young, ignorant, and superstitious, "No doubt in your country the dead can also walk without being zombis." From the depth of his bag he produced a withered fragment of kola nut, bit off one end to show it wasn't poisoned, and handed me the rest as a peace offering.

"Anyhow," I resumed, "Hamlet's dead father said that his own brother, the one who became chief, had poisoned him. He wanted Hamlet to avenge him. Hamlet believed this in his heart, for he did not like his father's brother." I took another swallow of beer. "In the country of the great chief, living in the same homestead, for it was a very large one, was an important elder who was often with the chief to advise and help him. His name was Polonius. Hamlet was courting his daughter, but her father and her brother . . . [I cast hastily about for some tribal analogy] warned her not to let Hamlet visit her when she was alone on her farm, for he would be a great chief and so could not marry her."

"Why not?" asked the wife, who had settled down on the edge of the old man's chair. He frowned at her for asking stupid questions and growled, "They lived in the same homestead."

"That was not the reason," I informed them. "Polonius was a stranger who lived in the homestead because he helped the chief, not because he was a relative."

"Then why couldn't Hamlet marry her?"

"He could have," I explained, "but Polonius didn't think he would. After all, Hamlet was a man of great importance who ought to marry a chief's daughter, for in his country a man could have only one wife. Polonius was afraid that if Hamlet made love to his daughter, then no one else would give a high price for her."

"That might be true," remarked one of the shrewder elders, "but a chief's son would give his mistress's father enough presents and patronage to more than make up the difference. Polonius sounds like a fool to me."

"Many people think he was," I agreed.

"Meanwhile Polonius sent his son Laertes off to Paris to learn the things of that country, for it was the homestead of a very great chief indeed. Because he was afraid that Laertes might waste a lot of money on beer and women and gambling, or get into trouble by fighting, he sent one of his servants to Paris secretly, to spy out what Laertes was doing. One day Hamlet came upon Polonius's daughter Ophelia. He behaved so oddly he frightened her. Indeed" —I was fumbling for words to express the dubious quality of Hamlet's madness—"the chief and many others had also noticed that when Hamlet talked one could understand the words but not what they meant. Many people thought that he had become mad." My audience suddenly became much more attentive. "The great chief wanted to know what was wrong with Hamlet, so he sent for two of Hamlet's age mates [school friends would have taken long explanation] to talk to Hamlet and find out what troubled his heart. Hamlet, seeing that they had been bribed by the chief to betray him, told them nothing. Polonius, however, insisted that Hamlet was mad because he had been forbidden to see Ophelia, whom he loved."

"Why," inquired a bewildered voice, "should anyone bewitch Hamlet on that account?"

"Bewitch him?"

"Yes, only witchcraft can make anyone mad, unless, of course, one sees the beings that lurk in the forest."

I stopped being a storyteller, took out my notebook and demanded to be told more about these two causes of madness. Even while they spoke and I jotted notes, I tried to calculate the effect of this new factor on the plot. Hamlet had not been exposed to the beings that lurk in the forest. Only his relatives in the male line could bewitch him. Barring relatives not mentioned by Shakespeare, it had to be Claudius who was at-

tempting to harm him. And, of course, it was.

For the moment I staved off questions by saying that the great chief also refused to believe that Hamlet was mad for the love of Ophelia and nothing else. "He was sure that something much more important was troubling Hamlet's heart."

"Now Hamlet's age mates," I continued, "had brought with them a famous storyteller. Hamlet decided to have this man tell the chief and all his homestead a story about a man who had poisoned his brother because he desired his brother's wife and wished to be chief himself. Hamlet was sure the great chief could not hear the story without making a sign if he was indeed guilty, and then he would discover whether his dead father had told him the truth."

The old man interrupted, with deep cunning, "Why should a father lie to his son?" he asked.

I hedged: "Hamlet wasn't sure that it really was his dead father." It was impossible to say anything, in that language, about devil-inspired visions.

"You mean," he said, "it actually was an omen, and he knew witches sometimes send false ones. Hamlet was a fool not to go to one skilled in reading omens and divining the truth in the first place. A man-who-sees-the-truth could have told him how his father died, if he really had been poisoned, and if there was witchcraft in it; then Hamlet could have called the elders to settle the matter."

The shrewd elder ventured to disagree. "Because his father's brother was a great chief, one-who-sees-the-truth might therefore have been afraid to tell it. I think it was for that reason that a friend of Hamlet's father—a witch and an elder—sent an omen so his friend's son would know. Was the omen true?"

"Yes," I said, abandoning ghosts and the devil; a witch-sent omen it would have to be.

"It was true, for when the storyteller was telling his tale before all the homestead, the great chief rose in fear. Afraid that Hamlet knew his secret he planned to have him killed."

The stage set of the next bit presented some difficulties of translation. I began cautiously. "The great chief told Hamlet's mother to find out from her son what he knew. But because a woman's children are always first in her heart, he had the important elder Polonius hide behind a cloth that hung against the wall of Hamlet's mother's sleeping hut. Hamlet started to scold his mother for what she had done."

There was a shocked murmur from everyone. A man should never scold his mother.

"She called out in fear, and Polonius moved behind the cloth. Shouting, 'A rat!' Hamlet took his machete and slashed through the cloth." I paused for dramatic effect. "He had killed Polonius!"

The old men looked at each other in supreme disgust. "That Polonius truly was a fool and a man who knew nothing! What child would not know enough to shout, 'It's me!'" With a pang, I remembered that these people are ardent hunters, always armed with bow, arrow, and machete; at the first rustle in the grass an arrow is aimed and ready, and the hunter shouts "Game!" If no human voice answers immediately, the arrow speeds on its way. Like a good hunter Hamlet shouted, "A rat!"

I rushed in to save Polonius's reputation. "Polonius did speak. Hamlet heard him. But he thought it was the chief and wished to kill him to avenge his father. He had meant to kill him earlier that evening. . . ." I broke down, unable to describe to these pagans, who had no belief in individual afterlife, the difference between dying at one's prayers and dying "unhousell'd, disappointed, unaneled."

This time I had shocked my audience seriously. "For a man to raise his hand against his father's brother and the one who

has become his father—that is a terrible thing. The elders ought to let such a man be bewitched."

I nibbled at my kola nut in some perplexity, then pointed out that after all the man had killed Hamlet's father.

"No," pronounced the old man, speaking less to me than to the young men sitting behind the elders. "If your father's brother has killed your father, you must appeal to your father's age mates; *they* may avenge him. No man may use violence against his senior relatives." Another thought struck him. "But if his father's brother had indeed been wicked enough to bewitch Hamlet and make him mad that would be a good story indeed, for it would be his fault that Hamlet, being mad, no longer had any sense and thus was ready to kill his father's brother."

There was a murmur of applause. *Hamlet* was again a good story to them, but it no longer seemed quite the same story to me. As I thought over the coming complications of plot and motive, I lost courage and decided to skim over dangerous ground quickly.

"The great chief," I went on, "was not sorry that Hamlet had killed Polonius. It gave him a reason to send Hamlet away, with his two treacherous age mates, with letters to a chief of a far country, saying that Hamlet should be killed. But Hamlet changed the writing on their papers, so that the chief killed his age mates instead." I encountered a reproachful glare from one of the men whom I had told undetectable forgery was not merely immoral but beyond human skill. I looked the other way.

"Before Hamlet could return, Laertes came back for his father's funeral. The great chief told him Hamlet had killed Polonius. Laertes swore to kill Hamlet because of this, and because his sister Ophelia, hearing her father had been killed by the man she loved, went mad and drowned in the river."

"Have you already forgotten what we told

you?" The old man was reproachful. "One cannot take vengeance on a madman; Hamlet killed Polonius in his madness. As for the girl, she not only went mad, she was drowned. Only witches can make people drown. Water itself can't hurt anything. It is merely something one drinks and bathes in."

I began to get cross. "If you don't like the story, I'll stop."

The old man made soothing noises and himself poured me some more beer. "You tell the story well, and we are listening. But it is clear that the elders of your country have never told you what the story really means. No, don't interrupt! We believe you when you say your marriage customs are different, or your clothes and weapons. But people are the same everywhere; therefore, there are always witches and it is we, the elders, who know how witches work. We told you it was the great chief who wished to kill Hamlet, and now your own words have proved us right. Who were Ophelia's male relatives?"

"There were only her father and her brother." Hamlet was clearly out of my hands.

"There must have been many more; this also you must ask of your elders when you get back to your country. From what you tell us, since Polonius was dead, it must have been Laertes who killed Ophelia, although I do not see the reason for it."

We had emptied one pot of beer, and the old men argued the point with slightly tipsy interest. Finally one of them demanded of me, "What did the servant of Polonius say on his return?"

With difficulty I recollected Reynaldo and his mission. "I don't think he did return before Polonius was killed."

"Listen," said the elder, "and I will tell you how it was and how your story will go, then you may tell me if I am right. Polonius knew his son would get into trouble, and so he did. He had many fines to pay for fighting, and debts from gambling. But

he had only two ways of getting money quickly. One was to marry off his sister at once, but it is difficult to find a man who will marry a woman desired by the son of a chief. For if the chief's heir commits adultery with your wife, what can you do? Only a fool calls a case against a man who will someday be his judge. Therefore Laertes had to take the second way: he killed his sister by witchcraft, drowning her so he could secretly sell her body to the witches."

I raised an objection. "They found her body and buried it. Indeed Laertes jumped into the grave to see his sister once more—so, you see, the body was truly there. Hamlet, who had just come back, jumped in after him."

"What did I tell you?" The elder appealed to the others. "Laertes was up to no good with his sister's body. Hamlet prevented him, because the chief's heir, like a chief, does not wish any other man to grow rich and powerful. Laertes would be angry, because he would have killed his sister without benefit to himself. In our country he would try to kill Hamlet for that reason. Is this not what happened?"

"More or less," I admitted. "When the great chief found Hamlet was still alive, he encouraged Laertes to try to kill Hamlet and arranged a fight with machetes between them. In the fight both the young men were wounded to death. Hamlet's mother drank the poisoned beer that the chief meant for Hamlet in case he won the fight. When he saw his mother die of poison, Hamlet, dying, managed to kill his father's brother with his machete."

"You see, I was right!" exclaimed the elder.

"That was a very good story," added the old man, "and you told it with very few mistakes. There was just one more error, at the very end. The poison Hamlet's mother drank was obviously meant for the survivor of the fight, whichever it was. If Laertes had won, the great chief would have poisoned him, for no one would know that he arranged Hamlet's death. Then, too, he need not fear Laertes' witchcraft; it takes a strong heart to kill one's only sister by witchcraft."

"Sometime," concluded the old man, gathering his ragged toga about him, "you must tell us some more stories of your country. We, who are elders, will instruct you in their true meaning, so that when you return to your own land your elders will see that you have not been sitting in the bush, but among those who know things and who have taught you wisdom."

Peter Abrahams

TELL FREEDOM

"And judgement is turned away backward, and justice standeth afar off: for truth is fallen in the street, and equity cannot enter." ISAIAH LIX, 14.

Wednesday was crackling day. On that day the children of the location made the long trek to Elsburg[2] siding for the squares of pig's rind that passed for our daily meat. We collected a double lot of cow dung the day before; a double lot of *moeroga* [wild spinach].

I finished my breakfast and washed up. Aunt Liza was at her wash-tub in the yard. A misty, sickly sun was just showing. And on the open veld the frost lay thick and white on the grass.

"Ready?" Aunt Liza called.

I went out to her. She shook the soapsuds off her swollen hands and wiped them on her apron. She lifted the apron and put her

2 Town in South Transvaal, Republic of South Africa.

hand through the slits of the many thin cotton dresses she wore. The dress nearest the skin was the one with the pocket. From this she pulled a sixpenny piece. She tied it in a knot in the corner of a bit of colored cloth.

"Take care of that. . . . Take the smaller piece of bread in the bin but don't eat it till you start back. You can have a small piece of crackling with it. Only a small piece, understand?"

"Yes, Aunt Liza."

"All right."

I got the bread and tucked it into the little canvas bag in which I would carry the crackling.

"Bye, Aunt Liza." I trotted off, one hand in my pocket, feeling the cloth where the money was. I paused at Andries's home.

"Andries!" I danced up and down while I waited. The cold was not so terrible on bare feet if one did not keep still.

Andries came trotting out of their yard. His mother's voice followed; desperate and plaintive:

"I'll skin you if you lose the money!"

"Women!" Andries said bitterly.

I glimpsed the dark, skinny woman at her wash-tub as we trotted across the veld. Behind, and in front of us, other children trotted in twos and threes.

There was a sharp bite to the morning air I sucked in; it stung my nose so that tears came to my eyes; it went down my throat like an icy draught; my nose ran. I tried breathing through my mouth but this was worse. The cold went through my shirt and shorts; my skin went pimply and chilled; my fingers went numb and began to ache; my feet felt like frozen lumps that did not belong to me, yet jarred and hurt each time I put them down. I began to feel sick and desperate.

"Jesus God in heaven!" Andries cried suddenly.

I looked at him. His eyes were rimmed in

red. Tears ran down his cheeks. His face was drawn and purple, a sick look on it.

"Faster," I said.

"Think it'll help?"

I nodded. We went faster. We passed two children, sobbing and moaning as they ran. We were all in the same desperate situation. We were creatures haunted and hounded by the cold. It was a cruel enemy who gave no quarter. And our means of fighting it were pitifully inadequate. In all the mornings and evenings of the winter months, young and old, big and small, were helpless victims of the bitter cold. Only towards noon and the early afternoon, when the sun sat high in the sky, was there a brief respite. For us, the children, the cold, especially the morning cold, assumed an awful and malevolent personality. We talk of "It." "It" was a half-human monster with evil thoughts, evil intentions, bent on destroying us. "It" was happiest when we were most miserable. Andries had told me how "It" had, last winter, caught and killed a boy.

Hunger was an enemy too, but one with whom we could come to terms, who had many virtues and values. Hunger gave our *pap*,[3] *moeroga*, and crackling a feast-like quality. We could, when it was not with us, think and talk kindly about it. Its memory could even give moments of laughter. But the cold winter was with us all the time. "It" never really eased up. There were only more bearable degrees of "It" at high noon and on mild days. "It" was the real enemy. And on this Wednesday morning, as we ran across the veld, winter was more bitterly, bitingly, freezingly, real than ever.

The sun climbed. The frozen earth thawed leaving the short grass looking wet and weary. Painfully, our feet and legs came alive. The aching numbness slowly left our fingers. We ran more slowly in the more bearable cold.

[3] A kind of porridge made with crushed maize.

In climbing, the sun lost some of its damp look and seemed a real, if cold, sun. When it was right overhead, we struck the sandy road which meant we were nearing the siding. None of the others were in sight. Andries and I were alone on the sandy road on the open veld. We slowed down to a brisk walk. We were sufficiently thawed to want to talk.

"How far?" I said.

"A few minutes," he said.

"I've got a piece of bread," I said.

"Me too," he said. "Let's eat it now."

"On the way back," I said. "With a bit of crackling."

"Good idea. . . . Race to the fork."

"All right."

"Go!" he said.

We shot off together, legs working like pistons. He soon pulled away from me. He reached the fork in the road some fifty yards ahead.

"I win!" he shouted gleefully, though his teeth still chattered.

We pitched stones down the road, each trying to pitch further than the other. I won and wanted to go on doing it. But Andries soon grew weary with pitching. We raced again. Again he won. He wanted another race but I refused. I wanted pitching, but he refused. So, sulking with each other, we reached the pig farm.

We followed a fenced-off pathway round sprawling white buildings. Everywhere about us was the grunt of pigs. As we passed an open doorway, a huge dog came bounding out, snarling and barking at us. In our terror, we forgot that it was fenced in and streaked away. Surprised, I found myself a good distance ahead of Andries. We looked back and saw a young white woman call the dog to heel.

"Damn Boer dog," Andries said.

"Matter with it?" I asked.

"They teach them to go for us. Never get caught by one. My old man's got a hole in his bottom where a Boer dog got him."

I remembered I had outstripped him.

"I won!" I said.

"Only because you were frightened," he said.

"I still won."

"Scare arse," he jeered.

"Scare arse, yourself!"

"I'll knock you!"

"I'll knock you back!"

A couple of white men came down the path and ended our possible fight. We hurried past them to the distant shed where a queue had already formed. There were grown-ups and children. All the grown-ups, and some of the children, were from places other than our location.

The line moved slowly. The young white man who served us did it in leisurely fashion, with long pauses for a smoke. Occasionally he turned his back.

At last, after what seemed hours, my turn came. Andries was behind me. I took the sixpenny piece from the square of cloth and offered it to the man.

"Well?" he said.

"Sixpence crackling, please."

Andries nudged me in the back. The man's stare suddenly became cold and hard. Andries whispered into my ear.

"Well?" the man repeated coldly.

"Please, *baas* [boss, master]," I said.

"What d'you want?"

"Sixpence crackling, please."

"What?"

Andries dug me in the ribs.

"Sixpence crackling, please, *baas*."

"What?"

"Sixpence crackling, please, *baas*."

"You new here?"

"Yes, *baas*." I looked at his feet while he stared at me.

At last he took the sixpenny piece from me. I held my bag open while he filled it with crackling from a huge pile on a large canvas sheet on the ground. Turning away,

I stole a fleeting glance at his face. His eyes met mine, and there was amused, challenging mockery in them. I waited for Andries at the back of the queue, out of the reach of the white man's mocking eyes.

The cold day was at its mildest as we walked home along the sandy road. I took out my piece of bread and, with a small piece of greasy crackling, still warm, on it, I munched as we went along. We had not yet made our peace, so Andries munched his bread and crackling on the other side of the road.

"Dumb fool!" he mocked at me for not knowing how to address the white man.

"Scare arse!" I shouted back.

Thus, hurling curses at each other, we reached the fork. Andries saw them first and moved over to my side of the road.

"White boys," he said.

There were three of them. Two of about our own size and one slightly bigger. They had school bags and were coming toward us up the road from the siding.

"Better run for it," Andries said.

"Why?"

"No, that'll draw them. Let's just walk along, but quickly."

"Why?" I repeated.

"Shut up," he said.

Some of his anxiety touched me. Our own scrap was forgotten. We marched side by side as fast as we could. The white boys saw us and hurried up the road. We passed the fork. Perhaps they would take the turning away from us. We dared not look back.

"Hear them?" Andries asked.

"No."

I looked over my shoulder.

"They're coming," I said.

"Walk faster," Andries said. "If they come closer, run."

"Hey, *Klipkop* [stonehead]!"

"Don't look back," Andries said.

"Hottentot!"

We walked as fast as we could.

"Bloody kaffir [infidel]!"

Ahead was a bend in the road. Behind the bend were bushes. Once there, we could run without them knowing it till it was too late.

"Faster," Andries said.

They began pelting us with stones.

"Run when we get to the bushes," Andries said.

The bend and the bushes were near. We would soon be there.

A clear young voice carried to us:

"Your fathers are dirty black bastards of baboons!"

"Run!" Andries called.

A violent, unreasoning anger suddenly possessed me. I stopped and turned.

"You're a liar!" I screamed it.

The foremost boy pointed at me:

"An ugly black baboon!"

In a fog of rage I went towards him.

"Liar!" I shouted. "My father was better than your father!"

I neared them. The bigger boy stepped between me and the one I was after.

"My father was better than your father! Liar!"

The big boy struck me a mighty clout on the side of the face. I staggered, righted myself, and leapt at the boy who had insulted my father. I struck him on the face, hard. A heavy blow on the back of my head nearly stunned me. I grabbed at the boy in front of me. We went down together.

"Liar!" I said through clenched teeth, hitting him with all my might.

Blows rained on me, on my head, my neck, the side of my face, my mouth, but my enemy was under me and I pounded him fiercely, all the time repeating:

"Liar! Liar! Liar!"

Suddenly, stars exploded in my head. Then there was darkness.

I emerged from the darkness to find Andries kneeling beside me.

"God, man! I thought they'd killed you."

I sat up. The white boys were nowhere to be seen. Like Andries, they'd probably thought me dead and run off in panic. The inside of my mouth felt sore and swollen. My nose was tender to the touch. The back of my head ached. A trickle of blood dripped from my nose. I stemmed it with the square of colored cloth. The greatest damage was to my shirt. It was ripped in many places. I remembered the crackling. I looked anxiously about. It was safe, a little off the road on the grass. I relaxed. I got up and brushed my clothes. I picked up the crackling.

"God, you're dumb!" Andries said. "You're going to get it! Dumb arse!"

I was too depressed to retort. Besides, I knew he was right. I was dumb. I should have run when he told me to.

"Come on," I said.

One of many small groups of children, each child carrying his little bag of crackling, we trod the long road home in the cold winter afternoon.

There was tension in the house that night. When I got back Aunt Liza had listened to the story in silence. The beating or scolding I expected did not come. But Aunt Liza changed while she listened, became remote and withdrawn. When Uncle Sam came home she told him what had happened. He, too, just looked at me and became more remote and withdrawn than usual. They were waiting for something; their tension reached out to me, and I waited with them, anxious, apprehensive.

The thing we waited for came while we were having our supper. We heard a trap pull up outside.

"Here it is," Uncle Sam said and got up.

Aunt Liza leaned back from the table and put her hands in her lap, fingers intertwined, a cold, unseeing look in her eyes.

Before Uncle Sam reached it, the door burst open. A tall, broad, white man strode in. Behind him came the three boys. The one I had attacked had swollen lips and a puffy left eye.

"Evening, *baas!*" Uncle Sam murmured.

"That's him," the bigger boy said, pointing at me.

The white man stared till I lowered my eyes.

"Well?" he said.

"He's sorry, *baas,*" Uncle Sam said quickly. "I've given him a hiding he won't forget soon. You know how it is, *baas.* He's new here, the child of a relative in Johannesburg and they don't all know how to behave there. You know how it is in the big towns, *baas.*" The plea in Uncle Sam's voice had grown more pronounced as he went on. He turned to me. "Tell the *baas* and young *basies* how sorry you are, Lee."

I looked at Aunt Liza and something in her lifelessness made me stubborn in spite of my fear.

"He insulted my father," I said.

The white man smiled.

"See, Sam, your hiding couldn't have been good."

There was a flicker of life in Aunt Liza's eyes. For a brief moment she saw me, looked at me, warmly, lovingly, then her eyes went dead again.

"He's only a child, *baas,*" Uncle Sam murmured.

"You stubborn too, Sam?"

"No, *baas.*"

"Good. . . . Then teach him, Sam. If you and he are to live here, you must teach him. Well. . . .?"

"Yes, *baas.*"

Uncle Sam went into the other room and returned with a thick leather thong. He wound it once round his hand and advanced on me. The man and boys leaned against the door, watching. I looked at Aunt Liza's face. Though there was no sign of life or feeling on it, I knew suddenly, instinctively, that she wanted me not to cry.

Bitterly, Uncle Sam said:

"You must never lift your hand to a white person. No matter what happens, you must never lift your hand to a white person . . ."

He lifted the strap and brought it down on my back. I clenched my teeth and stared at Aunt Liza. I did not cry with the first three strokes. Then, suddenly, Aunt Liza went limp. Tears showed in her eyes. The thong came down on my back, again and again. I screamed and begged for mercy. I grovelled at Uncle Sam's feet, begging him to stop, promising never to lift my hand to any white person. . . .

At last, the white man's voice said:

"All right, Sam."

Uncle Sam stopped. I lay whimpering on the floor. Aunt Liza sat like one in a trance.

"Is he still stubborn, Sam?"

"Tell the *baas* and *basies* you are sorry."

"I'm sorry," I said.

"Bet his father is one of those who believe in equality."

"His father is dead," Aunt Liza said.

"Good night, Sam."

"Good night, *baas.* Sorry about this."

"All right, Sam." He opened the door. The boys went out first, then he followed. "Good night, Liza."

Aunt Liza did not answer. The door shut behind the white folk, and soon we heard their trap moving away. Uncle Sam flung the thong viciously against the door, slumped down on the bench, folded his arms on the table, and buried his head on his arms. Aunt Liza moved away from him, came on the floor beside me and lifted me into her large lap. She sat rocking my body. Uncle Sam began to sob softly. After some time, he raised his head and looked at us.

"Explain to the child, Liza," he said.

"You explain," Aunt Liza said bitterly.

"You are the man. You did the beating. You are the head of the family. This is a man's world. You do the explaining."

"Please, Liza . . . ."

"You should be happy. The whites are satisfied. We can go on now."

With me in her arms, Aunt Liza got up. She carried me into the other room. The food on the table remained half eaten. She laid me on the bed on my stomach, smeared fat on my back, then covered me with the blankets. She undressed and got into bed beside me. She cuddled me close, warmed me with her own body. With her big hand on my cheek, she rocked me, first to silence, then to sleep.

For the only time of my stay there, I slept on a bed in Elsburg.

When I woke next morning Uncle Sam had gone. Aunt Liza only once referred to the beating he had given me. It was in the late afternoon, when I returned with the day's cow dung.

"It hurt him," she said. "You'll understand one day."

That night, Uncle Sam brought me an orange, a bag of boiled sweets, and a dirty old picture book. He smiled as he gave them to me, rather anxiously. When I smiled back at him, he seemed to relax. He put his hand on my head, started to say something, then changed his mind and took his seat by the fire.

Aunt Liza looked up from the floor where she dished out the food.

"It's all right, old man," she murmured.

"One day . . ." Uncle Sam said.

"It's all right," Aunt Liza repeated insistently.

The long winter passed. Slowly, day by day, the world of Elsburg became a warmer place. The cracks in my feet began to heal. The spells of bearable, noonday cold gave way to warmth. The noise of the veld at night became a din. The freezing nights changed, became bearable; changed again, became warm. Warm nights and hot days!

Summer had come, and with its coming the world became a softer, kindlier, more beautiful place. Sunflowers began blooming in people's yards. And people themselves began to relax and laugh. When, one evening, as I came in with some washing from the line, I heard Uncle Sam's voice raised in laughter, and saw him and Aunt Liza playing. I knew the summer had really come. Later that same evening he went into the other room and returned with a guitar. Aunt Liza beamed.

"Open the door?"

Uncle Sam nodded. He played. Soon people from the other houses came, in ones and twos, till our little room was crowded. Someone sang with his arms on his wife's shoulders, a love song:

> *I'll be your sweetheart,*
> *If you will be mine . . .*

Summer had come indeed.

In the long summer afternoons, after my day's work, I went down to the river. Sometimes Andries and some of the other children went with me. Often I went alone.

Often, with others, or alone, I climbed the short willows with their long drooping branches. The touch of willow leaf on the cheek gives a feeling of cool wonder. Often I jumped from stone to stone on the broad bed of the shallow, clear, fast-flowing river. Sometimes I found little pools of idle water, walled off by stones from the flow. I tickled long-tailed tadpoles in these. The sun on the water touched their bodies with myriad colors. Sometimes I watched the *springhaas* —the wild rabbit of the veld—go leaping across the land, almost faster than my eye could follow. And sometimes I lay on my back, on the green grass, on the bank of the river, and looked up at the distant sky, watching thin fleecy white clouds form and re-form and trying to associate the shapes with people and things I knew. I loved being alone by the river. It became my special world.

Each day I explored a little more of the river, going further up or down stream, extending the frontiers of my world. One day, going further downstream than I had been before, I came upon a boy. He was on the other side from me. We saw each other at the same time and stared. He was completely naked. He carried two finely carved sticks of equal size and shape, both about his own height. He was not light brown, like the other children of our location, but dark brown, almost black. I moved almost to the edge of the river. He called out in a strange language.

"Hello!" I shouted.

He called out again, and again I could not understand. I searched for a place with stones, then bounded across. I approached him slowly. As I drew near, he gripped his sticks more firmly. I stopped.

He spoke harshly, flung one stick on the ground at my feet, and held the other ready as though to fight.

"Don't want to fight," I said.

I reached down to pick up the stick and return it to him. He took a step forward and raised the one in his hand. I moved back quickly. He stepped back and pointed at the stick on the ground. I shook my head.

"Don't want to fight."

I pushed the stick toward him with my foot, ready to run at the first sign of attack. I showed my new, stubby teeth in a tentative smile. He said something that sounded less aggressive. I nodded, smiling more broadly. He relaxed, picked up the stick, and transferred both to his left hand. He smacked his chest.

"Joseph! Zulu!"

I smacked my own chest.

"Lee . . . ." But I didn't know what I was apart from that.

He held out his hand. We shook. His face lit up in a sunny smile. He said something and pointed downstream. Then he took my arm and led me down.

Far downstream, where the river skirted a hillside, hidden by a cluster of willows, we came on a large clear pool. Joseph flung his sticks on the ground and dived in. He shot through the water like a tadpole. He went down and came up. He shouted and beckoned me to come in. I undressed and went in more tentatively. Laughing, he pulled me under. I came up gasping and spluttering, my belly filled with water. He smacked me on the back and the water shot out of my mouth in a rush. When he realized I could not swim he became more careful. We spent the afternoon with Joseph teaching me to swim. At home, that evening, I stood beside Aunt Liza's wash-tub.

"Aunt Liza. . . ."

"Yes?"

"What am I?"

"What are you talking about?"

"I met a boy at the river. He said he was Zulu."

She laughed.

"You are Colored. There are three kinds of people: white people, Colored people and black people. The white people come first, then the Colored people, then the black people."

"Why?"

"Because it is so."

Next day, when I met Joseph, I smacked my chest and said: "Lee Colored!"

He clapped his hands and laughed.

Joseph and I spent most of the long summer afternoons together. He learnt some Afrikaans from me; I learnt some Zulu from him. Our days were full.

There was the river to explore.

There were my swimming lessons, and others.

I learnt to fight with sticks; to weave a

green hat of young willow wands and leaves; to catch frogs and tadpoles with my hands; to set a trap for the *springhaas;* to make the sounds of the river birds.

There was the hot sun to comfort us . . . .

There was the green grass to dry our bodies . . . .

There was the soft clay with which to build . . . .

There was the fine sand with which to fight . . . .

There were our giant grasshoppers to race . . . .

There were the locust swarms when the skies turned black and we caught them by the hundreds . . . .

There was the rare taste of crisp, brown, baked, salted locusts . . . .

There was the voice of the wind in the willows . . . .

There was the voice of the heaven in the thunderstorms . . . .

There were the voices of two children in laughter, ours . . . .

There were Joseph's tales of black kings who lived in days before the white man . . . .

At home, I said:

"Aunt Liza . . . ."

"Yes?"

"Did we have Colored kings before the white man?"

"No."

"Then where did we come from? Joseph and his mother come from the black kings who were before the white man."

And laughing, and ruffling my head, she said:

"You talk too much. . . . Go'n wash up."

And to Joseph, next day, I said:

"We didn't have Colored kings before the white man."

And he comforted me and said:

"It is of no moment. You are my brother. Now my kings will be your kings. Come: I have promised the mother to bring you home. She awaits you. I will race you to the hill."

From the top of the hill I looked into a long valley where cattle grazed. To the right, on the sloping land, nestled a cluster of mud huts. Round each hut was a wall built of mud.

"That is my home." Joseph pointed.

We veered right and went down to it. From a distance, we saw a woman at the gate of one of the huts.

"There is the mother!" He walked faster.

She was barefooted. She wore a slight skirt that came above her knees. A child was strapped to her back. The upper part of her body was naked except for the cloth across her chest that supported the child. Round her neck, arms, and legs were strings of white beads. As we drew near, I saw that she was young. And her broad, round face was beautiful. Her black eyes were liquid soft. She called out a greeting and smiled. Joseph pushed me forward.

"This is my brother, Lee of the Coloreds, little mother."

"Greetings, Mother," I said.

"I greet you, my son," she said softly, a twinkle in her eyes.

"As the man of my house has told you, food awaits. Come."

"See!" Joseph puffed out his chest. To his mother he said, "He would not believe when I told him I was the man in our house."

"He is indeed," she said.

Circling the hut was a raised platform. We sat on this while she brought us the food, salted fried locusts and corn on the cob. She sat nearby and watched us eating.

"Show the mother," Joseph said, and took another bite at the *mielies*. "Show the mother you are not circumcised yet."

I showed her.

"This is strange," she said. "Have you no initiation schools?"

"No!" Joseph said.

"Then when do you enter manhood?"

"He does not know."

"Is it true?" She looked at me.

I nodded.

"He's still a child!" Joseph cried. "So big and a child!"

Christmas came and it was a feast of eating and laughter. I spent half my time at home with Aunt Liza and Uncle Sam and the other half with Joseph and the little mother.

My sixth birthday came. Joseph and the little mother and I celebrated it by the river.

Then, early one morning, just as the first cold touches crept into the morning air, Joseph came to our location.

I was washing up when I heard young voices shouting:

"Look at the naked kaffir! Lee's kaffir!"

I rushed out. Joseph came gravely to me.

"I come to take leave, my brother. My father has died in the mines so we go back to our land."

He stood straight and stern, not heeding the shouts of the children about. He was a man. This was the burden of his manhood. I had learned much from him, so I said equally coldly:

"I must take leave of the little mother."

"She is a woman. She weeps."

We ran all the way there . . . .

When the little cart had taken them away, I climbed the hill and went down to the river. I carried Joseph's two sticks with me. These were his parting gift to his brother.

"Defend yourself," he had said. "I will make others."

I walked along the river that had been our kingdom. Now it was a desolate place. Joseph had been here with me; now Joseph had gone. Before I realized it, my tears flowed fast. There had been much between us.

So the summer passed. The autumn came. The leaves went brown on the willows by the river. They fluttered to the ground and turned to mould. The long days shortened suddenly. The cold came. Winter had come to torture us again.

André M. Tao-Kim-Hai

ORIENTALS ARE STOIC

The most peaceful moments of my first stay in an American hospital came just after my operation. Bandaged, half doped, faintly aching I lay flat on my back between smooth, clean sheets and hazily reflected that nothing is more annoying than a fresh incision with fresh stitches in one's abdomen except, of course, two fresh incisions with fresh stitches in one's abdomen. The thought, for some reason, made me chuckle, and the chuckle made me more than intellectually aware of the incisions—the result of that morning's operation for double hernia. But even pain did not quite touch me, and in the euphoria of ether intoxication I felt at one with the whole world, whose center for me was this New York hospital. I did not expect then that only a few days later I would commit there the most unpardonable sin for an Oriental (I am Vietnamese)—that of losing face through one's own bad behavior. But lose face I did, and to this day I wonder whether my shame was caused by the hypersensitivity of an ethnic minority group reduced to one specimen, or by my secret desire not to be treated as a foreigner in my wife's native land, or by my old, ill-suppressed Oriental prejudice against being openly pushed around by women, or simply by the fact that I had never been a hospital patient before and was hopelessly unprepared for the efficient, cold-blooded, and frequently, it seemed, nonsensical routines that are so familiar and so irritating to most convalescents. I still don't know, in short, whether my behavior was a display of just indignation or a childish tantrum.

I had a nurse, of course, after my operation—a woman whose white hair was ineffectually covered by a ridiculously small white bonnet, and who fluttered around my little private room with concentrated energy and, I am sure, efficiency. Despite a few minor differences, she reminded me of a Sister of Charity whom I had known twenty-eight years earlier in the Vietnamese town of Soctrang. My brother and I referred to this nun between ourselves as the *ange de charité*—a cliché we employed with no hint of irony because we knew she worked without salary and because the two huge, triangular white wings of her coif flapped over her shoulders angelically whenever she moved. On her flat chest she wore a black wooden cross with a worn metal Christ on it, and from her belt swung a long, heavy rosary. She was gentle and cheerful, as we imagined angels to be, although she sang in a French strongly tinged with a Marseille accent, which we somehow felt was not the true tone of angels. Did my New York nurse speak French? I was too weak in the hours following the operation to find out, and too weak even to try to identify her accent, which might have been that of Brooklyn. She was plump and there was none of the self-less gentleness of the nun about her. But a nurse is a nurse, I told myself, and therefore an angel. With this re-assuring conclusion, I closed my eyes and sank back into the fog of ether, thinking about how poorly my childhood had prepared me for modern medical care.

I was born in a small village on the banks of a canal, among the rich rice fields of South Vietnam. According to local standards, my father was a wealthy man, for he owned over a hundred and twenty hectares of rice fields, and our family lived in an enclosure containing a tile-roofed master house and several thatch-roofed outbuildings for farm hands, domestic servants, water buffaloes, and agricultural implements. This was an inviting world for a young boy, and I enjoyed it in an active, almost head-long fashion, collecting a vast assortment of cuts and bumps along the way. Whenever I hurt myself I would cry to get my mother's attention. She would come at once to scold not me but the object that hurt me, and then would rub my bruise or wash my cut with rain water, as the case might be (we had no clinic in our village, and no arnica or mercurochrome in our household), and tell me to forget about it. Then she would carry me across the yard to my favorite old water buffalo, and I would have an extra ride on his back all around our compound, to inspect the sparrow nests under the eaves of our red tile roof, to pass in review the dwarf coconut palms along the wide ditches where our barges were moored, or to pick hibiscus flowers from the hedge that separated our compound from the communal canal. Or, if it was raining, my mother would lay me in a hammock and swing it gently with one foot while she sat in a wicker chair beside me and read me passages from ancient stories that were full of heroes who suffered with equanimity—including a general who had a broken arrowhead removed from one arm and the wound cleansed with rice alcohol while playing Chinese chess with his free hand.

My older brother was, in his small way, another example to me. If he had a toothache, he would hold a spoonful of rice alcohol in his mouth—a Vietnamese remedy based on the principle of fighting pain with fire—without whimpering. He would even challenge me, in sign language, to one of the innumerable games Vietnamese children have played for generations, and, leering at me derisively over his mouthful of fire, beat me, no matter what the game. The fact that he was incapable of comment or small talk only added to his importance.

After my father's death, in 1910, my education fell temporarily to my mother and to one or another of her younger brothers. Maternal Uncle Number Three was a true scholar, whose philosophy was based on a mingling of native tradition, Taoism, Confucianism, and Buddhism. Along with my letters, he taught me our fundamental Vietnamese beliefs—among them the concept of man's three souls. The Superior Man, he often told me, pays little attention to his vegetative soul, restrains his animal soul under all circumstances, and strives to develop his spiritual soul as much as possible, in order to distinguish himself from cabbages, eggplants, coconut palms, cats, dogs, pigs, and water buffaloes. This uncle had a vegetative soul plagued by a number of minor tropical diseases—malaria and various skin eruptions—but he sternly refused to take notice of its sufferings. He classified his internal troubles into two categories—those caused by an excess of internal heat, to be treated with rhinoceros horn, and those caused by a deficiency of internal heat, to be treated with ginger. The first medicine is prepared by patiently rubbing a rhinoceros horn—from which the rhinoceros has been detached, of course—across the rough inner surface of an earthenware bowl containing cold water. When the water becomes milky, you drink it until your fever subsides. The second remedy is no more than a hot infusion of fresh ginger sweetened with rock sugar. You drink it until you feel warmer, which is very soon. My uncle had no quarrel with other local medicinal products, such as deer antler, dried bumblebees, tiger bones, ginseng, orange peel, and mint, but he saw no reason to complicate his life with them when he had a rhinoceros horn stored in a tin box and ginger growing in his own yard. As for surgical operations, he considered them sins against filial piety. Were they not mutilations of one's body, which was a precious gift from one's parents and not to be tampered with under any circumstances?

The concessions he did make to illness were rare and grudging. He bore his skin diseases without even scratching. He would drink rhinoceros-horn water and bathe himself with it from time to time, although he expected no rapid results. My mother used to bathe our mangy dogs in creosote diluted with water, and she urged my uncle to try the same cure for his skin troubles. "Of course, it must hurt a little," she said, "but it does the dogs a lot of good. You, Little Brother, have the same vegetative soul that dogs have, so why don't you try it?"

Little Brother resented this reminder of the least of his three souls. He was also an adult Vietnamese and only human, and was therefore suspicious of the creosote because it came in a bottle with a French label. But to prove to his elder sister that he did not shy away from pain he bathed himself once or twice with her dog medicine, proving simultaneously that it did not hasten the purging of his blood.

Malaria made him more coöperative with his vegetative soul. In some uncanny fashion, he knew when he was about to have a malarial seizure, and he would prepare his mat and his concoctions beforehand. As soon as he started to feel the chill, he would drink the ginger, lie down on his mat, and shake lamentably. After a time, the chill would pass, and there would be a little lull. Then the fever would seize him, and he would drink rhinoceros-horn water and perspire profusely for a while—a long while, it seemed to me. When the fever subsided he would sit up, give me a quizzical smile, half of apology and half of pride, and prepare himself a pot of Chinese tea while smoking one of the conical cigarettes he made out of black Vietnamese tobacco and the same coarse white paper I made kites with.

When I went off to a boarding school run by a group of Christian Brothers, I encountered another way of dealing with physical miseries. The *trés cher Frère Infirmier* [very dear Brother Medical Orderly] in charge of the school's infirmary was a fat man with a big red beard, and big blue eyes made bigger by thick lenses, who spoke French and Vietnamese with a Breton accent and who believed in Western medicine and Christian purgatory. Armed with a bottle of iodine and an applicator, he could make the smallest wound feel like a major abscess, and he classified our cuts and bruises as deserving, according to their size, one hundred days, two hundred days, or three hundred days of deliverance from purgatory, provided the patient offered his pain as a sacrifice to the Almighty and did not cry or whimper. Any rise in body temperature—checked with the *cher Frère's* oral thermometer—was followed by the administration of castor oil. The patients stood at attention in a row, and the *Frère Infirmier*, a huge bottle of castor oil in one hand and a teaspoon in the other, passed slowly down the line like a fatherly colonel, explaining to neophytes that they would receive three spoonfuls of the stuff, each worth one hundred days' remission from purgatory if the medicine was bravely offered to God. Sometimes a spoonful of castor oil, through no fault of the recipient, refused to stay down. The *Infirmier* would continue his distribution as though nothing unusual had happened, but he would keep the unfortunate boy after the others had been dismissed, to console him for his medicinal and spiritual loss.

As I lay now on my hard hospital bed and tried to remember the exact appearance of the *Infirmier's* face, my half-closed eyes were struck by a strong electric light switched on over my head. Another face, tanned and kind, seemed to be floating above me. I made an effort to focus on it, and recognized it as that of my surgeon. Behind him was a group of internes.

"How're you doing?" the surgeon asked me in a gentle voice.

"I'm doing all right, Doctor," I answered.

He uncovered me by pulling down the sheet and pulling up my hospital gown. My belly was warm, his fingers were cold, and at the best of times I am ticklish. The result was that I winced, and my face must have shown an inexplicable hilarity. The internes converged on me, watching me seriously. The cold fingers poked; I wiggled and giggled involuntarily. The soft voice asked "Does it hurt?" I answered "No," partly because my flesh was still numb and partly to reassure him that my wiggling was not due to pain. The internes looked on with intense gravity, from which I surmised that I was a rare sort of hospital patient, to be observed with special attention. The examination went on like this for some time, until at last the surgeon covered me again and departed with his solemn retinue.

I had full confidence in my surgeon and liked him, although many of our earlier encounters had been marked by this same kind of foolish misunderstanding. I must admit that at our first meeting, in 1948, I had disliked him. I had joined the United Nations staff in New York in 1946. Two years later, at the conclusion of a routine physical examination—the U.N. had its own clinic and its own staff of doctors giving regular physical checkups to all members of its Secretariat—a charming French-speaking woman doctor told me that she wanted me to see the specialist on hernia. "Just to make sure, you know," she added reassuringly. That was how I met my surgeon. He was nine years younger then, still under thirty and perhaps a little less gentle than he is now. I was far from patient with him, not because of my youth, since I was already forty-three, but because I spoke little English and he knew no French. When he asked me to uncover my middle, I started to explain to him in my slow English that I had never noticed anything wrong. He cut me short with an impatient "Yes, but—"

and plunged a long, firm finger into me. "Cough!" he commanded. I didn't feel like coughing, but I tried to oblige. "Louder!" he snapped. I did my best. He poked harder, and I began to giggle.

"There's nothing to laugh about," he said, and my blood pressure rose several points. After all, I was much older than he (in Vietnam he would have had to call me *ông*, which literally means "grandfather"), and we were of equal rank in the U.N. But my limited English prevented me from making a properly acid retort.

After a few more pokes, the doctor straightened up and asked, "How long have you had this double hernia?"

His tone was an accusation, as if I had known of the hernia all along and had willfully concealed it on my medical questionnaire. But again my English wouldn't come, and I could only answer him with a phrase I had learned from comic strips—"I dunno."

"Why don't you know?" he fired at me.

Nobody had asked me such a question since the days when I was a *soldat de deuxième classe* [second-class private] in the French Army. Sensing my rising temper at last, he tried to make me feel at ease. "You must be a real tough guy," he said.

This was no better. I had heard the epithet "tough guy," but I had always translated it to myself as *"mauvais garçon."* Again he must have seen my anger and incomprehension, because he modified his statement. "You don't pay much attention to minor pains, do you?"

After that, we got along better. He told me that there was no hurry about an operation, but I must come to him for an examination at least once a year. So for the next seven years I dutifully reported to his office, where he would poke and I would jump, and the operation would be postponed, because, he told me, it was only the beginnings of a hernia. Last year, however, I informed him of my decision to retire from the U.N.

and to move to Hawaii, and he said that the time had come for surgery. I was not getting any younger, he told me, and I might not find such good hospital facilities away from New York. My wife voted with the doctor and I reluctantly agreed. I did not then know what was in store for me.

One afternoon late last winter, I presented myself at the hospital, where my wife and I waited patiently and endlessly for a nurse in the admitting office to grant me an audience. At last she produced questionnaires and began to ask me a series of questions that reminded me of my first encounter with the Gestapo, in Marseille in 1943. My difficulties started with the very first questions: "What's your first name? What's your last name?"

Being intellectually scrupulous, I wanted clarification on what she meant by first and last. "First is what comes first. Last is what comes last," the bureaucrat-nurse said with infinite weariness.

My trouble was that we tradition-bound Vietnamese have been more reluctant than the Chinese to Westernize our way of writing our names, even when we live in a Western country, by reversing our usual order of family name first and given name last. My Vietnamese name is Tao-Kim-Hai, the family name Tao, coming first. But when I became a French citizen in 1929, I was required by law to add a Western given name in front of my old name. Thus my full name, André Marie Tao-Kim-Hai, now contains two first names first, then my family name, and then two first names *last*. After much explanation on my part and bored impatience on the nurse's part, my names were written down, but I reduced the name Marie to the initial M, in order to avoid confusing the nurse as to my sex.

"Country of birth?"

This was easy, or so I thought, and I answered without hesitation, "Vietnam."

The young lady held her pen poised but refused to write. "Never heard of it," she said, as if I had just invented a new country.

Vietnam is not a new country. Its first king is thought to have died in the year 2879 B.C. Perhaps an American lady, even a professional and educated lady, cannot be expected to know Vietnamese ancient history, because the name of the country has changed several times. But how about Bao-Dai, Ho Chi Minh, Ngo Dinh Diêm, Saigon, Hanoi, and Diên-Biên-Phu?

"Is it in China?" the nurse asked.

Now, that is a question calculated to drive any Vietnamese wild. The Vietnamese respect China as the seat of a very honorable culture, but they cannot forget the thousand years of war between China and Vietnam. Historically, ethnically, geographically, and politically the lady was wrong, but I drew a deep breath and held my temper. It took a long time, but eventually the nurse passed me, not *cum laude*, and turned me over to a male attendant, who turned me over to a cashier to pay in advance for private nurses. Finally, I was allowed to go to my room.

The room was small but comfortable and well located, with a balcony and a view over the city. When my sister-in-law was in the Soctrang hospital in 1929, she had a whole suite to herself on the ground floor, surrounded by a hedge of blooming hibiscus. Here in New York there was no blooming hibiscus but a hedge of dirty buildings, with a few skyscrapers in the background. Nevertheless, my room cost at least twenty times as much as the suite in the Soctrang hospital and at least twice as much as the room I had occupied in the Waldorf-Astoria in 1945. At that price, I decided, I could expect good service, some comfort, and a certain measure of privacy. I changed my business suit for pajamas and a robe, said goodbye to my wife, and eased myself comfortably into the one armchair and started to read.

The door opened suddenly and a voice boomed "Hi, André!" It was a Catholic priest, plump and jovial, complete with prayer book and stole. "How about Confession and Communion?"

I had told the admitting nurse expressly that although I was a Catholic, I did not want a priest, but here he was. He seemed a bit disappointed when I told him that it was not to be a serious operation, that I expected to survive, and that, anyway, I did not take death as seriously as many other Christians do. I tried to talk religion with him, but he did not seem particularly interested, and left after a few minutes.

Almost immediately, another man came in. He pointed an accusing finger at me and said with what I took to be a Middle European accent, "You have tuberculosis. You have venereal disease. You have—" There was not the slightest interrogative inflection in his voice.

"Who are you?" I interrupted.

"The anesthetist," he answered.

"Parlez-vous français?"

"Oui," he said, and resumed *"Vous avez la tuberculose. Vous avez des maladies vénériennes. Vous avez—"* as affirmatively as ever.

During that first afternoon in the hospital, many other unexpected and unknown visitors came in, always without knocking, without introducing themselves, and without stating their business—except for the man who came to rent me a television set. I was both annoyed and amused, assuming, rightly or wrongly, that all this was the normal routine of an American hospital.

There is nothing to report about the next morning, except that a man came in to prepare me for the operation and a nurse popped in to give me a hypodermic, the significance of which I did not realize until I woke in the afternoon and discovered the incisions in my abdomen.

That evening, when I was fast asleep,

somebody again turned on the light above my head. I looked at my watch and found that it was a few minutes after ten. Two young male internes and a young woman interne were sitting in chairs tilted back against the wall and looking at me. I recognized them as having been in the group that had visited me with the surgeon that afternoon. They smiled at me and I smiled back at them. We talked. One interne said that he had been surprised when I giggled during the surgeon's examination in the afternoon. "Orientals are stoic," he stated sententiously.

I decided that by "stoic" he meant tough, in the way my surgeon meant it when he said I was a tough guy, and I took it to be a compliment. But I wondered about "Orientals" and asked him for his interpretation of the word.

"Chinese, of course," he said.

I asked him if he thought the whole Orient—whatever geographical limits he gave to that word—was peopled by Chinese. To my astonishment, he said that he took it for granted that I was Chinese, and anyway, all yellow people were the same. I asked him if he thought all white people were the same. I saw that he was embarrassed, and I was aware that it was I who was embarrassing him. I tried to put him at ease—as if I were a host in this room, and not a man who had just had an operation and was hoping to be allowed to sleep—with the story of my adventure with some Canadian broadcasters.

A few years back, I told the interne, I had received a telephone call from Ottawa inviting me to go there as the guest of the Canadian Radiodiffusion and read a few pages of French text for a film sound track.

"Don't any of you in Canada speak French any more?" I asked.

"Yes, but we want somebody from the Orient to do it."

"What's the text?" I asked.

But it was a long-distance call, and they didn't want to go into details. I was glad to visit Canada at somebody else's expense and get paid for it besides. I flew to Ottawa, had an excellent French lunch, and was shown the film, which was about India, and I read their text aloud into a microphone. I read it in my own French accent, which had grown out of twenty-two years' residence in France, out of my study of French diction, and out of several years spent as an habitué of the Club du Faubourg, where Parisian orators discuss everything from Paul Valéry to colonialism. When I finished my recording, despair was on the faces of my Canadian hosts. I sensed that I was a complete failure, and said I was sorry.

A French-Canadian said, "*Mais c'est de la Comédie-Française!*[4] Couldn't you read French with an Oriental accent?"

"*Which* Oriental accent?" I replied. I explained that I did not know any of the dozens of languages spoken in India, any more than I knew Japanese or Chinese or Laotian or Cambodian or Malay or Siamese or Burmese, or whatever languages they speak in Afghanistan, Tibet, and Inner and Outer Mongolia. All I knew was Vietnamese, and my Vietnamese friends had told me that I spoke Vietnamese with an American accent, whatever that might be.

At the end of this story, the internes dropped the subject of race and tackled me on Oriental religions. I had a hard time explaining to them that neither Taoism nor Confucianism nor Buddhism is a religion in the Western sense of the word. They shrugged, and one of them said, "Tell us about Oriental food." But here again I had to say that I could find no common denominator for a Japanese *sukiyaki*, a Korean *pulgogi*, an Indonesian *nasi goreng*, a Siamese *mee kraub*, and an Indian curry. And so they left. They had not been unkind, but I had a feeling that they were disappointed by my inability to give them any general ideas and unhappy because they

4 "Your accent is as good as a French actor's."

were no longer sure of the general ideas they had had.

My real troubles started the next morning. Around five, a nurse came into my room and propped both doors wide open. I had never been awakened so early in my life except once in Oxford, where an English maid woke me before dawn to serve me early-morning tea. Here, in the New York hospital, my nurse served me an early-morning thermometer, without asking my consent or coöperation. I resolved to be patient, however, and tried, unsuccessfully, to go back to sleep. Around seven o'clock, I thought it was late enough to ask for a special favor, and I rang. Ten minutes later, a nurse in her late twenties whom I had never seen before came in. Before I had time to ask her please to bring me a cup of coffee or anything hot, and kindly to close the door when leaving, she shouted at me, "Whatsa matta, boy?"

I was nonplussed by the rudeness of her tone and her vocabulary, but I managed to lodge my double request. "Breakfast at eight-thirty," she snapped, and went out immediately—without closing the door.

She went out so fast that I had no time to formulate an appropriate reply. The word "boy" had stung me more than the nurse's tone and manner. I did remember that before my American father-in-law died, my mother-in-law used to explain his occasional absence from their cottage in Florida by saying "He must be out bowling with the boys"—by which she meant a group of gentlemen who were in their seventies. But I also could not forget my personal knowledge that the French in their colonies use the word "boy" to mean "servant." They even call a female servant a "boyesse." Suddenly angry, I wanted to ring for the nurse again and explain all this to her, but then I remembered my conversation with the internes and decided to live up to their high opinion of the stoicism of Orientals.

Around eight-thirty, several nurses invaded my room, all shockingly healthy and cheerful, and chattering like parakeets. I heard a jumble of overlapping greetings and questions, such as "Hi, boy!" "How do you feel this morning, sweetie?" "He looks wonderful!" "Where did you get this beautiful silk robe?" "Here's your breakfast." "Don't you like coffee? You prefer Chinese tea?" and "Soft-boiled eggs—no chop suey here!" I was confused, and I couldn't sort out the questions fast enough to answer any of them. Then a couple of male attendants walked into the crowded room, one of them shouting at me in Chinese, *Ni hau ma? Ni hau pu hau?* When I did not answer, he added, "You Chinese? What dialect you speak? . . . No Chinese? Jap?" The other attendant turned on the television, which responded with a blurred image and a blare of sound.

Suddenly my surgeon came in and the nurses and attendants became silent at once and filed out of the room. Gently he examined me. When he was through, he asked, "How do you feel?"

"Physically, as good as possible," I answered. "Mentally, not so good."

"Why?"

I explained to him that I had the impression of being a rare animal in a zoo. In fact, I added, this was worse than a zoo, because in a zoo the public is not supposed to excite the animals. The surgeon tried to cheer me up, telling me that there was a lack of privacy and social amenities in almost all hospitals. He went as far as to explain the psychology of nurses and hospital workers, who tend to become insensitive because they, fully clothed and able-bodied, habitually deal with more or less helpless patients who are stripped of their business suits and their vertical dignity.

This reasoning cheered me slightly, and I pondered over it later, when a nurse came to wash me. Her method was without consideration or kindness but efficient and thorough. No wonder nurses have a superiority complex, I reasoned as she rubbed my back, and no wonder I feel inferior, being babied like this. I quoted Spinoza to myself. "An emotion which is a passion ceases to be a passion as soon as we form a clear and distinct idea thereof."

But matters did not improve in the succeeding days. I was a "boy," I was a dumb Oriental. I was addressed in what sounded like pidgin English. I heard allusions to what the hospital staff thought of as Oriental ways and Oriental foods. Even my American wife was not spared rudeness, vexation, and humiliation. Although she had an M.A. in Greek before many of the nurses were born, these young ladies took it for granted that the wife of such a strange man could not amount to much. Several times I nearly exploded, but my wife, who can always guess my mood with accuracy, succeeded in calming me. I tried to remember my Maternal Uncle Number Three's teaching about the Superior Man. It was not my job, I told myself, to enlighten the hospital staff about world tolerance or the sensitiveness of one normal Oriental. My job was to restrain my animal, emotional soul and allow my physical, vegetative soul the best possible chance to heal my two incisions.

The moment of drama came unexpectedly. Its protagonist—the external, visible, and immediate cause—was a nurse, but as I think back on it, I realize she was no protagonist at all but only the last straw. Try as I may, I cannot even recall exactly what I said to her, or why I said it. I only remember her reply. "*I* am the supervisor," she said. "*I* am the head nurse here. *I* know my work and I know people like you!"

Jumping hastily and unnecessarily out of bed and fumbling with the telephone, I shouted to the operator, "I want my surgeon! I want him immediately!" Then I raved confusedly, incoherently, childishly, ridiculously. I don't remember most of what

I said; I remember only that the hand grasping the telephone shook and that my legs would barely hold me up. The nurse herself did not seem to trust her eyes; it must have been a scene she was not used to. I shouted at her, "I am a patient! I'm not a nurse! I'm not under your supervision!"

The surgeon came, and I poured out to him all my bitterness as a patient in general and as an Oriental patient in particular. In a loud, shrill tone I told him that a hospital should take care not only of the physical welfare of its patients but of their mental welfare as well, and that nurses should treat their patients as human beings, whatever their race, sex, religion, and state of health. In the middle of my ravings, I again saw the nurse staring at me, her eyes wide open, her mouth slightly ajar, and her arms hanging foolishly down. "If you have nothing to do, get out of here!" I shouted at her. "Get out of here!"

Abruptly, my excitation and exhilaration subsided, and I felt ashamed of myself. I was also angry—angry with myself, with all the nurses on my floor, with the whole hospital, with the entire United States of America, and with all the human stupidity in the world. The surgeon had listened to me in silence. When I had calmed down, he quietly asked me, "Would you like to change floors?"

His gentle suggestion made my anger flare up again, and I cried out, louder than necessary, that I would not retreat. Suddenly finding myself in command of the English language, I said that I wanted to stand my ground and fight it out, to shout back at those who shouted at me, to be sarcastic when I met sarcasm, and to make myself either respected or hated as a patient and as an Oriental.

Gently the doctor eased himself out, and my wife came in. She told me that I had been wrong. I knew she was right, but I shouted at her, too, angrier than ever. She left. I was alone for a long, long time. A feeling of shame overcame me—only shame, nothing more.

Someone knocked at my door—a thing I wasn't used to any more—and I managed a "Come in." A young nurse with red hair appeared with a tray. "Your dinner, sir," she said without any emphasis. It was the natural thing for her to say, but I felt embarrassed, as if I were being shown a special treatment that I did not deserve. Guardedly I smiled at her and thanked her. I readied myself for dinner, co-operating eagerly as she set up the collapsible table. I pointed out to her a box of liqueur chocolates from Holland and invited her to help herself. She did so with grace. I asked her if she spoke French, and—miracle!—she did. She spoke it with a Canadian accent, but it was French all the same. I felt like kissing her then and there, just as I had felt like kissing the first girl I saw in the Free Zone of France after I left Frontstalag[5] 152 in the Occupied Zone, in 1941. In both cases, however, I did not feel that I had won a battle.

From that day on, all the nurses I encountered treated me decently, finishing all their sentences with "sir"—even their supervisor, who reappeared discreetly the next day. I knew that I had behaved badly, that I had not been even faintly civilized, and that I had reacted in sheer animal passion. But I did not know how to apologize to the head nurse without embarrassing her. To make up for my inability to formulate an adequate apology, I coöperated with all the nurses and attendants beyond the call of a patient's duty. I took my own temperature. I took my own bath, sitting on the edge of the tub in my bathroom. I ate all my breakfast, although the eggs were never the way I liked them and the coffee was too American and too weak. I shared my gifts of candy and cookies with all the nurses. My guilt, nevertheless, lingered on, and I wondered if

[5] Prisoner-of-war camp near the front.

the head nurse now tolerated me as a spoiled and incurably ill-bred boy beyond redemption, whether she hated me or possibly even admired me for my outburst, whether future patients in this hospital would profit or suffer from my wild explosion, and whether Orientals would be received here from now on with special attentions or would not be admitted at all. These were some of the questions I was left with as a result of my first experience in a hospital, and I am afraid that I will not find satisfactory answers to them even after my scars fade and are forgotten.

Albert Camus

THE GUEST

The schoolmaster was watching the two men climb toward him. One was on horseback, the other on foot. They had not yet tackled the abrupt rise leading to the schoolhouse built on the hillside. They were toiling onward, making slow progress in the snow, among the stones, on the vast expanse of the high, deserted plateau. From time to time the horse stumbled. Without hearing anything yet, he could see the breath issuing from the horse's nostrils. One of the men, at least, knew the region. They were following the trail although it had disappeared days ago under a layer of dirty white snow. The schoolmaster calculated that it would take them half an hour to get onto the hill. It was cold; he went back into the school to get a sweater.

He crossed the empty, frigid classroom. On the blackboard the four rivers of France, drawn with four different colored chalks, had been flowing toward their estuaries for the past three days. Snow had suddenly fallen in mid-October after eight months of drought without the transition of rain, and the twenty pupils, more or less, who lived in the villages scattered over the plateau had stopped coming. With fair weather they would return. Daru now heated only the single room that was his lodging, adjoining the classroom and giving also onto the plateau to the east. Like the class windows, his window looked to the south too. On that side the school was a few kilometers from the point where the plateau began to slope toward the south. In clear weather could be seen the purple mass of the mountain range where the gap opened onto the desert.

Somewhat warmed, Daru returned to the window from which he had first seen the two men. They were no longer visible. Hence they must have tackled the rise. The sky was not so dark, for the snow had stopped falling during the night. The morning had opened with a dirty light which had scarcely become brighter as the ceiling of clouds lifted. At two in the afternoon it seemed as if the day were merely beginning. But still this was better than those three days when the thick snow was falling amidst unbroken darkness with little gusts of wind that rattled the double door of the classroom. Then Daru had spent long hours in his room, leaving it only to go to the shed and feed the chickens or get some coal. Fortunately the delivery truck from Tadjid,[6] the nearest village to the north, had brought his supplies two days before the blizzard. It would return in forty-eight hours.

Besides, he had enough to resist a siege, for the little room was cluttered with bags of wheat that the administration left as a stock to distribute to those of his pupils whose families had suffered from the drought. Actually they had all been victims because they were all poor. Every day Daru would distribute a ration to the children.

[6] The setting is Algeria, before it won independence from France.

They had missed it, he knew, during these bad days. Possibly one of the fathers or big brothers would come this afternoon and he could supply them with grain. It was just a matter of carrying them over to the next harvest. Now shiploads of wheat were arriving from France and the worst was over. But it would be hard to forget that poverty, that army of ragged ghosts wandering in the sunlight, the plateaus burned to a cinder month after month, the earth shriveled up little by little, literally scorched, every stone bursting into dust under one's foot. The sheep had died then by thousands and even a few men, here and there, sometimes without anyone's knowing.

In contrast with such poverty, he who lived almost like a monk in his remote schoolhouse, nonetheless satisfied with the little he had and with the rough life, had felt like a lord with his white-washed walls, his narrow couch, his unpainted shelves, his well, and his weekly provision of water and food. And suddenly this snow, without warning, without the foretaste of rain. This is the way the region was, cruel to live in, even without men—who didn't help matters either. But Daru had been born here. Everywhere else, he felt exiled.

He stepped out onto the terrace in front of the schoolhouse. The two men were now halfway up the slope. He recognized the horseman as Balducci, the old gendarme he had known for a long time. Balducci was holding on the end of a rope an Arab who was walking behind him with hands bound and head lowered. The gendarme waved a greeting to which Daru did not reply, lost as he was in contemplation of the Arab dressed in a faded blue jellaba [long blouse], his feet in sandals but covered with socks of heavy raw wool, his head surmounted by a narrow, short chèche [scarf]. They were approaching. Balducci was holding back his horse in order not to hurt the Arab, and the group was advancing slowly.

Within earshot, Balducci shouted: "One

hour to do the three kilometers from El Ameur!" Daru did not answer. Short and square in his thick sweater, he watched them climb. Not once had the Arab raised his head. "Hello," said Daru when they got up onto the terrace. "Come in and warm up." Balducci painfully got down from his horse without letting go the rope. From under his bristling mustache he smiled at the schoolmaster. His little dark eyes, deep-set under a tanned forehead, and his mouth surrounded with wrinkles made him look attentive and studious. Daru took the bridle, led the horse to the shed, and came back to the two men, who were now waiting for him in the school. He led them into his room. "I am going to heat up the classroom," he said. "We'll be more comfortable there." When he entered the room again, Balducci was on the couch. He had undone the rope tying him to the Arab, who had squatted near the stove. His hands still bound, the *chèche* pushed back on his head, he was looking toward the window. At first Daru noticed only his huge lips, fat, smooth, almost Negroid; yet his nose was straight, his eyes were dark and full of fever. The *chèche* revealed an obstinate forehead and, under the weathered skin now rather discolored by the cold, the whole face had a restless and rebellious look that struck Daru when the Arab, turning his face toward him, looked him straight in the eyes. "Go into the other room," said the schoolmaster, "and I'll make you some mint tea." "Thanks," Balducci said. "What a chore! How I long for retirement." And addressing his prisoner in Arabic: "Come on, you." The Arab got up and, slowly, holding his bound wrists in front of him, went into the classroom.

With the tea, Daru brought a chair. But Balducci was already enthroned on the nearest pupil's desk and the Arab had squatted against the teacher's platform facing the stove, which stood between the desk and the window. When he held out the glass of tea to the prisoner, Daru hesitated at the

sight of his bound hands. "He might perhaps be untied." "Sure," said Balducci. "That was for the trip." He started to get to his feet. But Daru, setting the glass on the floor, had knelt beside the Arab. Without saying anything, the Arab watched him with his feverish eyes. Once his hands were free, he rubbed his swollen wrists against each other, took the glass of tea, and sucked up the burning liquid in swift little sips.

"Good," said Daru. "And where are you headed?"

Balducci withdrew his mustache from the tea. "Here, son."

"Odd pupils! And you're spending the night?"

"No. I'm going back to El Ameur. And you will deliver this fellow to Tinguit. He is expected at police headquarters."

Balducci was looking at Daru with a friendly little smile.

"What's this story?" asked the schoolmaster. "Are you pulling my leg?"

"No, son. Those are the orders."

"The orders? I'm not . . ." Daru hesitated, not wanting to hurt the old Corsican. "I mean, that's not my job."

"What! What's the meaning of that? In wartime people do all kinds of jobs."

"Then I'll wait for the declaration of war!"

Balducci nodded.

"O.K. But the orders exist and they concern you too. Things are brewing, it appears. There is talk of a forthcoming revolt. We are mobilized, in a way."

Daru still had his obstinate look.

"Listen, son," Balducci said. "I like you and you must understand. There's only a dozen of us at El Ameur to patrol throughout the whole territory of a small department and I must get back in a hurry. I was told to hand this guy over to you and return without delay. He couldn't be kept there. His village was beginning to stir; they wanted to take him back. You must take him to Tinguit tomorrow before the day is over. Twenty kilometers shouldn't faze a husky fellow like you. After that, all will be over. You'll come back to your pupils and your comfortable life.''

Behind the wall the horse could be heard snorting and pawing the earth. Daru was looking out the window. Decidedly, the weather was clearing and the light was increasing over the snowy plateau. When all the snow was melted, the sun would take over again and once more would burn the fields of stone. For days, still, the unchanging sky would shed its dry light on the solitary expanse where nothing had any connection with man.

"After all,'' he said, turning around toward Balducci, "what did he do?'' And, before the gendarme had opened his mouth, he asked: "Does he speak French?''

"No, not a word. We had been looking for him for a month, but they were hiding him. He killed his cousin.''

"Is he against us?''

"I don't think so. But you can never be sure.''

"Why did he kill?''

"A family squabble, I think. One owed the other grain, it seems. It's not at all clear. In short, he killed his cousin with a bill-hook. You know, like a sheep, *kreezk!*''

Balducci made the gesture of drawing a blade across his throat and the Arab, his attention attracted, watched him with a sort of anxiety. Daru felt a sudden wrath against the man, against all men with their rotten spite, their tireless hates, their blood lust.

But the kettle was singing on the stove. He served Balducci more tea, hesitated, then served the Arab again, who, a second time, drank avidly. His raised arms made the jellaba fall open and the schoolmaster saw his thin, muscular chest.

"Thanks kid,'' Balducci said. "And now, I'm off.''

He got up and went toward the Arab, taking a small rope from his pocket.

"What are you doing?'' Daru asked dryly.

Balducci, disconcerted, showed him the rope.

"Don't bother.''

The old gendarme hesitated. "It's up to you. Of course, you are armed?''

"I have my shotgun.''

"Where?''

"In the trunk.''

"You ought to have it near your bed.''

"Why? I have nothing to fear.''

"You're crazy, son. If there's an uprising, no one is safe, we're all in the same boat.''

"I'll defend myself. I'll have time to see them coming.''

Balducci began to laugh, then suddenly the mustache covered the white teeth.

"You'll have time? O.K. That's just what I was saying. You have always been a little cracked. That's why I like you, my son was like that.''

At the same time he took out his revolver and put it on the desk.

"Keep it; I don't need two weapons from here to El Ameur.''

The revolver shone against the black paint of the table. When the gendarme turned toward him, the schoolmaster caught the smell of leather and horseflesh.

"Listen, Balducci,'' Daru said suddenly, "every bit of this disgusts me, and first of all your fellow here. But I won't hand him over. Fight, yes, if I have to. But not that.''

The old gendarme stood in front of him and looked at him severely.

"You're being a fool,'' he said slowly. "I don't like it either. You don't get used to putting a rope on a man even after years of it, and you're even ashamed—yes, ashamed. But you can't let them have their way.''

"I won't hand him over,'' Daru said again.

"It's an order, son, and I repeat it.''

"That's right. Repeat to them what I've said to you: I won't hand him over.''

Balducci made a visible effort to reflect. He looked at the Arab and at Daru. At last he decided.

"No, I won't tell them anything. If you want to drop us, go ahead; I'll not denounce you. I have an order to deliver the prisoner and I'm doing so. And now you'll just sign this paper for me."

"There's no need. I'll not deny that you left him with me."

"Don't be mean with me. I know you'll tell the truth. You're from hereabouts and you are a man. But you must sign, that's the rule."

Daru opened his drawer, took out a little square bottle of purple ink, the red wooden penholder with the "sergeant-major" pen he used for making models of penmanship, and signed. The gendarme carefully folded the paper and put it into his wallet. Then he moved toward the door.

"I'll see you off," Daru said.

"No," said Balducci. "There's no use being polite. You insulted me."

He looked at the Arab, motionless in the same spot, sniffed peevishly, and turned away toward the door. "Good-by, son," he said. The door shut behind him. Balducci appeared suddenly outside the window and then disappeared. His footsteps were muffled by the snow. The horse stirred on the other side of the wall and several chickens fluttered in fright. A moment later Balducci reappeared outside the window leading the horse by the bridle. He walked toward the little rise without turning around and disappeared from sight with the horse following him. A big stone could be heard bouncing down. Daru walked back toward the prisoner, who, without stirring, never took his eyes off him. "Wait," the schoolmaster said in Arabic and went toward the bedroom. As he was going through the door, he had a second thought, went to the desk, took the revolver, and stuck it in his pocket. Then, without looking back, he went into his room.

For some time he lay on his couch watching the sky gradually close over, listening to the silence. It was this silence that had seemed painful to him during the first days here, after the war. He had requested a post in the little town at the base of the foothills separating the upper plateaus from the desert. There, rocky walls, green and black to the north, pink and lavender to the south, marked the frontier of eternal summer. He had been named to a post farther north, on the plateau itself. In the beginning, the solitude and the silence had been hard for him on these wastelands peopled only by stones. Occasionally, furrows suggested cultivation, but they had been dug to uncover a certain kind of stone good for building. The only plowing here was to harvest rocks. Elsewhere a thin layer of soil accumulated in the hollows would be scraped out to enrich paltry village gardens. This is the way it was: bare rock covered three quarters of the region. Towns sprang up, flourished, then disappeared; men came by, loved one another or fought bitterly, then died. No one in this desert, neither he nor his guest, mattered. And yet, outside this desert neither of them, Daru knew, could have really lived.

When he got up, no noise came from the classroom. He was amazed at the unmixed joy he derived from the mere thought that the Arab might have fled and that he would be alone with no decision to make. But the prisoner was there. He had merely stretched out between the stove and the desk. With eyes open, he was staring at the ceiling. In that position, his thick lips were particularly noticeable, giving him a pouting look. "Come," said Daru. The Arab got up and followed him. In the bedroom, the schoolmaster pointed to a chair near the table under the window. The Arab sat down without taking his eyes off Daru.

"Are you hungry?"

"Yes," the prisoner said.

Daru set the table for two. He took flour and oil, shaped a cake in a frying-pan, and lighted the little stove that functioned on bottled gas. While the cake was cooking, he went out to the shed to get cheese, eggs, dates, and condensed milk. When the cake was done he set it on the window sill to cool, heated some condensed milk diluted with water, and beat up the eggs into an omelette. In one of his motions he knocked against the revolver stuck in his right pocket. He set the bowl down, went into the classroom, and put the revolver in his desk drawer. When he came back to the room, night was falling. He put on the light and served the Arab. "Eat," he said. The Arab took a piece of the cake, lifted it eagerly to his mouth, and stopped short.

"And you?" he asked.

"After you. I'll eat too."

The thick lips opened slightly. The Arab hesitated, then bit into the cake determinedly.

The meal over, the Arab looked at the schoolmaster. "Are you the judge?"

"No, I'm simply keeping you until tomorrow."

"Why do you eat with me?"

"I'm hungry."

The Arab fell silent. Daru got up and went out. He brought back a folding bed from the shed, set it up between the table and the stove, perpendicular to his own bed. From a large suitcase which, upright in a corner, served as a shelf for papers, he took two blankets and arranged them on the camp bed. Then he stopped, felt useless, and sat down on his bed. There was nothing more to do or to get ready. He had to look at this man. He looked at him, therefore, trying to imagine his face bursting with rage. He couldn't do so. He could see nothing but the dark yet shining eyes and the animal mouth.

"Why did you kill him?" he asked in a voice whose hostile tone surprised him.

The Arab looked away.

"He ran away. I ran after him."

He raised his eyes to Daru again and they were full of a sort of woeful interrogation. "Now what will they do to me?"

"Are you afraid?"

He stiffened, turning his eyes away.

"Are you sorry?"

The Arab stared at him openmouthed. Obviously he did not understand. Daru's annoyance was growing. At the same time he felt awkward and self-conscious with his big body wedged between the two beds.

"Lie down there," he said impatiently. "That's your bed."

The Arab didn't move. He called to Daru: "Tell me!"

The schoolmaster looked at him.

"Is the gendarme coming back tomorrow?"

"I don't know."

"Are you coming with us?"

"I don't know. Why?"

The prisoner got up and stretched out on top of the blankets, his feet toward the window. The light from the electric bulb shone straight into his eyes and he closed them at once.

"Why?" Daru repeated, standing beside the bed.

The Arab opened his eyes under the blinding light and looked at him, trying not to blink.

"Come with us," he said.

In the middle of the night, Daru was still not asleep. He had gone to bed after undressing completely; he generally slept naked. But when he suddenly realized that he had nothing on, he hesitated. He felt vulnerable and the temptation came to him to put his clothes back on. Then he shrugged his shoulders; after all, he wasn't a child and, if need be, he could break his adversary in two. From his bed he could observe him, lying on his back, still motionless with his eyes closed under the harsh light. When Daru turned out the light, the darkness seemed to coagulate all of a sudden. Little by little, the night came back to life in the window where the starless sky was stirring gently. The schoolmaster soon made out the body lying at his feet. The Arab still did not move, but his eyes seemed open. A faint wind was prowling around the schoolhouse. Perhaps it would drive away the clouds and the sun would reappear.

During the night the wind increased. The hens fluttered a little and then were silent. The Arab turned over on his side with his back to Daru, who thought he heard him moan. Then he listened for his guest's breathing, become heavier and more regular. He listened to that breath so close to him and mused without being able to go to sleep. In this room where he had been sleeping alone for a year, this presence bothered him. But it bothered him also by imposing on him a sort of brotherhood he knew well but refused to accept in the present circumstances. Men who share the same rooms, soldiers or prisoners, develop a strange alliance as if, having cast off their armor with their clothing, they fraternized every evening, over and above their differences, in the ancient community of dream and fatigue. But Daru shook himself; he didn't like such musings, and it was essential to sleep.

A little later, however, when the Arab stirred slightly, the schoolmaster was still not asleep. When the prisoner made a second move, he stiffened, on the alert. The Arab was lifting himself slowly on his arms with almost the motion of a sleepwalker. Seated upright in bed, he waited motionless without turning his head toward Daru, as if he were listening attentively. Daru did not stir; it had just occurred to him that the revolver was still in the drawer of his desk. It was better to act at once. Yet he continued to observe the prisoner, who, with the same slithery motion, put his feet on the ground, waited again, then began to stand up slowly. Daru was about to call out to him when the Arab began to walk, in a quite natural but extraordinarily silent way. He was heading toward the door at the end of the room that opened into the shed. He lifted the latch with precaution and went out, pushing the door behind him but without shutting it. Daru had not stirred. "He is running away," he merely thought. "Good riddance!" Yet he listened attentively. The hens were not fluttering; the guest must be on the plateau. A faint sound of water reached him, and he didn't know what it was until the Arab again stood framed in the doorway, closed the door carefully, and came back to bed without a sound. Then Daru turned his back on him and fell asleep. Still later he seemed, from the depths of his sleep, to hear furtive steps around the schoolhouse. "I'm dreaming! I'm dreaming!" he repeated to himself. And he went on sleeping.

When he awoke, the sky was clear; the loose window let in a cold, pure air. The Arab was asleep, hunched up under the blankets now, his mouth open, utterly relaxed. But when Daru shook him, he started dreadfully, staring at Daru with wild eyes as if he had never seen him and such a frightened expression that the schoolmaster stepped back. "Don't be afraid. It's me. You must eat." The Arab nodded his head and said yes. Calm had returned to his face, but his expression was vacant and listless.

The coffee was ready. They drank it seated together on the folding bed as they munched their pieces of the cake. Then Daru led the Arab under the shed and showed him the faucet where he washed. He went back into the room, folded the blankets and the bed, made his own bed and put the room in order. Then he went through the classroom and out onto the terrace. The sun was already rising in the blue sky; a soft, bright light was bathing the deserted plateau. On the ridge the snow was melting in spots. The stones were about to reappear. Crouched on the edge of the plateau, the schoolmaster looked at the deserted expanse. He thought of Balducci. He had hurt him, for he had sent him off in a way as if he didn't want to be associated with him. He could still hear the gendarme's farewell and, without knowing why, he felt strangely empty and vulnerable. At that moment, from the other side of the schoolhouse, the prisoner coughed. Daru listened to him almost despite himself and then, furious, threw a pebble that whistled through the air before sinking into the snow. That man's stupid crime revolted him, but to hand him over was contrary to honor. Merely thinking of it made him smart with humiliation. And he cursed at one and the same time his own people who had sent him this Arab and the Arab too who had dared to kill and not managed to get away. Daru got up, walked in a circle on the terrace, waited motionless, and then went back into the schoolhouse.

The Arab, leaning over the cement floor of the shed, was washing his teeth with two fingers. Daru looked at him and said: "Come." He went back into the room ahead of the prisoner. He slipped a hunting-jacket on over his sweater and put on walking-shoes. Standing, he waited until the Arab had put on his *chèche* and sandals. They went into the classroom and the schoolmaster pointed to the exit, saying: "Go ahead." The fellow didn't budge. "I'm coming," said Daru. The Arab went out. Daru went back into the room and made a package of pieces of rusk, dates, and sugar. In the classroom, before going out, he hesitated a second in front of his desk, then crossed the threshold and locked the door. "That's the way," he said. He started toward the east, followed by the prisoner. But, a short distance from the schoolhouse, he thought he heard a slight sound behind

them. He retraced his steps and examined the surroundings of the house; there was no one there. The Arab watched him without seeming to understand. "Come on," said Daru.

They walked for an hour and rested beside a sharp peak of limestone. The snow was melting faster and faster and the sun was drinking up the puddles at once, rapidly cleaning the plateau, which gradually dried and vibrated like the air itself. When they resumed walking, the ground rang under their feet. From time to time a bird rent the space in front of them with a joyful cry. Daru breathed in deeply the fresh morning light. He felt a sort of rapture before the vast familiar expanse, now almost entirely yellow under its dome of blue sky. They walked an hour more, descending toward the south. They reached a level height made up of crumbly rocks. From there on, the plateau sloped down, eastward, toward a low plain where there were a few spindly trees and, to the south, toward outcroppings of rock that gave the landscape a chaotic look.

Daru surveyed the two directions. There was nothing but the sky on the horizon. Not a man could be seen. He turned toward the Arab, who was looking at him blankly. Daru held out the package to him. "Take it," he said. "There are dates, bread, and sugar. You can hold out for two days. Here are a thousand francs too." The Arab took the package and the money but kept his full hands at chest level as if he didn't know what to do with what was being given him. "Now look," the schoolmaster said as he pointed in the direction of the east, "there's the way to Tinguit. You have a two-hour walk. At Tinguit you'll find the administration and the police. They are expecting you." The Arab looked toward the east, still holding the package and the money against his chest. Daru took his elbow and turned him rather roughly toward the south. At the foot of the height on which they stood could be seen a faint path. "That's the trail across the plateau. In a day's walk from here you'll find pasturelands and the first nomads. They'll take you in and shelter you according to their law." The Arab had now turned toward Daru and a sort of panic was visible in his expression. "Listen," he said. Daru shook his head: "No, be quiet. Now I'm leaving you." He turned his back on him, took two long steps in the direction of the school, looked hesitantly at the motionless Arab, and started off again. For a few minutes he heard nothing but his own step resounding on the cold ground and did not turn his head. A moment later, however, he turned around. The Arab was still there on the edge of the hill, his arms hanging now, and he was looking at the schoolmaster. Daru felt something rise in his throat. But he swore with impatience, waved vaguely, and started off again. He had already gone some distance when he again stopped and looked. There was no longer anyone on the hill.

Daru hesitated. The sun was now rather high in the sky and was beginning to beat down on his head. The schoolmaster retraced his steps, at first somewhat uncertainly, then with decision. When he reached the little hill, he was bathed in sweat. He climbed it as fast as he could and stopped, out of breath, at the top. The rock-fields to the south stood out sharply against the blue sky, but on the plain to the east a steamy heat was already rising. And in that slight haze, Daru, with heavy heart, made out the Arab walking slowly on the road to prison.

A little later, standing before the window of the classroom, the schoolmaster was watching the clear light bathing the whole surface of the plateau, but he hardly saw it. Behind him on the blackboard, among the winding French rivers, sprawled the clumsily chalked-up words he had just read: "You handed over our brother. You will pay for this." Daru looked at the sky, the plateau, and, beyond, the invisible lands stretching all the way to the sea. In this vast landscape he had loved so much, he was alone.

Flannery O'Connor

GREENLEAF

Mrs. May's bedroom window was low and faced on the east and the bull, silvered in the moonlight, stood under it, his head raised as if he listened—like some patient god come down to woo her—for a stir inside the room. The window was dark and the sound of her breathing too light to be carried outside. Clouds crossing the moon blackened him and in the dark he began to tear at the hedge. Presently they passed and he appeared again in the same spot, chewing steadily, with a hedge-wreath that he had ripped loose for himself caught in the tips of his horns. When the moon drifted into retirement again, there was nothing to mark his place but the sound of steady chewing. Then abruptly a pink glow filled the window. Bars of light slid across him as the venetian blind was slit. He took a step backward and lowered his head as if to show the wreath across his horns.

For almost a minute there was no sound from inside, then as he raised his crowned head again, a woman's voice, guttural as if addressed to a dog, said, "Get away from here, Sir!" and in a second muttered, "Some nigger's scrub bull."

The animal pawed the ground and Mrs. May, standing bent forward behind the blind, closed it quickly lest the light make him charge into the shrubbery. For a second she waited, still bent forward, her nightgown hanging loosely from her narrow shoulders. Green rubber curlers sprouted neatly over her forehead and her face beneath them was smooth as concrete with an egg-white paste that drew the wrinkles out while she slept.

She had been conscious in her sleep of a steady rhythmic chewing as if something were eating one wall of the house. She had been aware that whatever it was had been eating as long as she had had the place and had eaten everything from the beginning of her fence line up to the house and now was eating the house and calmly with the same steady rhythm would continue through the house, eating her and the boys, and then on, eating everything but the Greenleafs, on and on, eating everything until nothing was left but the Greenleafs on a little island all their own in the middle of what had been her place. When the munching reached her elbow, she jumped up and found herself, fully awake, standing in the middle of her room. She identified the sound at once: a cow was tearing at the shrubbery under her window. Mr. Greenleaf had left the lane gate open and she didn't doubt that the entire herd was on her lawn. She turned on the dim pink table lamp and then went to the window and slit the blind. The bull, gaunt and long-legged, was standing about four feet from her, chewing calmly like an uncouth country suitor.

For fifteen years, she thought as she squinted at him fiercely, she had been having shiftless people's hogs root up her oats, their mules wallow on her lawn, their scrub bulls breed her cows. If this one was not put up now, he would be over the fence, ruining her herd before morning—and Mr. Greenleaf was soundly sleeping a half mile down the road in the tenant house. There was no way to get him unless she dressed and got into her car and rode down there and woke him up. He would come but his expression, his whole figure, his every pause, would say, "Hit looks to me like one or both of them boys would not make their maw ride out in the middle of the night thisaway.

If hit was my boys, they would have got thet bull up theirself."

The bull lowered his head and shook it and the wreath slipped down to the base of his horns where it looked like a menacing prickly crown. She had closed the blind then; in a few seconds she heard him move off heavily.

Mr. Greenleaf would say, "If hit was my boys they would never have allowed their maw to go after hired help in the middle of the night. They would have did it theirself."

Weighing it, she decided not to bother Mr. Greenleaf. She returned to bed thinking that if the Greenleaf boys had risen in the world it was because she had given their father employment when no one else would have him. She had had Mr. Greenleaf fifteen years but no one else would have had him five minutes. Just the way he approached an object was enough to tell anybody with eyes what kind of a worker he was. He walked with a high-shouldered creep and he never appeared to come directly forward. He walked on the perimeter of some invisible circle and if you wanted to look him in the face, you had to move and get in front of him. She had not fired him because she had always doubted she could do better. He was too shiftless to go out and look for another job; he didn't have the initiative to steal, and after she had told him three of four times to do a thing, he did it; but he never told her about a sick cow until it was too late to call the veterinarian and if her barn had caught on fire, he would have called his wife to see the flames before he began to put them out. And of the wife, she didn't even like to think. Beside the wife, Mr. Greenleaf was an aristocrat.

"If it had been my boys," he would have said, "they would have cut off their right arm before they would have allowed their maw to. . . ."

"If your boys had any pride, Mr. Greenleaf," she would like to say to him some day, "there are many things that they would not *allow* their mother to do."

The next morning as soon as Mr. Greenleaf came to the back door, she told him there was a stray bull on the place and that she wanted him penned up at once.

"Done already been here three days." he said, addressing his right foot which he held forward, turned slightly as if he were trying to look at the sole. He was standing at the bottom of the three back steps while she leaned out the kitchen door, a small woman with pale near-sighted eyes and grey hair that rose on top like the crest of some disturbed bird.

"Three days!" she said in the restrained screech that had become habitual with her.

Mr. Greenleaf, looking into the distance over the near pasture, removed a package of cigarets from his shirt pocket and let one fall into his hand. He put the package back and stood for a while looking at the cigaret. "I put him in the bull pen but he torn out of there," he said presently. "I didn't see him none after that." He bent over the cigaret and lit it and then turned his head briefly in her direction. The upper part of his face sloped gradually into the lower which was long and narrow, shaped like a rough chalice. He had deep-set fox-colored eyes shadowed under a grey felt hat that he wore slanted forward following the line of his nose. His build was insignificant.

"Mr. Greenleaf," she said, "get that bull up this morning before you do anything else. You know he'll ruin the breeding schedule. Get him up and keep him up and the next time there's a stray bull on this place, tell me at once. Do you understand?"

"Where you want him put at?" Mr. Greenleaf asked.

"I don't care where you put him," she said. "You are supposed to have some sense.

Put him where he can't get out. Whose bull is he?"

For a moment Mr. Greenleaf seemed to hesitate between silence and speech. He studied the air to the left of him. "He must be somebody's bull," he said after a while.

"Yes, he must!" she said and shut the door with a precise little slam.

She went into the dining room where the two boys were eating breakfast and sat down on the edge of her chair at the head of the table. She never ate breakfast but she sat with them to see that they had what they wanted. "Honestly!" she said, and began to tell about the bull, aping Greenleaf saying, "It must be *somebody's* bull."

Wesley continued to read the newspaper folded beside his plate but Scofield interrupted his eating from time to time to look at her and laugh. The two boys never had the same reaction to anything. They were as different, she said, as night and day. The only thing they did have in common was that neither of them cared what happened on the place. Scofield was a business type and Wesley was an intellectual.

Wesley, the younger child, had had rheumatic fever when he was seven and Mrs. May thought that this was what had caused him to be an intellectual. Scofield, who had never had a day's sickness in his life, was an insurance salesman. She would not have minded his selling insurance if he had sold a nicer kind but he sold the kind that only Negroes buy. He was what Negroes call a "policy man." He said there was more money in nigger-insurance that any other kind, and before company, he was very loud about it. He would shout, "Mamma don't like to hear me say it but I'm the best nigger-insurance salesman in this county!"

Scofield was thirty-six and he had a broad pleasant smiling face but he was not married. "Yes," Mrs. May would say, "and if you sold decent insurance, some *nice* girl would be willing to marry you. What nice girl wants to marry a nigger-insurance man? You'll wake up some day and it'll be too late."

And at this Scofield would yodel and say, "Why Mamma, I'm not going to marry until you're dead and gone and then I'm going to marry me some nice fat farm girl that can take over this place!" And once he had added, "—some nice lady like Mrs. Greenleaf." When he had said this, Mrs. May had risen from her chair, her back stiff as a rake handle, and had gone to her room. There she had sat down on the edge of her bed for some time with her small face drawn. Finally she had whispered, "I work and slave, I struggle and sweat to keep this place for them and soon as I'm dead, they'll marry trash and bring it in here and ruin everything. They'll marry trash and ruin everything I've done," and she had made up her mind at that moment to change her will. The next day she had gone to her lawyer and had had the property entailed so that if they married, they could not leave it to their wives.

The idea that one of them might marry a woman even remotely like Mrs. Greenleaf was enough to make her ill. She had put up with Mr. Greenleaf for fifteen years, but the only way she had endured his wife had been by keeping entirely out of her sight. Mrs. Greenleaf was large and loose. The yard around her house looked like a dump and her five girls were always filthy; even the youngest one dipped snuff. Instead of making a garden or washing their clothes, her preoccupation was what she called "prayer healing."

Every day she cut all the morbid stories out of the newspaper—the accounts of women who had been raped and criminals who had escaped and children who had been burned and of train wrecks and plane crashes and the divorces of movie stars. She took these to the woods and dug a hole and buried them and then she fell on the ground over them and mumbled and groaned for

an hour or so, moving her huge arms back and forth under her and out again and finally just lying down flat and, Mrs. May suspected, going to sleep in the dirt.

She had not found out about this until the Greenleafs had been with her a few months. One morning she had been out to inspect a field that she had wanted planted in rye but that had come up in clover because Mr. Greenleaf had used the wrong seeds in the grain drill. She was returning through a wooded path that separated two pastures, muttering to herself and hitting the ground methodically with a long stick she carried in case she saw a snake. "Mr. Greenleaf," she was saying in a low voice, "I cannot afford to pay for your mistakes. I am a poor woman and this place is all I have. I have two boys to educate. I cannot . . . ."

Out of nowhere a guttural agonized voice groaned, "Jesus! Jesus!" In a second it came again with a terrible urgency. "Jesus! Jesus!"

Mrs. May stopped still, one hand lifted to her throat. The sound was so piercing that she felt as if some violent unleashed force had broken out of the ground and was charging toward her. Her second thought was more reasonable: somebody had been hurt on the place and would sue her for everything she had. She had no insurance. She rushed forward and turning a bend in the path, she saw Mrs. Greenleaf sprawled on her hands and knees off the side of the road, her head down.

"Mrs. Greenleaf!" she shrilled, "what's happened?"

Mrs. Greenleaf raised her head. Her face was a patchwork of dirt and tears and her small eyes, the color of two field peas, were red-rimmed and swollen, but her expression was as composed as a bulldog's. She swayed back and forth on her hands and knees and groaned, "Jesus, Jesus."

Mrs. May winced. She thought the word, Jesus, should be kept inside the church building like other words inside the bedroom. She was a good Christian woman with a large respect for religion, though she did not, of course, believe any of it was true. "What is the matter with you?" she asked sharply.

"You broken my healing," Mrs. Greenleaf said, waving her aside. "I can't talk to you until I finish."

Mrs. May stood, bent forward, her mouth open and her stick raised off the ground as if she were not sure what she wanted to strike with it.

"Oh Jesus, stab me in the heart!" Mrs. Greenleaf shrieked. "Jesus, stab me in the heart!" and she fell back flat in the dirt, a huge human mound, her legs and arms spread out as if she were trying to wrap them around the earth.

Mrs. May felt as furious and helpless as if she had been insulted by a child. "Jesus," she said, drawing herself back, "would be *ashamed* of you. He would tell you to get up from there this instant and go wash your children's clothes!" and she had turned and walked off as fast as she could.

Whenever she thought of how the Greenleaf boys had advanced in the world, she had only to think of Mrs. Greenleaf sprawled obscenely on the ground, and say to herself, "Well, no matter how far they *go*, they *came* from that."

She would like to have been able to put in her will that when she died, Wesley and Scofield were not to continue to employ Mr. Greenleaf. She was capable of handling Mr. Greenleaf; they were not. Mr. Greenleaf had pointed out to her once that her boys didn't know hay from silage. She had pointed out to him that they had other talents, that Scofield was a successful business man and Wesley a successful intellectual. Mr. Greenleaf did not comment, but he never lost an opportunity of letting her see, by his expression or some simple gesture, that he held the two of them in infinite contempt. As scrub-human as the Greenleafs were, he never hesitated to let her know that in any like circumstance in which his own boys

might have been involved, they—O. T. and E. T. Greenleaf—would have acted to better advantage.

The Greenleaf boys were two or three years younger than the May boys. They were twins and you never knew when you spoke to one of them whether you were speaking to O. T. or E. T., and they never had the politeness to enlighten you. They were long-legged and raw-boned and red-skinned, with bright grasping fox-colored eyes like their father's. Mr. Greenleaf's pride in them began with the fact that they were twins. He acted, Mrs. May said, as if this were something smart they had thought of themselves. They were energetic and hard-working and she would admit to anyone that they had come a long way—and that the Second World War responsible for it.

They had both joined the service and, disguised in their uniforms, they could not be told from other people's children. You could tell, of course, when they opened their mouths but they did that seldom. The smartest thing they had done was to get sent overseas and there to marry French wives. They hadn't married French trash either. They had married nice girls who naturally couldn't tell that they murdered the king's English or that the Greenleafs were who they were.

Wesley's heart condition had not permitted him to serve his country but Scofield had been in the army for two years. He had not cared for it and at the end of his military service, he was only a Private First Class. The Greenleaf boys were both some kind of sergeants, and Mr. Greenleaf, in those days, had never lost an opportunity of referring to them by their rank. They had both managed to get wounded and now they both had pensions. Further, as soon as they were released from the army, they took advantage of all the benefits and went to the school of agriculture at the university—the taxpayers meanwhile supporting their French wives. The two of them were living now about two miles down the highway on a piece of land that the government had helped them to buy and in a brick duplex bungalow that the government had helped to build and pay for. If the war had made anyone, Mrs. May said, it had made the Greenleaf boys. They each had three little children apiece, who spoke Greenleaf English and French, and who, on account of their mothers' background, would be sent to the convent school and brought up with manners. "And in twenty years," Mrs. May asked Scofield and Wesley, "do you know what those people will be?

"*Society*," she said blackly.

She had spent fifteen years coping with Mr. Greenleaf and, by now, handling him had become second nature with her. His disposition on any particular day was as much a factor in what she could and couldn't do as the weather was, and she had learned to read his face the way real country people read the sunrise and sunset.

She was a country woman only by persuasion. The late Mr. May, a business man, had bought the place when land was down, and when he died it was all he had to leave her. The boys had not been happy to move to the country to a broken-down farm, but there was nothing else for her to do. She had the timber on the place cut and with the proceeds had set herself up in the dairy business after Mr. Greenleaf had answered her ad. "i seen yor add and i will come have 2 boys," was all his letter said, but he arrived the next day in a pieced-together truck, his wife and five daughters sitting on the floor in back, himself and the two boys in the cab.

Over the years they had been on her place, Mr. and Mrs. Greenleaf had aged hardly at all. They had no worries, no responsibilities. They lived like the lilies of the field, off the fat that she struggled to put into the land. When she was dead and gone from overwork and worry, the Greenleafs, healthy and thriving, would be just ready to begin draining Scofield and Wesley.

Wesley said the reason Mrs. Greenleaf had not aged was because she released all her emotions in prayer healing. "You ought to start praying, Sweetheart," he had said in the voice that, poor boy, he could not help making deliberately nasty.

Scofield only exasperated her beyond endurance but Wesley caused her real anxiety. He was thin and nervous and bald and being an intellectual was a terrible strain on his disposition. She doubted if he would marry until she died but she was certain that then the wrong woman would get him. Nice girls didn't like Scofield but Wesley didn't like nice girls. He didn't like anything. He drove twenty miles every day to the university where he taught and twenty miles back every night, but he said he hated the twenty-mile drive and he hated the second-rate university and he hated the morons who attended it. He hated the country and he hated the life he lived; he hated living with his mother and his idiot brother and he hated hearing about the damn dairy and the damn help and the damn broken machinery. But in spite of all he said, he never made any move to leave. He talked about Paris and Rome but he never went even to Atlanta.

"You'd go to those places and you'd get sick," Mrs. May would say. "Who in Paris is going to see that you get a salt-free diet? And do you think if you married one of those odd numbers you take out that *she* would cook a salt-free diet for you? No indeed, she would not!" When she took this line, Wesley would turn himself roughly around in his chair and ignore her. Once when she had kept it up too long, he had snarled, "Well, why don't you do something practical, Woman? Why don't you pray for me like Mrs. Greenleaf would?"

"I don't like to hear you boys make jokes about religion," she had said. "If you would go to church, you would meet some nice girls."

But it was impossible to tell them anything. When she looked at the two of them

now, sitting on either side of the table, neither one caring the least if a stray bull
ruined her herd—which was their herd,
their future—when she looked at the two of
them, one hunched over a paper and the
other teetering back in his chair, grinning
at her like an idiot, she wanted to jump up
and beat her fist on the table and shout,
"You'll find out one of these days, you'll find
out what *Reality* is when it's too late!"

"Mamma," Scofield said, "don't you get
excited now but I'll tell you whose bull that
is." He was looking at her wickedly. He let
his chair drop forward and he got up. Then
with his shoulders bent and his hands held
up to cover his head, he tiptoed to the door.
He backed into the hall and pulled the door
almost to so that it hid all of him but his
face. "You want to know, Sugarpie?" he
asked.

Mrs. May sat looking at him coldly.

"That's O. T. and E. T.'s bull," he said.
"I collected from their nigger yesterday and
he told me they were missing it," and he
showed her an exaggerated expanse of teeth
and disappeared silently.

Wesley looked up and laughed.

Mrs. May turned her head forward again,
her expression unaltered. "I am the only
adult on this place," she said. She leaned
across the table and pulled the paper from
the side of his plate. "Do you see how it's
going to be when I die and you boys have to
handle him?" she began. "Do you see why
he didn't know whose bull that was? Because it was theirs. Do you see what I have to
put up with? Do you see that if I hadn't kept
my foot on his neck all these years, you boys
might be milking cows every morning at
four o'clock?"

Wesley pulled the paper back toward his
plate and staring at her full in the face, he
murmured, "I wouldn't milk a cow to save
your soul from hell."

"I know you wouldn't," she said in a
brittle voice. She sat back and began rapidly
turning her knife over at the side of her
plate. "O. T. and E. T. are fine boys," she
said. "They ought to have been my sons."
The thought of this was so horrible that her
vision of Wesley was blurred at once by a
wall of tears. All she saw was his dark shape,
rising quickly from the table. "And you
two," she cried, "you two should have belonged to that woman!"

He was heading for the door.

"When I die," she said in a thin voice, "I
don't know what's to become of you."

"You're always yapping about when-you-
die," he growled as he rushed out, "but you
look pretty healthy to me."

For some time she sat where she was, looking straight ahead through the window
across the room into a scene of indistinct
greys and greens. She stretched her face and
her neck muscles and drew in a long breath
but the scene in front of her flowed together
anyway into a watery grey mass. "They
needn't think I'm going to die any time
soon," she muttered, and some more defiant
voice in her added: I'll die when I get good
and ready.

She wiped her eyes with the table napkin
and got up and went to the window and
gazed at the scene in front of her. The cows
were grazing on two pale green pastures
across the road and behind them, fencing
them in, was a black wall of trees with a
sharp sawtooth edge that held off the indifferent sky. The pastures were enough to
calm her. When she looked out any window
in her house, she saw the reflection of her
own character. Her city friends said she was
the most remarkable woman they knew, to
go, practically penniless and with no experience, out to a rundown farm and make
a success of it. "Everything is against you,"
she would say, "the weather is against you
and the dirt is against you and the help is
against you. They're all in league against
you. There's nothing for it but an iron
hand!"

"Look at Mamma's iron hand!" Scofield
would yell and grab her arm and hold it up

so that her delicate blue-veined little hand would dangle from her wrist like the head of a broken lily. The company always laughed.

The sun, moving over the black and white grazing cows, was just a little brighter than the rest of the sky. Looking down, she saw a darker shape that might have been its shadow cast at an angle, moving among them. She uttered a sharp cry and turned and marched out of the house.

Mr. Greenleaf was in the trench silo, filling a wheelbarrow. She stood on the edge and looked down at him. "I told you to get that bull. Now he's in with the milk herd."

"You can't do two thangs at oncet," Mr. Greenleaf remarked.

"I told you to do that first."

He wheeled the barrow out of the open end of the trench toward the barn and she followed close behind him. "And you needn't think, Mr. Greenleaf," she said, "that I don't know exactly whose bull that is or why you haven't been in a hurry to notify me he was here. I might as well feed O. T. and E. T.'s bull as long as I'm going to have him here ruining my herd."

Mr. Greenleaf paused with the wheelbarrow and looked behind him. "Is that them boys' bull?" he asked in an incredulous tone.

She did not say a word. She merely looked away with her mouth taut.

"They told me their bull was out but I never known that was him," he said.

"I want that bull put up now," she said, "and I'm going to drive over to O. T. and E. T.'s and tell them they'll have to come and get him today. I ought to charge for the time he's been here—then it wouldn't happen again."

"They didn't pay but seventy-five dollars for him," Mr. Greenleaf offered.

"I wouldn't have had him as a gift," she said.

"They was just going to beef him," Mr. Greenleaf went on, "but he got loose and run his head into their pickup truck. He don't like cars and trucks. They had a time getting his horn out the fender and when they finally got him loose, he took off and they was too tired to run after him—but I never known that was him there."

"It wouldn't have paid to know, Mr. Greenleaf," she said, "But you know now. Get a horse and get him."

In a half hour, from her front window she saw the bull, squirrel-colored, with jutting hips and long light horns, ambling down the dirt road that ran in front of the house. Mr. Greenleaf was behind him on the horse. "That's a Greenleaf bull if I ever saw one," she muttered. She went out on the porch and called, "Put him where he can't get out."

"He likes to bust loose," Mr. Greenleaf said, looking with approval at the bull's rump. "This gentleman is a sport."

"If those boys don't come for him, he's going to be a dead sport," she said. "I'm just warning you."

He heard her but he didn't answer.

"That's the awfullest looking bull I ever saw," she called but he was too far down the road to hear.

It was mid-morning when she turned into O. T. and E. T.'s driveway. The house, a new red-brick, low-to-the-ground building that looked like a warehouse with windows, was on top of a treeless hill. The sun was beating down directly on the white roof of it. It was the kind of house that everybody built now and nothing marked it as belonging to Greenleafs except three dogs, part hound and part spitz, that rushed out from behind it as soon as she stopped her car. She reminded herself that you could always tell the class of people by the class of dog, and honked her horn. While she sat waiting for someone to come, she continued to study the house. All the windows were down and she wondered if the government could have air-conditioned the thing. No one came and she honked again. Presently a door opened and several children appeared in it and stood looking at her, making no move to come forward. She recognized this as a true Greenleaf trait—they could hang in a door, looking at you for hours.

"Can't one of you children come here?" she called.

After a minute they all began to move forward, slowly. They had on overalls and were barefooted but they were not as dirty as she might have expected. There were two or three that looked distinctly like Greenleafs; the others not so much so. The smallest child was a girl with untidy black hair. They stopped about six feet from the automobile and stood looking at her.

"You're mighty pretty," Mrs. May said, addressing herself to the smallest girl.

There was no answer. They appeared to share one dispassionate expression between them.

"Where's your Mamma?" she asked.

There was no answer to this for some time. Then one of them said something in French. Mrs. May did not speak French.

"Where's your daddy?" she asked.

After a while, one of the boys said, "He ain't hyar neither."

"Ahhhh," Mrs. May said as if something had been proven. "Where's the colored man?"

She waited and decided no one was going to answer. "The cat has six little tongues," she said. "How would you like to come home with me and let me teach you how to talk?" She laughed and her laugh died on the silent air. She felt as if she were on trial for her life, facing a jury of Greenleafs. "I'll go down and see if I can find the colored man," she said.

"You can go if you want to," one of the boys said.

"Well, thank you," she murmured and drove off.

The barn was down the lane from the house. She had not seen it before but Mr. Greenleaf had described it in detail, for it had been built according to the latest specifications. It was a milking parlor arrangement where the cows are milked from below. The milk ran in pipes from the machines to the milk house and was never carried in no bucket, Mr. Greenleaf said, by no human hand. "When you gonter get you one?" he had asked.

"Mr. Greenleaf," she had said, "I have to do for myself. I am not assisted hand and foot by the government. It would cost me $20,000 to install a milking parlor. I barely make ends meet as it is."

"My boys done it," Mr. Greenleaf had murmured, and then—"but all boys ain't alike."

"No indeed!" she had said. "I thank God for that!"

"I thank Gawd for ever-thang," Mr. Greenleaf had drawled.

You might as well, she had thought in the fierce silence that followed; you've never done anything for yourself.

She stopped by the side of the barn and honked but no one appeared. For several minutes she sat in the car, observing the various machines parked around, wondering how many of them were paid for. They had a forage harvester and a rotary hay baler. She had those too. She decided that since no one was here, she would get out and have a look at the milking parlor and see if they kept it clean.

She opened the milking room door and stuck her head in and for the first second she felt as if she were going to lose her breath. The spotless white concrete room was filled with sunlight that came from a row of windows head-high along both walls. The metal stanchions gleamed ferociously and she had to squint to be able to look at all. She drew her head out of the room quickly and closed the door and leaned against it, frowning. The light outside was not so bright but she was conscious that the sun was directly on top of her head, like a silver bullet ready to drop into her brain.

A Negro carrying a yellow calf-feed bucket appeared from around the corner of the machine shed and came toward her. He was a light yellow boy dressed in the cast-off army clothes of the Greenleaf twins. He stopped at a respectable distance and set the bucket on the ground.

"Where's Mr. O. T. and Mr. E. T.?" she asked.

"Mist O. T. he in town, Mist E. T. he off yonder in the field," the Negro said, pointing first to the left and then to the right as if he were naming the position of two planets.

"Can you remember a message?" she asked, looking as if she thought this doubtful.

"I'll remember it if I don't forget it," he said with a touch of sullenness.

"Well, I'll write it down then," she said. She got in her car and took a stub of pencil from her pocket book and began to write on the back of an empty envelope. The Negro came and stood at the window. "I'm Mrs. May," she said as she wrote. "Their bull is on my place and I want him off *today*. You can tell them I'm furious about it."

"That bull lef here Sareday," the Negro said, "and none of us ain't seen him since. We ain't knowed where he was."

"Well, you know now," she said, "and you can tell Mr. O. T. and Mr. E. T. that if they don't come get him today, I'm going to have their daddy shoot him the first thing in the morning. I can't have that bull ruining my herd." She handed him the note.

"If I knows Mist O. T. and Mist E. T.," he said, taking it, "they goin to say you go ahead and shoot him. He done busted up one of our trucks already and we glad to see the last of him."

She pulled her head back and gave him a look from slightly bleared eyes. "Do they expect me to take my time and my worker to shoot their bull?" she asked. "They don't want him so they just let him loose and expect somebody else to kill him? He's eating my oats and ruining my herd and I'm expected to shoot him too?"

"I speck you is," he said softly. "He done busted up . . ."

She gave him a very sharp look and said, "Well, I'm not surprised. That's just the way some people are," and after a second she asked, "Which is boss, Mr. O. T. or Mr. E. T.?" She had always suspected that they fought between themselves secretly.

"They never quarls," the boy said. "They like one man in two skins."

"Hmp. I expect you just never heard them quarrel."

"Nor nobody else heard them neither," he said, looking away as if this insolence were addressed to some one else.

"Well," she said, "I haven't put up with their father for fifteen years not to know a few things about Greenleafs."

The Negro looked at her suddenly with a gleam of recognition. "Is you my policy man's mother?" he asked.

"I don't know who your policy man is," she said sharply. "You give them that note and tell them if they don't come for that bull today, they'll be making their father shoot it tomorrow," and she drove off.

She stayed at home all afternoon waiting for the Greenleaf twins to come for the bull. They did not come. I might as well be working for them, she thought furiously. They are simply going to use me to the limit. At the supper table, she went over it again for the boys' benefit because she wanted them to see exactly what O. T. and E. T. would do. "They don't want the bull," she said, "—pass the butter—so they simply turn him loose and let somebody else worry about getting rid of him for them. How do you like that? I'm the victim. I've always been the victim."

"Pass the butter to the victim," Wesley said. He was in a worse humor than usual because he had had a flat tire on the way home from the university.

Scofield handed her the butter and said,

"Why Mamma, ain't you ashamed to shoot an old bull that ain't done nothing but give you a little scrub strain in your herd? I declare," he said, "with the Mamma I got it's a wonder I turned out to be such a nice boy!"

"You ain't her boy, Son," Wesley said.

She eased back in her chair, her fingertips on the edge of the table.

"All I know is," Scofield said, "I done mighty well to be as nice as I am seeing what I come from."

When they teased her they spoke Greenleaf English but Wesley made his own particular tone come through it like a knife edge. "Well lemme tell you one thang, Brother," he said, leaning over the table, "that if you had half a mind you would already know."

"What's that, Brother?" Scofield asked, his broad face grinning into the thin constricted one across from him.

"That is," Wesley said, "that neither you nor me is her boy . . . ," but he stopped abruptly as she gave a kind of hoarse wheeze like an old horse lashed unexpectedly. She reared up and ran from the room.

"Oh, for God's sake," Wesley growled, "what did you start her off for?"

"I never started her off," Scofield said. "You started her off."

"Hah."

"She's not as young as she used to be and she can't take it."

"She can only give it out," Wesley said. "I'm the one that takes it."

His brother's pleasant face had changed so that an ugly family resemblance showed between them. "Nobody feels sorry for a lousy bastard like you," he said and grabbed across the table for the other's shirtfront.

From her room she heard a crash of dishes and she rushed back through the kitchen into the dining room. The hall door was open and Scofield was going out of it. Wesley was lying like a large bug on his back with the edge of the over-turned table cutting him

across the middle and broken dishes scattered on top of him. She pulled the table off him and caught his arm to help him rise but he scrambled up and pushed her off with a furious charge of energy and flung himself out of the door after his brother.

She would have collapsed but a knock on the back door stiffened her and she swung around. Across the kitchen and back porch, she could see Mr. Greenleaf peering eagerly through the screenwire. All her resources returned in full strength as if she had only needed to be challenged by the devil himself to regain them. "I heard a thump," he called, "and I thought the plastering might have fell on you."

If he had been wanted someone would have had to go on a horse to find him. She crossed the kitchen and the porch and stood inside the screen and said, "No, nothing happened but the table turned over. One of the legs was weak," and without pausing, "the boys didn't come for the bull so tomorrow you'll have to shoot him."

The sky was crossed with thin red and purple bars and behind them the sun was moving down slowly as if it were descending a ladder. Mr. Greenleaf squatted down on the step, his back to her, the top of his hat on a level with her feet. "Tomorrow I'll drive him home for you," he said.

"Oh no, Mr. Greenleaf," she said in a mocking voice, "you drive him home tomorrow and next week he'll be back here. I know better than that." Then in a mournful tone, she said, "I'm surprised at O. T. and E. T. to treat me this way. I thought they'd have more gratitude. Those boys spent some mighty happy days on this place, didn't they, Mr. Greenleaf?"

Mr. Greenleaf didn't say anything.

"I think they did," she said. "I think they did. But they've forgotten all the nice little things I did for them now. If I recall, they wore my boys' old clothes and played with my boys' old toys and hunted with my boys' old guns. They swam in my pond and shot my birds and fished in my stream and I never forgot their birthday and Christmas seemed to roll around very often if I remember it right. And do they think of any of those things now?" she asked. "NOOOOO," she said.

For a few seconds she looked at the disappearing sun and Mr. Greenleaf examined the palms of his hands. Presently as if it had just occurred to her, she asked, "Do you know the real reason they didn't come for that bull?"

"Naw I don't," Mr. Greenleaf said in a surly voice.

"They didn't come because I'm a woman," she said. "You can get away with anything when you're dealing with a woman. If there was a man running this place . . ."

Quick as a snake striking Mr. Greenleaf said, "You got two boys. They know you got two men on the place."

The sun had disappeared behind the tree line. She looked down at the dark crafty face, upturned now, and at the wary eyes, bright under the shadow of the hatbrim. She waited long enough for him to see that she was hurt and then she said, "Some people learn gratitude too late, Mr. Greenleaf, and some never learn it at all," and she turned and left him sitting on the steps.

Half the night in her sleep she heard a sound as if some large stone were grinding a hole on the outside wall of her brain. She was walking on the inside, over a succession of beautiful rolling hills, planting her stick in front of each step. She became aware after a time that the noise was the sun trying to burn through the tree line and she stopped to watch, safe in the knowledge that it couldn't, that it had to sink the way it always did outside of her property. When she first stopped it was a swollen red ball, but as she stood watching it began to narrow and pale until it looked like a bullet. Then suddenly it burst through the tree line and raced down the hill toward her. She woke up with her hand over her mouth

and the same noise, diminished but distinct, in her ear. It was the bull munching under her window. Mr. Greenleaf had let him out.

She got up and made her way to the window in the dark and looked out through the slit blind, but the bull had moved away from the hedge and at first she didn't see him. Then she saw a heavy form some distance away, paused as if observing her. This is the last night I am going to put up with this, she said, and watched until the iron shadow moved away in the darkness.

The next morning she waited until exactly eleven o'clock. Then she got in her car and drove to the barn. Mr. Greenleaf was cleaning milk cans. He had seven of them standing up outside the milk room to get the sun. She had been telling him to do this for two weeks. "All right, Mr. Greenleaf," she said, "go get your gun. We're going to shoot that bull."

"I thought you wanted theseyer cans . . ."

"Go get your gun, Mr. Greenleaf," she said. Her voice and face were expressionless.

"That gentleman torn out of there last night," he murmured in a tone of regret and bent again to the can he had his arm in.

"Go get your gun, Mr. Greenleaf," she said in the same triumphant toneless voice. "The bull is in the pasture with the dry cows. I saw him from my upstairs window. I'm going to drive you up to the field and you can run him into the empty pasture and shoot him there."

He detached himself from the can slowly. "Ain't nobody ever ast me to shoot my boys' own bull!" he said in a high rasping voice. He removed a rag from his back pocket and began to wipe his hands violently, then his nose.

She turned as if she had not heard this and said, "I'll wait for you in the car. Go get your gun."

She sat in the car and watched him stalk off toward the harness room where he kept a gun. After he had entered the room, there was a crash as if he had kicked something out of his way. Presently he emerged again with the gun, circled behind the car, opened the door violently and threw himself onto the seat beside her. He held the gun between his knees and looked straight ahead. He'd like to shoot me instead of the bull, she thought, and turned her face away so that he could not see her smile.

The morning was dry and clear. She drove through the woods for a quarter of a mile and then out into the open where there were fields on either side of the narrow road. The exhilaration of carrying her point had sharpened her senses. Birds were screaming everywhere, the grass was almost too bright to look at, the sky was an even piercing blue. "Spring is here!" she said gaily. Mr. Greenleaf lifted one muscle somewhere near his mouth as if he found this the most asinine remark ever made. When she stopped at the second pasture gate, he flung himself out of the car door and slammed it behind him. Then he opened the gate and she drove through. He closed it and flung himself back in, silently, and she drove around the rim of the pasture until she spotted the bull, almost in the center of it, grazing peacefully among the cows.

"The gentleman is waiting on you," she said and gave Mr. Greenleaf's furious profile a sly look. "Run him into that next pasture and when you get him in, I'll drive in behind you and shut the gate myself."

He flung himself out again, this time deliberately leaving the car door open so that she had to lean across the seat and close it. She sat smiling as she watched him make his way across the pasture toward the opposite gate. He seemed to throw himself forward at each step and then pull back as if he were calling on some power to witness that he was being forced. "Well," she said aloud as if he were still in the car, "it's your own boys who are making you do this, Mr. Greenleaf." O. T. and E. T. were probably splitting their sides laughing at him now. She could hear their identical nasal voices

saying, "Made Daddy shoot our bull for us. Daddy don't know no better than to think that's a fine bull he's shooting. Gonna kill Daddy to shoot that bull!"

"If those boys cared a thing about you, Mr. Greenleaf," she said, "they would have come for that bull. I'm surprised at them."

He was circling around to open the gate first. The bull, dark among the spotted cows, had not moved. He kept his head down, eating constantly. Mr. Greenleaf opened the gate and then began circling back to approach him from the rear. When he was about ten feet behind him, he flapped his arms at his sides. The bull lifted his head indolently and then lowered it again and continued to eat. Mr. Greenleaf stooped again and picked up something and threw it at him with a vicious swing. She decided it was a sharp rock, for the bull leapt and then began to gallop until he disappeared over the rim of the hill. Mr. Greenleaf followed at his leisure.

"You needn't think you're going to lose him!" she cried and started the car straight across the pasture. She had to drive slowly over the terraces and when she reached the gate, Mr. Greenleaf and the bull were nowhere in sight. This pasture was smaller than the last, a green arena, encircled almost entirely by woods. She got out and closed the gate and stood looking for some sign of Mr. Greenleaf but he had disappeared completely. She knew at once that his plan was to lose the bull in the woods. Eventually, she would see him emerge somewhere from the circle of trees and come limping toward her and when he finally reached her, he would say, "If you can find that gentleman in them woods, you're better than me."

She was going to say, "Mr. Greenleaf, if I have to walk into those woods with you and stay all afternoon, we are going to find that bull and shoot him. You are going to shoot him if I have to pull the trigger for you." When he saw she meant business he would return and shoot the bull quickly himself.

She got back into the car and drove to the center of the pasture where he would not have so far to walk to reach her when he came out of the woods. At this moment she could picture him sitting on a stump, marking lines in the ground with a stick. She decided she would wait exactly ten minutes by her watch. Then she would begin to honk. She got out of the car and walked around a little and then sat down on the front bumper to wait and rest. She was very tired and she lay her head back against the hood and closed her eyes. She did not understand why she should be so tired when it was only midmorning. Through her closed eyes, she could feel the sun, red-hot overhead. She opened her eyes slightly but the white light forced her to close them again.

For some time she lay back against the hood, wondering drowsily why she was so tired. With her eyes closed, she didn't think of time as divided into days and nights but into past and future. She decided she was tired because she had been working continuously for fifteen years. She decided she had every right to be tired, and to rest for a few minutes before she began working again. Before any kind of judgement seat, she would be able to say: I've worked, I have not wallowed. At this very instant while she was recalling a lifetime of work, Mr. Greenleaf was loitering in the woods and Mrs. Greenleaf was probably flat on the ground, asleep over her holeful of clippings. The woman had got worse over the years and Mrs. May believed that now she was actually demented. "I'm afraid your wife has let religion warp her," she said once tactfully to Mr. Greenleaf. "Everything in moderation, you know."

"She cured a man oncet that half his gut was eat out with worms," Mr. Greenleaf said, and she had turned away, half-sickened. Poor souls, she thought now, so simple. For a few seconds she dozed.

When she sat up and looked at her watch, more than ten minutes had passed. She had not heard any shot. A new thought occurred to her: suppose Mr. Greenleaf had aroused the bull chunking stones at him and the animal had turned on him and run him up against a tree and gored him? The irony of it deepened: O. T. and E. T. would then get a shyster lawyer and sue her. It would be the fitting end to her fifteen years with the Greenleafs. She thought of it almost with pleasure as if she had hit on the perfect ending for a story she was telling her friends. Then she dropped it, for Mr. Greenleaf had a gun with him and she had insurance.

She decided to honk. She got up and reached inside the car window and gave three sustained honks and two or three shorter ones to let him know she was getting impatient. Then she went back and sat down on the bumper again.

In a few minutes something emerged from the tree line, a black heavy shadow that tossed its head several times and then bounded forward. After a second she saw it was the bull. He was crossing the pasture toward her at a slow gallop, a gay almost rocking gait as if he were overjoyed to find her again. She looked beyond him to see if Mr. Greenleaf was coming out of the woods too but he was not. "Here he is, Mr. Greenleaf!" she called and looked on the other side of the pasture to see if he could be coming out there but he was not in sight. She looked back and saw that the bull, his head lowered, was racing toward her. She remained perfectly still, not in fright, but in a freezing unbelief. She stared at the violent black streak bounding toward her as if she had no sense of distance, as if she could not decide at once what his intention was, and the bull had buried his head in her lap, like a wild tormented lover, before her expression changed. One of his horns sank until it pierced her heart and the other curved around her side and held her in an unbreakable grip. She continued to stare straight ahead but the entire scene in front of her had changed—the tree line was a dark wound in a world that was nothing but sky —and she had the look of a person whose sight has been suddenly restored but who finds the light unbearable.

Mr. Greenleaf was running toward her from the side with his gun raised and she saw him coming though she was not looking in his direction. She saw him approaching on the outside of some invisible circle, the tree line gaping behind him and nothing under his feet. He shot the bull four times through the eye. She did not hear the shots but she felt the quake in the huge body as it sank, pulling her forward on its head, so that she seemed, when Mr. Greenleaf reached her, to be bent over whispering some last discovery into the animal's ear.

Ted Poston

RAT JOINER ROUTS
THE KLAN

There had never been a Ku Klux Klan in Hopkinsville, Kentucky. So it was sort of surprising how our leading colored citizens got all worked up when they heard that *The Birth of a Nation* was coming to the Rex Theatre down on Ninth Street.

It was we young ones who brought them the news—although it didn't mean anything to us. And it was we young ones who got them out of it when the situation finally reached a stalemate.

The whole thing started one Saturday morning when Bronco Billy Anderson was being featured at the Rex in *The Revenge of the Ranger*. And, of course, not a one of us could afford to miss that.

Naturally, the Booker T. Washington Colored Grammar School was not open on Saturdays, but that meant only one extra hour's sleep. For all of us had to be at the Rex at 9 A.M. to be sure that we could get front row seats in the peanut gallery which was reserved for all of our colored citizens.

It was absolutely essential that we be there when the doors first opened or else the bigger boys would get there first and take the choice seats.

We always thought the big boys were unfair, but there was nothing we could do about it. No self-respecting young colored citizen would dream of squealing to the white folks about it. And furthermore, if we did, we knew the big boys would bop us for doing it.

But this was our problem: The Rex Theater charged only five cents admission for all of our colored citizens under ten years of age. But since Miss Lucy, the white ticket lady who took our nickels, was nearsighted, and saw us only through a peephole as we stood in line in the alley, there was a rumor around the colored community that none of us grew any older after we were nine years old until we suddenly reached twenty-one or more. For all you had to do was bend your knees, look up innocently, and slip your nickel through the slot, and she'd pass you right up the gallery stairs.

There was a story—which I never believed—that Jelly Roll Benson never paid more than a nickel to get into the Rex until he was about thirty-five years old.

"That's why he walks with a stoop in his shoulders and a bend in his knees to this day," Rat Joiner always insisted. "He got that way from fooling Miss Lucy. He'd still be doin' it now, but he forgot to shave one morning. And she suspected for the first time that he was over ten."

But all this happened before that historic Saturday when we all rushed to see Bronco Billy Anderson in *The Revenge of the Ranger*. All of us were crazy about Bronco Billy, but there was also another reason for going to see him. For in every picture, Bronco

Billy's main side-kick was a cowboy named Buffalo Pete. And, believe it or not, Buffalo Pete was as highly visible and 100 per cent colored as any citizen up on Billy Goat Hill.

He was the only colored cowboy or colored anything we ever saw in the movies in those days, and we wouldn't think of missing him. Our enthusiasm was not even dimmed by the cynicism of Rat Joiner, who observed one day: "They don't never let him kill none of them white mens, no matter how evil they is. Oh yeah, they let him knock off a Indian every now and then. But only Bronco Billy kills them white bad mens."

There was an unconfirmed rumor around town that another movie actor, named Noble Johnson, had Negro blood. But we didn't pay that no mind. We figured that the high-yallers in our colored community had dreamed up that story for prestige purposes. And anyway, Noble Johnson played in those silly love stories they showed at the Rex on weekday nights. And who would pay five cents to see one of them?

But *The Revenge of the Ranger* that Saturday was a real knock-down picture and we saw it eight times before they put us out at 5 P.M. in order to let the grownups in for the evening, at fifteen cents a head.

We got downstairs and out of the alley at just about the same time that the little white boys were being put out, and we noticed that they were all carrying handbills in their fists. Nobody had passed out any handbills upstairs, but we had no difficulty getting some when we found out that Tack Haired Baker had been paid twenty-five cents to stand by the front door in the lobby and pass them out.

We were a little disappointed when we read them, because it didn't mean anything

to us then. Bronco Billy and Buffalo Pete weren't even mentioned anywhere on the handbills. They read:

Special

Special

Special

THE SOUTH RISES AGAIN

Come See

B. W. Griffith's

"THE BIRTH OF A NATION"

Based on

"The Clansman"

Every night—Monday through Friday

Admission 25 cents

Most of us threw the handbills away before we got home, and I don't remember how I happened to hold on to mine.

But I still had it in my hand when I climbed up our front steps and tried to make my way through the usual Saturday crowd of elders and sporting men who were holding their weekly session with Papa. Papa was Professor E. Poston, dean of men at Kentucky State Industrial College for Negroes in Frankfort and the official arbiter of all bets and disputes which piled up during his two-weekly absences from home.

My sister Lillian, who is only three years older than I, was showing off by sitting next to Papa while he explained that a Negro jockey named Isaac Murphy was the first man to ride three winners in the Kentucky Derby, in 1884, 1890, and 1891. So as I stepped around Smoky Smith, our leading colored gambling man, who had raised the question, I handed Lillian the handbill. This *Birth of a Nation* thing sounded like one of those silly love-story movies she was always going to, so I thought I was doing her a favor.

But I was absolutely unprepared for the commotion that was raised when Mr. Freddie Williams, the first deacon of our Virginia Baptist Church, happened to glance at the handbill and let out a screech.

"Don't that say *The Birth of a Nation?*" he yelled as he snatched it out of Lillian's hands. "And coming to the Rex Theatre here?"

He thrust the crumpled handbill in Papa's face and said: "Professor Poston, you've got to do something about this right away."

I still had no idea what had caused the commotion, but Mr. J. B. Petty, our local insurance man-historian, very soon put me right.

It seemed that this novel, *The Clansman*, and the moving picture *The Birth of a Nation* were something about a bunch of peckerwoods who dressed up in sheets and went around whipping the heads of unsuspecting colored citizens and yelling about white supremacy. And there was one place in both things about some Negro—"played by a white man," Mr. J. B. Petty explained —who chased some poor white woman off the top of a rock quarry, with her yelling, "Death before dishonor."

Mr. Freddie Williams was putting it right up to Papa.

"You know what it will mean to show this sort of thing to these hillbillies and peckerwoods around here, Professor Poston," he kept saying. "And I'm sure that the quality white folks will agree with you if you put it up to them right. I'm surprised that Mr. Max Kaplan even thought of letting this happen."

Now even I knew that Mr. Max Kaplan, who owned the Rex was not exactly quality white folks in the eyes of Hopkinsville, Kentucky, even if he was a very popular white citizen in the colored community.

And neither was Judge Hezekiah Witherspoon, our veteran Republican leader, quality either. But he ran Hopkinsville, Kentucky, and it was to him that the group decided that Papa should make his first appeal.

Papa went right down to see him that Saturday night, but the meeting wasn't altogether successful. As I heard Papa explaining it to Mama when he finally got home, Judge Witherspoon started talking about private enterprise and what were the Negroes excited about anyhow? But Papa had one more weapon up his sleeve, he explained to Mama.

"So I finally said to him," Papa recalled, " 'I don't know if you read the book, Judge Witherspoon, but the whole thing is about the terrible things the scalawags and carpetbaggers did to the people of the South during Reconstruction. And although I didn't want to mention the subject, Judge, you must remember that all of those scalawags and carpetbaggers were Republicans, so I wonder if you want people reminded of that?' "

Papa chuckled as he recalled Judge Witherspoon's reaction.

" 'Eph, you damn Democrat,' he yelled at me," Papa said. " 'You keep your politics out of this.' But I could see that he was shaken, and I just let him rave for a few minutes."

"But finally he said: 'I'm not gonna get mixed up in this thing. But you go and see Max Kaplan and tell him how the colored people feel about this thing. And tell him I'll back him up if he feels he's got to do something about it.' "

Papa was very set up about the meeting. "I'm going out to see Mr. Max Kaplan tomorrow morning. After all, Sunday is not his Sabbath and he won't be averse to talking a little business."

I still didn't quite understand what the shouting was all about. But I had no doubt that Mr. Max Kaplan would side with our colored citizens if Papa asked him to. For Mr. Max Kaplan was quite an unusual citizen even in Hopkinsville, Kentucky. He had come there years before I was born and had got into hot water the minute he built the Rex Theatre, because he had planned only ground-floor seats for white and colored citizens alike.

Of course, the white folks, including the quality ones, had beaten him down on that, and he had been forced to spend extra money to fix the peanut gallery up for us.

Reaching Pete Washington, a classmate of mine in the Booker T. Washington Colored Grammar School, once said he was glad Mr. Max Kaplan lost that fight. Reaching Pete didn't have a nickel one Saturday when *The Clutching Hand* serial was playing the Rex, so he kept on up the alley and slipped through the fire-escape door on the ground floor where the white folks sat.

It was dark, of course, and nobody noticed that Reaching Pete had slipped in. But everybody knew it a few minutes later. For when Pete looked up, he was right under the screen and the pictures were twenty feet tall. And just at that moment, the Clutching Hand, a very mean crook who had a claw in place of his right hand, was reaching out for his next victim, and Pete thought he was reaching for him.

Pete closed his eyes and screamed so loud that they had to turn on the lights in the whole theatre to find out what was going on. The cops wanted to lock Reaching Pete up, but Mr. Max Kaplan wouldn't let them. He even let Reaching Pete go upstairs free of charge.

But that wasn't the only thing that endeared Mr. Max Kaplan to our colored community. There was the matter of Tapper Johnson, our motion-picture projectionist. When the white folks balked Mr. Max Kaplan and made him build a whole peanut gallery (after starting a whispering campaign that he was trying to bring his New York City ideas to Hopkinsville), he made up his mind to get even. So he decided to make his most highly paid employee one of our colored citizens. That was when he hired Tapper and trained him to be the only moving-picture-machine operator in all of Hopkinsville. And he paid Tapper thirty-five dollars each and every week.

And Tapper paid Mr. Max Kaplan back real nice too. He became the best moving-picture operator for his size and age in all of Kentucky, and there were rumors that he could have gotten five dollars more a week in Clarksville, Tennessee, if Mr. Kaplan had ever given him a vacation or a day off to go see about it.

But Tapper didn't want a day off. He had only two loves in his life—his motion-picture machine and little Cecelia Penrod with whom he had been in love long before he quit the fourth grade in the Booker T. Washington Colored Grammar School.

His love affair with the Rex Theatre moving-picture machine went along smoothly. But not his love affair with little Cecelia. For Cecelia was one of the nieces of Mrs. Nixola Green, our high-yaller social leader. And she felt that Tapper was too dark to become a member of her family.

In fact, my sister Lillian was always saying that Mrs. Nixola was trying to marry Cecelia off to Pat Slaker (who naturally was yaller), but that Pat and Cecelia weren't paying each other any mind. Cecelia was in love with Tapper, Lillian said, although there wasn't much she could do about it. She never got to go to the Rex Theatre alone. Mrs. Nixola always insisted on accompanying her.

Papa probably had all this in mind that

Sunday morning when he hopefully set out for Mr. Max Kaplan's home. But Papa was in for a disappointment. Mr. Kaplan wasn't in town. He'd left three weeks ago for California and he wasn't expected home until Wednesday.

Now *The Birth of a Nation* was due to start running Tuesday night. Time was running out as the elders of Freeman Methodist Chapel and the Virginia Street Baptist Church met that afternoon to receive Papa's report.

"Professor Poston," Mr. Freddie Williams finally said after the discussion had gone on for hours. "I know how you feel about poor white trash. But with Mr. Max Kaplan out of town, there's nothing we can do but appeal to S. J. Bolton."

It took some talking on the part of the elders, but Papa was finally persuaded to lay the matter before Mr. S. J. Bolton, Mr. Kaplan's manager of the Rex, and the results were disastrous, as he reported it to Mama later.

"This clay-eating cracker," Papa said later, in as near an approach to profanity as he ever permitted himself, "had the nerve to call me Eph. He said to me: 'Eph, what are you Nigras upset about? Why, my grandfather was one of the founders of the Klan. No Nigra who knows his place has anything to worry about in this glorious story of the re-rise of the South.'

"And then he added," Papa said, " 'Why Eph, you must know what my initials, S.J., stand for. Stonewall Jackson Bolton, of course.' "

Papa's indignation at the outcome of his conference was far exceeded by the reaction of the elders who met on our lawn that Sunday afternoon to hear his report.

But none of us young ones felt personally involved until Mr. Freddie Williams summed up the feelings of our elders.

"All right," he said, "if that is the way the white folks feel about it, let them. But I move that if *The Birth of a Nation* opens

at the Rex Tuesday evening, then 'The Death of the Rex' should set in that very night. Because if we don't patronize that peanut gallery Mr. Max Kaplan has for us, then they ain't gonna make enough money each week to pay even Tapper's salary. And that means not only us staying away, but our kids as well—Bronco Billy and Buffalo Pete notwithstanding."

Now this created a very desperate situation indeed, as I explained to my classmates at the Booker T. Washington Colored Grammar School the next morning.

But what could we do about it? We were all pretty downcast until Rat Joiner said: "I think I got an idea." And then he explained.

And as soon as school was out that day, we all went to work to raise the fifteen cents Rat said was necessary for the success of his plan. Coco-Cola bottles, scrap wire, everything went into the pot until we had the fifteen cents.

There was no picket line at the Rex the next night, but some of our most responsible colored citizens were loitering around the alley from the minute the evening tickets went on sale. And most of them were very upset when Rat Joiner, the pride of Billy Goat Hill, showed up as the only colored customer that night who plunked down fifteen cents and requested a peanut-gallery ticket from Miss Lucy.

In fact, there was talk about mentioning the fact to Reverend Timberlake, and having him read Roosevelt Alonzo Taylor Joiner out of the congregation of the Dirt's Avenue Methodist Church.

But that was before they found out the nature of Rat's mission.

For Rat entered the Rex just thirty minutes before the main feature was to go on, just when Tapper was preparing to rewind the film for Hopkinsville's first showing of *The Birth of a Nation*.

Rat knocked on the door of the projection room, then came right to the matter at hand.

"Tapper," he said, "Mrs. Nixola Green has finally persuaded Cecelia to run off and marry Pat Slaker. They're up at Mrs. Nixola's house on First Street and they're going to head for Clarksville any minute. I know it ain't none of my business, but you always been fair to us and—"

Tapper waited to hear no more. He dashed out of the projection room and headed first for Mrs. Nixola's house on First Street.

Of course, Cecelia wasn't there; the whole family was over in Earlington, Kentucky, attending a family reunion.

But Tapper didn't know this. He rushed down to Irving's Livery Stable and rented the fastest horse and rig for an emergency dash to Clarksville, Tennessee, where he hoped to head off the nuptials.

Well, the downstairs section of the Rex Theatre was crowded (with only Rat in the peanut gallery) before Mr. S. J. Bolton learned that Hopkinsville's only movie projectionist was no longer in the Rex Theatre. He tried to stall the showing for a half hour, but when Tapper didn't show up then, Mr. S. J. Bolton tried to run the machine himself.

Rat, who had decided to stay inside since he had paid an unheard-of fifteen cents to be there anyway, explained to us later what happened.

"Tapper had started rewinding the film backwards to get to the front," he said, "but Mr. S. J. Bolton didn't know that. So he picked up the first film roll he saw and started running it on that picture thing.

"Well, it turned out that it was the middle of the picture and backwards besides. So, instead of that colored gentleman (played by some white man) chasing that white lady off the top of the quarry, it started with the white lady at the bottom of the quarry. And she was leaping to the top of the quarry so that the colored gentleman (who was really a white man) could grab her.

"The white folks didn't see much of the picture, because Mr. S. J. Bolton yanked that part off so fast that he tore up the whole thing. I waited another half hour and nothing else came on, so all of us went home."

So Hopkinsville, Kentucky, never got to see *The Birth of a Nation*. Mr. Max Kaplan came back the next day and substituted another film for *The Birth of a Nation*. There were always two schools of thought in the colored community after that—and even Papa couldn't settle the dispute.

One school held that Mr. Max Kaplan would never have let *The Birth of a Nation* be booked for the Rex if he had known anything about it and if he hadn't been in Los Angeles. And the other school contended that Mr. S. J. Bolton had so messed up the original print in trying to run it without Tapper that it couldn't have been shown anyway.

In any case, Mr. Max Kaplan took steps to see that a certain situation never obtained again. He had little Cecelia Penrod smuggled out of her house while Mrs. Nixola wasn't watching. And he took her and Tapper down to Judge Hezekiah Witherspoon who married both of them on the spot. Mrs. Nixola Green collapsed at the news and went over to Clarksville, Tennessee, to recuperate at the home of some of her high-yaller relatives.

When she came back she boasted that she had passed for white and had seen *The Birth of a Nation* at the Princess Theatre there.

"And it was a very good picture," she said, "I don't know what all the fuss over here was about."

John Milton

ON THE LATE MASSACRE
IN PIEDMONT

Avenge, O Lord, thy slaughtered saints, whose
    bones
  Lie scattered on the Alpine mountains cold;
  Even them who kept thy truth so pure of old,
  When all our fathers worshipped stocks and
    stones,
Forget not: in thy book record their groans
  Who were thy sheep, and in their ancient fold
  Slain by the bloody Piedmontese, that rolled
  Mother with infant down the rocks. Their
    moans
The vales redoubled to the hills, and they
  To heaven. Their martyred blood and ashes
    sow   10
  O'er all the Italian fields, where still doth
    sway
The triple tyrant; that from these may grow
  A hundred fold, who, having learnt thy way,
  Early may fly the Babylonian woe.

ON THE LATE MASSACRE IN PIEDMONT: The massacre
was perpetrated in 1655 by the Duke of Savoy upon
the Waldensians, a Protestant sect in the Italian
Alps who for centuries had worshipped according
to the austere customs of the primitive Christians.
12 *tyrant:* the Pope, who wears a three-tiered crown.
14 *woe:* the punishment that Protestants believed
would be visited upon the Church of Rome; see
Revelations XIV, 8.

William Blake

THE LITTLE BLACK BOY

My mother bore me in the southern wild,
And I am black, but O my soul is white;
White as an angel is the English child,
But I am black, as if bereaved of light.

My mother taught me underneath a tree,
And sitting down before the heat of day,
She took me on her lap and kissed me,
And, pointing to the east, began to say:

"Look on the rising sun—there God does live,
And gives his light, and gives his heat
    away;   10
And flowers and trees and beasts and men receive
Comfort in morning, joy in the noonday.

"And we are put on earth a little space,
That we may learn to bear the beams of love;
And these black bodies and this sunburnt face
Is but a cloud, and like a shady grove.

"For when our souls have learned the heat to
    bear,
The cloud will vanish; we shall hear his voice,
Saying: 'Come out from the grove, my love and
    care,
And round my golden tent like lambs
    rejoice.' "   20

Thus did my mother say, and kissèd me;
And thus I say to little English boy.
When I from black and he from white cloud
    free,
And round the tent of God like lambs we joy,

I'll shade him from the heat, till he can bear
To lean in joy upon our father's knee;
And then I'll stand and stroke his silver hair,
And be like him, and he will then love me.

William Blake

THE CHIMNEY SWEEPER (I)

When my mother died I was very young,
And my father sold me while yet my tongue
Could scarcely cry " 'weep! 'weep! 'weep! 'weep!"
So your chimneys I sweep, and in soot I sleep.

There's little Tom Dacre, who cried when his
     head,
That curled like a lamb's back, was shaved: so I
     said
"Hush, Tom! never mind it, for when your
     head's bare
You know that the soot cannot spoil your white
     hair."

And so he was quiet, and that very night,
As Tom was a-sleeping, he had such a
     sight!   10
That thousands of sweepers, Dick, Joe, Ned, and
     Jack,
Were all of them locked up in coffins of black.

And by came an angel who had a bright key,
And he opened the coffins and set them all free;
Then down a green plain leaping, laughing, they
     run,
And wash in a river, and shine in the sun.

Then naked and white, all their bags left
     behind,
They rise upon clouds and sport in the wind;
And the angel told Tom, if he'd be a good boy,
He'd have God for his father, and never want
     joy.   20

And so Tom awoke; and we rose in the dark,

THE CHIMNEY SWEEPER (I): This and the poem
before it first appeared in *Songs of Innocence*,
1789. Notice the irony of the last line.
  3 *" 'weep!"*: the child's pronunciation of the
street-cry "Sweep!" by which he hopes to be hired.
The double meaning is plain.

And got with our bags and our brushes to work.
Though the morning was cold, Tom was happy
     and warm:
So if all do their duty they need not fear harm.

William Blake

THE CHIMNEY SWEEPER (II)

A little black thing among the snow,
     Crying " 'weep! 'weep!" in notes of woe!
"Where are thy father and mother? say?"
     "They are both gone up to the church to pray.

"Because I was happy upon the heath,
     And smiled among the winter's snow,
They clothèd me in the clothes of death,
     And taught me to sing the notes of woe.

"And because I am happy and dance and sing,
     They think they have done me no injury,   10
And are gone to praise God and his priest and
     king,
     Who make up a heaven of our misery."

THE CHIMNEY SWEEPER (II): From *Songs of Experience,* 1794.

Percy Bysshe Shelley

SONG TO THE MEN OF ENGLAND

Men of England, wherefore plough
For the lords who lay ye low?
Wherefore weave with toil and care
The rich robes your tyrants wear?

Wherefore feed, and clothe, and save,
From the cradle to the grave,

Those ungrateful drones who would
Drain your sweat—nay, drink your blood?

Wherefore, Bees of England, forge
Many a weapon, chain, and scourge,   10
That these stingless drones may spoil
The forcèd produce of your toil?

Have ye leisure, comfort, calm,
Shelter, food, love's gentle balm?
Or what is it ye buy so dear
With your pain and with your fear?

The seed ye sow, another reaps;
The wealth ye find, another keeps;
The robes ye weave, another wears;
The arms ye forge, another bears.   20

Sow seed—but let no tyrant reap;
Find wealth—let no impostor heap;
Weave robes—let not the idle wear;
Forge arms—in your defense to bear.

Shrink to your cellars, holes, and cells;
In halls ye deck another dwells.
Why shake the chains ye wrought?
Ye see
The steel ye tempered glance on ye.

With plough and spade, and hoe and loom,
Trace your grave, and build your tomb,   30
And weave your winding-sheet, till fair
England be your sepulchre.

Percy Bysshe Shelley

SONNET: ENGLAND IN 1819

An old, mad, blind, despised, and dying king,—
Princes, the dregs of their dull race, who flow
Through public scorn—mud from a muddy
        spring—
Rulers who neither see, nor feel, nor know,

1 *king:* George III (1738–1820), declared mentally
incompetent in 1811.

But leech-like to their fainting country cling,
Till they drop, blind in blood, without a blow—
A people starved and stabbed in the untilled
        field—
An army, which liberticide and prey
Makes as a two-edged sword to all who wield—
Golden and sanguine laws which tempt and
        slay;   10
Religion Christless, Godless—a book sealed;
A Senate—Time's worst statute unrepealed—
Are graves, from which a glorious phantom may
Burst, to illumine our tempestuous day.

Gwendolyn Brooks

THE BALLAD OF RUDOLF REED

Rudolph Reed was oaken.
His wife was oaken too.
And his two good girls and his good little man
Oakened as they grew.

"I am not hungry for berries.
I am not hungry for bread.
But hungry hungry for a house
Where at night a man in bed.

"May never hear the plaster
Stir as if in pain.
May never hear the roaches
Falling like fat rain.

"Where never wife and children need
Go blinking through the gloom.
Where every room of many rooms
Will be full of room.

"Oh my home may have its east or west
Or north or south behind it.
All I know is I shall know it,
And fight for it when I find it."

It was in a street of bitter white

That he made his application.
For Rudolph Reed was oakener
Than others in the nation.

The agent's steep and steady stare
Corroded to a grin.
Why, you black old, tough old hell of a man,
Move your family in!

Nary a grin grinned Rudolph Reed,
Nary a curse cursed he,
But moved in his house, with his dark little
    wife,
And his dark little children three.

A neighbor would *look*, with a yawning eye
That squeezed into a slit.
But the Rudolph Reeds and the children three
Were too joyous to notice it.

For were they not firm in a home of their own
With windows everywhere
And a beautiful banistered stair
And a front yard for flowers and a back yard for
    grass?

The first night, a rock, big as two fists.
The second, a rock big as three.
But nary a curse cursed Rudolph Reed.
(Though oaken as man could be.)

The third night, a silvery ring of glass.
Patience ached to endure.
But he looked, and lo! small Mabel's blood
Was staining her gaze so pure.

Then up did rise our Rudolph Reed
And pressed the hand of his wife,
And went to the door with a thirty-four
And a beastly butcher knife.

He ran like a mad thing into the night.
And the words in his mouth were stinking.
By the time he had hurt his first white man
He was no longer thinking.

By the time he had hurt his fourth white man

Rudolph Reed was dead.
His neighbors gathered and kicked his corpse.
"Nigger—" his neighbors said.

Small Mabel whimpered all night long,
For calling herself the cause.
Her oak-eyed mother did no thing
But change the bloody gauze.

Gwendolyn Brooks

THE CHICAGO *DEFENDER* SENDS A MAN TO LITTLE ROCK FALL, 1957

In Little Rock the people bear
Babes, and comb and part their hair
And watch the want ads, put repair
To roof and latch. While wheat toast burns
A woman waters multiferns.

Time upholds or overturns
The many, tight, and small concerns.

In Little Rock the people sing
Sunday hymns like anything,
Through Sunday pomp and polishing.

And after testament and tunes,
Some soften Sunday afternoons
With lemon tea and Lorna Doones.

I forecast
And I believe
Come Christmas Little Rock will cleave
To Christmas tree and trifle, weave,
From laugh and tinsel, texture fast.

DEFENDER: A weekly newspaper, appealing especially to Black readers, which would have been particularly interested in the disorders that occurred in September, 1957 when a high school in the capital of Arkansas was integrated.

In Little Rock is baseball; Barcarolle.
That hotness in July . . . the uniformed figures
	raw and implacable
And not intellectual,
Batting the hotness or clawing the suffering dust.
The Open Air Concert, on the special twilight
	green . . .
When Beethoven is brutal or whispers to
	lady-like air.
Blanket-sitters are solemn, as Johann troubles to
	lean
To tell them what to mean. . . .

There is love, too, in Little Rock. Soft women
	softly
Opening themselves in kindness,
Or, pitying one's blindness,
Awaiting one's pleasure
In azure
Glory with anguished rose at the root. . . .
To wash away old semi-discomfitures.
They re-teach purple and unsullen blue.
The wispy soils go. And uncertain
Half-havings have they clarified to sures.

In Little Rock they know
Not answering the telephone is a way of
	rejecting life,

That it is our business to be bothered, is our
	business
To cherish bores or boredom, be polite
To lies and love and many-faceted fuzziness.

I scratch my head, massage the hate-I-had.
I blink across my prim and pencilled pad.
The saga I was sent for is not down.
Because there is a puzzle in this town.
The biggest News I do not dare
Telegraph to the Editor's chair:
"They are like people everywhere."

The angry Editor would reply
In hundred harryings of Why.

And true, they are hurling spittle, rock,
Garbage and fruit in Little Rock.
And I saw coiling storm a-writhe
On bright madonnas. And a scythe
Of men harassing brownish girls.
(The bows and barrettes in the curls
And braids declined away from joy.)

I saw a bleeding brownish boy. . . .

The lariat lynch-wish I deplored.

The loveliest lynchee was our Lord.

Chapter 7

PEACE AND WAR

Warfare—one of the oldest, most widespread, and continuous of human institutions—commends itself to writers because the intensity of its conflicts affords unparalleled opportunities for the revelation of human nature. The literature of war, from Homer to our day, presents action that is overt, violent, exciting, and large in scale; passions are strong, and certain fundamental human traits, both virtues and weaknesses, are thrown into sharp relief. Hate, in all its forms and qualities, may fascinate a writer as much as love; and war is the institutionalizing and the expression of hate. That is its dark side. But war also can call forth, as William James points out, some of the nobler aspects of human beings: courage, self-sacrifice, loyalty, and devotion to duty.

The works in this chapter offer many aspects of war for consideration. James's "Moral Equivalent of War," "An Irish Airman Foresees his Death," and "Dulce et Decorum Est" center on the motives that drive men to fight. "The Room" and "An Episode of War" show the impact of war upon the soldier; "An Occurrence at Owl Creek Bridge," and "September 1939" show its impact on those who wait at home. Wars have of course differed enormously: in the purposes for which they were fought, the

scope of their terror, the quality of the typical experiences they afforded. The one-act play in this chapter, "Botticelli," captures certain of the most significant features of fighting in our own most recent, and longest, war.

For those who would grasp the larger implications of war, its literature offers much to reflect upon. Several profoundly different points of view emerge, as writers relate themselves in various ways to the events they describe, or imagine their characters trying to understand what is happening to them. To Stephen Crane's lieutenant, fighting is simply the job he has been given to do. To the speaker of "The Charge of the Light Brigade," war is a glorious activity. The rejection of war as inherently immoral, absurd, unworthy of humankind may be presented in forceful arguments, as by William James, in the vivid realism of "The Room," or in the satirical tone of "The Fable of the Vultures," "The War-Song of Dinas Vawr," and "Channel Firing." Militarism has been defended and attacked in various terms; these writings become literature when they rise above the level of polemics and propaganda, penetrate the surface of warfare, embody the writer's passionate convictions about it, and illuminate its implications for human life.

Samuel Johnson

THE FABLE OF
THE VULTURES

Many naturalists are of opinion that the animals which we commonly consider as mute have the power of imparting their thoughts to one another. That they can express general sensations is very certain; every being that can utter sounds has a different voice for pleasure and for pain. The hound informs his fellows when he scents his game; the hen calls her chickens to their food by her cluck and drives them from danger by her scream.

Birds have the greatest variety of notes; they have indeed a variety which seems almost sufficient to make a speech adequate to the purposes of a life which is regulated by instinct and can admit little change or improvement. To the cries of birds, curiosity or superstition has been always attentive; many have studied the language of the feathered tribes, and some have boasted that they understood it.

The most skillful or most confident interpreters of the sylvan dialogues have been commonly found among the philosophers of the East, in a country where the calmness of the air and the mildness of the seasons allow the student to pass a great part of the year in groves and bowers. But what may be done in one place by peculiar opportunities may be performed in another by peculiar diligence. A shepherd of Bohemia has, by long abode in the forests, enabled himself to understand the voice of birds; at least he relates with great confidence a story of which the credibility is left to be considered by the learned.

"As I was sitting," said he, "within a hol-

THE FABLE OF THE VULTURES: THE IDLER, No. 22, 16 September 1758.

low rock and watching my sheep that fed in the valley, I heard two vultures interchangeably crying on the summit of the cliff. Both voices were earnest and deliberate. My curiosity prevailed over my care of the flock; I climbed slowly and silently from crag to crag, concealed among the shrubs, till I found a cavity where I might sit and listen without suffering or giving disturbance.

"I soon perceived that my labor would be well repaid; for an old vulture was sitting on a naked prominence with her young about her, whom she was instructing in the arts of a vulture's life, and preparing by the last lecture for their final dismission to the mountains and the skies.

" 'My children,' said the old vulture, 'you will the less want my instructions because you have had my practice before your eyes; you have seen me snatch from the farm the household fowl; you have seen me seize the leveret in the bush and the kid in the pasture; you know how to fix your talons and how to balance your flight when you are laden with your prey. But you remember the taste of more delicious food; I have often regaled you with the flesh of man.' 'Tell us,' said the young vultures, 'where man may be found and how he may be known; his flesh is surely the natural food of a vulture. Why have you never brought a man in your talons to the nest?' 'He is too bulky,' said the mother; 'when we find a man, we can only tear away his flesh and leave his bones upon the ground.' 'Since man is so big,' said the young ones, 'how do you kill him? You are afraid of the wolf and of the bear; by what power are vultures superior to man? Is man more defenseless than a sheep?' 'We have not the strength of man,' returned the mother, 'and I am sometimes in doubt whether we have the subtlety; and the vultures would seldom feast upon his flesh, had not nature, that devoted him to our uses, infused into him a strange ferocity which I have never observed in any other being that feeds upon the earth. Two herds of men will often meet and shake the earth with noise and fill the air with fire. When you hear noise and see fire, with flashes along the ground, hasten to the place with your swiftest wing, for men are surely destroying one another; you will then find the ground smoking with blood and covered with carcasses, of which many are dismembered and mangled for the convenience of the vulture.' 'But when men have killed their prey,' said the pupil, 'why do they not eat it? When the wolf has killed a sheep, he suffers not the vulture to touch it till he has satisfied himself. Is not man another kind of wolf?' 'Man,' said the mother, 'is the only beast who kills that which he does not devour, and this quality makes him so much a benefactor to our species.' 'If men kill our prey and lay it in our way,' said the young one, 'what need shall we have of laboring for ourselves?' 'Because man will sometimes,' replied the mother, 'remain for a long time quiet in his den. The old vultures will tell you when you are to watch his motions. When you see men in great numbers moving close together like a flight of storks, you may conclude that they are hunting and that you will soon revel in human blood.' 'But still,' said the young one, 'I would gladly know the reason of this mutual slaughter. I could never kill what I could not eat.' 'My child,' said the mother, 'this is a question which I cannot answer, though I am reckoned the most subtle bird of the mountain. When I was young, I used frequently to visit the aerie of an old vulture who dwelt upon the Carpathian rocks; he had made many observations; he knew the places that afforded prey round his habitation as far in every direction as the strongest wing can fly between the rising and setting of the summer sun; he had fed year after year on the entrails of men. His opinion was that men had only the appearance of animal life, being really vegetables with a power of motion; and that as the boughs of an oak are dashed together by the storm that swine

may fatten upon the falling acorns, so men are by some unaccountable power driven one against another till they lose their motion that vultures may be fed. Others think they have observed something of contrivance and policy among these mischievous beings; and those that hover more closely round them pretend that there is in every herd one that gives directions to the rest, and seems to be more eminently delighted with a wide carnage. What is it that entitles him to such pre-eminence we know not; he is seldom the biggest or the swiftest, but he shows by his eagerness and diligence that he is, more than any of the others, a friend to vultures.' "

William James

THE MORAL EQUIVALENT OF WAR

The war against war is going to be no holiday excursion or camping party. The military feelings are too deeply grounded to abdicate their place among our ideals until better substitutes are offered than the glory and shame that come to nations as well as to individuals from the ups and downs of politics and the vicissitudes of trade. There is something highly paradoxical in the modern man's relation to war. Ask all our millions, north and south, whether they would vote now (were such a thing possible) to have our war for the Union expunged from history, and the record of a peaceful transition to the present time substituted for that of its marches and battles, and probably hardly a handful of eccentrics would say yes. Those ancestors, those efforts, those memories and legends, are the most ideal part of what we now own together, a sacred spiritual possession worth more than all the blood poured out. Yet ask those same people whether they would be willing in cold blood to start another civil war now to gain another similar possession, and not one man or woman would vote for the proposition. In modern eyes, precious though wars may be, they must not be waged solely for the sake of the ideal harvest. Only when forced upon one, only when an enemy's injustice leaves us no alternative, is war now thought permissible.

It was not thus in ancient times. The earlier men were hunting men, and to hunt a neighboring tribe, kill the males, loot the villages, and possess the females, was the most profitable as well as the most exciting way of living. Thus were the more martial tribes selected, and in chiefs and peoples a pure pugnacity and love of glory came to mingle with the more fundamental appetite for plunder.

Modern war is so expensive that we feel trade to be a better avenue to plunder; but modern man inherits all the innate pugnacity and all the love of glory of his ancestors. Showing war's irrationality and horror is of no effect upon him. The horrors make the fascination. War is the *strong* life; it is life *in extremis*; war-taxes are the only ones men never hesitate to pay, as the budgets of all nations show us.

History is a bath of blood. The *Iliad* is one long recital of how Diomedes and Ajax, Sarpedon and Hector *killed*. No detail of the wounds they made is spared us, and the Greek mind fed upon the story. Greek history is a panorama of jingoism and imperialism—war for war's sake, all the citizens being warriors. It is horrible reading, because of the irrationality of it all—save for the purpose of making "history"—and the history is that of the utter ruin of a civilization in intellectual respects perhaps the highest the earth has ever seen.

Those wars were purely piratical. Pride, gold, women, slaves, excitement were their only motives. In the Peloponnesian war, for example, the Athenians ask the inhabitants of Melos (the island where the "Venus of Milo" was found), hitherto neutral, to own their lordship. The envoys meet, and hold a debate which Thucydides gives in full,[1] and which, for sweet reasonableness of form, would have satisfied Matthew Arnold. "The powerful exact what they can," said the Athenians, "and the weak grant what they must." When the Meleans say that sooner than be slaves they will appeal to the gods, the Athenians reply: "Of the gods we believe and of men we know that, by a law of their nature, wherever they can rule they will. This law was not made by us, and we are not the first to have acted upon it; we did but inherit it, and we know that you and all mankind, if you were as strong as we are, would do as we do. So much for the gods; we have told you why we expect to stand as high in their good opinion as you." Well, the Meleans still refused, and their town was taken. "The Athenians," Thucydides quietly says, "thereupon put to death all who were of military age and made slaves of the women and children. They then colonized the island, sending thither five hundred settlers of their own."

Alexander's career was piracy pure and simple, nothing but an orgy of power and plunder, made romantic by the character of the hero. There was no rational principle in it, and the moment he died his generals and governors attacked one another. The cruelty of those times is incredible. When Rome finally conquered Greece, Paulus Æmilius was told by the Roman Senate to reward his soldiers for their toil by "giving" them the old kingdom of Epirus. They sacked seventy cities and carried off a hundred and fifty thousand inhabitants as slaves. How many they killed I know not; but in Etolia they killed all the senators, five

[1] *History of the Peloponnesian War*, V, 89–116, translated by Benjamin Jowett. Melos surrendered in 416 B.C.

hundred and fifty in number. Brutus was "the noblest Roman of them all," but to reanimate his soldiers on the eve of Philippi he similarly promises to give them the cities of Sparta and Thessalonica to ravage, if they win the fight.

Such was the gory nurse that trained societies to cohesiveness. We inherit the warlike type; and for most of the capacities of heroism that the human race is full of we have to thank this cruel history. Dead men tell no tales, and if there were any tribes of other type than this they have left no survivors. Our ancestors have bred pugnacity into our bone and marrow, and thousands of years of peace won't breed it out of us. The popular imagination fairly fattens on the thought of wars. Let public opinion once reach a certain fighting pitch, and no ruler can withstand it. In the Boer War both governments began with bluff, but couldn't stay there, the military tension was too much for them. In 1898 our people had read the word WAR in letters three inches high for three months in every newspaper. The pliant politician McKinley was swept away by their eagerness, and our squalid war with Spain became a necessity.

At the present day, civilized opinion is a curious mental mixture. The military instincts and ideals are as strong as ever, but are confronted by reflective criticisms which sorely curb their ancient freedom. Innumerable writers are showing up the bestial side of military service. Pure loot and mastery seem no longer morally avowable motives, and pretexts must be found for attributing them solely to the enemy. England and we, our army and navy authorities repeat without ceasing, arm solely for "peace," Germany and Japan it is who are bent on loot and glory. "Peace" in military mouths today is a synonym for "war expected." The word has become a pure provocative, and no government wishing peace sincerely should allow it ever to be printed in a newspaper.

Every up-to-date dictionary should say that "peace" and "war" mean the same thing, now *in posse*, now *in actu*.[2] It may even reasonably be said that the intensely sharp competitive *preparation* for war by the nations *is the real war*, permanent, unceasing; and that the battles are only a sort of public verification of the mastery gained during the "peace" interval.

It is plain that on this subject civilized man has developed a sort of double personality. If we take European nations, no legitimate interest of any one of them would seem to justify the tremendous destructions which a war to compass it would necessarily entail. It would seem as though common sense and reason ought to find a way to reach agreement in every conflict of honest interests. I myself think it our bounden duty to believe in such international rationality as possible. But, as things stand, I see how desperately hard it is to bring the peace-party and the war-party together, and I believe that the difficulty is due to certain deficiencies in the program of pacificism which set the militarist imagination strongly, and to a certain extent justifiably, against it. In the whole discussion both sides are on imaginative and sentimental ground. It is but one utopia against another, and everything one says must be abstract and hypothetical. Subject to this criticism and caution, I will try to characterize in abstract strokes the opposite imaginative forces, and point out what to my own very fallible mind seems the best utopian hypothesis, the most promising line of conciliation.

In my remarks, pacificist though I am, I will refuse to speak of the bestial side of the war-régime (already done justice to by many writers) and consider only the higher aspects of militaristic sentiment. Patriotism no one thinks discreditable; nor does anyone deny

[2] I.e., "peace" means war in prospect, "war" means war in actuality.

that war is the romance of history. But inordinate ambitions are the soul of every
patriotism, and the possibility of violent
death the soul of all romance. The militarily
patriotic and romantic-minded everywhere,
and especially the professional military
class, refuse to admit for a moment that war
may be a transitory phenomenon in social
evolution. The notion of a sheep's paradise
like that revolts, they say, our higher imagination. Where then would be the steeps of
life? If war had ever stopped, we should
have to re-invent it, on this view, to redeem
life from flat degeneration.

Reflective apologists for war at the present day all take it religiously. It is a sort of
sacrament. Its profits are to the vanquished
as well as to the victor; and quite apart from
any question of profit, it is an absolute good,
we are told, for it is human nature at its
highest dynamic. Its "horrors" are a cheap
price to pay for rescue from the only alternative supposed, of a world of clerks and
teachers, of co-education and zoophily,[3] of
"consumer's leagues" and "associated char-
ities," of industrialism unlimited, and feminism unabashed. No scorn, no hardness, no
valor any more! Fie upon such a cattleyard
of a planet!

So far as the central essence of this feeling
goes, no healthy-minded person, it seems to
me, can help to some degree partaking of it.
Militarism is the great preserver of our
ideals of hardihood, and human life with no
use for hardihood would be contemptible.
Without risks or prizes for the darer, history
would be insipid indeed; and there is a type
of military character which everyone feels
that the race should never cease to breed, for
everyone is sensitive to its superiority. The
duty is incumbent on mankind, of keeping
military characters in stock—of keeping
them, if not for use, then as ends in themselves and as pure pieces of perfection—so

3 I.e., keeping pet animals.

that Roosevelt's weaklings and molly-
coddles[4] may not end by making everything
else disappear from the face of nature.

This natural sort of feeling forms, I
think, the innermost soul of army writings.
Without any exception known to me,
militarist authors take a highly mystical
view of their subject, and regard war as a
biological or sociological necessity, uncontrolled by ordinary psychological checks and
motives. When the time of development is
ripe the war must come, reason or no reason,
for the justifications pleaded are invariably
fictitious. War is, in short, a permanent
human *obligation*. General Homer Lea, in
his recent book *The Valor of Ignorance*,
plants himself squarely on this ground.
Readiness for war is for him the essence of
nationality, and ability in it the supreme
measure of the health of nations.

Nations, General Lea says, are never stationary—they must necessarily expand or
shrink, according to their vitality or decrepitude. Japan now is culminating; and by the
fatal law in question it is impossible that
her statesmen should not long since have
entered, with extraordinary foresight, upon
a vast policy of conquest—the game in
which the first moves were her wars with
China and Russia and her treaty with England, and of which the final objective is the
capture of the Philippines, the Hawaiian Islands, Alaska, and the whole of our coast west
of the Sierra passes. This will give Japan
what her ineluctable vocation as a state
absolutely forces her to claim, the possession
of the entire Pacific Ocean; and to oppose
these deep designs we Americans have, according to our author, nothing but our conceit, our ignorance, our commercialism, our
corruption, and our feminism. General Lea
makes a minute technical comparison of the

4 Theodore Roosevelt (1858–1919) advocated "the
strenuous life"—and in 1897, as Assistant Secretary
of the Navy, war with Spain.

military strength which we at present could oppose to the strength of Japan, and concludes that the islands, Alaska, Oregon, and southern California would fall almost without resistance, that San Francisco must surrender in a fortnight to a Japanese investment, that in three or four months the war would be over, and our republic, unable to regain what it had heedlessly neglected to protect sufficiently, would then "disintegrate," until perhaps some Caesar should arise to weld us again into a nation.

A dismal forecast indeed! Yet not unplausible, if the mentality of Japan's statesmen be of the Caesarian type of which history shows so many examples, and which is all that General Lea seems able to imagine. But there is no reason to think that women can no longer be the mothers of Napoleonic or Alexandrian characters; and if these come in Japan and find their opportunity, just such surprises as *The Valor of Ignorance* paints may lurk in ambush for us. Ignorant as we still are of the innermost recesses of Japanese mentality, we may be foolhardy to disregard such possibilities.

Other militarists are more complex and more moral in their considerations. The *Philosophie des Krieges* [*Philosophy of War*], by S. R. Steinmetz is a good example. War, according to this author, is an ordeal instituted by God, who weighs the nations in its balance. It is the essential form of the state, and the only function in which peoples can employ all their powers at once and convergently. No victory is possible save as the resultant of a totality of virtues, no defeat for which some vice or weakness is not responsible. Fidelity, cohesiveness, tenacity, heroism, conscience, education, inventiveness, economy, wealth, physical health and vigor—there isn't a moral or intellectual point of superiority that doesn't tell, when God holds his assizes and hurls the peoples upon one another. *Die Welt-*

geschichte ist das Weltgericht; [5] and Dr. Steinmetz does not believe that in the long run chance and luck play any part in apportioning the issues.

The virtues that prevail, it must be noted, are virtues anyhow, superiorities that count in peaceful as well as in military competition; but the strain on them, being infinitely intenser in the latter case, makes war infinitely more searching as a trial. No ordeal is comparable to its winnowings. Its dread hammer is the welder of men into cohesive states, and nowhere but in such states can human nature adequately develop its capacity. The only alternative is "degeneration."

Dr. Steinmetz is a conscientious thinker, and his book, short as it is, takes much into account. Its upshot can, it seems to me, be summed up in Simon Patten's word, that mankind was nursed in pain and fear, and that the transition to a "pleasure-economy" may be fatal to a being wielding no powers of defense against its disintegrative influences. If we speak of the *fear of emancipation from the fear-régime*, we put the whole situation into a single phrase; fear regarding ourselves now taking the place of the ancient fear of the enemy.

Turn the fear over as I will in my mind, it all seems to lead back to two unwillingnesses of the imagination, one esthetic and the other moral: unwillingness, first to envisage a future in which army life, with its many elements of charm, shall be forever impossible, and in which the destinies of peoples shall nevermore be decided quickly, thrillingly, and tragically, by force, but only gradually and insipidly by "evolution"; and, secondly, unwillingness to see the supreme theater of human strenuousness closed, and the splendid military aptitudes

[5] World history is the world's court of law—i.e., makes the final judgments on nations.

of men doomed to keep always in a state of latency and never show themselves in action. These insistent unwillingnesses, no less than other esthetic and ethical insistencies have, it seems to me, to be listened to and respected. One cannot meet them effectively by mere counter-insistency on war's expensiveness and horror. The horror makes the thrill; and when the question is of getting the extremest and supremest out of human nature, talk of expense sounds ignominious. The weakness of so much merely negative criticism is evident—pacificism makes no converts from the military party. The military party denies neither the bestiality nor the horror, nor the expense; it only says that these things tell but half the story. It only says that war is *worth* them; that, taking human nature as a whole, its wars are its best protection against its weaker and more cowardly self, and that mankind cannot *afford* to adopt a peace economy.

Pacificists ought to enter more deeply into the esthetical and ethical point of view of their opponents. Do that first in any controversy, says J. J. Chapman, *then move the point*, and your opponent will follow. So long as anti-militarists propose no substitute for war's disciplinary function, no *moral equivalent* of war, analogous, as one might say, to the mechanical equivalent of heat, so long they fail to realize the full inwardness of the situation. And as a rule they do fail. The duties, penalties, and sanctions pictured in the utopias they paint are all too weak and tame to touch the military-minded. Tolstoy's pacificism is the only exception to this rule, for it is profoundly pessimistic as regards all this world's values, and makes the fear of the Lord furnish the moral spur provided elsewhere by the fear of the enemy. But our socialistic peace-advocates all believe absolutely in this world's values; and instead of the fear of the Lord and the fear of the enemy, the only fear they reckon with is the fear of poverty if one be lazy. This weakness pervades all the socialistic literature with which I am acquainted. Even in Lowes Dickinson's exquisite dialogue,[6] high wages and short hours are the only forces invoked for overcoming man's distaste for repulsive kinds of labor. Meanwhile men at large still live as they always have lived, under a pain-and-fear economy—for those of us who lived in an ease-economy are but an island in the stormy ocean—and the whole atmosphere of present-day utopian literature tastes mawkish and dishwatery to people who still keep a sense for life's more bitter flavors. It suggests, in truth, ubiquitous inferiority.

Inferiority is always with us, and merciless scorn of it is the keynote of the military temper. "Dogs, would you live forever?" shouted Frederick the Great. "Yes," say our utopians, "let us live forever, and raise our level gradually." The best thing about our "inferiors" today is that they are as tough as nails, and physically and morally almost as insensitive. Utopianism would see them soft and squeamish, while militarism would keep their callousness but transfigure it into a meritorious characteristic, needed by "the service" and redeemed by that from the suspicion of inferiority. All the qualities of a man acquire dignity when he knows that the service of the collectivity that owns him needs them. If proud of the collectivity, his own pride rises in proportion. No collectivity is like an army for nourishing such pride; but it has to be confessed that the only sentiment which the image of pacific cosmopolitan industrialism is capable of arousing in countless worthy breasts is shame at the idea of belonging to *such* a collectivity. It is obvious that the United States of America as they exist today impress a mind like

6 *Justice and Liberty* (New York, 1909).

General Lea's as so much human blubber. Where is the sharpness and precipitousness, the contempt for life, whether one's own, or another's? Where is the savage "yes" and "no," the unconditional duty? Where is the conscription? Where is the blood-tax? Where is anything that one feels honored by belonging to?

Having said thus much in preparation, I will now confess my own utopia. I devoutly believe in the reign of peace and in the gradual advent of some sort of a socialistic equilibrium. The fatalistic view of the war-function is to me nonsense, for I know that war-making is due to definite motives and subject to prudential checks and reasonable criticisms, just like any other form of enterprise. And when whole nations are the armies, and the science of destruction vies in intellectual refinement with the sciences of production, I see that war becomes absurd and impossible from its own monstrosity. Extravagant ambitions will have to be replaced by reasonable claims, and nations must make common cause against them. I see no reason why all this should not apply to yellow as well as to white countries, and I look forward to a future when acts of war shall be formally outlawed as between civilized peoples.

All these beliefs of mine put me squarely into the anti-militarist party. But I do not believe that peace either ought to be or will be permanent on this globe unless the states pacifically organized preserve some of the old elements of army discipline. A permanently successful peace-economy cannot be a simple pleasure-economy. In the more or less socialistic future towards which mankind seems drifting we must still subject ourselves collectively to those severities which answer to our real position upon this only partly hospitable globe. We must make new energies and hardihoods continue the manliness to which the military mind so faithfully clings. Martial virtues must be the enduring cement; intrepidity, contempt of

softness, surrender of private interest, obedience to command must still remain the rock upon which states are built—unless, indeed, we wish for dangerous reactions against commonwealths fit only for contempt, and liable to invite attack whenever a center of crystallization for military-minded enterprise gets formed anywhere in their neighborhood.

The war-party is assuredly right in affirming and reaffirming that the martial virtues, although originally gained by the race through war, are absolute and permanent human goods. Patriotic pride and ambition in their military form are, after all, only specifications of a more general competitive passion. They are its first form, but that is no reason for supposing them to be its last form. Men now are proud of belonging to a conquering nation, and without a murmur they lay down their persons and their wealth, if by so doing they may fend off subjection. But who can be sure that *other aspects of one's country* may not, with time and education and suggestion enough, come to be regarded with similarly effective feelings of pride and shame? Why should men not some day feel that it is worth a blood-tax to belong to a collectivity superior in *any* ideal respect? Why should they not blush with indignant shame if the community that owns them is vile in any way whatsoever? Individuals, daily more numerous, now feel this civic passion. It is only a question of blowing on the spark till the whole population gets incandescent, and on the ruins of the old morals of military honor, a stable system of morals of civic honor builds itself up. What the whole community comes to believe in grasps the individual as in a vise. The war-function has grasped us so far; but constructive interests may some day seem no less imperative, and impose on the individual a hardly lighter burden.

Let me illustrate my idea more concretely. There is nothing to make one indignant in the mere fact that life is hard, that men should toil and suffer pain. The planetary conditions once for all are such, and we can stand it. But that so many men, by mere accidents of birth and opportunity, should have a life of *nothing else* but toil and pain and hardness and inferiority imposed upon them, should have *no* vacation, while others natively no more deserving never get any taste of this campaigning life at all—*this* is capable of arousing indignation in reflective minds. It may end by seeming shameful to all of us that some of us have nothing but campaigning, and others nothing but unmanly ease. If now—and this is my idea—there were, instead of military conscription, a conscription of the whole youthful population to form for a certain number of years a part of the army enlisted against *nature*, the injustice would tend to be evened out, and numerous other goods to the commonwealth would follow. The military ideals of hardihood and discipline would be wrought into the growing fiber of the people; no one would remain blind, as the luxurious classes now are blind, to man's real relations to the globe he lives on and to the permanently sour and hard foundations of his higher life. To coal and iron mines, to freight trains, to fishing fleets in December, to dishwashing, clothes-washing and window-washing, to road-building and tunnel-making, to foundries and stoke-holes, and to the frames of skyscrapers would our gilded youths be drafted off, according to their choice, to get the childishness knocked out of them and to come back into society with healthier sympathies and soberer ideas. They would have paid their blood-tax, done their own part in the immemorial human warfare against nature, they would tread the earth more proudly, the women would value them more highly, they would be better fathers and teachers of the following generation.

Such a conscription, with the state of public opinion that would have required it, and the many moral fruits it would bear,

would preserve in the midst of a pacific civilization the manly virtues which the military party is so afraid of seeing disappear in peace. We should get toughness without callousness, authority with as little criminal cruelty as possible, and painful work done cheerily because the duty is temporary, and threatens not, as now, to degrade the whole remainder of one's life. I spoke of the "moral equivalent" of war. So far, war has been the only force that can discipline a whole community, and until an equivalent discipline is organized, I believe that war must have its way. But I have no serious doubt that the ordinary prides and shames of social man, once developed to a certain intensity, are capable of organizing such a moral equivalent as I have sketched, or some other just as effective for preserving manliness of type. It is but a question of time, of skillful propagandism, and of opinion-making men seizing historic opportunities.

The martial type of character can be bred without war. Strenuous honor and disinterestedness abound elsewhere. Priests and medical men are in a fashion educated to it, and we should all feel some degree of it imperative if we were conscious of our work as an obligatory service to the state. We should be *owned*, as soldiers are by the army, and our pride would rise accordingly. We could be poor, then, without humiliation, as army officers now are. The only thing needed henceforward is to inflame the civic temper as past history has inflamed the military temper. H. G. Wells, as usual, sees the center of the situation. "In many ways," he says, "military organization is the most peaceful of activities. When the contemporary man steps from the street, of clamorous insincere advertisement, push, adulteration, under-selling and intermittent employment, into the barrack-yard, he steps on to a higher social plane, into an atmosphere of service and cooperation and of infinitely more honorable emulations. Here at least men are not flung out of employment to degenerate because there is no immediate work for them to do. They are fed and drilled and trained for better services. Here at least a man is supposed to win promotion by self-forgetfulness, and not by self-seeking. And beside the feeble and irregular endowment of research by commercialism, its little short-sighted snatches at profit by innovation and scientific economy, see how remarkable is the steady and rapid development of method and appliances in naval and military affairs! Nothing is more striking than to compare the progress of civil conveniences which has been left almost entirely to the trader, to the progress in military apparatus during the last few decades. The house-appliances of today, for example, are little better than they were fifty years ago. A house of today is still almost as ill-ventilated, badly heated by wasteful fires, clumsily arranged and furnished as the house of 1858. Houses a couple of hundred years old are still satisfactory places of residence, so little have our standards risen. But the rifle or battleship of fifty years ago was beyond all comparison inferior to those we possess; in power, in speed, in convenience alike. No one has a use now for such super-annuated things." [7]

Wells adds[8] that he thinks that the conceptions of order and discipline, the tradition of service and devotion, of physical fitness, unstinted exertion and universal responsibility, which universal military duty is now teaching European nations, will remain a permanent acquisition, when the last ammunition has been used in the fireworks that celebrate the final peace. I believe as he does. It would be simply preposterous if the only force that could work ideals of honor and standards of efficiency into English or American natures should be the fear of being killed by the Germans or the Japanese. Great indeed is fear, but it is

not, as our military enthusiasts believe and try to make us believe, the only stimulus known for awakening the higher ranges of men's spiritual energy. The amount of alteration in public opinion which my utopia postulates is vastly less than the difference between the mentality of those black warriors who pursued Stanley's party on the Congo with their cannibal war-cry of "Meat! meat" and that of the "general staff" of any civilized nation. History has seen the latter interval bridged over: the former one can be bridged over much more easily.

Ambrose Bierce

AN OCCURRENCE AT OWL CREEK BRIDGE

A man stood upon a railroad bridge in northern Alabama, looking down into the swift water twenty feet below. The man's hands were behind his back, the wrists bound with a cord. A rope closely encircled his neck. It was attached to a stout cross-timber above his head and the slack fell to the level of his knees. Some loose boards laid upon the sleepers supporting the metals of the railway supplied a footing for him and his executioners—two private soldiers of the Federal army, directed by a sergeant who in civil life may have been a deputy sheriff. At a short remove upon the same temporary platform was an officer in the uniform of his rank, armed. He was a captain. A sentinel at each end of the bridge stood with his rifle in the position known as "support," that is to say, vertical in front of the left shoulder, the hammer resting on the forearm thrown straight across the chest—a formal and unnatural position, enforcing an erect carriage of the body. It did not appear to be the duty of

[7] *First and Last Things* (1908), p. 215.
[8] *Ibid.*, p. 226.

these two men to know what was occurring at the center of the bridge; they merely blockaded the two ends of the foot planking that traversed it.

Beyond one of the sentinels nobody was in sight; the railroad ran straight away into a forest for a hundred yards, then, curving, was lost to view. Doubtless there was an outpost farther along. The other bank of the stream was open ground—a gentle acclivity topped with a stockade of vertical tree trunks, loopholed for rifles, with a single embrasure through which protruded the muzzle of a brass cannon commanding the bridge. Midway of the slope between the bridge and fort were the spectators—a single company of infantry in line, at "parade rest," the butts of the rifles on the ground, the barrels inclining slightly backward against the right shoulder, the hands crossed upon the stock. A lieutenant stood at the right of the line, the point of his sword upon the ground, his left hand resting upon his right. Excepting the group of four at the center of the bridge, not a man moved. The company faced the bridge, staring stonily, motionless. The sentinels, facing the banks of the stream, might have been statues to adorn the bridge. The captain stood with folded arms, silent, observing the work of his subordinates, but making no sign. Death is a dignitary who when he comes announced is to be received with formal manifestations of respect, even by those most familiar with him. In the code of military etiquette silence and fixity are forms of deference.

The man who was engaged in being hanged was apparently about thirty-five years of age. He was a civilian, if one might judge from his habit, which was that of a planter. His features were good—a straight nose, firm mouth, broad forehead, from which his long, dark hair was combed straight back, falling behind his ears to the collar of his well-fitting frock coat. He wore a mustache and pointed beard, but no whiskers; his eyes were large and dark gray, and had a kindly expression which one would hardly have expected in one whose neck was in the hemp. Evidently this was no vulgar assassin. The liberal military code makes provision for hanging many kinds of persons, and gentlemen are not excluded.

The preparations being complete, the two private soldiers stepped aside, and each drew away the plank upon which he had been standing. The sergeant turned to the captain, saluted, and placed himself immediately behind that officer, who in turn moved apart one pace. These movements left the condemned man and the sergeant standing on the two ends of the same plank, which spanned three of the crossties of the bridge. The end upon which the civilian stood almost, but not quite, reached a fourth. This plank had been held in place by the weight of the captain; it was now held by that of the sergeant. At a signal from the former the latter would step aside, the plank would tilt, and the condemned man go down between two ties. The arrangement commended itself to his judgment as simple and effective. His face had not been covered nor his eyes bandaged. He looked a moment at his "unsteadfast footing," [9] then let his gaze wander to the swirling water of the stream racing madly beneath his feet. A piece of dancing driftwood caught his attention, and his eyes followed it down the current. How slowly it appeared to move! What a sluggish stream!

He closed his eyes in order to fix his last thoughts upon his wife and children. The water, touched to gold by the early sun, the brooding mists under the banks at some distance down the stream, the fort, the soldiers, the piece of drift—all had distracted him. And now he became conscious of a new disturbance. Striking through the thought of his dear ones was a sound which he could neither ignore nor understand, a sharp, dis-

9 *I Henry IV*, I, III.

tinct, metallic percussion like the stroke of a blacksmith's hammer upon the anvil; it had the same ringing quality. He wondered what it was, and whether immeasurably distant or near by—it seemed both. Its recurrence was regular, but as slow as the tolling of a death knell. He awaited each stroke with impatience and—he knew not why—apprehension. The intervals of silence grew progressively longer; the delays became maddening. With their greater infrequency the sounds increased in strength and sharpness. They hurt his ear like the thrust of a knife; he feared he would shriek. What he heard was the ticking of his watch.

He unclosed his eyes and saw again the water below him. "If I could free my hands," he thought, "I might throw off the noose and spring into the stream. By diving I could evade the bullets and, swimming vigorously, reach the bank, take to the woods and get away home. My home, thank God, is as yet outside their lines; my wife and little ones are still beyond the invader's farthest advance."

As these thoughts, which have here to be set down in words, were flashed into the doomed man's brain rather than evolved from it, the captain nodded to the sergeant. The sergeant stepped aside.

Peyton Farquhar was a well-to-do planter, of an old and highly respected Alabama family. Being a slave owner and like other slave owners a politician, he was naturally an original secessionist and ardently devoted to the Southern cause. Circumstances of an imperious nature, which it is unnecessary to relate here, had prevented him from taking service with the gallant army that had fought the disastrous campaigns ending with the fall of Corinth, and he chafed under the inglorious restraint, longing for the release of his energies, the larger life of the soldier, the opportunity for distinction. That opportunity, he felt, would come, as it comes to all in wartime. Meanwhile he did

what he could. No service was too humble for him to perform in aid of the South, no adventure too perilous for him to undertake if consistent with the character of a civilian who was at heart a soldier and who in good faith and without too much qualification assented to at least a part of the frankly villainous dictum that all is fair in love and war.

One evening while Farquhar and his wife were sitting on a rustic bench near the entrance to his grounds, a gray-clad soldier rode up to the gate and asked for a drink of water. Mrs. Farquhar was only too happy to serve him with her own white hands. While she was fetching the water her husband approached the dusty horseman and inquired eagerly for news from the front.

"The Yanks are repairing the railroads," said the man, "and are getting ready for another advance. They have reached the Owl Creek bridge, put it in order, and built a stockade on the north bank. The commandant has issued an order, which is posted everywhere, declaring that any civilian caught interfering with the railroad, its bridges, tunnels, or trains will be summarily hanged. I saw the order."

"How far is it to the Owl Creek bridge?" Farquhar asked.

"About thirty miles."

"Is there no force on this side the creek?"

"Only a picket post half a mile out, on the railroad, and a single sentinel at this end of the bridge."

"Suppose a man—a civilian and student of hanging—should elude the picket post and perhaps get the better of the sentinel," said Farquhar, smiling, "what could he accomplish?"

The soldier reflected. "I was there a month ago," he replied. "I observed that the flood of last winter had lodged a great quantity of driftwood against the wooden pier at this end of the bridge. It is now dry and would burn like tow."

The lady had now brought the water, which the soldier drank. He thanked her ceremoniously, bowed to her husband, and rode away. An hour later, after nightfall, he repassed the plantation, going northward in the direction from which he had come. He was a Federal scout.

As Peyton Farquhar fell straight downward through the bridge he lost consciousness and was as one already dead. From this state he was awakened—ages later, it seemed to him—by the pain of a sharp pressure upon his throat, followed by a sense of suffocation. Keen, poignant agonies seemed to shoot from his neck downward through every fiber of his body and limbs. These pains appeared to flash along well-defined lines of ramification and to beat with an inconceivably rapid periodicity. They seemed like streams of pulsating fire heating him to an intolerable temperature. As to his head, he was conscious of nothing but a feeling of fullness—of congestion. These sensations were unaccompanied by thought. The intellectual part of his nature was already effaced; he had power only to feel, and feeling was torment. He was conscious of motion. Encompassed in a luminous cloud, of which he was now merely the fiery heart, without material substance, he swung through unthinkable arcs of oscillation, like a vast pendulum. Then all at once, with terrible suddenness, the light about him shot upward with the noise of a loud plash; a frightful roaring was in his ears, and all was cold and dark. The power of thought was restored; he knew that the rope had broken and he had fallen into the stream. There was no additional strangulation; the noose about his neck was already suffocating him and kept the water from his lungs. To die of hanging at the bottom of a river!—the idea seemed to him ludicrous. He opened his eyes in the darkness and saw above him a gleam of light, but how distant, how inaccessible! He was still sinking, for the light became fainter and fainter until it was a mere glimmer. Then it began to grow and brighten, and he knew that he was rising toward the surface—knew it with reluctance, for he was now very comfortable. "To be hanged and drowned," he thought, "that is not so bad; but I do not wish to be shot. No; I will not be shot; that is not fair."

He was not conscious of an effort, but a sharp pain in his wrist apprised him that he was trying to free his hands. He gave the struggle his attention, as an idler might observe the feat of a juggler, without interest in the outcome. What splendid effort! What magnificent, what superhuman strength! Ah, that was a fine endeavor! Bravo! The cord fell away; his arms parted and floated upward, the hands dimly seen on each side in the growing light. He watched them with a new interest as first one and then the other pounced upon the noose at his neck. They tore it away and thrust it fiercely aside, its undulations resembling those of a water snake. "Put it back, put it back!" He thought he shouted these words to his hands, for the undoing of the noose had been succeeded by the direst pang that he had yet experienced. His neck ached horribly; his brain was on fire; his heart, which had been fluttering faintly, gave a great leap, trying to force itself out at his mouth. His whole body was racked and wrenched with an insupportable anguish! But his disobedient hands gave no heed to the command. They beat the water vigorously with quick, downward strokes, forcing him to the surface. He felt his head emerge; his eyes were blinded by the sunlight; his chest expanded convulsively, and with a supreme and crowning agony his lungs engulfed a great draught of air, which instantly he expelled in a shriek!

He was now in full possession of his physical senses. They were, indeed, preternaturally keen and alert. Something in the awful disturbance of his organic system had so exalted and refined them that they made record of things never before perceived. He felt the ripples upon his face and heard their separate sounds as they struck. He looked at the forest on the bank of the stream, saw the individual trees, the leaves, and the veining of each leaf—saw the very insects upon them: the locusts, the brilliant-bodied flies, the gray spiders stretching their webs from twig to twig. He noted the prismatic colors in all the dewdrops upon a million blades of grass. The humming of the gnats that danced above the eddies of the stream, the beating of the dragonflies' wings, the strokes of the water spiders' legs, like oars which have lifted their boat—all these made audible music. A fish slid along beneath his eyes and he heard the rush of its body parting the water.

He had come to the surface facing down the stream; in a moment the visible world seemed to wheel slowly round, himself the pivotal point, and he saw the bridge, the fort, the soldiers upon the bridge, the captain, the sergeant, the two privates, his executioners. They were in silhouette against the blue sky. They shouted and gesticulated, pointing at him. The captain had drawn his pistol, and did not fire; the others were unarmed. Their movements were grotesque and horrible, their forms gigantic.

Suddenly he heard a sharp report and something struck the water smartly within a few inches of his head, spattering his face with spray. He heard a second report, and saw one of the sentinels with his rifle at his shoulder, a light cloud of blue smoke rising from the muzzle. The man in the water saw the eye of the man on the bridge gazing into his own through the sights of the rifle. He observed that it was a gray eye and remembered having read that gray eyes were keenest, and that all famous marksmen had them. Nevertheless, this one had missed.

A counter-swirl had caught Farquhar and turned him half round; he was again looking into the forest on the bank opposite the fort. The sound of a clear, high voice in a monotonous sing-song now rang out behind him and came across the water with a distinctness that pierced and subdued all other sounds, even the beating of the ripples in his ears. Although no soldier, he had frequented camps enough to know the dread significance of that deliberate, drawling, aspirated chant; the lieutenant on shore was taking a part in the morning's work. How coldly and pitilessly—with what an even, calm intonation, presaging and enforcing tranquillity in the men—with what accurately measured intervals fell those cruel words:

"Attention, company! . . . Shoulder arms! . . . Ready! . . . Aim! . . . Fire!"

Farquhar dived—dived as deeply as he could. The water roared in his ears like the voice of Niagara, yet he heard the dulled thunder of the volley and, rising again toward the surface, met shining bits of metal, singularly flattened, oscillating slowly downward. Some of them touched him on the face and hands, then fell away, continuing their descent. One lodged between his collar and neck; it was uncomfortably warm and he snatched it out.

As he rose to the surface, gasping for breath, he saw that he had been a long time under water; he was perceptibly farther down stream—nearer to safety. The soldiers had almost finished reloading; the metal ramrods flashed all at once in the sunshine as they were drawn from the barrels, turned in the air, and thrust into their sockets. The two sentinels fired again, independently and ineffectually.

The hunted man saw all this over his shoulder; he was now swimming vigorously with the current. His brain was as energetic as his arms and legs; he thought with the rapidity of lightning.

"The officer," he reasoned, "will not make that martinet's error a second time. It is as easy to dodge a volley as a single shot. He has probably already given the command to fire at will. God help me, I cannot dodge them all!"

An appalling plash within two yards of him was followed by a loud, rushing sound, *diminuendo,* which seemed to travel back through the air to the fort and died in an explosion which stirred the very river to its deeps! A rising sheet of water curved over him, fell down upon him, blinded him, strangled him! The cannon had taken a hand in the game. As he shook his head free from the commotion of the smitten water he heard the deflected shot humming through the air ahead, and in an instant it was cracking and smashing the branches in the forest beyond.

"They will not do that again," he thought; "the next time they will use a charge of grape. I must keep my eye upon the gun; the smoke will apprise me—the report arrives too late; it lags behind the missile. That is a good gun."

Suddenly he felt himself whirled round and round—spinning like a top. The water, the banks, the forests, the now distant bridge, fort and men—all were commingled and blurred. Objects were represented by their colors only; circular horizontal streaks of color—that was all he saw. He had been caught in a vortex and was being whirled on with a velocity of advance and gyration that made him giddy and sick. In a few moments he was flung upon the gravel at the foot of the left bank of the stream—the southern bank—and behind a projecting point which concealed him from his enemies. The sudden arrest of his motion, the abrasion of one of his hands on the gravel, restored him, and he wept with delight. He dug his fingers into the sand, threw it over himself in handfuls, and audibly blessed it. It looked like diamonds, rubies, emeralds; he could think of nothing beautiful which it did not resemble. The trees upon the bank were giant garden plants; he noted a definite order in their arrangement, inhaled the fragrance of their blooms. A strange, roseate light shone through the spaces among their trunks, and the wind made in their branches the music of Æolian harps. He had no wish to perfect his escape—was content to remain in that enchanting spot until retaken.

A whiz and rattle of grapeshot among the branches high above his head roused him from his dream. The baffled cannoneer had fired him a random farewell. He sprang to his feet, rushed up the sloping bank, and plunged into the forest.

All that day he traveled, laying his course by the rounding sun. The forest seemed interminable; nowhere did he discover a break in it, not even a woodman's road. He had not known that he lived in so wild a region. There was something uncanny in the revelation.

By nightfall he was fatigued, footsore, famishing. The thought of his wife and children urged him on. At last he found a road which led him in what he knew to be the right direction. It was as wide and straight as a city street, yet it seemed untraveled. No fields bordered it, no dwelling anywhere. Not so much as the barking of a dog suggested human habitation. The black bodies of the trees formed a straight wall on both sides, terminating on the horizon in a point, like a diagram in a lesson in perspective. Overhead, as he looked up through this rift in the wood, shone great golden stars looking unfamiliar and grouped in strange constellations. He was sure they were arranged in some order which had a secret and malign significance. The wood on either side was full of singular noises, among which—once, twice, and again—he distinctly heard whispers in an unknown tongue.

His neck was in pain, and lifting his hand to it he found it horribly swollen. He knew that it had a circle of black where the rope had bruised it. His eyes felt congested; he could no longer close them. His tongue was swollen with thirst; he relieved its fever by thrusting it forward from between his teeth into the cold air. How softly the turf had carpeted the untraveled avenue—he could no longer feel the roadway beneath his feet!

Doubtless, despite his suffering, he had fallen asleep while walking, for now he sees another scene—perhaps he has merely recovered from a delirium. He stands at the gate of his own home. All is as he left it, and all bright and beautiful in the morning sunshine. He must have traveled the entire night. As he pushes open the gate and passes up the wide white walk, he sees a flutter of female garments; his wife, looking fresh and cool and sweet, steps down from the veranda to meet him. At the bottom of the steps she stands waiting, with a smile of ineffable joy, an attitude of matchless grace and dignity. Ah, how beautiful she is! He springs forward with extended arms. As he is about to clasp her he feels a stunning blow upon the back of the neck; a blinding white light blazes all about him with a sound like the shock of a cannon—then all is darkness and silence!

Peyton Farquhar was dead; his body, with a broken neck, swung gently from side to side beneath the timbers of the Owl Creek bridge.

Stephen Crane

AN EPISODE OF WAR

The lieutenant's rubber blanket lay on the ground, and upon it he had poured the company's supply of coffee. Corporals and other representatives of the grimy and hot-throated men who lined the breastwork had come for each squad's portion.

The lieutenant was frowning and serious at this task of division. His lips pursed as he drew with his sword various crevices in the heap, until brown squares of coffee, astoundingly equal in size, appeared on the blanket. He was on the verge of a great triumph in mathematics, and the corporals were thronging forward, each to reap a little square, when suddenly the lieutenant cried out and looked quickly at a man near him as if he suspected it was a case of personal assault. The others cried out also when they saw blood upon the lieutenant's sleeve.

He had winced like a man stung, swayed dangerously, and then straightened. The sound of his hoarse breathing was plainly audible. He looked sadly, mystically, over the breastwork at the green face of a wood, where now were many little puffs of white smoke. During this moment the men about him gazed statue-like and silent, astonished and awed by this catastrophe which happened when catastrophes were not expected —when they had leisure to observe it.

As the lieutenant stared at the wood, they too swung their heads, so that for another instant all hands, still silent, contemplated the distant forest as if their minds were fixed upon the mystery of a bullet's journey.

The officer had, of course, been compelled to take his sword into his left hand. He did not hold it by the hilt. He gripped it at the middle of the blade, awkwardly. Turning his eyes from the hostile wood, he looked at the sword as he held it there, and seemed puzzled as to what to do with it, where to put it. In short, this weapon had of a sudden become a strange thing to him. He looked at it in a kind of stupefaction, as if he had been endowed with a trident, a sceptre, or a spade.

Finally he tried to sheathe it. To sheathe a sword held by the left hand, at the middle of the blade, in a scabbard hung at the left hip, is a feat worthy of a sawdust ring. This wounded officer engaged in a desperate struggle with the sword and the wobbling scabbard, and during the time of it he breathed like a wrestler.

But at this instant the men, the spectators, awoke from their stone-like poses and
crowded forward sympathetically. The
orderly-sergeant took the sword and tenderly placed it in the scabbard. At the time,
he leaned nervously backward, and did not
allow even his finger to brush the body of
the lieutenant. A wound gives strange dignity to him who bears it. Well men shy
from this new and terrible majesty. It is as
if the wounded man's hand is upon the curtain which hangs before the revelations of
all existence—the meaning of ants, poten-
tates, wars, cities, sunshine, snow, a feather
dropped from a bird's wing; and the power
of it sheds radiance upon a bloody form, and
makes the other men understand sometimes
that they are little. His comrades look at
him with large eyes thoughtfully. Moreover,
they fear vaguely that the weight of a finger
upon him might send him headlong, precipitate the tragedy, hurl him at once into the
dim, grey unknown. And so the orderly-
sergeant, while sheathing the sword, leaned
nervously backward.

There were others who proffered assistance. One timidly presented his shoulder
and asked the lieutenant if he cared to lean
upon it, but the latter waved him away
mournfully. He wore the look of one who
knows he is the victim of a terrible disease
and understands his helplessness. He again
stared over the breastwork at the forest, and
then, turning, went slowly rearward. He
held his right wrist tenderly in his left hand
as if the wounded arm was made of very
brittle glass.

And the men in silence stared at the
wood, then at the departing lieutenant;
then at the wood, then at the lieutenant.

As the wounded officer passed from the
line of battle, he was enabled to see many
things which as a participant in the fight
were unknown to him. He saw a general on
a black horse gazing over the lines of blue
infantry at the green woods which veiled
his problems. An aide galloped furiously,

dragged his horse suddenly to a halt, saluted, and presented a paper. It was, for a
wonder, precisely like a historical painting.

To the rear of the general and his staff a
group, composed of a bugler, two or three
orderlies, and the bearer of the corps standard, all upon maniacal horses, were working like slaves to hold their ground, preserve
their respectful interval, while the shells
boomed in the air about them, and caused
their chargers to make furious quivering
leaps.

A battery, a tumultuous and shining
mass, was swirling toward the right. The
wild thud of hoofs, the cries of the riders
shouting blame and praise, menace and encouragement, and, last, the roar of the
wheels, the slant of the glistening guns,
brought the lieutenant to an intent pause.
The battery swept in curves that stirred the
heart; it made halts as dramatic as the crash
of a wave on the rocks, and when it fled onward this aggression of wheels, levers,
motors, had a beautiful unity, as if it were a
missile. The sound of it was a war-chorus
that reached into the depths of man's emotion.

The lieutenant, still holding his arm as
if it were of glass, stood watching this battery until all detail of it was lost, save the
figures of the riders, which rose and fell and
waved lashes over the black mass.

Later, he turned his eyes toward the battle, where the shooting sometimes crackled
like bush-fires, sometimes sputtered with
exasperating irregularity, and sometimes reverberated like the thunder. He saw the
smoke rolling upward and saw crowds of
men who ran and cheered, or stood and
blazed away at the inscrutable distance.

He came upon some stragglers, and they
told him how to find the field hospital. They
described its exact location. In fact, these
men, no longer having part in the battle,
knew more of it than others. They told the
performance of every corps, every division,
the opinion of every general. The lieuten-

ant, carrying his wounded arm rearward, looked upon them with wonder.

At the roadside a brigade was making coffee and buzzing with talk like a girls' boarding school. Several officers came out to him and inquired concerning things of which he knew nothing. One, seeing his arm, began to scold. "Why, man, that's no way to do. You want to fix that thing." He appropriated the lieutenant and the lieutenant's wound. He cut the sleeve and laid bare the arm, every nerve of which softly fluttered under his touch. He bound his handkerchief over the wound, scolding away in the meantime. His tone allowed one to think that he was in the habit of being wounded every day. The lieutenant hung his head, feeling, in this presence, that he did not know how to be correctly wounded.

The low white tents of the hospital were grouped around an old schoolhouse. There was here a singular commotion. In the foreground two ambulances interlocked wheels in the deep mud. The drivers were tossing the blame of it back and forth, gesticulating and berating, while from the ambulances, both crammed with wounded, there came an occasional groan. An interminable crowd of bandaged men was coming and going. Great numbers sat under the trees nursing heads or arms or legs. There was a dispute of some kind raging on the steps of the schoolhouse. Sitting with his back against a tree a man with a face as grey as a new army blanket was serenely smoking a corn-cob pipe. The lieutenant wished to rush forward and inform him that he was dying.

A busy surgeon was passing near the lieutenant. "Good morning," he said, with a friendly smile. Then he caught sight of the lieutenant's arm, and his face at once changed. "Well, let's have a look at it." He seemed possessed suddenly of a great contempt for the lieutenant. This wound evidently placed the latter on a very low social plane. The doctor cried out impatiently:

"What mutton-head had tied it up that way anyhow?" The lieutenant answered, "Oh, a man."

When the wound was disclosed the doctor fingered it disdainfully. "Humph," he said. "You come along with me and I'll 'tend to you." His voice contained the same scorn as if he were saying: "You will have to go to jail."

The lieutenant had been very meek, but now his face flushed, and he looked into the doctor's eyes. "I guess I won't have it amputated," he said.

"Nonsense, man! Nonsense! Nonsense!" cried the doctor. "Come along, now. I won't amputate it. Come along. Don't be a baby."

"Let go of me," said the lieutenant, holding back wrathfully, his glance fixed upon the door of the old schoolhouse, as sinister to him as the portals of death.

And this is the story of how the lieutenant lost his arm. When he reached home, his sisters, his mother, his wife, sobbed for a long time at the sight of the flat sleeve. "Oh, well," he said, standing shamefaced amid these tears, "I don't suppose it matters so much as all that."

Victor Kolpacoff

THE ROOM

There were the six of us and the prisoner in a room that was thirty feet long and half as wide, and the table took up a quarter of the space. It was made out of heavy sheet metal and had strong vises at either end, as if it had once been a workbench. Above it was a low ceiling of corrugated tin, sagging in the middle where the rusted sheets had been bolted together. All the heat in the room seemed to come from that ceiling. It leaked in under the sagging plates like lava.

The walls, too, were made of tin sheets. The ruts of the corrugated surface did not look comfortable, but I had a prisoner's instinct to keep my back against something, and I marked the hot corners of the room as a retreat. On the wall opposite the door there was a tool rack that stood as high as a man's head. It was divided into thick plywood boxes, black with grease, and each box was marked with a number that had been burned into the wood. The tools had been thrown in on top of each other by the last occupants of the room, but I could see the gleaming black handles of wrenches and metal hammers. Deeper back, where the electric light did not reach, there were dark coils of rope and wire cable. The floor was dirt, hard-packed from use, and as dry as the parade ground. Only the cots were new. For the moment they gave the room an odor of new wood and canvas that almost covered the musty smell of tin and human sweat.

Then there were the faces: Cowley's heavy, ugly face, squinting up at the light; and McGruder, as ugly as Cowley, but with no humor around his eyes or mouth, watching the prisoner; and Buckley's handsome pink face, clean-shaven, with his pale blue eyes moving from place to place; and finally Nguyen, whose impassive, patient eyes were fixed on Buckley. Only the prisoner seemed to want to see nothing. He kept his face lowered out of the light and fixed his eyes on a long streak of rust that ran down a leg from the top of the table, as if the metal were slowly bleeding.

When I saw that, I wanted to get out, but I had been carefully taught that escape from Quai Dong was impossible. I tried not to think about it. The soldier, Russell, was still holding his carbine at the ready. He looked frightened and dangerous, as if he might squeeze the trigger and shoot through the ceiling.

Not that he wanted to hurt anyone. For the time being, I didn't think that any of them wanted that. They only seemed frightened or unaccountably angry.

Buckley and Nguyen began to argue quietly between themselves about how to begin with the boy. Buckley was in a hurry, but Nguyen was telling him that "such things" took time. Finally Buckley turned his back to the light and looked at us. "You all know why you're here," he said, "and what we have to do."

"Let's get it started," McGruder said.

"No, we're going to do it properly," Buckley replied sternly, and McGruder moved away with a shrug and watched the crack of sunlight under the door.

"Now listen to me," Buckley said, raising his voice, though we had heard him perfectly well before; "we're a rest camp and a military stockade. We don't have the right people to do this kind of job, but we're going to do the best we can and get it over with. Now," he added, stepping forward and dropping his voice, "I've got a Vietnamese interpreter who says this thing will take a long time. Do any of you think you can do better than that?"

"Let me have him, Lieutenant," McGruder said, and he turned toward the boy hopefully—but Buckley was looking only at me and seemed not to hear.

"Kreuger?" he asked.

"I don't know what you want," I said.

Cowley dug his fingers into the back of my arm. "Keep out of it!" he whispered.

I wanted to tell Buckley that I did not know why I was there at all, but Cowley was right; it was safer to be quiet and I said nothing. Among the six of us in the room nothing seemed clear. I did not know if Cowley and I were counted with the interrogators or as convicts. We still wore our prison uniforms. Our position was awkward, and if something went wrong it could be dangerous, for we would be witnesses to whatever took place. Buckley knew it as well as I did, but he tried to hide it from us.

"You're here as an officer," he said.

"What about Cowley?" I asked.

Buckley shifted his feet and did not answer for a moment, then he frowned up at the light. "We've had trouble from a local guerrilla outfit for a month. We need your help. Forget the stockade."

"I thought the district was pacified."

"It is officially pacified," he said, tightening his lips, "and we want it to stay that way."

"What does the boy have to do with it?" I asked, despite the pressure of Cowley's fingers on my arm. Finally I felt his hand slide down, and he let me go.

McGruder turned around slowly and looked at me. "We took him off the Weichu Road," he said. "He was trying to get through our patrols."

I watched McGruder for a moment. He looked at me full of hate, as if he thought that I was somehow a threat to him or to what he wanted to do. I wanted only to stay clear, but there was no way to tell him that.

"What will happen to the boy?" I asked Buckley.

"Leave that to us," he replied quickly. "You do your job and you'll come out all right."

I agreed with him, since there was nothing else for me to do, and I retreated to one of the cots along the walls and sat down where I would be able to watch what happened from the farthest possible distance. Cowley followed me. All that puzzled me was what my "job" was supposed to be. It was not until I looked up across the room at Buckley that I realized that I had turned my back to an officer and walked away. I had taken a seat, in spite of my prison khaki, and had not been immediately jabbed with a swagger stick and ordered to get back on my feet. That had never happened to me before at Quai Dong. Only then did I realize how much of our punishment in the stockade had been made up of simple humiliation. Already, somehow, I had acquired this simple privilege. I was grateful to Buckley. I couldn't help it, and that made me distrust him.

Still, it seemed that we had been granted a reprieve for as long as the interrogation lasted. At the moment that was all that mattered. I thought of the other prisoners still working on the beach, trudging from the hollow to the shore with their sacks full of sand. The corrugated shed would be a diversion, at the very worst. All that remained was to make the most of it, and to keep out of the way of whatever was about to happen.

Cowley, however, put another face on our good luck. He leaned close to me and asked me if I knew why they had brought me to the hut instead of taking someone from the regular camp.

"I know some Vietnamese," I said, watching the prisoner's head.

"They've got a translator," he whispered. "What the hell do they need you for?"

I shrugged. "We'll find out soon enough."

"Use your head," he said. "Guys in the rest camp go back to the States after a year out here. They can talk and make trouble. We're easy to keep quiet because we aren't going anywhere."

He added that he had seen interrogations before; and then he grinned ruefully, as if to make the best of a bad thing.

I began to ask him what he meant, though I understood it well enough, when Lieutenant Buckley suddenly turned impatiently away from Nguyen, with whom he had again been arguing about the prisoner, and rapped the table angrily with his knuckles to silence us.

"This is no joke," he said, raising his voice again, but now to an official tone, as if he were about to address a staff meeting. "We need definite information about these guerrillas, and we need it fast. We've finally got a prisoner of war that can tell us everything we need to know, and our Vietnamese ally says that he'll need at least a day to make him talk."

McGruder said, in a very matter-of-fact way, that the guerrillas might attack again somewhere during the night.

"You don't need to tell me that," Buckley replied.

He was so earnest that he couldn't stand still. Yet it was what he said, not the way he moved, that made me uneasy, for certainly McGruder and Nguyen knew perfectly well what they had come to do. Therefore Buckley was speaking only to me, which was either dangerous or foolish, depending on what he meant by it.

"They've hit us everywhere," he said. "Fuel dumps, quartermaster convoys, rest camps. Last week they mined the road to Doc Thieu. At dawn we lost a jeep and three men."

He added that all the attacks had come at night. It seemed to be a personal affront to him. "In six weeks they've cost us fifty casualties, and as far as we know we haven't killed one of them yet—or if we have, they carry their dead with them. This is a little peasant outfit. Saigon says there isn't a hard-core Viet Cong in the district. All the help they're getting from the outside is equipment, and they're careful with that. They don't take on combat units. Only isolated patrols or a single vehicle. They like to win," he added, "and so far they've had it all their way."

He looked angrily at the boy—the prisoner—and said that he was one of the guerrillas. He called them Victor Charlies as was the custom at staff briefings. I glanced up at the broken tin roof, thinking more about the heat than what Buckley was saying. He turned around and looked down at me as if to gauge the effect of his words. Of course none of it meant anything to me, and I didn't try to hide it. Buckley frowned with disapproval and nodded to McGruder.

"Show the lieutenant what the prisoner was carrying," he said. He used the title that was no longer mine, as if to place me still further in his debt. I began to hate Buckley a little.

McGruder swung a string of grenades off his shoulder and held them up to the light. "They were rolled inside the little bastard's blanket," he said, and, for the first time, he seemed satisfied that things were going the way they should.

I recognized the grenades, as they doubtless knew that I would. They were Chinese, in a North Vietnamese Army sling. I felt a dim memory of anger, of ambushes and night patrols, but I did not let McGruder see it.

"It's clear that he was running supplies for the guerrillas," Buckley continued, as though he were satisfied with his evidence. "The patrol that took him off the road found drugs on him as well as grenades. Now all we have to do is make him tell us where he was meeting his contact, and our job is finished." He cast one last official look around the room. For a second he even looked at Russell, but Russell only gripped his carbine tighter and stared back at him.

"Saigon says that this zone is a military backwater," Buckley said quietly, watching the boy's lowered head. "A rest and recreation camp and a stockade. The entire district stinks of it. According to the brass, we have nothing to do out here but sit on our ass and play cards. We're a joke in Saigon bars. I've heard it. Well now," he said, "we've got a little operation of our own, a tough little guerrilla outfit that just asks to be cut up—and we're going to do the job without any outside help, no interpreters from division, no Special Forces people butting in where they don't belong. This kid is our first break," he concluded, looking at each of us in turn. "He can lead us to their base and supplies, and by God we're going to make him do just that."

Cowley and I sat perfectly still. We had

nothing to say. It seemed simple enough, to hear Buckley tell it, though it was their job and not ours. I wondered why they had sent for us at all, since they already had an interpreter who knew more Vietnamese than I did. There seemed nothing for me to do, and even less for Cowley, who was good for nothing but fighting.

However, Buckley told McGruder to untie the prisoner without offering us any further explanation, and the boy was brought under the light. The interrogation got under way.

Nguyen began the questioning slowly. Buckley was almost immediately moving back and forth from one wall to the next as if he could not control himself now that his ignorance of the language had forced him to surrender the proceedings to Nguyen. He seemed to consider the business an urgent affair that had to be finished in the shortest possible time. Within the hour, if Nguyen could do it; before sundown, at the latest. Buckley chain-smoked, but the cigarettes didn't help him and he kept pacing around the room. Now and then he glanced down at me, as if I had somehow let him down; but he said nothing.

We waited. There were no provisions for the night in the room—only the heavy table, the bare light bulb, and the three cots without blankets. Not even drinking water had been brought in. The walls were bare except for the tool crib, but the tools were no part of the interrogation, as far as I could see. We seemed to be locked in alone with the prisoner.

Nguyen asked him where he had gotten the grenades. When I listened to the Vietnamese, which only Nguyen and the prisoner and I could understand, I felt even more alone than I had before. Buckley, McGruder, and even Cowley could not follow me as far as my understanding of the language forced me to go. I didn't like it, for it made me feel a party to anything that

Nguyen said, but there was no escaping the sound of his voice in that small room.

I looked up to see what the boy's answer would be—and it was then, for the second time, that I felt the uneasy certainty that something unreasonable was going to happen. It was happening. I could not connect the frail-looking boy with Buckley's account of guerrilla raids and dead Americans. I knew better, but I could not do it. And yet Buckley, and McGruder, and even the quiet Nguyen looked at the prisoner as if he were unquestionably the enemy, and were all waiting only to hear his confession, not to hear the truth, whatever it was.

When I looked up at the boy's face, caught under the cruel light, I saw only the stiff black hair, the delicate forehead, the high cheekbones, the small brown eyes that hardly moved behind their tightly drawn lids, the full, impassive mouth, and the narrow chin where the blood had dried and turned black—and stamped on it all was a look of immovable fear, as though he were staring at death, without hope. I knew that face. It bore sisters and daughters who were beautiful—for the face was inherently feminine—and who now filled the brothels in Saigon. And I had seen it, and a hundred of its brothers, in the quick glimpses of highland skirmishes; and once, the last time, I had not been able to see the enemy. Only the face itself. Disembodied. Waiting. I was kneeling in tall grass at the mouth of a valley near Darlac when it happened to me. Barren hills rose on three sides of us. Our captain had been killed in the morning, and I was left in command of two hundred men. Four other companies of infantry were dug in on the ridges on top of the hills, ready to open fire on the remnants of a Viet Cong outfit that we had trapped on the floor of the valley. My job was simple. When the company commander on the hilltops had his machine guns and mortars in position— the anvil—I was to give the order for my men to move in. We were the hammer: machine guns, grenades, flame throwers, automatic rifles, and finally bayonets. There would be no survivors, unless we took one or two prisoners out of the valley for questioning. The Montagnard tribesmen who would move through the valley after we had gone would see to that. I watched the Vietnamese trying to dig in, sweeping my field glasses from one knot of them to another; and then, perhaps because the sun was hot on my back, or because I was tired, I began to see, not the enemy, but faces. Only faces. Here and there I would glimpse them for a fleeting second, unreal through my glasses, enlarged, yet tense, expectant, certain of death. Suddenly two mortar shells exploded among them, taking the range. My radioman signaled me. I took the receiver and heard the order to attack when the barrage lifted. My company was braced, waiting. I waited too, kneeling in the sunlight, listening to the whirring of insects in the tall grass, gazing at the small figures of the men we were about to kill—and then I pulled my company back. The men were veterans and they obeyed my order. We opened up one end of the valley like a hinged door and withdrew up the side of the hill to our left. The Vietnamese were quick and they fled through the gap before the outfits on the hills understood what had happened. There were one or two mortar hits. A few men were killed. But that was all.

At my court-martial I was accused of refusing to obey an order under fire, and of "aiding and abetting the enemies of the United States." I was given legal counsel, an Army lawyer from the Military Justice Division. He pleaded that I had suffered a nervous breakdown; "combat fatigue," he called it, and cited my past record to show that I had been a good soldier and, as he put it, a patriot. He was a hard-working man and I bore him no ill-will. The court found me guilty of willfully failing to obey an

order under fire, which was only right, and was about to sentence me when a colonel dropped in—I don't remember his name— and discovered that I knew two thousand words of Vietnamese. He asked me if that was true, and I said that it was. Then he decided that I was Army property, and too valuable to be disposed of entirely; and thus it was that they only broke me to the ranks and sentenced me to hard labor in the camp at Quai Dong, where my two thousand words would be available if anyone wanted to use them.

Once or twice during the first weeks of my imprisonment I was called to the major's quarters to interpret. A village headman complained that his chickens had been stolen; the mother of a dead child wanted compensation for its funeral. Then they seemed to forget about me, and my days went on undisturbed. No doubt someone mislaid my file; or, which seemed more reasonable to me, they had decided that I was unreliable, and could not be trusted.

Now I was expected, once again, to look at a boy's face and see the face of my enemy. It was very remote from my life after so long a time at Quai Dong, where there were no enemies and no friends, but only endless days of waiting. Still, Buckley and the others showed no doubt. Obviously, I was expected to follow their lead and to make my stand with them. We were to show solidarity in the face of the enemy. Yet it seemed a difficult question, and it was one, moreover, on which the Army could no longer force me to give an answer.

The other questions that Nguyen asked the boy, the simple ones that centered around concrete facts like hand grenades and medicines, were always the same; the boy's answers, too, were identical each time. It puzzled me at first, then it became tiring to hear. But Nguyen seemed undisturbed by it, as if he had expected it. The prisoner's replies were made in a voice so low that it was barely audible. That, too, was irritating to hear, for, though I did not want to listen to any part of it, I could not keep from straining to catch his words. Only later did I realize that it was difficult for him to speak through his broken lips.

"Where did you get the grenades?" Nguyen asked. He spoke with a razor's edge to his voice, though his voice remained quiet. Unlike Buckley, he did not have to shout.

"From the dead soldier," the boy replied humbly.

"Was he American?"

"North Vietnamese."

"Where was he?"

"On the road to Weichu."

"There are no dead soldiers there."

"He was in a ditch."

"Why did you take the grenades?"

"To protect myself."

"Where did you get the medicine?"

"From the dead soldier."

"Soldiers of the Democratic Republic of North Vietnam do not carry penicillin and morphine!"

"This one did, sir."

"Where were you taking your supplies?"

"I was going to Saigon, to my sister."

"The Weichu Road does not go to Saigon."

"There was fighting on the other side of the hills. I was afraid to go that way."

"You will tell me now," Nguyen said, "where you were told to meet your comrades."

"I am alone, sir. I was only going to my sister. Our parents are dead."

Nguyen studied the boy's lowered head for a moment, then he turned to Buckley. "You see," he said, "he is obstinate."

McGruder approached with a business-like expression on his face, but Buckley waved him back before he could reach the table. He told Nguyen to begin again. "Keep after him," he said.

Nguyen put the same list of questions to the boy. Buckley began to pace back and forth between the close walls of the room. I watched him, for I was already tired of watching Nguyen. It seemed reasonable enough, I thought, for him to want to find out where the guerrillas were meeting to launch their raids. He was impatient and angry, but he looked honest. I supposed that if he broke the prisoner's resistance he would be able to save some lives and do his career some credit. There was little enough chance for that at Quai Dong.

But when I looked back from Buckley to the boy, who had been dragged off the Weichu Road and locked in a windowless room with four Americans and a Vietnamese that he could not trust, it all seemed more questionable, somehow, than when I looked at Buckley alone.

"There's no way of knowing whether he's a guerrilla or not," I observed quietly.

"What do you mean by that?" Buckley snapped, looking at me for the first time as if I were a convict.

Cowley nudged me hard, and I said nothing more.

But McGruder was aroused. He looked at me vengefully, as if he had been waiting for me to make a mistake, and said that you could never tell one Vietnamese from another until he shot you. "But we caught this little son of a bitch red-handed, and we ain't gonna let him off!"

I admitted that he was right, but still he wasn't satisfied, and told Buckley that Nguyen was wasting time. "Throw the Chinaman out of here, Lieutenant," he begged. "Let's do it our way."

I saw the boy's arms stiffen when Mc-Gruder raised his voice; and I knew then how his mouth had been covered with blood.

McGruder saw his involuntary motion too, and a look of pleasure came into his eyes. "I can make him squeal like a monkey," he said, and took up a threatening position behind the boy, not quite touching him but so close that he must have felt his breath. McGruder's head nearly touched the hot bulb, but he was too interested in the boy to feel anything. For a moment I hated him. I was fascinated and sickened by the thought of driving my fist into his unshaven jaw. But I stopped myself, for I did not want to get involved, and I leaned cautiously back and listened to the droning sound of Nguyen's voice, which went on undisturbed in spite of McGruder.

By three o'clock the interrogation had made no visible progress. I passed the time watching a cockroach moving in the shadows along the floor. It was pushing its snout against the wall behind Cowley's foot, trying to find its way out. The floor was dirt, but the metal walls had been driven in too deep for it to have a chance. Still the bug felt up and down, inching along. But it was going in the opposite direction from the door, where it must have come in. There seemed no reason to step on it. If it was patient and went all the way round, behind the heels of the other men in the room, it might find its way out; if not, it was its own fault.

From time to time I listened to the questioning. It remained unchanged, and the prisoner's answers remained identical. Finally I saw that Nguyen was forcing the boy to repeat his meaningless replies by quietly menacing him if he varied them in the slightest way from the answers that he had first given. The word-for-word repetition puzzled me. It was wearing on everyone's nerves. But I supposed that there was a ritual that they would observe before the boy would tell us anything, since they were both Vietnamese in the presence of Americans, however much they might hate one another.

Certainly, after the first hour, the boy looked tired. Probably he had not slept for a long time. If he had been trying to get to Saigon he had most likely been walking for days. Of course, if he were a Quai Dong guerrilla, it didn't matter; but I began to number the uses that a peasant might have for hand grenades, and especially for medicine, without being a Viet Cong. I could imagine several—the black market in Saigon for one—but it was none of my business, and I kept quiet. It didn't seem to be Nguyen's business either, for he had not asked the prisoner about it. He simply went down his original set of questions, as methodically as if he were performing a mass.

Buckley, however, was not taking it with Nguyen's equanimity. He dropped one half-smoked cigarette after another, ground them angrily under his heel, and told Nguyen to hurry up.

"We're wasting time!" he complained.

McGruder grunted and looked at the back of the boy's head. "He's afraid to hurt him," he said.

Nguyen denied it—he seemed to fear that accusation above all others—but he was silenced by a wave of Buckley's hand and told to continue in whatever way he thought was best.

"Only be quick," Buckley repeated. "We don't know when the guerrillas will attack again."

Buckley looked down at me and added that every minute that we lost might cost an American his life. I said nothing, and Nguyen turned back to the prisoner and began over again from the beginning, but he warned Buckley to be patient.

"He is very strong," he said, gazing at the boy's lowered face.

McGruder began to swear under his breath.

"I do not mean physical strength," Nguyen said, looking at McGruder with contempt and speaking in his slow but strangely fluent English, the tone of which seemed to aggravate McGruder even more than what Nguyen said. "I mean a stubborn spirit, which is much stronger. That is why you must not injure him again. Pain will not break his spirit. It will only kill his body. We must exhaust him, then he will be willing to betray his comrades."

"If I hit him," McGruder muttered, "he'll talk."

"No, he will only die, and thus escape us."

McGruder turned red and made a motion toward the fragile-looking Nguyen, but Buckley told him to keep away. Then he turned to Nguyen and asked him how much longer it would take.

"Two, maybe three days," Nguyen answered, studying the boy's face intently.

"But you said it would only be a day and a night!" Buckley shouted.

"I did not know then how strong he was," Nguyen said, straightening up and facing him.

Buckley ran his fingers through his hair and moved away from the light. "We can't wait that long," he said, shaking his head and shoving his hands into his hip pockets. "The major will never stand for it."

Again McGruder asked to be put in Nguyen's place. Buckley ignored him, lit another cigarette, and sat down. And then, without warning, he turned to me.

"What do you think?" he asked.

I shook my head, and told him that it was none of my business.

"I'm only asking your opinion."

"I don't have one," I replied, suddenly hating Buckley for trying to draw me into his game again, whatever it was going to be. Silence was my only defense. I refused to say anything more. Buckley glanced up at the boy's head, then he looked back at me and shrugged, as if to say that he had done his part and given me my chance and that now anything that happened to the boy would be my fault, not his.

"Do what you can, Nguyen," he said, and settled back against the wall.

McGruder moved quietly away from the light, apparently satisfied from the tone of Buckley's voice that his time would come,

and Nguyen began his interrupted questions from the beginning. Now I understood more of his method, and I feared the room in a way that I had not before. Nguyen was not angry at anything that the boy might say—the answers themselves became meaningless when they had been repeated a hundred times. Even the words lost their accustomed sense and were reduced to nonsense syllables, like a chant in an alien tongue. Nguyen asked him, for the hundredth time and with no change whatever in the expression of his voice, where he had found the dead soldier. And the boy answered, for the hundredth time, "On the road to Weichu."

"There are no dead soldiers there."

"He was in a ditch."

"Why did you take the grenades?"

"To protect myself."

"Where did you get the medicine?"

"From the dead soldier."

"Soldiers of the Democratic Republic of North Vietnam do not carry penicillin and morphine!"

"This one did."

Nguyen stopped. Slowly his hand came up, and the boy said, "This one did, *sir*."

"Where were you taking your supplies?"

"I was going to Saigon, to my sister."

"The Weichu Road does not go to Saigon."

"There was fighting on the other side of the hills. I was afraid to go that way."

"You will tell me how you were instructed to meet your comrades!"

"I am alone, sir. I was only going to my sister."

Then Nguyen, without allowing a second's rest to mark the completion of the cycle of questions, asked again where he had gotten the grenades. The boy answered as he had always answered, and the rhythm of the questions was repeated. It was maddening to listen to, and I tried to ignore it, for I saw now that Nguyen's purpose was not intelligence, but simple exhaustion. He would wear the boy down until he was too weak to give any answer at all. Then, I supposed, he would have a way of extracting whatever he wanted from him. They would beat the boy's mind into a shapeless mass, and in it, like splinters of broken glass, they would find what they had been looking for. But the end was a long way off, and it was obvious that someone would have to relieve Nguyen from time to time. The strain was more than one man could bear—and with a sudden halt in my thoughts I realized why I had been taken from the stockade into that room, for I, who had escaped a military prison because I spoke two thousand words of Vietnamese, was Nguyen's replacement.

I got up instantly and crossed the room. "Am I supposed to interrogate him?" I asked Buckley.

He looked up at me and seemed pleased, as if he had known that I would come to ask him that question, sooner or later. "Not entirely," he answered, and moved over to offer me a place to sit down next to him.

"I won't question the boy," I said. I warned him that I'd go back to the stockade first. The hut looked less like a reprieve than it had at the beginning. I didn't know if they could do anything more than send me back to the stockade, but I was ready to risk it.

To my surprise Buckley gave me a friendly look and told me to sit down. When I did, he lowered his voice and spoke under the steady droning of Nguyen's questions.

"Can you understand what they're saying to each other?" he asked.

I listened for a moment. "Yes," I said reluctantly, "I can."

Buckley was pleased with me then. "Good. All I want you to do for the present is listen to what they say. Don't let a word slip by, not one word." He squinted up into the light and said, "We'd be fools to trust Nguyen."

"They're only repeating the same thing," I said. "It's meaningless."

"I don't care. We'll let him do it his way for now; but they're both Vietnamese and they'll try to stick together."

"I doubt it," I murmured, yet there was no way for me to know whether Nguyen was in earnest with his interrogation or not, since I had never seen an interrogation before and had no idea how one was carried on. I glanced at Buckley. Something had changed in the room. It had somehow become smaller. It seemed to give me less room in which to hide. Gradually I realized that the cost of my simple act of crossing from one wall to the other had been the loss of my immunity. I had wanted only to defend myself, and to warn Buckley that I would not interrogate the boy, but something had gone wrong. Perhaps, if I did what Buckley wanted, I would gain a degree of power. But I did not want the power. I wanted only to stay clear. Cowley was scowling at me from across the room, and Buckley was smiling, as if he understood perfectly what was in my mind and had been counting on it. Now he thought that I was his man.

"If Nguyen doesn't break him soon," he said, "we may have to do this by ourselves."

Buckley watched the two figures who stood under the light, but he was leaning so close to me that our shoulders touched. Some treacherous idea was fixed in his mind. That much was clear to me, and I drew away from him. But it was not clear to me how I was supposed to convince him that he was wrong. The only way for me to stay clear now was to stop the interrogation, but I had no way of doing it. Perhaps Buckley was right and Nguyen was protecting the boy. It meant nothing to me in either case, and that, at any other time, should have been enough to keep me out of it—but it was not difficult to see that if Buckley lost confidence in Nguyen entirely he would be left with no one to carry on the interrogation but myself, unless he gave the boy to McGruder. I glanced at Buckley's face. His eyes were fixed on the boy, waiting, and it was then that I realized that it was he, and not I, who had gained a degree of power. I was deep in the trap with him now, with no way out.

But of course there was no need for apprehension. Thus far everything was under control.

Another hour passed. The voices of Nguyen and the boy went on with the deadly regularity of a ticking clock. McGruder sat on the cot along the back wall, apparently passive, with his head covered by his hands and only his knuckles visible. Nguyen stood in front of the table with his back to us, his round shoulders and his short-cropped head in the light, and went on with his even and methodical questioning as though he were conscious of no threat to his position. The walls of the tin hut creaked in the heat. The boy's voice was a weak whisper, into which Nguyen jabbed each question before he could recover his breath from the last answer. The boy was allowed no rest, and he seemed to be losing ground. The torture was mental, a slow dulling of the senses. I found myself becoming fascinated by it; then, looking up, I saw that Russell was no longer in the room.

"He's outside," Buckley said, "standing guard duty."

"Why?" I asked, getting off the cot.

Buckley looked at me, and shrugged. "We have a prisoner," he said.

"There's a fence around the motor pool, and there's barbed wire around the entire compound. Nobody's going to get away."

"It's normal security. Why does it bother you so much?" Then he added, with a grin, "You should be used to barbed wire by now."

I walked to the door, but I did not open it, nor could I look out. There were no windows in the hut, not even an air vent through which I might have seen the sky, or the stars, if it was already night. We were entirely sealed in. The heat was suddenly unbearable. I wanted badly to see what was outside, for in that closed place I seemed unable to trust my memory of what I had left behind. I thought of the beach, but it was far away, beyond reach. I hated the thought of sentries outside the door, though I had never felt it so strongly before. But then I saw that Buckley was watching me with too much interest, and I moved away from the door.

Suddenly I heard Cowley shout, "Look out!" Instantly there was a loud crash behind me and a wild cry of anger.

When I turned around I saw the prisoner lying on his back in the dirt six feet from the table. McGruder, who had knocked his cot over to get at him, was standing alone under the light, panting, as if he couldn't breathe.

"He'll talk now, by God," he whispered.

Nguyen had been thrown aside, but he was already accusing McGruder at the top of his lungs. "You are a fool, you are a fool, Sergeant McGruder!" he yelled, losing his self-control. "You are a barbarian!"

"You're chicken-livered," McGruder grunted. "I swear to God I'll kill him if you don't get it over with."

"And do you think you can make him talk then?" Nguyen shouted.

McGruder turned slowly away from the boy and Nguyen backed out of his reach. Buckley stood up. For the first time since the interrogation began he looked calm and untroubled. He quietly told McGruder to get out of the hut. "If you attack the prisoner again," he said, "I'll have you put in detention."

To my surprise McGruder turned his back and went outside without a word. There was a flash of sunlight when he opened the door, and I saw that it was not yet night.

"Kreuger," Buckley said, without looking at me, "see if the prisoner is all right."

I should not have moved, but I had been conditioned too thoroughly in the stockade not to obey—at least once—and I went past Cowley, who had jumped to his feet when

McGruder hit the boy and was standing in a corner, ready to fight his way out of the room if he had to. When I bent over the boy I saw that his eyes were open, but dazed.

Nguyen leaned over my shoulder. His face was inexpressive again, as if nothing had happened. He reached down and took the boy by the chin and turned his head sharply from side to side. A thick swelling was rising on his left temple, but it was not bleeding.

"He is all right," Nguyen said quietly, and helped me pull him to his feet. The boy weighed less than a girl, and I pulled too hard and nearly upset him. Nguyen took him away from me and dragged him back under the light, but when he released him his knees buckled and he collapsed on the floor. We picked him up again, but he couldn't stand by himself. Nguyen finally left him sitting in the dirt with his head leaning to one side, and looked up at Buckley. "You see that we cannot go on," he said bitterly.

"Stand him up," Buckley ordered.

"It is no use if he cannot speak," Nguyen answered.

Buckley turned around. "All right," he said, and rubbed his hand across his mouth, "bring a medic."

I didn't look at anyone in the room. Not even the boy. My only instinct was to keep my head down, no matter what happened.

Finally it was Cowley who spoke up. "They're all down in the stockade giving shots."

"Get one up here then," Buckley answered impatiently.

Cowley hesitated. "It's outside the gate," he said.

"Damn it, I don't care where it is! I gave you an order! Do you know who you're talking to? I want a medic in here, and I want him fast!"

Cowley left without another word, and Buckley controlled himself. The three of us remained in silence, staring at the prisoner's face, waiting for a sign of life. Somehow I did not expect Cowley to come back—if I had gone I would not have come back—but he did. I suppose that he could think of no way of getting out either. He brought Finley with him. Cowley remained next to the door and Finley looked around the room, still blinded by the sun's light, as if he saw none of us.

"Revive him," Buckley said, pointing to the boy, who still sat in the dirt with his back slumped against one of the heavy legs of the table.

Finley glanced at me, but when he received no sign of recognition he knelt beside the prisoner and began to examine his mouth and jaw, where he could see the dried blood.

That irritated Buckley. "It's his forehead that's hurt," he snapped.

Finley saw his error then, and he left the boy's mouth alone and cleaned and bandaged his temple. Then he gave him a shot of something that looked like water, but which made his head begin to roll from side to side.

"All right," Buckley said, "can he stand up?"

"Yes sir, I guess so," Finley answered, stepping back cautiously, as though the floor were mined.

Again the boy was pulled to his feet. This time he kept his balance, although his eyes were open abnormally wide and his breathing was shallow and hard. Then the drug seemed to wear off and his head fell into its lowered position once more. All that I could see was the pressure bandage on his temple and his eyes, which were blinking rapidly, as if he were dizzy or afraid. He looked smaller, as if something had broken inside him, but he stayed on his feet.

"Get back to work," Buckley ordered, and returned to his cot, where he picked up the cigarette that he had carefully laid aside when McGruder had knocked the boy down. "You may find the prisoner more willing to talk now," he added, and leaned back against the wall to watch.

Buckley looked satisfied, as though things had finally taken a turn for the better. Nguyen didn't say a word to any of us. He simply began his interrupted questions again. The only difference was that now there was a new sense of urgency in his voice, as if he too felt that his time was running out.

At first the boy did not answer, for the rhythm of the interrogation had been broken. McGruder's fist had allowed him to rest. Only when Nguyen's voice fell across his face like a whiplash, again and again, without mercy, did his broken lips open and begin to form the ritual phrases once more. He spoke now as if he were in a trance, but after a few moments his answers and Nguyen's questions slowly fell into their accustomed pattern.

The sound of it was worse now than before, when it had looked as if it would go on undisturbed for days. Now we could see that it was only an interlude, and that at the end of it the boy would be hurt again. Yet the combined sound of their voices was almost worse than the sight of the boy's damaged head lying face down in the dirt. McGruder's attack had freed us from the sounds of the interrogation, if only for a moment. Now the deadening murmur of it filled the room again—and I wondered, with a dropping in the pit of my stomach, how many times the prisoner could recover and go on.

Finley moved noiselessly around the room, keeping his back near the wall and staying out of the circle of light where Nguyen worked the boy. He sat down next to me on my cot, where I had taken refuge when the interrogation got under way again. Soon Cowley joined us, and the three of us sat together. Cowley was very quiet now, and seemed to be waiting only to see what direction things would go. Finley glanced about the room nervously. "What's this all about?" he whispered.

"Nothing," I said; then I added, "Guerrillas—they think the kid was on his way to meet the guerrillas with supplies. Nguyen's trying to find out where."

"Oh," Finley answered, as if it made sense to him, then he stared up at the boy and at the ugly string of grenades that McGruder had left on the table under the light. "Is he really a guerrilla?"

I shrugged. "Most likely."

Finley said that he had never seen a guerrilla before. He studied the fragile neck and shoulders of the boy.

I was sick of Finley. His innocence was worse than McGruder's sadism. I stood up and moved deliberately toward the door.

All that I wanted now was to get out. Nothing else mattered. I saw that Cowley had been right; they had used us because we were convicts and they thought we had no choice. But they were wrong. We had nothing more to fear and, being outsiders, nothing whatever to gain from the interrogation. They did not understand that only men who still had something to hope for could be made to do such things. They could send me back to the stockade, under the harmless muzzle of Russell's carbine, as they had brought me to the room. Cowley and the medic could take care of themselves.

I was past Nguyen and the boy, who faced each other under the hard light, chanting their litany of question and answer as if they could keep it up for weeks. Then I was beyond Buckley, who made no move to stop me, and I held the door knob. To my relief it turned in my hand. I stepped out into the heat and the blinding sunlight without looking back, and turned away toward the jeep and the open gate.

And then I saw the barbed wire. Russell and three new guards were pulling it up throat-high around all sides of the hut. Now there was a third ring of barbed wire, and we were alone inside of it. In the sunlight it looked black, like a barren hedge of thorns, but metal, impassable. Only a six-foot zone of free ground remained between it and the tin walls. McGruder was there, sitting to my right with his back against the shed, regarding his heavy boots, waiting with doglike tenacity. Outside the fence I saw Russell watching me. Four carbines were stacked within his reach, with fixed bayonets, ready; and far away, through the coils of the second fence at the motor pool, were the distant tents of the stockade and the guard towers, shimmering patiently in the heat.

John Milton

TO THE LORD GENERAL CROMWELL

Cromwell, our chief of men, who through a
    cloud
Not of war only, but detractions rude,
Guided by faith and matchless fortitude,
To peace and truth thy glorious way hast plowed,
And on the neck of crownèd Fortune proud
Hast reared God's trophies, and his work
    pursued,
While Darwen stream, with blood of Scots
    imbrued,
And Dunbar field, resounds thy praises loud,
And Worcester's laureate wreath. Yet much
    remains
To conquer still; peace hath her victories   10
No less renowned than war: new foes arise,
Threatening to bind our souls with secular
    chains.
Help us to save free conscience from the paw
Of hireling wolves whose gospel is their maw.

7 *Darwen stream:* near Preston, where in 1648 Cromwell defeated a Scottish army. 8–9 *Dunbar, Worcester:* scenes of other victories over the Scots, 1650–1651, leading to the peace mentioned in line 4. 11 *foes:* John Owen and other members of a Parliamentary committee who favored a state-supported, state-controlled church.

Thomas Love Peacock

THE WAR-SONG OF DINAS VAWR

The mountain sheep are sweeter,
But the valley sheep are fatter;
We therefore deemed it meeter
To carry off the latter.
We made an expedition;
We met a host and quelled it;
We forced a strong position
And killed the men who held it.

On Dyfed's richest valley,
Where herds of kine were browsing,   10
We made a mighty sally,
To furnish our carousing.
Fierce warriors rushed to meet us;
We met them, and o'erthrew them:
They struggled hard to beat us,
But we conquered them and slew them.

As we drove our prize at leisure,
The king marched forth to catch us:
His rage surpassed all measure,
But his people could not match us.   20
He fled to his hall-pillars;
And, ere our force we led off,
Some sacked his house and cellars,
While others cut his head off.

We there, in strife bewild'ring,
Spilt blood enough to swim in:
We orphaned many children
And widowed many women.
The eagles and the ravens
We glutted with our foemen;   30
The heroes and the cravens,
The spearmen and the bowmen.

We brought away from battle,
And much their land bemoaned them,

9 *Dyfed:* ancient name of what is now Pembrokeshire, southwest Wales.

Two thousand head of cattle
And the head of him who owned them:
Ednyfed, kind of Dyfed,
His head was borne before us;
His wine and beasts supplied our feasts
And his overthrow, our chorus.

Alfred, Lord Tennyson

THE CHARGE OF THE LIGHT BRIGADE

I

Half a league, half a league,
Half a league onward,
All in the valley of Death
    Rode the six hundred.
"Forward, the Light Brigade!
Charge for the guns!" he said.
Into the valley of Death
    Rode the six hundred.

II

"Forward, the Light Brigade!"
Was there a man dismayed?   10
Not though the soldier knew
    Someone had blundered.
Theirs not to make reply,
Theirs not to reason why,
Theirs but to do and die.
Into the valley of Death
    Rode the six hundred.

III

Cannon to right of them,
Cannon to left of them,
Cannon in front of them   20
    Volleyed and thundered;
Stormed at with shot and shell,
Boldly they rode and well,

Into the jaws of death,
Into the mouth of hell
    Rode the six hundred.

IV

Flashed all their sabres bare,
Flashed as they turned in air,
Sabring the gunners there,
Charging an army, while   30
    All the world wondered.
Plunged in the battery-smoke
Right through the line they broke;
Cossack and Russian
Reeled from the sabre-stroke
    Shattered and sundered.
Then they rode back, but not,
    Not the six hundred.

V

Cannon to right of them,
Cannon to left of them,   40
Cannon behind them
    Volleyed and thundered;
Stormed at with shot and shell,
While horse and hero fell,
They that had fought so well
Came through the jaws of Death,
Back from the mouth of hell,
All that was left of them,
    Left of six hundred.

VI

When can their glory fade?   50
O the wild charge they made!
    All the world wondered.
Honor the charge they made!
Honor the Light Brigade,
    Noble six hundred!

Thomas Hardy

CHANNEL FIRING

That night your great guns, unawares,
Shook all our coffins as we lay,
And broke the chancel window-squares,
We thought it was the Judgment Day

And sat upright. While drearisome
Arose the howl of wakened hounds;
The mouse let fall the altar-crumb,
The worms drew back into the mounds,

The glebe cow drooled. Till God called, "No;
It's gunnery practice out at sea   10
Just as before you went below;
The world is as it used to be:

"All nations striving strong to make
Red war yet redder. Mad as hatters
They do no more for Christès sake
Than you who are helpless in such matters.

"That this is not the judgment-hour
For some of them's a blessed thing,
For if it were they'd have to scour
Hell's floor for so much threatening. . . .   20

"Ha, ha. It will be warmer when
I blow the trumpet (if indeed
I ever do; for you are men,
And rest eternal sorely need)."

So we lay down again. "I wonder
Will the world ever saner be,"
Said one, "than when He sent us under
In our indifferent century!"

And many a skeleton shook his head.
"Instead of preaching forty year,"   30
My neighbor Parson Thirdly said,
"I wish I had stuck to pipes and beer."

Again the guns disturbed the hour,
Roaring their readiness to avenge,
As far inland as Stourton Tower,
And Camelot, and starlit Stonehenge.

35 *Tower:* Alfred's Tower at Stourton, Wiltshire,
near the site of Cadbury Castle, which is said to be
the legendary Camelot.

A. E. Housman

MY DREAMS ARE OF
A FIELD AFAR

My dreams are of a field afar
    And blood and smoke and shot.
There in their graves my comrades are,
    In my grave I am not.

I too was taught the trade of man
    And spelt the lesson plain;
But they, when I forgot and ran,
    Remembered and remain.

Wilfred Owen

DULCE ET DECORUM EST

Bent double, like old beggars under sacks,
Knock-kneed, coughing like hags, we cursed
        through sludge,
Till on the haunting flares we turned our backs,
And towards our distant rest began to trudge.

Men marched asleep. Many had lost their boots,
But limped on blood-shod. All went lame, all
        blind;
Drunk with fatigue; deaf even to the hoots
Of gas-shells dropping softly behind.

Gas! Gas! Quick, boys!—An ecstasy of fumbling,
Fitting the clumsy helmets just in time,　　10
But someone still was yelling out and stumbling
And floundering like a man in fire or lime.—
Dim through the misty panes and thick green
　　　light,
As under a green sea, I saw him drowning.

In all my dreams before my helpless sight
He plunges at me, guttering, choking, drowning.

If in some smothering dreams, you too could
　　　pace
Behind the wagon that we flung him in,
And watch the white eyes writhing in his face,
His hanging face, like a devil's sick of sin;　　20
If you could hear, at every jolt, the blood
Come gargling from the froth-corrupted lungs,
Bitter as the cud
Of vile, incurable sores on innocent tongues,—
My friend, you would not tell with such high zest
To children ardent for some desperate glory,
The old Lie: *Dulce et decorum est*
Pro patria mori.

　27 *Dulce, etc.:* It is sweet and fitting to die for
one's country. Horace, *Odes* III, 2, 13.

William Butler Yeats

AN IRISH AIRMAN FORESEES
HIS DEATH

I know that I shall meet my fate
Somewhere among the clouds above;
Those that I fight I do not hate,
Those that I guard I do not love;
My country is Kiltartan Cross,
My countrymen Kiltartan's poor,
No likely end could bring them loss
Or leave them happier than before.
Nor law, nor duty bade me fight,

　5 *Kiltartan:* village near Coole Park, the home of
Yeats's friend, Lady Gregory, in County Galway.

Nor public men, nor cheering crowds,　　10
A lonely impulse of delight
Drove to this tumult in the clouds;
I balanced all, brought all to mind,
The years to come seemed waste of breath,
A waste of breath the years behind
In balance with this life, this death.

W. H. Auden

SEPTEMBER 1, 1939

I sit in one of the dives
On Fifty-Second Street
Uncertain and afraid
As the clever hopes expire
Of a low dishonest decade:
Waves of anger and fear
Circulate over the bright
And darkened lands of the earth,
Obsessing our private lives;
The unmentionable odor of death　　10
Offends the September night.

Accurate scholarship can
Unearth the whole offence
From Luther until now
That has driven a culture mad,
Find what occurred at Linz,
What huge imago made
A psychopathic god:
I and the public know
What all school children learn,　　20
Those to whom evil is done
Do evil in return.

Exiled Thucydides knew
All that a speech can say
About Democracy,

　2 *Street:* in New York City. 16 *Linz:* The
schooldays of Adolf Hitler at Linz (1900–1902) were
marked by conflicts with the teachers and with his
father. 23 *Thucydides:* whose *History of the Peloponnesian War* (431–404 B.C.) reports the eulogy of
the Athenian war-dead by Pericles; II, 35–46.

And what dictators do,
The elderly rubbish they talk
To an apathetic grave;
Analyzed all in his book,
The enlightenment driven away,   30
The habit-forming pain,
Mismanagement and grief:
We must suffer them all again.

Into this neutral air
Where blind skyscrapers use
Their full height to proclaim
The strength of Collective Man,
Each language pours its vain
Competitive excuse:
But who can live for long   40
In an euphoric dream;
Out of the mirror they stare,
Imperialism's face
And the international wrong.

Faces along the bar
Cling to their average day:
The lights must never go out,
The music must always play,
All the conventions conspire
To make this fort assume   50
The furniture of home;
Lest we should see where we are,
Lost in a haunted wood,
Children afraid of the night
Who have never been happy or good.

The windiest militant trash
Important Persons shout
Is not so crude as our wish:
What mad Nijinsky wrote
About Diaghilev   60
Is true of the normal heart;
For the error bred in the bone
Of each woman and each man
Craves what it cannot have,
Not universal love
But to be loved alone.

From the conservative dark
Into the ethical life
The dense commuters come,

Repeating their morning vow;   70
"I *will* be true to the wife,
I'll concentrate more on my work,"
And helpless governors wake
To resume their compulsory game:
Who can release them now,
Who can reach the deaf,
Who can speak for the dumb?

All I have is a voice
To undo the folded lie,
The romantic lie in the brain   80
Of the sensual man-in-the-street
And the lie of Authority
Whose buildings grope the sky:
There is no such thing as the State
And no one exists alone;
Hunger allows no choice
To the citizen or the police;
We must love one another or die.

Defenceless under the night
Our world in stupor lies;   90
Yet, dotted everywhere,
Ironic points of light
Flash out wherever the Just
Exchange their messages:
May I, composed like them
Of Eros and of dust,
Beleaguered by the same
Negation and despair,
Show an affirming flame.

Robert Graves

THE PERSIAN VERSION

Truth-loving Persians do not dwell upon
The trivial skirmish fought near Marathon.
As for the Greek theatrical tradition
Which represents that summer's expedition
Not as a mere reconnaissance in force

3 *tradition:* e.g., *The Persians* (472 B.C.), by
Aeschylus.

By three brigades of foot and one of horse
(Their left flank covered by some obsolete
Light craft detached from the main Persian
    fleet)
But as a grandiose, ill-starred attempt
To conquer Greece—they treat it with
    contempt;   10
And only incidentally refute
Major Greek claims, by stressing what repute
The Persian monarch and the Persian nation
Won by this salutary demonstration:
Despite a strong defence and adverse weather
All arms combined magnificently together.

  13 *monarch:* Darius I, 558?–486 B.C.

Robert Lowell

CHRISTMAS EVE UNDER HOOKER'S STATUE

Tonight a blackout. Twenty years ago
I hung my stocking on the tree, and hell's
Serpent entwined the apple in the toe
To sting the child with knowledge. Hooker's
    heels

Kicking at nothing in the shifting snow,
A cannon and a cairn of cannon balls
Rusting before the blackened Statehouse, know
How the long horn of plenty broke like glass
In Hooker's gauntlets. Once I came from Mass;

Now storm-clouds shelter Christmas, once
    again   10
Mars meets his fruitless stars with open arms,
His heavy saber flashes with the rime,
The war-god's bronzed and empty forehead
    forms
Anonymous machinery from raw men;

  HOOKER'S STATUE: The statue of Major General Joseph Hooker (1814–1879) stands in the public square, the Common, across from the Statehouse in Boston, Mass. Hooker was defeated at Chancellorsville (line 24).

The cannon on the Common cannot stun
The blundering butcher as he rides on Time—
The barrel clinks with holly. I am cold:
I ask for bread, my father gives me mould;

His stocking is full of stones. Santa in red
Is crowned with wizened berries. Man of
    war,   20
Where is the summer's garden? In its bed
The ancient speckled serpent will appear,
And black-eyed susan with her frizzled head.
When Chancellorsville mowed down the
    volunteer,
"All wars are boyish," Herman Melville said;
But we are old, our fields are running wild:
Till Christ again turn wanderer and child.

  25 *Melville said:* In "The March into Virginia," line 6.

Terrance McNally

BOTTICELLI

Jungle foliage. Afternoon sun and shadows. Insect noises. Two soldiers, Wayne and Stu, crouching with rifles.

CHARACTERS

WAYNE
STU
MAN

WAYNE.   No, I'm not Marcel Proust.
STU.   Proust was a stylist.
WAYNE.   And he died *after* World War I.

  BOTTICELLI: A game in which one player professes to be a famous person, and announces the initial of the person's last name. (In the play, Wayne has announced that his name begins with P.) The other player or players try to guess who the person is by questions formulated in the manner used by Stu. When the first player cannot answer such a question he must answer a direct one: e.g., "Are you living?"

STU. You sure?

WAYNE. 1922.

STU. Yeah?

WAYNE. November 4, 19—

STU. All right! (*Then.*) What's up?

WAYNE. (*Stiffening.*) I thought I heard something. (*Relaxes.*)   10

STU. Are you a . . . let's see . . . are you a
Polish concert pianist who donated a large
part of the proceeds from his concerts to the
cause of Polish nationalism?

WAYNE. Oh that's a real brain-crusher, that
one is!

STU. Well are you?

WAYNE. No I'm not Paderewski.

STU. Are you sure you're dead?

WAYNE. Oh brother!   20

STU. A dead European male in the arts beginning with "P"?

WAYNE. Why don't you write it down?

STU. Got it! You're a controversial Russian
poet, novelist, dramatist and short story
writer.

WAYNE. Sorry. I'm not Pushkin.

STU. Pushkin wasn't considered controversial.

WAYNE. Who says?

STU. I do.   30

WAYNE. He was part Negro.

STU. What's controversial about that?

WAYNE. Dumas *père*?

STU. Don't change the subject. Controversial
Russian writer. Come on. I've got you
stumped, hunh? Look at you. Drew a blank.
Hunh? Hunh?

WAYNE. I hope it's not Boris Pasternak you're
crowing about.

STU. Drop dead, will you?   40

WAYNE. Then give up, hunh? (*Tenses.*) Sshh!
(*Relaxes.*) Not yet.

STU. You'd think he'd starve in there by now.

WAYNE. Maybe he has. Why don't you go see?

STU. And get a grenade in the face. That tunnel
could be half a mile long for all we know.

He's buried in there like a ground-hog. No,
sir, I'm holding tight, staying right where I
am, sergeant's orders. I got all the time in the
world to wait for that bugger to stick his head
out. (*Wayne starts making cigarette.*) Are
you a . . . ? I'm running dry. P's the hardest
letter in the alphabet.

WAYNE. Wanna turn on?

STU. How much we got left?

WAYNE. If he's not out of there by tonight
we're in trouble.

STU. Do you keep a diary?

WAYNE. Sure. Every night.

STU. No, who you are! Does he keep a diary?

WAYNE. I'm not Samuel Pepys.

STU. Smart ass! (*They smoke.*) Would you say
this is the best part of the whole war?

WAYNE. What is?

STU. This. Pot.

WAYNE. No. I'd say Raquel Welch.

STU. Yeah.

WAYNE. What'd you think of her?

STU. I didn't.

WAYNE. Those goddam white leather boots up
to here . . . and that yellow miniskirt . . .

STU. Hey, are you the outstanding English
Baroque composer?

WAYNE. I'm not Henry Purcell. I thought
Raquel Welch looked like a sexy . . . ostrich.

STU. Do the words "Rape of the Lock" mean
anything to you?

WAYNE. No, and they don't mean anything to
Alexander Pope either.

STU. Nuts!

WAYNE. Look, let me tell you who I am, hunh?

STU. No I said.

WAYNE. Brother, you're stubborn.

STU. And *you're* a Victorian playwright!

WAYNE. I'm not Arthur Wing Pinero.

STU. Sir.

WAYNE. Hunh?

STU. Sir Arthur Wing Pinero.

WAYNE. I know!

STU.　You didn't say it.　　　　　　　　　90

WAYNE.　I'd rather talk about Raquel Welch.

STU.　Sure you would. You're getting stoned.

WAYNE.　I'm not getting anything else.

STU.　You still worrying about that letter from Susan?

WAYNE.　Not since Raquel Welch I'm not.

STU.　I bet.

WAYNE.　Let her get a divorce. I don't care. Hell, the only mistake I made was thinking I had to marry her. I should've sent her to Puerto Rico. She could've had a vacation on me, too.

STU.　Only you had scruples.

WAYNES.　Leave me alone.

STU.　Jesuit high school, Dominican college scruples.

WAYNE. God, you're insensitive. Wait'll *you* get married.

STU.　Maybe I never will.

WAYNE.　Yeah!　　　　　　　　　　　　110

STU.　I might not.

WAYNE.　You'd marry the first girl who looked twice at you. Yours is one wedding I wouldn't want to miss. There's always Marlene Schroll.

STU.　As You Desire Me!

WAYNE.　What the—?

STU.　You wrote As You Desire Me.

WAYNE.　I'm not Luigi Pirandello.

STU.　Okay, but simmer down, hunh?

WAYNE.　It's a dumb game.　　　　　　120

STU.　Your idea.

WAYNE.　I was trying to kill time.

STU.　Well if we had something intelligent to discuss . . .

WAYNE.　What's wrong with Raquel Welch?

STU.　Nothing. She's the quintessence of intelligence.

WAYNE.　I'm gonna bust you in the mouth. (*Pause.*) I wish I'd burned my draft card.

STU.　Are you a Russian composer?　　　130

WAYNE.　I'm not Prokofiev.

STU.　An Italian composer?

WAYNE.　I'm not Puccini.

STU.　An Italian composer?

WAYNE.　I'm not Ponchielli.

STU.　An Italian composer?

WAYNE.　What are you, a record?

STU.　An Italian composer?

WAYNE.　All right, who?

STU.　Pizzarella.　　　　　　　　　　140

WAYNE.　Go to hell.

STU.　What's wrong with Pizzarella?

WAYNE.　There's no Italian composer named Pizzarella.

STU.　How do you know?

WAYNE.　I know!

STU.　Well maybe there is.

WAYNE.　Yeah and you just made him up. Pizzarella. Look, if you're gonna play, play fair. Boy, you haven't changed since college. Even in charades you'd try to put something over.

STU.　Like when?

WAYNE.　Like when you did "The Brothers Karamazov." Only you did it in Russian. How could anyone guess the "Brothers Karamazov" in a game of charades when *you* were doing it in Russian?

STU.　It would've been too easy in English.

WAYNE.　No wonder you never made the chess and bridge teams. Those are precise games. You don't muck with the rules in *them*. (*Pause.*) Typical. Sulk now.

STU.　I'm thinking.

WAYNE.　(*Rolls over on back, looks up at sky.*) You know what I can't get over?

STU.　Mmmmmm.

WAYNE.　Poor Father Reilly.

STU.　Yeah.

WAYNE.　I mean just dropping dead like that. God, we were lucky having him for a teacher. And of all places to drop dead. He loved Rome the same way some men love women. I think he lived for his summer vacations. As much as he gave his students, his heart was always in Rome on the Spanish Steps or the Pincio. And I guess it was all those steps and hills that finally killed him. A great man.

STU. Wayne? 180

WAYNE. Yeah?

STU. An Italian composer?

WAYNE. You see this fist?

STU. I just thought of two more.

WAYNE. Real ones?

STU. Give up, you'll see.

WAYNE. If they're not, buddy . . . !

STU. (*Looking at watch.*) You've got fifteen seconds.

WAYNE. Unh . . . unh . . . unh . . . quit making me nervous . . . unh . . .

STU. Ten!

WAYNE. Palestrina!

STU. Who else?

WAYNE. Palestrina and . . . unh . . .

STU. Pizzarella?

WAYNE. Can it! Palestrina and . . .

STU. Five seconds.

WAYNE. Pergolesi. Giovanni Pergolesi! (*Burst of machine gun fire, they both flatten out.*) That dirty little . . . (*Aims, ready to fire.*)

STU. (*Terse whisper.*) Homosexual Greek philosopher.

WAYNE. Brother, are you warped. I mean that's disgusting.

STU. Come on.

WAYNE. Plato wasn't homosexual.

STU. You were right there, climbing the Acropolis.

WAYNE. Your mind is really sick. A remark like that turns my stomach.

STU. Who made any remarks?

WAYNE. It's not even funny. (*Firing stops.*) Where the hell is he? Come on, buster, stick your neck out. He's shooting to see if anybody's out here. We'll just have to sit tight.

STU. Apropos the Parthenon, did you by any chance supervise the re-building of it?

WAYNE. I'm not Phidias. What are we on now? Your Greek kick? 220

STU. You're a fine one to talk about *that*.

WAYNE. There's something crawling on you.

STU. Hey! What the hell is it? This country. Bugs in your shoes, bugs in your hair, bugs in your food. Look at him go. Eight legs . . . no, ten! . . . I guess those are wings . . . nice antennae . . . I used to be scared of bugs.

WAYNE. Do you have to have a conversation with him?

STU. Bonsoir, bug. (*Crushes bug.*) 230

WAYNE. I could never do that.

STU. Bugs have souls now, too?

WAYNE. Shut up about all that, will you?

STU. I don't suppose you're an Italian poet?

WAYNE. I'm not Petrarch, Einstein.

STU. It was just a wild guess.

WAYNE. You're never going to get me.

STU. I'm not going to give up either.

WAYNE. Stubborn, stubborn, stubborn!

STU. I'd lose all self-respect if I weren't. 240

WAYNE. Sshh.

STU. I mean the only reason to begin a game is to win it.

WAYNE. I said shut up! (*The Man has come out of the tunnel. He's young, emaciated. He pauses at the entrance, quivering like a frightened rabbit. Spot on him.*) Look at the little bugger.

STU. Not so little through these sights.

WAYNE. Not yet! He has to come this way. Wait'll he's closer.

STU. You're not a French painter? A great master of the classical school?

WAYNE. I'm not Poussin.

STU. I've got another one. Impressionist.

WAYNE. French.

STU.   Yeah.

WAYNE.   I'm not Pisaro.

STU.   I can't think of any more P's.

WAYNE.   All right, *you* gave up, I'm—   260

STU.   No! (*Man has begun to move cautiously away from tunnel opening.*)

WAYNE.   Here he comes. Quiet now.

STU.   Were you an Italian sculptor working with Giotto on the campanile in Florence?

WAYNE.   I'm not Pisano. Get ready.

STU.   Okay, and this is it, Wayne. Did you write a famous "Lives"?

WAYNE.   I'm not Plutarch. Let's go. (*Man's face contorts with pain as he is cut down by a seemingly endless volley of gunfire. He falls, twitches, finally lies still. Wayne and Stu approach.*)

STU.   Is he dead? I just asked!

WAYNE.   Let's get back to camp.

STU.   Okay, I give up. Who are you?

WAYNE.   Pollaiuolo.

STU.   Who?

WAYNE.   Pollaiuolo. Antonio del Pollaiuolo.

STU.   That's like Pizzarella. (*They start moving off. Spot stays on Man's face.*)

WAYNE.   Italian painter, sculptor and goldsmith, 1432–1498.

STU. Well I never heard of him.

WAYNE.   Famous for his landscapes and the movement he put into the human body.

STU.   Never heard of him.

WAYNE.   He influenced Dürer, Signorelli and Verrocchio. (*They are just voices now.*)

STU.   *Them* I've heard of.   290

WAYNE.   Portrait of a Man? The Labors of Hercules? David? The Martyrdom of St. Sebastian? Tobias and the Angel?

STU.   Never heard of him.

WAYNE.   The tomb of Sixtus IV?

STU.   Never heard of him.

WAYNE.   Good God, he was a contemporary of Botticelli!

STU.   Never heard of him.

WAYNE.   Christ, you're dumb.   300

STU.   I NEVER HEARD OF HIM. (*Spot stays on Man's face. Slow fade.*)

Chapter 8

ARTS
AND
THE MAN

In virtually all cultures, and at every stage of history, human beings create works of art—objects of beauty or of aesthetic interest. This aspect of human life is the focus of this chapter. Since a dramatist, poet, or short-story writer is himself an artist in words, the nature and significance of his craft (and hence of art in general, of which literary works are a species) will be of special concern to him. He may be puzzled about the mysterious sources of its power to move and delight. If he takes a theoretical interest in his own art or another, he may be able to show or tell us much that enables us to understand and enjoy that art more fully: for example, the art of acting ("Duse and Bernhardt"), of country music ("Believing in Bluegrass"), of constructing visual images ("Nude Descending a Staircase"), or of poetry itself ("In Search of Fundamental Values").

In the process of creation, the artist faces problems: those raised by the inherent character of his medium, by his own passionate and sometimes obsessive need to create, by the economic conditions under which he lives, by the obstacles that an indifferent or hostile society may place in his path. Society's indifference to art may be inimical to its own interests, as the essay "Economics and Art" argues, in discussing the role that good design can play in our economy. Society's hostility may be tragic for the artist, as is suggested in "The Albatross" and portrayed in "Sonny's Blues." But even lack of understanding and formidable technical difficulties may be overcome by the tremendous will of an artist, such as Cellini reveals himself to be, in his reminiscence of "Casting the Perseus."

The deepest and most perplexing question about the arts lurks in the background of many of these selections and comes to the fore in some: What is the ultimate point of creating art, after all? This question has numerous corollaries: Are the social costs of art worth paying? Would the death of art leave humankind poorer in some essential way? Could we imagine a satisfying human life in which there was no poetry, no song, no dance, no harmony of color and shape? W. H. Auden finds in painting, Housman and Marianne Moore in poetry, Browning in music, a commentary on man's fate—bitter, perhaps, but sustaining. "The Real Thing" suggests that art, the realm of imagined possibility, is distinct from nature, the realm of fact—and at least as necessary to human beings. "Sonny's Blues" says much about the healing effect of art on its creators and its audiences. More questions are raised than answered here; but these works should help the student to think more deeply and clearly toward his own answers, tentative and incomplete though they may have to be.

Benvenuto Cellini

CASTING THE PERSEUS

I

Having succeeded so well with the cast of the Medusa,[1] I had great hope of bringing my Perseus through; for I had laid the wax on, and felt confident that it would come out in bronze as perfectly as the Medusa. The waxen model produced so fine an effect that when the Duke[2] saw it and was struck with its beauty—whether somebody had persuaded him it could not be carried out with the same finish in metal, or whether he thought so for himself—he came to visit me more frequently than usual, and on one occasion said: "Benvenuto, this figure cannot succeed in bronze; the laws of art do not admit of it." These words of his Excellency stung me so sharply that I answered: "My lord, I know how very little confidence you have in me; and I believe the reason of this is that your most illustrious Excellency lends too ready an ear to my calumniators, or else indeed that you do not understand my art." He hardly let me close the sentence when he broke in: "I profess myself a connoisseur, and understand it very very well indeed." I replied: "Yes, like a prince, not like an artist; for if your Excellency understood my trade as well as you imagine, you

would trust me on the proofs I have already given. These are, first, the colossal bronze bust of your Excellency, which is now in Elba;[3] secondly, the restoration of the Ganymede in marble, which offered so many difficulties and cost me so much trouble, that I would rather have made the whole statue new from the beginning; thirdly, the Medusa, cast by me in bronze, here now before your Excellency's eyes, the execution of which was a greater triumph of strength and skill than any of my predecessors in this fiendish art have yet achieved. Look you, my lord! I constructed that furnace anew on principles quite different from those of other founders; in addition to many technical improvements and ingenious devices, I supplied it with two issues for the metal, because this difficult and twisted figure could not otherwise have come out perfect. It is only owing to my intelligent insight into means and appliances that the statue turned out as it did; a triumph judged impossible by all the practitioners of this art. I should like you furthermore to be aware, my lord, for certain, that the sole reason why I succeeded with all those great and arduous works in France under his most admirable Majesty King Francis, was the high courage which that good monarch put into my heart by the liberal allowances he made me, and the multitude of workpeople he left at my disposal. I could have as many as I asked for, and employed at times above forty, all chosen by myself. These were the causes of my having there produced so many masterpieces in so short a space of time. Now then, my lord, put trust in me; supply me with the aid I need. I am confident of being able to complete a work which will delight your soul. But if your Excellency goes on disheartening me, and does not advance me the assistance which is absolutely required, neither I nor any man alive upon

---

[1] The Gorgon slain by Perseus, who was represented as holding up her head.

[2] Cosimo de' Medici (1519–1574), ruler of Florence.

[3] At Portoterraio. It came afterwards to Florence. [Symonds]

this earth can hope to achieve the slightest thing of value."

II

It was as much as the Duke could do to stand by and listen to my pleadings. He kept turning first this way and then that; while I, in despair, poor wretched I, was calling up remembrance of the noble state I held in France, to the great sorrow of my soul. All at once he cried: "Come, tell me, Benvenuto, how is it possible that yonder splendid head of Medusa, so high up there in the grasp of Perseus, should ever come out perfect?" I replied upon the instant: "Look you now, my lord! If your Excellency possessed that knowledge of the craft which you affirm you have, you would not fear one moment for the splendid head you speak of. There is good reason, on the other hand, to feel uneasy about this right foot, so far below and at a distance from the rest." When he heard these words, the Duke turned, half in anger, to some gentlemen in waiting and exclaimed: "I verily believe that this Benvenuto prides himself on contradicting everything one says." Then he faced round to me with a touch of mockery, upon which his attendants did the like, and began to speak as follows: "I will listen patiently to any argument you can possibly produce in explanation of your statement, which may convince me of its probability." I said in answer: "I will adduce so sound an argument that your Excellency shall perceive the full force of it." So I began: "You must know, my lord, that the nature of fire is to ascend, and therefore I promise you that Medusa's head will come out famously; but since it is not in the nature of fire to descend, and I must force it downwards six cubits by artificial means, I assure your Excellency upon this most convincing ground of proof that the foot cannot possibly come out. It will, however, be quite easy for me to restore it." "Why, then," said the Duke,

"did you not devise it so that the foot should come out as well as you affirm the head will?" I answered: "I must have made a much larger furnace, with a conduit as thick as my leg; and so I might have forced the molten metal by its own weight to descend so far. Now, my pipe, which runs six cubits to the statue's foot, as I have said, is not thicker than two fingers. However, it was not worth the trouble and expense to make a larger; for I shall easily be able to mend what is lacking. But when my mould is more than half full, as I expect, from this middle point upwards, the fire ascending by its natural property, then the heads of Perseus and Medusa will come out admirably; you may be quite sure of it." After I had thus expounded these convincing arguments, together with many more of the same kind, which it would be tedious to set down here, the Duke shook his head and departed without further ceremony.

III

Abandoned thus to my own resources, I took new courage, and banished the sad thoughts which kept recurring to my mind, making me often weep bitter tears of repentance for having left France; for though I did so only to revisit Florence, my sweet birthplace, in order that I might charitably succor my six nieces, this good action, as I well perceived, had been the beginning of my great misfortune. Nevertheless, I felt convinced that when my Perseus was accomplished, all these trials would be turned to high felicity and glorious well-being.

Accordingly I strengthened my heart, and with all the forces of my body and my purse, employing what little money still remained to me, I set to work. First I provided myself with several loads of pinewood from the forests of Serristori, in the neighborhood of Montelupo. While these were on their way, I clothed my Perseus with the clay which I had prepared many months beforehand, in order that it might be duly seasoned. After making its clay tunic (for that is the term used in this art) and properly arming it and fencing it with iron girders, I began to draw the wax out by means of a slow fire. This melted and issued through numerous air-vents I had made; for the more there are of these, the better will the mould fill. When I had finished drawing off the wax, I constructed a funnel-shaped furnace all round the model of my Perseus.[4] It was built of bricks, so interlaced, the one above the other, that numerous apertures were left for the fire to exhale at. Then I began to lay on wood by degrees, and kept it burning two whole days and nights. At length, when all the wax was gone, and the mould was well baked, I set to work at digging the pit in which to sink it. This I performed with scrupulous regard to all the rules of art. When I had finished that part of my work, I raised the mould by windlasses and stout ropes to a perpendicular position, and suspending it with the greatest care one cubit above the level of the furnace, so that it hung exactly above the middle of the pit, I next lowered it gently down into the very bottom of the furnace, and had it firmly placed with every possible precaution for its safety. When this delicate operation was accomplished, I began to bank it up with the earth I had excavated; and, ever as the earth grew higher, I introduced its proper air-vents, which were little tubes of earthenware, such as folk use for drains and suchlike purposes.[5] At length, I felt sure that it

[4] This furnace, called *manica*, was like a grain-hopper, so that the mould could stand upright in it as in a cup. The word *manica* is the same as our *manuch*, an antique form of sleeve. [Symonds]

[5] These air-vents, or *sfiatatoi*, were introduced into the outer mould, which Cellini calls the *tonaca*, or clay tunic laid upon the original model of baked clay and wax. They served the double purpose of drawing off the wax, whereby a space was left for the molten bronze to enter, and also of facilitating the penetration of this molten metal by allowing a free escape of air and gas from the outer mould. [Symonds]

was admirably fixed, and that the filling-in of the pit and the placing of the air-vents had been properly performed. I also could see that my workpeople understood my method, which differed very considerably from that of all the other masters in the trade. Feeling confident, then, that I could rely upon them, I next turned to my furnace, which I had filled with numerous pigs of copper and other bronze stuff. The pieces were piled according to the laws of art, that is to say, so resting one upon the other that the flames could play freely through them, in order that the metal might heat and liquefy the sooner. At last I called out heartily to set the furnace going. The logs of pine were heaped in, and, what with the unctuous resin of the wood and the good draught I had given, my furnace worked so well that I was obliged to rush from side to side to keep it going. The labor was more than I could stand; yet I forced myself to strain every nerve and muscle. To increase my anxieties, the workshop took fire, and we were afraid lest the roof should fall upon our heads; while, from the garden, such a storm of wind and rain kept blowing in, that it perceptibly cooled the furnace.

Battling thus with all these untoward circumstances for several hours, and exerting myself beyond even the measure of my powerful constitution, I could at last bear up no longer, and a sudden fever of the utmost possible intensity attacked me. I felt absolutely obliged to go and fling myself upon my bed. Sorely against my will having to drag myself away from the spot, I turned to my assistants, about ten or more in all, what with master-founders, hand-workers, country-fellows, and my own special journeymen, among whom was Bernardino Mannellini of Mugello, my apprentice through several years. To him in particular I spoke: "Look, my dear Bernardino, that you observe the rules which I have taught you; do your best with all despatch, for the metal will soon be fused. You cannot go wrong; these honest men will get the channels ready; you will easily be able to drive back the two plugs with this pair of iron crooks; and I am sure that my mould will fill miraculously. I feel more ill than I ever did in all my life, and verily believe that it will kill me before a few hours are over." [6] Thus, with despair at heart, I left them, and betook myself to bed.

IV

No sooner had I got to bed, than I ordered my serving-maids to carry food and wine for all the men into the workshop; at the same time I cried: "I shall not be alive tomorrow." They tried to encourage me, arguing that my illness would pass over, since it came from excessive fatigue. In this way I spent two hours battling with the fever, which steadily increased, and calling out continually: "I feel that I am dying." My housekeeper, who was named Mona Fiore da Castel del Rio, a very notable manager and no less warmhearted, kept chiding me for my discouragement; but, on the other hand, she paid me every kind attention which was possible. However, the sight of my physical pain and moral dejection so affected her, that, in spite of that brave heart of hers, she could not refrain from

---

[6] Some technical terms require explanation in this sentence. The *canali* or channels were sluices for carrying the molten metal from the furnace into the mould. The *mandriani*, which I have translated by *iron crooks*, were poles fitted at the end with curved irons, by which the openings of the *furnace*, *plugs*, or in Italian *spine*, could be partially or wholly driven back, so as to let the molten metal flow through the channels into the mould. When the metal reached the mould, it entered in a red-hot stream between the *tonaca*, or outside mould, and the *anima*, or inner block, filling up exactly the space which had previously been occupied by the wax extracted by a method of slow burning alluded to above. I believe that the process is known as casting *à cire perdue*. The *forma*, or mould, consisted of two pieces; one hollow (*la tonaca*), which gave shape to the bronze; one solid and rounded (*la anima*), which stood at a short interval within the former, and regulated the influx of the metal. [Symonds]

shedding tears; and yet, so far as she was able, she took good care I should not see them. While I was thus terribly afflicted, I beheld the figure of a man enter my chamber, twisted in his body into the form of a capital S. He raised a lamentable, doleful voice, like one who announces their last hour to men condemned to die upon the scaffold, and spoke these words: "O Benvenuto! your statue is spoiled, and there is no hope whatever of saving it." No sooner had I heard the shriek of that wretch than I gave a howl which might have been heard from the sphere of flame. Jumping from my bed, I seized my clothes and began to dress. The maids, and my lad, and everyone who came around to help me, got kicks or blows of the fist, while I kept crying out in lamentation: "Ah! traitors! enviers! This is an act of treason, done by malice prepense! But I swear by God that I will sift it to the bottom, and before I die will leave such witness to the world of what I can do as shall make a score of mortals marvel."

When I had got my clothes on, I strode with soul bent on mischief toward the workshop; there I beheld the men, whom I had left erewhile in such high spirits, standing stupefied and downcast. I began at once and spoke: "Up with you! Attend to me! Since you have not been able or willing to obey the directions I gave you, obey me now that I am with you to conduct my work in person. Let no one contradict me, for in cases like this we need the aid of hand and hearing, not of advice." When I had uttered these words, a certain Maestro Alessandro Lastricati broke silence and said: "Look you, Benvenuto, you are going to attempt an enterprise which the laws of art do not sanction, and which cannot succeed." I turned upon him with such fury and so full of mischief, that he and all the rest of them exclaimed with one voice: "On then! Give orders! We will obey your least commands, so long as life is left in us." I believe they spoke thus feelingly because they thought I must fall shortly dead upon the ground. I went immediately to inspect the furnace, and found that the metal was all curdled; an accident which we express by "being caked." I told two of the hands to cross the road and fetch from the house of the butcher Capretta a load of young oak-wood, which had lain dry for above a year; this wood had been previously offered me by Madame Ginevra, wife of the said Capretta. So soon as the first armfuls arrived, I began to fill the grate beneath the furnace. Now oak-wood of that kind heats more powerfully than any other sort of tree; and for this reason, where a slow fire is wanted, as in the case of gun-foundry, alder or pine is preferred. Accordingly, when the logs took fire, oh! how the cake began to stir beneath that awful heat, to glow and sparkle in a blaze! At the same time I kept stirring up the channels, and sent men upon the roof to stop the conflagration, which had gathered force from the increased combustion in the furnace; also I caused boards, carpets, and other hangings to be set up against the garden, in order to protect us from the violence of the rain.

V

When I had thus provided against these several disasters, I roared out first to one man and then to another: "Bring this thing here! Take that thing there!" At this crisis, when the whole gang saw the cake was on the point of melting, they did my bidding, each fellow working with the strength of three. I then ordered half a pig of pewter to be brought, which weighed about sixty pounds, and flung it into the middle of the cake inside the furnace. By this means, and by piling on wood and stirring now with pokers and now with iron rods, the curdled mass rapidly began to liquefy. Then, knowing I had brought the dead to life again, against the firm opinion of those ignoramuses, I felt such vigor fill my veins, that all those pains of fever, all those fears of death, were quite forgotten.

All of a sudden an explosion took place, attended by a tremendous flash of flame, as though a thunderbolt had formed and been discharged amongst us. Unwonted and appalling terror bewildered everyone, and me more even than the rest. When the din was over and the dazzling light extinguished, we began to look each other in the face. Then I discovered that the cap of the furnace had blown up, and the bronze was bubbling over from its source beneath. So I had the mouths of my mould immediately opened, and at the same time drove in the two plugs which kept back the molten metal. But I noticed that it did not flow as rapidly as usual, the reason being probably that the fierce heat of the fire we kindled had consumed its base alloy. Accordingly I sent for all my pewter platters, porringers, and dishes, to the number of some two hundred pieces, and had a portion of them cast, one by one, into the channels, the rest into the furnace. This expedient succeeded, and every one could now perceive that my bronze was in most perfect liquefaction, and my mould was filling; whereupon they all with heartiness and happy cheer assisted and obeyed my bidding, while I, now here, now there, gave orders, helped with my own hands, and cried aloud: "O God! Thou that by Thy immeasurable power didst rise from the dead, and in Thy glory didst ascend to heaven!" . . . even thus in a moment my mould was filled; and seeing my work finished, I fell upon my knees, and with all my heart gave thanks to God.

After all was over, I turned to a plate of salad on a bench there, and ate with hearty appetite, and drank together with the whole crew. Afterwards I retired to bed, healthy and happy, for it was now two hours before morning, and slept as sweetly as though I had never felt a touch of illness. My good housekeeper, without my giving any orders, had prepared a fat capon for my repast. So that, when I rose, about the hour for breaking fast, she presented herself with a smiling countenance, and said: "Oh! is that the man who felt that he was dying? Upon my word, I think the blows and kicks you dealt us last night, when you were so enraged, and had that demon in your body as it seemed, must have frightened away your mortal fever! The fever feared that it might catch it too, as we did!" All my poor household, relieved in like measure from anxiety and overwhelming labor, went at once to buy earthen vessels in order to replace the pewter I had cast away. Then we dined together joyfully; nay, I cannot remember a day in my whole life when I dined with greater gladness or a better appetite.

After our meal I received visits from the several men who had assisted me. They exchanged congratulations, and thanked God for our success, saying they had learned and seen things done which other masters judged impossible. I too grew somewhat glorious; and deeming I had shown myself a man of talent, indulged in boastful humor. So I thrust my hand into my purse, and paid them all to their full satisfaction.

That evil fellow, my mortal foe, Messer Pier Francesco Ricci, majordomo of the Duke, took great pains to find out how the affair had gone. In answer to his questions, the two men whom I suspected of having caked my metal for me said I was no man, but of a certainty some powerful devil, since I had accomplished what no craft of the art could do; indeed they did not believe a mere ordinary fiend could work such miracles as I in other ways had shown. They exaggerated the whole affair so much, possibly in order to excuse their own part in it, that the majordomo wrote an account to the Duke, who was then in Pisa, far more marvelous and full of thrilling incidents than what they had narrated.

VI

After I had let my statue cool for two whole days, I began to uncover it by slow degrees. The first thing I found was that the head of Medusa had come out most admir-

ably, thanks to the air-vents; for, as I had told the Duke, it is the nature of fire to ascend. Upon advancing farther, I discovered that the other head, that, namely, of Perseus, had succeeded no less admirably; and this astonished me far more, because it is at a considerably lower level than that of the Medusa. Now the mouths of the mould were placed above the head of Perseus and behind his shoulders; and I found that all the bronze my furnace contained had been exhausted in the head of this figure. It was a miracle to observe that not one fragment remained in the orifice of the channel, and that nothing was wanting to the statue. In my great astonishment I seemed to see in this the hand of God arranging and controlling all.

I went on uncovering the statue with success, and ascertained that everything had come out in perfect order, until I reached the foot of the right leg on which the statue rests. There the heel itself was formed, and going farther, I found the foot apparently complete. This gave me great joy on the one side, but was half unwelcome to me on the other, merely because I had told the Duke that it could not come out. However, when I reached the end, it appeared that the toes and a little piece above them were unfinished, so that about half the foot was wanting. Although I knew that this would add a trifle to my labor, I was very well pleased, because I could now prove to the Duke how well I understood my business. It is true that far more of the foot than I expected had been perfectly formed; the reason of this was that, from causes I have recently described, the bronze was hotter than our rules of art prescribe; also that I had been obliged to supplement the alloy with my pewter cups and platters, which no one else, I think, had ever done before.

Having now ascertained how successfully my work had been accomplished, I lost no time in hurrying to Pisa, where I found the Duke. He gave me a most gracious reception, as did also the Duchess; and although the majordomo had informed them of the whole proceedings, their Excellencies deemed my performance far more stupendous and astonishing when they heard the tale from my own mouth. When I arrived at the foot of Perseus, and said it had not come out perfect, just as I previously warned his Excellency, I saw an expression of wonder pass over his face, while he related to the Duchess how I had predicted this beforehand. Observing the princes to be so well disposed toward me, I begged leave from the Duke to go to Rome. He granted it in most obliging terms, and bade me return as soon as possible to complete his Perseus; giving me letters of recommendation meanwhile to his ambassador, Averardo Serristori.

Bernard Shaw

DUSE AND BERNHARDT

This week began with the relapse of Sarah Bernhardt[7] into her old profession of serious actress. She played Magda in Sudermann's *Heimat* [*Home*], and was promptly challenged by Duse[8] in the same part at Drury Lane[9] on Wednesday. The contrast between the two Magdas is as extreme as any contrast could possibly be between artists who have finished their twenty years' apprenticeship to the same profession under closely similar conditions. Madame Bernhardt has the charm of a jolly maturity, rather spoilt and petulant, perhaps, but always ready with a sunshine-through-the-clouds smile if only she is made much of. Her dresses and diamonds, if not exactly splendid, are at least

[7] French actress, 1844–1923, known as "the divine Sarah."
[8] Eleanora Duse, 1859–1924, Italian actress.
[9] Theatre on Russell Street, London.

splendacious; her figure, far too scantily upholstered in the old days, is at its best; and her complexion shows that she has not studied modern art in vain. Those charming roseate effects which French painters produce by giving flesh the pretty color of strawberries and cream, and painting the shadows pink and crimson, are cunningly reproduced by Madame Bernhardt in the living picture. She paints her ears crimson and allows them to peep enchantingly through a few loose braids of her auburn hair. Every dimple has its dab of pink; and her fingertips are so delicately incarnadined that you fancy they are transparent like her ears, and that the light is shining through their delicate blood-vessels. Her lips are like a newly painted pillar box; her cheeks, right up to the languid lashes, have the bloom and surface of a peach; she is beautiful with the beauty of her school, and entirely inhuman and incredible. But the incredibility is pardonable, because, though it is all the greatest nonsense, nobody believing in it, the actress herself least of all, it is so artful, so clever, so well recognized a part of the business, and carried off with such a genial air, that it is impossible not to accept it with good-humor. One feels, when the heroine bursts on the scene, a dazzling vision of beauty, that instead of imposing on you, she adds to her own piquancy by looking you straight in the face, and saying, in effect: "Now who would ever suppose that I am a grandmother?" That, of course, is irresistible; and one is not sorry to have been coaxed to relax one's notions of the dignity of art when she gets to serious business and shows how ably she does her work. The coaxing suits well with the childishly egotistical character of her acting, which is not the art of making you think more highly or feel more deeply, but the art of making you admire her, pity her, champion her, weep with her, laugh at her jokes, follow her fortunes breathlessly, and applaud her wildly when the curtain falls. It is the art of finding out all your weaknesses and practising on them—cajoling you, harrowing you, exciting you—on the whole, fooling you. And it is always Sarah Bernhardt in her own capacity who does this to you. The dress, the title of the play, the order of the words may vary; but the woman is always the same. She does not enter into the leading character: she substitutes herself for it.

All this is precisely what does not happen in the case of Duse, whose every part is a separate creation. When she comes on the stage, you are quite welcome to take your opera-glass and count whatever lines time and care have so far traced on her. They are the credentials of her humanity; and she knows better than to obliterate that significant handwriting beneath a layer of peach-bloom from the chemist's. The shadows on her face are grey, not crimson; her lips are sometimes nearly grey also; there are neither dabs nor dimples; her charm could never be imitated by a barmaid with unlimited pin money and a row of footlights before her instead of the handles of a beer-engine. The result is not so discouraging as the patrons of the bar might suppose. Wilkes,[10] who squinted atrociously, boasted that he was only quarter of an hour behind the handsomest man in Europe: Duse is not in action five minutes before she is quarter of a century ahead of the handsomest woman in the world. I grant that Sarah's elaborate Mona Lisa smile, with the conscious droop of the eyelashes and the long carmined lips coyly disclosing the brilliant row of teeth, is effective of its kind—that it not only appeals to your susceptibilities, but positively jogs them. And it lasts quite a minute, sometimes longer. But Duse, with a tremor of the lip which you feel rather than see, and which lasts half an instant, touches you straight on the very heart; and there is not a line in the face or a cold tone in the grey shadow that does not give poignancy to that tremor. As to youth and age, who can associate purity and delicacy of emotion, and simplicity of expression, with the sordid craft that repels us in age; or voluptuous appeal and egotistical self-insistence with the candor and generosity that attract us in youth? Who ever thinks of Potiphar's wife as a young woman, or St. Elizabeth of Hungary as an old one? [11] These associations are horribly unjust to age, and undeserved by youth: they belong of right to differences of character, not of years; but they rule our imaginations; and the great artist profits by them to appear eternally young. However, it would be a critical blunder as well as a personal folly on my part to suggest that Duse, any more than Sarah Bernhardt, neglects any art that could heighten the effect of her acting when she is impersonating young and pretty women. The truth is that in the art of being beautiful, Madame Bernhardt is a child beside her. The French artist's stock of attitudes and facial effects could be catalogued as easily as her stock of dramatic ideas: the counting would hardly go beyond the fingers of both hands. Duse produces the illusion of being infinite in variety of beautiful pose and motion. Every idea, every shade of thought and mood, expresses itself delicately but vividly to the eye; and yet, in an apparent million of changes and inflections, it is impossible to catch any line at an awkward angle, or any strain interfering with the perfect abandonment of all the limbs to what appears to be their natural gravitation towards the finest grace. She is ambidextrous and supple, like a gymnast or a panther; only the multitude of ideas which find physical expression in her movements are all of that high quality which marks off humanity from the animals, and, I fear I must add, from a good many

---

10 John Wilkes (1727–1797), British politician. He was cross-eyed.

11 The first attempted to seduce Joseph in *Genesis* xxxix, 7–12; the second (1207–1231), a princess, devoted her life to the care of the sick.

gymnasts. When it is remembered that the majority of tragic actors excel only in explosions of those passions which are common to man and brute, there will be no difficulty in understanding the indescribable distinction which Duse's acting acquires from the fact that behind every stroke of it is a distinctively human idea. In nothing is this more apparent than in the vigilance in her of that high human instinct which seeks to awaken the deepest responsive feeling without giving pain. In *La Dame aux Camélias*,[12] for instance, it is easy for an intense actress to harrow us with her sorrows and paroxysms of phthisis, leaving us with a liberal pennyworth of sensation, not fundamentally distinguishable from that offered by a public execution, or any other evil in which we still take a hideous delight. As different from this as light from darkness is the method of the actress who shows us how human sorrow can express itself only in its appeal for the sympathy it needs, whilst striving by strong endurance to shield others from the infection of its torment. That is the charm of Duse's interpretation of the stage poem of Marguerite Gautier. It is unspeakably touching because it is exquisitely considerate: that is, exquisitely sympathetic. No physical charm is noble as well as beautiful unless it is the expression of a moral charm; and it is because Duse's range includes these moral high notes, if I may so express myself, that her compass, extending from the depths of a mere predatory creature like Claude's wife[13] up to Marguerite Gautier at her kindest or Magda at her bravest, so immeasurably dwarfs the poor little octave and a half on which Sarah Bernhardt plays such pretty canzonets and stirring marches.

[12] *The Lady of Camellias* (1852), better known in English as *Camille*, a play by Alexander Dumas the Younger. Its heroine, Marguerite Gautier, dies of tuberculosis.

[13] In the play (1873) of that name, also by Dumas.

Obvious as the disparity of the two famous artists has been to many of us since we first saw Duse, I doubt whether any of us realized, after Madame Bernhardt's very clever performance as Magda on Monday night, that there was room in the nature of things for its annihilation within forty-eight hours by so comparatively quiet a talent as Duse's. And yet annihilation is the only word for it. Sarah was very charming, very jolly when the sun shone, very petulant when the clouds covered it, and positively angry when they wanted to take her child away from her. And she did not trouble us with any fuss about the main theme of Sudermann's play, the revolt of the modern woman against that ideal of home which exacts the sacrifice of her whole life to its care, not by her grace, and as its own sole help and refuge, but as a right which it has to the services of all females as abject slaves. In fact, there is not the slightest reason to suspect Madame Bernhardt of having discovered any such theme in the play; though Duse, with one look at Schwartze, the father, nailed it to the stage as the subject of the impending dramatic struggle before she had been five minutes on the scene. Before long, there came a stroke of acting which will probably never be forgotten by those who saw it, and which explained at once why those artifices of the dressing-table which help Madame Bernhardt would hinder Duse almost as much as a screen placed in front of her. I should explain, first, that the real name of the play is not *Magda* but *Home*. Magda is a daughter who has been turned out of doors for defying her father, one of those outrageous persons who mistake their desire to have everything their own way in the house for a sacred principle of home life. She has a hard time of it, but at last makes a success as an opera singer, though not until her lonely struggles have thrown her for sympathy on a fellow student, who in due time goes his way and leaves her to face motherhood as best she can. In the fullness of her fame she returns to her native town, and in an attack of homesickness makes advances to her father, who consents to receive her again. No sooner is she installed in the house than she finds that one of the most intimate friends of the family is the father of her child. In the third act of the play she is on the stage when he is announced as a visitor. It must be admitted that Sarah Bernhardt played this scene very lightly and pleasantly: there was genuine good fellowship in the way in which she reassured the embarrassed gallant and made him understand that she was not going to play off the sorrows of Gretchen[14] on him after all those years, and that she felt that she owed him the priceless experience of maternity, even if she did not particularly respect him for it. Her self-possession at this point was immense: the peach-bloom never altered by a shade. Not so with Duse. The moment she read the card handed her by the servant, you realized what it was to have to face a meeting with the man. It was interesting to watch how she got through it when he came in, and how, on the whole, she got through it pretty well. He paid his compliments and offered his flowers; they sat down; and she evidently felt that she had got it safely over and might allow herself to think at her ease, and to look at him to see how much he had altered. Then a terrible thing happened to her. She began to blush; and in another moment she was conscious of it, and the blush was slowly spreading and deepening until, after a few vain efforts to avert her face or to obstruct his view of it without seeming to do so, she gave up and hid the blush in her hands. After that feat of acting I did not need to be told why Duse does not paint an inch thick. I could detect no trick in it: it seemed to me a perfectly genuine effect of the dramatic imagination. In the third act of *La Dame aux Camélias,* where she produces a touching effect by throwing herself down, and presently rises with her face changed and flushed with weeping, the flush is secured by the preliminary plunge to a stooping attitude, imagination or no imagination; but Magda's blush did not admit of that explanation; and I must confess to an intense professional curiosity as to whether it always comes spontaneously.

I shall make no attempt to describe the rest of that unforgettable act. To say that it left the house not only frantically applauding, but actually roaring, is to say nothing; for had we not applauded Sarah as Gismonda and roared at Mrs. Patrick Campbell as Fedora? [15] But there really was something to roar at this time. There was a real play, and an actress who understood the author and was a greater artist than he. And for me, at least, there was a confirmation of my sometimes flagging faith that a dramatic critic is really the servant of a high art, and not a mere advertiser of entertainments of questionable respectability of motive.

John Kenneth Galbraith

ECONOMICS AND ART

I

Several years ago at a leading eastern university the case arose of a young assistant professor of economics. He was an able and even brilliant teacher. He had written a number of good papers. One or two in particular showed originality, technical virtuosity, and incomprehensibility, a com-

14 The deserted girl in *Faust*, Part I (1808), by J. W. von Goethe. She kills her child and is sentenced to death.

15 In the plays (1882, 1894) of those names by Victorien Sardou. Mrs. Campbell, née Beatrice Tanner, lived from 1865 to 1940.

bination which is held in the highest professional regard. But he had grave drawbacks. These included a passion for music and painting and a morbid lack of interest in the ordinary manifestations of material well-being. He lived in evident contentment in a small house heated by a coal stove. It was sensibly decided—though it must be said not without discussion—that he had no future as an economist. He was not promoted.

The incident illustrates the traditional relationship between art and economics. There is none. Art has nothing to do with the sterner preoccupations of the economist. The artist's values—his splendid and often splenetic insistence on the supremacy of aesthetic goals—are subversive of the straightforward materialist concerns of the economist. He makes the economist feel dull, routine, philistine, and uncomfortable and also sadly unappreciated for his earthy concern for bread and butter, including that which nourishes the artist. Not only do the two worlds not meet, but the regret in each is evidently negligible.

This alienation, though unregretted, is unfortunate. The economist can perhaps say something useful to the artist about his environment and what nourishes the artistic imagination. And the artist stands in far more important relation to economics, and indirectly to politics, than we have yet realized. I will end this essay by arguing that one of the more important problems of our day—the weakening of the American balance of international payments and the complex of foreign and domestic issues which follow in its train—is partly the result of the alienation of the artist from our economic life. But first a word or two of explanation.

The amateur venturing into the world of art is soon made to feel the perils of his path. Art is the creation of beauty and its language. But art and how to deal with Russia have this in common: that subjectivity is the parent of both certainty and emotion. One man's beauty, it is clear, is another man's missed opportunity; had the critics been present at the time, there would have been some highly deprecatory words about the Lord's creative instinct. I shall not venture to say what is beauty; and fortunately for the purposes of this chapter, I need only to be allowed a certain band within which it will be agreed that it occurs. Whether a particular artist or work belongs within this band is not something I need decide.

I have need to refer not only to the artist but to those for whom his language has meaning. This is the community which shares the artist's imagination and responds to it. Its size and the depth and discernment of its response are matters of much importance. I shall refer to it simply as the aesthetic response.

II

The economic myth of the artist is of the man devoid of material baggage and indifferent to pecuniary reward. It is not a myth that can be reconciled entirely with reality. In the Greco-Roman epoch, the painter or sculptor soiled his hands at a wearisome and hence unbecoming toil. Accordingly, and unlike the poet, he was identified with the artisan and the slave, and his pay was that of a worker.[16] This was only slightly less so of the early Renaissance artists—Hauser describes them as "economically on a footing with the petty bourgeois tradesman." [17] However, by the latter part of the fifteenth century, the great painters had, financially speaking, come into their own. Raphael and Titian lived handsomely on ample incomes. Michelangelo was a wealthy man; it was because of his wealth

16 Arnold Hauser, *The Social History of Art* (New York: Alfred A. Knopf, Inc., 1951), I, 124.
17 *Ibid.*, p. 315.

that he was able to decline payment for the design of St. Peter's. Leonardo ultimately received a handsome salary.

In later times it is difficult to make a rule. The Dutch masters, as a consequence of heavy overproduction, had a hard time. Rembrandt, Hals, and Vermeer led a financially precarious existence. For what we would now call reasons of economic security, van Goyen traded in tulips, Hobbema was a tax collector, and Jan Steen was an innkeeper. In modern times Van Gogh, Gauguin, and Toulouse-Lautrec were vagabonds because this was implicit in their alienation from bourgeois civilization. But interspersed through the history of Western painting from Rubens to Picasso have been others who have earned great fortunes. This has included Americans. Copley was rich enough to speculate in real estate and owned much of Beacon Hill. Winslow Homer lived a very comfortable life. The most popular of the abstract expressionists are being handsomely rewarded by any standards. It is not clear that wealth, for the artist, has been or is an insuperable obstacle.

What is not in doubt is that the aesthetic response is nourished by secure well-being. From classical Athens through the princes, bankers, and popes of the Renaissance, the Dutch bourgeois of the seventeenth century, the courtly patrons of the seventeenth and eighteenth centuries to the collectors and connoisseurs of modern times, wealth has been the unmistakable companion of art. Perhaps it has not always brought a discerning interest. But if it has not been a sufficient, it certainly has been a facilitating influence. The artist may transcend hunger and privation—conceivably his senses are honed by his suffering. But not so his audience. It turns to art after it has had dinner. At first glance, such a philistine assertion will seem surely suspect. But, subject always to individual exceptions, it will hardly be argued that the aesthetic response has been as strong from the poor and the insecure as

from the rich and established. "Great periods in art have traditionally come with stability in government, with prosperity and leisure." [18] "The overworked, driven person or class is seldom creative, while leisure, even wasteful leisure, may end creatively." [19]

III

One can bring these matters within the scope of a simple hypothesis. It is that pecuniary motivation—roughly the desire for money income—has a marked tendency to pre-empt the individual's emotions. Only as it releases its grip is there opportunity for artistic, or, for that matter, for any cultural or intellectual interest not immediately related to income. As Alfred Marshall observed, "The business by which a person earns his livelihood generally fills his thoughts during by far the greater part of those hours in which his mind is at its best." [20] If he and his family live under the threat of hunger, cold, or exposure, this preoccupation will be total. By the same token, to remove the threat of physical hardship will be, other things equal, to weaken the role of pecuniary motivation and allow other influences to enter the pattern of life.

The fear of hardship, we may assume, will play somewhat the same pre-emptive role as hardship itself. And fear is not confined to physical hardship. As most people are constituted, they will be perturbed by any serious threat to existing levels of well-being. They defend accustomed living standards with considerable tenacity. Accordingly, if people are so circumstanced that

18 Edward Durrell Stone, "The Case Against the Tailfin Age," *New York Times*, October 18, 1959.
19 Bernard Berenson, *One Year's Reading for Fun: 1942* (New York: Alfred A. Knopf, Inc., 1960), p. 93.
20 *Principles of Economics* (London: Macmillan. 8th edition, 1927), p. 1.

they live under the threat of a reduction in income—of being plunged into some dark and half-imagined abyss—pecuniary motivation will be strong. The gods are waiting to hurl the unwary man to his doom; they can only be propitiated by unremitting vigilance. The secure man, in contrast, can turn his thoughts to other matters.

Until comparatively recent times the preferred model of a nonsocialist society was one of marked uncertainty. Production was for a common market made by many sellers; in this market, prices moved freely in response to changes in consumer taste or need or changes in cost and output. Incomes, at least, in the form of profits, salaries, or wages were inherently insecure.[21] Favorable profits, for example, would attract new participants. This was possible, for entry into any business was assumed to be inexpensive and easy. The resulting increase in supply would lower prices and therewith profits, and, in practice, the unco-ordinated response of numerous new entrants could easily cause profits to disappear. Profits could also disappear as the result of unexpected or inexplicable shifts in consumer taste or changes in technology which gave other producers a sudden and substantial advantage in cost. Wages and salaries shared the uncertainty of the income from which they came.

The uncertainty of this model, it should be noted, was not only intrinsic but a virtue. It was what punished sloth and kept producers on their toes. This is almost exactly to say that the system was designed to make pecuniary motivation as nearly preemptive as possible.[22] It was meant to be artistically barren, for it rewarded a full-time concern with making money and it drove its participants with the omnipresent possibility of failure.

The nearest approach to the competitive model in the American economy is agriculture. Here many comparatively small producers do supply a common market under conditions which, in the past at least, have been characterized by marked uncertainty. In this industry earnings often have suddenly and disastrously disappeared for many participants. Without stopping to consider the reason, we expect the modern practising farmer to be beyond the reach of the aesthetic response. That the successful lawyer should have a concern for painting does not surprise us. But not the successful cattleman. He is the man for whom the calendars and *The Saturday Evening Post* covers are drawn. As his income increases, he may develop an interest in a better automobile, possibly in an airplane, and certainly in an array of consumer goods. That he should develop a serious concern for painting or sculpture or even for domestic architecture is not expected. A farmer has too many other worries. He cannot be frivolous or eccentric. Unlike the more secure lawyer, it is in fact taken for granted that his pecuniary concerns are pre-emptive.[23]

As with the farmer, so generally with the small businessman—the dealer, salesman, contractor, and small merchant. His income may be handsome by any past standards. But he is a man who has to hustle. Accordingly, the arts are not for him. George

---

[21] The case of income accruing from rent is rather different. And it is proof of the point that the more secure and leisurely landlord has long been considered accessible by the artist.

[22] It did not, of course, exclude religious motivation. But this is not in conflict with pecuniary motivation. It nowise interferes with the work week and, as in the case of Calvinism, it provides a moral sanction and reinforcement for economic achievement.

[23] I am here characterizing an attitude. It is one to which, I would certainly assume, there are many individual exceptions. And one reason for wishing for a greater security of farm income is to enlarge the number of exceptions. That an increase in the amount and security of income should bring an artistic and cultural renaissance on the farms should not strike us as odd. That is what income is for. Yet even those who are at first moved to think all this an aspersion on the agrarian soul will think it odd.

Babbitt,[24] who in secret moments hungered for something with slightly more magic, knew in the end that he had to keep his thoughts on the real estate business. The competitive economy still imposes this requirement.

IV

Were ours still an economy of insecure small producers, we would have therein a sufficient explanation of the alienation of art from economic life. The insecurity of such a society is pre-emptive; the aesthetic response will only be strong where it is somehow protected from the dominant economic motivation.

But modern economic society does not conform to the competitive model. The centerpiece of the modern capitalist economy is the great corporation. It is an institution which is arranged to provide a rather large number of people rather large and secure incomes. Through control of its prices and of its sources of supply, by diversification of its products, by research which insures that technological innovation does not catch it unawares and, in degree, by the management of consumer tastes, the modern corporation has either eliminated or much reduced the main sources of insecurity of the competitive firm. Consequently earnings are highly reliable; of the one hundred largest industrial firms in the United States, not one failed to earn a profit in 1957, and this was a year of mild recession.[25]

As a result the modern corporate executive enjoys a security of income and tenure comparable with that of a college professor. In examining the protection which a vocation accords to the individual, one should examine the fate not of the successful but of the unsuccessful. The benign and protective character of government employment is indicated by the decorative sinecures into which the inadequate can be sidetracked with appropriate ceremony. Ambassadorships in untroubled countries, assistant secretaryships for public affairs or membership on the Federal Communications Commission are all available. In colleges and universities, compassion is similarly manifested by establishing research projects of reviewing progress in behavioral sciences or international relations, by appointments as deans for relations with parents, wives, or the local churches or to committees to reconsider the curriculum. But the modern corporation is peculiarly rich in its arrangements for cushioning the fall of the man who stumbles in mid-career. Not only are a wide variety of posts—public relations, staff relations, community liaison, charitable contributions, supervision of office festivities—available with honorific titles, but there is also in most firms an understanding not present in the university that all will deny fiercely that any featherbedding is involved.

Accordingly, the comparatively secure and remunerative life provided by the modern corporation should be hospitable to the arts. Eventually it will be—and for the good of the economy, it must so become. However, the myth of the insecure, tough, competitive enterprise has outlasted the reality. Business is assumed still to require a total concentration of energies; anything less is still deemed to be out of character. And men are still treated by their commitment, or their simulation of a commitment, to what is held to be a demanding, no-nonsense, nose-to-the-grindstone, hard-driving existence. To suppose that the requirements of a business career are secondary, or supplementary, to artistic or cultural interests or a means of supporting them is still the exception. There are distinguished exceptions, but

24 In the novel *Babbitt* (1922), by Sinclair Lewis.
25 *Fortune*, August 1958. Of the largest two hundred, only one, an automobile manufacturer, failed to turn in a profit. Size is here measured by volume of sales.

they depart from the general rule. At the turn of the century, Charles Lang Freer made his business, as a builder of railroad cars, the servant of his interest in Whistler and Oriental art. His industrialist friends complained that he preferred talking about the tariff on paintings to discussing the price of steel.[26] Such talk might still cause question about his effectiveness as a businessman.

Indeed one senses that there has even been a partial reversal of form. Two generations ago, with the highly interested assistance of Duveen,[27] the great tycoons proved by their art collections that they were not mere money-grubbers. A few million dollars invested in Botticelli, Fra Angelico, Rembrandt, or Vermeer showed, as nothing else, that the investor was identified with the secure and aristocratic leisured classes from the Renaissance on. Now the organization man may seek to prove the opposite. In his single-minded devotion to his enterprise, he shows that he is identified in spirit with the hard-bitten entrepreneurship but not the other interests of Henry Clay Frick, Andrew Mellon, and J. Pierpont Morgan.

Modern Soviet painting—the socialist realism which depicts strong maidens looking over the high-yielding wheat to the sun —asserts that art is the handmaiden of economics. Its goal is to help organize the country for the maximum of aesthetically static output. Those who insist on the total primacy of economic motivation in our economic life come out at curiously near the same point. They too are likely to insist on forthright realism—and defend it, not without indignation, as "what the people want." They may also, on occasion, be suspicious of what unduly taxes the imagination. The precise painting which official Communist critics characterize as bourgeois degeneracy, the down-to-earth American conservative condemns as Communist-inspired. Both, we may imagine, find it difficult to reconcile such art with pre-emptive pecuniary motivation. Although the need to defend this no longer exists, the habit persists.

V

To the extent that the business firm still insists on the primacy and inviolability of economic goals, it excludes and alienates the artist and narrows the aesthetic response normal to a society of secure well-being. There are three other ways in which the model of a competitive society, as it affects its corporate successor, is at odds with the artist. One of these, of particular importance to the architect, is its tendency to deny him control of the aesthetic environment. In the competitive model, the role of the state is slight. It is meant to be a self-regulating economic society in which the best government, in economic matters, governs the least. The modern corporate economy has found it convenient to assert the same rule wherever it is reasonably plausible, for it keeps public authority from intruding on the not unwelcome exercise of private authority. In the years following World War II, and partly no doubt as reaction to the wartime controls and the individuals who administered them, we had a strong reaction against anything seeming to smack of centralized guidance of economic activity. Planning became an evil word. The uncontrolled development of economic activity was justified not only on grounds of efficiency. It became a moral good.

In Cambridge, Massachusetts, near the banks of the Charles, there are two buildings—an auditorium and a chapel—by Eero Saarinen.[28] They are, one imagines, beauti-

26 Aline Saarinen, *The Proud Possessors* (New York: Random House, 1958), p. 125.

27 Joseph Duveen (1869–1939), British art dealer known for his ability to interest millionaires in collecting valuable paintings.

28 American architect (1910–1961), known for his modernism.

ful buildings, but no one can really know. For on one side is an early Norman apartment house and on the other a dingy and decayed four-story brick. In front is a parking lot filled with multicolored and rather dirty cars; behind are a candy factory, a fireproof storage warehouse, and a large sign advertising the 57 Varieties. Down the road are purveyors of fried foods and gasoline. St. Mark's might well lose some of its charm were the Piazza San Marco[29] surrounded by Gulf, Esso, and Texaco stations and a Donut shop, with Howard Johnson's at the end. But such grotesque arrangements are strongly defended by the competitive ideology. They are the natural and valued consequence of competitive enterprise. The man who questions the outcome runs the risk of being called an impractical aesthete who has not properly grasped the principles which have made the system what it is today.

The second problem is advertising—not all of it but an important part. As people are less persuaded of their desires by physical need, someone is certain to seek to persuade them. The essence of this persuasion is to attract attention. This advertising does in one successful form by allowing beauty to attract our eyes or ears and then introducing a contrasting, which is to say, in practice, a jarring note. Thus advertising cannot seek harmony with its environment. The most beautiful billboards would be those that blended into the landscape—and were not seen. The most agreeable commercials would be those that did not interfere with the play or music—and were not heard. Such advertising, it will be contended, would be ineffective. But then it cannot be argued that the jarring alternatives are a contribution to beauty. In speaking of the pre-emptive tendencies of pecuniary motivation, I have been speaking of a force which

[29] The large open square before the Cathedral of St. Mark, in Venice.

alienates industry from the artist. Advertising—that which is juxtaposed to beauty—has the equal but opposite effect. It alienates the artist from industry. Possibly it is the most important influence determining the reaction of the artist to economic life.

Finally there is the conflict in which the modern industrial firm finds itself, under the best of circumstances, between the pursuit of sales and the pursuit of excellence. Few would wish to argue that the popular taste is the best taste, that it reflects the highest aesthetic response. And it is quite clear that the ordinary industrial firm must produce for the popular market. There may be thus, by the artist's standards, a deliberate preference for commonplace or banal design. But the businessman, in the first instance at least, is hardly to be blamed. When the Court and a few cultivated Parisians provided the principal market for French craftsmen, the standard of artistic excellence could be high. The standard would certainly have fallen if France had suddenly become a prosperous, egalitarian democracy.

However, it seems probable that modern industrial design has managed to get the worst of a bad bargain. Taste is not static. And change begins with those who are in communication with the artist—who have a strong aesthetic response. Industry, alienated from the artist and with its eyes fixed by way of the market researchers on the popular taste, has regularly failed to perceive those advances in taste which were rendering its designs banal and otiose. Instead of being a little ahead, it has been a little behind.

Progress toward better design has also been handicapped by planned obsolescence. To offset the excessive durability of products and the inhibiting effects of this on demand, many of them must be constantly restyled. These constant changes cannot but have an exhausting effect on the artistic resources of the industry. In the past, good design lasted for a long time—and this, one imagines, was one reason it was good.

VI

In a diverse society such as ours, economic institutions are not coterminous with life; there is much room for development in the interstices. Accordingly, the pre-emptive role of economic motivation and the associated problems of the competitive society are not fatally damaging to the artist or to the aesthetic response. Certainly they are far less damaging than in the Communist countries.

We have seen, moreover, that part of the hostility—the determined preoccupation with down-to-earth pecuniary concerns in the modern large corporation—is based not on necessity but on the perpetuation of a myth. The myth is not invulnerable. Without question, its hold is weakening. Of all artists, the architect is the most dependent on the aesthetic response. Its absence brings us an enormous amount of very bad building with which, no doubt, we will have to put up for a very long time. The glass beehives and shoddy metal boxes which disfigure Manhattan, long our proudest architectural exhibit, are perhaps the greatest tragedy. But even here there are brilliant exceptions, although—if there is need to prove a rule—they have been mostly cases where, fortuitously or otherwise, pecuniary motivation was not predominant. Rockefeller Center was built by a noted affluent family of marked aesthetic response and at least partly as a demonstration piece. In the United Nations group, commercial motivations were absent and the architects had an exceptionally free hand. The Lever Brothers Building was built by a company headed by an architect[30] temporarily miscast as a businessman. The Seagram Building no doubt reflects the greater need of a distillery for ultimate distinction than for immediate gain, and also the sensitivity of an influential daughter to the work of Mies van der Rohe.[31] And there are many instances—the General Motors Technical Center, Connecticut General's new building, and others—where corporations in the ordinary course of business have given rein to the artistic imagination.

It is not the artist who has suffered from the alienation of art from economics but the reverse. For the economic system the alienation is serious, more serious certainly than is imagined. In recent years there has been a sharp decline in the export of American goods. There has been an even more dramatic increase in the import of European-made products. As one result, the American balance of payments is weak—a brief episode in 1932-33 apart—for the first time in our modern history. In largest part the problem is one of cost; for a considerable range of our goods, we have been pricing ourselves out of world markets including our own. But in no small measure it is a matter of design; our goods have fallen below both European standards and our own tastes. Edward Durrell Stone observed not long ago that "the American people can afford everything but beauty."[32] But, in fact, they have been searching for it with no small diligence. And they have been finding it in Italian, French, German, and Swedish products far more than in their own. The automobile is the most important and also the most publicized example. But in a host of other products—furniture, glass, ceramics, leather, metalware—Americans have turned to foreign designs as foreigners have turned away from American products. And as Stone has also pointed out, in their

[30] Charles Luckman (b. 1909), who now heads the architectural firm of Charles Luckman Associates. Lever House was designed by Gordon Bunshaft of Skidmore, Owings & Merrill.

[31] American architect, b. 1886 in Aachen, Germany.

[32] See note 18.

search for beauty, our people have been turning away from the disorderly and bill-board-studded American scene. This lies behind part of the annual tourist migration which also has an effect on the balance of payments.

Our failure has not been general. There is much good American design. Industry in many fields has come into communication with the artist—it has shown itself capable of a strong aesthetic response. But in an alarming number of instances this, clearly, is not the case. In these industries it is supposed that industry is something apart from art, or, at best, that the artistic imagination must be kept carefully subordinate to popular appeal. And here the customers have been responding to the closer identification of the European industry with the artist and vice versa, and the superior product that results.

That design is one dimension of quality no one will question. But that it is a dimension of growing importance must still be stressed. A poor society may ask only that its products be well engineered. But a richer one is certain to require that they have beauty as well. In the earlier stages of industrialization the engineer is important. In the later stages he yields place to the artist. The practical man who holds that this is a lot of precious nonsense may, like the automobile makers, have to learn the truth the hard and expensive way.

Indeed one already senses that the learning is causing pain. One senses a kind of angry impatience over the rejection of various of our own products and the popularity of European replacements. This is something that is being put over by the highbrows and the cultural snobs. If the honest American had been left alone he would have remained with his honest chrome. We are a brass-rail-and-cuspidor folk; we welcome a nice dashboard, and a fancy decanter for our grain neutral spirits. The mark of an American is that he rises above any precious tendencies to look for beauty, especially in useful things. There is not much future in this kind of cultural protectionism. Self-criticism will probably stand us in better stead.

VII

To summarize, then: in a simple society, pecuniary motivation can be powerful and indeed transcendent. And perhaps it must be, for the earning of bread, where bread is scarce, has to be a preoccupying concern. But one of the happy consequences of security and reasonable well-being is that people have time and thought and emotion for other things. Economic institutions must in turn be responsive to this change. At least partly under the influence of the earlier myth, our institutions are less responsive than they should be. We are still reluctant, moreover, to accept the social and political arrangements, notably the planning, which would allow harmony between the artist and his environment. We are tolerant of the destruction of beauty if it sells the goods. Those who assail our senses or disfigure our landscape for commercial purposes can still presume to claim that they are serving the paramount goal of the society.

The artistic imagination enters only rather furtively into economic life. Artistic truth is still revealed not by the artist but by the market researcher. In a community of developing taste, he may be a guide only to the obsolescent.

The remedies are not simple. Pecuniary goals are unequivocal and direct. To avow and pursue them is an uncomplicated matter. To create beauty is anything but simple. The goals are highly equivocal—indeed it will regularly precipitate an awkward struggle over the nature of beauty. To recognize, as now we must, that society must assume responsibility for the protection of the aesthetic standards of the environment will bring bitter debate. So will

the need to subordinate jarring salesman-
ship to aesthetic goals. And the American
businessman, having accommodated himself to the scientist in the course of accom-
modating himself to the twentieth century,
must now come to terms with the artist.
Artistic perception is as necessary to the
modern manufacturer of consumer goods as
engineering skill. Indeed now more so. How
it is brought to bear is another and long
story. But as a start, we can reject the myth
that still holds that it has no place.

L. C. Knights

IN SEARCH OF
FUNDAMENTAL VALUES

When one is asked for a short statement of
critical beliefs and principles there are a
good many generalizations ready to hand:
for example, literature increases our range
of understanding of ourselves, of other
people, of our world. But this and similar
formulations of the functions of literature
belong to Coleridge's class of "truths . . .
considered as *so* true, that they lose all the
life and efficiency of truth"; they are likely
to get no more than a perfunctory nod of
recognition. When I cast around for the
fundamental value of literature, recognizable in the smallest instance where delight
announces its presence and from which all
else springs, the point on which the edifice
of "criticism" is raised, I find it in the energy
of mind and imagination released by the
creative use of words. Wordsworth's sonnet
"Composed upon Westminster Bridge" will
serve for an example:

Earth has not anything to show more fair;
Dull would he be of soul who could pass by
A sight so touching in its majesty . . .

The peculiar pleasure of that last line—
though the pleasure is independent of conscious recognition of the source—comes
from the movement of mind by which we
bring together in one apprehension "touching" and "majesty": feelings and attitudes
springing from our experience of what is
young and vulnerable, that we should like
to protect, fuse with our sense of things towards which we feel awe, in respect of which
it is we who are young, inexperienced, or
powerless. That is London as Wordsworth
saw it on an early autumn morning in 1803
and (to adapt his own words on another
occasion) "planted, for immortality, . . . in
the celestial soil of the imagination."
The whole poem grows from a similar fu-
sion of opposites: the buildings momentarily appear as right—as proportioned,
inviting and composed—as nature's valleys
and hills; the old and shackled city ("Near
where the chartered Thames does flow" [33])
is as new as the morning. There is no self-
deception: beauty that is "like a garment"
can, we know, be put off; the "smokeless
air" will soon be smoke-filled; and the supreme quiet contains the pulse of life about
to resume its course. It is simply that paradox and hyperbole, recognizing themselves
for what they are, so activate the mind that,
as we read this most beautiful poem, new
powers of vision and apprehension come
into being.

I am not putting forward the view that
paradox is the essential characteristic of
poetry: I am simply pointing towards that
energizing of the mind that poetry can
achieve in an infinity of ways. The exact
descriptive word; the surprising figure of
speech that levers new recognitions ("Like a
green thought . . ." [34]); naked simplicity
("How fast has brother followed brother,

[33] William Blake, "London"; see p. 161.
[34] Andrew Marvell, "The Garden"; see p. 126.

From sunshine to the sunless land!" [35]); the alignment of a few objects or events so that the presented experience comes to stand for something as wide as human life itself (Blake's "Echoing Green" or Frost's "The Pasture"); slight shifts of tone (as in the last two lines of Frost's "Come in")—these are only random examples of the ways in which the poet can enlist that active collaboration of the reader through which a specific experience is realized.

I have referred so far to lyric poetry because that is easier to speak of in a short space than prose literature and the longer forms. But whether we read a short lyric, a play, or a novel—supposing each to be good of its kind—the same principles are at work: in varied ways the mind's energies are evoked and directed in a single "realizing intuition." In the larger works, of course, the scope is wider and the perceptions are likely to be related in more complex ways. In *King Lear* we not only respond with delight to the ever-changing local realizations—"Strike flat the thick rotundity of the world" (the reverberations of thunder in a blank verse line); "women's weapons, water drops" (a range of mistaken assumptions compressed into a phrase)—we bring together the varied and even contradictory meanings of "need," "justice," "folly," and so on, as imagery and action enforce. In this way routine notions and attitudes are broken down, and a new direction of consciousness emerges from the interplay of meanings: not meanings, so to speak, "out there," as though we were trying to understand a legal document, but meanings in which the reader or spectator is involved as a person, simply because movements of sympathy or antipathy, or assent or dissent—in short, of judgment from a personal center—are a necessary part of them. A simple example is Lear's assumption that punishment is an essential function of justice:

> Tremble, thou wretch
> That hast within thee undivulgèd crimes,
> Unwhipped of justice . . .

The way we take this is finally determined by our reaction to such things as the picture of the social outcast who is "whipped from tithing to tithing, and stock-punished, and imprisoned," and of the "rascal beadle," society's representative, lashing the whore with her blood on his hands. When the mind really attends to what Shakespeare says or implies about legal justice in *King Lear* it is forced to make strides across the convenient areas of obscurity in which our ignorance and hypocrisy habitually take refuge; it is compelled to make connections, and its thinking about "justice," about man's relation to justice, is correspondingly enriched. It is the same with all the other central themes (those who dislike the word are at liberty to use another) of which *King Lear* is composed. Different aspects of experience are held together in what is virtually a single act of attention, and a new direction of thought emerges from the resulting tensions. But because the thinking is in terms of images, not abstract concepts, it is in the fullest possible relation to the intimate personal life of the reader or spectator: the knowledge gained is, as we say, brought home to him—in Keats's phrase, it is "proved on the pulses." [36]

The philosopher may raise an eyebrow at the use of "knowledge" in this context, and indeed there is much defining that even an unphilosophical critic needs to do. I can only say briefly and parenthetically what seem to me the main features of response to literature considered as an activity of knowing. First, what is known is not an object

[35] William Wordsworth, "Extempore Effusion on the Death of James Hogg."

[36] Letter to J. H. Reynolds, 3 May 1818.

existing independently of the reader: he is himself directly involved in the creative process, and without that involvement there would be no knowledge. In the experience of poetry there is, therefore, a paradoxical union of particularity (we submit to the discipline of what is "so, and not otherwise") with a spread of meanings that will vary with each individual; for what we have to deal with is not a cut-and-dried experience, but one that lives and, as it were, reverberates in the receiving mind. That is why literature can so powerfully affect the quality of our relations with the world. Secondly, the knowledge in question can never be completely conceptualized: partly because of the subtle intricacy of the texture of the work (even in a "classical" work, deliberately avoiding vagueness, there is bound to be a more or less large area of connotation); partly—and more important—because there are, it seems, matters of great concern that can only be known with the cooperation of mental powers below the level of full consciousness. Eliot, like Valéry, has testified that a poem "may tend to realize itself first as a particular rhythm before it reaches expression in words," and it may be assumed that unless the reader, in turn, is responsive to effects of rhythm that are ultimately unanalyzable—as to other non-discursive elements of meaning such as poetic symbols—he will not fully enter into the presented experience. Knowledge of poetry—the knowledge that comes through poetry—demands not only an active but a relaxed and receptive mind.

Attention, collaboration, realization—these are the three basic activities (or, rather, phases or aspects of the same activity) that make up the critical, the fully engaged, response to literature. It is this realizing activity that often makes one want to speak of literature in terms of the depth and presentness of some given object (a person, an action, a landscape), and in a sense one is

right to do so: after reading Keats's ode[37] we do know autumn as never before. But of course there is no object except the poem itself, which, as Susanne Langer insists,[38] offers not ordinary experience but a virtual experience, a symbolic structure of meanings held in the mind. The contradiction, however, is only apparent. When we have undergone the experience of great poetry, of great literature, the world *is* present because the mind, the imagination, is present to the world. It is in this sense that the poet, as Edwin Muir says, releases us from the language—and therefore the world—of the third person and the onlooker, the world of generalities, and continually brings us back to direct confrontation with the particular. The importance of this at a time when, as Muir also points out in his book, *The Estate of Poetry*, so many agencies tempt us to a merely generalized apprehension of life— this needs no stressing. But perhaps it should be added that the sphere of unrealized experience is also the sphere of corrupting fantasy. Literature is a great cleanser, simply because, through language, it energizes the mind. As Coleridge said of Shakespeare's *Venus and Adonis:* "The reader is forced into too much action to sympathize with the merely passive of our nature." [39] It was of course also Coleridge who spoke of "the beneficial after-effects of verbal precision in the preclusion of fanaticism, which masters the feelings more especially by indistinct watch-words."

It is, then, simply in the growth and strengthening of the imagination that the value of literature resides. Imagination, as I have used the term, is simultaneously the central creative drive of human beings and the organ of all knowledge in which the

37 "To Autumn"; see p. 129.
38 Especially in *Feeling and Form* (1953) and *Problems of Art: Ten Philosophic Lectures* (1957).
39 *Biographia Literaria* (1817), ch. xv.

individual is involved as more than a detached observer. It is an active, relating, realizing power, through which the limited self, with its unlimited desires and its abysmal ignorance of everything that cannot be used or manipulated, grows into a person, freely moving in a world of values and relationships. It is the mediator between the unknown depths within and the so little-known world without ("Every symbol is two-edged," says Tillich;[40] "it opens up reality and it opens up the soul.") As a unifying power it simultaneously works towards the integrity and wholeness of the person and the creation of a cosmos from the world of mere experience which, without it, would remain fragmentary and deceptive. The importance of literature is therefore that indicated by Martin Foss[41] when he speaks of "the work of art . . . giving to everybody and releasing in everybody the power of a creative spiritual life." But as Foss also reminds us, "what art brings to the surface is everywhere at work where men think and feel." Imaginative literature is simply one of the ways through which life comes to consciousness; and the claim that the teacher of literature may justifiably make for his vocation is only possible because what underlies and justifies his activities is what underlies and justifies all the arts and humane studies. To be sure, those who profess other "subjects" could often, one feels, profit from the insights that a familiarity with literature brings: there is clear profit for the psychologist in Shakespeare and Blake as well as in George Eliot and Henry James; and theologians could perhaps learn something from the symbolic language of great poetry. But then the critic and teacher of literature, in his turn, needs to know something of other

ways of eliciting meanings from the world. The study of literature cannot remain self-enclosed. Indeed it is my own conviction that there is important work waiting to be done "on the frontiers," where the study of literature joins hands with the study of history, philosophy, theology, etc. But it will need to be done by those who really know what literature is, not by specialists in other subjects who merely look to literature for documentation.

From what has been said there follow certain practical implications, only one of which can be dealt with here. The job of the teacher of literature calls for a peculiar tact. Just as scholarship, necessary as a tool, can become a barrier between living works and the potentially receptive and responsive mind, so "practical criticism," an even more urgent necessity in any English course, can inhibit growth from the living center. Thirty or forty years ago the situation was different; then the need was to free the study of literature from a mere accumulation of dead opinions, fossilized in histories of literature, gilded over with a vague "appreciation." The direct confrontation of the pupil with "the words on the page" was a necessary tactic in a war of liberation. Today one senses danger from the over-anxiety of some teachers to train their pupils in close reading. I hope I shall not be misunderstood on this point: intelligent understanding of literature is what the teacher aims to foster; understanding involves personal judgment; and sensibility can be trained. But intelligence and sensibility may be inhibited by too great a stress on conscious understanding: "explication" as a formal teaching method can turn the poem into an object almost as effectively as the museum-catalogue techniques of the past. Poetry of any depth may be intuitively apprehended before the experience can be critically defined; wide and voracious reading is as necessary—especially for the young

40 Paul Tillich (1886–1965), author of *The Courage to Be* (1952) and many other works.
41 Author of *Symbol and Metaphor in Human Experience* (1949) and other works.

—as the ability to concentrate all one's powers for an hour; and even in the most concentrated act of attention to literature there is a quality of relaxed absorption that makes activity like rest.

Robert Cantwell

BELIEVING IN BLUEGRASS

Bill Monroe's Fifth Annual Bluegrass Music Festival last summer in Bean Blossom, Indiana, drew more people than even Bill Monroe could have anticipated. Bill Monroe, in case you didn't know, is a direct descendant of President James Monroe and the man credited with the "invention" of bluegrass music. If you ask Bill Monroe just what bluegrass music is, he will say simply that it is "the best music in the world." I doubt that anyone at Bean Blossom much minded the hyperbole. Those of us who love bluegrass love it obsessively. I got my money's worth right at the gate, where Bill Monroe, who had never seen me before in his life, said "Howdy!" and smiled like a senator.

When Bill Monroe thirty years ago began to sing and play the traditional string band music of the Appalachian range, he was able, by a subtle and sensitive control of immense exertions, to focus its diverse energies into a formal style as rich as the blues in its powers of personal expression. His ringing, athletic mandolin-picking and his unearthly tenor voice, which sounds something like the wind, have made him a sort of Leadbelly or Bessie Smith of mountain music. And because his band hailed from Kentucky, he called them "The Blue Grass Boys," and so named a renewed tradition of folk music which is, remarkably, still in the hands of its own folk.

We came to Bean Blossom to hear bluegrass music, and to see it. In the park the commerce of guitars, banjos, fiddles, mandolins, and tenor voices could be heard from six o'clock one morning until three the next. Bluegrass bands are as exciting to watch as hockey games, and cannot be fully appreciated except in person. I discovered at Bean Blossom that because I had never seen Bill Monroe in person I had never really heard him. The most sophisticated recording instruments cannot reproduce the drama generated by the corporate creation of a tune. First, there is the choreography of performance, the regularly changing relationship of each member of the band to the microphone—or simply to the foreground—which a group must master in order to render a piece coherently. The lead singer, who most often plays mandolin or guitar, lingers near the center and is joined by one, two, three, or all of the others for choruses in harmony. Meanwhile, a vastly complicated interplay of melodies is embroidered in the background by fiddle, mandolin, and banjo. At the end of a chorus the singers abruptly disperse to make way for the solo instrument —banjo, fiddle, mandolin, and more recently the guitar—on which the soloist displays his often incredible virtuosity with variations on the theme. At the end of his break he will either sail away on a river of notes or suddenly swoon into a void behind the lead singer, who has returned to the point of focus. All of this is done, by professionals at least, with fluidity and ease, but with scrupulous care as well. Part of the effect of the music is the tension one feels between what is heard, with its energy and movement, and what is seen, the absolute concentration required of a performer in the execution of a break. While the music may make you want to jump out of your skin, the band itself, especially the banjo-player, is stonesteady and pokerfaced. For the musician, performance is an opportunity to be both wholly himself—to display his particular abilities and ideas—and to submerge himself wholly in the identity of the group.

Just what the "identity of the group" is makes an interesting question. One highly proficient professional group, The Country Gentlemen, who have been playing bluegrass for at least fifteen years, recently had a rather sweeping change in personnel: of the original quartet, three have been replaced. Yet they are, in some fundamental way, the same people that they have always been. Similarly, Bill Monroe's Bluegrass Boys, with whom practically every well-known bluegrass musician has played at one time or another, retains that quality which Bill Monroe once sought and obviously found. Like oral epic literature, if I may be allowed a somewhat academic analogy, bluegrass music is formulaic, being primarily a fund of instrumental licks and runs, traditional melodies and songs which are transmitted not only in live performance, as it was for epic in the days of Homer, but also by means of phonograph records. In fact, all songs and instrumental breakdowns, whether traditional or originally composed, enter the bluegrass "tradition" once they are recorded, yet change, grow, and influence one another in authentic oral fashion.

At Bean Blossom perfect strangers could form bands and in moments be making fine music together. Even though a bluegrass musician develops himself largely in solitary, he cannot fully display or even realize his musical abilities until he participates with other individuals in a band. Thus he is not fully an individual, musically at least, until he is swept up in the operations of that tiny but very real community. I believe anyone who has ever played in a bluegrass band will testify that it can be a deeply satisfying and elevating experience, and at times—in those moments of transcendent coopera-

tion—sublime. Consequently the music is largely participatory, and those who came to Bean Blossom were seeking, I think, something more than diversion, stimulation or entertainment. I was astonished to find that even while Bill Monroe performed in the park pavilion, intrepid pickers and fiddlers, in and out of tents, campers, and house trailers, were making bluegrass.

On Tuesday, "Barbecue Bean Day" and the first day of the festival, there were flash floods forty miles away, where two inches of rain had fallen in forty-five minutes. In the remote areas of the park, now filling up as more and more people arrived, cars and pickup trucks with campers were settling complacently into the mud and declaring that spot their campsite. Not until the following day, when attendance began to exceed expectations, did it become necessary to move the automobiles and park them in neat rows to make room for newcomers, who were arriving at all hours of the day and night. In this mild crisis there was, of course, an elated conviviality as strangers cooperated to push out of the mud the most absurdly marooned Oldsmobiles, Buicks, and Chevys—not all showroom iron. A brightly painted pickup with chrome wheel covers, two or three American flag decals on the back window, and a richly laden shotgun rack behind the driver's seat arose from the mud with the aid of four or five grunting, groaning, laughing hippies with shoulder-length hair, tie-dyed shirts, and mottled jeans, and a braless girlfriend standing by.

Throughout Wednesday and Thursday the society in Bill Monroe's Jamboree Park shifted and settled, each newcomer orienting himself to the somewhat elusive water supplies, to the geography of the park, and to the IGA store a quarter of a mile down Indiana 135. Being neighborly seemed much easier in the more perfect democracy of a camping ground, where outward signs of social differences are minimized, and unwitting judgments happily retarded. Nearly everyone was cooking on a Sears or Coleman cookstove, lighting his way with a Sears or Coleman lantern, sleeping in a Sears cotton-twill wax-finish cabin tent—what did it matter that some folks had campers with built-in stoves and real beds? It was all a kind of circus, and it was difficult to feel anything but innocent delight.

Walking from one end of the camp to the other, perhaps from the phone booth out on the highway or from the grocery store back through the main gate, across the flat plain of the parking area, down the hill and into the woods, then onto the mud road leading back to a second, recently bulldozed clearing one could hear, in fluid sequence, bluegrass bands, first one, then a hint of the next, then a new band several yards ahead, one band never interfering with another. Occasionally one would stop to hear some exceptionally good fiddler or banjo-picker or to catch the last verse or two of a favorite song. I stopped once to listen to the sharp tenor singing of a man in a fishing hat, who leaned laconically against his camper where a sign read: "Business? Gone to Hell!" and strummed his mandolin. One morning we were attracted to an unusually large crowd in a grove of trees near the park pavilion. In their midst was a wholesome-looking family seated in lawn chairs making some breathtakingly clean bluegrass: father on guitar, sisters on bass and mandolin, and junior on banjo. Junior, a lad of about thirteen whose glasses kept slipping down his nose, was picking a series of riffs and runs and slides and chord changes that were literally beyond belief. "He's fantastic!" I said spontaneously to no one in particular.

"He shore is," a rather large man in front of me said dolefully, turning away and heading, I supposed, back to his banjo.

A few came to Bean Blossom, it seemed, only to say that they had been there. A squirrel-hunter from Indianapolis who nearly mowed down our tent when he arrived in the middle of the night hung around his truck, with a bottle of beer perpetually in hand, and never once, for three days, went up to hear the performing bands. "This is mah fift yer at Bean Blossom," he said proudly. "Used t'be held up awn Birch Monroe's farm up chere the road bout two mile. You know got too big fer thet." Birch Monroe was Bill's older brother and on the previous night he had fiddled his way through a veritable briar patch of oldtimey tunes. "Ahm from Kentuck, originally," the squirrel-hunter added, redundantly.

On Thursday afternoon one of the first major events, the banjo-pickers' contest, was held in the pavilion. The youngest contestant, about nine, whose banjo was perhaps an inch shorter than he was, raced through "Reuben" as nimbly as a typist typing. A mustachioed college dropout who had built his own banjo, including the delicately cut mother-of-pearl inlays, the carved neck, and the inlaid presidential eagle on the back, appeared on stage alone (the others brought guitar accompaniment) and played an original piece called, I think, "Fox Run."

Every bluegrass banjo-picker is ultimately indebted to the man who played banjo with Bill Monroe's original Bluegrass Boys—Earl Scruggs. Scruggs had developed out of the old "drop-thumb" style of banjo-picking a three-finger syncopated style so compelling that audiences still bounce on their haunches listening to it, even youngsters nurtured on electric rock. At Bean Blossom nearly every competitor played at least one tune worked into the style from traditional melodies by Earl Scruggs himself, and although the Scruggs-style of banjo-picking has been much elaborated since the early days of the music, specialization having overtaken even bluegrass, it seemed to me that the contest was won almost solely on the winner's capacity—and it was considerable—to bring Earl Scruggs to mind.

Through Thursday, Friday, and well into midafternoon on Saturday, people continued to arrive. Tight but adequate parking spaces appeared for them as if by magic. Bill Monroe and his fiddler Kenny Baker, along with some volunteers, worked most of the day digging postholes and stringing new fence in order to expand the available camping space. By Friday at suppertime, when the park was filled with people and with music, a sense of rich promise pervaded everything. A walk to the gate would show that the name bands—Ralph Stanley and the Clinch Mountain Boys, Don Reno, Bill Harrell and the Tennessee Cut-Ups, Jim and Jesse and the Virginia Boys, Jimmy Martin and the Sunny Mountain Boys—had begun to arrive in their lettered buses. All the young banjo-pickers, mandolin-chunkers, and high lonesome screamers of the preceding three days took on the obsolescence of a just-read novel. Even the Brown County Boys, a group of fifteen-year-olds from five miles down the road who had astonished everyone with their cool skill, faded behind the presence of storied professionals, who might be seen walking about, or standing in conversation (often slightly plumper than record album covers showed), or signing autographs. Lester Flatt ambled by me wearing a red-white-and-blue hand-painted tie. Don Reno, whom I had seen at the University of Chicago Folk Festival three years before with silver-white hair, now sported a wavy auburn pompadour. He still had those fancy white cowboy boots that I recall were the envy of a Blackstone Ranger who happened to be hanging around the university coffee shop.

The authentic beginnings of the festival took place that evening around the gate of the park. Bill Monroe had organized what in five years had become a tradition—he called it the "sunset jam session." Everyone who dreams of playing bluegrass with Bill Monroe here found his opportunity. In the confines of a small grassy area defined by a clothesline hung across temporary posts, Bill had gathered with upwards of one hundred and twenty guitar-, banjo-, and mandolin-pickers, fiddlers, and singers to play and sing, into three widely spaced mikes wired to a sound truck, songs and tunes from the Bill Monroe canon which *everyone* knew by heart. Knew, that is, in an absolute, liturgical sense. Clustered around Bill in his gleaming white jacket and white cowboy hat were the very young, amateurs and professionals, musicians who had learned under Monroe, played in his band, and had gone off to make their own reputations, and those who hoped eventually to record and carry on Bill Monroe's music themselves. Bill administered each number, singing and playing into one of the mikes, dropping behind and inviting a stranger or a friend to sing or play a bit, or with the palm of his hand gently prodding a shy and thrilled youngster to play a hesitating but thoroughly satisfying instrumental solo. "I call you all my children," Bill said, and suddenly it became clear that this bluegrass festival was nothing more or less than an old-time camp meeting, an evangelical retreat of the very kind that rural folk a century ago waited all summer for, yet now somehow enlightened beyond dogma, hellfire, and exploitation. And here was Bill Monroe the teacher, founder of the brotherhood and sisterhood, standing among all the picking and singing like John Wesley on the green of an eighteenth-century English village. That night, when someone in the audience asked the highly talented mandolin-picker for the Brown County Boys to play "Rawhide," an instrumental created by Bill Monroe and requiring incredible dexterity in both hands, the young man drawled, "Naw, let's leave that one for the Master."

And why shouldn't it be so? It is the province of a religious teacher to restore a private and inward dimension to people whose lives have become dominated by outward forms and thus by the hypocrisy and cant which inevitably result—to freshen "the individual value of every soul." This is, I believe, what Bill Monroe accomplished for his people through the agency of their music, music being their most characteristic and most articulate mode of expression, the prime embodiment of the mountain imagination. Thus he became for mountain people, who, like other rural societies, have tended to move more slowly and deliberately through history than the rest of the world, the first modern man.

I hesitate to use the sociological term "subculture," since the people out of whom bluegrass music originated and to whom it is addressed are not, in my opinion, subordinate to American culture as a whole (assuming there is such a thing as American culture as a whole). They are certainly a "people," however, with ties more fundamental than the music itself, though the music may be, *like* a religion, that common body of knowledge, ceremony, and experience which makes their unity self-conscious and serviceable because it has been outwardly expressed. In the broadest sense, inclusive of the gospel and string music which preceded it, bluegrass music is perhaps one of the largest surviving finds of traditional knowledge in the country outside of Indian lore and religion itself. As such it is bound up with larger attitudes and beliefs axiomatic with the people and especially with their special, almost heretical variety of protestant Christianity which, along with the music, reveals the unique way of appreciating life they as individuals hold in common.

Over fifty bands, amateur and professional, not to mention a great number of individual fiddlers, banjo- and guitar-pickers, appeared on stage at Bean Blossom. Many more performed who never stepped onto the stage but who entertained hundreds passing by. Every novice and amateur band, even some of the plodders, was received with enthusiasm. Bill Monroe's

people are warmly hospitable and emotional, deeply appreciative of fellow feeling.

These emotional qualities are still more pronounced in bluegrass musicians themselves, who have a reputation for intensity and unpredictability. I heard of one accomplished guitarist who abandoned the instrument altogether when his guitar was stolen, insisting that it would be a kind of betrayal to play a strange guitar, and took up mandolin. Another fine singer of my acquaintance refuses to sing anything but sacred songs. In short, there is a kind of mysticism in bluegrass music. In its subject matter, in its performers and their performances, even in its most antic moods, it is pervaded by death. Often it is actually about death, in pious, morbid, or sentimental ways; murder ballads and tales of death on the railroad or highway are, of course, nearly synonymous with traditional music. One of Bill Monroe's most famous songs, "Footprints in the Snow," seems even to celebrate death, since it foretells of the reunion in heaven of a man with his departed wife, whom he met "when the snow was on the ground." The symbolic association of snow and death is, I think, lost on no one; yet the tune is lilting, joyous—confidence in the promised land is so lucid and steadfast that it is the implied subject of nearly every "sacred" number, and seems to underlie every serious treatment of life. Bill Monroe's voice, with its high lonesome pang, seems sometimes to come from beyond the grave, not from some dreary underworld, but from some bright, bucolic mountain paradise.

One man seems most significant of all in this respect: Ralph Stanley. If Bill Monroe's voice sounds like the wind, Ralph Stanley's sounds like the woods. He and his brother Carter came out of the Clinch Mountains in the late forties playing and singing in a style strangely steeped in an ancient mountain modality which persisted even after they had acquired the habits of bluegrass. Not long after a performance at

Bean Blossom several years ago, Carter Stanley died; Ralph continues to play the music of the Stanley Brothers and the Clinch Mountain Boys, and has found a series of guitarists who can virtually duplicate Carter's singing and playing, so that to hear Ralph's new band is to feel that Carter has been reincarnated.

But the queer phenomenon of calling up the dead past goes still further in Ralph's band. Two young Kentucky musicians, aged seventeen and eighteen, who last year created a sensation by playing and singing in an absolutely perfect imitation of the early Stanley Brothers, are now regular members of the Clinch Mountain Boys. To hear the whole group, then, is to hear not only Ralph and Carter Stanley but also a kind of geological record of their career, collapsed into some of the most hair-raising and beautiful harmonies in any music. Ralph's voice is not perfect; there is a slight quaver in it, and a laurel twig. But it can stir up matter at the primitive floor of the soul with as much authority as a Navajo chant.

Ralph is an earnest man, showing the kind of steady watchfulness and complete absence of frivolity that we associate either with deep piety or with fear. In concert he makes much of Carter's grave, its situation on a hillside, the headstone, the epitaph— his interest is almost medieval in its fondness. At Bean Blossom he did a monologue about their musical life together, backed up by a weird reincarnation of the old Stanley Brothers singing a gospel song. Ralph seems to sing in the expectation of death, with dread nobly penetrated by creative necessity. Or it is possible that his zeal arises out of a slender doubt:

As the years roll by, I often wonder—
Will we all be together someday?
Each night as I wander through the graveyard
Darkness finds me as I kneel to pray.[42]

[42] From "White Dove," Copyright 1949 by Peer International Corporation. Used by permission.

At its worst the death motif in bluegrass music acquires an effete morbidity. A most interesting and appropriately named group, James Monroe and the Midnight Ramblers, capture in their music a funereal quality highlighted by a range of imagery reminiscent of Petrarch's Tuscany. Replete with fields of lilies, bloodstained veils, and dark impulses, it is a world of the dead.

James Monroe has a corpselike pallor and shadowy eyes; his music has the eerie loveliness of an Easter basket or a funeral wreath. Unlike most bluegrass bands, his is unaggressive and obsequious, the fiddler offering mournful, sustained condolences, the banjo-picker politely lingering in the background. His lyrics are ambiguously situated between dream and reality, and thus symbolic: virginal figures drift through in white, wanderers recline on green lawns or pause at crossroads. In one moving ballad called "I Haven't Seen Mary in Years," the singer is led after a life of profligacy to a meadow where a family reunion is being held. There he sees his father, who does not recognize him because of his changed appearance, and his mother, whom the singer cannot recognize, explaining in the concluding line of the song, "I haven't seen mother in years." Mother! All along we have assumed that Mary is a lost *wife*, but now wife and mother are confounded with all the straightforwardness of a textbook in intermediate psychology. James Monroe's ladies are almost always named Mary, recalling Anglo-Saxon hymns to the Virgin; when we expect him to sing "my life," he sings "my dream," and in many respects he himself seems a dream, a ghost. Incidentally, he is Bill Monroe's son.

The deepest allegiances in bluegrass, then, are to Mother and Dad, to home, in a way that few of us have had the privilege of feeling. Some of the most frequent subjects in serious pieces are the death of parents and of children, the regret over having left home, the reunion in heaven. All are, of course, one, and together make a kind of rude cosmology. The imagination of a poor and isolated people ranges only as far as their own experience, so that the natural life provides material for their deepest insights. It is thrifty and practical, intellectually speaking, to associate eternity with the better world of childhood; the stories in traditional music of lost souls who return home only to find parents gone, pathways overgrown, and the fields turned brown make good figures for life itself, "life's railway to heaven," with its drift away from innocence. Death, being wholly dark behind, becomes a kind of twist in the fabric of things by which everything returns to itself. There is the less mysterious explanation, of course, that when life is wretched— as it no doubt was (and is) for many poor mountain folk—the mind clings to fantasy worlds. A sense of individuality also implies a sense of one's own finiteness. But the themes of bluegrass music transcend simple otherworldliness, and at best they are genuinely metaphysical. The same sentiments churned out in Nashville and hawked on the air by sincere-sounding disc jockeys can turn the stomach.

I suspect, however, that many of Bill Monroe's people are suffering a subtle death they can't detect, a gradual impoverishment different from the kind which, over the generations, they have learned to live with. As technology penetrates their isolation, and American prosperity, however hollow it may be, their poverty, the way of life which created the music and which continued to cultivate an imagination receptive to it eventually dissolves and disappears. They are dying as a people as they become assimilated into the great mass of middle-class Americans who crowd the roads and parks in the summertime and who have discovered that one way to relieve some of the pang of existence is to diminish the intensity of life. And as the scope and depth of their lives shrink, so will the music seem more distant: too emotional, too rigid, too . . . well, hill-

billy. The ecstasy of which the music is often capable will be gone too.

The fact is that Bill Monroe's people themselves feel that they are preserving something of the past. They call it the "old-time music." Bluegrass musicians are constantly giving awards to one another for preserving it. Possessed in this way of a historical sense, death, time's instrument, becomes a matter of intense interest to them. As the late Johan Huizinga pointed out in *The Waning of the Middle Ages*, a consciousness of the past, awakened in the medieval mind by scholarship, produced a pervasive melancholy over the transitory quality in men and the world. Artistically this meant an obsession with death, in its early physical signs and in the corruption of the flesh which follows. Bluegrass folk, surrounded by a civilization which advertises its material advantages and falsely represents its values as the same ones they hold dear, are secretly persuaded by it, and so indulge the waning habits like an old clock or a failing grandparent. The sublime becomes quaint. The essential becomes recreation, and it's a proud man who can make up a bluegrass band out of mere children, with a six-year-old on the five-string.

Yet in all this there is a massive contradiction. Though death is often present in the music, Bean Blossom was astonishingly alive. Bluegrass music is as fresh as if it had been born yesterday, and full of surprises. In fact, it must be said that the show was deftly stolen by a brand-new group out of Louisville who call themselves The Bluegrass Alliance. More children? Nope. Hippies. Hippies, that is, with the one exception of Lonnie Peerce, a twenty-year veteran of the fiddle. "I suppose you folks wonder why Lonnie here is playing with a bunch of freaks," the bassist, Ebo Walker, asked the audience. Hoots, howls, and hollers. "I'm their social worker," Lonnie answered, and started fiddling. They all started in, banjo-picker picking, mandolin-picker picking and jiving around the stage, hair hanging to his shoulders, making it seem as though we were watching the Jefferson Airplane and not some bluegrass group. Finally the lead singer, who from a distance might have been a prim old maid with hair severely tied behind her head, opened up with a voice that was pure gold bullion, something like three trumpets blowing two octaves above middle C in a tiled shower room. The crowd went wild. "We'll be selling some albums back at our bus," Ebo said. "Bring 'em back if you have any trouble with 'em—they're on Oral Roberts label, and we have a little problem with the holes healing up." Laughter, some muffled protests. "I see we got both sides here tonight."

The folks loved them on Thursday night, on Friday night; and on Saturday, when they were not originally scheduled to play, they brought the house, or rather the treetops, down with "One Tin Soldier," a song very different from most in bluegrass:

> Go ahead and hate your neighbor
> Go ahead and cheat your friend
> Do it in the name of heaven
> Justify it in the end.
> There won't be trumpets blowin'
> On the Judgment Day:
> On the bloody morning after
> One tin soldier rides away.[43]

The point is that while some folks may be growing away from the music, others are growing toward it, and it may be that even those for whom it is a native idiom are beginning to awaken to their own traditions, the way blacks and American Indians are to theirs, to what they created while the business of living went steadily on. However at odds the members of the Bluegrass Al-

liance may be with their audience upon any other issue but bluegrass, on that one they have come to a profound agreement. Bluegrass music is the traditional life, a kind of knowing many of us have difficulty in understanding, and the traditional life is the sacramental life. We who live among dead things should wonder at a people who, though they dwell upon death, have not forgotten how to live.

Henry James

THE REAL THING

I

When the porter's wife (she used to answer the house-bell) announced, "A gentleman—with a lady, sir," I had, as I often had in those days, for the wish was father to the thought, an immediate vision of sitters. Sitters my visitors in this case proved to be; but not in the sense I should have preferred. However, there was nothing at first to indicate that they might not have come for a portrait. The gentleman, a man of fifty, very high and very straight, with a moustache slightly grizzled and a dark grey walking-coat admirably fitted, both of which I noted professionally—I don't mean as a barber or yet as a tailor—would have struck me as a celebrity if celebrities often were striking. It was a truth of which I had for some time been conscious that a figure with a good deal of frontage was, as one might say, almost never a public institution. A glance at the lady helped to remind me of this paradoxical law: she also looked too distinguished to be a "personality." Moreover one would scarcely come across two variations together.

Neither of the pair spoke immediately—they only prolonged the preliminary gaze which suggested that each wished to give the other a chance. They were visibly shy; they stood there letting me take them in— which, as I afterwards perceived, was the most practical thing they could have done. In this way their embarrassment served their cause. I had seen people painfully reluctant to mention that they desired anything so gross as to be represented on canvas; but the scruples of my new friends appeared almost insurmountable. Yet the gentleman might have said, "I should like a portrait of my wife," and the lady might have said, "I should like a portrait of my husband." Perhaps they were not husband and wife—this naturally would make the matter more delicate. Perhaps they wished to be done together—in which case they ought to have brought a third person to break the news.

"We come from Mr. Rivet," the lady said at last, with a dim smile which had the effect of a moist sponge passed over a "sunk" piece of painting, as well as of a vague allusion to vanished beauty. She was as tall and straight, in her degree, as her companion, and with ten years less to carry. She looked as sad as a woman could look whose face was not charged with expression; that is her tinted oval mask showed friction as an exposed surface shows it. The hand of time had played over her freely, but only to simplify. She was slim and stiff, and so well-dressed, in dark blue cloth, with lappets and pockets and buttons, that it was clear she employed the same tailor as her husband. The couple had an indefinable air of prosperous thrift—they evidently got a good deal of luxury for their money. If I was to be one of their luxuries it would behove me to consider my terms.

"Ah, Claude Rivet recommended me?" I inquired; and I added that it was very kind of him, though I could reflect that, as he only painted landscape, this was not a sacrifice.

The lady looked very hard at the gentleman, and the gentleman looked round the room. Then staring at the floor a moment and stroking his moustache, he rested his pleasant eyes on me with the remark: "He said you were the right one."

"I try to be, when people want to sit."

"Yes, we should like to," said the lady anxiously.

"Do you mean together?"

My visitors exchanged a glance. "If you could do anything with *me*, I suppose it would be double," the gentleman stammered.

"Oh yes, there's naturally a higher charge for two figures than for one."

"We should like to make it pay," the husband confessed.

"That's very good of you," I returned, appreciating so unwonted a sympathy—for I supposed he meant pay the artist.

A sense of strangeness seemed to dawn on the lady. "We mean for the illustrations— Mr. Rivet said you might put one in."

"Put one in—an illustration?" I was equally confused.

"Sketch her off, you know," said the gentleman, coloring.

It was only then that I understood the service Claude Rivet had rendered me; he had told them that I worked in black and white, for magazines, for story-books, for sketches of contemporary life, consequently had frequent employment for models. These things were true, but it was not less true (I may confess it now—whether because the aspiration was to lead to everything or to nothing I leave the reader to guess), that I couldn't get the honors, to say nothing of the emoluments, of a great painter of portraits out of my head. My "illustrations" were my pot-boilers; I looked to a different branch of art (far and away the most interesting it had always seemed to me), to perpetuate my fame. There was no shame in looking to it also to make my fortune; but that fortune was by so much further from being made from the moment my visitors wished to be "done" for nothing. I was disappointed; for in the pictorial sense I had immediately *seen* them. I had seized their type—I had already settled what I would do with it. Something that wouldn't absolutely have pleased them, I afterwards reflected.

"Ah, you're—you're—a—?" I began, as soon as I had mastered my surprise. I couldn't bring out the dingy word "models"; it seemed to fit the case so little.

"We haven't had much practice," said the lady.

"We've got to *do* something, and we've thought that an artist in your line might perhaps make something of us," her husband threw off. He further mentioned that they didn't know many artists and that they had gone first, on the off-chance (he painted views of course, but sometimes put in figures—perhaps I remembered), to Mr. Rivet, whom they had met a few years before at a place in Norfolk where he was sketching.

"We used to sketch a little ourselves," the lady hinted.

"It's very awkward, but we absolutely *must* do something," her husband went on.

"Of course, we're not so *very* young," she admitted, with a wan smile.

With the remark that I might as well know something more about them, the husband had handed me a card extracted from a neat new pocket-book (their appurtenances were all of the freshest) and inscribed with the words "Major Monarch." Impressive as these words were they didn't carry my knowledge much further; but my visitor presently added: "I've left the army, and we've had the misfortune to lose our money. In fact our means are dreadfully small."

"It's an awful bore," said Mrs. Monarch.

They evidently wished to be discreet—to take care not to swagger because they were gentlefolks. I perceived they would have been willing to recognize this as something of a drawback, at the same time that I guessed at an underlying sense—their consolation in adversity—that they *had* their points. They certainly had; but these advantages struck me as preponderantly social; such for instance as would help to make a drawing-room look well. However, a drawing-room was always, or ought to be, a picture.

In consequence of his wife's allusion to their age Major Monarch observed: "Naturally, it's more for the figure that we thought of going in. We can still hold ourselves up." On the instant I saw that the figure was indeed their strong point. His "naturally" didn't sound vain, but it lighted up the question. "*She* has got the best," he continued, nodding at his wife, with a pleasant after-dinner absence of circumlocution. I could only reply, as if we were in fact sitting over our wine, that this didn't prevent his own from being very good; which led him in turn to rejoin: "We thought that if you ever have to do people like us, we might be something like it. *She*, particularly —for a lady in a book, you know."

I was so amused by them that, to get more of it, I did my best to take their point of view; and though it was an embarrassment to find myself appraising physically, as if they were animals on hire or useful blacks, a pair whom I should have expected to meet only in one of the relations in which criticism is tacit, I looked at Mrs. Monarch judicially enough to be able to exclaim, after a moment, with conviction: "Oh yes, a lady in a book!" She was singularly like a bad illustration.

"We'll stand up, if you like," said the Major; and he raised himself before me with a really grand air.

I could take his measure at a glance—he was six feet two and a perfect gentleman. It would have paid any club in process of formation and in want of a stamp to engage him at a salary to stand in the principal window. What struck me immediately was that in coming to me they had rather missed their vocation; they could surely have been turned to better account for advertising purposes. I couldn't of course see the thing in detail, but I could see them make someone's fortune—I don't mean their own. There was something in them for a waistcoat-maker, an hotel-keeper or a soap-vendor. I could imagine "We always use it" pinned on their bosoms with the greatest effect; I had a vision of the promptitude with which they would launch a table d'hôte.

Mrs. Monarch sat still, not from pride but from shyness, and presently her husband said to her: "Get up, my dear, and show how smart you are." She obeyed, but she had no need to get up to show it. She walked to the end of the studio, and then she came back blushing with her fluttered eyes on her husband. I was reminded of an incident I had accidentally had a glimpse of in Paris—being with a friend there, a dramatist about to produce a play—when an actress came to him to ask to be entrusted with a part. She went through her paces before him, walked up and down as Mrs. Monarch was doing. Mrs. Monarch did it quite as well, but I abstained from applauding. It was very odd to see such people apply for such poor pay. She looked as if she had ten thousand a year. Her husband had used the word that described her: she was, in the London current jargon, essentially and typically "smart." Her figure was, in the same order of ideas, conspicuously and irreproachably "good." For a woman of her age her waist was surprisingly small; her elbow moreover had the orthodox crook. She held her head at the conventional angle; but why did she come to *me?* She ought to have tried on jackets at a big shop. I feared my visitors were not only destitute, but "artistic"—which would be a great complication. When she sat down I thanked her, observing that what a draughtsman most valued in his model was the faculty of keeping quiet.

"Oh, *she* can keep quiet," said Major

Monarch. Then he added, jocosely: "I've always kept her quiet."

"I'm not a nasty fidget, am I?" Mrs. Monarch appealed to her husband.

He addressed his answer to me. "Perhaps it isn't out of place to mention—because we ought to be quite business-like, oughtn't we? —that when I married her she was known as the Beautiful Statue."

"Oh dear!" said Mrs. Monarch, ruefully.

"Of course I shall want a certain amount of expression," I rejoined.

"Of *course!*" they both exclaimed.

"And then I suppose you know that you'll get awfully tired."

"Oh, we *never* get tired!" they eagerly cried.

"Have you had any kind of practice?"

They hesitated—they looked at each other. "We've been photographed, *immensely*," said Mrs. Monarch.

"She means the fellows have asked us," added the Major.

"I see—because you're so good-looking."

"I don't know what they thought, but they were always after us."

"We always got our photographs for nothing," smiled Mrs. Monarch.

"We might have brought some, my dear," her husband remarked.

"I'm not sure we have any left. We've given quantities away," she explained to me.

"With our autographs and that sort of thing," said the Major.

"Are they to be got in the shops?" I inquired, as a harmless pleasantry.

"Oh, yes; *hers*—they used to be."

"Not now," said Mrs. Monarch, with her eyes on the floor.

II

I could fancy the "sort of thing" they put on the presentation-copies of their photographs, and I was sure they wrote a beautiful hand. It was odd how quickly I was sure of everything that concerned them. If they were now so poor as to have to earn shillings and pence, they never had had much of a margin. Their good looks had been their capital, and they had good-humoredly made the most of the career that this resource marked out for them. It was in their faces, the blankness, the deep intellectual repose of the twenty years of country-house visiting which had given them pleasant intonations. I could see the sunny drawing-rooms, sprinkled with periodicals she didn't read, in which Mrs. Monarch had continuously sat; I could see the wet shrubberies in which she had walked, equipped to admiration for either exercise. I could see the rich covers the Major had helped to shoot and the wonderful garments in which, late at night, he repaired to the smoking-room to talk about them. I could imagine their leggings and waterproofs, their knowing tweeds and rugs, their rolls of sticks and cases of tackle and neat umbrellas; and I could evoke the exact appearance of their servants and the compact variety of their luggage on the platforms of country stations.

They gave small tips, but they were liked; they didn't do anything themselves, but they were welcome. They looked so well everywhere; they gratified the general relish for stature, complexion and "form." They knew it without fatuity or vulgarity, and they respected themselves in consequence. They were not superficial; they were thorough and kept themselves up—it had been their line. People with such a taste for activity had to have some line. I could feel how, even in a dull house, they could have been counted upon for cheerfulness. At present something had happened—it didn't matter what, their little income had grown less, it had grown least—and they had to do something for pocket-money. Their friends liked them, but didn't like to support them. There was something about them that represented credit—their clothes, their

manners, their type; but if credit is a large empty pocket in which an occasional chink reverberates, the chink at least must be audible. What they wanted of me was to help to make it so. Fortunately they had no children—I soon divined that. They would also perhaps wish our relations to be kept secret: this was why it was "for the figure" —the reproduction of the face would betray them.

I liked them—they were so simple; and I had no objection to them if they would suit. But, somehow, with all their perfections I didn't easily believe in them. After all they were amateurs, and the ruling passion of my life was the detestation of the amateur. Combined with this was another perversity —an innate preference for the represented subject over the real one: the defect of the real one was so apt to be a lack of representation. I liked things that appeared; then one was sure. Whether they *were* or not was a subordinate and almost always a profitless question. There were other considerations, the first of which was that I already had two or three people in use, notably a young person with big feet, in alpaca, from Kilburn, who for a couple of years had come to me regularly for my illustrations and with whom I was still—perhaps ignobly—satisfied. I frankly explained to my visitors how the case stood; but they had taken more precautions than I supposed. They had reasoned out their opportunity, for Claude Rivet had told them of the projected *édition de luxe* of one of the writers of our day—the rarest of the novelists—who, long neglected by the multitudinous vulgar and dearly prized by the attentive (need I mention Philip Vincent?) had had the happy fortune of seeing, late in life, the dawn and then the full light of a higher criticism—an estimate in which, on the part of the public, there was something really of expiation. The edition in question, planned by a publisher of taste, was practically an act of high reparation; the wood-cuts with which it was to be enriched were the homage of English art to one of the most independent representatives of English letters. Major and Mrs. Monarch confessed to me that they had hoped I might be able to work *them* into my share of the enterprise. They knew I was to do the first of the books, "Rutland Ramsay," but I had to make clear to them that my participation in the rest of the affair—this first book was to be a test—was to depend on the satisfaction I should give. If this should be limited my employers would drop me without a scruple. It was therefore a crisis for me, and naturally I was making special preparations, looking about for new people, if they should be necessary, and securing the best types. I admitted however that I should like to settle down to two or three good models who would do for everything.

"Should we have often to—a—put on special clothes?" Mrs. Monarch timidly demanded.

"Dear, yes—that's half the business."

"And should we be expected to supply our own costumes?"

"Oh, no; I've got a lot of things. A painter's models put on—or put off—anything he likes."

"And do you mean—a—the same?"

"The same?"

Mrs. Monarch looked at her husband again.

"Oh, she was just wondering," he explained, "if the costumes are in *general* use." I had to confess that they were, and I mentioned further that some of them (I had a lot of genuine, greasy last-century things), had served their time, a hundred years ago, on living, world-stained men and women. "We'll put on anything that *fits*," said the Major.

"Oh, I arrange that—they fit in the pictures."

"I'm afraid I should do better for the modern books. I would come as you like," said Mrs. Monarch.

"She has got a lot of clothes at home: they might do for contemporary life," her husband continued.

"Oh, I can fancy scenes in which you'd be quite natural." And indeed I could see the slipshod rearrangements of stale properties—the stories I tried to produce pictures for without the exasperation of reading them—whose sandy tracts the good lady might help to people. But I had to return to the fact that for this sort of work—the daily mechanical grind—I was already equipped; the people I was working with were fully adequate.

"We only thought we might be more like *some* characters," said Mrs. Monarch mildly, getting up.

Her husband also rose; he stood looking at me with a dim wistfulness that was touching in so fine a man. "Wouldn't it be rather a pull sometimes to have—a—to have—?" He hung fire; he wanted me to help him by phrasing what he meant. But I couldn't—I didn't know. So he brought it out, awkwardly: "The *real* thing; a gentleman, you know, or a lady." I was quite ready to give a general assent—I admitted that there was a great deal in that. This encouraged Major Monarch to say, following up his appeal with an unacted gulp: "It's awfully hard—we've tried everything." The gulp was communicative; it proved too much for his wife. Before I knew it Mrs. Monarch had dropped again upon a divan and burst into tears. Her husband sat down beside her, holding one of her hands; whereupon she quickly dried her eyes with the other, while I felt embarrassed as she looked up at me. "There isn't a confounded job I haven't applied for —waited for—prayed for. You can fancy we'd be pretty bad at first. Secretaryships and that sort of thing? You might as well ask for a peerage. I'd be *anything*—I'm strong; a messenger or a coalheaver. I'd put on a gold-laced cap and open carriage-doors in front of the haberdasher's; I'd hang about a station, to carry portmanteaus; I'd be a postman. But they won't *look* at you; there are thousands, as good as yourself, already on the ground. *Gentlemen,* poor beggars, who have drunk their wine, who have kept their hunters!"

I was as reassuring as I knew how to be, and my visitors were presently on their feet again while, for the experiment, we agreed on an hour. We were discussing it when the door opened and Miss Churm came in with a wet umbrella. Miss Churm had to take the omnibus to Maida Vale and then walk half-a-mile. She looked a trifle blowsy and slightly splashed. I scarcely ever saw her come in without thinking afresh how odd it was that, being so little in herself, she should yet be so much in others. She was a meagre little Miss Churm, but she was an ample heroine of romance. She was only a freckled cockney, but she could represent everything, from a fine lady to a shepherdess; she had the faculty, as she might have had a fine voice or long hair. She couldn't spell, and she loved beer, but she had two or three "points," and practice, and a knack, and mother-wit, and a kind of whimsical sensibility, and a love of the theatre, and seven sisters, and not an ounce of respect, especially for the *h.* The first thing my visitors saw was that her umbrella was wet, and in their spotless perfection they visibly winced at it. The rain had come on since their arrival.

"I'm all in a soak; there *was* a mess of people in the 'bus. I wish you lived near a stytion," said Miss Churm. I requested her to get ready as quickly as possible, and she passed into the room in which she always changed her dress. But before going out she asked me what she was to get into this time.

"It's the Russian princess, don't you know?" I answered; "the one with the 'golden eyes,' in black velvet, for the long thing in the *Cheapside.*"

"Golden eyes? I *say!*" cried Miss Churm, while my companions watched her with intensity as she withdrew. She always arranged herself, when she was late, before I could turn round; and I kept my visitors a little, on purpose, so that they might get an idea, from seeing her, what would be expected of themselves. I mentioned that she was quite my notion of an excellent model—she was really very clever.

"Do you think she looks like a Russian princess?" Major Monarch asked, with lurking alarm.

"When I make her, yes."

"Oh, if you have to *make* her—!" he reasoned, acutely.

"That's the most you can ask. There are so many that are not makeable."

"Well now, *here's* a lady"—and with a persuasive smile he passed his arm into his wife's—"who's already made!"

"Oh, I'm not a Russian princess," Mrs. Monarch protested, a little coldly. I could see that she had known some and didn't like them. There, immediately, was a complication of a kind that I never had to fear with Miss Churm.

This young lady came back in black velvet—the gown was rather rusty and very low on her lean shoulders—and with a Japanese fan in her red hands. I reminded her that in the scene I was doing she had to look over someone's head. "I forget whose it is; but it doesn't matter. Just look over a head."

"I'd rather look over a stove," said Miss Churm; and she took her station near the fire. She fell into position, settled herself into a tall attitude, gave a certain backward inclination to her head and a certain forward droop to her fan, and looked, at least to my prejudiced sense, distinguished and charming, foreign and dangerous. We left her looking so, while I went downstairs with Major and Mrs. Monarch.

"I think I could come about as near it as that," said Mrs. Monarch.

"Oh, you think she's shabby, but you must allow for the alchemy of art."

However, they went off with an evident increase of comfort, founded on their demonstrable advantage in being the real thing. I could fancy them shuddering over Miss Churm. She was very droll about them when I went back, for I told her what they wanted.

"Well, if *she* can sit I'll tyke to book-keeping," said my model.

"She's very lady-like," I replied, as an innocent form of aggravation.

"So much the worse for *you.* That means she can't turn round."

"She'll do for the fashionable novels."

"Oh yes, she'll *do* for them!" my model humorously declared. "Ain't they bad enough without her?" I had often sociably denounced them to Miss Churm.

III

It was for the elucidation of a mystery in one of these works that I first tried Mrs. Monarch. Her husband came with her, to be useful if necessary—it was sufficiently clear that as a general thing he would prefer to come with her. At first I wondered if this were for "propriety's" sake—if he were going to be jealous and meddling. The idea was too tiresome, and if it had been confirmed it would speedily have brought our acquaintance to a close. But I soon saw there was nothing in it and that if he accompanied Mrs. Monarch it was (in addition to the chance of being wanted), simply because he had nothing else to do. When she was away from him his occupation was gone—she never *had* been away from him. I judged, rightly, that in their awkward situation their close union was

their main comfort and that this union had no weak spot. It was a real marriage, an encouragement to the hesitating, a nut for pessimists to crack. Their address was humble (I remember afterwards thinking it had been the only thing about them that was really professional), and I could fancy the lamentable lodgings in which the Major would have been left alone. He could bear them with his wife—he couldn't bear them without her.

He had too much tact to try and make himself agreeable when he couldn't be useful; so he simply sat and waited, when I was too absorbed in my work to talk. But I liked to make him talk—it made my work, when it didn't interrupt it, less sordid, less special. To listen to him was to combine the excitement of going out with the economy of staying at home. There was only one hindrance: that I seemed not to know any of the people he and his wife had known. I think he wondered extremely, during the term of our intercourse, whom the deuce I *did* know. He hadn't a stray sixpence of an idea to fumble for; so we didn't spin it very fine—we confined ourselves to questions of leather and even of liquor (saddlers and breeches-makers and how to get good claret cheap), and matters like "good trains" and the habits of small game. His lore on these last subjects was astonishing, he managed to interweave the stationmaster with the ornithologist. When he couldn't talk about greater things he could talk cheerfully about smaller, and since I couldn't accompany him into reminiscences of the fashionable world he could lower the conversation without a visible effort to my level.

So earnest a desire to please was touching in a man who could so easily have knocked one down. He looked after the fire and had an opinion on the draught of the stove, without my asking him, and I could see that he thought many of my arrangements not half clever enough. I remember telling him that if I were only rich I would offer him a salary to come and teach me how to live. Sometimes he gave a random sigh, of which the essence was: "Give me even such a bare old barrack as *this*, and I'd do something with it!" When I wanted to use him he came alone; which was an illustration of the superior courage of women. His wife could bear her solitary second floor, and she was in general more discreet; showing by various small reserves that she was alive to the propriety of keeping our relations markedly professional—not letting them slide into sociability. She wished it to remain clear that she and the Major were employed, not cultivated, and if she approved of me as a superior, who could be kept in his place, she never thought me quite good enough for an equal.

She sat with great intensity, giving the whole of her mind to it, and was capable of remaining for an hour almost as motionless as if she were before a photographer's lens. I could see she had been photographed often, but somehow the very habit that made her good for that purpose unfitted her for mine. At first I was extremely pleased with her lady-like air, and it was a satisfaction, on coming to follow her lines, to see how good they were and how far they could lead the pencil. But after a few times I began to find her too insurmountably stiff; do what I would with it my drawing looked like a photograph or a copy of a photograph. Her figure had no variety of expression—she herself had no sense of variety. You may say that this was my business, was only a question of placing her. I placed her in every conceivable position, but she managed to obliterate their differences. She was always a lady certainly, and into the bargain was always the same lady. She was the real thing, but always the same thing. There were moments when I was oppressed by the serenity of her confidence that she *was* the real thing. All her dealings with me and all her husband's were an implication that this was lucky for *me*. Meanwhile I found myself trying to invent types that approached her own, instead of making her own transform itself—in the clever way that was not impossible, for instance, to poor Miss Churm. Arrange as I would and take the precautions I would, she always, in my pictures, came out too tall—landing me in the dilemma of having represented a fascinating woman as seven feet high, which, out of respect perhaps to my own very much scantier inches, was far from my idea of such a personage.

The case was worse with the Major—nothing I could do would keep *him* down, so that he became useful only for the representation of brawny giants. I adored variety and range, I cherished human accidents, the illustrative note; I wanted to characterize closely, and the thing in the world I most hated was the danger of being ridden by a type. I had quarreled with some of my friends about it—I had parted company with them for maintaining that one *had* to be, and that if the type was beautiful (witness Raphael and Leonardo), the servitude was only a gain. I was neither Leonardo nor Raphael; I might only be a presumptuous young modern searcher, but I held that everything was to be sacrificed sooner than character. When they averred that the haunting type in question could easily *be* character, I retorted, perhaps superficially: "Whose?" It couldn't be everybody's—it might end in being nobody's.

After I had drawn Mrs. Monarch a dozen times I perceived more clearly than before that the value of such a model as Miss Churm resided precisely in the fact that she had no positive stamp, combined of course with the other fact that what she did have was a curious and inexplicable talent for imitation. Her usual appearance was like a curtain which she could draw up at request for a capital performance. This performance was simply suggestive; but it was a word to the wise—it was vivid and pretty. Sometimes, even, I thought it, though she was plain herself, too insipidly pretty; I made it a reproach to her that the figures drawn from her were monotonously (*bête-ment* [stupidly], as we used to say) graceful. Nothing made her more angry; it was so much her pride to feel that she could sit for characters that had nothing in common with each other. She would accuse me at such moments of taking away her "reputy-tion."

It suffered a certain shrinkage, this queer quantity, from the repeated visits of my new friends. Miss Churm was greatly in demand, never in want of employment, so I had no scruple in putting her off occa-sionally, to try them more at my ease. It was certainly amusing at first to do the real thing—it was amusing to do Major Monarch's trousers. They *were* the real thing, even if he did come out colossal. It was amusing to do his wife's back hair (it was so mathematically neat), and the par-ticular "smart" tension of her tight stays. She lent herself especially to positions in which the face was somewhat averted or blurred; she abounded in lady-like back views and *profils perdus* [lost profiles]. When she stood erect she took naturally one of the attitudes in which court-painters represent queens and princesses; so that I found myself wondering whether, to draw out this accomplishment, I couldn't get the editor of the *Cheapside* to publish a really royal romance, "A Tale of Buckingham Palace." Sometimes, however, the real thing and the make-believe came into contact; by which I mean that Miss Churm, keeping an appointment or coming to make one on days when I had much work in hand, en-countered her invidious rivals. The en-counter was not on their part, for they noticed her no more than if she had been the housemaid; not from intentional lofti-ness, but simply because, as yet, profes-sionally, they didn't know how to fraternize, as I could guess that they would have liked —or at least that the Major would. They

couldn't talk about the omnibus—they al-ways walked; and they didn't know what else to try—she wasn't interested in good trains or cheap claret. Besides, they must have felt—in the air—that she was amused at them, secretly derisive of their ever know-ing how. She was not a person to conceal her scepticism if she had had a chance to show it. On the other hand Mrs. Monarch didn't think her tidy; for why else did she take pains to say to me (it was going out of the way, for Mrs. Monarch), that she didn't like dirty women?

One day when my young lady happened to be present with my other sitters (she even dropped in, when it was convenient, for a chat), I asked her to be so good as to lend a hand in getting tea—a service with which she was familiar and which was one of a class that, living as I did in a small way, with slender domestic resources, I often appealed to my models to render. They liked to lay hands on my property, to break the sitting, and sometimes the china—I made them feel Bohemian. The next time I saw Miss Churm after this incident she surprised me greatly by making a scene about it—she accused me of having wished to humiliate her. She had not resented the outrage at the time, but had seemed obliging and amused, enjoying the comedy of asking Mrs. Monarch, who sat vague and silent, whether she would have cream and sugar, and put-ting an exaggerated simper into the ques-tion. She had tried intonations—as if she too wished to pass for the real thing; till I was afraid my other visitors would take offence.

Oh, *they* were determined not to do this; and their touching patience was the measure of their great need. They would sit by the hour, uncomplaining, till I was ready to use them; they would come back on the chance of being wanted and would walk away cheerfully if they were not. I used to go to the door with them to see in what magni-ficent order they retreated. I tried to find other employment for them—I introduced them to several artists. But they didn't "take," for reasons I could appreciate, and I became conscious, rather anxiously, that after such disappointments they fell back upon me with a heavier weight. They did me the honor to think that it was I who was most *their* form. They were not picturesque enough for the painters, and in those days there were not so many serious workers in black and white. Besides, they had an eye to the great job I had mentioned to them— they had secretly set their hearts on supplying the right essence for my pictorial vindication of our fine novelist. They knew that for this undertaking I should want no costume-effects, none of the frippery of past ages—that it was a case in which everything would be contemporary and satirical and, presumably, genteel. If I could work them into it their future would be assured, for the labor would of course be long and the occupation steady.

One day Mrs. Monarch came without her husband—she explained his absence by his having had to go to the City. While she sat there in her usual anxious stiffness there came, at the door, a knock which I immediately recognized as the subdued appeal of a model out of work. It was followed by the entrance of a young man whom I easily perceived to be a foreigner and who proved in fact an Italian acquainted with no English word but my name, which he uttered in a way that made it seem to include all others. I had not then visited his country, nor was I proficient in his tongue; but as he was not so meanly constituted—what Italian is?—as to depend only on that member for expression, he conveyed to me, in familiar but graceful mimicry, that he was in search of exactly the employment in which the lady before me was engaged. I was not struck with him at first, and while I continued to draw I emitted rough sounds of discouragement and dismissal. He stood his ground, however, not importunately, but with a

dumb, dog-like fidelity in his eyes which amounted to innocent impudence—the manner of a devoted servant (he might have been in the house for years), unjustly suspected. Suddenly I saw that this very attitude and expression made a picture, whereupon I told him to sit down and wait till I should be free. There was another picture in the way he obeyed me, and I observed as I worked that there were others still in the way he looked wonderingly, with his head thrown back, about the high studio. He might have been crossing himself in St. Peter's. Before I finished I said to myself: "The fellow's a bankrupt orange-monger, but he's a treasure."

When Mrs. Monarch withdrew he passed across the room like a flash to open the door for her, standing there with the rapt, pure gaze of the young Dante spellbound by the young Beatrice. As I never insisted, in such situations, on the blankness of the British domestic, I reflected that he had the making of a servant (and I needed one, but couldn't pay him to be only that), as well as of a model; in short I made up my mind to adopt my bright adventurer if he would agree to officiate in the double capacity. He jumped at my offer, and in the event my rashness (for I had known nothing about him), was not brought home to me. He proved a sympathetic though a desultory ministrant, and had in a wonderful degree the *sentiment de la pose* [feeling for posing]. It was uncultivated, instinctive; a part of the happy instinct which had guided him to my door and helped him to spell out my name on the card nailed to it. He had had no other introduction to me than a guess, from the shape of my high north window, seen outside, that my place was a studio, and that as a studio it would contain an artist. He had wandered to England in search of fortune, like other itinerants, and had embarked, with a partner and a small green handcart, on the sale of penny ices. The ices had melted away and the partner had dissolved in their train. My young man wore tight yellow trousers with reddish stripes and his name was Oronte. He was sallow but fair, and when I put him into some old clothes of my own he looked like an Englishman. He was as good as Miss Churm, who could look, when required, like an Italian.

IV

I thought Mrs. Monarch's face slightly convulsed when, on her coming back with her husband, she found Oronte installed. It was strange to have to recognize in a scrap of a lazzarone [vagabond] a competitor to her magnificent Major. It was she who scented danger first, for the Major was anecdotically unconscious. But Oronte gave us tea, with a hundred eager confusions (he had never seen such a queer process), and I think she thought better of me for having at last an "establishment." They saw a couple of drawings that I had made of the establishment, and Mrs. Monarch hinted that it never would have struck her that he had sat for them. "Now the drawings you make from *us*, they look exactly like us," she reminded me, smiling in triumph; and I recognized that this was indeed just their defect. When I drew the Monarchs I couldn't, somehow, get away from them— get into the character I wanted to represent; and I had not the least desire my model should be discoverable in my picture. Miss Churm never was, and Mrs. Monarch thought I hid her, very properly, because she was vulgar; whereas if she was lost it was only as the dead who go to heaven are lost —in the gain of an angel the more.

By this time I had got a certain start with "Rutland Ramsay," the first novel in the great projected series; that is, I had produced a dozen drawings, several with the help of the Major and his wife, and I had sent them in for approval. My understanding with the publishers, as I have already hinted, had been that I was to be left to do my work, in this particular case, as I liked, with the whole book committed to me; but my connection with the rest of the series was only contingent. There were moments when, frankly, it *was* a comfort to have the real thing under one's hand; for there were characters in "Rutland Ramsay" that were very much like it. There were people presumably as straight as the Major and women of as good a fashion as Mrs. Monarch. There was a great deal of country-house life— treated, it is true, in a fine, fanciful, ironical, generalized way—and there was a considerable implication of knickerbockers and kilts. There were certain things I had to settle at the outset; such things for instance as the exact appearance of the hero, the particular bloom of the heroine. The author of course gave me a lead, but there was a margin for interpretation. I took the Monarchs into my confidence, I told them frankly what I was about, I mentioned my embarrassments and alternatives. "Oh, take *him!*" Mrs. Monarch murmured sweetly, looking at her husband; and "What could you want better than my wife?" the Major inquired, with the comfortable candor that now prevailed between us.

I was not obliged to answer these remarks —I was only obliged to place my sitters. I was not easy in mind, and I postponed, a little timidly perhaps, the solution of the question. The book was a large canvas, the other figures were numerous, and I worked off at first some of the episodes in which the hero and the heroine were not concerned. When once I had set *them* up I should have to stick to them—I couldn't make my young man seven feet high in one place and five feet nine in another. I inclined on the whole to the latter measurement, though the Major more than once reminded me that *he* looked about as young as anyone. It was indeed quite possible to arrange him, for the figure, so that it would have been difficult to detect his age. After the spontaneous Oronte had been with me a month, and after I had given him to understand several different times that his native exuberance would presently constitute an insurmountable barrier to our further intercourse, I waked to a sense of his heroic capacity. He was only five feet seven, but the remaining inches were latent. I tried him almost secretly at first, for I was really rather afraid of the judgment my other models would pass on such a choice. If they regarded Miss Churm as little better than a snare, what would they think of the representation by a person so little the real thing as an Italian street-vendor of a protagonist formed by a public school?[44]

If I went a little in fear of them it was not because they bullied me, because they had got an oppressive foothold, but because in their really pathetic decorum and mysteriously permanent newness they counted on me so intensely. I was therefore very glad when Jack Hawley came home: he was always of such good counsel. He painted badly himself, but there was no one like him for putting his finger on the place. He had been absent from England for a year; he had been somewhere—I don't remember where —to get a fresh eye. I was in a good deal of dread of any such organ, but we were old friends; he had been away for months and a sense of emptiness was creeping into my life. I hadn't dodged a missile for a year.

He came back with a fresh eye, but with the same old black velvet blouse, and the first evening he spent in my studio we smoked cigarettes till the small hours. He had done no work himself, he had only got the eye; so the field was clear for the production of my little things. He wanted to see what I had done for the *Cheapside*, but he was disappointed in the exhibition. That at least seemed the meaning of two or three comprehensive groans which, as he lounged on my big divan, on a folded leg, looking at

44 Eton, Rugby, or some other fashionable private school.

my latest drawings, issued from his lips with the smoke of the cigarette.

"What's the matter with you?" I asked.

"What's the matter with *you*?"

"Nothing save that I'm mystified."

"You are indeed. You're quite off the hinge. What's the meaning of this new fad?" And he tossed me, with visible irreverence, a drawing in which I happened to have depicted both my majestic models. I asked if he didn't think it good, and he replied that it struck him as execrable, given the sort of thing I had always represented myself to him as wishing to arrive at; but I let that pass, I was so anxious to see exactly what he meant. The two figures in the picture looked colossal, but I supposed this was *not* what he meant, inasmuch as, for aught he knew to the contrary, I might have been trying for that. I maintained that I was working exactly in the same way as when he last had done me the honor to commend me. "Well, there's a big hole somewhere," he answered; "wait a bit and I'll discover it." I depended upon him to do so: where else was the fresh eye? But he produced at last nothing more luminous than, "I don't know —I don't like your types." This was lame, for a critic who had never consented to discuss with me anything but the question of execution, the direction of strokes and the mystery of values.

"In the drawing you've been looking at I think my types are very handsome."

"Oh, they won't do!"

"I've had a couple of new models."

"I see you have. *They* won't do."

"Are you very sure of that?"

"Absolutely—they're stupid."

"You mean *I* am—for I ought to get round that."

"You *can't*—with such people. Who are they?"

I told him, as far as was necessary, and he declared, heartlessly: "*Ce sont des gens qu'il faut mettre à la porte*" [They are people that must be got rid of].

"You've never seen them; they're awfully good," I compassionately objected.

"Not seen them? Why, all this recent work of yours drops to pieces with them. It's all I want to see of them."

"No one else has said anything against it —the *Cheapside* people are pleased."

"Everyone else is an ass, and the *Cheapside* people the biggest asses of all. Come, don't pretend, at this time of day, to have pretty illusions about the public, especially about publishers and editors. It's not for *such* animals you work—it's for those who know, *coloro che sanno;* so keep straight for *me* if you can't keep straight for yourself. There's a certain sort of thing you tried for from the first—and a very good thing it is. But this twaddle isn't *in* it." When I talked with Hawley later about "Rutland Ramsay" and its possible successors he declared that I must get back into my boat again or I would go to the bottom. His voice in short was the voice of warning.

I noted the warning, but I didn't turn my friends out of doors. They bored me a good deal; but the very fact that they bored me admonished me not to sacrifice them—if there was anything to be done with them— simply to irritation. As I look back at this phase they seem to me to have pervaded my life not a little. I have a vision of them as most of the time in my studio, seated, against the wall, on an old velvet bench to be out of the way, and looking like a pair of patient courtiers in a royal ante-chamber. I am convinced that during the coldest weeks of the winter they held their ground because it saved them fire. Their newness was losing its gloss, and it was impossible not to feel that they were objects of charity. Whenever Miss Churm arrived they went away, and after I was fairly launched in "Rutland Ramsay" Miss Churm arrived pretty often. They managed to express to me tacitly that they supposed I wanted her for the low life of the book, and I let them

suppose it, since they had attempted to study the work—it was lying about the studio—without discovering that it dealt only with the highest circles. They had dipped into the most brilliant of our novelists without deciphering many passages. I still took an hour from them, now and again, in spite of Jack Hawley's warning: it would be time enough to dismiss them, if dismissal should be necessary, when the rigor of the season was over. Hawley had made their acquaintance—he had met them at my fireside—and thought them a ridiculous pair. Learning that he was a painter they tried to approach him, to show him too that they were the real thing; but he looked at them, across the big room, as if they were miles away: they were a compendium of everything that he most objected to in the social system of his country. Such people as that, all convention and patent-leather, with ejaculations that stopped conversation, had no business in a studio. A studio was a place to learn to see, and how could you see through a pair of feather beds?

The main inconvenience I suffered at their hands was that, at first, I was shy of letting them discover how my artful little servant had begun to sit to me for "Rutland Ramsay." They knew that I had been odd enough (they were prepared by this time to allow oddity to artists) to pick a foreign vagabond out of the streets, when I might have had a person with whiskers and credentials; but it was some time before they learned how high I rated his accomplishments. They found him in an attitude more than once, but they never doubted I was doing him as an organ-grinder. There were several things they never guessed, and one of them was that for a striking scene in the novel, in which a footman briefly figured, it occurred to me to make use of Major Monarch as the menial. I kept putting this off, I didn't like to ask him to don the livery —besides the difficulty of finding a livery to fit him. At last, one day late in the winter, when I was at work on the despised Oronte (he caught one's idea in an instant), and was in the glow of feeling that I was going very straight, they came in, the Major and his wife, with their society laugh about nothing (there was less and less to laugh at), like country-callers—they always reminded me of that—who have walked across the park after church and are presently persuaded to stay to luncheon. Luncheon was over, but they could stay to tea—I knew they wanted it. The fit was on me, however, and I couldn't let my ardor cool and my work wait, with the fading daylight, while my model prepared it. So I asked Mrs. Monarch if she would mind laying it out—a request which, for an instant, brought all the blood to her face. Her eyes were on her husband's for a second, and some mute telegraphy passed between them. Their folly was over the next instant; his cheerful shrewdness put an end to it. So far from pitying their wounded pride, I must add, I was moved to give it as complete a lesson as I could. They bustled about together and got out the cups and saucers and made the kettle boil. I know they felt as if they were waiting on my servant, and when the tea was prepared I said: "He'll have a cup, please—he's tired." Mrs. Monarch brought him one where he stood, and he took it from her as if he had been a gentleman at a party, squeezing a crush-hat with an elbow.

Then it came over me that she had made a great effort for me—made it with a kind of nobleness—and that I owed her a compensation. Each time I saw her after this I wondered what the compensation could be. I couldn't go on doing the wrong thing to oblige them. Oh, it *was* the wrong thing, the stamp of the work for which they sat—Hawley was not the only person to say it now. I sent in a large number of the drawings I had made for "Rutland Ramsay," and I received

a warning that was more to the point than Hawley's. The artistic adviser of the house for which I was working was of opinion that many of my illustrations were not what had been looked for. Most of these illustrations were the subjects in which the Monarchs had figured. Without going into the question of what *had* been looked for, I saw at this rate I shouldn't get the other books to do. I hurled myself in despair upon Miss Churm, I put her through all her paces. I not only adopted Oronte publicly as my hero, but one morning when the Major looked in to see if I didn't require him to finish a figure for the *Cheapside*, for which he had begun to sit the week before, I told him that I had changed my mind—I would do the drawing from my man. At this my visitor turned pale and stood looking at me. "Is *he* your idea of an English gentleman?" he asked.

I was disappointed, I was nervous, I wanted to get on with my work; so I replied with irritation: "Oh, my dear Major—I can't be ruined for *you!*"

He stood another moment; then, without a word, he quitted the studio. I drew a long breath when he was gone, for I said to myself that I shouldn't see him again. I had not told him definitely that I was in danger of having my work rejected, but I was vexed at his not having felt the catastrophe in the air, read with me the moral of our fruitless collaboration, the lesson that, in the deceptive atmosphere of art, even the highest respectability may fail of being plastic.

I didn't owe my friends money, but I did see them again. They reappeared together, three days later, and under the circumstances there was something tragic in the fact. It was a proof to me that they could find nothing else in life to do. They had threshed the matter out in a dismal conference—they had digested the bad news that they were not in for the series. If they were not useful to me even for the *Cheap-*

side their function seemed difficult to determine, and I could only judge at first that they had come, forgivingly, decorously, to take a last leave. This made me rejoice in secret that I had little leisure for a scene; for I had placed both my other models in position together and I was pegging away at a drawing from which I hoped to derive glory. It had been suggested by the passage in which Rutland Ramsay, drawing up a chair to Artemisia's piano-stool, says extraordinary things to her while she ostensibly fingers out a difficult piece of music. I had done Miss Churm at the piano before—it was an attitude in which she knew how to take on an absolutely poetic grace. I wished the two figures to "compose" together, intensely, and my little Italian had entered perfectly into my conception. The pair were vividly before me, the piano had been pulled out; it was a charming picture of blended youth and murmured love, which I had only to catch and keep. My visitors stood and looked at it, and I was friendly to them over my shoulder.

They made no response, but I was used to silent company and went on with my work, only a little disconcerted (even though exhilarated by the sense that *this* was at least the ideal thing), at not having got rid of them after all. Presently I heard Mrs. Monarch's sweet voice beside, or rather above me: "I wish her hair was a little better done." I looked up and she was staring with a strange fixedness at Miss Churm, whose back was turned to her. "Do you mind my just touching it?" she went on—a question which made me spring up for an instant, as with the instinctive fear that she might do the young lady a harm. But she quieted me with a glance I shall never forget—I confess I should like to have been able to paint *that*—and went for a moment to my model. She spoke to her softly, laying a hand upon her shoulder and bending over her; and as the girl, understanding, gratefully assented, she disposed her rough curls, with a few

quick passes, in such a way as to make Miss Churm's head twice as charming. It was one of the most heroic personal services I have ever seen rendered. Then Mrs. Monarch turned away with a low sigh and, looking about her as if for something to do, stooped to the floor with a noble humility and picked up a dirty rag that had dropped out of my paint-box.

The Major meanwhile had also been looking for something to do and, wandering to the other end of the studio, saw before him my breakfast things, neglected, unremoved. "I say, can't I be useful *here?*" he called out to me with an irrepressible quaver. I assented with a laugh that I fear was awkward and for the next ten minutes, while I worked, I heard the light clatter of china and the tinkle of spoons and glass. Mrs. Monarch assisted her husband—they washed up my crockery, they put it away. They wandered off into my little scullery, and I afterwards found that they had cleaned my knives and that my slender stock of plate had an unprecedented surface. When it came over me, the latent eloquence of what they were doing, I confess that my drawing was blurred for a moment—the picture swam. They had accepted their failure, but they couldn't accept their fate. They had bowed their heads in bewilderment to the perverse and cruel law in virtue of which the real thing could be so much less precious than the unreal; but they didn't want to starve. If my servants were my models, my models might be my servants. They would reverse the parts—the others would sit for the ladies and gentlemen, and *they* would do the work. They would still be in the studio—it was an intense dumb appeal to me not to turn them out. "Take us on," they wanted to say—"we'll do *anything*."

When all this hung before me the *afflatus* vanished—my pencil dropped from my hand. My sitting was spoiled and I got rid of my sitters, who were also evidently rather mystified and awestruck. Then, alone with the Major and his wife, I had a most uncomfortable moment. He put their prayer into a single sentence: "I say, you know— just let *us* do for you, can't you?" I couldn't —it was dreadful to see them emptying my slops; but I pretended I could, to oblige them, for about a week. Then I gave them a sum of money to go away; and I never saw them again. I obtained the remaining books, but my friend Hawley repeats that Major and Mrs. Monarch did me a permanent harm, got me into a second-rate trick. If it be true I am content to have paid the price —for the memory.

James Baldwin

SONNY'S BLUES

I read about it in the paper, in the subway, on my way to work. I read it, and I couldn't believe it, and I read it again. Then perhaps I just stared at it, at the newsprint spelling out his name, spelling out the story. I stared at it in the swinging lights of the subway car, and in the faces and bodies of the people, and in my own face, trapped in the darkness which roared outside.

It was not to be believed and I kept telling myself that, as I walked from the subway station to the high school. And at the same time I couldn't doubt it. I was scared, scared for Sonny. He became real to me again. A great block of ice got settled in my belly and kept melting there slowly all day long, while I taught my classes algebra. It was a special kind of ice. It kept melting, sending trickles of ice water all up and down my veins, but it never got less. Sometimes it hardened and seemed to expand until I felt my guts were going to come spilling out or that I was going to choke or scream. This would always be at a moment when I was remembering some specific thing Sonny had once said or done.

When he was about as old as the boys in my classes his face had been bright and open, there was a lot of copper in it; and he'd had wonderfully direct brown eyes, and great gentleness and privacy. I wondered what he looked like now. He had been picked up, the evening before, in a raid on an apartment downtown, for peddling and using heroin.

I couldn't believe it: but what I mean by that is that I couldn't find any room for it anywhere inside me. I had kept it outside me for a long time. I hadn't wanted to know. I had had suspicions, but I didn't name them, I kept putting them away. I told myself that Sonny was wild but he wasn't crazy. And he'd always been a good boy, he hadn't ever turned hard or evil or disrespectful, the way kids can, so quick, so quick, especially in Harlem. I didn't want to believe that I'd ever see my brother going down, coming to nothing, all that light in his face gone out, in the condition I'd already seen so many others. Yet it had happened and here I was, talking about algebra to a lot of boys who might, every one of them for all I knew, be popping off needles every time they went to the head. Maybe it did more for them than algebra could.

I was sure that the first time Sonny had ever had horse, he couldn't have been much older than these boys were now. These boys, now, were living as we'd been living then, they were growing up with a rush and their heads bumped abruptly against the low ceiling of their actual possibilities. They were filled with rage. All they really knew were two darknesses, the darkness of their lives, which was now closing in on them, and the darkness of the movies, which had blinded them to that other darkness, and in which they now, vindictively, dreamed, at once more together than they were at any other time, and more alone.

When the last bell rang, the last class ended, I let out my breath. It seemed I'd been holding it for all that time. My clothes were wet—I may have looked as though I'd been sitting in a steam bath, all dressed up, all afternoon. I sat alone in the classroom a long time. I listened to the boys outside, downstairs, shouting and cursing and laughing. Their laughter struck me for perhaps the first time. It was not the joyous laughter which—God knows why—one associates with children. It was mocking and insular, its intent was to denigrate. It was disenchanted, and in this, also, lay the authority of their curses. Perhaps I was listening to them because I was thinking about my brother and in them I heard my brother. And myself.

One boy was whistling a tune, at once very complicated and very simple, it seemed to be pouring out of him as though he were a bird, and it sounded very cool and moving through all that harsh, bright air, only just holding its own through all those other sounds.

I stood up and walked over to the window and looked down into the courtyard. It was the beginning of the spring and the sap was rising in the boys. A teacher passed through them every now and again, quickly, as though he or she couldn't wait to get out of that courtyard, to get those boys out of their sight and off their minds. I started collecting my stuff. I thought I'd better get home and talk to Isabel.

The courtyard was almost deserted by the time I got downstairs. I saw this boy standing in the shadow of a doorway, looking just like Sonny. I almost called his name. Then I saw that it wasn't Sonny, but somebody we used to know, a boy from around our block. He'd been Sonny's friend. He'd never been mine, having been too young for me, and anyway, I'd never liked him. And now, even though he was a grown-up man, he still hung around that block, still spent hours on the street corners, was always high and raggy. I used to run into him from time to

time and he'd often work around to asking me for a quarter or fifty cents. He always had some real good excuse, too, and I always gave it to him, I don't know why.

But now, abruptly, I hated him. I couldn't stand the way he looked at me, partly like a dog, partly like a cunning child. I wanted to ask him what the hell he was doing in the school courtyard.

He sort of shuffled over to me, and he said, "I see you got the papers. So you already know about it."

"You mean about Sonny? Yes, I already know about it. How come they didn't get you?"

He grinned. It made him repulsive and it also brought to mind what he'd looked like as a kid. "I wasn't there. I stay away from them people."

"Good for you." I offered him a cigarette and I watched him through the smoke. "You come all the way down here just to tell me about Sonny?"

"That's right." He was sort of shaking his head and his eyes looked strange, as though they were about to cross. The bright sun deadened his damp dark brown skin and it made his eyes look yellow and showed up the dirt in his kinked hair. He smelled funky. I moved a little away from him and I said, "Well, thanks. But I already know about it and I got to get home."

"I'll walk you a little ways," he said. We started walking. There were a couple of kids still loitering in the courtyard, and one of them said goodnight to me and looked strangely at the boy beside me.

"What're you going to do?" he asked me. "I mean, about Sonny?"

"Look. I haven't seen Sonny for over a year, I'm not sure I'm going to do anything. Anyway, what the hell *can* I do?"

"That's right," he said quickly, "ain't nothing you can do. Can't much help old Sonny no more, I guess."

It was what I was thinking and so it seemed to me he had no right to say it.

"I'm surprised at Sonny, though," he

went on—he had a funny way of talking, he looked straight ahead as though he were talking to himself—"I thought Sonny was a smart boy, I thought he was too smart to get hung."

"I guess he thought so too," I said sharply, "and that's how he got hung. And how about you? You're pretty goddamn smart, I bet."

Then he looked directly at me, just for a minute. "I ain't smart," he said. "If I was smart, I'd have reached for a pistol a long time ago."

"Look. Don't tell *me* your sad story, if it was up to me, I'd give you one." Then I felt guilty—guilty, probably, for never having supposed that the poor bastard *had* a story of his own, much less a sad one, and I asked, quickly, "What's going to happen to him now?"

He didn't answer this. He was off by himself some place. "Funny thing," he said, and from his tone we might have been discussing the quickest way to get to Brooklyn. "When I saw the papers this morning, the first thing I asked myself was if I had anything to do with it. I felt sort of responsible."

I began to listen more carefully. The subway station was on the corner, just before us, and I stopped. He stopped, too. We were in front of a bar and he ducked slightly, peering in, but whoever he was looking for didn't seem to be there. The juke box was blasting away with something black and bouncy and I half watched the barmaid as she danced her way from the juke box to her place behind the bar. And I watched her face as she laughingly responded to something someone said to her, still keeping time to the music. When she smiled one saw a little girl, one sensed the doomed, still-struggling woman beneath the battered face of the semi-whore.

"I never *give* Sonny nothing," the boy said finally, "but a long time ago I come to school high and Sonny asked me how it felt." He paused, I couldn't bear to watch him, I watched the barmaid, and I listened to the music which seemed to be causing the pavement to shake. "I told him it felt great." The music stopped, the barmaid paused and watched the juke box until the music began again. "It did."

All this was carrying me some place I didn't want to go. I certainly didn't want to know how it felt. It filled everything, the people, the houses, the music, the dark, quicksilver barmaid, with menace; and this menace was their reality.

"What's going to happen to him now?" I asked again.

"They'll send him away some place and they'll try to cure him." He shook his head. "Maybe he'll even think he's kicked the habit. Then they'll let him loose"—he gestured, throwing his cigarette into the gutter. "That's all."

"What do you mean, that's *all?*"

But I knew what he meant.

"I *mean*, that's *all.*" He turned his head and looked at me, pulling down the corners of his mouth. "Don't you know what I mean?" he asked, softly.

"How the hell *would* I know what you mean?" I almost whispered it, I don't know why.

"That's right," he said to the air, "how would *he* know what I mean?" He turned toward me again, patient and calm, and yet I somehow felt him shaking, shaking as though he were going to fall apart. I felt that ice in my guts again, the dread I'd felt all afternoon; and again I watched the barmaid, moving about the bar, washing glasses, and singing. "Listen. They'll let him out and then it'll just start all over again. That's what I mean."

"You mean—they'll let him out. And then he'll just start working his way back in again. You mean he'll never kick the habit. Is that what you mean?"

"That's right," he said, cheerfully. "*You* see what I mean."

"Tell me," I said at last, "why does he want to die? He must want to die, he's killing himself, why does he want to die?"

He looked at me in surprise. He licked his lips. "He don't want to die. He wants to live. Don't nobody want to die, ever."

Then I wanted to ask him—too many things. He could not have answered, or if he had, I could not have borne the answers. I started walking. "Well, I guess it's none of my business."

"It's going to be rough on old Sonny," he said. We reached the subway station. "This is your station?" he asked. I nodded. I took one step down. "Damn!" he said, suddenly. I looked up at him. He grinned again. "Damn it if I didn't leave all my money home. You ain't got a dollar on you, have you? Just for a couple of days, is all."

All at once something inside gave and threatened to come pouring out of me. I didn't hate him any more. I felt that in another moment I'd start crying like a child.

"Sure," I said. "Don't sweat." I looked in my wallet and didn't have a dollar, I only had a five. "Here," I said. "That hold you?"

He didn't look at it—he didn't want to look at it. A terrible, closed look came over his face, as though he were keeping the number on the bill a secret from him and me. "Thanks," he said, and now he was dying to see me go. "Don't worry about Sonny. Maybe I'll write him or something."

"Sure," I said. "You do that. So long."

"Be seeing you," he said. I went on down the steps.

And I didn't write Sonny or send him anything for a long time. When I finally did, it was just after my little girl died; he wrote me back a letter which made me feel like a bastard.

Here's what he said:

Dear brother,

You don't know how much I needed to hear from you. I wanted to write you many a time but I dug how much I must have hurt you and so I didn't write. But now I feel like a man who's been trying to climb up out of some deep, real deep and funky hole and just saw the sun up there, outside. I got to get outside.

I can't tell you much about how I got here. I mean I don't know how to tell you. I guess I was afraid of something or I was trying to escape from something and you know I have never been very strong in the head (smile). I'm glad Mama and Daddy are dead and can't see what's happened to their son and I swear if I'd known what I was doing I would never have hurt you so, you and a lot of other fine people who were nice to me and who believed in me.

I don't want you to think it had anything to do with me being a musician. It's more than that. Or maybe less than that. I can't get anything straight in my head down here and I try not to think about what's going to happen to me when I get outside again. Sometime I think I'm going to flip and *never* get outside and sometime I think I'll come straight back. I tell you one thing, though, I'd rather blow my brains out than go through this again. But that's what they all say, so they tell me. If I tell you when I'm coming to New York and if you could meet me, I sure would appreciate it. Give my love to Isabel and the kids and I was sure sorry to hear about little Gracie. I wish I could be like Mama and say the Lord's will be done, but I don't know it seems to me that trouble is the one thing that never does get stopped and I don't know what good it does to blame it on the Lord. But maybe it does some good if you believe it.

Your brother,
Sonny

Then I kept in constant touch with him and I sent him whatever I could and I went to meet him when he came back to New York. When I saw him many things I thought I had forgotten came flooding back to me. This was because I had begun, finally, to wonder about Sonny, about the life that Sonny lived inside. This life, whatever it was, had made him older and thinner and it had deepened the distant stillness in which he had always moved. He looked very unlike my baby brother. Yet, when he smiled, when we shook hands, the baby brother I'd never known looked out from the depths of his private life, like an animal waiting to be coaxed into the light.

"How you been keeping?" he asked me.

"All right. And you?"

"Just fine." He was smiling all over his face. "It's good to see you again."

"It's good to see you."

The seven years' difference in our ages lay between us like a chasm: I wondered if these years would ever operate between us as a bridge. I was remembering, and it made it hard to catch my breath, that I had been there when he was born; and I had heard the first words he had ever spoken. When he started to walk, he walked from our mother straight to me. I caught him just before he fell when he took the first steps he ever took in this world.

"How's Isabel?"

"Just fine. She's dying to see you."

"And the boys?"

"They're fine, too. They're anxious to see their uncle."

"Oh, come on. You know they don't remember me."

"Are you kidding? Of course they remember you."

He grinned again. We got into a taxi. We had a lot to say to each other, far too much to know how to begin.

As the taxi began to move, I asked, "You still want to go to India?"

He laughed. "You still remember that. Hell, no. This place is Indian enough for me."

"It used to belong to them," I said.

And he laughed again. "They damn sure knew what they were doing when they got rid of it."

Years ago, when he was around fourteen, he'd been all hipped on the idea of going to India. He read books about people sitting on rocks, naked, in all kinds of weather, but mostly bad, naturally, and walking barefoot through hot coals and arriving at wisdom. I used to say that it sounded to me as though they were getting away from wisdom as fast as they could. I think he sort of looked down on me for that.

"Do you mind," he asked, "if we have the driver drive alongside the park? On the west side— I haven't seen the city in so long."

"Of course not," I said. I was afraid that I might sound as though I were humoring him, but I hoped he wouldn't take it that way.

So we drove along, between the green of the park and the stony, lifeless elegance of hotels and apartment buildings, toward the vivid, killing streets of our childhood. These streets hadn't changed, though housing projects jutted up out of them now like rocks in the middle of a boiling sea. Most of the houses in which we had grown up had vanished, as had the stores from which we had stolen, the basements in which we had first tried sex, the rooftops from which we had hurled tin cans and bricks. But houses exactly like the houses of our past yet dominated the landscape, boys exactly like the boys we once had been found themselves smothering in these houses, came down into the streets for light and air, and found themselves encircled by disaster. Some escaped the trap, most didn't. Those who got out always left something of themselves behind, as some animals amputate a leg and leave it in the trap. It might be said, perhaps, that I had escaped, after all, I was a school teacher; or that Sonny had, he hadn't lived in Harlem for years. Yet, as the cab moved uptown through streets which seemed, with the rush, to darken with dark people, and as I covertly studied Sonny's face, it came to me that what we both were seeking through our separate cab windows was that part of ourselves which had been left behind. It's always at the hour of trouble and confrontation that the missing member aches.

We hit 110th Street and started rolling up Lenox Avenue. And I'd known this avenue all my life, but it seemed to me again, as it had seemed on the day I'd first heard about Sonny's trouble, filled with a hidden menace which was its very breath of life.

"We almost there," said Sonny.

"Almost." We were both too nervous to say anything more.

We live in a housing project. It hasn't been up long. A few days after it was up it seemed uninhabitably new, now, of course, it's already rundown. It looks like a parody of the good, clean, faceless life—God knows the people who live in it do their best to make it a parody. The beat-looking grass lying around isn't enough to make their lives green, the hedges will never hold out the streets, and they know it. The big windows fool no one, they aren't big enough to make space out of no space. They don't bother with the windows, they watch the TV screen instead. The playground is most popular with the children who don't play at jacks, or skip rope, or roller skate, or swing, and they can be found in it after dark. We moved in partly because it's not too far from where I teach, and partly for the kids; but it's really just like the houses in which Sonny and I grew up. The same things happen, they'll have the same things to remember. The moment Sonny and I started into the house I had the feeling that I was simply bringing him back into the danger he had almost died trying to escape.

Sonny has never been talkative. So I don't know why I was sure he'd be dying to talk to me when supper was over the first night. Everything went fine, the oldest boy remembered him, and the youngest boy liked him, and Sonny had remembered to bring something for each of them; and Isabel, who is really much nicer than I am, more open and giving, had gone to a lot of trouble about

dinner and was genuinely glad to see him. And she's always been able to tease Sonny in a way that I haven't. It was nice to see her face so vivid again and to hear her laugh and watch her make Sonny laugh. She wasn't, or, anyway, she didn't seem to be, at all uneasy or embarrassed. She chatted as though there were no subject which had to be avoided and she got Sonny past his first, faint stiffness. And thank God she was there, for I was filled with that icy dread again. Everything I did seemed awkward to me, and everything I said sounded freighted with hidden meaning. I was trying to remember everything I'd heard about dope addiction and I couldn't help watching Sonny for signs. I wasn't doing it out of malice. I was trying to find out something about my brother. I was dying to hear him tell me he was safe.

"Safe!" my father grunted, whenever Mama suggested trying to move to a neighborhood which might be safer for children. "Safe, hell! Ain't no place safe for kids, nor nobody."

He always went on like this, but he wasn't, ever, really as bad as he sounded, not even on weekends, when he got drunk. As a matter of fact, he was always on the lookout for "something a little better," but he died before he found it. He died suddenly, during a drunken weekend in the middle of the war, when Sonny was fifteen. He and Sonny hadn't ever got on too well. And this was partly because Sonny was the apple of his father's eye. It was because he loved Sonny so much and was frightened for him, that he was always fighting with him. It doesn't do any good to fight with Sonny. Sonny just moves back, inside himself, where he can't be reached. But the principal reason that they never hit it off is that they were so much alike. Daddy was big and rough and loud-talking, just the opposite of Sonny, but they both had—that same privacy.

Mama tried to tell me something about this, just after Daddy died. I was home on leave from the army.

This was the last time I ever saw my mother alive. Just the same, this picture gets all mixed up in my mind with pictures I had of her when she was younger. The way I always see her is the way she used to be on a Sunday afternoon, say, when the old folks were talking after the big Sunday dinner. I always see her wearing pale blue. She'd be sitting on the sofa. And my father would be sitting in the easy chair, not far from her. And the living room would be full of church folks and relatives. There they sit, in chairs all around the living room, and the night is creeping up outside, but nobody knows it yet. You can see the darkness growing against the window-panes and you hear the street noises every now and again, or maybe the jangling beat of a tambourine from one of the churches close by, but it's real quiet in the room. For a moment nobody's talking, but every face looks darkening, like the sky outside. And my mother rocks a little from the waist, and my father's eyes are closed. Everyone is looking at something a child can't see. For a minute they've forgotten the children. Maybe a kid is lying on the rug, half asleep. Maybe somebody's got a kid in his lap and is absent-mindedly stroking the kid's head. Maybe there's a kid, quiet and big-eyed, curled up in a big chair in the corner. The silence, the darkness coming, and the darkness in the faces frightens the child obscurely. He hopes that the hand which strokes his forehead will never stop—will never die. He hopes that there will never come a time when the old folks won't be sitting around the living room, talking about where they've come from, and what they've seen, and what's happened to them and their kinfolk.

But something deep and watchful in the child knows that this is bound to end, is already ending. In a moment someone will get up and turn on the light. Then the old folks will remember the children and they won't talk any more that day. And when light fills the room, the child is filled with darkness. He knows that every time this happens he's moved just a little closer to that darkness outside. The darkness outside is what the old folks have been talking about. It's what they've come from. It's what they endure. The child knows that they won't talk any more because if he knows too much about what's happened to *them*, he'll know too much too soon, about what's going to happen to *him*.

The last time I talked to my mother, I remember I was restless. I wanted to get out and see Isabel. We weren't married then and we had a lot to straighten out between us.

There Mama sat, in black, by the window. She was humming an old church song, *Lord you brought me from a long ways off*. Sonny was out somewhere. Mama kept watching the streets.

"I don't know," she said, "if I'll ever see you again, after you go off from here. But I hope you'll remember the things I tried to teach you."

"Don't talk like that," I said, and smiled. "You'll be here a long time yet."

She smiled, too, but she said nothing. She was quiet for a long time. And I said, "Mama, don't you worry about nothing. I'll be writing all the time, and you be getting the checks. . . ."

"I want to talk to you about your brother," she said, suddenly. "If anything happens to me he ain't going to have nobody to look out for him."

"Mama," I said, "ain't nothing going to happen to you *or* Sonny. Sonny's all right. He's a good boy and he's got good sense."

"It ain't a question of his being a good boy," Mama said, "nor of his having good sense. It ain't only the bad ones, nor yet the dumb ones that gets sucked under." She stopped, looking at me. "Your Daddy once had a brother," she said, and she smiled in a way that made me feel she was in pain. "You didn't never know that, did you?"

"No," I said, "I never knew that," and I watched her face.

"Oh, yes," she said, "your Daddy had a brother." She looked out of the window again. "I know you never saw your Daddy cry. But *I* did—many a time, through all these years."

I asked her, "What happened to his brother? How come nobody's ever talked about him?"

This was the first time I ever saw my mother look old.

"His brother got killed," she said, "when he was just a little younger than you are now. I knew him. He was a fine boy. He was maybe a little full of the devil, but he didn't mean nobody no harm."

Then she stopped and the room was silent, exactly as it had sometimes been on those Sunday afternoons. Mama kept looking out into the streets.

"He used to have a job in the mill," she said, "and, like all young folks, he just liked to perform on Saturday nights. Saturday nights, him and your father would drift around to different places, go to dances and things like that, or just sit around with people they knew, and your father's brother would sing, he had a fine voice, and play along with himself on his guitar. Well, this particular Saturday night, him and your father was coming home from some place, and they were both a little drunk and there was a moon that night, it was bright like day. Your father's brother was feeling kind of good, and he was whistling to himself, and he had his guitar slung over his shoulder. They was coming down a hill and beneath them was a road that turned off from the highway. Well, your father's brother, being always kind of frisky, decided to run down this hill, and he did, with that guitar banging and clanging behind him,

and he ran across the road, and he was making water behind a tree. And your father was sort of amused at him and he was still coming down the hill, kind of slow. Then he heard a car motor and that same minute his brother stepped from behind the tree, into the road, in the moonlight. And he started to cross the road. And your father started to run down the hill, he says he don't know why. This car was full of white men. They was all drunk, and when they seen your father's brother they let out a great whoop and holler and they aimed the car straight at him. They was having fun, they just wanted to scare him, the way they do sometimes, you know. But they was drunk. And I guess the boy, being drunk, too, and scared, kind of lost his head. By the time he jumped it was too late. Your father says he heard his brother scream when the car rolled over him, and he heard the wood of that guitar when it give, and he heard them strings go flying, and he heard them white men shouting, and the car kept on a-going and it ain't stopped till this day. And, time your father got down the hill, his brother weren't nothing but blood and pulp."

Tears were gleaming on my mother's face. There wasn't anything I could say.

"He never mentioned it," she said, "because I never let him mention it before you children. Your Daddy was like a crazy man that night and for many a night thereafter. He says he never in his life seen anything as dark as the road after the lights of that car had gone away. Weren't nothing, weren't nobody on that road, just your Daddy and his brother and that busted guitar. Oh, yes. Your Daddy never did really get right again. Till the day he died he weren't sure but that every white man he saw was the man that killed his brother."

She stopped and took out her handkerchief and dried her eyes and looked at me.

"I ain't telling you all this," she said, "to make you scared or bitter or to make you hate nobody. I'm telling you this because you got a brother. And the world ain't changed."

I guess I didn't want to believe this. I guess she saw this in my face. She turned away from me, toward the window again, searching those streets.

"But I praise my Redeemer," she said at last, "that He called your Daddy home before me. I ain't saying it to throw no flowers at myself, but, I declare, it keeps me from feeling too cast down to know I helped your father get safely through this world. Your father always acted like he was the roughest, strongest man on earth. And everybody took him to be like that. But if he hadn't had *me* there—to see his tears!"

She was crying again. Still, I couldn't move. I said, "Lord, Lord, Mama, I didn't know it was like that."

"Oh, honey," she said, "there's a lot that you don't know. But you are going to find it out." She stood up from the window and came over to me. "You got to hold on to your brother," she said, "and don't let him fall, no matter what it looks like is happening to him and no matter how evil you gets with him. You going to be evil with him many a time. But don't you forget what I told you, you hear?"

"I won't forget," I said. "Don't you worry, I won't forget. I won't let nothing happen to Sonny."

My mother smiled as though she were amused at something she saw in my face. Then, "You may not be able to stop nothing from happening. But you got to let him know you's *there*."

Two days later I was married, and then I was gone. And I had a lot of things on my mind and I pretty well forgot my promise to Mama until I got shipped home on a special furlough for her funeral.

And, after the funeral, with just Sonny and me alone in the empty kitchen, I tried to find out something about him.

"What do you want to do?" I asked him.

"I'm going to be a musician," he said.

For he had graduated, in the time I had been away, from dancing to the juke box to finding out who was playing what, and what they were doing with it, and he had bought himself a set of drums.

"You mean, you want to be a drummer?" I somehow had the feeling that being a drummer might be all right for other people but not for my brother Sonny.

"I don't think," he said, looking at me very gravely, "that I'll ever be a good drummer. But I think I can play a piano."

I frowned. I'd never played the role of the older brother quite so seriously before, had scarcely ever, in fact, *asked* Sonny a damn thing. I sensed myself in the presence of something I didn't really know how to handle, didn't understand. So I made my frown a little deeper as I asked: "What kind of musician do you want to be?"

He grinned. "How many kinds do you think there are?"

"Be *serious*," I said.

He laughed, throwing his head back, and then looked at me. "I *am* serious."

"Well, then, for Christ's sake, stop kidding around and answer a serious question. I mean, do you want to be a concert pianist, you want to play classical music and all that, or—or what?" Long before I finished he was laughing again. "For Christ's *sake*, Sonny!"

He sobered, but with difficulty. "I'm sorry. But you sound so—*scared!*" and he was off again.

"Well, you may think it's funny now, baby, but it's not going to be so funny when you have to make your living at it, let me tell you *that*." I was furious because I knew he was laughing at me and I didn't know why.

"No," he said, very sober now, and afraid, perhaps, that he'd hurt me, "I don't want to be a classical pianist. That isn't what interests me. I mean"—he paused, looking hard at me, as though his eyes would help me to understand, and then gestured helplessly, as though perhaps his hand would help—"I mean, I'll have a lot of studying to do, and I'll have to study *everything*, but, I mean, I want to play *with*—jazz musicians." He stopped. "I want to play jazz," he said.

Well, the word had never before sounded as heavy, as real, as it sounded that afternoon in Sonny's mouth. I just looked at him and I was probably frowning a real frown by this time. I simply couldn't see why on earth he'd want to spend his time hanging around nightclubs, clowning around on bandstands, while people pushed each other around a dance floor. It seemed—beneath him, somehow. I had never thought about it before, had never been forced to, but I suppose I had always put jazz musicians in a class with what Daddy called "good-time people."

"Are you *serious*?"

"Hell, *yes*, I'm serious."

He looked more helpless than ever, and annoyed, and deeply hurt.

I suggested, helpfully: "You mean—like Louis Armstrong?"

His face closed as though I'd struck him. "No. I'm not talking about none of that old-time, down home crap."

"Well, look, Sonny, I'm sorry, don't get mad. I just don't altogether get it, that's all. Name somebody—you know, a jazz musician you admire."

"Bird."

"Who?"

"Bird! Charlie Parker! Don't they teach you nothing in the goddamn army?"

I lit a cigarette. I was surprised and then a little amused to discover that I was trembling. "I've been out of touch," I said. "You'll have to be patient with me. Now, Who's this Parker character?"

"He's just one of the greatest jazz musicians alive," said Sonny, sullenly, his hands in his pockets, his back to me. "Maybe *the* greatest," he added, bitterly, "that's probably why *you* never heard of him."

"All right," I said, "I'm ignorant. I'm sorry. I'll go out and buy all the cat's records right away, all right?"

"It don't," said Sonny, with dignity, "make any difference to me. I don't care what you listen to. Don't do me no favors."

I was beginning to realize that I'd never seen him so upset before. With another part of my mind I was thinking that this would probably turn out to be one of those things kids go through and that I shouldn't make it seem important by pushing it too hard. Still, I didn't think it would do any harm to ask: "Doesn't all this take a lot of time? Can you make a living at it?"

He turned back to me and half leaned, half sat, on the kitchen table. "Everything takes time," he said, "and—well, yes, sure, I can make a living at it. But what I don't seem to be able to make you understand is that it's the only thing I want to do."

"Well, Sonny," I said, gently, "you know people can't always do exactly what they *want* to do—"

"*No*, I don't know that," said Sonny, surprising me. "I think people *ought* to do what they want to do, what else are they alive for?"

"You getting to be a big boy," I said desperately, "it's time you started thinking about your future."

"I'm thinking about my future," said Sonny, grimly. "I think about it all the time."

I gave up. I decided, if he didn't change his mind, that we could always talk about it later. "In the meantime," I said, "you got to finish school." We had already decided that he'd have to move in with Isabel and her folks. I knew this wasn't the ideal arrangement because Isabel's folks are inclined to be dicty and they hadn't especially wanted Isabel to marry me. But I didn't know what else to do. "And we have to get you fixed up at Isabel's."

There was a long silence. He moved from the kitchen table to the window. "That's a terrible idea. You know it yourself."

"Do you have a *better* idea?"

He just walked up and down the kitchen for a minute. He was as tall as I was. He had started to shave. I suddenly had the feeling that I didn't know him at all.

He stopped at the kitchen table and picked up my cigarettes. Looking at me with a kind of mocking, amused defiance, he put one between his lips. "You mind?"

"You smoking already?"

He lit the cigarette and nodded, watching me through the smoke. "I just wanted to see if I'd have the courage to smoke in front of you." He grinned and blew a great cloud of smoke to the ceiling. "It was easy." He looked at my face. "Come on, now. I bet you was smoking at my age, tell the truth."

I didn't say anything but the truth was on my face, and he laughed. But now there was something very strained in his laugh. "Sure. And I bet that ain't all you was doing."

He was frightening me a little. "Cut the crap," I said. "We already decided that you was going to go and live at Isabel's. Now what's got into you all of a sudden?"

"*You* decided it," he pointed out. "*I* didn't decide nothing." He stopped in front of me, leaning against the stove, arms loosely folded. "Look, brother, I don't want to stay in Harlem no more, I really don't." He was very earnest. He looked at me, then over toward the kitchen window. There was something in his eyes I'd never seen before, some thoughtfulness, some worry all his own. He rubbed the muscle of one arm. "It's time I was getting out of here."

"Where do you want to *go*, Sonny?"

"I want to join the army. Or the navy, I don't care. If I say I'm old enough, they'll believe me."

Then I got mad. It was because I was so scared. "You must be crazy. You goddamn fool, what the hell do you want to go and join the *army* for?"

"I just told you. To get out of Harlem."

"Sonny, you haven't even finished *school*. And if you really want to be a musician, how do you expect to study if you're in the *army*?"

He looked at me, trapped, and in anguish. "There's ways. I might be able to work out some kind of deal. Anyway, I'll have the G.I. Bill when I come out."

"*If* you come out." We stared at each other. "Sonny, please. Be reasonable. I know the setup is far from perfect. But we got to do the best we can."

"I ain't learning nothing in school," he said. "Even when I go." He turned away from me and opened the window and threw his cigarette out into the narrow alley. I watched his back. "At least, I ain't learning nothing you'd want me to learn." He slammed the window so hard I thought the glass would fly out, and turned back to me. "And I'm sick of the stink of these garbage cans!"

"Sonny," I said, "I know how you feel. But if you don't finish school now, you're going to be sorry later that you didn't." I grabbed him by the shoulders. "And you only got another year. It ain't so bad. And I'll come back and I swear I'll help you do *whatever* you want to do. Just try to put up with it till I come back. Will you please do that? For me?"

He didn't answer and he wouldn't look at me.

"Sonny. You hear me?"

He pulled away. "I hear you. But you never hear anything *I* say."

I didn't know what to say to that. He looked out of the window and then back at me. "OK," he said, and sighed. "I'll try."

Then I said, trying to cheer him up a little, "They got a piano at Isabel's. You can practice on it."

And as a matter of fact, it did cheer him up for a minute. "That's right," he said to himself. "I forgot that." His face relaxed a little. But the worry, the thoughtfulness, played on it still, the way shadows play on a face which is staring into the fire.

But I thought I'd never hear the end of that piano. At first, Isabel would write me, saying how nice it was that Sonny was so serious about his music and how, as soon as he came in from school, or wherever he had been when he was supposed to be at school, he went straight to that piano and stayed there until suppertime. And, after supper, he went back to that piano and stayed there until everybody went to bed. He was at the piano all day Saturday and all day Sunday. Then he bought a record player and started playing records. He'd play one record over and over again, all day long sometimes, and he'd improvise along with it on the piano. Or he'd play one section of the record, one chord, one change, one progression, then he'd do it on the piano. Then back to the record. Then back to the piano.

Well, I really don't know how they stood it. Isabel finally confessed that it wasn't like living with a person at all, it was like living with sound. And the sound didn't make any sense to her, didn't make any sense to any of them—naturally. They began, in a way, to be afflicted by this presence that was living in their home. It was as though Sonny were some sort of god, or monster. He moved in an atmosphere which wasn't like theirs at all. They fed him and he ate, he washed himself, he walked in and out of their door; he certainly wasn't nasty or unpleasant or rude, Sonny isn't any of those things; but it was as though he were all wrapped up in some cloud, some fire, some vision all his own; and there wasn't any way to reach him.

At the same time, he wasn't really a man yet, he was still a child, and they had to watch out for him in all kinds of ways. They certainly couldn't throw him out. Neither did they dare to make a great scene about that piano because even they dimly sensed, as I sensed, from so many thousands of miles away, that Sonny was at that piano playing for his life.

But he hadn't been going to school. One day a letter came from the school board and Isabel's mother got it—there had, apparently, been other letters but Sonny had torn them up. This day, when Sonny came in, Isabel's mother showed him the letter and asked where he'd been spending his time. And she finally got it out of him that he'd been down in Greenwich Village, with musicians and other characters, in a white girl's apartment. And this scared her and she started to scream at him and what came up, once she began—though she denies it to this day—was what sacrifices they were making to give Sonny a decent home and how little he appreciated it.

Sonny didn't play the piano that day. By evening, Isabel's mother had calmed down but then there was the old man to deal with, and Isabel herself. Isabel says she did her best to be calm but she broke down and started crying. She says she just watched Sonny's face. She could tell, by watching him, what was happening with him. And what was happening was that they penetrated his cloud, they had reached him. Even if their fingers had been a thousand times more gentle than human fingers ever are, he could hardly help feeling that they had stripped him naked and were spitting on that nakedness. For he also had to see that his presence, that music, which was life or death to him, had been torture for them and that they had endured it, not at all for his sake, but only for mine. And Sonny couldn't take that. He can take it a little better today than he could then but he's still not very good at it and, frankly, I don't know anybody who is.

The silence of the next few days must have been louder than the sound of all the music ever played since time began. One morning, before she went to work, Isabel was in his room for something and she suddenly realized that all of his records were gone. And she knew for certain that he was gone. And he was. He went as far as the navy would carry him. He finally sent me a post-card from some place in Greece and that was the first I knew that Sonny was still alive. I didn't see him any more until we were both back in New York and the war had long been over.

He was a man by then, of course, but I wasn't willing to see it. He came by the house from time to time, but we fought almost every time we met. I didn't like the way he carried himself, loose and dreamlike all the time, and I didn't like his friends, and his music seemed to be merely an excuse for the life he led. It sounded just that weird and disordered.

Then we had a fight, a pretty awful fight, and I didn't see him for months. By and by I looked him up, where he was living, in a furnished room in the Village, and I tried to make it up. But there were lots of other people in the room and Sonny just lay on his bed and he wouldn't come downstairs with me, and he treated these other people as though they were his family and I weren't. So I got mad and then he got mad, and then I told him that he might just as well be dead as live the way he was living. Then he stood up and he told me not to worry about him any more in life, that he *was* dead as far as I was concerned. Then he pushed me to the door and the other people looked on as though nothing were happening, and he slammed the door behind me. I stood in the hallway, staring at the door. I heard some-body laugh in the room and then the tears came to my eyes. I started down the steps, whistling to keep from crying. I kept whis-tling to myself. *You going to need me, baby, one of these cold, rainy days.*

I read about Sonny's trouble in the spring. Little Grace died in the fall. She was a beau-tiful little girl. But she only lived a little over two years. She died of polio and she suffered. She had a slight fever for a couple of days, but it didn't seem like anything and we just kept her in bed. And we would certainly have called the doctor, but the fever drop-ped, she seemed to be all right. So we thought it had just been a cold. Then, one day, she was up, playing, Isabel was in the kitchen fixing lunch for the two boys when they'd come in from school, and she heard Grace fall down in the living room. When you have a lot of children you don't always start run-ning when one of them falls, unless they start screaming or something. And, this time, Grace was quiet. Yet, Isabel says that when she heard that *thump* and then that silence, something happened in her to make her afraid. And she ran to the living room and there was little Grace on the floor, all twisted up, and the reason she hadn't screamed was that she couldn't get her breath. And when she did scream, it was the worst sound, Isabel says, that she'd ever heard in all her life, and she still hears it sometimes in her dreams. Isabel will sometimes wake me up with a low, moaning, strangled sound and I have to be quick to awaken her and hold her to me and where Isabel is weeping against me seems a mortal wound.

I think I may have written Sonny the very day that little Grace was buried. I was sitting in the living room in the dark, by myself, and I suddenly thought of Sonny. My trouble made his real.

One Saturday afternoon, when Sonny had been living with us, or, anyway, been in our house, for nearly two weeks, I found myself wandering aimlessly about the living room, drinking from a can of beer, and trying to work up the courage to search Sonny's room. He was out, he was usually out whenever I was home, and Isabel had taken the children to see their grandparents. Suddenly I was standing still in front of the living-room window, watching Seventh Avenue. The idea of searching Sonny's room made me still. I scarcely dared to admit to myself what I'd be searching for. I didn't know what I'd do if I found it. Or if I didn't.

On the sidewalk across from me, near the entrance to a barbecue joint, some people were holding an old-fashioned revival meeting. The barbecue cook, wearing a dirty white apron, his conked hair reddish and metallic in the pale sun, and a cigarette between his lips, stood in the doorway, watching them. Kids and older people paused in their errands and stood there, along with some older men and a couple of very tough-looking women who watched everything that happened on the avenue, as though they owned it, or were maybe owned by it. Well, they were watching this, too. The revival was being carried on by three sisters in black, and a brother. All they had were their voices and their Bibles and a tambourine. The brother was testifying and while he testified two of the sisters stood together, seeming to say, amen, and the third sister walked around with the tambourine outstretched and a couple of people dropped coins into it. Then the brother's testimony ended and the sister who had been taking up the collection dumped the coins into her palm and transferred them to the pocket of her long black robe. Then she raised both hands, striking the tambourine against the air, and then against one hand, and she started to sing. And the two other sisters and the brother joined in.

It was strange, suddenly, to watch, though I had been seeing these street meetings all my life. So, of course, had everybody else down there. Yet, they paused and watched and listened and I stood still at the window. *"'Tis the old ship of Zion,"* they sang, and the sister with the tambourine kept a steady, jangling beat, *"it has rescued many a thousand!"* Not a soul under the sound of their voices was hearing this song for the first time, not one of them had been rescued. Nor had they seen much in the way of rescue work being done around them. Neither did they

especially believe in the holiness of the three sisters and the brother, they knew too much about them, knew where they lived, and how. The woman with the tambourine, whose voice dominated the air, whose face was bright with joy, was divided by very little from the woman who stood watching her, a cigarette between her heavy, chapped lips, her hair a cuckoo's nest, her face scarred and swollen from many beatings, and her black eyes glittering like coal. Perhaps they both knew this, which was why, when, as rarely, they addressed each other, they addressed each other as Sister. As the singing filled the air the watching, listening faces underwent a change, the eyes focusing on something within; the music seemed to soothe a poison out of them; and time seemed, nearly, to fall away from the sullen, belligerent, battered faces, as though they were fleeing back to their first condition, while dreaming of their last. The barbecue cook half shook his head and smiled, and dropped his cigarette and disappeared into his joint. A man fumbled in his pockets for change and stood holding it in his hand impatiently, as though he had just remembered a pressing appointment further up the avenue. He looked furious. Then I saw Sonny, standing on the edge of the crowd. He was carrying a wide, flat notebook with a green cover, and it made him look, from where I was standing, almost like a schoolboy. The coppery sun brought out the copper in his skin, he was very faintly smiling, standing very still. Then the singing stopped, the tambourine turned into a collection plate again. The furious man dropped in his coins and vanished, so did a couple of the women, and Sonny dropped some change in the plate, looking directly at the woman with a little smile. He started across the avenue, toward the house. He has a slow, loping walk, something like the way Harlem hipsters walk, only he's imposed on this his own half-beat. I had never really noticed it before.

I stayed at the window, both relieved and apprehensive. As Sonny disappeared from my sight, they began singing again. And they were still singing when his key turned in the lock.

"Hey," he said.

"Hey, yourself. You want some beer?"

"No. Well, maybe." But he came up to the window and stood beside me, looking out. "What a warm voice," he said.

They were singing *If I could only hear my mother pray again!*

"Yes," I said, "and she can sure beat that tambourine."

"But what a terrible song," he said, and laughed. He dropped his notebook on the sofa and disappeared into the kitchen. "Where's Isabel and the kids?"

"I think they went to see their grandparents. You hungry?"

"No." He came back into the living room with his can of beer. "You want to come some place with me tonight?"

I sensed, I don't know how, that I couldn't possibly say no. "Sure. Where?"

He sat down on the sofa and picked up his notebook and started leafing through it. "I'm going to sit in with some fellows in a joint in the Village."

"You mean, you're going to play, tonight?"

"That's right." He took a swallow of his beer and moved back to the window. He gave me a sidelong look. "If you can stand it."

"I'll try," I said.

He smiled to himself and we both watched as the meeting across the way broke up. The three sisters and the brother, heads bowed, were singing *God be with you till we meet again*. The faces around them were very quiet. Then the song ended. The small crowd dispersed. We watched the three women and the lone man walk slowly up the avenue.

"When she was singing before," said Sonny, abruptly, "her voice reminded me for a minute of what heroin feels like sometimes —when it's in your veins. It makes you feel sort of warm and cool at the same time. And distant. And—and sure." He sipped his beer, very deliberately not looking at me. I watched his face. "It makes you feel—in control. Sometimes you've got to have that feeling."

"Do you?" I sat down slowly in the easy chair.

"Sometimes." He went to the sofa and picked up his notebook again. "Some people do."

"In order," I asked, "to play?" And my voice was very ugly, full of contempt and anger.

"Well"—he looked at me with great, troubled eyes, as though, in fact, he hoped his eyes would tell me things he could never otherwise say—"they *think* so. And *if* they think so—!"

"And what do *you* think?" I asked.

He sat on the sofa and put his can of beer on the floor. "I don't know," he said, and I couldn't be sure if he were answering my question or pursuing his thoughts. His face didn't tell me. "It's not so much to *play*. It's to *stand* it, to be able to make it at all. On any level." He frowned and smiled: "In order to keep from shaking to pieces."

"But these friends of yours," I said, "they seem to shake themselves to pieces pretty goddamn fast."

"Maybe." He played with the notebook. And something told me that I should curb my tongue, that Sonny was doing his best to talk, that I should listen. "But of course you only know the ones that've gone to pieces. Some don't—or at least they haven't *yet* and that's just about all *any* of us can say." He paused. "And then there are some who just live, really, in hell, and they know it and they see what's happening and they go right on. I don't know." He sighed, dropped the notebook, folded his arms. "Some guys, you can tell from the way they play, they on something *all* the time. And you can see that, well, it makes something real for them. But of course," he picked up his beer from the floor and sipped it and put the can down again, "they *want* to, too, you've got to see that. Even some of them that say they don't —*some*, not all."

"And what about you?" I asked—I couldn't help it. "What about you? Do *you* want to?"

He stood up and walked to the window and remained silent for a long time. Then he sighed. "Me," he said. Then: "While I was downstairs before, on my way here, listening to that woman sing, it struck me all of a sudden how much suffering she must have had to go through—to sing like that. It's *repulsive* to think you have to suffer that much."

I said: "But there's no way not to suffer— is there, Sonny?"

"I believe not," he said and smiled, "but that's never stopped anyone from trying." He looked at me. "Has it?" I realized, with this mocking look, that there stood between us, forever, beyond the power of time or forgiveness, the fact that I had held silence—so long!—when he had needed human speech to help him. He turned back to the window. "No, there's no way not to suffer. But you try all kinds of ways to keep from drowning in it, to keep on top of it, and to make it seem—well, like *you*. Like you did something, all right, and now you're suffering for it. You know?" I said nothing. "Well you know," he said, impatiently, "why *do* people suffer? Maybe it's better to do something to give it a reason, *any* reason."

"But we just agreed," I said, "that there's no way not to suffer. Isn't it better, then, just to—take it?"

"But nobody just takes it," Sonny cried, "that's what I'm telling you! *Everybody* tries not to. You're just hung up on the *way* some people try—it's not *your* way!"

The hair on my face began to itch, my face felt wet. "That's not true," I said, "that's not true. I don't give a damn what other people

do, I don't even care how they suffer. I just care how *you* suffer." And he looked at me. "Please believe me," I said, "I don't want to see you—die—trying not to suffer."

"I won't," he said, flatly, "die trying not to suffer. At least, not any faster than anybody else."

"But there's no need," I said, trying to laugh, "is there? in killing yourself."

I wanted to say more, but I couldn't. I wanted to talk about will power and how life could be—well, beautiful. I wanted to say that it was all within; but was it? or, rather, wasn't that exactly the trouble? And I wanted to promise that I would never fail him again. But it would all have sounded— empty words and lies.

So I made the promise to myself and prayed that I would keep it.

"It's terrible sometimes, inside," he said, "that's what's the trouble. You walk these streets, black and funky and cold, and there's not really a living ass to talk to, and there's nothing shaking, and there's no way of getting it out—that storm inside. You can't talk it and you can't make love with it, and when you finally try to get with it and play it, you realize *nobody's* listening. So *you're* got to listen. You got to find a way to listen."

And then he walked away from the window and sat on the sofa again, as though all the wind had suddenly been knocked out of him. "Sometimes you'll do *anything* to play, even cut your mother's throat." He laughed and looked at me. "Or your brother's." Then he sobered. "Or your own." Then: "Don't worry. I'm all right now and I think I'll *be* all right. But I can't forget—where I've been. I don't mean just the physical place I've been, I mean where I've *been*. And *what* I've been."

"What have you been, Sonny?" I asked.

He smiled—but sat sideways on the sofa, his elbow resting on the back, his fingers playing with his mouth and chin, not looking at me. "I've been something I didn't recognize, didn't know I could be. Didn't know anybody could be." He stopped, looking inward, looking helplessly young, looking old. "I'm not talking about it now because I feel *guilty* or anything like that—maybe it would be better if I did, I don't know. Anyway, I can't really talk about it. Not to you, not to anybody," and now he turned and faced me. "Sometimes, you know, and it was actually when I was most *out* of the world, I felt that I was in it, that I was *with* it, really, and I could play or I didn't really have to *play*, it just came out of me, it was there. And I don't know how I played, thinking about it now, but I know I did awful things, those times, sometimes, to people. Or it wasn't that I *did* anything to them—it was that they weren't real." He picked up the beer can; it was empty; he rolled it between his palms: "And other times—well, I needed a fix, I needed to find a place to lean, I needed to clear a space to *listen*—and I couldn't find it, and I—went crazy, I did terrible things to *me*, I was terrible *for* me." He began pressing the beer can between his hands, I watched the metal begin to give. It glittered, as he played with it, like a knife, and I was afraid he would cut himself, but I said nothing. "Oh well. I can never tell you. I was all by myself at the bottom of something, stinking and sweating and crying and shaking, and I smelled it, you know? *my* stink, and I thought I'd die if I couldn't get away from it and yet, all the same, I knew that everything I was doing was just locking me in with it. And I didn't know," he paused, still flattening the beer can, "I didn't know, I still *don't* know, something kept telling me that maybe it was good to smell your own stink, but I didn't think that *that* was what I'd been trying to do—and—who can stand it?" and he abruptly dropped the ruined beer can, looking at me with a small, still smile, and then rose, walking to the window as though it were the lodestone rock. I watched his face, he watched the avenue. "I couldn't tell you when Mama died—but the reason I wanted to leave Harlem so bad was to get away from drugs. And then, when I ran away, that's what I was running from—really. When I came back, nothing had changed, *I* hadn't changed, I was just—older." And he stopped, drumming with his fingers on the windowpane. The sun had vanished, soon darkness would fall. I watched his face. "It can come again," he said, almost as though speaking to himself. Then he turned to me. "It can come again," he repeated. "I just want you to know that.

"All right," I said, at last. "So it can come again. All right."

He smiled, but the smile was sorrowful. "I had to try to tell you," he said.

"Yes," I said. "I understand that."

"You're my brother," he said, looking straight at me, and not smiling at all.

"Yes," I repeated, "yes. I understand that."

He turned back to the window, looking out. "All that hatred down there," he said, "all that hatred and misery and love. It's a wonder it doesn't blow the avenue apart."

We went to the only nightclub on a short, dark street, downtown. We squeezed through the narrow, chattering, jam-packed bar to the entrance of the big room, where the bandstand was. And we stood there for a moment, for the lights were very dim in this room and we couldn't see. Then, "Hello, boy," said a voice and an enormous black man, much older than Sonny or myself, erupted out of all that atmospheric lighting and put an arm around Sonny's shoulder. "I been sitting right here," he said, "waiting for you."

He had a big voice, too, and heads in the darkness turned toward us.

Sonny grinned and pulled a little away, and said, "Creole, this is my brother. I told you about him."

Creole shook my hand. "I'm glad to meet you, son," he said, and it was clear that he was glad to meet me *there*, for Sonny's sake. And he smiled, "You got a real musician in *your* family," and he took his arm from Sonny's shoulder and slapped him, lightly, affectionately, with the back of his hand.

"Well. Now I've heard it all," said a voice behind us. This was another musician, and a friend of Sonny's, a coal-black, cheerful-looking man, built close to the ground. He immediately began confiding to me, at the top of his lungs, the most terrible things about Sonny, his teeth gleaming like a lighthouse and his laugh coming up out of him like the beginning of an earthquake. And it turned out that everyone at the bar knew Sonny, or almost everyone; some were musicians, working there, or nearby, or not working, some were simply hangers-on, and some were there to hear Sonny play. I was introduced to all of them and they were all very polite to me. Yet, it was clear that, for them, I was only Sonny's brother. Here, I was in Sonny's world. Or, rather: his kingdom. Here, it was not even a question that his veins bore royal blood.

They were going to play soon and Creole installed me, by myself, at a table in a dark corner. Then I watched them, Creole, and the little black man, and Sonny, and the others, while they horsed around, standing just below the bandstand. The light from the bandstand spilled just a little short of them and, watching them laughing and gesturing and moving about, I had the feeling that they, nevertheless, were being most careful not to step into that circle of light too suddenly: that if they moved into the light too suddenly, without thinking, they would perish in flame. Then, while I watched, one of them, the small, black man, moved into the light and crossed the bandstand and started fooling around with his drums. Then—being funny and being, also, extremely ceremonious—Creole took Sonny by the arm and led him to the piano. A woman's voice called Sonny's name and a few hands started clapping. And Sonny, also being funny and being ceremonious, and so touched, I think that he could have cried,

but neither hiding it nor showing it, riding it like a man, grinned, and put both hands to his heart and bowed from the waist.

Creole then went to the bass fiddle and a lean, very bright-skinned brown man jumped upon the bandstand and picked up his horn. So there they were, and the atmosphere on the bandstand and in the room began to change and tighten. Someone stepped up to the microphone and announced them. Then there were all kinds of murmurs. Some people at the bar shushed others. The waitress ran around, frantically getting in the last orders, guys and chicks got closer to each other, and the lights on the bandstand, on the quartet, turned to a kind of indigo. Then they all looked different there. Creole looked about him for the last time, as though he were making certain that all his chickens were in the coop, and then he—jumped and struck the fiddle. And there they were.

All I know about music is that not many people ever really hear it. And even then, on the rare occasions when something opens within, and the music enters, what we mainly hear, or hear corroborated, are personal, private, vanishing evocations. But the man who creates the music is hearing something else, is dealing with the roar rising from the void and imposing order on it as it hits the air. What is evoked in him, then, is of another order, more terrible because it has no words, and triumphant, too, for that same reason. And his triumph, when he triumphs, is ours. I just watched Sonny's face. His face was troubled, he was working hard, but he wasn't with it. And I had the feeling that, in a way, everyone on the bandstand was waiting for him, both waiting for him and pushing him along. But as I began to watch Creole, I realized that it was Creole who held them all back. He had them on a short rein. Up there, keeping the beat with his whole body, wailing on the fiddle, with his eyes half closed, he was listening to everything, but he was listening to Sonny. He was having a dialogue with Sonny. He wanted Sonny to leave the shoreline and strike out for the deep water. He was Sonny's witness that deep water and drowning were not the same thing—he had been there, and he knew. And he wanted Sonny to know. He was waiting for Sonny to do the things on the keys which would let Creole know that Sonny was in the water.

And, while Creole listened, Sonny moved, deep within, exactly like someone in torment. I had never before thought of how awful the relationship must be between the musician and his instrument. He has to fill it, this instrument, with the breath of life, his own. He has to make it do what he wants it to do. And a piano is just a piano. It's made out of so much wood and wires and little hammers and big ones, and ivory. While there's only so much you can do with it, the only way to find this out is to try; to try and make it do everything.

And Sonny hadn't been near a piano for over a year. And he wasn't on much better terms with his life, not the life that stretched before him now. He and the piano stammered, started one way, got scared, stopped; started another way, panicked, marked time, started again; then seemed to have found a direction, panicked again, got stuck. And the face I saw on Sonny I'd never seen before. Everything had been burned out of it, and, at the same time, things usually hidden were being burned in, by the fire and fury of the battle which was occurring in him up there.

Yet, watching Creole's face as they neared the end of the first set, I had the feeling that something had happened, something I hadn't heard. Then they finished, there was scattered applause, and then, without an instant's warning, Creole started into something else, it was almost sardonic, it was *Am I Blue*. And, as though he commanded, Sonny began to play. Something began to happen. And Creole let out the reins. The dry, low, black man said something awful on the drums, Creole answered, and the drums talked back. Then the horn insisted, sweet and high, slightly detached perhaps, and Creole listened, commenting now and then, dry, and driving, beautiful and calm, and old. Then they all came together again, and Sonny was part of the family again. I could tell this from his face. He seemed to have found, right there beneath his fingers, a damn brand-new piano. It seemed that he couldn't get over it. Then, for awhile, just being happy with Sonny, they seemed to be agreeing with him that brand-new pianos certainly were a gas.

Then Creole stepped forward to remind them that what they were playing was the blues. He hit something in all of them, he hit something in me, myself, and the music tightened and deepened, apprehension began to beat the air. Creole began to tell us what the blues were all about. They were not about anything very new. He and his boys up there were keeping it new, at the risk of ruin, destruction, madness, and death, in order to find new ways to make us listen. For, while the tale of how we suffer, and how we are delighted, and how we may triumph is never new, it always must be heard. There isn't any other tale to tell, it's the only light we've got in all this darkness.

And this tale, according to the face, that body, those strong hands on those strings, has another aspect in every country, and a new depth in every generation. Listen, Creole seemed to be saying, listen. Now these are Sonny's blues. He made the little black man on the drums know it, and the bright, brown man on the horn. Creole wasn't trying any longer to get Sonny in the water. He was wishing him Godspeed. Then he stepped back, very slowly, filling the air with the immense suggestion that Sonny speak for himself.

Then they all gathered around Sonny and Sonny played. Every now and again one of them seemed to say, amen. Sonny's fingers filled the air with life, his life. But that life contained so many others. And Sonny went all the way back, he really began with the spare, flat statement of the opening phrase of the song. Then he began to make it his. It was very beautiful because it wasn't hurried and it was no longer a lament. I seemed to hear with what burning he had made it his, with what burning we had yet to make it ours, how we could cease lamenting. Freedom lurked around us and I understood, at last, that he could help us to be free if we would listen, that he would never be free until we did. Yet, there was no battle in his face now. I heard what he had gone through, and would continue to go through until he came to rest in earth. He had made it his: that long line, of which we knew only Mama and Daddy. And he was giving it back, as everything must be given back, so that, passing through death, it can live forever. I saw my mother's face again, and felt, for the first time, how the stones of the road she had walked on must have bruised her feet. I saw the moonlit road where my father's brother died. And it brought something else back to me, and carried me past it. I saw my little girl again and felt Isabel's tears again, and I felt my own tears begin to rise. And I was yet aware that this was only a moment, that the world waited outside, as hungry as a tiger, and that trouble stretched above us, longer than the sky.

Then it was over. Creole and Sonny let out their breath, both soaking wet, and grinning. There was a lot of applause and some of it was real. In the dark, the girl came by and I asked her to take drinks to the bandstand. There was a long pause, while they talked up there in the indigo light and after awhile I saw the girl put a Scotch and milk on top of the piano for Sonny. He didn't seem to notice it, but just before they started playing again, he sipped from it and looked toward me, and nodded. Then he put it back on top of the piano. For me, then, as they began to play again, it glowed and shook above my brother's head like the very cup of trembling.

Samuel Taylor Coleridge

KUBLA KHAN

In Xanadu did Kubla Khan
A stately pleasure-dome decree:
Where Alph, the sacred river, ran
Through caverns measureless to man
Down to a sunless sea.
So twice five miles of fertile ground
With walls and towers were girdled round:
And there were gardens bright with sinuous rills,
Where blossomed many an incense-bearing tree;
And here were forests ancient as the hills,   10
Enfolding sunny spots of greenery.

But oh! that deep romantic chasm which slanted
Down the green hill athwart a cedarn cover!
A savage place! as holy and enchanted
As e'er beneath a waning moon was haunted
By woman wailing for her demon-lover!
And from this chasm, with ceaseless turmoil
   seething,
As if this earth in fast thick pants were breathing,
A mighty fountain momently was forced:
Amid whose swift half-intermitted burst   20
Huge fragments vaulted like rebounding hail,
Or chaffy grain beneath the thresher's flail:
And 'mid these dancing rocks at once and ever
It flung up momently the sacred river.
Five miles meandering with a mazy motion
Through wood and dale the sacred river ran,
Then reached the caverns measureless to man,
And sank in tumult to a lifeless ocean:
And 'mid this tumult Kubla heard from far
Ancestral voices prophesying war!   30

   The shadow of the dome of pleasure
   Floated midway on the waves;
   Where was heard the mingled measure
   From the fountain and the caves.
It was a miracle of rare device,
A sunny pleasure-dome with caves of ice!

1 *Xanadu:* in Tartary.

A damsel with a dulcimer
In a vision once I saw:
It was an Abyssinian maid,
And on her dulcimer she played,   40
Singing of Mount Abora.
Could I revive within me
Her symphony and song,
To such a deep delight 'twould win me,
That with music loud and long,
I would build that dome in air,
That sunny dome! those caves of ice!
And all who heard should see them there,
And all should cry, Beware! Beware!
His flashing eyes, his floating hair!   50
Weave a circle round him thrice
And close your eyes with holy dread,
For he on honey-dew hath fed
And drunk the milk of Paradise.

John Keats

ON FIRST LOOKING INTO CHAPMAN'S HOMER

Much have I travelled in the realms of gold
    And many goodly states and kingdoms seen;
    Round many western islands have I been
Which bards in fealty to Apollo hold.
Oft of one wide expanse had I been told
    That deep-browed Homer ruled as his
        demesne;
    Yet did I never breathe its pure serene
Till I heard Chapman speak out loud and bold.

Then felt I like some watcher of the skies
    When a new planet swims into his ken;   10
Or like stout Cortez when with eagle eyes
    He stared at the Pacific, and all his men
Looked at each other with a wild surmise—
    Silent, upon a peak in Darien.

4 *Apollo:* As god of poetry he is here considered
overlord of the poems already read. 8 *Chapman:*
George Chapman (1559?–1634?) published his translations of Homer's poems from 1598 to 1624.

Robert Browning

"TRANSCENDENTALISM: A POEM IN TWELVE BOOKS"

Stop playing, poet! May a brother speak?
'Tis you speak, that's your error. Song's our art:
Whereas you please to speak these naked
        thoughts
Instead of draping them in sights and sounds.
—True thoughts, good thoughts, thoughts fit to
        treasure up!
But why such long prolusion and display,
Such turning and adjustment of the harp
And taking it upon your breast, at length,
Only to speak dry words across its strings?
Stark-naked thought is in request enough: 10
Speak prose and hollo it till Europe hears!
The six-foot Swiss tube, braced about with bark,
Which helps the hunter's voice from Alp to
        Alp—
Exchange our harp for that, who hinders you?

    But here's your fault; grown men want
        thought, you think;
Thought's what they mean by verse, and seek in
        verse.
Boys seek for images and melody,
Men must have reason—so, you aim at men.
Quite otherwise! Objects throng our youth, 'tis
        true;
We see and hear and do not wonder much: 20
If you could tell us what they mean, indeed!
As German Boehme never cared for plants
Until it happed, a-walking in the fields,
He noticed all at once that plants could speak,
Nay, turned with loosened tongue to talk with
        him.
That day the daisy had an eye indeed—
Colloquized with the cowslip on such themes!

1 *poet:* an imagined one, intent on producing
poems full of philosophy rather than poetry. 12
tube: wooden megaphone. 22 *Boehme:* Jacob
Boehme (1575–1624), German mystic and philos-
pher.

We find them extant yet in Jacob's prose.
But by the time youth slips a stage or two
While reading prose in that tough book he
    wrote   30
(Collating and emendating the same
And settling on the sense most to our mind),
We shut the clasps and find life's summer past.
Then, who helps more, pray, to repair our loss—
Another Boehme with a tougher book
And subtler meanings of what roses say
Or some stout mage like him of Halberstadt,
John, who made things Boehme wrote thoughts
    about?
He with a "look you!" vents a brace of rhymes,
And in there breaks the sudden rose herself,   40
Over us, under, round us every side,
Nay, in and out the tables and the chairs
And musty volumes, Boehme's book and all—
Buries us with a glory, young once more,
Pouring heaven into this shut house of life.

So come, the harp back to your heart again!
You are a poem, though your poem's naught.
The best of all you showed before, believe,
Was your own boy-face o'er the finer chords
Bent, following the cherub at the top   50
That points to God with his paired half-moon
    wings.

40 *sudden rose: Wonders of the Little World*
(1678), by Nathaniel Wanley, ascribes this miracle
to Johannes Teutonicus, a canon of Halberstadt
Cathedral.

Robert Browning

A TOCCATA OF GALUPPI'S

I

Oh Galuppi, Baldassaro, this is very sad to find!
I can hardly misconceive you; it would prove me
    deaf and blind;

A TOCCATA OF GALUPPI'S: Toccatas are rapid, free-
flowing musical compositions. In this poem the
speaker hears or plays one by Baldasarre Galuppi,
1706–1785.

But although I take your meaning, 'tis with such
    a heavy mind!

II

Here you come with your old music, and here's
    all the good it brings.
What, they lived once thus at Venice where the
    merchants were the kings,
Where Saint Mark's is, where the Doges used to
    wed the sea with rings?

III

Ay, because the sea's the street there, and 'tis
    arched by . . . what you call
. . . Shylock's bridge with houses on it, where
    they kept the carnival:
I was never out of England—it's as if I saw it all.

IV

Did young people take their pleasure when the
    sea was warm in May?   10
Balls and masks begun at midnight, burning
    ever to mid-day,
When they made up fresh adventures for the
    morrow, do you say?

V

Was a lady such a lady, cheeks so round and lips
    so red,
On her neck the small face buoyant, like a
    bell-flower on its bed,
O'er the breast's superb abundance where a man
    might base his head?

VI

Well, and it was graceful of them—they'd break
    talk off and afford
—She, to bite her mask's black velvet—he, to
    finger on his sword,
While you sat and played toccatas, stately at the
    clavichord?

VII

What? Those lesser thirds so plaintive, sixths
    diminished, sigh on sigh,
Told them something? Those suspensions, those
    solutions—"Must we die?"   20
Those commiserating sevenths—"Life might
    last! we can but try!"

VIII

"Were you happy?"—"Yes,"—"And are you still
    as happy?"—"Yes, And you?"
—"Then, more kisses!"—"Did *I* stop them,
    when a million seemed so few?"
Hark, the dominant's persistence till it must be
    answered to!

IX

So, an octave struck the answer. Oh, they praised
    you, I dare say!
"Brave Galuppi! that was music! good alike at
    grave and gay!
I can always leave off talking when I hear a
    master play!"

X

Then they left you for their pleasure: till in due
    time, one by one,
Some with lives that came to nothing, some with
    deeds as well undone,
Death stepped tacitly and took them where
    they never see the sun.   30

XI

But when I sit down to reason, think to take my
    stand nor swerve,
While I triumph o'er a secret wrung from
    nature's close reserve,
In you come with your cold music till I creep
    through every nerve.

XII

Yes, you, like a ghostly cricket, creaking where
    a house was burned:

"Dust and ashes, dead and done with, Venice
    spent what Venice earned.
The soul, doubtless, is immortal—where a soul
    can be discerned.

XIII

"Yours for instance: you know physics,
    something of geology,
Mathematics are your pastime; souls shall rise in
    their degree;
Butterflies may dread extinction,—you'll not
    die, it cannot be!

XIV

"As for Venice and her people, merely born to
    bloom and drop,   40
Here on earth they bore their fruitage, mirth and
    folly were the crop:
What of soul was left, I wonder, when the kissing
    had to stop?

XV

"Dust and ashes!" So you creak it, and I want the
    heart to scold.
Dear dead women, with such hair, too—what's
    become of all the gold
Used to hang and brush their bosoms? I feel
    chilly and grown old.

Charles Baudelaire

THE ALBATROSS

Often, for pastime, mariners will ensnare
The albatross, that vast sea-bird who sweeps
On high companionable pinion where
Their vessel glides upon the bitter deeps.

Torn from his native space, this captive king
Flounders upon the deck in stricken pride,
And pitiably lets his great white wing
Drag like a heavy paddle at his side.

This rider of winds, how awkward he is, and
    weak!
How droll he seems, who lately was all
    grace!   10
A sailor pokes a pipestem into his beak;
Another, hobbling, mocks his trammeled pace.

The Poet is like this monarch of the clouds,
Familiar of storms, of stars, and of all high
    things;
Exiled on earth amidst its hooting crowds,
He cannot walk, borne down by his giant wings.

A. E. Housman

TERENCE, THIS IS STUPID STUFF

"Terence, this is stupid stuff:
You eat your victuals fast enough;
There can't be much amiss, 'tis clear,
To see the rate you drink your beer.
But oh, good Lord, the verse you make,
It gives a chap the belly-ache.
The cow, the old cow, she is dead;
It sleeps well, the hornèd head:
We poor lads, 'tis our turn now
To hear such tunes as killed the cow.   10
Pretty friendship 'tis to rhyme
Your friends to death before their time
Moping melancholy mad:
Come, pipe a tune to dance to, lad."

Why, if 'tis dancing you would be,
There's brisker pipes than poetry.
Say, for what were hop-yards meant,
Or why was Burton built on Trent?
Oh, many a peer of England brews

Livelier liquor than the Muse,   20
And malt does more than Milton can
To justify God's ways to man.
Ale, man, ale's the stuff to drink
For fellows whom it hurts to think:
Look into the pewter pot
To see the world as the world's not.
And faith, 'tis pleasant till 'tis past:
The mischief is that 'twill not last.
Oh, I have been to Ludlow fair
And left my necktie God knows where,   30
And carried halfway home, or near,
Pints and quarts of Ludlow beer:
Then the world seemed none so bad,
And I myself a sterling lad;
And down in lovely muck I've lain,
Happy till I woke again.
Then I saw the morning sky:
Heigho, the tale was all a lie;
The world, it was the old world yet,
I was I, my things were wet,   40
And nothing now remained to do
But begin the game anew.

Therefore, since the world has still
Much good, but much less good than ill,
And while the sun and moon endure
Luck's a chance, but trouble's sure,
I'd face it as a wise man would,
And train for ill and not for good.
'Tis true, the stuff I bring for sale
Is not so brisk a brew as ale: 50
Out of a stem that scored the hand
I wrung it in a weary land.
But take it: if the smack is sour,
The better for the embittered hour;
It should do good to heart and head
When your soul is in my soul's stead;
And I will friend you, if I may,
In the dark and cloudy day.

There was a king reigned in the East:
There, when kings will sit to feast,   60

1 *this:* the poetry of Terence, who is fictitious but whose melancholy resembles Housman's. From line 15 on he speaks in his own defense. 18 *Burton:* city in Staffordshire, known for its breweries. The next couplet is a gibe at those who owe their titles to fortunes made there.

22 *To justify, etc.:* an allusion to Paradise Lost I, 26. 29 *Ludlow:* in Shropshire, the usual setting of Housman's poems. 59 *king:* Mithridates ruled Pontus c. 115–63 B.C.

They get their fill before they think
With poisoned meat and poisoned drink.
He gathered all that springs to birth
From the many-venomed earth;
First a little, thence to more,
He sampled all her killing store;
And easy, smiling, seasoned sound,
Sate the king when healths went round.
They put arsenic in his meat
And stared aghast to watch him eat;   70
They poured strychnine in his cup
And shook to see him drink it up:
They shook, they stared as white's their shirt:
Them it was their poison hurt.
—I tell the tale that I heard told.
Mithridates, he died old.

76 *old:* and so well immunized that to avoid capti-
vity he had to order a slave to stab him.

W. H. Auden

MUSÉE DES BEAUX ARTS

About suffering they were never wrong,
The Old Masters: how well they understood
Its human position; how it takes place
While someone else is eating or opening a
        window or just walking dully along;
How, when the aged are reverently, passionately
        waiting
For the miraculous birth, there always must be
Children who did not specially want it to
        happen, skating
On a pond at the edge of the wood:
They never forgot

That even the dreadful martyrdom must run its
        course   10
Anyhow in a corner, some untidy spot

MUSÉE DES BEAUX ARTS: Museum of Fine Arts, the
gallery in Brussels which owns *The Fall of Icarus,*
by Pieter Brueghel the Elder (1520?–1569).

Where the dogs go on with their doggy life and
        the torturer's horse
Scratches its innocent behind on a tree.

In Brueghel's *Icarus,* for instance: how
        everything turns away
Quite leisurely from the disaster; the ploughman
        may
Have heard the splash, the forsaken cry,
But for him it was not an important failure; the
        sun shone
As it had to on the white legs disappearing
        into the green
Water; and the expensive delicate ship that
        must have seen
Something amazing, a boy falling out of the
        sky,   20
Had somewhere to get to and sailed calmly on.

X. J. Kennedy

NUDE DESCENDING A STAIRCASE

Toe upon toe, a snowing flesh,
A gold of lemon, root and rind,
She sifts in sunlight down the stairs
With nothing on. Nor on her mind.

We spy beneath the banister
A constant thresh of thigh on thigh—
Her lips imprint the swinging air
That parts to let her parts go by.

One-woman waterfall, she wears
Her slow descent like a long cape   10
And pausing, on the final stair
Collects her motions into shape.

NUDE DESCENDING A STAIRCASE. Painting by Marcel
Duchamp, 1887–1968.

Galway Kinnell

THE CORRESPONDENCE SCHOOL INSTRUCTOR SAYS GOODBYE TO HIS POETRY STUDENTS

Goodbye, lady in Bangor, who sent me
snapshots of yourself, after definitely hinting
you were beautiful; goodbye,
Miami Beach urologist, who enclosed plain
brown envelopes for the return of your *very*
"Clinical Sonnets"; goodbye, manufacturer
of brassieres on the Coast, whose eclogues
give the fullest treatment in literature yet
to the sagging breast motif; goodbye, you in
    San Quentin,
who wrote, "Being German my hero is
    Hitler,"   10
instead of "Sincerely yours," at the end of long,
neat-scripted letters demolishing
the pre-Raphaelites:

I swear to you, it was just my way
of cheering myself up, as I licked
the stamped, self-addressed envelopes,
the game I had
of trying to guess which one of you, this time,
had poisoned his glue. I did care.
I did read each poem entire.   20
I did say what I thought was the truth
in the mildest words I knew. And now,
in this poem, or chopped prose, not any better,
I realize, than those troubled lines
I kept sending back to you,
I have to say I am relieved it is over:
at the end I could feel only pity
for that urge toward more life
your poems kept smothering in words, the smell
of which, days later, would tingle   30
in your nostrils as new, God-given impulses
to write.

Goodbye,
you who are, for me, the postmarks again
of shattered towns — Xenia, Burnt Cabins,
    Hornell —
their loneliness
given away in poems, only their solitude kept.

Marianne Moore

POETRY

I, too, dislike it: there are things that are important beyond all this fiddle.
    Reading it, however, with a perfect contempt for it, one discovers in
      it after all, a place for the genuine.
        Hands that can grasp, eyes
          that can dilate, hair that can rise
            if it must, these things are important not because a

high-sounding interpretation can be put upon them but because they are
    useful. When they become so derivative as to became unintelligible,
      the same thing may be said for all of us, that we
        do not admire what   10
          we cannot understand: the bat
            holding on upside down or in quest of something to

eat, elephants pushing, a wild horse taking a roll, a tireless wolf under
    a tree, the immovable critic twitching his skin like a horse that feels a flea, the
    baseball fan, the statistician—
        nor is it valid
            to discriminate against "business documents and

school-books"; all these phenomena are important. One must make a distinction
    however: when dragged into prominence by half-poets, the result is not poetry,
    nor till the poets among us can be
        "literalists of
        the imagination"—above
            insolence and triviality and can present

for inspection, imaginary gardens with real toads in them, shall we have
    it. In the meantime, if you demand on the one hand,
    the raw material of poetry in
        all its rawness and
        that which is on the other hand
            genuine, then you are interested in poetry.

20

Chapter 9

THE SCIENTIFIC ENTERPRISE

Placed in a natural setting whose overwhelming powers, though often menacing, can also be benign, mankind is understandably curious and apprehensive about the workings of nature, its underlying order, its secret springs of force. When this curiosity is strong and persistent, and the effort to satisfy is sustained and methodical, we have science. To many people the word "science" suggests the application of knowledge in the control of nature—engineering or medical research. To others, it suggests a systematic body of propositions—of laws and theories—in mathematical form: the results of scientific inquiry. But more basically, science is the enterprise itself that yields such knowledge and makes possible such technology. It is an activity, a search, that can call upon some of the highest capacities and noblest qualities of human beings, extraordinary intelligence and concentration, selfless dedication to the truth, great patience and stubborn courage in the face of countless discouragements.

Though not all of us are scientists in the professional sense, whenever we undertake a serious effort to find the answer to some question, we can share a little of the scientific spirit. Literature that takes for its material the experience of scientific inquiry can give us further insight into the quality of that experience. The joy of sheer discovery, of coming to understand, is celebrated in Cowley's "Ode upon Dr. Harvey" and in several vivid scenes of Brecht's play *Life of Galileo*. Some of the frustrations of research are shown in "Troublesome Molluscs" and "S. Miami." The scientist's commitment to truth, whatever it may turn out to be, is shown in Huxley's letter to Kingsley and in "The Blood of the Martyrs."

Not all reflections on science as a human enterprise have led to so affirmative a view of it. Some criticism of science seems to be based on a confusion of it with technology, which is not science but its fruit; a good deal of science fiction joins in this theme with writing on the ecological perils of unbridled technological exploitation. Sometimes the scientist has been accused of social irresponsibility and inhumanity—an ethical question that comes to concern Brecht's Galileo at the end of the play. Such poets as Blake, Poe, Whitman, E. E. Cummings—like the Cadi whose letter William James quotes—have mocked or deplored scientific experiment and the mechanistic view of nature to which the work of Galileo and Newton led. The literary artist has sometimes felt the spirit of the scientist to be alien and inhumane. Yet just as scientists (for example, Huxley) have sometimes written eloquently of their work and helped us to see in what ways it is like literary creation, so literary artists have done much to bridge the gap between the "Two Cultures," as the realms of natural science and the humanities have been called.

Berton Roueché

S. MIAMI

Around five o'clock on Friday morning, June 4, 1954, an Upton, Massachusetts, garage mechanic whom I'll call Alfred Edison—a married man and the father of a three-year-old daughter—was wrenched from sleep by a grinding pain in the stomach. It doubled him up and turned him over and almost took his breath away. He began to groan, and his groans awakened his wife. He heard her asking what had happened, but before he could answer, a wave of nausea and diarrhea overwhelmed him. When he emerged from the bathroom some ten minutes later, the light was on in the nursery. His wife was holding the baby in her arms. The child was flushed and whimpering, and she had vomited in her bed. She was also, it soon developed, diarrheic. Frightened into a fleeting convalescence, Edison helped his wife calm and comfort the child, and presently she fell asleep. The Edisons then headed back to bed. At the door of their room, Mrs. Edison stopped. Her face went green. She turned and ran for the bathroom. Edison got as far as the nearest chair. He tumbled into it, gagging and retching, with another seizure of cramps. The baby awoke again and began to cry. There was no more sleep for anyone in the Edison house that night. Even the baby only dozed. Finally, toward seven o'clock, they decided to call the doctor. Edison dragged himself downstairs and telephoned a general practitioner named Bernard F. McKernan.

"Not that he had much choice," Dr. McKernan says. "I mean, if they wanted a doctor. Upton is a fair-sized village. It has a population of around three thousand. But I'm the only physician in town. Don't ask me why. It isn't my doing. I could use some help—in fact, I'd welcome it. I'd be more than happy to share the strain. I certainly would have been, back there in June of 1954. However, I'm the doctor, and he called me. I was up and dressed—you have to get up early to handle a practice like mine—and was just sitting down to breakfast. It wasn't hard to get the picture. The symptoms told the story. I couldn't see much cause for alarm, but I already had one house call to make in that neighborhood, so I told him I'd drop around. I got there a little after eight. I found no reason to change my first impression. It looked like a routine gastroenteritis. What I call summer diarrhea. Moreover, by then the worst appeared to be over. No more cramps and no more vomiting. Nobody had any fever. The only remaining symptom was diarrhea. I gave them each a dose of kaolin for that, and prescribed the usual bland diet and rest. Then, as a matter of course, I asked them what they had been eating in the past twenty-four hours or so. They couldn't think of anything unusual. They couldn't think of anything at all. Just what they always ate, they said. I let it go at that. I told them to give me a ring the following day if the diarrhea continued, and went on to the next call on my list. They didn't call me on Saturday, so I put them out of my mind.

"Until Sunday. Sunday is nominally my day of rest. I realize that people can't always arrange their illnesses to suit my convenience, but I don't have office hours on Sunday, and I'm very much obliged when nobody calls me at home. Needless to say, that seldom happens. And it didn't happen that Sunday. My holiday ended at about three o'clock in the afternoon with a call from a man named, I'll say, Smith. He sounded pretty frantic. Could I come over right away? Both of his children—an eight-year-old boy and a girl of four—were violently ill. So was his wife. So were two members of her family who were spending the weekend with them—her father and one of her brothers. I asked him what seemed to be the trouble. Cramps, he said, terrible stomach cramps. Nausea and vomiting. Diarrhea. That made me perk up my ears. Summer diarrhea is a common complaint, but it isn't all that common. Two family outbreaks in less than three days in a village this size was something to think about. I told him I was on my way. I saw Mrs. Smith and the children first. Smith hadn't exaggerated. They were sick—really sick. Far sicker than the Edisons had ever been. Along with everything else, they were flat on their backs, too weak to lift a hand, and running quite a fever. Both children had a temperature of a hundred and three, and Mrs. Smith's was almost that high. I then had a look at her brother. The old man, it turned out, wasn't there. He didn't believe in doctors. When he heard I was coming, he left and went home—to Hopkinton, as I recall. No matter. His is another story. He died a week or two later, but not of gastroenteritis, although that might have been a contributing factor. The cause of death was a tibial-artery thrombosis. Well, to get back to the Smiths—I did what I could to make them comfortable. I also revised my original diagnosis. This was obviously no mere summer diarrhea. It was a full-fledged case of food poisoning—bacterial food poisoning, most likely.

"In the first place, it couldn't be chemical poisoning. That usually comes on within minutes of ingestion, and the time lapse is never much more than a couple of hours. These people, however, took sick before breakfast. They didn't eat any breakfast. Their last meal was dinner on Saturday night. And the dinner menu eliminated the possibility that they had been poisoned by some inherently poisonous plant or animal substance. Toxic mushrooms, for example. Dinner was steak and fried potatoes, bread and butter, carrots and peas, and coleslaw, with milk for the children and watermelon for dessert. It had to be some form of bacterial poisoning. To judge from the clinical picture, the organism responsible could be either a staphylococcus or one of the salmonella group. My guess, in view of the onset time, was the latter. The staphylococcus toxin makes itself felt within two to seven hours. Salmonella takes from twelve to thirty-six hours. The next step was to try to determine just what food had served as the vehicle of infection. At a glance, there were three possibilities—the milk, the coleslaw, and the steak. But only at a glance. The children didn't eat any coleslaw, and they alone drank milk. That left the steak. Meat is an excellent medium for the growth of salmonella. Raw or rare meat, that is. Thorough cooking will safely destroy the organism. The Smith steak was fried to a crisp. Well, maybe the trouble went back to an earlier meal. I took up Saturday lunch and Saturday breakfast and dinner on Friday night. Lunch was out of the question. The boy had lunched at a neighbor's house, and the brother had also eaten somewhere else. Breakfast was completely innocuous. It consisted of fruit juice, doughnuts, and coffee. The children drank milk. Friday-night dinner was even less promising than the dinner on Saturday night—fried fish and boiled potatoes, bread and butter, and string beans, with the usual milk for the children. Dessert, as on the following night, was watermelon.

"I've seldom felt so stumped. Or, a moment later, so stupid. I was just about ready to call it quits when the obvious suddenly dawned. The children were sick. Mrs. Smith was sick. Her brother was sick. And so, apparently, was her father. But Smith himself was well. How come? There was only one reasonable explanation. He hadn't eaten something that all the others ate. I was right. I asked him and he told me. It was watermelon. He never ate watermelon. He simply didn't like it. I don't know what I expected, but I'm sure it wasn't that. I'd never heard of watermelon as a vehicle for food poisoning. Nobody ever had. Nevertheless, it had to be considered. I asked Smith a few more questions and got a few more answers. They had bought the watermelon—it was half a melon, actually—at the supermarket in Milford, about five miles southeast of here, on Friday. There was some of it left. It was out in the refrigerator, if I wanted to take a look. I told him to keep it there. I'd probably want to have it analyzed.

"I got back home a little after four. I put the car away and went in the house and dropped my bag, and the doorbell rang. It was a woman I knew—Mrs. Brown, I'll call her. She and her husband and their four young children lived just down the street. Well, she hated to bother me on Sunday, but it couldn't be helped. It was mostly on account of the children. They had been sick and vomiting since nine o'clock that morning. And now they were violently diarrheic. So was she, but it was the children that really concerned her. What did I think was the matter? I let that go for a moment. I had some questions of my own that I wanted answered first. She hadn't mentioned her husband. Did that mean that he wasn't sick? No, she said. Or, rather, yes— he was fine. I began to get a rather creepy feeling. Had they by any chance eaten any watermelon recently? She gave me a very odd look. Why, yes; they'd had watermelon for dinner only last night. I wondered if it might have come from the supermarket at Milford. It did—yes. That's where they always traded. And they had all eaten some of it? No. She and the children had, but not her husband. He didn't like watermelon.

Neither did she, particularly. They had really bought it mainly for the children. I picked up my bag and opened the door and followed her out of the house.

"The first thing Monday morning, I put in a call to the Milford supermarket. I identified myself to the manager, and told him I had an outbreak of food poisoning on my hands that was tentatively traced to watermelon bought at his store within the past two or three days. Until the matter was settled, I'd be much obliged if he would withhold all watermelon still in stock from sale. All things considered, he took it very well. He didn't try to argue. He stuttered and stammered a little, but that was largely from shock. Or maybe just plain disbelief. If so, I could hardly blame him. I didn't entirely believe it myself. The idea of watermelon as a source of infection in food poisoning still seemed a trifle farfetched. There was reason to suspect it, but the evidence was purely circumstantial, and it was based on just two sets of circumstances. It could be a mere coincidence. I don't mean I really thought so, but it was possible to wonder. It was possible on Monday morning. By Monday afternoon, however, it was wholly out of the question. Two things accounted for the change. One was that I saw the Edison family again. I was called back there around noon. The kaolin hadn't seemed to help. They were all still miserably diarrheic. In view of what I now suspected, that wasn't too surprising. An attack of salmonellosis can hang on for four or five days. In fact, I've known of cases where the symptoms kept recurring for weeks, and even months. I did what I could—what I'd done for others. I prescribed another absorbent, and a regime of penicillin and sulfasuxidine. I then brought up the subject of food again. With a little prompting, their memory revived. Enough to recall that on Thursday night they'd had watermelon for dessert. It was all gone now—they had only bought a slice. But, yes, it had come from the supermarket at Milford. Then came another outbreak—a young couple I'll call Miller. The Millers had been sick since Sunday with cramps, vomiting, and diarrhea. Mrs. Miller had a temperature of a hundred and two. On Saturday night, they had entertained another couple at dinner. Dessert was a slice of watermelon, from the Milford supermarket. There was some of it left in the refrigerator. Their guests, as it happened, hadn't eaten any. I took down the name of their friends, and when I got back to the office I gave them a ring. The wife answered the phone. Her husband was at work—and quite well. So was she.

"Well, that was the end of the argument. The watermelon was clearly in the picture. It was also clear that I had gone as far as I could alone. The rest was up to the State Department of Public Health. Food poisoning is a reportable disease in Massachusetts. I filled out a notification form and sent it off to the health officer for this district, in Worcester."

The district health officer to whom Dr. McKernan addressed his report was a physician named Gilbert E. Gayler. It reached Dr. Gayler on Tuesday. The following morning, he drove down to Upton for a preliminary survey of the outbreak. He first conferred with Dr. McKernan. There were now, he learned, not four but five stricken families. The fifth was an elderly couple named (I'll say) Green. They had shared a slice of watermelon from the Milford supermarket on Friday night, they had become ill on Saturday, and on Tuesday, after nearly four days of misery, they had summoned Dr. McKernan. The Greens brought the number of cases to a total—the final total, as it turned out—of seventeen. Dr. Gayler spent the rest of the morning on a round of clinical calls. Accompanied by Dr. McKernan, he visited the Greens, the Smiths, and the Millers, and left with each of the several patients an enteric-specimen kit. The pa-

tients were instructed to mail the kits as soon as possible to the Diagnostic Laboratory of the Massachusetts Department of Public Health, in Boston. In addition, Dr. Gayler obtained from the Millers the remains of their Saturday-night watermelon. His next stop, after a hurried lunch with Dr. McKernan, was the supermarket at Milford. He interviewed the manager, the assistant manager, and three clerks assigned to the fruit-and-vegetable department. All five were in their normal state of health. None were, or recently had been, afflicted with any sort of skin, respiratory, or gastro-intestinal trouble. An examination of the fruit-and-vegetable department indicated that it was, if anything, better kept and cleaner than that of the average market. As requested by Dr. McKernan, the store's stock of watermelons—both whole and sliced—had been withdrawn from sale, but all the cut melons were still meticulously wrapped in cellophane, as they had been all along. Dr. Gayler took one of the slices with him to be analyzed along with the Miller sample. He then returned to his car, and headed for Boston and the Diagnostic Laboratory.

Dr. Robert A. MacCready, the director in charge, was not at the laboratory that afternoon when Dr. Gayler turned up with his samples of melon. He was attending a conference at the State House. It was not until his return the next day that he learned of the visit and its purpose. He heard the news from his senior bacteriologist, Mrs. Marion B. Holmes, and he heard it with incredulity.

"I had no opinion of Dr. McKernan," Dr. MacCready says. "I didn't know him. I did know Dr. Gayler, though. I knew him well enough to know that he was a sound and sensible man. That's about all that kept me from scoffing at Dr. McKernan's hunch. There are innumerable vehicles of salmonella infection. The literature is full of outbreaks spread by almost any food you can name—meat, poultry, fish, eggs, milk, cheese, salads, pastries. Almost any food, that is, except fresh fruit. The incidence of salmonella in fresh fruit is so rare as to be almost negligible. Especially watermelon! That thick hide! The notion was almost whimsical. Mrs. Holmes thought so, too. Or, rather, she did at first. But now, after thinking it over, she wasn't entirely sure. She didn't attempt to explain just how a watermelon might come to harbor a colony of salmonellae. She simply pointed out that watermelon is rich in sugar and moisture. It could thus serve the organism very nicely as a medium for growth and proliferation. Which, of course, was perfectly true. I had to agree that watermelon was within the range of possibility. In my opinion, however, it still seemed quite unlikely. The inside of a whole watermelon is presumably sterile, and the cut melons had been carefully wrapped by clerks who were all in good health. I'd believe the implication when I saw some proof—when and if the laboratory could demonstrate the presence of salmonella in those melons. The procedure involved in such a test is a standard one. Specimens of the suspected material are planted in certain culture mediums that especially favor the growth of salmonella. Then nature takes its course. The results, if any, can usually be obtained in two or three days. This was Thursday. We should have an answer by Saturday or Sunday. Meanwhile, there was nothing to do but wait.

"The only trouble was I didn't feel like just waiting. It wasn't impatience. I got over that long ago. It was simple curiosity. I was intrigued. Watermelon or no watermelon, it was a most unusual case, and I wanted to know a good deal more about it than Mrs. Holmes had learned from Dr. Gayler. That meant a trip to the scene. I made the necessary arrangements that afternoon, and drove down on Friday morning. For company, among other reasons, I took along a colleague—Joseph P. Reardon. He was, and is, the epidemiologist in the De-partment's Division of Communicable Diseases. As it turned out, Dr. Reardon more than paid his way. Our first stop was Dr. McKernan's office. Dr. Gayler joined us there. They gave us a full report. Dr. Gayler's contribution was a poll of the other doctors in the Milford area. I don't remember just how many he called, and it doesn't matter. The responses were all the same. None of the doctors had seen a case of acute gastroenteritis in the past ten days or two weeks. So the outbreak was confined to Upton. Before moving on to Milford, we had a look at some of the patients. That was mere routine. We didn't expect any revelations and we didn't find any. We did pick up another sample for the laboratory—the melon that Dr. McKernan had instructed the Smiths to save. Dr. Gayler had been favorably impressed by the look of the supermarket. So were Dr. Reardon and I. We inspected it practically foot by foot. There was no evidence of rats or mice. Animal droppings—particularly those of rodents—are a frequent salmonella reservoir. The store was as clean as good management could make it. Then we settled down in the fruit-and-vegetable department. We talked with the clerks and arranged for sample stools. The watermelons were still under embargo—some of them whole and some sliced and covered with cellophane. We were shown the knife that was used to slice them, and I took a sample swab of the blade for laboratory analysis. Dr. Reardon suggested a swab of the shelf where the knife was kept. I thought that was pretty futile—there was nothing there but dust. The possibility of salmonella's even existing there—let alone multiplying —was exceedingly remote. But I humored him. There was no harm in one more sample. We had little enough to show for the day.

"We left Dr. Gayler at Milford, and Dr. Reardon and I drove back to Boston. After dropping him off, I stopped by the office.

The only news from Mrs. Holmes was the arrival of the first lot of stool samples. I handed over our harvest of swabs and melon and went home. I wasn't exactly depressed. I just didn't feel quite comfortable. It was obvious that Dr. McKernan had done an excellent job. So good, in fact, that I hardly knew what to think. I still had certain misgivings about the watermelon theory. It still went against my grain. And yet, if the melon wasn't responsible, what was? The answer to that was: Nothing. There wasn't anything else. It had to be the melon.

"Our laboratory is on a skeleton basis over the weekend. We don't have the funds to function at full strength seven days a week. As a rule, however, there's always somebody there—the bacteriologists take turns—and this weekend it was Mrs. Holmes. She kept me in touch with developments. As expected, there were several, and, as hoped, they told the story—the only possible story. Dr. McKernan was right. By Sunday night, the laboratory had confirmed him on every point. It confirmed his clinical diagnosis of salmonellosis. All of the patient stools were teeming with salmonellae. So were the Smith and Miller watermelon samples. That confirmed the melon as the vehicle of infection. It also pretty definitely linked the outbreak to the Milford supermarket. Then, thanks to Dr. Reardon, the shelf swab completed the chain. It produced a magnificent culture. I still find that hard to believe. The odds against it were literally astronomical. It was an extraordinary stroke of luck. And a very fortunate one, as well. Because the swab I'd taken of the knife itself was negative. What happened, I suppose, was that the knife had been washed after Dr. McKernan embargoed the melons. The knife was our only disappointment. We got one other negative culture—from the melon slice that Dr. Gayler had picked up at the store—but that was hardly a blow. Just the reverse, as a matter of fact. It provided an acceptable answer to one of the

two big questions that the positive cultures raised. It explained why the outbreak was confined to just those seventeen customers of the Milford supermarket. Dr. Gayler's melon was clean because the bulk of the melons were clean. If all, or most, or even many of the melons had been contaminated, the outbreak pattern would have been quite different. There would have been cases scattered all over the Milford area. But none of the doctors polled by Dr. Gayler had seen a sign of gastroenteritis. The conclusion was practically unavoidable. There must have been only two or three contaminated melons, and by some streak of circumstance they ended up in Upton.

"The other question was, of course, the essence of the problem. It was also the essence of my discontent—the root of all my misgivings. How did the contaminated melons get that way? How *could* something with so thick a hide have ever got contaminated? To answer that—to even attempt an answer—we needed to know a little more about the organism involved. We knew it was salmonella, but we didn't know the serotype—the species. When we did, we might have a lead. However, serotyping calls for antigenic analyses that most laboratories—including ours at that time—are not equipped to perform. We relied for such work on the New York Salmonella Center, at Beth Israel Hospital in Manhattan. Accordingly, on Monday morning we prepared a sample culture and sent it off to the Center for specific identification. If all went well, we would have a report in a couple of days or so.

"The salmonella is a curious group of pathogens. It differs in many important respects from the other bacteria commonly associated with food poisoning—such as the staphylococci and *Clostridium botulinum*, the botulism organism. For one thing, salmonella is inherently infectious to man. The ingestion of food containing a quantity of living salmonellae commonly results in illness. Moreover, because salmonella is perfectly adapted for growth and reproduction within the human body, the quantity need not be an enormous one. With the others, the mechanism is quite different. Botulism and staphylococcus food poisoning are intoxications rather than infections. Their cause is not the living organism but a toxin excreted in the food by the organism in the course of its proliferation there. In other words, the food itself is poisonous. That largely explains why staphylococcus food poisoning comes on so much faster than salmonellosis. Botulism takes longer—sometimes three or four days—but it isn't a gastroenteritis. It's primarily a disease of the central nervous system. And an extremely serious one. Fortunately, it is easily controlled. *C. botulinum* lives in the soil and can grow and elaborate its toxin only in a total absence of oxygen. Most outbreaks of botulism in this country are traced to home-canned vegetables inexpertly washed and processed and eaten without further cooking. Although heat has little or no effect on the botulism organism itself, proper cooking will safely destroy the toxin. The staphylococci enterotoxin, on the other hand, is highly heat-resistant. In addition, the staphylococcus organism is ubiquitous in nature. It's even been isolated from the air of rooms. And it is perhaps the commonest cause of boils and other skin and wound infections. Nevertheless, the control of staphylococcus food poisoning is not—at least potentially—too difficult. Refrigeration will prevent the development of the toxin, and good common-sense hygiene on the part of food handlers will do the rest. Salmonellosis would seem to be as easily controlled. Cooking, refrigeration, and cleanliness are all helpful precautions. The first will destroy the organism, and the others will retard its growth. But the problem is more complicated than that. Infected human beings are not alone responsible for the spread of salmonellosis. Salmonella can live in the intestinal tract of almost any animal, including those that are closest to man—dogs, rats, mice, cows, chickens. And, to make matters worse, it appears to be a perfect parasite. It can live and propagate in most such animals without any visible signs of harm to the animal.

"Nor is that all. New species of salmonella turn up every year. Since 1885, when the first member of the group was described —by an American pathologist named Daniel E. Salmon—literally hundreds of species have been identified. The total now known is well in excess of four hundred. So far, I'm glad to say, most of them don't exhibit any unusual pathogenic powers. They produce a disagreeable but not usually fatal illness. But that doesn't mean they never will. A more virulent species might emerge tomorrow. The multitude of species is not in itself particularly disturbing. It actually had a certain epidemiological value. Many apparently unrelated outbreaks of salmonellosis have been linked through identification of the species involved. It also sometimes happens that the identity of the species will indicate the ultimate source of the trouble. It has been the custom for many years to name a newly discovered species for the place where it first was found. The names of some no longer have any geographical significance. In the intervening years, the species they denote have been found in many different places. *Salmonella montevideo* is one of that increasingly widespread group. So, among others, are *S. oranienburg, S. newport, S. derby, S. bareilly,* and *S. panama.* A good many more, however, are still essentially regional species. Such as, to mention just a few, *S. dares-selaam, S. moscow, S. bronx, S. israel, S. marylebone, S. ndola, S. oslo,* and *S. fresno.* Another is *S. miami.* And that was the one we got. That was the Upton organism.

"I had a telegram from Dr. Ivan Saphra, the chief bacteriologist at the New York Salmonella Center, around four o'clock on

Tuesday. The late Dr. Saphra, I should say —he died in 1957. A great pity. He was a fine man, and an outstanding one in his field, as his work in this case plainly testifies. Our culture didn't reach him until sometime Tuesday morning, but he had it typed that afternoon. It often takes longer than that to identify a relatively common species. To even think of *S. miami* in this part of the country was remarkable. The implications of his report were even more so. *S. miami*, as its name suggests, is a Florida organism. It has been recovered in several human outbreaks in that area, and from many different animals. We could hardly have hoped for a more provocative lead. Or one that so comfortably simplified the problem. It was only necessary to find a link between Florida and Massachusetts. What might have transported *S. miami* from way down there to here? An animal host? Not likely. Our examination of the supermarket had produced no evidence of rodent infestation. A human carrier? The answer to that was on my desk in a laboratory report on the specimen stools from the fruit-and-vegetable clerks. They were negative for salmonella. What else? Well, unless I was very much mistaken, Florida was a major source of produce for the Northeastern market in the spring and early summer. I put in a call to the supermarket at Milford and had a word with the manager. He was most cooperative. Their melons were Florida melons.

"That seemed to tell the story—the only reasonable story. We could scratch the store off the list. The trouble didn't originate there. It came up with the melons from Florida. To be sure, that was largely an inference, but it had the ring of truth. No other explanation was warranted by the facts. It wasn't, of course, the whole story. It didn't tell us how the contaminated melons got contaminated. That basic question still loomed. But it helped. We had sufficient data now to at least make a stab

at an answer. We began with a train of assumptions. Suppose a melon had come in contact with infected animal droppings down there in some Florida field. Or, for that matter, after it was harvested and stacked in the local jobber's warehouse. Suppose some of the material adhered to the skin of the melon. Suppose it was still there when the melon arrived at the store. And suppose it was still there when the clerk took his knife and sliced up the melon for sale. What then? It was easy enough to find out. All we needed was a watermelon.

"I picked one up on the way to the office on Thursday. We lugged it into the laboratory, and Mrs. Holmes prepared a dilute suspension of *S. miami* from one of the positive cultures. She swabbed some of the material on the skin of the melon. Then, using a clean knife, she cut a slice out of the melon at that point. That pretty well reproduced our hypothetical situation. The next step was to demonstrate the result. We made two sets of cultures from the meat where it had come in contact with the knife. The first was made immediately after the melon was cut, and the second a few hours later—when the organism would have had time to establish itself better. We then tried a different approach. We deliberately contaminated the knife with our *S. miami* suspension and cut off another slice of melon and made a culture from that. The idea, of course, was to see if a knife could spread the infection from one melon to another. At that point, we called it a day. For good measure, however, we left the original slice of melon overnight on the laboratory table. Fifteen hours or so at room temperature would give the remaining *S. miami* a really good chance to grow. The following day, we made a culture from that exposed slice.

"We got the first results on Saturday. They weren't exactly discouraging. I went down to the laboratory and read them myself. On the other hand, they fell a bit short of convincing. The first set, made right after the first slice was cut, was practically nothing—just a hint of *S. miami*. There was a little more life in the two other Thursday cultures. They each produced a colony or two. That left the overnight culture. I won't pretend that we waited for Sunday with bated breath. The results of the other cultures were an indication that we might expect something fairly conclusive. So I was fully prepared for the best. But I wasn't prepared for what we actually got. It wasn't just a good solid cluster of colonies. It was any number of colonies—innumerable colonies. It was an *S. miami* metropolis."

Thomas Henry Huxley

THE FAITH OF A SCIENTIST

14 Waverley Place, Sept. 23, 1860.

My dear Kingsley—I cannot sufficiently thank you, both on my wife's account and my own, for your long and frank letter, and for all the hearty sympathy which it[1] exhibits—and Mrs. Kingsley will, I hope, believe that we are no less sensible of her kind thought of us. To myself your letter was especially valuable, as it touched upon what I thought even more than upon what I said in my letter to you. My convictions, positive and negative, on all the matters of which you speak, are of long and slow growth and are firmly rooted. But the great blow which fell upon me seemed to stir them to their foundation, and had I lived a couple of centuries earlier I could have fancied a devil scoffing at me and them—and asking me what profit it was to have stripped myself of the hopes and consolations of the mass

of mankind? To which my only reply was and is, Oh devil! truth is better than much profit. I have searched over the grounds of my belief, and if wife and child and name and fame were all to be lost to me one after the other as the penalty, still I will not lie.

And now I feel that it is due to you to speak as frankly as you have done to me. An old and worthy friend of mine tried some three or four years ago to bring us together —because, as he said, you were the only man who would do me any good. Your letter leads me to think he was right, though not perhaps in the sense he attached to his own words.

To begin with the great doctrine you discuss, I neither deny nor affirm the immortality of man. I see no reason for believing in it, but, on the other hand, I have no means of disproving it.

Pray understand that I have no *a priori* objections to the doctrine. No man who has to deal daily and hourly with nature can trouble himself about *a priori* difficulties. Give me such evidence as would justify me in believing anything else, and I will believe that. Why should I not? It is not half so wonderful as the conservation of force, or the indestructibility of matter. Whoso clearly appreciates all that is implied in the falling of a stone can have no difficulty about any doctrine simply on account of its marvellousness. But the longer I live, the more obvious it is to me that the most sacred act of man's life is to say and to feel, "I believe such and such to be true." All the greatest rewards and all the heaviest penalties of existence cling about that act. The universe is one and the same throughout; and if the condition of my success in unravelling some little difficulty of anatomy or physiology is that I shall rigorously refuse to put faith in that which does not rest on sufficient evidence, I cannot believe that the great mysteries of existence will be laid open to me on other terms. It is no use to talk to me of analogies and probabilities. I know what I

---

[1] The Rev. Charles Kingsley (1819–1875), clergyman and novelist, had attempted to console Huxley for the death of his four-year-old son.

mean when I say I believe in the law of the inverse squares, and I will not rest my life and my hopes upon weaker convictions. I dare not if I would.

Measured by this standard, what becomes of the doctrine of immortality?

You rest in your strong conviction of your personal existence, and in the instinct of the persistence of that existence which is so strong in you as in most men.

To me this is as nothing. That my personality is the surest thing I know—may be true. But the attempt to conceive what it is leads me into mere verbal subtleties. I have champed up all that chaff about the ego and the non-ego, about noumena and phenomena, and all the rest of it, too often not to know that in attempting even to think of these questions, the human intellect flounders at once out of its depth.

It must be twenty years since, a boy, I read Hamilton's essay on the unconditioned,[2] and from that time to this, ontological speculation has been a folly to me. When Mansel[3] took up Hamilton's argument on the side of orthodoxy (!) I said he reminded me of nothing so much as the man who is sawing off the sign on which he is sitting, in Hogarth's picture.[4] But this by the way.

I cannot conceive of my personality as a thing apart from the phenomena of my life. When I try to form such a conception I discover that, as Coleridge would have said, I only hypostatize a word, and it alters nothing if, with Fichte, I suppose the universe to be nothing but a manifestation of my personality. I am neither more nor less eternal than I was before.

Nor does the infinite difference between myself and the animals alter the case. I do not know whether the animals persist after they disappear or not. I do not even know whether the infinite difference between us and them may not be compensated by *their* persistence and *my* cessation after apparent death, just as the humble bulb of an annual lives, while the glorious flowers it has put forth die away.

Surely it must be plain that an ingenious man could speculate without end on both sides, and find analogies for all his dreams. Nor does it help me to tell me that the aspirations of mankind—that my own highest aspirations even—lead me towards the doctrine of immortality. I doubt the fact, to begin with, but if it be so even, what is this but in grand words asking me to believe a thing because I like it?

Science has taught to me the opposite lesson. She warns me to be careful how I adopt a view which jumps with my preconceptions, and to require stronger evidence for such belief than for one to which I was previously hostile.

My business is to teach my aspirations to conform themselves to fact, not to try and make facts harmonize with my aspirations.

Science seems to me to teach in the highest and strongest manner the great truth which is embodied in the Christian conception of entire surrender to the will of God. Sit down before fact as a little child, be prepared to give up every preconceived notion, follow humbly wherever and to whatever abysses nature leads, or you shall learn nothing. I have only begun to learn content and peace of mind since I have resolved at all risks to do this.

There are, however, other arguments commonly brought forward in favor of the immortality of man, which are to my mind not only delusive but mischievous. The one is the notion that the moral government of the world is imperfect without a system of future rewards and punishments. The other is that such a system is indispensable to practical morality. I believe that both these dogmas are very mischievous lies.

[2] It appeared in 1829. Sir William Hamilton (1788–1856) was a Scottish philosopher.

[3] Henry L. Mansel, 1820–1871.

[4] "The Election: Canvassing for Votes" (1757), by William Hogarth.

With respect to the first, I am no optimist, but I have the firmest belief that the Divine Government (if we may use such a phrase to express the sum of the "customs of matter") is wholly just. The more I know intimately of the lives of other men (to say nothing of my own), the more obvious it is to me that the wicked does *not* flourish nor is the righteous punished. But for this to be clear we must bear in mind what almost all forget, that the rewards of life are contingent upon obedience to the *whole* law—physical as well as moral—and that moral obedience will not atone for physical sin, or vice versa.

The ledger of the Almighty is strictly kept, and every one of us has the balance of his operations paid over to him at the end of every minute of his existence.

Life cannot exist without a certain conformity to the surrounding universe; that conformity involves a certain amount of happiness in excess of pain. In short, as we live we are paid for living.

And it is to be recollected in view of the apparent discrepancy between men's acts and their rewards that Nature is juster than we. She takes into account what a man brings with him into the world, which human justice cannot do. If I, born a bloodthirsty and savage brute, inheriting these qualities from others, kill you, my fellowmen will very justly hang me, but I shall not be visited with the horrible remorse which would be my real punishment if, my nature being higher, I had done the same thing.

The absolute justice of the system of things is as clear to me as any scientific fact. The gravitation of sin to sorrow is as certain as that of the earth to the sun, and more so—for experimental proof of the fact is within reach of us all—nay, is before us all in our own lives, if we had but the eyes to see it.

Not only, then, do I disbelieve in the need for compensation, but I believe that the seeking for rewards and punishments out of this life leads men to a ruinous ignorance of the fact that their inevitable rewards and punishments are here.

If the expectation of hell hereafter can keep me from evil-doing, surely *a fortiori* the certainty of hell now will do so? If a man could be firmly impressed with the belief that stealing damaged him as much as swallowing arsenic would do (and it does), would not the dissuasive force of that belief be greater than that of any based on mere future expectations?

And this leads me to my other point.

As I stood behind the coffin of my little son the other day, with my mind bent on anything but disputation, the officiating minister read, as a part of his duty, the words, "If the dead rise not again, let us eat and drink, for tomorrow we die." [5] I cannot tell you how inexpressibly they shocked me. Paul had neither wife nor child, or he must have known that his alternative involved a blasphemy against all that was best and noblest in human nature. I could have laughed with scorn. What! because I am face to face with irreparable loss, because I have given back to the source whence it came the cause of great happiness, still retaining through all my life the blessings which have sprung and will spring from that cause, I am to renounce my manhood, and, howling, grovel in bestiality? Why, the very apes know better, and if you shoot their young, the poor brutes grieve their grief out and do not immediately seek distraction in a gorge.

Kicked into the world a boy without guide or training, or with worse than none, I confess to my shame that few men have drunk deeper of all kinds of sin than I. Happily, my course was arrested in time—before I had earned absolute destruction—and for long years I have been slowly and painfully climbing, with many a fall, towards better things. And when I look back,

5 St. Paul's *First Letter to the Corinthians* xv, 32.

what do I find to have been the agents of my redemption? The hope of immortality or of future reward? I can honestly say that for these fourteen years such a consideration has not entered my head. No, I can tell you exactly what has been at work. *Sartor Resartus*[6] led me to know that a deep sense of religion was compatible with the entire absence of theology. Secondly, science and her methods gave me a resting-place independent of authority and tradition. Thirdly, love opened up to me a view of the sanctity of human nature, and impressed me with a deep sense of responsibility.

If at this moment I am not a worn-out, debauched, useless carcass of a man, if it has been or will be my fate to advance the cause of science, if I feel that I have a shadow of a claim on the love of those about me, if in the supreme moment when I looked down into my boy's grave my sorrow was full of submission and without bitterness, it is because these agencies have worked upon me, and not because I have ever cared whether my poor personality shall remain distinct for ever from the All from whence it came and whither it goes.

And thus, my dear Kingsley, you will understand what my position is. I may be quite wrong, and in that case I know I shall have to pay the penalty for being wrong. But I can only say with Luther, "Gott helfe mir, ich kann nichts anders." [God help me, I can do nothing else].

I know right well that ninety-nine out of a hundred of my fellows would call me atheist, infidel, and all the other usual hard names. As our laws stand, if the lowest thief steals my coat, my evidence (my opinions being known) would not be received against him.

But I cannot help it. One thing people shall not call me with justice and that is—a liar. As you say of yourself, I too feel that I lack courage; but if ever the occasion arises when I am bound to speak, I will not shame my boy.

I have spoken more openly and distinctly to you than I ever have to any human being except my wife.

If you can show me that I err in premises or conclusion, I am ready to give up these as I would any other theories. But at any rate you will do me the justice to believe that I have not reached my conclusions without the care befitting the momentous nature of the problems involved.

And I write this the more readily to you, because it is clear to me that if that great and powerful instrument for good or evil, the Church of England, is to be saved from being shivered into fragments by the advancing tide of science—an event I should be very sorry to witness, but which will infallibly occur if men like Samuel of Oxford[7] are to have the guidance of her destinies—it must be by the efforts of men who, like yourself, see your way to the combination of the practice of the Church with the spirit of science. Understand that all the younger men of science whom I know intimately are *essentially* of my way of thinking. (I know not a scoffer or an irreligious or an immoral man among them, but they all regard orthodoxy as you do Brahmanism.) Understand that this new school of the prophets is the only one that can work miracles, the only one that can constantly appeal to nature for evidence that it is right, and you will comprehend that it is of no use to try to barricade us with shovel hats and aprons,[8] or to talk about our doctrines being "shocking."

I don't profess to understand the logic of

[6] By Thomas Carlyle, published in 1833.

[7] Bishop Samuel Wilberforce ("Soapy Sam," 1805–1873) who in 1860 debated at Oxford with Huxley concerning the truth of evolution.

[8] The costume of Anglican bishops.

yourself, Maurice,[9] and the rest of your school, but I have always said I would swear by your truthfulness and sincerity, and that good must come of your efforts. The more plain this was to me, however, the more obvious the necessity to let you see where the men of science are driving, and it has often been in my mind to write to you before.

If I have spoken too plainly anywhere, or too abruptly, pardon me, and do the like to me.

My wife thanks you very much for your volume of sermons.—Ever yours very faithfully,

T. H. Huxley

William James

FOOTNOTE ON SCIENCE

The aspiration to be "scientific" is such an idol of the tribe[10] to the present generation, is so sucked in with his mother's milk by every one of us, that we find it hard to conceive of a creature who should not feel it and harder still to treat it freely as the altogether peculiar and one-sided subjective interest which it is. But as a matter of fact, few even of the cultivated members of the race have shared it; it was invented but a generation or two ago. In the Middle Ages it meant only impious magic; and the way in which it even now strikes Orientals is charmingly shown in the letter of a Turkish cadi to an English traveller asking him for statistical information, which Sir A. Layard prints at the end of his *Nineveh and Baby-*

---

[9] Frederick Denison Maurice (1805–1872), British theologian who worked with Kingsley to found the Christian Socialistic movement.
[10] See *Novum Organum* I, 39 (1620), by Sir Francis Bacon.

lon. The document is too full of edification not to be given in full. It runs thus:

My Illustrious Friend, and Joy of my Liver!

The thing you ask of me is both difficult and useless. Although I have passed all my days in this place, I have neither counted the houses nor inquired into the number of the inhabitants; and as to what one person loads on his mules and the other stows away in the bottom of his ship, that is no business of mine. But, above all, as to the previous history of this city, God only knows the amount of dirt and confusion that the infidels may have eaten before the coming of the sword of Islam. It were unprofitable for us to inquire into it.

O my soul! O my lamb! seek not after the things which concern thee not. Thou camest unto us and we welcomed thee; go in peace.

Of a truth thou hast spoken many words; and there is no harm done, for the speaker is one and the listener is another. After the fashion of thy people thou hast wandered from one place to another, until thou art happy and content in none. We (praise be to God) were born here, and never desire to quit it. Is it possible, then, that the idea of a general intercourse between mankind should make any impression on our understandings? God forbid!

Listen, O my son! There is no wisdom equal unto the belief in God! He created the world, and shall we liken ourselves unto Him in seeking to penetrate into the mysteries of His creation? Shall we say, "Behold this star spinneth round that star, and this other star with a tail goeth and cometh in so many years!" Let it go! He from whose hand it came will guide and direct it.

But thou wilt say unto me, "Stand aside, O man, for I am more learned than thou art, and have seen more things." If thou thinkest that thou art in this respect better than I am, thou art welcome. I praise God that I seek not that which I require not. Thou art learned in the things I care not for; and as for that which thou hast seen, I spit upon it. Will much knowledge create thee a double belly, or wilt thou seek Paradise with thine eyes?

O my friend! if thou wilt be happy, say, "There is no God but God!" Do no evil, and thus wilt thou fear neither man nor death; for surely thine hour will come!

The meek in spirit (El Fakir),

Imaum Ali Zadi

E. M. Forster

TROUBLESOME MOLLUSCS

Thirty years have passed, and Voltaire, now at the height of his fame, holds a pair of scissors in one hand and a slug in the other. Let me repeat: in the one hand he holds a large brown slug, and in the other a pair of scissors. The slug is of Swiss extraction, and comes off one of his estates, where it has been eating the lettuces. *Ecrasez l'infâme?*[11] But no: he reserves it for another purpose. Looking into its face, he surveys the gloomy, unresponsive snout which is all a slug offers; he compares it with the face of a snail, so much more piquant, and both with the face of a man. All three are different, but all are faces, and he does not know whether he trembles at the edge of a great discovery or of a joke. Beneath him are the blue waters of the Lake Leman, beyond them the walls of Mont Blanc; he stands with one foot in Genevan territory to escape the French, and the other in France, to be safe from the Swiss. He stands triumphant, all his possessions are around him, thousands of his trees grow, his conten-

ted peasantry work, his invalid cousin dozes, the bells of the church he built chime —and he cuts off the slug's head.

His niece, Madame Denis, keeps house for him now—or rather houses, for he possesses three. Awkward and torpid, Madame Denis holds at bay the ambassadors, savants, mountebanks, princesses, who have come from all over Europe to see her uncle. He is researching, he must not be disturbed. The scissors approach again, and a second slug is decapitated, and a third, until there are twelve. Nor does this conclude the gruesome tale: in a box hard by seethes a clot of headless snails. Voltaire surveys his victims with affability. He does not like the slugs much but has great sympathy with the snails; he finds their courtships gallant if curious, their contours intelligent, and their taste delightful. Nevertheless, he continues to snip off their heads. It is Science. He is trying to find out whether heads grow again.

Once more, the results are conflicting. As in the case of fire, it is as if all Nature combines to conceal the truth. Slugs behave differently to snails, which might be expected, but they also behave differently among themselves. All molluscs lack earnestness of purpose, so to speak—sometimes they die when their heads are removed, sometimes they grow fresh heads and live, sometimes they live without heads. Voltaire is delighted, but puzzled. On the whole, slugs grow new heads, snails don't; though snails when mutilated merely between the horns repair the damage more frequently than do slugs whose heads have been removed entirely. What may we deduce from this? Well —not much, and at the end of one of his solemn works (his *Questions on the Encyclopaedia*) he suddenly exclaims, "Retraction! I retract the scissors with which I cut off the snails' heads." For they had grown in 1772 but not in 1773, and what can one build on such creatures? He can only say that Nature is always admirable, and that what we call

---

[11] Stamp out the shame: Voltaire's war-cry in his battles against dogmatic religion.

"Nature" is really an art that we have not yet understood. "All is art, from Zodiac down to my snails."

To retract and to relinquish are, however, different things, and Voltaire had the happy idea of turning his failures into a joke, and fathering them on the unfortunate clergy. He invents a charming monk, Père l'Escarbotier, who is also a cook, and causes him to pour out his difficulties to Père Elie, who is a Doctor in Theology in another convent. The correspondence between the two is superb. "People used to talk about Jesuits, but now they are completely occupied with snails," begins Père l'Escarbotier with modest pride, and he goes on to describe his own inconclusive experiments in the kitchen; he has often mentioned them in his sermons: "I could compare certain of my snails only to Saint Denis, who, after his head had been cut off, carried it tenderly for six miles in his arms." Père Elie receives this miracle in silence. In a second letter the reverend cook asks what, when the heads are cut off, happens to the souls. He replies to this readily enough: the question is simple, though it requires a different answer in the case of snails and of slugs, for the souls of snails are in their heads, but slugs have their souls anywhere. But a third letter, raising the question of a "vital germ," from which all species have developed, elicits a sharp rebuke; Père Elie reminds Père l'Escarbotier that "corruption is the mother of all things" and warns him against heretical speculations which lead to no good. "Adieu!" he concludes, on a kinder note. "May the snails who are set beneath you and the insects who accompany you ever bless your reverence." And there is a further conclusion as from the pen of Voltaire himself: "We must marvel and be silent." Gaily and charmingly he has turned his foolish scientific experiments into a humorous pamphlet: he has begun as a goose and ended as a mockingbird.

Since Madame du Châtelet's death he had taken science less seriously. He had never married, and his niece urged him towards the drama, if anywhere, for she enjoyed acting. Now and then the old ardor would break out: he would wonder whether Hannibal had really dissolved the Alps with hot vinegar, as the historian Livy reports, so he heated some vinegar and poured it on a piece of Mont Blanc. As soon as Mont Blanc adequately cracked, his mind was at rest, and he went on to other matters. The fact is that his seriousness was taking another direction: all his wit and wisdom were being marshaled for his struggle against the Church. He believed in God, he even built a church: but he loathed the Church, and the depth of his hatred appears in the extraordinary difficulties into which he got over sea-shells.

Sea-shells do not, to the outsider, seem more troublesome than other molluscs, but Voltaire regarded them from a very special point of view: they were traitors, who attempted to demonstrate the truth of revealed religion instead of advancing the cause of Liberty, as natural objects should. Had they remained in the sea, all would have been well, but straying from their proper element they appeared in large heaps in the middle of Touraine and elsewhere, or in fossil forms, or on the tops of mountains. Why, you may ask, did this disconcert Voltaire? Why, because it suggested that they had been left when the waters of the Flood subsided, so that Genesis was true. He could not allow this, and he set out with his usual energy and ingenuity to put shells in their places. He had not been trained by the Jesuits for nothing, and the arguments he brought forward are rather too conclusive to be convincing.

In the first place, he argued that the shells in question are not from the sea at all, but are either the shells of fresh-water oysters or the property of his old friends the snails. "In a rainy year, there are more snails in a space of thirty miles than there are men in the whole earth," and this being so, the deposits in Touraine and elsewhere can be easily accounted for. Then he argues that the shells were engendered spontaneously in the earth, "and grew just as stones do." A correspondent of his, a gentleman who had property near Chinon, had actually watched empty shells growing; twice in eighty years a heavy crop had been produced; they were microscopic at first, and gradually swelled and stuck against one another until they formed a soft stone, suitable for building; there were five or six species of these empty shells, and since the tenants and neighbors of the gentleman had seen them too, doubt was impossible. Indeed, we can all of us watch the process for ourselves, for the reason that the so-called Ammonite fossils vary in size: the curves of their spirals must obviously increase the longer they lie in the earth. And, finally, let us grant, for the sake of argument, that all the above arguments are false, and that the shells which have given such support to superstition really did originate in the sea. No matter—all is not lost: they can still be accounted for in three ways. Firstly, since so many of them are cockles, they may have dropped from the hats of Palmers who were going to the shrine of St. James at Compostella in the Middle Ages. Secondly, since so many are edible, they may be the debris of picnic parties. And thirdly, since so many of them are different, they may have come from the collections of dead conchologists. To this last argument—which leaves us almost more breathless than its companions—Voltaire returns more than once. He was vexed by the bones of a reindeer and of a hippopotamus which were found near Etampes. "Are we to conclude from this," he asks, "that the Nile and Lapland once shared the Orleans-Paris road?" Surely, it is simpler to suppose that the bones once adorned the cabinet of a connoisseur!

His anxiety over shells led him even further than we should expect. He feared that if once a flood was admitted Noah's ark would come sailing in, and consequently had to ridicule all theories of the universe that emphasized water. There was the fish Oannes, who came out of the Euphrates to preach to the Babylonians.[12] There was Thales, who thought that the stars lived on mist. There was Buffon, who ascribes mountains to the action of waves. There was Maillet,[13] who deduced from a heap of shells at Cairo that Egypt had once been under the sea and the Egyptians fish. Voltaire mocks them all indiscriminately. "In spite of the present passion for genealogies, there are not many people who would claim descent from a turbot or a cod." Then the coral insects strike his eye, and seeing that they may give trouble he makes short work of their claims. They must not be allowed to build coral reefs, or the land will appear once to have been under the sea. "Certainly, one does find little insects in coral, but where does one not find little insects? Old walls are full of them, but no one supposes that they build the old walls. So is old cheese—but no one argues that the cheese has been made by the mites." One way and another, the sea is prevented from encroaching on human destiny; not even in the name of science may it cover the earth, lest when the waters decrease Mount Ararat should appear and our race again enter into bondage. Voltaire's attitude here is, in a cruder form, the attitude of certain unorthodox people today, who are disquieted by the work of Eddington and Jeans, because of the support for Christianity that may be extracted from it. He hated religion, having witnessed the misery it caused, and he was not detached enough to admit that because a thing is baneful it is not necessarily un-

[12] As related by the Babylonian priest Berossus, third century B.C.
[13] Benoît de Maillet, author of *Discourses on the Shrinking of the Sea* . . . , 1748.

true. Indeed, he was not detached at all, and if we think he was we misread both him and his age; he loved freedom, not truth, so that when the coral insects appeared to be helping the Jesuits he used casuistry to discredit them. Never, never, if he could help it, should Noah's ark sail over the world again. And if he had lived today, and been told that in the opinion of many biologists all life, including human life, had a marine or intertidal origin, he would once more bring up his armory and produce arguments which, alas! we should no longer find devastating. For Voltaire, today, would seem a much smaller figure than he was in the eighteenth century; we should admire his personality, fear his tongue, and adore his short stories, but dismiss his "serious" utterances as journalism.

Probably he could have been an eminent scientist if he liked—he was intelligent enough for anything, and while he was under Madame du Châtelet's influence he showed powers of application: his treatise on Newton proves this. But after her death he became desultory and a tease; his mistrust of theories led him to the theory that other people's conclusions must be wrong. He was hampered by his need of fun; both scientists and their pursuits can be irresistibly amusing, and Voltaire was not the man to check his own mirth. He came, he saw, he laughed, and the slugs and snails that might have led a serious anatomist towards the discovery of the pharyngeal ring, suggested instead a correspondence between two comic monks.

Nevertheless, he did science one good turn: he impressed the general public with her importance. This is all that a literary man can do for science, and perhaps only a literary man can do it. The expert scientist is too conscious of the difficulties of his subject; he knows that he can only communicate his discoveries to us by simplifying and therefore falsifying them, and that even when he can state a fact correctly we receive it incorrectly, because we cannot relate it to the thousands of other facts relevant. The literary man has no such misgivings. His imagination is touched by the infinite variety of the natural world; he reads books about it, skipping the statistics, he forgets most of what he does read, and perhaps he performs a few experiments in order to grasp the meaning of research. Then, in the course of his other activities, he writes about science, with a spurious lucidity that makes the expert smile. Spurious, but stimulating; the public does not realize, from the remarks of such men as Lucretius, Voltaire, Charles Kingsley, Samuel Butler, Mr. Aldous Huxley, Mr. Gerald Heard,[14] that something is happening. It does get a misty idea of the expanding empire of mankind.

"Certainly, one must admit that Nature is varied." said the traveller.
"Yes, Nature is like a bed of flowers, where—"
"Oh, never mind the bed of flowers!"
"She is," the secretary continued, "like an assemblage of blondes and of brunettes, whose tresses—"
"Oh, bother the blondes and brunettes!"
"Well, she is like a picture gallery, where the features—"
"No no; Nature is like Nature; why introduce similes?"
"To amuse you!" the secretary replied.
"I don't want to be amused," said the traveller; "I want to learn!"

In this passage—it comes from his charming fantasy *Micromégas*—Voltaire neatly contrasts the literary man and the scientist. The literary man loves images, and as soon as he has found a vivid one, his interest in the truth it is supposed to illustrate is apt to cease. But the scientist knows that Nature is Nature. Voltaire himself was literary, yet he had enough sense of science to perceive

14 Author of *The Ascent of Humanity*, 1929.

his own limitations, and though he amuses us and is amused by hot iron and slugs, he has realized—perhaps through Madame du Châtelet—that the universe has not been created for our stylistic exercises. For what, then, has it been created? He cannot say, *"cultiver son jardin"* [15] is a reaction, not a reply. But he could ask the question, he could cause others to ask it, and if "popular interest in science" has any importance (for my own part, I think it has immense importance), he must be honored as an early popularizer.

Jonathan Swift

THE FLYING ISLAND

This next day I sailed to another island and thence to a third and fourth, sometimes using my sail, and sometimes my paddles. But not to trouble the reader with a particular account of my distresses, let it suffice that on the fifth day I arrived at the last island in my sight, which lay south-southeast to the former.

The island was at a greater distance than I expected, and I did not reach it in less than five hours. I encompassed it almost round before I could find a convenient place to land in, which was a small creek, about three times the wideness of my canoe. I found the island to be all rocky, only a little intermingled with tufts of grass and sweet-smelling herbs. I took out my small provisions, and after having refreshed myself, I secured the remainder in a cave, whereof there were great numbers. I gathered plenty of eggs upon the rocks and got a quantity of dry seaweed and parched grass, which I de-

signed to kindle the next day and roast my eggs as well as I could. (For I had about me my flint, steel, match, and burning-glass.) I lay all night in the cave where I had lodged my provisions. My bed was the same dry grass and seaweed which I intended for fuel. I slept very little, for the disquiets of my mind prevailed over my weariness and kept me awake. I considered how impossible it was to preserve my life in so desolate a place and how miserable my end must be. Yet I found myself so listless and desponding that I had not the heart to rise, and before I could get spirits enough to creep out of my cave, the day was far advanced. I walked a while among the rocks; the sky was perfectly clear and the sun so hot that I was forced to turn my face from it: when all on a sudden it became obscured, as I thought, in a manner very different from what happens by the interposition of a cloud. I turned back and perceived a vast opaque body between me and the sun, moving forwards towards the island: it seemed to be about two miles high, and hid the sun six or seven minutes, but I did not observe the air to be much colder or the sky more darkened than if I had stood under the shade of a mountain. As it approached nearer over the place where I was, it appeared to be a firm substance, the bottom flat, smooth, and shining very bright from the reflection of the sea below. I stood upon a height about two hundred yards from the shore and saw this vast body descending almost to a parallel with me, at less than an English mile distance. I took out my pocket-perspective[16] and could plainly discover numbers of people moving up and down the sides of it, which appeared to be sloping, but what those people were doing I was not able to distinguish.

The natural love of life gave me some inward motions of joy, and I was ready to entertain a hope that this adventure might

15 [One must] cultivate one's garden—the resigned conclusion of Voltaire's novel *Candide* (1759).

16 Small telescope.

converse with them. I was soon able to call for bread and drink or whatever else I wanted.

After dinner my company withdrew, and a person was sent to me by the King's order, attended by a flapper. He brought with him pen, ink, and paper, and three or four books, giving me to understand by signs that he was sent to teach me the language. We sat together four hours, in which time I wrote down a great number of words in columns with the translations over against them. I likewise made a shift to learn several short sentences. For my tutor would order one of my servants to fetch something, to turn about, to make a bow, to sit, or stand, or walk and the like. Then I took down the sentence in writing. He showed me also in one of his books the figures of the sun, moon, and stars, the zodiac, the tropics, and polar circles, together with the denominations of many figures of planes and solids. He gave me the names and descriptions of all the musical instruments and the general terms of art in playing on each of them. After he had left me I placed all my words with their interpretations in alphabetical order. And thus in a few days, by the help of a very faithful memory, I got some insight into their language.

The word which I interpret the *Flying* or *Floating Island* is in the original *Laputa*, whereof I could never learn the true etymology. *Lap* in the old obsolete language signifieth *high*, and *untuh* a *governor*, from which they say by corruption was derived *Laputa*, from *Lapuntuh*. But I do not approve of this derivation, which seems to be a little strained. I ventured to offer to the learned among them a conjecture of my own, that *Laputa* was *quasi Lap outed; Lap* signifying properly the dancing of the sunbeams in the sea, and *outed* a wing, which however I shall not obtrude, but submit to the judicious reader.

Those to whom the King had entrusted me, observing how ill I was clad, ordered a tailor to come next morning and take my measure for a suit of clothes. This operator did his office after a different manner from those of this trade in Europe. He first took my altitude by a quadrant, and then, with rule and compasses, described the dimensions and outlines of my whole body, all which he entered upon paper, and in six days brought my clothes very ill made and quite out of shape, by happening to mistake a figure in the calculation. But my comfort was that I observed such accidents very frequent and little regarded.

During my confinement for want of clothes, and by an indisposition that held me some days longer, I much enlarged my dictionary; and when I went next to court, was able to understand many things the King spoke and to return him some kind of answers. His Majesty had given orders that the island should move northeast and by east to the vertical point over Lagado, the metropolis of the whole kingdom below upon the firm earth. It was about ninety leagues distant, and our voyage lasted four days and a half. I was not in the least sensible of the progressive motion made in the air by the island. On the second morning about eleven o'clock, the King himself in person, attended by his nobility, courtiers, and officers, having prepared all their musical instruments, played on them for three hours without intermission, so that I was quite stunned with the noise; neither could I possibly guess the meaning till my tutor informed me. He said that the people of their island had their ears adapted to hear the music of the spheres,[18] which always played at certain periods, and the court was now prepared to bear their part in whatever instrument they most excelled.

In our journey towards Lagado, the capital city, his Majesty ordered that the island should stop over certain towns and villages,

[18] The harmonious sounds supposedly produced by the moving crystal globes thought to support the heavenly bodies.

from whence he might receive the petitions of his subjects. And to this purpose several packthreads were let down with small weights at the bottom. On these packthreads the people strung their petitions, which mounted up directly like the scraps of paper fastened by schoolboys at the end of the string that holds their kite. Sometimes we received wine and victuals from below, which were drawn up by pulleys.

The knowledge I had in mathematics gave me great assistance in acquiring their phraseology, which depended much upon that science and music; and in the latter I was not unskilled. Their ideas are perpetually conversant in[19] lines and figures. If they would, for example, praise the beauty of a woman or any other animal, they describe it by rhombs, circles, parallelograms, ellipses, and other geometrical terms, or else by words of art drawn from music, needless here to repeat. I observed in the King's kitchen all sorts of mathematical and musical instruments, after the figures of which they cut up the joints that were served to his Majesty's table.

Their houses were very ill built, the walls bevel, without one right angle in any apartment, and this defect ariseth from the contempt they bear for practical geometry, which they despise as vulgar and mechanic, those instructions they give being too refined for the intellectuals of their workmen, which occasions perpetual mistakes. And although they are dexterous enough upon a piece of paper in the management of the rule, the pencil, and the divider, yet in the common actions and behavior of life I have not seen a more clumsy, awkward, and unhandy people, nor so slow and perplexed in their conceptions upon all other subjects except those of mathematics and music. They are very bad reasoners and vehemently given to opposition unless when they happen to be of the right opinion, which is

[19] Involved with.

seldom their case. Imagination, fancy, and invention they are wholly strangers to nor have any words in their language by which those ideas can be expressed, the whole compass of their thoughts and mind being shut up within the two forementioned sciences.

Most of them, and especially those who deal in the astronomical part, have great faith in judicial astrology, although they are ashamed to own it publicly. But what I chiefly admired and thought altogether unaccountable was the strong disposition I observed in them towards news and politics, perpetually enquiring into public affairs, giving their judgments in matters of state, and passionately disputing every inch of a party opinion. I have indeed observed the same disposition among most of the mathematicians I have known in Europe, although I could never discover the least analogy between the two sciences, unless those people suppose that because the smallest circle hath as many degrees as the largest, therefore the regulation and management of the world require no more abilities than the handling and turning of a globe. But I rather take this quality to spring from a very common infirmity of human nature, inclining us to be more curious and conceited in matters where we have least concern and for which we are least adapted either by study or nature.

These people are under continual disquietudes, never enjoying a minute's peace of mind; and their disturbances proceed from causes which very little affect the rest of mortals. Their apprehensions arise from several changes they dread in the celestial bodies. For instance that the earth by the continual approaches of the sun towards it must in course of time be absorbed or swallowed up. That the face of the sun will by degrees be encrusted with its own effluvia and give no more light to the world. That the earth very narrowly escaped a brush from the tail of the last comet, which would have infallibly reduced it to ashes; and that the next, which they have calculated for one-and-thirty years hence, will probably destroy us. For, if in its perihelion it should approach within a certain degree of the sun (as by their calculations they have reason to dread), it will conceive a degree of heat ten thousand times more intense than that of red-hot glowing iron; and in its absence from the sun, carry a blazing tail ten hundred thousand and fourteen miles long, through which if the earth should pass at the distance of one hundred thousand miles from the nucleus or main body of the comet, it must in its passage be set on fire and reduced to ashes. That the sun daily spending its rays without any nutriment to supply them, will at last be wholly consumed and annihilated, which must be attended with the destruction of this earth and of all the planets that receive their light from it.

They are so perpetually alarmed with the apprehensions of these and the like impending dangers that they can neither sleep quietly in their beds or have any relish from the common pleasures or amusements of life. When they meet an acquaintance in the morning, the first question is about the sun's health, how he looked at his setting and rising, and what hopes they have to avoid the stroke of the approaching comet. This conversation they are apt to run into with the same temper that boys discover in delighting to hear terrible stories of sprites and hobgoblins, which they greedily listen to and dare not go to bed for fear.

The women of the island have abundance of vivacity; they contemn their husbands and are exceedingly fond of strangers, whereof there is always a considerable number from the continent below, attending at court, either upon affairs of the several towns and corporations of their own particular occasions, but are much despised because they want the same endowments.[20]

20 I.e., the Laputan husbands scorn the strangers for not having the same talents as themselves.

Among these the ladies choose their gallants: but the vexation is that they act with too much ease and security, for the husband is always so rapt in speculation that the mistress and lover may proceed to the greatest familiarities before his face, if he be but provided with paper and implements, and without his flapper at his side.

The wives and daughters lament their confinement to the island, although I think it the most delicious spot of ground in the world; and although they live here in the greatest plenty and magnificence and are allowed to do whatever they please, they long to see the world and take the diversions of the metropolis, which they are not allowed to do without a particular licence from the King; and this is not easy to be obtained because the people of quality have found by frequent experience how hard it is to persuade their women to return from below. I was told that a great court lady, who had several children, is married to the prime minister, the richest subject in the kingdom, a very graceful person, extremely fond of her, and lives in the finest palace of the island, went down to Lagado on the pretence of health, there hid herself for several months, till the King sent a warrant to search for her, and she was found in an obscure eating house all in rags, having pawned her clothes to maintain an old deformed footman who beat her every day and in whose company she was taken much against her will. And although her husband received her with all possible kindness and without the least reproach, she soon after contrived to steal down again with all her jewels, to the same gallant, and hath not been heard of since.

This may perhaps pass with the reader rather for a European or English story than for one of a country so remote. But he may please to consider that the caprices of womankind are not limited by any climate or nation and that they are much more uniform than can be easily imagined.

In about a month's time I had made a tolerable proficiency in their language and was able to answer most of the King's questions when I had the honor to attend him. His Majesty discovered not the least curiosity to enquire into the laws, government, history, religion, or manners of the countries where I had been, but confined his questions to the state of mathematics, and received the account I gave him with great contempt and indifference, though often roused by his flapper on each side.

Stephen Vincent Benét

THE BLOOD OF THE MARTYRS

The man who expected to be shot lay with his eyes open, staring at the upper left-hand corner of his cell. He was fairly well over his last beating, and they might come for him any time now. There was a yellow stain in the cell corner near the ceiling; he had liked it at first, then disliked it; now he was coming back to liking it again.

He could see it more clearly with his glasses on, but he only put on his glasses for special occasions now—the first thing in the morning, and when they brought the food in, and for interviews with the General. The lenses of the glasses had been cracked in a beating some months before, and it strained his eyes to wear them too long. Fortunately, in his present life he had very few occasions demanding clear vision. But, nevertheless, the accident to his glasses worried him, as it worries all near-sighted people. You put your glasses on the first thing in the morning and the world leaps into proportion; if it

THE BLOOD OF THE MARTYRS: ". . . is the seed of the Church"—Tertullian, *Apologeticus*, L.

does not do so, something is wrong with the world.

The man did not believe greatly in symbols, but his chief nightmare, nowadays, was an endless one in which, suddenly and without warning, a large piece of glass would drop out of one of the lenses and he would grope around the cell, trying to find it. He would grope very carefully and gingerly, for hours of darkness, but the end was always the same—the small, unmistakable crunch of irreplaceable glass beneath his heel or his knee. Then he would wake up sweating, with his hands cold. This dream alternated with the one of being shot, but he found no great benefit in the change.

As he lay there, you could see that he had an intellectual head—the head of a thinker or a scholar, old and bald, with the big, domed brow. It was, as a matter of fact, a well-known head; it had often appeared in the columns of newspapers and journals, sometimes when the surrounding text was in a language Professor Malzius could not read. The body, though stooped and worn, was still a strong peasant body and capable of surviving a good deal of ill-treatment, as his captors had found out. He had fewer teeth than when he came to prison, and both the ribs and the knee had been badly set, but these were minor matters. It also occurred to him that his blood count was probably poor. However, if he could ever get out and to a first-class hospital, he was probably good for at least ten years more of work. But, of course, he would not get out. They would shoot him before that, and it would be over.

Sometimes he wished passionately that it would be over—tonight—this moment; at other times he was shaken by the mere blind fear of death. The latter he tried to treat as he would have treated an attack of malaria, knowing that it was an attack, but not always with success. He should have been able to face it better than most—he was Gregor Malzius, the scientist—but that did not always help. The fear of death persisted, even when one had noted and classified it as a purely physical reaction. When he was out of here, he would be able to write a very instructive little paper on the fear of death. He could even do it here, if he had writing materials, but there was no use asking for those. Once they had been given him and he had spent two days quite happily. But they had torn up the work and spat upon it in front of his face. It was a childish thing to do, but it discouraged a man from working.

It seemed odd that he had never seen anybody shot, but he never had. During the war, his reputation and his bad eyesight had exempted him from active service. He had been bombed a couple of times when his reserve battalion was guarding the railway bridge, but that was quite different. You were not tied to a stake, and the airplanes were not trying to kill you as an individual. He knew the place where it was done here, of course. But prisoners did not see the executions, they merely heard, if the wind was from the right quarter.

He had tried again and again to visualize how it would be, but it always kept mixing with an old steel engraving he had seen in boyhood—the execution of William Walker, the American filibuster, in Honduras. William Walker was a small man with a white, semi-Napoleonic face. He was standing, very correctly dressed, in front of an open grave, and before him a ragged line of picturesque natives were raising their muskets. When he was shot he would instantly and tidily fall into the grave, like a man dropping through a trap door; as a boy, the extreme neatness of the arrangement had greatly impressed Gregor Malzius. Behind the wall there were palm trees, and, somewhere off to the right, blue and warm, the Caribbean Sea. It would not be like that at all, for his own execution; and yet, whenever he thought of it, he thought of it as being like that.

Well, it was his own fault. He could have

accepted the new regime; some respectable people had done that. He could have fled the country; many honorable people had. A scientist should be concerned with the eternal, not with transient political phenomena; and a scientist should be able to live anywhere. But thirty years at the university were thirty years, and after all, he was Malzius, one of the first biochemists in the world. To the last, he had not believed that they would touch him. Well, he had been wrong about that.

The truth, of course, was the truth. One taught it or one did not teach it. If one did not teach it, it hardly mattered what one did. But he had no quarrel with any established government; he was willing to run up a flag every Tuesday, as long as they let him alone. Most people were fools, and one government was as good as another for them—it had taken them twenty years to accept his theory of cell mutation. Now, if he'd been like his friend Bonnard—a fellow who signed protests, attended meetings for the cause of world peace, and generally played the fool in public—they'd have had some reason to complain. An excellent man in his field, Bonnard—none better—but outside of it, how deplorably like an actor, with his short gray beard, his pink cheeks, and his impulsive enthusiasm! Any government could put a fellow like Bonnard in prison—though it would be an injury to science and, therefore, wrong. For that matter, he thought grimly, Bonnard would enjoy being a martyr. He'd walk gracefully to the execution post with a begged cigarette in his mouth, and some theatrical last quip. But Bonnard was safe in his own land—doubtless writing heated and generous articles on The Case of Professor Malzius—and he, Malzius, was the man who was going to be shot. He would like a cigarette, too, on his way to execution; he had not smoked in five months. But he certainly didn't intend to ask for one, and they wouldn't think of offering him any. That was the difference between him and Bonnard.

His mind went back with longing to the stuffy laboratory and stuffier lecture hall at the university; his feet yearned for the worn steps he had climbed ten thousand times, and his eyes for the long steady look through the truthful lens into worlds too tiny for the unaided eye. They had called him "The Bear" and "Old Prickly," but they had fought to work under him, the best of the young men. They said he would explain the Last Judgment in terms of cellular phenomena, but they had crowded to his lectures. It was Williams, the Englishman, who had made up the legend that he carried a chocolate éclair and a set of improper postcards in his battered briefcase. Quite untrue, of course —chocolate always made him ill, and he had never looked at an improper postcard in his life. And Williams would never know that he knew the legend, too; for Williams had been killed long ago in the war. For a moment, Professor Malzius felt blind hate at the thought of an excellent scientific machine like Williams being smashed in a war. But blind hate was an improper emotion for a scientist, and he put it aside.

He smiled grimly again; they hadn't been able to break up his classes—lucky he was The Bear! He'd seen one colleague hooted from his desk by a band of determined young hoodlums—too bad, but if a man couldn't keep order in his own classroom, he'd better get out. They'd wrecked his own laboratory, but not while he was there.

It was so senseless, so silly. "In God's name," he said reasonably, to no one, "what sort of conspirator do you think I would make? A man of my age and habits! I am interested in cellular phenomena!" And yet they were beating him because he would not tell about the boys. As if he had even paid attention to half the nonsense! There were certain passwords and greetings—a bar of music you whistled, entering a restaurant; the address of a firm that specialized, osten-

sibly, in vacuum cleaners. But they were not his own property. They belonged to the young men who had trusted The Bear. He did not know what half of them meant, and the one time he had gone to a meeting, he had felt like a fool. For they were fools and childish—playing the childish games of conspiracy that people like Bonnard enjoyed. Could they even make a better world than the present? He doubted it extremely. And yet, he could not betray them; they had come to him, looking over their shoulders, with darkness in their eyes.

A horrible, an appalling thing—to be trusted. He had no wish to be a guide and counselor of young men. He wanted to do his work. Suppose they were poor and ragged and oppressed; he had been a peasant himself, he had eaten black bread. It was by his own efforts that he was Professor Malzius. He did not wish the confidences of boys like Gregopolous and the others—for, after all what was Gregopolous? An excellent and untiring laboratory assistant—and a laboratory assistant he would remain to the end of his days. He had pattered about the laboratory like a fox terrier, with a fox terrier's quick bright eyes. Like a devoted dog, he had made a god of Professor Malzius. "I don't want your problems, man. I don't want to know what you are doing outside the laboratory." But Gregopolous had brought his problems and his terrible trust none the less, humbly and proudly, like a fox terrier with a bone. After that—well, what was a man to do?

He hoped they would get it over with, and quickly. The world should be like a chemical formula, full of reason and logic. Instead, there were all these young men, and their eyes. They conspired, hopelessly and childishly, for what they called freedom against the new regime. They wore no overcoats in winter and were often hunted and killed. Even if they did not conspire, they had miserable little love affairs and ate the wrong food—yes, even before, at the university, they had been the same. Why the devil would they not accept? Then they could do their work. Of course, a great many of them would not be allowed to accept—they had the wrong ideas or the wrong politics—but then they could run away. If Malzius, at twenty, had had to run from his country, he would still have been a scientist. To talk of a free world was a delusion; men were not free in the world. Those who wished got a space of time to get their work done. That was all. And yet, he had not accepted—he did not know why.

Now he heard the sound of steps along the corridor. His body began to quiver and the places where he had been beaten hurt him. He noted it as an interesting reflex. Sometimes they merely flashed the light in the cell and passed by. On the other hand, it might be death. It was a hard question to decide.

The lock creaked, the door opened. "Get up, Malzius!" said the hard, bright voice of the guard. Gregor Malzius got up, a little stiffly, but quickly.

"Put on your glasses, you old fool!" said the guard, with a laugh. "You are going to the General."

Professor Malzius found the stone floors of the corridor uneven, though he knew them well enough. Once or twice the guard struck him, lightly and without malice, as one strikes an old horse with a whip. The blows were familiar and did not register on Professor Malzius' consciousness; he merely felt proud of not stumbling. He was apt to stumble; once he had hurt his knee.

He noticed, it seemed to him, an unusual tenseness and officiousness about his guard. Once, even, in a brightly lighted corridor the guard moved to strike him, but refrained. However, that, too, happened occasionally, with one guard or another, and Professor Malzius merely noted the fact. It was a small fact, but an important one in the economy in which he lived.

But there could be no doubt that something unusual was going on in the castle. There were more guards than usual, many of them strangers. He tried to think, carefully, as he walked, if it could be one of the new national holidays. It was hard to keep track of them all. The General might be in a good humor. Then they would merely have a cat-and-mouse conversation for half an hour and nothing really bad would happen. Once, even, there had been a cigar. Professor Malzius, the scientist, licked his lips at the thought.

Now he was being turned over to a squad of other guards, with salutings. This was really unusual; Professor Malzius bit his mouth, inconspicuously. He had the poignant distrust of a monk or an old prisoner at any break in routine. Old prisoners are your true conservatives; they only demand that the order around them remains exactly the same.

It alarmed him as well that the new guards did not laugh at him. New guards almost always laughed when they saw him for the first time. He was used to the laughter and missed it—his throat felt dry. He would have liked, just once, to eat at the university restaurant before he died. It was bad food, ill cooked and starchy, food good enough for poor students and professors, but he would have liked to be there, in the big smoky room that smelt of copper boilers and cabbage, with a small cup of bitter coffee before him and a cheap cigarette. He did not ask for his dog or his notebooks, the old photographs in his bedroom, his incomplete experiments, or his freedom. Just to lunch once more at the university restaurant and have people point out The Bear. It seemed a small thing to ask, but of course, it was quite impossible.

"Halt!" said a voice, and he halted. There were, for the third time, salutings. Then the door of the General's office opened and he was told to go in.

He stood, just inside the door, in the posture of attention, as he had been taught.

The crack in the left lens of his glasses made a crack across the room, and his eyes were paining him already, but he paid no attention to that. There was the familiar figure of the General, with his air of a well-fed and extremely healthy tomcat, and there was another man, seated at the General's desk. He could not see the other man very well—the crack made him bulge and waver —but he did not like his being there.

"Well, professor," said the General, in an easy, purring voice.

Malzius' entire body jerked. He had made a fearful, an unpardonable omission. He must remedy it at once. "Long live the state," he shouted in a loud thick voice, and saluted. He knew, bitterly, that his salute was ridiculous and that he looked ridiculous, making it. But perhaps the General would laugh—he had done so before. Then everything would be all right, for it was not quite as easy to beat a man after you had laughed at him.

The General did not laugh. He made a half turn instead, toward the man at the desk. The gesture said, "You see, he is well trained." It was the gesture of a man of the world, accustomed to deal with unruly peasants and animals—the gesture of a man fitted to be General.

The man at the desk paid no attention to the General's gesture. He lifted his head, and Malzius saw him more clearly and with complete unbelief. It was not a man but a picture come alive. Professor Malzius had seen the picture a hundred times; they had made him salute and take off his hat in front of it, when he had had a hat. Indeed, the picture had presided over his beatings. The man himself was a little smaller, but the picture was a good picture. There were many dictators in the world, and this was one type. The face was white, beaky, and semi-Napoleonic; the lean, military body sat squarely in its chair. The eyes dominated the face, and the mouth was rigid. I remember also a hypnotist and a woman Charcot showed me, at his clinic in Paris, thought Professor Malzius. But there is also, obviously, an endocrine unbalance. Then his thoughts stopped.

"Tell the man to come closer," said the man at the desk. "Can you hear me? Is he deaf?"

"No, Your Excellency," said the General, with enormous, purring respect. "But he is a little old, though perfectly healthy. . . . Are you not, Professor Malzius?"

"Yes, I am perfectly healthy. I am very well treated here," said Professor Malzius, in his loud thick voice. They were not going to catch him with traps like that, not even by dressing up somebody as the Dictator. He fixed his eyes on the big old-fashioned inkwell on the General's desk—that, at least, was perfectly sane.

"Come closer," said the man at the desk to Professor Malzius, and the latter advanced till he could almost touch the inkwell with his fingers. Then he stopped with a jerk, hoping he had done right. The movement removed the man at the desk from the crack in his lenses, and Professor Malzius knew suddenly that it was true. This was, indeed, the Dictator, this man with the rigid mouth. He began to talk.

"I have been very well treated here and the General has acted with the greatest consideration," he said. "But I am Professor Gregor Malzius—professor of biochemistry. For thirty years I have lectured at the university; I am a fellow of the Royal Society, a corresponding member of the Academy of Sciences at Berlin, at Rome, at Boston, at Paris, and Stockholm. I have received the Nottingham Medal, the Lamarck Medal, the Order of St. John of Portugal, and the Nobel Prize. I think my blood count is low, but I have received a great many degrees and my experiments on the migratory cells are not finished. I do not wish to complain of my treatment, but I must continue my experiments."

He stopped, like a clock that has run down, surprised to hear the sound of his own voice. He noted, in one part of his mind, that the General had made a move to silence him, but had himself been silenced by the Dictator.

"Yes, Professor Malzius," said the man at the desk, in a harsh, toneless voice. "There has been a regrettable error." The rigid face stared at Professor Malzius. Professor Malzius stared back. He did not say anything.

"In these days," said the Dictator, his voice rising, "the nation demands the submission of every citizen. Encircled by jealous foes, our reborn land yet steps forward toward her magnificent destiny." The words continued for some time, the voice rose and fell. Professor Malzius listened respectfully; he had heard the words many times before and they had ceased to have meaning to him. He was thinking of certain cells of the body that rebel against the intricate processes of Nature and set up their own bellicose state. Doubtless they, too, have a destiny, he thought, but in medicine it is called cancer.

"Jealous and spiteful tongues in other countries have declared that it is our purpose to wipe out learning and science," concluded the Dictator. "That is not our purpose. After the cleansing, the rebirth. We mean to move forward to the greatest science in the world—our own science, based on the enduring principles of our nationhood." He ceased abruptly, his eyes fell into their dream. Very like the girl Charcot showed me in my young days, thought Professor Malzius; there was first the ebullition, then the calm.

"I was part of the cleansing? You did not mean to hurt me?" he asked timidly.

"Yes, Professor Malzius," said the General, smiling, "you were part of the cleansing. Now that is over. His Excellency has spoken."

"I do not understand," said Professor Malzius, gazing at the fixed face of the man behind the desk.

"It is very simple," said the General. He spoke in a slow careful voice, as one speaks to a deaf man or a child. "You are a distinguished man of science—you have received the Nobel Prize. That was a service to the state. You became, however, infected by the wrong political ideas. That was treachery to the state. You had, therefore, as decreed by His Excellency, to pass through a certain period for probation and rehabilitation. But that, we believe, is finished."

"You do not wish to know the names of the young men any more?" said Professor Malzius. "You do not want the addresses?"

"That is no longer of importance," said the General patiently. "There is no longer opposition. The leaders were caught and executed three weeks ago."

"There is no longer opposition," repeated Professor Malzius.

"At the trial, you were not even involved."

"I was not even involved," said Professor Malzius. "Yes."

"Now," said the General, with a look at the Dictator, "we come to the future. I will be frank—the new state is frank with its citizens."

"It is so," said the Dictator, his eyes still sunk in his dream.

"There has been—let us say—a certain agitation in foreign countries regarding Professor Malzius," said the General, his eyes still fixed on the Dictator. "That means nothing, of course. Nevertheless, your acquaintance, Professor Bonnard, and others have meddled in matters that do not concern them."

"They asked after me?" said Professor

Malzius, with surprise. "It is true, my experiments were reaching a point that—"

"No foreign influence could turn us from our firm purpose," said the Dictator. "But it is our firm purpose to show our nation first in science and culture as we have already shown her first in manliness and statehood. For that reason, you are here, Professor Malzius." He smiled.

Professor Malzius stared. His cheeks began to tremble.

"I do not understand," said Professor Malzius. "You will give me my laboratory back?"

"Yes," said the Dictator, and the General nodded as one nods to a stupid child.

Professor Malzius passed a hand across his brow.

"My post at the university?" he said. "My experiments?"

"It is the purpose of our regime to offer the fullest encouragement to our loyal sons of science," said the Dictator.

"First of all," said Professor Malzius, "I must go to a hospital. My blood count is poor. But that will not take long." His voice had become impatient and his eyes glowed. "Then—my notebooks were burned, I suppose. That was silly, but we can start in again. I have a very good memory, an excellent memory. The theories are in my head, you know," and he tapped it. "I must have assistants, of course; little Gregopolous was my best one—"

"The man Gregopolous has been executed," said the General, in a stern voice. "You had best forget him."

"Oh," said Professor Malzius. "Well, then, I must have someone else. You see, these are important experiments. There must be some young men—clever ones—they cannot all be dead. I will know them." He laughed a little, nervously. "The Bear always got the pick of the crop," he said. "They used to call me The Bear, you know." He stopped and looked at them for a mo-

ment with ghastly eyes. "You are not fooling me?" he said. He burst into tears.

When he recovered he was alone in the room with the General. The General was looking at him as he himself had looked once at strange forms of life under the microscope, with neither disgust nor attraction, but with great interest.

"His Excellency forgives your unworthy suggestion," he said. "He knows you are overwrought."

"Yes," said Professor Malzius. He sobbed once and dried his glasses.

"Come, come," said the General, with a certain bluff heartiness. "We mustn't have our new president of the National Academy crying. It would look badly in the photographs."

"President of the Academy?" said Professor Malzius quickly. "Oh, no; I mustn't be that. They make speeches; they have administrative work. But I am a scientist, a teacher."

"I'm afraid you can't very well avoid it," said the General, still heartily, though he looked at Professor Malzius. "Your induction will be quite a ceremony. His Excellency himself will preside. And you will speak on the new glories of our science. It will be a magnificent answer to the petty and jealous criticisms of our neighbors. Oh, you needn't worry about the speech," he added quickly. "It will be prepared; you will only have to read it. His Excellency thinks of everything."

"Very well," said Professor Malzius; "and then may I go back to my work?"

"Oh, don't worry about that," said the General smiling. "I'm only a simple soldier; I don't know about those things. But you'll have plenty of work."

"The more the better," said Malzius eagerly. "I still have ten good years."

He opened his mouth to smile, and a shade of dismay crossed the General's face.

"Yes," he said, as if to himself. "The teeth

must be attended to. At once. And a rest, undoubtedly, before the photographs are taken. Milk. You are feeling sufficiently well, Professor Malzius?"

"I am very happy," said Professor Malzius. "I have been very well treated and I come of peasant stock."

"Good," said the General. He paused for a moment, and spoke in a more official voice.

"Of course, it is understood, Professor Malzius—" he said.

"Yes?" said Professor Malzius. "I beg your pardon. I was thinking of something else."

"It is understood, Professor Malzius," repeated the General, "that your—er—rehabilitation in the service of the state is a permanent matter. Naturally, you will be under observation, but, even so, there must be no mistake."

"I am a scientist," said Professor Malzius impatiently. "What have I to do with politics? If you wish me to take oaths of loyalty, I will take as many as you wish."

"I am glad you take that attitude," said the General, though he looked at Professor Malzius curiously. "I may say that I regret the unpleasant side of our interview. I trust you bear no ill will."

"Why should I be angry?" said Professor Malzius. "You were told to do one thing. Now you are told to do another. That is all."

"It is not quite so simple as that," said the General rather stiffly. He looked at Professor Malzius for a third time. "And I'd have sworn you were one of the stiff-necked ones," he said. "Well, well, every man has his breaking point, I suppose. In a few moments you will receive the final commands of His Excellency. Tonight you will go to the capitol and speak over the radio. You will have no difficulty there—the speech is written. But it will put a quietus on the activities of our friend Bonnard and

the question that has been raised in the British Parliament. Then a few weeks of rest by the sea and the dental work, and then, my dear president of the National Academy, you will be ready to undertake your new duties. I congratulate you and hope we shall meet often under pleasant auspices." He bowed from the waist to Malzius, the bow of a man of the world, though there was still something feline in his moustaches. Then he stood to attention, and Malzius, too, for the Dictator had come into the room.

"It is settled?" said the Dictator. "Good. Gregor Malzius, I welcome you to the service of the new state. You have cast your errors aside and are part of our destiny."

"Yes," said Professor Malzius, "I will be able to do my work now."

The Dictator frowned a little.

"You will not only be able to continue your invaluable researches," he said, "but you will also be able—and it will be part of your duty—to further our national ideals. Our reborn nation must rule the world for the world's good. There is a fire within us that is not in other stocks. Our civilization must be extended everywhere. The future wills it. It will furnish the subject of your first discourse as president of the Academy."

"But," said Professor Malzius, in a low voice, "I am not a soldier. I am a biochemist. I have no experience in these matters you speak of."

The Dictator nodded. "You are a distinguished man of science," he said. "You will prove that our women must bear soldiers, our men abandon this nonsense of republics and democracies for trust in those born to rule them. You will prove by scientific law that certain races—our race in particular—are destined to rule the world. You will prove they are destined to rule by the virtues of war, and that war is part of our heritage."

"But," said Professor Malzius, "it is not

like that. I mean," he said, "one looks and watches in the laboratory. One waits for a long time. It is a long process, very long. And then, if the theory is not proved, one discards the theory. That is the way it is done. I probably do not explain it well. But I am a biochemist; I do not know how to look for the virtues of one race against another, and I can prove nothing about war, except that it kills. If I said anything else, the whole world would laugh at me."

"Not one in this nation would laugh at you," said the Dictator.

"But if they do not laugh at me when I am wrong, there is no science," said Professor Malzius, knotting his brows. He paused. "Do not misunderstand me," he said earnestly. "I have ten years of good work left; I want to get back to my laboratory. But, you see, there are the young men—if I am to teach the young men."

He paused again, seeing their faces before him. There were many. There was Williams, the Englishman, who had died in the war, and little Gregopolous with the fox-terrier eyes. There were all who had passed through his classrooms, from the stupidest to the best. They had shot little Gregopolous for treason, but that did not alter the case. From all over the world they had come —he remembered the Indian student and the Chinese. They wore cheap overcoats, they were hungry for knowledge; they ate the bad, starchy food of the poor restaurants, they had miserable little love affairs and played childish games of politics, instead of doing their work. Nevertheless, a few were promising—all must be given the truth. It did not matter if they died, but they must be given the truth. Otherwise there could be no continuity and no science.

He looked at the Dictator before him— yes, it was a hysteric face. He would know how to deal with it in his classroom—but such faces should not rule countries or young men. One was willing to go through a great many meaningless ceremonies in order to do one's work—wear a uniform or salute or be president of the Academy. That did not matter; it was part of the due to Caesar. But not to tell lies to young men on one's subject. After all, they had called him The Bear and said he carried improper postcards in his briefcase. They had given him their terrible confidence—not for love or kindness, but because they had found him honest. It was too late to change.

The Dictator looked sharply at the General. "I thought this had been explained to Professor Malzius," he said.

"Why, yes," said Professor Malzius. "I will sign any papers. I assure you I am not interested in politics—a man like myself, imagine! One state is as good as another. And I miss my tobacco—I have not smoked in five months. But, you see, one cannot be a scientist and tell lies."

He looked at the two men.

"What happens if I do not?" he said, in a low voice. But, looking at the Dictator, he had his answer. It was a fanatic face.

"Why, we shall resume our conversations, Professor Malzius," said the General, with a simper.

"Then I shall be beaten again," said Professor Malzius. He stated what he knew to be a fact.

"The process of rehabilitation is obviously not quite complete," said the General, "but perhaps, in time—"

"It will not be necessary," said Professor Malzius. "I cannot be beaten again." He stared wearily around the room. His shoulders straightened—it was so he had looked in the classroom when they had called him The Bear. "Call your other officers in," he said in a clear voice. "There are papers for me to sign. I should like them all to witness."

"Why—" said the General. "Why—" He looked doubtfully at the Dictator.

An expression of gratification appeared

on the lean, semi-Napoleonic face. A white hand, curiously limp, touched the hand of Professor Malzius.

"You will feel so much better, Gregor," said the hoarse, tense voice. "I am so very glad you have given in."

"Why, of course, I give in," said Gregor Malzius. "Are you not the Dictator? And besides, if I do not, I shall be beaten again. And I cannot—you understand?—I cannot be beaten again."

He paused, breathing a little. But already the room was full of other faces. He knew them well, the hard faces of the new regime. But youthful some of them too.

The Dictator was saying something with regard to receiving the distinguished scientist, Professor Gregor Malzius, into the service of the state.

"Take the pen," said the General in an undertone. "The inkwell is there, Professor Malzius. Now you may sign."

Professor Malzius stood, his fingers gripping the big, old-fashioned inkwell. It was full of ink—the servants of the Dictator were very efficient. They could shoot small people with the eyes of fox terriers for treason, but their trains arrived on time and their inkwells did not run dry.

"The state," he said, breathing. "Yes. But science does not know about states. And you are a little man—a little, unimportant man."

Then, before the General could stop him, he had picked up the inkwell and thrown it in the Dictator's face. The next moment the General's fist caught him on the side of the head and he fell behind the desk to the floor. But lying there, through his cracked glasses, he could still see the grotesque splashes of ink on the Dictator's face and uniform, and the small cut above his eye where the blood was gathering. They had not fired; he had thought he would be too close to the Dictator for them to fire in time.

"Take that man out and shoot him. At once," said the Dictator in a dry voice. He did not move to wipe the stains from his uniform—and for that Professor Malzius admired him. They rushed then, each anxious to be first. But Professor Malzius made no resistance.

As he was being hustled along the corridors, he fell now and then. On the second fall, his glasses were broken completely, but that did not matter to him. They were in a great hurry, he thought, but all the better —one did not have to think while one could not see.

Now and then he heard his voice make sounds of discomfort, but his voice was detached from himself. There was little Gregopolous—he could see him very plainly—and Williams, with his fresh English coloring —and all the men whom he had taught.

He had given them nothing but work and the truth; they had given him their terrible trust. If he had been beaten again, he might have betrayed them. But he had avoided that.

He felt a last weakness—a wish that someone might know. They would not, of course; he would have died of typhoid in the castle and there would be regretful notices in the newspapers. And then he would be forgotten, except for his work, and that was as it should be. He had never thought much of martyrs—hysterical people in the main. Though he'd like Bonnard to have known about the ink; it was in the coarse vein of humor that Bonnard could not appreciate. But then, he was a peasant; Bonnard had often told him so.

They were coming out into an open courtyard now; he felt the fresh air of outdoors. "Gently," he said. "A little gently. What's the haste?" But already they were tying him to the post. Someone struck him in the face and his eyes watered. "A schoolboy covered with ink," he muttered through his lost teeth. "A hysterical schoolboy too. But you cannot kill truth."

They were not good last words, and he knew that they were not. He must try to think of better ones—not shame Bonnard. But now they had a gag in his mouth; just as well; it saved him the trouble.

His body ached, bound against the post, but his sight and his mind were clearer. He could make out the evening sky, gray with fog, the sky that belonged to no country, but to all the world.

He could make out the gray high buttress of the castle. They had made it a jail, but it would not always be a jail. Perhaps in time it would not even exist. But if a little bit of truth were gathered, that would always exist, while there were men to remember and rediscover it. It was only the liars and the cruel who always failed.

Sixty years ago, he had been a little boy, eating black bread and thin cabbage soup in a poor house. It had been a bitter life, but he could not complain of it. He had had some good teachers and they had called him The Bear.

The gag hurt his mouth—they were getting ready now. There had been a girl called Anna once; he had almost forgotten her. And his rooms had smelt a certain way and he had had a dog. It did not matter what they did with the medals. He raised his head and looked once more at the gray foggy sky. In a moment there would be no thought, but, while there was thought, one must remember and note. His pulse rate was lower than he would have expected and his breathing oddly even, but those were not the important things. The important thing was beyond, in the gray sky that had no country, in the stones of the earth and the feeble human spirit. The important thing was truth.

"Ready!" called the officer. "Aim! Fire!" But Professor Malzius did not hear the three commands of the officer. He was thinking about the young men.

Abraham Cowley

ODE UPON DR. HARVEY

I

Coy Nature (which remained, though agèd
    grown,
A beauteous virgin still, enjoyed by none
   Nor seen unveiled by anyone)
When Harvey's violent passion she did see,
Began to tremble and to flee,
Took sanctuary like Daphne in a tree.
There Daphne's lover stopped, and thought it
    much
   The very leaves of her to touch,
But Harvey, our Apollo, stopped not so:
Into the bark and root he after her did go.   10
   No smallest fibres of a plant
For which the eyebeam's point doth sharpness
    want
   His passage after her withstood.
What should she do? Through all the moving
    wood
Of lives endowed with sense she took her flight;
Harvey pursues, and keeps her still in sight.
But as the deer long-hunted takes a flood,
She leapt at last into the winding streams of
    blood;
Of man's Meander all the purple reaches made,
   Till at the heart she stayed,   20
    Where, turning head and at a bay,
Thus, by well purgèd ears, was she o'erheard
    to say:

II

"Here sure shall I be safe," said she;
"None will be able, sure, to see
   This my retreat, but only He
   Who made both it and me.

HARVEY: William Harvey, 1578–1657.

The heart of man what art can e'er reveal?
  A wall impervious between
  Divides the very parts within
And doth the heart of man even from itself
        conceal."   30
    She spoke, but e'er she was aware
    Harvey was with her there
And held this slippery Proteus in a chain
Till all her mighty mysteries she descried,
Which from his wit the attempt before to hide
Was the first thing that Nature did in vain.

III

  He the young practice of new life did see,
  Whilst, to conceal its toilsome poverty,
It for a living wrought, both hard and privately.
    Before the liver understood   40
    The noble scarlet dye of blood,
    Before one drop was by it made
Or brought into it to set up the trade;
Before the untaught heart began to beat
The tuneful march to vital heat,
From all the souls that living buildings rear,
Whether implied for earth or sea or air,
Whether it in the womb or egg be wrought,
A strict account to him is hourly brought
    How the great fabric does proceed,   50
What time and what materials it does need.
He so exactly does the work survey
As if he hired the workers by the day.

IV

Thus Harvey sought for truth in truth's own
        book—
    The creatures, which by God himself was writ,
      And wisely thought 'twas fit
Not to read comments only upon it
But on the original itself to look.

Methinks in art's great circle others stand
    Locked up together, hand in hand.   60
    Everyone leads as he is led;
    The same bare path they tread,
A dance like fairies', a fantastic round,
But neither change their motion nor their
        ground.
Had Harvey to this road confined his wit
His noble circle of the blood had been
        untrodden yet.
Great doctor! The art of curing's cured by thee:
    We now thy patient, physic, see
From all inveterate diseases free;
    Purged of old errors by thy care,   70
New dieted, put forth to clearer air,
    It now will strong and healthful prove.
Itself before lethargic lay and could not move.

V

These useful secrets to his pen we owe,
And thousands more 'twas ready to bestow,
Of which a barbarous war's unlearnèd rage
      Has robbed the ruined age.
O cruel loss! as if the Golden Fleece,
    With so much cost and labor bought
And from afar by a great hero brought,   80
      Had sunk even in the ports of Greece.
O cursèd war! Who can forgive thee this?
    Houses and towns may rise again,
        And ten times easier it is
To rebuild Paul's than any work of his.
That mighty task none but himself can do—
      Nay, scarce himself too now,
For though his wit the force of age withstand,
His body, alas, and time it must command;
And Nature now, so long by him surpassed,   90
Will sure have her revenge on him at last.

---

34 *descried:* disclosed. 37 *new life:* Harvey's *Essays on the Generation of Animals* appeared in 1651.

59 *others:* i.e., other scientists are paralyzed as though by enchantment, because they accept authority instead of engaging in research as Harvey did. 76 *war's unlearnèd rage:* the Civil War, 1642–1646; Harvey sided with Charles I. 85 *Paul's:* St. Paul's Cathedral, burned in 1666.

William Blake

MOCK ON, MOCK ON, VOLTAIRE, ROUSSEAU

Mock on, mock on, Voltaire, Rousseau;
Mock on, mock on; 'tis all in vain!
You throw the sand against the wind,
And the wind blows it back again.

And every sand becomes a gem
Reflected in the beams divine;
Blown back they blind the mocking eye,
But still in Israel's paths they shine.

The atoms of Democritus
And Newton's particles of light   10
Are sands upon the Red Sea shore,
Where Israel's tents do shine so bright.

Edgar Allan Poe

SONNET—TO SCIENCE

SCIENCE! true daughter of old time thou art!
   Who alterest all things with thy peering eyes.
Why preyest thou thus upon the poet's heart,
   Vulture, whose wings are dull realities?
How should he love thee? or how deem thee wise
   Who wouldst not leave him in his wandering
To seek for treasure in the jeweled skies,
   Albeit he soared with an undaunted wing?
Hast thou not dragged Diana from her car?
   And driven the hamadryad from the wood   10
To seek a shelter in some happier star?
   Hast thou not torn the naiad from her flood,
The elfin from the green grass, and from me
The summer dream beneath the tamarind tree?

13 *elfin:* elf.

Alfred, Lord Tennyson

NATURE, RED IN TOOTH AND CLAW

"So careful of the type?" but no.
   From scarpèd cliff and quarried stone
   She cries, "A thousand types are gone;
I care for nothing, all shall go.

"Thou makest thine appeal to me.
   I bring to life, I bring to death;
   The spirit does but mean the breath.
I know no more." And he, shall he,

Man, her last work, who seemed so fair,
   Such splended purpose in his eyes,   10
   Who rolled the psalm to wintry skies,
Who built him fanes of fruitless prayer,

Who trusted God was love indeed
   And love creation's final law—
   Though Nature, red in tooth and claw
With ravine, shrieked against his creed—

Who loved, who suffered countless ills,
   Who battled for the true, and just,
   Be blown about the desert dust,
Or sealed within the iron hills?   20

No more? A monster then, a dream,
   A discord. Dragons of the prime,
   That tare each other in their slime,
Were mellow music matched with him.

O life as futile, then, as frail!
   O for thy voice to soothe and bless!
   What hope of answer, or redress?
Behind the veil, behind the veil.

1 *type:* genus, species. 3 *she:* Nature. 22 *Dragons:* primeval monsters. 26 *thy voice:* that of Arthur Henry Hallam, who had died in 1833.

Robert Browning

THE LABORATORY

Ancien Régime

Now that I, tying thy glass mask tightly,
May gaze through these faint smokes curling
    whitely,
As thou pliest thy trade in this devil's-smithy—
Which is the poison to poison her, prithee?

He is with her, and they know that I know
Where they are, what they do; they believe my
    tears flow
While they laugh, laugh at me, at me fled to the
    drear
Empty church, to pray God in, for them!—I am
    here.

Grind away, moisten and mash up thy paste,
Pound at thy powder—I am not in haste!   10
Better sit thus and observe thy strange things
Than go where men wait me and dance at the
    King's.

That in the mortar—you call it a gum?
Ah, the brave tree whence such gold oozings
    come!
And yonder soft phial, the exquisite blue,
Sure to taste sweetly—is that poison too?

Had I but all of them, thee and thy treasures,
What a wild crowd of invisible pleasures!
To carry pure death in an earring, a casket,
A signet, a fan-mount, a filigree basket!   20

Soon, at the King's, a mere lozenge to give,
And Pauline should have just thirty minutes to
    live!
But to light a pastille and Elise, with her head

And her breast and her arms and her hands,
    should drop dead!

Quick—is it finished? The color's too grim!
Why not soft like the phial's, enticing and dim?
Let it brighten her drink, let her turn it and stir,
And try it and taste, ere she fix and prefer!

What a drop! She's not little, no minion like me!
That's why she ensnared him: this never will
    free   30
The soul from those masculine eyes, say "no!"
To that pulse's magnificent come-and-go.

For only last night, as they whispered, I brought
My own eyes to bear on her so that I thought
Could I keep them one half-minute fixed, she
    would fall
Shrivelled; she fell not; yet this does it all!

Not that I bid you spare her the pain;
Let death be felt and the proof remain:
Brand, burn up, bite into its grace—
He is sure to remember her dying face!   40

Is it done? Take my mask off! Nay, be not
    morose;
It kills her, and this prevents seeing it close:
The delicate droplet, my whole fortune's fee!
If it hurts her, beside, can it ever hurt me?

Now, take all my jewels, gorge gold to your fill;
You may kiss me, old man, on my mouth if you
    will!
But brush this dust off me, lest horror it brings
Ere I know it—next moment I dance at the
    King's!

28 *ere, etc.:* before deciding whether she likes it.

---

1 *glass mask:* for protection from heat, worn in glassworks.

Thomas Hardy

NATURE'S QUESTIONING

When I look forth at dawning, pool,
   Field, flock, and lonely tree,
   All seem to gaze at me
Like chastened children sitting silent in a
   school;

Their faces dulled, constrained, and worn,
   As though the master's ways
   Through the long teaching days
Had cowed them till their early zest was
   overborne.

Upon them stirs in lippings mere
   (As if once clear in call,   10
   But now scarce breathed at all)—
"We wonder, ever wonder, why we find us
   here!

"Has some Vast Imbecility,
   Mighty to build and blend
   But impotent to tend,
Framed us in jest, and left us now to hazardry?

"Or come we of an Automaton
   Unconscious of our pains? . . .
   Or are we live remains
Of Godhead dying downwards, brain and eye
   now gone?   20

"Or is it that some high Plan betides,
   As yet not understood,
   Of Evil stormed by Good,
We the Forlorn Hope over which Achievement
   strides?"

Thus things around. No answer I. . . .
   Meanwhile the winds, and rains,
   And Earth's old glooms and pains
Are still the same, and Life and Death are
   neighbors nigh.

9 *lippings:* lip movements, murmurings.

E. E. Cummings

PITY THIS BUSY MONSTER

pity this busy monster, manunkind,

not. Progress is a comfortable disease:
your victim (death and life safely beyond)
plays with the bigness of his littleness
—electrons deify one razorblade
into a mountainrange; lenses extend

unwish through curving wherewhen till
   unwish
returns on its unself.
                A world of made
is not a world of born—pity poor flesh

and trees, poor stars and stones, but never
   this   10
fine specimen of hypermagical

ultraomnipotence. We doctors know

a hopeless case if—listen: there's a hell
of a good universe next door; let's go

Walt Whitman

WHEN I HEARD THE
LEARNED ASTRONOMER

When I heard the learned astronomer,
When the proofs, the figures, were ranged in columns before me,
When I was shown the charts and diagrams, to add, divide, and measure them,
When I sitting heard the astronomer where he lectured with much applause in the
    lecture-room,
How soon unaccountable I became tired and sick,
Till rising and gliding out I wandered off by myself,
In the mystical moist night-air, and from time to time,
Looked up in perfect silence at the stars.

Bertolt Brecht

LIFE OF GALILEO

CHARACTERS

GALILEO GALILEI
ANDREA SARTI
MRS. SARTI, Galileo's housekeeper, Andrea's
    mother
LUDOVICO MARSILI, a rich young man
MR. PRIULI, procurator of the University of
    Padua
SAGREDO, Galileo's friend
VIRGINIA, Galileo's daughter
FEDERZONI, a lens grinder, Galileo's collab-
    orator
THE DOGE
SENATORS
COSMO DE' MEDICI, Grand Duke of Florence
THE LORD CHAMBERLAIN
THE THEOLOGIAN
THE PHILOSOPHER
THE MATHEMATICIAN

LIFE OF GALILEO: Translated by Wolfgang Sauer-
lauder and Ralph Manheim.

THE OLDER LADY-IN-WAITING
THE YOUNGER LADY-IN-WAITING
A LACKEY at the Grand Duke's court
TWO NUNS
TWO SOLDIERS
THE OLD WOMAN
A FAT PRELATE
TWO SCHOLARS
TWO MONKS
TWO ASTRONOMERS
A VERY THIN MONK
THE VERY OLD CARDINAL
FATHER CHRISTOPHER CLAVIUS, an astron-
    omer
THE LITTLE MONK
THE CARDINAL INQUISITOR
CARDINAL BARBERINI, later Pope Urban VIII
CARDINAL BELLARMINE
TWO ECCLESIASTICAL SECRETARIES
TWO YOUNG LADIES
FILIPPO MUCIUS, a scholar
MR. GAFFONE, rector of the University of
    Pisa
THE BALLAD SINGER
HIS WIFE
VANNI, an iron founder
AN ATTENDANT
A HIGH OFFICIAL

A Shady Individual
A Monk
A Peasant
A Border Guard
A Clerk
Men, Women, Children

1

Galileo Galilei, teacher of mathematics in Padua, sets out to demonstrate the new Copernican system.

In the year sixteen hundred and nine
Science' light began to shine.
At Padua city, in a modest house
Galileo Galilei set out to prove
The sun is still, the earth is on the move.

Galileo's modest study in Padua. It is morning. A boy, Andrea, the housekeeper's son, brings in a glass of milk and a roll.

GALILEO (*washing his torso, puffing and happy*). Put the milk on the table, but don't shut any books.

ANDREA.   Mother says we've got to pay the milkman. Or he'll make a circle around our house, Mr. Galilei.

GALILEO.   You must say, "describe a circle," Andrea.

ANDREA.   Of course. If we don't pay he'll describe a circle around us, Mr. Galilei.

GALILEO.   And Mr. Cambione, the bailiff, will head for us in a straight line, covering what sort of distance between two points?

ANDREA (*grinning*). The shortest.

GALILEO.   Good. I've got something for you. Look behind the star charts.
(*Andrea fishes a large wooden model of the Ptolemaic system from behind the star charts*)

ANDREA.   What is it?

GALILEO.   An armillary sphere. It shows how the stars move around the earth, in the opinion of the ancients.

ANDREA.   How?

GALILEO.   Let's examine it. First of all: description.

ANDREA.   There's a little stone in the middle.

GALILEO.   That's the earth.

ANDREA.   There are rings around it, one inside another.

GALILEO.   How many?

ANDREA.   Eight.

GALILEO.   Those are the crystal spheres.

ANDREA.   There are balls fastened to the rings . . .

GALILEO.   The stars.

ANDREA.   There are tags with words painted on them.

GALILEO.   What kind of words?

ANDREA.   Names of stars.

GALILEO.   Such as?

ANDREA.   The bottommost ball is the moon, it says. The one above it is the sun.

GALILEO.   Now spin the sun around.

ANDREA (*sets the rings in motion*). That's pretty. But we're so shut in.

GALILEO (*drying himself*).   Yes, that's just what I felt when I saw the thing for the first time. Some people feel that way. (*Throws Andrea the towel, meaning that he should rub his back*) Walls and rings and immobility. For two thousand years men believed that the sun and all the stars of heaven were circling around them. The pope, the cardinals, princes and scholars, the captains, merchants, fishwives and schoolchildren, all thought they were sitting motionless inside this crystal sphere. But now we'll get out of it, Andrea, we're in full sail. Because the old times are gone, and this is a new age. For the last hundred years mankind has seemed to be expecting something.

Cities are narrow, and so are minds. Superstition and plague. But now we say: Since things are thus and so, they will not remain thus and so. Because, my friend, everything is in motion.

I like to think that it all started with ships.

From time immemorial ships had hugged the shores, but suddenly they abandoned the shores, and sailed out upon the oceans.

A rumor has sprung up on our old continent —that there are new continents. And now that our ships have been going there, people on all the laughing continents are saying that the big dreaded ocean is nothing but a small lake. And a great desire has arisen to find the causes of all things: Why a stone falls when it's released and how it goes up when it's thrown into the air. Every day something new is being discovered. Even men a hundred years old let youngsters shout in their ears to tell them about the latest discoveries.

A great deal has been discovered, but there's much more to be discovered. Plenty of work for future generations.

When I was a young man in Siena I saw some masons, after arguing for five minutes, discard an age-old method of moving granite blocks in favor of a new and more practical arrangement of the ropes. Then and there I realized that the old times are over and that this is a new day. Some men will know all about their habitat, this heavenly body they live on. They're no longer satisfied with what it says in the ancient books.

Because where faith had ruled for a thousand years, doubt has now set in. Today everybody is saying: Yes, that's what the books tell us, but we want to see for ourselves. The most sacred truths are being looked into. Things that were never held in doubt are being doubted now.

All this has stirred up a breeze that lifts even the gold-braided coats of princes and prelates, revealing stout or spindly legs, legs just the same as ours. The heavens, we know now, are empty. And that has given rise to joyous laughter.

The waters of the earth supply power to the new spinning wheels, and in shipyards and the workshops of ropers and sailmakers new methods enable five hundred hands to work together.

I foresee that in our lifetime people will talk astronomy in the market place. Even the sons of fishwives will go to school. The people of our cities are always eager for novelty, they will be glad to hear that in our new astronomy the earth moves too. It has always been taught that the stars are pinned to a crystal vault, which prevents them from falling down. Now we've mustered the courage to let them float free, with nothing to hold them; they're in full sail, just as our ships are in full sail.

And the earth rolls merrily around the sun, and all the fishwives, merchants, princes and cardinals, and even the pope, roll with it.

Overnight, the universe has lost its center and now in the morning it has any number of centers. Now any point in the universe may be taken as a center. Because, suddenly, there's plenty of room.

Our ships sail far out into the ocean, our planets revolve far out in space, and even in chess nowadays the rooks range over many fields.

What does the poet say? "Oh, early morning . . ."

ANDREA
"Oh, early morning of beginning!
Oh, breath of wind that
Comes from new-found shores!"
And you'd better drink your milk. There'll be people coming in a minute.

GALILEO. Did you figure out what I told you yesterday?

ANDREA. What? You mean Kippernick and all that turning business?

GALILEO. Yes.

ANDREA. No. Why do you want me to figure it out? It's too hard for me, I'll only be eleven in October.

GALILEO. I want you to understand it, you in particular. To make everybody understand, that's why I work and buy expensive books instead of paying the milkman.

ANDREA. But I can see that the sun's not in the same place in the evening and morning. So it can't stand still. It just can't.

GALILEO. You "see"! What do you see? You see nothing at all. You're just gaping. Gaping isn't seeing. (*He places the iron washstand in the center of the room*) Now, that's the sun. Sit down. (*Andrea sits down in the only chair. Galileo stands behind him*) Where is the sun, right or left?

ANDREA. Left.

GALILEO. And how does it get to the right?

ANDREA. When you carry it over to the right. Naturally.

GALILEO. Only then? (*He picks up the chair with him in it and turns it halfway around*) Where's the sun now?

ANDREA. On the right.

GALILEO. Has it moved?

ANDREA. I guess it hasn't.

GALILEO. What moved?

ANDREA. Me.

GALILEO (*roars*). Wrong! Stupid! the chair!

ANDREA. But me with it!

GALILEO. Obviously. The chair is the earth. You're sitting on it.

MRS. SARTI (*has come in to make the bed. She has watched the scene*). Mr. Galilei, what on earth are you doing with my boy?

GALILEO. I'm teaching him how to see, Mrs. Sarti.

MRS. SARTI. By carrying him around the room?

ANDREA. Never mind, mother. You don't understand.

MRS. SARTI. Is that so? But of course you understand. A young gentleman is here, he wants to take lessons. Very well dressed, and he has a letter of recommendation. (*Hands over the letter*) When you get through with my Andrea, he'll be saying that two times two make five. You've got him all mixed up. Last night he tried to prove to me that the earth moves around the sun. He says some fellow by the name of Kippernick figured it out.

ANDREA. Didn't that Kippernick figure it out, Mr. Galilei? You tell her.

MRS. SARTI. Do you really tell him such nonsense? He blabs it out in school and the priests come running to me because of all the sinful stuff he says. You should be ashamed of yourself, Mr. Galilei.

GALILEO (*eating his breakfast*). Mrs. Sarti, as a result of our investigations, and after heated arguments, Andrea and I have made discoveries which we can no longer keep secret from the world. The new age has dawned, a great age, and it's a joy to be alive.

MRS. SARTI. I see. I hope we'll be able to pay the milkman in the new age, Mr. Galilei. (*Pointing at the letter*) Just do me a favor and don't turn this one away. I'm thinking of the milk bill. (*Out*)

GALILEO (*laughing*). Just give me time to finish my milk!—(*To Andrea*) Well, you seem to have understood something yesterday after all.

ANDREA. I only told her to get a rise out of her. But it's not true. You only turned the chair with me in it around sideways, but not like this. (*He moves his arm in a circle to the front*) Because I'd have fallen off the chair, and that's a fact. Why didn't you turn the chair over? Because that would prove I'd fall off the earth if it moved that way. There.

GALILEO. But I proved to you . . .

ANDREA. But last night I figured out that if the earth turned that way I'd hang down head first at night, and that's a fact.

GALILEO (*takes an apple from the table*). Look here. This is the earth.

ANDREA. Don't always use that kind of example, Mr. Galilei. That way you can prove anything.

GALILEO (*putting the apple back*). Very well.

ANDREA. You can do anything with examples if you're clever. But I can't carry my mother around in a chair like that. So you see, it was a bad example. And what would happen if the apple were the earth? Nothing would happen.

GALILEO (*laughs*). I thought you weren't interested.

ANDREA. All right, take the apple. What would keep me from hanging head down at night?

GALILEO. Well, here's the earth, and you're standing here. (*He sticks a splinter from a log into the apple*) And now the earth turns.

ANDREA. And now I'm hanging head down.

GALILEO. What do you mean? Look closely! Where's the head?

ANDREA (*shows on the apple*). There. Below.

GALILEO. Sure? (*Turns the apple back*) Isn't the head still in the same place? Aren't the feet still below it? When I turn it, do you stand like this? (*He takes the splinter out and turns it upside down*)

ANDREA. No. Then, why don't I notice the turning?

GALILEO. Because you're turning too. You and the air above you and everything else on the globe.

ANDREA. But why does it look as if the sun were moving?

GALILEO (*again turns the apple with the splinter*). Look, you see the earth underneath, it stays that way, it's always underneath and as far as you're concerned it doesn't move. Now look up. The lamp is over your head. But now that I've turned it, what's over your head, in other words, above?

ANDREA (*making the same turn*). The stove.

GALILEO. And where's the lamp?

ANDREA. Below.

GALILEO. Aha!

ANDREA. That's great. That'll get a rise out of her.
(*Ludovico Marsili, a rich young man, enters*)

GALILEO. This place is as busy as a pigeon house.

LUDOVICO. Good morning, sir. My name is Ludovico Marsili.

GALILEO (*examining the letter of recommendation*). You've been in Holland?

LUDOVICO. Where I heard a great deal about you, Mr. Galilei.

GALILEO. Your family owns property in the Campagna?

LUDOVICO. My mother wanted me to look around and see what's going on in the world. That kind of thing.

GALILEO. And in Holland they told you that in Italy, for instance, I was going on?

LUDOVICO. And since mother also wanted me to take a look at the sciences . . .

GALILEO. Private lessons: Ten scudi a month.

LUDOVICO. Very well, sir.

GALILEO. What are your interests?

LUDOVICO. Horses.

GALILEO. I see.

LUDOVICO. I have no head for science, Mr. Galilei.

GALILEO. I see. In that case it'll be fifteen scudi a month.

LUDOVICO. Very well, Mr. Galilei.

GALILEO. I'll have to take you first thing in the morning. You'll be the loser, Andrea. Naturally I'll have to drop you. You understand, you don't pay.

ANDREA. All right. I'm going. Can I take the apple?

GALILEO. Yes.
(*Andrea leaves*)

LUDOVICO. You'll have to be patient with me. Mostly because in science everything's the opposite of common sense. Take that crazy tube they're selling in Amsterdam. I've examined it carefully. A green leather casing and two lenses, one like this (*he indicates a concave lens*) and one like this (*indicates a convex lens*). As far as I know, one magnifies and the other reduces. Any sensible person would expect them to cancel each other out. But they don't. When you look through the thing everything's five times as big. That's science for you.

GALILEO. What do you see five times as big?

LUDOVICO. Steeples, pigeons, anything far away.

GALILEO. Have you seen these magnified steeples?

LUDOVICO.   Certainly, sir.

GALILEO.   You say the tube has two lenses? (*He makes a sketch on a sheet of paper*) Like this? (*Ludovico nods*) How old is this invention?

LUDOVICO.   I believe it wasn't much more than a few days old when I left Holland, at least it hadn't been on the market any longer than that.

GALILEO (*almost friendly*).   Why do you insist on physics? Why not horse breeding?
(*Enter Mrs. Sarti, unnoticed by Galileo*)

LUDOVICO.   Mother thinks a little science won't hurt me. Everybody's eating and drinking science nowadays, you know.

GALILEO.   Why not try a dead language or theology? They're easier. (*Sees Mrs. Sarti*) All right, come Tuesday morning.
(*Ludovico leaves*)

GALILEO.   Don't look at me like that, I've accepted him.

MRS. SARTI.   Because you saw me in the nick of time. The procurator[21] of the university is here.

GALILEO.   Bring him in. He's important. It might mean five hundred scudi. Then I wouldn't have to take pupils.
(*Mrs. Sarti shows the procurator in. Galileo has completed dressing while scribbling figures on a slip of paper*)

GALILEO.   Good morning, lend me half a scudo. (*Gives the coin the procurator has fished out of his purse to Mrs. Sarti*) Sarti, would you send Andrea to the spectacle maker for some lenses? Here are the measurements.
(*Mrs. Sarti goes out with the slip of paper*)

THE PROCURATOR.   I've come in regard to your request for a raise of salary. You have asked for a thousand scudi. Unfortunately I cannot recommend such an increase to the university. You are aware, I am sure, that courses in mathematics don't attract students to the university. Mathematics doesn't pay. Not that the republic doesn't value it highly. It may

21 Governor; i.e., president.

not be as important as philosophy or as useful as theology; still, it gives endless pleasure to the connoisseur.

GALILEO (*immersed in his papers*).   My dear man, I can't get along on five hundred scudi.

THE PROCURATOR.   But, Mr. Galilei, all you do is give a two-hour lecture twice a week. Surely your extraordinary reputation must attract any number of students who can afford private lessons. Haven't you got private pupils?

GALILEO.   Sir, I have too many! I'm teaching all the time. When am I to learn? Good God, man, I'm not as clever as the gentlemen of the philosophical faculty. I'm stupid. I don't understand a thing. I've got to plug the holes in my knowledge. And where am I to find time for that? When am I to study and experiment? My knowledge, sir, is thirsty for more knowledge. In all the biggest problems we still have nothing but hypotheses to go by. What we need is proofs. How can I get anywhere if, to keep my household going, I have to drum it into the head of every idiot who can pay that parallel lines meet in infinity?

THE PROCURATOR.   The republic may not pay as much as certain princes, but don't forget, it guarantees freedom of inquiry. We in Padua even admit Protestants as students. And we grant them doctor's degrees. Did we hand Mr. Cremonini over to the Inquisition when we had proof—proof, Mr. Galilei!—that he had made sacrilegious statements? No, we even granted him an increase in salary. As far away as Holland, Venice is known as the republic where the Inquisition has nothing to say. That ought to be worth something to an astronomer like you, working in a field where the doctrines of the church have not been held in due respect of late.

GALILEO.   You handed Giordano Bruno over to Rome. Because he professed the teachings of Copernicus.

THE PROCURATOR.   Not because he professed the teachings of Mr. Copernicus which, incidentally, are wrong, but because he was not a citizen of Venice and was not employed here. You can leave him out of it, even if they did burn him. And by the by, for all our liberties I shouldn't advise you to make too free with a name that has been expressly anathematized by the church, not even here, no, not even here.

GALILEO. Your protection of freedom of thought is rather good business, isn't it? You get good teachers for low pay by pointing out that other towns are run by the Inquisition, which burns people. In return for protection from the Inquisition, your professors work for next to nothing.

THE PROCURATOR. You're being unfair. What good would it do you to have all the time you want for research if any witless monk of the Inquisition could simply suppress your ideas? No rose without thorns, Mr. Galilei, no prince without monks!

GALILEO. And what's the use of free investigation without free time to investigate? What happens to the results? Why don't you submit my work on the laws of falling bodies (*He points at a sheaf of manuscript*) to the gentlemen of the signoria and ask them if it's not worth a few scudi more.

THE PROCURATOR. It's worth infinitely more, Galilei.

GALILEO. Not infinitely more, sir, but five hundred scudi more.

THE PROCURATOR. Only what brings in scudi is worth scudi. If you want money, you'll have to come up with something different. If you have knowledge to sell, you can ask only as much as it earns the purchaser. For instance, the philosophy Mr. Colombe is selling in Florence brings the prince at least ten thousand scudi a year. Granted, your laws of falling bodies raised some dust. They're applauding you in Paris and Prague. But the gentlemen who applaud don't pay the university of Padua what you cost it. Your misfortune, Mr. Galilei, is your field.

GALILEO. I get it: free trade, free research. Free trade in research, is that it?

THE PROCURATOR. But Mr. Galilei! How can you say such a thing? Permit me to observe that I don't fully appreciate your witticism. The flourishing trade of the republic is hardly to be sneered at. Much less can I, as long-time procurator of the university, countenance the, I must say, frivolous tone in which you speak of research. (*While Galileo sends longing glances toward his worktable*) Think of the world around us! The whip of slavery under which science is groaning at certain universities—where old leather-bound tomes have been cut into whips. Where no one cares how the pebble falls, but only what Aristotle writes about it. The eyes have only one purpose: reading. What use are the new laws of gravity when the law of suavity is all that matters? And then think of the immense joy with which our republic accepts your ideas. Here you can do research! Here you can work! Nobody spies on you, nobody oppresses you. Our merchants, who know the importance of better linen in their competition with Florence, listen with interest to your cry for "Better physics!" And don't forget how much physics owes to the campaign for better looms! Our most eminent citizens—men for whom time is money—take an interest in your work, they come to see you and watch demonstrations of your discoveries. Don't despise trade, Mr. Galilei! None of us here would ever allow your work to be interfered with or permit outsiders to create difficulties for you. You've got to admit, Mr. Galilei, that this is the ideal place for you to work!

GALILEO (*in despair*). Yes.

THE PROCURATOR. Then the financial aspect: All you have to do is come up with another invention as clever as that splendid proportional compass of yours which a person ignorant of mathematics can use (*He counts on his fingers*) —trace a line, compute compound interest, reproduce a land survey in enlarged or reduced scale, and determine the weight of cannon balls.

GALILEO. Flimflam.

THE PROCURATOR. An invention that delighted and amazed our leading citizens and brought in money—you call that flimflam. I'm told that even General Stefano Gritti can do square roots with it.

GALILEO. Quite a gadget—all the same, Priuli, you've given me an idea. Priuli, I may have something along those lines for you. (*He picks up the sheet with his sketch*)

THE PROCURATOR. Really? That would be the solution. (*Gets up*) Mr. Galilei, we know you are a great man. A great but dissatisfied man, if I may say so.

GALILEO. Yes, I am dissatisfied and that's what you should be paying me for if you had any sense. Because I'm dissatisfied with myself. But you do everything to make me dissatisfied with you. I admit it amuses me to do my bit for my Venetian friends, working in your great arsenal with its shipyards and armories. But you leave me no time to follow up the speculations which result from this work. You muzzle the ox that does your threshing. I'm forty-six years old and I've accomplished nothing that satisfies me.

THE PROCURATOR. In that case I won't disturb you any longer.

GALILEO. Thank you.
(*The procurator leaves. Galileo remains alone for a few moments and begins to work. Then Andrea comes running in*)

GALILEO (*at work*). Why didn't you eat the apple?

ANDREA. I need it to show her that the earth turns.

GALILEO. I must tell you something, Andrea. Don't mention our ideas to other people.

ANDREA. Why not?

GALILEO. Our rulers have forbidden it.

ANDREA. But it's the truth.

GALILEO. Even so, they forbid it.—And there's another reason. We still have no proofs for what we know to be right. Even the doctrine of the great Copernicus is not yet proven. It's only a hypothesis. Give me the lenses.

ANDREA. Half a scudo wasn't enough. I had to leave him my jacket as a pledge.

GALILEO. How will you get through the winter without a jacket?
(*Pause. Galileo arranges the lenses on the sheet with the sketch*)

ANDREA. What's a hypothesis?

GALILEO. It's when we consider something probable but have no facts. We assume that Felice, nursing her baby down there outside the basket weaver's shop, is giving milk to the baby and not getting milk from it. That's a hypothesis as long as we can't go and see for ourselves and prove it. In the face of the heavenly bodies we're like worms with dim eyes that see very little. The ancient doctrines that have been accepted for a thousand years are rickety. There's less solid timber in those immense edifices than in the props needed to keep them from collapsing. Too many laws that explain too little, whereas our new hypothesis has few laws that explain a great deal.

ANDREA. But you've proved it all to me.

GALILEO. Only that it's possible. You see, the hypothesis is a very elegant one and there's no evidence to the contrary.

ANDREA. I want to be a physicist, too, Mr. Galilei.

GALILEO. Very sensible in view of all the problems remaining to be solved in our field. (*He has gone to the window and looked through the lenses. Mildly interested*) Take a look, Andrea.

ANDREA. Holy Mary! Everything comes close. The bells of the campanile are right here. I can even read the copper letters: GRACIA DEI.

GALILEO. It'll get us five hundred scudi.

2

Galileo presents a new invention to the republic of Venice.

> No one's virtue is complete:
> Great Galileo liked to eat.

> You will not resent, we hope,
> The truth about his telescope.

The great arsenal of Venice near the harbor. Senators, headed by the doge. On one side Galileo's friend Sagredo and Virginia Galilei, fifteen; she is holding a velvet cushion on which lies a telescope about two feet long, encased in red leather. Galileo is standing on a dais. Behind him the tripod for the telescope; the lens grinder Federzoni is in charge of it.

GALILEO.   Your Excellency, august signoria! As professor of mathematics at your university in Padua and director of the great arsenal here in Venice, I have always felt it incumbent upon me not only to fulfill my duties as a teacher but also to produce special advantages to the republic of Venice by means of useful inventions. With great satisfaction and in all due humility, I shall demonstrate and present to you today an entirely new instrument, my spyglass or telescope, manufactured in your world-famous great arsenal in accordance with the highest scientific and Christian principles, the fruit of seventeen years of your obedient servant's patient labors. *(Galileo leaves the dais and stands next to Sagredo)*
(Applause, Galileo takes a bow)

GALILEO.   *(softly to Sagredo)*   What a waste of time!

SAGREDO *(softly)*.   You'll be able to pay the butcher, old friend.

GALILEO.   Yes, they'll make money on it. (Makes *another bow*)

THE PROCURATOR *(steps up on the dais)*.   Your Excellency, august signoria! Once again a glorious page in the great book of human accomplishments is being written in Venetian characters. *(Polite applause)* A scholar of world renown is presenting to you, and to you alone, a highly salable tube for you to manufacture and market at your pleasure. *(Stronger applause)* Has it occurred to you that in the event of war this instrument will enable us to recognize the nature and number of the enemy's

ships at least two hours before they have a clear view of ours and, in full cognizance of its strength, decide whether to pursue, engage or withdraw? *(Loud applause)* And now, Your Excellency, august signoria, Mr. Galilei bids you accept this instrument of his invention, this evidence of his genius, from the hands of his charming daughter.
(Music. Virginia steps forward, bows, hands the telescope to the procurator, who passes it on to Federzoni. Federzoni places it on the tripod and adjusts it. The doge and the senators mount the dais and look through the tube)

GALILEO *(softly)*.   I can't promise to go through with this farce. They think they're getting a profitable gadget, but it's much more than that. Last night I turned the tube on the moon.

SAGREDO.   What did you see?

GALILEO.   It has no light of its own.

SAGREDO.   What?

SENATOR.   Mr. Galilei, I can see the fortifications of Santa Rosita.—Over there on that boat they're having lunch. Fried fish. I'm getting hungry.

GALILEO.   I tell you, astronomy has been marking time for a thousand years for lack of a telescope.

SENATOR.   Mr. Galilei!

SAGREDO.   You're wanted.

SENATOR.   One sees too well with that thing. I'll have to warn my ladies to stop bathing on the roof.

GALILEO.   Do you know what the Milky Way consists of?

SAGREDO.   No.

GALILEO.   I do.

SENATOR.   A thing like that is worth its ten scudi, Mr. Galilei.
(Galileo bows)

VIRGINIA *(takes Ludovico to her father)*.   Ludovico wants to congratulate you, father.

LUDOVICO *(embarrassed)*.   Congratulations, sir.

GALILEO.   I've improved on it.

LUDOVICO. So I see, sir. You made the casing red. In Holland it was green.

GALILEO (*turns to Sagredo*). I wonder if I couldn't prove a certain doctrine with that thing.

SAGREDO. Watch your step!

THE PROCURATOR. Your five hundred scudi are in the bag, Mr. Galilei.

GALILEO (*paying no attention to him*). Of course, I'm always wary of rash conclusions.
(*The doge, a fat, modest man, has approached Galileo and is attempting, with clumsy dignity, to address him*)

THE PROCURATOR. Mr. Galilei, His Excellency the doge.
(*The doge shakes Galileo's hand*)

GALILEO. Oh yes, the five hundred! Are you satisfied, Your Excellency?

DOGE. Unfortunately our city fathers always need some sort of pretext before they can do anything for our scholars.

THE PROCURATOR. Otherwise, where would the incentive be, Mr. Galilei?

DOGE (*smiling*). This is our pretext.
(*The doge and the procurator lead Galileo to the senators, who surround him. Virginia and Ludovico slowly go away*)

VIRGINIA. Did I do it all right?

LUDOVICO. It seemed all right to me.

VIRGINIA. What's the matter?

LUDOVICO. Oh, nothing. A green casing might have done just as well.

VIRGINIA. I think they're all very pleased with father.

LUDOVICO. And I think I'm beginning to understand something about science.

3

January 10, 1610: By means of the telescope Galileo discovers celestial phenomena which prove the Copernican system. Warned by his friends of the possible consequences of his investigations, Galileo affirms his faith in reason.

> January ten, sixteen ten:
> Galileo Galilei abolishes heaven.

Galileo's study in Padua. Night. Galileo and Sagredo, both in heavy overcoats, at the telescope.

SAGREDO (*looking through the telescope, in an undertone*). The edge of the crescent is quite irregular, rough and serrated. In the dark part near the luminous edge there are luminous points. They are emerging, one after another. From these points the light spreads out over wider and wider areas and finally merges with the larger luminous part.

GALILEO. How do you account for those luminous points?

SAGREDO. It can't be.

GALILEO. But it is. They're mountains.

SAGREDO. On a star?

GALILEO. Gigantic mountains. Their peaks are gilded by the rising sun while the surrounding slopes are still deep in darkness. You can see the light descending from the highest peaks into the valleys.

SAGREDO. But that contradicts all the astronomy of two thousand years.

GALILEO. True. No mortal has ever seen what you are seeing, except me. You're the second.

SAGREDO. But the moon can't be another earth with mountains and valleys, any more than the earth can be a planet.

GALILEO. The moon can be an earth with mountains and valleys, and the earth can be a planet. Simply another heavenly body, one among thousands. Take another look. Is the dark part of the moon entirely dark?

SAGREDO. No. When I look closely, I see a feeble gray light on it.

GALILEO. What can that light be?

SAGREDO. ?

GALILEO. It's from the earth.

SAGREDO. Nonsense. How can the earth with its mountains and forests and oceans—a cold body—give light?

GALILEO. The same way the moon sheds light. Because both bodies are illuminated by the sun, that's why they shed light. What the moon is to us we are to the moon. The moon sees us by turns as a crescent, as a half-circle, as full, and then not at all.

SAGREDO. Then there's no difference between moon and earth?

GALILEO. Apparently not.

SAGREDO. Less than ten years ago a man was burned in Rome. His name was Giordano Bruno and he had said the same thing.

GALILEO. I know. But we can see it. Keep your eyes to the tube. What you see is that there's no difference between heaven and earth. This is the tenth of January, 1610. Humanity notes in its diary: Heaven abolished.

SAGREDO. It's terrifying.

GALILEO. I've discovered something else. Perhaps something even more amazing.

MRS. SARTI (comes in). The procurator.
(The procurator rushes in)

THE PROCURATOR. I apologize for the late hour. I'd be much obliged if we could talk privately.

GALILEO. Mr. Sagredo can hear anything I can hear, Mr. Priuli.

THE PROCURATOR. It might embarrass you to have the gentleman hear what has happened. Unfortunately, it's something quite incredible.

GALILEO. Mr. Sagredo is used to hearing incredible things in my presence.

THE PROCURATOR. I wonder. (pointing at the telescope) There it is, your splendid gadget. You might as well throw it away. It's worthless, absolutely worthless.

SAGREDO (who has been restlessly pacing the floor). What do you mean?

THE PROCURATOR. Do you realize that this invention of yours, "the fruit of seventeen years of patient labor," is for sale on every street corner in Italy for a couple of scudi? Made in Holland, I might add. At this very moment a Dutch freighter is unloading five hundred telescopes in the harbor.

GALILEO. You don't say.

THE PROCURATOR. Your equanimity, sir, is beyond me.

SAGREDO. I fail to see what's troubling you. Let me tell you that just in these last few days Mr. Galilei—with this very instrument—has made the most revolutionary discoveries concerning heavenly bodies.

GALILEO (laughing). Have a look for yourself, Priuli.

THE PROCURATOR. Let me tell you that after having Mr. Galilei's salary doubled on the strength of this worthless gadget I'm quite satisfied with the discovery I've already made. It's sheer accident that when the gentlemen of the signoria first looked through your tube, confident of having acquired something for the republic that could be manufactured only here, they failed to see—seven times magnified—a common peddler on the next corner hawking the same tube for a song.
(Galileo roars with laughter)

SAGREDO. Dear Mr. Priuli, I may not be able to judge the instrument's value to the economy, but its value to philosophy is so enormous that . . .

THE PROCURATOR. To philosophy! What business has Mr. Galilei, a mathematician, meddling with philosophy? Mr. Galilei, you once invented a very respectable pump for the city; your irrigation system functions. The weavers, too, are very pleased with your machine. How on earth could I have anticipated anything like this?

GALILEO. Not so fast, Priuli. Sea routes are still long, unsafe and expensive We lack a dependable clock in the sky. A guide to navigation. I have reason to believe that with the telescope we can very clearly perceive certain stars with very regular motions. New star charts, Mr. Priuli, could save the shipping interests millions of scudi.

THE PROCURATOR. Forget it. I've heard more than enough. In return for my kindness you've made me the laughingstock of the city. I'll be remembered as the procurator who fell for a worthless telescope. You have every reason to laugh. You've got your five hundred scudi. But I'm telling you, and I speak as an honest man: This world makes me sick! (*He leaves, banging the door behind him*)

GALILEO. He's rather likable when he gets angry. Did you hear what he said: A world where you can't do business makes him sick.

SAGREDO. Did you know about the Dutch instruments?

GALILEO. Of course. From hearsay. But the one I made for those skinflints in the signoria is twice as good. How can I do my work with the bailiff at the door? And Virginia will need her trousseau soon, she's not bright. Besides, I like to buy books, and not only about physics, and I like to eat well. I get my best ideas over a good meal. A rotten time to live in! They weren't paying me as much as the teamster who carts their wine barrels. Four cords of firewood for two courses in mathematics. I've wormed five hundred scudi out of them, but I've got debts, some of them twenty years old. Give me five years of leisure and I'll prove everything. Let me show you something else.

SAGREDO (*hesitates to go to the telescope*). I almost think I'm afraid, Galileo.

GALILEO. I want to show you a milky-white patch of luminous mist in the galaxy. Tell me what it's made of.

SAGREDO. Why, stars, countless stars.

GALILEO. In the constellation of Orion alone there are five hundred fixed stars. Those are the many worlds, the countless other worlds, the stars beyond stars that the man they burned talked about. He didn't see them, but he knew they would be there.

SAGREDO. Even if our earth is a star, it's still a long way to Copernicus' contention that the earth revolves around the sun. There isn't any star in the heavens with another revolving around it. And the earth, you will have to admit, has the moon revolving around it.

GALILEO. Sagredo, I wonder. I've been wondering for two days. There's Jupiter. (*He adjusts the telescope*) Now, near it there are four smaller stars that you can only make out through the tube. I saw them on Monday but I didn't pay too much attention to their positions. Yesterday I looked again. I could have sworn that all four had moved. I recorded their positions. Now they're different again. What's that now? There were four of them. (*Getting excited*) You look!

SAGREDO. I see three.

GALILEO. Where's the fourth? Here are the tables. We must compute the movements they can have made.

(*Agitated, they sit down to work. The stage turns dark, but on a cyclorama Jupiter and its satellites remain visible. When it grows light again, they are still sitting there in their winter coats*)

GALILEO. Now we have proof. The fourth must have moved behind Jupiter where we can't see it. There you have a star with another revolving around it.

SAGREDO. But the crystal sphere that Jupiter is fastened to?

GALILEO. Where is it indeed? How can Jupiter be fastened to anything if other stars revolve around it? There is no scaffolding in the sky. There's nothing holding the universe up! There you have another sun!

SAGREDO. Calm down. You're thinking too fast.

GALILEO. Fast, hell! Man, get excited! You're seeing something that nobody ever saw before. They were right!

SAGREDO. Who? The Copernicans?

GALILEO. Yes, and you know who. The whole world was against them, and yet they were right. That's something for Andrea! (*Beside himself, he runs to the door and shouts*) Mrs. Sarti! Mrs. Sarti!

SAGREDO. Galileo, please calm yourself!

GALILEO. Sagredo, please get excited! Mrs. Sarti!

SAGREDO (*turning the telescope aside*) Will you stop yelling like a fool?

GALILEO. Will you stop standing there like a stockfish when we've discovered the truth?

SAGREDO. I'm not standing here like a stockfish, I'm trembling for fear it's the truth.

GALILEO. What?

SAGREDO. Have you taken leave of your senses? Don't you realize what you're getting into if what you see is really true? And if you go shouting all over town that the earth is a planet and not the center of the universe?

GALILEO. Yes, and that the whole enormous cosmos with all its stars doesn't revolve around our tiny earth, as anyone could have guessed anyway.

SAGREDO. So that there's nothing but stars!— But where does that put God?

GALILEO. What do you mean?

SAGREDO. God! Where's God?

GALILEO (*furious*). Not out there! Any more than He'd be on earth if somebody out there started looking for Him here.

SAGREDO. Where is God then?

GALILEO. Am I a theologian? I'm a mathematician.

SAGREDO. First of all you're a human being. And I ask you: Where is God in your world system?

GALILEO. Inside us or nowhere!

SAGREDO (*shouting*). As the man who was burned said?

GALILEO. As the man who was burned said!

SAGREDO. That's why he was burned! Less than ten years ago!

GALILEO. Because he couldn't prove it! Because all he could do was say so! Mrs. Sarti!

SAGREDO. Galileo, I know you're a clever man. For three years in Pisa and seventeen here in Padua you've patiently instructed hundreds of students in the Ptolemaic system as ad-

vocated by the church and confirmed by the scriptures on which the church is grounded. Like Copernicus you thought it was wrong, but you taught it.

GALILEO. Because I couldn't prove anything.

SAGREDO (*incredulous*). You think that makes a difference?

GALILEO. All the difference in the world! Look here, Sagredo! I believe in man and that means I believe in reason. Without that belief I wouldn't have the strength to get out of bed in the morning.

SAGREDO. Then let me tell you this: I don't believe in reason. Forty years' experience has taught me that human beings are not accessible to reason. Show them a comet with a red tail, put dark fear into them, and they'll rush out of their houses and break their legs. But make a reasonable statement, prove it with seven good reasons, and they'll just laugh at you.

GALILEO. That's all wrong and it's slander. I don't see how you can love science if you believe that. Only the dead are impervious to argument.

SAGREDO. How can you mistake their contemptible cunning for reason?

GALILEO. I'm not talking about their cunning. I know they call a donkey a horse when they're selling and a horse a donkey when they're buying. That's their cunning. But the old woman with calloused hands who gives her mule an extra bunch of hay the night before setting out on a trip; the sea captain who allows for storms and doldrums when he lays in his stores; the child who puts on his cap when he realizes that it may rain—these people are my hope, they accept the law of cause and effect. Yes, I believe in the gentle force of reason, in the long run no one can resist it. Nobody can watch me drop (*He lets a pebble fall from his hand to the floor*) a pebble and say: It doesn't fall. Nobody can do that. The seduction of proof is too strong. Most people will succumb to it and in time they all will. Thinking is one of the greatest pleasures of the human race.

MRS. SARTI (*comes in*). Did you want something, Mr. Galilei?

GALILEO (*back at the telescope, scribbling notes, very kindly*). Yes, I want Andrea.

MRS. SARTI. Andrea? But he's in bed, he's sound asleep.

GALILEO. Can't you wake him?

MRS. SARTI. What do you want him for, may I ask?

GALILEO. I want to show him something that'll please him. He's going to see something that no one but us has ever seen since the earth began.

MRS. SARTI. Something through your tube?

GALILEO. Something through my tube, Mrs. Sarti.

MRS. SARTI. And for that you want me to wake him in the middle of the night? Are you out of your mind? He needs his sleep. I wouldn't think of waking him.

GALILEO. Not a chance?

MRS. SARTI. Not a chance.

GALILEO. Mrs. Sarti, in that case maybe you can help me. You see, a question has come up that we can't agree on, perhaps because we've read too many books. It's a question about the sky, involving the stars. Here it is: Which seems more likely, that large bodies turn around small bodies or small bodies around large ones?

MRS. SARTI (*suspiciously*). I never know what you are up to, Mr. Galilei. Is this a serious question or are you pulling my leg again?

GALILEO. A serious question.

MRS. SARTI. Then I can give you a quick answer. Do I serve your dinner or do you serve mine?

GALILEO. You serve mine. Yesterday it was burned.

MRS. SARTI. And why was it burned? Because you made me get your shoes while I was cooking it. Didn't I bring you your shoes?

GALILEO. I presume you did.

MRS. SARTI. Because it's you who went to school and can pay.

GALILEO. I see. I see there's no difficulty. Good morning, Mrs. Sarti.
(*Mrs. Sarti, amused, goes out*)

GALILEO. And such people are supposed not to be able to grasp the truth? They snatch at it.
(*The matins bell has begun to peal. In comes Virginia in a cloak, carrying a shaded candle*)

VIRGINIA. Good morning, father.

GALILEO. Up so early?

VIRGINIA. I'm going to matins with Mrs. Sarti. Ludovico will be there too. How was the night, father?

GALILEO. Clear.

VIRGINIA. May I look through it?

GALILEO. What for? (*Virginia has no answer*) It's not a toy.

VIRGINIA. I know, father.

GALILEO. By the way, the tube's a big flop. You'll hear all about it soon. It's being sold on the street for three scudi, it was invented in Holland.

VIRGINIA. Didn't you find anything new in the sky with it?

GALILEO. Nothing for you. Only a few dim specks on the left side of a big star, I'll have to find a way of calling attention to them. (*speaking to Sagredo over his daughter's head*) Maybe I'll call them the "Medicean Stars" to please the grand duke of Florence. (*Again to Virginia*) It may interest you, Virginia, to know that we'll probably move to Florence. I've written to ask if the grand duke can use me as court mathematician.

VIRGINIA (*radiant*). At court?

SAGREDO. Galileo!

GALILEO. I need leisure, old friend. I need proofs. And I want the fleshpots. With a position like that I won't have to ram the Ptolemaic system down the throats of private students, I'll have time—time, time, time, time!—to work out my proofs. What I've got now isn't enough. It's nothing, it's just bits and pieces. I can't stand up to the whole world with that. There's still no proof that any heavenly body revolves around the sun. But I'm going to find the proofs, proofs for everybody from Mrs. Sarti to the pope. The only thing that worries me is that the court may not want me.

VIRGINIA. Oh, I'm sure they'll take you, father, with your new stars and all.

GALILEO. Go to your mass.

(*Virginia leaves*)

GALILEO. I'm not used to writing letters to important people. (*He hands Sagredo a letter*) Do you think this will do?

SAGREDO (*reading aloud the end of the letter which Galileo has handed him*). "Withal I am yearning for nothing so much as to be nearer to Your Highness, the rising sun which will illuminate this age." The grand duke of Florence is nine years old.

GALILEO. I know. I see, you think my letter is too servile. I wonder if it's servile enough, not too formal, as if I were lacking in genuine devotion. A more restrained letter might be all right for someone with the distinction of having proved the truth of Aristotle, not for me. A man like me can only get a halfway decent position by crawling on his belly. And you know I despise men whose brains are incapable of filling their stomachs.

(*Mrs. Sarti and Virginia walk past the two men on their way to mass*)

SAGREDO. Don't go to Florence, Galileo.

GALILEO. Why not?

SAGREDO. Because it's ruled by monks.

GALILEO. There are distinguished scholars at the Florentine court.

SAGREDO. Toadies.

GALILEO. I'll take them by the scruff of their necks and drag them to my tube. Even monks are human beings, Sagredo. Even monks can be seduced by proofs. Copernicus—don't forget that—wanted them to trust his figures, I'm only asking them to trust the evidence of their eyes. When truth is too weak to defend itself, it has to attack. I'll take them by the scruff of their necks and make them look through the tube.

SAGREDO. Galileo, you're on a dangerous path. It's bad luck when a man sees the truth. And delusion when he believes in the rationality of the human race. Who do we say walks with open eyes? The man who's headed for perdition. How can the mighty leave a man at large who knows the truth, even if it's only about the remotest stars? Do you think the pope will hear your truth when you tell him he's wrong? No, he'll hear only one thing, that you've said he's wrong. Do you think he will calmly write in his diary: January 10, 1610, Heaven abolished? How can you want to leave the republic with the truth in your pocket and walk straight into the trap of the monks and princes with your tube in your hands? You may be very skeptical in your science, but you're as gullible as a child about anything that looks like a help in pursuing it. You may not believe in Aristotle, but you believe in the grand duke of Florence. A moment ago when I saw you at your tube looking at the new stars I thought I saw you on a flaming pyre and when you said you believed in proofs I smelled burnt flesh. I love science, but I love you more, my friend. Galileo, don't go to Florence!

GALILEO. If they'll have me I'll go.

(*On a curtain appears the last page of the letter*)

In assigning the sublime name of the Medicean line to the stars newly discovered by me I am fully aware that when gods and heroes were elevated to the starry skies they were thereby glorified, but that in the present case it is the stars that will be glorified by receiving the name of the Medici. With this I recommend myself as one among the number of your most faithful and obedient servants, who holds it the highest honor to have been born your subject.

Withal I yearn for nothing so much as to be nearer to Your Highness, the rising sun which will illuminate this age.

Galileo Galilei

4

Galileo has exchanged the Venetian republic for the court of Florence. The discoveries he has made with the help of the telescope are met with disbelief by the court scholars.

The old says: What I've always done I'll always do.
The new says: If you're useless you must go.

Galileo's house in Florence. Mrs. Sarti is getting Galileo's study ready to receive guests. Her son Andrea is seated, putting celestial charts away.

MRS. SARTI. Ever since we arrived in this marvelous Florence I've seen nothing but bowing and scraping. The whole town files past this tube and I can scrub the floor afterwards. But it won't do us a bit of good. If these discoveries amounted to anything, the reverend fathers would know it, wouldn't they? For four years I was in the service with Monsignor Filippo, I never managed to dust the whole of his library. Leather-bound volumes up to the ceiling and no love poems either. And the good monsignor had two pounds of boils on his behind from poring over all that learning. Wouldn't a man like that know what's what? The big demonstration today will be another flop and tomorrow I won't be able to look the milkman in the face. I knew what I was saying when I told him to give the gentlemen a good dinner first, a nice piece of lamb, before they start in on his tube. Oh no! (*She imitates Galileo*) "I've got something better for them." (*Knocking downstairs*)

MRS. SARTI (*looks in the window-mirror*). Goodness, there's the grand duke already. And Galileo still at the university! (*She runs downstairs and admits Cosmo de' Medici, grand duke of Tuscany, accompanied by the lord chamberlain and two ladies-in-waiting*)

COSMO. I want to see the tube.

THE LORD CHAMBERLAIN. Perhaps your Highness would prefer to wait until Mr. Galilei and the other gentlemen have returned from the university. (*To Mrs. Sarti*) Mr. Galilei wanted the professors of astronomy to examine the newly discovered stars which he calls the Medicean stars.

COSMO. They don't believe in the tube, far from it. Where is it?

MRS. SARTI. Upstairs, in his workroom.
(*The boy nods, points to the staircase, and upon a nod from Mrs. Sarti dashes up the stairs*)

THE LORD CHAMBERLAIN (*a very old man*). Your Highness! (*To Mrs. Sarti*) Must we go up there? I only came because the tutor is ill.

MRS. SARTI. Nothing can happen to the young gentleman. My boy's upstairs.

COSMO (*entering above*). Good evening.
(*The two boys ceremoniously bow to each other. Pause. Then Andrea goes back to his work*)

ANDREA (*much like his teacher*). This place is as busy as a pigeon house.

COSMO. Lots of visitors?

ANDREA. Stumble about and gape and don't know beans.

COSMO. I see. Is that . . . ? (*Points at the tube*)

ANDREA. Yes, that's it. But don't touch it. It's not allowed.

COSMO. And what's that? (*He indicates the wooden model of the Ptolemaic system*)

ANDREA. That's the Ptolemaic system.

COSMO. It shows how the sun moves, doesn't it?

ANDREA. Yes, so they say.

COSMO (*sitting down in a chair, he takes the model on his knees*). My tutor has a cold. So I was able to get away early. It's nice here.

ANDREA (*is restless, ambles about irresolutely,*

throwing suspicious glances at the strange boy, and at last, unable to resist the temptation any longer, takes from behind the star charts another wooden model representing the Copernican system). But of course it's really like this.

COSMO. What's like this?

ANDREA *(pointing at the model on Cosmo's knees).* That's the way people think it is and that's *(pointing at his model)* the way it really is. The earth turns around the sun. See?

COSMO. You really think so?

ANDREA. Of course. It's been proven.

COSMO. You don't say!—I wish I knew why they didn't let me go in to see the old man. Last night he was at dinner as usual.

ANDREA. You don't seem to believe it, or do you?

COSMO. Why certainly, I do.

ANDREA *(pointing at the model on Cosmo's knees).* Give it back, you don't even understand that one!

COSMO. But you don't need two.

ANDREA. Give it back this minute. It's not a toy for little boys.

COSMO. I don't mind giving it back but you ought to be a little more polite, you know.

ANDREA. You're stupid and I don't care about being polite. Give it back or you'll see.

COSMO. Hands off, do you hear?

(They start fighting and are soon rolling on the floor)

ANDREA. I'll show you how to treat a model. Give up!

COSMO. You've broken it. You're twisting my hand.

ANDREA. We'll see who's right and who isn't. Say it turns or I'll box your ears.

COSMO. I won't. Ouch, you redhead. I'll teach you good manners.

ANDREA. Redhead? Am I a redhead?

(They continue to fight in silence. Below, Galileo and several university professors enter. Behind them Federzoni)

THE LORD CHAMBERLAIN. Gentlemen, a slight illness has prevented Mr. Suri, His Highness' tutor, from accompanying His Highness.

THE THEOLOGIAN. Nothing serious, I hope.

THE LORD CHAMBERLAIN. No, no, by no means.

GALILEO *(disappointed).* Isn't His Highness here?

THE LORD CHAMBERLAIN. His Highness is upstairs. May I ask you gentlemen to proceed. The court is so very anxious to hear the opinion of our illustrious university about Mr. Galilei's extraordinary instrument and those marvelous new stars.

(They go upstairs)

(The boys lie still. They have heard sounds downstairs)

COSMO. Here they come. Let me up.

(They quickly get up)

THE GENTLEMEN *(as they file upstairs).* No. No, there's nothing to worry about.—The faculty of medicine has declared that the cases in the inner city can't possibly be plague. The miasma would freeze at the present temperature.—The worst danger in these situations is panic.—We can always expect an epidemic of colds at this time of year.—No ground for suspicion.—Nothing to worry about.

(Salutations upstairs)

GALILEO. Your Highness, I am extremely pleased that you should be present while I communicate our new discoveries to the gentlemen of our university.

(Cosmo makes formal bows to all, including Andrea)

THE THEOLOGIAN *(seeing the broken Ptolemaic model on the floor).* There seems to have been some breakage here.

(Cosmo stoops quickly and hands the model politely to Andrea. At the same time Galileo slyly puts away the other model)

GALILEO *(at the telescope).* As Your Highness no doubt knows, we astronomers have for some time been encountering great difficulties in our calculations. We are using a very old system which seems to be in agreement with philosophy but unfortunately not with the facts. According to this old system, the Ptolemaic system, the movements of the planets are extremely complicated. Venus, for instance, is supposed to move something like this. (*He sketches on a blackboard the epicyclic course of Venus according to Ptolemy*) But if we predicate these complicated movements, we are unable to calculate the position of any star accurately in advance. We do not find it in the place where it should be. Furthermore there are stellar motions for which the Ptolemaic system has no explanation at all. According to my observations, certain small stars I have discovered describe motions of this kind around the planet Jupiter. If you gentlemen are agreeable, we shall begin with the inspection of the satellites of Jupiter, the Medicean stars.

ANDREA (*pointing to the stool in front of the telescope*). Kindly sit here.

THE PHILOSOPHER. Thank you, my child. I'm afraid it will not be so simple. Mr. Galilei, before we apply ourselves to your famous tube, we should like to request the pleasure of a disputation: Can such planets exist?

THE MATHEMATICIAN. A formal disputation.

GALILEO. I thought you'd just look through the telescope and see for yourselves.

ANDREA. Here, if you please.

THE MATHEMATICIAN. Yes, yes.—You are aware, of course, that in the view of the ancients no star can revolve around any center other than the earth and that there can be no stars without firm support in the sky.

GALILEO. Yes.

THE PHILOSOPHER. And, regardless of whether such stars are possible, a proposition which the mathematician (*he bows to the mathematician*) seems to doubt, I as a philosopher should like with all due modesty to raise this question: Are such stars necessary? Aristotelis divini universum[22] . . .

[22] The cosmos of the divine Aristotle . . . The philosopher finishes his sentence several speeches later.

GALILEO. Oughtn't we to continue in the vernacular? My colleague, Mr. Federzoni, doesn't understand Latin.

THE PHILOSOPHER. Does it matter whether he understands us?

GALILEO. Yes.

THE PHILOSOPHER. I beg your pardon. I thought he was your lens grinder.

ANDREA. Mr. Federzoni is a lens grinder and a scholar.

THE PHILOSOPHER. Thank you, my child. If Mr. Federzoni insists . . .

GALILEO. I insist.

THE PHILOSOPHER. The debate will lose in brilliance, but this is your house.—The cosmos of the divine Aristotle with its spheres and their mystical music, with its crystal vaults and the circular courses of its heavenly bodies, with the oblique angle of the sun's course and the mysteries of its tables of satellites and the wealth of stars in the catalog of the southern hemisphere and the inspired construction of the celestial globe is an edifice of such order and beauty that we shall be well advised not to disturb its harmony.

GALILEO. Your Highness, would you care to observe those impossible and unnecessary stars through the telescope?

THE MATHEMATICIAN. One might be tempted to reply that if your tube shows something that cannot exist it must be a rather unreliable tube.

GALILEO. What do you mean by that?

THE MATHEMATICIAN. It certainly would be much more to the point, Mr. Galilei, if you were to tell us your reasons for supposing that there can be free-floating stars moving about in the highest sphere of the immutable heavens.

THE PHILOSOPHER. Reasons, Mr. Galilei, reasons!

GALILEO. My reasons? When I look at these stars and my calculations demonstrate the phenomenon? This debate is getting absurd, sir.

THE MATHEMATICIAN. If it were not to be feared that you would get even more excited than you are, one might suggest that what is in your tube and what is in the sky might be two different things.

THE PHILOSOPHER. It would be difficult to put it more politely.

FEDERZONI. They think we painted the Medician stars on the lens!

GALILEO. You accuse me of fraud?

THE PHILOSOPHER. We wouldn't dream of it! In the presence of His Highness!

THE MATHEMATICIAN. Your instrument, whether we call it your own or your adoptive child, has doubtless been very cleverly constructed.

THE PHILOSOPHER. And we are convinced, Mr. Galilei, that neither you nor anyone else would dare to grace stars with the illustrious name of the ruling house if there were the slightest doubt of their existence.
(*All bow deeply to the grand duke*)

COSMO (*turning to the ladies-in-waiting*). Is there something wrong with my stars?

THE OLDER LADY-IN-WAITING (*to the grand duke*). Your Highness' stars are fine. The gentlemen are only wondering whether they really and truly exist.
(*Pause*)

THE YOUNGER LADY-IN-WAITING. They say you can see the scales of the Dragon with this instrument.

FEDERZONI. Yes, and you can see all sorts of things on the Bull.

GALILEO. Are you gentlemen going to look through it, or not?

THE PHILOSOPHER. Certainly, certainly.

THE MATHEMATICIAN. Certainly.
(*Pause. Suddenly Andrea turns around and walks stiffly out through the length of the room. His mother intercepts him*)

MRS. SARTI. What's got into you?

ANDREA. They're stupid. (*Tears himself loose and runs away*)

THE PHILOSOPHER. A deplorable child.

THE LORD CHAMBERLAIN. Your Highness, gentlemen, may I remind you that the state ball is due to start in forty-five minutes?

THE MATHEMATICIAN. Why beat about the bush? Sooner or later Mr. Galilei will have to face up to the facts. His moons of Jupiter would pierce the crystal sphere. That's all there is to it.

FEDERZONI. You'll be surprised, but there is no crystal sphere.

THE PHILOSOPHER. Any textbook will tell you there is, my good man.

FEDERZONI. Then we need new textbooks.

THE PHILOSOPHER. Your Highness, my esteemed colleague and I are supported by no less an authority than the divine Aristotle.

GALILEO (*almost abjectly*). Gentlemen, belief in the authority of Aristotle is one thing, observable facts are another. You say that according to Aristotle there are crystal spheres up there and that certain motions are impossible because the stars would have to pierce the spheres. But what if you observed these motions? Wouldn't that suggest to you that the spheres do not exist? Gentlemen, I humbly beseech you to trust your own eyes.

THE MATHEMATICIAN. My dear Galilei, though it may seem dreadfully old-fashioned to you, I'm in the habit of reading Aristotle now and then, and I can assure you that when I read Aristotle I do trust my eyes.

GALILEO. I'm used to seeing the gentlemen of all faculties close their eyes to all facts and act as if nothing had happened. I show them my calculations, and they smile; I make my telescope available to help them see for themselves, and they quote Aristotle.

FEDERZONI. The man had no telescope!

THE MATHEMATICIAN. Exactly.

THE PHILOSOPHER (*grandly*). If Aristotle, an authority acknowledged not only by all the scientists of antiquity but by the church fathers themselves, is to be dragged through the mire, a continuation of this discussion seems superfluous, at least to me. I refuse to take part in irrelevant arguments. Basta. [Enough].

GALILEO. Truth is the child of time, not of authority. Our ignorance is infinite, let's whittle away just one cubic millimeter. Why should we still want to be so clever when at long last we have a chance of being a little less stupid? I've had the good fortune to lay hands on a new instrument with which we can observe a tiny corner of the universe a little more closely, not much though. Make use of it.

THE PHILOSOPHER. Your Highness, ladies and gentlemen, I can only wonder what all this will lead to.

GALILEO. I submit that as scientists we have no business asking what the truth may lead to.

THE PHILOSOPHER (*in wild alarm*). Mr. Galilei, the truth can lead to all sorts of things!

GALILEO. Your Highness. In these nights telescopes are being directed at the sky all over Italy. The moons of Jupiter don't lower the price of milk. But they have never been seen before, and yet they exist. The man in the street will conclude that a good many things may exist if only he opens his eyes. And you ought to back him up. It's not the motions of some remote stars that make Italy sit up and take notice, but the news that doctrines believed to be unshakeable are beginning to totter, and we all know that of these there are far too many. Gentlemen, we oughtn't to be defending shaky doctrines!

FEDERZONI. You are teachers, you ought to be doing the shaking.

THE PHILOSOPHER. I wish your man there would keep out of a scientific debate.

GALILEO. Your Highness! My work in the great arsenal of Venice brought me into daily contact with draftsmen, architects and instrument makers. Those people taught me many new ways of doing things. They don't read books but they trust the testimony of their five senses, most of them without fear as to where it will lead them . . .

THE PHILOSOPHER. Fancy that!

GALILEO. Very much like our seamen who left our shores a hundred years ago, without the slightest idea of what other shores, if any, they might reach. It looks as if we had to go to the shipyards nowadays to find the high curiosity that was the glory of ancient Greece.

THE PHILOSOPHER. After what we have heard here today, I have no doubt that Mr. Galilei will find admirers in the shipyards.

THE LORD CHAMBERLAIN. Your Highness, I note to my great dismay that this exceedingly instructive conversation has taken a little longer than foreseen. Your Highness must rest a while before the court ball.

(*At a signal, the grand duke bows to Galileo. The court quickly prepares to leave*)

MRS. SARTI (*stepping in the way of the grand duke and offering him a plate of pastry*). A bun, Your Highness?

(*The older lady-in-waiting leads the grand duke away*)

GALILEO (*running after them.*) But all you gentlemen need do is look through the instrument.

THE LORD CHAMBERLAIN. His Highness will not fail to obtain an expert opinion on your statements by consulting our greatest living astronomer, Father Christopher Clavius, astronomer-in-chief at the papal college in Rome.

5

Undaunted even by the plague, Galileo continues his investigations.

a)

Early morning. Galileo bending over his notes at the telescope. Virginia comes in with a traveling bag.

GALILEO. Virginia! Is anything wrong?

VIRGINIA. The convent is closed. They sent us home. There are five cases of plague in Arcetri.

GALILEO (*calls out*). Sarti!

VIRGINIA. And last night our market was roped off. They say two people have died in the old city, and there are three more dying in the hospital.

GALILEO. As usual, they've hushed it up until the last minute.

MRS. SARTI (*comes in*). What are you doing here?

VIRGINIA. The plague.

MRS. SARTI. My God! I'd better pack. (*Sits down*)

GALILEO. No need to pack. Take Virginia and Andrea. I'll go get my notes.
(*He hurries back to the table and gathers his papers in great haste. Mrs. Sarti puts a coat on Andrea as he runs in, and goes to get some food and bedding. One of the grand duke's lackeys enters*)

LACKEY. His Highness has left the city for Bologna because of the raging disease. Before leaving he insisted that Mr. Galilei should be given an opportunity to escape. The coach will be here in two minutes.

MRS. SARTI (*to Virginia and Andrea*). Go right outside, you two. Here, take this.

ANDREA. Why? If you don't tell me why, I won't go.

MRS. SARTI. It's the plague, my child.

VIRGINIA. We'll wait for father.

MRS. SARTI. Mr. Galilei, are you ready?

GALILEO (*wrapping the telescope in a tablecloth*). Put Virginia and Andrea in the coach. I'll join you in a minute.

VIRGINIA. No, we won't leave without you. You'll never be ready if you start packing your books.

MRS. SARTI. The carriage is here.

GALILEO. Be reasonable, Virginia. If no one gets in, the coachman will just drive away. The plague is no joke.

VIRGINIA (*protesting as Mrs. Sarti leads her and Andrea out*). Help him with his books or he won't come.

MRS. SARTI (*calls out from the house door*). Mr. Galilei! The coachman says he won't wait.

GALILEO. Mrs. Sarti, I don't think I should leave. Everything is in such a muddle here, you know, all my notes of the last three months, I might as well throw them away if I don't go on with them for a night or two. And anyway the plague is everywhere.

MRS. SARTI. Mr. Galilei! Come this minute! You're out of your mind.

GALILEO. You go with Virginia and Andrea. I'll come later.

MRS. SARTI. In another hour they won't let anyone leave the city. You must come! (*Listens*) He's driving off! I've got to stop him. (*Out*)
(*Galileo walks back and forth. Mrs. Sarti returns, very pale, without her bundle*)

GALILEO. Don't stand around like that! The coach with the children will leave without you.

MRS. SARTI. They've left. They had to hold Virginia down. The children will be taken care of in Bologna. But who'd get you your meals?

GALILEO. You're crazy. Staying in the city to cook! . . . (*Takes up his papers*) You mustn't take me for a fool, Mrs. Sarti. I can't interrupt my observations. I have powerful enemies, I've got to supply proofs for certain propositions.

MRS. SARTI. You needn't apologize. But it's not reasonable.

b)
Outside Galileo's house in Florence. Galileo comes out of the door and looks down the street. Two nuns are passing by.

GALILEO (*addresses them*). Sisters, could you tell me where I can buy milk? This morning the milk woman didn't come, and my housekeeper is away.

THE FIRST NUN. Only the shops in the lower city are open.

THE OTHER NUN. Did you come out of this house? (*Galileo nods*) This is the street!

(*The two nuns cross themselves, mumble an Ave Maria and run. A man passes*)

GALILEO (*addresses him*).   Aren't you the baker who brings us our bread? (*The man nods*) Have you seen my housekeeper? She must have gone out last night. She hasn't been here all morning.

(*The man shakes his head. A window across the street is opened and a woman looks out*)

THE WOMAN (*screams*).   Run! Quick! They've got the plague! (*Frightened, the man runs away*)

GALILEO.   Do you know anything about my housekeeper?

THE WOMAN.   Your housekeeper collapsed in the street. Up there. She must have known. That's why she left you. How can people be so inconsiderate? (*She bangs the window shut*)

(*Children come down the street. When they see Galileo they run away screaming. As Galileo turns around, two soldiers in full armour come rushing in*)

THE SOLDIERS.   Get back in that house! (*With their long lances they push Galileo back into his house. They bolt the door behind him*)

GALILEO (*at a window*).   Can you tell me what's happened to the woman?

THE SOLDIERS.   They take 'em to potter's field.

THE WOMAN (*appears at the window again*). The whole street back there's infected. Why don't you close it off?

(*The soldiers stretch a rope across the street*)

THE WOMAN.   But now nobody can get into our house! Don't put your rope there. We're all well up here. Stop! Stop! Can't you hear? My husband's gone to the city, he won't be able to get back. You beasts! You beasts!

(*Her sobbing and screaming are heard from inside. The soldiers leave. An old woman appears at another window*)

GALILEO.   There seems to be a fire back there.

THE OLD WOMAN.   The firemen won't touch it if there's any suspicion of plague. All they can think about is the plague.

GALILEO.   Just like them! Their whole system of government is like that. They cut us off like a withered fig branch that's stopped bearing fruit.

THE OLD WOMAN.   You mustn't say that. They're helpless, that's all.

GALILEO.   Are you alone in your house?

THE OLD WOMAN.   Yes. My son sent me a note. Thank God he heard last night that someone had died around here, so he didn't come home. There've been eleven cases in the neighborhood during the night.

GALILEO.   I can't forgive myself for not sending my housekeeper away in time. I had urgent work to finish, but she had no reason to stay.

THE OLD WOMAN.   We can't go away either. Who would take us in? You mustn't reproach yourself. I saw her. She left this morning, at about seven o'clock. She was sick, because when she saw me step out to bring in the bread she circled around me. I suppose she didn't want your house to be sealed off. But they get wise to everything.

(*A rattling sound is heard*)

GALILEO.   What's that?

THE OLD WOMAN.   They're making noise to drive away the clouds that carry seeds of the plague.

(*Galileo roars with laughter*)

THE OLD WOMAN.   How can you laugh?

(*A man comes down the street and finds it roped off*)

GALILEO.   Hey, you! The street's closed and there's nothing to eat in the house.

(*The man has already run away*)

GALILEO.   You can't just let us starve here! Hey! Hey!

THE OLD WOMAN.   Maybe they'll bring us something. If they don't, I can put a pitcher of milk on your doorstep, if you're not afraid, but not until after dark.

GALILEO.   Hey! Hey! Somebody ought to hear us.

(*Suddenly Andrea stands at the rope. His face is stained with tears*)

GALILEO.   Andrea! How did you get here?

ANDREA. I was here this morning. I knocked, but you didn't open. People told me . . .

GALILEO. Didn't you go away?

ANDREA. I did. But I managed to jump out. Virginia went on. Can I come in?

THE OLD WOMAN. No, you can not. You must go to the Ursulines. Maybe your mother is there too.

ANDREA. I've been there. But they wouldn't let me see her. She's too sick.

GALILEO. Did you walk the whole way back? You've been gone for three days.

ANDREA. That's how long it took, don't be angry. And once they caught me.

GALILEO (*helplessly*). Don't cry, Andrea. You know, I've found out a few things in the meantime. Shall I tell you? (*Andrea nods, sobbing*) But listen carefully, or you won't understand. Remember when I showed you the planet Venus? Don't listen to that noise, it's nothing. Remember? You know what I saw? It's like the moon. I saw it as a half-circle and I saw it as a crescent. What do you think of that? I can show you the whole thing with a little ball and a lamp. It proves that Venus has no light of its own either. And it describes a simple circle around the sun, isn't that marvelous?

ANDREA (*sobbing*). Yes, and that's a fact.

GALILEO (*softly*). I didn't stop her from leaving. (*Andrea is silent*)

GALILEO. But of course if I hadn't stayed it wouldn't have happened.

ANDREA. Will they have to believe you now?

GALILEO. I've got all the proofs I need. You know what? When all this is over, I'll go to Rome and show them. (*Two muffled men with long poles and buckets come down the street. With the poles they hold out bread to Galileo and the old woman in their windows*)

THE OLD WOMAN. There's a woman with three children over there. Give her some too.

GALILEO. I've nothing to drink. There's no water in the house. (*The two shrug their shoulders*) Will you be back tomorrow?

THE MAN (*with muffled voice, his mouth covered by a cloth*). Who knows what tomorrow will bring?

GALILEO. If you do come, could you reach up to me a little book that I need for my work?

THE MAN (*with a muffled laugh*). A book won't do you any good now. Lucky if you get bread.

GALILEO. This boy, my pupil, will be here to give it to you. It's a table showing the period of Mercury, Andrea. I've mislaid mine. Will you find me one at school? (*The men have already moved on*)

ANDREA. Sure. I'll get it for you, Mr. Galilei. (*Out*) (*Galileo retires. The old woman steps out of the house opposite and places a pitcher at Galileo's door*)

6

1616: The Collegium Romanum, the research institute of the Vatican, confirms Galileo's discoveries.

> Things take indeed a wondrous turn
> When learned men do stoop to learn.
> Clavius, we are pleased to say
> Upheld Galileo Galilei.

Large hall in the Collegium Romanum, Rome. It is night. High ecclesiastics, monks, scholars, in groups. Galileo on one side, alone. Great merriment. Before the scene opens, boisterous laughter is heard.

A FAT PRELATE (*holds his belly for laughter*). Oh stupidity! Oh stupidity! Can anyone tell me of a proposition that has *not* been believed?

A SCHOLAR. What about the proposition that you have an unconquerable aversion to food, monsignor!

THE FAT PRELATE. Will be believed, never fear. Only reasonable statements are not believed. The existence of the devil is being doubted. But that the earth spins around like a marble in a gutter, that's being believed. Sancta simplicitas! [Holy simplicity!]

A MONK (*acting out a comedy*).   I'm dizzy. The earth is turning too fast. Permit me to hold on to you, professor. (*He pretends to stagger and holds on to a scholar*)

THE SCHOLAR (*joining in the fun*).   Yes, she's dead drunk again, the old hag.

THE MONK.   Stop, stop! We're sliding off! Stop, I say!

ANOTHER SCHOLAR.   Venus is listing badly. I can only see half of her behind. Help!
(*A cluster of monks is forming who with much laughter pretend to be on a storm-tossed ship, struggling to avoid being thrown overboard*)

ANOTHER MONK.   If only we don't get thrown on the moon. Brothers, they say it bristles with sharp mountain peaks!

THE FIRST SCHOLAR.   Plant your foot against it.

THE FIRST MONK.   And don't look down. I feel as sick as a monkey.

THE FAT PRELATE (*pointedly loud in Galileo's direction*).   What! Monkey business in the Collegium Romanum?
(*Loud laughter. Two astronomers of the Collegium come out of a door. Quiet sets in*)

A MONK.   Still investigating? That's a scandal!

THE FIRST ASTRONOMER (*angrily*).   Not us!

THE SECOND ASTRONOMER.   Where's this going to end? I can't understand Clavius . . . Are all the claims made in the last fifty years to be taken at face value? In 1572 a new star appeared in the highest sphere, the eighth, the sphere of the fixed stars. It was rather larger and brighter than its neighbors and a year and a half later it was gone, overtaken by perdition. Is that any reason to question the eternal immutability of the heavens?

THE PHILOSOPHER.   If we let them, they'd smash up the whole universe.

THE FIRST ASTRONOMER.   Yes, what's the world coming to! Five years later, Tycho Brahe, a Dane, determined the trajectory of a comet. It started above the moon and broke through all

the spheres, the material carriers of all movable celestial bodies. It met with no resistance, its light was not deflected. Is that any reason to doubt the existence of the spheres?

THE PHILOSOPHER.   Out of the question! How can Christopher Clavius, the greatest astronomer of Italy and of the church, lower himself to investigating such stuff!

THE FAT PRELATE.   Scandalous!

THE FIRST ASTRONOMER.   But there he is, investigating. There he sits, gaping through that devil's tube.

THE SECOND ASTRONOMER.   Principiis obsta! [Resist the beginnings!] The whole trouble began years ago when we started using the tables of Copernicus—a heretic—for calculating such things as the length of the solar year, the dates of solar and lunar eclipses, the positions of the celestial bodies.

A MONK.   I ask you: What is better, to get a lunar eclipse three days behind schedule or to miss out on eternal salvation altogether?

A VERY THIN MONK (*steps forward with an open Bible, fanatically stabbing his finger at a passage*).   What does the Book say? "Sun, stand thou still upon Gibeon; and thou, moon, in the valley of Ajalon." [23] How can the sun stand still if it never moves as these heretics claim? Does the Book lie?

THE FIRST ASTRONOMER.   No, and that's why we're leaving.

THE SECOND ASTRONOMER.   Yes, there *are* phenomena that perplex us astronomers, but must man understand everything?
(*Both go out*)

THE VERY THIN MONK.   They degrade the home of mankind, a planet they call it. They load man, animal, plant and soil on a cart and chase it in circles through the empty sky. Heaven and earth, they claim, have ceased to exist. The earth because it's a star in the sky, and the sky because it consists of many earths. There's no longer any difference between

---

23 *Joshua* x, 12.

above and below, between eternal and transient. That we are transient, that we know. But now they tell us that heaven itself is transient. There are sun, moon and stars, but we live on this earth, that's what we've learned and what the Book says; but now, according to them, the earth is just another star. One day they'll be saying there's no difference between man and beast, that man himself is an animal and only animals exist.

THE FIRST SCHOLAR (*to Galileo*). Mr. Galilei, you've dropped something.

GALILEO (*who had taken his pebble out of his pocket during the preceding speech and dropped it on the floor, as he stoops to pick it up*). It didn't drop, monsignor, it rose.

THE FAT PRELATE (*turns his back on him*). The insolence of the man!

(*A very old cardinal comes in, supported by a monk. The others reverentially make room for him*)

THE VERY OLD CARDINAL. Are they still in there? Can't they get this foolishness over with? Surely Clavius knows his astronomy. I hear this Mr. Galilei has moved man from the center of the universe to somewhere on the edge. Obviously he's an enemy of mankind. And ought to be treated as such. Man is the crown of creation, every child knows that, he's God's highest and most beloved creature. Would God have put his most marvelous work, his supreme effort on a little far-away star that's constantly on the move? Would he have sent His Son to such a place? How can there be men so perverse as to believe these slaves of their mathematical tables? How can one of God's creatures put up with such a thing?

THE FAT PRELATE (*in an undertone*). The gentleman is present.

THE VERY OLD CARDINAL (*to Galileo*). Oh, you're the man? You know, I don't see too well any more, but I can see that you look remarkably like the man—what was his name again?—whom we burned a few years ago.

THE MONK. Your Eminence, you mustn't excite yourself. The doctor . . .

THE VERY OLD CARDINAL (*brushing him off, to Galileo*). You want to degrade our earth, though you live on it and receive everything from it. You're fouling your own nest! But I for one will not stand for it. (*He pushes the monk out of the way and struts proudly back and forth*) I'm not some nondescript being on some little star that briefly circles around somewhere. I walk with assurance on a firm earth, it stands still, it is the center of the universe, I am in the center, and the Creator's eye rests on me, on me alone. Around me, fixed to eight crystal spheres, revolve the fixed stars and the mighty sun, which was created to illumine my surroundings. And myself as well, in order that God may see me. Hence obviously and irrefutably, everything depends on me, man, the supreme work of God, the creature in the center, the image of God, imperishable and . . . (*He collapses*)

THE MONK. Your Eminence, you have overtaxed yourself!

(*At this moment the door in the rear is opened and the great Clavius comes in at the head of his astronomers. Quickly, without a word or a glance aside, he traverses the hall and, near the exit, says to a monk*)

CLAVIUS. He's right.

(*He goes out, followed by the astronomers. The door in the rear remains open. Deadly silence. The very old cardinal revives*)

THE VERY OLD CARDINAL. What happened? Has there been a decision?

(*No one dares to tell him*)

THE MONK. Your Eminence, you must let them take you home.

(*The old man is helped out. All leave the hall, perturbed. A little monk, a member of Clavius' investigating commission, stops at Galileo's side*)

THE LITTLE MONK (*furtively*). Mr. Galilei, before he left Father Clavius said: Now the theologians can see about setting the heavenly spheres right again. You have prevailed. (*Out*)

GALILEO (*trying to hold him back*). It has prevailed. Not I, reason has prevailed!

(The little monk has gone. Galileo is leaving too. In the doorway he meets a tall cleric, the cardinal inquisitor, accompanied by an astronomer. Galileo bows. Before going out, he whispers a question to a doorkeeper)

DOORKEEPER *(whispering back).* His Eminence the cardinal inquisitor.

(The astronomer leads the cardinal inquisitor to the telescope)

7

But the Inquisition places the Copernican doctrine on the Index (March 5, 1616).

> When Galileo was in Rome
> A cardinal asked him to his home.
> He wined and dined him as his guest
> And only made one small request.

The house of Cardinal Bellarmine in Rome. A ball is in progress. In the vestibule, where two ecclesiastical secretaries are playing chess and exchanging observations about the guests, Galileo is received by an applauding group of masked ladies and gentlemen. He is accompanied by his daughter Virginia and her fiancé Ludovico Marsili.

VIRGINIA. I won't dance with anyone else, Ludovico.

LUDOVICO. Your shoulder clasp is loose.

GALILEO.
> "Your tucker, Thaïs, is askew. Don't
> Set it straight, for preciously it shows me
> And others too some deeper disorder.
> In the candlelight of the swirling ballroom
> It makes them dream of
> Darker coigns in the expectant park."

VIRGINIA. Feel my heart.

GALILEO *(places his hand on her heart).* It's beating.

VIRGINIA. I want to look beautiful.

GALILEO. You'd better, or else they'll start doubting again that the earth revolves.

LUDOVICO. It doesn't revolve at all. *(Galileo laughs)* All Rome is talking of nothing but you, sir. After tonight Rome will be talking about your daughter.

GALILEO. Everybody agrees that it's easy to look beautiful in the Roman spring. I myself probably look like a paunchy Adonis. *(To the secretaries)* I'm to wait here for the cardinal. *(To the couple)* Run along and enjoy yourselves!

(Before they reach the ballroom in the rear Virginia skips back once more)

VIRGINIA. Father, the hairdresser on Via del Trionfo took me first and made four ladies wait. He knew your name right away. *(Out)*

GALILEO *(to the secretaries playing chess).* How can you go on playing chess the old way? Too confined. As it's played now, the larger pieces can range over many fields. The rook goes like this *(he demonstrates it)* and the bishop like this, and the queen like this and this. That gives you plenty of room and you can plan ahead.

THE FIRST SECRETARY. It doesn't fit in with our small salaries. We can only afford to move like this. *(He makes a short move)*

GALILEO. It's the other way round, my friend. If you live grandly, you can get away with anything. You must go with the times, gentlemen. You mustn't keep hugging the shore, one fine day you must venture out on the high seas.

(The very old cardinal of the previous scene crosses the stage, steered by his monk. He notices Galileo, passes him by, then turns uncertainly and greets him. Galileo sits down. The beginning of Lorenzo de' Medici's famous poem about the transience of the world is heard from the ballroom, sung by boys)

> "I who have seen the summer's roses die
> And all their petals pale and shriveled lie
> Upon the chilly ground, I know the truth:
> How evanescent is the flower of youth."

GALILEO. Rome.—Big party?

THE FIRST SECRETARY. The first carnival after

the years of plague. All the great families of Italy are represented here tonight. The Orsinis, the Villanis, the Nuccolis, the Soldanieris, the Canes, the Lecchis, the Estensis, the Colombinis . . .

THE SECOND SECRETARY (*interrupts*). Their Eminences, Cardinals Bellarmine and Barberini.

(*Enter Cardinal Bellarmine and Cardinal Barberini. They hold, respectively, a lamb's and a dove's mask mounted on sticks before their faces*)

BARBERINI (*pointing his index finger at Galileo*). "The sun also ariseth, and the sun goeth down, and hasteth to his place where he arose." [24] So says Solomon, and what does Galileo say?

GALILEO. When I was this big (*he shows with his hand*), Your Eminence, I was on a ship, and I cried out: The shore's moving away.— Today I know that the shore stood still and the ship was moving.

BARBERINI. Clever, clever. What we see, Bellarmine, to wit, that the stars in heaven are turning, need not be so, witness ship and shore. And what is true, to wit, that the earth turns, cannot be observed! Very clever. On the other hand, his satellites of Jupiter are hard nuts for our astronomers. Unfortunately, I too once read a little astronomy, Bellarmine. It clings to you like the itch.

BELLARMINE. We must go with the times, Barberini. If star charts based on a new hypothesis make navigation easier for our seamen, let's use them. We disapprove only of doctrines that put scripture in the wrong. (*He waves a greeting to the ballroom*)

GALILEO. Scripture.—"He that withholdeth corn, the people shall curse him." Proverbs of Solomon.

BARBERINI. "A prudent man concealeth knowledge." Proverbs of Solomon.

GALILEO. "Where no oxen are, the crib is clean: but much increase is by the strength of the ox."

BARBERINI. "He that ruleth his spirit is better than he that taketh a city."

GALILEO. "But a broken spirit drieth the bones." (*Pause*) "Doth not wisdom cry?"

BARBERINI. "Can one go upon hot coals, and his feet not be burned?" [25]—Welcome to Rome, my dear Galileo. You remember the founding of Rome? Two little boys, the story goes, received milk and shelter from a she-wolf. Ever since then all the she-wolf's children have had to pay for their milk. In return, the she-wolf provides all manner of pleasures, spiritual and worldly, from conversations with my learned friend Bellarmine to three or four ladies of international repute, would you like to see them? (*He leads Galileo toward the rear to show him the ballroom. Galileo follows reluctantly*) No? He prefers a serious discussion. Very well. Are you sure, friend Galilei, that you astronomers aren't just trying to make astronomy a little easier for yourselves? (*He leads him back to the front*) You like to think in circles or ellipses and in uniform velocities, in simple motions commensurate with your minds. But what if God had been pleased to make His stars move like this? (*He moves his finger through the air in a very complicated course with varying velocity in the air*) What would become of your calculations?

GALILEO. Your Eminence, if God had created the world like this (*He retraces Barberini's course*) He would have constructed our minds like this too (*He repeats the same course*) to enable them to recognize these courses as the simplest. I believe in reason.

BARBERINI. I consider reason inadequate. No answer. He's too polite to say he considers mine inadequate. (*Laughs and returns to the balustrade*)

BELLARMINE. Reason, my friend, doesn't go very far. All around us we see nothing but falsehood, crime and weakness. Where is the truth?

[24] *Ecclesiastes* I, 5. Solomon was thought to be the author.

[25] In order, *Proverbs* XI, 26; XII, 23; XIV, 4; XVI, 32; XVII, 22; VIII, 1; and VI, 28.

GALILEO (*angrily*).   I believe in reason.

BARBERINI (*to the secretaries*).   Don't take anything down. This is a scientific discussion among friends.

BELLARMINE.   Consider for a moment the intellectual effort it cost the church fathers and many after them to make some sense out of this world (abominable, isn't it?). Consider the cruelty of those who have their peasants whipped half-naked around their estates in the Campagna and the stupidity of the wretches who kiss their feet in return.

GALILEO.   Shameful! On my way here I saw . . .

BELLARMINE.   We've transferred the responsibility for such conditions (the very stuff of life) which we cannot understand to a higher being, we say that certain purposes are served thereby, that a master plan is being followed. Not that our minds are set entirely at ease. But now you come along and accuse this supreme being of not knowing how the planets move, when it's perfectly clear to you. Is that wise?

GALILEO (*launching into an explanation*).   I'm a faithful son of the church . . .

BARBERINI.   He's really dreadful. In all innocence he accuses God of the juiciest boners in astronomy! I suppose God didn't work hard enough at His astronomy before He wrote Holy Scripture? My *dear* friend!

BELLARMINE.   Don't you think it likely that the Creator knows more about His creation than any of His creatures?

GALILEO.   But, gentlemen, after all we can misinterpret not only the movements of the heavenly bodies, but the Bible as well.

BELLARMINE.   But wouldn't you say that after all the interpretation of the Bible is the business of the Holy Church?
(*Galileo is silent*)

BELLARMINE.   You see, you don't answer. (*He makes a sign to the secretaries*) Mr. Galilei, the Holy Office has decided tonight that the doctrine of Copernicus, according to which the sun is the center of the cosmos and motionless, whereas the earth moves and is not the center of the cosmos, is inane, absurd, and heretical. I have been charged to admonish you to relinquish this opinion. (*To the first secretary*) Please repeat.

FIRST SECRETARY.   His Eminence, Cardinal Bellarmine, to the aforementioned Galileo Galilei: The Holy Office has decided that the doctrine of Copernicus, according to which the sun is the center of the cosmos and motionless, whereas the earth moves and is not the center of the cosmos, is inane, absurd, and heretical. I have been charged to admonish you to relinquish this opinion.

GALILEO.   What does this mean?
(*From the ballroom another verse of the poem is heard, sung by boys*)
"I said, the seasons do not stay.
Pluck the roses while it's May."
(*Barberini motions Galileo to keep quiet while the singing continues. They all listen*)

GALILEO.   What about the facts? I understand that the astronomers of the Collegium Romanum have confirmed my observations.

BELLARMINE.   And expressed their profound satisfaction, in a manner most complimentary to you.

GALILEO.   But the satellites of Jupiter, the phases of Venus . . .

BELLARMINE.   The Holy Congregation has arrived at its decision without taking these particulars into account.

GALILEO.   In other words, all further scientific research . . .

BELLARMINE.   Is guaranteed, Mr. Galilei. In keeping with the church tenet that we cannot know but may investigate. (*Again he salutes a guest in the ballroom*) You are at liberty to deal with this doctrine as a mathematical hypothesis. Science is the legitimate and most beloved daughter of the church, Mr. Galilei. None of us seriously believes that you wish to undermine man's trust in the church.

GALILEO (*angrily*).   To invoke trust is to exhaust it.

BARBERINI.   Really? (*Laughing heartily, he slaps*

his shoulder. Then with a sharp look he says, not unkindly) Don't throw the baby out with the bath water, my friend. Nor shall we. We need you more than you need us.

BELLARMINE.   I can't wait to introduce Italy's greatest mathematician to the commissioner of the Holy Office who has the highest regard for you.

BARBERINI *(taking Galileo's other arm)*.   Whereupon he changes back into a lamb. You too, my friend, should have come here in disguise—as a respectable doctor of scholastic philosophy. It's my mask that allows me a little freedom tonight. When I wear it, you may even hear me murmuring: If God did not exist, we should have to invent Him. Well, let's put our masks on again. Poor Galilei hasn't got one.
(They take Galileo between them and lead him into the ballroom)

FIRST SECRETARY.   Have you got the last sentence?

SECOND SECRETARY.   Putting it down. *(They write eagerly)* What was that about his believing in reason?
(Enter the cardinal inquisitor)

THE INQUISITOR.   Has the interview taken place?

FIRST SECRETARY *(mechanically)*.   First Mr. Galilei arrived with his daughter. She was betrothed today to Mr. . . . *(The inquisitor motions him to skip it)* Mr. Galilei went on to tell us about the new method of playing chess in which, contrary to the rules, the pieces are moved over many squares.

THE INQUISITOR *(again beckons "no")*.   The minutes.
(A secretary hands him the minutes and the cardinal sits down to skim through them. Two young ladies in masks cross the stage and curtsy to the cardinal)

THE FIRST LADY.   Who's that?

THE SECOND LADY.   The cardinal inquisitor.
(They giggle and leave. Enter Virginia, looking around for someone)

THE INQUISITOR *(from his corner)*.   Well, my daughter?

VIRGINIA *(with a little start as she has not seen him)*.   Oh, Your Eminence!
(The inquisitor, without looking up, tenders his right hand. She approaches, kneels down, and kisses his ring)

THE INQUISITOR.   Glorious night! Allow me to congratulate you on your engagement. Your fiancé comes of a distinguished family. Will you stay in Rome?

VIRGINIA.   Not for the present, Your Eminence. There's so much to be done for a wedding.

THE INQUISITOR.   Then you'll go back to Florence with your father. I'm glad to hear it. I imagine your father needs you. Mathematics is a cold housewife, I should say. A woman of flesh and blood in such surroundings makes all the difference. It's so easy to lose oneself in the universe which is so very immense if one happens to be a great man.

VIRGINIA *(breathless)*.   You're very kind, Your Eminence. I really know practically nothing about these things.

THE INQUISITOR.   Indeed? *(He laughs)* Well, I suppose they don't eat fish in the fisherman's house. It will amuse your father to hear that, come right down to it, you learned what you know about the heavenly bodies from me. *(Leafing through the minutes)* I read here that our innovators, whose acknowledged leader is your father—a great man, one of the greatest—regard our present ideas about the importance of our good earth as somewhat exaggerated. Well then, from the age of Ptolemy, a sage of antiquity, to the present day, the whole of creation, that is, the entire crystal globe with the earth at its center, has been computed to measure approximately two thousand earth diameters. Quite a lot of space, but not enough, not nearly enough, for the innovators. They maintain, so I hear, that the universe extends further than we can imagine, that the distance between earth and sun—a rather considerable distance, we always thought—is so negligibly small when compared with the distance between our poor earth and the fixed stars on the outermost crystal sphere, that there is no need whatever to consider it in our calculations. Yes, our innovators live on a very grand scale. (*Virginia laughs. The inquisitor, too, laughs*)

THE INQUISITOR. And indeed, certain gentlemen of the Holy Office, not so long ago, came very close to taking offence at such a picture of the world, compared to which our old picture is a mere miniature that might well be hanging from the charming neck of a certain young lady. The gentlemen of the Holy Office are worried that a prelate or even a cardinal might get lost in such spaces. The Almighty might even lose sight of the pope himself. Yes, it's all very amusing. But even so, my dear child, I'm glad that you'll be staying with your eminent father, whom we all hold in the highest esteem. I wonder if I know your father confessor . . .

VIRGINIA. Father Christopher of St. Ursula.

THE INQUISITOR. Well then, I'm glad you'll be going with your father. He will need you, perhaps you can't conceive of such a thing, but the time will come. You're very young and very much alive and greatness is not always an easy thing to bear for those to whom God has given it, no, not always. No mortal is too great to be included in a prayer. But I'm keeping you, dear child, and I'm making your fiancé jealous and perhaps your father too by telling you something about the heavenly bodies—which may, to be sure, be quite obsolete. Hurry back to the ball, but don't forget to give Father Christopher my regards. (*Virginia, after a deep curtsy, leaves quickly*)

8

A Conversation

> Galileo, feeling grim
> A young monk came to visit him.
> The monk was born of common folk.
> It was of science that they spoke.

In the palace of the Florentine ambassador to Rome, Galileo listens to the little monk, who after the session of the Collegium Romanum

repeated Father Clavius' remark to him in a whisper.

GALILEO. Speak up, speak up! The cloth you wear entitles you to say what you please.

THE LITTLE MONK. I've studied mathematics, Mr. Galilei.

GALILEO. That might be a good thing if it led you to admit that two times two is sometimes four.

THE LITTLE MONK. For three nights I haven't been able to sleep, Mr. Galilei. I can't figure out how to reconcile the decree which I've read with the satellites of Jupiter which I've seen. So I decided to read mass this morning and come and see you.

GALILEO. To tell me that Jupiter has no satellites?

THE LITTLE MONK. No. I recognized the wisdom of the decree. It showed me how dangerous unrestricted inquiry can be to mankind, and I've decided to give up astronomy. Still, I felt I had to acquaint you with the motives which compel me, even though I'm an astronomer, to desist from pursuing a certain doctrine.

GALILEO. I can assure you that such motives are well known to me.

THE LITTLE MONK. I understand your bitterness. You're thinking of certain exceptional means of pressure exerted by the church.

GALILEO. Don't beat about the bush: instruments of torture.

THE LITTLE MONK. Yes, but I'd like to speak of other motives. Forgive me if I talk about myself. I grew up in the Campagna. My parents are peasants, simple folk. They knew all about olive trees, but very little else. As I observe the phases of Venus, I can see my parents sitting by the stove with my sister, eating lasagna. I see the beams over their heads, blackened by the smoke of centuries, I see distinctly their work-worn old hands and the little spoons they hold in them. They're very poor, but even in their misery there is a certain order. There are cyclic rhythms, scrubbing the floor, tending the olive trees in their seasons, paying taxes. There's a regularity in the calamities that descend on them. My father's back wasn't bowed all at once, no, a little more with every spring in the olive grove, just as the child-bearing that has made my mother more and more sexless occurred at regular intervals. What gives them the strength to sweat their way up stony paths with heavy baskets, to bear children, even to eat, is the feeling of stability and necessity they get from the sight of the soil, of the trees, turning green every year, of their little church standing there, and from hearing Bible verses read every Sunday. They have been assured that the eye of God is upon them, searching and almost anxious, that the whole world-wide stage is built around them in order that they, the players, may prove themselves in their great or small roles. What would my people say if I were to tell them they were living on a small chunk of stone that moves around another star, turning incessantly in empty space, one among many and more or less significant? What would be the good or necessity of their patience, of their acquiescence in their misery? What would be the good of the Holy Scripture which explains everything and demonstrates the necessity of all their sweat, patience, hunger and submission, if it turns out to be full of errors? No, I can see their eyes waver, I can see them rest their spoons on the table, I can see how cheated and betrayed they feel. In that case, they will say, no one is watching over us. Must we, un-taught, old and exhausted as we are, look out for ourselves? No one has given us a part to play, only this wretched role on a tiny star which is wholly dependent, around which nothing turns? There is no sense in our misery, hunger means no more than going without food, it is no longer a test of strength; effort means no more than bending and carrying, there is no virtue in it. Can you understand now that in the decree of the Holy Congregation I discern a noble motherly compassion, a great goodness of soul?

GALILEO. Goodness of soul! Don't you simply mean that there's nothing left, the wine's been drunk, their lips are parched, so let them kiss the cassock. But why is nothing left? Why is there no order in this country but the order in an empty drawer, and no necessity but the necessity of working oneself to death? Amid overflowing vineyards and wheat fields? Your peasants in the Campagna are paying for the wars which the vicar of gentle Jesus is waging in Spain and Germany. Why does he put the earth at the center of the universe? Because he wants the See of St. Peter to be in the center of the world! That's the crux of the matter. You're right; the question is not the planets, but the peasants of the Campagna. And don't talk to me about the beauty of phenomena in the golden glow of old age. Do you know how the Margaritifera oyster produces pearls? By contracting a near-fatal disease, by enveloping an unassimilable foreign body, a grain of sand, for instance, in a ball of mucus. It almost dies in the process. To hell with the pearl, give me the healthy oyster. Virtue is not bound up with misery, my friend. If your people were prosperous and happy, they could develop the virtues of prosperity and happiness. But today the virtues of exhausted people derive from exhausted fields, and I reject those virtues. Yes, sir, my new water pumps can work more miracles than your preposterous superhuman toil.—"Be fruitful and multiply," [26] because your fields are barren and you are decimated by wars. You want me to lie to your people?

THE LITTLE MONK (in great agitation). The very highest motives bid us keep silent: the peace of mind of the wretched and lowly!

GALILEO. Would you care to see a Cellini clock that Cardinal Bellarmine's coachman left here this morning? You see, my friend, as a reward for my letting your good parents have their peace of mind, the government offers me the wine which they press in the sweat of their countenance, which as you know was fashioned in the image of God. If I agreed to keep silent, my motives would undoubtedly be rather sordid: an easy life, no persecution, and so on.

26 Genesis I, 28.

THE LITTLE MONK.   Mr. Galilei, I'm a priest.

GALILEO.   You're also a physicist. And you can see that Venus has phases. Look out there. (*He point out the window*) Can you see the little Priapus by the laurel tree at the well? The god of gardens, birds, and thieves, rustic, obscene, two thousand years old. He wasn't so much of a liar. All right, we'll skip that, I too am a son of the church. But do you know the *Eighth Satire* of Horace? I've been reread-ing him lately, he gives me a certain balance. (*He reaches for a small book*) He puts words in the mouth of this same Priapus, a little statue that used to stand in the Esquiline Gardens. Here's how it starts:

"I was a figtree stump, wood of little use
When once a carpenter, pondering whether
To fashion a Priapus or a footstool
Decided on the god . . ."

Do you think Horace would have let anyone forbid him the footstool and put a table in the poem instead? Sir, a cosmology in which Venus has no phases violates my esthetic sense! We can't invent machines for pumping river water if we're forbidden to study the greatest machine before our eyes, the mechanism of the heavenly bodies. The sum total of the an-gles in a triangle can't be changed to suit the requirements of the curia. Nor can I calculate the courses of flying bodies in such a way as to account for witches riding on broom-sticks.

THE LITTLE MONK.   Don't you think the truth will prevail, even without us, if it is the truth?

GALILEO.   No, no, no. Truth prevails only when we make it prevail! The triumph of reason can only be the triumph of reasoning men. You describe your peasants in the Campagna as if they were moss on their huts. How can anyone imagine that the sum of the angles of a triangle runs counter to *their* needs! But if they don't rouse themselves and learn how to think, the best irrigation systems in the world won't do them any good. Damn it, I see the divine patience of your people, but where is their divine wrath?

THE LITTLE MONK.   They're tired.

GALILEO (*throws a bundle of manuscripts in front of him*).   Are you a physicist, my son? Here you'll find the reasons for the ocean's tides. But don't read it, do you hear. Ah, reading already? I see you're a physicist.
(*The little monk has immersed himself in the papers*)

GALILEO.   An apple from the tree of knowledge. He gobbles it up. He'll be damned for all eternity, but he's got to bolt it down, the hap-less glutton. Sometimes I think I'd gladly be locked up in a dungeon ten fathoms below ground, if in return I could find out one thing: What is light? And the worst of it is: What I know I must tell others. Like a lover, a drunkard, a traitor. It's a vice, I know, and leads to ruin. But how long can I go on shout-ing into empty air—that is the question.

THE LITTLE MONK (*points at a passage in the papers*).   I don't understand this sentence.

GALILEO.   I'll explain it to you, I'll explain it to you.

9

After a silence of eight years Galileo feels encouraged by the enthronement of a new pope, himself a scientist, to resume his re-search in the forbidden field. The sunspots.

Eight long years with tongue in cheek
Of what he knew he did not speak.
The temptations grew too great
And Galileo challenged fate.

Galileo's house in Florence. Galileo's pupils, Federzoni, the little monk and Andrea Sarti, now a young man, are gathered for an experi-ment. Galileo, standing, is reading a book.— Virginia and Mrs. Sarti are sewing bridal linen.

VIRGINIA.   Sewing a trousseau is fun. This is for the long dining table, Ludovico loves to have company. But it has got to be right, his mother notices every stitch. She isn't happy about father's books. Any more than Father Christopher.

MRS. SARTI. He hasn't written a book in years.

VIRGINIA. I think he saw he was mistaken. In Rome, a very high ecclesiastic told me a lot of things about astronomy. The distances are too great.

ANDREA (writes the program for the day on a blackboard and reads aloud). "Thursday afternoon: Floating bodies."—That means ice again; bucket of water; scales, iron needle; Aristotle. (He fetches the objects)
(The others are looking up things in books. Enter Filippo Mucius, a scholar in his middle years. He appears to be upset)

MUCIUS. Would you tell Mr. Galilei he must see me? He has condemned me without a hearing.

MRS. SARTI. I've told you he doesn't wish to see you.

MUCIUS. God will reward you if you ask him again. I must speak to him.

VIRGINIA (goes to the staircase). Father!

GALILEO. What is it?

VIRGINIA. Mr. Mucius!

GALILEO (looks up brusquely, goes to the head of the stairs, his pupils trailing behind him). What do you want?

MUCIUS. Mr. Galilei, I request permission to explain the passages in my book which seem to indicate a condemnation of the Copernican doctrine that the earth revolves. I've . . .

GALILEO. What is there to explain? You are in full agreement with the Holy Congregation's decree of 1616. You are perfectly within your rights. It's true, you studied mathematics with us, but we have no authority to make you say that two times two is four. You have every right to say that this stone (He takes a pebble from his pocket and throws it down to the ground floor) has just flown up to the ceiling.

MUCIUS. Mr. Galilei. I . . .

GALILEO. Don't talk about difficulties! The plague didn't prevent me from going on with my observations.

MUCIUS. Mr. Galilei, the plague is not the worst.

GALILEO. Let me tell you this: Not to know the truth is just stupid. To know the truth and call it a lie is criminal! Leave my house at once!

MUCIUS (tonelessly). You are right. (He goes out)
(Galileo returns to his study)

FEDERZONI. That's how it is, I'm afraid. He doesn't amount to much and no one could pay any attention to him if he hadn't been your pupil. But now of course they all say: He's heard everything Galileo had to say and is forced to admit that it's all wrong.

MRS. SARTI. I feel sorry for the gentleman.

VIRGINIA. Father was very fond of him.

MRS. SARTI. I wanted to talk to you about your marriage, Virginia. You're such a young thing, and you have no mother, and your father just puts little pieces of ice in water, Anyway, I wouldn't ask him questions about your marriage if I were you. He would say the most dreadful things for a week, naturally at meals when the young people are there, because he hasn't half a scudo's worth of shame in him, never did have. That's not what I had in mind, I'm thinking of what the future has in store. Not that I know anything, I'm only an ignorant woman. But this is a very serious thing, you mustn't go into it blindly. I do think you should go to a real astronomer at the university and consult him about your horoscope. Then you'll know what to expect. Why are you laughing?

VIRGINIA. Because I've been.

MRS. SARTI (very curious). What did he say?

VIRGINIA. For three months I must be careful because the sun will be in Aries, but then I get a very good ascendant and the clouds will part. As long as I don't lose sight of Jupiter, I can go on any journey I please, because I'm an Aries.

MRS. SARTI.   And Ludovico?

VIRGINIA.   He's a Leo. *(After a little pause)* That means sensual, I think.
(Pause)

VIRGINIA.   I know that step. It's Mr. Gaffone, the rector.[27]
(Enter Mr. Gaffone, the rector of the university)

GAFFONE.   Just thought I'd bring you a book that might be of interest to your father. For heaven's sake don't disturb Mr. Galilei. I can't help feeling that every minute taken from that great man is a minute taken from Italy. I'll just put the book in your little hands, and disappear, on tiptoe.
(He goes out. Virginia hands the book to Federzoni)

GALILEO.   What's it about?

FEDERZONI.   I don't know. *(Spelling it out)* "De maculis in sole."

ANDREA.   On the sunspots. Another one!
(Federzoni angrily hands it to him)

ANDREA.   Listen to this dedication! "To the greatest living authority on physics, Galileo Galilei."
(Galileo has immersed himself once more in his book)

ANDREA.   I've read the treatise by Fabricius in Holland. He believes the spots are clusters of stars passing between the earth and the sun.

THE LITTLE MONK.   Isn't that doubtful, Mr. Galilei?
(Galileo does not answer)

ANDREA.   In Paris and Prague they think they're vapors from the sun.

FEDERZONI.   Hm.

ANDREA.   Federzoni has his doubts.

FEDERZONI.   Kindly leave me out of it. I said "Hm," that's all. I'm the lens grinder, I grind lenses, you people look through them and observe the sky, and what you see is not spots, but "maculis." How can I doubt anything?

[27] I.e., the president of the university.

How many times do I have to tell you I can't read these books, they're in Latin.
(In his anger he gesticulates with the scales. A pan falls to the floor. Galileo walks over and silently picks it up)

THE LITTLE MONK.   It's blissful to doubt; I wonder why.

ANDREA.   Every sunny day in the last two weeks I've climbed up to the attic, right under the roof. A thin beam of light comes down through a tiny crack in the tiles. With that beam you can catch the reverse image of the sun on a sheet of paper. I saw a spot as big as a fly and blurred like a small cloud. It moved. Why don't we investigate those spots, Mr. Galilei?

GALILEO.   Because we're working on floating bodies.

ANDREA.   Mother has whole baskets full of letters. All Europe wants your opinion. With the reputation you've built up, you can't be silent.

GALILEO.   Rome has allowed me to build up a reputation because I've kept silent.

FEDERZONI.   But you can't afford to be silent any more.

GALILEO.   Nor can I afford to be roasted over a wood fire like a ham.

ANDREA.   Do you think the spots come into it?
(Galileo does not answer)

ANDREA.   All right, let's stick to our little pieces of ice. They can't hurt you.

GALILEO.   Exactly.—Our proposition, Andrea!

ANDREA.   We assume that whether a body floats or not depends essentially not on its shape, but on whether it is lighter or heavier than water.

GALILEO.   What does Aristotle say?

THE LITTLE MONK.   "Discus latus platique . . ."

GALILEO.   Translate, translate!

THE LITTLE MONK.   "A broad, flat disk of ice floats in water, whereas an iron needle sinks."

GALILEO.   Why then, according to Aristotle, doesn't ice sink?

THE LITTLE MONK.   Because, being broad and flat, it cannot divide the water.

GALILEO.   Very well. (*A piece of ice is handed to him and he puts it into the bucket*) Now I press the ice firmly down to the bottom of the bucket. I remove the pressure of my hands. What happens?

THE LITTLE MONK.   It rises to the surface.

GALILEO.   Correct. In rising it seems to be able to divide the water, Fulganzio!

THE LITTLE MONK.   But why then does it float at all? Ice is heavier than water, because it is condensed water.

GALILEO.   What if it were diluted water?

ANDREA.   It must be lighter than water, or it wouldn't float.

GALILEO.   Aha!

ANDREA.   Just as an iron needle can't float. Everything lighter than water floats, everything heavier sinks. Which was to be proved.

GALILEO.   Andrea, you must learn to think carefully. Give me the iron needle. A sheet of paper. Is iron heavier than water?

ANDREA.   Yes.
(*Galileo places the needle on a sheet of paper and floats it in the water. Pause*)

GALILEO.   What happens?

FEDERZONI.   The needle floats! Holy Aristotle, they never checked up on him!
(*They laugh*)

GALILEO.   One of the main reasons for the poverty of science is that it is supposed to be so rich. The aim of science is not to open the door to everlasting wisdom, but to set a limit to everlasting error. Take that down.

VIRGINIA.   What's the matter?

MRS. SARTI.   Every time they laugh, a fright comes over me. I wonder what they're laughing about.

VIRGINIA.   Father says theologians have their church bells and physicists have their laughter.

MRS. SARTI.   At least I'm glad he doesn't look through his tube so much any more. That was much worse.

VIRGINIA.   No, he only puts pieces of ice in water. No harm can come of that.

MRS. SARTI.   Who knows?
(*Enter Ludovico Marsili in traveling garb, followed by a manservant with luggage. Virginia runs toward him and embraces him*)

VIRGINIA.   Why didn't you let us know you were coming?

LUDOVICO.   I was near here inspecting our vineyards, and I just couldn't stay away.

GALILEO (*as though nearsighted*).   Who's that?

VIRGINIA.   Ludovico.

THE LITTLE MONK.   Can't you see him?

GALILEO.   Oh yes, Ludovico. (*Goes toward him*) How are the horses?

LUDOVICO.   They're fine, sir.

GALILEO.   Sarti, let's celebrate. Bring us a jug of that old Sicilian wine!
(*Mrs. Sarti goes out with Andrea*)

LUDOVICO (*to Virginia*).   You look pale. Country life will do you good. Mother is expecting you in September.

VIRGINIA.   Wait, I want to show you my wedding dress. (*Runs out*)

GALILEO.   Sit down.

LUDOVICO.   I hear you have more than a thousand students in your lectures at the university, sir. What are you working on at the moment?

GALILEO.   Routine stuff. Did you come through Rome?

LUDOVICO.   Yes.—Before I forget, mother congratulates you on your admirable tact in connection with all that fuss over the sunspots in Holland.

GALILEO (*dryly*).   That's kind of her.
(*Mrs. Sarti and Andrea bring wine and glasses. All gather around the table*)

LUDOVICO.   Rome has found a topic of conversation for February. Christopher Clavius said he was afraid the whole earth-around-the-sun circus would flare up again because of those sunspots.

ANDREA.   Don't let it worry you.

GALILEO.   Any other news from the Holy City, apart from hopes for new sins on my part?

LUDOVICO. You heard, of course, that the Holy Father is dying?

THE LITTLE MONK. Oh.

GALILEO. Who's mentioned as successor?

LUDOVICO. Mostly Barberini.

GALILEO. Barberini.

ANDREA. Mr. Galilei knows Barberini personally.

THE LITTLE MONK. Cardinal Barberini is a mathematician.

FEDERZONI. A scientist in the chair of St. Peter! (*Pause*)

GALILEO. I see, now they need men like Barberini who've read a little mathematics. Things will start moving, Federzoni, we may live to see the day when we won't have to glance over our shoulders like criminals every time we say that two times two is four. (*To Ludovico*) I like this wine, Ludovico. What do you think of it?

LUDOVICO. It's good.

GALILEO. I know the vineyard. The slope is steep and stony, the grapes are almost blue. I love this wine.

LUDOVICO. Yes, sir.

GALILEO. There are little shadows in it. And it's almost sweet but stops at the "almost."— Andrea, put the stuff away, the ice and bucket and needle.—I value the consolations of the flesh. I have no patience with cowardly souls who speak of weakness. I say: To enjoy yourself is an achievement.

THE LITTLE MONK. What are you taking up next?

FEDERZONI. We're starting in again on the earth-around-the-sun circus.

ANDREA (*singing in an undertone*)
The Book says it stands still and so
Each learned doctor proves.
The Holy Father takes it by the ears
And holds it fast. And yet it moves.
(*Andrea, Federzoni and the little monk hurry to the workbench and clear it*)

ANDREA. We might even find out that the sun revolves too. How would you like that, Marsili?

LUDOVICO. What's the excitement about?

MRS. SARTI. You're not going back to those abominations, Mr. Galilei?

GALILEO. Now I know why your mother sent you here. Barberini is on the rise. Knowledge will be a passion and research a delight. Clavius is right, the sunspots do interest me. You like my wine, Ludovico?

LUDOVICO. I said I did, sir.

GALILEO. You really like it?

LUDOVICO (*stiffly*). I like it.

GALILEO. Would you go so far as to accept a man's wine or his daughter without asking him to give up his profession? What has my astronomy got to do with my daughter? The phases of Venus don't affect my daughter's rear end.

MRS. SARTI. Don't be vulgar. I'll go get Virginia.

LUDOVICO (*holds her back*). In families like mine marriages are not decided by sexual considerations alone.

GALILEO. Did they prevent you from marrying my daughter for the last eight years because I was on probation?

LUDOVICO. My wife will also have to cut a figure in the village church.

GALILEO. You mean, your peasants won't pay their rent if the lady of the manor is insufficiently saintly?

LUDOVICO. In a way.

GALILEO. Andrea, Fulganzio, get the brass mirror and the screen! We'll project the sun's image on it to protect our eyes. That's your method, Andrea.
(*Andrea and the little monk get mirror and screen*)

LUDOVICO. Years ago in Rome, sir, you signed a pledge to stay away from this earth-around-the-sun business.

GALILEO. Oh well. We had a reactionary pope in those days.

MRS. SARTI. Had! His Holiness isn't even dead yet.

GALILEO. Pretty near, pretty near!—Put a grid over the screen. We'll proceed methodically. And we'll be able to answer all those letters, won't we, Andrea?

MRS. SARTI. "Pretty near!" Fifty times that man weighs his pieces of ice, but when something happens that suits his purposes he believes it blindly!

(*The screen is put up*)

LUDOVICO. Mr. Galilei, if His Holiness should die, the next pope—no matter who he is or how much he loves science—will have to take account of how much the country's leading families love him.

THE LITTLE MONK. God made the physical world, Ludovico; God made the human brain; God will allow physics.

MRS. SARTI. Galileo, let me tell you something. I've watched my son fall into sin for the sake of these "experiments" and "theories" and "observations," and I haven't been able to do anything about it. You set yourself against the authorities and they gave you a warning. The greatest cardinals spoke to you the way you'd speak to a sick horse. It worked for a while, but two months ago, right after the Immaculate Conception,[28] I caught you sneaking back to your "observations." In the attic! I didn't say anything, but I knew. I ran out and lit a candle for St. Joseph. It's more than I can bear. When we're alone you show some sense, you say you've got to behave because it's dangerous, but two days of "experiments" and you're as bad as ever. If I lose my eternal salvation because I stand by a heretic, that's my business, but you have no right to trample your daughter's happiness with your big feet!

GALILEO (*gruffly*). Get the telescope!

LUDOVICO. Giuseppe, put the luggage back in the coach.

(*The manservant goes out*)

28 December 8, an ecclesiastical feast day.

MRS. SARTI. She'll never get over this. You can tell her yourself.

(*She runs out, still holding the pitcher*)

LUDOVICO. I see you've made up your mind. Mr. Galilei, three quarters of the year mother and I live on our estate in the Campagna and I can assure you that our peasants lose no sleep over your treatises on the moons of Jupiter. They work too hard in the fields. It might upset them, though, if they heard that attacks on the holy doctrine of the church were going unpunished. Don't forget that those poor brutalized wretches get everything mixed up. They really are brutes, you have no idea. A rumor that somebody's seen a pear growing on an apple tree makes them run away from their work to gab about it.

GALILEO (*with interest*). Really?

LUDOVICO. Animals. When they come to the manor with a trifling complaint, mother has to have a dog whipped in front of them to remind them of discipline and order and good manners. You, Mr. Galilei, you may occasionally see flowering corn fields from your traveling coach, or absent-mindedly eat our olives and our cheese, but you have no idea how much effort it takes to raise all these things—all the supervision!

GALILEO. Young man, I never eat my olives absent-mindedly. (*Rudely*) You're wasting my time. (*Calls toward outside*) Is the screen ready?

ANDREA. Yes. Are you coming?

GALILEO. You whip more than dogs to keep discipline, don't you, Marsili?

LUDOVICO. Mr. Galilei, you have a marvelous brain. Too bad.

THE LITTLE MONK (*amazed*). He's threatening you.

GALILEO. Yes, I might stir up his peasants to think new thoughts. And his servants and his overseers.

FEDERZONI. How, they don't know Latin.

GALILEO. I could write in the vernacular for the many instead of in Latin for the few. For our new ideas we need people who work with their hands. Who else wants to know the causes of everything? People who never see bread except on their tables have no desire to know how it's baked; those bastards would rather thank God than the baker. But the men who bake the bread will understand that nothing can move unless something moves it. Fulganzio, your sister at the olive press won't be much surprised—she'll probably laugh—when she hears that the sun is not a gold escutcheon, but a lever: The earth moves because the sun moves it.

LUDOVICO. You'll always be a slave to your passions. Convey my apologies to Virginia. It's better, I think, if I don't see her now.

GALILEO. The dowry is at your disposal. At any time.

LUDOVICO. Good day. (*He goes*)

ANDREA. Our regards to all the Marsilis!

FEDERZONI. Who tell the earth to stand still so their castles won't fall off.

ANDREA. And to the Cencis and Villanis!

FEDERZONI. The Cervillis!

ANDREA. The Lecchis!

FEDERZONI. The Pierleonis!

ANDREA. Who'll only kiss the pope's foot as long as he tramples the people with it.

THE LITTLE MONK. (*also at the instruments*) The new pope will be an enlightened man.

GALILEO. And now let's start observing these spots in the sun which interest us—at our own risk, not counting too much on the protection of a new pope . . .

ANDREA (*interrupting*). But fully confident of dispelling Mr. Fabricius' star shadows and the solar vapors of Prague and Paris, and proving that the sun rotates.

GALILEO. Reasonably confident that the sun rotates. My aim is not to prove that I've been right, but to find out whether or not I have been. I say: Abandon hope, all ye who enter upon observation. Maybe it's vapors, maybe it's spots, but before we assume that they're

spots, though it would suit us if they were, we'd do better to assume they're fishtails. Yes, we shall start all over again from scratch. And we won't rush ahead with seven-league boots, but crawl at snail's pace. And what we find today we'll wipe from the blackboard tomorrow, and not write it down again until we find it a second time. And if there's something we hope to find, we'll regard it with particular distrust when we do find it. Accordingly let us approach our observation of the sun with the inexorable resolve to prove that the earth *stands still!* Only after we have failed, after we have been totally and hopelessly defeated and are licking our wounds in utter dejection, only then shall we begin to ask whether the earth does not indeed move! (*With a twinkle*) But then, when every other hypothesis has gone up in smoke, then no mercy for those who have never observed anything, yet go on talking. Take the cloth off the tube and focus it on the sun! (*He adjusts the brass mirror*)

THE LITTLE MONK. I knew you had taken up your work again. I knew it when you didn't recognize Mr. Marsili.

(*In silence they begin their examinations. When the flaming image of the sun appears on the screen Virginia in her bridal gown runs in*)

VIRGINIA. You've sent him away! (*She faints. Andrea and the little monk rush to her aid*)

GALILEO. I've got to know.

10

In the course of the next ten years Galileo's doctrine is disseminated among the common people. Pamphleteers and ballad singers everywhere seize upon the new ideas. In the carnival of 1632 the guilds in many Italian cities take astronomy as the theme for their carnival processions.

A half-starved couple of show people with a five-year-old girl and an infant enter a market place where many people, some with masks,

are awaiting the carnival procession. They carry
bundles, a drum and other props.

THE BALLAD SINGER (*drumming*). Citizens,
ladies, and gentlemen! Before the great carnival procession of the guilds arrives we bring
you the latest Florentine song which is being
sung all over northern Italy. We've imported
it at great expense. The title is: The horren-
dous doctrine and teaching of Mr. Galileo
Galilei, court physicist, or, A Foretaste of the
Future. (*He sings*)

When the Almighty made the universe
He made the earth and then he made the sun.
Then round the earth he bade the sun to turn—
That's in the Bible, Genesis, Chapter One.
And from that time all beings here below
Were in obedient circles meant to go.

They all began to turn around
The little fellows round the big shots
And the hindmost round the foremost
On earth as it is in heaven.
Around the popes the cardinals
Around the cardinals the bishops
Around the bishops the secretaries
Around the secretaries the aldermen
Around the aldermen the craftsmen
Around the craftsmen the servants
Around the servants the dogs, the chickens and
the beggars.

That, my friends, is the great order, ordo ordi-
num [order of orders], as the theologians call it,
regula aeternis, the rule of rules. And then, my
friends, what happened then? (*He sings*)

Up stood the learned Galileo
(Chucked the Bible, pulled out his telescope,
and took a look at the universe)
And told the sun: Stand still!
From this time on, the wheels
Shall turn the other way.
Henceforth the mistress, ho!
Shall turn around the maid.

Now that was rash, my friends, it is no matter
small:
For heresy will spread today like foul diseases.
Change Holy Writ, forsooth? What will be left
at all?
Why: each of us would say and do just what he
pleases!

Esteemed citizens, such doctrines are utterly im-
possible. (*He sings*)
Good people, what will come to pass
If Galileo's teachings spread?
The server will not serve at mass
No servant girl will make the bed.
Now that is grave, my friends, it is no matter
small:
For independent spirit spreads like foul dis-
eases!
Yet life is sweet and man is weak and after
all—
How nice it is, for once, to do just as one
pleases!

Now, my good friends, here, look to the future
and see what the most learned doctor Galileo
Galilei predicts. (*He sings*)

Two ladies at a fishwife's stall
Are in for quite a shock
The fishwife takes a loaf of bread
And gobbles up all her stock.
The carpenters take wood and build
Houses for themselves, not pews
And members of the cobblers' guild
Now walk around in shoes!
Is this permitted? No, it is no matter small:
For independent spirit spreads like foul dis-
eases!
Yet life is sweet and man is weak and after
all—
How nice it is, for once, to do just as one
pleases!

The tenant kicks his noble master
Smack in the ass like that
The tenant's wife now gives her children

Milk that made the parson fat.

No, no my friends, for the Bible is no matter
   small:

For independent spirit spreads like foul diseases!

Yet life is sweet and man is weak and after
   all—

How nice it is for once to do just as one
   pleases!

THE SINGER'S WIFE.

   The other day I tried it too
   And did my husband frankly tell
   Let's see now if what you can do
   Other stars can do as well.

BALLAD SINGER.

   No, no, no, no, no, no, stop, Galileo, stop!
   For independent spirit spreads like foul dis-
      eases.
   People must keep their place, some down and
      some on top!
   Though it is nice for once to do just as one
      pleases.

BOTH.

   Good people who have trouble here below
   In serving cruel lords and gentle Jesus
   Who bids you turn the other cheek just so
   While they prepare to strike the second blow:
   Obedience will never cure your woe
   So each of you wake up and do just as he
      pleases!

THE BALLAD SINGER.   Esteemed citizens, behold
Galileo Galilei's phenomenal discovery: The
earth revolving around the sun!
(*He belabors the drum violently. His wife and
child step forward. The wife holds a crude
replica of the sun, and the child, holding a
gourd, image of the earth, over her head, circles
around the woman. The singer excitedly points
at the little girl as if she were performing a
dangerous acrobatic feat in jerkily taking step*

*after step in rhythm with the drumbeats.
Then drumming from the rear*)

A DEEP VOICE (*calls out*).   The procession!
(*Enter two men in rags drawing a little cart.
The "Grand Duke of Florence," a figure in
sackcloth with a cardboard crown, sits on a
ridiculous throne and peers through a telescope. Over the throne a painted sign "Looking
for trouble." Next, four masked men march
in carrying a huge tarpaulin. They stop and
bounce a large doll representing a cardinal. A
dwarf has posted himself to one side with a
sign "The New Age." Among the crowd a
beggar raises himself by his crutches and
stomps the ground in a dance until he collapses. Enter a stuffed figure, more than life-
size, Galileo Galilei, which bows to the audience. In front of it a child displays a giant
open Bible with crossed-out pages.*)

THE BALLAD SINGER.   Galileo Galilei, the Bible-
smasher!
(*An outburst of laughter among the crowd*)

11

1633. The inquisition summons the world-
famous scholar to Rome

   The depths are hot, the heights are chill
   The streets are loud, the court is still.

*Antechamber and staircase of the Medici
Palace, Florence. Galileo and his daughter are
waiting to be admitted to the grand duke.*

VIRGINIA.   It's been a long wait.

GALILEO.   Yes.

VIRGINIA.   There's that man again who's been
following us. (*She points at a shady individual
who passes by without paying attention to
them*)

GALILEO (*whose eyesight is impaired*).   I don't
know him.

VIRGINIA.   I've seen him several times lately.
He gives me the shivers.

GALILEO. Nonsense. We're in Florence, not among Corsican robbers.

VIRGINIA. There's Rector Gaffone.

GALILEO. *He* frightens *me*. The blockhead will draw me into another interminable conversation.

(*Mr. Gaffone, the rector of the university, descends the stairs. He is visibly startled when he sees Galileo and walks stiffly past the two, with rigidly averted head and barely nodding.*)

GALILEO. What's got into him? My eyes are bad again. Did he greet us at all?

VIRGINIA. Just barely.—What have you said in your book? Can they think it's heretical?

GALILEO. You hang around church too much. Getting up before dawn and running to mass is ruining your complexion. You pray for me, don't you?

VIRGINIA. There's Mr. Vanni, the iron founder. The one you designed the smelting furnace for. Don't forget to thank him for the quails.

(*A man has come down the stairs*)

VANNI. How did you like the quails I sent you, Mr. Galileo?

GALILEO. Maestro Vanni, the quails were excellent. Again many thanks.

VANNI. They're talking about you upstairs. They claim you're responsible for those pamphlets against the Bible that are being sold all over.

GALILEO. I know nothing about pamphlets. My favorite books are the Bible and Homer.

VANNI. Even if that were not the case: Let me take this opportunity of assuring you that we manufacturers are on your side. I don't know much about the movement of stars, but the way I look at it, you're the man who is fighting for the freedom to teach new knowledge. Just take that mechanical cultivator from Germany that you described to me. Last year alone five works on agriculture were published in London. Here we'd be grateful for one book about the Dutch canals. It's the same people who are making trouble for you and preventing the physicians in Bologna from dissecting corpses for research.

GALILEO. Your vote counts, Vanni.

VANNI. I hope so. Do you know that in Amsterdam and London they have money markets? And trade schools too. And newspapers that appear regularly. Here we're not even free to make money. They're against iron foundries because they claim too many workers in one place promote immorality. I swim or sink with men like you, Mr. Galilei! If ever they try to harm you, please remember that you have friends in every branch of industry. The cities of northern Italy are behind you, sir.

GALILEO. As far as I know no one has any intention of harming me.

VANNI. Really?

GALILEO. Really.

VANNI. I believe you'd be better off in Venice. Not so many cassocks. You'd be free to carry on the fight. I have a coach and horses, Mr. Galilei.

GALILEO. I can't see myself as a refugee. I love comfort.

VANNI. I understand. But to judge by what I heard up there, there's no time to be lost. I got the impression that right now they'd prefer not to have you in Florence.

GALILEO. Nonsense. The grand duke is a pupil of mine, not to mention the fact that if anyone tries to trip me up the pope himself will tell him where to get off.

VANNI. You don't seem able to distinguish your friends from your enemies, Mr. Galilei.

GALILEO. I'm able to distinguish power from lack of power. (*He brusquely steps away*)

VANNI. Well, I wish you luck. (*Goes out*)

GALILEO (*back at Virginia's side*). Every Tom, Dick and Harry with a grievance picks me as his spokesman, especially in places where it doesn't exactly help me. I've written a book on the mechanism of the universe, that's all. What people make or don't make of it is no concern of mine.

VIRGINIA (*in a loud voice*).   If people only knew how you condemned the goings-on at last year's carnival.

GALILEO.   Yes. Give a bear honey if it's hungry and you'll lose your arm.

VIRGINIA (*in an undertone*).   Did the grand duke send for you today?

GALILEO.   No, but I've sent in my name. He wants the book, he's paid for it. Ask somebody, complain about the long wait.

VIRGINIA (*goes to talk to an attendant, followed by the individual*). Mr. Mincio, has His Highness been informed that my father wishes to speak to him?

THE ATTENDANT.   How should I know?

VIRGINIA.   That's no answer.

THE ATTENDANT.   Really?

VIRGINIA.   You ought to be polite.
(*The attendant half turns his back on her and yawns while looking at the shady individual*)

VIRGINIA (*has come back*).   He says the grand duke is still busy.

GALILEO.   I heard you say something about "polite." What was it?

VIRGINIA.   I thanked him for his polite answer, that's all. Can't you just leave the book for him? You're wasting your time.

GALILEO.   I'm beginning to wonder what my time is worth. Maybe I should accept Sagredo's invitation to go to Padua for a few weeks. My health hasn't been up to snuff.

VIRGINIA.   You couldn't live without your books.

GALILEO.   We could take some of the Sicilian wine, one, two cases.

VIRGINIA.   You always say it doesn't travel. And the court owes you three months' salary. They won't forward it.

GALILEO.   That's true.

VIRGINIA (*whispers*).   The cardinal inquisitor!
(*The cardinal inquisitor descends the stairs. Passing them, he bows low to Galileo*)

VIRGINIA.   What's the cardinal inquisitor doing in Florence, father?

GALILEO.   I don't know. His attitude was re-

spectful, I think. I knew what I was doing when I came to Florence and held my peace all these years. Their praises have raised me so high that they have to take me as I am.

THE ATTENDANT (*announces*).   His Highness, the grand duke!
(*Cosmo de' Medici comes down the stairs. Galileo approaches him. Cosmo, slightly embarrassed, stops*)

GALILEO.   May I present Your Highness with my *Dialogues on the Two Chief Syst* . . .

COSMO.   I see, I see. How are your eyes?

GALILEO.   Not too good, Your Highness. With Your Highness' permission, I should like to present my . . .

COSMO.   The state of your eyes alarms me. Yes, it alarms me a good deal. Haven't you been using your splendid tube a little too much?
(*He walks off without accepting the book*)

GALILEO.   He didn't take the book, did he?

VIRGINIA.   Father, I'm afraid.

GALILEO (*subdued but firmly*).   Don't show your feelings. We are not going home, but to Volpi, the glass cutter's. I've arranged with him to have a cart with empty wine casks ready in the tavern yard next door, to take me away at any time.

VIRGINIA.   Then you knew . . .

GALILEO.   Don't look back.
(*They start to leave*)

A HIGH OFFICIAL (*descending the stairs*).   Mr. Galilei, I have orders to inform you that the court of Florence is no longer in a position to oppose the request of the Holy Inquisition for your interrogation in Rome. Mr. Galilei, the coach of the Holy Inquisition is waiting for you.

12

The Pope

A room in the Vatican. Pope Urban VIII (formerly Cardinal Barberini) has received the cardinal inquisitor. During the audience the pope is being dressed. From outside the shuffling of many feet is heard.

THE POPE (*very loud*).   No! No! No!

THE INQUISITOR.   Then Your Holiness really means to tell the doctors of all the faculties, the representatives of all the religious orders and of the entire clergy, who have come here guided by their childlike faith in the word of God as recorded in scripture to hear Your Holiness confirm them in their faith—you mean to inform them that scripture can no longer be considered true?

THE POPE.   I won't permit the multiplication tables to be broken. No!

THE INQUISITOR.   Yes, these people say it is only a matter of the multiplication tables, not of the spirit of rebellion and doubt. But it is not the multiplication tables. It is an alarming unrest that has come over the world. It is the unrest of their own minds, which they transfer to the immovable earth. They cry out: The figures force our hands! But where do these figures come from? Everyone knows they come from doubt. These people doubt everything. Is our human community to be built on doubt and no longer on faith? "You are my master, but I doubt whether that is a good arrangement." "This is your house and your wife, but I doubt whether they should not be mine." On the other hand, as we can read on the house walls of Rome, disgraceful interpretations are being put on Your Holiness' great love for art, to which we owe such marvelous collections: "The Barberinis are stripping Rome of what the barbarians failed to take." And abroad? It has pleased God to visit heavy tribulation upon the Holy See. Your Holiness' policy in Spain is misunderstood by persons lacking in insight, your rift with the emperor is deplored. For fifteen years Germany has been a shambles, people have been slaughtering one another with Bible quotations on their lips. And at a time when under the onslaught of plague, war and reformation, Christianity is being reduced to a few disorganized bands, a rumor is spreading through Europe that you are in secret league with Lutheran Sweden to weaken the Catholic emperor. This is the moment these mathematicians, these worms, choose to turn their tubes to the sky and inform the world that even here, the one place where your authority is not yet contested, Your Holiness is on shaky ground. Why, is one tempted to ask, this sudden interest in so recondite a science as astronomy? Does it make any difference how these bodies move? Yet, thanks to the bad example of that Florentine, all Italy, down to the last stableboy, is prattling about the phases of Venus and thinking at the same time of many irksome things which are held in our schools and elsewhere to be immutable. Where will it end, if all these people, weak in the flesh and inclined to excess, come to rely exclusively on their own reason, which this madman declares to be the ultimate authority? They begin by doubting whether the sun stood still at Gibeon[29] and end up directing their unclean doubts at the church collections. Since they began sailing the high seas—to which I have no objection—they have been putting their trust in a brass sphere that they call a compass, and no longer in God. Even as a young man this Galileo wrote about machines. With machines they expect to work miracles. What kind of miracles? Of course they have no more use for God, but what is to be the nature of these miracles? For one thing, they expect to do away with Above and Below. They don't need it any more. Aristotle, whom in other respects they regard as a dead dog, said—and this they quote—: If the shuttle were to weave by itself and the plectron to pluck by itself, masters would no longer need apprentices nor lords servants. They believe that this time has come. This evil man knows what he is doing when he writes his astronomical works not in Latin but in the idiom of fishwives and wool merchants.

29 *Joshua x*, 13.

THE POPE. It's certainly in bad taste. I'll tell him.

THE INQUISITOR. Some he incites, others he bribes. The north Italian ship owners keep clamoring for Mr. Galiliei's star charts. We shall have to yield to them, since material interests are involved.

THE POPE. But these star charts are based on his heretical statements, on the movements of certain heavenly bodies which become impossible if his doctrine is rejected. You can't reject the doctrine and accept the star charts.

THE INQUISITOR. Why not? It's the only solution.

THE POPE. This shuffling makes me nervous. Forgive me if I seem distracted.

THE INQUISITOR. Perhaps it speaks to you more clearly than I can, Your Holiness. Are all these people to go home with doubts in their hearts?

THE POPE. After all the man is the greatest physicist of our time, a beacon for Italy, and not some good-for-nothing crank. He has friends. There's Versailles.[30] There's the court in Vienna. They will call the church a cesspool of rotten prejudices. Hands off!

THE INQUISITOR. Actually, we wouldn't have to go very far in his case. He is a man of the flesh. He would cave in very quickly.

THE POPE. He gets pleasure out of more things than any man I ever met. Even his thinking is sensual. He can never say no to an old wine or a new idea. I will not stand for any condemning of physical facts, any battle cry of "church" against "reason." I gave him leave to write his book provided it ended with a statement that the last word is not with science but with faith. He has complied.

THE INQUISITOR. But how did he comply? His book is an argument between a simpleton who —naturally—propounds the opinions of Aristotle, and an intelligent man, just as naturally

voicing Mr. Galilei's opinions; and the concluding remark, Your Holiness, is made by whom?

THE POPE. What was that again? Who states our opinion?

THE INQUISITOR. Not the intelligent one.

THE POPE. This is impudence. This stamping in the halls is insufferable. Is the whole world coming here?

THE INQUISITOR. Not the whole world, but the best part of it. (*Pause. The pope is now fully robed*).

THE POPE. At the very most the instruments may be shown to him.

THE INQUISITOR. That will suffice, Your Holiness. Mr. Galilei is well versed in instruments.

13

On June 22, 1633, Galileo Galilei abjures his doctrine of the motion of the earth before the Inquisition.

> June twenty-second, sixteen thirty-three
> A momentous day for you and me.
> Of all the days that was the one
> An age of reason could have begun.

Palace of the Florentine ambassador in Rome. Galileo's pupils are waiting for news. The little monk and Federzoni are playing the new chess with its sweeping movements. Virginia kneels in a corner saying an Ave Maria.

THE LITTLE MONK. The pope refused to see him. No more scientific debates.

FEDERZONI. The pope was his last hope. I guess Cardinal Barberini was right when he said to him years ago: We need you. Now they've got him.

ANDREA. They'll kill him. The *Discorsi*[31] will never be finished.

---

[30] I.e., the court of France—an anachronism, since Versailles did not become the seat of government till 1682.

[31] *Discourses and Mathematical Demonstrations on Two New Sciences*, mechanics and the science of motion, published at Leiden, the Netherlands, in 1638.

FEDERZONI (*with a furtive glance at him*). You think so?

ANDREA. Because he'll never recant.
(*Pause*)

THE LITTLE MONK. When you lie awake at night you chew on the most useless ideas. Last night I couldn't get rid of the thought that he should never have left the republic of Venice.

ANDREA. He couldn't write his book there.

FEDERZONI. And in Florence he couldn't publish it.
(*Pause*)

THE LITTLE MONK. I also kept wondering whether they'd let him keep the stone he always carries in his pocket. His touchstone.

FEDERZONI. Where they're taking him people don't wear pockets.

ANDREA (*screaming*). They won't dare! And even if they do, he'll never recant. "Not to know the truth is just stupid. To know the truth and call it a lie is criminal."

FEDERZONI. I don't think so either, and I wouldn't want to go on living if he did, but they have the power.

ANDREA. Power isn't everything.

FEDERZONI. Maybe not.

THE LITTLE MONK (*softly*). He's been in prison for twenty-three days. Yesterday was the great interrogation. Today the judges are in session. (*As Andrea is listening, he raises his voice*) When I came to see him here two days after the decree, we were sitting over there; he showed me the little Priapus by the sundial in the garden—you can see it from here—and compared his own work with a poem by Horace, in which it is also impossible to change anything. He spoke of his esthetic sense, which compels him to look for the truth. And he told me his motto: Hieme et aestate, et prope et procul, usque dum vivam et ultra. [In winter and summer, both near and far, as long as I live and afterward.] He was referring to the truth.

ANDREA (*to the little monk*). Did you tell him what he did in the Collegium Romanum while they were examining his tube? Tell him! (*The little monk shakes his head*) He acted the same as always. He put his hands on his hams, stuck out his belly and said: Gentlemen, I beg for reason! (*Laughingly he imitates Galileo*)
(*Pause*)

ANDREA (*referring to Virginia*). She's praying for him to recant.

FEDERZONI. Let her pray. She's all mixed up since they talked to her. They brought her confessor down from Florence.
(*Enter the shady individual from the grand ducal palace in Florence*)

THE SHADY INDIVIDUAL. Mr. Galilei will be here soon. He may want a bed.

FEDERZONI. Has he been released?

THE SHADY INDIVIDUAL. Mr. Galilei is expected to recant at five o'clock before the plenary session of the Inquisition. The big bell of St. Mark's will be rung and the wording of the abjuration will be proclaimed publicly.

ANDREA. I don't believe it.

THE SHADY INDIVIDUAL. Because of the crowds in the streets, Mr. Galilei will be conducted to the postern on this side of the palace. (*Out*)

ANDREA (*suddenly in a loud voice*). The moon is an earth and has no light of its own. And Venus has no light of its own either and is like the earth and moves around the sun. And four moons revolve around the planet Jupiter which is as far away as the fixed stars and not fastened to any sphere. And the sun is the center of the universe and immovable in its place, and the earth is not the center and not immovable. And he was the man who proved it.

THE LITTLE MONK. No force can make what has been seen unseen.
(*Silence*)

FEDERZONI (*looks at the sundial in the garden*). Five o'clock.
(*Virginia prays louder*)

ANDREA. I can't stand it! They're beheading the truth! (*He holds his hands to his ears, so does the little monk. The bell is not rung.*

After a pause filled with Virginia's murmured prayers Federzoni shakes his head in the negative. The others drop their hands)

FEDERZONI *(hoarsely)*. Nothing. It's three minutes past five.

ANDREA. He's resisting.

THE LITTLE MONK. He hasn't recanted!

FEDERZONI. No. Oh, my friends!
(They embrace. They are wildly happy)

ANDREA. You see: They can't do it with force! Force isn't everything! Hence: Stupidity is defeated, it's not invulnerable! Hence: Man is not afraid of death!

FEDERZONI. Now the age of knowledge will begin in earnest. This is the hour of its birth. Just think! If he had recanted!

THE LITTLE MONK. I didn't say anything but I was very worried. I was faint of heart.

ANDREA. I knew it.

FEDERZONI. It would have been as if morning had turned back to night.

ANDREA. As if the mountain said: I'm water.

THE LITTLE MONK *(kneels down in tears)*. Lord, I thank Thee.

ANDREA. But now everything has changed. Man is lifting his head, tormented man, and saying: I can live. All this is accomplished when one man gets up and says No!
(At this moment the big bell of St. Mark's begins to boom. All stand transfixed)

VIRGINIA *(getting up)*. The bell of St. Mark's. He hasn't been condemned!
(From the street the announcer is heard reciting Galileo's recantation)

ANNOUNCER'S VOICE. "I, Galileo Galilei, professor of mathematics and physics in Florence, hereby abjure what I have taught, to wit, that the sun is the center of the world and motionless in its place, and the earth is not the center and not motionless. Out of a sincere heart and unfeigned faith, I abjure, condemn and execrate all these errors and heresies as I do all other errors and all other opinions in opposition to the Holy Church."
(Darkness)

(When it grows light again, the bell is still booming, then it stops. Virginia has left. Galileo's pupils are still there)

FEDERZONI. He never paid you properly for your work. You couldn't buy a pair of pants or publish anything. You had to put up with all that because you were "working for science"!

ANDREA *(loudly)*. Unhappy the land that has no heroes!
(Galileo has come in, completely, almost unrecognizably, changed by the trial. He has heard Andrea's exclamation. For a few moments he hesitates at the door, expecting a greeting. As none is forthcoming and his pupils shrink back from him, he goes slowly and because of his bad eyesight uncertainly to the front where he finds a footstool and sits down)

ANDREA. I can't look at him. I wish he'd go away.

FEDERZONI. Calm yourself.

ANDREA *(screams at Galileo)*. Wine barrel! Snail eater! Have you saved your precious skin? *(Sits down)* I feel sick.

GALILEO *(calmly)*. Get him a glass of water.
(The little monk goes out to get Andrea a glass of water. The others pay no attention to Galileo who sits on his footstool, listening. From far off the announcer's voice is heard again)

ANDREA. I can walk now if you'll help me.
(They lead him to the door. When they reach it, Galileo begins to speak)

GALILEO. No. Unhappy the land that needs a hero.

A reading in front of the curtain:
Is it not obvious that a horse falling from a height of three or four ells will break its legs, whereas a dog would not suffer any damage, nor would a cat from a height of eight or nine ells, or a cricket from a tower, or an ant even if it were to fall from the moon? And just as smaller animals are comparatively stronger than larger ones, so small plants too stand up

better: an oak tree two hundred ells high cannot sustain its branches in the same proportion as a small oak tree, nor can nature let a horse grow as large as twenty horses or produce a giant ten times the size of man unless it changes all the proportions of the limbs and especially of the bones, which would have to be strengthened far beyond the size demanded by mere proportion.—The common assumption that large and small machines are equally durable is apparently erroneous.

Galileo, *Discorsi*

14

1633–1642. Galileo Galilei spends the rest of his life in a villa near Florence, as a prisoner of the Inquisition. The *Discorsi*.

Sixteen hundred thirty-three to
sixteen hundred forty-two
Galileo Galilei remains a prisoner
of the church until his death.

A large room with a table, a leather chair and a globe. Galileo, now old and almost blind, is experimenting carefully with a small wooden ball rolling on a curved wooden rail. In the anteroom a monk is sitting on guard. A knock at the door. The monk opens and a peasant comes in carrying two plucked geese. Virginia emerges from the kitchen. She is now about forty years old.

THE PEASANT. I'm supposed to deliver these.

VIRGINIA. Who from? I didn't order any geese.

THE PEASANT. I was told to say from someone that's passing through. (*Out*)
(*Virginia looks at the geese in astonishment. The monk takes them from her and examines them suspiciously. Satisfied, he gives them back and she carries them by the necks to Galileo in the large room*)

VIRGINIA. A present, dropped off by someone who's passing through.

GALILEO. What is it?

VIRGINIA. Can't you see?

GALILEO. No. (*He goes closer*) Geese. Was there any name?

VIRGINIA. No.

GALILEO (*taking one goose from her*). Heavy. Maybe I'll have some.

VIRGINIA. You can't be hungry again. You just finished dinner. And what's wrong with your eyes today? You ought to be able to see them from where you are.

GALILEO. You're standing in the shadow.

VIRGINIA. I'm not in the shadow. (*She carries the geese out*)

GALILEO. Put in thyme and apples.

VIRGINIA (*to the monk*). We must send for the eye doctor. Father couldn't see the geese.

THE MONK. I'll need permission from Monsignor Carpula.—Has he been writing again?

VIRGINIA. No. He's dictating his book to me, you know that. You have pages 131 and 132, they were the last.

THE MONK. He's an old fox.

VIRGINIA. He doesn't do anything against the rules. His repentance is real. I keep an eye on him. (*She gives him the geese*) Tell them in the kitchen to fry the liver with an apple and an onion. (*She comes back into the large room*) And now we're going to think of our eyes and stop playing with that ball and dictate a little more of our weekly letter to the archbishop.

GALILEO. I don't feel up to it. Read me some Horace.

VIRGINIA. Only last week Monsignor Carpula, to whom we owe so much—those vegetables the other day—told me the archbishop keeps asking him what you think of the questions and quotations he's been sending you. (*She has sat down ready for dictation*)

GALILEO. Where was I?

VIRGINIA. Section four: Concerning the reaction of the church to the unrest in the arsenal in Venice, I agree with Cardinal Spoletti's at-

titude concerning the rebellious rope makers
. . .

GALILEO. Yes. *(Dictates)* . . . agree with Cardinal Spoletti's attitude concerning the rebellious rope makers, to wit, that it is better to dispense soup to them in the name of Christian charity than to pay them more for their ship's cables and bell ropes. All the more so, since it seems wiser to strengthen their faith than their greed. The Apostle Paul says: Charity never faileth.—How does that sound?

VIRGINIA. It's wonderful, father.

GALILEO. You don't think it could be mistaken for irony?

VIRGINIA. No, the archbishop will be very pleased. He's a practical man.

GALILEO. I rely on your judgment. What's the next point?

VIRGINIA. A very beautiful saying: "When I am weak then I am strong."

GALILEO. No comment.

VIRGINIA. Why not?

GALILEO. What's next?

VIRGINIA. "And to know the love of Christ, which passeth knowledge." Paul to the Ephesians three nineteen.

GALILEO. I must especially thank Your Eminence for the magnificent quotation from the epistle to the Ephesians. Inspired by it, I found the following in our incomparable "Imitation";[32] *(He quotes from memory)* "He to whom speaketh the eternal word is free from much questioning." May I seize this opportunity to say something on my own behalf? To this day I am being reproached for once having written a book on celestial bodies in the language of the market place. In so doing, I did not mean to suggest, or to express my approval of the writing of books on such important subjects as theology in the jargon of spaghetti vendors. The argument in favor of the service in Latin—that the universality

of this language enables all nations to hear mass in exactly the same way—seems less than fortunate since the scoffers, who are never at a loss, may well argue that the use of this language prevents all nations from understanding the text. I for my part prefer to forego the cheap intelligibility of things holy. The Latin tongue, which protects the eternal verities of the church from the prying of the ignorant, inspires confidence when recited by priests, sons of the lower classes, in the pronunciation of their local dialects.—No, strike that out.

VIRGINIA. The whole thing?

GALILEO. Everything after the spaghetti vendors.

(A knocking at the door. Virginia goes into the anteroom. The monk opens the door. Andrea Sarti appears. He is a man in his middle years)

ANDREA. Good evening. I am leaving Italy. To do scientific work in Holland. I was asked to see him on my way through and bring the latest news of him.

VIRGINIA. I don't know if he'll want to see you. You never came to visit us.

ANDREA. Ask him.

(Galileo has recognized the voice. He sits motionless. Virginia goes in to him)

GALILEO. Is it Andrea?

VIRGINIA. Yes. Should I send him away?

GALILEO *(after a pause)*. Bring him in.

(Virginia leads Andrea inside)

VIRGINIA *(to the monk)*. He's harmless. He was his pupil. So now he's his enemy.

GALILEO. Leave us alone, Virginia.

VIRGINIA. I want to hear what he says. *(She sits down)*

ANDREA *(cool)*. How are you?

GALILEO. Come closer. What are you doing? Tell me about your work. I hear you're on hydraulics.

ANDREA. Fabricius in Amsterdam has asked me to inquire about your health.

(Pause)

[32] *The Imitation of Christ*, reputedly by Thomas à Kempis (1380–1471).

GALILEO.   I'm well. I receive every attention.

ANDREA.   I shall be glad to report that you are well.

GALILEO.   Fabricius will be glad to hear it. And you may add that I am living in reasonable comfort. The depth of my repentance has moved my superiors to allow me limited scientific pursuits under clerical control.

ANDREA.   Oh yes. We too have heard that the church is pleased with you. Your total submission has borne fruit. The authorities, I am told, are most gratified to note that since your submission no work containing any new hypothesis has been published in Italy.

GALILEO (*listening in the direction of the anteroom*).   Unfortunately there are countries which elude the protection of the church. I fear the condemned doctrines are being perpetuated in those countries.

ANDREA.   There too your recantation has resulted in a setback most gratifying to the church.

GALILEO.   You don't say. (*Pause*) Nothing from Descartes?[33] No news from Paris?

ANDREA.   Oh yes. When he heard you had recanted he stuffed his treatise on the nature of light in his desk drawer.
(*Long pause*)

GALILEO.   I keep worrying about some of my scientific friends whom I led down the path of error. Has my recantation helped them to mend their ways?

ANDREA.   I am going to Holland to carry on my work. The ox is not allowed to do what Jupiter denies himself.

GALILEO.   I understand.

ANDREA.   Federzoni is back at his lens grinding, in some shop in Milan.

GALILEO (*laughs*).   He doesn't know Latin.
(*Pause*)

ANDREA.   Fulganzio, our little monk, has given up science and returned to the fold.

33 René Descartes (1596–1650), French philosopher, mathematician, and physicist.

GALILEO.   Yes. (*Pause*) My superiors are looking forward to my complete spiritual recovery. I'm making better progress than expected.

ANDREA.   I see.

VIRGINIA.   The Lord be praised.

GALILEO (*gruffly*).   Attend to the geese, Virginia. (*Virginia leaves angrily. In passing she is addressed by the monk*)

THE MONK.   I don't like that man.

VIRGINIA.   He's harmless. You heard what he said. (*On her way out*) We've got fresh goat cheese.
(*The monk follows her out*)

ANDREA.   I'm going to travel through the night so as to cross the border by morning. May I go now?

GALILEO.   I can't see why you've come, Sarti. To stir me up? I've been living prudently and thinking prudently since I came here. I have my relapses even so.

ANDREA.   I have no desire to upset you, Mr. Galilei.

GALILEO.   Barberini called it the itch. He wasn't entirely free from it himself. I've been writing again.

ANDREA.   You have?

GALILEO.   I've finished the *Discorsi*.

ANDREA.   What? The *Discourses Concerning Two New Sciences: Mechanics and Local Motion*? Here?

GALILEO.   Oh, they let me have paper and pen. My superiors aren't stupid. They know that ingrained vices can't be uprooted overnight. They protect me from unpleasant consequences by locking up page after page.

ANDREA.   Oh God!

GALILEO.   Did you say something?

ANDREA.   They let you plow water! They give you pen and paper to quiet you! How could you ever write under such conditions?

GALILEO.   Oh, I'm a slave of habit.

ANDREA.   The *Discorsi* in the hands of monks! When Amsterdam and London and Prague are clamoring for them!

GALILEO.   I can just hear Fabricius wailing, demanding his pound of flesh, while he himself sits safely in Amsterdam.

ANDREA.   Two new branches of science as good as lost!

GALILEO.   No doubt he and some others will feel uplifted when they hear that I jeopardized the last pitiful remnants of my comfort to make a copy, behind my own back so to speak, for six months using up the last ounces of light on the clearer nights.

ANDREA.   You have a copy?

GALILEO.   So far my vanity has prevented me from destroying it.

ANDREA.   Where is it?

GALILEO.   "If thine eye offend thee, pluck it out." [34] Whoever wrote that knew more about comfort than I do. I'm sure it's the height of folly to let it out of my hands. But since I've been unable to leave science alone, you may just as well have it. The copy is in the globe. Should you consider taking it to Holland, you would of course have to bear full responsibility. You'd say you bought it from someone with access to the Holy Office.
(*Andrea has gone to the globe. He takes out the copy*)

ANDREA.   The *Discorsi!* (*He leafs through the manuscript. He reads*) "It is my purpose to establish an entirely new science in regard to a very old problem, namely, motion. By means of experiments I have discovered some of its properties, which are worth knowing."

GALILEO.   I had to do something with my time.

ANDREA.   This will be the foundation of a new physics.

GALILEO.   Put it under your coat.

ANDREA.   And we thought you had deserted us! My voice was the loudest against you!

GALILEO.   You were absolutely right. I taught you science and I denied the truth.

ANDREA.   That changes everything. Everything.

GALILEO.   You think so?

[34] *Gospel of St. Matthew* v, 29.

ANDREA.   You were hiding the truth. From the enemy. Even in ethics you were centuries ahead of us.

GALILEO.   Explain that to me, Andrea.

ANDREA.   With the man on the street we said: He'll die, but he'll never recant.—You came back and said: I've recanted but I shall live. —Your hands are stained, we said.—You said: Better stained than empty.

GALILEO.   Better stained than empty. Sounds realistic. Sounds like me. A new science, a new ethics.

ANDREA.   I should have known—better than anyone else. I was eleven when you sold another man's telescope to the senate in Venice. And I watched you make immortal use of that instrument. Your friends shook their heads when you humbled yourself to that child in Florence: But science found an audience. You've always laughed at heroes. "People who suffer bore me," you said. "Bad luck comes from faulty calculations," and "If there are obstacles the shortest line between two points may well be a crooked line."

GALILEO.   I remember.

ANDREA.   And in thirty-three when you decided to abjure a popular item of your doctrine, I should have known that you were merely withdrawing from a hopeless political brawl in order to further the true interests of science.

GALILEO.   Which consist in . . .

ANDREA.   . . . the study of the properties of motion, the mother of machines, which alone will make the earth so good to live on that we shall be able to do without heaven.

GALILEO.   Hm.

ANDREA.   You won the leisure to write a scientific work which you alone could write. Had you perished in the fiery halo of the stake, the others would have been the victors.

GALILEO.   They are the victors. Besides, there is no scientific work that one man alone can write.

ANDREA.   Then why did you recant?

GALILEO.   I recanted because I was afraid of physical pain.

ANDREA.   No!

GALILEO.   They showed me the instruments.

ANDREA.   Then it was not premeditated?

GALILEO.   It was not.
(Pause)

ANDREA (loud).   In science only one thing counts: contribution to knowledge.

GALILEO.   And that I have supplied. Welcome to the gutter, brother in science and cousin in treason! You like fish? I have fish. What stinks is not my fish, it's me. I'm selling out, you are the buyer. Oh, irresistible sight of a book, that hallowed commodity. The mouth waters, the curses are drowned. The great Babylonian whore, the murderous beast, the scarlet woman, opens her thighs, and everything is different! Hallowed be our haggling, whitewashing, death-shunning community!

ANDREA.   To shun death is human. Human weaknesses are no concern of science.

GALILEO.   No?!—My dear Sarti, even in my present condition I believe I can give you a few hints about the science you are devoting yourself to.
(A short pause)

GALILEO (in lecture style, hands folded over his paunch).   In my free time, and I've got plenty of that, I have reviewed my case and asked myself how the world of science, of which I no longer consider myself a member, will judge it. Even a wool merchant, in addition to buying cheap and selling dear, has to worry about the obstacles that may be put in the way of the wool trade itself. In this sense, the pursuit of science seems to call for special courage. Science trades in knowledge distilled from doubt. Providing everybody with knowledge of everything, science aims at making doubters of everybody. But princes, landlords and priests keep the majority of the people in a pearly haze of superstition and outworn words to cover up their own machinations. The misery of the many is as old as the hills and is proclaimed in church and lecture hall to be as indestructible as the hills. Our new art of doubting delighted the common people.

They grabbed the telescope out of our hands and focused it on their tormentors—princes, landlords, priests. Those self-seeking violent men greedily exploited the fruits of science for their own ends but at the same time they felt the cold stare of science focused upon the millennial, yet artificial miseries which mankind could obviously get rid of by getting rid of them. They showered us with threats and bribes, which weak souls cannot resist. But can we turn our backs on the people and still remain scientists? The movements of the heavenly bodies have become more comprehensible; but the movements of their rulers remain unpredictable to the people. The battle to measure the sky was won by doubt; but credulity still prevents the Roman housewife from winning her battle for milk. Science, Sarti, is involved in both battles. If mankind goes on stumbling in a pearly haze of superstition and outworn words and remains too ignorant to make full use of its own strength, it will never be able to use the forces of nature which science has discovered. What end are you scientists working for? To my mind, the only purpose of science is to lighten the toil of human existence. If scientists, browbeaten by selfish rulers, confine themselves to the accumulation of knowledge for the sake of knowledge, science will be crippled and your new machines will only mean new hardships. Given time, you may well discover everything there is to discover, but your progress will be a progression away from humanity. The gulf between you and humanity may one day be so wide that the response to your exultation about some new achievement will be a universal outcry of horror.—As a scientist, I had a unique opportunity. In my time astronomy reached the market place. Under these very special circumstances, one man's steadfastness might have had tremendous repercussions. If I had held out, scientists might have developed something like the physicians' Hippocratic oath, the vow to use their knowledge only for the good of mankind. As things stand now, the best we can hope for is a generation of inventive dwarfs who can be hired for any purpose. Furthermore, I have come to the conclusion, Sarti, that I was never in any real danger. For a few years I was as strong as the authorities. And yet I handed the powerful my knowledge to use, or not to use, or to misuse as served their purposes.

(*Virginia has come in with a dish and stops now*)

I have betrayed my calling. A man who does what I have done, cannot be tolerated in the ranks of science.

VIRGINIA.   You have been received in the ranks of the faithful.

(*She walks on and sets the dish on the table*)

GALILEO.   Yes.—I must eat now.

(*Andrea offers him his hand. Galileo sees it but does not take it*)

GALILEO.   You are teaching now yourself. Can you afford to shake a hand such as mine? (*He goes to the table*) Somebody on the way through has sent me two geese. I still like to eat.

ANDREA.   Then you no longer believe that a new era has dawned?

GALILEO.   I do.—Take good care of yourself when you pass through Germany with the truth under your coat.

ANDREA (*unable to leave*).   Regarding your opinion of the author we discussed I cannot answer you. But I refuse to believe that your devastating analysis can be the last word.

GALILEO.   Thank you, sir. (*He begins to eat*)

VIRGINIA (*seeing Andrea out*).   We don't like visitors from the past. They upset him.

(*Andrea leaves. Virginia comes back*)

GALILEO.   Any idea who could have sent the geese?

VIRGINIA.   Not Andrea.

GALILEO.   Maybe not. How is the night?

VIRGINIA (*at the window*).   Clear.

15

1637. Galileo's book *Discorsi* crosses the Italian border.

The great book o'er the border went
And, good folk, that was the end.
But we hope you'll keep in mind
You and I were left behind.
May you now guard science's light
Keep it up and use it right
Lest it be a flame to fall
One day to consume us all.

A small Italian border town. Early morning. Children are playing by the turnpike near the guard house. Andrea, beside a coachman, is waiting for his papers to be examined by the guards. He is sitting on a small box reading in Galileo's manuscript. The coach is on the far side of the turnpike.

THE CHILDREN (*sing*).

Mary sat upon a stone
Had a pink shift of her own
The shift was full of shit.
But when cold weather came along
Mary put her shift back on
Shitty is better than split.

THE BORDER GUARD.   Why are you leaving Italy?

ANDREA.   I'm a scholar.

THE BORDER GUARD (*to the clerk*).   Write under "Reason for Leaving": Scholar.

(*The clerk does so*)

THE FIRST BOY (*to Andrea*).   Don't sit there. (*He points at the hut in front of which Andrea is sitting*) A witch lives there.

THE SECOND BOY.   Old Marina isn't a witch.

THE FIRST BOY.   Want me to twist your arm?

THE THIRD BOY.   She is too. She flies through the air at night.

THE FIRST BOY.   If she's not a witch, why can't she get any milk anywhere in town?

THE SECOND BOY.   How can she fly through the air? Nobody can do that. (*To Andrea*) Or can they?

THE FIRST BOY (*referring to the second boy*). That's Giuseppe. He doesn't know anything, because he doesn't go to school, because his pants are torn.

THE BORDER GUARD. What's that book?

ANDREA (*without looking up*). It's by Aristotle, the great philosopher.

THE BORDER GUARD (*suspiciously*). What's he up to?

ANDREA. He's dead.
(*To tease Andrea, the boys walk around him in a way indicating that they too are reading books*)

THE BORDER GUARD (*to the clerk*). See if there's anything about religion in it.

THE CLERK (*turning leaves*). Can't see anything.

THE BORDER GUARD. Anyway there's no point in looking. Nobody'd be so open about anything he wanted to hide. (*To Andrea*) You'll have to sign a paper saying we examined everything.
(*Andrea hesitantly gets up and reading all the time goes into the house with the guards*)

THE THIRD BOY (*to the clerk, pointing at the box*). Look, there's something else.

THE CLERK. Wasn't it here before?

THE THIRD BOY. The devil's put it there. It's a box.

THE SECOND BOY. No, it belongs to the traveler.

THE THIRD BOY. I wouldn't go near it. She's bewitched Passi the coachman's horses. I looked through the hole in the roof that the snowstorm made, and I heard them coughing.

THE CLERK (*almost at the box hesitates and goes back*). Witchery, ha? Well, we can't examine everything. We'd never get through.
(*Andrea returns with a pitcher of milk. He sits down on the box again and continues to read*)

THE BORDER GUARD (*following him with papers*). Close the boxes. Is that all?

THE CLERK. Yes.

THE SECOND BOY (*to Andrea*). You say you're a scholar. Then tell me: Can people fly through the air?

ANDREA. Just a moment.

THE BORDER GUARD. You may proceed.

(*The luggage has been picked up by the coachman. Andrea takes his box and prepares to go*)

THE BORDER GUARD. Wait! What's in that box?

ANDREA (*taking up his book again*). Books.

THE FIRST BOY. It's the witch's box.

THE BORDER GUARD. Nonsense. How could she hex a box?

THE THIRD BOY. If the devil's helping her!

THE BORDER GUARD (*laughs*). Not in our rule book. (*To the clerk*) Open it.
(*The box is opened*)

THE BORDER GUARD (*listlessly*). How many?

ANDREA. Thirty-four.

THE BORDER GUARD (*to the clerk*). How long will it take you?

THE CLERK (*who has started rummaging superficially through the box*). All printed stuff. You'd have no time for breakfast, and when do you expect me to collect the overdue toll from Passi the coachman when his house is auctioned off, if I go through all these books?

THE BORDER GUARD. You're right, we've got to get that money. (*He kicks at the books*) What could be in them anyway? (*To the coachman*) Pfftt!
(*Andrea and the coachman, who carries the box, cross the border. Beyond it Andrea puts Galileo's manuscript in his bag*)

THE THIRD BOY (*points at the pitcher which Andrea had left behind*). Look!

THE FIRST BOY. And the box is gone! Now do you see it was the devil?

ANDREA (*turning around*). No, it was me. You must learn to use your eyes. The milk and the pitcher are paid for. Give them to the old woman. Oh yes, Giuseppe, I haven't answered your question. No one can fly through the air on a stick. Unless it has some sort of machine attached to it. Such machines don't exist yet. Maybe they never will because man is too heavy. But of course, we don't know. We don't know nearly enough, Giuseppe. We've hardly begun.

Chapter 10

THE
VOYAGE
WITHIN

One of the primary marks of maturity is a fairly high degree of self-understanding: to mature as a person is not just to grow older, but to become more deeply aware of one's abilities and limitations, hopes and fears, values and obligations. To this process, of course, all experience can contribute, but it is one of the main functions of literature to help us in just this way. In reading of and entering into the problems of others, their conflicts and dilemmas, their victories and defeats, we can objectify our own thoughts and feelings and contemplate them with greater penetration.

But some literary works are more centrally concerned with self-knowledge than are others. Such works direct our attention to various ways in which human beings seek to answer the persistent questions of self-identity: Who am I? Why am I here? Where am I to go? One person may seek himself in the history of his parents and ancestors, like the speaker of "My Furthest-Back Person—The African." Another may turn to the scientific study of human beings, the work of the psychologist or psychiatrist, as in "The Schizophrenic Experience." Another may be guided by faith in a supernatural religion to consider deeply his place in the scheme of things and to face ultimate questions about the universe—as in the poems by Donne and Hopkins included here.

The theme of self-discovery and of self-revelation takes many literary forms, of which several are illustrated in this chapter. There is the recurrent mystery of the abiding duality between the inner and outer aspect of human nature, as we see it explored humorously in "The Secret Life of Walter Mitty," compassionately in "The Blind Man," and fearfully in "Young Goodman Brown." The central plot may be one in which a character comes gradually or suddenly to realize an important truth about himself that had hitherto been hidden from him; compare the rabbi in "I Place My Reliance on No Man" with the priest in "After Cortes." A poem may take on the character of a meditation on the meaning of life, or of the speaker's life, as in "Sunday Morning" and "The Abyss"; and this meditation may lead to a terrifying realization of the extent to which one's life is not meaningful, as in "The Roofwalker" and "The Hollow Men." Such works as these help us to see, too, that literature itself is R. D. Laing's "language of experience," the language for talking about these important things, and especially "the infinite reaches of inner space."

496

Alex Haley

MY FURTHEST-BACK PERSON
—THE AFRICAN

My Grandma Cynthia Murray Palmer lived in Henning, Tennessee (pop. 500), about fifty miles north of Memphis. Each summer as I grew up there, we would be visited by several women relatives who were mostly around Grandma's age, such as my Great Aunt Liz Murray, who taught in Oklahoma, and Great Aunt Till Merriwether from Jackson, Tennessee, or their considerably younger niece, Cousin Georgia Anderson from Kansas City, Kansas, and some others. Always after the supper dishes had been washed, they would go out to take seats and talk in the rocking chairs on the front porch, and I would scrunch down, listening, behind Grandma's squeaky chair, with the dusk deepening into night and the lightning bugs flicking on and off above the now shadowy honeysuckles. Most often they talked about our family—the story had been passed down for generations—until the whistling blur of lights of the southbound Panama Limited train whooshing through Henning at 9:05 P.M. signaled our bedtime.

So much of their talking of people, places and events I didn't understand: For instance, what was an "Ol' Massa," an "Ol' Missus" or a "plantation"? But early I gathered that white folks had done lots of bad things to our folks, though I couldn't figure out why. I guessed that all that they talked about had happened a long time ago, as now or then Grandma or another, speaking of someone in the past, would excitedly thrust a finger toward me, exclaiming, "Wasn't big as *this* young 'un!" And it would astound me that anyone as old and grey-haired as they could relate to my age. But in time my head began both a recording and picturing of the more graphic scenes they would describe, just as I also visualized David killing Goliath with his slingshot, Old Pharaoh's army drowning, Noah and his ark, Jesus feeding that big multitude with nothing but five loaves and two fishes, and other wonders that I heard in my Sunday-school lessons at our New Hope Methodist Church.

The furthest-back person Grandma and the others talked of—always in tones of awe, I noticed—they would call "The African." They said that some ship brought him to a place that they pronounced " 'Naplis." They said that then some "Mas' John Waller" bought him for his plantation in "Spotsylvania County, Virginia." This African kept on escaping, the fourth time trying to kill the "hateful po' cracker" slave-catcher, who gave him the punishment choice of castration or of losing one foot. This African took a foot being chopped off with an ax against a tree stump, they said, and he was about to die. But his life was saved by "Mas' John's" brother—"Mas' William Waller," a doctor, who was so furious about what had happened that he bought the African for himself and gave him the name "Toby."

Crippling about, working in "Mas' William's" house and yard, the African in time met and mated with "the big house cook named Bell," and there was born a girl named Kizzy. As she grew up her African daddy often showed her different kinds of things, telling her what they were in his native tongue. Pointing at a banjo, for example, the African uttered, "*ko*"; or pointing at a river near the plantation, he would say, "*Kamby Bolong*." Many of his strange words started with a "*k*" sound, and the little, growing Kizzy learned gradually that they identified different things.

When addressed by other slaves as "Toby," the master's name for him, the African said angrily that his name was "*Kintay*." And as he gradually learned English, he told young Kizzy some things about himself—for instance, that he was not far from his village, chopping wood to make himself a drum, when four men had surprised, overwhelmed, and kidnaped him.

So Kizzy's head held much about her African daddy when at age sixteen she was sold away onto a much smaller plantation in North Carolina. Her new "Mas' Tom Lea" fathered her first child, a boy she named George. And Kizzy told her boy all about his African grandfather. George grew up to be such a gamecock fighter that he was called "Chicken George," and people would come from all over and "bet big money" on his cockfights. He mated with Matilda, another of Lea's slaves; they had seven children, and he told them the stories and strange sounds of their African great-grandfather. And one of those children, Tom, became a blacksmith who was bought away by a "Mas' Murray" for his tobacco plantation in Alamance County, North Carolina.

Tom mated there with Irene, a weaver on the plantation. She also bore seven children, and Tom now told them all about their African great-great-grandfather, the faithfully passed-down knowledge of his sounds and stories having become by now the family's prideful treasure.

The youngest of that second set of seven children was a girl, Cynthia, who became my maternal Grandma (which today I can only see as fated). Anyway, all of this is how I was growing up in Henning at Grandma's, listening from behind her rocking chair as she and the other visiting old women talked of that African (never then comprehended as *my* great-great-great-great-grandfather) who said his name was *"Kintay,"* and said *"ko"* for banjo, *"Kamby Bolong"* for river, and a jumble of other *"k"*-beginning sounds that Grandma privately muttered, most often while making beds or cooking, and who also said that near his village he was kidnaped while chopping wood to make himself a drum.

The story had become nearly as fixed in my head as in Grandma's by the time Dad and Mama moved me and my two younger brothers, George and Julius, away from Henning to be with them at the small black agricultural and mechanical college in Normal, Alabama, where Dad taught.

To compress my next twenty-five years: When I was seventeen Dad let me enlist as a mess boy in the U.S. Coast Guard. I became a ship's cook out in the South Pacific during World War II, and at night down by my bunk I began trying to write sea adventure stories, mailing them off to magazines and collecting rejection slips for eight years before some editors began purchasing and publishing occasional stories. By 1949 the Coast Guard had made me its first "journalist"; finally with twenty years' service, I retired at the age of thirty-seven, determined to make a full time career of writing. I wrote mostly magazine articles; my first book was *The Autobiography of Malcolm X.*

Then one Saturday in 1965 I happened to be walking past the National Archives building in Washington. Across the interim years I had thought of Grandma's old stories—otherwise I can't think what diverted me up the Archives' steps. And when a main reading room desk attendant asked if he could help me, I wouldn't have dreamed of admitting to him some curiosity hanging on from boyhood about my slave forebears. I kind of bumbled that I was interested in census records of Alamance County, North Carolina, just after the Civil War.

The microfilm rolls were delivered, and I turned them through the machine with a building sense of intrigue, viewing in different census takers' penmanship an endless parade of names. After about a dozen microfilmed rolls, I was beginning to tire, when in utter astonishment I looked upon the names of Grandma's parents: Tom Murray,

Irene Murray . . . older sisters of Grandma's as well—every one of them a name that I'd heard countless times on her front porch.

It wasn't that I hadn't believed Grandma. You just *didn't* not believe my Grandma. It was simply so uncanny actually seeing those names in print and in official U.S. Government records.

During the next several months I was back in Washington whenever possible, in the Archives, the Library of Congress, the Daughters of the American Revolution Library. (Whenever black attendants understood the idea of my search, documents I requested reached me with miraculous speed.) In one source or another during 1966 I was able to document at least the highlights of the cherished family story. I would have given anything to have told Grandma, but, sadly, in 1949 she had gone. So I went and told the only survivor of those Henning front-porch storytellers: Cousin Georgia Anderson, now in her eighties in Kansas City, Kansas. Wrinkled, bent, not well herself, she was so overjoyed, repeating to me the old stories and sounds; they were like Henning echoes: "Yeah, boy, that African say his name was 'Kin-tay'; he say the banjo was 'ko,' an' the river 'Kamby-Bolong,' an' he was off choppin' some wood to make his drum when they grabbed 'im!" Cousin Georgia grew so excited we had to stop her, calm her down, 'You go' head, boy! Your grandma an' all of 'em—they up there watching what you do!"

That week I flew to London on a magazine assignment. Since by now I was steeped in the old, in the past, scarcely a tour guide missed me—I was awed at so many historical places and treasures I'd heard of and read of. I came upon the Rosetta stone in the British Museum, marveling anew at how Jean Champollion, the French archaeologist, had miraculously deciphered its ancient demotic and hieroglyphic texts.

The thrill of that just kept hanging around in my head. I was on a jet returning to New York when a thought hit me. Those strange, unknown-tongue sounds, always part of our family's old story . . . they were obviously bits of our original African "Kintay's" native tongue. What specific tongue? Could I somehow find out?

Back in New York, I began making visits to the United Nations Headquarters lobby; it wasn't hard to spot Africans. I'd stop any I could, asking if my bits of phonetic sounds held any meaning for them. A couple of dozen Africans quickly looked at me, listened, and took off—understandably dubious about some Tennesseean's accent alleging "African" sounds.

My research assistant, George Sims (we grew up together in Henning), brought me some names of ranking scholars of African linguistics. One was particularly intriguing: a Belgian- and English-educated Dr. Jan Vansina; he had spent his early career living in West African villages, studying and tape-recording countless oral histories that were narrated by certain very old African men; he had written a standard textbook, *The Oral Tradition*.

So I flew to the University of Wisconsin to see Dr. Vansina. In his living room I told him every bit of the family story in the fullest detail that I could remember it. Then, intensely, he queried me about the story's relay across the generations, about the gibberish of "*k*" sounds Grandma had fiercely muttered to herself while doing her housework, with my brothers and me giggling beyond her hearing at what we had dubbed "Grandma's noises."

Dr. Vansina, his manner very serious, finally said, "These sounds your family has kept sound very probably of the tongue called 'Mandinka.' "

I'd never heard of any "Mandinka." Grandma just told of the African saying "*ko*" for banjo, or "*Kamby Bolong*" for a Virginia river.

Among Mandinka stringed instruments, Dr. Vansina said, one of the oldest was the *"kora."*

"Bolong," he said, was clearly Mandinka for "river." Preceded by *"Kamby,"* it very likely meant "Gambia River."

Dr. Vansina telephoned an eminent Africanist colleague, Dr. Philip Curtin. He said that the phonetic *"Kin-tay"* was correctly spelled *"Kinte,"* a very old clan that had originated in Old Mali. The Kinte men traditionally were blacksmiths, and the women were potters and weavers.

I knew I must get to the Gambia River.

The first native Gambian I could locate in the U.S. was named Ebou Manga, then a junior attending Hamilton College in upstate Clinton, New York. He and I flew to Dakar, Senegal, then took a smaller plane to Yundum Airport, and rode in a van to Gambia's capital, Bathurst. Ebou and his father assembled eight Gambia government officials. I told them Grandma's stories, every detail I could remember, as they listened intently, then reacted. " *'Kamby Bolong'* of course is Gambia River!" I heard. "But more clue is your forefather's saying his name was *'Kinte.'* " Then they told me something I would never even have fantasized—that in places in the back country lived very old men, commonly called *griots,* who could tell centuries of the histories of certain very old family clans. As for *Kintes,* they pointed out to me on a map some family villages, Kinte-Kundah, and Kinte-Kundah Janneh-Ya, for instance.

The Gambian officials said they would try to help me. I returned to New York dazed. It is embarrassing to me now, but despite Grandma's stories, I'd never been concerned much with Africa, and I had the routine images of African people living mostly in exotic jungles. But a compulsion now laid hold of me to learn all I could, and I began devouring books about Africa, especially about the slave trade. Then one Thursday's mail contained a letter from one of the Gambian officials, inviting me to return there.

Monday I was back in Bathurst. It galvanized me when the officials said that a *griot* had been located who told the *Kinte* clan history—his name was Kebba Kanga Fofana. To reach him, I discovered, required a modified safari: renting a launch to get upriver, two land vehicles to carry supplies by a roundabout land route, and employing finally, fourteen people, including three interpreters and four musicians, since a *griot* would not speak the revered clan histories without background music.

The boat Baddibu vibrated upriver, with me acutely tense: Were these Africans maybe viewing me as but another of the pith-helmets? After about two hours, we put in at James Island, for me to see the ruins of the once British-operated James Fort. Here two centuries of slave ships had loaded thousands of cargoes of Gambian tribespeople. The crumbling stones, the deeply oxidized swivel cannon, even some remnant links of chain seemed all but impossible to believe. Then we continued upriver to the left-bank village of Albreda, and there put ashore to continue on foot to Juffure, village of the *griot.* Once more we stopped, for me to see *toubob kolong,* "the white man's well," now almost filled in, in a swampy area with abundant, tall, saw-toothed grass. It was dug two centuries ago to "seventeen men's height deep" to insure survival drinking water for long-driven, famishing coffles of slaves.

Walking on, I kept wishing that Grandma could hear how her stories had led me to the *"Kamby Bolong."* (Our surviving storyteller Cousin Georgia died in a Kansas City hospital during this same morning, I would learn later.) Finally, Juffure village's playing children, sighting us, flashed an alert. The seventy-odd people came rushing from their circular, thatch-roofed, mud-walled huts, with goats bounding up and about, and parrots squawking from up in the palms. I sensed him in advance some-how, the small man amid them, wearing a pillbox cap and an off-white robe—the *griot*. Then the interpreters went to him, as the villagers thronged around me.

And it hit me like a gale wind: every one of them, the whole crowd, was *jet black*. An enormous sense of guilt swept me—a sense of being some kind of hybrid . . . a sense of being impure among the pure. It was an aw-ful sensation.

The old *griot* stepped away from my interpreters and the crowd quickly swarmed around him—all of them buzzing. An inter-preter named A. B. C. Salla came to me; he whispered: "Why they stare at you so, they have never seen here a black American." And that hit me: I was symbolizing for them twenty-five millions of us they had never seen. What did they think of me—of us?

Then abruptly the old *griot* was briskly walking toward me. His eyes boring into mine, he spoke in Mandinka, as if instinc-tively I should understand—and A. B. C. Salla translated:

"Yes . . . we have been told by the fore-fathers . . . that many of us from this place are in exile . . . in that place called America . . . and in other places."

I suppose I physically wavered, and they thought it was the heat; rustling whispers went through the crowd, and a man brought me a low stool. Now the whispering hushed —the musicians had softly begun playing *kora* and *balafon,* and a canvas sling lawn seat was taken by the *griot,* Kebba Kanga Fofana, aged seventy-three "rains" (one rainy season each year). He seemed to gather himself into a physical rigidity, and he be-gan speaking the *Kinte* clan's ancestral oral history; it came rolling from his mouth across the next hours . . . 17th- and 18th cen-tury *Kinte* lineage details, predominantly what men took wives; the children they "be-got," in the order of their births; those children's mates and children.

Events frequently were dated by some proximate singular physical occurrence. It was as if some ancient scroll were printed indelibly within the *griot's* brain. Each few sentences or so, he would pause for an inter-preter's translation to me. I distill here the essence:

The *Kinte* clan began in Old Mali, the men generally blacksmiths " . . . who con-quered fire," and the women potters and weavers. One large branch of the clan moved to Mauretania, from where one son of the clan, Kairaba Kunta Kinte, a Moslem Mar-about holy man, entered Gambia. He lived first in the village of Pakali N'Ding; he moved next to Jiffarong village; " . . . and then he came here, into our own village of Juffure."

In Juffure, Kairaba Kunta Kinte took his first wife, " . . . a Mandinka maiden, whose name was Sireng. By her, he begot two sons, whose names were Janneh and Saloum. Then he got a second wife, Yaisa. By her, he begot a son, Omoro."

The three sons became men in Juffure. Janneh and Saloum went off and founded a new village, Kinte-Kundah Janneh-Ya. "And then Omoro, the youngest son, when he had thirty rains, took as a wife a maiden, Binta Kebba.

"And by her, he begot four sons—Kunta, Lamin, Suwadu, and Madi . . ."

Sometimes, a "begotten," after his nam-ing, would be accompanied by some later-occurring detail, perhaps as " . . . in time of big water (flood), he slew a water buffalo." Having named those four sons, now the *griot* stated such a detail.

"About the time the king's soldiers came, the eldest of these four sons, Kunta, when he had about sixteen rains, went away from this village, to chop wood to make a drum . . . and he was never seen again . . ."

Goose-pimples the size of lemons seemed to pop all over me. In my knapsack were my cumulative notebooks, the first of them including how in my boyhood, my Grand-ma, Cousin Georgia and the others told of the African *"Kin-tay"* who always said he was kidnapped near his village—while chopping wood to make a drum . . .

I showed the interpreter, he showed and told the *griot,* who excitedly told the people; they grew very agitated. Abruptly then they formed a human ring, encircling me, dancing and chanting. Perhaps a dozen of the women carrying their infant babies rushed in toward me, thrusting the infants into my arms—conveying, I would later learn, "the laying on of hands . . . through this flesh which is us, we are you, and you are us." The men hurried me into their mosque, their Arabic praying later being translated outside: "Thanks be to Allah for returning the long lost from among us." Direct descendants of Kunta Kinte's blood brothers were hastened, some of them from nearby villages, for a family portrait to be taken with me, surrounded by actual ancestral sixth cousins. More symbolic acts filled the remaining day.

When they would let me leave, for some reason I wanted to go away over the African land. Dazed, silent in the bumping Land Rover, I heard the cutting staccato of talking drums. Then when we sighted the next village, its people came thronging to meet us. They were all—little naked ones to wizened elders—waving, beaming, amid a cacophony of crying out; and then my ears identified their words: *"Meester Kinte! Meester Kinte!"*

Let me tell you something: I am a man. But I remember the sob surging up from my feet, flinging up my hands before my face and bawling as I had not done since I was a baby . . . the jet-black Africans were jostling, staring . . . I didn't care, with the feelings surging. If you really knew the odyssey of us millions of black Americans, if you really knew how we came in the seeds of our forefathers, captured, driven, beaten, inspected, bought, branded, chained in foul ships, if you really knew, you needed weeping . . .

Back home, I knew that what I must write, really, was our black saga, where any individual's past is the essence of the millions'. Now flat broke, I went to some editors I knew, describing the Gambian miracle, and my desire to pursue the research; Doubleday contracted to publish, and Reader's Digest to condense the projected book; then I had advances to travel further.

What ship brought Kinte to Grandma's " 'Naplis" (Annapolis, Maryland, obviously)? The old *griot's* time reference to "king's soldiers" sent me flying to London. Feverish searching at last identified, in British Parliament records, "Colonel O'Hare's Forces," dispatched in mid-1767 to protect the then British-held James Fort, whose ruins I'd visited. So Kunta Kinte was down in some ship probably sailing later that summer from the Gambia River to Annapolis.

Now I feel it was fated that I had taught myself to write in the U.S. Coast Guard. For the sea dramas I had concentrated on had given me years of experience searching among yellowing old U.S. maritime records. So now in English 18th Century marine records I finally tracked ships reporting themselves in and out to the Commandant of the Gambia River's James Fort. And then early one afternoon I found that a Lord Ligonier under a Captain Thomas Davies had sailed on the Sabbath of July 5, 1767. Her cargo: 3,265 elephants' teeth, 3,700 pounds of beeswax, 800 pounds of cotton, 32 ounces of Gambian gold, and 140 slaves; her destination: "Annapolis."

That night I recrossed the Atlantic. In the Library of Congress the Lord Ligonier's arrival was one brief line in "Shipping In The Port Of Annapolis—1748-1785." I located the author, Vaughan W. Brown, in his Baltimore brokerage office. He drove to Historic Annapolis, the city's historical society, and found me further documentation of her arrival on Sept. 29, 1767. (Exactly two centuries later, Sept. 29, 1967, standing, staring seaward from an Annapolis pier, again I knew tears). More help came in the Maryland Hall of Records. Archivist Phebe Jacobsen found the Lord Ligonier's arriving customs declaration listing, "98 Negroes"— so in her eighty-six-day crossing, forty-two Gambians had died, one among the survivors being sixteen-year-old Kunta Kinte. Then the microfilmed October 1, 1767, *Maryland Gazette* contained, on page two, an announcement to prospective buyers from the ship's agents, Daniel of St. Thos. Jenifer and John Ridout (the Governor's secretary): "from the River GAMBIA, in AFRICA . . . a cargo of choice, healthy SLAVES . . ."

R. D. Laing

THE SCHIZOPHRENIC EXPERIENCE

JONES (*laughs loudly, then pauses*): I'm Mc-Dougal myself. (*This actually is not his name.*)

SMITH: What do you do for a living, little fellow? Work on a ranch or something?

J: No, I'm a civilian seaman. Supposed to be high muckamuck society.

S: A singing recording machine, huh? I guess a recording machine sings sometimes. If they're adjusted right. Mm-hm. I thought that was it. My towel, mm-hm. We'll be going back to sea in about—eight or nine months though. Soon as we get our—destroyed parts repaired. (*Pause*)

J: I've got lovesickness, secret love.

S: Secret love, huh? (*Laughs*)

J: Yeah.

S: I ain't got any secret love.

J: I fell in love, but I don't feed any woo—that sits over—looks something like me—walking around over there.

S: My, oh, my only one, my only love is the shark. Keep out of the way of him.

J: Don't they know I have a life to live? (*Long pause*)

S: Do you work at the air base? Hm?

J: You know what I think of work. I'm thirty-three in June, do you mind?

S: June?

J: Thirty-three years old in June. This stuff goes out the window after I live this, uh—leave this hospital. So I lay off cigarettes, I'm a spatial condition, from outer space myself, no shit.

S (*laughs*): I'm a real space ship from across.

J: A lot of people talk, uh—that way, like crazy, but Believe It or Not by Ripley, take it or leave it—alone it's in the *Examiner*, it's in the comic section, Believe It or Not by Ripley, Robert E. Ripley, Believe It or Not, but we don't have to believe anything, unless I feel like it. (*Pause*) Every little rosette—too much alone. (*Pause*)

S: Could be possible. (*Phrase inaudible because of airplane noise*)

J: I'm a civilian seaman.

S: Could be possible. (*Sighs*) I take my bath in the ocean.

J: Bathing stinks. You know why? 'Cause you can't quit when you feel like it. You're in the service.

S: I can quit whenever I feel like quitting. I can get out when I feel like getting out.

J (*talking at the same time*): Take me. I'm a civilian, I can quit.

S: Civilian?

J: Go my—my way.

S: I guess we have, in port, civilian. (*Long pause*)

J: What do they want with us?

S: Hm?

J: What do they want with you and me?

S: What do they want with you and me? How do I know what they want with you? I know what they want with me. I broke the law, so I have to pay for it. (*Silence*)[1]

[1] J. Haley, *Strategies of Psychotherapy* (New York: Grune and Stratton, 1963), pages 99–100.

This is a conversation between two persons diagnosed as schizophrenic. What does this diagnosis mean?

To regard the gambits of Smith and Jones as due *primarily* to some psychological deficit is rather like supposing that a man doing a handstand on a bicycle on a tightrope one hundred feet up with no safety net is suffering from an inability to stand on his own two feet. We may well ask why these people have to be, often brilliantly, so devious, so elusive, so adept at making themselves unremittingly incomprehensible.

In the last decade, a radical shift of outlook has been occurring in psychiatry. This has entailed the questioning of old assumptions, based on the attempts of nineteenth-century psychiatrists to bring the frame of clinical medicine to bear on their observations. Thus the subject matter of psychiatry was thought of as mental illness; one thought of mental physiology and mental pathology, one looked for signs and symptoms, made one's diagnosis, assessed prognosis and prescribed treatment. According to one's philosophical bias, one looked for the etiology of these mental illnesses in the mind, in the body, in the environment, or in inherited propensities.

The term "schizophrenia" was coined by a Swiss psychiatrist, Bleuler, who worked within this frame of reference. In using the term schizophrenia, I am not referring to any condition that I suppose to be mental rather than physical, or to an illness, like pneumonia, but to a label that some people pin on other people under certain social circumstances. The "cause" of "schizophrenia" is to be found by the examination, not of the prospective diagnosee alone, but of the whole social context in which the psychiatric ceremonial is being conducted.[2]

2 See H. Garfinkel, "Conditions of Successful Degradation Ceremonies," *American Journal of Sociology*, Volume LXI (March, 1956), pages 420–4; also R. D. Laing, "Ritualization in Abnormal Behavior" in *Ritualization of Behavior in Animals and Man* (Royal Society, Philosophical Transactions, Series B [in press]).

Once demystified, it is clear, at least, that some people come to behave and to experience themselves and others in ways that are strange and incomprehensible to most people, including themselves. If this behavior and experience fall into certain broad categories, they are liable to be diagnosed as subject to a condition called schizophrenia. By present calculation almost one in every one hundred children born will fall into this category at some time or other before the age of forty-five, and in the United Kingdom at the moment there are roughly 60,000 men and women in mental hospitals, and many more outside hospitals, who are termed schizophrenic.

A child born today in the United Kingdom stands a ten times greater chance of being admitted to a mental hospital than to a university, and about one-fifth of mental hospital admissions are diagnosed schizophrenic. This can be taken as an indication that we are driving our children mad more effectively than we are genuinely educating them. Perhaps it is our way of educating them that is driving them mad.

Most but not all psychiatrists still think that people they call schizophrenic suffer from an inherited predisposition to act in predominantly incomprehensible ways, that some as yet undetermined genetic factor (possibly a genetic morphism) transacts with a more or less ordinary environment to induce biochemical-endocrinological changes which in turn generate what we observe as the behavioral signs of a subtle underlying organic process.

But it is wrong to impute a hypothetical disease of unknown etiology and undiscovered pathology to someone unless *he* can prove otherwise.[3]

The schizophrenic is someone who has queer experiences and/or is acting in a queer way,

3 See T. Szasz, *The Myth of Mental Illness* (New York: Harper & Row, 1961; London: Secker & Warburg, 1962).

from the point of view usually of his relatives and of ourselves. . . .

That the diagnosed patient is suffering from a pathological process is either a fact, or an hypothesis, an assumption, or a judgement.

To regard it as fact is unequivocally false. To regard it as an hypothesis is legitimate. It is unnecessary either to make the assumption or to pass judgement.

The psychiatrist, adopting his clinical stance in the presence of the pre-diagnosed person, whom he is already looking at and listening to as a patient, has tended to come to believe that he is in the presence of the "fact" of schizophrenia. He acts as if its existence were an established fact. He then has to discover its cause or multiple etiological factors, to assess its prognosis, and to treat its course. The heart of the illness then resides outside the agency of the person. That is, the illness is taken to be a process that the person is subject to or undergoes, whether genetic, constitutional, endogenous, exogenous, organic or psychological, or some mixture of them all.[4]

Many psychiatrists are now becoming much more cautious about adopting this starting point. But what might take its place?

In understanding the new viewpoint on schizophrenia, we might remind ourselves of the six blind men and the elephant: one touched its body and said it was a wall, another touched an ear and said it was a fan, another a leg and thought it was a pillar, and so on. The problem is sampling, and the error is incautious extrapolation.

The old way of sampling the behavior of schizophrenics was by the method of clinical examination. The following is an example of the type of examination conducted at the turn of the century. The account is given by the German psychiatrist Emil Kraepelin in his own words.

Gentlemen, the cases that I have to place before you today are peculiar. First of all, you see a servant-girl, aged twenty-four, upon whose features and frame traces of great emaciation can be plainly seen. In spite of this, the patient is in continual movement, going a few steps forward, then back again; she plaits her hair, only to unloose it the next minute. *On attempting to stop her movement*, we meet with unexpectedly strong resistance; *if I place myself in front of her with my arms spread out* in order to stop her, if she cannot push me on one side, she suddenly turns and slips through under my arms, so as to continue her way. *If one takes firm hold* of her, she distorts her usually rigid, expressionless features with deplorable weeping, that only ceases so soon as one lets her have her own way. We notice besides that she holds a crushed piece of bread spasmodically clasped in the fingers of the left hand, which she absolutely *will not allow to be forced from her*. The patient does not trouble in the least about her surroundings so long as you leave her alone. *If you prick her in the forehead with a needle*, she scarcely winces or turns away, and leaves the needle quietly sticking there without letting it disturb her restless, beast-of-prey-like wandering backwards and forwards. *To questions* she answers almost nothing, at the most shaking her head. But from time to time she wails: 'O dear God! O dear God! O dear mother! O dear mother!', always repeating uniformly the same phrases.[5]

Here are a man and a young girl. If we see the situation purely in terms of Kraepelin's point of view, it all immediately falls into place. He is sane, she is insane; he is rational, she is irrational. This entails looking at the patient's actions out of the context of the situation as she experienced it. But if we take Kraepelin's actions (in italics)—he tries to stop her movements, stands in front of her with arms outspread, tries to force a piece of bread out of her hand, sticks a

[4] R. D. Laing and A. Esterson, *Sanity, Madness and the Family*, Volume I, *Families of Schizophrenics* (London: Tavistock Publications, 1964; New York: Basic Books, 1965), page 4.

[5] E. Kraepelin, *Lectures on Clinical Psychiatry*, edited by T. Johnstone (London: Baillière, Tindall and Cox, 1906), pages 30–31.

needle in her forehead, and so on—out of the context of the situation as experienced and defined by him, how extraordinary *they* are!

A feature of the interplay between psychiatrist and patient is that if the patient's part is taken out of context, as is done in the clinical description, it might seem very odd. The psychiatrist's part, however, is taken as the very touchstone for our common-sense view of normality. The psychiatrist, as *ipso facto* sane, shows that the patient is out of contact with him. The fact that he is out of contact with the patient shows that there is something wrong with the patient, but not with the psychiatrist.

But if one ceases to identify with the clinical posture and looks at the psychiatrist-patient couple without such presuppositions, then it is difficult to sustain this naïve view of the situation.

Psychiatrists have paid very little attention to the *experience* of the patient. Even in psychoanalysis there is an abiding tendency to suppose that the schizophrenic's experiences are somehow unreal or invalid; one can make sense out of them only by interpreting them; without truth-giving interpretations the patient is enmeshed in a world of delusions and self-deception. Kaplan, an American psychologist, in an introduction to an excellent collection of self-reports on the experience of being psychotic, says very justly:

With all virtue on his side, he (the psychiatrist or psychoanalyst) reaches through the subterfuges and distortions of the patient and exposes them to the light of reason and insight. In this encounter between the psychiatrist and patient, the efforts of the former are linked with science and medicine, with understanding and care. What the patient experiences is tied to illness and irreality, to perverseness and distortion. The process of psychotherapy consists in large part of the patient's abandoning his false subjective perspectives for the therapist's objective

ones. But the essence of this conception is that the psychiatrist understands what is going on, and the patient does not.[6]

H. S. Sullivan used to say to young psychiatrists when they came to work with him, "I want you to remember that in the present state of our society, the patient is right, and you are wrong." This is an outrageous simplification. I mention it to loosen any fixed ideas that are no less outrageous, that the psychiatrist is right, and the patient wrong. I think, however, that schizophrenics have more to teach psychiatrists about the inner world than psychiatrists their patients.

A different picture begins to develop if the interaction between patients themselves is studied without presuppositions. One of the best accounts here is by the American sociologist Erving Goffman.

Goffman spent a year as an assistant physical therapist in a large mental hospital of some 7,000 beds, near Washington. His lowly staff status enabled him to fraternize with the patients in a way that upper echelons of the staff were unable to do. One of his conclusions is:

There is an old saw that no clearcut line can be drawn between normal people and mental patients; rather there is a continuum with the well-adjusted citizen at one end and the full-fledged psychotic at the other. I must argue that after a period of acclimatization in a mental hospital, the notion of a continuum seems very presumptuous. A community is a community. Just as it is bizarre to those not in it, so it is natural, even if unwanted, to those who live it from within. The system of dealings that patients have with one another does not fall at one end of anything, but rather provides one example of human association, to be avoided, no doubt, but also to be filed by the student in

6 Bert Kaplan (ed.), *The Inner World of Mental Illness* (New York and London: Harper and Row, 1964), page vii.

a circular cabinet along with all the other examples of association that he can collect.[7]

A large part of his study is devoted to a detailed documentation of how it comes about that a person, in being put in the role of patient, tends to become defined as a nonagent, as a nonresponsible object, to be treated accordingly, and even comes to regard himself in this light.

Goffman shows also that by shifting one's focus from seeing the person out of context, to seeing him in his context, behavior that might seem quite unintelligible, at best explained as some intrapsychic regression or organic deterioration, can make quite ordinary human sense. He does not just describe such behavior "in" mental hospital patients, he describes it within the context of personal interaction and the system in which it takes place.

. . . there is a vicious circle process at work. Persons who are lodged on "bad" wards find that very little equipment of any kind is given them —clothes may be taken away from them each night, recreational materials may be withheld, and only heavy wooden chairs and benches provided for furniture. Acts of hostility against the institution have to rely on limited, ill-designed devices, such as banging a chair against the floor or striking a sheet of newspaper sharply so as to make an annoying explosive sound. And the more inadequate this equipment is to convey rejection of the hospital, the more the act appears as a psychotic symptom, and the more likely it is that management feels justified in assigning the patient to a bad ward. When a patient finds himself in seclusion, naked and without visible means of expression, he may have to rely on tearing up his mattress, if he can, or writing with faeces on the wall—actions

management takes to be in keeping with the kind of person who warrants seclusion.[8]

It is on account of their behavior outside hospitals, however, that people get diagnosed as schizophrenic and admitted to hospitals in the first place.

There have been many studies of social factors in relation to schizophrenia. These include attempts to discover whether schizophrenia occurs more or less frequently in one or other ethnic group, social class, sex, ordinal position in the family and so on. The conclusion from such studies has often been that social factors do not play a significant role in the "etiology of schizophrenia." This begs the question, and moreover such studies do not get close enough to the relevant situation. If the police wish to determine whether a man has died of natural causes, or has committed suicide, or has been murdered, they do not look up prevalence or incidence figures. They investigate the circumstances attendant upon each single case in turn. Each investigation is an original research project, and it comes to an end when enough evidence has been gathered to answer the relevant questions.

It is only in the last ten years that the immediate interpersonal environment of "schizophrenics" has come to be studied in its interstices. This work was prompted, in the first place, by psychotherapists who formed the impression that, if their patients were *disturbed*, their families were often very *disturbing*. Psychotherapists, however, remained committed by their technique not to study the families directly. At first the focus was mainly on the mothers (who are always the first to get the blame for everything), and a "schizophrenogenic" mother was postulated, who was supposed to generate disturbance in her child.

Next, attention was paid to the husbands of these undoubtedly unhappy women,

[7] E. Goffman, *Asylums. Essays on the Social Situation of Mental Patients and Other Inmates* (New York: Doubleday Anchor Books, 1961), page 303.

[8] E. Goffman, op. cit., page 306.

then to the parental and parent-child inter-
actions (rather than to each person in the
family separately), then to the nuclear family
group of parents and children, and finally to
the whole relevant network of people in and
around the family, including the grandparents of patients. By the time our own
researches started, this methodological
breakthrough had been made and, in addition, a major theoretical advance had been
achieved.

This was the "double-bind" hypothesis,
whose chief architect was the anthropologist
Gregory Bateson. The theory[9], first published in 1956, represented a theoretical
advance of the first order. The germ of the
idea developed in Bateson's mind while
studying New Guinea in the 1930s. In New
Guinea the culture had, as all cultures have,
built-in techniques for maintaining its own
inner balance. One technique, for example,
that served to neutralize dangerous rivalry
was sexual transvestism. However, mis-
sionaries and the occidental government
tended to object to such practices. The culture was therefore caught between the risk
of external extermination or internal dis-
ruption.

Together with research workers in California, Bateson brought this paradigm of an
insoluble "can't win" situation, specifically
destructive of self-identity, to bear on the
internal communication pattern of families
of diagnosed schizophrenics.

The studies of the families of schizophrenics conducted at Palo Alto, California,
Yale University, the Pennsylvania Psychiatric Institute and the National Institute
of Mental Health, among other places, have
all shown that the person who gets diagnosed
is part of a wider network of extremely disturbed and disturbing patterns of communication. In all these places, to the best

of my knowledge, *no* schizophrenic has been
studied whose disturbed pattern of communication has not been shown to be a reflection of, and reaction to, the disturbed
and disturbing pattern characterizing his or
her family of origin. This is matched in our
own researches.[10]

In over one hundred cases where we[11]
studied the actual circumstances around the
social event when one person comes to be
regarded as schizophrenic, it seems to us
that *without exception* the experience and
behavior that gets labeled schizophrenic is
*a special strategy that a person invents in
order to live in an unlivable situation*. In
his life situation the person has come to feel
he is in an untenable position. He cannot
make a move, or make no move, without
being beset by contradictory and paradoxical
pressures and demands, pushes and pulls,
both internally from himself, and externally
from those around him. He is, as it were,
in a position of checkmate.

This state of affairs may not be perceived
as such by any of the people in it. The man
at the bottom of the heap may be being
crushed and suffocated to death without
anyone noticing, much less intending it.
The situation here described is impossible
to see by studying the different people in it
singly. The social system, not single individuals extrapolated from it, must be the object of study.

We know that the biochemistry of the
person is highly sensitive to social circumstance. That a checkmate situation
occasions a biochemical response which, in
turn, facilitates or inhibits certain types of
experience and behavior is plausible *a
priori*.

The behavior of the diagnosed patient is
part of a much larger network of disturbed

---

[9] G. Bateson, D. D. Jackson, J. Haley, J. and J.
Weakland, "Towards a theory of schizophrenia,"
Behavioral Science, Volume I, Number 251, 1956.

[10] R. D. Laing and A. Esterson, *Sanity, Madness
and the Family* (London: Tavistock Publications,
1964; New York: Basic Books, 1965).

[11] Drs. David Cooper, A. Esterson and myself.

behavior. The contradictions and confusions "internalized" by the individual must
be looked at in their larger social contexts.

Something is wrong somewhere, but it can
no longer be seen exclusively or even primarily "in" the diagnosed patient.

Nor is it a matter of laying the blame at
anyone's door. The untenable position, the
"can't win" double-bind, the situation of
checkmate, is by definition *not obvious* to
the protagonists. Very seldom is it a question
of contrived, deliberate, cynical lies or a
ruthless intention to drive someone crazy,
although this occurs more commonly than is
usually supposed. We have had parents tell
us that they would rather their child was
mad than that he or she realize the truth.
Though even here, they say "it is a mercy"
that the person is "out of his mind." A
checkmate position cannot be described in
a few words. The whole situation has to be
grasped before it can be seen that no move
is possible, and making no move is equally
unlivable.

With these reservations, the following is
an example of an interaction given in *The
Self and Others*[12] between a father, mother,
and son of twenty recovering from a schizophrenic episode.

In this session the patient was maintaining that he was selfish, while his parents
were telling him that he was not. The psychiatrist asked the patient to give an example of what he meant by "selfish."

SON. Well, when my mother sometimes makes
me a big meal and I won't eat it if I don't feel
like it.

FATHER. But he wasn't always like that, you
know. He's always been a good boy.

MOTHER. That's his illness, isn't it, doctor? He
was never ungrateful. He was always most
polite and well brought up. We've done our
best by him.

[12] R. D. Laing (London: Tavistock Publications,
1961; Chicago: Quadrangle Press, 1962).

SON. No, I've always been selfish and ungrateful. I've no self-respect.

FATHER. But you have.

SON. I could have, if you respected me. No one
respects me. Everyone laughs at me. I'm the
joke of the world. I'm the joker all right.

FATHER. But, son, I respect you, because I respect a man who respects himself.

It is hardly surprising that the person in
his terror may stand in curious postures in
an attempt to control the irresolvably contradictory social "forces" that are controlling him, that he projects the inner on to
the outer, introjects the outer on to the inner, that he tries in short to protect himself
from destruction by every means that he
has, by projection, introjection, splitting,
denial and so on.

Gregory Bateson, in a brilliant introduction to a nineteenth-century autobiograph-
ical account of schizophrenia, said this:

It would appear that once precipitated into
psychosis the patient has a course to run. He is, as
it were, embarked upon a voyage of discovery
which is only completed by his return to the
normal world, to which he comes back with insights different from those of the inhabitants
who never embarked on such a voyage. Once
begun, a schizophrenic episode would appear
to have as definite a course as an initiation ceremony—a death and rebirth—into which the
novice may have been precipitated by his family
life or by adventitious circumstances, but which
in its course is largely steered by endogenous
process.

In terms of this picture, spontaneous remission is no problem. This is only the final and
natural outcome of the total process. What
needs to be explained is the failure of many
who embark upon this voyage to return from
it. *Do these encounter circumstances either in
family life or in institutional care so grossly
maladaptive that even the richest and best orga-*

nized hallucinatory experience cannot save them?[13]

I am in substantial agreement with this view.

A revolution is currently going on in relation to sanity and madness, both inside and outside psychiatry. The clinical point of view is giving way before a point of view that is both existential and social.

From an ideal vantage point on the ground, a formation of planes may be observed in the air. One plane may be out of formation. But the whole formation may be off course. The plane that is "out of formation" may be abnormal, bad or "mad," from the point of view of the formation. But the formation itself may be bad or mad from the point of view of the ideal observer. The plane that is out of formation may also be more or less off course than the formation itself is.

The "out of formation" criterion is the clinical positivist criterion.

The "off course" criterion is the ontological. One needs to make two judgements along these different parameters. In particular, it is of fundamental importance not to confuse the person who may be "out of formation" by telling him he is "off course" if he is not. It is of fundamental importance not to make the positivist mistake of assuming that, because a group are "in formation," this means they are necessarily "on course." This is the Gadarene swine* fallacy. Nor is it necessarily the case that the person who is "out of formation" is more "on course" than the formation. There is no need to idealize someone just because he is labeled "out of formation." Nor is there any need to persuade the person who is "out of formation" that cure consists in getting back into formation. The person who is "out of formation" is often full of hatred toward the formation and of fears about being the odd man out.

If the formation is itself off course, then the man who is really to get "on course" must leave the formation. But it is possible to do so, if one desires, without screeches and screams, and without terrorizing the already terrified formation that one has to leave.

In the diagnostic category of schizophrenic are many different types of sheep and goats.

"Schizophrenia" is a diagnosis, a label applied by some people to others. This does not prove that the labeled person is subject to an essentially pathological process, of unknown nature and origin, going on *in* his or her body. It does not mean that the process is, primarily or secondarily, a *psycho*-pathological one, going on *in* the *psyche* of the person. But it does establish as a social fact that the person labeled is one of Them. It is easy to forget that the process is a hypothesis, to assume that it is a fact, then to pass the judgement that it is biologically maladaptive and, as such, pathological. But social adaptation to a dysfunctional society may be very dangerous. The perfectly adjusted bomber pilot may be a greater threat to species survival than the hospitalized schizophrenic deluded that the Bomb is inside him. Our society may itself have become biologically dysfunctional, and some forms of schizophrenic alienation from the alienation of society may have a sociobiological function that we have not recognized. This holds even if a genetic factor predisposes to some kinds of schizophrenic behavior. Recent critiques of the work on genetics[14] and the most recent

---

[13] G. Bateson (ed.), *Perceval's Narrative. A Patient's Account of his Psychosis* (Stanford, California: Stanford University Press, 1961), pages xiii–xiv; italics mine [Laing's].

* According to *The Gospel of St. Luke* VIII, 26–33 Jesus cured a man of Gadara, who was possessed, by casting his devils into a herd of swine. The swine then ran into a lake and were drowned. [Ed.]

[14] See for instance: Pekka Tienari, *Psychiatric Illnesses in Identical Twins* (Copenhagen: Munksgaard, 1963).

empirical genetic studies, leave this matter open.

Jung suggested some years ago that it would be an interesting experiment to study whether the syndrome of psychiatry runs in families. A pathological process called "psychiatrosis" may well be found, by the same methods, to be a delineable entity, with somatic correlates and psychic mechanisms, with an inherited or at least constitutional basis, a natural history, and a doubtful prognosis.

The most profound recent development in psychiatry has been to redefine the basic categories and assumptions of psychiatry itself. We are now in a transitional stage where to some extent we still continue to use old bottles for new wine. We have to decide whether to use old terms in a new way, or abandon them to the dustbin of history.

There is no such "condition" as "schizophrenia," but the label is a social fact and the social fact a *political event*.[15] This political event, occurring in the civic order of society, imposes definitions and consequences on the labeled person. It is a social prescription that rationalizes a set of social actions whereby the labeled person is annexed by others, who are legally sanctioned, medically empowered and morally obliged, to become responsible for the person labeled. The person labeled is inaugurated not only into a role, but into a career of patient, by the concerted action of a coalition (a "conspiracy") of family, G.P., mental health officer, psychiatrists, nurses, psychiatric social workers, and often fellow patients. The "committed" person labeled as patient, and specifically as "schizophre-

nic," is degraded from full existential and legal status as human agent and responsible person to someone no longer in possession of his own definition of himself, unable to retain his own possessions, precluded from the exercise of his discretion as to whom he meets, what he does. His time is no longer his own and the space he occupies is no longer of his choosing. After being subjected to a degradation ceremonial[16] known as psychiatric examination, he is bereft of his civil liberties in being imprisoned in a total institution[17] known as a "mental" hospital. More completely, more radically than anywhere else in our society, he is invalidated as a human being. In the mental hospital he must remain, until the label is rescinded or qualified by such terms as "remitted" or "readjusted." Once a "schizophrenic," there is a tendency to be regarded as always a "schizophrenic."

Now, why and how does this happen? And what functions does this procedure serve for the maintenance of the civic order? These questions are only just beginning to be asked, much less answered. Questions and answers have so far been focused on the family as a social subsystem. Socially, this work must now move to further understanding, not only of the internal disturbed and disturbing patterns of communication within families, of the double-binding procedures, the pseudo-mutuality, of what I have called the mystifications and the untenable positions, but also to the meaning of all this within the larger context of the civic order of society—that is, of the *political* order, of the ways persons exercise control and power over one another.

Some people labeled schizophrenic (not

[15] T. Scheff, "Social Conditions for Rationality: How Urban and Rural Courts Deal with the Mentally Ill," *Amer. Behav. Scient.*, March, 1964. Also T. Scheff, "The Societal Reaction to Deviants: Ascriptive Elements in the Psychiatric Screening of Mental Patients in a Midwestern State," *Social Problems*, No. 4, Spring, 1964.

[16] H. Garfinkel, "Conditions of Successful Degradation Ceremonies," *American Journal of Sociology*, Volume LXI (March, 1956).

[17] E. Goffman, *Asylums. Essays on the Social Situation of Mental Patients and Other Inmates* (New York: Doubleday Anchor Books, 1961).

all, and not necessarily) manifest behavior in words, gestures, actions (linguistically, paralinguistically and kinetically) that is unusual. Sometimes (not always and not necessarily) this unusual behavior (manifested to us, the others, as I have said, by sight and sound) expresses, wittingly or unwittingly, unusual experiences that the person is undergoing. Sometimes (not always and not necessarily) these unusual experiences expressed by unusual behavior appear to be part of a potentially orderly, natural sequence of experiences.

This sequence is very seldom allowed to occur because we are so busy "treating" the patient, whether by chemotherapy, shock therapy, *milieu* therapy, group therapy, psychotherapy, family therapy—sometimes now, in the very best, most advanced places, by the lot.

What we see sometimes in *some* people whom we label and "treat" as schizophrenics are the behavioral expressions of an experiential drama. But we see this drama in a distorted form that our therapeutic efforts tend to distort further. The outcome of this unfortunate dialectic is a *forme frustre* [distortion] of a potentially *natural* process, that we do not allow to happen.

In characterizing this sequence in general terms, I shall write *entirely* about a sequence of experience. I shall therefore have to use the language of experience. So many people feel they have to translate "subjective" events into "objective" terms in order to be scientific. To be genuinely scientific means to have valid knowledge of a chosen domain of reality. So in the following I shall use the language of experience to describe the events of experience. Also, I shall not so much be describing a series of different discrete events as describing a unitary sequence, from different points of view, and using a variety of idioms to do so. I suggest that this natural process, which our labeling and well-intentioned therapeutic efforts distort and arrest, is as follows.

We start again from the split of our experience into what seems to be two worlds, inner and outer.

The normal state of affairs is that we know little of either and are alienated from both, but that we know perhaps a little more of the outer than the inner. However, the very fact that it is necessary to speak of outer and inner at all implies that an historically conditioned split has occurred, so that the inner is already as bereft of substance as the outer is bereft of meaning.

We need not be unaware of the "inner" world. We do not realize its existence most of the time. But many people enter it—unfortunately without guides, confusing outer with inner realities, and inner with outer—and generally lose their capacity to function competently in ordinary relations.

This need not be so. The process of entering into *the other* world from this world, and returning to *this* world from the other world, is as natural as death and giving birth or being born. But in our present world, which is both so terrified and so unconscious of the other world, it is not surprising that when "reality," the fabric of this world, bursts, and a person enters the other world, he is completely lost and terrified and meets only incomprehension in others.

Some people wittingly, some people unwittingly, enter or are thrown into more or less total inner space and time. We are socially conditioned to regard total immersion in outer space and time as normal and healthy. Immersion in inner space and time tends to be regarded as antisocial withdrawal, a deviation, invalid, pathological *per se*, in some sense discreditable.

Sometimes, having gone through the looking glass, through the eye of the needle, the territory is recognized as one's lost home, but most people now in inner space and time are, to begin with, in unfamiliar territory and are frightened and confused. They are lost. They have forgotten that they have been there before. They clutch at chimeras. They try to retain their bearings by compounding their confusion, by projection (putting the inner on to the outer), and introjection (importing outer categories into the inner). They do not know what is happening, and no one is likely to enlighten them.

We defend ourselves violently even from the full range of our egoically limited experience. How much more are we likely to react with terror, confusion and "defenses" against ego-loss experience. There is nothing intrinsically pathological in the experience of ego-loss, but it may be very difficult to find a living context for the journey one may be embarked upon.

The person who has entered this inner realm (if only he is allowed to experience this) will find himself going, or being conducted—one cannot clearly distinguish active from passive here—on a journey.

This journey is experienced as going further "in," as going back through one's personal life, in and back and through and beyond into the experience of all mankind, of the primal man, of Adam and perhaps even further into the beings of animals, vegetables and minerals.

In this journey there are many occasions to lose one's way, for confusion, partial failure, even final shipwreck; many terrors, spirits, demons to be encountered, that may or may not be overcome.

We do not regard it as pathologically deviant to explore a jungle or to climb Mount Everest. We feel that Columbus was entitled to be mistaken in his construction of what he discovered when he came to the New World. We are far more out of touch with even the nearest approaches of the infinite reaches of inner space than we now are with the reaches of outer space. We respect the voyager, the explorer, the climber, the space man. It makes far more sense to me as a valid project—indeed, as a desperately and urgently required project for our time—to explore the inner space and time of consciousness. Perhaps this is one of the few things that still make sense in our historical context. We are so out of touch with this realm that many people can now argue seriously that it does not exist. Small wonder that it is perilous indeed to explore such a lost realm. The situation I am suggesting is precisely as though we all had almost total lack of any knowledge whatever of what we call the outer world. What would happen if some of us then started to see, hear, touch, smell, taste things? We would hardly be more confused than the person who first has vague intimations of, and then moves into, inner space and time. This is where the person labeled catatonic has often gone. He is not at all here: he is all there. He is frequently very mistaken about what he is experiencing, and he probably does not want to experience it. He may indeed be lost. There are very few of us who know the territory in which he is lost, who know how to reach him and how to find the way back.

No age in the history of humanity has perhaps so lost touch with this natural *healing* process that implicates *some* of the people whom we label schizophrenic. No age has so devalued it, no age has imposed such prohibitions and deterrences against it, as our own. Instead of the mental hospital, a sort of reservicing factory for human breakdowns, we need a place where people who have traveled further and, consequently, may be more lost than psychiatrists and other sane people, can find their way *further* into inner space and time, and back again. Instead of the *degradation* ceremonial of psychiatric examination, diagnosis and prognostication, we need, for those who are ready for it (in psychiatric terminology, often those who are about to go into a schizophrenic breakdown), an *initiation* ceremonial, through which the person will be guided with full social encouragement and sanction into inner space and time, by people who have been there and back again. Psychiatrically, this would appear as ex-patients helping future patients to go mad.

What is entailed then is:

(i) a voyage from outer to inner,
(ii) from life to a kind of death,
(iii) from going forward to going back,
(iv) from temporal movement to temporal standstill,
(v) from mundane time to eonic time,
(vi) from the ego to the self,
(vii) from outside (post-birth) back into the womb of all things (pre-birth),

and then subsequently a return voyage from

(1) inner to outer,
(2) from death to life,
(3) from the movement back to a movement once more forward,
(4) from immortality back to mortality,
(5) from eternity back to time,
(6) from self to a new ego,
(7) from a cosmic fetalization to an existential rebirth.

I shall leave it to those who wish to translate the above elements of this perfectly natural and necessary process into the jargon of psychopathology and clinical psychiatry. This process may be one that all of us need, in one form or another. This process could have a central function in a truly sane society.

I have listed very briefly little more than the headings for an extended study and understanding of a natural sequence of experiential stepping stones that, in some instances, is submerged, concealed, distorted and arrested by the label "schizo-phrenia" with its connotations of pathology and consequences of an illness-to-be-cured.

Perhaps we will learn to accord to so-called schizophrenics who have come back to us, perhaps after years, no less respect than the often no less lost explorers of the Renaissance. If the human race survives, future men will, I suspect, look back on our enlightened epoch as a veritable Age of Darkness. They will presumably be able to savor the irony of this situation with more amusement than we can extract from it. The laugh's on us. They will see that what we call "schizophrenia" was one of the forms in which, often through quite ordinary people, the light began to break through the cracks in our all-too-closed minds.

Schizophrenia used to be a new name for dementia praecox—a slow, insidious illness that was supposed to overtake young people in particular and to be liable to go on to a terminal dementia.

Perhaps we can still retain the now old name, and read into it its etymological meaning: *Schiz*—"broken"; *Phrenos*—"soul" or "heart."

The schizophrenic in this sense is one who is brokenhearted, and even broken hearts have been known to mend, if we have the heart to let them.

But "schizophrenia," in this existential sense, has little to do with the clinical examination, diagnosis, prognosis and prescriptions for therapy of "schizophrenia."

Nathaniel Hawthorne

YOUNG GOODMAN BROWN

Young Goodman Brown came forth at sunset into the street at Salem village, but put his head back, after crossing the threshold, to exchange a parting kiss with his young wife. And Faith, as the wife was aptly named, thrust her own pretty head into the street, letting the wind play with the pink ribbons of her cap while she called to Goodman Brown.

"Dearest heart," whispered she, softly and rather sadly, when her lips were close to his ear, "prithee put off your journey until sunrise and sleep in your own bed tonight. A lone woman is troubled with such dreams and such thoughts that she's afeard of herself sometimes. Pray tarry with me this night, dear husband, of all nights in the year."

"My love and my Faith," replied young Goodman Brown, "of all nights in the year, this one night must I tarry away from thee. My journey, as thou callest it, forth and back again, must needs be done 'twixt now and sunrise. What, my sweet, pretty wife, dost thou doubt me already, and we but three months married?"

"Then God bless you!" said Faith, with the pink ribbons, "and may you find all well when you come back."

"Amen!" cried Goodman Brown. "Say thy prayers, dear Faith, and go to bed at dusk, and no harm will come to thee."

So they parted; and the young man pursued his way until, being about to turn the corner by the meeting-house, he looked back and saw the head of Faith still peeping after him with a melancholy air, in spite of her pink ribbons.

"Poor little Faith!" thought he, for his heart smote him. "What a wretch am I to leave her on such an errand! She talks of dreams, too. Methought as she spoke there was trouble in her face, as if a dream had warned her what work is to be done tonight. But no, no; 't would kill her to think it. Well, she's a blessed angel on earth; and after this one night I'll cling to her skirts and follow her to heaven."

With this excellent resolve for the future, Goodman Brown felt himself justified in making more haste on his present evil purpose. He had taken a dreary road, darkened by all the gloomiest trees of the forest, which barely stood aside to let the narrow path creep through and closed immediately behind. It was all as lonely as could be; and there is this peculiarity in such a solitude, that the traveller knows not who may be concealed by the innumerable trunks and the thick boughs overhead; so that with lonely footsteps he may yet be passing through an unseen multitude.

"There may be a devilish Indian behind every tree," said Goodman Brown to himself; and he glanced fearfully behind him as he added, "What if the devil himself should be at my very elbow!"

His head being turned back, he passed a crook of the road and, looking forward again, beheld the figure of a man, in grave and decent attire, seated at the foot of an old tree. He arose at Goodman Brown's approach and walked onward side by side with him.

"You are late, Goodman Brown," said he. "The clock of the Old South[18] was striking as I came through Boston, and that is full fifteen minutes agone."

"Faith kept me back a while," replied the young man, with a tremor in his voice caused by the sudden appearance of his companion, though not wholly unexpected.

It was now deep dusk in the forest, and deepest in that part of it where these two were journeying. As nearly as could be discerned, the second traveller was about fifty years old, apparently in the same rank of life as Goodman Brown, and bearing a considerable resemblance to him, though perhaps more in expression than features. Still they might have been taken for father and son. And yet, though the elder person was as simply clad as the younger, and as simple in manner too, he had an indescribable air of one who knew the world and who would not have felt abashed at the governor's dinner table or in King William's court,[19] were it possible that his affairs

[18] The Church or Meeting House, built in 1729.
[19] William III was King of England from 1689 to 1702.

should call him thither. But the only thing about him that could be fixed upon as remarkable was his staff, which bore the likeness of a great black snake, so curiously wrought that it might almost be seen to twist and wriggle itself like a living serpent. This, of course, must have been an ocular deception, assisted by the uncertain light.

"Come, Goodman Brown," cried his fellow traveller, "this is a dull pace for the beginning of a journey. Take my staff, if you are so soon weary."

"Friend," said the other, exchanging his slow pace for a full stop, "having kept covenant by meeting thee here, it is my purpose now to return whence I came. I have scruples touching the matter thou wot'st of."

"Sayest thou so?" replied he of the serpent, smiling apart. "Let us walk on, nevertheless, reasoning as we go; and if I convince thee not thou shalt turn back. We are but a little way in the forest yet."

"Too far! too far!" exclaimed the goodman, unconsciously resuming his walk. "My father never went into the woods on such an errand, nor his father before him. We have been a race of honest men and good Christians since the days of the martyrs; and shall I be the first of the name of Brown that ever took this path and kept. . . ."

"Such company, thou wouldst say," observed the elder person, interpreting his pause. "Well said, Goodman Brown! I have been as well acquainted with your family as with ever a one among the Puritans; and that's no trifle to say. I helped your grandfather, the constable, when he lashed the Quaker woman so smartly through the streets of Salem; and it was I that brought your father a pitch-pine knot, kindled at my own hearth, to set fire to an Indian village, in King Philip's war. They were my good friends, both; and many a pleasant walk have we had along this path,

and returned merrily after midnight. I would fain be friends with you for their sake."

"If it be as thou sayest," replied Goodman Brown, "I marvel they never spoke of these matters; or, verily, I marvel not, seeing that the least rumor of the sort would have driven them from New England. We are a people of prayer, and good works to boot, and abide no such wickedness."

"Wickedness or not," said the traveller with the twisted staff, "I have a very general acquaintance here in New England. The deacons of many a church have drunk the communion wine with me; the selectmen of divers towns make me their chairman; and a majority of the Great and General Court[20] are firm supporters of my interest. The governor and I, too—But these are state secrets."

"Can this be so?" cried Goodman Brown, with a stare of amazement at his undisturbed companion. "Howbeit, I have nothing to do with the governor and council; they have their own ways and are no rule for a simple husbandman like me. But were I to go on with thee, how should I meet the eye of that good old man, our minister, at Salem village? Oh, his voice would make me tremble both Sabbath day and lecture day."

Thus far the elder traveller had listened with due gravity; but now burst into a fit of irrepressible mirth, shaking himself so violently that his snakelike staff actually seemed to wriggle in sympathy.

"Ha! ha! ha!" shouted he again and again; then composing himself, "Well, go on, Goodman Brown, go on; but, prithee, don't kill me with laughing."

"Well, then, to end the matter at once," said Goodman Brown, considerably nettled, "there is my wife, Faith. It would break her dear little heart; and I'd rather break my own."

[20] Governing body of the Massachusetts Colony.

"Nay, if that be the case," answered the other, "e'en go thy ways, Goodman Brown. I would not for twenty old women like the one hobbling before us that Faith should come to any harm."

As he spoke he pointed his staff at a female figure on the path, in whom Goodman Brown recognized a very pious and exemplary dame, who had taught him his catechism in youth and was still his moral and spiritual adviser, jointly with the minister and Deacon Gookin.

"A marvel, truly, that Goody Cloyse should be so far in the wilderness at nightfall," said he. "But with your leave, friend, I shall take a cut through the woods until we have left this Christian woman behind. Being a stranger to you, she might ask whom I was consorting with and whither I was going."

"Be it so," said his fellow traveller. "Betake you to the woods, and let me keep the path."

Accordingly the young man turned aside, but took care to watch his companion, who advanced softly along the road until he had come within a staff's length of the old dame. She, meanwhile, was making the best of her way, with singular speed for so aged a woman, and mumbling some indistinct words—a prayer, doubtless—as she went. The traveller put forth his staff and touched her withered neck with what seemed the serpent's tail.

"The devil!" screamed the pious old lady.

"Then Goody Cloyse knows her old friend?" observed the traveller, confronting her and leaning on his writhing stick.

"Ah, forsooth, and is it your worship indeed?" cried the good dame. "Yea, truly is it, and in the very image of my old gossip, Goodman Brown, the grandfather of the silly fellow that now is. But—would your worship believe it?—my broomstick hath strangely disappeared, stolen, as I suspect, by that unhanged witch, Goody Cory, and that, too, when I was all anointed with the juice of smallage, and cinquefoil, and wolf's bane—"

"Mingled with fine wheat and the fat of a newborn babe," said the shape of old Goodman Brown.

"Ah, your worship knows the recipe," cried the old lady, cackling aloud. "So, as I was saying, being all ready for the meeting, and no horse to ride on, I made up my mind to foot it; for they tell me there is a nice young man to be taken into communion tonight. But now your good worship will lend me your arm, and we shall be there in a twinkling."

"That can hardly be," answered her friend. "I may not spare you my arm, Goody Cloyse; but here is my staff, if you will."

So saying, he threw it down at her feet, where, perhaps, it assumed life, being one of the rods which its owner had formerly lent to the Egyptian magi.[21] Of this fact, however, Goodman Brown could not take cognizance. He had cast up his eyes in astonishment and, looking down again, beheld neither Goody Cloyse nor the serpentine staff, but his fellow traveller alone, who waited for him as calmly as if nothing had happened.

"That old woman taught me my catechism," said the young man; and there was a world of meaning in this simple comment.

They continued to walk onward, while the elder traveller exhorted his companion to make good speed and persevere in the path, discoursing so aptly that his arguments seemed rather to spring up in the bosom of his auditor than to be suggested by himself. As they went, he plucked a branch of maple to serve for a walking stick, and began to strip it of the twigs and little boughs, which were wet with evening dew. The moment his fingers touched them they became strangely withered and dried up as

21 I.e., Pharaoh's magicians; *Exodus* VII, 12.

with a week's sunshine. Thus the pair proceeded at a good free pace, until suddenly, in a gloomy hollow of the road, Goodman Brown sat himself down on the stump of a tree and refused to go any farther.

"Friend," said he stubbornly, "my mind is made up. Not another step will I budge on this errand. What if a wretched old woman do choose to go to the devil when I thought she was going to heaven: is that any reason why I should quit my dear Faith and go after her?"

"You will think better of this by and by," said his acquaintance composedly. "Sit here and rest yourself a while; and when you feel like moving again, there is my staff to help you along."

Without more words, he threw his companion the maple stick, and was as speedily out of sight as if he had vanished into the deepening gloom. The young man sat a few moments by the roadside, applauding himself greatly and thinking with how clear a conscience he should meet the minister in his morning walk, nor shrink from the eye of good old Deacon Gookin. And what calm sleep would be his that very night, which was to have been spent so wickedly, but so purely and sweetly now, in the arms of Faith! Amidst these pleasant and praiseworthy meditations, Goodman Brown heard the tramp of horses along the road and deemed it advisable to conceal himself within the verge of the forest, conscious of the guilty purpose that had brought him thither, though now so happily turned from it.

On came the hoof tramps and the voices of the riders, two grave old voices, conversing soberly as they drew near. These mingled sounds appeared to pass along the road, within a few yards of the young man's hiding-place; but, owing doubtless to the depth of the gloom at that particular spot, neither the travellers nor their steeds were visible. Though their figures brushed the small boughs by the wayside, it could not

be seen that they intercepted, even for a moment, the faint gleam from the strip of bright sky athwart which they must have passed. Goodman Brown alternately crouched and stood on tiptoe, pulling aside the branches and thrusting forth his head as far as he durst, without discerning so much as a shadow. It vexed him the more, because he could have sworn, were such a thing possible, that he recognized the voices of the minister and Deacon Gookin, jogging along quietly, as they were wont to do, when bound to some ordination or ecclesiastical council. While yet within hearing one of the riders stopped to pluck a switch.

"Of the two, reverend sir," said the voice like the deacon's, "I had rather miss an ordination dinner than tonight's meeting. They tell me that some of our community are to be here from Falmouth and beyond, and others from Connecticut and Rhode Island, besides several of the Indian pow-wows, who, after their fashion, know almost as much deviltry as the best of us. Moreover, there is a goodly young woman to be taken into communion."

"Mighty well, Deacon Gookin!" replied the solemn old tones of the minister. "Spur up, or we shall be late. Nothing can be done, you know, until I get on the ground."

The hoofs clattered again; and the voices, talking so strangely in the empty air, passed on through the forest where no church had ever been gathered or solitary Christian prayed. Whither, then, could these holy men be journeying so deep into the heathen wilderness? Young Goodman Brown caught hold of a tree for support, being ready to sink down on the ground, faint and overburdened with the heavy sickness of his heart. He looked up to the sky, doubting whether there really was a heaven above him. Yet there was the blue arch, and the stars brightening in it.

"With heaven above and Faith below, I will yet stand firm against the devil!" cried Goodman Brown.

While he still gazed upward into the deep arch of the firmament and had lifted his hands to pray, a cloud, though no wind was stirring, hurried across the zenith and hid the brightening stars. The blue sky was still visible, except directly overhead, where this black mass of cloud was sweeping swiftly northward. Aloft in the air, as if from the depths of cloud, came a confused and doubtful sound of voices. Once the listener fancied that he could distinguish the accents of townspeople of his own, men and women, both pious and ungodly, many of whom he had met at the communion table, and had seen others rioting at the tavern. The next moment, so indistinct were the sounds, he doubted whether he had heard aught but the murmur of the old forest, whispering without a wind. Then came a stronger swell of those familiar tones, heard daily in the sunshine at Salem village but never until now from a cloud of night. There was one voice of a young woman uttering lamentations, yet with an uncertain sorrow, and entreating for some favor which, perhaps, it would grieve her to obtain; and all the unseen multitude, both saints and sinners, seemed to encourage her onward.

"Faith!" shouted Goodman Brown, in a voice of agony and desperation; and the echoes of the forest mocked him, crying "Faith! Faith!" as if bewildered wretches were seeking her all through the wilderness.

The cry of grief, rage, and terror was yet piercing the night, when the unhappy husband held his breath for a response. There was a scream, drowned immediately in a louder murmur of voices, fading into far-off laughter as the dark cloud swept away, leaving the clear and silent sky above Goodman Brown, but something fluttered lightly down through the air and caught on the branch of a tree. The young man seized it and beheld a pink ribbon.

"My Faith is gone!" cried he after one stupefied moment. "There is no good on earth, and sin is but a name. Come, devil, for to thee is this world given."

And maddened with despair, so that he laughed loud and long, did Goodman Brown grasp his staff and set forth again, at such a rate that he seemed to fly along the forest path rather than to walk or run. The road grew wilder and drearier and more faintly traced, and vanished at length, leaving him in the heart of the dark wilderness, still rushing onward with the instinct that guides mortal men to evil. The whole forest was peopled with frightful sounds— the creaking of the trees, the howling of wild beasts, and the yell of Indians; while sometimes the wind tolled like a distant church bell, and sometimes gave a broad roar around the traveller, as if all nature were laughing him to scorn. But he was himself the chief horror of the scene, and shrank not from its other horrors.

"Ha! ha! ha!" roared Goodman Brown when the wind laughed at him. "Let us hear which will laugh loudest. Think not to frighten me with your deviltry. Come witch, come wizard, come Indian powwow, come devil himself, and here comes Goodman Brown. You may as well fear him as he fear you."

In truth, all through the haunted forest there could be nothing more frightful than the figure of Goodman Brown. On he flew among the black pines, brandishing his staff with frenzied gestures, now giving vent to an inspiration of horrid blasphemy and now shouting forth such laughter as set all the echoes of the forest laughing like demons around him. The fiend in his own shape is less hideous than when he rages in the breast of man. Thus sped the demoniac on his course, until, quivering among the trees, he saw a red light before him, as when the felled trunks and branches of a clearing have been set on fire and throw up their lurid blaze against the sky, at the hour of midnight. He paused in a lull of the tempest that had driven him onward and heard the swell of what seemed a hymn, rolling solemnly from a distance with the weight of many voices. He knew the tune; it was a familiar one in the choir of the village meeting-house. The verse died heavily away and was lengthened by a chorus, not of human voices but of all the sounds of the benighted wilderness pealing in awful harmony together. Goodman Brown cried out, and his cry was lost to his own ear by its unison with the cry of the desert.

In the interval of silence he stole forward until the light glared full upon his eyes. At one extremity of an open space, hemmed in by the dark wall of the forest, arose a rock bearing some rude, natural resemblance either to an altar or a pulpit, and surrounded by four blazing pines, their tops aflame, their stems untouched, like candles at an evening meeting. The mass of foliage that had overgrown the summit of the rock was all on fire, blazing high into the night and fitfully illuminating the whole field. Each pendant twig and leafy festoon was in a blaze. As the red light arose and fell, a numerous congregation alternately shone forth, then disappeared in shadow, and again grew, as it were, out of the darkness, peopling the heart of the solitary woods at once.

"A grave and dark-clad company," quoth Goodman Brown.

In truth they were such. Among them, quivering to and fro between gloom and splendor, appeared faces that would be seen next day at the council board of the province, and others which, Sabbath after Sabbath, looked devoutly heavenward, and benignantly over the crowded pews, from the holiest pulpits in the land. Some affirm that the lady of the governor was there. At least there were high dames well known to her, and wives of honored husbands, and widows, a great multitude, and ancient maidens, all of excellent repute, and fair young girls, who trembled lest their mothers should espy them. Either the sudden gleams of light flashing over the obscure field bedazzled Goodman Brown, or he recognized a score of the church members of Salem village famous for their especial sanctity. Good old Deacon Gookin had arrived and waited at the skirts of that venerable saint, his revered pastor. But, irreverently consorting with these grave, reputable, and pious people, these elders of the church, these chaste dames and dewy virgins, there were men of dissolute lives and women of spotted fame, wretches given over to all mean and filthy vice, and suspected even of horrid crimes. It was strange to see that the good shrank not from the wicked, nor were the sinners abashed by the saints. Scattered also among their pale-faced enemies were the Indian priests, or powwows, who had often scared their native forest with more hideous incantations than any known to English witchcraft.

"But where is Faith?" thought Goodman Brown; and, as hope came into his heart, he trembled.

Another verse of the hymn arose, a slow and mournful strain such as the pious love, but joined to words expressed all that our nature can conceive of sin, and darkly hinted at far more. Unfathomable to mere mortals is the lore of fiends. Verse after verse was sung; and still the chorus of the desert swelled between like the deepest tone of a mighty organ; and with the final peal of that dreadful anthem there came a sound as if the roaring wind, the rushing streams, the howling beasts, and every other voice of the unconcerted wilderness were mingling and according with the voice of guilty man in homage to the prince of all. The four blazing pines threw up a loftier flame and obscurely discovered shapes and visages of horror on the smoke wreaths above the impious assembly. At the same moment the fire on the rock shot redly forth and formed a glowing arch above its base, where now appeared a figure. With reverence be it spoken, the figure bore no slight similitude both in garb and manner to some grave divine of the New England churches.

"Bring forth the converts!" cried a voice that echoed through the field and rolled into the forest.

At the word, Goodman Brown stepped forth from the shadow of the trees and approached the congregation, with whom he felt a loathful brotherhood by the sympathy of all that was wicked in his heart. He could have well-nigh sworn that the shape of his own dead father beckoned him to advance, looking downward from a smoke wreath, while a woman with dim features of despair threw out her hand to warn him back. Was it his mother? But he had no power to retreat one step, nor to resist, even in thought, when the minister and good old Deacon Gookin seized his arms and led him to the blazing rock. Thither came also the slender form of a veiled female led between Goody Cloyse, that pious teacher of the catechism, and Martha Carrier, who had received the devil's promise to be a queen of hell. A rampant hag was she. And there stood the proselytes beneath the canopy of fire.

"Welcome, my children," said the dark figure, "to the communion of your race. Ye have found thus young your nature and your destiny. My children, look behind you!"

They turned; and flashing forth, as it were, in a sheet of flame, the fiend worshippers were seen; the smile of welcome gleamed darkly on every visage.

"There," resumed the sable form, "are all whom ye have reverenced from youth. Ye deemed them holier than yourselves and shrank from your own sin, contrasting it with their lives of righteousness and prayerful aspirations heavenward. Yet here are they all in my worshipping assembly. This night it shall be granted you to know their secret deeds: how hoary-bearded elders of the church have whispered wanton words to the young maids of their households; how many a woman, eager for widow's weeds, has given her husband a drink at bedtime and let him sleep his last sleep in her bosom; how beardless youths have made haste to inherit their fathers' wealth; and how fair damsels—blush not, sweet ones—have dug little graves in the garden, and bidden me, the sole guest, to an infant's funeral. By the sympathy of your human hearts for sin ye shall scent out all the places—whether in church, bedchamber, street, field, or forest—where crime has been committed, and shall exult to behold the whole earth one stain of guilt, one mighty blood spot. Far more than this. It shall be yours to penetrate, in every bosom, the deep mystery of sin, the fountain of all wicked arts, and which inexhaustibly supplies more evil impulses than human power—than my power at its utmost—can make manifest in deeds. And now, my children, look upon each other."

They did so; and by the blaze of the hell-kindled torches the wretched man beheld his Faith, and the wife her husband, trembling before that unhallowed altar.

"Lo, there ye stand, my children," said the figure in a deep and solemn tone, almost sad with its despairing awfulness, as if his once angelic nature could yet mourn for our miserable race. "Depending upon one another's hearts, ye had still hoped that virtue were not all a dream. Now are ye undeceived. Evil is the nature of mankind. Evil must be your only happiness. Welcome again, my children, to the communion of your race."

"Welcome," repeated the fiend worshippers, in one cry of despair and triumph.

And there they stood, the only pair, as it seemed, who were yet hesitating on the verge of wickedness in this dark world. A basin was hollowed, naturally, in the rock. Did it contain water, reddened by the lurid light? or was it blood? or, perchance, a liquid flame? Herein did the shape of evil dip his hand and prepare to lay the mark of baptism upon their foreheads, that they might be partakers of the mystery of sin, more conscious of the secret guilt of others, both in deed and thought, than they could now be of their own. The husband cast one look at his pale wife, and Faith at him. What polluted wretches would the next glance show them to each other, shuddering alike at what they disclosed and what they saw!

"Faith! Faith!" cried the husband, "look up to heaven, and resist the wicked one."

Whether Faith obeyed he knew not. Hardly had he spoken when he found himself amid calm night and solitude, listening to a roar of the wind which died heavily away through the forest. He staggered against the rock and felt it chill and damp; while a hanging twig that had been all on fire besprinkled his cheek with the coldest dew.

The next morning young Goodman Brown came slowly into the street of Salem village, staring around him like a bewildered man. The good old minister was taking a walk along the graveyard to get an appetite for breakfast and meditate his sermon, and bestowed a blessing as he passed on Goodman Brown. He shrank from the venerable saint as if to avoid an anathema. Old Deacon Gookin was at domestic worship, and the holy words of his prayer were heard through the open window. "What God doth the wizard pray to?" quoth Goodman Brown. Goody Cloyse, that excellent old Christian, stood in the early sunshine at her own lattice, catechizing a little girl who had brought her a pint of morning's milk. Goodman Brown snatched away the child as from the grasp of the fiend himself. Turning the corner by the meeting-house, he spied the head of Faith, with the pink ribbons, gazing anxiously forth and bursting into such joy at sight of him that she skipped along the street and almost kissed her husband before the whole village. But Goodman Brown looked sternly and sadly into her face and passed on without a greeting.

Had Goodman Brown fallen asleep in the forest and only dreamed a wild dream of a witch-meeting?

Be it so if you will; but, alas! it was a dream of evil omen for young Goodman Brown. A stern, a sad, a darkly meditative, a distrustful if not a desperate man did he become from the night of that fearful dream. On the Sabbath day, when the congregation were singing a holy psalm, he could not listen because an anthem of sin rushed loudly upon his ear and drowned all the blessed strain. When the minister spoke from the pulpit with power and fervid eloquence, and, with his hand on the open Bible, of the sacred truths of our religion, and of saintlike lives and triumphant deaths, and of future bliss or misery unutterable, then did Goodman Brown turn pale, dreading lest the roof should thunder down upon the gray blasphemer and his hearers. Often, waking suddenly at midnight, he shrank from the bosom of Faith; and at morning or eventide, when the family knelt down at prayer, he scowled and muttered to himself, and gazed sternly at his wife, and turned away. And when he had lived long, and was borne to his grave a hoary corpse, followed by Faith, an aged woman, and children and grandchildren, a goodly procession, besides neighbors not a few, they carved no hopeful verse upon his tombstone, for his dying hour was gloom.

D. H. Lawrence

THE BLIND MAN

Isabel Pervin was listening for two sounds —for the sound of wheels on the drive outside and for the noise of her husband's footsteps in the hall. Her dearest and oldest friend, a man who seemed almost indispensable to her living, would drive up in the rainy dusk of the closing November day. The trap had gone to fetch him from the station. And her husband, who had been blinded in Flanders, and who had a disfiguring mark on his brow, would be coming in from the outhouses.

He had been home for a year now. He was totally blind. Yet they had been very happy. The Grange was Maurice's own place. The back was a farmstead, and the Wernhams, who occupied the rear premises, acted as farmers. Isabel lived with her husband in the handsome rooms in front. She and he had been almost entirely alone together since he was wounded. They talked and sang and read together in a wonderful and unspeakable intimacy. Then she reviewed books for a Scottish newspaper, carrying on her old interest, and he occupied himself a good deal with the farm. Sightless, he could still discuss everything with Wernham, and he could also do a good deal of work about the place—menial work, it is true, but it gave him satisfaction. He milked the cows, carried in the pails, turned the separator, attended to the pigs and horses. Life was still very full and strangely serene for the blind man, peaceful with the almost incomprehensible peace of immediate contact in darkness. With his wife he had a whole world, rich and real and invisible.

They were newly and remotely happy. He did not even regret the loss of his sight in these times of dark, palpable joy. A certain exultance swelled his soul.

But as time wore on, sometimes the rich glamor would leave them. Sometimes, after months of this intensity, a sense of burden overcame Isabel, a weariness, a terrible ennui, in that silent house approached between a colonnade of tall-shafted pines. Then she felt she would go mad, for she could not bear it. And sometimes he had devastating fits of depression, which seemed to lay waste his whole being. It was worse than depression—a black misery, when his

own life was a torture to him, and when his presence was unbearable to his wife. The dread went down to the roots of her soul as these black days recurred. In a kind of panic she tried to wrap herself up still further in her husband. She forced the old spontaneous cheerfulness and joy to continue. But the effort it cost her was almost too much. She knew she could not keep it up. She felt she would scream with the strain, and would give anything, anything, to escape. She longed to possess her husband utterly; it gave her inordinate joy to have him entirely to herself. And yet, when again he was gone in a black and massive misery, she could not bear him, she could not bear herself; she wished she could be snatched away off the earth altogether, anything rather than live at this cost.

Dazed, she schemed for a way out. She invited friends, she tried to give him some further connection with the outer world. But it was no good. After all their joy and suffering, after their dark, great year of blindness and solitude and unspeakable nearness, other people seemed to them both shallow, prattling, rather impertinent. Shallow prattle seemed presumptuous. He became impatient and irritated, she was wearied. And so they lapsed into their solitude again. For they preferred it.

But now, in a few weeks' time, her second baby would be born. The first had died, an infant, when her husband first went out to France. She looked with joy and relief to the coming of the second. It would be her salvation. But also she felt some anxiety. She was thirty years old, her husband was a year younger. They both wanted the child very much. Yet she could not help feeling afraid. She had her husband on her hands, a terrible joy to her, and a terrifying burden. The child would occupy her love and attention. And then, what of Maurice? What would he do? If only she could feel that he, too, would be at peace and happy when the child came!

She did so want to luxuriate in a rich, physical satisfaction of maternity. But the man, what would he do? How could she provide for him, how avert those shattering black moods of his, which destroyed them both?

She sighed with fear. But at this time Bertie Reid wrote to Isabel. He was her old friend, a second or third cousin, a Scotchman, as she was a Scotchwoman. They had been brought up near to one another, and all her life he had been her friend, like a brother, but better than her own brothers. She loved him—though not in the marrying sense. There was a sort of kinship between them, an affinity. They understood one another instinctively. But Isabel would never have thought of marrying Bertie. It would have seemed like marrying in her own family.

Bertie was a barrister and a man of letters, a Scotchman of the intellectual type, quick, ironical, sentimental, and on his knees before the woman he adored but did not want to marry. Maurice Pervin was different. He came of a good old country family—the Grange was not a very great distance from Oxford. He was passionate, sensitive, perhaps over-sensitive, wincing—a big fellow with heavy limbs and a forehead that flushed painfully. For his mind was slow, as if drugged by the strong provincial blood that beat in his veins. He was very sensitive to his own mental slowness, his feelings being quick and acute. So that he was just the opposite to Bertie, whose mind was much quicker than his emotions, which were not so very fine.

From the first the two men did not like each other. Isabel felt that they ought to get on together. But they did not. She felt that if only each could have the clue to the other there would be such a rare understanding between them. It did not come off, however. Bertie adopted a slightly ironical attitude, very offensive to Maurice, who returned the Scotch irony with English re-

sentment, a resentment which deepened sometimes into stupid hatred.

This was a little puzzling to Isabel. However, she accepted it in the course of things. Men were made freakish and unreasonable. Therefore, when Maurice was going out to France for the second time, she felt that, for her husband's sake, she must discontinue her friendship with Bertie. She wrote to the barrister to this effect. Bertram Reid simply replied that in this, as in all other matters, he must obey her wishes, if these were indeed her wishes.

For nearly two years nothing had passed between the two friends. Isabel rather gloried in the fact; she had no compunction. She had one great article of faith, which was that husband and wife should be so important to one another that the rest of the world simply did not count. She and Maurice were husband and wife. They loved one another. They would have children. Then let everybody and everything else fade into insignificance outside this connubial felicity. She professed herself quite happy and ready to receive Maurice's friends. She was happy and ready: the happy wife, the ready woman in possession. Without knowing why, the friends retired abashed and came no more. Maurice, of course, took as much satisfaction in this connubial absorption as Isabel did.

He shared in Isabel's literary activities, she cultivated a real interest in agriculture and cattle-raising. For she, being at heart perhaps an emotional enthusiast, always cultivated the practical side of life and prided herself on her mastery of practical affairs. Thus the husband and wife had spent the five years of their married life. The last had been one of blindness and unspeakable intimacy. And now Isabel felt a great indifference coming over her, a sort of lethargy. She wanted to be allowed to bear her child in peace, to nod by the fire and drift vaguely, physically, from day to day. Maurice was like an ominous thundercloud. She had to keep waking up to re-member him.

When a little note came from Bertie, asking if he were to put up a tombstone to their dead friendship and speaking of the real pain he felt on account of her hus-band's loss of sight, she felt a pang, a flut-tering agitation of reawakening. And she read the letter to Maurice.

"Ask him to come down," he said.

"Ask Bertie to come here!" she re-echoed.

"Yes—if he wants to."

Isabel paused for a few moments.

"I know he wants to—he'd only be too glad," she replied. "But what about you, Maurice? How would you like it?"

"I should like it."

"Well—in that case— But I thought you didn't care for him—"

"Oh, I don't know. I might think dif-ferently of him now," the blind man re-plied. It was rather abstruse to Isabel.

"Well, dear," she said, "if you're quite sure—"

"I'm sure enough. Let him come," said Maurice.

So Bertie was coming, coming this even-ing, in the November rain and darkness. Isabel was agitated, racked with her old restlessness and indecision. She had always suffered from this pain of doubt, just an agonizing sense of uncertainty. It had begun to pass off, in the lethargy of maternity. Now it returned, and she resented it. She struggled as usual to maintain her calm, composed, friendly bearing, a sort of mask she wore over all her body.

A woman had lighted a tall lamp beside the table and spread the cloth. The long dining room was dim, with its elegant but rather severe pieces of old furniture. Only the round table glowed softly under the light. It had a rich, beautiful effect. The white cloth glistened and dropped its heavy, pointed lace corners almost to the carpet, the china was old and handsome, creamy-yellow, with a blotched pattern of harsh red and deep blue, the cups large and bell-shaped, the teapot gallant. Isabel looked at it with superficial appreciation.

Her nerves were hurting her. She looked automatically again at the high, uncur-tained windows. In the last dusk she could just perceive outside a huge fir-tree swaying its boughs: it was as if she thought it rather than saw it. The rain came flying on the windowpanes. Ah, why had she no peace? These two men, why did they tear at her? Why did they not come—why was there this suspense?

She sat in a lassitude that was really sus-pense and irritation. Maurice, at least, might come in—there was nothing to keep him out. She rose to her feet. Catching sight of her reflection in a mirror, she glanced at herself with a slight smile of recognition, as if she were an old friend to herself. Her face was oval and calm, her nose a little arched. Her neck made a beautiful line down to her shoulder. With hair knotted loosely behind, she had something of a warm, maternal look. Thinking this of her-self, she arched her eyebrows and her rather heavy eyelids, with a little flicker of a smile, and for a moment her grey eyes looked amused and wicked, a little sardonic, out of her transfigured Madonna face.

Then, resuming her air of womanly patience—she was really fatally self-deter-mined—she went with a little jerk towards the door. Her eyes were slightly reddened.

She passed down the wide hall and through a door at the end. Then she was in the farm premises. The scent of dairy, and of farm kitchen, and of farmyard and of leather almost overcame her: but parti-cularly the scent of dairy. They had been scalding out the pans. The flagged passage in front of her was dark, puddled, and wet. Light came out from the open kitchen door. She went forward and stood in the doorway. The farm people were at tea, seated at a little distance from her, round a long, nar-row table, in the center of which stood a white lamp. Ruddy faces, ruddy hands holding food, red mouths working, heads bent over the teacups: men, land-girls, boys: it was teatime, feeding time. Some faces caught sight of her. Mrs. Wernham, going round behind the chairs with a large black teapot, halting slightly in her walk, was not aware of her for a moment. Then she turned suddenly.

"Oh, is it Madam!" she exclaimed. "Come in, then, come in! We're at tea." And she dragged forward a chair.

"No, I won't come in," said Isabel. "I'm afraid I interrupt your meal."

"No—no—not likely, Madam, not likely."

"Hasn't Mr. Pervin come in, do you know?"

"I'm sure I couldn't say! Missed him, have you, Madam?"

"No, I only wanted him to come in," laughed Isabel, as if shyly.

"Wanted him, did ye? Get up, boy—get up, now—"

Mrs. Wernham knocked one of the boys on the shoulder. He began to scrape to his feet, chewing largely.

"I believe he's in top stable," said another face from the table.

"Ah! No, don't get up. I'm going myself," said Isabel.

"Don't you go out of a dirty night like this. Let the lad go. Get along wi' ye, boy," said Mrs. Wernham.

"No, no," said Isabel, with a decision that was always obeyed. "Go on with your tea, Tom. I'd like to go across to the stable, Mrs. Wernham."

"Did ever you hear tell!" exclaimed the woman.

"Isn't the trap late?" asked Isabel.

"Why, no," said Mrs. Wernham, peering into the distance at the tall, dim clock. "No, Madam—we can give it another quarter or twenty minutes yet, good—yes, every bit of a quarter."

"Ah! It seems late when darkness falls so early," said Isabel.

"It do, that it do. Bother the days, that they draw in so," answered Mrs. Wernham. "Proper miserable!"

"They are," said Isabel, withdrawing.

She pulled on her overshoes, wrapped a large tartan shawl around her, put on a man's felt hat, and ventured out along the causeways of the first yard. It was very dark. The wind was roaring in the great elms behind the outhouses. When she came to the second yard the darkness seemed deeper. She was unsure of her footing. She wished she had brought a lantern. Rain blew against her. Half she liked it, half she felt unwilling to battle.

She reached at last the just-visible door of the stable. There was no sign of a light anywhere. Opening the upper half, she looked in: into a simple well of darkness. The smell of horses and ammonia, and of warmth was startling to her, in that full night. She listened with all her ears but could hear nothing save the night, and the stirring of a horse.

"Maurice!" she called, softly and musically, though she was afraid. "Maurice—are you there?"

Nothing came from the darkness. She knew the rain and wind blew in upon the horses, the hot animal life. Feeling it wrong, she entered the stable and drew the lower half of the door shut, holding the upper part close. She did not stir, because she was aware of the presence of the dark hindquarters of the horses, though she could not see them, and she was afraid. Something wild stirred in her heart.

She listened intensely. Then she heard a small noise in the distance—far away, it seemed—the chink of a pan, and a man's voice speaking a brief word. It would be Maurice, in the other part of the stable. She stood motionless, waiting for him to come through the partition door. The horses were so terrifyingly near to her, in the invisible.

The loud jarring of the inner door-latch made her start; the door was opened. She could hear and feel her husband entering and invisibly passing among the horses near to her, in darkness as they were, actively intermingled. The rather low sound of his voice as he spoke to the horses came velvety to her nerves. How near he was, and how invisible! The darkness seemed to be in a strange swirl of violent life, just upon her. She turned giddy.

Her presence of mind made her call quietly and musically:

"Maurice! Maurice—dea-ar!"

"Yes," he answered. "Isabel?"

She saw nothing, and the sound of his voice seemed to touch her.

"Hello!" she answered cheerfully, straining her eyes to see him. He was still busy, attending to the horses near her, but she saw only darkness. It made her almost desperate.

"Won't you come in, dear?" she said.

"Yes, I'm coming. Just half a minute. Stand over—now! Trap's not come, has it?"

"Not yet," said Isabel.

His voice was pleasant and ordinary, but it had a slight suggestion of the stable to her. She wished he would come away. Whilst he was so utterly invisible, she was afraid of him.

"How's the time?" he asked.

"Not yet six," she replied. She disliked to answer into the dark. Presently he came very near to her, and she retreated out of doors.

"The weather blows in here," he said, coming steadily forward, feeling for the doors. She shrank away. At last she could dimly see him.

"Bertie won't have much of a drive," he said, as he closed the doors.

"He won't indeed!" said Isabel calmly, watching the dark shape at the door.

"Give me your arm, dear," she said.

She pressed his arm close to her, as she went. But she longed to see him, to look at him. She was nervous. He walked erect, with face rather lifted, but with a curious tentative movement of his powerful, muscular legs. She could feel the clever, careful, strong contact of his feet with the earth, as she balanced against him. For a moment he was a tower of darkness to her, as if he rose out of the earth.

In the house-passage he wavered and went cautiously, with a curious look of silence about him as he felt for the bench. Then he sat down heavily. He was a man with rather sloping shoulders but with heavy limbs, powerful legs that seemed to know the earth. His head was small, usually carried high and light. As he bent down to unfasten his gaiters and boots he did not look blind. His hair was brown and crisp, his hands were large, reddish, intelligent, the veins stoood out in the wrists; and his thighs and knees seemed massive. When he stood up his face and neck were surcharged with blood, the veins stood out on his temples. She did not look at his blindness.

Isabel was always glad when they had passed through the dividing door into their own regions of repose and beauty. She was a little afraid of him, out there in the animal grossness of the back. His bearing also changed, as he smelt the familiar indefinable odor that pervaded his wife's surroundings, a delicate, refined scent, very faintly spicy. Perhaps it came from the potpourri bowls.

He stood at the foot of the stairs, arrested, listening. She watched him, and her heart sickened. He seemed to be listening to fate.

"He's not here yet," he said. "I'll go up and change."

"Maurice," she said, "you're not wishing he wouldn't come, are you?"

"I couldn't quite say," he answered. "I feel myself rather on the qui vive."

"I can see you are," she answered. And she reached up and kissed his cheek. She saw his mouth relax into a slow smile.

"What are you laughing at?" she said roguishly.

"You consoling me," he answered.

"Nay," she answered. "Why should I console you? You know we love each other —you know how married we are! What does anything else matter?"

"Nothing at all, my dear."

He felt for her face and touched it, smiling.

"You're all right, aren't you?" he asked anxiously.

"I'm wonderfully all right, love," she answered. "It's you I am a little troubled about, at times."

"Why me?" he said, touching her cheeks delicately with the tips of his fingers. The touch had an almost hypnotizing effect on her.

He went away upstairs. She saw him mount into the darkness, unseeing and unchanging. He did not know that the lamps on the upper corridor were unlighted. He went on into the darkness with unchanging step. She heard him in the bathroom.

Pervin moved about almost unconsciously in his familiar surroundings, dark though everything was. He seemed to know the presence of objects before he touched them. It was a pleasure to him to rock thus through a world of things, carried on the flood in a sort of blood-prescience. He did not think much or trouble much. So long as he kept this sheer immediacy of blood-contact with the substantial world he was happy, he wanted no intervention of visual consciousness. In this state there was a certain rich positivity, bordering sometimes on rapture. Life seemed to move in him like a tide lapping, lapping, and advancing, enveloping all things darkly. It was a pleasure to stretch forth the hand and meet the unseen object, clasp it, and possess it in pure contact. He did not try to remember, to visualize. He did not want to. The new way of consciousness substituted itself in him.

The rich suffusion of this state generally kept him happy, reaching its culmination in the consuming passion for his wife. But at times the flow would seem to be checked and thrown back. Then it would beat inside him like a tangled sea, and he was tortured in the shattered chaos of his own blood. He grew to dread this arrest, this throwback, this chaos inside himself, when he seemed merely at the mercy of his own powerful and conflicting elements. How to get some measure of control or surety, this was the question. And when the question rose maddening in him, he would clench his fists as if he would compel the whole universe to submit to him. But it was in vain. He could not even compel himself.

Tonight, however, he was still serene, though little tremors of unreasonable exasperation ran through him. He had to handle the razor very carefully, as he shaved, for it was not at one with him, he was afraid of it. His hearing also was too much sharpened. He heard the woman lighting the lamps on the corridor and attending to the fire in the visitor's room. And then, as he went to his room, he heard the trap arrive. Then came Isabel's voice, lifted and calling, like a bell ringing:

"Is it you, Bertie? Have you come?"

And a man's voice answered out of the wind:

"Hello, Isabel! There you are."

"Have you had a miserable drive? I'm so sorry we couldn't send a closed carriage. I can't see you at all, you know."

"I'm coming. No, I liked the drive—it was like Perthshire. Well, how are you? You're looking fit as ever, as far as I can see."

"Oh, yes" said Isabel. "I'm wonderfully well. How are you? Rather thin, I think—"

"Worked to death—everybody's old cry. But I'm all right, Ciss. How's Pervin?—isn't he here?"

"Oh, yes, he's upstairs changing. Yes, he's awfully well. Take off your wet things; I'll send them to be dried."

"And how are you both, in spirits? He doesn't fret?"

"No—no, not at all. No, on the contrary, really. We've been wonderfully happy, incredibly. It's more than I can understand—so wonderful: the nearness, and the peace—"

"Ah! Well, that's awfully good news—"

They moved away. Pervin heard no more. But a childish sense of desolation had come over him, as he heard their brisk voices. He seemed shut out—like a child that is left out. He was aimless and excluded, he did not know what to do with himself. The helpless desolation came over him. He fumbled nervously as he dressed himself, in a state almost of childishness. He disliked the Scotch accent in Bertie's speech, and the slight response it found on Isabel's tongue. He disliked the slight purr of complacency in the Scottish speech. He disliked intensely the glib way in which Isabel spoke of their happiness and nearness. It made him recoil. He was fretful and beside himself like a child, he had almost a childish nostalgia to be included in the life circle. And at the same time he was a man, dark and powerful and infuriated by his own weakness. By some fatal flaw, he could not be by himself, he had to depend on the support of another. And this very dependence enraged him. He hated Bertie Reid, and at the same time he knew the hatred was nonsense, he knew it was the outcome of his own weakness.

He went downstairs. Isabel was alone in the dining-room. She watched him enter, head erect, his feet tentative. He looked so strong-blooded and healthy and, at the same time, cancelled. Cancelled—that was

the word that flew across her mind. Perhaps it was his scar suggested it.

"You heard Bertie come, Maurice?" she said.

"Yes—isn't he here?"

"He's in his room. He looks very thin and worn."

"I suppose he works himself to death."

A woman came in with a tray—and after a few minutes Bertie came down. He was a little dark man, with a very big forehead, thin, wispy hair, and sad, large eyes. His expression was inordinately sad—almost funny. He had odd, short legs.

Isabel watched him hesitate under the door and glance nervously at her husband. Pervin heard him and turned.

"Here you are, now," said Isabel. "Come, let us eat."

Bertie went across to Maurice.

"How are you, Pervin?" he said as he advanced.

The blind man stuck his hand out into space, and Bertie took it.

"Very fit. Glad you've come," said Maurice. Isabel glanced at them and glanced away, as if she could not bear to see them.

"Come," she said. "Come to table. Aren't you both awfully hungry? I am, tremendously."

"I'm afraid you waited for me," said Bertie, as they sat down.

Maurice had a curious monolithic way of sitting in a chair, erect and distant. Isabel's heart always beat when she caught sight of him thus.

"No," she replied to Bertie. "We're very little later than usual. We're having a sort of high tea, not dinner. Do you mind? It gives us such a nice long evening, uninterrupted."

"I like it," said Bertie.

Maurice was feeling, with curious little movements, almost like a cat kneading her bed, for his plate, his knife and fork, his napkin. He was getting the whole geography of his cover into his consciousness. He sat erect and inscrutable, remote-seeming. Bertie watched the static figure of the blind man, the delicate tactile discernment of the large, ruddy hands, and the curious mindless silence of the brow, above the scar. With difficulty he looked away and, without knowing what he did, picked up a little crystal bowl of violets from the table and held them to his nose.

"They are sweet-scented," he said. "Where do they come from?"

"From the garden—under the windows," said Isabel.

"So late in the year—and so fragrant! Do you remember the violets under Aunt Bell's south wall?"

The two friends looked at each other and exchanged a smile, Isabel's eyes lighting up.

"Don't I?" she replied. "Wasn't she queer!"

"A curious old girl," laughed Bertie. "There's a streak of freakishness in the family, Isabel."

"Ah—but not in you and me, Bertie," said Isabel. "Give them to Maurice, will you?" she added, as Bertie was putting down the flowers. "Have you smelled the violets, dear? Do!—they are so scented."

Maurice held out his hand, and Bertie placed the tiny bowl against his large, warm-looking fingers. Maurice's hand closed over the thin white fingers of the barrister. Bertie carefully extricated himself. Then the two watched the blind man smelling the violets. He bent his head and seemed to be thinking. Isabel waited.

"Aren't they sweet, Maurice?" she said at last, anxiously.

"Very," he said. And he held out the bowl. Bertie took it. Both he and Isabel were a little afraid, and deeply disturbed.

The meal continued. Isabel and Bertie chatted spasmodically. The blind man was silent. He touched his food repeatedly, with quick, delicate touches of his knife-point, then cut irregular bits. He could not bear to be helped. Both Isabel and Bertie suffered: Isabel wondered why. She did not suffer when she was alone with Maurice. Bertie made her conscious of a strangeness.

After the meal the three drew their chairs to the fire and sat down to talk. The decanters were put on a table near at hand. Isabel knocked the logs on the fire, and clouds of brilliant sparks went up the chimney. Bertie noticed a slight weariness in her bearing.

"You will be glad when your child comes now, Isabel?" he said.

She looked up to him with a quick wan smile.

"Yes, I shall be glad," she answered. "It begins to seem long. Yes, I shall be very glad. So will you, Maurice, won't you?" she added.

"Yes, I shall," replied her husband.

"We are both looking forward so much to having it," she said.

"Yes, of course," said Bertie.

He was a bachelor, three or four years older than Isabel. He lived in beautiful rooms overlooking the river, guarded by a faithful Scottish manservant. And he had his friends among the fair sex—not lovers, friends. So long as he could avoid any danger of courtship or marriage, he adored a few good women with constant and unfailing homage, and he was chivalrously fond of quite a number. But if they seemed to encroach on him, he withdrew and detested them.

Isabel knew him very well, knew his beautiful constancy, and kindness, also his incurable weakness, which made him unable ever to enter into close contact of any sort. He was ashamed of himself because he could not marry, could not approach women physically. He wanted to do so. But he could not. At the center of him he was afraid, helplessly and even brutally afraid. He had given up hope, had ceased to expect any more that he could escape his own weakness. Hence he was a brilliant and successful barrister, also a *littérateur* of high repute, a rich man, and a great social success. At the center he felt himself neuter, nothing.

Isabel knew him well. She despised him even while she admired him. She looked at his sad face, his little short legs, and felt contempt of him. She looked at his dark grey eyes, with their uncanny, almost child-like, intuition, and she loved him. He understood amazingly—but she had no fear of his understanding. As a man she patronized him.

And she turned to the impassive, silent figure of her husband. He sat leaning back with folded arms and face a little uptilted. His knees were straight and massive. She sighed, picked up the poker, and again began to prod the fire, to rouse the clouds of soft brilliant sparks.

"Isabel tells me," Bertie began suddenly, "that you have not suffered unbearably from the loss of sight."

Maurice straightened himself to attend but kept his arms folded.

"No," he said, "not unbearably. Now and again one struggles against it, you know. But there are compensations."

"They say it is much worse to be stone deaf," said Isabel.

"I believe it is," said Bertie. "Are there compensations?" he added to Maurice.

"Yes. You cease to bother about a great many things." Again Maurice stretched his figure, stretched the strong muscles of his back, and leaned backwards, with uplifted face.

"And that is a relief," said Bertie. "But what is there in place of the bothering? What replaces the activity?"

There was a pause. At length the blind man replied, as out of a negligent, unattentive thinking:

"Oh, I don't know. There's a good deal when you're not active."

"Is there?" said Bertie. "What, exactly? It always seems to me that when there is no thought and no action, there is nothing."

Again Maurice was slow in replying.

"There is something," he replied. "I couldn't tell you what it is."

And the talk lapsed once more, Isabel and Bertie chatting gossip and reminiscence, the blind man silent.

At length Maurice rose restlessly, a big obtrusive figure. He felt tight and hampered. He wanted to go away.

"Do you mind," he said, "if I go and speak to Wernham?"

"No—go along, dear," said Isabel.

And he went out. A silence came over the two friends. At length Bertie said:

"Nevertheless, it is a great deprivation, Cissie."

"It is, Bertie. I know it is."

"Something lacking all the time," said Bertie.

"Yes, I know. And yet—and yet—Maurice is right. There is something else, something there, which you never knew was there, and which you can't express."

"What is there?" asked Bertie.

"I don't know—it's awfully hard to define it—but something strong and immediate. There's something strange in Maurice's presence—indefinable—but I couldn't do without it. I agree that it seems to put one's mind to sleep. But when we're alone I miss nothing, it seems awfully rich, almost splendid, you know."

"I'm afraid I don't follow," said Bertie.

They talked desultorily. The wind blew loudly outside, rain chattered on the window-panes, making a sharp drum-sound because of the closed, mellow-golden shutters inside. The logs burned slowly, with hot, almost invisible small flames. Bertie seemed uneasy; there were dark circles round his eyes. Isabel, rich with her approaching maternity, leaned looking into the fire. Her hair curled in odd, loose strands, very pleasing to the man. But she had a curious feeling of old woe in her heart, old timeless night woe.

"I suppose we're all deficient somewhere," said Bertie.

"I suppose so," said Isabel wearily.

"Damned, sooner or later."

"I don't know," she said, rousing herself. "I feel quite all right, you know. The child coming seems to make me indifferent to everything, just placid. I can't feel that there's anything to trouble about, you know."

"A good thing, I should say," he replied slowly.

"Well, there it is. I suppose it's just nature. If only I felt I needn't trouble about Maurice, I should be perfectly content—"

"But you feel you must trouble about him?"

"Well—I don't know—" She even resented this much effort.

The night passed slowly. Isabel looked at the clock. "I say," she said. "It's nearly ten o'clock. Where can Maurice be? I'm sure they're all in bed at the back. Excuse me a moment."

She went out, returning almost immediately.

"It's all shut up and in darkness," she said. "I wonder where he is. He must have gone out to the farm—"

Bertie looked at her.

"I suppose he'll come in," he said.

"I suppose so," she said. "But it's unusual for him to be out now."

"Would you like me to go out and see?"

"Well—if you wouldn't mind. I'd go, but—" She did not want to make the physical effort.

Bertie put on an old overcoat and took a lantern. He went out from the side door. He shrank from the wet and roaring night. Such weather had a nervous effect on him: too much moisture everywhere made him feel almost imbecile. Unwilling, he went

through it all. A dog barked violently at him. He peered in all the buildings. At last, as he opened the upper door of a sort of intermediate barn, he heard a grinding noise, and looking in, holding up his lantern, saw Maurice, in his shirtsleeves, standing listening, holding the handle of a turnip-pulper. He had been pulping sweet roots, a pile of which lay dimly heaped in a corner behind him.

"That you, Wernham?" said Maurice, listening.

"No, it's me," said Bertie.

A large, half-wild grey cat was rubbing at Maurice's leg. The blind man stooped to rub its sides. Bertie watched the scene, then unconsciously entered and shut the door behind him. He was in a high sort of barn-place, from which, right and left, ran off the corridors in front of the stalled cattle. He watched the slow, stooping motion of the other man, as he caressed the great cat.

Maurice straightened himself.

"You came to look for me?" he said.

"Isabel was a little uneasy," said Bertie.

"I'll come in. I like messing about doing these jobs."

The cat had reared her sinister, feline length against his leg, clawing at his thigh affectionately. He lifted her claws out of his flesh.

"I hope I'm not in your way at all at the Grange here," said Bertie, rather shy and stiff.

"My way? No, not a bit. I'm glad Isabel has somebody to talk to. I'm afraid it's I who am in the way. I know I'm not very lively company. Isabel's all right, don't you think? She's not unhappy, is she?"

"I don't think so."

"What does she say?"

"She says she's very content—only a little troubled about you."

"Why me?"

"Perhaps afraid that you might brood," said Bertie, cautiously.

"She needn't be afraid of that," He continued to caress the flattened grey head of the cat with his fingers. "What I am a bit afraid of," he resumed, "is that she'll find me a dead weight, always alone with me down here."

"I don't think you need think that," said Bertie, though this was what he feared himself.

"I don't know," said Maurice. "Sometimes I feel it isn't fair that she's saddled with me." Then he dropped his voice curiously. "I say," he asked, secretly struggling, "is my face much disfigured? Do you mind telling me?"

"There is the scar," said Bertie, wondering. "Yes, it is a disfigurement. But more pitiable than shocking."

"A pretty bad scar, though," said Maurice.

"Oh, yes."

There was a pause.

"Sometimes I feel I am horrible," said Maurice, in a low voice, talking as if to himself. And Bertie actually felt a quiver of horror.

"That's nonsense," he said.

Maurice again straightened himself, leaving the cat.

"There's no telling," he said. Then again, in an odd tone, he added: "I don't really know you, do I?"

"Probably not," said Bertie.

"Do you mind if I touch you?"

The lawyer shrank away instinctively. And yet, out of very philanthropy, he said, in a small voice: "Not at all."

But he suffered as the blind man stretched out a strong, naked hand to him. Maurice accidentally knocked off Bertie's hat.

"I thought you were taller," he said, starting. Then he laid his hand on Bertie Reid's head, closing the dome of the skull in a soft, firm grasp, gathering it, as it were; then, shifting his grasp and softly closing again, with a fine, close pressure, till he had covered the skull and the face of the smaller man, tracing the brows and touching the full, closed eyes, touching the small nose and the nostrils, the rough, short moustache, the mouth, the rather strong chin. The hand of the blind man grasped the shoulder, the arm, the hand of the other man. He seemed to take him, in the soft, travelling grasp.

"You seem young," he said quietly, at last.

The lawyer stood almost annihilated, unable to answer.

"Your head seems tender, as if you were young," Maurice repeated. "So do your hands. Touch my eyes, will you?—touch my scar."

Now Bertie quivered with revulsion. Yet he was under the power of the blind man, as if hypnotized. He lifted his hand and laid the fingers on the scar, on the scarred eyes. Maurice suddenly covered them with his own hand, pressed the fingers of the other man upon his disfigured eye-sockets, trembling in every fibre and rocking slightly, slowly, from side to side. He remained thus for a minute or more, whilst Bertie stood as if in a swoon, unconscious, imprisoned.

Then suddenly Maurice removed the hand of the other man from his brow and stood holding it in his own.

"Oh, my God," he said, "we shall know each other now, shan't we? We shall know each other now."

Bertie could not answer. He gazed mute and terror-struck, overcome by his own weakness. He knew he could not answer. He had an unreasonable fear, lest the other man should suddenly destroy him. Whereas Maurice was actually filled with hot, poignant love, the passion of friendship.

Perhaps it was this very passion of friendship which Bertie shrank from most.

"We're all right together now, aren't we?" said Maurice. "It's all right now, as long as we live, so far as we're concerned?"

"Yes," said Bertie, trying by any means to escape.

Maurice stood with head lifted, as if listening. The new delicate fulfilment of mortal friendship had come as a revelation and surprise to him, something exquisite and unhoped-for. He seemed to be listening to hear if it were real.

Then he turned for his coat.

"Come," he said, "we'll go to Isabel."

Bertie took the lantern and opened the door. The cat disappeared. The two men went in silence along the causeways. Isabel, as they came, thought their footsteps sounded strange. She looked up pathetically and anxiously for their entrance. There seemed a curious elation about Maurice. Bertie was haggard, with sunken eyes.

"What is it?" she asked.

"We've become friends," said Maurice, standing with his feet apart, like a strange colossus.

"Friends!" re-echoed Isabel. And she looked again at Bertie. He met her eyes with a furtive, haggard look; his eyes were as if glazed with misery.

"I'm so glad," she said, in sheer perplexity.

"Yes," said Maurice.

He was indeed so glad. Isabel took his hand with boths hers and held it fast.

"You'll be happier now, dear," she said.

But she was watching Bertie. She knew that he had one desire—to escape from this intimacy, this friendship, which had been thrust upon him. He could not bear it that he had been touched by the blind man, his insane reserve broken in. He was like a mollusc whose shell is broken.

James Thurber

THE SECRET LIFE OF WALTER MITTY

"We're going through!" The Commander's voice was like thin ice breaking. He wore his full-dress uniform, with the heavily braided white cap pulled down rakishly over one cold gray eye. "We can't make it, sir. It's spoiling for a hurricane, if you ask me." "I'm not asking you, Lieutenant Berg," said the Commander. "Throw on the power lights! Rev her up to 8,500! We're going through!" The pounding of the cylinders increased: tapocketa-pocketa-pocketa-*pocketa-pocketa*. The Commander stared at the ice forming on the pilot window. He walked over and twisted a row of complicated dials. "Switch on No. 8 auxiliary!" he shouted "Switch on No. 8 auxiliary!" repeated Lieutenant Berg. "Full strength in No. 3 turret!" shouted the Commander. "Full strength in No. 3 turret!" The crew, bending to their various tasks in the huge, hurtling eight-engined Navy hydroplane, looked at each other and grinned. "The Old Man'll get us through," they said to one another. "The Old Man ain't afraid of Hell!" . . .

"Not so fast! You're driving too fast!" said Mrs. Mitty. "What are you driving so fast for?"

"Hmm?" said Walter Mitty. He looked at his wife, in the seat beside him, with shocked astonishment. She seemed grossly unfamiliar, like a strange woman who had yelled at him in a crowd. "You were up to fifty-five," she said. "You know I don't like to go more than forty. You were up to fifty-five." Walter Mitty drove on toward Waterbury in silence, the roaring of the SN202 through the worst storm in twenty years of Navy flying fading in the remote, intimate airways of his mind. "You're tensed up again," said Mrs. Mitty. "It's one of your days. I wish you'd let Dr. Renshaw look you over."

Walter Mitty stopped the car in front of the building where his wife went to have her hair done. "Remember to get those overshoes while I'm having my hair done," she said. "I don't need overshoes," said Mitty. She put her mirror back into her bag. "We've been all through that," she said, getting out of the car. "You're not a young man any longer." He raced the engine a little. "Why don't you wear your gloves? Have you lost your gloves?" Walter Mitty reached in a pocket and brought out the gloves. He put them on, but after she had turned and gone into the building and he had driven on to a red light, he took them off again. "Pick it up, brother!" snapped a cop as the light changed, and Mitty hastily pulled on his gloves and lurched ahead. He drove around the streets aimlessly for a time, and then he drove past the hospital on his way to the parking lot.

. . . "It's the millionaire banker, Wellington McMillan," said the pretty nurse. "Yes?" said Walter Mitty, removing his gloves slowly. "Who has the case?" "Dr. Renshaw and Dr. Benbow, but there are two specialists here, Dr. Remington from New York and Mr. Pritchard-Mitford from London. He flew over." A door opened down a long, cool corridor and Dr. Renshaw came out. He looked distraught and haggard. "Hello, Mitty," he said. "We're having the devil's own time with McMillan, the millionaire banker and close personal friend of Roosevelt. Obstreosis of the ductal tract. Tertiary. Wish you'd take a look at him." "Glad to," said Mitty.

In the operating room there were whispered introductions: "Dr. Remington, Dr. Mitty. Mr. Pritchard-Mitford, Dr. Mitty." "I've read your book on streptothricosis," said Pritchard-Mitford, shaking hands. "A brilliant performance, sir." "Thank you," said Walter Mitty. "Didn't know you were

in the States, Mitty," grumbled Remington. "Coals to Newcastle, bringing Mitford and me here for a tertiary." "You are very kind," said Mitty. A huge, complicated machine, connected to the operating table, with many tubes and wires, began at this moment to go pocketa-pocketa-pocketa. "The new anesthetizer is giving way!" shouted an interne. "There is no one in the East who knows how to fix it!" "Quiet, man!" said Mitty, in a low, cool voice. He sprang to the machine, which was now going pocketa-pocketa-queep-pocketa-queep. He began fingering delicately a row of glistening dials. "Give me a fountain pen!" he snapped. Someone handed him a fountain pen. He pulled a faulty piston out of the machine and inserted the pen in its place. "That will hold for ten minutes," he said. "Get on with the operation." A nurse hurried over and whispered to Renshaw, and Mitty saw the man turn pale. "Coreopsis has set in," said Renshaw nervously. "If you would take over, Mitty?" Mitty looked at him and at the craven figure of Benbow, who drank, and at the grave, uncertain faces of the two great specialists. "If you wish," he said. They slipped a white gown on him; he adjusted a mask and drew on thin gloves; nurses handed him shining. . . .

"Back it up, Mac! Look out for that Buick!" Walter Mitty jammed on the brakes. "Wrong lane, Mac," said the parking-lot attendant, looking at Mitty closely. "Gee. Yeh," muttered Mitty. He began cautiously to back out of the lane marked "Exit Only." "Leave her sit there," said the attendant. "I'll put her away." Mitty got out of the car. "Hey, better leave the key." "Oh," said Mitty, handing the man the ignition key. The attendant vaulted into the car, backed it up with insolent skill, and put it where it belonged.

They're so damn cocky, thought Walter Mitty, walking along Main Street; they think they know everything. Once he had tried to take his chains off, outside New Milford, and he had got them wound around the axles. A man had had to come out in a wrecking car and unwind them, a young, grinning garageman. Since then Mrs. Mitty always made him drive to a garage to have the chains taken off. The next time, he thought, I'll wear my right arm in a sling; they won't grin at me then. I'll have my right arm in a sling and they'll see I couldn't possibly take the chains off myself. He kicked at the slush on the sidewalk. "Overshoes," he said to himself, and he began looking for a shoe store.

When he came out into the street again, with the overshoes in a box under his arm, Walter Mitty began to wonder what the other thing was his wife had told him to get. She had told him twice, before they set out from their house for Waterbury. In a way he hated these weekly trips to town— he was always getting something wrong. Kleenex, he thought, Squibb's, razor blades? No. Toothpaste, toothbrush, bicarbonate, carborundum, initiative and referendum? He gave it up. But she would remember it. "Where's the what's-its-name?" she would ask. "Don't tell me you forgot the what's-its-name?" A newsboy went by shouting something about the Waterbury trial.

. . . "Perhaps this will refresh your memory." The District Attorney suddenly thrust a heavy automatic at the quiet figure on the witness stand. "Have you ever seen this before?" Walter Mitty took the gun and examined it expertly. "This is my Webley-Vickers 50.80," he said calmly. An excited buzz ran around the courtroom. The judge rapped for order. "You are a crack shot with any sort of firearms, I believe?" said the District Attorney, insinuatingly. "Objection!" shouted Mitty's attorney. "We have shown that the defendant could not have fired the shot. We have shown that he wore his right arm in a sling on the night of the fourteenth of July." Walter Mitty raised his hand briefly and the bickering attorneys were stilled. "With any known

make of gun," he said evenly, "I could have killed Gregory Fitzhurst at three hundred feet *with my left hand*." Pandemonium broke loose in the courtroom. A woman's scream rose above the bedlam and suddenly a lovely, dark-haired girl was in Walter Mitty's arms. The District Attorney struck at her savagely. Without rising from his chair, Mitty let the man have it on the point of the chin. "You miserable cur!" . . .

"Puppy biscuit," said Walter Mitty. He stopped walking and the buildings of Waterbury rose up out of the misty courtroom and surrounded him again. A woman who was passing laughed. "He said 'Puppy biscuit,'" she said to her companion. "That man said 'Puppy biscuit' to himself." Walter Mitty hurried on. He went into an A. & P., not the first one he came to but a smaller one farther up the street. "I want some biscuit for small, young dogs," he said to the clerk. "Any special brand, sir?" The greatest pistol shot in the world thought a moment. "It says 'Puppies Bark for It' on the box," said Walter Mitty.

His wife would be through at the hairdresser's in fifteen minutes, Mitty saw in looking at his watch, unless they had trouble drying it; sometimes they had trouble drying it. She didn't like to get to the hotel first; she would want him to be there waiting for her as usual. He found a big leather chair in the lobby, facing a window, and he put the overshoes and the puppy biscuit on the floor beside it. He picked up an old copy of *Liberty* and sank down into the chair. "Can Germany Conquer the World Through the Air?" Walter Mitty looked at the pictures of bombing planes and of ruined streets.

. . . "The cannonading has got the wind up in young Raleigh, sir," said the sergeant. Captain Mitty looked up at him through tousled hair. "Get him to bed," he said wearily. "With the others. I'll fly alone." "But you can't, sir," said the sergeant anxiously. "It takes two men to handle that bomber and the Archies are pounding hell out of the air. Von Richtman's circus is between here and Saulier." "Somebody's got to get that ammunition dump," said Mitty. "I'm going over. Spot of brandy?" He poured a drink for the sergeant and one for himself. War thundered and whined around the dugout and battered at the door. There was a rending of wood and splinters flew through the room. "A bit of a near thing," said Captain Mitty carelessly. "The box barrage is closing in," said the sergeant. "We only live once, Sergeant," said Mitty, with his faint, fleeting smile. "Or do we?" He poured another brandy and tossed it off. "I never see a man could hold his brandy like you sir," said the sergeant. "Begging your pardon, sir." Captain Mitty stood up and strapped on his huge Webley-Vickers automatic. "It's forty kilometers through hell, sir," said the sergeant. Mitty finished one last brandy. "After all," he said softly, "what isn't?" The pounding of the cannon increased; there was the rat-tat-tatting of machine guns, and from somewhere came the menacing pocketa-pocketa-pocketa of the new flame-throwers. Walter Mitty walked to the door of the dugout humming "Auprès de Ma Blonde." He turned and waved to the sergeant. "Cheerio!" he said. . . .

Something struck his shoulder. "I've been looking all over this hotel for you," said Mrs. Mitty. "Why do you have to hide in this old chair? How did you expect me to find you?" "Things close in," said Walter Mitty vaguely. "What?" Mrs. Mitty said. "Did you get the what's-its-name? The puppy biscuit? What's in the box?" "Overshoes," said Mitty. "Couldn't you have put them on in the store?" "I was thinking," said Walter Mitty. "Does it ever occur to you that I am sometimes thinking?" She looked at him. "I'm going to take your temperature when I get you home," she said.

They went out through the revolving doors that made a faintly derisive whistling sound when you pushed them. It was two blocks to the parking lot. At the drugstore on the corner she said "Wait here for me. I forgot something. I won't be a minute." She was more than a minute. Walter Mitty lighted a cigarette. It began to rain, rain with sleet in it. He stood up against the wall of the drugstore, smoking. . . . He put his shoulders back and his heels together. "To hell with the handkerchief," said Walter Mitty scornfully. He took one last drag on his cigarette and snapped it away. Then, with that faint, fleeting smile playing about his lips, he faced the firing squad; erect and motionless, proud and disdainful, Walter Mitty the Undefeated, inscrutable to the last.

Isaac Bashevis Singer

I PLACE MY RELIANCE ON NO MAN

I

From the day people began to talk about his becoming the rabbi at Yavrov, Rabbi Jonathan Danziger of Yampol[22] didn't have a minute's peace. His Yampol enemies begrudged his going to the bigger city, though they couldn't wait for him to leave Yampol because they already had someone to take his place. The Yampol elders wanted the rabbi to leave Yampol without being able to go to Yavrov. They tried to ruin his chances for the Yavrov appointment by spreading rumors about him. They intended to treat him the way they had treated the previous rabbi: he was to leave

22 Both are towns in the southwestern Ukraine, formerly part of Poland.

town in disgrace riding in an ox-drawn cart. But why? What evil had he done? He had hurt no one's honor; he was invariably friendly to everyone. Yet they all had private grudges against him. One claimed that the rabbi gave a wrong interpretation of the Talmud; another had a son-in-law who wanted to take over the rabbi's position; a third thought Rabbi Jonathan should follow a Hasidic leader. The butchers whined that the rabbi found too many cows unkosher, the ritual slaughterer that the rabbi asked to check his knife twice a week. The bathhouse attendant complained because once, on the eve of a holy day, the rabbi had declared the ritual bath impure, and thus the women could not copulate with their husbands.

On Bridge Street the mob insisted that the rabbi spent too much time at his books, that he didn't pay attention to the common people. In taverns ruffians made fun of the way the rabbi shouted when reciting "Hear, O Israel," and how he spat when he mentioned the idols. The enlightened proved that the rabbi made mistakes in Hebrew grammar. The rabbi's wife was mocked by the ladies because she spoke in the accent of Great Poland and because she drank her chicory and coffee without sugar. There was nothing they didn't make fun of. They didn't like it when the rabbi's wife baked bread every Thursday rather than once every three weeks. They looked askance at the rabbi's daughter, Yentl the widow, who, they said, spent too much time knitting and embroidering. Before each Passover there was a row because of the Passover matzohs, and the rabbi's enemies ran to his house to break his windows. After Succoth,[23] when many children fell ill, the pious matrons screamed that the rabbi hadn't cleansed the town of sins, that he had allowed the young women to go about with uncovered hair,

---

[23] Feast of Tabernacles, autumn festival.

and that the Angel of Death was thus punishing innocent infants with his sword. One way or another, every faction carped and found fault. With all this, the rabbi received the lowly salary of five gulden a week; he lived in the direst need.

As if he wasn't burdened enough with enemies, even his friends behaved like enemies. They relayed every petty accusation to him. The rabbi told them that this was a sin, quoting from the Talmud that gossip hurts all three parties: the gossiper, the one who receives the gossip, and the one gossiped about. It breeds anger, hatred, desecration of the Holy Name. The rabbi begged his followers not to trouble him with slander; but every word his enemies uttered was reported to him. If the rabbi expressed disapproval of the messenger of evil, then that person would immediately defect to the hostile camp. The rabbi could no longer pray and study in peace. He would plead with God: How long can I endure this Gehenna? Even condemned men don't suffer more than twelve months. . . .

Now that Rabbi Jonathan was about to take over the office in Yavrov, he could see that it was very much like Yampol. There was already an opposition in Yavrov, too. There, as well, was a rich man whose son-in-law coveted the rabbi's post. Besides, though the Yavrov rabbi made his living by selling candles and yeast, a few merchants had taken the forbidden merchandise into their stores, even after being threatened with excommunication.

The rabbi was barely fifty, but he was already gray. His tall figure was bent. The beard which once had been the color of straw had become white and sparse like that of an old man. His eyebrows were bushy, and below his eyes hung mossy, brownish-blue bags. He suffered from all sorts of ailments. He coughed, winter and summer. His body was mere skin and bone; he was so light that when he walked in the wind, his coattails almost lifted him into the air. His wife lamented that he didn't eat enough, drink enough, sleep enough. Racked by nightmares he would wake from sleep with a start. He dreamed of persecutions and pogroms and because of these he often had to fast. The rabbi believed that he was being punished for his sins. Sometimes he would say harsh words against his tormentors; he would question the ways of God and even doubt His mercy. He would put on his prayer shawl and phylacteries and the thought would suddenly flash through his mind: Suppose there is no Creator? After such blasphemy, the rabbi would not allow himself to taste food all day, until the stars came out. "Woe is me, where shall I run?" the rabbi sighed. "I'm a lost man."

In the kitchen sat mother and daughter and each one kept her own counsel. Ziporah the rabbi's wife, came from a wealthy family. As a girl she had been considered beautiful, but the years of poverty had ruined her looks. In her unbecoming old-fashioned bonnet and dress from the time of King Sobieski, she seemed stooped and emaciated; her face was wrinkled and had taken on the rustiness of an unripe pear. Her hands had grown large and full of veins like those of a man. But Ziporah found one consolation in all her misery: work. She washed, chopped wood, carried water from the well, scoured the floors. People in Yampol joked that she scrubbed the dishes so hard that she made holes in them. She darned the table cloths and sheets so thickly that not a thread remained of the original weave. She even repaired the rabbi's slippers. Of the six children to which she had given birth, only Yentl had survived.

Yentl took after her father: her hair was yellowish, she was tall, fair-skinned, freckled, flat-chested. Yentl was no less diligent than her mother, but her mother would not al-low her to touch any housework. Yentl's husband Ozer, a yeshiva[24] student, had died of consumption. Yentl now sewed, knitted, read books which she borrowed from peddlers. At first she had received many marriage offers, but she managed to discourage the matchmakers. She never stopped mourning her husband. As soon as someone began arranging a match for her, she suddenly began to suffer from cramps. People in Yampol spread the rumor that she had given Ozer an oath on his deathbed that she would never marry again. She didn't have a single girl friend in Yampol. Summers she would take a basket, a rope, and go off into the woods to pick berries and mushrooms. Such behavior was considered highly improper for a rabbi's daughter.

The move to Yavrov seemed a good prospect, but the rabbi's wife and Yentl worried more than they rejoiced. Neither mother nor daughter had a decent stitch of clothing or piece of jewelry. During the years at Yampol, they had become so destitute that the rabbi's wife wailed to her husband that she had forgotten how to speak to people. She prayed at home, avoiding escorting brides to the synagogue or taking part in a circumcision ceremony. But Yavrov was a different matter. There, ladies decked themselves out in fashionable dresses, costly furs, silken wigs, shoes with high heels and pointed toes. The young married women went to the synagogue in feathered hats. Each had a golden chain or brooch. How could one come to such a place in rags, with broken-down furniture and patched linen? Yentl simply refused to move. What would she do in Yavrov? She was neither a girl nor a married woman; at least in Yampol she had a mound of earth and a gravestone.

Rabbi Jonathan listened and shook his

24 Rabbinical seminary.

head. He had been sent a contract from
Yavrov, but had not as yet received any
advance. Was that the custom, or were they
treating him this way because they considered him naive? He was ashamed to ask
for money. It went against his nature to use
the Torah for profit. The rabbi paced back
and forth in his study; "Father in heaven,
save me. 'I am come into deep waters, where
the floods overflow me!' "

II

It was the rabbi's custom to pray in the
synagogue rather than in the study house,
for among the poor Jews he had fewer
enemies. He prayed at sunrise with the first
quorum. It was after Pentecost. At three-
thirty the morning star rose. At four the
sun was already shining. The rabbi loved
the stillness of the morning when most of
the townfolk were still sleeping behind
closed shutters. He never tired of watching
the sun come up: purple, golden, washed
in the waters of the Great Sea. The rising
sun always brought the same thought to his
mind: unlike the sun, the son of man never
renews himself; that is why he is doomed
to death. Man has memories, regrets, resent-
ments. They collect like dust, they block
him up so he can't receive the light and
life that descends from heaven. But God's
creation is constantly renewing itself. If the
sky becomes cloudy, it clears up again. The
sun sets, but is reborn every morning. There
is no blemish of the past on the moon or
stars. The ceaselessness of nature's creation
is never so obvious as at dawn. Dew is falling, the birds twitter, the river catches fire,
the grass is moist and fresh. Happy is the
man who can renew himself together with
creation "when all the stars of the morning
sing together." [25]

[25] Cf. *Job* xxxviii, 7.

This morning was like any other morning. The rabbi rose early in order to be first
in the synagogue. He knocked on the oak
door to warn the spirits who pray there of
his arrival. Then he went into the dark antechamber. The synagogue was hundreds of
years old, but it remained almost as it was
on the day it was built. Everything exuded
eternity: the gray walls, the high ceiling, the
brass candelabras, the copper washbasin,
the lectern with the four pillars, the carved
high Ark with the tables of the Commandments and the two gilded lions. Streams of
sun moats passed through the oval, stained-
glass windows. Even though the ghosts who
pray there usually leave it at cockcrow to
make room for the living, there remained
behind them a breathlessness and stillness.
The rabbi began to pace up and down and
to recite the "Lord of the Universe." The
rabbi repeated the words, "And after all
things shall have had an end. He alone
shall reign," several times. The rabbi imagined the family of man perishing, houses
crumbling, everything evil melting away
and God's light again inhabiting all space.
The shrinking of His power, the unholy
forces, everything mean and filthy would
cease. Time, accidents, passions, struggles
would vanish, for these were but illusion
and deception. The real truth was sheer
goodness.

The rabbi said his prayers, contemplating
the inner meaning of the words. Little by
little the worshipers began to arrive: the
first quorum was of hardworking men who
rise at the rooster's crow—Leibush the
carter, Chaim Jonah the fish merchant,
Avrom the saddlemaker, Shloime Meyer
who grows orchards outside Yampol. They
greeted the rabbi, then put on their phylacteries and prayer shawls. It occurred to the
rabbi that his enemies in the town were
either the rich or the lazy idlers. The poor
and hardworking, all those who made an
honest living, were on his side. "Why didn't

it ever occur to me?" the rabbi wondered. "Why didn't I realize it?" He felt a sudden love for these Jews who deceived no one, who knew nothing of swindling and grabbing, but followed God's sentence: "From the sweat of thy brow thou shalt eat bread. . . ." [26] Now they thoughtfully wrapped the phylactery thongs around their arms, kissed the fringes of the prayer shawls, and assumed the heavy yoke of the Kingdom of Heaven. A morning tranquillity rested on their faces and beards. Their eyes shone with the mildness of those who have been burdened from childhood on.

It was Monday. After confession the scroll was taken from the Ark while the rabbi recited "Blessed be Thy Name." The opening of the Holy Ark always moved him. Here they stood, the pure scrolls, the Torah of Moses, silken-skirted and decorated with chains, crowns, silver plates— all similar, but each with its separate destiny. Some scrolls were read on weekdays, others on the Sabbath, still others were taken out only on the Day of the Rejoicing of the Law. There were also several worn books of the Law with faded letters and mouldering parchment. Every time the rabbi thought about these holy ruins, he felt a pain in his heart. He swayed back and forth, mumbling the Aramaic words, "Thou rulest over all . . . I, the servant of the Holy One, blessed be He, bow down before Him and the splendor of His law. . . ." [27] When the rabbi came to the words, "I place my reliance on no man," he stopped. The words stuck in his throat.

For the first time he realized that he was lying. No one relied on people more than he. The whole town gave him orders, he depended on everyone. Anyone could do him harm. Today it happened in Yampol,

tomorrow it would happen in Yavrov. He, the rabbi, was a slave to every powerful man in the community. He must hope for gifts, for favors, and must always seek supporters. The rabbi began to examine the other worshipers. Not one of them needed allies. No one else worried about who might be for or against him. No one cared a penny for the tales of rumor-mongers. "Then what's the use of lying?" the rabbi thought. "Whom am I cheating? The Almighty?" The rabbi shuddered and covered his face in shame. His knees buckled. They had already put the scroll on the reading table, but the rabbi had not noticed this. Suddenly something inside the rabbi laughed. He lifted his hand as if swearing an oath. A long forgotten joy came over him, and he felt an unexpected determination. In one moment everything became clear to him. . . .

They called the rabbi to the reading and he mounted the steps to the lectern. He placed a fringe on the parchment, touched it to his brow, and kissed it. He recited the benediction in a loud voice. Then he listened to the reader. It was the chapter, "Send thou men. . . ." [28] It told of the spies who went to search the land of Canaan and who returned frightened by the sons of Anak. Cowardice had destroyed the generation of the desert, Rabbi Jonathan said to himself. And if they were not supposed to fear giants, why should I tremble before midgets? It's worse than cowardice; it's nothing but pride. I'm afraid to lose my rabbinical vestments. The co-worshipers gaped at the rabbi. He seemed transformed. A mysterious strength emanated from him. It's probably because he's moving to Yavrov, they explained to themselves.

After praying, the men began to disperse. Shloime Meyer took his prayer shawl, ready to leave. He was a small man, wide-boned, with a yellow beard, yellow eyes, yellow

[26] *Genesis* III, 19.

[27] The prayer, part of the Sha-harith or morning service, is found in the Zohar, a collection of cabalistic writings and commentaries on the Bible.

[28] *Numbers* XIII.

freckles. His canvas cap, his gabardine coat, and his coarse boots were parched yellow by the sun. The rabbi made a sign to him. "Shloime Meyer, please wait a minute."

"Yes, Rabbi."

"How are your orchards?" the rabbi asked. "Is the harvest good?"

"Thank God. If there are no winds, then it will be good."

"Do you have men to do the picking?"

Shloime Meyer thought it over for a moment. "They're hard to get, but we manage."

"Why are they hard to get?"

"The work isn't easy. They have to stand on ladders all day and sleep in the barn at night."

"How much do you pay?"

"Not much."

"Enough to live on?"

"I feed them."

"Shloime Meyer, take me on. I'll pick fruit for you."

Shloime Meyer's yellow eyes filled with laughter. "Why not?"

"I'm not joking."

Shloime Meyer's eyes saddened. "I don't know what the Rabbi means."

"I'm not a rabbi any more."

"What? Why is that?"

"If you have a minute, I'll tell you."

Shloime Meyer listened while the rabbi spoke. The quorum had left and the two men remained alone. They stood near the pulpit. Although the rabbi spoke quietly, each word echoed back as though someone unseen were repeating it after him.

"What do you say, Shloime Meyer?" the rabbi finally asked.

Shloime Meyer made a face as though he had swallowed something sour. He shook his head from side to side.

"What can I say? I'm afraid I'll be excommunicated."

"You must not fear anyone. 'Ye shall not fear the face of man.' That's the essence of Jewishness."

"What will your wife say?"

"She'll help me with my work."

"It's not for the likes of you."

"They that wait on the Lord shall renew their strength."

"Well, well . . ."

"You agree, then?"

"If the Rabbi wants . . ."

"Don't call me Rabbi anymore. From now on I'm your employee. And I'll be an honest worker."

"I'm not worried about that."

"When do you leave for the orchards?"

"In a couple of hours."

"Come by with your cart. I'll be waiting."

"Yes, Rabbi."

Shloime Meyer waited a while longer and then left. Near the door to the antechamber he glanced back. The rabbi stood alone, his hands clasped, his gaze wandering from wall to wall. He would make his departure from the synagogue where he had prayed for so many years. It was all so familiar: the twelve signs of the zodiac, the seven stars, the figures of the lion, the stag, the leopard and the eagle, the unutterable Name of God, painted in red. The gilded lions on the top of the Ark stared at the rabbi with their amber eyes while their curved tongues supported the tables with the Ten Commandments. It seemed to the rabbi that these sacred beasts were asking: Why did you wait so long? Couldn't you see from the start that one cannot serve God and man at the same time? Their open mouths seemed to laugh with benign ferocity. The rabbi clutched at his beard. "Well, it is never too late. Eternity is still before one. . . ." He walked backwards until he reached the threshold. There is no mezuzah in a synagogue, but the rabbi touched the jamb with his index finger and then his lips.

In Yampol, in Yavrov, the strange news soon spread. Rabbi Jonathan, his wife, and Yentl, his daughter, had gone off to pick fruit in Shloime Meyer's orchards.

Helen Hudson

AFTER CORTES

The road from Mérida to Chichén Itzá runs with a dull persistence between the fields of cactus and henequen. Even in the rainy season the land is hot and dry, a harsh, hostile country bristling with deprivations. Father Cheney, panting on the back seat of the Ford, let his huge body flop helplessly and wondered if he should have sat up front with the guide. In Mexico City, he had noticed, passengers always sat up with the driver. But in such heat, truth goes naked and the fact was that Father Cheney preferred empty spaces about him whenever possible. Besides, he always wore mufti on vacation and he allowed himself to put off certain minor mortifications along with his round collar. For a man of his size and temperament and calling, it was enough just to be in Mexico in August: Mexico with its fierce anti-clericalism, its pagan Christianity, and the heat making the medal of St. Damian a burning coal around his neck. In Chamula he had seen rouged saints with stone jaguars peeping out from beneath their skirts and at Guadalupe there were raised platforms where Indian worshipers danced in rattles and paint before the carved doors of the Cathedral. Across the road, the sun, too low for comfort, seemed to be melting into the parched fields. No wonder the Indians thought it might someday fall to earth and had fed it a steady diet of human hearts to keep it where it was. Father Cheney sighed while the hot breeze lifted his thin, blond hair and the ends of his flowered shirt.

As far as the eye could see there was only the straight road and the coarse brush and the henequen with leaves like raised swords. Occasionally they passed a lone Indian walking along the side of the road, though there was no village for miles around. The load on his back was held by a strap around his forehead so that he kept his head bent while the car raced by, making a wall of dust around him. Once in a great while they drove through a village, its back to the road, its life hidden behind adobe walls— silent, secret as Mexico itself with its hidden patios and enclosed squares and the slow figures wrapped in the serape and the shawl. Silent, secret—except for the churches. The car would come upon one suddenly rising like a fountain above the flat, dry landscape—or a shout of triumph. And Father Cheney would smile to see it there.

He was new to the priesthood, having come to his calling late, as though he had tried first to find a place for his large frame in the world below the altar. But he always felt squeezed in the pews, and the lumps of human flesh bobbing up and down repelled him. He had longed for the dignity and distinction of black cloth and the empty calm about the altar. Once ordained, he looked down on his congregation with some compassion, though he could not avoid a certain distaste for them at the Communion rail when the mouths all fell open and the tongues flopped out.

For the past few years he had spent his summer vacations in Mexico. He liked to sit alone in the best restaurants, served by small, silent men whose ancestors had built huge temples to their gods and kept their altars damp with the blood of their enemies. But their temples lay buried now and they served him his enchilladas with an obsequious grace. Here in Yucatán they were smaller, more silent than usual, with the soft, round faces of children. Where was it he had read that the women wore nothing under their ankle-length *huipils*? But there was so little wind here. A civilization built without wind or water or wheel, he thought sleepily. He was beginning to doze now, dreaming of the tequila sour they would offer him at the hotel "with the compliments of the management."

Suddenly the driver shouted something and the car stopped abruptly. Father Cheney opened his eyes and saw her standing directly in front of the car, her arms raised. She was wearing a white shirt and tight white pants with blue lacing up the front, like a sailor he thought vaguely. She came around to his window and stood there for a minute laughing, showing big, strong teeth. "Breakdown," she said, jerking her head toward the Volkswagen parked at the side of the road. "Give me a lift?"

"Sure," Father Cheney said. "Where to?"

"Wherever you're going."

"Hotel Maya."

"Sounds beautiful. Tell your guide to stay with my car and I'll drive. I don't dare leave it alone. In this country *stealing* is the oldest profession." She had straight black hair pulled back and held by a rubber band, except for a few strands that hung in a skimpy bang on her forehead. She had a long nose and a big mouth but she spoke in a high, little-girl voice. "Okay?"

"Okay," Father Cheney said. "But *I'll* drive." He watched her run around the car to the guide, in her tight slightly soiled pants. The guide was a fiercely built little man from Mérida with incongruous red hair who called himself, for the benefit of American tourists Father Cheney suspected, Señor Camera. There was contempt in the foreshortened name—for the tourists and for himself—as though he knew that the pride he had inherited from his Spanish ancestors was as inappropriate in his present circumstances as his full name. It made him arrogant to tourists and cruel to natives. He smoked incessantly and drove through the villages at top speed, scattering women and children. But the girl was

neither tourist nor native. She spoke to him in Spanish through the car window and pointed to the Volkswagen. Father Cheney saw Señor Camera's head jerk up for a moment. Then he nodded while the back of his neck grew quite red. They left him there in the Volkswagen at the side of the road with the wide, prickly fields around him.

All the way to Chichén Itzá the girl talked and laughed and stroked her trousered thighs. To Father Cheney her image seemed to decompose into discrete and unrelated parts: the high, little-girl voice, the sailor suit and the coarse black hair in the ambiguous style—which sometimes reminded him less of a girl of the twentieth century than a boy of the eighteenth. He felt slightly uneasy.

Her name was Carla and she had driven all the way from Los Angeles in the Volkswagen. The only other time she had had any trouble with it, six Mexicans had towed it through the streets of the village while she sat behind the wheel honking the horn. "My God, I felt like the Virgin Mary," she said. "They do that, you know. Move an image of the Virgin from one church to another—but they put *her* in a Cadillac, and I think only people in a state of grace are allowed to pull it. And those boys were in another state entirely."

Father Cheney felt inside his shirt for the medal on his chest. "Did you drive all the way from Los Angeles alone?" he asked.

"Oh, no. I had a girl friend with me part of the way. But she saw something she liked in Guadalajara and decided to stay for a while."

"Something she liked?"

"Yeah. A big, blond German with a private swimming pool and a glass eye. My friend is just crazy about glass eyes."

Carla taught school in the winter and hated it. "Mostly Mexican kids who come every other Tuesday and don't speak a word of English. You can't teach them anything. All you can do is keep the seat of their pants where it belongs and an eye on your purse. Christ, what a life!"

Father Cheney smiled, for her lack of sentimentality pleased him. Yet he feared her too, battening down his defenses and shifting closer to the door.

"Where are you from?" Carla asked. He could feel her examining his large frame. "Texas?"

"No. New York."

"New York. God, you're lucky. Someday, somehow," she said slapping her thighs, "I'm going to get to New York and stay there."

"Quite a place," Father Cheney said. But he thought of his church in the East Bronx, squeezed between the fat new apartment houses, with its poor, crooked spire like a thumb groping for the sky. He remembered how carefully his mother walked across the cracked pavement of the church-yard when she came to visit and how she sat through Mass with her veil down as though she did not care to be recognized by her Maker in such surroundings. His father wore his I'll-speak-to-the-Bishop expression. Yet Father Cheney had been careful to hide from them how much he really hated it. To constantly mortify so much flesh in the squalor of St. Aedan's Parish was, he felt, a high price to pay for the ready-made dignity of the black cloth and the privacy of the stiff round collar.

He had chosen the priesthood for practical rather than pious considerations as a man might choose a career in the army or the navy for reasons that have nothing at all to do with killing. A fastidious, bookish man, bachelorhood suited him and the vow of celibacy was a positive relief. The duties of a priest protected him from certain facts and allowed him to contemplate

others. It was a good life, or might have been in another parish with a more comfortable rectory in which he might have settled his body and released his soul. But that was impossible at St. Aedan's, where the furniture seemed stuffed with old poker chips and the windows looked out on the eternal essences of the A. & P. "Very handy both ways, Father," he had been told, for the worshipers could park there on Sundays and the shoppers could slip in for quick devotions. Father Cheney was sure that someday he would find a bargain-happy housewife pushing a grocery cart down the central nave. But the humiliation to his spirit was worst of all. He felt no Father to this slovenly, loose-lipped flock. It pained him to force his mind to meet theirs, to reduce the intricacy and beauty and mystery of Catholic dogma to the simple act and the blunt command, like limiting *Hamlet* to its plot. He read late at night and since there was no one with whom to share his thoughts, he took them to Mexico each summer. There the mating of mind and eye helped to carry him through the next winter.

The sunlight was receding now, leaving pools of darkness scattered across the fields, but the road and the heat continued, the henequen spearing the air with its pointed leaves and the cactus needles poised for any stray thread of wind. Soon they would be only black shapes like ink blots against the absorbent sky. Next to him the girl had drawn up her legs and gone to sleep. He glanced at her untidy hair and the rumpled pants and wondered where she had slept last night. She was a girl, he thought, who invited that question constantly. He remembered how she had looked standing so boldly before the car with her hands raised and her head high. He wondered if she did that sort of thing often, for one reason or another. At night with her black hair loose and that white outfit, she might be taken for the legendary La Malinche, "the wicked one," Cortes's Indian mistress who had betrayed her own people and still wandered the roads at night leading men to sudden death.

At last, when the light was only a thin rim on the horizon, they reached Chichén. On the left, Father Cheney could just make out a huge, dim shape like a draped figure. It gave him a strange feeling, as though it had been waiting for him.

"That's one of the ruins," Carla said, sitting up and rubbing her eyes. "Good of the Mayans to build it so handy to the hotel, wasn't it? There's the hotel, right across the road. All that pink stone laid out like a hacienda."

"It's supposed to be jammed full of Mormons right now," Father Cheney said. "They told me in Mérida. Sixty of them touring Latin America. Examining the remnants of the lost tribes, no doubt." He smiled faintly. "Have you got a reservation?"

"Are you kidding? At twenty-five dollars a day—not counting drinks? Besides, I've never had a reservation in my life. I was *born* impromptu. My mother had me in the kitchen in the middle of a late beer. She just lay down on the floor for a while and then got up and finished the can— hey," she shouted suddenly, "there's Manuel."

A slim young Mexican with polished hair and white cotton shirt and pants was standing on the steps of the hotel blowing cigarette smoke into the dusk. Carla jumped out of the car and ran up to him. "What in hell are you doing here? I thought you were supposed to be taking care of the *touristi* in Uxmal."

He smiled and stepped back with a slight bow. "But of course, I am here to welcome you to Chichén."

"Marvelous. Just what I need. A nice, wet welcome." She took his arm.

"Hey," Father Cheney called from the car. "What about Señor Camera and the Volkswagen?"

"My God," Carla said. "I forgot all about them. Be an angel and let Manuel and me have the Ford. Manuel's marvelous with machines."

"All right," Father Cheney said. "But be sure you bring it back tonight. *And* Señor Camera. I'm paying twelve dollars a day for the pair of them." He smiled at her weakly and lifted himself and his suitcase out of the car. He felt slightly ashamed, as though there were more of him than was proper.

Carla began to pull Manuel toward the car. "A moment, please," he said. "I am not dressed for the Volkswagen."

"All right," Carla said. "Go change your beautiful clothes. I'll meet you in the bar." She fell into step beside Father Cheney. "By the way," she said, "I don't know your name."

"Charles."

"Shall we have a drink, Charlie?"

He followed her across the patio to the terrace of the bar and they fitted themselves behind a tiny, three-legged table that bobbed like a cork between them. Father Cheney, overlapping the dainty, wrought-iron chair, felt that he was sitting mostly on air. He could feel his thin, fine hair waving like tendrils in the hot breeze. Carla leaned back, crossed her legs, and smiled at him. Her eyes across the table were black obsidian. She wanted a double bourbon; it was such a thirsty country, wasn't it? Father Cheney nodded, his mouth dry with resignation. Carla smoked unfiltered cigarettes and kept one eye on the waiter, to shorten the time between drinks. Father Cheney leaned forward to light her cigarette. His medal swayed between them.

A man at the next table got up from behind a bottle of Seven-Up. He was a tiny man with an enormous gold watch like a shackle around his wrist. "Father Cheney?" he said. "Welcome to Chichén Itzá. They told me about you at the desk. Glad to have you with us." He was Elder Briggs from Ogden, Utah, with all of Latin America at his back. He stared up at Father Cheney blinking magnanimously and offered his hand in consolation. "If you'd care to join us in prayer, Father, in the lounge at . . ." he glanced at his watch. "In five minutes. Good heavens." He nodded swiftly and hurried off, his wide trousers flapping anxiously about his ankles.

Father Cheney sat down.

"Father?" Carla said and lifted her eyebrows. "Father . . . Time? Christmas? Not . . . ?"

He nodded.

"You didn't tell me."

"You didn't ask." His hands crept into the dark privacy of his pockets.

"Well I'll be damned." And then she threw back her head and laughed as Father Cheney knew she would. He saw the wide tunnel of her mouth, big enough to hold his fist, and the strong white teeth and the thick tongue. Inside his pockets, Father Cheney's fingers curled into his dry palms as though squeezing from the moment the last hot drops of humiliation. But the rest of him sat high above the glasses, stiff and exposed while the small table rocked between their knees. He reached for his drink.

"I'm sorry," Carla said at last. "But all that flowered shirt. It came as quite a surprise. Not to say shock. You must be *huge* in a cassock. You must *back* into the confessional." She looked at his hand wrapped around the highball glass as though trying to imagine it lifted in benediction. She frowned at the flowered shirt. "But why the disguise?" she said.

"It's not a 'disguise.' I'm on vacation."

"I didn't know priests were ever 'on vacation'—like teamsters or schoolteachers."

"They're not." He spoke slowly, precisely, sharpening his words to a fine point. "But we are, occasionally, released for short periods from routine parish duties."

"I'll bet the Mayan priests never had a vacation."

"Maybe not. Maybe they enjoyed their work too much." He smiled, but the back of his mouth felt raw.

"Cutting out hearts is a lot easier than saving souls, isn't it? And sometimes, I'll bet, much more satisfying too."

Father Cheney lifted his glass to ease his burning throat. And then Manuel who was "marvelous with machines" appeared at the edge of the patio, neat in blue denims with placid hair. Carla got up and shook hands and thanked Father Cheney for the drink. Her palm was moist and Father Cheney rubbed his hand on his trousers. She swung her black handbag over her shoulder and grinned. "See you in church," she said.

Father Cheney sat over his drinks for a long time after that. The terrace of the bar faced the swimming pool, where two plump teen-age blondes were cavorting with a heavy-footed young man in purple trunks. They kept screaming about not getting their hair wet, in thick Texan accents, while the man dunked them methodically, one after the other, chasing them with his head down and panting heavily like a bull caught with two matadors. Father Cheney wished they would shut up and let him listen to the silences of Mexico. Far down, through the arched entrance of the hotel, he could see the ruin, swathed in gray against the sky, framed in the doorway like a saint in a niche—or a mummy in a box.

"Beautiful, isn't it?" an elderly man at the next table said softly. "That's the Castillo, you know. The perfect pyramid." He spoke gently with an accent Father Cheney could not identify. In the darkness only a bit of white hair and a white shirt were visible. The two men sat side by side in silence, clinking the ice in their glasses. After a while the stranger got up and walked quietly away.

The blondes climbed out of the pool at

last, complaining, between screams of
laughter, of their wet heads. They would
appear at dinner with enormous rollers in
their hair, only partially covered by
flowered kerchiefs. They would frown over
the menu and pull the straps of their cotton dresses further down off their shoulders
and say, over and over, that it was hot. And
when the food came they would eat steadily,
wordlessly, with a bored petulant air, no
doubt wishing they were having hambur-
gers and cokes at the corner drugstore in
Houston, with the local swains eying them
from the door. My God, how fatuous they
were, Father Cheney thought, and their
indulgent father with the face like a but-
tered scone, dripping complacency, and
their stubbornly blond mother who would
price everything in the gift shop after dinner. They would have piles of money and
not an unselfish thought to pass among
them from one Sunday to the next.

Yet they were probably no worse than
the rest—all of them with their vision
blocked by the palms of their hands. They
treated their God like a desk clerk with
whom they lodged requests and complaints.
And they behaved as though he, Father
Cheney, were a mere funnel into which they
poured their banal confessions not so much
for penance as for pity. Even in a flowered
shirt he seemed to attract endless confidences as though he had nothing to do
with his life but hang it over the back of
his chair and sit with his eyes shut and his
hands drooping between his thighs, listening. That woman on the plane from Mexico
City, for instance. Hadn't she looked a
thoroughly nice woman, her hair in a net,
her hands in mesh gloves, a proper, self-
contained little woman from Pottsville,
Pennsylvania, about whom the neighbors
would certainly say that Mrs. Prouty was
"a fine person"? Then why, at the sight of
him, had she launched into the most intimate details of her life as soon as her son
went off to flirt with the stewardess? Did

she think he had come all the way to Mexico
to hear about Aunt Alice and Freddie and
an ex-husband who spent his evenings
sawing wood in the basement? Father Cheney had rubbed his palms in despair and
escaped, at last, to the men's room. But
they were all alike inside their personalized
clothes, all like Carla really, interested only
in themselves and what they could grab,
though they probably washed their hands
more often.

Father Cheney closed his eyes. He would
not think of them. He would think of the
Castillo instead. He opened his eyes and
saw it faintly in the doorway, cloaked and
waiting. But even as he watched, it withdrew, stepping slowly back into the night.

Tomorrow he would go to the ruins
where the temples sat high on their mounds
like thrones above the dry land, waiting for
the high priests with their human offerings
and the moisture of human blood. He
would haul his huge bulk up to the tops
of the pyramids in the broiling sun, remembering that each stone had been carried for miles by small, dark men with bare
feet. And standing on the high temple he
would see the world spread out about him
and the Hotel Maya low and crooked as a
snake among the trees.

"Well, o' course, Mother always used to
keep everything locked up but I'm forever
losing keys, and Freddie gets so cross with
me. But o' course, down here . . . well, I've
got all our travelers' checks rolled up in my
nylons." It was little Mrs. Prouty on her
way to the bar to have one tiny weak one,
just to be sociable. Father Cheney got up
quietly and went to dress for dinner.

Carla did not appear in the dining room
as Father Cheney knew she would not for
she was not a guest of the hotel, only of
Manuel or Señor Camera or anyone else on
the other side of a drink. She went to hotels
as some people go to church, for the free,
fringe benefits—to rest, or use the facilities,
or contemplate the good life. Father Che-

ney sat alone at a table for two sipping iced tea with limes and smoking little cigars. A mariachi band played lively tunes on a small balcony and a huge mural depicting Mexican gods painted to look like American football players, stared benignly out over the guests. The dining room was warm and crowded, filled mostly with the touring Mormons, the men dressed as if for rocking on the back porch, the women plump and red-faced with tight curls, eating chocolate cake and bringing the atmosphere of the church supper to the Hotel Maya. Little Indian waiters and waitresses in native dress rushed among the tables with enormous trays, mixing up the orders, banging down the dishes, and letting the sweat gather on their silent, sober faces.

After dinner Father Cheney avoided the Mormon hymn-singing in the lounge though they had pressed him, as a man of God, to join them: "We're all Christians together, Father," smiling indulgently and folding their arms over their own superior brand. Instead he walked through the grounds of the hotel. There was no moon and a single fat star stared boldly at a tiny dim one across the empty sky. He saw Carla sitting at a table on the terrace with three men. Her back was toward him, a broad, white back with the little pony tail sticking out straight behind her. Next to her Manuel was holding a guitar and across the table Señor Camera sat behind his own smoke, tilting back in his chair as though for greater distance. The third man, paying for the drinks, was Mrs. Prouty's Freddie. "Ptomaine Paradise. That's what they ought to call this place," he was saying. Father Cheney could see his face screwed up in an effort to get his wallet out—or keep his dinner down.

He walked on, past old trees and flowers that crowded to the path's edge like children. They embarrassed him slightly, perhaps because he did not know their names. Further on the path wound back to the road, black as a ravine except for the scattered lights of the servants' huts that lay in the wake of the hotel. Through an open door he could see a small room lit by a single naked bulb, completely bare except for a hammock stretched across the center. Beyond the huts there was nothing. Once a truck rushed by with startled eyes as though it feared the dark road and La Malinche, who might be waiting just beyond the headlights. Father Cheney could imagine her rising up in front of it, all in white, arms high in a gesture of command. And across the road were the ruins, tall, shrouded, waiting. He turned and walked quickly back to the hotel.

In the patio he could hear Carla's voice across the pool. "And then, by God, the police came," she was saying. "They wanted to know what the hell I was doing there at four A.M. I could have asked them the same question but by then everyone in the place was awake and shouting out the windows." She was still at the same table with the same three men. No one noticed Father Cheney. He hurried to his room and shut the door.

Inside it was close and hot, making him feel smothered in his own flesh. The bed, wrapped in mosquito netting, looked very small and airtight. He sat down and took off his shoes and began to read about the ruins. But the lamp was dim and hung about with bugs, and every now and then he could hear the shouts of Carla and the men breaking through the words on the page. He read on doggedly while the bugs nibbled at his skin and the heat held him in a clammy embrace. He read on until the words on the page pounded in his head and the sounds of the hotel died away. "The theme is a large eagle holding a human heart in his claw, alternating with a warrior carrying the decapitated head of his opponent. The whole frieze has a beautiful, rhythmic pattern . . ." He was stifling.

He shut the book, put on his shoes, and went outside. The air was cooler here. He began to walk slowly, watching the sky covered with stars now, like dots in a child's puzzle which have only to be connected to make a picture. The hotel was completely quiet. The bar was closed and even the space behind the desk was empty. Carla was still on the terrace but there was only one man there now, someone Father Cheney did not recognize, someone fast asleep with his cheek on the table behind the empty glasses. Suddenly Carla turned and saw him. "Hi, Charlie," she shouted. She got up and walked slowly toward him. She seemed quite drunk and her hair was soaking wet. She raised her hands and patted her head gently and giggled. "We've been swimming. Skinny. Shhhhh." She put a finger over her lips. "Don't tell the management. Managements upset very easy." She took his arm and led him down the path. "Let's me and you go to the ruins together."

"Now?"

"Now."

"But it's too dark now."

"Tomorrow then."

"What about your pals?"

"Them?" She laughed. "They won't be able to lift their heads tomorrow, the bastards. Besides, I want to go with you. I like you. You're smart. I'll bet you know all about the ruins. I'll bet you know more than the guides even. I'll bet you go to bed with a good book about ruins every night."

Her arm was through his and her head rested against his shoulder. He looked down at her with distaste. Her black eyes bulged up at him and her wet hair lay flat as a second skin. He knew exactly how she would behave at the ruins once she let him pay her entrance fee. She would be as noisy as a child at a playground, attracting attention and treating the ruins like a jungle gym, as though they were nothing but masses to be climbed.

Her hand closed around his arm. She swayed slightly and she seemed to have difficulty moving her lips. "You haven't seen Manuel or Camera or any of those bastards around, have you? They've left me, the bastards. Just went off and left me. But you won't leave me, will you Father?" She smiled up at him and quietly passed out.

He caught her as she fell and picked her up. She was surprisingly heavy. He stood bracing himself for a moment, wondering what in hell to do with her. The hotel was completely still and the circles of light beneath the lamps were empty. Silence filled the chairs and the space behind the desk and lay across the warm, still waters of the pool. He was alone in the middle of the night with a strange girl in his arms inside a ring of unattractive alternatives. He could think of nothing to do that would not raise endless sniggering questions and every eyebrow in the hotel. He could imagine the manager accepting his explanations courteously at two in the morning with a barely perceptible smile. "Sí, Señor. Of course. We will find a room for her. But we are quite filled up, as you know." Or the Mormons, nodding their heads at breakfast at what Mabel saw coming out of that priest's room just after her early morning swim. His big body shrank from the merest touch of scandal. Yet he could hardly leave her lying there in the middle of the patio as though she were some stray cat, a consort to darkness and at home with night.

He walked slowly out through the arch and stood under the crowded sky, the girl heavy in his arms. He wished that somehow he could give her to the night, could empty his arms of her and let the darkness gather her up. He sighed and turned and noticed a car parked at the side of the hotel. The door was unlocked and he put her on the back seat quickly, awkwardly. He left her there with one hand dangling to the floor and her head turned sharply as though something were broken. Then he walked swiftly back through the hotel, swinging his empty arms.

He stopped at the desk and left a note to be called at five-thirty the next morning. He would do the ruins alone, before the others were up: Carla or Camera or the Mormons or the Texans or any of them. He would take one quick, glorious gulp all alone in the cool, early morning when the jaguars and the eagles and the serpents would prance and writhe just for him, and the temples, atop their high pyramids sat waiting, their steps lowered, just for him. After that he would catch the next plane back to Mexico City.

He slept badly. His feet hung over the end of the bed and sometime during the night the mosquito netting collapsed, covering him like a fish in a trap. He awoke early, before the knock on his door, with his skin moist and his throat dry.

Outside the air was still cool with a sky like a tinted shell. An elderly Indian woman with bare feet was sweeping the walk. She gave him a shy smile. "*Buene*, Señor."

He went quickly through the arched doorway and up the road. He felt excited and pleased with himself as he saw the top of the Castillo, square and sturdy in the morning light with a symmetry so perfect that it seemed to order the space around it. He was looking up so that he did not see what lay on the side of the road until he was almost upon it. He saw the empty sandal first, and the black bag, its handles covered with dust. And then he saw the heap of white clothes and the spread arms and the short pony tail that would never grow any longer. She lay with her face in the dirt and he knew without touching her that she was dead.

He stood beside her for a moment and stared down. He noticed the way the loose hair curled against her neck, saw the dark mole just below one ear. He remembered

her easy walk and her laugh full of teeth and her little-girl voice. "You won't leave me, will you Father?" And he wondered why she should have ended like this, like her Volkswagen, alone on the side of the road at the edge of the bristling fields. How had it happened? When had she come to enough to get out of the car? And where was she going? To find Manuel or Señor Camera or just an empty hammock? Somebody, no doubt some frightened Indian boy, driving his truck down that dark, lonely road had thought he saw La Malinche waiting for him at the end of the headlights and pressed his foot closer to the floor. Father Cheney had willed her to the night and the night had taken her. But this time he knew what to do. He picked her up carefully and started back to the hotel. His vacation was over. He would never take another.

Though it was only a short way, it seemed to him that he walked for a long time. The sun crawled slowly up over the horizon and clung, fierce and swollen, to the edge of the sky. It bent the cactus and curled the henequen. He could feel it prick his skin, making the perspiration and the freckles come. He felt dazed. The weight in his arms was heavy and warm, and he had the strange sensation that he was carrying, not only the body of a woman, but an armful of sun as well.

He walked on with the ruins at his back and the highway ahead, straight and empty without a shadow or a curve. His head hung low beneath the sun and the medal seared his chest, but he moved on through the burning dust carrying a dead girl to a decent rest. Yet for a second, just for one blazing second between the raising and the lowering of a foot, the sun seemed to have fallen into the brush and he was a high priest bearing a human sacrifice to set it back again. The sweat poured from his face and fell upon the dead girl in his arms.

Author Unknown

EDWARD

"Why dois your brand sae drap wi bluid,
  Edward, Edward,
Why dois your brand sae drap wi bluid,
  And why sae sad gang yee O?"
"O I hae killed my hauke sae guid,
  Mither, mither,
O I hae killed my hauke sae guid,
  And I had nae mair bot hee O."

"Your haukis bluid was nevir sae reid,
  Edward, Edward,   10
Your haukis bluid was nevir sae reid,
  My deir son I tell thee O."
"O I hae killed my reid-roan steid,
  Mither, mither,
O I hae killed my reid-roan steid,
  That erst was sae fair and frie O."

"Your steid was auld, and ye hae got mair,
  Edward, Edward,
Your steid was auld and ye hae got mair,
  Sum other dule ye drie O."   20
"O I hae killed my fadir deir,
  Mither, mither,
O I hae killed my fadir deir,
  Alas, and wae is mee O!"

"And whatten penance wul ye drie for that?
  Edward, Edward,
And whatten penance wul ye drie for that?
  My deir son, now tell me O."
"Ile set my feit in yonder boat,
  Mither, mither,   30
Ile set my feit in yonder boat,
  And Ile fare ovir the sea O."

"And what wul ye doe wi your towirs and your
  ha,

---

1 *brand:* sword; *sae:* so. 4 *gang:* go. 5 *guid:*
good. 8 *nae mair bot hee:* no others. 20 *dule:*
grief; *drie:* suffer. 33 *ha:* hall, house.

  Edward, Edward,
And what wul ye doe wi your towirs and your ha,
  That were sae fair to see O?"
"Ile let thame stand tul they doun fa,
  Mither, mither,
Ile let thame stand tul they doun fa,
  For here nevir mair maun I bee O."   40

"And what wul ye leive to your bairns and your
  wife,
  Edward, Edward,
And what wul ye leive to your bairns and your
  wife,
  Whan ye gang ovir the sea O?"
"The warldis room, late them beg thrae life,
  Mither, mither,
The warldis room, late them beg thrae life
  For thame nevir mair wul I see O."

"And what wul ye leive to your ain mither deir,
  Edward, Edward,   50
And what wul ye leive to your ain mither deir?
  My deir son, now tell me O."
"The curse of hell frae me sall ye beir,
  Mither, mither,
The curse of hell frae me sall ye beir,
  Sic counseils ye gave to me O."

---

37 *thame:* them; *doun fa:* fall down. 40 *maun:*
must. 45 *warldis:* world's; *thrae:* through. 53
frae: from. 56 *Sic:* such.

Author Unknown

LORD RANDAL

"O where ha you been, Lord Randal, my son?
And where ha you been, my handsome young
  man?"
"I ha been at the greenwood; mother, mak my
  bed soon,
For I'm wearied wi huntin, and fain wad lie
  down."

"And wha met ye there, Lord Randal, my son?
And wha met you there, my handsome young
    man?"
"I met wi my true-love; mother, mak my bed
    soon,
For I'm wearied wi huntin, and fain wad lie
    down."

"And what did she give you, Lord Randal, my
    son?
And what did she give you, my handsome young
    man?"   10
"Eels fried in a pan; mother, mak my bed soon,
For I'm wearied wi huntin, and fain wad lie
    down."

"And wha gat your leavins, Lord Randal, my
    son?
And wha gat your leavins, my handsome young
    man?"
"My hawks and my hounds; mother, mak my
    bed soon,
For I'm wearied wi huntin, and fain wad lie
    down."

"And what becam of them, Lord Randal, my
    son?
And what becam of them, my handsome young
    man?"
"They stretched their legs out and died; mother,
    make my bed soon,
For I'm wearied wi huntin, and fain wad lie
    down."   20

"O I fear you are poisoned, Lord Randal, my
    son!
I fear you are poisoned, my handsome young
    man!"
"O yes, I am poisoned; mother, mak my bed
    soon,
For I'm sick at the heart, and I fain wad lie
    down."

"What d' ye leave to your mother, Lord Randal,
    my son?

5 *wha:* who.

What d' ye leave to your mother, my handsome
    young man?"
"Four-and-twenty milk kye; mother, mak my
    bed soon,
For I'm sick at the heart, and I fain wad lie
    down."

"What d' ye leave to your sister, Lord Randal,
    my son?
What d' ye leave to your sister, my handsome
    young man?"   30
"My gold and my silver; mother, mak my bed
    soon,
For I'm sick at the heart, and I fain wad lie
    down."

"What d' ye leave to your brother, Lord Randal,
    my son?
What d' ye leave to your brother, my handsome
    young man?"
"My houses and my lands; mother, mak my bed
    soon,
For I'm sick at the heart, and I fain wad lie
    down."

"What d' ye leave to your true-love, Lord
    Randal, my son?
What d' ye leave to your true-love, my handsome
    young man?"
"I leave her hell and fire; mother, mak my bed
    soon,
For I'm sick at the heart, and I fain wad lie
    down."   40

27 *kye:* kine, cows.

William Shakespeare

POOR SOUL, THE CENTER

Poor soul, the center of my sinful earth,
Rebuke these rebel powers that thee array!
Why dost thou pine within and suffer dearth,

1 *earth:* body. 2 *powers, etc.:* appetites, the
essence of your bodily dress. *array:* dress up;
(ironically) disfigure.

Painting thy outward walls so costly gay?
Why so large cost, having so short a lease,
Dost thou upon thy fading mansion spend?
Shall worms, inheritors of this excess,
Eat up thy charge? Is this thy body's end?
Then, soul, live thou upon thy servant's loss
And let that pine to aggravate thy store;   10
Buy terms divine in selling hours of dross;
Within be fed, without be rich no more:
So shalt thou feed on Death, that feeds on men,
And Death once dead, there's no more dying
          then.

  8 *charge:* expenditure; *Is:* i.e., Is not. 10 *aggravate, etc.:* increase your wealth. 11 *terms divine:*
eternity.   12 *feed on Death, etc.:* consume your own
mortal elements and thus gain immortality.

John Donne

AT THE ROUND EARTH'S
IMAGINED CORNERS

At the round earth's imagined corners, blow
Your trumpets, angels; and arise, arise
From death, you numberless infinities
Of souls, and to your scattered bodies go;
All whom the flood did, and fire shall, o'erthrow,
All whom war, dearth, age, agues, tyrannies,
Despair, law, chance hath slain, and you whose
          eyes
Shall behold God and never taste death's woe.
But let them sleep, Lord, and me mourn a
          space;
For if above all these my sins abound,   10
'Tis late to ask abundance of Thy grace
When we are there. Here on this lowly ground,
Teach me how to repent; for that's as good
As if Thou hadst sealed my pardon with Thy
          blood.

  7 *you, etc.:* See *Gospel of St. Luke* IX, 27.

John Donne

BATTER MY HEART,
THREE-PERSONED GOD

Batter my heart, three-personed God; for You
As yet but knock, breathe, shine, and seek to
          mend;
That I may rise and stand, o'erthrow me, and
          bend
Your force, to break, blow, burn, and make me
          new.
I, like a usurped town to another due,
Labor to admit You, but oh! to no end;
Reason, Your viceroy in me, me should defend,
But is captived and proves weak or untrue.
Yet dearly I love You, and would be loved fain,
But am betrothed unto Your enemy.   10
Divorce me, untie, or break that knot again;
Take me to You, imprison me, for I,
Except You enthrall me, never shall be free,
Nor ever chaste, except You ravish me.

  5 *due:* rightly belonging.

John Keats

ODE TO A NIGHTINGALE

My heart aches, and a drowsy numbness pains
     My sense, as though of hemlock I had drunk,
Or emptied some dull opiate to the drains
     One minute past, and Lethe-wards had sunk:
'Tis not through envy of thy happy lot,
     But being too happy in thine happiness—
          That thou, light-wingèd Dryad of the
               trees,
               In some melodious plot

  3 *drains:* dregs. 4 *Lethe-wards:* to oblivion.

Of beechen green, and shadows numberless,
  Singest of summer in full-throated ease.   10

O for a draught of vintage! that hath been
  Cooled a long age in the deep-delvèd earth,
Tasting of Flora and the country green,
  Dance, and Provençal song, and sunburnt
    mirth!
O for a beaker full of the warm South,
  Full of the true, the blushful Hippocrene,
    With beaded bubbles winking at the brim,
      And purple-stainèd mouth;
  That I might drink, and leave the world
    unseen,
    And with thee fade away into the forest
      dim: 20

Fade far away, dissolve, and quite forget
  What thou among the leaves hast never
    known,
The weariness, the fever, and the fret
  Here, where men sit and hear each other
    groan;
Where palsy shakes a few, sad, last grey hairs,
  Where youth grows pale, and specter-thin,
    and dies;
    Where but to think is to be full of sorrow
      And leaden-eyed despairs,
  Where beauty cannot keep her lustrous eyes,
    Or new love pine at them beyond
      tomorrow.   30

Away! away! for I will fly to thee,
  Not charioted by Bacchus and his pards,
But on the viewless wings of poesy,
  Though the dull brain perplexes and retards:
Already with thee! tender is the night,
  And haply the Queen-Moon is on her throne,
    Clustered around by all her starry fays;
      But here there is no light,
  Save what from heaven is with the breezes
    blown
    Through verdurous glooms and winding
      mossy ways.   40

32 *pards:* leopards, which supposedly drew the
chariot of the god of wine.

I cannot see what flowers are at my feet,
  Nor what soft incense hangs upon the boughs,
But, in embalmèd darkness, guess each sweet
  Wherewith the seasonable month endows
The grass, the thicket, and the fruit-tree wild;
  White hawthorn and the pastoral eglantine,
    Fast fading violets covered up in leaves,
      And mid-May's eldest child,
  The coming musk-rose, full of dewy wine,
    The murmurous haunt of flies on summer
      eves.   50

Darkling I listen, and for many a time
  I have been half in love with easeful death,
Called him soft names in many a musèd rhyme,
  To take into the air my quiet breath;
Now more than ever seems it rich to die,
  To cease upon the midnight with no pain,
    While thou art pouring forth thy soul
      abroad
      In such ecstasy!
  Still wouldst thou sing, and I have ears in
    vain—
    To thy high requiem become a sod.   60

Thou wast not born for death, immortal bird!
  No hungry generations tread thee down;
The voice I hear this passing night was heard
  In ancient days by emperor and clown:
Perhaps the self-same song that found a path
  Through the sad heart of Ruth, when sick for
    home,
    She stood in tears amid the alien corn;
      The same that oft-times hath
  Charmed magic casements, opening on the
    foam
    Of perilous seas, in faery lands
      forlorn.   70

Forlorn! the very word is like a bell
  To toll me back from thee to my sole self!
Adieu! the fancy cannot cheat so well
  As she is famed to do, deceiving elf.
Adieu! adieu! thy plaintive anthem fades

64 *clown:* peasant. 67 *corn:* grain; see *The
Book of Ruth* II, 2–3. Ruth's homesickness is Keats's
invention.

Past the near meadows, over the still stream,
    Up the hillside; and now 'tis buried deep
        In the next valley-glades:
    Was it a vision, or a waking dream?
        Fled is that music.—Do I wake or
            sleep?   80

George Meredith

LUCIFER IN STARLIGHT

On a starred night Prince Lucifer uprose.
Tired of his dark dominion swung the fiend
Above the rolling ball in cloud part screened,
Where sinners hugged their specter of repose.

Poor prey to his hot fit of pride were those.
And now upon his western wing he leaned,
Now his huge bulk o'er Afric's sands careened,
Now the black planet shadowed Arctic snows.
Soaring through wider zones that pricked his
        scars
With memory of the old revolt from Awe,   10
He reached a middle height, and at the stars,
Which are the brain of heaven, he looked, and
        sank.
Around the ancient track marched, rank on
        rank,
The army of unalterable law.

Gerard Manley Hopkins

SPRING AND FALL: TO A YOUNG CHILD

Márgarét, are you gríeving
Over Goldengrove unleaving?
Léaves, líke the things of man, you
With your fresh thoughts care for, can you?
Áh! ás the heart grows older
It will come to such sights colder

By and by, nor spare a sigh
Though worlds of wanwood leafmeal lie.
And yet you wíll weep and know why.
Now no matter, child, the name: 10
Sórrow's spríngs are the same.
Nor mouth had, no nor mind, expressed
What heart heard of, ghost guessed:
It ís the blight man was born for,
It is Margaret you mourn for.

T. S. Eliot

THE HOLLOW MEN

Mistah Kurtz—he dead.

                    A penny for the Old Guy.

I

We are the hollow men
We are the stuffed men
Leaning together
Headpiece filled with straw. Alas!
Our dried voices, when
We whisper together
Are quiet and meaningless
As wind in dry grass
Or rats' feet over broken glass
In our dry cellar   10

Shape without form, shade without color,
Paralyzed force, gesture without motion;

Those who have crossed
With direct eyes, to death's other Kingdom
Remember us—if at all—not as lost
Violent souls, but only
As the hollow men
The stuffed men.

Epigraphs: (1) The words announcing the death of the main character in *Heart of Darkness*, by Joseph Conrad; (2) the cry with which English children beg for pennies on Guy Fawkes Day, November 5.

II

Eyes I dare not meet in dreams
In death's dream kingdom   20
These do not appear:
There, the eyes are
Sunlight on a broken column
There, is a tree swinging
And voices are
In the wind's singing
More distant and more solemn
Than a fading star.

Let me be no nearer
In death's dream kingdom   30
Let me also wear
Such deliberate disguises
Rat's coat, crowskin, crossed staves
In a field
Behaving as the wind behaves
No nearer—

Not that final meeting
In the twilight kingdom.

III

This is the dead land
This is cactus land   40
Here the stone images
Are raised, here they receive
The supplication of a dead man's hand
Under the twinkle of a fading star.

Is it like this
In death's other kingdom
Waking alone
At the hour when we are
Trembling with tenderness
Lips that would kiss   50
Form prayers to broken stone.

IV

The eyes are not here
There are no eyes here
In this valley of dying stars

In this hollow valley
This broken jaw of our lost kingdoms

In this last of meeting places
We grope together
And avoid speech
Gathered on this beach of the tumid river   60

Sightless, unless
The eyes reappear
As the perpetual star
Multifoliate rose
Of death's twilight kingdom
The hope only
Of empty men.

V

Here we go round the prickly pear
Prickly pear prickly pear
Here we go round the prickly pear   70
At five o'clock in the morning.

Between the idea
And the reality
Between the motion
And the act
Falls the shadow
      For Thine is the Kingdom

Between the conception
And the creation
Between the emotion   80
And the response
Falls the Shadow
      Life is very long

Between the desire
And the spasm
Between the potency
And the existence
Between the essence
And the descent
Falls the Shadow   90
      For Thine is the Kingdom

For Thine is
Life is
For Thine is the

This is the way the world ends
This is the way the world ends
This is the way the world ends
Not with a bang but a whimper.

Robert Frost

DESERT PLACES

Snow falling and night falling fast, oh, fast
In a field I looked into going past,
And the ground almost covered smooth in snow,
But a few weeds and stubble showing last.

The woods around it have it—it is theirs.
All animals are smothered in their lairs.
I am too absent-spirited to count;
The loneliness includes me unawares.

And lonely as it is that loneliness
Will be more lonely ere it will be less—   10
A blanker whiteness of benighted snow
With no expression, nothing to express.

They cannot scare me with their empty spaces
Between stars—on stars where no human race is.
I have it in me so much nearer home
To scare myself with my own desert places.

Wallace Stevens

SUNDAY MORNING

I

Complacencies of the peignoir, and late
Coffee and oranges in a sunny chair,
And the green freedom of a cockatoo
Upon a rug mingle to dissipate
The holy hush of ancient sacrifice.

She dreams a little, and she feels the dark
Encroachment of that old catastrophe,
As a calm darkens among water-lights.
The pungent oranges and bright, green wings
Seem things in some procession of the
    dead,   10
Winding across wide water, without sound.
The day is like wide water, without sound,
Stilled for the passing of her dreaming feet
Over the seas, to silent Palestine,
Dominion of the blood and sepulchre.

II

Why should she give her bounty to the dead?
What is divinity if it can come
Only in silent shadows and in dreams?
Shall she not find in comforts of the sun,
In pungent fruit and bright, green wings, or
    else   20
In any balm or beauty of the earth,
Things to be cherished like the thought of
    heaven?
Divinity must live within herself:
Passions of rain, or moods in falling snow;
Grievings in loneliness, or unsubdued
Elations when the forest blooms; gusty
Emotions on wet roads on autumn nights;
All pleasures and all pains, remembering
The bough of summer and the winter branch.
These are the measures destined for her
    soul.   30

III

Jove in the clouds had his inhuman birth.
No mother suckled him, no sweet land gave
Large-mannered motions to his mythy mind.
He moved among us, as a muttering king,
Magnificent, would move among his hinds,
Until our blood, commingling, virginal,
With heaven, brought such requital to desire
The very hinds discerned it, in a star.

31 *Jove:* Zeus or Jupiter, King of the gods: here
used to mean generalized Deity. 38 *hinds:* apparently the shepherds of *Gospel of St. Luke* ii, 8—
but it was the Wise Men who saw the star (*St.
Matthew* ii, 9).

Shall our blood fail? Or shall it come to be
The blood of paradise? And shall the
    earth   40
Seem all of paradise that we shall know?
The sky will be much friendlier then than now,
A part of labor and a part of pain,
And next in glory to enduring love,
Not this dividing and indifferent blue.

IV

She says, "I am content when wakened birds,
Before they fly, test the reality
Of misty fields, by their sweet questionings;
But when the birds are gone, and their warm
    fields
Return no more, where, then, is paradise?"   50
There is not any haunt of prophecy,
Nor any old chimera of the grave,
Neither the golden underground, nor isle
Melodious, where spirits gat them home,
Nor visionary south, nor cloudy palm
Remote on heaven's hill, that has endured
As April's green endures; or will endure
Like her remembrance of awakened birds,
Or her desire for June and evening, tipped
By the consummation of the swallow's
    wings.   60

V

She says, "But in contentment I still feel
The need of some imperishable bliss."
Death is the mother of beauty; hence from her,
Alone, shall come fulfilment to our dreams
And our desires. Although she strews the leaves
Of sure obliteration on our paths,
The path sick sorrow took, the many paths
Where triumph rang its brassy phrase, or love
Whispered a little out of tenderness,
She makes the willow shiver in the sun   70
For maidens who were wont to sit and gaze
Upon the grass, relinquished to their feet.

53 *underground, nor isle:* Greek ideas of paradise; cf. "Ulysses," by Tennyson, lines 63–64.

She causes boys to pile new plums and pears
On disregarded plate. The maidens taste
And stray impassioned in the littering leaves.

VI

Is there no change of death in paradise?
Does ripe fruit never fall? Or do the boughs
Hang always heavy in that perfect sky,
Unchanging, yet so like our perishing earth,
With rivers like our own that seek for seas   80
They never find, the same receding shores
That never touch with inarticulate pang?
Why set the pear upon those river-banks
Or spice the shores with odors of the plum?
Alas, that they should wear our colors there,
The silken weavings of our afternoons,
And pick the strings of our insipid lutes!
Death is the mother of beauty, mystical,
Within whose burning bosom we devise
Our earthly mothers waiting, sleeplessly.   90

VII

Supple and turbulent, a ring of men
Shall chant in orgy on a summer morn
Their boisterous devotion to the sun,
Not as a god, but as a god might be,
Naked among them, like a savage source.
Their chant shall be a chant of paradise,
Out of their blood, returning to the sky;
And in their chant shall enter, voice by voice,
The windy lake wherein their lord delights,
The trees, like serafin, and echoing hills,   100
That choir among themselves long afterward.
They shall know well the heavenly fellowship
Of men that perish and of summer morn.
And whence they came and whither they shall
    go
The dew upon their feet shall manifest.

VIII

She hears, upon that water without sound,
A voice that cries, "The tomb in Palestine

100 *Serafin:* seraphim, angels.

Is not the porch of spirits lingering.
It is the grave of Jesus, where he lay."
We live in an old chaos of the sun,   110
Or old dependency of day and night,
Or island solitude, unsponsored, free,
Of that wide water, inescapable.
Deer walk upon our mountains, and the quail
Whistle about us their spontaneous cries;
Sweet berries ripen in the wilderness;
And, in the isolation of the sky,
At evening, casual flocks of pigeons make
Ambiguous undulations as they sink,
Downward to darkness, on extended
       wings.   120

Philip Larkin

CHURCH GOING

Once I am sure there's nothing going on
I step inside, letting the door thud shut.
Another church: matting, seats, and stone,
And little books; sprawling of flowers, cut
For Sunday, brownish now; some brass and stuff
Up at the holy end; the small neat organ;
And a tense, musty, unignorable silence,
Brewed God knows how long. Hatless, I take off
My cycle-clips in awkward reverence.

Move forward, run my hand around the
       font.   10
From where I stand, the roof looks almost new—
Cleaned, or restored? Someone would know: I
       don't.
Mounting the lectern, I peruse a few
Hectoring large-scale verses, and pronounce
"Here endeth" much more loudly than I'd
       meant.
The echoes snigger briefly. Back at the door
I sign the book, donate an Irish sixpence,
Reflecting the place was not worth stopping for.
Yet stop I did: in fact I often do,
And always end much at a loss like this,   20

Wondering what to look for; wondering, too,
When churches fall completely out of use
What we shall turn them into; if we shall keep
A few cathedrals chronically on show,
Their parchment, plate, and pyx in locked cases,
And let the rest rent-free to rain and sheep.
Shall we avoid them as unlucky places?

Or, after dark, will dubious women come
To make their children touch a particular
       stone;
Pick simples for a cancer; or on some   30
Advised night see walking a dead one?
Power of some sort or other will go on
In games, in riddles, seemingly at random;
But superstition, like belief, must die,
And what remains when disbelief has gone?
Grass, weedy pavement, brambles, buttress, sky,

A shape less recognizable each week,
A purpose more obscure. I wonder who
Will be the last, the very last, to seek
This place for what it was; one of the
       crew   40
That tap and jot and know what rood-lofts
       were?
Some ruin-bibber, randy for antique,
Or Christmas-addict, counting on a whiff
Of gown-and-bands and organ-pipes and myrrh?
Or will he be my representative

Bored, uninformed, knowing the ghostly silt
Dispersed, yet tending to this cross of ground
Through suburb scrub because it held unspilt
So long and equably what since is found
Only in separation—marriage, and birth,   50
And death, and thoughts of these—for whom
       was built
This special shell? For, though I've no idea
What this accoutred frowsty barn is worth,
It pleases me to stand in silence here;

A serious house on serious earth it is,
In whose blent air all our compulsions meet,

42 *randy:* sexually excited.

Are recognized, and robed as destinies.
And that much never can be obsolete,
Since someone will forever be surprising
A hunger in himself to be more serious, 60

And gravitating with it to this ground,
Which, he once heard, was proper to grow wise
   in,
If only that so many dead lie round.

Theodore Roethke

THE ABYSS

1

Is the stair here?
Where's the stair?
"The stair's right there,
But it goes nowhere."

And the abyss? the abyss?
"The abyss you can't miss:
It's right where you are—
A step down the stair."

Each time ever
There always is
Noon of failure,
Part of a house. 10

In the middle of,
Around a cloud,
On top a thistle
The wind's slowing.

2

I have been spoken to variously
But heard little.
My inward witness is dismayed
By my unguarded mouth.
I have taken, too often, the dangerous path, 20
The vague, the arid,
Neither in nor out of this life.

Among us, who is holy?
What speech abides?
I hear the noise of the wall.

They have declared themselves,
Those who despise the dove.

Be with me, Whitman, maker of catalogues:
For the world invades me again,   30
And once more the tongues begin babbling.
And the terrible hunger for objects quails me:
The sill trembles.
And there on the blind
A furred caterpillar crawls down a string.
My symbol!
For I have moved closer to death, lived with death;
Like a nurse he sat with me for weeks, a sly surly attendant,
Watching my hands, wary.
Who sent him away?   40
I'm no longer a bird dipping a beak into rippling water
But a mole winding through earth,
A night-fishing otter.

3

Too much reality can be a dazzle, a surfeit;
Too close immediacy an exhaustion:
As when the door swings open in a florist's storeroom—
The rush of smells strikes like a cold fire, the throat freezes,
And we turn back to the heat of August,
Chastened.

So the abyss—   50
The slippery cold heights,
After the blinding misery,
The climbing, the endless turning,
Strike like a fire,
A terrible violence of creation,
A flash into the burning heart of the abominable;
Yet if we wait, unafraid, beyond the fearful instant,
The burning lake turns into a forest pool,
The fire subsides into rings of water,
A sunlit silence.   60

4

How can I dream except beyond this life?
Can I outleap the sea—
The edge of all the land, the final sea?
I envy the tendrils, their eyeless seeking,
The child's hand reaching into the coiled smilax,

And I obey the wind at my back
Bringing me home from the twilight fishing.

   In this, my half-rest,
   Knowing slows for a moment,
   And not-knowing enters, silent,   70
   Bearing being itself,
   And the fire dances
   To the stream's
   Flowing.

Do we move toward God, or merely another condition?
By the salt waves I hear a river's undersong,
In a place of mottled clouds, a thin mist morning and evening.
I rock between dark and dark,
My soul nearly my own,
My dead selves singing.   80
And I embrace this calm—
Such quiet under the small leaves!—
Near the stem, whiter at root,
A luminous stillness.

   The shade speaks slowly:
   "Adore and draw near.
   Who knows this—
   Knows all."

5

I thirst by day. I watch by night.
I receive! I have been received!   90
I hear the flowers drinking in their light,
I have taken counsel of the crab and the sea-urchin,
I recall the falling of small waters,
The stream slipping beneath the mossy logs,
Winding down to the stretch of irregular sand,
The great logs piled like matchsticks.

I am most immoderately married:
The Lord God has taken my heaviness away;
I have merged, like the bird, with the bright air,
And my thought flies to the place by the bo-tree.   100

Being, not doing, is my first joy.

   100 *bo-tree:* fig tree, sacred to Buddhists, under
which the Gautama received heavenly inspiration.

Adrienne Rich

THE ROOFWALKER

for Denise Levertov

Over the half-finished houses
night comes. The builders
stand on the roof. It is
quiet after the hammers,
the pulleys hang slack.
Giants, the roofwalkers,
on a listening deck, the wave
of darkness about to break
on their heads. The sky
is a torn sail where figures   10
pass magnified, shadows
on a burning deck.

I feel like them up there:

exposed, larger than life,
and due to break my neck.

Was it worth while to lay—
with infinite exertion—
a roof I can't live under?
—All those blueprints,
closing of gaps,   20
measurings, calculations?
A life I didn't choose
chose me: even
my tools are the wrong ones
for what I have to do.
I'm naked, ignorant,
a naked man fleeing
across the roofs
who could with a shade of difference
be sitting in the lamplight   30
against the cream wallpaper
reading—not with indifference—
about a naked man
fleeing across the roofs.

Chapter 11

AT THE
END OF
LIFE

Man, the existential philosophers have taught us, is the animal that knows he must die. This knowledge gives to his existence a unique character, though not necessarily the anxiety that some existentialists have emphasized. The young person, though often deeply moved and changed by the deaths of others, does not normally think much about his own. In later years, the abstract certainty of dying becomes a new knowledge: that death is not far off. And this gives special significance to the experience of old age.

These fundamental and inescapable features of human life have always presented some of the greatest challenges and opportunities to the literary artist. They present profound mysteries that we strive to understand; and sensitive treatments of them in literary works are one of our greatest sources of understanding. They represent facts to be faced and spiritual threats to be overcome; and literature, by objectifying them for contemplation and bringing them home to us, strengthens our capacity to live with them. Old age and death offer the writer endless themes for literary exploitation.

Human character and personality, in all their vast variety, are often starkly revealed in people's attitudes toward death, as the works in this chapter reveal. Confronted with the death of another, one may be sad-dened, like the speaker in "Tears, Idle Tears"; or ironically detached, like the speaker in "Dead Boy"; moved to reflection on the human condition, like John Donne and the speaker in "On Wenlock Edge"; or brought half-comprehendingly closer to maturity, as are the two children in "The Grave." Confronted with the nearness of one's own death, one may feel the resignation of Chuan in "An Odyssey of Birds"; the calm acceptance with which O'Flaherty's old woman makes her preparations; the terror of Claudio in *Measure for Measure;* the hope of eternal blessedness expressed by John Donne.

"Call no man happy until dead," said the ancient Greeks—meaning that the judgment of a life, of its meaning and its reach, cannot be made until it is over. The thoughts occasioned by death—thoughts of what is lost or destroyed by it—bring correlative reflection on what made a life worth living in the first place. Death brings home the ultimate question of what really matters. Thus Shakespeare's song "Fear No More" presents life simply as a "worldly task," to be concluded, one hopes, by a quiet consummation; Browning's bishop and the speaker in "Adieu, Farewell Earth's Bliss" regard the pleasures of life so ambiguously that more than a trace of sardonic humor pervades their utterances; "Tithonus" and "Asphodel, That Greeny Flower" suggest that the very values of life itself may depend on its having the limits and finality imposed by death.

John Donne

A DISCOURSE OF BELLS

We have a convenient[1] author who writ a discourse of bells, when he was prisoner in Turkey.[2] How would he have enlarged himself if he had been my fellow-prisoner in this sick bed, so near to that steeple,[3] which never ceases, no more than the harmony of the spheres, but is more heard. When the Turks took Constantinople, they melted the bells into ordnance; I have heard both bells and ordnance, but never been so much affected with those, as with these bells. I have lain [lodged] near a steeple in which there are said to be more than thirty bells,[4] and near another where there is one so big as that the clapper is said to weigh more than six hundred pound,[5] yet [was I] never so affected as here. Here the bells can scarce solemnize the funeral of any person but that I knew him, or knew that he was my neighbor: we dwelt in houses near to one another before, but now he is gone into that house, into which I must follow him.

There is a way of correcting the children of great persons, that other children are corrected in their behalf and in their names, and this works upon them, who indeed had

more deserved it. And when these bells tell me that now one and now another is buried, must not I acknowledge that they have the correction due to me and paid the debt that I owe? There is a story of a bell in a monastery which, when any of the house was sick to death, rung always voluntarily, and they knew the inevitableness of the danger by that. It rung once, when no man was sick; but the next day one of the house fell from the steeple and died, and the bell held the reputation of a prophet still.

If these bells that warn to a funeral now were appropriated to none, may not I, by the hour of the funeral, supply? How many men that stand at an execution, if they would ask, for what dies that man, should hear their own faults condemned and see themselves executed, by attorney? We scarce hear of any man preferred, but we think of ourselves, that we might very well have been that man; why might not I have been that man that is carried to his grave now? Could I fit myself to stand or sit in any man's place and not to lie in any man's grave? I may lack much of the good parts of the meanest, but I lack nothing of the mortality of the weakest; they may have acquired better abilities than I, but I was born to as many infirmities as they. To be an incumbent by lying down in a grave, to be a doctor by teaching mortification by example, by dying, though I may have seniors, others may be elder than I, yet I have proceeded apace in a good university, and gone a great way in a little time, by the furtherance of a vehement fever; and whomsoever these bells bring to the ground today, if he and I had been compared yesterday, perchance I should have been thought likelier to come to this preferment, then, than he.

God hath kept the power of death in his own hands, lest any man should bribe death. If man knew the gain of death, the ease of death, he would solicit, he would provoke death to assist him, by any hand which he might use. But as when men see many of

---

[1] Contemporary.

[2] Girolamo Maggi, captured at the fall of Famagusta, Cyprus, in 1571. His *De Tintinabulis* was published in 1608.

[3] Of St. Paul's Cathedral, of which Donne was Dean from 1621 to 1631. His illness occurred in 1623.

[4] That of Antwerp Cathedral.

[5] The Amboise bell in Rouen Cathedral.

their own professions preferred, it ministers a hope that that may light upon them; so when these hourly bells tell me of so many funerals of men like me, it presents, if not a desire that it may, yet a comfort whensoever mine shall come.

John Donne

NO MAN IS AN ISLAND

Perchance he for whom this bell tolls may be so ill as that he knows not it tolls for him; and perchance I may think myself so much better than I am as that they who are about me and see my state may have caused it to toll for me, and I know not that. The church is catholic, universal, so are all her actions; all that she does belongs to all. When she baptizes a child, that action concerns me; for that child is thereby connected to that head which is my head too and ingrafted into that body whereof I am a member. And when she buries a man, that action concerns me. All mankind is of one author and is one volume; when one man dies, one chapter is not torn out of the book, but translated into a better language; and every chapter must be so translated. God employs several translators; some pieces are translated by age, some by sickness, some by war, some by justice; but God's hand is in every translation, and his hand shall bind up all our scattered leaves again for that library where every book shall lie open to one another. As therefore the bell that rings to a sermon calls not upon the preacher only but upon the congregation to come, so this bell calls us all; but how much more me who am brought so near the door by this sickness!

There was a contention as far as a suit—in which piety and dignity, religion and estimation, were mingled—which of the re-

ligious orders should ring to prayers first in the morning; and it was determined that they should ring first that rose earliest. If we understand aright the dignity of this bell that tolls for our evening prayer, we would be glad to make it ours by rising early, in that application, that it might be ours as well as his whose indeed it is. The bell doth toll for him that thinks it doth; and though it intermit again, yet from that minute that that occasion wrought upon him he is united to God. Who casts not up his eye to the sun when it rises? But who takes off his eye from a comet when that breaks out? Who bends not his ear to any bell which upon any occasion rings? But who can remove it from that bell which is passing a piece of himself out of this world? No man is an island entire of itself; every man is a piece of the continent, a part of the main. If a clod be washed away by the sea, Europe is the less, as well as if a promontory were, as well as if a manor of thy friend's or of thine own were. Any man's death diminishes me, because I am involved in mankind, and therefore never send to know for whom the bell tolls; it tolls for thee.

Neither can we call this a begging of misery or a borrowing of misery, as though we were not miserable enough of ourselves but must fetch in more from the next house, in taking upon us the misery of our neighbors. Truly it were an excusable covetousness if we did, for affliction is a treasure, and scarce any man hath enough of it. No man hath affliction enough that is not matured and ripened by it and made fit for God by that affliction. If a man carry treasure in bullion or in a wedge of gold and have none coined into current money, his treasure will not defray him as he travels. Tribulation is treasure in the nature of it, but it is not current money in the use of it, except we get nearer and nearer our home, heaven, by it. Another man may be sick too, and sick to death, and this affliction may lie in his bowels as gold in a mine and be of no use to him; but this bell that tells me of his affliction digs out and applies that gold to me, if by this consideration of another's danger I take mine own into contemplation and so secure myself by making my recourse to my God, who is our only security.

Georges Blond

AN ODYSSEY OF BIRDS

The man was bracing himself against a wall of rock which rose vertically more than six hundred feet above him. His crushing load, whose weight was at least as great as his own, was jammed against the wall. He could just manage to maintain this position by the wide spread of his spindly legs, which were already trembling in a pair of blue cotton trousers, and indeed were visibly on the point of giving way. He wore tattered, rope-soled, canvas shoes, which had held out only by a miracle this far, and his torn trousers flapped like a flag in the freezing wind that blew over the whole width of the mountain pass. It was only August and the wind came from the south, but for all that it was icy. The caravan, with its bearers and horses, was making its way slowly and painfully over the mountains, battling against the wind, and the man leaning his back against the wall of rock surveyed it with an impenetrable expression.

He might have been thirty-five years old, or else sixty—how is one to guess at the age of a Chinaman? This human machine, worn down to the thread, had no age whatsoever. His skinny forearms emerged from the amputated sleeves of an American army jacket, which had incredibly bargained and bartered its way to the heart of Asia. The caravan was traveling from Qulja to Aqsu, on the edge of the desert, three hundred miles as the crow flies, and the horses seemed as near the point of collapse as the men. From Qulja to the Muzart Pass, they had covered two hundred miles, most of it through the mountains.

The man leaning against the rock, whose knees were now slightly bent so that he was even less erect than before, had covered the two hundred miles in the following manner: first he took fifty short, quick steps, with his back bent under his load at a forty-five-degree angle; then he stopped, stuck his stick into the ground or ice, spread his two hands over the top and let his stomach rest upon them, while he breathed heavily, making a noise like that of a pair of defective bellows. Two to five seconds later, he began the cycle again with fifty more steps. For at least two hundred years, as every traveler's account tells us, the technique has been exactly the same, and caravan bearers have carried as much as two hundred and fifty pounds of tea on their backs. Naturally, they do not live to a ripe old age; but then, in most of Asia, the care and feeding of a man is less expensive than that of a horse.

The Muzart Pass is in the middle of the high central range of the Tien Shan Mountains: a vast agglomeration in Turkestan, whose area is greater than that of France. These mountains are never in the newspapers; they hold no interest for famous climbers, because their highest peak is only about twenty-four thousand feet above sea level. Indeed, the topography of the central range is in many places uncertainly defined, for few geographers are tempted to haul their instruments to this far-away and chaotic region. And any pilot who flies over it watches his dials and listens to his motors with particular attention, knowing that a landing is impossible and a parachute jump would unquestionably be the prelude to slow death from exposure. The Muzart Pass crosses this range at an altitude of twelve thousand feet, rimmed by glaciers which sweep down from the surrounding mountains, every one of them higher than the Mont Blanc. For three quarters of the year, violent winds raise tempests of snow. The whole length of the pass and some distance to either side are littered with bones, but snow conceals them most of the time from view.

The man leaning against the rock watched as the caravan passed slowly before him. Every now and then a bearer, with his back bent at a forty-five degree angle, stopped to rest on his stick. The furious blast of the wind and the chatter of a mountain stream smothered the bearers' groaning sighs and the tread of the horses, which other men, bending their bodies to meet the wind's impact, were leading by their bridles. The men moved like so many pale ghosts, and indeed their whole existence had something unreal and ghostlike about it.

For convenience, let us give the man leaning against the rock a name. Let us call him Chuan. It is more than likely that neither this name or any other which the reader may choose was ever entered in the birth records of a village or town. A peasant family from the borderland of Chinese Turkestan has little legal existence, and for years no one had had occasion to call Chuan anything at all. A caravan bearer doesn't wait to be called; he is there, with fifty ghostly companions, and if he is not there no one is going to miss him. He may be dead, or he may be curled up in a corner, smoking remnants of opium; it doesn't really matter.

Chuan felt himself slipping and closed his eyes. His legs had crumpled, and finally he sat on his haunches, with his load resting partially on the ground although the straps still dug into his shoulders. From this sloping position he could no longer see the stooping men of the caravan pass before him. His head was turned slightly to the

right, and beyond the pass, to the southeast, between two snow-clad mountains, he saw a slope, slightly lower than the rest, covered with pines. The dark green trees, with a ray of sunlight upon them, stood in closed ranks, like the soldiers of a motionless army. Neither poverty nor wind had bent them over; they carried no load and stood marvelously straight, just as they had grown, pointing toward the sky. The picture they made was one of dignity and freedom and power.

Chuan relaxed his legs and stretched them out in front of him. Still feeling the straps cut into the area between his chest and his shoulders, he threw back the upper part of his body and at once obtained relief. The pine forest was now lower in his line of vision, and without moving his head he could see a large part of the snowy mountain summits. Twenty times or more he had crossed the Tien Shan Mountains, and his eyes had been blinded by the dazzling whiteness of the plateaus, but never for more than a fleeting second had he been able to lift them to see the jagged, white peaks stand out against the sky. For a bearer marches bent over at an angle of forty-five degrees.

Chuan looked, then, upon the jagged, white peaks. The mountains ceased to form the infernally hostile world to which a bearer must return over and over again in order to make his wretched living; they seemed now like the immobile waves of a majestic white ocean, tinged here and there with rose and blue lights. Chuan no longer saw the caravan pass by or wondered whether one of the ghostly figures would come to a halt before him; the caravan and its ghostly figures had gone out of his mind. The cold had dangerously invaded his thin, ill-protected body, but he did not feel either the cold or the bite of the wind on his parchment-like skin. Only the great snowy waves rolled over and penetrated him. By now he was lying alongside his load, flat on the ground. For a long moment he closed his eyes, and when he opened them he saw the sky filled with birds.

The infinite depth of the sky was pale blue and absolutely cloudless, and the wild geese, flying at a single level, cut it horizontally in two. There were dozens and dozens of groups of birds, all of them in chevron or V formation, flying straight from north to south. As far as Chuan could see, the birds filled the sky, flying in the rarefied air high above the mountain pass. The air was so clear that Chuan could make out every bird, every neck outstretched parallel to the one next to it and every pair of wings making the same regular, powerful rowing motion. Although the wind was blowing from the south and the geese were flying against it, their pace was faultlessly even. Each chevron was like a compass, with unequally long legs; the compasses were all open at exactly the same angle, but without rigidity. They might be compared, also, to large, lightweight, flexible kites, pulled by invisible strings in the same direction.

The rays of the setting sun lit up the ranks of wild geese from below, and those on the western side seemed to be of a lighter color than the rest, a pale gray very close to white. Chuan knew their exact shading, for as a child he had watched them go by, once in spring and once at the end of summer. At dawn he had seen them fly low over the plains, and occasionally his father had got him out of bed at night and led him into the dark and silent fields in order that he might hear the strange whirring noise produced by the beat of thousands of wings. Sometimes, he remembered, the noise had continued for hours on end, and long after he had gone back to bed the geese were still flying over.

How many years had gone by since these dawn and midnight vigils? How long had it been since the stooped caravan bearer had looked up to see the great migration of the graylag geese, high in the sky? All this time the birds had continued, at the same seasons, to fly over. The bearer's body had become more and more bent, and turned into a rag more miserable than the rags which covered it; the insectlike steps he took under his killing load were increasingly jerky, and his hoarse breathing was very painful to the ear. And yet the movement of the birds was just what it had been before. Now the intermediate period of time was contracted and wiped out, and the birds' motion seemed to Chuan like a part of himself which had been preserved from age and poverty and degradation. A great peace came over him. Probably none of the bearers or the men who were leading the horses through the windswept pass had noticed that the flight of the geese had begun. Only Chuan, to all appearances a still, parchment-skinned mummy, discolored by the icy cold but delivered forever of the crushing load it had been his lot to carry, was aware of what was going on. As long as he liked he would gaze upon this unparalleled sight, yes, just as long as the child Chuan, for whom the passage of time had no meaning.

The graylag geese were flying over the Tien Shan Mountains; soon they would cross the Desert of Takla Makan, the wild Altyn Tagh, the stifling Tibetan plateau, and finally, at an altitude of twenty-six thousand feet, the Himalayas, which no other migrant birds are known to pass. Just now their first line was passing over the Muzart Pass, above the only human face turned in their direction, the face of a miserable caravan bearer, whose stare was gradually congealing. Chuan's eyes no longer moved, but he could still see the passage of the great flexible kites overhead. The sky was beginning to darken, but still the wild geese flew over. Their great flight across the high heaven was the last movement registered by the retinas of the poor bearer, who had for so long bent nearly double over the ground.

Katherine Anne Porter

THE GRAVE

The grandfather, dead for more than thirty years, had been twice disturbed in his long repose by the constancy and possessiveness of his widow. She removed his bones first to Louisiana and then to Texas as if she had set out to find her own burial place, knowing well she would never return to the places she had left. In Texas she set up a small cemetery in a corner of her first farm, and as the family connection grew and oddments of relations came over from Kentucky to settle, it contained at last about twenty graves. After the grandmother's death, part of her land was to be sold for the benefit of certain of her children, and the cemetery happened to lie in the part set aside for sale. It was necessary to take up the bodies and bury them again in the family plot in the big new public cemetery, where the grandmother had been buried. At last her husband was to lie beside her for eternity, as she had planned.

The family cemetery had been a pleasant small neglected garden of tangled rose bushes and ragged cedar trees and cypress, the simple flat stones rising out of uncropped sweet-smelling wild grass. The graves were lying open and empty one burning day when Miranda and her brother Paul, who often went together to hunt rabbits and doves, propped their twenty-two Winchester rifles carefully against the rail fence, climbed over, and explored among the graves. She was nine years old and he was twelve.

They peered into the pits all shaped alike with such purposeful accuracy, and looking at each other with pleased adventurous eyes, they said in solemn tones: "These were graves!" trying by words to shape a special, suitable emotion in their minds, but they felt nothing except an agreeable thrill of wonder: they were seeing a new sight, doing something they had not done before. In them both there was also a small disappointment at the entire commonplaceness of the actual spectacle. Even if it had once contained a coffin for years upon years, when the coffin was gone a grave was just a hole in the ground. Miranda leaped into the pit that had held her grandfather's bones. Scratching around aimlessly and pleasurably as any young animal, she scooped up a lump of earth and weighed it in her palm. It had a pleasantly sweet, corrupt smell, being mixed with cedar needles and small leaves, and as the crumbs fell apart, she saw a silver dove no larger than a hazel nut, with spread wings and a neat fan-shaped tail. The breast had a deep round hollow in it. Turning it up to the fierce sunlight, she saw that the inside of the hollow was cut in little whorls. She scrambled out, over the pile of loose earth that had fallen back into one end of the grave, calling to Paul that she had found something, he must guess what. . . . His head appeared smiling over the rim of another grave. He waved a closed hand at her. "I've got something too!" They ran to compare treasures, making a game of it, so many guesses each, all wrong, and a final showdown with opened palms. Paul had found a thin wide gold ring carved with intricate flowers and leaves. Miranda was smitten at sight of the ring and wished to have it. Paul seemed more impressed by the dove. They made a trade, with some little bickering. After he had got the dove in his hand, Paul said, "Don't you know what this is? This is a screw head for a coffin! . . . I'll bet nobody else in the world has one like this!"

Miranda glanced at it without covetousness. She had the gold ring on her thumb; it fitted perfectly. "Maybe we ought to go now," she said, "maybe one of the niggers 'll see us and tell somebody." They knew the land had been sold, the cemetery was no longer theirs, and they felt like trespassers. They climbed back over the fence, slung their rifles loosely under their arms—they had been shooting at targets with various kinds of firearms since they were seven years old—and set out to look for the rabbits and doves or whatever small game might happen along. On these expeditions Miranda always followed at Paul's heels along the path, obeying instructions about handling her gun when going through fences; learning how to stand it up properly so it would not slip and fire unexpectedly; how to wait her time for a shot and not just bang away in the air without looking, spoiling shots for Paul, who really could hit things if given a chance. Now and then, in her excitement at seeing birds whizz up suddenly before her face, or a rabbit leap across her very toes, she lost her head, and almost without sighting she flung her rifle up and pulled the trigger. She hardly ever hit any sort of mark. She had no proper sense of hunting at all. Her brother would be often completely disgusted with her. "You don't care whether you get your bird or not," he said. "That's no way to hunt." Miranda could not understand his indignation. She had seen him smash his hat and yell with fury when he had missed his aim. "What I like about shooting," said Miranda, with exasperating inconsequence, "is pulling the trigger and hearing the noise."

"Then, by golly," said Paul, "whyn't you go back to the range and shoot at bullseyes?"

"I'd just as soon," said Miranda, "only like this, we walk around more."

"Well, you just stay behind and stop spoiling my shots," said Paul, who, when he made a kill, wanted to be certain he had made it. Miranda, who alone brought down a bird once in twenty rounds, always claimed as her own any game they got when they fired at the same moment. It was tiresome and unfair and her brother was sick of it.

"Now, the first dove we see, or the first rabbit, is mine," he told her. "And the next will be yours. Remember that and don't get smarty."

"What about snakes?" asked Miranda idly. "Can I have the first snake?"

Waving her thumb gently and watching her gold ring glitter, Miranda lost interest in shooting. She was wearing her summer roughing outfit: dark blue overalls, a light blue shirt, a hired-man's straw hat, and thick brown sandals. Her brother had the same outfit except his was a sober hickory-nut color. Ordinarily Miranda preferred her overalls to any other dress, though it was making rather a scandal in the countryside, for the year was 1903, and in the back country the law of female decorum had teeth in it. Her father had been criticized for letting his girls dress like boys and go careering around astride barebacked horses. Big sister Maria, the really independent and fearless one, in spite of her rather affected ways, rode at a dead run with only a rope knotted around her horse's nose. It was said the motherless family was running down, with the Grandmother no longer there to hold it together. It was known that she had discriminated against her son Harry in her will, and that he was in straits about money. Some of his old neighbors reflected with vicious satisfaction that now he would probably not be so stiffnecked, nor have any more high-stepping horses either. Miranda knew this, though she could not say how. She had met along the road old women of the kind who smoked corn-cob pipes, who had treated her grandmother with most sincere respect. They slanted their gummy old eyes sideways at the granddaughter and said, "Ain't you ashamed of yoself, Missy? It's against the Scriptures to dress like that. Whut yo Pappy thinkin about?" Miranda, with her powerful social sense, which was like a fine set of antennae radiating from every pore of her skin, would feel ashamed because she knew well it was rude and ill-bred to shock anybody, even bad-tempered old crones, though she had faith in her father's judgment and was perfectly comfortable in the clothes. Her father had said, "They're just what you need, and they'll save your dresses for school. . . ." This sounded quite simple and natural to her. She had been brought up in rigorous economy. Wastefulness was vulgar. It was also a sin. These were truths; she had heard them repeated many times and never once disputed.

Now the ring, shining with the serene purity of fine gold on her rather grubby thumb, turned her feelings against her overalls and sockless feet, toes sticking through the thick brown leather straps. She wanted to go back to the farmhouse, take a good cold bath, dust herself with plenty of Maria's violet talcum powder—provided Maria was not present to object, of course —put on the thinnest, most becoming dress she owned, with a big sash, and sit in a wicker chair under the trees. . . . These things were not all she wanted, of course; she had vague stirrings of desire for luxury and a grand way of living which could not take precise form in her imagination but were founded on family legend of past wealth and leisure. These immediate comforts were what she could have, and she wanted them at once. She lagged rather far behind Paul, and once she thought of just turning back without a word and going home. She stopped, thinking that Paul would never do that to her, and so she would have to tell him. When a rabbit leaped, she let Paul have it without dispute. He killed it with one shot.

When she came up with him, he was already kneeling, examining the wound, the rabbit trailing from his hands. "Right through the head," he said complacently, as if he had aimed for it. He took out his sharp, competent bowie knife and started to skin the body. He did it very cleanly and quickly. Uncle Jimbilly knew how to pre-

pare the skins so that Miranda always had fur coats for her dolls, for though she never cared much for her dolls she liked seeing them in fur coats. The children knelt facing each other over the dead animal. Miranda watched admiringly while her brother stripped the skin away as if he were taking off a glove. The flayed flesh emerged dark scarlet, sleek, firm; Miranda with thumb and finger felt the long fine muscles with the silvery flat strips binding them to the joints. Brother lifted the oddly bloated belly. "Look," he said, in a low amazed voice. "It was going to have young ones."

Very carefully he slit the thin flesh from the center ribs to the flanks, and a scarlet bag appeared. He slit again and pulled the bag open, and there lay a bundle of tiny rabbits, each wrapped in a thin scarlet veil. The brother pulled these off and there they were, dark gray, their sleek wet down lying in minute even ripples, like a baby's head just washed, their unbelievably small delicate ears folded close, their little blind faces almost featureless.

Miranda said, "Oh, I want to *see*," under her breath. She looked and looked—excited but not frightened, for she was accustomed to the sight of animals killed in hunting— filled with pity and astonishment and a kind of shocked delight in the wonderful little creatures for their own sakes, they were so pretty. She touched one of them ever so carefully. "Ah, there's blood running over them," she said and began to tremble without knowing why. Yet she wanted most deeply to see and to know. Having seen, she felt at once as if she had known all along. The very memory of her former ignorance faded, she had always known just this. No one had ever told her anything outright, she had been rather unobservant of the animal life around her because she was so accustomed to animals. They seemed simply disorderly and unaccountably rude in their habits, but altogether natural and not very interesting. Her brother had spoken as if he had known about everything all along. He may have seen all this before. He had never said a word to her, but she knew now a part at least of what he knew. She understood a little of the secret, formless intuitions in her own mind and body, which had been clearing up, taking form, so gradually and so steadily she had not realized that she was learning what she had to know. Paul said cautiously, as if he were talking about something forbidden: "They were just about ready to be born." His voice dropped on the last word. "I know," said Miranda, "like kittens. I know, like babies." She was quietly and terribly agitated, standing again with her rifle under her arm, looking down at the bloody heap. "I don't want the skin," she said, "I won't have it." Paul buried the young rabbits again in their mother's body, wrapped the skin around her, carried her to a clump of sage bushes, and hid her away. He came out again at once and said to Miranda, with an eager friendliness, a confidential tone quite unusual in him, as if he were taking her into an important secret on equal terms: "Listen, now. Now you listen to me, and don't ever forget. Don't you ever tell a living soul that you saw this. Don't tell a soul. Don't tell Dad because I'll get into trouble. He'll say I'm leading you into things you ought not to do. He's always saying that. So now don't you go and forget and blab out sometime the way you're always doing. . . . Now, that's a secret. Don't you tell."

Miranda never told, she did not even wish to tell anybody. She thought about the whole worrisome affair with confused unhappiness for a few days. Then it sank quietly into her mind and was heaped over by accumulated thousands of impressions, for nearly twenty years. One day she was picking her path among the puddles and crushed refuse of a market street in a strange city of a strange country, when without warning, plain and clear in its true colors as if she looked through a frame upon a scene that had not stirred nor changed since the moment it happened, the episode of that far-off day leaped from its burial place before her mind's eye. She was so reasonlessly horrified she halted suddenly staring, the scene before her eyes dimmed by the vision back of them. An Indian vendor had held up before her a tray of dyed sugar sweets, in the shapes of all kinds of small creatures: birds, baby chicks, baby rabbits, lambs, baby pigs. They were in gay colors and smelled of vanilla, maybe. . . . It was a very hot day and the smell in the market, with its piles of raw flesh and wilting flowers, was like the mingled sweetness and corruption she had smelled that other day in the empty cemetery at home: the day she had remembered always until now vaguely as the time she and her brother had found treasure in the opened graves. Instantly upon this thought the dreadful vision faded, and she saw clearly her brother, whose childhood face she had forgotten, standing again in the blazing sunshine, again twelve years old, a pleased sober smile in his eyes, turning the silver dove over and over in his hands.

Liam O'Flaherty

THE OLD WOMAN

Maggie Crampton was coming down the path that led to the back yard of Julia Duggan's house. She was so stooped and feeble that she had to keep her hands on her knees as she walked. Her prone back was almost level with the tops of the low stone fences that bound the lane. She thrust her bare feet forward with the extreme slowness of a huge tortoise. She grunted every time she struck her toe against one of the loose stones that lay on the ground.

A small white bag hung from her neck by

a black cord. It was quite clean, in striking contrast with the filthy condition of her ragged grey dress and of her body. It swung to and fro gently with each step, like the heavy pendulum of a big clock.

She halted when she came to the stile that led into Julia Duggan's back yard. Grunting loudly, she straightened her back and gripped the top of the stile with both hands. There she rested for a little while, with her face turned towards the sky. Her lips moved in prayer. Strands of white hair hung down on either side of her wrinkled yellow cheeks. The color had almost completely faded from the pupils of her eyes. She had no teeth left.

As she began to climb over the stile, a yellow dog came running around the gable end of the house. He was barking furiously, with his tail and his mane on end. He stopped barking and slowed down to a walk on catching sight of the old woman. Then he put his tail between his legs and began to whine as he approached her. He crawled right up to her and put his snout against her naked right foot. He sniffed hungrily.

The old woman sat down to rest on a stone after getting over the stile. She struck at the dog with her fist and cursed. The animal darted away a short distance. There he stood watching her intently. When she resumed her journey around the gable end of the house, he followed close at her heels, with his mane on end and his tail under his belly. Now and again, as he crawled after her, he laid his snout against her dirty flesh and shuddered violently.

Nellie Duggan, a little girl of seven, came out of the house as the old woman approached the door. She had pretty flaxen hair and blue eyes. She wore a neat white pinafore and there was an orange bow at the end of her plaited hair. Her bare feet were spotlessly clean. She ran indoors after staring in fright for a few seconds at Maggie Crampton.

"She is coming," she whispered to her mother as she crossed the floor to the chimney corner at full speed. "She is nearly at the door."

Mrs. Duggan was kneading dough for a cake on the kitchen table. She turned and looked at her daughter.

"Who is coming?" she said.

"Maggie Crampton," Nellie said as she sat down on a blue stool. "She is outside in the yard."

"I never saw such a girl," Mrs. Duggan said with a smile. "You are afraid of everybody."

Nellie put her feet close together and her hands behind her back. She kept her eyes fixed on the open doorway.

"I don't know what to do with you," Mrs. Duggan said, as she resumed her work. "You are so nervous. I'm worried about you."

Nellie almost leaped to her feet again as the old woman's grunting became audible in the kitchen.

"Here she comes," she whispered in horror. "She's at the door now."

"Stop that," Mrs. Duggan said. "You should respect old age. It's against the law of God to be afraid of a good Christian."

The old woman waddled into the kitchen and halted near the doorway.

"God save all here," she said.

"You, too," Julia Duggan said. "You are welcome in God's name. Draw down to the fire."

"I'll be all right here near the door," Maggie Crampton said.

"Don't behave like a stranger in my house," Julia Duggan said, raising her voice. "Draw down to the hearth, I tell you."

Maggie waddled down to the hearth and sat on a black stool in the corner opposite to the little girl. Then she began to fumble with the cord to which the white bag was attached.

"I want you to look at it again for me," she said to Julia. "Today I got afraid that the moths might have got into the bag since you looked at it last time. That was in March and now we're at the end of July. I'm terribly worried about it, Julia."

"I'll look at it for you and welcome," Julia said, "as soon as this cake is in the oven."

"God spare your health," Maggie said. "My hour might strike at any moment now."

"It's our Christian duty to help the old," Julia said.

"I want to be sure that everything is in proper order," Maggie said in a loud voice. "I don't want to look untidy and I laid out."

At that moment, the dog thrust his head slowly around the corner of the doorway. He looked towards Maggie with hunger in his bloodshot yellow eyes. He sniffed and began to whine on a low note.

Julia turned her head quickly on hearing him whine. Her face clouded with anger when she caught sight of him in the doorway. She spat.

"Get out of here," she shouted. "You filthy creature!"

The dog disappeared at once.

"Bah!" Julia continued. "What horrid things there are in God's world."

"Don't say that, Julia," the old woman said as she detached the little white bag from the cord. "There are only lovely things in God's world."

"There are horrid things in it, too," Julia said. "There are things in it that frighten me."

"Everything that God made has a divine purpose," the old woman said.

"I know there are ugly things," Julia said. "Many ugly things."

"How could a divine thing frighten a Christian?" Maggie said.

"I have seen many ugly things that frighten me," Julia said.

Maggie put the little bag down carefully beside her on a red stool.

"Nothing that God made could be ugly,"

she shouted in an arrogant tone. "I'm telling you that now, Julia, because I know it's the truth."

"It's easy for the old to be wise," Julia said. "Their blood is nearly cold. It's only the young that suffer."

"They suffer because they are sinful," the old woman said.

"Their blood is warm," Julia shouted. "How can they be wise when their blood is warm?"

"It's only sin that's ugly," Maggie said. "It was the devil made sin."

"The old only see what pleases them," Julia said. "When the blood is hot, many ugly things are seen."

She suddenly turned her head and looked out the doorway.

"Ah! Woe!" she cried plaintively. "Why should there be such ugly things in God's world?"

The old woman took a clay pipe from the pocket of her skirt and lit the tobacco in the bowl with a sod of turf from the fire. She smoked for a little while, grunting with pleasure. Then she removed the pipe from her lips and turned towards Julia Duggan.

"There are no ugly things in God's world," she cried at the top of her voice. "I'm telling you that, Julia, because I know it's the truth. God has a reason for everything."

During the silence that followed, Nellie raised her eyes timidly and looked at Maggie Crampton's feet. She shuddered when she saw the enormous size to which they had swollen. The lower parts were quite black with dirt. The upper parts were red, with greyish patches here and there, like the scales on a rockfish. Then she raised her eyes still further and looked at the old woman's face. To her surprise, she saw that it was kindly and wise, whereas she had expected to see the horrid countenance of an ogress.

Trembling with delight, the little girl looked into the fire and her cheeks flushed crimson. She had suddenly become infinitely happy, because she had got rid of a terror that oppressed her from infancy. Ever since then, older people had frightened her by saying that Maggie Crampton would come and put her in a sack and take her away to a dark cave unless she behaved. So that the existence of the old woman had always been, until this moment, the most horrid fact in her consciousness. She had once gone with an old cousin to the one-roomed hut where Maggie Crampton lived, at the northern end of the village. The two children had stood hand in hand by the open doorway of the hut, peering into the smoky gloom, until they heard the old woman grunt. Then they had fled in terror. From that day, little Nellie never again dared look at Maggie Crampton's face, until this happy moment of deliverance.

Now it was fondness that she felt for the old woman, instead of fear. As she stared into the fire, she kept thinking how wonderful it was not to be afraid any more.

"I have seen many things that frightened me," Julia Duggan said as she was putting the kneaded dough into the oven. "I have seen many horrible things in God's world."

The old woman knocked the ashes out of her pipe and said:

"Only sin is ugly. It was the devil made sin."

"There are many ugly things," Julia Duggan said. "I have seen them and they frightened me."

"It's only now when my hour approaches," the old woman said as she put the pipe into the pocket of her skirt, "that I understand the loveliness of God's world. Sometimes I can hardly bear the pain of longing for it. When I'm alone on a lovely summer day like this in my little house, saying my prayers, I hear the shouting of children at their play, or the song of a bird. Then I can pray no more and I hate the thought of death. I long for my own loveliness. I long for my youth, when I shouted and

danced and picked cowslips in the fields of May beneath the singing larks. Aye! Aye! There are times when the loveliness of God's world gives me pain."

After she had put the oven on the fire, Julia scrubbed and dried the table. Then she laid a clean white cloth over the board.

"Give me the bag now," she said to Maggie.

"Be careful with it," the old woman said nervously as Julia took the little white bag to the table. "My sight is nearly all gone now, so I can't look at it myself. I can't touch it, either, because my hands are hardly ever clean enough."

"You poor creature!" Julia said, as she opened the bag. "You are to be pitied, all alone and your hour approaching, without anybody to look after you."

"Oh! I have good neighbors," the old woman said. "They look after me. It's hard, though, to keep an old person clean. I keep groping things. So my hands get dirty. That's why I'm afraid to open the bag myself."

Julia took a dark brown burial dress from the bag and spread it on the table. It was made of cheap cotton cloth. There was a narrow lace frill around the neck and silk braiding down the front, in two parallel lines. A strip of white linen was stitched over the breast, with a red heart in the center of the strip. A religious motto was embroidered in black on the white linen, encircling the red heart.

She also took a pair of white cotton gloves and white cotton stockings from the little bag.

"They look all right," she said, after having examined them carefully.

"Thank God," the old woman said fervently. "It would be terrible if I looked untidy when I faced God for my judgment."

"I'll touch them with the iron," Julia Duggan said.

"God spare your health," Maggie Crampton said. "You're the only one I'd let touch them, because you have holy hands. When I had my sight, I loved watching your hands."

"You say the queerest things," Julia Duggan said as she blushed slightly.

Her touch was extremely delicate. Her long, slender fingers moved ever so daintily over the coarse fabric of the burial dress. They caressed it gently as if it were made of the most precious stuff.

Little Nellie suddenly jumped to her feet and ran out of the house. She clasped her hands over her head and skipped down the yard.

"There are only lovely things in God's world," she cried gaily as she ran. "There are no ugly things."

After having ironed the burial robes, Julia Duggan folded them neatly and put them back into the bag. Then she tied the bag and gave it to the old woman.

"God spare your health, Julia," the old woman said.

"It's only kindness that saves us from damnation," Julia said, "in a world where there are so many wicked things."

"Don't say that, Julia," the old woman said as she attached the little white bag to the black cord. "Everything has a divine purpose."

She got to her feet when the bag was attached and waddled to the doorway with her hands on her knees. There she halted and turned her face towards Julia Duggan.

"There are only lovely things in God's world," she shouted in an arrogant tone. "I'm telling you that now, Julia, because it's the truth."

Then she waddled out of the house.

"There are many wicked things," Julia Duggan shouted from the hearth in a forlorn voice. "I have seen them and they frightened me."

The old woman halted and raised her head when she was near the gable end.

"It was the devil made sin," she shouted. "Remember that now and say no more."

The yellow dog came loping cautiously through the back yard as the old woman was going up the lane. He had his tail under his belly and his mane stood on end. He climbed to the top of the stile and crouched there, sniffing the air hungrily in her direction.

"There are only lovely things in God's world," she kept muttering as she advanced slowly up the lane with her hands on her knees.

The little white bag swung gently to and fro with each step.

Chidiock Tichborne

ELEGY

My prime of youth is but a frost of cares,
  My feast of joy is but a dish of pain,
My crop of corn is but a field of tares,
  And all my good is but vain hope of gain;

Elegy: Tichborne was convicted in 1586 of plotting against the life of Queen Elizabeth I. According to tradition, he wrote his "Elegy" in the Tower of London, the night before his execution.

The day is past, and yet I saw no sun,
And now I live, and now my life is done.

My tale was heard and yet it was not told,
My fruit is fallen and yet my leaves are green,
My youth is spent and yet I am not old,
I saw the world and yet I was not seen;
My thread is cut and yet it is not spun,
And now I live, and now my life is done. 10

I sought my death and found it in my womb,
I looked for life and saw it was a shade,
I trod the earth and knew it was my tomb,
And now I die, and now I was but made;
My glass is full, and now my glass is run.
And now I live, and now my life is done.

William Shakespeare

FEAR NO MORE

Fear no more the heat o' the sun
  Nor the furious winter's rages;
Thou thy worldly task hast done,
  Home art gone and ta'en thy wages;
Golden lads and girls all must,
As chimney-sweepers, come to dust.

Fear no more the frown o' the great:
  Thou art past the tyrant's stroke;
Care no more to clothe and eat:
  To thee the reed is as the oak: 10
The sceptre, learning, physic must
All follow this, and come to dust.

Fear no more the lightning-flash
  Nor the all-dreaded thunder-stone;
Fear not slander, censure rash;
  Thou hast finished joy and moan;
All lovers young, all lovers must
Consign to thee, and come to dust.

No exorciser harm thee!
  Nor no witchcraft charm thee! 20
Ghost unlaid forbear thee!
  Nothing ill come near thee!
Quiet consummation have;
And renownèd be thy grave!

William Shakespeare

AY, BUT TO DIE

Ay, but to die, and go we know not where;
To lie in cold obstruction and to rot;
This sensible warm motion to become
A kneaded clod; and the delighted spirit
To bathe in fiery floods, or to reside
In thrilling region of thick-ribbèd ice;
To be imprisoned in the viewless winds
And blown with restless violence round about
The pendent world; or to be worse than worst
Of those that lawless and uncertain
    thoughts 10

11 *physic:* medicine. 12 *this:* this law. 14 *thunder-stone:* thunderbolt. 18 *consign to thee:* submit to the same terms.

AY, BUT TO DIE: From *Measure for Measure*, III, I.
2 *obstruction:* cessation of vital functions.

Imagine howling:—'tis too horrible!
The weariest and most loathed worldly life
That age, ache, penury, and imprisonment
Can lay on nature is a paradise
To what we fear of death.

Thomas Nashe

ADIEU, FAREWELL EARTH'S BLISS

Adieu, farewell earth's bliss,
This world uncertain is;
Fond are life's lustful joys,
Death proves them all but toys,
None from his darts can fly.
I am sick, I must die.
　　Lord, have mercy on us!

Rich men, trust not in wealth,
Gold cannot buy you health;
Physic himself must fade,   10
All things to end are made.
The plague full swift goes by;
I am sick, I must die.
　　Lord, have mercy on us!

Beauty is but a flower
Which wrinkles will devour:
Brightness falls from the air,
Queens have died young and fair,
Dust has closèd Helen's eye.
I am sick, I must die.   20
　　Lord, have mercy on us!

Strength stoops unto the grave,
Worms feed on Hector brave,
Swords may not fight with fate.
Earth still holds ope her gate;
Come! come! the bells do cry.
I am sick, I must die.
　　Lord, have mercy on us!

Wit with his wantonness
Tasteth death's bitterness;   30
Hell's executioner
Hath no ears for to hear
What vain art can reply.
I am sick, I must die.
　　Lord, have mercy on us!

Haste, therefore, each degree,
To welcome destiny.
Heaven is our heritage,
Earth but a player's stage;
Mount we unto the sky.   40
I am sick, I must die.
　　Lord, have mercy on us!

John Donne

DEATH, BE NOT PROUD

Death, be not proud, though some have callèd
　　thee
Mighty and dreadful, for thou art not so;
For those whom thou think'st thou dost
　　overthrow
Die not, poor Death, nor yet canst thou kill me.
From rest and sleep, which but thy pictures be,
Much pleasure, then from thee much more must
　　flow,
And soonest our best men with thee do go,
Rest of their bones, and soul's delivery.
Thou art slave to fate, chance, kings, and
　　desperate men,
And dost with poison, war, and sickness
　　dwell,   10
And poppy or charms can make us sleep as well
And better than thy stroke; why swell'st thou
　　then?
One short sleep past, we wake eternally,
And Death shall be no more; Death, thou shalt
　　die.

　　11 *poppy:* opium.

Alfred, Lord Tennyson

TITHONUS

The woods decay, the woods decay and fall,
The vapors weep their burthen to the ground,
Man comes and tills the field and lies beneath,
And after many a summer dies the swan.
Me only cruel immortality
Consumes; I wither slowly in thine arms
Here at the quiet limit of the world,
A white-haired shadow roaming like a dream
The ever-silent spaces of the East,
Far-folded mists, and gleaming halls of morn.   10
  Alas! for this gray shadow, once a man—
So glorious in his beauty and thy choice,
Who madest him thy chosen, that he seemed
To his great heart none other than a god!
I asked thee, "Give me immortality."
Then didst thou grant mine asking with a smile,
Like wealthy men who care not how they give.
But thy strong Hours indignant worked their
      wills,
And beat me down and marred and wasted me,
And though they could not end me, left me
      maimed   20
To dwell in presence of immortal youth,
Immortal age beside immortal youth,
And all I was in ashes. Can thy love,
Thy beauty, make amends, though even now,
Close over us, the silver star, thy guide,
Shines in those tremulous eyes that fill with tears
To hear me? Let me go; take back thy gift.
Why should a man desire in any way
To vary from the kindly race of men,
Or pass beyond the goal of ordinance   30

Where all should pause, as is most meet for all?
  A soft air fans the cloud apart; there comes
A glimpse of that dark world where I was born.
Once more the old mysterious glimmer steals
From thy pure brows, and from thy shoulders
      pure,
And bosom beating with a heart renewed.
Thy cheek begins to redden through the gloom,
Thy sweet eyes brighten slowly close to mine,
Ere yet they blind the stars, and the wild team
Which love thee, yearning for thy yoke, arise   40
And shake the darkness from their loosened
      manes,
And beat the twilight into flakes of fire.
  Lo! ever thus thou growest beautiful
In silence, then before thine answer given
Departest, and thy tears are on my cheek.
  Why wilt thou ever scare me with thy tears
And make me tremble lest a saying learnt,
In days far-off, on that dark earth, be true?
"The gods themselves cannot recall their gifts."
  Ay me! ay me! with what another heart   50
In days far-off, and with what other eyes
I used to watch—if I be he that watched—
The lucid outline forming round thee; saw
The dim curls kindle into sunny rings;
Changed with thy mystic change, and felt my
      blood
Glow with the glow that slowly crimsoned all
Thy presence and thy portals, while I lay,
Mouth, forehead, eyelids, growing dewy-warm
With kisses balmier than half-opening buds
Of April, and could hear the lips that kissed   60
Whispering I knew not what of wild and sweet,
Like that strange song I heard Apollo sing,
While Ilion like a mist rose into towers.
  Yet hold me not for ever in thine East;
How can my nature longer mix with thine?
Coldly thy rosy shadows bathe me, cold
Are all thy lights, and cold my wrinkled feet
Upon thy glimmering thresholds, when the
      steam

---

4 *swan:* swans are proverbially long-lived; they were once thought to live more than a century. 6 *thine:* those of Eos, or Aurora, goddess of dawn, who, according to Greek legend, fell in love with Tithonus, a mortal. She successfully begged unending life for him, but neglected to have him given eternal youth. 18 *Hours:* the goddesses in charge of the cycle of birth, growth, and death. 25 *star:* Venus, the star of morning. 30 *goal of ordinance:* ordained limit, normal span of life.

33 *glimpse:* the poem begins just before daylight. 39 *team:* Eos will shortly visit earth in a chariot drawn by swift horses. 63 *Ilion:* Troy, built to Apollo's music; Tithonus' brother, Priam, was King of Troy.

Floats up from those dim fields about the homes
Of happy men that have the power to die,   70
And grassy barrows of the happier dead.
Release me, and restore me to the ground.
Thou seest all things, thou wilt see my grave;
Thou wilt renew thy beauty morn by morn,
I earth in earth forget these empty courts,
And thee returning on thy silver wheels.

Alfred, Lord Tennyson

TEARS, IDLE TEARS

Tears, idle tears, I know not what they mean,
Tears from the depth of some divine despair
Rise in the heart, and gather to the eyes,
In looking on the happy autumn fields,
And thinking of the days that are no more.

Fresh as the first beam glittering on a sail
That brings our friends up from the underworld,
Sad as the last which reddens over one
That sinks with all we love below the verge;
So sad, so fresh, the days that are no more.   10

Ah, sad and strange as in dark summer dawns
The earliest pipe of half-awakened birds
To dying ears, when unto dying eyes
The casement slowly grows a glimmering square;
So sad, so strange, the days that are no more.

Dear as remembered kisses after death,
And sweet as those by hopeless fancy feigned
On lips that are for others; deep as love,
Deep as first love, and wild with all regret;
O Death in Life, the days that are no more.   20

Robert Browning

THE BISHOP ORDERS HIS TOMB AT SAINT PRAXED'S CHURCH

Vanity, saith the preacher, vanity!
Draw round my bed: is Anselm keeping back?
Nephews—sons mine . . . ah God, I know not!
    Well—
She, men would have to be your mother once,
Old Gandolf envied me, so fair she was!
What's done is done, and she is dead beside,
Dead long ago, and I am Bishop since,
And as she died so must we die ourselves,
And thence ye may perceive the world's a dream.
Life, how and what is it? As here I lie   10
In this state chamber, dying by degrees,
Hours and long hours in the dead night, I ask
"Do I live, am I dead?" Peace, peace seems all.
Saint Praxed's ever was the church for peace;
And so, about this tomb of mine. I fought
With tooth and nail to save my niche, ye know;
—Old Gandolf cozened me, despite my care;
Shrewd was that snatch from out the corner
    south
He graced his carrion with, God curse the same!
Yet still my niche is not so cramped but thence   20
One sees the pulpit o' the epistle-side,
And somewhat of the choir, those silent seats,
And up into the aery dome where live
The angels, and a sunbeam's sure to lurk:
And I shall fill my slab of basalt there,
And 'neath my tabernacle take my rest,
With those nine columns round me, two and
    two,

THE BISHOP ORDERS HIS TOMB AT SAINT PRAXED'S CHURCH: The speaker is supposed to typify church-men of the Renaissance. The Church of S. Prassede, in Rome, commemorates a first-century senator's daughter, canonized for giving aid to Christians.
1 *preacher*: see *Ecclesiastes* I, 2. 21 *epistle-side*: left side of the altar, from which the epistle is read. 26 *tabernacle*: canopy.

The odd one at my feet where Anselm stands;
Peach-blossom marble all, the rare, the ripe
As fresh-poured red wine of a mighty pulse.   30
—Old Gandolf with his paltry onion-stone,
Put me where I may look at him! True peach,
Rosy and flawless: how I earned the prize!
Draw close: that conflagration of my church
—What then? So much was saved if aught were
    missed!
My sons, ye would not be my death? Go dig
The white-grape vineyard where the oil-press
    stood,
Drop water gently till the surface sink,
And if ye find . . . Ah God, I know not, I! . . .
Bedded in store of rotten fig-leaves soft,   40
And corded up in a tight olive-frail,
Some lump, ah God, of lapis lazuli,
Big as a Jew's head cut off at the nape,
Blue as a vein o'er the Madonna's breast. . . .
Sons, all have I bequeathed you, villas, all,
That brave Frascati villa with its bath,
So, let the blue lump poise between my knees,
Like God the Father's globe on both his hands
Ye worship in the Jesu Church so gay,
For Gandolf shall not choose but see and
    burst!   50
Swift as a weaver's shuttle fleet our years:
Man goeth to the grave, and where is he?
Did I say basalt for my slab, sons? Black—
'Twas ever antique-black I meant! How else
Shall ye contrast my frieze to come beneath?
The bas-relief in bronze ye promised me,
Those Pans and nymphs ye wot of, and per-
    chance
Some tripod, thyrsus, with a vase or so,
The Savior at his sermon on the mount,
Saint Praxed in a glory, and one Pan   60
Ready to twitch the nymph's last garment off,
And Moses with the tables. . . . But I know
Ye mark me not! What do they whisper thee,
Child of my bowels, Anselm? Ah, ye hope
To revel down my villas while I gasp

Bricked o'er with beggar's mouldy travertine
Which Gandolf from his tomb-top chuckles at!
Nay, boys, ye love me—all of jasper, then!
'Tis jasper ye stand pledged to, lest I grieve.
My bath must needs be left behind, alas!   70
One block, pure green as a pistachio-nut;
There's plenty jasper somewhere in the world—
And have I not Saint Praxed's ear to pray
Horses for ye, and brown Greek manuscripts,
And mistresses with great smooth marbly limbs?
—That's if ye carve my epitaph aright,
Choice Latin, picked phrase, Tully's every word,
No gaudy ware like Gandolf's second line—
Tully, my masters? Ulpian serves his need!
And then how I shall lie through centuries   80
And hear the blessed mutter of the mass,
And see God made and eaten all day long,
And feel the steady candle-flame, and taste
Good strong thick stupefying incense-smoke!
For as I lie here, hours of the dead night,
Dying in state and by such slow degrees,
I fold my arms as if they clasped a crook,
And stretch my feet forth straight as stone can
    point,
And let the bedclothes, for a mortcloth, drop
Into great laps and folds of sculptor's work: 90
And as yon tapers dwindle, and strange thoughts
Grow, with a certain humming in my ears,
About the life before I lived this life,
And this life too, popes, cardinals, and priests,
Saint Praxed at his sermon on the mount,
Your tall pale mother with her talking eyes,
And new-found agate urns as fresh as day,
And marble's language, Latin pure, discreet,
—Aha, ELUCESCEBAT quoth our friend?
No Tully, said I, Ulpian at the best!   100
Evil and brief hath been my pilgrimage.
All lapis, all, sons! Else I give the Pope
My villas! Will ye ever eat my heart?
Ever your eyes were as a lizard's quick.

---

31 *onion-stone:* inferior marble. 46 *Frascati:* suburb of Rome. 49 *Jesu Church:* Church of the Jesuits, in Rome. 51 *Swift, etc.:* see *The Book of Job* VII, 6. 62 *tables:* tablets inscribed with the Ten Commandments, as in *Exodus* XXXII, 15.

79 *Ulpian:* whose Late Latin style is considered degenerate compared with the classic purity of Cicero's. 82 *God made and eaten:* i.e., in the mass. 89 *mort-cloth:* funeral pall. 95 *Saint Praxed, etc.:* a confused echo, perhaps, of line 59; Saint Praxed was a woman. 99 ELUCESCEBAT: he was illustrious; *elucebat* is the classic form.

They glitter like your mother's for my soul,
Or ye would heighten my impoverished frieze,
Piece out its starved design, and fill my vase
With grapes, and add a visor and a Term,
And to the tripod ye would tie a lynx
That in his struggle throws the thyrsus down, 110
To comfort me on my entablature
Whereon I am to lie till I must ask
"Do I live, am I dead?" There, leave me, there!
For ye have stabbed me with ingratitude
To death—ye wish it—God, ye wish it! Stone—
Gritstone, a-crumble! Clammy squares which
    sweat
As if the corpse they keep were oozing through—
And no more *lapis* to delight the world!
Well, go! I bless ye. Fewer tapers there,
But in a row: and, going, turn your backs   120
—Ay, like departing altar-ministrants.—
And leave me in my church, the church for
    peace,
That I may watch at leisure if he leers,
Old Gandolf, at me, from his onion-stone,
As still he envied me, so fair she was!

    108 *visor:* death-mask (?). 116 *gritstone:* coarse
sandstone.

Emily Dickinson

BECAUSE I COULD NOT STOP FOR DEATH

Because I could not stop for Death
He kindly stopped for me;
The carriage held but just ourselves
And immortality.

We slowly drove, he knew no haste,
And I had put away
My labor, and my leisure too,
For his civility.

We passed the school where children played
At wrestling in a ring;   10

We passed the fields of gazing grain,
We passed the setting sun.

He paused before a house that seemed
A swelling of the ground;
The roof was scarcely visible,
The cornice but a mound.

Since then 'tis centuries; but each
Feels shorter than the day
I first surmised the horses' heads
Were toward eternity.   20

A. E. Housman

ON WENLOCK EDGE

On Wenlock Edge the wood's in trouble;
    His forest fleece the Wrekin heaves;
The gale, it plies the saplings double,
    And thick on Severn snow the leaves.

'Twould blow like this through holt and hanger
    When Uricon the city stood:
'Tis the old wind in the old anger,
    But then it threshed another wood.

Then, 'twas before my time, the Roman
    At yonder heaving hill would stare: 10
The blood that warms an English yeoman,
    The thoughts that hurt him, they were there.

There, like the wind through woods in riot,
    Through him the gale of life blew high;
The tree of man was never quiet:
    Then 'twas the Roman, now 'tis I.

The gale, it plies the saplings double,
    It blows so hard, 'twill soon be gone:
Today the Roman and his trouble
    Are ashes under Uricon.   20

    1 *Wenlock Edge:* range of hills in Shropshire,
south of the Severn River. 2 *Wrekin:* volcanic hill
to the north. 5 *hanger:* wood on a hillside. 6
Uricon: Uriconium, Roman town in what is now
central Shropshire.

Edwin Arlington Robinson

MR. FLOOD'S PARTY

Old Eben Flood, climbing alone one night
Over the hill between the town below
And the forsaken upland hermitage
That held as much as he should ever know
On earth again of home, paused warily.
The road was his with not a native near;
And Eben, having leisure, said aloud,
For no man else in Tilbury Town to hear:

"Well, Mr. Flood, we have the harvest moon
Again, and we may have many more;   10
The bird is on the wing, the poet says,
And you and I have said it here before.
Drink to the bird." He raised up to the light
The jug that he had gone so far to fill,
And answered huskily: "Well, Mr. Flood,
Since you propose it, I believe I will."

Alone, as if enduring to the end
A valiant armor of scarred hopes outworn,
He stood there in the middle of the road
Like Roland's ghost winding a silent horn.   20
Below him, in the town among the trees,
Where friends of other days had honored him,
A phantom salutation of the dead
Rang thinly till old Eben's eyes were dim.

Then, as a mother lays her sleeping child
Down tenderly, fearing it may awake,
He set the jug down slowly at his feet
With trembling care, knowing that most things
      break;
And only when assured that on firm earth
It stood, as the uncertain lives of men   30

8 *Tilbury:* imaginary New England town, in
which many of Robinson's poems are set. 11 *poet:*
Edward Fitzgerald, in *The Rubáiyát of Omar
Khayyam,* line 28. 20 *Roland's:* in *The Song of
Roland (c.* 1100) the hero decides too late to blow
his horn and summon aid, and is overcome by the
Saracens.

Assuredly did not, he paced away,
And with his hand extended paused again.

"Well, Mr. Flood, we have not met like this
In a long time; and many a change has come
To both of us, I fear, since last it was
We had a drop together. Welcome home!"
Convivially returning with himself,
Again he raised the jug up to the light
And with an acquiescent quaver said:
"Well, Mr. Flood, if you insist, I might."   40

"Only a very little, Mr. Flood—
For auld lang syne. No more, sir; that will do."
So, for the time, apparently it did,
And Eben evidently thought so too;
For soon amid the silver loneliness
Of night he lifted up his voice and sang,
Secure, with only two moons listening,
Until the whole harmonious landscape rang—

"For auld lang syne." The weary throat gave out,
The last word wavered; and the song being
      done,   50
He raised again the jug regretfully
And shook his head, and was again alone.
There was not much that was ahead of him,
And there was nothing in the town below—
Where strangers would have shut the many doors
That many friends had opened long ago.

William Butler Yeats

SAILING TO BYZANTIUM

That is no country for old men. The young
In one another's arms, birds in the trees,
—Those dying generations—at their song,
The salmon-falls, the mackerel-crowded seas,
Fish, flesh, or fowl, commend all summer long
Whatever is begotten, born, and dies.

1 *That:* the physical world, as described in the
next sentence. 3 *generations:* compare "Ode to a
Nightingale," lines 61–62.

Caught in that sensual music all neglect
Monuments of unaging intellect.

An aged man is but a paltry thing,
A tattered coat upon a stick, unless   10
Soul clap its hands and sing, and louder sing
For every tatter in its mortal dress,
Nor is there singing school but studying
Monuments of its own magnificence;
And therefore I have sailed the seas and come
To the holy city of Byzantium.

O sages standing in God's holy fire
As in the gold mosaic of a wall,
Come from the holy fire, perne in a gyre,
And be the singing-masters of my soul.   20
Consume my heart away; sick with desire
And fastened to a dying animal
It knows not what it is; and gather me
Into the artifice of eternity.

Once out of nature I shall never take
My bodily form from any natural thing,
But such a form as Grecian goldsmiths make
Of hammered gold and gold enameling
To keep a drowsy Emperor awake;
Or set upon a golden bough to sing   30
To lords and ladies of Byzantium
Of what is past, or passing, or to come.

17 *sages:* Byzantium, or Constantinople, is famous
for its mosaics depicting religious leaders. 19 *perne:*
whirl, come alive to me. 27 *form:* Yeats's note: "I
have read somewhere [perhaps in the letter of Liud-
prand, Bishop of Cremona, to the Emperor Otto I
in 968] that in the emperor's palace at Byzantium
was a tree made of gold and silver, and artificial birds
that sang."

John Crowe Ransom

DEAD BOY

The little cousin is dead, by foul subtraction,
A green bough from Virginia's aged tree,
And none of the county kin like the transaction,
Nor some of the world of outer dark, like me.

A boy not beautiful, nor good, nor clever,
A black cloud full of storms too hot for keeping,
A sword beneath his mother's heart—yet never
Woman bewept her babe as this is weeping.

A pig with a pasty face, so I had said,
Squealing for cookies, kinned by poor pretense 10
With a noble house. But the little man quite
          dead,
I see the forebears' antique lineaments.

The elder men have strode by the box of death
To the wide flag porch, and muttering low send
          round
The bruit of the day. O friendly waste of breath!
Their hearts are hurt with a deep dynastic
          wound.

He was pale and little, the foolish neighbors say;
The first fruits, saith the preacher, the Lord hath
          taken;
But this was the old tree's late branch wrenched
          away,
Grieving the sapless limbs, the shorn and
          shaken.   20

18 *saith:* perhaps on the text *Leviticus* XXIII, 10–
11.

Archibald Macleish

THE END OF THE WORLD

Quite unexpectedly as Vasserot
The armless ambidextrian was lighting
A match between his great and second toe
And Ralph the lion was engaged in biting
The neck of Madame Sossman while the drum

Pointed, and Teeny was about to cough
In waltz-time swinging Jocko by the thumb—
Quite unexpectedly the top blew off:
And there, there overhead, there, there, hung
    over
Those thousands of white faces, those dazed
    eyes,   10
There in the starless dark the poise, the hover,
There with vast wings across the canceled skies,
There in the sudden blackness the black pall
Of nothing, nothing, nothing—nothing at all.

Theodore Roethke

ELEGY FOR JANE
MY STUDENT, THROWN BY
A HORSE

I remember the neckcurls, limp and damp as tendrils;
And her quick look, a sidelong pickerel smile;
And how, once startled into talk, the light syllables leaped for her,
And she balanced in the delight of her thought,
A wren, happy, tail into the wind,
Her song trembling the twigs and small branches.
The shade sang with her;
The leaves, their whispers turned to kissing;
And the mold sang in the bleached valleys under the rose.

Oh, when she was sad, she cast herself down into such a pure depth,   10
Even a father could not find her:
Scraping her cheek against straw;
Stirring the clearest water.

My sparrow, you are not here,
Waiting like a fern, making a spiny shadow.
The sides of wet stones cannot console me,
Nor the moss, wound with the last light.

If only I could nudge you from this sleep,
My maimed darling, my skittery pigeon.
Over this damp grave I speak the words of my love: 20
I, with no rights in this matter,
Neither father nor lover.

William Carlos Williams

ASPHODEL, THAT GREENY FLOWER: CODA

Inseparable from the fire
            its light
                        takes precedence over it.
Then follows
            what we have dreaded—
                        but it can never
overcome what has gone before.
            In the huge gap
                        between the flash
and the thunderstroke   10
            spring has come in
                        or a deep snow fallen.
Call it old age.
            In that stretch
                        we have lived to see
a colt kick up his heels.
            Do not hasten
                        laugh and play
in an eternity
            the heat will not overtake the light   20
                        That's sure.
That gelds the bomb,
            permitting
                        that the mind contain it.
This is that interval,
            that sweetest interval,
                        when love will blossom,
come early, come late
            and give itself to the lover.
Only the imagination is real!   30
            I have declared it
                        time without end.
If a man die
            it is because death

has first
possessed his imagination.
            But if he refuse death—
                        no greater evil
can befall him
            unless it be the death of love   40
                        meet him
in full career.
            Then indeed
                        for him
the light has gone out.
But love and the imagination
            are of a piece,
                        swift as the light
to avoid destruction.
            So we come to watch time's flight   50
                        as we might watch
summer lightning
            or fireflies, secure,
                        by grace of the
                                    imagination,
safe in its care.
            For if
                        the light itself
has escaped,
            the whole edifice opposed to it
                        goes down.   60
Light, the imagination
            and love,
                        in our age,
by natural law,
            which we worship,
                        maintain
all of a piece
            their dominance.
So let us love
            confident as is the light   70
                        in its struggle with
                                    darkness
that there is as much to say
            and more
                        for the one side
and that not the darker
            which John Donne
                        for instance
among many men
            presents to us.

ASPHODEL, THAT GREENY FLOWER: CODA: The concluding section of a long poem, written when Williams was seventy-two, and addressed to Florence
Herman Williams, whom he had married forty-
three years earlier. In Greek mythology the happy
dead walk through fields of asphodel.

In the controversy   80
touching the younger
        and the older Tolstoi,
                Villon, St. Anthony, Kung
                        [Confucius],
Rimbaud, Buddha
        and Abraham Lincoln
                the palm goes
always to the light;
        Who most shall advance the light—
                call it what you may!
The light   90
        for all time shall outspeed
                the thunder crack.
Medieval pageantry
        is human and we enjoy
                the rumor of it
as in our world we enjoy
        the reading of Chaucer,
                likewise
a priest's raiment
        (or that of a savage chieftain) .   100
                It is all
a celebration of the light.
        All the pomp and ceremony
                of weddings,
"Sweet Thames, run softly
        till I end
                my song,"—
are of an equal sort.
For our wedding, too,
        the light was wakened   110
                and shone. The light!
the light stood before us
        waiting!
                I thought the world
stood still.
        At the altar
                so intent was I
before my vows,
        so moved by your presence
                a girl so pale   120
and ready to faint
        that I pitied

105 *Sweet Thames . . .* Edmund Spenser, "Pro-
thalaminm," refrain.

and wanted to protect you.
As I think of it now,
        after a lifetime,
                it is as if
a sweet-scented flower
        were poised
                and for me did open.
Asphodel   130
        has no odor
                save to the imagination
but it too
        celebrates the light.
                It is late
but an odor
        as from our wedding
                has revived for me
and begun again to penetrate
        into all crevices   140
                of my world.

William Carlos Williams

TRACT

I will teach you my townspeople
how to perform a funeral—
for you have it over a troop
of artists—

unless one should scour the world—
you have the ground sense necessary.

See! the hearse leads.
I begin with a design for a hearse.
For Christ's sake not black—
nor white either—and not polished!   10
Let it be weathered—like a farm wagon—
with gilt wheels (this could be
applied fresh at small expense)
or no wheels at all:
a rough dray to drag over the ground.

Knock the glass out!
My God—glass, my townspeople!

For what purpose? Is it for the dead
to look out or for us to see
how well he is housed or to see   20
the flowers or the lack of them—
or what?
To keep the rain and snow from him?
He will have a heavier rain soon:
pebbles and dirt and what not.
Let there be no glass—
and no upholstery phew!
and no little brass rollers
and small easy wheels on the bottom—
my townspeople what are you thinking of?   30

A rough plain hearse then
with gilt wheels and no top at all.
On this the coffin lies
by its own weight.

        No wreaths please—
especially no hot house flowers.
Some common memento is better,
something he prized and is known by:
his old clothes—a few books perhaps—
God knows what! You realize
how we are about these things   40
my townspeople—
something will be found—anything
even flowers if he had come to that.
So much for the hearse.

For heaven's sake though see to the driver!
Take off the silk hat! In fact
that's no place at all for him—
up there unceremoniously
dragging our friend out to his own dignity!
Bring him down—bring him down!   50
Low and inconspicuous! I'd not have him ride
on the wagon at all—damn him—
the undertaker's understrapper!
Let him hold the reins
and walk at the side
and inconspicuously too!

Then briefly as to yourselves:
Walk behind—as they do in France,
seventh class, or if you ride

Hell take curtains! Go with some show   60
of inconvenience; sit openly—
to the weather as to grief.
Or do you think you can shut grief in?
What—from us? We who have perhaps
nothing to lose? Share with us
share with us—it will be money
in your pockets.
          Go now
I think you are ready.

Chapter 12

ACHIEVEMENT AND REALIZATION

Special circumstances, crises that force momentous choices, changes in fortune that call for high courage, can make us ask the most searching and serious practical questions about ourselves: What kind of life should I aim to live? What have I done with my talents and abilities? What are, or ought to be, the most important things in my life? Such questions, if they are kept in view for a time, lead to reflection upon our hopes and our accomplishments, our successes and failures, the drive or drift of our everyday existence. Such reflection is much enriched by comparison of ourselves with others—including the characters we encounter in literature and often know, through the writer's art, more deeply than real persons.

What gives meaning to a life is the extent to which it is imbued with purpose. A purpose may be common and humble, circumscribed and modest, yet if firmly held to, carried out with care or zest, it may illumine and even transfigure a life. We can see this in various works in earlier chapters of this book. At the other extreme, a purpose may be ambitious to the point of megalomania, possessing its possessor and driving him to extravagant and self-destructive deeds—as we see in such historical figures as Alexan-

der the Great, Napoleon, Hitler. On an intermediate scale, works of fiction, as well as history, present to us images of truly heroic lives, in which great purposes are carried out despite dismaying obstacles. Cromwell as portrayed by Marvell, Ulysses as portrayed by Tennyson, Oedipus as portrayed by Sophocles, are characters of this kind.

A person's achievement is something to be objectively measured by others; his realization of himself is relative to the capacities he happens to have been born with. When these fall apart we may perceive an ironic contrast—as when a person betrays his deepest values for what he takes (at least for a time) to be a high and unselfish motive. Or there may be pathos in using to the full one's limited abilities. Such concepts as success and failure, fame and fortune, ambition and glory—which we apply in appraising the quality and worth of a life—take on many meanings in complex human situations. We admire the unconquerable spirit of the bullfighter in "The Undefeated"; the devotion to duty of Sir Patrick Spens and Oliver Cromwell; the ability of the ship's captain in "The Secret Sharer" to surmount the first great test of his career. How far these lives are from the suspended animation, pointless motions, and idle fantasies depicted in "At the End of the Mechanical Age."

Joseph Conrad

THE SECRET SHARER

On my right hand there were lines of fishing stakes resembling a mysterious system of half-submerged bamboo fences, incomprehensible in its division of the domain of tropical fishes, and crazy of aspect as if abandoned forever by some nomad tribe of fishermen now gone to the other end of the ocean; for there was no sign of human habitation as far as the eye could reach. To the left a group of barren islets, suggesting ruins of stone walls, towers, and blockhouses, had its foundations set in a blue sea that itself looked solid, so still and stable did it lie below my feet; even the track of light from the westering sun shone smoothly, without that animated glitter which tells of an imperceptible ripple. And when I turned my head to take a parting glance at the tug which had just left us anchored outside the bar, I saw the straight line of the flat shore joined to the stable sea, edge to edge, with a perfect and unmarked closeness, in one leveled floor half brown, half blue under the enormous dome of the sky. Corresponding in their insignificance to the islets of the sea, two small clumps of trees, one on each side of the only fault in the impeccable joint, marked the mouth of the river Meinam[1] we had just left on the first preparatory stage of our homeward journey; and, far back on the inland level, a larger and loftier mass,

the grove surrounding the great Paknam[2] pagoda, was the only thing on which the eye could rest from the vain task of exploring the monotonous sweep of the horizon. Here and there gleams as of a few scattered pieces of silver marked the windings of the great river; and on the nearest of them, just within the bar, the tug steaming right into the land became lost to my sight, hull and funnel and masts, as though the impassive earth had swallowed her up without an effort, without a tremor. My eye followed the light cloud of her smoke, now here, now there, above the plain, according to the devious curves of the stream, but always fainter and farther away, till I lost it at last behind the miter-shaped hill of the great pagoda. And then I was left alone with my ship, anchored at the head of the Gulf of Siam.

She floated at the starting point of a long journey, very still in an immense stillness, the shadows of her spars flung far to the eastward by the setting sun. At that moment I was alone on her decks. There was not a sound in her—and around us nothing moved, nothing lived, not a canoe on the water, not a bird in the air, not a cloud in the sky. In this breathless pause at the threshold of a long passage we seemed to be measuring our fitness for a long and arduous enterprise, the appointed task of both our existences to be carried out, far from all human eyes, with only sky and sea for spectators and for judges.

There must have been some glare in the air to interfere with one's sight, because it was only just before the sun left us that my roaming eyes made out beyond the highest ridge of the principal islet of the group something which did away with the solemnity of perfect solitude. The tide of darkness flowed on swiftly; and with tropical suddenness a swarm of stars came out above the shadowy earth, while I lingered yet, my

---

[1] Principal river of Thailand, now usually spelled Menam.

[2] The town of Samutprakan, in Thailand.

hand resting lightly on my ship's rail as if on the shoulder of a trusted friend. But, with all that multitude of celestial bodies staring down at one, the comfort of quiet communion with her was gone for good. And there were also disturbing sounds by this time—voices, footsteps forward; the steward flitted along the main deck, a busily ministering spirit; a hand bell tinkled urgently under the poop deck. . . .

I found my two officers waiting for me near the supper table, in the lighted cuddy. We sat down at once, and as I helped the chief mate, I said:

"Are you aware that there is a ship anchored inside the islands? I saw her mastheads above the ridge as the sun went down."

He raised sharply his simple face, overcharged by a terrible growth of whisker, and emitted his usual ejaculations: "Bless my soul, sir! You don't say so!"

My second mate was a round-cheeked, silent young man, grave beyond his years, I thought; but as our eyes happened to meet I detected a slight quiver on his lips. I looked down at once. It was not my part to encourage sneering on board my ship. It must be said, too, that I knew very little of my officers. In consequence of certain events of no particular significance, except to myself, I had been appointed to the command only a fortnight before. Neither did I know much of the hands forward. All these people had been together for eighteen months or so, and my position was that of the only stranger on board. I mention this because it has some bearing on what is to follow. But what I felt most was my being a stranger to the ship; and if all the truth must be told, I was somewhat of a stranger to myself. The youngest man on board (barring the second mate), and untried as yet by a position of the fullest responsibility, I was willing to take the adequacy of the others for granted. They had simply to be equal to their tasks; but I wondered how

far I should turn out faithful to that ideal conception of one's own personality every man sets up for himself secretly.

Meantime the chief mate, with an almost visible effect of collaboration on the part of his round eyes and frightful whiskers, was trying to evolve a theory of the anchored ship. His dominant trait was to take all things into earnest consideration. He was of a painstaking turn of mind. As he used to say, he "liked to account to himself" for practically everything that came in his way, down to a miserable scorpion he had found in his cabin a week before. The why and the wherefore of that scorpion— how it got on board and came to select his room rather than the pantry (which was a dark place and more what a scorpion would be partial to), and how on earth it managed to drown itself in the inkwell of his writing desk—had exercised him infinitely. The ship within the islands was much more easily accounted for; and just as we were about to rise from the table he made his pronouncement. She was, he doubted not, a ship from home lately arrived. Probably she drew too much water to cross the bar except at the top of spring tides. Therefore she went into that natural harbor to wait for a few days in preference to remaining in an open roadstead.

"That's so," confirmed the second mate, suddenly, in his slightly hoarse voice. "She draws over twenty feet. She's the Liverpool ship *Sephora* with a cargo of coal. Hundred and twenty-three days from Cardiff."

We looked at him in surprise.

"The tugboat skipper told me when he came on board for your letters, sir," explained the young man. "He expects to take her up the river the day after tomorrow."

After thus overwhelming us with the extent of his information he slipped out of the cabin. The mate observed regretfully that he "could not account for that young fellow's whims." What prevented him telling us about it at once, he wanted to know.

I detained him as he was making a move. For the last two days the crew had had plenty of hard work, and the night before they had very little sleep. I felt painfully that I—a stranger—was doing something unusual when I directed him to let all hands turn in without setting an anchor watch. I proposed to keep on deck myself till one o'clock or thereabouts. I would get the second mate to relieve me at that hour.

"He will turn out the cook and the steward at four," I concluded, "and then give you a call. Of course at the slightest sign of any sort of wind we'll have the hands up and make a start at once."

He concealed his astonishment. "Very well, sir." Outside the cuddy he put his head in the second mate's door to inform him of my unheard-of caprice to take a five hours' anchor watch on myself. I heard the other raise his voice incredulously: "What? The captain himself?" Then a few more murmurs, a door closed, then another. A few moments later I went on deck.

My strangeness, which had made me sleepless, had prompted that unconventional arrangement, as if I had expected in those solitary hours of the night to get on terms with the ship of which I knew nothing, manned by men of whom I knew very little more. Fast alongside a wharf, littered like any ship in port with a tangle of unrelated things, invaded by unrelated shore people, I had hardly seen her yet properly. Now, as she lay cleared for sea, the stretch of her main deck seemed to me very fine under the stars. Very fine, very roomy for her size, and very inviting. I descended the poop and paced the waist, my mind picturing to myself the coming passage through the Malay Archipelago, down the Indian Ocean, and up the Atlantic. All its phases were familiar enough to me, every characteristic, all the alternatives which were likely to face me on the high seas—everything! . . . except the novel responsibility of command. But I

took heart from the reasonable thought that the ship was like other ships, the men like other men, and that the sea was not likely to keep any special surprises expressly for my discomfiture.

Arrived at that comforting conclusion, I bethought myself of a cigar and went below to get it. All was still down there. Everybody at the after end of the ship was sleeping profoundly. I came out again on the quarterdeck, agreeably at ease in my sleeping suit on that warm breathless night, barefooted, a glowing cigar in my teeth, and, going forward, I was met by the profound silence of the fore end of the ship. Only as I passed the door of the forecastle I heard a deep, quiet, trustful sigh of some sleeper inside. And suddenly I rejoiced in the great security of the sea as compared with the unrest of the land, in my choice of that untempted life presenting no disquieting problems, invested with an elementary moral beauty by the absolute straightforwardness of its appeal and by the singleness of its purpose.

The riding light in the fore-rigging burned with a clear, untroubled, as if symbolic, flame, confident and bright in the mysterious shades of the night. Passing on my way aft along the other side of the ship, I observed that the rope side ladder, put over, no doubt, for the master of the tug when he came to fetch away our letters, had not been hauled in as it should have been. I became annoyed at this, for exactitude in small matters is the very soul of discipline. Then I reflected that I had myself peremptorily dismissed my officers from duty, and by my own act had prevented the anchor watch being formally set and things properly attended to. I asked myself whether it was wise ever to interfere with the established routine of duties even from the kindest of motives. My action might have made me appear eccentric. Goodness only knew how that absurdly whiskered mate would "account" for my conduct, and what the whole ship thought of that informality of their new captain. I was vexed with myself.

Not from compunction certainly, but, as it were mechanically, I proceeded to get the ladder in myself. Now a side ladder of that sort is a light affair and comes in easily, yet my vigorous tug, which should have brought it flying on board, merely recoiled upon my body in a totally unexpected jerk. What the devil! . . . I was so astounded by the immovableness of that ladder that I remained stock-still, trying to account for it to myself like that imbecile mate of mine. In the end, of course, I put my head over the rail.

The side of the ship made an opaque belt of shadow on the darkening glassy shimmer of the sea. But I saw at once something elongated and pale floating very close to the ladder. Before I could form a guess a faint flash of phosphorescent light, which seemed to issue suddenly from the naked body of a man, flickered in the sleeping water with the elusive, silent play of summer lightning in a night sky. With a gasp I saw revealed to my stare a pair of feet, the long legs, a broad livid back immersed right up to the neck in a greenish cadaverous glow. One hand, awash, clutched the bottom rung of the ladder. He was complete but for the head. A headless corpse! The cigar dropped out of my gaping mouth with a tiny plop and a short hiss quite audible in the absolute stillness of all things under heaven. At that I suppose he raised up his face, a dimly pale oval in the shadow of the ship's side. But even then I could only barely make out down there the shape of his black-haired head. However, it was enough for the horrid, frost-bound sensation which had gripped me about the chest to pass off. The moment of vain exclamations was past, too. I only climbed on the spare spar and leaned over the rail as far as I could, to bring my eyes nearer to that mystery floating alongside.

As he hung by the ladder, like a resting swimmer, the sea lightning played about his limbs at every stir; and he appeared in it ghastly, silvery, fishlike. He remained as mute as a fish, too. He made no motion to get out of the water, either. It was inconceivable that he should not attempt to come on board, and strangely troubling to suspect that perhaps he did not want to. And my first words were prompted by just that troubled incertitude.

"What's the matter?" I asked in my ordinary tone; speaking down to the face upturned exactly under mine.

"Cramp," it answered, no louder. Then slightly anxious, "I say, no need to call anyone."

"I was not going to," I said.

"Are you alone on deck?"

"Yes."

I had somehow the impression that he was on the point of letting go the ladder to swim away beyond my ken—mysterious as he came. But, for the moment, this being appearing as if he had risen from the bottom of the sea (it was certainly the nearest land to the ship) wanted only to know the time. I told him. And he, down there, tentatively:

"I suppose your captain's turned in?"

"I am sure he isn't," I said.

He seemed to struggle with himself, for I heard something like the low, bitter murmur of doubt. "What's the good?" His next words came out with a hesitating effort.

"Look here, my man. Could you call him out quietly?"

I thought the time had come to declare myself.

"*I* am the captain."

I heard a "By Jove!" whispered at the level of the water. The phosphorescence flashed in the swirl of the water all about his limbs; his other hand seized the ladder.

"My name's Leggatt."

The voice was calm and resolute. A good voice. The self-possession of that man had somehow induced a corresponding state in myself. It was very quietly that I remarked:

"You must be a good swimmer."

"Yes. I've been in the water practically since nine o'clock. The question for me now is whether I am to let go this ladder and go on swimming till I sink from exhaustion, or—to come on board here."

I felt this was no mere formula of desperate speech, but a real alternative in the view of a strong soul. I should have gathered from this that he was young; indeed, it is only the young who are ever confronted by such clear issues. But at the time it was pure intuition on my part. A mysterious communication was established already between us two—in the face of that silent, darkened tropical sea. I was young, too, young enough to make no comment. The man in the water began suddenly to climb up the ladder, and I hastened away from the rail to fetch some clothes.

Before entering the cabin I stood still, listening in the lobby at the foot of the stairs. A faint snore came through the closed door of the chief mate's room. The second mate's door was on the hook, but the darkness in there was absolutely soundless. He, too, was young and could sleep like a stone. Remained the steward, but he was not likely to wake up before he was called. I got a sleeping suit out of my room and, coming back on deck, saw the naked man from the sea sitting on the main hatch, glimmering white in the darkness, his elbows on his knees and his head in his hands. In a moment he had concealed his damp body in a sleeping suit of the same gray-stripe pattern as the one I was wearing and followed me like my double on the poop. Together we moved right aft, barefooted, silent.

"What is it?" I asked in a deadened voice, taking the lighted lamp out of the binnacle and raising it to his face.

"An ugly business."

He had rather regular features; a good mouth; light eyes under somewhat heavy, dark eyebrows; a smooth, square forehead; no growth on his cheeks; a small, brown mustache, and a well-shaped, round chin. His expression was concentrated, meditative, under the inspecting light of the lamp I held up to his face; such as a man thinking hard in solitude might wear. My sleeping suit was just right for his size. A well-knit young fellow of twenty-five at most. He caught his lower lip with the edge of white, even teeth.

"Yes," I said replacing the lamp in the binnacle. The warm, heavy tropical night closed upon his head again.

"There's a ship over there," he murmured.

"Yes, I know. The *Sephora*. Did you know of us?"

"Hadn't the slightest idea. I am the mate of her—" He paused and corrected himself. "I should say I *was*."

"Aha! Something wrong?"

"Yes. Very wrong indeed. I've killed a man."

"What do you mean? Just now?"

"No, on the passage. Weeks ago. Thirty-nine south. When I say a man—"

"Fit of temper," I suggested, confidently.

The shadowy, dark head, like mine, seemed to nod imperceptibly above the ghostly gray of my sleeping suit. It was, in the night, as though I had been faced by my own reflection in the depths of a somber and immense mirror.

"A pretty thing to have to own up to for a *Conway*[3] boy," murmured my double, distinctly.

"You're a *Conway* boy?"

"I am," he said as if startled. Then, slowly . . . "Perhaps you too—"

It was so; but being a couple of years older I had left before he joined. After a quick interchange of dates a silence fell; and

[3] A ship on which officer candidates for the merchant marine were trained.

I thought suddenly of my absurd mate with his terrific whiskers and the "Bless my soul —you don't say so" type of intellect. My double gave me an inkling of his thoughts by saying:

"My father's a parson in Norfolk. Do you see me before a judge and jury on that charge? For myself I can't see the necessity. There are fellows that an angel from heaven—And I am not that. He was one of those creatures that are just simmering all the time with a silly sort of wickedness. Miserable devils that have no business to live at all. He wouldn't do his duty and wouldn't let anybody else do theirs. But what's the good of talking! You know well enough the sort of ill-conditioned snarling cur—"

He appealed to me as if our experiences had been as identical as our clothes. And I knew well enough the pestiferous danger of such a character where there are no means of legal repression. And I knew well enough also that my double there was no homicidal ruffian. I did not think of asking him for details, and he told me the story roughly in brusque, disconnected sentences. I needed no more. I saw it all going on as though I were myself inside that other sleeping suit.

"It happened while we were setting a reefed foresail, at dusk. Reefed foresail! You understand the sort of weather. The only sail we had left to keep the ship running; so you may guess what it had been like for days. Anxious sort of job, that. He gave me some of his cursed insolence at the sheet. I tell you I was overdone with this terrific weather that seemed to have no end to it. Terrific, I tell you—and a deep ship. I believe the fellow himself was half crazed with funk. It was no time for gentlemanly reproof, so I turned round and felled him like an ox. He up and at me. We closed just as an awful sea made for the ship. All hands saw it coming and took to the rigging, but I had him by the throat, and went on shaking him like a rat, the men above us yelling, 'Look out! look out!' Then a crash as if the sky had fallen on my head. They say that for over ten minutes hardly anything was to be seen of the ship —just the three masts and a bit of the forecastle head and of the poop all awash driving along in a smother of foam. It was a miracle that they found us, jammed together behind the forebits. It's clear that I meant business, because I was holding him by the throat still when they picked us up. He was black in the face. It was too much for them. It seems they rushed us aft together, gripped as we were, screaming 'Murder!' like a lot of lunatics, and broke into the cuddy. And the ship running for her life, touch and go all the time, any minute her last in a sea fit to turn your hair gray only a-looking at it. I understand that the skipper, too, started raving like the rest of them. The man had been deprived of sleep for more than a week, and to have this sprung on him at the height of a furious gale nearly drove him out of his mind. I wonder they didn't fling me overboard after getting the carcass of their precious shipmate out of my fingers. They had rather a job to separate us, I've been told. A sufficiently fierce story to make an old judge and a respectable jury sit up a bit. The first thing I heard when I came to myself was the maddening howling of that endless gale, and on that the voice of the old man. He was hanging on to my bunk, staring into my face out of his sou'wester.

"'Mr. Leggatt, you have killed a man. You can act no longer as chief mate of this ship.'"

His care to subdue his voice made it sound monotonous. He rested a hand on the end of the skylight to steady himself with, and all that time did not stir a limb, so far as I could see. "Nice little tale for a quiet tea party," he concluded in the same tone.

One of my hands, too, rested on the end of the skylight; neither did I stir a limb, so far as I knew. We stood less than a foot from each other. It occurred to me that if old "Bless my soul—you don't say so" were to put his head up the companion and catch sight of us, he would think he was seeing double, or imagine himself come upon a scene of weird witchcraft; the strange captain having a quiet confabulation by the wheel with his own gray ghost. I became very much concerned to prevent anything of the sort. I heard the other's soothing undertone.

"My father's a parson in Norfolk," it said. Evidently he had forgotten he had told me this important fact before. Truly a nice little tale.

"You had better slip down into my stateroom now," I said, moving off stealthily. My double followed my movements; our bare feet made no sound; I let him in, closed the door with care, and, after giving a call to the second mate, returned on deck for my relief.

"Not much sign of any wind yet," I remarked when he approached.

"No, sir. Not much," he assented, sleepily, in his hoarse voice, with just enough deference, no more, and barely suppressing a yawn.

"Well, that's all you have to look out for. You have got your orders."

"Yes, sir."

I paced a turn or two on the poop and saw him take up his position face forward with his elbow in the ratlines of the mizzen-rigging before I went below. The mate's faint snoring was still going on peacefully. The cuddy lamp was burning over the table on which stood a vase with flowers, a polite attention from the ship's provision merchant—the last flowers we should see for the next three months at the very least. Two bunches of bananas hung from the beam symmetrically, one on each side of the rudder casing. Everything was as before in the ship—except that two of her captain's sleeping suits were simultaneously in use, one motionless in the cuddy, the other keeping very still in the captain's stateroom.

It must be explained here that my cabin had the form of the capital letter L, the door being within the angle and opening into the short part of the letter. A couch was to the left, the bed-place to the right; my writing desk and the chronometers' table faced the door. But anyone opening it, unless he stepped right inside, had no view of what I call the long (or vertical) part of the letter. It contained some lockers surmounted by a bookcase; and a few clothes, a thick jacket or two, caps, oilskin coat, and such like, hung on hooks. There was at the bottom of that part a door opening into my bathroom, which could be entered also directly from the saloon. But that way was never used.

The mysterious arrival had discovered the advantage of this particular shape. Entering my room, lighted strongly by a big bulkhead lamp swung on gimbals above my writing desk, I did not see him anywhere till he stepped out quietly from behind the coats hung in the recessed part.

"I heard somebody moving about, and went in there at once," he whispered.

I, too, spoke under my breath.

"Nobody is likely to come in here without knocking and getting permission."

He nodded. His face was thin and the sunburn faded, as though he had been ill. And no wonder. He had been, I heard presently, kept under arrest in his cabin for nearly seven weeks. But there was nothing sickly in his eyes or in his expression. He was not a bit like me, really; yet, as we stood leaning over my bed-place, whispering side by side, with our dark heads together and our backs to the door, anybody bold enough to open it stealthily would have been treated to the uncanny sight of a double captain busy talking in whispers with his other self.

"But all this doesn't tell me how you

came to hang on to our side ladder," I inquired, in the hardly audible murmurs we
used, after he had told me something more
of the proceedings on board the *Sephora*
once the bad weather was over.

"When we sighted Java Head I had had
time to think all those matters out several
times over. I had six weeks of doing nothing
else, and with only an hour or so every
evening for a tramp on the quarter-deck."

He whispered, his arms folded on the
side of my bed-place, staring through the
open port. And I could imagine perfectly
the manner of this thinking out—a stubborn if not a steadfast operation; something
of which I should have been perfectly incapable.

"I reckoned it would be dark before we
closed with the land," he continued, so low
that I had to strain my hearing, near as we
were to each other, shoulder touching
shoulder almost. "So I asked to speak to the
old man. He always seemed very sick when
he came to see me—as if he could not look
me in the face. You know, that foresail
saved the ship. She was too deep to have
run long under bare poles. And it was I
that managed to set it for him. Anyway, he
came. When I had him in my cabin—he
stood by the door looking at me as if I had
the halter around my neck already—I asked
him right away to leave my cabin door unlocked at night while the ship was going
through Sunda Straits. There would be the
Java coast within two or three miles, off
Angier Point. I wanted nothing more. I've
had a prize for swimming my second year
in the *Conway*."

"I can believe it," I breathed out.

"God only knows why they locked me in
every night. To see some of their faces
you'd have thought they were afraid I'd go
about at night strangling people. Am I a
murdering brute? Do I look it? By Jove! if
I had been he wouldn't have trusted himself like that into my room. You'll say I
might have chucked him aside and bolted
out, there and then—it was dark already.
Well, no. And for the same reason I
wouldn't think of trying to smash the door.
There would have been a rush to stop me
at the noise, and I did not mean to get into a confounded scrimmage. Somebody
else might have got killed—for I would not
have broken out only to get chucked back,
and I did not want any more of that work.
He refused, looking more sick than ever. He
was afraid of the men, and also of the old
second mate of his who had been sailing
with him for years—a gray-headed old
humbug; and his steward, too, had been
with him devil knows how long—seventeen
years or more—a dogmatic sort of loafer
who hated me like poison, just because I
was the chief mate. No chief mate ever
made more than one voyage in the *Sephora*,
you know. Those two old chaps ran the
ship. Devil only knows what the skipper
wasn't afraid of (all his nerve went to pieces
altogether in that hellish spell of bad
weather we had)—of what the law would
do to him—of his wife, perhaps. Oh, yes!
she's on board. Though I don't think she
would have meddled. She would have been
only too glad to have me out of the ship in
any way. The 'brand of Cain' business, don't
you see. That's all right. I was ready enough
to go off wandering on the face of the
earth—and that was price enough to pay
for an Abel of that sort. Anyhow, he
wouldn't listen to me. 'This thing must
take its course. I represent the law here.'
He was shaking like a leaf. 'So you won't?'
'No!' 'Then I hope you will be able to sleep
on that,' I said, and turned my back on
him. 'I wonder that *you* can,' cries he, and
locks the door.

"Well, after that, I couldn't. Not very
well. That was three weeks ago. We have
had a slow passage through the Java Sea;
drifted about Carimata for ten days. When
we anchored here they thought, I suppose,
it was all right. The nearest land (and that's
five miles) is the ship's destination; the

consul would soon set about catching me; and there would have been no object in bolting to these islets there. I don't suppose there's a drop of water on them. I don't know how it was, but tonight that steward, after bringing me my supper, went out to let me eat it, and left the door unlocked. And I ate it—all there was, too. After I had finished I strolled out on the quarter-deck. I don't know that I meant to do anything. A breath of fresh air was all I wanted, I believe. Then a sudden temptation came over me. I kicked off my slippers and was in the water before I had made up my mind fairly. Somebody heard the splash and they raised an awful hullabaloo. 'He's gone! Lower the boats! He's committed suicide! No, he's swimming.' Certainly I was swimming. It's not so easy for a swimmer like me to commit suicide by drowning. I landed on the nearest islet before the boat left the ship's side. I heard them pulling about in the dark, hailing, and so on, but after a bit they gave up. Everything quieted down and the anchorage became as still as death. I sat down on a stone and began to think. I felt certain they would start searching for me at daylight. There was no place to hide on those stony things—and if there had been, what would have been the good? But now I was clear of that ship, I was not going back. So after a while I took off all my clothes, tied them up in a bundle with a stone inside, and dropped them in the deep water on the other side of that islet. That was suicide enough for me. Let them think what they liked, but I didn't mean to drown myself. I meant to swim till I sank—but that's not the same thing. I struck out for another of these little islands, and it was from that one that I first saw your riding light. Something to swim for. I went on easily, and on the way I came upon a flat rock a foot or two above water. In the daytime, I dare say, you might make it out with a glass from your poop. I scrambled up

on it and rested myself for a bit. Then I made another start. That last spell must have been over a mile."

His whisper was getting fainter and fainter, and all the time he stared straight out through the porthole, in which there was not even a star to be seen. I had not interrupted him. There was something that made comment impossible in his narrative, or perhaps in himself; a sort of feeling, a quality, which I can't find a name for. And when he ceased, all I found was a futile whisper: "So you swam for our light?"

"Yes—straight for it. It was something to swim for. I couldn't see any stars low down because the coast was in the way, and I couldn't see the land, either. The water was like glass. One might have been swimming in a confounded thousand-feet deep cistern with no place for scrambling out anywhere; but what I didn't like was the notion of swimming round and round like a crazed bullock before I gave out; and as I didn't mean to go back . . . No. Do you see me being hauled back, stark naked, off one of these little islands by the scruff of the neck and fighting like a wild beast? Somebody would have got killed for certain, and I did not want any of that. So I went on. Then your ladder—"

"Why didn't you hail the ship?" I asked, a little louder.

He touched my shoulder lightly. Lazy footsteps came right over our heads and stopped. The second mate had crossed from the other side of the poop and might have been hanging over the rail, for all we knew.

"He couldn't hear us talking—could he?" My double breathed into my very ear, anxiously.

His anxiety was an answer, a sufficient answer, to the question I had put to him. An answer containing all the difficulty of that situation. I closed the porthole quietly, to make sure. A louder word might have been overheard.

"Who's that?" he whispered then.

"My second mate. But I don't know much more of the fellow than you do."

And I told him a little about myself. I had been appointed to take charge while I least expected anything of the sort, not quite a fortnight ago. I didn't know either the ship or the people. Hadn't had the time in port to look about me or size anybody up. And as to the crew, all they knew was that I was appointed to take the ship home. For the rest, I was almost as much of a stranger on board as himself, I said. And at the moment I felt it most acutely. I felt that it would take very little to make me a suspect person in the eyes of the ship's company.

He had turned about meantime; and we, the two strangers in the ship, faced each other in identical attitudes.

"Your ladder—" he murmured, after a silence. "Who'd have thought of finding a ladder hanging over at night in a ship anchored out here! I felt just then a very unpleasant faintness. After the life I've been leading for nine weeks, anybody would have got out of condition. I wasn't capable of swimming round as far as your rudder chains. And, lo and behold! there was a ladder to get hold of. After I gripped it I said to myself, 'What's the good?' When I saw a man's head looking over I thought I would swim away presently and leave him shouting—in whatever language it was. I didn't mind being looked at. I—I liked it. And then you speaking to me so quietly— as if you had expected me—made me hold on a little longer. It had been a confounded lonely time—I don't mean while swimming. I was glad to talk a little to somebody that didn't belong to the *Sephora*. As to asking for the captain, that was a mere impulse. It could have been no use, with all the ship knowing about me and the other people pretty certain to be round here in the morning. I don't know—I wanted to be seen, to talk with somebody, before I went on. I don't know what I would have said. . . . 'Fine night, isn't it?' or something of the sort."

"Do you think they will be round here presently?" I asked with some incredulity.

"Quite likely," he said faintly.

He looked extremely haggard all of a sudden. His head rolled on his shoulders.

"H'm. We shall see then. Meantime get into that bed," I whispered. "Want help? There."

It was a rather high bed-place with a set of drawers underneath. This amazing swimmer really needed the lift I gave him by seizing his leg. He tumbled in, rolled over on his back, and flung one arm across his eyes. And then, with his face nearly hidden, he must have looked exactly as I used to look in that bed. I gazed upon my other self for a while before drawing across carefully the two green serge curtains which ran on a brass rod. I thought for a moment of pinning them together for greater safety, but I sat down on the couch, and once there I felt unwilling to rise and hunt for a pin. I would do it in a moment. I was extremely tired, in a peculiarly intimate way, by the strain of stealthiness, by the effort of whispering and the general secrecy of this excitement. It was three o'clock by now and I had been on my feet since nine, but I was not sleepy; I could not have gone to sleep. I sat there, fagged out, looking at the curtains, trying to clear my mind of the confused sensation of being in two places at once, and greatly bothered by an exasperating knocking in my head. It was a relief to discover suddenly that it was not in my head at all, but on the outside of the door. Before I could collect myself the words "Come in" were out of my mouth, and the steward entered with a tray, bringing in my morning coffee. I had slept, after all, and I was so frightened that I shouted, "This way! I am here, steward," as though he had been miles away. He put down the tray on the table next the couch and only then said, very quietly, "I can see you are here, sir." I felt him give me a keen look, but I dared not meet his eyes just then. He must have wondered why I had drawn the curtains of my bed before going to sleep on the couch. He went out, hooking the door open as usual.

I heard the crew washing decks above me. I knew I would have been told at once if there had been any wind. Calm, I thought, and I was doubly vexed. Indeed, I felt dual more than ever. The steward reappeared suddenly in the doorway. I jumped up from the couch so quickly that he gave a start.

"What do you want here?"

"Close your port, sir—they are washing decks."

"It is closed," I said, reddening.

"Very well, sir." But he did not move from the doorway and returned my stare in an extraordinary, equivocal manner for a time. Then his eyes wavered, all his expression changed, and in a voice unusually gentle, almost coaxingly:

"May I come in to take the empty cup away, sir?"

"Of course!" I turned my back on him while he popped in and out. Then I unhooked and closed the door and even pushed the bolt. This sort of thing could not go on very long. The cabin was as hot as an oven, too. I took a peep at my double and discovered that he had not moved, his arm was still over his eyes; but his chest heaved; his hair was wet; his chin glistened with perspiration. I reached over him and opened the port.

"I must show myself on deck," I reflected.

Of course, theoretically, I could do what I liked, with no one to say nay to me within the whole circle of the horizon; but to lock my cabin door and take the key away I did not dare. Directly I put my head out of the companion I saw the group of my two officers, the second mate barefooted, the chief mate in long india-rubber boots, near the break of the poop, and the steward halfway down the poop ladder talking to them eagerly. He happened to catch sight of me and dived, the second ran down on the main deck shouting some order or other, and the chief mate came to meet me, touching his cap.

There was a sort of curiosity in his eye that I did not like. I don't know whether the steward had told them that I was "queer" only, or downright drunk, but I know the man meant to have a good look at me. I watched him coming with a smile which, as he got into point-blank range, took effect and froze his very whiskers. I did not give him time to open his lips.

"Square the yards by lifts and braces before the hands go to breakfast."

It was the first particular order I had given on board that ship; and I stayed on deck to see it executed, too. I had felt the need of asserting myself without loss of time. That sneering young cub got taken down a peg or two on that occasion, and I also seized the opportunity of having a good look at the face of every fore-mast man as they filed past me to go to the after braces. At breakfast time, eating nothing myself, I presided with such frigid dignity that the two mates were only too glad to escape from the cabin as soon as decency permitted; and all the time the dual working of my mind distracted me almost to the point of insanity. I was constantly watching myself, my secret self, as dependent on my actions as my own personality, sleeping in that bed, behind that door which faced me as I sat at the head of the table. It was very much like being mad, only it was worse because one was aware of it.

I had to shake him for a solid minute, but when at last he opened his eyes it was in the full possession of his senses, with an inquiring look.

"All's well so far," I whispered. "Now you must vanish into the bathroom."

He did so, noiseless as a ghost, and I then rang for the steward, and facing him boldly, directed him to tidy up my stateroom while I was having my bath—"and be quick about it." As my tone admitted of no excuses, he said, "Yes, sir," and ran off to fetch his dustpan and brushes. I took a bath and did most of my dressing, splashing, and whistling softly for the steward's edification, while the secret sharer of my life stood drawn up bolt upright in that little space, his face looking very sunken in daylight, his eyelids lowered under the stern, dark line of his eyebrows drawn together by a slight frown.

When I left him there to go back to my room the steward was finishing dusting. I sent for the mate and engaged him in some insignificant conversation. It was, as it were, trifling with the terrific character of his whiskers; but my object was to give him an opportunity for a good look at my cabin. And then I could at last shut, with a clear conscience, the door of my stateroom and get my double back into the recessed part. There was nothing else for it. He had to sit still on a small folding stool, half smothered by the heavy coats hanging there. We listened to the steward going into the bathroom out of the saloon, filling the water bottles there, scrubbing the bath, setting things to rights, whisk, bang, clatter—out again into the saloon—turn the key—click. Such was my scheme for keeping my second self invisible. Nothing better could be contrived under the circumstances. And there we sat; I at my writing desk ready to appear busy with some papers, he behind me, out of sight of the door. It would not have been prudent to talk in daytime; and I could not have stood the excitement of that queer sense of whispering to myself. Now and then, glancing over my shoulder, I saw him far back there, sitting rigidly on the low stool, his bare feet close together, his arms folded, his head hanging on his breast—and perfectly still. Anybody would have taken him for me.

I was fascinated by it myself. Every moment I had to glance over my shoulder. I was looking at him when a voice outside the door said:

"Beg pardon, sir."

"Well!" . . . I kept my eyes on him, and so, when the voice outside the door announced, "There's a ship's boat coming our way, sir," I saw him give a start—the first movement he had made for hours. But he did not raise his bowed head.

"All right. Get the ladder over."

I hesitated. Should I whisper something to him? But what? His immobility seemed to have been never disturbed. What could I tell him he did not know already? . . . Finally I went on deck.

II

The skipper of the *Sephora* had a thin red whisker all round his face, and the sort of complexion that goes with hair of that color; also the particular, rather smeary shade of blue in the eyes. He was not exactly a showy figure; his shoulders were high, his stature but middling—one leg slightly more bandy than the other. He shook hands, looking vaguely around. A spiritless tenacity was his main characteristic, I judged. I behaved with a politeness which seemed to disconcert him. Perhaps he was shy. He mumbled to me as if he were ashamed of what he was saying; gave his name (it was something like Archbold—but at this distance of years I hardly am sure), his ship's name, and a few other particulars of that sort, in the manner of a criminal making a reluctant and doleful confession. He had had terrible weather on the passage out—terrible—terrible—wife aboard, too.

By this time we were seated in the cabin

and the steward brought in a tray with a bottle and glasses. "Thanks! No." Never took liquor. Would have some water, though. He drank two tumblerfuls. Terrible thirsty work. Ever since daylight had been exploring the islands round his ship.

"What was that for—fun?" I asked, with an appearance of polite interest.

"No!" He sighed. "Painful duty."

As he persisted in his mumbling and I wanted my double to hear every word, I hit upon the notion of informing him that I regretted to say I was hard of hearing.

"Such a young man, too!" he nodded, keeping his smeary-blue, unintelligent eyes fastened upon me. What was the cause of it—some disease? he inquired, without the least sympathy and as if he thought that, if so, I'd got no more than I deserved.

"Yes; disease," I admitted in a cheerful tone which seemed to shock him. But my point was gained, because he had to raise his voice to give me his tale. It is not worth while to record that version. It was just over two months since all this had happened, and he had thought so much about it that he seemed completely muddled as to its bearings, but still immensely impressed.

"What would you think of such a thing happening on board your own ship? I've had the *Sephora* for these fifteen years. I am a well-known shipmaster."

He was densely distressed—and perhaps I should have sympathized with him if I had been able to detach my mental vision from the unsuspected sharer of my cabin as though he were my second self. There he was on the other side of the bulkhead, four or five feet from us, no more, as we sat in the saloon. I looked politely at Captain Archbold (if that was his name), but it was the other I saw, in a gray sleeping suit, seated on a low stool, his bare feet close together, his arms folded, and every word

said between us falling into the ears of his dark head bowed on his chest.

"I have been at sea now, man and boy, for seven-and-thirty years, and I've never heard of such a thing happening in an English ship. And that it should be my ship. Wife on board, too."

I was hardly listening to him.

"Don't you think," I said, "that the heavy sea, which, you told me, came aboard just then might have killed the man? I have seen the sheer weight of a sea kill a man very neatly, by simply breaking his neck."

"Good God!" he uttered impressively, fixing his smeary-blue eyes on me. "The sea! No man killed by the sea ever looked like that." He seemed positively scandalized at my suggestion. And as I gazed at him, certainly not prepared for anything original on his part, he advanced his head close to mine and thrust his tongue out at me so suddenly that I couldn't help starting back.

After scoring over my calmness in this graphic way he nodded wisely. If I had seen the sight, he assured me, I would never forget it as long as I lived. The weather was too bad to give the corpse a proper sea burial. So next day at dawn they took it up on the poop, covering its face with a bit of bunting; he read a short prayer, and then, just as it was, in its oilskins and long boots, they launched it amongst those mountainous seas that seemed ready every moment to swallow up the ship herself and the terrified lives on board of her.

"That reefed foresail saved you," I threw in.

"Under God—it did," he exclaimed fervently. "It was by a special mercy, I firmly believe, that it stood some of those hurricane squalls."

"It was the setting of that sail which—" I began.

"God's own hand in it," he interrupted me. "Nothing less could have done it. I don't mind telling you that I hardly dared give the order. It seemed impossible that we could touch anything without losing it, and then our last hope would have been gone."

The terror of that gale was on him yet. I let him go on for a bit, then said, casually —as if returning to a minor subject:

"You were very anxious to give up your mate to the shore people, I believe?"

He was. To the law. His obscure tenacity on that point had in it something incomprehensible and a little awful; something, as it were, mystical, quite apart from his anxiety that he should not be suspected of "countenancing any doings of that sort." Seven-and-thirty virtuous years at sea, of which over twenty of immaculate command, and the last fifteen in the *Sephora*, seemed to have laid him under some pitiless obligation.

"And you know," he went on, groping shamefacedly amongst his feelings, "I did not engage that young fellow. His people had some interest with my owners. I was in a way forced to take him on. He looked very smart, very gentlemanly, and all that. But do you know—I never liked him, somehow. I am a plain man. You see, he wasn't exactly the sort for the chief mate of a ship like the *Sephora*."

I had become so connected in thoughts and impressions with the secret sharer of my cabin that I felt as if I, personally, were being given to understand that I, too, was not the sort that would have done for the chief mate of a ship like the *Sephora*. I had no doubt of it in my mind.

"Not at all the style of man. You understand," he insisted, superfluously, looking hard at me.

I smiled urbanely. He seemed at a loss for a while.

"I suppose I must report a suicide."

"Beg pardon?"

"Sui-cide! That's what I'll have to write to my owners directly I get in."

"Unless you manage to recover him before tomorrow," I assented, dispassionately. . . . "I mean alive."

He mumbled something which I really did not catch, and I turned my ear to him in a puzzled manner. He fairly bawled:

"The land—I say, the mainland is at least seven miles off my anchorage."

"About that."

My lack of excitement, of curiosity, of surprise, of any sort of pronounced interest, began to arouse his distrust. But except for the felicitous pretense of deafness I had not tried to pretend anything. I had felt utterly incapable of playing the part of ignorance properly, and therefore was afraid to try. It is also certain that he had brought some ready-made suspicions with him, and that he viewed my politeness as a strange and unnatural phenomenon. And yet how else could I have received him? Not heartily! That was impossible for psychological reasons, which I need not state here. My only object was to keep off his inquiries. Surlily? Yes, but surliness might have provoked a point-blank question. From its novelty to him and from its nature, punctilious courtesy was the manner best calculated to restrain the man. But there was the danger of his breaking through my defense bluntly. I could not, I think, have met him by a direct lie, also for psychological (not moral) reasons. If he had only known how afraid I was of his putting my feeling of identity with the other to the test! But, strangely enough—(I thought of it only afterward)—I believe that he was not a little disconcerted by the reverse side of that weird situation, by something in me that reminded him of the man he was seeking—suggested a mysterious similitude to the young fellow he had distrusted and disliked from the first.

However that might have been, the silence was not very prolonged. He took another oblique step.

"I reckon I had no more than a two-mile pull to your ship. Not a bit more."

"And quite enough, too, in this awful heat," I said.

Another pause full of mistrust followed. Necessity, they say, is mother of invention, but fear, too, is not barren of ingenious suggestions. And I was afraid he would ask me point-blank for news of my other self.

"Nice little saloon, isn't it?" I remarked, as if noticing for the first time the way his eyes roamed from one closed door to the other. "And very well fitted out, too. Here, for instance," I continued, reaching over the back of my seat negligently and flinging the door open, "is my bathroom."

He made an eager movement, but hardly gave it a glance. I got up, shut the door of the bathroom, and invited him to have a look round, as if I were very proud of my accommodation. He had to rise and be shown round, but he went through the business without any raptures whatever.

"And now we'll have a look at my stateroom," I declared, in a voice as loud as I dared to make it, crossing the cabin to the starboard side with purposely heavy steps.

He followed me in and gazed around. My intelligent double had vanished. I played my part.

"Very convenient—isn't it?"

"Very nice. Very comf . . ." He didn't finish, and went out brusquely as if to escape from some unrighteous wiles of mine. But it was not to be. I had been too frightened not to feel vengeful; I felt I had him on the run, and I meant to keep him on the run. My polite insistence must have had something menacing in it, because he gave in suddenly. And I did not let him off a single item; mate's room, pantry, storerooms, the very sail locker which was also under the poop—he had to look into them all. When at last I showed

him out on the quarter-deck he drew a long, spiritless sigh, and mumbled dismally that he must really be going back to his ship now. I desired my mate, who had joined us, to see to the captain's boat.

The man of whiskers gave a blast on the whistle which he used to wear hanging round his neck, and yelled, "*Sephora* away!" My double down there in my cabin must have heard, and certainly could not feel more relieved than I. Four fellows came running out from somewhere forward and went over the side, while my own men, appearing on deck too, lined the rail. I escorted my visitor to the gangway ceremoniously, and nearly overdid it. He was a tenacious beast. On the very ladder he lingered, and in the unique, guiltily conscientious manner of sticking to the point:

"I say . . . you . . . you don't think that—"

I covered his voice loudly:

"Certainly not. . . . I am delighted. Goodby."

I had an idea of what he meant to say, and just saved myself by the privilege of defective hearing. He was too shaken generally to insist, but my mate, close witness of that parting, looked mystified and his face took on a thoughtful cast. As I did not want to appear as if I wished to avoid all communication with my officers, he had the opportunity to address me.

"Seems a very nice man. His boat's crew told our chaps a very extraordinary story, if what I am told by the steward is true. I suppose you had it from the captain, sir?"

"Yes. I had a story from the captain."

"A very horrible affair—isn't it, sir?"

"It is."

"Beats all these tales we hear about murders in Yankee ships."

"I don't think it beats them. I don't think it resembles them in the least."

"Bless my soul—you don't say so! But of course I've no acquaintance whatever with American ships, not I, so I couldn't go against your knowledge. It's horrible enough for me. . . . But the queerest part is that those fellows seemed to have some idea the man was hidden aboard here. They had really. Did you ever hear of such a thing?"

"Preposterous—isn't it?"

We were walking to and fro athwart the quarter-deck. No one of the crew forward could be seen (the day was Sunday), and the mate pursued:

"There was some little dispute about it. Our chaps took offense. 'As if we would harbor a thing like that,' they said. 'Wouldn't you like to look for him in our coal hole?' Quite a tiff. But they made it up in the end. I suppose he did drown himself. Don't you, sir?"

"I don't suppose anything."

"You have no doubt in the matter, sir?"

"None whatever."

I left him suddenly. I felt I was producing a bad impression, but with my double down there it was most trying to be on deck. And it was almost as trying to be below. Altogether a nerve-trying situation. But on the whole I felt less torn in two when I was with him. There was no one in the whole ship whom I dared take into my confidence. Since the hands had got to know his story, it would have been impossible to pass him off for anyone else, and an accidental discovery was to be dreaded now more than ever. . . .

The steward being engaged in laying the table for dinner, we could talk only with our eyes when I first went down. Later in the afternoon we had a cautious try at whispering. The Sunday quietness of the ship was against us; the stillness of air and water around her was against us; the elements, the men were against us—everything was against us in our secret partnership; time itself—for this could not go on forever. The very trust in Providence was, I suppose, denied to his guilt. Shall I confess that this thought cast me down very much? And as to the chapter of accidents which counts for so much in the book of success, I

could only hope that it was closed. For what favorable accident could be expected?

"Did you hear everything?" were my first words as soon as we took up our position side by side, leaning over my bed-place.

He had. And the proof of it was his earnest whisper, "The man told you he hardly dared to give the order."

I understood the reference to be to that saving foresail.

"Yes. He was afraid of it being lost in the setting."

"I assure you he never gave me the order. He may think he did, but he never gave it. He stood there with me on the break of the poop after the maintopsail blew away, and whimpered about it and nothing else— and the night coming on! To hear one's skipper go on like that in such weather was enough to drive any fellow out of his mind. It worked me up into a sort of desperation. I just took it into my own hands and went away from him, boiling, and—But what's the use telling you? *You* know! . . . Do you think that if I had not been pretty fierce with them I should have got the men to do anything? Not it! The bosun perhaps? Perhaps! It wasn't a heavy sea—it was a sea gone mad! I suppose the end of the world will be something like that; and a man may have the heart to see it coming once and be done with it—but to have to face it day after day—I don't blame anybody. I was precious little better than the rest. Only— I was an officer of that old coal-wagon, anyhow—"

"I quite understand," I conveyed that sincere assurance into his ear. He was out of breath with whispering; I could hear him pant slightly. It was all very simple. The same strung-up force which had given twenty-four men a chance, at least, for their lives, had, in a sort of recoil, crushed an unworthy mutinous existence.

But I had no leisure to weigh the merits of the matter—footsteps in the saloon, a heavy knock. "There's enough wind to get under way with, sir." Here was the call of a new claim upon my thoughts and even upon my feelings.

"Turn the hands up," I cried through the door. "I'll be on deck directly."

I was going out to make the acquaintance of my ship. Before I left the cabin our eyes met—the eyes of the only two strangers on board. I pointed to the recessed part where the little campstool awaited him and laid my finger on my lips. He made a gesture— somewhat vague—a little mysterious, accompanied by a faint smile, as if of regret.

This is not the place to enlarge upon the sensations of a man who feels for the first time a ship move under his feet to his own independent word. In my case they were not unalloyed. I was not wholly alone with my command; for there was that stranger in my cabin. Or rather, I was not completely and wholly with her. Part of me was absent. That mental feeling of being in two places at once affected me physically as if the mood of secrecy had penetrated my very soul. Before an hour had elapsed since the ship had begun to move, having occasion to ask the mate (he stood by my side) to take a compass bearing of the Pagoda, I caught myself reaching up to his ear in whispers. I say I caught myself, but enough had escaped to startle the man. I can't describe it otherwise than by saying that he shied. A grave, preoccupied manner, as though he were in possession of some perplexing intelligence, did not leave him henceforth. A little later I moved away from the rail to look at the compass with such a stealthy gait that the helmsman noticed it—and I could not help noticing the unusual roundness of his eyes. These are trifling instances, though it's to no commander's advantage to be suspected of ludicrous eccentricities. But I was also more seriously affected. There are to a seaman certain words, gestures, that should in given conditions come as naturally, as instinctively as the winking of a menaced eye. A certain

order should spring on to his lips without thinking; a certain sign should get itself made, so to speak, without reflection. But all unconscious alertness had abandoned me. I had to make an effort of will to recall myself back (from the cabin) to the conditions of the moment. I felt that I was appearing an irresolute commander to those people who were watching me more or less critically.

And, besides, there were the scares. On the second day out, for instance, coming off the deck in the afternoon (I had straw slippers on my bare feet) I stopped at the open pantry door and spoke to the steward. He was doing something there with his back to me. At the sound of my voice he nearly jumped out of his skin, as the saying is, and incidentally broke a cup.

"What on earth's the matter with you?" I asked, astonished.

He was extremely confused. "Beg pardon, sir. I made sure you were in your cabin."

"You see I wasn't."

"No, sir. I could have sworn I had heard you moving in there not a moment ago. It's most extraordinary . . . very sorry, sir."

I passed on with an inward shudder. I was so identified with my secret double that I did not even mention the fact in those scanty, fearful whispers we exchanged. I suppose he had made some slight noise of some kind or other. It would have been miraculous if he hadn't at one time or another. And yet, haggard as he appeared, he looked always perfectly self-controlled, more than calm—almost invulnerable. On my suggestion he remained almost entirely in the bathroom, which, upon the whole, was the safest place. There could be really no shadow of an excuse for anyone ever wanting to go in there, once the steward had done with it. It was a very tiny place. Sometimes he reclined on the floor, his legs bent, his head sustained on one elbow. At others I would find him on the campstool, sitting in his gray sleeping suit and with his cropped dark hair like a patient, un-moved convict. At night I would smuggle him into my bed-place, and we would whis-per together, with the regular footfalls of the officer of the watch passing and repas-sing over our heads. It was an infinitely miserable time. It was lucky that some tins of fine preserves were stowed in a locker in my stateroom; hard bread I could always get hold of; and so he lived on stewed chicken, pâté de foie gras, asparagus, cooked oysters, sardines—on all sorts of abominable sham delicacies out of tins. My early morn-ing coffee he always drank; and it was all I dared do for him in that respect.

Every day there was the horrible man-euvering to go through so that my room and then the bathroom should be done in the usual way. I came to hate the sight of the steward, to abhor the voice of that harm-less man. I felt that it was he who would bring on the disaster of discovery. It hung like a sword over our heads.

The fourth day out, I think (we were then working down the east side of the Gulf of Siam, tack for tack, in light winds and smooth water)—the fourth day, I say, of this miserable juggling with the unavoid-able, as we sat at our evening meal, that man, whose slightest movement I dreaded, after putting down the dishes ran upon deck busily. This could not be dangerous. Presently he came down again; and then it appeared that he had remembered a coat of mine which I had thrown over a rail to dry after having been wetted in a shower which had passed over the ship in the after-noon. Sitting stolidly at the head of the table I became terrified at the sight of the garment on his arm. Of course he made for my door. There was no time to lose.

"Steward," I thundered. My nerves were so shaken that I could not govern my voice and conceal my agitation. This was the sort of thing that made my terrifically whiskered mate tap his forehead with his forefinger. I

had detected him using that gesture while talking on deck with a confidential air to the carpenter. It was too far to hear a word, but I had no doubt that this pantomime could only refer to the strange new captain.

"Yes, sir," the pale-faced steward turned resignedly to me. It was this maddening course of being shouted at, checked with-out rhyme or reason, arbitrarily chased out of my cabin, suddenly called into it, sent flying out of his pantry on incomprehen-sible errands, that accounted for the grow-ing wretchedness of his expression.

"Where are you going with that coat?"

"To your room, sir."

"Is there another shower coming?"

"I'm sure I don't know, sir. Shall I go up again and see, sir?"

"No! never mind."

My object was attained, as of course my other self in there would have heard every-thing that passed. During this interlude my two officers never raised their eyes off their respective plates; but the lip of that con-founded cub, the second mate, quivered visibly.

I expected the steward to hook my coat on and come out at once. He was very slow about it; but I dominated my nervousness sufficiently not to shout after him. Suddenly I became aware (it could be heard plainly enough) that the fellow for some reason or other was opening the door of the bath-room. It was the end. The place was liter-ally not big enough to swing a cat in. My voice died in my throat and I went stony all over. I expected to hear a yell of sur-prise and terror, and made a movement, but had not the strength to get on my legs. Everything remained still. Had my second self taken the poor wretch by the throat? I don't know what I would have done next moment if I had not seen the steward come out of my room, close the door, and then stand quietly by the sideboard.

Saved, I thought. But, no! Lost! Gone! He was gone!

I laid my knife and fork down and leaned back in my chair. My head swam. After a while, when sufficiently recovered to speak in a steady voice, I instructed my mate to put the ship round at eight o'clock himself.

"I won't come on deck," I went on. "I think I'll turn in, and unless the wind shifts I don't want to be disturbed before midnight. I feel a bit seedy."

"You did look middling bad a little while ago," the chief mate remarked without showing any great concern.

They both went out, and I stared at the steward clearing the table. There was nothing to be read on that wretched man's face. But why did he avoid my eyes? I asked myself. Then I thought I should like to hear the sound of his voice.

"Steward!"

"Sir!" Startled as usual.

"Where did you hang up that coat?"

"In the bathroom, sir." The usual anxious tone. "It's not quite dry yet, sir."

For some time longer I sat in the cuddy. Had my double vanished as he had come? But of his coming there was an explanation, whereas his disappearance would be inexplicable. . . . I went slowly into my dark room, shut the door, lighted the lamp, and for a time dared not turn round. When at last I did I saw him standing bolt upright in the narrow recessed part. It would not be true to say I had a shock, but an irresistible doubt of his bodily existence flitted through my mind. Can it be, I asked myself, that he is not visible to other eyes than mine? It was like being haunted. Motionless, with a grave face, he raised his hands slightly at me in a gesture which meant clearly, "Heavens! what a narrow escape!" Narrow indeed. I think I had come creeping quietly as near insanity as any man who has not actually gone over the border. That gesture restrained me, so to speak.

The mate with the terrific whiskers was now putting the ship on the other tack. In the moment of profound silence which follows upon the hands going to their stations I heard on the poop his raised voice: "Hard alee!" and the distant shout of the order repeated on the main deck. The sails, in that light breeze, made but a faint fluttering noise. It ceased. The ship was coming round slowly; I held my breath in the renewed stillness of expectation; one wouldn't have thought that there was a single living soul on her decks. A sudden brisk shout, "Mainsail haul!" broke the spell, and in the noisy cries and rush overhead of the men running away with the main brace we two, down in my cabin, came together in our usual position by the bed-place.

He did not wait for my question. "I heard him fumbling here and just managed to squat myself down in the bath," he whispered to me. "The fellow only opened the door and put his arm in to hang the coat up. All the same—"

"I never thought of that," I whispered back, even more appalled than before at the closeness of the shave, and marveling at that something unyielding in his character which was carrying him through so finely. There was no agitation in his whisper. Whoever was being driven distracted, it was not he. He was sane. And the proof of his sanity was continued when he took up the whispering again.

"It would never do for me to come to life again."

It was something that a ghost might have said. But what he was alluding to was his old captain's reluctant admission of the theory of suicide. It would obviously serve his turn—if I had understood at all the view which seemed to govern the unalterable purpose of his action.

"You must maroon me as soon as ever you can get amongst these islands off the Cambodje shore," he went on.

"Maroon you! We are not living in a boy's adventure tale," I protested. His scornful whispering took me up.

"We aren't indeed! There's nothing of a boy's tale in this. But there's nothing else for it. I want no more. You don't suppose

I am afraid of what can be done to me? Prison or gallows or whatever they may please. But you don't see me coming back to explain such things to an old fellow in a wig and twelve respectable tradesmen, do you? What can they know whether I am guilty or not—or of *what* I am guilty, either? That's my affair. What does the Bible say? 'Driven off the face of the earth.' Very well. I am off the face of the earth now. As I came at night so shall I go."

"Impossible!" I murmured. "You can't."

"Can't? . . . Not naked like a soul on the Day of Judgment. I shall freeze on to this sleeping suit. The Last Day is not yet—and . . . you have understood thoroughly. Didn't you?"

I felt suddenly ashamed of myself. I may say truly that I understood—and my hesitation in letting that man swim away from my ship's side had been a mere sham sentiment, a sort of cowardice.

"It can't be done now till next night," I breathed out. "The ship is on the offshore tack and the wind may fail us."

"As long as I know that you understand," he whispered. "But of course you do. It's a great satisfaction to have got somebody to understand. You seem to have been there on purpose." And in the same whisper, as if we two whenever we talked had to say things to each other which were not fit for the world to hear, he added, "It's very wonderful."

We remained side by side talking in our secret way—but sometimes silent or just exchanging a whispered word or two at long intervals. And as usual he stared through the port. A breath of wind came now and again into our faces. The ship might have been moored in dock, so gently and on an even keel she slipped through the water, that did not murmur even at our passage, shadowy and silent like a phantom sea.

At midnight I went on deck, and to my mate's great surprise put the ship round on the other tack. His terrible whiskers flitted round me in silent criticism. I certainly should not have done it if it had been only a question of getting out of that sleepy gulf as quickly as possible. I believe he told the second mate, who relieved him, that it was a great want of judgment. The other only yawned. That intolerable cub shuffled about so sleepily and lolled against the rails in such a slack, improper fashion that I came down on him sharply.

"Aren't you properly awake yet?"

"Yes, sir! I am awake."

"Well, then, be good enough to hold yourself as if you were. And keep a lookout. If there's any current we'll be closing with some islands before daylight."

The east side of the gulf is fringed with islands, some solitary, others in groups. On the blue background of the high coast they seem to float on silvery patches of calm water, arid and gray, or dark green and rounded like clumps of evergreen bushes, with the larger ones, a mile or two long, showing the outlines of ridges, ribs of gray rock under the dark mantle of matted leafage. Unknown to trade, to travel, almost to geography, the manner of life they harbor is an unsolved secret. There must be villages—settlements of fishermen at least —on the largest of them, and some communication with the world is probably kept up by native craft. But all that forenoon, as we headed for them, fanned along by the faintest of breezes, I saw no sign of man or canoe in the field of the telescope I kept on pointing at the scattered group.

At noon I gave no orders for a change of course, and the mate's whiskers became much concerned and seemed to be offering themselves unduly to my notice. At last I said:

"I am going to stand right in. Quite in —as far as I can take her."

The stare of extreme surprise imparted an air of ferocity also to his eyes, and he looked truly terrific for a moment.

"We're not doing well in the middle of the gulf," I continued, casually. "I am going to look for the land breezes tonight."

"Bless my soul! Do you mean, sir, in the dark amongst the lot of all them islands and reefs and shoals?"

"Well—if there are any regular land breezes at all on this coast one must get close inshore to find them, mustn't one?"

"Bless my soul!" he exclaimed again under his breath. All that afternoon he wore a dreamy, contemplative appearance which in him was a mark of perplexity. After dinner I went into my stateroom as if I meant to take some rest. There we two bent our dark heads over a half-unrolled chart lying on my bed.

"There," I said. "It's got to be Koh-ring. I've been looking at it ever since sunrise. It has got two hills and a low point. It must be inhabited. And on the coast opposite there is what looks like the mouth of a big-gish river—with some town, no doubt, not far up. It's the best chance for you that I can see."

"Anything. Koh-ring let it be."

He looked thoughtfully at the chart as if surveying chances and distances from a lofty height—and following with his eyes his own figure wandering on the blank land of Cochin-China, and then passing off that piece of paper clean out of sight into uncharted regions. And it was as if the ship had two captains to plan her course for her. I had been so worried and restless running up and down that I had not had the patience to dress that day. I had remained in my sleeping suit, with straw slippers and a soft floppy hat. The closeness of the heat in the gulf had been most oppressive, and the crew were used to see me wandering in that airy attire.

"She will clear the south point as she heads now," I whispered into his ear. "Goodness only knows when, though, but certainly after dark. I'll edge her in to half a mile, as far as I may be able to judge in the dark—"

"Be careful," he murmured, warningly—and I realized suddenly that all my future,

the only future for which I was fit, would perhaps go irretrievably to pieces in any mishap to my first command.

I could not stop a moment longer in the room. I motioned him to get out of sight and made my way on the poop. That unplayful cub had the watch. I walked up and down for a while thinking things out, then beckoned him over.

"Send a couple of hands to open the two quarter-deck ports," I said, mildly.

He actually had the impudence, or else so forgot himself in his wonder at such an incomprehensible order, as to repeat:

"Open the quarter-deck ports! What for, sir?"

"The only reason you need concern yourself about is because I tell you to do so. Have them open wide and fastened properly."

He reddened and went off, but I believe made some jeering remark to the carpenter as to the sensible practice of ventilating a ship's quarter-deck. I know he popped into the mate's cabin to impart the fact to him because the whiskers came on deck, as it were by chance, and stole glances at me from below—for signs of lunacy or drunkenness, I suppose.

A little before supper, feeling more restless than ever, I rejoined, for a moment, my second self. And to find him sitting so quietly was surprising, like something against nature, inhuman.

I developed my plan in a hurried whisper.

"I shall stand in as close as I dare and then put her round. I shall presently find means to smuggle you out of here into the sail locker, which communicates with the lobby. But there is an opening, a sort of square for hauling the sails out, which gives straight on the quarter-deck and which is never closed in fine weather, so as to give air to the sails. When the ship's way is deadened in stays and all the hands are aft at the main braces you shall have a clear road to slip out and get overboard through the open quarter-deck port. I've had them both fastened up. Use a rope's end to lower yourself into the water so as to avoid a splash—you know. It could be heard and cause some beastly complication."

He kept silent for a while, then whispered, "I understand."

"I won't be there to see you go," I began with an effort. "The rest . . . I only hope I have understood, too."

"You have. From first to last," and for the first time there seemed to be a faltering, something strained in his whisper. He caught hold of my arm, but the ringing of the supper bell made me start. He didn't, though; he only released his grip.

After supper I didn't come below again till well past eight o'clock. The faint, steady breeze was loaded with dew; and the wet, darkened sails held all there was of propelling power in it. The night, clear and starry, sparkled darkly, and the opaque, lightless patches shifting slowly against the low stars were the drifting islets. On the port bow there was a big one more distant and shadowily imposing by the great space of sky it eclipsed.

On opening the door I had a back view of my very own self looking at a chart. He had come out of the recess and was standing near the table.

"Quite dark enough," I whispered.

He stepped back and leaned against my bed with a level, quiet glance. I sat on the couch. We had nothing to say to each other. Over our heads the officer of the watch moved here and there. Then I heard him move quickly. I knew what that meant. He was making for the companion; and presently his voice was outside my door.

"We are drawing in pretty fast, sir. Land looks rather close."

"Very well," I answered, "I am coming on deck directly."

I waited till he was gone out of the cuddy, then rose. My double moved too. The time had come to exchange our last whispers, for neither of us was ever to hear each other's natural voice.

"Look here!" I opened a drawer and took out three sovereigns. "Take this, anyhow. I've got six and I'd give you the lot, only I must keep a little money to buy some fruit and vegetables for the crew from native boats as we go through Sunda Straits."

He shook his head.

"Take it," I urged him, whispering desperately. "No one can tell what—"

He smiled and slapped meaningly the only pocket of the sleeping jacket. It was not safe, certainly. But I produced a large old silk handkerchief of mine, and tying the three pieces of gold in a corner, pressed it on him. He was touched, I suppose, because he took it at last and tied it quickly round his waist under the jacket, on his bare skin.

Our eyes met; several seconds elapsed, till, our glances still mingled, I extended my hand and turned the lamp out. Then I passed through the cuddy, leaving the door of my room wide open. . . . "Steward!"

He was still lingering in the pantry in the greatness of his zeal, giving a rub-up to a plated cruet stand the last thing before going to bed. Being careful not to wake up the mate, whose room was opposite, I spoke in an undertone.

He looked round anxiously. "Sir!"

"Can you get me a little hot water from the galley?"

"I am afraid, sir, the galley fire's been out for some time now."

"Go and see."

He fled up the stairs.

"Now," I whispered, loudly, into the saloon—too loudly, perhaps, but I was afraid I couldn't make a sound. He was by my side in an instant—the double captain slipped past the stairs—through a tiny dark passage . . . a sliding door. We were in the sail locker, scrambling on our knees over the sails. A sudden thought struck me. I saw myself wandering barefooted, bareheaded, the sun beating on my dark poll. I snatched off my floppy hat and tried hurriedly in the dark to ram it on my other self. He dodged and fended off silently. I wonder what he thought had come to me before he understood and suddenly desisted. Our hands met gropingly, lingered united in a steady, motionless clasp for a second. . . . No word was breathed by either of us when they separated.

I was standing quietly by the pantry door when the steward returned.

"Sorry, sir. Kettle barely warm. Shall I light the spirit lamp?"

"Never mind."

I came out on deck slowly. It was now a matter of conscience to shave the land as close as possible—for now he must go overboard whenever the ship was put in stays. Must! There could be no going back for him. After a moment I walked over to leeward and my heart flew into my mouth at the nearness of the land on the bow. Under any other circumstances I would not have held on a minute longer. The second mate had followed me anxiously.

I looked on till I felt I could command my voice.

"She will weather," I said then in a quiet tone.

"Are you going to try that, sir?" he stammered out incredulously.

I took no notice of him and raised my tone just enough to be heard by the helmsman.

"Keep her good full."

"Good full, sir."

The wind fanned my cheek, the sails slept, the world was silent. The strain of watching the dark loom of the land grow bigger and denser was too much for me. I had shut my eyes—because the ship must go closer. She must! The stillness was intolerable. Were we standing still?

When I opened my eyes the second view started my heart with a thump. The black southern hill of Koh-ring seemed to hang right over the ship like a towering fragment of the everlasting night. On that enormous mass of blackness there was not a gleam to be seen, not a sound to be heard. It was gliding irresistibly toward us and yet seemed already within reach of the hand. I saw the vague figures of the watch grouped in the waist, gazing in awed silence.

"Are you going on, sir?" inquired an unsteady voice at my elbow.

I ignored it. I had to go on.

"Keep her full. Don't check her way. That won't do now," I said warningly.

"I can't see the sails very well," the helmsman answered me, in strange, quavering tones.

Was she close enough? Already she was, I won't say in the shadow of the land, but in the very blackness of it, already swallowed up as it were, gone too close to be recalled, gone from me altogether.

"Give the mate a call," I said to the young man who stood at my elbow as still as death. "And turn all hands up."

My tone had a borrowed loudness reverberated from the height of the land. Several voices cried out together: "We are all on deck, sir."

Then stillness again, with the great shadow gliding closer, towering higher, without a light, without a sound. Such a hush had fallen on the ship that she might have been a bark of the dead floating in slowly under the very gate of Erebus.

"My God! Where are we?"

It was the mate moaning at my elbow. He was thunderstruck, and as it were deprived of the moral support of his whiskers. He clapped his hands and absolutely cried out, "Lost!"

"Be quiet," I said sternly.

He lowered his tone, but I saw the shadowy gesture of his despair. "What are we doing here?"

"Looking for the land wind."

He made as if to tear his hair, and addressed me recklessly.

"She will never get out. You have done it, sir. I knew it'd end in something like this. She will never weather, and you are too close now to stay. She'll drift ashore before she's round. O my God!"

I caught his arm as he was raising it to batter his poor devoted head, and shook it violently.

"She's ashore already," he wailed, trying to tear himself away.

"Is she? . . . Keep good full there!"

"Good full, sir," cried the helmsman in a frightened, thin, childlike voice.

I hadn't let go the mate's arm and went on shaking it. "Ready about, do you hear? You go forward"—shake—"and stop there" —shake—"and hold your noise"—shake— "and see these head sheets properly over-hauled"—shake, shake—shake.

And all the time I dared not look toward the land lest my heart should fail me. I released my grip at last and he ran forward as if fleeing for dear life.

I wondered what my double there in the sail locker thought of this commotion. He was able to hear everything—and perhaps he was able to understand why, on my conscience, it had to be thus close—no less. My first order, "Hard alee!" re-echoed ominously under the towering shadow of Koh-ring as if I had shouted in a mountain gorge. And then I watched the land intently. In that smooth water and light wind it was impossible to feel the ship coming-to. No! I could not feel her. And my second self was making now ready to slip out and lower himself overboard. Perhaps he was gone already . . . ?

The great black mass brooding over our very mastheads began to pivot away from the ship's side silently. And now I forgot the secret stranger ready to depart, and re-membered only that I was a total stranger to the ship. I did not know her. Would she do it? How was she to be handled?

I swung the mainyard and waited help-lessly. She was perhaps stopped, and her very fate hung in the balance, with the black mass of Koh-ring like the gate of the ever-lasting night towering over her taffrail. What would she do now? Had she way on her yet? I stepped to the side swiftly, and on the shadowy water I could see nothing except a faint phosphorescent flash reveal-ing the glassy smoothness of the sleeping surface. It was impossible to tell—and I had not learned yet the feel of my ship. Was she moving? What I needed was something easily seen, a piece of paper, which I could throw overboard and watch. I had nothing on me. To run down for it I didn't dare. There was no time. All at once my strained, yearning stare distinguished a white object floating within a yard of the ship's side. White on the black water. A phosphorescent flash passed under it. What was that thing? . . . I recognized my own floppy hat. It must have fallen off his head . . . and he didn't bother. Now I had what I wanted—the saving mark for my eyes. But I hardly thought of my other self, now gone from the ship, to be hidden forever from all friendly faces, to be a fugitive and a vaga-bond on the earth, with no brand of the curse on his sane forehead to stay a slaying hand . . . too proud to explain.

And I watched the hat—the expression of my sudden pity for his mere flesh. It had been meant to save his homeless head from the dangers of the sun. And now—behold —it was saving the ship, by serving me for a mark to help out the ignorance of my strangeness. Ha! It was drifting forward, warning me just in time that the ship had gathered sternway.

"Shift the helm," I said in a low voice to the seaman standing still like a statue.

The man's eyes glistened wildly in the binnacle light as he jumped round on the other side and spun round the wheel.

I walked to the break of the poop. On the overshadowed deck all hands stood by the forebraces waiting for my order. The stars ahead seemed to be gliding from right to left. And all was so still in the world that I heard the quiet remark, "She's round," passed in a tone of intense relief between two seamen.

"Let go and haul."

The foreyards ran round with a great noise, amidst cheery cries. And now the frightful whiskers made themselves heard giving various orders. Already the ship was drawing ahead. And I was alone with her. Nothing! no one in the world should stand now between us, throwing a shadow on the way of silent knowledge and mute affection, the perfect communion of a seaman with his first command.

Walking to the taffrail, I was in time to make out, on the very edge of a darkness thrown by a towering black mass like the very gateway of Erebus—yes, I was in time to catch an evanescent glimpse of my white hat left behind to mark the spot where the secret sharer of my cabin and of my thoughts, as though he were my second self, had lowered himself into the water to take his punishment: a free man, a proud swimmer striking out for a new destiny.

Ernest Hemingway

THE UNDEFEATED

Manuel Garcia climbed the stairs to Don Miguel Retana's office. He set down his suitcase and knocked on the door. There was no answer. Manuel, standing in the hallway, felt there was someone in the room. He felt it through the door.

"Retana," he said, listening.

There was no answer.

He's there, all right, Manuel thought.

"Retana," he said and banged the door.

"Who's there?" said someone in the office.

"Me, Manolo," Manuel said.

"What do you want?" asked the voice.

"I want to work," Manuel said.

Something in the door clicked several times and it swung open. Manuel went in, carrying his suitcase.

A little man sat behind a desk at the far side of the room. Over his head was a bull's head, stuffed by a Madrid taxidermist; on the walls were framed photographs and bullfight posters.

The little man sat looking at Manuel.

"I thought they'd killed you," he said.

Manuel knocked with his knuckles on the desk. The little man sat looking at him across the desk.

"How many corridas [bullfights] you had this year?" Retana asked.

"One," he answered.

"Just that one?" the little man asked.

"That's all."

"I read about it in the papers," Retana said. He leaned back in the chair and looked at Manuel.

Manuel looked up at the stuffed bull. He had seen it often before. He felt a certain family interest in it. It had killed his brother, the promising one, about nine years ago. Manuel remembered the day. There was a brass plate on the oak shield the bull's head was mounted on. Manuel could not read it, but he imagined it was in memory of his brother. Well, he had been a good kid.

The plate said: "The Bull 'Mariposa' of the Duke of Veragua, which accepted 9 varas [spears] for 7 caballos [horses], and caused the death of Antonio Garcia, Novillero [fighter of young bulls], April 27, 1909."

Retana saw him looking at the stuffed bull's head.

"The lot the Duke sent me for Sunday will make a scandal," he said. "They're all bad in the legs. What do they say about them at the Café?"

"I don't know," Manuel said. "I just got in."

"Yes," Retana said. "You still have your bag."

He looked at Manuel, leaning back behind the big desk.

"Sit down," he said. "Take off your cap."

Manuel sat down; his cap off, his face was changed. He looked pale, and his coleta [pig-tail] pinned forward on his head, so that it would not show under the cap, gave him a strange look.

"You don't look well," Retana said.

"I just got out of the hospital," Manuel said.

"I heard they'd cut your leg off," Retana said.

"No," said Manuel. "It got all right."

Retana leaned forward across the desk and pushed a wooden box of cigarettes toward Manuel.

"Have a cigarette," he said.

"Thanks."

Manuel lit it.

"Smoke?" he said, offering the match to Retana.

"No," Retana waved his hand, "I never smoke."

Retana watched him smoking.

"Why don't you get a job and go to work?" he said.

"I don't want to work," Manuel said. "I am a bullfighter."

"There aren't any bullfighters any more," Retana said.

"I'm a bullfighter," Manuel said.

"Yes, while you're in there," Retana said.

Manuel laughed.

Retana sat, saying nothing and looking at Manuel.

"I'll put you in a nocturnal if you want," Retana offered.

"When?" Manuel asked.

"Tomorrow night."

"I don't like to substitute for anybody," Manuel said. That was the way they all got killed. That was the way Salvador got killed. He tapped with his knuckles on the table.

"It's all I've got," Retana said.

"Why don't you put me on next week?" Manuel suggested.

"You wouldn't draw," Retana said. "All they want is Litri and Rubito and La Torre. Those kids are good."

"They'd come to see me get it," Manuel said, hopefully.

"No, they wouldn't. They don't know who you are any more."

"I've got a lot of stuff," Manuel said.

"I'm offering to put you on tomorrow night," Retana said. "You can work with young Hernandez and kill two novillos [young bulls] after the Charlots." [4]

"Whose novillos?" Manuel asked.

"I don't know. Whatever stuff they've got in the corrals. What the veterinaries won't pass in the daytime."

"I don't like to substitute," Manuel said.

"You can take it or leave it," Retana said. He leaned forward over the papers. He was no longer interested. The appeal that Manuel had made to him for a moment when he thought of the old days was gone. He would like to get him to substitute for Larita because he could get him cheaply. He could get others cheaply too. He would like to help him though. Still he had given him the chance. It was up to him.

"How much do I get?" Manuel asked. He was still playing with the idea of refusing. But he knew he could not refuse.

"Two hundred and fifty pesetas," Retana said. He had thought of five hundred, but when he opened his mouth it said two hundred and fifty.

"You pay Villalta seven thousand," Manuel said.

"You're not Villalta," Retana said.

"I know it," Manuel said.

"He draws it, Manolo," Retana said in explanation.

"Sure," said Manuel. He stood up. "Give me three hundred, Retana."

"All right," Retana agreed. He reached in the drawer for a paper.

"Can I have fifty now?" Manuel asked.

"Sure," said Retana. He took a fifty-peseta note out of his pocketbook and laid it, spread out flat, on the table.

---

[4] Burlesque acts—from the French nickname for Charlie Chaplin.

Manuel picked it up and put it in his pocket.

"What about a cuadrilla [crew]?" he asked.

"There's the boys that always work for me nights," Retana said. "They're all right."

"How about picadors?" Manuel asked.

"They're not much," Retana admitted.

"I've got to have one good pic," Manuel said.

"Get him then," Retana said. "Go and get him."

"Not out of this," Manuel said. "I'm not paying for any cuadrilla out of sixty duros." [5]

Retana said nothing but looked at Manuel across the big desk.

"You know I've got to have one good pic," Manuel said.

Retana said nothing but looked at Manuel from a long way off.

"It isn't right," Manuel said.

Retana was still considering him, leaning back in his chair, considering him from a long way away.

"They're the regular pics," he offered.

"I know," Manuel said. "I know your regular pics."

Retana did not smile. Manuel knew it was over.

"All I want is an even break," Manuel said reasoningly. "When I go out there I want to be able to call my shots on the bull. It only takes one good picador."

He was talking to a man who was no longer listening.

"If you want something extra," Retana said, "go and get it. There will be a regular cuadrilla out there. Bring as many of your own pics as you want. The charlotada[6] is over by 10.30."

"All right," Manuel said. "If that's the way you feel about it."

"That's the way," Retana said.

"I'll see you tomorrow night," Manuel said.

"I'll be out there," Retana said.

Manuel picked up his suitcase and went out.

"Shut the door," Retana called.

Manuel looked back. Retana was sitting forward looking at some papers. Manuel pulled the door tight until it clicked.

He went down the stairs and out of the door into the hot brightness of the street. It was very hot in the street and the light on the white buildings was sudden and hard on the eyes. He walked down the shady side of the steep street toward the Puerta del Sol.[7] The shade felt solid and cool as running water. The heat came suddenly as he crossed the intersecting streets. Manuel saw no one he knew in all the people he passed.

Just before the Puerta del Sol he turned into a café.

It was quiet in the café. There were a few men sitting at tables against the wall. At one table four men played cards. Most of the men sat against the wall smoking, empty coffee cups and liqueur glasses before them on the tables. Manuel went through the long room to a small room in back. A man sat at a table in the corner asleep. Manuel sat down at one of the tables.

A waiter came in and stood beside Manuel's table.

"Have you seen Zurito?" Manuel asked him.

"He was in before lunch," the waiter answered. "He won't be back before five o'clock."

"Bring me some coffee and milk and a shot of the ordinary," Manuel said.

The waiter came back into the room carrying a tray with a big coffee glass and a liqueur glass on it. In his left hand he held a bottle of brandy. He swung these down to the table and a boy who had followed him

---

[5] Pesos; one peso equals five pesetas.
[6] Charlot act; see note 4.

[7] Public square in downtown Madrid.

poured coffee and milk into the glass from two shiny, spouted pots with long handles.

Manuel took off his cap and the waiter noticed his pigtail pinned forward on his head. He winked at the coffee boy as he poured out the brandy into the little glass beside Manuel's coffee. The coffee boy looked at Manuel's pale face curiously.

"You fighting here?" asked the waiter, corking up the bottle.

"Yes," Manuel said. "Tomorrow."

The waiter stood there, holding the bottle on one hip.

"You in the Charlie Chaplins?" he asked.

The coffee boy looked away, embarrassed.

"No. In the ordinary."

"I thought they were going to have Chaves and Hernandez," the waiter said.

"No. Me and another."

"Who? Chaves or Hernandez?"

"Hernandez, I think."

"What's the matter with Chaves?"

"He got hurt."

"Where did you hear that?"

"Retana."

"Hey, Looie," the waiter called to the next room, "Chaves got cogida [tossed]."

Manuel had taken the wrapper off the lumps of sugar and dropped them into his coffee. He stirred it and drank it down, sweet, hot, and warming in his empty stomach. He drank off the brandy.

"Give me another shot of that," he said to the waiter.

The waiter uncorked the bottle and poured the glass full, slopping another drink into the saucer. Another waiter had come up in front of the table. The coffee boy was gone.

"Is Chaves hurt bad?" the second waiter asked Manuel.

"I don't know," Manuel said. "Retana didn't say."

"A hell of a lot he cares," the tall waiter said. Manuel had not seen him before. He must have just come up.

"If you stand in with Retana in this town, you're a made man," the tall waiter said. "If you aren't in with him, you might just as well go out and shoot yourself."

"You said it," the other waiter who had come in said. "You said it then."

"You're right I said it," said the tall waiter. "I know what I'm talking about when I talk about that bird."

"Look what he's done for Villalta," the first waiter said.

"And that ain't all," the tall waiter said. "Look what he's done for Màrcial Lalanda. Look what he's done for Nacional."

"You said it, kid," agreed the short waiter.

Manuel looked at them, standing talking in front of his table. He had drunk his second brandy. They had forgotten about him. They were not interested in him.

"Look at that bunch of camels," the tall waiter went on. "Did you ever see this Nacional II?"

"I seen him last Sunday didn't I?" the original waiter said.

"He's a giraffe," the short waiter said.

"What did I tell you?" the tall waiter said. "Those are Retana's boys."

"Say, give me another shot of that," Manuel said. He had poured the brandy the waiter had slopped over in the saucer into his glass and drank it while they were talking.

The original waiter poured his glass full mechanically, and the three of them went out of the room talking.

In the far corner the man was still asleep, snoring slightly on the intaking breath, his head back against the wall.

Manuel drank his brandy. He felt sleepy himself. It was too hot to go out into the town. Besides there was nothing to do. He wanted to see Zurito. He would go to sleep while he waited. He kicked his suitcase under the table to be sure it was there. Perhaps it would be better to put it back under the seat, against the wall. He leaned down and shoved it under. Then he leaned forward on the table and went to sleep.

When he woke there was someone sitting across the table from him. It was a big man with a heavy brown face like an Indian. He had been sitting there some time. He had waved the waiter away and sat reading the paper and occasionally looking down at Manuel, asleep, his head on the table. He read the paper laboriously, forming the words with his lips as he read. When it tired him he looked at Manuel. He sat heavily in the chair, his black Cordoba hat tipped forward.

Manuel sat up and looked at him.

"Hello, Zurito, " he said.

"Hello, kid," the big man said.

"I've been asleep." Manuel rubbed his forehead with the back of his fist.

"I thought maybe you were."

"How's everything?"

"Good. How is everything with you?"

"Not so good."

They were both silent. Zurito, the picador, looked at Manuel's white face. Manuel looked down at the picador's enormous hands folding the paper to put away in his pocket.

"I got a favor to ask you, Manos," Manuel said.

Manosduros [Hard hands] was Zurito's nickname. He never heard it without thinking of his huge hands. He put them forward on the table self-consciously.

"Let's have a drink," he said.

"Sure," said Manuel.

The waiter came and went and came again. He went out of the room looking back at the two men at the table.

"What the matter, Manolo?" Zurito set down his glass.

"Would you pic two bulls for me tomorrow night?" Manuel asked, looking up at Zurito across the table.

"No," said Zurito. "I'm not pic-ing."

Manuel looked down at his glass. He had expected that answer; now he had it. Well, he had it.

"I'm sorry, Manolo, but I'm not pic-ing." Zurito looked at his hands.

"That's all right," Manuel said.

"I'm too old," Zurito said.

"I just asked you," Manuel said.

"Is it the nocturnal tomorrow?"

"That's it. I figured if I had just one good pic, I could get away with it."

"How much are you getting?"

"Three hundred pesetas."

"I get more than that for pic-ing."

"I know," said Manuel. "I didn't have any right to ask you."

"What do you keep on doing it for?" Zurito asked. "Why don't you cut off your coleta, Manolo?"

"I don't know," Manuel said.

"You're pretty near as old as I am," Zurito said.

"I don't know," Manuel said. "I got to do it. If I can fix it so that I get an even break, that's all I want. I got to stick with it, Manos."

"No, you don't."

"Yes I do. I've tried keeping away from it."

"I know how you feel. But it isn't right. You ought to get out and stay out."

"I can't do it. Besides, I've been going good lately."

Zurito looked at his face.

"You've been in the hospital."

"But I was going great when I got hurt."

Zurito said nothing. He tipped the cognac out of his saucer into his glass.

"The papers said they never saw a better faena [working of a bull]," Manuel said.

Zurito looked at him.

"You know when I get going I'm good," Manuel said.

"You're too old," the picador said.

"No," said Manuel. "You're ten years older than I am."

"With me it's different."

"I'm not too old," Manuel said.

They sat silent, Manuel watching the picador's face.

"I was going great till I got hurt," Manuel offered.

"You ought to have seen me, Manos," Manuel said, reproachfully.

"I don't want to see you," Zurito said. "It makes me nervous."

"You haven't seen me lately."

"I've seen you plenty."

Zurito looked at Manuel, avoiding his eyes.

"You ought to quit it, Manolo."

"I can't," Manuel said. "I'm going good now, I tell you."

Zurito leaned forward, his hands on the table.

"Listen. I'll pic for you and if you don't go big tomorrow night, you'll quit. See? Will you do that?"

"Sure."

Zurito leaned back, relieved.

"You got to quit," he said. "No monkey business. You got to cut the coleta."

"I won't have to quit," Manuel said. "You watch me. I've got the stuff."

Zurito stood up. He felt tired from arguing.

"You got to quit," he said. "I'll cut your coleta myself."

"No, you won't," Manuel said. "You won't have a chance."

Zurito called the waiter.

"Come on," said Zurito. "Come on up to the house."

Manuel reached under the seat for his suitcase. He was happy. He knew Zurito would pic for him. He was the best picador living. It was all simple now.

"Come on up to the house and we'll eat," Zurito said.

Manuel stood in the patio de caballos waiting for the Charlie Chaplins to be over. Zurito stood beside him. Where they stood it was dark. The high door that led into the bull ring was shut. Above them they heard a shout, then another shout of laughter. Then there was silence. Manuel liked the smell of the stables about the patio de caballos. It smelt good in the dark. There was another roar from the arena and then applause, prolonged applause, going on and on.

"You ever seen these fellows?" Zurito asked, big and looming beside Manuel in the dark.

"No," Manuel said.

"They're pretty funny," Zurito said. He smiled to himself in the dark.

The high, double, tight-fitting door into the bull ring swung open and Manual saw the ring in the hard light of the arc lights, the plaza, dark all the way around, rising high; around the edge of the ring were running and bowing two men dressed like tramps, followed by a third in the uniform of a hotel bellboy who stooped and picked up the hats and canes thrown down onto the sand and tossed them back up into the darkness.

The electric light went on in the patio.

"I'll climb onto one of those ponies while you collect the kids," Zurito said.

Behind them came the jingle of the mules, coming out to go into the arena and be hitched onto the dead bull.

The members of the cuadrilla, who had been watching the burlesque from the runway between the barrera [fence] and the seats, came walking back and stood in a group talking, under the electric light in the patio. A good-looking lad in a silver-and-orange suit came up to Manuel and smiled.

"I'm Hernandez," he said and put out his hand.

Manuel shook it.

"They're regular elephants we've got tonight," the boy said cheerfully.

"They're big ones with horns," Manuel agreed.

"You drew the worst lot," the boy said.

"That's all right," Manuel said. "The bigger they are, the more meat for the poor."

"Where did you get that one?" Hernandez grinned.

"That's an old one," Manuel said. "You line up your cuadrilla, so I can see what I've got."

"You've got some good kids," Hernandez said. He was very cheerful. He had been on twice before in nocturnals and was beginning to get a following in Madrid. He was happy the fight would start in a few minutes.

"Where are the pics?" Manuel asked.

"They're back in the corrals fighting about who gets the beautiful horses," Hernandez grinned.

The mules came through the gate in a rush, the whips snapping, bells jangling, and the young bull ploughing a furrow of sand.

They formed up for the paseo [procession] as soon as the bull had gone through. Manuel and Hernandez stood in front. The youths of the cuadrillas were behind, their heavy capes furled over their arms. In back, the four picadors, mounted, holding their steel-tipped push-poles erect in the half-dark of the corral.

"It's a wonder Retana wouldn't give us enough light to see the horses by," one picador said.

"He knows we'll be happier if we don't get too good a look at these skins," another pic answered.

"This thing I'm on barely keeps me off the ground," the first picador said.

"Well, they're horses."

"Sure, they're horses."

They talked, sitting their gaunt horses in the dark.

Zurito said nothing. He had the only steady horse of the lot. He had tried him, wheeling him in the corrals, and he responded to the bit and the spurs. He had taken the bandage off his right eye and cut the strings where they had tied his ears tight shut at the base. He was a good, solid horse, solid on his legs. That was all he needed. He intended to ride him all through the corrida. He had already, since he had mounted, sitting in the half-dark in the big, quilted saddle, waiting for the paseo, pic-ed through the whole corrida in his mind. The other picadors went on talking on both sides of him. He did not hear them.

The two matadors stood together in front of their three peones [helpers], their capes furled over their left arms in the same fashion. Manuel was thinking about the three lads in back of him. They were all three Madrilenos [natives of Madrid], like Hernandez, boys about nineteen. One of them, a gypsy, serious, aloof, and dark-faced, he liked the look of. He turned.

"What's your name, kid?" he asked the gypsy.

"Fuentes," the gypsy said.

"That's a good name," Manuel said.

The gypsy smiled, showing his teeth.

"You take the bull and give him a little run when he comes out," Manuel said.

"All right," the gypsy said. His face was serious. He began to think about just what he would do.

"Here she goes," Manuel said to Hernandez.

"All right. We'll go."

Heads up, swinging with the music, their right arms swinging free, they stepped out, crossing the sanded arena under the arc lights, the cuadrillas opening out behind, the picadors riding after; behind came the bullring servants and the jingling mules. The crowd applauded Hernandez as they marched across the arena. Arrogant, swinging, they looked straight ahead as they marched.

They bowed before the president, and the procession broke up into its component parts. The bullfighters went over to the barrera and changed their heavy mantles for the light fighting capes. The mules went out. The picadors galloped jerkily around the ring, and two rode out the gate they had come in by. The servants swept the sand smooth.

Manuel drank a glass of water poured for him by one of Retana's deputies, who was acting as his manager and sword-handler. Hernandez came over from speaking with his own manager.

"You got a good hand, kid," Manuel complimented him.

"They like me," Hernandez said happily.

"How did the paseo go?" Manuel asked Retana's man.

"Like a wedding," said the handler. "Fine. You came out like Joselito and Belmonte."

Zurito rode by, a bulky equestrian statue. He wheeled his horse and faced him toward the toril [bullpen] on the far side of the ring where the bull would come out. It was strange under the arc light. He pic-ed in the hot afternoon sun for big money. He didn't like this arc-light business. He wished they would get started.

Manuel went up to him.

"Pic him, Manos," he said. "Cut him down to size for me."

"I'll pic him, kid," Zurito spat on the sand. "I'll make him jump out of the ring."

"Lean on him, Manos," Manuel said.

"I'll lean on him," Zurito said. "What's holding it up?"

"He's coming now," Manuel said.

Zurito sat there, his feet in the box-stirrups, his great legs in the buckskin-covered armor gripping the horse, the reins in his left hand, the long pic held in his right hand, his broad hat well down over his eyes to shade them from the lights, watching the distant door of the toril. His horse's ears quivered. Zurito patted him with his left hand.

The red door of the toril swung back and for a moment Zurito looked into the empty passageway far across the arena. Then the bull came out in a rush, skidding on his four legs as he came out under the lights, then charging in a gallop, moving softly in a fast gallop, silent except as he woofed through wide nostrils as he charged, glad to be free after the dark pen.

In the first row of seats, slightly bored, leaning forward to write on the cement wall in front of his knees, the substitute bullfight critic of *El Heraldo* scribbled: "Campagnero, Negro,[8] 42, came out at 90 miles an hour with plenty of gas—"

Manuel, leaning against the barrera, watching the bull, waved his hand and the gypsy ran out, trailing his cape. The bull, in full gallop, pivoted and charged the cape, his head down, his tail rising. The gypsy moved in a zigzag, and as he passed, the bull caught sight of him and abandoned the cape to charge the man. The gyp sprinted and vaulted the red fence of the barrera as the bull struck it with his horns. He tossed into it twice with his horns, banging into the wood blindly.

The critic of *El Heraldo* lit a cigarette and tossed the match at the bull, then wrote in his notebook, "large and with enough horns to satisfy the cash customers, Campagnero showed a tendency to cut into the terrain of the bullfighters."

Manuel stepped out on the hard sand as the bull banged into the fence. Out of the corner of his eye he saw Zurito sitting the white horse close to the barrera, about a quarter of the way around the ring to the left. Manuel held the cape close in front of him, a fold in each hand, and shouted at the bull. "Huh! Huh!" The bull turned, seemed to brace against the fence as he charged in a scramble, driving into the cape as Manuel side-stepped, pivoted on his heels with the charge of the bull, and swung the cape just ahead of the horns. At the end of the swing he was facing the bull again and held the cape in the same position close in front of his body, and pivoted again as the bull recharged. Each time, as he swung, the crowd shouted.

Four times he swung with the bull, lifting the cape so it billowed full, and each time bringing the bull around to charge again.

---

[8] Black; 42 appears to be the bull's number.

Then, at the end of the fifth swing, he held the cape against his hip and pivoted, so the cape swung out like a ballet dancer's skirt and wound the bull around himself like a belt, to step clear, leaving the bull facing Zurito on the white horse, come up and planted firm, the horse facing the bull, its ears forward, its lips nervous, Zurito, his hat over his eyes, leaning forward, the long pole sticking out before and behind in a sharp angle under his right arm, held halfway down, the triangular iron point facing the bull.

El Heraldo's second-string critic, drawing on his cigarette, his eyes on the bull, wrote: "the veteran Manolo designed a series of acceptable veronicas, ending in a very Belmontistic recorte[9] that earned applause from the regulars, and we entered the tercio of the cavalry." [10]

Zurito sat his horse, measuring the distance between the bull and the end of the pic. As he looked, the bull gathered himself together and charged, his eyes on the horse's chest. As he lowered his head to hook, Zurito sunk the point of the pic in the swelling hump of muscle above the bull's shoulder, leaned all his weight on the shaft, and with his left hand pulled the white horse into the air, front hoofs pawing, and swung him to the right as he pushed the bull under and through so the horns passed safely under the horse's belly and the horse came down, quivering, the bull's tail brushing his chest as he charged the cape Hernandez offered him.

Hernandez ran sideways, taking the bull out and away with the cape, toward the other picador. He fixed him with a swing of the cape, squarely facing the horse and rider, and stepped back. As the bull saw the horse he charged. The picador's lance slid

along his back, and as the shock of the charge lifted the horse, the picador was already halfway out of the saddle, lifting his right leg clear as he missed with the lance and falling to the left side to keep the horse between him and the bull. The horse, lifted and gored, crashed over with the bull driving into him; the picador gave a shove with his boots against the horse and lay clear, waiting to be lifted and hauled away and put on his feet.

Manuel let the bull drive into the fallen horse; he was in no hurry, the picador was safe; besides, it did a picador like that good to worry. He'd stay on longer next time. Lousy pics! He looked across the sand at Zurito a little way out from the barrera, his horse rigid, waiting.

"Huh!" he called to the bull, "Tomar [Take]!" holding the cape in both hands so it would catch his eye. The bull detached himself from the horse and charged the cape, and Manuel, running sideways and holding the cape spread wide, stopped, swung on his heels, and brought the bull sharply around facing Zurito.

"Campagnero accepted a pair of varas for the death of one rosinante, with Hernandez and Manolo at the quites," [11] *El Heraldo's* critic wrote. "He pressed on the iron and clearly showed he was no horse-lover. The veteran Zurito resurrected some of his old stuff with the pike-pole, notably the suerte[12]—"

"Olé! Olé!" the man sitting beside him shouted. The shout was lost in the roar of the crowd, and he slapped the critic on the back. The critic looked up to see Zurito, directly below him, leaning far out over his horse, the length of the pic rising in a sharp angle under his armpit, holding the pic almost by the point, bearing down with all his weight, holding the bull off, the bull

---

[9] Gestures with the cape, climaxed by avoidance of the bull in the style of the famous bullfighter Juan Belmonte.

[10] That third of the exhibition which is dominated by the mounted picadors.

[11] Maneuvers by which the bull is distracted from a fallen bullfighter.

[12] Maneuver by which the picador keeps the bull from hurting his horse.

pushing and driving to get at the horse, and Zurito, far out, on top of him, holding him, holding him, and slowly pivoting the horse against the pressure, so that at last he was clear. Zurito felt the moment when the horse was clear and the bull could come past, and relaxed the absolute steel lock of his resistance, and the triangular steel point of the pic ripped in the bull's hump of shoulder muscle as he tore loose to find Hernandez's cape before his muzzle. He charged blindly into the cape and the boy took him out into the open arena.

Zurito sat patting his horse and looking at the bull charging the cape that Hernandez swung for him out under the bright light while the crowd shouted.

"You see that one?" he said to Manuel.

"It was a wonder," Manuel said.

"I got him that time," Zurito said. "Look at him now."

At the conclusion of a closely turned pass of the cape the bull slid to his knees. He was up at once, but far out across the sand Manuel and Zurito saw the shine of the pumping flow of blood, smooth against the black of the bull's shoulder.

"I got him that time," Zurito said.

"He's a good bull," Manuel said.

"If they gave me another shot at him, I'd kill him," Zurito said.

"They'll change the thirds on us," Manuel said.

"Look at him now," Zurito said.

"I got to go over there," Manuel said, and started on a run for the other side of the ring, where the monos [clowns] were leading a horse out by the bridle toward the bull, whacking him on the legs with rods and all, in a procession, trying to get him toward the bull, who stood, dropping his head, pawing, unable to make up his mind to charge.

Zurito, sitting his horse, walking him toward the scene, not missing any detail, scowled.

Finally the bull charged, the horse leaders ran for the barrera, the picador hit too far back, and the bull got under the horse, lifted him, threw him onto his back.

Zurito watched. The monos, in their red shirts, running out to drag the picador clear. The picador, now on his feet, swearing and flopping his arms. Manuel and Hernandez standing ready with their capes. And the bull, the great, black bull, with a horse on his back, hooves dangling, the bridle caught in the horns. Black bull with a horse on his back, staggering short-legged, then arching his neck and lifting, thrusting, charging to slide the horse off, horse sliding down. Then the bull into a lunging charge at the cape Manuel spread for him.

The bull was slower now, Manuel felt. He was bleeding badly. There was a sheen of blood all down his flank.

Manuel offered him the cape again. There he came, eyes open, ugly, watching the cape. Manuel stepped to the side and raised his arms, tightening the cape ahead of the bull for the veronica.

Now he was facing the bull. Yes, his head was going down a little. He was carrying it lower. That was Zurito.

Manuel flopped the cape; there he comes; he side-stepped and swung in another veronica. He's shooting awfully accurately, he thought. He's had enough fight, so he's watching now. He's hunting now. Got his eye on me. But I always gave him the cape.

He shook the cape at the bull; there he comes; he side-stepped. Awful close that time. I don't want to work that close to him.

The edge of the cape was wet with blood where it had swept along the bull's back as he went by.

All right, here's the last one.

Manuel, facing the bull, having turned with him each charge, offered the cape with his two hands. The bull looked at him. Eyes watching, horns straight forward, the bull looked at him, watching.

"Huh!" Manuel said, "Toro!" and leaning back, swung the cape forward. Here he comes. He side-stepped, swung the cape in back of him, and pivoted, so the bull followed a swirl of cape and then was left with nothing, fixed by the pass, dominated by the cape. Manuel swung the cape under his muzzle with one hand, to show the bull was fixed, and walked away.

There was no applause.

Manuel walked across the sand toward the barrera, while Zurito rode out of the ring. The trumpet had blown to change the act to the planting of the banderillas [spears with pennants] while Manuel had been working with the bull. He had not consciously noticed it. The monos were spreading canvas over the two dead horses and sprinkling sawdust around them.

Manuel came up to the barrera for a drink of water. Retana's man handed him the heavy porous jug.

Fuentes, the tall gypsy, was standing holding a pair of banderillas, holding them together, slim, red sticks, fish-hook points out. He looked at Manuel.

"Go on out there," Manuel said.

The gypsy trotted out. Manuel set down the jug and watched. He wiped his face with his handkerchief.

The critic of *El Heraldo* reached for the bottle of warm champagne that stood between his feet, took a drink, and finished his paragraph.

"—the aged Manolo rated no applause for a vulgar series of lances with the cape and we entered the third of the palings."

Alone in the center of the ring the bull stood, still fixed. Fuentes, tall, flat-backed, walking toward him arrogantly, his arms spread out, the two slim, red sticks, one in each hand, held by the fingers, points straight forward. Fuentes walked forward. Back of him and to one side was a peon with a cape. The bull looked at him and was no longer fixed.

His eyes watched Fuentes, now standing still. Now he leaned back, calling to him.

Fuentes twitched the two banderillas and the light on the steel points caught the bull's eye.

His tail went up and he charged.

He came straight, his eyes on the man. Fuentes stood still, leaning back, the banderillas pointing forward. As the bull lowered his head to hook, Fuentes leaned backward, his arms came together and rose, his two hands touching, the banderillas two descending red lines, and leaning forward drove the points into the bull's shoulder, leaning far in over the bull's horns and pivoting on the two upright sticks, his legs tight together, his body curving to one side to let the bull pass.

"Olé!" from the crowd.

The bull was hooking wildly, jumping like a trout, all four feet off the ground. The red shafts of the banderillas tossed as he jumped.

Manuel, standing at the barrera, noticed that he hooked always to the right.

"Tell him to drop the next pair on the right," he said to the kid who started to run out to Fuentes with the new banderillas.

A heavy hand fell on his shoulder. It was Zurito.

"How do you feel, kid?" he asked.

Manuel was watching the bull.

Zurito leaned forward on the barrera, leaning the weight of his body on his arms. Manuel turned to him.

"You're going good," Zurito said.

Manuel shook his head. He had nothing to do now until the next third. The gypsy was very good with the banderillas. The bull would come to him in the next third in good shape. He was a good bull. It had all been easy up to now. The final stuff with the sword was all he worried over. He did not really worry. He did not even think about it. But standing there he had a heavy sense of apprehension. He looked out at the bull, planning his faena, his work with the red cloth that was to reduce the bull, to make him manageable.

The gypsy was walking out toward the bull again, walking heel-and-toe, insultingly, like a ballroom dancer, the red shafts of the banderillas twitching with his walk. The bull watched him, not fixed now, hunting him, but waiting to get close enough so he could be sure of getting him, getting the horns into him.

As Fuentes walked forward the bull charged. Fuentes ran across the quarter of a circle as the bull charged and, as he passed running backward, stopped, swung forward, rose on his toes, arms straight out, and sunk the banderillas straight down into the tight of the big shoulder muscles as the bull missed him.

The crowd were wild about it.

"That kid won't stay in this night stuff long," Retana's man said to Zurito.

"He's good," Zurito said.

"Watch him now."

They watched.

Fuentes was standing with his back against the barrera. Two of the cuadrilla were back of him, with their capes ready to flop over the fence to distract the bull.

The bull, with his tongue out, his barrel heaving, was watching the gypsy. He thought he had him now. Back against the red planks. Only a short charge away. The bull watched him.

The gypsy bent back, drew back his arms, the banderillas pointing at the bull. He called to the bull, stamped one foot. The bull was suspicious. He wanted the man. No more barbs in the shoulder.

Fuentes walked a little closer to the bull. Bent back. Called again. Somebody in the crowd shouted a warning.

"He's too damn close," Zurito said.

"Watch him," Retana's man said.

Leaning back, inciting the bull with the banderillas, Fuentes jumped, both feet off the ground. As he jumped the bull's tail rose and he charged. Fuentes came down on his toes, arms straight out, whole body arching forward, and drove the shafts straight down as he swung his body clear of the right horn.

The bull crashed into the barrera where the flopping capes had attracted his eye as he lost the man.

The gypsy came running along the barrera toward Manuel, taking the applause of the crowd. His vest was ripped where he had not quite cleared the point of the horn. He was happy about it, showing it to the spectators. He made the tour of the ring. Zurito saw him go by, smiling, pointing at his vest. He smiled.

Somebody else was planting the last pair of banderillas. Nobody was paying any attention.

Retana's man tucked a baton inside the red cloth of a muleta, folded the cloth over it, and handed it over the barrera to Manuel. He reached in the leather sword-case, took out a sword, and holding it by its leather scabbard, reached it over the fence to Manuel. Manuel pulled the blade out by the red hilt and the scabbard fell limp.

He looked at Zurito. The big man saw he was sweating.

"Now you get him, kid," Zurito said.

Manuel nodded.

"He's in good shape," Zurito said.

"Just like you want him," Retana's man assured him.

Manuel nodded.

The trumpeter, up under the roof, blew for the final act, and Manuel walked across the arena toward where, up in the dark boxes, the president must be.

In the front row of seats the substitute bullfight critic of *El Heraldo* took a long drink of the warm champagne. He had decided it was not worth while to write a running story and would write up the corrida back in the office. What the hell was it anyway? Only a nocturnal. If he missed anything he would get it out of the morning papers. He took another drink of the champagne. He had a date at Maxim's at twelve. Who were these bullfighters anyway? Kids and bums. A bunch of bums. He put his pad of paper in his pocket and looked over toward Manuel, standing very much alone in the ring, gesturing with his hat in a salute toward a box he could not see high up in the dark plaza. Out in the ring the bull stood quiet, looking at nothing.

"I dedicate this bull to you, Mr. President, and to the public of Madrid, the most intelligent and generous of the world," was what Manuel was saying. It was a formula. He said it all. It was a little long for nocturnal use.

He bowed at the dark, straightened, tossed his hat over his shoulder, and, carrying the muleta in his left hand and the sword in his right, walked out toward the bull.

Manuel walked toward the bull. The bull looked at him; his eyes were quick. Manuel noticed the way the banderillas hung down on his left shoulder and the steady sheen of blood from Zurito's pic-ing. He noticed the way the bull's feet were. As he walked forward, holding the muleta in his left hand and the sword in his right, he watched the bull's feet. The bull could not charge without gathering his feet together. Now he stood square on them, dully.

Manuel walked toward him, watching his feet. This was all right. He could do this. He must work to get the bull's head down, so he could go in past the horns and kill him. He did not think about the sword, not about killing the bull. He thought about one thing at a time. The coming things oppressed him, though. Walking forward, watching the bull's feet, he saw successively his eyes, his wet muzzle, and the wide, forward-pointing spread of his horns. The bull had light circles about his eyes. His eyes watched Manuel. He felt he was going to get this little one with the white face.

Standing still now and spreading the red cloth of the muleta with the sword, pricking the point into the cloth so that the sword, now held in his left hand, spread the

red flannel like the jib of a boat, Manuel noticed the points of the bull's horns. One of them was splintered from banging against the barrera. The other was sharp as a porcupine quill. Manuel noticed while spreading the muleta that the white base of the horn was stained red. While he noticed these things he did not lose sight of the bull's feet. The bull watched Manuel steadily.

He's on the defensive now, Manuel thought. He's reserving himself. I've got to bring him out of that and get his head down. Always get his head down. Zurito had his head down once, but he's come back. He'll bleed when I start him going and that will bring it down.

Holding the muleta, with the sword in his left hand widening it in front of him, he called to the bull.

The bull looked at him.

He leaned back insultingly and shook the widespread flannel.

The bull saw the muleta. It was a bright scarlet under the arc light. The bull's legs tightened.

Here he comes. Whoosh! Manuel turned as the bull came and raised the muleta so that it passed over the bull's horns and swept down his broad back from head to tail. The bull had gone clean up in the air with the charge. Manuel had not moved.

At the end of the pass the bull turned like a cat coming around a corner and faced Manuel.

He was on the offensive again. His heaviness was gone. Manuel noted the fresh blood shining down the black shoulder and dripping down the bull's leg. He drew the sword out of the muleta and held it in his right hand. The muleta held low down in his left hand, leaning toward the left, he called to the bull. The bull's legs tightened, his eyes on the muleta. Here he comes, Manuel thought. Yuh!

He swung with the charge, sweeping the muleta ahead of the bull, his feet firm, the sword following the curve, a point of light under the arcs.

The bull recharged as the pase natural finished and Manuel raised the muleta for a pase de pecho.[13] Firmly planted, the bull came by his chest under the raised muleta. Manuel leaned his head back to avoid the clattering banderilla shafts. The hot, black bull body touched his chest as it passed.

Too damn close, Manuel thought. Zurito, leaning on the barrera, spoke rapidly to the gypsy, who trotted out toward Manuel with a cape. Zurito pulled his hat down low and looked out across the arena at Manuel.

Manuel was facing the bull again, the muleta held low and to the left. The bull's head was down as he watched the muleta.

"If it was Belmonte doing that stuff, they'd go crazy," Retana's man said.

Zurito said nothing. He was watching Manuel out in the center of the arena.

"Where did the boss dig this fellow up?" Retana's man asked.

"Out of the hospital," Zurito said.

"That's where he's going damn quick," Retana's man said.

Zurito turned on him.

"Knock on that," he said, pointing to the barrera.

"I was just kidding, man," Retana's man said.

"Knock on the wood."

Retana's man leaned forward and knocked three times on the barrera.

"Watch the faena," Zurito said.

Out in the center of the ring, under the lights, Manuel was kneeling, facing the bull, and as he raised the muleta in both hands the bull charged, tail up.

Manuel swung his body clear and, as the bull recharged, brought around the muleta in a half-circle that pulled the bull to his knees.

---

[13] After the "ordinary pass" Manuel prepares for a "chest pass," in which he must hold the muleta high and close to his chest.

"Why, that one's a great bullfighter," Retana's man said.

"No, he's not," said Zurito.

Manuel stood up and, the muleta in his left hand, the sword in his right, acknowledged the applause from the dark plaza.

The bull had humped himself up from his knees and stood waiting, his head hung low.

Zurito spoke to two of the other lads of the cuadrilla and they ran out to stand back of Manuel with their capes. There were four men back of him now. Hernandez had followed him since he first came out with the muleta. Fuentes stood watching, his cape held against his body, tall, in repose, watching lazy-eyed. Now the two came up. Hernandez motioned them to stand one at each side. Manuel stood alone, facing the bull.

Manuel waved back the men with the capes. Stepping back cautiously, they saw his face was white and sweating.

Didn't they know enough to keep back? Did they want to catch the bull's eye with the capes after he was fixed and ready? He had enough to worry about without that kind of thing.

The bull was standing, his four feet square, looking at the muleta. Manuel furled the muleta in his left hand. The bull's eyes watched it. His body was heavy on his feet. He carried his head low, but not too low.

Manuel lifted the muleta at him. The bull did not move. Only his eyes watched.

He's all lead, Manuel thought. He's all square. He's framed right. He'll take it.

He thought in bullfight terms. Sometimes he had a thought and the particular piece of slang would not come into his mind and he could not realize the thought. His instincts and his knowledge worked automatically, and his brain worked slowly and in words. He knew all about bulls. He did not have to think about them. He just did the right thing. His eyes noted things and his body performed the necessary measures without thought. If he thought about it, he would be gone.

Now, facing the bull, he was conscious of many things at the same time. There were the horns, the one splintered, the other smoothly sharp, the need to profile himself toward the left horn, lance himself short and straight, lower the muleta so the bull would follow it, and, going in over the horns, put the sword all the way into a little spot about as big as a five-peseta piece straight in back of the neck, between the sharp pitch to the bull's shoulders. He must do all this and must then come out from between the horns. He was conscious he must do all this, but his only thought was in words: "Corto y derecho."

"Corto y derecho," he thought, furling the muleta. Short and straight. Corto y derecho, he drew the sword out of the muleta, profiled on the splintered left horn, dropped the muleta across his body, so his right hand with the sword on the level with his eye made the sign of the cross, and, rising on his toes, sighted along the dipping blade of the sword at the spot high up between the bull's shoulders.

Corto y derecho he launched himself on the bull.

There was a shock, and he felt himself go up in the air. He pushed on the sword as he went up and over, and it flew out of his hand. He hit the ground and the bull was on him. Manuel, lying on the ground, kicked at the bull's muzzle with his slippered feet. Kicking, kicking, the bull after him, missing him in his excitement, bumping him with his head, driving the horns into the sand. Kicking like a man keeping a ball in the air, Manuel kept the bull from getting a clean thrust at him.

Manuel felt the wind on his back from the capes flopping at the bull, and then the bull was gone, gone over him in a rush. Dark, as his belly went over. Not even stepped on.

Manuel stood up and picked up the muleta. Fuentes handed him the sword. It was bent where it had struck the shoulder-blade. Manuel straightened it on his knee and ran toward the bull, standing now beside one of the dead horses. As he ran, his jacket flopped where it had been ripped under his armpit.

"Get him out of there," Manuel shouted to the gypsy. The bull had smelled the blood of the dead horse and ripped into the canvas cover with his horns. He charged Fuentes's cape, with the canvas hanging from his splintered horn, and the crowd laughed. Out in the ring, he tossed his head to rid himself of the canvas. Hernandez, running up from behind him, grabbed the end of the canvas and neatly lifted it off the horn.

The bull followed it in a half-charge and stopped still. He was on the defensive again. Manuel was walking toward him with the sword and muleta. Manuel swung the muleta before him. The bull would not charge.

Manuel profiled toward the bull, sighting along the dipping blade of the sword. The bull was motionless, seemingly dead on his feet, incapable of another charge.

Manuel rose to his toes, sighting along the steel, and charged.

Again there was the shock and he felt himself being borne back in a rush, to strike hard on the sand. There was no chance of kicking this time. The bull was on top of him. Manuel lay as though dead, his head on his arms, and the bull bumped him. Bumped his back, bumped his face in the sand. He felt the horn go into the sand between his folded arms. The bull hit him in the small of the back. His face drove into the sand. The horn drove through one of his sleeves and the bull ripped it off. Manuel was tossed clear and the bull followed the capes.

Manuel got up, found the sword and muleta, tried the point of the sword with his thumb, and then ran toward the barrera for a new sword.

Retana's man handed him the sword over the edge of the barrera.

"Wipe off your face," he said.

Manuel, running again toward the bull, wiped his bloody face with his handkerchief. He had not seen Zurito. Where was Zurito?

The cuadrilla had stepped away from the bull and waited with their capes. The bull stood, heavy and dull again after the action.

Manuel walked toward him with the muleta. He stopped and shook it. The bull did not respond. He passed it right and left, left and right before the bull's muzzle. The bull's eyes watched it and turned with the swing, but he would not charge. He was waiting for Manuel.

Manuel was worried. There was nothing to do but go in. Corto y derecho. He profiled close to the bull, crossed the muleta in front of his body and charged. As he pushed in the sword, he jerked his body to the left to clear the horn. The bull passed him and the sword shot up in the air, twinkling under the arc lights, to fall red-hilted on the sand.

Manuel ran over and picked it up. It was bent and he straightened it over his knee.

As he came running toward the bull, fixed again now, he passed Hernandez standing with his cape.

"He's all bone," the boy said encouragingly.

Manuel nodded, wiping his face. He put the bloody handkerchief in his pocket.

There was the bull. He was close to the barrera now. Damn him. Maybe he was all bone. Maybe there was not any place for the sword to go in. The hell there wasn't! He'd show them.

He tried a pass with the muleta and the bull did not move. Manuel chopped the muleta back and forth in front of the bull. Nothing doing.

He furled the muleta, drew the sword out, profiled, and drove in on the bull. He felt the sword buckle as he shoved it in, leaning his weight on it, and then it shot high in the air, end-over-ending into the crowd. Manuel had jerked clear as the sword jumped.

The first cushions thrown down out of the dark missed him. Then one hit him in the face, his bloody face looking toward the crowd. They were coming down fast. Spotting the sand. Somebody threw an empty champagne bottle from close range. It hit Manuel on the foot. He stood there watching the dark, where the things were coming from. Then something whished through the air and struck by him. Manuel leaned over and picked it up. It was his sword. He straightened it over his knee and gestured with it to the crowd.

"Thank you," he said. "Thank you."

Oh, the dirty bastards! Dirty bastards! Oh, the lousy, dirty bastards! He kicked into a cushion as he ran.

There was the bull. The same as ever. All right, you dirty, lousy bastard!

Manuel passed the muleta in front of the bull's black muzzle.

Nothing doing.

You won't! All right. He stepped close and jammed the sharp peak of the muleta into the bull's damp muzzle.

The bull was on him as he jumped back, and as he tripped on a cushion he felt the horn go into him, into his side. He grabbed the horn with his two hands and rode backward, holding tight onto the place. The bull tossed him and he was clear. He lay still. It was all right. The bull was gone.

He got up coughing and feeling broken and gone. The dirty bastards!

"Give me the sword," he shouted. "Give me the stuff."

Fuentes came up with the muleta and the sword.

Hernandez put his arm around him.

"Go on to the infirmary, man," he said. "Don't be a damn fool."

"Get away from me," Manuel said. "Get to hell away from me."

He twisted free. Hernandez shrugged his shoulders. Manuel ran toward the bull.

There was the bull standing, heavy, firmly planted.

All right, you bastard! Manuel drew the sword out of the muleta, sighted with the same movement, and flung himself onto the bull. He felt the sword go in all the way. Right up to the guard. Four fingers and his thumb into the bull. The blood was hot on his knuckles, and he was on top of the bull.

The bull lurched with him as he lay on, and seemed to sink; then he was standing clear. He looked at the bull going down slowly over on his side, then suddenly four feet in the air.

Then he gestured at the crowd, his hand warm from the bull blood.

All right, you bastards! He wanted to say something, but he started to cough. It was hot and choking. He looked down for the muleta. He must go over and salute the president. President hell! He was sitting down looking at something. It was the bull. His four feet up. Thick tongue out. Things crawling around on his belly and under his legs. Crawling where the hair was thin. Dead bull. To hell with the bull! To hell with them all! He started to get to his feet and commenced to cough. He sat down again, coughing. Somebody came and pushed him up.

They carried him across the ring to the infirmary, running with him across the sand, standing blocked at the gate as the mules came in, then around under the dark passageway, men grunting as they took him up the stairway, and then laid him down.

The doctor and two men in white were waiting for him. They laid him out on the table. They were cutting away his shirt. Manuel felt tired. His whole chest felt scalding inside. He started to cough and they held something to his mouth. Everybody was very busy.

There was an electric light in his eyes. He shut his eyes.

He heard someone coming very heavily up the stairs. Then he did not hear it. Then he heard a noise far off. That was the crowd. Well, somebody would have to kill his other bull. They had cut away all his shirt. The doctor smiled at him. There was Retana.

"Hello, Retana!" Manuel said. He could not hear his voice.

Retana smiled at him and said something. Manuel could not hear it.

Zurito stood beside the table, bending over where the doctor was working. He was in his picador clothes, without his hat.

Zurito said something to him. Manuel could not hear it.

Zurito was speaking to Retana. One of the men in white smiled and handed Retana a pair of scissors. Retana gave them to Zurito. Zurito said something to Manuel. He could not hear it.

To hell with this operating table. He'd been on plenty of operating tables before. He was not going to die. There would be a priest if he was going to die.

Zurito was saying something to him. Holding up the scissors.

That was it. They were going to cut off his coleta. They were going to cut off his pigtail.

Manuel sat up on the operating table. The doctor stepped back, angry. Some one grabbed him and held him.

"You couldn't do a thing like that, Manos," he said.

He heard suddenly, clearly, Zurito's voice.

"That's all right," Zurito said. "I won't do it. I was joking."

"I was going good," Manuel said. "I didn't have any luck. That was all."

Manuel lay back. They had put something over his face. It was all familiar. He inhaled deeply. He felt very tired. He was very, very tired. They took the thing away from his face.

"I was going good," Manuel said weakly. "I was going great."

Retana looked at Zurito and started for the door.

"I'll stay here with him," Zurito said.

Retana shrugged his shoulders.

Manuel opened his eyes and looked at Zurito.

"Wasn't it going good, Manos?" he asked, for confirmation.

"Sure," said Zurito. "You were going great."

The doctor's assistant put the cone over Manuel's face and he inhaled deeply. Zurito stood awkwardly, watching.

Donald Barthelme

AT THE END OF THE MECHANICAL AGE

I went to the grocery store to buy some soap. I stood for a long time before the soaps in their attractive boxes, RUB and FAB and TUB and suchlike, I couldn't decide so I closed my eyes and reached out blindly and when I opened my eyes I found her hand in mine.

Her name was Mrs. Davis, she said, and TUB was best for important cleaning experiences, in her opinion. So we went to lunch at a Mexican restaurant which as it happened she owned, she took me into the kitchen and showed me her stacks of handsome beige tortillas and the steam tables which were shiny-brite. I told her I wasn't very good with women and she said it didn't matter, few men were, and that nothing mattered, now that Jake was gone, but I would do as an interim project and sit down and have a Carta Blanca. So I sat down and had a cool Carta Blanca, God was standing in the basement reading the meters to see how much grace had been used up in the month of June. Grace is electricity science

has found, it is not *like* electricity, it *is* electricity and God was down in the basement reading the meters in His blue jump suit with the flashlight stuck in the back pocket.

"The mechanical age is drawing to a close," I said to her.

"Or has already done so," she replied.

"It was a good age," I said. "I was comfortable in it, relatively. Probably I will not enjoy the age to come quite so much. I don't like its look."

"One must be fair. We don't know yet what kind of an age the next one will be. Although I feel in my bones that it will be an age inimical to personal well-being and comfort, and that is what I like, personal well-being and comfort."

"Do you suppose there is something to be done?" I asked her.

"Huddle and cling," said Mrs. Davis. "We can huddle and cling. It will pall, of course, everything palls, in time . . ."

Then we went back to my house to huddle and cling, most women are two different colors when they remove their clothes especially in summer but Mrs. Davis was all one color, an ocher. She seemed to like huddling and clinging, she stayed for many days. From time to time she checked the restaurant keeping everything shiny-brite and distributing sums of money to the staff, returning with tortillas in sacks, cases of Carta Blanca, buckets of guacamole, but I paid her for it because I didn't want to feel obligated.

There was a song I sang her, a song of great expectations.

"Ralph is coming," I sang, *"Ralph is striding in his suit of lights over moons and mountains, over parking lots and fountains, toward your silky side. Ralph is coming, he has a coat of many colors and all major credit cards and he is striding to meet you and culminate your foggy dreams in an explosion of blood and soil, at the end of the mechanical age. Ralph is coming preceded*

by fifty running men with spears and fifty dancing ladies who are throwing leaf spinach out of little baskets, in his path. Ralph is perfect," I sang, *"but he is also full of interesting tragic flaws, and he can drink fifty running men under the table without breaking his stride and he can have congress with fifty dancing ladies without breaking his stride, even his socks are ironed, so natty is Ralph, but he is also right down in the mud with the rest of us, he markets the mud at high prices for specialized industrial uses and he is striding, striding, striding, toward your waiting heart. Of course you may not like him, some people are awfully picky . . . Ralph is coming,"* I sang to her, *"he is striding over dappled plains and run-mad rivers and he will change your life for the better, probably, you will be fainting with glee at the simple touch of his grave gentle immense hand although I am aware that some people can't stand prosperity, Ralph is coming, I hear his hoofsteps on the drumhead of history, he is striding as he has been all his life toward you, you, you."*

"Yes," Mrs. Davis said, when I had finished singing, "that is what I deserve, all right. But probably I will not get it. And in the meantime, there is you."

* * *

God then rained for forty days and forty nights, when the water tore away the front of the house we got into the boat, Mrs. Davis liked the way I maneuvered the boat off the trailer and out of the garage, she was provoked into a memoir of Jake.

"Jake was a straight-ahead kind of man," she said, "he was simpleminded and that helped him to be the kind of man that he was." She was staring into her Scotch-and-floodwater rather moodily I thought, debris bouncing on the waves all around us but she paid no attention. "That is the type of man I like," she said, "a strong and simpleminded man. The case-study method was not Jake's method, he went right

through the middle of the line and never failed to gain yardage, no matter what the game was. He had a lust for life, and life had a lust for him, I was inconsolable when Jake passed away." Mrs. Davis was drinking the Scotch for her nerves, she had no nerves of course, she was nerveless and possibly heartless also but that is another question, gutless she was not, she had a gut and a very pretty one ocher in color but that was another matter. God was standing up to His neck in the raging waters with a smile of incredible beauty on His visage, He seemed to be enjoying His creation, the disaster, the waters all around us were raging louder now, raging like a mighty tractor-trailer tailgating you on the highway.

Then Mrs. Davis sang to me, a song of great expectations.

"Maude is waiting for you," Mrs. Davis sand to me, *"Maude is waiting for you in all her seriousness and splendor, under her gilded onion dome, in that city which I cannot name at this time, Maude waits. Maude is what you lack, the profoundest of your lacks. Your every yearn since the first yearn has been a yearn for Maude, only you did not know it until I, your dear friend, pointed it out. She is going to heal your scrappy and generally unsatisfactory life with the balm of her Maudeness, luckiest of dogs, she waits only for you. Let me give you just one instance of Maude's inhuman sagacity. Maude named the tools. It was Maude who thought of calling the rattail file a rattail file. It was Maude who christened the needle-nose pliers. Maude named the rasp. Think of it. What else could a rasp be but a rasp? Maude in her wisdom went right to the point, and called it* rasp. *It was Maude who named the maul. Similarly the sledge, the wedge, the ball-peen hammer, the adz, the shim, the hone, the strop. The handsaw, the hacksaw, the bucksaw, and the fretsaw were named by Maude, peering into each saw and in-*

tuiting at once its specialness. The scratch awl, the scuffle hoe, the prick punch and the countersink—I could go on and on. The tools came to Maude, tool by tool in a long respectful line, she gave them their names. The vise. The gimlet. The cold chisel. The reamer, the router, the gouge. The plumb bob. How could she have thought up the rough justice of these wonderful cognomens? Looking languidly at a pair of tin snips, and then deciding to call them tin snips—*what a burst of glory! And I haven't even cited the bush hook, the grass snath, or the plumber's snake, or the C-clamp, or the nippers, or the scythe. What a tall achievement, naming the tools! And this is just one of Maude's contributions to our worldly estate, there are others. What delights will come crowding,"* Mrs. Davis sang to me, *"delight upon delight, when the epithalamium is ground out by the hundred organ grinders who are Maude's constant attendants, on that good-quality day of her own choosing, which you have desperately desired all your lean life, only you weren't aware of it until I, your dear friend, pointed it out. And Maude is young but not too young,"* Mrs. Davis sang to me, *"she is not too old either, she is* just right *and she is waiting for you with her tawny limbs and horse sense, when you receive Maude's nod your future and your past will begin."*

There was a pause, or pall.

"Is that true," I asked, "that song?"

"It is a metaphor," said Mrs. Davis, "it has metaphorical truth."

"And the end of the mechanical age," I said, "is that a metaphor?"

"The end of the mechanical age," said Mrs. Davis, "is in my judgment an actuality straining to become a metaphor. One must wish it luck, I suppose. One must cheer it on. Intellectual rigor demands that we give these damned metaphors every chance, even if they are inimical to personal well-being and comfort. We have a duty to under-

stand everything, whether we like it or not —a duty I would scant if I could." At that moment the water jumped into the boat and sank us.

* * *

At the wedding Mrs. Davis spoke to me kindly.

"Tom," she said, "you are not Ralph, but you are all that is around at the moment. I have taken in the whole horizon with a single sweep of my practiced eye, no giant figure looms there and that is why I have decided to marry you, temporarily, with Jake gone and an age ending. It will be a marriage of convenience all right, and when Ralph comes, or Maude nods, then our arrangement will automatically self-destruct, like the tinted bubble that it is. You were very kind and considerate, when we were drying out, in the tree, and I appreciated that. That counted for something. Of course kindness and consideration are not what the great songs, the Ralph-song and the Maude-song, promise. They are merely flaky substitutes for the terminal experience. I realize that and want you to realize it. I want to be straight with you. That is one of the most admirable things about me, that I am always straight with people, from the sweet beginning to the bitter end. Now I will return to the big house where my handmaidens will proceed with the robing of the bride."

It was cool in the meadow by the river, the meadow Mrs. Davis had selected for the travesty, I walked over to the tree under which my friend Blackie was standing, he was the best man in a sense.

"This disgusts me," Blackie said, "this hollow pretense and empty sham and I had to come all the way from Chicago."

God came to the wedding and stood behind a tree with just part of His effulgence showing, I wondered whether He was planning to bless this makeshift construct with His grace, or not. It's hard to imagine what He was thinking of in the beginning when He planned everything that was ever going to happen, planned everything exquisitely right down to the tiniest detail such as what I was thinking at this very moment, my thought about His thought, planned the end of the mechanical age and detailed the new age to follow, and then the bride emerged from the house with her train, all ocher in color and very lovely.

"And do you, Anne," the minister said, "promise to make whatever mutually satisfactory accommodations necessary to reduce tensions and arrive at whatever previously agreed-upon goals both parties have harmoniously set in the appropriate planning sessions?"

"I do," said Mrs. Davis.

"And do you, Thomas, promise to explore all differences thoroughly with patience and inner honesty ignoring no fruitful avenues of discussion and seeking at all times to achieve rapprochement while eschewing advantage in conflict situations?"

"Yes," I said.

"Well, now we are married," said Mrs. Davis, "I think I will retain my present name if you don't mind, I have always been Mrs. Davis and your name is a shade graceless, no offense, dear."

"OK," I said.

Then we received the congratulations and good wishes of the guests, who were mostly employees of the Mexican restaurant, Raul was there and Consuelo, Pedro, and Pepe came crowding around with outstretched hands and Blackie came crowding around with outstretched hands, God was standing behind the caterer's tables looking at the enchiladas and chalupas and chile con queso and chicken mole as if He had never seen such things before but that was hard to believe.

I started to speak to Him as all of the world's great religions with a few exceptions urge, from the heart, I started to say, "Lord, Little Father of the Poor and all that, I was just wondering now that an age, the mechanical age, is ending and a new age beginning or so they say, I was just wondering if You could give me a hint, sort of, not a Sign, I'm not asking for a Sign, but just the barest hint as to whether what we have been told about Your nature and our nature is, forgive me and I know how You feel about doubt or rather what we have been told You feel about it, but if You could just let drop the slightest indication as to whether what we have been told is authentic or just a bunch of apocryphal heterodoxy—"

But He had gone away with an insanely beautiful smile on His lighted countenance, gone away to read the meters and get a line on the efficacy of grace in that area, I surmised, I couldn't blame Him, my question had not been so very elegantly put, had I been able to express it mathematically He would have been more interested, maybe, but I have never been able to express anything mathematically.

* * *

After the marriage Mrs. Davis explained marriage to me.

Marraige, she said, an institution deeply enmeshed with the mechanical age.

Pairings smiled upon by law were but reifications of the laws of mechanics, inspired by unions of a technical nature, such as nut with bolt, wood with woodscrew, aircraft with Plane-Mate.

Permanence or impermanence of the bond a function of (1) materials and (2) technique.

Growth of literacy a factor, she said.

Growth of illiteracy also.

The center will not hold if it has been spotwelded by an operator whose deepest concern is not with the weld but with his lottery ticket.

God interested only in grace—keeping things humming.

Blackouts, brownouts, temporary dimmings of household illumination all portents not of Divine displeasure but of Divine indifference to executive development programs at middle-management levels.

He likes to get out into the field Himself, she said. With his flashlight. He is doing the best He can.

We two, she and I, no exception to general ebb/flow of world juice and its concomitant psychological effects, she said.

Bitter with the sweet, she said.

* * *

After the explanation came the divorce.

"Will you be wanting to contest the divorce?" I asked Mrs. Davis.

"I think not," she said calmly, "although I suppose one of us should, for the fun of the thing. An uncontested divorce always seems to me contrary to the spirit of divorce."

"That is true," I said, "I have had the same feeling myself, not infrequently."

After the divorce the child was born. We named him A. F. of L. Davis and sent him to that part of Russia where people live to be one hundred and ten years old. He is living there still, probably, growing in wisdom and beauty. Then we shook hands, Mrs. Davis and I, and she set out Ralphward, and I, Maudeward, the glow of hope not yet extinguished, the fear of pall not yet triumphant, standby generators ensuring the flow of grace to all of God's creatures at the end of the mechanical age.

Author Unknown

SIR PATRICK SPENS

The king sits in Dumferling toune,
   Drinking the blude-reid wine:
"O whar will I get guid sailor,
   To sail this schip of mine?"

Up and spak an eldern knicht,
   Sat at the kings richt kne:
"Sir Patrick Spens is the best sailor,
   That sails upon the se."

The king has written a braid letter,
   And signed it wi his hand,   10
And sent it to Sir Patrick Spens
   Was walking on the sand.

The first line that Sir Patrick red,
   A loud lauch lauchèd he;
The next line that Sir Patrick red,
   The teir blinded his ee.

"O wha is this has don this deid,
   This ill deid don to me,
To send me out this time o' the yeir,
   To sail upon the se!   20

"Mak haste, mak haste, my mirry men all,
   Our guid schip sails the morne."
"O say no sae, my master deir,
   For I feir a deadlie storme.

"Late, late yestreen I saw the new moone,
   Wi the auld moone in hir arme,
And I feir, I feir, my deir master,
   That we will cum to harme."

O our Scots nobles were richt laith
   To weet their cork-heild schoone;   30
Bot lang owre a' the play wer playd,
   Thair hats they swam aboone.

O lang, lang may their ladies sit,
   Wi thar fans into their hand,
Or eir they se Sir Patrick Spens
   Cum sailing to the land.

O lang, lang may the ladies stand
   Wi thar gold kems in their hair,
Waiting for thair ain deir lords,
   For they'll se thame na mair.   40

1 *Dumferling:* Dunfermline, in southeast Scotland. 3 *guid:* good.

5 *eldern knicht:* elderly knight. 6 *richt:* right. 9 *braid:* broad, on large paper. 14 *lauch:* laugh.

Haf owre, haf owre to Aberdour,
  It's fiftie fadom deip,
And thair lies guid Sir Patrick Spens,
  Wi the Scots lords at his feit.

John Milton

ON HIS BLINDNESS

When I consider how my light is spent
Ere half my days in this dark world and wide,
And that one talent which is death to hide
Lodged with me useless, though my soul more
    bent
To serve therewith my Maker and present
My true account, lest He returning chide,

"Doth God exact day-labor, light denied?"
I fondly ask. But Patience, to prevent
That murmur, soon replies, "God doth not need
Either man's work or his own gifts. Who best   10
Bear his mild yoke, they serve him best. His state
Is kingly: thousands at his bidding speed
And post o'er land and ocean without rest;
They also serve who only stand and wait."

  1 *spent:* Milton's sight began to fail when he
was in his thirties. 3 *hide:* as in the parable, *Gospel of St. Matthew* xxv, 14–29. 8 *fondly:* foolishly.
11 *yoke:* "My yoke is easy": ibid., xi, 30. 12 *thousands:* i.e., of angels.

Andrew Marvell

AN HORATIAN ODE UPON CROMWELL'S RETURN FROM IRELAND

The forward youth that would appear
Must now forsake his muses dear,
  Nor in the shadows sing
  His numbers languishing:

RETURN: In 1650, after subduing the Irish rebels.
  1 *forward:* ambitious; *appear:* become known.

'Tis time to leave the books in dust
And oil the unused armor's rust,
  Removing from the wall
  The corselet of the hall.

So restless Cromwell would not cease
In the inglorious arts of peace,   10
  But through adventurous war
  Urgèd his active star,

And, like the three-forked lightning, first
Breaking the clouds where it was nursed,
  Did thorough his own side
  His fiery way divide;

For 'tis all one to courage high,
The emulous or enemy,
  And with such to enclose,
  Is more than to oppose.   20

Then burning through the air he went,
And palaces and temples rent;
  And Caesar's head at last
  Did through his laurels blast.

'Tis madness to resist or blame
The force of angry heaven's flame;
  And, if we would speak true,
  Much to the man is due

Who from his private gardens, where
He lived reservèd and austere,   30
  As if his highest plot
  To plant the bergamot,

Could by industrious valor climb
To ruin the great work of time
  And cast the kingdoms old
  Into another mold,

Though Justice against Fate complain,
And plead the ancient rights in vain;
  But those do hold or break
  As men are strong or weak.   40

  9 *cease:* rest. 16 *divide:* i.e., forced military re-
forms on his own party. 18 *emulous:* rival on
one's own side. 20 *more:* more dangerous. 23
head: that of Charles I, who lost it in 1649.

Nature, that hateth emptiness,
Allows of penetration less,
   And therefore must make room
   Where greater spirits come.

What field of all the civil war
Where his were not the deepest scar?
   And Hampton shows what part
   He had of wiser art,

Where, twining subtle fears with hope,
He wove a net of such a scope   50
   That Charles himself might chase
   To Carisbrooke's narrow case,

That thence the royal actor borne
The tragic scaffold might adorn,
   While round the armèd bands
   Did clap their bloody hands.

He nothing common did, or mean,
Upon that memorable scene,
   But with his keener eye
   The ax's edge did try;   60

Nor called the gods with vulgar spite
To vindicate his helpless right,
   But bowed his comely head
   Down, as upon a bed.

This was that memorable hour
Which first assured the forcèd power;
   So, when they did design
   The Capitol's first line,

A bleeding head, where they begun,
Did fright the architects to run;   70
   And yet in that the state
   Foresaw its happy fate.

And now the Irish are ashamed
To see themselves in one year tamed;

So much one man can do,
   That does both act and know.

They can affirm his praises best,
And have, though overcome, confessed
   How good he is, how just,
   And fit for highest trust;   80

Nor yet grown stiffer with command,
But still in the republic's hand,
   How fit he is to sway
   That can so well obey!

He to the Commons' feet presents
A kingdom for his first year's rents;
   And, what he may, forbears
   His fame, to make it theirs;

And has his sword and spoils ungirt,
To lay them at the public's skirt: 90
   So when the falcon high
   Falls heavy from the sky,

She, having killed, no more doth search
But on the next green bough to perch;
   Where, when he first does lure,
   The falconer has her sure.

What may not then our isle presume
While victory his crest does plume?
   What may not others fear
   If thus he crowns each year?   100

A Caesar he, ere long, to Gaul,
To Italy a Hannibal,
   And to all states not free
   Shall climacteric be.

The Pict no shelter now shall find
Within his parti-colored mind,
   But from this valor sad
   Shrink underneath the plaid,

42 *penetration:* presence of two things in one place.
47 *Hampton:* Marvell thought Cromwell influenced
the King's disastrous decision to flee from his palace
of Hampton Court to Carisbrooke Castle in the
Isle of Wight. 54 *scaffold:* a pun on the meanings
"stage" and "execution platform." 66 *power:* the
Commonwealth, established by war. 67 *they:* the
Romans; "Capitol" comes from Latin *caput,* "head."

86 *kingdom:* Ireland. 87 *what:* as much as; *forbears:* belittles. 92 *heavy:* because carrying her
prey. 104 *climacteric:* decisive. 105 *Pict:* Scot; in
1650 Cromwell was preparing for war in the north.
106 *parti-colored:* i.e., like his plaid; hence, change-
able. 107 *sad:* firm.

Happy if in the tufted brake
The English hunter him mistake   110
  Nor lay his hounds in near
  The Caledonian deer.

But thou, the war's and Fortune's son,
March undefatigably on
  And for the least effect
  Still keep the sword erect;

Besides the force it has to fright
The spirits of the shady night,
  The same arts that did gain
  A power must it maintain.   120

110 *mistake:* overlook.   111 *lay:* send.

John Keats

ODE ON A GRECIAN URN

Thou still unravished bride of quietness,
  Thou foster-child of silence and slow time,
Sylvan historian, who canst thus express
  A flowery tale more sweetly than our rhyme:

What leaf-fringed legend haunts about thy shape
  Of deities or mortals, or of both,
    In Tempe or the dales of Arcady?
  What men or gods are these? What maidens
      loth?
What mad pursuit? What struggle to escape?
  What pipes and timbrels? What wild
      ecstasy?   10

Heard melodies are sweet, but those unheard
  Are sweeter; therefore, ye soft pipes, play on;
Not to the sensual ear, but, more endeared,
  Pipe to the spirit ditties of no tone:
Fair youth, beneath the trees, thou canst not
    leave

13 *sensual:* sensory, physical.

Thy song, nor ever can those trees be bare;
  Bold lover, never, never canst thou kiss,
Though winning near the goal—yet do not
    grieve;
  She cannot fade, though thou hast not thy
    bliss;
  Forever wilt thou love, and she be fair!   20

Ah, happy, happy boughs! that cannot shed
  Your leaves, nor ever bid the spring adieu;
And, happy melodist, unwearièd,
  Forever piping songs forever new;
More happy love! more happy, happy love!
  Forever warm and still to be enjoyed,
    Forever panting, and forever young;
All breathing human passion far above,
  That leaves a heart high-sorrowful and cloyed,
    A burning forehead and a parching tongue.

Who are these coming to the sacrifice?
  To what green altar, O mysterious priest,
Lead'st thou that heifer lowing at the skies,
  And all her silken flanks with garlands
      dressed?
What little town by river or seashore,
  Or mountain-built with peaceful citadel,
    Is emptied of this folk, this pious morn?
And, little town, thy streets forevermore
  Will silent be; and not a soul to tell
    Why thou art desolate can e'er return.   40

O Attic shape! Fair attitude! with brede
  Of marble men and maidens overwrought,
With forest branches and the trodden weed;
  Thou, silent form, dost tease us out of thought
As doth eternity: Cold Pastoral!
  When old age shall this generation waste,
    Thou shalt remain, in midst of other woe
  Than ours, a friend to man, to whom thou
      say'st,
Beauty is truth, truth beauty—that is all
  Ye know on earth, and all ye need to know.

41 *brede:* braid, embroidery.

John Keats

WHEN I HAVE FEARS

When I have fears that I may cease to be
Before my pen has gleaned my teeming brain,
Before high-pilèd books, in charactery,
Hold like rich garners the full-ripened grain;
When I behold, upon the night's starred face
Huge cloudy symbols of a high romance,
And think that I may never live to trace
Their shadows, with the magic hand of chance;
And when I feel, fair creature of an hour,
That I shall never look upon thee more,   10
Never have relish in the faery power
Of unreflecting love;—then on the shore
Of the wide world I stand alone, and think
Till love and fame to nothingness do sink.

Alfred, Lord Tennyson

ULYSSES

It little profits that an idle king,
By this still hearth, among these barren crags,
Matched with an agèd wife, I mete and dole
Unequal laws unto a savage race
That hoard, and sleep, and feed, and know not
    me.
I cannot rest from travel: I will drink
Life to the lees: all times I have enjoyed
Greatly, have suffered greatly, both with those
That loved me, and alone; on shore, and when
Through scudding drifts the rainy Hyades   10
Vexed the dim sea: I am become a name;
For always roaming with a hungry heart
Much have I seen and known; cities of men
And manners, climates, councils, governments,
Myself not least, but honored of them all;
And drunk delight of battle with my peers,

2 *crags:* those of Ithaca, an island off the western
coast of Greece.

Far on the ringing plains of windy Troy.
I am a part of all that I have met;
Yet all experience is an arch wherethrough
Gleams that untraveled world, whose margin
    fades   20
Forever and forever when I move.
How dull it is to pause, to make an end,
To rust unburnished, not to shine in use!
As though to breathe were life. Life piled on life
Were all too little, and of one to me
Little remains: but every hour is saved
From that eternal silence, something more,
A bringer of new things; and vile it were
For some three suns to store and hoard myself,
And this gray spirit yearning in desire   30
To follow knowledge like a sinking star,
Beyond the utmost bound of human thought.

    This is my son, mine own Telemachus,
To whom I leave the scepter and the isle—
Well-loved of me, discerning to fulfil
This labor, by slow prudence to make mild
A rugged people, and through soft degrees
Subdue them to the useful and the good.
Most blameless is he, centered in the sphere
Of common duties, decent not to fail   40
In offices of tenderness, and pay
Meet adoration to my household gods
When I am gone. He works his work, I mine.

    There lies the port; the vessel puffs her sail;
There gloom the dark broad seas. My mariners,
Souls that have toiled, and wrought, and thought
    with me—
That ever with a frolic welcome took
The thunder and the sunshine, and opposed
Free hearts, free foreheads—you and I are old;
Old age hath yet his honor and his toil;   50
Death closes all: but something ere the end,
Some work of noble note, may yet be done,
Not unbecoming men that strove with gods.
The lights begin to twinkle from the rocks:
The long day wanes: the slow moon climbs: the
    deep
Moans round with many voices. Come, my
    friends,

19 *arch:* rainbow.

'Tis not too late to seek a newer world.
Push off, and sitting well in order smite
The sounding furrows; for my purpose holds
To sail beyond the sunset and the baths   60
Of all the western stars, until I die.
It may be that the gulfs will wash us down:
It may be we shall touch the Happy Isles
And see the great Achilles, whom we knew.
Though much is taken, much abides; and
     though
We are not now that strength which in old days
Moved earth and heaven, that which we are, we
     are;
One equal temper of heroic hearts,
Made weak by time and fate, but strong in will
To strive, to seek, to find, and not to yield.   70

63 *Happy Isles:* one of the Greek ideas of
Paradise.

Guy Wetmore Carryl

THE SYCOPHANTIC FOX AND THE GULLIBLE RAVEN

A raven sat upon a tree,
     And not a word he spoke, for
His beak contained a piece of Brie,
     Or maybe it was Roquefort.
          We'll make it any kind you please—
          At all events, it was a cheese.

Beneath the tree's umbrageous limb
     A hungry fox sat smiling;
He saw the raven watching him,
     And spoke in words beguiling: 10
          "*J'admire,*" said he, "*ton beau plumage*"
          (The which was simply persiflage).

Two things there are, no doubt you know,
     To which a fox is used:

11 *J'admire, etc.:* Your fine feathers fill me with
admiration.

A rooster that is bound to crow,
     A crow that's bound to roost;
          And whichsoever he espies
          He tells the most unblushing lies.

"Sweet fowl," he said, "I understand
     You're more than merely natty,   20
I hear you sing to beat the band
     And Adelina Patti.
          Pray render with your liquid tongue
          A bit from *Götterdämmerung.*"

This subtle speech was aimed to please
     The crow, and it succeeded;
He thought no bird in all the trees
     Could sing as well as he did.
          In flattery completely doused,
          He gave the "Jewel Song" from *Faust.*   30

But gravitation's law, of course,
     As Isaac Newton showed it,
Exerted on the cheese its force
     And elsewhere soon bestowed it.
          In fact, there is no need to tell
          What happened when to earth it fell.

I blush to add that when the bird
     Took in the situation
He said one brief, emphatic word
     Unfit for publication.   40
          The fox was greatly startled, but
          He only sighed and answered "Tut."

THE MORAL is: A fox is bound
     To be a shameless sinner.
And also: When the cheese comes round
     You know it's after dinner.
          But (what is only known to few)
          The fox is after dinner, too.

15 *rooster:* in another version of the fable, a fox
flatters a rooster into crowing; see "The Nun's
Priest's Tale," by Geoffrey Chaucer. 22 *Adelina
Patti:* Italian coloratura soprano, 1843–1919.

A. E. Housman

TO AN ATHLETE DYING YOUNG

The time you won your town the race
We chaired you through the market place;
Man and boy stood cheering by,
And home we brought you shoulder-high.

Today, the road all runners come,
Shoulder-high we bring you home
And set you at your threshold down,
Townsman of a stiller town.

Smart lad, to slip betimes away
From fields where glory does not stay,   10
And early though the laurel grows
It withers quicker than the rose.

Eyes the shady night has shut
Cannot see the record cut,
And silence sounds no worse than cheers
After earth has stopped the ears.

Now you will not swell the rout
Of lads that wore their honors out,
Runners whom renown outran,
And the name died before the man.   20

So set, before its echoes fade,
The fleet foot on the sill of shade,
And hold to the low lintel up
The still-defended challenge-cup.

And round that early-laureled head
Will flock to gaze the strengthless dead,
And find unwithered on its curls
The garland briefer than a girl's.

William Butler Yeats

THE SECOND COMING

Turning and turning in the widening gyre
The falcon cannot hear the falconer;
Things fall apart; the centre cannot hold;
Mere anarchy is loosed upon the world,
The blood-dimmed tide is loosed, and every-
    where
The ceremony of innocence is drowned;
The best lack all conviction, while the worst
Are full of passionate intensity.

Surely some revelation is at hand;
Surely the Second Coming is at hand.   10
The Second Coming! Hardly are those words out
When a vast image out of *Spiritus Mundi*
Troubles my sight: somewhere in sands of the
    desert
A shape with lion body and the head of a man,
A gaze blank and pitiless as the sun,
Is moving its slow thighs, while all about it
Reel shadows of the indignant desert birds.
The darkness drops again; but now I know
That twenty centuries of stony sleep
Were vexed to nightmare by a rocking cradle,
And what rough beast, its hour come round at
    last,
Slouches toward Bethlehem to be born?

    12 *Spiritus Mundi:* World's Spirit, the race's
memory.

Sophocles

OEDIPUS THE KING

THE LEGEND

The dialogue of Oedipus the King *abounds in ironies arising from* OEDIPUS' *ignorance of his identity. According to a legend well known to the ancient Greek audience, he is the son of Laïos, King of Thebes, and Laïos' queen,* IOCASTÊ, *who have been warned that if ever they have a son, that son will one day kill his father and marry his mother. Therefore when* IOCASTÊ *bears a son, Laïos has his ankles pierced and orders a shepherd to leave him to die on Mount Kithairon, south of Thebes. But a Corinthian shepherd takes him to Corinth, beyond the mountain, where he is named Oedipus ("swollen foot") and reared as the son of King Polybos and Queen Meropê.*

One day, after OEDIPUS *reaches manhood, a drunken reveler taunts him with being a foundling, and this drives him to consult the oracle at Delphi, west of Thebes, as to his real identity. Instead of answering directly, the oracle tells him that he is to be his father's murderer and his mother's husband.* OEDIPUS *then determines never to return to Corinth, but, when he comes to the place where the highway forks, to take the road to Thebes. At this crossroads he quarrels with another traveler and deals him a fatal blow. The other traveler is King Laïos.*

In order to reach Thebes, OEDIPUS *has to encounter the Sphinx, a she-monster who is harassing the city by killing all passers-by unable to answer her riddle: "What goes on four legs, then on two, and then on three?"* OEDIPUS *answers correctly, "Man" (man crawls, then walks, then in old age walks with a cane), and the Sphinx kills herself. The grateful Thebans marry him to the widowed* IOCASTÊ *and make him their* tyrannos, *a ruler who has not acquired the throne by royal descent.* OEDIPUS *and* IOCASTÊ *have two sons, Eteocles and Polyneices, and later two daughters,* ANTIGONE *and* ISMENE.

In Scene I of the play, OEDIPUS *betrays some uneasiness at not being (he thinks) of the line of Kadmos, Polydoros, Labdakos, and Laïos. Kadmos, son of Agenor, King of Tyre, founded Thebes; hence Thebes is referred to as "the house of Kadmos."*

CHARACTERS

in the order of their appearance

PRIEST
SUPPLIANTS
OEDIPUS, *King of Thebes*
CHORUS *and* CHORAGOS, *old men of Thebes*
CREON, *brother of* IOCASTÊ
TEIRESIAS, *a seer*
PAGE OF TEIRESIAS
IOCASTÊ, *Queen of Thebes*
MESSENGER, *formerly a Corinthian shepherd*
SHEPHERD *of Laïos*
SECOND MESSENGER
ANTIGONE *and* ISMENE, *daughters of* OEDIPUS *and* IOCASTÊ
ATTENDANTS

SCENE. *Before the palace of* OEDIPUS, *King of Thebes. A central door and two lateral doors open onto a platform which runs the length of the façade. On the platform, right and left, are altars; and three steps lead down into the "orchestra," or chorus-ground. At the beginning of the action these steps are crowded by suppliants who have brought branches and chaplets of olive leaves and who lie in various attitudes of despair.* OEDIPUS *enters.*

PROLOGUE

OEDIPUS.   My children, generations of the living
In the line of Kadmos, nursed at his ancient hearth:
Why have you strewn yourselves before these altars
In supplication, with your boughs and garlands?

The breath of incense rises from the city
With a sound of prayer and lamentation.
                                    Children,
I would not have you speak through messengers,
And therefore I have come myself to hear you—
I, Oedipus, who bear the famous name.
                            [*To a* PRIEST
You, there, since you are eldest in the company,
Speak for them all, tell me what preys upon you,
Whether you come in dread, or crave some
    blessing:
Tell me, and never doubt that I will help you
In every way I can; I should be heartless
Were I not moved to find you suppliant here.

PRIEST.   Great Oedipus, O powerful King of
    Thebes!
You see how all the ages of our people
Cling to your altar steps: here are boys
Who can barely stand alone, and here are priests
By weight of age, as I am a priest of God,   20
And young men chosen from those yet
    unmarried;
As for the others, all that multitude,
They wait with olive chaplets in the squares,
At the two shrines of Pallas, and where Apollo
Speaks in the glowing embers.
                            Your own eyes
Must tell you: Thebes is tossed on a murdering
    sea
And cannot lift her head from the death surge.
A rust consumes the buds and fruits of the earth;
The herds are sick; children die unborn.
And labor is vain. The god of plague and pyre
Raids like detestable lightning through the city,
And all the house of Kadmos is laid waste,
All emptied, and all darkened: Death alone
Battens upon the misery of Thebes.

You are not one of the immortal gods, we know;
Yet we have come to make our prayer
As to the man surest in mortal ways
And wisest in the ways of God. You saved us
From the Sphinx, that flinty singer, and the
    tribute
We paid to her so long; yet you were never   40
Better informed than we, nor could we teach
    you:
It was some god breathed in you to set us free.

Therefore, O mighty King, we turn to you:
Find us our safety, find us a remedy,
Whether by counsel of the gods or men.
A king of wisdom tested in the past
Can act in a time of troubles, and act well.
Noblest of men, restore
Life to your city! Think how all men call you
Liberator for your triumph long ago;   50
Ah, when your years of kingship are remembered,
Let them not say *We rose, but later fell*—
Keep the State from going down in the storm!
Once, years ago, with happy augury,
You brought us fortune; be the same again!
No man questions your power to rule the land:
But rule over men, not over a dead city!
Ships are only hulls, citadels are nothing,
When no life moves in the empty passageways.

OEDIPUS.   Poor children! You may be sure I
    know   60
All that you longed for in your coming here.
I know that you are deathly sick; and yet,
Sick as you are, not one is as sick as I.
Each of you suffers in himself alone
His anguish, not another's; but my spirit
Groans for the city, for myself, for you.

I was not sleeping, you are not waking me.
No, I have been in tears for a long while
And in my restless thought walked many ways.
In all my search, I found one helpful course,   70
And that I have taken: I have sent Creon,
Son of Menoikeus, brother of the Queen,
To Delphi, Apollo's place of revelation,
To learn there, if he can,
What act or pledge of mine may save the city.
I have counted the days, and now, this very day,
I am troubled, for he has overstayed his time.
What is he doing? He has been gone too long.
Yet whenever he comes back, I should do ill
To scant whatever duty God reveals.   80

PRIEST.   It is a timely promise. At this instant
They tell me Creon is here.

OEDIPUS.   O Lord Apollo!
May his news be fair as his face is radiant!

PRIEST.   It could not be otherwise: he is
    crowned with bay;

72 *brother:* i.e., Creon and Iocastê are the children of Menoikeus.

The chaplet is thick with berries.

OEDIPUS.   We shall soon know;
He is near enough to hear us now.

[*Enter* CREON

O Prince:

Brother: son of Menoikeus:
What answer do you bring us from the god?

CREON.   A strong one. I can tell you, great afflictions
Will turn out well, if they are taken well.   90

OEDIPUS.   What was the oracle? These vague words
Leave me still hanging between hope and fear.

CREON.   Is it your pleasure to hear me with all these
Gathered around us? I am prepared to speak,
But should we not go in?

OEDIPUS.   Let them all hear it.
It is for them I suffer, more than for myself.

CREON.   Then I will tell you what I heard at Delphi.

In plain words
The god commands us to expel from the land of Thebes
An old defilement we are sheltering.   100
It is a deathly thing, beyond cure;
We must not let it feed upon us longer.

OEDIPUS.   What defilement? How shall we rid ourselves of it?

CREON.   By exile or death, blood for blood. It was
Murder that brought the plague-wind on the city.

OEDIPUS.   Murder of whom? Surely the god has named him?

CREON.   My lord: long ago Laïos was our king,
Before you came to govern us.

OEDIPUS.   I know;
I learned of him from others; I never saw him.

CREON.   He was murdered; and Apollo commands us now   110
To take revenge upon whoever killed him.

OEDIPUS.   Upon whom? Where are they? Where shall we find a clue
To solve that crime, after so many years?

CREON.   Here in this land, he said.

                                        If we make enquiry,
We may touch things that otherwise escape us.

OEDIPUS.   Tell me: Was Laïos murdered in his house,
Or in the fields, or in some foreign country?

CREON.   He said he planned to make a pilgrimage.
He did not come home again.

OEDIPUS.   And was there no one,
No witness, no companion, to tell what
happened?   120

CREON.   They were all killed but one, and he got away
So frightened that he could remember one thing only.

OEDIPUS.   What was that one thing? One may be the key
To everything, if we resolve to use it.

CREON.   He said that a band of highwaymen attacked them,
Outnumbered them, and overwhelmed the King.

OEDIPUS.   Strange, that a highwayman should be so daring—
Unless some faction here bribed him to do it.

CREON.   We thought of that. But after Laïos' death
New troubles arose and we had no avenger.   130

OEDIPUS.   What troubles could prevent your hunting down the killers?

CREON.   The riddling Sphinx's song
Made us deaf to all mysteries but her own.

OEDIPUS.   Then once more I must bring what is dark to light.
It is most fitting that Apollo shows,
As you do, this compunction for the dead.
You shall see how I stand by you, as I should,
To avenge the city and the city's god,
And not as though it were for some distant friend,
But for my own sake, to be rid of evil.   140
Whoever killed King Laïos might—who knows?—
Decide at any moment to kill me as well.
By avenging the murdered king I protect myself.

Come, then, my children: leave the altar steps,
Lift up your olive boughs!
                          One of you go
And summon the people of Kadmos to gather
  here.
I will do all that I can; you may tell them that.
                          [*Exit a* PAGE
So, with the help of God,
We shall be saved—or else indeed we are lost.

PRIEST.   Let us rise, children. It was for this we
  came,   150
And now the King has promised it himself.
Phoibos has sent us an oracle; may he descend
Himself to save us and drive out the plague.
[*Exeunt* OEDIPUS *and* CREON *into the palace by
the central door. The* PRIEST *and the* SUPPLIANTS
disperse right and left. After a short pause the
                          CHORUS *enters the orchestra.*

152 *Phoibos:* the bright one, an epithet of Apollo,
the sun-god.   *orchestra:* see description of the Scene,
p. 644.

Párodos

                                    [STROPHE 1
CHORUS.   What is God singing in his profound
Delphi of gold and shadow?
What oracle for Thebes, the sunwhipped city?

Fear unjoints me, the roots of my heart tremble.

Now I remember, O Healer, your power, and
  wonder:
Will you send doom like a sudden cloud, or
  weave it
Like nightfall of the past?

Speak, speak to us, issue of holy sound:
Dearest to our expectancy: be tender!

                          [ANTISTROPHE 1
Let me pray to Athenê, the immortal daughter
  of Zeus,   10
And to Artemis her sister

PÁRODOS: entrance-song of the CHORUS. STROPHE,
ANTISTROPHE: formal divisions, sung antiphonally,
of the choric ode.

Who keeps her famous throne in the market
  ring,
And to Apollo, bowman at the far butts of
  heaven—

O gods, descend! Like three streams leap against
The fires of our grief, the fires of darkness;
Be swift to bring us rest!

As in the old time from the brilliant house
Of air you stepped to save us, come again!

                                    [STROPHE 2
Now our afflictions have no end,
Now all our stricken host lies down   20
And no man fights off death with his mind;

The noble plowland bears no grain,
And groaning mothers cannot bear—

See, how our lives like birds take wing,
Like sparks that fly when a fire soars,
To the shore of the god of evening.

                                    [ANTISTROPHE 2
The plague burns on, it is pitiless,
Though pallid children laden with death
Lie unwept in the stony ways,

And old gray women by every path   30
Flock to the strand about the altars

There to strike their breasts and cry
Worship of Phoibos in wailing prayers:
Be kind, God's golden child!

                                    [STROPHE 3
There are no swords in this attack by fire,
No shields, but we are ringed with cries.
Send the besieger plunging from our homes
Into the vast sea-room of the Atlantic
Or into the waves that foam eastward of
  Thrace—

For the day ravages what the night spares—   40

Destroy our enemy, lord of the thunder!
Let him be riven by lightning from heaven!

                                    [ANTISTROPHE 3
Phoibos Apollo, stretch the sun's bowstring,

That golden cord, until it sings for us,
Flashing arrows in heaven!

                       Artemis, huntress,
Race with flaring lights upon our mountains!

O scarlet god, O golden-banded brow,
O Theban Bacchos in a storm of Maenads,
               [*Enter* OEDIPUS, *center*
Whirl upon Death, that all the Undying hate!
Come with blinding torches, come in joy!   50

   49 *Undying:* gods and goddesses.

SCENE I

OEDIPUS. Is this your prayer? It may be an-
    swered. Come,
Listen to me, act as the crisis demands,
And you shall have relief from all these evils.

Until now I was a stranger to this tale,
As I had been a stranger to the crime.
Could I track down the murderer without a
    clue?
But now, friends,
As one who became a citizen after the murder,
I make this proclamation to all Thebans:
If any man knows by whose hand Laïos, son of
    Labdakos,   10
Met his death, I direct that man to tell me
    everything,
No matter what he fears for having so long
    withheld it.
Let it stand as promised that no further trouble
Will come to him, but he may leave the land in
    safety.

Moreover: If anyone knows the murderer to be
    foreign,
Let him not keep silent: he shall have his reward
    from me.
However, if he does conceal it; if any man
Fearing for his friend or for himself disobeys this
    edict,
Hear what I propose to do:

I solemnly forbid the people of this country, 20
Where power and throne are mine, ever to re-
    ceive that man

Or speak to him, no matter who he is, or let him
Join in sacrifice, lustration, or in prayer.
I decree that he be driven from every house,
Being, as he is, corruption itself to us: the
    Delphic
Voice of Zeus has pronounced this revelation.
Thus I associate myself with the oracle
And take the side of the murdered king.

As for the criminal, I pray to God—
Whether it be a lurking thief, or one of a num-
    ber—   30
I pray that that man's life be consumed in evil
    and wretchedness,
And as for me, this curse applies no less
If it should turn out that the culprit is my guest
    here,
Sharing my hearth.

                  You have heard the penalty.
I lay it on you now to attend to this
For my sake, for Apollo's, for the sick
Sterile city that heaven has abandoned.
Suppose the oracle had given you no command:
Should this defilement go uncleansed for ever?
You should have found the murderer: your
    king,   40
A noble king, had been destroyed!

                      Now I,
Having the power that he held before me,
Having his bed, begetting children there
Upon his wife, as he would have, had he lived—
Their son would have been my children's
    brother,
If Laïos had had luck in fatherhood!
(But surely ill luck rushed upon his reign)—
I say I take the son's part, just as though
I were his son, to press the fight for him
And see it won! I'll find the hand that brought
Death to Labdakos' and Polydoros' child,
Heir of Kadmos' and Agenor's line.
And as for those who fail me,
May the gods deny them the fruit of the earth,
Fruit of the womb, and may they rot utterly!
Let them be wretched as we are wretched, and
    worse!
For you, for loyal Thebans, and for all
Who find my actions right, I pray the favor
Of justice, and of all the immortal gods.

CHORAGOS.   Since I am under oath, my lord, I swear   60
I did not do the murder, I cannot name
The murderer. Might not the oracle
That has ordained the search tell where to find him?

OEDIPUS.   An honest question. But no man in the world
Can make the gods do more than the gods will.

CHORAGOS.   There is one last expedient—

OEDIPUS.   Tell me what it is.
Though it seem slight, you must not hold it back.

CHORAGOS.   A lord clairvoyant to the lord Apollo,
As we all know, is the skilled Teiresias.
One might learn much about this from him, Oedipus.   70

OEDIPUS.   I am not wasting time:
Creon spoke of this, and I have sent for him—
Twice, in fact; it is strange that he is not here.

CHORAGOS.   The other matter—that old report
—seems useless.

OEDIPUS.   Tell me. I am interested in all reports.

CHORAGOS.   The King was said to have been killed by highwaymen.

OEDIPUS.   I know. But we have no witnesses to that.

CHORAGOS.   If the killer can feel a particle of dread,
Your curse will bring him out of hiding!

OEDIPUS.   No.
The man who dared that act will fear no curse.
[*Enter the blind seer* TEIRESIAS, *led by a* PAGE

CHORAGOS.   But there is one man who may detect the criminal.
This is Teiresias, this is the holy prophet
In whom, alone of all men, truth was born.

OEDIPUS.   Teiresias: seer: student of mysteries,
Of all that's taught and all that no man tells,
Secrets of heaven and secrets of the earth:

60 CHORAGOS: leader of the CHORUS; he sometimes speaks as an individual.

Blind though you are, you know the city lies
Sick with plague; and from this plague, my lord,
We find that you alone can guard or save us.

Possibly you did not hear the messengers?   90
Apollo, when we sent to him,
Sent us back word that this great pestilence
Would lift, but only if we established clearly
The identity of those who murdered Laïos.
They must be killed or exiled.
                              Can you use
Birdflight or any art of divination
To purify yourself, and Thebes, and me
From this contagion? We are in your hands.
There is no fairer duty
Than that of helping others in distress.   100

TEIRESIAS.   How dreadful knowledge of the truth can be
When there's no help in truth! I knew this well,
But made myself forget. I should not have come.

OEDIPUS.   What is troubling you? Why are your eyes so cold?

TEIRESIAS.   Let me go home. Bear your own fate, and I'll
Bear mine. It is better so: trust what I say.

OEDIPUS.   What you say is ungracious and unhelpful
To your native country. Do not refuse to speak.

TEIRESIAS.   When it comes to speech, your own is neither temperate
Nor opportune. I wish to be more prudent.   110

OEDIPUS.   In God's name, we all beg you—

TEIRESIAS.   You are all ignorant.
No; I will never tell you what I know.
Now it is my misery; then, it would be yours.

OEDIPUS.   What! You do know something, and will not tell us?
You would betray us all and wreck the State?

TEIRESIAS.   I do not intend to torture myself, or you.
Why persist in asking? You will not persuade me.

OEDIPUS.   What a wicked old man you are! You'd try a stone's
Patience! Out with it! Have you no feeling at all?

TEIRESIAS.   You call me unfeeling. If you could
only see   120
The nature of your own feelings . . .

OEDIPUS.   Why,
Who would not feel as I do? Who could endure
Your arrogance toward the city?

TEIRESIAS.   What does it matter!
Whether I speak or not, it is bound to come.

OEDIPUS.   Then, if "it" is bound to come, you
are bound to tell me.

TEIRESIAS.   No, I will not go on. Rage as you
please.

OEDIPUS.   Rage? Why not!
                        And I'll tell you what I think:
You planned it, you had it done, you all but
Killed him with your own hands: if you had
eyes,
I'd say the crime was yours, and yours alone. 130

TEIRESIAS.   So? I charge you, then,
Abide by the proclamation you have made:
From this day forth
Never speak again to these men or to me;
You yourself are the pollution of this country.

OEDIPUS.   You dare say that! Can you possibly
think you have
Some way of going free, after such insolence?

TEIRESIAS.   I have gone free. It is the truth sustains me.

OEDIPUS.   Who taught you shamelessness? It
was not your craft.

TEIRESIAS.   You did. You made me speak. I did
not want to.   140

OEDIPUS.   Speak what? Let me hear it again
more clearly.

TEIRESIAS.   Was it not clear before? Are you
tempting me?

OEDIPUS.   I did not understand it. Say it again.

TEIRESIAS.   I say that you are the murderer
whom you seek.

OEDIPUS.   Now twice you have spat out infamy.
You'll pay for it!

TEIRESIAS.   Would you care for more? Do you
wish to be really angry?

OEDIPUS.   Say what you will. Whatever you say
is worthless.

TEIRESIAS.   I say you live in hideous shame with
those
Most dear to you. You cannot see the evil.

OEDIPUS.   It seems you can go on mouthing
like this for ever.   150

TEIRESIAS.   I can, if there is power in truth.

OEDIPUS.   There is:
But not for you, not for you,
You sightless, witless, senseless, mad old man!

TEIRESIAS.   You are the madman. There is no
one here
Who will not curse you soon, as you curse me.

OEDIPUS.   You child of endless night! You cannot hurt me
Or any other man who sees the sun.

TEIRESIAS.   True: it is not from me your fate
will come.
That lies within Apollo's competence,
As it is his concern.

OEDIPUS.   Tell me: 160
Are you speaking for Creon, or for yourself?

TEIRESIAS.   Creon is no threat. You weave your
own doom.

OEDIPUS.   Wealth, power, craft of statesman-
ship!
Kingly position, everywhere admired!
What savage envy is stored up against these,
If Creon, whom I trusted, Creon my friend,
For this great office which the city once
Put in my hands unsought—if for this power
Creon desires in secret to destroy me!

He has bought this decrepit fortune-teller, this
Collector of dirty pennies, this prophet fraud—
Why, he is no more clairvoyant than I am!
                                                  Tell us:
Has your mystic mummery ever approached the
truth?
When that hellcat the Sphinx was performing
here,
What help were you to these people?
Her magic was not for the first man who came
along:
It demanded a real exorcist. Your birds—

What good were they? or the gods, for the matter of that?

But I came by,

Oedipus, the simple man, who knows nothing—

I thought it out for myself, no birds helped me!

And this is the man you think you can destroy,

That you may be close to Creon when he's king!

Well, you and your friend Creon, it seems to me,

Will suffer most. If you were not an old man,

You would have paid already for your plot.

CHORAGOS.   We cannot see that his words or
yours

Have been spoken except in anger, Oedipus,

And of anger we have no need. How can God's
will

Be accomplished best? That is what most con-
cerns us.   190

TEIRESIAS.   You are a king. But where argument's concerned

I am your man, as much a king as you.

I am not your servant, but Apollo's.

I have no need of Creon to speak for me.

Listen to me. You mock my blindness, do you?

But I say that you, with both your eyes, are
blind:

You cannot see the wretchedness of your life,

Nor in whose house you live, no, nor with whom.

Who are your father and mother? Can you tell
me?

You do not even know the blind wrongs   200

That you have done them, on earth and in the
world below.

But the double lash of your parents' curse will
whip you

Out of this land some day, with only night

Upon your precious eyes.

Your cries then—where will they not be heard?

What fastness of Kithairon will not echo them?

And that bridal-descant of yours—you'll know
it then,

The song they sang when you came here to
Thebes

And found your misguided berthing.

All this, and more, that you cannot guess at
now,   210

Will bring you to yourself among your children.

Be angry, then. Curse Creon. Curse my words.

I tell you, no man that walks upon the earth

Shall be rooted out more horribly than you.

OEDIPUS.   Am I to bear this from him?—Damnation

Take you! Out of this place! Out of my sight!

TEIRESIAS.   I would not have come at all if you
had not asked me.

OEDIPUS.   Could I have told that you'd talk
nonsense, that

You'd come here to make a fool of yourself, and
of me?

TEIRESIAS.   A fool? Your parents thought me
sane enough.   220

OEDIPUS.   My parents again!—Wait: who were
my parents?

TEIRESIAS.   This day will give you a father, and
break your heart.

OEDIPUS.   Your infantile riddles! Your damned
abracadabra!

TEIRESIAS.   You were a great man once at solving riddles.

OEDIPUS.   Mock me with that if you like; you
will find it true.

TEIRESIAS.   It was true enough. It brought
about your ruin.

OEDIPUS.   But if it saved this town?

TEIRESIAS [to the PAGE].   Boy, give me your
hand.

OEDIPUS.   Yes, boy; lead him away.

                                             —While you are here

We can do nothing. Go; leave us in peace.   230

TEIRESIAS.   I will go when I have said what I
have to say.

How can you hurt me? And I tell you again:

The man you have been looking for all this
time,

The damned man, the murderer of Laïos,

That man is in Thebes. To your mind he is
foreign-born,

But it will soon be shown that he is a Theban,

A revelation that will fail to please.

                                             A blind man,

Who has his eyes now; a penniless man, who is
rich now;

And he will go tapping the strange earth with his staff
To the children with whom he lives now he will be
Brother and father—the very same; to her   240
Who bore him, son and husband—the very same
Who came to his father's bed, wet with his father's blood.

Enough. Go think that over.
If later you find error in what I have said,
You may say that I have no skill in prophecy.

[*Exit* TEIRESIAS, *led by his* PAGE. OEDIPUS
goes into the palace.

ODE I

[STROPHE 1

CHORUS.   The Delphic stone of prophecies
Remembers ancient regicide
And a still bloody hand.
That killer's hour of flight has come.
He must be stronger than riderless
Coursers of untiring wind,
For the son of Zeus armed with his father's thunder
Leaps in lightning after him;
And the Furies follow him, the sad Furies.

[ANTISTROPHE 1

Holy Parnassos' peak of snow   10
Flashes and blinds that secret man,
That all shall hunt him down:
Though he may roam the forest shade
Like a bull gone wild from pasture
To rage through glooms of stone.
Doom comes down on him; flight will not avail him;
For the world's heart calls him desolate,
And the immortal Furies follow, forever follow.

[STROPHE 2

But now a wilder thing is heard
From the old man skilled at hearing Fate in the wing-beat of a bird.   20
Bewildered as a blown bird, my soul hovers and cannot find

7 *son of Zeus:* Apollo.

Foothold in this debate, or any reason or rest of mind.
But no man ever brought—none can bring
Proof of strife between Thebes' royal house,
Labdakos' line, and the son of Polybos;
And never until now has any man brought word
Of Laïos' dark death staining Oedipus the King.

[ANTISTROPHE 2

Divine Zeus and Apollo hold
Perfect intelligence alone of all tales ever told;
And well though this diviner works, he works in his own night;   30
No man can judge that rough unknown or trust in second sight,
For wisdom changes hands among the wise.
Shall I believe my great lord criminal
At a raging word that a blind old man let fall?
I saw him, when the carrion woman faced him of old,
Prove his heroic mind! These evil words are lies.

SCENE II

CREON.   Men of Thebes:
I am told that heavy accusations
Have been brought against me by King Oedipus.

I am not the kind of man to bear this tamely.

If in these present difficulties
He holds me accountable for any harm to him
Through anything I have said or done—why, then,
I do not value life in this dishonor.
It is not as though this rumor touched upon
Some private indiscretion. The matter is grave.
The fact is that I am being called disloyal
To the State, to my fellow-citizens, to my friends.

CHORAGOS.   He may have spoken in anger, not from his mind.

CREON.   But did you not hear him say I was the one
Who seduced the old prophet into lying?

35 *carrion woman:* the Sphinx.

CHORAGOS. The thing was said; I do not know how seriously.

CREON. But you were watching him! Were his eyes steady?
Did he look like a man in his right mind?

CHORAGOS.   I do not know.
I can not judge the behavior of great men.
But here is the King himself.   20

[Enter OEDIPUS

OEDIPUS.   So you dared come back.
Why? How brazen of you to come to my house,
You murderer!
                    Do you think I do not know
That you plotted to kill me, plotted to steal my throne?
Tell me, in God's name: am I coward, a fool,
That you should dream you could accomplish this?
A fool who could not see your slippery game?
A coward, not to fight back when I saw it?
You are the fool, Creon, are you not? hoping
Without support or friends to get a throne?
Thrones may be won or bought: you could do neither.   30

CREON. Now listen to me. You have talked; let me talk, too.
You cannot judge unless you know the facts.

OEDIPUS. You speak well: there is one fact; but I find it hard
To learn from the deadliest enemy I have.

CREON. That above all I must dispute with you.

OEDIPUS. That above all I will not hear you deny.

CREON. If you think there is anything good in being stubborn
Against all reason, then I say you are wrong.

OEDIPUS. If you think a man can sin against his own kind
And not be punished for it, I say you are mad.

CREON. I agree. But tell me: what have I done to you?

OEDIPUS. You advised me to send for that wizard, did you not?

CREON. I did. I should do it again.

OEDIPUS.   Very well. Now tell me:
How long has it been since Laïos—

CREON.   What of Laïos?

OEDIPUS. Since he vanished in that onset by the road?

CREON. It was long ago, a long time.

OEDIPUS.   And this prophet,
Was he practicing here then?

CREON.   He was; and with honor, as now.

OEDIPUS. Did he speak of me at that time?   50

CREON.   He never did;
At least, not when I was present.

OEDIPUS.   But . . . the enquiry?
I suppose you held one?

CREON.   We did, but we learned nothing.

OEDIPUS. Why did the prophet not speak against me then?

CREON. I did not know; and I am the kind of man
Who holds his tongue when he has no facts to go on.

OEDIPUS. There's one fact that you know, and you could tell it.

CREON. What fact is that? If I know it, you shall have it.

OEDIPUS. If he were not involved with you, he could not say
That it was I who murdered Laïos.   60

CREON. If he says that, you are the one that knows it!—
But now it is my turn to question you.

OEDIPUS. Put your questions. I am no murderer.

CREON. First, then: You married my sister?

OEDIPUS.   I married your sister.

CREON. And you rule the kingdom equally with her?

OEDIPUS. Everything that she wants she has from me.

CREON. And I am the third, equal to both of you?

OEDIPUS. That is why I call you a bad friend.

CREON.   No. Reason it out, as I have done.   70
Think of this first: Would any sane man prefer
Power, with all a king's anxieties,
To that same power and the grace of sleep?
Certainly not I.
I have never longed for the king's power—only
   his rights.
Would any wise man differ from me in this?
As matters stand, I have my way in everything
With your consent, and no responsibilities.
If I were king, I should be a slave to policy.

How could I desire a scepter more   80
Than what is now mine—untroubled influence?
No, I have not gone mad; I need no honors,
Except those with the perquisites I have now.
I am welcome everywhere; every man salutes me,
And those who want your favor seek my ear,
Since I know how to manage what they ask.
Should I exchange this ease for that anxiety?
Besides, no sober mind is treasonable.
I hate anarchy
And never would deal with any man who likes it.

Test what I have said. Go to the priestess
At Delphi, ask if I quoted her correctly.
And as for this other thing: if I am found
Guilty of treason with Teiresias,
Then sentence me to death! You have my word
It is a sentence I should cast my vote for—
But not without evidence!

                            You do wrong
When you take good men for bad, bad men for
   good.
A true friend thrown aside—why, life itself
Is not more precious!   100
               In time you will know this well:
For time, and time alone, will show the just man,
Though scoundrels are discovered in a day.

CHORAGOS.   This is well said, and a prudent
   man would ponder it.
Judgments too quickly formed are dangerous.

OEDIPUS.   But is he not quick in his duplicity?
And shall I not be quick to parry him?
Would you have me stand still, hold my peace,
   and let
This man win everything, through my inaction?

CREON.   And you want—what is it, then? To
   banish me?

OEDIPUS.   No, not exile. It is your death I
   want,   110
So that all the world may see what treason
means.

CREON.   You will persist, then? You will not believe me?

OEDIPUS.   How can I believe you?

CREON.   Then you are a fool.

OEDIPUS.   To save myself?

CREON.   In justice, think of me.

OEDIPUS.   You are evil incarnate.

CREON.   But suppose that you are wrong?

OEDIPUS.   Still I must rule.

CREON.   But not if you rule badly.   120

OEDIPUS.   O city, city!

CREON.   It is my city, too!

CHORAGOS.   Now, my lords, be still. I see the
   Queen,
Iocastê, coming from her palace chambers;
And it is time she came, for the sake of you both.
This dreadful quarrel can be resolved through
   her.

                            [Enter IOCASTÊ

IOCASTÊ.   Poor foolish men, what wicked din is
this?
With Thebes sick to death, is it not shameful
That you should rake some private quarrel up?
[To OEDIPUS]
Come into the house.   130
                —And you, Creon, go now:
Let us have no more of this tumult over nothing.

CREON.   Nothing? No, sister: what your husband plans for me
Is one of two great evils: exile or death.

OEDIPUS.   He is right.
          Why, woman I have caught him squarely
Plotting against my life.

CREON.   No! Let me die
Accurst if ever I have wished you harm!

IOCASTÊ.   Ah, believe it, Oedipus!
In the name of the gods, respect this oath of his
For my sake, for the sake of these people here!

[STROPHE 1

CHORAGOS.   Open your mind to her, my lord.
Be ruled by her, I beg you!   140

OEDIPUS.   What would you have me do?

CHORAGOS.   Respect Creon's word. He has never
spoken like a fool,
And now he has sworn an oath.

OEDIPUS.   You know what you ask?

CHORAGOS.   I do.

OEDIPUS.   Speak on, then.

CHORAGOS.   A friend so sworn should not be
baited so,
In blind malice, and without final proof.

OEDIPUS.   You are aware, I hope, that what you
say
Means death for me, or exile at the least.   150

[STROPHE 2

CHORAGOS.   No, I swear by Helios, first in
Heaven!
May I die friendless and accurst,
The worst of deaths, if ever I meant that!
   It is the withering fields
      That hurt my sick heart:
   Must we bear all these ills,
      And now your bad blood as well?

OEDIPUS.   Then let him go. And let me die, if I
must,
Or be driven by him in shame from the land of
Thebes.
It is your unhappiness, and not his talk,   160
That touches me.
                  As for him—
Wherever he goes, hatred will follow him.

CREON.   Ugly in yielding, as you were ugly in
rage!
Natures like yours chiefly torment themselves.

OEDIPUS.   Can you not go? Can you not leave
me?

CREON.   I can.
You do not know me: but the city knows me,
And in its eyes I am just, if not in yours.
                                    [Exit CREON

151 *Helios:* the sun.

[ANTISTROPHE 1

CHORAGOS.   Lady Iocastê, did you not ask the
King to go to his chambers?

IOCASTÊ.   First tell me what has happened.

CHORAGOS.   There was suspicion without evidence: yet it rankled   170
As even false charges will.

IOCASTÊ.   On both sides?

CHORAGOS.   On both.

IOCASTÊ.   But what was said?

CHORAGOS.   Oh let it rest, let it be done with!
Have we not suffered enough?

OEDIPUS.   You see to what your decency has
brought you:
You have made difficulties where my heart saw
none.

[ANTISTROPHE 2

CHORAGOS.   Oedipus, it is not once only I have
told you—
You must know I should count myself unwise
To the point of madness, should I now forsake
you—
You, under whose hand,
   In the storm of another time,
Our dear land sailed out free.
   But now stand fast at the helm!

IOCASTÊ.   In God's name, Oedipus, inform your
wife as well:
Why are you so set in this hard anger?

OEDIPUS.   I will tell you, for none of these men
deserves
My confidence as you do. It is Creon's work,
His treachery, his plotting against me.   190

IOCASTÊ.   Go on, if you can make this clear to
me.

OEDIPUS.   He charges me with the murder of
Laïos.

IOCASTÊ.   Has he some knowledge? Or does he
speak from hearsay?

OEDIPUS.   He would not commit himself to such
a charge,
But he has brought in that damnable sooth-
sayer
To tell his story.

IOCASTÊ.   Set your mind at rest.

If it is a question of soothsayers, I tell you

That you will find no man whose craft gives
   knowledge

Of the unknowable.

                Here is my proof: 200

An oracle was reported to Laïos once

(I will not say from Phoibos himself, but from

His appointed ministers, at any rate)

That his doom would be death at the hands of
   his own son—

His son, born of his flesh and of mine!

Now, you remember the story: Laïos was killed

By marauding strangers where three highways
   meet;

But his child had not been three days in this
   world

Before the King had pierced the baby's ankles

And let him die on a lonely mountainside.   210

Thus, Apollo never caused that child

To kill his father, and it was not Laïos' fate

To die at the hands of his son, as he had feared.

This is what prophets and prophecies are worth!

Have no dread of them.

              It is God himself

Who can show us what he wills, in his own way.

OEDIPUS.   How strange a shadowy memory
   crossed my mind,

Just now while you were speaking; it chilled my
   heart.

IOCASTÊ.   What do you mean? What memory
   do you speak of?

OEDIPUS.   If I understand you, Laïos was
   killed   220

At a place where three roads meet.

IOCASTÊ.   So it was said;

We have no later story.

OEDIPUS.   Where did it happen?

IOCASTÊ.   Phokis, it is called: at a place where
   the Theban Way

Divides into the roads toward Delphi and
   Daulia.

224 *Phokis:* kingdom in which the towns of Delphi and Daulia are situated.

OEDIPUS.   When?

IOCASTÊ.   We had the news not long before you
   came

And proved the right to your succession here.

OEDIPUS.   Ah, what net has God been weaving
   for me?

IOCASTÊ.   Oedipus! Why does this trouble
   you?   230

OEDIPUS.   Do not ask me yet.

First, tell me how Laïos looked, and tell me

How old he was.

IOCASTÊ.   He was tall, his hair just touched

With white; his form was not unlike your own.

OEDIPUS.   I think that I myself may be accurst

By my own ignorant edict.

IOCASTÊ.   You speak strangely.

It makes me tremble to look at you, my King.

OEDIPUS.   I am not sure that the blind man
   cannot see.

But I should know better if you were to tell
   me—   240

IOCASTÊ.   Anything—though I dread to hear
   you ask it.

OEDIPUS.   Was the King lightly escorted, or did
   he ride

With a large company, as a ruler should?

IOCASTÊ.   There were five men with him in all:
   one was a herald,

And a single chariot, which he was driving.

OEDIPUS.   Alas, that makes it plain enough!

                 But who—

Who told you how it happened?

IOCASTÊ.   A household servant,

The only one to escape.

OEDIPUS.   And is he still

A servant of ours?   250

IOCASTÊ.   No; for when he came back at last

And found you enthroned in place of the dead
   king,

He came to me, touched my hand with his, and
   begged

That I would send him away to the frontier
   district

Where only the shepherds go—

As far away from the city as I could send him.
I granted his prayer; for although the man was
  a slave,
He had earned more than this favor at my
  hands.

OEDIPUS.   Can he be called back quickly?

IOCASTÊ.   Easily.
But why?   260

OEDIPUS.   I have taken too much upon myself
Without enquiry; therefore I wish to consult
  him.

IOCASTÊ.   Then he shall come.
                          But am I not one also
To whom you might confide these fears of yours?

OEDIPUS.   That is your right; it will not be
  denied you,
Now least of all; for I have reached a pitch
Of wild foreboding. Is there anyone
To whom I should sooner speak?

Polybos of Corinth is my father.
My mother is a Dorian: Meropê.   270
I grew up chief among the men of Corinth
Until a strange thing happened—
Not worth my passion, it may be, but strange.

At a feast, a drunken man maundering in his
  cups
Cries out that I am not my father's son!

I contained myself that night, though I felt
  anger
And a sinking heart. The next day I visited
My father and mother, and questioned them.
  They stormed,
Calling it all the slanderous rant of a fool;
And this relieved me. Yet the suspicion   280
Remained always aching in my mind;
I knew there was talk; I could not rest;
And finally, saying nothing to my parents,
I went to the shrine at Delphi.
The god dismissed my question without reply;
He spoke of other things.
                          Some were clear,
Full of wretchedness, dreadful, unbearable:
As, that I should lie with my own mother, breed

Children from whom all men would turn their
  eyes:
And that I should be my father's murderer.   290

I heard all this, and fled. And from that day
Corinth to me was only in the stars
Descending in that quarter of the sky,
As I wandered farther and farther on my way
To a land where I should never see the evil
Sung by the oracle. And I came to this country
Where, so you say, King Laïos was killed.

I will tell you all that happened there, my lady.

There were three highways
Coming together at a place I passed;   300
And there a herald came towards me, and a
  chariot
Drawn by horses, with a man such as you
  describe
Seated in it. The groom leading the horses
Forced me off the road at his lord's command;
But as this charioteer lurched over towards me
I struck him in my rage. The old man saw me
And brought his double goad down upon my
  head
As I came abreast.
                    He was paid back, and more!
Swinging my club in this right hand I knocked
  him
Out of his car, and he rolled on the ground.
                          I killed him.   310
I killed them all.
Now if that stranger and Laïos were—kin,
Where is a man more miserable than I?
More hated by the gods? Citizen and alien alike
Must never shelter me or speak to me—
I must be shunned by all.
                          And I myself
Pronounced this malediction upon myself!

Think of it: I have touched you with these
  hands,
These hands that killed your husband. What
  defilement!

Am I all evil, then? It must be so,   320
Since I must flee from Thebes, yet never again
See my own countrymen, my own country,

For fear of joining my mother in marriage
And killing Polybos, my father.

                              Ah,
If I was created so, born to this fate,
Who could deny the savagery of God?
O holy majesty of heavenly powers!
May I never see that day! Never!
Rather let me vanish from the race of men
Than know the abomination destined me!   330

CHORAGOS.   We too, my lord, have felt dismay
  at this.
But there is hope: you have yet to hear the
  shepherd.

OEDIPUS.   Indeed, I fear no other hope is left
  me.

IOCASTÊ.   What do you hope from him when he
  comes?

OEDIPUS.   This much:
If his account of the murder tallies with yours,
Then I am cleared.

IOCASTÊ.   What was it that I said
Of such importance?

OEDIPUS.   Why, "marauders," you said,
Killed the King, according to this man's story.
If he maintains that still, if there were several,
Clearly the guilt is not mine: I was alone.
But if he says one man, singlehanded, did it,
Then the evidence all points to me.

IOCASTÊ.   You may be sure that he said there
  were several;
And can he call back that story now? He cannot.
The whole city heard it as plainly as I.
But suppose he alters some detail of it:
He cannot ever show that Laïos' death
Fulfilled the oracle: for Apollo said
My child was doomed to kill him; and my
  child—
Poor baby!—it was my child that died first.   350

No. From now on, where oracles are concerned,
I would not waste a second thought on any.

OEDIPUS.   You may be right.
                              But come: let someone go
For the shepherd at once. This matter must be
  settled.

IOCASTÊ.   I will send for him.
I would not wish to cross you in anything,
And surely not in this.—Let us go in.

                              [*Exeunt into the palace*

ODE II

                                        [STROPHE 1

CHORUS.   Let me be reverent in the ways of
  right,
Lowly the paths I journey on;
Let all my words and actions keep
The laws of the pure universe
From highest heaven handed down.
For heaven is their bright nurse,
Those generations of the realms of light;
Ah, never of mortal kind were they begot,
Nor are they slaves of memory, lost in sleep:
Their Father is greater than Time, and ages
  not.   10

                                     [ANTISTROPHE 1

The tyrant is a child of Pride
Who drinks from his great sickening cup
Recklessness and vanity,
Until from his high crest headlong
He plummets to the dust of hope.
That strong man is not strong.
But let no fair ambition be denied;
May God protect the wrestler for the State
In government, in comely policy,
Who will fear God, and on His ordinance wait.

                                        [STROPHE 2

Haughtiness and the high hand of disdain
Tempt and outrage God's holy law;
And any mortal who dares hold
No immortal power in awe
Will be caught up in a net of pain:
The price for which his levity is sold.
Let each man take due earnings, then,
And keep his hands from holy things,
And from blasphemy stand apart—
Else the crackling blast of heaven   30
Blows on his head, and on his desperate heart;
Though fools will honor impious men,
In their cities no tragic poet sings.

                                     [ANTISTROPHE 2

Shall we lose faith in Delphi's obscurities,

We who have heard the world's core
Discredited, and the sacred wood
Of Zeus at Elis praised no more?
The deeds and the strange prophecies
Must make a pattern yet to be understood.
Zeus, if indeed you are lord of all,   40
Throned in light over night and day,
Mirror this in your endless mind:
Our masters call the oracle
Words on the wind, and the Delphic vision
   blind!
Their hearts no longer know Apollo,
And reverence for the gods has died away.

SCENE III

                        [*Enter* IOCASTÊ

IOCASTÊ.   Princes of Thebes, it has occurred to
   me
To visit the altars of the gods, bearing
These branches as a suppliant, and this incense.
Our King is not himself: his noble soul
Is overwrought with fantasies of dread,
Else he would consider
The new prophecies in the light of the old.
He will listen to any voice that speaks disaster,
And my advice goes for nothing.
               [*She approaches the altar, right*
                        To you, then, Apollo,
Lycean lord, since you are nearest, I turn in
   prayer.   10
Receive these offerings, and grant us deliverance
From defilement. Our hearts are heavy with fear
When we see our leader distracted, as helpless
   sailors
Are terrified by the confusion of their helmsman.
                        [*Enter* MESSENGER

MESSENGER.   Friends, no doubt you can direct
   me:
Where shall I find the house of Oedipus,
Or, better still, where is the King himself?

CHORAGOS.   It is this very place, stranger; he is
   inside.
This is his wife and mother of his children.

35 *world's core:* i.e., the oracle; Delphi was considered the *omphalos* (navel) of the earth.   37 *Elis:*
there was another oracle at the Temple of Olym-
pian Zeus in Elis, a region of the Peloponnesus.

MESSENGER.   I wish her happiness in a happy
   house,   20
Blest in all the fulfillment of her marriage.

IOCASTÊ.   I wish as much for you: your courtesy
Deserves a like good fortune. But now, tell me:
Why have you come? What have you to say to
   us?

MESSENGER.   Good news, my lady, for your
   house and your husband.

IOCASTÊ.   What news? Who sent you here?

MESSENGER.   I am from Corinth.
The news I bring ought to mean joy for you,
Though it may be you will find some grief in it.

IOCASTÊ.   What is it? How can it touch us in
   both ways?

MESSENGER.   The word is that the people of the
   Isthmus   30
Intend to call Oedipus to be their king.

IOCASTÊ.   But old King Polybos—is he not
   reigning still?

MESSENGER.   No. Death holds him in his sepulchre.

IOCASTÊ.   What are you saying? Polybos is
   dead?

MESSENGER.   If I am not telling the truth, may
   I die myself.

IOCASTÊ [*To a* MAIDSERVANT].   Go in, go quickly:
   tell this to your master.
O riddles of God's will, where are you now!
This was the man whom Oedipus, long ago,
Feared so, fled so, in dread of destroying him—
But it was another fate by which he died.   40
                        [*Enter* OEDIPUS, *center*

OEDIPUS.   Dearest Iocastê, why have you sent
   for me?

IOCASTÊ.   Listen to what this man says, and
   then tell me
What has become of the solemn prophecies.

OEDIPUS.   Who is this man? What is his news
   for me?

IOCASTÊ.   He has come from Corinth to announce your father's death!

OEDIPUS.   Is it true, stranger? Tell me in your
   own words.

MESSENGER. I cannot say it more clearly: the King is dead.

OEDIPUS. Was it by treason? Or by an attack of illness?

MESSENGER. A little thing brings old men to their rest.

OEDIPUS. It was sickness, then?   50

MESSENGER.   Yes, and his many years.

OEDIPUS. Ah!
Why should a man respect the Pythian hearth, or
Give heed to the birds that jangle above his head?
They prophesied that I should kill Polybos,
Kill my own father; but he is dead and buried,
And I am here—I never touched him, never,
Unless he died of grief for my departure,
And thus, in a sense, through me. No. Polybos
Has packed the oracles off with him underground.
They are empty words.   60

IOCASTÊ.   Had I not told you so?

OEDIPUS. You had; it was my faint heart that betrayed me.

IOCASTÊ. From now on never think of those things again.

OEDIPUS. And yet—must I not fear my mother's bed?

IOCASTÊ. Why should anyone in this world be afraid,
Since Fate rules us and nothing can be foreseen?
A man should live only for the present day.
Have no more fear of sleeping with your mother:
How many men, in dreams, have lain with their mothers!
No reasonable man is troubled by such things.

OEDIPUS. That is true; only—
If only my mother were not still alive!
But she is alive. I cannot help my dread.

IOCASTÊ. Yet this news of your father's death is wonderful.

OEDIPUS. Wonderful. But I fear the living woman.

52 *Pythian hearth:* i.e., the oracle of Apollo.

MESSENGER. Tell me, who is this woman that you fear?

OEDIPUS. It is Meropê, man; the wife of King Polybos.

MESSENGER. Meropê? Why should you be afraid of her?

OEDIPUS. An oracle of the gods, a dreadful saying.

MESSENGER. Can you tell me about it or are you sworn to silence?   80

OEDIPUS. I can tell you, and I will.
Apollo said through his prophet that I was the man
Who should marry his own mother, shed his father's blood
With his own hands. And so, for all these years
I have kept clear of Corinth, and no harm has come—
Though it would have been sweet to see my parents again.

MESSENGER. And this is the fear that drove you out of Corinth?

OEDIPUS. Would you have me kill my father?

MESSENGER.   As for that
You must be reassured by the news I gave you.

OEDIPUS. If you could reassure me, I would reward you.   90

MESSENGER. I had that in mind, I will confess: I thought
I could count on you when you returned to Corinth.

OEDIPUS. No: I will never go near my parents again.

MESSENGER. Ah, son, you still do not know what you are doing—

OEDIPUS. What do you mean? In the name of God tell me!

MESSENGER.—If these are your reasons for not going home.

OEDIPUS. I tell you, I fear the oracle may come true.

MESSENGER. And guilt may come upon you through your parents?

OEDIPUS. That is the dread that is always in my heart.

MESSENGER. Can you not see that all your fears are groundless? 100

OEDIPUS. How can you say that? They are my parents, surely?

MESSENGER. Polybos was not your father.

OEDIPUS.   Not my father?

MESSENGER. No more your father than the man speaking to you.

OEDIPUS. But you are nothing to me!

MESSENGER.   Neither was he.

OEDIPUS. Then why did he call me son?

MESSENGER.   I will tell you:
Long ago he had you from my hands, as a gift.

OEDIPUS. Then how could he love me so, if I was not his? 110

MESSENGER. He had no children, and his heart turned to you.

OEDIPUS. What of you? Did you buy me? Did you find me by chance?

MESSENGER. I came upon you in the crooked pass of Kithairon.

OEDIPUS. And what were you doing there?

MESSENGER.   Tending my flocks.

OEDIPUS. A wandering shepherd?

MESSENGER.   But your savior, son, that day.

OEDIPUS. From what did you save me?

MESSENGER. Your ankles should tell you that.

OEDIPUS. Ah, stranger, why do you speak of that childhood pain? 120

MESSENGER. I cut the bonds that tied your ankles together.

OEDIPUS. I have had the mark as long as I can remember.

MESSENGER. That was why you were given the name you bear.

OEDIPUS. God! Was it my father or my mother who did it? Tell me!

MESSENGER. I do not know. The man who gave you to me
Can tell you better than I.

OEDIPUS. It was not you that found me, but another?

MESSENGER. It was another shepherd gave you to me.

OEDIPUS. Who was he? Can you tell me who he was?

MESSENGER. I think he was said to be one of Laïos' people. 130

OEDIPUS. You mean the Laïos who was king here years ago?

MESSENGER. Yes; King Laïos; and the man was one of his herdsmen.

OEDIPUS. Is he still alive? Can I see him?

MESSENGER.   These men here
Know best about such things.

OEDIPUS.   Does anyone here
Know this shepherd that he is talking about?
Have you seen him in the fields, or in the town?
If you have, tell me. It is time things were made plain.

CHORAGOS. I think the man he means is that same shepherd 140
You have already asked to see. Iocastê perhaps
Could tell you something.

OEDIPUS.   Do you know anything
About him, Lady? Is he the man we have summoned?
Is that the man this shepherd means?

IOCASTÊ.   Why think of him?
Forget this herdsman. Forget it all.
This talk is a waste of time.

OEDIPUS.   How can you say that,
When the clues to my true birth are in my hands? 150

IOCASTÊ. For God's love, let us have no more questioning!
Is your life nothing to you?
My own is pain enough for me to bear.

OEDIPUS. You need not worry. Suppose my mother a slave,
And born of slaves: no baseness can touch you.

IOCASTÊ. Listen to me, I beg you: do not do this thing!

OEDIPUS. I will not listen; the truth must be
made known.

IOCASTÊ. Everything that I say is for your own
good!

OEDIPUS.   My own good
Snaps my patience, then; I want none of it.   160

IOCASTÊ. You are fatally wrong! May you never
learn who you are!

OEDIPUS. Go, one of you, and bring the shepherd here.
Let us leave this woman to brag of her royal
name.

IOCASTÊ. Ah, miserable!
That is the only word I have for you now.
That is the only word I can ever have.

                        [*Exit into the palace*

CHORAGOS. Why has she left us, Oedipus? Why
has she gone
In such a passion of sorrow? I fear this silence:
Something dreadful may come of it.

OEDIPUS.   Let it come!   170
However base my birth, I must know about it.
The·Queen, like a woman, is perhaps ashamed
To think of my low origin. But I
Am a child of Luck; I cannot be dishonored.
Luck is my mother; the passing months, my
brothers,
Have seen me rich and poor.

                        If this is so,
How could I wish that I were someone else?
How could I not be glad to know my birth?

Ode III

                                  [STROPHE

CHORUS. If ever the coming time were known
To my heart's pondering,
Kithairon, now by heaven I see the torches
At the festival of the next full moon,
And see the dance, and hear the choir sing
A grace to your gentle shade:
Mountain where Oedipus was found,
O mountain guard of a noble race!
May the god who heals us lend his aid,

  9 *god:* Apollo.

And let that glory come to pass   10
For our king's cradling-ground.

                              [ANTISTROPHE
Of the nymphs that flower beyond the years,
Who bore you, royal child,
To Pan of the hills or the timberline Apollo,
Cold in delight where the upland clears,
Or Hermês for whom Kyllenê's heights are piled?
Or flushed as evening cloud,
Great Dionysos, roamer of mountains,
He—was it he who found you there,
And caught you up in his own proud   20
Arms from the sweet god-ravisher
Who laughed by the Muses' fountains?

SCENE IV

OEDIPUS. Sirs: though I do not know the man,
I think I see him coming, this shepherd we want:
He is old, like our friend here, and the men
Bringing him seem to be servants of my house.
But you can tell, if you have ever seen him.
            [*Enter* SHEPHERD *escorted by servants*

CHORAGOS. I know him, he was Laïos' man. You
can trust him.

OEDIPUS. Tell me first, you from Corinth: is
this the shepherd
We were discussing?

MESSENGER.   This is the very man.

OEDIPUS. [*To* SHEPHERD]
Come here. No, look at me. You must answer   10
Everything I ask.—You belonged to Laïos?

SHEPHERD. Yes: born his slave, brought up in
his house.

OEDIPUS. Tell me: what kind of work did you
do for him?

SHEPHERD. I was a shepherd of his, most of my
life.

OEDIPUS. Where mainly did you go for pas-
turage?

  10 *glory:* i.e., let Kithairon become famous as
Oedipus' birthplace. 16 *Kyllenê:* mountain in
Arcadia, birthplace of Hermês. 21 *god-ravisher:*
the CHORUS imagines that OEDIPUS is the offspring of
a mountain nymph and one of the gods.

SHEPHERD. Sometimes Kithairon, sometimes the hills near by.

OEDIPUS. Do you remember ever seeing this man out there?

SHEPHERD. What would he be doing there? This man?

OEDIPUS. This man standing here. Have you ever seen him before?

SHEPHERD. No. At least, not to my recollection. 20

MESSENGER. And that is not strange, my lord.
But I'll refresh
His memory: he must remember when we two
Spent three whole seasons together, March to September,
On Kithairon or thereabouts. He had two flocks;
I had one. Each autumn I'd drive mine home
And he would go back with his to Laïos' sheepfold.—
Is this not true, just as I have described it?

SHEPHERD. True, yes; but it was all so long ago.

MESSENGER. Well, then: do you remember, back in those days,
That you gave me a baby boy to bring up as my own? 30

SHEPHERD. What if I did? What are you trying to say?

MESSENGER. King Oedipus was once that little child.

SHEPHERD. Damn you, hold your tongue!

OEDIPUS. No more of that!
It is your tongue needs watching, not this man's.

SHEPHERD. My king, my master, what is it I have done wrong?

OEDIPUS. You have not answered his question about the boy.

SHEPHERD. He does not know . . . He is only making trouble . . .

OEDIPUS. Come, speak plainly, or it will go hard with you.

SHEPHERD. In God's name, do not torture an old man!

OEDIPUS. Come here, one of you; bind his arms behind him. 40

SHEPHERD. Unhappy king! What more do you wish to learn?

OEDIPUS. Did you give this man the child he speaks of?

SHEPHERD. I did.
And I would to God I had died that very day.

OEDIPUS. You will die now unless you speak the truth.

SHEPHERD. Yet if I speak the truth, I am worse than dead.

OEDIPUS. Very well; since you insist upon delaying—

SHEPHERD. No! I have told you already that I gave him the boy.

OEDIPUS. Where did you get him? From your house? From somewhere else?

SHEPHERD. Not from mine, no. A man gave him to me.

OEDIPUS. Is that man here? Do you know whose slave he was? 50

SHEPHERD. For God's love, my king, do not ask me any more!

OEDIPUS. You are a dead man if I have to ask you again.

SHEPHERD. Then . . . Then the child was from the palace of Laïos.

OEDIPUS. A slave child? or a child from his own line?

SHEPHERD. Ah, I am on the brink of dreadful speech!

OEDIPUS. And I of dreadful hearing. Yet I must hear.

SHEPHERD. If you must be told, then . . .
They said it was Laïos' child;
But it is your wife who can tell you about that.

OEDIPUS. My wife!—Did she give it to you?

SHEPHERD. My lord, she did. 60

OEDIPUS. Do you know why?

SHEPHERD. I was told to get rid of it.

OEDIPUS. An unspeakable mother!

SHEPHERD. There had been prophecies . . .

OEDIPUS. Tell me.

SHEPHERD. It was said that the boy would kill his own father.

OEDIPUS.   Then why did you give him over to
this old man?

SHEPHERD.   I pitied the baby, my king.
And I thought that this man would take him
far away
To his own country.   70
                 He saved him—but for what a fate!
For if you are what this man says you are,
No man living is more wretched than Oedipus.

OEDIPUS.   Ah God!
It was true!
             All the prophecies!
                         —Now,
O Light, may I look on you for the last time!
I, Oedipus,
Oedipus, damned in his birth, in his marriage
damned,   80
Damned in the blood he shed with his own
hand!

             [*He rushes into the palace*

Ode IV

                                   [STROPHE 1
CHORUS.   Alas for the seed of men.

What measure shall I give these generations
That breathe on the void and are void
And exist and do not exist?

Who bears more weight of joy
Than mass of sunlight shifting in images,
Or who shall make his thought stay on
That down time drifts away?

Your splendor is all fallen.

O naked brow of wrath and tears,   10
O change of Oedipus!
I who saw your days call no man blest—
Your great days like ghosts gone.

                              [ANTISTROPHE 1
That mind was a strong bow.

Deep, how deep you drew it then, hard archer,
At a dim fearful range,
And brought dear glory down!

15 *archer:* Apollo.

You overcame the stranger—
The virgin with her hooking lion claws—
And though death sang, stood like a tower   20
To make pale Thebes take heart.

Fortress against our sorrow!

True king, giver of laws,
Majestic Oedipus!
No prince in Thebes had ever such renown,
No prince won such grace of power.

                                   [STROPHE 2
And now of all men ever known
Most pitiful is this man's story:
His fortunes are most changed, his state
Fallen to a low slave's   30
Ground under bitter fate.

O Oedipus, most royal one!
The great door that expelled you to the light
Gave at night—ah, gave night to your glory:
As to the father, to the fathering son.

All understood too late.

How could that queen whom Laïos won,
The garden that he harrowed at his height,
Be silent when that act was done?

                              [ANTISTROPHE 2
But all eyes fail before time's eye,   40
All actions come to justice there.
Though never willed, though far down the
deep past,
Your bed, your dread sirings,
Are brought to book at last.

Child by Laïos doomed to die,
Then doomed to lose that fortunate little death,
Would God you never took breath in this air
That with my wailing lips I take to cry:

For I weep the world's outcast.

I was blind, and now I can tell why: 50
Asleep, for you had given ease of breath
To Thebes, while the false years went by.

18 *stranger: the   Sphinx.* 33 *door:* IOCASTÊ's
womb. 35 *father . . . son:* i.e., by giving birth to
OEDIPUS, IOCASTÊ destroyed both LAÏOS and him.
39 *act:* the mating of OEDIPUS and IOCASTÊ.

Exodus

[Enter, from the palace, SECOND MESSENGER

SECOND MESSENGER. Elders of Thebes, most
  honored in this land,
What horrors are yours to see and hear, what
  weight
Of sorrow to be endured if, true to your birth,
You venerate the line of Labdakos!
I think neither Istros nor Phasis, those great
  rivers,
Could purify this place of the corruption
It shelters now, or soon must bring to light—
Evil now done unconsciously, but willed.

The greatest griefs are those we cause ourselves.

CHORAGOS.   Surely, friend, we have grief enough
  already;   10
What new sorrow do you mean?

SECOND MESSENGER.   The Queen is dead.

CHORAGOS.   Iocastê? Dead? But at whose hand?

SECOND MESSENGER.   Her own.
The full horror of what happened you cannot
  know,
For you did not see it; but I, who did, will tell
  you
As clearly as I can how she met her death.

When she had left us,
In passionate silence, passing through the court,
She ran to her apartment in the house,
Her hair clutched by the fingers of both hands.
She closed the doors behind her; then, by that
  bed
Where long ago the fatal son was conceived—
That son who should bring about his father's
  death—
We heard her call upon Laïos, dead so many
  years,
And heard her wail for the double fruit of her
  marriage,
A husband by her husband, children by her
  child.
Exactly how she died I do not know:
For Oedipus burst in moaning and would not
  let us

ÉXODOS: Conclusion.

Keep vigil to the end: it was by him
As he stormed about the room that our eyes
  were caught.   30
From one to another of us he went, begging a
  sword,
Cursing the wife who was not his wife, the
  mother
Whose womb had carried his own children and
  himself.
I do not know: it was none of us aided him,
But surely one of the gods was in control!
For with a dreadful cry
He hurled his weight, as though wrenched out
  of himself,
At the twin doors: the bolts gave, and he rushed
  in.
And there we saw her hanging, her body swaying
From the cruel cord she had noosed about her
  neck.   40
A great sob broke from him, heartbreaking to
  hear,
As he loosed the rope and lowered her to the
  ground.

I would blot out from my mind what happened
  next!
For the King ripped from her gown the golden
  brooches
That were her ornament, and raised them, and
  plunged them down
Straight into his own eyeballs, crying, "No more,
No more shall you look on the misery about me,
The horrors of my own doing! Too long you
  have known
The faces of those whom I should never have
  seen,
Too long been blind to those for whom I was
  searching!   50
From this hour, go in darkness!" And as he
  spoke,
He struck at his eyes—not once, but many times;
And the blood spattered his beard,
Bursting from his ruined sockets like red hail.

So from the unhappiness of two this evil has
  sprung,
A curse on the man and woman alike. The old
Happiness of the house of Labdakos

Was happiness enough: where is it today?
It is all wailing and ruin, disgrace, death—all
The misery of mankind that has a name—   60
And it is wholly and for ever theirs.

CHORAGOS.   Is he in agony still? Is there no rest
for him?

SECOND MESSENGER.   He is calling for someone
to lead him to the gates
So that all the children of Kadmos may look
upon
His father's murderer, his mother's—no,
I cannot say it!
                    And then he will leave Thebes,
Self-exiled, in order that the curse
Which he himself pronounced may depart from
the house.
He is weak, and there is none to lead him,
So terrible is his suffering.
                          But you will see: 70
Look, the doors are opening; in a moment
You will see a thing that would crush a heart of
stone.

            [*The central door is opened;* OEDIPUS,
                            blinded, is led in

CHORAGOS.   Dreadful indeed for men to see.
Never have my own eyes
Looked on a sight so full of fear.

Oedipus!
What madness came upon you, what demon
Leaped on your life with heavier
Punishment than a mortal man can bear?
No: I cannot even   80
Look at you, poor ruined one.
And I would speak, question, ponder,
If I were able. No.
You make me shudder.

OEDIPUS. God.   God.
Is there a sorrow greater?
Where shall I find harbor in this world?
My voice is hurled far on a dark wind.
What has God done to me?

CHORAGOS.   Too terrible to think of, or to see.

                                    [STROPHE 1

OEDIPUS.   O cloud of night,

Never to be turned away; night coming on,
I cannot tell how: night like a shroud!

My fair winds brought me here.
                                    O God. Again
The pain of the spikes where I had sight,
The flooding pain
Of memory, never to be gouged out.

CHORAGOS.   This is not strange.
You suffer it all twice over, remorse in pain,
Pain in remorse.   100

                                    [ANTISTROPHE 1

OEDIPUS.   Ah dear friend
Are you faithful even yet, you alone?
Are you still standing near me, will you stay
here,
Patient, to care for the blind?
                                    The blind man!
Yet even blind I know who it is attends me,
By the voice's tone—
Though my new darkness hide the comforter.

CHORAGOS.   Oh fearful act!
What god was it drove you to rake black
Night across your eyes?   110

                                    [STROPHE 2

OEDIPUS.   Apollo. Apollo. Dear
Children, the god was Apollo.
He brought my sick, sick fate upon me.
But the blinding hand was my own!
How could I bear to see
When all my sight was horror everywhere?

CHORAGOS.   Everywhere; that is true.

OEDIPUS.   And now what is left?
Images? Love? A greeting even,
Sweet to the senses? Is there anything?   120
Ah, no, friends: lead me away.
Lead me away from Thebes.
                                    Lead the great wreck
And hell of Oedipus, whom the gods hate.

CHORAGOS.   Your fate is clear, you are not blind
to that.
Would God you had never found it out!

                                    [ANTISTROPHE 2

OEDIPUS.   Death take the man who unbound
My feet on that hillside

And delivered me from death to life! What life?
If only I had died,
This weight of monstrous doom 130
Could not have dragged me and my darlings
  down.

CHORAGOS.   I would have wished the same.

OEDIPUS.   Oh never to have come here
With my father's blood upon me! Never
To have been the man they call his mother's
  husband!
Oh accurst! Oh child of evil,
To have entered that wretched bed—
                        the selfsame one!
More primal than sin itself, this fell to me.

CHORAGOS.   I do not know how I can answer
  you.
You were better dead than alive and blind.

OEDIPUS.   Do not counsel me any more. This
  punishment
That I have laid upon myself is just.
If I had eyes,
I do not know how I could bear the sight
Of my father, when I came to the house of
  Death,
Or my mother: for I have sinned against them
  both
So vilely that I could not make my peace
By strangling my own life.
                        Or do you think my children,
Born as they were born, would be sweet to my
  eyes?
Ah never, never! Nor this town with its 150
  high walls,
Nor the holy images of the gods.
                        For I,
Thrice miserable!—Oedipus, noblest of all the
  line
Of Kadmos, have condemned myself to enjoy
These things no more, by my own malediction
Expelling that man whom the gods declared
To be a defilement in the house of Laïos.
After exposing the rankness of my own guilt,
How could I look men frankly in the eyes?
No, I swear it,
If I could have stifled my hearing at its source,
I would have done it and made all this body

A tight cell of misery, blank to light and sound:
So I should have been safe in a dark agony
Beyond all recollection.
                        Ah Kithairon!
Why did you shelter me? When I was cast upon
  you,
Why did I not die? Then I should never
Have shown the world my execrable birth.

Ah Polybos! Corinth, city that I believed
The ancient seat of my ancestors: how fair
I seemed, your child! and all the while this evil
Was cancerous within me!
                        For I am sick
In my daily life, sick in my origin.

O three roads, dark ravine, woodland and way
Where three roads met: you, drinking my
  father's blood,
My own blood, spilled by my own hand: can
  you remember
The unspeakable things I did there, and the
  things
I went on from there to do?
                        O marriage, marriage!
The act that engendered me, and again the act
Performed by the son in the same bed—
                        Ah, the net
Of incest, mingling fathers, brothers, sons, 180
With brides, wives, mothers: the last evil
That can be known by men: no tongue can say
How evil!
                        No. For the love of God, conceal me
Somewhere far from Thebes; or kill me; or hurl
  me
Into the sea, away from men's eyes for ever.

Come, lead me. You need not fear to touch me.
Of all men, I alone can bear this guilt.
                        [Enter CREON

CHORAGOS.   We are not the ones to decide; but
  Creon here
May fitly judge of what you ask. He only
Is left to protect the city in your place. 190

OEDIPUS.   Alas, how can I speak to him? What
  right have I
To beg his courtesy whom I have deeply
  wronged?

CREON.   I have not come to mock you, Oedipus,
Or to reproach you, either.

> [*To* ATTENDANTS:
> —You, standing there:

If you have lost all respect for man's dignity,
At least respect the flame of Lord Helios:
Do not allow this pollution to show itself
Openly here, an affront to the earth
And heaven's rain and the light of day. No,
     take him
Into the house as quickly as you can.   200
For it is proper
That only the close kindred see his grief.

OEDIPUS.   I pray you in God's name, since your
     courtesy
Ignores my dark expectation, visiting
With mercy this man of all men most execrable:
Give me what I ask—for your good, not for
     mine.

CREON.   And what is it that you would have me
     do?

OEDIPUS.   Drive me out of this country as
     quickly as may be
To a place where no human voice can ever greet
     me.

CREON.   I should have done that before now—
     only,   210
God's will had not been wholly revealed to me.

OEDIPUS.   But his command is plain: the par-
     ricide
Must be destroyed. I am that evil man.

CREON.   That is the sense of it, yes; but as
     things are,
We had best discover clearly what is to be done.

OEDIPUS.   You would learn more about a man
     like me?

CREON.   You are ready now to listen to the god.

OEDIPUS.   I will listen. But it is to you
That I must turn for help. I beg you, hear me.

The woman in there—   220
Give her whatever funeral you think proper:
She is your sister.
               —But let me go, Creon!
Let me purge my father's Thebes of the pol-
     lution
Of my living here, and go out to the wild hills,
To Kithairon, that has won such fame with me,
The tomb my mother and father appointed for
     me,
And let me die there, as they willed I should.
And yet I know
Death will not ever come to me through sickness
Or in any natural way: I have been preserved
For some unthinkable fate. But let that be.

As for my sons, you need not care for them.
They are men, they will find some way to live.
But my poor daughters, who have shared my
     table,
Who never before have been parted from their
     father—
Take care of them, Creon; do this for me.
And will you let me touch them with my hands
A last time, and let us weep together?
Be kind, my lord,
Great prince, be kind!   240

               Could I but touch them,
They would be mine again, as when I had my
     eyes.

          [*Enter* ANTIGONE *and* ISMENE, *attended*
Ah, God!
Is it my dearest children I hear weeping?
Has Creon pitied me and sent my daughters?

CREON.   Yes, Oedipus: I knew that they were
     dear to you
In the old days, and know you must love them
     still.

OEDIPUS.   May God bless you for this—and be
     a friendlier
Guardian to you than he has been to me!
Children, where are you?
Come quickly to my hands: they are   250
     your brother's—
Hands that have brought your father's once
     clear eyes
To this way of seeing—
               Ah dearest ones,
I had neither sight nor knowledge then, your
     father
By the woman who was the source of his own
     life!
And I weep for you—having no strength to see
     you—,
I weep for you when I think of the bitterness

That men will visit upon you all your lives.
What homes, what festivals can you attend
Without being forced to depart again in tears?
And when you come to marriageable age,   260
Where is the man, my daughters, who would
    dare
Risk the bane that lies on all my children?
Is there any evil wanting? Your father killed
His father; sowed the womb of her who bore
    him;
Engendered you at the fount of his own exis-
    tence!
That is what they will say of you.

                                  Then, whom
Can you ever marry? There are no bridegrooms
    for you,
And your lives must wither away in sterile
    dreaming.
O Creon, son of Menoikeus!
You are the only father my daughters have,   270
Since we, their parents, are both of us gone for-
    ever.
They are your own blood: you will not let them
Fall into beggary and loneliness;
You will keep them from the miseries that are
    mine!
Take pity on them; see, they are only children,
Friendless except for you. Promise me this,
Great prince, and give me your hand in token
    of it.

                    [CREON *clasps his right hand*
Children:
I could say much, if you could understand me,
But as it is, I have only this prayer for you: 280
Live where you can, be as happy as you can—
Happier, please God, than God has made your
    father!

CREON.   Enough. You have wept enough. Now
    go within.

OEDIPUS.   I must; but it is hard.

CREON.   Time eases all things.

OEDIPUS.   But you must promise—

CREON.   Say what you desire.

OEDIPUS.   Send me from Thebes!

CREON.   God grant that I may!

OEDIPUS.   But since God hates me . . .   290

CREON.   No, he will grant your wish.

OEDIPUS.   You promise?

CREON.   I cannot speak beyond my knowledge.

OEDIPUS.   Then lead me in.

CREON.   Come now, and leave your children.

OEDIPUS.   No! Do not take them from me!

CREON.   Think no longer
That you are in command here, but rather
    think
How, when you were, you served your own de-
    struction.
    [*Exeunt into the house all but the* CHORUS;
    the CHORAGOS *chants directly to the audience*

CHORAGOS.   Men of Thebes: look upon Oedi-
    pus.

This is the king who solved the famous riddle
And towered up, most powerful of men.
No mortal eyes but looked on him with envy,
Yet in the end ruin swept over him.

Let every man in mankind's frailty
Consider his last day; and let none
Presume on his good fortune until he find
Life, at his death, a memory without pain.

READING
AN
ESSAY

In "The Study of Literature," the introduction to this book, the distinguishing and characteristic features of each of the four basic modes of literature are briefly considered. In the following pages, we shall discuss in more detail the nature of each mode, beginning with the essay, and illustrating each discussion by reference to a particular example from this book. Though essays come in a very large variety, certain principles apply to all, and these can be made clear by the analysis of a single example: Walter Lippmann's "The Indispensable Opposition" (p. 177).

SUBJECT AND THESIS

The essential feature of an essay is that it solicits the reader's belief and purports to tell him what he did not already know or did not understand well. It is, in short, not fiction, even if it happens to be false: what counts is its claim to truth. Even if an essay is fanciful, like "The Fable of the Vultures," or comic, like "Shakespeare in the Bush," it must have a point to make, a proposition or cluster of propositions to assert. And this point, whether single or plural, whether explicitly stated or left to the pondering reader to elicit, is the *thesis* of the essay.

Like all literary works, an essay has a

subject (what it is about) and a speaker (who may represent the opinion of the author), and it shows the speaker's *attitude* toward the subject—which includes his opinions or convictions, that is, the beliefs he offers to share with the reader.[1] The subject may be plainly designated by the title, as in "Of Marriage and Single Life," or alluded to figuratively or symbolically, as in "The Price of Amphibians." The substance of the essay is what the speaker has to say about that subject.

Many comparatively simple essays have the form of a *narrative*; they present a piece of biography, like "The Figgerin' of Aunt Wilma," or of history, like "My Furthest-Back Person." Other essays have a *reflective* character: they range from straightforward description, like "The Headlong Wave," through definition and explanation, like "Nature Fights Back," to sustained argument, like "The Moral Equivalent of War." In an argument, the thesis is not merely stated, illustrated, clarified—it is supported by reasons, which are set forth to convince the reader, that is, to produce or strengthen his acceptance of the thesis as true. "The Indispensable Opposition" is an argument.

[1] Words in italics are defined in the Index of Critical Terms.

The thesis of "The Indispensable Opposition" is stated explicitly, and indeed reiterated; and it is a weighty one, since it is presented as a fundamental principle underlying the democratic form of government. In one of its formulations it is argued that freedom to dissent from government policies and majority opinions is essential to the existence of democratic self-government. This thesis is presented, explained, illustrated, and argued for in an essay that is remarkably short, considering the far-reaching significance of what it says. The general shape of the essay, like that of all reflective essays, can be considered from two points of view: it has a *logical structure* and a *rhetorical structure*.

LOGICAL STRUCTURE

The logical structure of an essay consists in the logical relationships among the key propositions it contains. The central structure may be an argument, in which the propositions are connected according to the rules of reasoning in such a way as to support the argument's conclusion. The argument has a logical form: it may be deductive or inductive, or it may combine deductive and inductive reasoning in complex patterns. But even if an essay is not an argument, it may perform other logical operations that give it structure: for example, it may provide a classification of some kind, a definition of some important concept, an explanation of how something works. "The Indispensable Opposition," quite apart from its argument, is partly built on a basic pair of contrasts—one might say, of oppositions that illustrate the importance of opposition. Section I contrasts two ways of justifying the toleration of dissent in a democracy:

A.1 that people have a "right" to say what they please (paragraph 3);
A.2 that the majority benefits from hearing dissenting views, even when they are unwelcome.

Section II contrasts two concepts of freedom of speech:

B.1 that it consists merely in self-expression, whether or not anyone is listening;
B.2 that it consists in engaging in open public debate in which both sides are heard—and also listen.

If the essay had done no more than clarify these two distinctions for us, it would still have a logical structure, and would have had something important to say. But of course in this context the distinctions become part of the argument: the second one serves to clarify the thesis, the first one to clarify the reasoning that supports the thesis. The structure of this argument consists essentially of two steps: Proposition P is true, therefore Q is true, therefore R is true. Or, to put it in reverse order: Why should we tolerate dissent? Because "in a democracy the opposition not only is tolerated as constitutional but must be maintained because it is in fact indispensable" (paragraph 25). Why is it indispensable? Because without it, a government (or dominant majority) cannot obtain adequate "knowledge of forgotten facts, hidden feelings, neglected truths, and practical suggestions" (paragraph 10). This outline gives, of course, only the bare skeleton of the argument, but it is this skeleton that underlies the details in which the argument is worked out.

It is evident that, like all arguments, this one makes certain tacit assumptions: it assumes, for example, without argument, that democratic self-government is desirable. Every argument must start somewhere, with certain premises; its job is, first, to select sound premises and, second, to show us what follows once we accept them. Lippmann's argument can be analyzed, then, as having the basic form of an end-means argument, in which an action or policy is justified as a necessary means to a supposedly desirable end. The first premise is presupposed (hence placed in brackets):

1. [Democratic self-government should be maintained.]
2. Therefore: whatever is required to maintain democratic self-government is to be encouraged.
3. Freedom to dissent is required to maintain democratic self-government.
4. Therefore: freedom to dissent is to be encouraged.

The movement from (1) to (2) invokes a method of ethical reasoning that raises important questions on its own; the three propositions (2), (3), and (4) constitute a deductive argument of the form known as the syllogism.

Once the reader of an essay is alerted to the fact that it is indeed an argument (and the word "because" in the quotation from paragraph 25 is a signal of this), it becomes his task to make sure that he grasps the structure of the argument: its conclusion, its basic premises, and the (alleged) logical connections between them.

KINETIC (RHETORICAL) STRUCTURE

An argument or exposition cannot be presented all at once; it is developed discursively, that is, in a series of sentences. This development consists of thought in motion, so to speak, and the course of the development may have its own noteworthy qualities, like those of a story or drama. An essay may not only interest us intellectually in its argument; it may catch us up in its movement. We feel suspense. We find ourselves anticipating how the argument will move, and we are surprised, disappointed, or pleased as it unfolds, step by step. An argument may have its own quality, which we can savor: its boldness of speculative

leap, its cleverness, subtlety, zest, its tight rigor and air of inevitability as the conclusion is reached. Two arguments that have basically the same logical structure may develop in very different ways: one, perhaps, announcing its conclusion at the start and then carefully building up the reasons to clinch it; the other starting with some casual remarks, gradually picking up power, and only toward the end revealing its unexpected point.

The rhetorical or kinetic structure of an essay is just the pattern of its movement: its direction, its variations of emotional intensity, its modulations of tone, its shifts of emphasis, its rise to a climax, and so on. This structure often marks the distinctive character of a writer's thought and mind. It is the way he tends to dramatize his thinking, and marks his essay as unmistakably the work of, say, Walter Lippmann, Bertrand Russell, Paul Tillich, Hannah Arendt.

In analyzing the rhetorical structure of an essay, we may want to ask such questions as these:

1. How does the discussion open? The first paragraph, even the first sentence, may set the terms of the discussion, establish a relationship between speaker and reader, give away the speaker's assumptions or conceal them (sometimes illegitimately) from the reader. The opening of "The Indispensable Opposition" does a remarkable number of things at once: it announces the thesis, however vaguely; it concedes that this thesis is doubted by most people (so we think of the speaker as himself a dissenter from majority opinion, and sympathize with him for his uphill work); it slips in a definition of "political freedom," which we need as early as possible in the essay; it adopts a calm, judicious, reasoned tone that promises a thoughtful discussion ahead. All this in the first sentence!

2. How does the argument (if there is an argument) proceed? The steps of the argument may be clearly marked and placed in

an orderly progression so that it moves with ineluctable force; or the argument may wander carelessly and lose its way, so that it requires some effort to keep track of, and never reaches a firm conclusion. "The Indispensable Opposition" is carefully composed; its main movements of thought are clearly posted; we sense that it is under the control of a skillful and disciplined thinker. It inspires confidence—but that is also something for the reader to be wary of, for his respect for the speaker must not make him uncritical in accepting what is said.

3. Where is the climax of the argument? An argument may reach a point at which its force is most strongly felt, or there is a sudden sense of illumination. The speaker, though centrally concerned to develop his ideas, may show his feelings, too: his sense of moral indignation at actions he is attacking, or his genuine enthusiasm for the subject he is writing about. "The Indispensable Opposition" moves, on the whole, on an even emotional level; the speaker is clearly concerned about what he is saying, yet he is aiming to be reasonable and to appeal to reason rather than to feeling. However, the allusion to Socrates (paragraph 24) seems to heighten the speaker's involvement, and brings Section II to a kind of climax. At this point the argument is really complete; Section III turns to review what has been said, and to restate it with new emphasis and greater eloquence.

PERSPECTIVE AND STYLE

The basic human relationship projected by an essay—that of the speaker to his ostensible or putative reader—implies more or less clearly a background of ideas and situations within which it unfolds and finds its place. The essay appears at a particular time and place, and what it has to say may have a special relevance to that time and place. Especially if it enters into a continuing dispute of some sort (as a present-day essay might deal with problems about abortion-rights or school busing or Watergate), it can only be fully understood and rightly judged if it is seen in relationship to what has gone before and what is going on in the world around. "The Indispensable Opposition," it is important to note, was first published in 1939. Some of Lippmann's incidental references—to the Italy of Mussolini, the Germany of Hitler, the Russia of Stalin —require that we keep the date in mind. Moreover, the essay appeared on the eve of World War II, which was to prove a very serious test for the survival of Western democracies in their struggle with various forms of totalitarianism. And it is worthwhile to see the essay in this broader setting as well.

But on a higher level, the essay is by no means time-bound. For the thesis is not applied to the contemporary situation alone; it is set forth, and defended, as a timeless, or universal, truth about the necessary conditions of democratic self-government. In this light, the essay may be said to be addressed to an audience far wider than the author's contemporaries—which is why we can read it with profit today, long after it was written. For the author is concerned not with a temporary or passing political problem, but with a perennial one; and if his argument holds, it holds not just for 1939, but for as long as there are, or can be, democracies to understand and sustain.

These considerations have to do with the basic *perspective*, or what may also be called the rhetorical stance, of the essay: what it shows us (mostly implicitly rather than by overt telling) about the speaker–reader relationship. And we can say a good deal more about what kind of speaker is projected here, and what kind of audience he assumes (or hopes to have). The speaker is a thoughtful, literate, political philosopher (at least he is cast in that role here), deeply committed to democracy as a form of government, but concerned that others who are equally committed may not understand its necessary conditions well enough to preserve democracy effectively. He addresses himself to an intelligent, reflective audience that is capable of grasping his distinctions and is open to persuasion by rational argument. He does not preach or harangue, but sits the reader down in another armchair, drawing him into a serious conversation, in which he hopes to bring the reader to realize (or realize more clearly) the importance of permitting, indeed fostering, dissent.

The speaker's attitude toward the situation and toward his reader determines the *tone* of an essay: here a serious, somewhat professorial tone, patient and a bit repetitious. There is no humor, no levity; there is no declamation, scolding, patronizing, cajoling. Tone is largely conveyed by *style*. It is a distinctive style that marks the first-rate essayist such as Bacon or Thoreau; for the details of syntax, diction, sentence rhythm, turn of phrase express his individual outlook on the world and on whatever may be the specific subject of a particular essay. The style of "The Indispensable Opposition" is marked by rather elaborate, carefully constructed sentences, in which the balance and opposition of ideas (reflecting, so to speak, in the very texture of the essay the central theme of political balance and opposition) is frequently brought out by syntax:

> . . . it would be difficult to say whether we are tolerant because we are magnanimous or because we are lazy, because we have strong principles or because we lack serious conviction (paragraph 5).

> . . . not that it is a system for the tolerating of error, but that it is a system for finding the truth (paragraph 9).

The measured movement of the sentences reflects the speaker's serious concern; his syntactic structures reflect his continuous effort to be judicious, to take other opinions into account, to avoid one-sidedness.

EVALUATION

The question of value remains to be discussed. There are many qualities that may help to make an essay a good one; only a few of the most important ones can be noted here. When we are judging an essay, we must ask various questions about it. Some of these are internal to the essay itself: they are answered by studying the essay and the relationships among its various features. Three of these internal questions are particularly important:

1. Is the essay clear? That is, is the thesis clearly discernible; are the reasons marked as such; are the logical connections indicated? No essay whose thesis is ambiguous or vague can be very well written. "The Indispensable Opposition" states (and restates) its thesis so that no attentive reader can be in doubt about what the thesis is; and the reasons supporting it are set forth in an orderly way.

2. Is the argument cogent? We must be alert for digressions from the argument, for inconsistencies, for unfair methods of persuasion, for logical weaknesses and fallacies. As far as the main line of Lippmann's argument is concerned, it seems quite sound; the premises do give support to the conclusion —though we might, of course, wish to question the premises themselves. There is one argument from analogy (paragraph 6) that might strike a reader as shaky: that in which the government's (or majority's) allowing dissent is likened to a person's going to the doctor to find out what's wrong with him. Lippmann suggests that one who publicly defends an unpopular cause—such as complete amnesty for those who refused to participate in the Vietnam war, or the abolition of censorship or of prisons—performs a service very like that of the doctor who gives

us the unpleasant diagnosis that we have ulcers and must cut out hoagies and beer. But one might argue in reply that the doctor is after all an expert in medicine, whereas the supporter of amnesty may be no more of an expert on amnesty than those he disagrees with. If this difference is crucial, the analogy is weakened, and so is the argument. The issue is complex, of course, and cannot be settled here—but it will serve as an example of how a dispute over the cogency of an essay can arise.

3. Is the essay unified as a total experience? Sometimes the rhetorical structure of an essay works at cross-purposes to the logical structure: as when the writer has an implausible thesis which he tosses at the reader before preparing him to understand it. The style is sometimes incongruous with the subject or thesis—imagine "The Indispensable Opposition" rewritten in a flippant, wisecracking tone, despite the seriousness of the matters it deals with. In this essay, there is a fine fitness of tone and topic, of rhetorical structure and rhetorical stance, of style and thesis.

An essay, in short, may do more than merely present a thesis or construct an argument—and it must do more, if it is to be considered a work of literature. It may, as it were, enact its argument, giving it dramatic shape, placing it in a human context, convey the emotions of the logical chase, the excitement of discovery, the agony of doubting, the joy of learning. Such essays include qualities that are enjoyable for their own sakes: wit, passion, pathos, ingenuity, force. Thus they become works of art which, unlike a typical report or memorandum or scholarly footnote, can do more than inform and convince: they can afford an experience that is at once complex and unified and intensely human. When we can say this of an essay, we may be sure that it is literature.

Beyond these internal matters are external questions that must be asked, in the end, of a reflective essay. We shall want to consider how seriously to take it as a piece of argument or exposition. If it gives us truth, how important is that truth in relation to what we already know or reasonably believe? Even if the thesis turns out to be false, the essay may still be interesting and valuable to us, for it may give us insight into the point of view of someone with whom we disagree (as Lippmann says dissent does, even when it is mistaken); and it may contain important information, even if the conclusions drawn from that information do not really follow. An essay that is profoundly in error may challenge some of our deepest preconceptions, and make us re-examine them—as Socrates sometimes made people re-examine their beliefs by arguing for views they knew were untrue but found hard to refute.

Surely "The Indispensable Opposition" is quite successful in these ways, at least; many readers will also see in it the expression and defense of a fundamental political truth. Of course so short an essay could hardly be expected to give a complete and conclusive proof of its thesis. If it shows that its thesis is important and reasonable, that may be the most it can accomplish. From that point on, the thesis belongs to the reader to think about and put to his own tests. When we read "The Indispensable Opposition" today we may think of contemporary conflicts—such as government threats against newspapers that publish materials the government wishes to keep secret or attempts by student groups to prevent a scientist from giving a lecture because he claims to have evidence of connections between I. Q. and race. How would Lippmann's central principle of political freedom apply to these cases? We must decide for ourselves whether that principle is still valid, and, if so, what it teaches us about the rights and wrongs of these difficult and vital problems.

READING
A
STORY

In "Reading an Essay" we saw that all essays, whether reflective or narrative, have this characteristic: They are composed of statements purporting to be true or valid, and the reader's estimate of the worth of an essay depends greatly on whether or not he can accept its claim to be believed, in this rudimentary sense. Essays thus differ from the other modes of literature. Short stories, novels, plays, and poems are fictions; they cannot be truthful in the way that essays are, for their actions, characters, and other elements are invented. Although the writer of a fiction may closely model his actions and characters on events and persons supplied by his memory or by history, he recombines and reshapes these materials, and so, to this extent at least, the actions and characters in his work are his inventions. Therefore, what he offers his reader is not an account of actuality but an imaginative experience. The ultimate test of a fiction is not whether it is true but whether it is moving, in a valid and enduring way.

It may be clearer that plays and poems are inventions, or artifices, than that prose fictions are, because short stories and novels are written to resemble news reports, biographies, memoirs, and other varieties of narrative essays. The writer and the reader agree to pretend for a while that these fic-

tions are accounts of actual occurrences; and it is perfectly proper, on first reading a story, to be mainly intent on what happens in it. Prose fiction is, above all else, a representation of human actions. Typically its people walk, run, ride, play, work, fight, make love —in short, engage in the multifarious activities that involve movement of the human body. The characters in fiction may also, and regularly do, speak and think and fall into reveries, but the main business of stories and novels is to depict action—that is, human beings in motion.

This concern with action explains why stories and novels are the most popular forms of fiction, for many readers say that they read fictions simply to find out what happens in them. But since that can normally be done in a single reading, such readers miss the heightened pleasure obtainable from rereading a story that only gradually reveals the fullness of its meaning. Students of fiction have devised a number of terms for its important elements, and knowing these terms greatly assists our efforts to understand a fictional work in its entirety. Some of these terms—for example, *plot* and *character*—are probably old acquaintances; others may be less familiar. Since all of them become more understandable when they are defined with the help of concrete illustrations, let us discuss them in respect to Robert Penn Warren's story "Blackberry Winter," page 27.

As "The Study of Literature" points out, prose fiction is told for the most part in the past tense, as though its events were already concluded. The narrator has apparently lived through these events; he knows their outcome and seems to have brooded over it in an effort to find its meaning. Fiction is make-believe history, but the imagined events constitute only one of its elements. Like all other literary works, a story consists of a *speaker* and a *situation* toward which the speaker reveals an *attitude*. While the events are normally the most important component of the situation, the attitude of the speaker is at least as important as they are. To say that a story is an artifice means that all its elements have been arranged to elicit a continuous flow of feelings and judgments from its readers. Thus, in our total impression of it, the events may be subordinate to their appraisal or interpretation. A story is like an essay in this respect.

But one of the ways in which stories differ from essays is that some of them purport to be told by one of their characters. The narrator or speaker in "Blackberry Winter" is not Robert Penn Warren but a forty-four-year-old man named Seth. The actions that he recalls are rather trifling: His mother hires a tramp to bury some drowned chickens; he sees a dead cow in a flooded creek; a woman slaps her child; and so on. But these impressions combine to produce the situation, which is the world of Seth's childhood with its precarious stability and threatened destruction—a situation that has immense importance for him. His attitude combines affection for that vanished world with grief at its passing, and the narrative method being *dramatic*—that is, the story pretends that one of its characters narrates it—helps to set attitude above action in significance.

In distinguishing the elements of a story we must keep two warnings in mind: First, the short story is such a varied form that not all our terms will apply equally well to every story. Second, the separation of a story into its elements, though useful for analysis, is an artificial process. They cannot in reality be separated, for each of them derives its existence from its relationship to the others. Action creates character, for instance, and is mainly determined by character. The elements of a successful story, like those of any other work of art, compose an organic unity that makes the reading of it a single, harmonious experience.

PLOT AND SCENE

Plot is conventionally defined as the chain of events that make up a fiction. What links these events is that they are brought into being by a character forming or revealing a purpose, as in "Blackberry Winter" Seth purposes to walk barefoot to the creek. Human purposes regularly encounter obstacles, just as Seth's purpose does; the complications of the plot consist of these encounters; and the plot concludes when the main character's purpose has either succeeded or failed irretrievably. In a story emphasizing plot the events are always connected in this way. But the metaphor of a chain suggests a linking of each event to the next, which is not found in all stories. In "Blackberry Winter," if Seth had worn his shoes he would not have gone into Dellie's cabin—these events are linked as cause and effect; but the arrival of the tramp is not caused by the flood or any other event, nor does it produce the events at the creek or those in the cabin and the barn. It is a coincidence like those that we encounter in real life. By complicating the other events of the day, it sharpens their meaning; but the breakup of Seth's world would occur just the same if no stranger had entered it. The two sets of happenings harmonize to suggest the theme of the story; they are not otherwise chained together. The term *plot*, however, usefully describes that part of the situation that consists of events connected by their relationship to the purposes revealed by the characters.

Although a short story may be physically divided into parts as a book is divided into chapters, most stories are told in unbroken sequence. But they rely on two different methods of telling, which frequently alternate and form a pattern in the narrative. One of these is the summarizing of the action, wholly in the past tense; the other is the presentation of action by means of *scenes*. In a scene, the action is described concretely, not summarized; it is presented in sharp focus, with enough detail to suggest the way in which an event actually happens, and a scene normally includes *dialogue*, or conversation in the form that real talk has when we hear it. The effect of a scene is to dramatize that part of the action and thus give it particular emphasis. A story consists of its scenes together with the narrative summary needed to connect them. "Blackberry Winter" begins with a scene of a boy standing before a fireplace, arguing with his mother about going barefoot. The scene ends as he sees a tramp appear from the woods. Then follows a scene in the kitchen, as the boy and his mother discuss the meaning of what has just happened. Thus the narrative is developed step by step. As these examples suggest, the first stage in analyzing a short story is to distinguish its different scenes, for they are the units out of which the situation is developed.

PROGRESSION AND CONFLICT

A story may of course include as many events as the writer wishes, whether they are caused by previous events or not. But the writer is restrained by two expectations on the part of the reader: one, that the events shall be related to the other elements of the story, as the actions of the tramp and of Dellie, though neither knows of the other's existence, are related to the theme. Second, the reader expects that each event shall contribute to the story's *progression:* the sense that it is moving steadily forward, without undue repetition of effect, and approaching its conclusion. The need for progression results from the fact that any good narrative creates suspense: doubt and curiosity as to its outcome. Its development causes questions to arise in our minds; and, though suspense is one of its most enjoyable qualities, we paradoxically wish to arrive at the answers to these questions so that the suspense will be ended.

What sort of questions should the development of the narrative produce? They are those that arise from its contrasts and *conflicts*. A contrast is a difference made striking by its presence in the same or similar persons or things or ideas; conflict results when a character's purpose encounters opposition. The arrival of the tramp in "Blackberry Winter" creates suspense simply because he is a stranger. The first of the many conflicts in which he is involved occurs when the dogs try to prevent him from approaching the house. This conflict is based upon the contrast that precedes it. Later on, the conflict of the tramp and Seth's father is underscored by the contrast between their shoes. As these examples show, the related elements of contrast and conflict give rise to the suspense that accompanies the progression of the story to its conclusion.

Not all of the conflicts in a story are marked by such tension as these, nor do they contribute so richly to the meaning of the story. The argument between Seth and his mother, though it helps to establish both the setting and the theme, has little effect on the action that follows. It is but a slightly humorous incident of a happy, somewhat idealized childhood. The conflict of the tramp and Seth's father, on the other hand, is full of danger and causes anxiety about its outcome. When a conflict having great significance to the plot comes to a head, that point in the plot is called a *climax*. Obviously, a story may have more than one climax: the tramp's yielding before Seth's father is one, and his threatening Seth at the end of the story is another.

CHARACTERS

Characters are at least as vital a part of the situation as the plot is; the reader is interested not only in what happens, but in the sort of persons to whom it happens. The persons in a story may be characterized by assertion as well as by action. That is, the writer may tell us what sort of persons they are as well as cause them to reveal themselves by what they do. But it is to be noted that assertions have little force unless supported by action. When Seth tells us that his mother "was clear and brisk about everything she did," her insistence on his wearing shoes has prepared for this assertion, and her behavior to the tramp clinches the truth of it. In contrast, the character of the father is made known entirely by his actions. The reader should distinguish between these ways of depicting character, for nothing strengthens or weakens the credibility of a story more than the degree of congruity between what the characters do and what the writer asserts about their personalities. At such points, the inseparability of plot and character is most clearly seen.

Many longer works of fiction—novels and plays—depict the evolution of character: Othello, for instance, is transformed from the lover of Desdemona to her destroyer. To trace such a development requires space, however; and as a rule, the characters of a short story are static. The impression they make on the reader may be and often is complex, but it tends to be constant. The characters may also be partially revealed, and rightly so: if Seth's childhood seems somewhat idealized, it is because his parents are shown as entirely admirable, without any of the weaknesses that are found in real persons. But a worshipful attitude toward his parents is quite credible in a boy of nine —or for that matter in an adult whose parents have died young. This sort of characterization is in keeping with the restricted point of view of the story.

SETTING AND SYMBOLS

The farmyard, the bank of the creek, Dellie's cabin, and the driveway are the places where the most important events of "Blackberry Winter" occur, but its setting is more than the sum of these places. It comprises the chilly June day, the flooded creek, the ruined fields—and beyond these tangible elements, it is rural Tennessee in the year 1910, with all that this can imply about farm wages, the relation of whites and Negroes, the consequences of a crop failure, and so on. *Setting*, in short, means whatever encompasses the plot and characters: not only the physical environment, but also customs, laws, and other conditions of life so far as these are present in the story. The short story, having come to maturity in comparatively recent times, mirrors the modern interest in the way these conditions influence character. Thus the setting may receive as much attention as the characters themselves, and many stories—"Blackberry Winter," for example—stress the importance of their settings by deriving their titles from them.

Closely related to the setting and equally worthy of attention are the objects to which the action gives prominence. In a carefully constructed story like "Blackberry Winter," such objects as the knife carried by the tramp and the dead cow floating down the creek play a vital part in establishing impressions and meanings. The knife, drawn against the dogs, characterizes the tramp once and for all as ugly and menacing. The grotesque description of the cow's body impresses upon us the havoc wrought by the unseasonable weather, which symbolizes the forces of change that are at the heart of the story's theme. As this example shows, the most conspicuous objects in a story tend to become *symbols* of its deepest meaning. A symbol is a tangible thing or event that brings to mind an abstract force or entity not otherwise associated with it. The reflections on Time in the fourth paragraph, together with the final summary of Seth's later life, expand the meaning of the flood and the objects associated with it. Because these other passages in the story endow the objects with a generalized significance, we call the objects symbols; they symbolize the forces of change that sweep away the ordered world of Seth's childhood. Thus the objects made prominent in fiction regularly have richer significance than most of the things by which we are surrounded in real life. The reader must be alert for their meanings, and the writer, too, has a special obligation toward them. The great Russian short-story writer, Anton Chekov, observed that if a gun is hanging on the wall in the first part of a story, it must be fired or otherwise used before the story ends.

POINT OF VIEW

As plot, characters, and setting make up the subject of the story, so other aspects of it—point of view, attitude, tone—are related to the narrator. Fiction would have little value if it merely presented a subject; its value arises from ordering and interpreting the experience that it creates. The writer begins to impose order on his material as soon as he decides on the *point of view* from which the story shall be told. "Blackberry Winter" exemplifies the most restricted possible point of view, that of a narrator who is also a character. In such stories, the reader can learn only what the narrator knows and reveals; "Blackberry Winter," for instance, leaves the tramp's past and his future almost blank. And although the narrator may be the most important character, it is hard to characterize him clearly, should that be necessary. We learn nothing of Seth's appearance, and his stubbornness and curiosity are traits of almost any little boy.

It may be wondered why the writer should invite such restrictions, when other points of view are at his command. He may, while restricting himself to what is experienced by one character, tell the story from outside that character, so that the character can be individualized as much as any other. Or the point of view may be external to all the characters, which is the way that we see incidents in real life that do not involve ourselves. Or the narrator may be "omniscient" (all-knowing), so that he passes at will from presenting the characters externally to revealing their inner lives.

In the face of these other possibilities, the point of view of the first-person narrator is one of the most common. It has the immediacy of the "eyewitness account," and its very limitations may be advantages. As we saw in discussing the characters of "Blackberry Winter," the point of view justifies the apparent perfection of Seth's parents, which is closely related to the theme. The lack of information about the tramp and Seth makes their encounter readily universalized, as it is in the last sentence of the story. Since the point of view helps to determine the form and therefore the meaning of the story, the choice depends upon the nature of the subject and the attitude that is to be implied toward it.

ATTITUDE AND TONE

We have seen that a literary work that merely presented a situation, without making an evaluation of it, would have little point, though the evaluation may be and regularly is implied rather than expressed. It would, in fact, be impossible for the writer to exclude all values from his presentation, for each of its events and characters would arouse feelings in the reader, much as the actions and words of the persons we meet in real life cause us to feel one way or another about them. The artistry of a story, however, consists in so arranging the situation that a rational, unified *attitude* toward it is implied.

To say that the speaker's attitude must be a rational one means that his feelings should be understandable—that is, adequately motivated by the circumstances given in the story. At the same time, however, circumstances may not be so manipulated that they outrage our sense of fact; otherwise we should condemn the story as sentimental. "Blackberry Winter" expresses Seth's affection for the rural world of his childhood, but it does so without suppressing the hard facts of farm life: the flood will cause many of the farmers to be hungry by Christmas, and Seth's father dies from an accident involving a mowing machine. The speaker does not falsify his subject; his feelings are firmly grounded in things as they are. And his attitude is not only rational but unified: it combines affection for his childhood world with regret for its passing, and these feelings are, of course, consistent with one another.

Identifying the attitude implicit in a story makes it necessary to discuss the speaker's *tone*. When we hear words spoken in a special manner, we can usually identify the attitude that lies behind them. But it can be easily shown that printed words may have a tone as well as spoken ones. Consider the following sentence from "Blackberry Winter": "He glared at me for an instant out of the bloodshot eyes, then demanded in a low, harsh voice, 'What you looking at?'" If we were reading this sentence aloud, we should know approximately how to pronounce the question even if the phrase "in a low, harsh voice" had not been included. The preceding words, with their strong sug-

gestion of the tramp's hostility, determine the tone of his question. Suppose the sentence had begun, "He glanced at me briefly, then asked. . . ." Its tone would then be neutral, expressive of no attitude, and we should not be sure how to read the question aloud.

Tone, then, results from the choice and arrangement of words—from their very rhythm. It is thus a function of the writer's style, as the style is made to express the attitude of the speaker toward the subject. The last sentence of "Blackberry Winter"—"But I did follow him, all the years"—affords two examples of the connection between tone and style. First, the choice of the country phrase "all the years" recalls the speaker's attachment to his childhood. Second, the statement that Seth has followed the tramp is not literally true. It is a *metaphor*, expressive of Seth's regret for the rootless life that has been his as a result of the changes that Time has brought. Because metaphors and other *figures of speech* almost always convey sharp feelings, they often provide the key to the speaker's attitude.

THEME

Such experiences as passing from childhood to maturity are common to most human beings, and so a work in which a particular character undergoes one of these recurrent experiences strikes us as having a point or meaning larger than the specific situation presented in the work. This kind of "universal" meaning, arising from the interaction of the different elements in the work, is called its *theme*. It strikes us as latent in the situation, not bluntly stated but implied by the narrative elements in organic combination. Since the theme grows out of these elements, we have already referred to the theme of "Blackberry Winter" in discussing its plot, characters, and settings. It is a story about the destruction of the world of childhood by the forces of change, which Seth recognizes as he grows to maturity. As the abstract form of this statement shows, the meaning of the story is not confined to Seth; it touches on the common experience of mankind. A great many readers, therefore, will find analogies between their own experience and that of Seth, even if they regard their childhoods with feelings different from his. Some persons are driven by circumstances into environments different in kind from the ones in which they grew up; others, although remaining where they were born, encounter such changes there and in themselves that they feel as lost as though they had left their native places forever. Both groups of readers will, as the saying is, see in the story something of themselves.

Theme has been discussed last because themes emerge from the interrelationships among the concrete elements of the work. But this does not mean that the quality of a work depends upon the novelty of its theme.

As the example of "Blackberry Winter" suggests, many a successful story rings variations on a familiar theme. The value of the story may be to remind the reader powerfully of a universal truth. Its power derives not from its theme alone, however, but from the organic development of the theme by means of all the other elements. Our judgment is not to be determined by the universality of the theme either, yet the pleasure of reading stories results partly from the recognition of likenesses between the experiences of their characters and our own experience of reality. Stating the theme helps us to decide whether or not the story accords with what we know of life.

READING
A
PLAY

Since both plays and stories are representations of human action, in a broad sense, plays are made up of the same basic elements: plot, character, setting, and theme. Likewise, many of the terms introduced in the discussion of "Blackberry Winter"—*exposition, conflict, climax,* and the others—can usefully be applied to plays. But stories and plays also differ from each other in fundamental ways, and these differences make it necessary to give attention to the special characteristics of drama.

In the first place, we cannot say that the presentation of action, in the strictest sense of men moving and doing things, dominates a play as it does a story or a novel. What a play represents, characteristically, is men and women talking. A dramatic work having dialogue and no action would still be a play, but a work that had action and no dialogue would be called not a play but a pantomime. The characters mainly talk, of course, about their actions—past, present, and especially those to come. But since a theater of any kind is physically limited, plays cannot present great numbers of actions as stories and novels can. In *Oedipus the King,* for instance, we are told that one character hangs herself and another puts out his eyes, but we do not witness these actions. Plays of the modern theater—modern in the broad sense, from Shakespeare's time to our own—directly present much more action than ancient Greek plays did, and Bertolt Brecht's *Life of Galileo* is unusually "active" even for a contemporary play. Yet its audience only hears of Galileo's trial and recantation; it does not witness them. Like Shakespeare, Brecht expects you to

Think when we talk of horses that you see them
Printing their proud hoofs i' the receiving earth.

It follows that the acid test of a playwright is his skill with language, his ability to provide the actors with lines that are eloquent and stirring. It follows too that when reading a play we must in imagination hear the dialogue spoken, with all the force and expressiveness that trained actors can bring to it.

Most plays, then, though written to be staged, can be read with the same profit and pleasure that novels and biographies afford. Plays belong to the reader as well as to the audience. Those by Shakespeare, for instance, are read by many more people than ever see them performed; and modern playwrights—Bernard Shaw, Eugene O'Neill, Bertolt Brecht—often prepare special texts of their works for the reader. The text of

Galileo in this book is a reading text, as is shown by the title given each scene and the bits of doggerel rhyme that introduce most of them. When an experienced reader enjoys a play in his armchair, he makes himself into an imaginary audience and acts out the play in his mind, visualizing it on a stage as though he were present in a theater where it was being produced. The reading text is designed to help him to do this. The differences between it and the acting text are not shown in dialogue but in the stage directions, which describe the appearance of the stage in detail, and indicate the way in which many of the characters' words should be spoken. The text of *Galileo* affords examples of both these aids to the reader's imagination. After one has read a few plays, it becomes almost automatic to visualize them on the stage of one's mind.

A second distinguishing trait of drama is that normally a play has no narrator. The *speaker*, in the technical sense of the creator of the *situation*, remains hidden. We must therefore ask how we can know what we are expected to feel, what judgments we are being asked to make—what, in short, the speaker's *attitude* is toward the action and the characters. The characters often comment on each other and on themselves, but since these comments are *dramatic* (not proceeding from the author) they are not necessarily trustworthy. When characters disagree, and those in plays do continually disagree, which one, if either or any, is supposed to be right?

These questions are related, we shall see, to a third essential characteristic of drama: the perspective in which the playwright presents his action. Whereas stories are narrated predominantly in the past tense, the action of a play occurs in the present; past action has only secondary importance, for our attention is fixed on what is happening *now*, and on the future as it becomes the present. Yet some knowledge of earlier events must be given. The playwright may not in his own person provide a summary of past action nor of happenings that are supposed to connect the incidents of the present, any more than he can himself tell us what sort of persons his characters are. We are made to know them almost entirely by what they say, what they do, and what other characters say about them.

We have now distinguished three characteristics that differentiate drama from prose fiction: A play primarily shows us characters talking rather than doing; second, since no narrator is present to express his attitudes, we must guess how we are expected to feel about the situation and how we are to judge it; and third, dramatic action appears to take place in the present, not the past. A play thus makes more demands upon one's attention than a comparable story does, and the reader of a play, if he is to respond appropriately, must imagine it in production. And this imaginative creation of the play as it would be produced on a stage is assisted by all that the reader knows about the elements of dramatic technique.

ACTS AND SCENES

Nearly all modern plays, those of the past four centuries, are divided into acts; these are the major divisions, corresponding to the chapters of a book. The acts may be subdivided into scenes. Shakespeare's plays are made up of many short scenes; a century later the scenes of each play were grouped into five acts, as was the custom then and long afterward. Most recent plays have three acts, sometimes subdivided, with the action restricted to one, two, or three places; but *Galileo* is Shakespearean in its freedom of movement, which gives it no fewer than fifteen scenes. The division into acts and scenes emphasizes the structure of the play, enhancing its sense of development, its dramatic rhythm. The divisions are also convenient because, whenever the place represented by the stage is changed, or more time is supposed to pass than that taken up by the action, the action must of course be suspended—usually by lowering the curtain. A division may or may not be followed by the representation of a new place; it nearly always means a lapse of time.

The term *scene*, however, is also applied, much as it is in discussing a story, to the unit of action marked off by the coming-in or going-out of an important character, even when the action is not otherwise interrupted. Thus we should say that Scene 1 of *Galileo* begins with a scene between Galileo and Andrea, followed by a scene with Andrea's mother and other scenes with Ludovico and the Procurator. Each of these has its own point to make about the leading character: his scientific genius, his optimism about the acceptance of his discoveries, his poverty and love of creature comforts, and the threat of opposition to his ideas. By this time nearly all of the leading concerns of the play have been established. In any play the succession of scenes, in this second meaning of the term, marks the progress of the action. Hence it deserves the same close attention that we give to the successive scenes of a story.

ACTION AND PROPERTIES

The people who attend a production of a play are its hearers, etymologically speaking —its *audience*; and, as we have seen, the most important part of a play is its dialogue. But the hearers are also appropriately called the spectators, for a good playwright addresses the eyes of the audience as well as their ears. The plays of our theatrical tradition, going back to medieval times, find means of supporting and accentuating their dialogue with action directly presented on the stage. The action of a modern (post-medieval) play, although necessarily more restricted than that of a story or a film, is no less essential to the total impression. And yet the action need not be violent: Andrea's rubbing Galileo's back is as much an action as Andrea's scuffle with Cosmo—and it has more significance, suggesting as it does the human, earthy side of Galileo's character.

Closely connected with the action are the *properties*, the tangible objects that the characters use in the course of it. Properties are distinct from the scenery, costumes, and furniture, though these also perform important parts in the visual impact of the play; properties are things small enough to be moved about, and frequently attention is drawn to them—and their significance emphasized—by the actors' moving them here and there. Like the objects that are named and discussed in stories and poems, stage properties are inclined to take on the multiple meanings of *symbols*. Scene 1 of *Galileo* is particularly rich in properties: Galileo's breakfast, his models of the solar system, the apple and other objects with which he demonstrates the motions of the heavenly bodies, the lenses that he fashions into a telescope. Clearly the presence of these properties does more than merely keep the actors busy; their significance lies in helping to unfold the complexity of Galileo's character as Brecht conceives it. Galileo's mind is both practical and theoretical; he is equally gifted at producing inventions having immediate usefulness, and at making discoveries involving the most abstract conceptions. He can explain his abstruse observations so that a boy of ten can understand them, and he is withal a recognizable human being, devoted to bodily pleasures and (later) fearful of bodily torture. The presence of the properties on the stage, where at the proper time each becomes the focus of the audience's eyes, is vital to their success in conveying these meanings.

EXPOSITION

Because of the physical limitations of the stage, a play must establish many of the circumstances of its story by indirect means. We need information about the characters' supposed lives before the action begins, and usually about what is supposedly happening outside the action and in the intervals of the action. The process of imparting such information to the reader or audience is called *exposition*. The narrator of a story attends to his exposition largely by speaking directly to the reader. In a play the exposition must be smuggled in as an inconspicuous part of the dialogue. The situation at the beginning of *Galileo* is quickly established: Galileo is an underpaid professor who stands on the brink of great discoveries, which he knows will mark the opening of a new scientific age. This information is conveyed chiefly through Galileo's teacher–pupil relationship with Andrea; it seems plausible that Galileo should impart his knowledge, both of current beliefs about the heavens and of the truth about them, to the boy whom he is training as his disciple. But of course the audience is equally the target of his discourses. Brecht's ability to convey such necessary information, much of it already well known to the characters involved, is demonstrated in other scenes as well: the skepticism of the Florentine scholars, for instance, or the particulars of the plague, or the treatment of Galileo by the Vatican. The skill of a playwright may often be judged by the way he manages his exposition without appearing to be intent upon it.

PLOT

As the play begins and the necessary exposition is being supplied, the playwright must at the same time set his narrative in motion, developing simultaneously its interdependent parts: plot, characters, and setting. Although these may seem identical with the corresponding parts of a story, the fact that drama presents its actions in present time makes necessary some special considerations of them as they figure in plays.

For several reasons, a noticeable amount of artifice enters into the plot of a play. Except where Destiny takes a hand, which rarely happens in modern plays, the plot must proceed from the purposes and decisions of the characters, and these must appear to be motivated with a clarity seldom found in life. Second, the evolution of the plot proceeds with preternatural rapidity: for example, in the middle of Scene 1 Galileo first hears of a telescope, and by the end of it (twenty minutes later?) he has procured the necessary materials and constructed one, by which Andrea reads the letters on the campanile. Third, the *resolution* occurs with a clear-cut decisiveness that is likewise seldom matched by reality. Prose fiction, presenting as it does a summation of events that supposedly have already occurred, approaches nearer to the often leisurely development of events in reality. In a play the dramatization of present action must proceed with dispatch if the attention of the audience is to be held. During almost every scene more time seems to elapse than really does elapse. None of these departures from realism are to be regarded as faults, however; they are the very breath of life to a play.

CHARACTERS

The interdependence of plot and characters is even more apparent in a play than in a story. As the events of a play proceed from the characters' purposes and decisions, so its characters are established by what they say and do. There is no one to *tell* us that Galileo is a commanding figure, a towering genius, but we readily infer it from his manner with Sarti, Ludovico, and the Procurator, and especially from his long speech on the new scientific age. The Procurator in effect labels Galileo a trickster, but we already know from the action how he has profited from his plagiarism of the telescope. Dramatic characterizations thus depend less upon assertion than upon action and speech. As a result, plays seldom attempt to present more than half a dozen important characters, and these are individualized by two or three striking traits at most. Galileo's character is exceptionally rich and complicated, as we have seen, and he dominates the play, for he is surrounded by other characters of exceptional simplicity. Few of them can be distinguished from one another, and none is endowed with more than a single characteristic or so. Although the genius of Shakespeare made possible a greater range of characterization, the playwright must as a rule content himself with fewer and more simply drawn characters than those of the novelist.

SETTING

Many playwrights, in their reading texts at least, provide detailed descriptions of the rooms and other places in which their scenes are to be enacted. Brecht's stage directions of this kind are even sketchier than those that Sophocles' translators have provided for the setting of *Oedipus the King*. This brevity, probably reflecting Brecht's recognition of the difficulties created by a play of fifteen scenes, nearly all with different settings, should not mislead us into supposing that the settings are unimportant. They contribute just as the properties do to the total meaning of the play. *Galileo* is a work dealing with the conflict between powerful authority and the lonely individual, and its settings underscore that conflict. Galileo's study is "modest," as befits an impoverished professor, and his other habitations stand in equal contrast to such edifices of the rich and powerful as the Grand

Duke's palace and Cardinal Bellarmine's residence in Rome. The reader must exercise his imagination to realize this contrast as vividly as he can.

The term *setting* may also be used in the broader, less tangible sense of the world that surrounds the characters: in *Galileo*, the world of late-Renaissance Italy, dominated by the Church and religious belief, but stirred by the excitement of new discoveries and the shocks they have given to the foundations on which the Church is built. It is an authoritarian world, a world of poverty and plague, but also one in which discoveries and inventions spread rapidly from country to country. The setting of the play is not only the physical surroundings of the action but also the mercantile, political, and economic conditions of the time, the beliefs and preconceptions of the people, their general ways of thinking and feeling. Brecht seems to be saying that only in this particular setting, this milieu, can the career of Galileo be imagined.

CONFLICT

When the purposes of two or more characters are opposed, or a character's purposes collide with some impersonal force such as war or Destiny, the result is *conflict*, the tension existing between a purpose and an obstacle to its fulfillment. Conflict is so peculiarly characteristic of the drama that we often praise stories and other literary works for being dramatic when we mean that they are based on conflicts that are strong and interesting. Bernard Shaw, in one of his prefaces, points out that "every drama is the artistic presentation of a conflict. The end may be reconciliation or destruction, or, as in life itself, there may be no end; but the conflict is indispensable: no conflict, no drama." In a well-constructed play, the arrival on the stage of each new character supplies a new element in the conflict, so that the action of the play is advanced and developed in every scene. Reading a play with thorough understanding means not only awareness of the dominant conflict and its outcome, by which the major themes of the work are expressed, but awareness also of the slight tensions between the characters by which a playwright as skillful as Brecht maintains the interest of his audience continuously. Surely no reader of *Galileo* could overlook the clash between Galileo and the Church authorities, but one should also consider such minor effects as the dialogue between Galileo and Andrea at the play's beginning. Andrea is intent upon their debts while Galileo is intent upon geometry, and even this is a situation of conflict, for the characters are at cross-purposes.

What are the reasons underlying the law formulated in Shaw's words, "No conflict, no drama"? The answer to this question is first of all a technical one. Conflict produces what is known as an *unstable situation:* the action cannot rest where it is, for the tension felt by the characters concerned leads on to further action as they struggle to gain the upper hand. But in addition to this structural function, the omnipresence of conflict in the drama reflects its inner meaning, the particular interpretation of life with which drama is concerned. For a play, even one so overshadowed by Destiny as the *Oedipus* of Sophocles, portrays life as the action of characters who possess at least the illusion that their wills are free. Having purposes, they make decisions—or believe they make them —in order to realize their purposes, and their decisions inevitably bring them into collision with the purposes and decisions of others. Situations of conflict impel the characters, like real persons, toward a loss of control. They tend to drop their masks, to disclose the realities of their being, much more than when they are calm and collected. The conflicts in the play thus enable the playwright to reveal the human values that he thinks are admirable or detestable,

secure or fragile, and likely to be victorious or doomed in the long run.

ATTITUDES

A play, as we have seen, invites a continuous flow of judgments and *attitudes* from its audience or reader, exactly as a story does. But unlike a story, a play must indicate wholly by implication what judgments it demands, and its success will depend upon the ability of its situation to evoke these judgments. If the play succeeds in doing this, the reader will find it moving and rewarding. If it fails, he will condemn it for the incoherence it has produced in his feelings.

How, then, in the absence of a narrator, does a play indicate what judgments of its actions and characters are appropriate? Without pretending to completeness, we may discern several principles that operate sometimes alone, sometimes in combination.

In establishing the heroic quality of its main character, *Galileo* of course makes its chief appeal to our instinct for truth and reason. Most people believe, or think they believe, that things should be seen as they in fact are, and the play at once establishes Galileo as the proponent of views that the modern reader knows to be correct. In this process, a familiar conflict arises between the practical or mundane and the idealistic, with the ideal—the pursuit of truth—presented so attractively that Galileo's debts, his trickery, and even the shipwreck of his daughter's hopes seem trivial by comparison. However mundane the reader's normal outlook may be, a literary work can induce him to adopt a "higher," more idealistic view of its subject matter.

Thus far the play has invited judgments of a fairly familiar sort. When Galileo surrenders to the Inquisition, however, he apparently betrays the very ideal that until then has made him heroic; and the reader participates in the scorn that Andrea and his other disciples feel toward him. But this climactic moment in the play prepares for one of the two reversals of attitude that will be called for at its conclusion: the recantation is shown to have been in the service of scientific progress after all. The other reversal, of course, is Galileo's perception of the menace to humanity of the ideal to which he has devoted his life.

Notice how greatly these developments heighten the interest of the play. At first the judgments that it invites proceed from values that the reader shares or at least finds familiar. But as Galileo's career reaches its climax, the play demands that the reader adopt new, unexpected attitudes, requiring a readjustment of the values that he may be assumed to have possessed originally.

THEME

The definition of a play as "the artistic presentation of a conflict" implies that the interaction of plot, characters, and setting shall result in an implied point or meaning, for to the extent that the conflict is pre-sented artistically it will become meaningful. That meaning consists of a *theme* or cluster of themes. In *Galileo* the action evolves with such complexity that it would be hard to say which of its themes is the dominant one. It is a play about faith in reason, about the collision between reason and mental inertia, about the strength of authority and the weakness—or is it the triumph?—of the individual mind. But *Galileo* is also about a specifically modern kind of heroism, and about what a people's need for heroes reveals about their condition. In the end these themes are seen to be related ironically, for Galileo, whose work has so often brought him to certainty, arrives in the end at a certain uncertainty—though Andrea, his devoted disciple once again, seems not to be aware of it. Galileo is an intensely realized, recognizably human character; the events of his life and the world surrounding them are presented in richly concrete detail. And yet the ultimate interest of Brecht's *Life of Galileo*, for some readers at least, may lie in its more abstract meanings, its themes, which are not so much directly expressed as implied by the interrelationships of all its visible elements.

READING
A
POEM

Discussing poetry as a literary mode in "The Study of Literature" (p. xxv) , we suggested that *verse*, rather than *poetry*, is the term to use for discourses in which the *texture* and the *structure* of sounds are more conspicuous than they ordinarily are in prose. All works having *rhyme* and *meter* (including "Thirty Days Hath September") are verse, but not all of them are poems; *blank verse* has meter but not rhyme; *free verse*, which has neither meter nor rhyme, employs other means of calling attention to the sounds of its words. If a work of literature, one in which a *speaker* reveals an *attitude* toward a *situation*, is written in verse instead of prose, it is a poem, regardless of its quality.

The distinction between verse and prose, and therefore between poetry and prose, is a relative and not an absolute one. The term *poetic prose* is applied to prose passages that remind us of poems by emphasizing the sounds of words, by being suffused with feeling, and by having a significant amount of implied meaning. Donne's "No Man Is an Island" is rich in rhythmic patterns and formal stylistic devices. In sound-texture it resembles "When I Heard the Learned Astronomer" and other specimens of free verse. Meter and rhyme, though they regularly characterize poetry as song, are not essential to poetry in general. Those who would recognize poetry by their presence are right in seeking to identify it by means of sounds; they err only in defining a poetic sound-texture too narrowly.

From the time of Homer until at least that of Chaucer, the word *poem* brought to mind a versified narrative, a representation of human actions. Poems may also be *dramatic*, like "My Last Duchess" and Browning's other *dramatic monologues*; these are representations of persons speaking. To the modern reader, however, *poem* normally suggests a lyric or meditative work. A poem of this kind can most usefully be thought of as a representation of a reverie or daydream; and when the word occurs in this section, it is mainly this kind of poem that is meant. Good poems are far better organized than actual reveries are, but the two possess an important structural similarity. The content of a reverie is seldom a connected narrative, and still less is it an argument supporting a thesis or "idea"; yet many students seem to approach a poem as though it were a story or an essay. Perhaps the popularity of poetry has waned because of these mistaken expectations. If a work does not offer us the kind of meaning we suppose it will, we may be led to conclude too hastily that it is incomprehensible.

690

At the same time, however, poetry in some forms is as popular as ever, and the modern reader who expresses a distaste for it is usually not expressing his feelings accurately. The words of popular songs are poems, though not often admirable ones; and comic verse, whether printable or not, has as good a chance of popularity as any prose production. When we find pleasure in the lyrics of a popular song or Dryden's epitaph for his wife ("Here lies my wife, here let her lie! / Now she's at rest, and so am I") we are responding in large measure to the sound-texture, the distinctively poetic quality of these lines. A reader who says he dislikes poetry means the poems he has been asked to admire in the classroom. Yet these are the very ones that, instead of being quickly forgotten, continue to interest at least a few readers from one age to the next. Let us see how a reader of this kind reads a poem when he first encounters it.

SOUND AND EMOTION

An experienced reader hardly expects to understand a great poem after reading it only once. The concentration of meaning that poetic technique makes possible requires that the poem be read slowly and often if it is to be fully comprehended. What would occupy many pages if it could be expressed in prose cannot be grasped in a few minutes. Can we then say anything about the order in which the elements of a poem are mastered during the successive readings?

Though readers differ tremendously, it is likely that most of them on first reading a poem respond mainly to its sound-texture. They recognize the individual words, of course, and so understand some portions of the sense, but at this stage they are mainly aware of the rhymes, if there are any, and the rhythm, or pattern of stressed syllables, together with the support that these give to the fragments of the sense that are being taken in. A second reading will advance one's understanding of the sense, while at the same time one begins to identify the sound-structure: the *rhyme-scheme* and *verse-form*, if these are present. In subsequent readings, keeping in mind the likelihood that it is a reverie that is being represented, one may perceive the feelings more clearly, analyze the experiences that motivate them, notice the order (if any) of ideas from one stage of the poem to the next, and —last of all, perhaps—work out the complete implications of the *figures of speech* and their relevance to the subject. In some such way does the experienced reader arrive gradually at an understanding of the poem in all its organic complexity. While he is analyzing its parts, his awareness of its whole is maintained by the structure of its sound, which he remembers from his first readings.

Poetry differs from prose, then, chiefly in the greater organization of its sound. But since the meaning of words in combination is somewhat affected by their sound, it follows that the meaning of a poem cannot be duplicated in prose. It will always differ from even the closest paraphrase, chiefly because, as some of the famous descriptions of poetry suggest, one of the most important aspects of its subject matter is emotion.[1] This is especially the part of the meaning that eludes paraphrase, for the rendering of emotion is bound up with the more conspicuous sound-texture of poetry.

Poetry must not be thought of, however, merely as emotional language, for emotions are important in most prose works, and actions, ideas, and other elements found in prose enter into the subject matter of many poems. Just as there is no absolute distinction where sound is concerned, so poetry

---

[1] Milton, for instance, observed that poetry is more simple, sensuous, and passionate (i.e., emotional) than rhetoric; and Wordsworth stated that "poetry is the spontaneous overflow of powerful feelings; it takes its origin from emotion recollected in tranquillity."

and prose cannot be absolutely distinguished with respect to subject. Yet poetry tends to be more concerned with emotion, so that to read a poem without regard to the emotions present in it is to overlook one of the most characteristic elements in its meaning.

RHYTHM

English sentences have rhythm because our words are made up of syllables that are not stressed equally when the words are spoken. One syllable, for example, in almost every noun, verb, and adjective—the words that contribute most to the meaning—receives major stress, whereas articles and connectives are usually unstressed or receive only minor stress. In short, we tend to stress the important words and not the less important ones. Readers who are unable to distinguish major from minor stresses will find it helpful to notice in which syllables they clearly pronounce the vowel sounds, for these syllables have major stresses: the sentence before this one is pronounced almost as though it were written thus: *'n short, w'tend t'stress th'mport'nt words 'nd not th'un'mport'nt ones.* A less barbarous-looking method of indicating the major stresses, however, is to mark them with accents: *In short, we ténd to stréss . . .* etc.

As words are arranged into sentences, most of the major stresses will be separated by one or more minor ones. If the words are arranged so that the stresses support the meaning rather than hinder it, the result will be pleasing though not perfectly regular. It will be rhythmical: that is, possess a quality somewhat like the beat in music or the motion of the waves of the sea. In an ordinary sentence, the stresses are not evenly spaced, not so much as musical beats or the motion of the waves; but in an emotional passage like parts of "No Man Is an Island," they become more than ordinarily regular—

The béll doth tóll for hím that thínks it dóth . . .

without destroying the essential prose character of the passage.

How, then, is its rhythm related to that of poetry? Arranging the passage in approximately equal groups of words, each with about the same number of stresses, would make the reader much more aware of its sound:

The béll doth tóll for hím that thínks it dóth;

and though it intermít agáin,

yet fróm that mínute that that occásion

wrought upón him hé is united to Gód.

Who cásts not úp his éye to the sún when it ríses?

But whó takes óff his éye from a cómet when

that breaks óut?

Although the sequence and the sense of the words are unchanged, it is now apparent that their sounds have been ordered so that they have as much regularity as is found in many poems. Compare, for instance, the opening lines of "Musee des Beaux Arts":

About súffering théy were néver wróng,

The Óld Másters: how wéll they understóod

Its húman position; how it tákes pláce . . .

The poem is not more rhythmical than the prose passage, but it has been printed in a way that accentuates its sound-structure. Donne's passage is so nearly regular that its units of sound can almost be measured. That is, it comes near being metered.

METER

Under such entries as *free verse, meter, rhyme,* and *verse-forms,* the Index of Critical Terms defines the principal terms used in analyzing the sound-texture of verse.

Meter also lists the most common variations in the standard metrical patterns. The reader should, however, guard himself against the tendency to think of the topic as more complicated than it really is, and keep the following commonsense principles in mind.

1. By far the most common English verse-form is the ten-syllable line with major stresses on the even-numbered syllables. The next most common is the eight-syllable line with the same pattern of stresses.

2. No poem is entirely regular; meter is an imaginary pattern that actual poems do not precisely conform to but approximate more or less closely. Most of the variations are predictable.

3. Meter is important because it may make a real though not very specific contribution to the meaning of a poem. The situation presented in a metrical poem, such as Milton's sonnet "On His Blindness," will seem to have been ordered and mastered, and thus set apart from the chaos of actual experience. This poem is about the power of patience to suppress Milton's anger against God; hence the regular meter is wholly appropriate to the stated meaning. When meter becomes irregular or is absent, as in free verse, the effect is often one of agitation, as though the speaker found his experience baffling, absurd, or not altogether within his control.

The relation of meter to meaning, then, is an auxiliary one. Skillfully employed, meter can reinforce whatever meaning the words of the poem establish in their context, but the various meters have no independent meanings. Poems of widely differing meanings have been written in every one of them.

SPEAKER, SUBJECT, ATTITUDE

Poems, then, differ from prose works in respect to sound: Their rhythm is more pronounced, and most of them exhibit features involving the repetition of sounds, such as meter. But a poem is like any other literary work in consisting of a situation presented by a speaker who reveals an attitude toward that situation. What the reader of this book has learned about the content of stories and other prose works will therefore assist him in understanding poems. Accordingly, without repeating the explanation of terms introduced earlier, let us examine a specific poem that presents some difficulties of understanding: "Fern Hill," by Dylan Thomas, page 44.

On first reading a poem, as we have seen, the reader is apt to be more concerned with its sound than its sense. If he is wise, he will start by reading it aloud; and if it is "Fern Hill," he can assist his own reading by first listening to the admirable recording of it made by the poet himself. The long, flowing lines with which the stanzas begin will probably establish his first impression of "Fern Hill"; he will particularly notice the "liquid" quality of the rhythm, which results in part from the number of syllables with minor stress that precede the major stresses. There are few if any clusters of consonants or of stresses to arrest the voice; the sounds, urging the reader onward, contribute to the feeling of zest with which the poem celebrates the joys of childhood. As to the sense, the reader will probably gather at this first reading that Fern Hill is the name of a farm, that the poem represents a reverie about the speaker's childhood pleasures there (the games he played and the delights of simply going to sleep and waking up), and that the prominent words "dying" and "chains" in the final lines convey a wholly different emotion, one that will complete the basic contrast of the poem. Thus, even at this early stage, the reader begins to grasp the character of the speaker, the main outlines of the situation, and the contrasting emotions that enter into the speaker's attitude. If, later on, the structure of the stanzas is analyzed, it will be noticed that the contrast is reinforced by the meter: in general, the long, flowing lines are concerned with the joys of childhood, whereas the pathos of its passing is concentrated in the short six-syllable lines, three of which begin with the word "Time."

Further readings make the reader's awareness of the remembered pleasures much more vivid and concrete. The speaker's claim that he was "happy as the grass was green" is supported by a series of images in which he describes the games that he played, the sensation of falling asleep while "the owls were bearing the farm away," the joy of waking to a world that seemed as fresh and new as on the day it was created. The poem, so far as it is a hymn to the delights of childhood, must stand or fall by the success with which it provides a solid basis for this emotion. But these remembered pleasures constitute only a part of the theme; for, paradoxically, the greater the happiness of childhood, the greater its pathos—the sadder is its passing. Like "Blackberry Winter," which it resembles in theme, "Fern Hill" asserts that for a child Time does not exist. Alas, however, Time is all the while carrying him out of his childhood, as later it will carry him from life to death. Yet the child is mercifully unconscious of what is happening to him. These reflections are suggested by the references to Time in the poem, though it is only after many readings that the full implications of such figures as "Time let me play and be/Golden in the mercy of his means" can be grasped.

At some point in his reading, the reader will do well to notice the likenesses between the poem and a short story, for these will assist his understanding. The *setting* of "Fern Hill," as we have already seen, is essential to its meaning; except for Time, the *characters* are restricted to the speaker, as is usual in reverie; and a sort of *plot* is provided by the succession of *scenes* full of action and movement ("I was huntsman and herdsman"; "it was running"; "I ran my heedless ways"), which convey the intense though transitory vitality of the main

character. The *point of view*, the recollection of boyhood from the vantage point of maturity, is the same as that of "Blackberry Winter"—as might be expected from the likeness of their *themes*. Finally, a consideration of the *progression* in "Fern Hill" leads to an appreciation of its two most striking passages.

We have said that working out all the implications of the *metaphors* and *symbols* in a poem is one of the last stages in its reading. It is the symbols in the concluding stanza of "Fern Hill," particularly in the line "Up to the swallow-thronged loft by the shadow of my hand," that suggest the analogy between passing from childhood to maturity and passing from life to death. But this aspect of the theme is not introduced abruptly in the last stanza: it has been prepared for by the progression that occurs at the middle of the poem. Having established the joyousness of childhood by mentioning its games and the sensations of sleeping and waking, the speaker sums up in the striking metaphor, "it was Adam and maiden." The world of childhood, that is, resembles the Garden of Eden: all freshness and innocence, for the child knows neither sin nor death. Time will lead him out of this realm of grace, as the angel led Adam and Eve from Paradise, but he is as unaware of this fate as they were of theirs before their fall. Instead of resting in its expression of childish joys and the pathos of their passing, the poem proceeds to link these emotions with the joy and sorrow that are seemingly central to man's condition. And the reader's understanding is prepared for the wider dimension that the concluding stanza will give to the subject; instead of merely repeating what has already been established, the final lines suggest that the poem is concerned not only with childhood, but with the whole cycle of human life and death.

We have suggested that some modern readers approach a poem with mistaken expectations. If a reader were to ask what the "thought" or "idea" of "Fern Hill" is, we should have to answer that it is merely that the child is unaware of the brevity of life, an answer that would probably cause disappointment. Such a reader has asked the wrong question. The reading of a poem is a complex experience in which understanding the idea may play only a minor part, as it does in reading "Fern Hill." Its fifty-four lines typify the concentration of meaning that characterizes all good poetry; and though we have discussed its sound, its speaker and situation, its figures of speech and the emotions that are interwoven with them, these prose paragraphs only begin to explore its riches. The essence of "Fern Hill" is not its thought, but the universal ironic contrast that the poem realizes by its concrete presentation of childhood pleasures and the sharp, subtle metaphors that ring in the reader's memory and unfold new meanings as he turns them over in his mind. The poem is pervaded by a feeling of controlled wild energy, by a joyous acceptance of the paradox of growth; and it is the intensity of these qualities, along with the complex, interrelated structure of its symbols, that makes the reading of "Fern Hill" a moving, satisfying experience.

INDEX OF CRITICAL TERMS

Aesthetic. Pertaining to those aspects of an object—either a man-made object, such as a literary work, or a natural one—by virtue of which it affords the kind of satisfaction characteristic of works of art. These aesthetic aspects are generally held to include its form, qualities, and symbolic significance; and aesthetic value is held to be distinct from economic, scientific, moral, religious, and other values. Cf. p. xxxiv.

Allegory. Narrative in which the concrete elements—the incidents, characters, settings, and so forth—bring to mind abstract conceptions systematically related. "Young Goodman Brown" is at least partly allegorical; e.g., Brown's wife, Faith, personifies religious belief.

Allusion. In general, an implied or covert reference; in a literary work, a reminder of another work or of a person, place, or idea, known from another document. "A new nation, . . . dedicated to the proposition that all men are created equal" contains an allusion to *The Declaration of Independence;* "Ode to a Nightingale," lines 66–67, alludes to *The Book of Ruth;* "The Conversion of the Jews" and "If I Forget Thee, O Earth" are allusive titles. Such a reminder enlarges the meaning of the work in which it occurs. See **Multiple meaning,** p. xxxi.

Attitude. Disposition arising from one's beliefs and emotions to feel and judge in a particular way; the attitude of the **speaker** in a literary work is his appraisal or evaluation of the **situation** he presents.

Auditor. In a poem or prose fiction in **dramatic** form, the implied listener to the narrative. This may be one person (Eos in "Tithonus") or more than one ("Why I Live at the P. O."). Cf. p. xxvii.

Ballad. A narrative poem, distinguished from an epic by its brevity and its verse-form; and from a lyric by the speaker's emphasis on the action almost to the point of self-effacement ("Edward," "Sir Patrick Spens").

Ballad-stanza. See **Verse-forms.**

Blank verse. See **Meter.**

Climax. A point of maximum intensity in a plot, the culmination of a **conflict.**

Conflict. Encounter between a character's purposes and obstacles to their fulfilment. These may consist of others' purposes, the forces of a hostile environment, or warring impulses within the character himself. Conflict is essential to plot, to drama, and to the dramatic element in prose fiction. Cf. pp. xxviii–xxix.

Dialogue. Conversation represented directly, not summarized. Plays consist of dialogue almost entirely, and the scenes in prose fiction characteristically include it. See **Scene** (3).

Dramatic. Besides its usual meaning—pertaining to the literary mode called drama (p. xxxiii)—"dramatic" means "spoken by someone who is distinctly not the author." See the two terms following **Auditor.**

Dramatic monologue. A work, usually a poem, supposed to be entirely spoken by an imagined character, whose identity, as in "Tithonus" and "The Bishop Orders His Tomb at St. Praxed's Church," is ordinarily indicated by the title.

Dramatic soliloquy. A work similar to a **dramatic monologue** but purporting to represent a character's feelings and thoughts directly rather than through speech by him ("Ulysses," "The Love Song of J. Alfred Prufrock").

Essay. A work in which statements purporting to be true of the actual world predominate; characteristically, a work designed to support a thesis. Also, the literary mode comprising such works. A **reflective essay** ("The Headlong Wave") is an overt argument; a **narrative essay** ("Tell Freedom") devotes most of its space to action and may only imply its **thesis or theme.** Cf. p. xxxiii.

Exposition. In narrative, including plays, the process of imparting information about what has supposedly happened before the narrative opens—or outside the **scenes** that are narrated directly. Cf. p. 686.

Fiction. (1) Imaginative literature (prose narratives, plays, and poems) in which the events, characters, and other elements are either invented or imaginatively recreated from those supplied by experience or history; (2) short stories and novels collectively (also **prose fiction**—an awkward usage, since plays of the past three hundred years have mainly been written in prose). Cf. p. xxxii.

Figures of speech (also **figurative language, trope**). If words are to be understood in their primary meanings they are used *literally;* otherwise they are used *figuratively,* and this is properly done to express meanings for which literal speech will not suffice. At least as long

ago as Aristotle's *Poetics* it was recognized that the most important figure of speech is **metaphor,** which "demands originality and is a sign of genius; for to make good metaphors is to perceive similarity" (Ch. 22). Metaphor expresses this perception by substituting a similar thing, which may be called the **surrogate,** for the thing referred to (the **referent**). In the statement "the seas are the heart's blood of the earth" ("The Headlong Wave"), blood is made to stand for the life-sustaining functions of the oceans. (Referent and surrogate correspond, respectively but roughly, to what are sometimes called **tenor** and **vehicle.**) **Trope,** a synonym of "metaphor," suggests by its etymology how such expressions make themselves understood: the reader "turns" to another meaning when he sees that the literal meaning is impossible. P. xxxi.

Figures of speech have been elaborately catalogued and labeled; but, as the *Poetics* (Ch. 21) suggests when it illustrates *metaphor* with "Ten thousand brave deeds has Odysseus done," most of them are metaphorical; they entail substitution and identification. The statement about Odysseus may be called **hyperbole** (expressive, not deceptive, exaggeration). The opposite figures are **understatement** (as one might say that Odysseus led a rather active life), and its subspecies **litotes** or **meiosis:** in "Duse and Bernhardt" Shaw writes that when watching Sara Bernhardt act "one is *not sorry* . . . to relax one's notions of the dignity of art." (These shade off into **irony.**) The surrogate and referent of **metonymy** are closely associated things; in "still keep the sword erect" (Marvell's "Horatian Ode") we must understand that "sword" means "military posture." This instance may equally well be called a **personification**—speaking of inanimate things as though they were animate—which suggests the close kinship of all these modes of metaphor. **Synecdoche,** substituting a part for the whole or vice versa, is distinguished rather arbitrarily from metonymy; the sword is, after all, one of the weapons of seventeenth-century warfare.

The ability to make distinctions among the modes of metaphor is less important than understanding the two following facts: first, figurative language is an attribute of all language, prose as well as verse—and slang in particular. It occurs more densely in poems, but all the examples above—except Aristotle's —originated in essays and other specimens of everyday prose. Secondly, a good figure cannot be paraphrased without some change of meaning, for it expresses what literal speech will not express. It is especially necessary, as the examples show, in discriminating shades of feeling and emotion. A precise reference to feeling, writes Susanne Langer, "is usually made by mentioning the circumstance that suggests it—'a mood of autumn evening,' 'a holiday feeling.'"

Form. The relationship among the parts of a work; distinguished from **substance**. See **Structure; Texture; pp. xxx–xxxi.**

Free verse. Verse "freed" of equal numbers of syllables from line to line and of accented syllables recurring regularly. It remains verse by virtue of some rhythmic organization that employs the sounds of words to a greater extent that ordinary language does. In some free verse, broken metrical patterns appear ("Dover Beach," "The Love Song of J. Alfred Prufrock"). Other examples are characterized by balance and repetition ("When I heard the Learned Astronomer").

Hyperbole. See **Figures of speech.**

Image. The verbal imitation of a visual impression; a word-picture; by extension, the imitation in words of any sense-impression. Sometimes **visual image** is used to distinguish the first from **auditory image, kinesthetic image,** etc. But the predominance of sight causes **image** to mean **visual image** unless otherwise qualified. Either literal or figurative language can create images, but **figures of speech** nearly always do.

Irony. (1) **Irony of situation** is a quality perceived in the consequences of an action, when those consequences are the opposite of what was expected. The attempt of Oedipus to avoid his destiny is the very act which causes that destiny to overtake him. (2) **Verbal irony** is a quality of a discourse in which the meaning is different from—often the opposite of— the apparent meaning. Verbal irony is usually critical but not necessarily so, and is distinct from sarcasm. "A shepherd of Bohemia . . . relates with great confidence a story, of which the credibility is left to be considered by the learned," a sentence near the beginning of "The Fable of the Vultures," suggests that the story will be fantastic, which it is, and yet full of truth. Verbal irony, it is said, "postulates a double audience": in this example, one that expects the story to be credible and one that understands the warning implicit in the irony. **Dramatic irony** characterizes the words of a speaker who sees less meaning in them than his hearers do: as when Oedipus, in *Oedipus the King*, orders that no one shall associate with Laïos's murderer when he is found.

Litotes. See **Figures of speech.**

Lyric. A short poem, identified in this book as the representation of a reverie, the content of which is normally a state of affairs or an arrested stage of an event; e.g., "On Wenlock Edge." The speaker's feelings tend to be more than usually intense. A narrative poem, like a story, appears to create a series of past events ("Out, Out—"); a dramatic poem, like a play, appears to create a future disclosing itself in the present ("The Bishop Orders His Tomb at St. Praxed's Church"). A lyric, however, suggests a timeless confrontation of a speaker and a situation. Nowadays when anyone speaks of poetry it is generally the lyric to which he is referring.

Meiosis. See **Figures of speech.**

Metaphor. See **Figures of speech; p. 697.**

Meter. The pattern of sounds in a discourse divided into lines having equal numbers of syllables, with the words so ordered that major stresses occur at equal intervals. Since meter is a pattern, it may be apparent in a series of lines no one of which is wholly regular, as long as regularity is noticeably approximated. Syllabic equality may itself form a pattern, as in "My Dreams Are of a Field Afar": 8–6–8–6, 8–6–8–6.

By far the most common division of English verse is into lines of ten syllables, which are called **decasyllabics**; eight-syllable lines, **octosyllabics,** are next. By far the most common stress-pattern is arrangement of the words so that the even-numbered syllables receive major stresses:

When I con·sid·er how my light is spent,
1　2　3　4　5　6　7　8　9　10
(On His Blindness")

The time you won your town the race
1　2　3　4　5　6　7　8
("To an Athlete Dying Young")

The most admired poems in English are decasyllabic, with this stress-pattern—the form that is usually called **blank verse** when it is unrhymed.

Much verse, however, has other stress-patterns, of which three are most common. The major stresses may fall on the odd-numbered syllables:

Men of Eng·land, where·fore plough
1　2　3　4　5　6　7
("Song to the Men of England")

(Most verse of this pattern is octosyllabic.) Or the major stresses may be separated by two minor ones, with major stress on either the first or the last syllable of the line:

Half a league, half a league,
1　2　3　4　5　6
("The Charge of the Light Brigade")

O say, can you see, by the dawn's ear·ly light,
1　2　3　4　5　6　7　8　9　10　11
("The Star-Spangled Banner")

Since the pattern is determined by the position of the stresses, it is tempting to think of the unit of meter as being a group of syllables with a major stress as its nucleus. Such a unit is called a **foot.** The kinds of metrical feet already exemplified are these:

iamb or **iambus** (^{x} /; adjective, **iambic**):

The time | you won | your town | the race

trochee (/ ^{x}; adjective, **trochaic**):

Men of | Eng·land, | where·fore | plough

dactyl (/ $^{x\,x}$; adjective, **dactylic**):

Half a league, | half a league,

anapest ($^{x\,x}$ /; adjective, **anapestic**):

O say, | can you see, | by the dawn's | ear·ly

light,[1]

There are also these three feet:

amphibrach (^{x} / ^{x}; adjective, **amphibrachic**):

And thought of | con·vinc·ing | while they

thought | of din·ing;
("Epitaph for Edmund Burke")

spondee (/ /; adjective, **spondaic**):

That night | your great | guns, un·|a·wares,
("Channel Firing")

[1] The first foot is a spondee in place of the anapest; see **substitutions,** below. Notice that the lines are accented by the *principle of relative stress*: i.e., the x-marks denote, not unstressed syllables, but minor stresses—syllables having lighter stress than those nearest them. To mark "O say, can you see . . ." to show actual pronunciation, we should have to use a system such as this:

O say, | can you see, | by the dawn's | ear·ly light . . .
But since "can" and "you" have lighter stress than "see," it is metrically irrelevant whether they have any at all, and whether one has more than the other. So they are given x-marks. The major stresses on "say," "see," "dawn's," and "light" establish the anapestic meter.

pyrrhic (ˣ ˣ; adjective, **pyrrhic**):

x   x
Will the | world ev•er san•er be

(Ibid., line 26)

The last two kinds, as the examples suggest, almost never appear except as **substitutions** for the other five. Having no major stress, the pyrrhic is not always considered a foot.

The number of feet in a line may be denoted thus:

1	monometer	5	pentameter
2	dimeter	6	hexameter
3	trimeter	7	heptameter
4	tetrameter	8	octameter.

By this system, blank verse is called **iambic pentameter unrhymed**; "To an Athlete Dying Young," is **iambic tetrameter**; "The Charge of the Light Brigade" begins as **dactylic dimeter**; "The Star-Spangled Banner" is **anapestic tetrameter**.

The art of versification, including such related sound-effects as **rhyme**, is called **prosody**. To analyze verse in order to discover its meter is to **scan** it; and the immediate object of scansion is to discover the *prevailing* meter, ignoring substitutions, as when we call "The Star-Spangled Banner" anapestic tetrameter, despite its opening spondee. Since a meter is an abstract pattern, few if any poems follow it slavishly. Prosody consists equally of establishing a sound-pattern and of introducing artful variations upon it. To appreciate the harmonious effects of these, the reader must first apprehend the pattern that is being varied. If irregularities make scansion difficult for him at first, he will soon find that the possible variations, without destruction of the meter, are limited. The following are most to be expected:

In iambics,

(1) **inversion**, especially of the first foot:

/   x   x   /   x   /   x /
Just as | be•fore | you went | be•low;

("Channel Firing," line 11)

(2) addition of a minor stress, especially at end:

x   x   /   x   /   x /   x
Said one, | "than when | He sent | us un•|der

(Ibid., line 27)

(3) regrouping, especially at first:

x   x   /   / x /   x /
Will the | world ev•|er san•|er be,"

(Ibid., line 26)

(We might say, "Substitution of a pyrrhic and a spondee for the first two iambs.")

The markedly irregular line 16 has three variations:

x   /   x x   /   x x   /
Than you | who are help•|less in | such

/   x
mat•|ters.

In trochaics, omission of the last syllable:

/ x   /   x   /   x /   x   /   x
What of soul was left, I won•der, when the

/ x   / x /
kis•sing had to stop?

("A Toccata of Galuppi's," line 42)

In dactylic and anapestic verse,

(1) omission of syllables:

/   x x   / x x   /
All in the | val•ley of | Death,

("The Charge of the Light Brigade," line 3)

(2) substitution of spondees:

/ /   x   x   /
O say, | can you see . . .

Metonymy. See **Figures of speech.**

Multiple meaning. Enrichment of meaning by implication; p. xxxi.

Narrative. Story-telling; a story; an account of events that purportedly happen to human beings or imaginary beings with human characteristics. See **Plot; Structure;** pp. xxix–xxx.

Ode. A poem that praises someone or something, similar in feeling to a hymn. Whether or not such a poem is entitled an ode appears to be arbitrary: "To Autumn," by John Keats, is generally considered along with "Ode to a Nightingale" and his other odes. The verse-form of the ode is also indefinable: when it consists of long, irregular stanzas resembling those of Pindar (522?–433 B.C.), these may be called **strophes** ("Ode upon Dr. Harvey"). Keats wrote odes in regular stanzas that he invented by combining parts of **sonnets**. "Ode to the West Wind" is **terza rima** (see **Verse-forms**).

Personification. See **Figures of speech.**

Perspective. See **Point of view.**

Plot. The representation in fiction of a character's efforts to achieve a purpose in the face of obstacles, concluding with his decisive success or failure. Cf. pp. 677 and 686.

Plot structure. See **Structure.**

Poetry. Metrical or free-verse discourse characterized by situations presented with feeling, expressed or implied, and by complication and enrichment of language. Pp. xxxi–xxxii.

Point of view. In narrative, the temporal or spatial vantage-point of the narrator. Since his time-perspective is that of one who knows the story in its entirety, he tells it in the past tense. His spatial perspective may be omniscient—knowing everything, including the thoughts and feelings of all the characters—or restricted in one of these ways: (1) the story may seem a report of events that the narrator has observed but not engaged in; (2) it may seem a personal experience in which the narrator has played an important part; (3) writing in the third person, he may seem to know the story only as one of its characters has experienced it. Some of these methods may be combined. The omniscient method, which now seems somewhat old-fashioned, is exemplified by "The Girl in Arles." The restricted methods are exemplified respectively by "The Undefeated," "The Real Thing," and "After Cortes." Pp. xxxiii, 680.

Progression. The sense that a narrative is moving toward its resolution. Cf. p. 678.

Properties. Movable objects in a play. Cf. p. 685.

Reflective essay. See **Essay.**

Refrain. See **Verse-forms.**

Resolution (also **denouement**). The point in a narrative at which a character's dominant purpose has been either fulfilled or decisively frustrated.

Rhyme. The syllables of the word "hodge-podge" rhyme because the full vowel-sound in each and all the sounds after it are identical, and the sounds before it are different. A full vowel-sound is one in a stressed syllable—which may not be the last one, or even in the same word: "hurly-burly," "best of us, rest of us." (These are called **feminine rhymes**.) Rhyme is wholly a matter of sound: "burly" rhymes with "early" but not with "sourly"—nor, of course, with "burley." In verse, most rhyme is **end-rhyme,** but **internal rhyme** is also found: "But now and then they grow to men." The greater the differences between two rhyming combinations, the more striking will be their identity of sound. The least interesting rhymes are those involving the same parts of speech having the same terminal spellings: "rang, sang." Such rhymes as "debt, sweat" are more surprising.

Poets of the past were expected to rhyme strictly if at all, except that by "poetic license" a few **near-rhymes** ("never, river"; "even, heaven") were admitted. But since the number of rhymes in English is limited compared with the number in some other languages, many of them came to seem hackneyed; and recent poets have expanded the resources of the rhymer by admitting near-rhymes to equal status with strict ones ("Sailing to Byzantium"). Most near-rhymes vary the vowel-sound while retaining the consonant-sound ("seas, dies") or else ignore the rule of stress ("sing, studying"). Only seldom are the final consonant-sounds varied ("time, climbs"). To be more precise, one may speak of **assonance** and **consonance**: repetition of vowel-sounds and of consonant-sound respectively. Poets find near-rhymes, though they are sometimes mistaken for clumsiness, a middle course between repeating the familiar rhymes of earlier poems and abandoning rhyme entirely.

Most **verse-forms** (which see) are determined by a combination of a meter and a **rhyme-scheme.**

Scene. (1) A division of a play, shorter than an act; (2) **setting,** which see; (3) in a narrative, a passage consisting of action described in detail, a definite setting, and usually dialogue; opposed to narrative summary, by which the scenes are connected. Cf. pp. 677, 684.

Setting. In literature, whatever encompasses the plot and characters: the physical scene, the time, the customs and laws of that milieu, etc. Setting may so influence the characters as to rank with them in importance; in "Blackberry Winter," for instance, it represents both the world of childhood and its destroyer.

Simile. "When a thing happens it ... stands solid in Time like the tree that you can walk around" ("Blackberry Winter") contains a simile—commonly defined as "an explicit comparison of two dissimilar things" or "things of different classes." But there is no simile in "They didn't take the trouble to have a vegetable patch like Dellie and Jebb" (*ibid.*), which satisfies this definition. The difficulty lies in the indefiniteness of the terms "dissimilar" and "different classes." It seems less arbitrary to call a simile an expressed comparison having some unexpressed meaning: the meaning of the second example is stated, but the similarity of a happening and a tree is partly left to the reader to discover.

Situation. The events, objects, ideas, relationships, and all else that a speaker describes and presents attitudes toward, considered collectively. Pp. xxvi–xxvii.

Sonnet. See **Verse-forms.**

Speaker. The fictitious person who purports to utter the sentences making up a literary work: e.g., the "I" of the work or the ostensible narrator.

Stanza. See **Verse-forms.**

Structure. The relationship among the dominant parts of a work; distinct from **texture**

p. xxx. A pattern of emotional development toward a climax, or a system of such patterns, is a **kinetic** or **rhetorical structure;** pp. xxx, 672–73. **Logical structure,** characteristic of essays, consists of such relationships as that between a thesis and its supporting reasons, or a system of classification, or chronological development; pp. 671–72. **Plot structure** connects the origin of a conflict in a character's purposes with the resolution of the conflict; see **Plot.**

Style. The quality in a discourse that results from recurring features of its texture; p. xxx.

Subject. Of a literary work, what the work is about, as "To His Coy Mistress" is a love-poem; p. xxvi. The events, characters, places, and all else forming the situation constitute the **concrete subject;** the themes of the work are its **abstract subjects.** P. xxviii.

Symbol. The Yale bulldog, Mercury's profile, the American eagle, and the cross are tangible objects that have been made to suggest intangible realities or ideals: the determined spirit of a university or its teams, the speed and power of an automobile, and so on. Therefore they are symbols. Literary works often create such objects by means of words: the million-yen cracker in "Three Million Yen," the Texas ponies in "Spotted Horses." The sharp difference between the symbol and the thing symbolized should be noticed. The immense value of symbolism is that it enables us to talk in concrete terms of abstract conceptions—and thus charge them with feeling. It is one of the chief methods by which a writer achieves **multiple meaning** (p. xxxi).

Synecdoche. See **Figures of speech.**

Texture. The particular characteristics of the words in a discourse, especially their qualities of sound, levels of usage, grammatical relationships, and figurative character; distinguished from **structure.** Cf. p. xxx.

Theme. A conception about the states, qualities, processes, etc., of human experience, suggested by the **concrete subject** of a work. Cf. p. xxviii.

Thesis. An arguable proposition, consisting of an expressed or implied belief of the speaker. Theses are characteristic of essays, but are also common in other literary modes. Cf. p. xxviii.

Tone. The quality of a speaker's words that reveals his feelings and attitudes about the situation that he presents. Cf. xxvii–xxviii.

Trope. See **Figures of speech.**

Understatement. See **Figures of speech.**

Unstable situation. A point in a narrative at which the conflict is so far from its resolution that additional action must follow. Cf. p. 688.

Verse. Metrical and other discourse in which the sounds of words are more conspicuous than is normally the case in prose. See **Meter; Free verse;** p. xxxi.

Verse-forms. A passage of verse may be divided into paragraphs, as "There Was a Boy" is, or into **stanzas,** which are units normally having the same number of lines. Division into paragraphs follows the meaning, as in prose; division into stanzas is a sound-effect and may not correspond to the meaning at all. To call a stanza a "verse" is confusing, both because of the word's general meaning and because in old-fashioned usage a verse is a single line. A poem may be written in a newly invented stanza-form, as "Fern Hill" is, or in an established one, as most stanzaic poems are; and a few poems (e.g., "Poetry") have stanzas of unequal length. When the lines in a stanza-form have different numbers of syllables, the differences may themselves form a pattern that appears in every stanza. Thus the **ballad-stanza** ("Sir Patrick Spens") has a pattern of 8–6–8–6 syllables, to which may be added a **refrain,** a more or less exactly repeated line. Almost any stanza-form may be combined with a refrain, as in "Adieu, Farewell Earth's Bliss."

The terms **couplet, tercet,** and **quatrain** signify divisions of two, three, and four lines, as in "Morning," "Ode to the West Wind,"

and "On Wenlock Edge" respectively. These effects may be created by rhymes as well as by spaces; if a stanza rhymes, the pattern is its **rhyme-scheme.** For descriptive purposes the first rhyming line and all other lines that rhyme with it are denoted by *a*'s; the next set by *b*'s, and so on. An *x* stands for an unrhymed line. The rhyme-scheme of "Sir Patrick Spens" is *xaxa;* of "My Dreams Are of a Field Afar," also a ballad-stanza, *abab.*

Unrhymed verse is called **blank verse,** though the term usually suggests unrhymed decasyllabics (see **Meter**). So many prominent poems in English are decasyllabic that this form has been called its **heroic meter** (suitable for epics). Decasyllabic lines rhyming in pairs are called **heroic couplets** ("Morning"). Most of the verse-forms that are known as the **fixed forms** are determined by rhyme; and most of them, except the ballad-stanza, have decasyllabic lines. The most prominent of these is the **sonnet,** all varieties of which have fourteen lines.

An **English (Elizabethan, Shakespearean) sonnet** consists of three quatrains and a couplet; it rhymes *abab cdcd efef gg.* Five of Shakespeare's sonnets appear in this book; a modern example of an English sonnet is "The End of the World."

An **Italian (Petrarchan) sonnet** consists of an **octave** rhyming *abbaabba* and a **sestet** rhyming *cdcdcd, cdecde,* or some such combination—as long as a couplet does not conclude. The eighth line of the octave brings a segment of the meaning to a conclusion, and the meaning then takes a new direction in the sestet. The "Holy Sonnets" of John Donne are examples. The rigor of the octave's rhyme-scheme is sometimes relaxed. A rarer exception is "The Windhover": not all its lines are decasyllabic.

A **Miltonic sonnet** has the Italian rhyme-scheme, but the meaning, instead of being divided after the octave, develops steadily to the conclusion ("On His Blindness," "On the Late Massacre in Piedmont").

Two other celebrated fixed forms are represented in this book:

ottava rima, stanzas rhyming *abababcc* ("Women in Love," "Sailing to Byzantium");

terza rima (the verse-form of Dante's *Divine Comedy*), tercets having interlocking rhymes, *aba bcb cdc.* . . . The poet makes his escape by omitting the middle line of the last tercet and thus concluding with a couplet: . . . *yzy zz* ("Ode to the West Wind").

INDEX OF AUTHORS AND TITLES